CANADIAN EDITION

Global Business Today

CHARLES W. L. HILL
University of Washington

THOMAS McKAIG
Ryerson University and University of Guelph
(Adjunct Professor, Department of Marketing and Consumer Studies)

Contributor

TIM RICHARDSON
Seneca College of Applied Arts and Technology and
University of Toronto

McGraw-Hill Ryerson

Toronto Montréal Boston Burr Ridge, IL Dubuque, IA Madison, WI New York San Francisco
St. Louis Bangkok Bogotá Caracas Kuala Lumpur Lisbon London Madrid Mexico City Milan
New Delhi Santiago Seoul Singapore Sydney Taipei

For June and Mike Hill, my parents.
To my mother and father, Dorothy and Russell M^c^Kaig.

The McGraw·Hill Companies

McGraw-Hill Ryerson

Global Business Today, Canadian Edition

ISBN-13: 978-0-07-094709-2
ISBN-10: 0-07-094709-0

2 3 4 5 6 7 8 9 10 CTPS 0 9 8 7

Printed and bound in China

Publisher: *Nicole Lukach*
Sponsoring Editor: *Kim Brewster*
Senior Marketing Manager: *Kelly Smyth*
Managing Editor, Development: *Jennifer DiDomenico*
Developmental Editor: *Sarah Dann*
Copy Editor: *Erin Moore*
Production Coordinator: *Paula Brown*
Permissions and Photo Research: *Craig Saunders*
Cover Design: *Sharon Lucas*
Interior Design: *Jennifer McQueen and Amanda Kavanagh, Ark Design*
Cover Image Credit: © *Photodisc Green/Ken Usami*
Page Layout: *Sharon Lucas*
Printer: *China Translation & Printing Services Ltd.*

Library and Archives Canada Cataloguing in Publication

Hill, Charles W. L.
Global business today / Charles W.L. Hill, Thomas McKaig. – Canadian ed.
Includes bibliographical references and index.
ISBN 0-07-094709-0
1. International business enterprises–Management–Textbooks. 2. International trade–Textbooks. 3. Investments, Foreign–Textbooks. 4. Capital market–Textbooks.
I. McKaig, Thomas II. Title.
HD62.4.H54 2006 658'.049 C2005-906074-3

ABOUT THE AUTHORS

Charles W. L. Hill is the Hughes M. Blake Professor of International Business at the School of Business, University of Washington. Professor Hill received his Ph.D. in industrial organization economics in 1983 from the University of Manchester's Institute of Science and Technology (UMIST) in Great Britain. In addition to the University of Washington, he has served on the faculties of UMIST, Texas A&M University, and Michigan State University.

Professor Hill has published more than 40 articles in peer-reviewed academic journals. He also has published two textbooks, one on strategic management and the other on international business. Professor Hill serves on the editorial boards of several academic journals and previously served as consulting editor at the *Academy of Management Review*.

Professor Hill teaches in the MBA and executive MBA programs at the University of Washington and has received awards for teaching excellence in both programs. He has also taught on several customized executive programs.

Thomas McKaig is Adjunct Professor at the Department of Marketing and Consumer Studies at the University of Guelph and teaches international business studies at Ryerson University. He has also taught at the University of Saskatchewan. He earned his Diplôme for his thesis on *Canada – EEC Trade Relations* and Certificat majoring in International Relations and minoring in European Economics, also at the Institut des Hautes Études Européennes of the Université de Strasbourg III (now Université Robert Schuman). He earned his Honours BA in Political Science from the University of Ottawa at which time he was selected by the World University Service of Canada for study sessions that took place at the University of the West Indies in Mona, Jamaica and in Cave Hill, Barbados.

Thomas McKaig also provides advisory services in diverse industries, pinpointing and delivering strategic realignment solutions in areas of business development, operations and management reviews, international trade research, and training. He is Principal in Thomas McKaig International Inc. (TMI), an international development firm (www.tm-int.com). Some of his past clients include the United States Treasury Department's Bureau of the United States Mint and the Montreal Exchange. His work has been repeatedly acknowledged and praised within the Canadian House of Commons.

BRIEF CONTENTS

PREFACE xi

PART ONE Globalization 2

- CHAPTER ONE — Globalization 2

PART TWO Country Differences 40

- CHAPTER TWO — Country Differences in Political Economy 40
- CHAPTER THREE — The Cultural Environment 84
- CHAPTER FOUR — Ethics in International Business 122

PART THREE Cross-Border Trade and Investment 160

- CHAPTER FIVE — International Trade Theories 160
- CHAPTER SIX — The Political Economy of International Trade 192
- CHAPTER SEVEN — Foreign Direct Investment 224
- CHAPTER EIGHT — Regional Economic Integration 258

PART FOUR Global Money System 294

- CHAPTER NINE — The Foreign Exchange Market 294
- CHAPTER TEN — The Global Monetary System 322

PART FIVE Competing in a Global Marketplace 362

- CHAPTER ELEVEN — Global Strategy 362
- CHAPTER TWELVE — Entering Foreign Markets 398
- CHAPTER THIRTEEN — Exporting, Importing, and Countertrade 426
- CHAPTER FOURTEEN — Global Marketing and R&D 450
- CHAPTER FIFTEEN — Global Manufacturing and Materials Management 484
- CHAPTER SIXTEEN — Global Human Resource Management 508

GLOSSARY 535

END NOTES 541

NAME/COMPANY INDEX 560

SUBJECT INDEX 564

CONTENTS

PREFACE xi

PART ONE Globalization 2

CHAPTER ONE
Globalization 2
Opening Case: The Global Grocer 2
Introduction 5
What Is Globalization? 7
The Globalization of Markets 7
The Globalization of Production 8
The Emergence of Global Institutions 8
Drivers of Globalization 10
Declining Trade and Investment Barriers 10
The Role of Technological Change 13
The Changing Demographics of the Global Economy 16
The Changing World Output and World Trade Picture 16
The Changing Foreign Direct Investment Picture 20
The Changing Nature of the Multinational Enterprise 23
The Changing World Order 24
The Global Economy of the Twenty-First Century 25
The Globalization Debate 26
Antiglobalization Protests 26
Globalization, Jobs, and Incomes 28
Globalization, Labour Policies, and the Environment 29
Globalization and National Sovereignty 30
Globalization and the World's Poor 31
Managing in the Global Marketplace 32
Implications for Business 33
The North–South Divide 34
The Role of Technology in International Trade 34
Key Terms 34
Summary 35
Critical Thinking and Discussion Questions 35
Research Task 36
Closing Case: The Canadian Beef Industry and Mad Cow Disease 36
Sustainability in Practice: Adidas-Salomon: Supply-Chain Management 38

PART TWO Country Differences 40

CHAPTER TWO
Country Differences in Political Economy 40
Opening Case: The Changing Political Economy of India 40
Introduction 42
Political Systems 44
Collectivism and Individualism 44
Democracy and Totalitarianism 46
Economic Systems 48
Market Economy 48
Command Economy 49
Mixed Economy 49
Legal Systems 49
Different Legal Systems 50
Differences in Contract Law 51
Property Rights 52
The Protection of Intellectual Property 55
Product Safety and Product Liability 60
The Determinants of Economic Development 60
Differences in Economic Development 60
Broader Conceptions of Development: Amartya Sen 62
Political Economy and Economic Progress 62
Geography, Education, and Economic Development 66
States in Transition 67
The Spread of Democracy 67
The New World Order? 69

The Spread of Market-Based Systems 70
The Nature of Economic Transformation 71
Implications 75
Implications for Business 75
Attractiveness 75
Ethics and Regulations 78
Key Terms 80
Summary 80
Critical Thinking and Discussion Questions 81
Research Task 81
Closing Case: Delivering Electricity in Canada 82

CHAPTER THREE
The Cultural Environment 84
Opening Case: Guanxi—Ties that Bind 84
Introduction 86
What Is Culture? 88
Values and Norms 88
Culture, Society, and the Nation-State 89
The Determinants of Culture 90
Social Structure 91
Individuals and Groups 91
Social Stratification 94
Religious and Ethical Systems 96
Christianity 98
Islam 99
Hinduism 101
Buddhism 103
Confucianism 104
Language 105
Spoken Language 105
Unspoken Language 106
Education 107
Culture and the Workplace 109
Cultural Change 112
Implications for Business 115
Cross-Cultural Literacy 115
Culture and Competitive Advantage 115
Culture and Business Ethics 117
Key Terms 119
Summary 119
Critical Thinking and Discussion Questions 120
Research Task 120
Closing Case: Disney in France 120

CHAPTER FOUR
Ethics in International Business 122
Opening Case: Imagine No Metal 122
Introduction 125
Ethics, as Effected by the "Environments" 125
Ethical Issues in International Business 126
Ethics, as Effected by the "Technological Environments" 126
Employment Practices 127
Human Rights 127
Environmental Pollution 130
Corruption 131
Moral Obligations 134
Ethical Dilemmas 135
The Roots of Unethical Behaviour 136
Philosophical Approaches to Ethics 141
Straw Men 141
Utilitarian and Kantian Ethics 144
Rights Theories 145
Justice Theories 146
Ethical Decision Making 147
Hiring and Promotion 148
Organization Culture and Leadership 148
Decision-Making Processes 149
Ethics Officers 151
Moral Courage 152
Summary of Decision-Making Steps 152
Implications for Business 152
Benefits 153
Costs 153
Risks 153
Key Terms 154
Summary 154
Critical Thinking and Discussion Questions 155
Research Task 155
Closing Case: Etch-A-Sketch Ethics 156

Sustainability in Practice: B.C. Hydro's Aboriginal Relations Program 158

PART THREE Cross-Border Trade and Investment 160

CHAPTER FIVE
International Trade Theories 160
Opening Case: The Gains from Trade: Ghana and South Korea 160
Introduction 163
An Overview of Trade Theory 163
The Benefits of Trade 163
The Pattern of International Trade 164
Trade Theory and Government Policy 166
Mercantilism 166
Absolute Advantage 167
Comparative Advantage 169
The Gains from Trade 170
Qualifications and Assumptions 172
Trade and Simple Extensions of the Ricardian Model 172
Heckscher–Ohlin Theory 174
The Leontief Paradox 175
The Product Life-Cycle Theory 176
The New Trade Theory 176
The Aerospace Example 178
Implications 179
National Competitive Advantage: Porter's Diamond 181
Factor Endowments 182
Demand Conditions 182
Related and Supporting Industries 183
Firm Strategy, Structure, and Rivalry 183
Evaluating Porter's Theory 185

Implications for Business 185
Location Implications 186
First-Mover Implications 186
Policy Implications 187
Key Terms 187
Summary 188
Critical Thinking and Discussion Questions 188
Research Task 189
Closing Case: The Rise of the Indian Software Industry 189

CHAPTER SIX
The Political Economy of International Trade 192
Opening Case: The Great Banana Wars 192
Introduction 194
Instruments of Trade Policy 195
Tariffs 195
Subsidies 198
Import Quotas and Voluntary Export Restraints 199
Local Content Requirements 200
Administrative Policies 200
Antidumping Policies 202
The Case for Government Intervention 202
Political Arguments for Intervention 203
Economic Arguments for Intervention 206
The Revised Case for Free Trade 208
Retaliation and Trade War 208
Domestic Politics 209
Development of the World Trading System 209
From Smith to the Great Depression 210
1947–1979: GATT, Trade Liberalization, and Economic Growth 210
1980–1993: Disturbing Trends 211
The Uruguay Round and the World Trade Organization 212
The Future of the WTO: Unresolved Issues and the Doha Round 214
Implications for Business 217
Trade Barriers and Firm Strategy 217
Policy Implications 218
Key Terms 219
Summary 219
Critical Thinking and Discussion Questions 220
Research Task 220
Closing Case: When Do Government Tax Incentives Become Export Subsidies? 221

CHAPTER SEVEN
Foreign Direct Investment 224
Opening Case: Starbucks' Foreign Direct Investment 224
Introduction 226
Foreign Direct Investment in the World Economy 227
The Growth of FDI 227
The Form of FDI: Acquisitions versus Green-Field Investments 231
Canada's Case 231
The Theory of Foreign Direct Investment 234
Why Foreign Direct Investment? 234
The Pattern of Foreign Direct Investment 238
Political Ideology and Foreign Direct Investment 240
The Radical View 241
The Free Market View 241
Pragmatic Nationalism 242
Shifting Ideology 243
Costs and Benefits of FDI to the Nation-State 243
Host-Country Effects: Benefits 243
Host-Country Effects: Costs 245
Home-Country Effects: Benefits 247
Home-Country Effects: Costs 247
International Trade Theory and Foreign Direct Investment 248
Government Policy Instruments and FDI 248
Home-Country Policies 248
Host-Country Policies 249
International Institutions and the Liberalization of FDI 250
Implications for Business 251
The Theory of FDI 251
Government Policy 253
Key Terms 254
Summary 254
Critical Thinking and Discussion Questions 255
Research Task 255
Closing Case: Manulife Financial Buys John Hancock 255

CHAPTER EIGHT
Regional Economic Integration 258
Opening Case: Changes in the European Insurance Market 258
Introduction 260
Levels of Economic Integration 262
The Case for Regional Integration 264
The Economic Case for Integration 264
The Political Case for Integration 265
Impediments to Integration 265
The Case against Regional Integration 267
Regional Economic Integration in Europe 269
Evolution of the European Union 269
Political Structure of the European Union 270
The Single European Act 272
The Establishment of the Euro 273
Fortress Europe? 276
Regional Economic Integration in the Americas 277
The North American Free Trade Agreement 277
The Andean Pact 281
MERCOSUR 282
Central American Common Market and CARICOM 283
Free Trade Area of the Americas 283
Regional Economic Integration Elsewhere 283
Association of Southeast Asian Nations 284
Asia-Pacific Economic Cooperation 284

Regional Trade Blocs in Africa 285
Implications for Business 286
Opportunities 286
Threats 287
Key Terms 288
Summary 288
Critical Thinking and Discussion Questions 289
Research Task 289
Closing Case: Deutsche Bank's pan-European Retail Banking Strategy 290
Sustainability in Practice: Foreign Investment for Sustainable Community Development 292

PART FOUR Global Money System 294

CHAPTER NINE
The Foreign Exchange Market 294
Opening Case: Foreign Exchange Losses at JAL 294
Introduction 295
The Functions of the Foreign Exchange Market 297
Currency Conversion 297
The World and the Canadian Dollar 296
Insuring against Foreign Exchange Risk 299
The Nature of the Foreign Exchange Market 303
Economic Theories of Exchange Rate Determination 305
Prices and Exchange Rates 306
Interest Rates and Exchange Rates 311
Investor Psychology and Bandwagon Effects 312
Summary 313
Exchange Rate Forecasting 313
The Efficient Market School 313
The Inefficient Market School 313
Approaches to Forecasting 314
Currency Convertibility 316
Convertibility and Government Policy 316
Countertrade 317
Implications for Business 318
Key Terms 318
Summary 319
Critical Thinking and Discussion Questions 319
Research Task 320
Closing Case: Is Bigger Always Better? 320

CHAPTER TEN
The Global Monetary System 322
Opening Case: Turkey's 18th IMF Program 322
Introduction 324
The Gold Standard 326
Mechanics of the Gold Standard 327
Strength of the Gold Standard 327
The Period between the Wars: 1918–1939 327
The Bretton Woods System 329
The Role of the IMF 329
The Role of the World Bank 330
The Collapse of the Fixed Exchange Rate System 331
The Floating Exchange Rate Regime 332
The Jamaica Agreement 332
Exchange Rates since 1973 332
Fixed versus Floating Exchange Rates 334
The Case for Floating Exchange Rates 334
The Case for Fixed Exchange Rates 335
Who Is Right? 336
Exchange Rate Regimes in Practice 337
Pegged Exchange Rates 337
Currency Boards 338
Crisis Management by the IMF 339
Financial Crises in the Post-Bretton Woods Era 339
Third World Debt Crisis 343
Mexican Currency Crisis of 1995 344
Russian Ruble Crisis 344
The Asian Crisis 348
Evaluating the IMF's Policy Prescriptions 352
Implications for Business 355
Currency Management 355
Business Strategy 355
Corporate–Government Relations 356
Key Terms 356
Summary 357
Critical Thinking and Discussion Questions 357
Research Task 358
Closing Case: Caterpillar Inc. 358
Sustainability in Practice: A Tax on Currency Speculation to Finance Sustainable Development and Other Suggestions for a Sustainable Global Economy 360

PART FIVE Competing in a Global Marketplace 362

CHAPTER ELEVEN
Global Strategy 362
Opening Case: Global Strategy at MTV Networks 362
Introduction 365
Strategy and the Firm 365
Value Creation 366
The Firm as a Value Chain 367
The Role of Strategy 369
Profiting from Global Expansion 370
Location Economies 371
Experience Effects 372
Leveraging Core Competencies 375
Leveraging Subsidiary Skills 376
Pressures for Cost Reductions and Local Responsiveness 376
Pressures for Cost Reductions 377
Pressures for Local Responsiveness 378
Strategic Choices 380
International Strategy 381
Multidomestic Strategy 383
Global Strategy 384
Transnational Strategy 386
Summary 387
Strategic Alliances 388
The Advantages of Strategic Alliances 388
The Disadvantages of Strategic Alliances 389

Making Alliances Work 390
Partner Selection 390
Alliance Structure 391
Managing the Alliance 392
Implications for Business 393
International Business Requirements 393
Key Terms 394
Summary 394
Critical Thinking and Discussion Questions 395
Research Task 395
Closing Case: General Motors' Global Strategy Includes Canada 396

CHAPTER TWELVE
Entering Foreign Markets 398
Opening Case: ING Group 398
Introduction 400
Basic Entry Decisions 401
Which Foreign Markets? 401
Timing of Entry 402
Scale of Entry and Strategic Commitments 403
Summary 406
Entry Modes 407
Exporting 407
Turnkey Projects 408
Licensing 408
Franchising 410
Joint Ventures 412
Wholly Owned Subsidiaries 413
Selecting an Entry Mode 414
Core Competencies and Entry Mode 414
Pressures for Cost Reductions and Entry Mode 415
Establishing a Wholly Owned Subsidiary: Green-Field Venture or Acquisition? 416
Pros and Cons of Acquisitions 416
Pros and Cons of Green-Field Ventures 419
Green-Field Venture or Acquisition? 420
Implications for Business 421
Contractual Joint Ventures 421
Critical Success Factor Issues When Doing Business in China and Beyond 422
Key Terms 422
Summary 423
Critical Thinking and Discussion Questions 424
Research Task 424
Closing Case: Canadian Banks in the U.S.A. 424

CHAPTER THIRTEEN
Exporting, Importing, and Countertrade 426
Opening Case: Megahertz Communications 426
Introduction 428
The Promise and Pitfalls of Exporting 428
Improving Export Performance 430
An International Comparison 430
Utilizing Export Management Companies 430
Exporting Strategy 431
Export and Import Financing 434
Lack of Trust 434
Letter of Credit 436
Draft 437
Bill of Lading 437
A Typical International Trade Transaction 438
Export Information Sources 440
Countertrade 441
The Growth of Countertrade 441
Types of Countertrade 442
The Pros and Cons of Countertrade 443
Implications for Business 444
Key Terms 445
Summary 446
Critical Thinking and Discussion Questions 446
Research Task 447
Closing Case: CAE Takes on the World 447

CHAPTER FOURTEEN
Global Marketing and R&D 450
Opening Case: Procter & Gamble in Japan: From Marketing Failure to Success 450
Introduction 452
The Globalization of Markets and Brands 453
Market Segmentation 455
Product Attributes 457
Cultural Differences 457
Economic Development 458
Product and Technical Standards 459
Distribution Strategy 459
A Typical Distribution System 459
Differences between Countries 460
Choosing a Distribution Strategy 462
Communication Strategy 463
Barriers to International Communication 463
Push versus Pull Strategies 464
Global Advertising 481
Pricing Strategy 469
Price Discrimination 469
Strategic Pricing 472
Regulatory Influences on Prices 474
Configuring the Marketing Mix 474
New-Product Development 475
The Location of R&D 476
Integrating R&D, Marketing, and Production 477
Cross-Functional Teams 478
Implications for Business 479
Key Terms 480
Summary 481
Critical Thinking and Discussion Questions 481
Research Task 482
Closing Case: Celestica—On a Rebound? 482

CHAPTER FIFTEEN
Global Manufacturing and Materials Management 484
Opening Case: Managing Timberland's Global Supply Chain 484
Introduction 486
Strategy, Manufacturing, and Logistics 487
Where to Manufacture 489
Country Factors 489
Technological Factors 490
Product Factors 494
Locating Manufacturing Facilities 494
The Strategic Role of Foreign Factories 496
Make-or-Buy Decisions 498
The Advantages of Make 498
The Advantages of Buy 500
Trade-offs 502
Strategic Alliances with Suppliers 502
Implications for Business 503
Coordinating a Global Manufacturing System 503
The Power of Just-in-Time 504
The Role of Information Technology and the Internet 504
Key Terms 505
Summary 505
Critical Thinking and Discussion Questions 506
Research Task 506
Closing Case: Foreign Direct Investment at the Source of Raw Materials 507

CHAPTER SIXTEEN
Global Human Resource Management 508
Opening Case: Molex 508
Introduction 510
The Strategic Role of International HRM 511
Staffing Policy 512
Types of Staffing Policy 512
Expatriate Managers 515
Training and Management Development 519
Training for Expatriate Managers 519
Repatriation of Expatriates 520
Management Development and Strategy 521
Performance Appraisal 521
Performance Appraisal Problems 521
Guidelines for Performance Appraisal 523
Compensation 523
National Differences in Compensation 523
Expatriate Pay 525
Implications for Business 527
International Labour Relations 527
The Concerns of Organized Labour 528
The Strategy of Organized Labour 528
Approaches to Labour Relations 529
Key Terms 530
Summary 530
Critical Thinking and Discussion Questions 531
Research Task 531
Closing Case: How Coca-Cola Retains Employees 532
Sustainability in Practice: An Environmentally Sustainable Commitment to Business and Material Management 533

GLOSSARY 535

END NOTES 541

NAME/COMPANY INDEX 560

SUBJECT INDEX 564

PREFACE

THE *GLOBAL BUSINESS TODAY* APPROACH

Global Business Today is intended for the first international business course at either the undergraduate or the MBA level. Our goal in writing this Canadian edition has been to set a new standard for international business textbooks. We have attempted to write a book that (1) integrates the Canadian perspective on international business and Canada's place within the international business environment, (2) is comprehensive and up-to-date, (3) goes beyond an uncritical presentation and shallow explanation of the body of knowledge, (4) focuses on implications for business and makes important theories, issues, and practices accessible and interesting to Canadian students.

INTEGRATED COVERAGE OF THE CANADIAN PERSPECTIVE

Although this book is geared to the Canadian reader, this does not mean that all examples within are Canadian examples. The author has written about those realities and examples that best portray chapter topical themes, as well as writing about what the market wants, based upon market research in the academic field. The textbook pays particular attention to small- and medium-sized enterprises and their push onto the international business scene.

COMPREHENSIVE AND UP-TO-DATE COVERAGE

To be comprehensive, an international business textbook must clearly communicate:

- How and why the world's countries differ
- Why a comprehensive review of economics and politics of international trade and investment is necessary in understanding international trade
- How the functions and form of the global monetary system are tied into global trade
- How the strategies, objectives, and international structures of international business need to conform to certain guidelines set out by international organizations and other bodies
- The special roles of an international business's activities

This book pays close attention to these issues. Ultimately, a successful business is an informed business. It is our intention to cover, in an in-depth manner, the linkages between success and knowledge on the global business stage. As time moves forward, an increasing number of students will become international managers, and this book will better equip them with knowledge about the strategies, operations, and functions of small and large businesses alike.

The theories behind international trade help students to grasp the scope and execution of international business. Many books convey an adequate task of communicating long established theories (e.g., the theory of comparative advantage and Vernon's product life-cycle theory) but they ignore important newer works included in *Global Business Today*, such as:

- The new trade theory and strategic trade policy
- The work of Nobel prize-winning economist Amartya Sen on economic development
- Samuel Huntington's influential thesis on the "clash of civilizations"
- The new growth of economic development championed by Paul Romer and Gene Grossman
- Recent empirical work by Jeffrey Sachs and others on the relationship between international trade and economic growth
- Michael Porter's theory of the competitive advantage of nations

- Robert Reich's work on national competitive advantage
- The work of Douglass North and others on national institutional structures and the protection of property rights
- The market imperfections approach to foreign direct investment that has grown out of Ronald Coase and Oliver Williamson's work on transaction cost economics
- Bartlett and Ghoshal's research on the transnational corporation
- The writings of C.K. Prahalad and Gary Hamel on core competencies, global competition, and global strategic alliances

In addition to cutting-edge theory and the exponentially quickening pace of the international business environment, every effort has been made to ensure that this book is as current as possible when it goes to press. This Canadian edition contains current data from the World Trade Organization, The Organization for Economic Cooperation and Development (OECD), the United Nations Commission on Trade and Development (UNCTAD), Statistics Canada, and Export Development Canada, among others. This book provides readers with a fresh insight into factors influencing Canada and other countries in the world of international trade, Canadian businesses' forays into world markets, and reactions to ongoing economic structural readjustments in 2006 and beyond. For example:

- Chapter 1, "Globalization," looks at the changing global economy and uses Bombardier and Embraer as examples of Canadian companies competing globally and locally.
- The Management Focus, "Working in China," in Chapter 3, "The Cultural Environment," presents some cultural guidelines from a Canadian business student while working and travelling in China.
- Chapter 6, "The Political Economy of International Trade," provides an example of how a Canadian company has brought a global perspective to the fishing industry.
- In Chapter 8, "Regional Economic Integration," we can see that Canadian companies are breaking through the challenges brought forth by the NAFTA agreement and are achieving excellence in exporting.
- In Chapter 10, "The Global Monetary System," an example is given to show how currency exchange rates, among other factors, have bolstered the Canadian film industry.
- Chapter 12, "Entering Foreign Markets," offers insight into reactions in other countries to privatization issues, as described in the Country Focus, "What Privatization Means to the Residents of Bolivia."
- Chapter 13, "Exporting, Importing, and Countertrade" provides hands-on perspectives into the "logistics" of international trade, e.g., letters of credit, along with other areas where export advice can be received. One such world-class export training program is offered through the Forum for International Trade Training (FITT) in Ottawa, where learning modules in eight fields of international trade are taught at higher learning institutes across Canada.
- Chapter 14, "Global Marketing and R&D," highlights the current stalemate in the Canadian–U.S. softwood lumber negotiations in the Country Focus, "Lumberjacks or Robber Barons."

BEYOND UNCRITICAL PRESENTATION AND SHALLOW EXPLANATION

Many issues in international business are complex and thus necessitate considerations of pros and cons. To demonstrate this to students, we have adopted a critical approach that presents the arguments for and against economic theories, government policies, business strategies, organizational structures, and so on.

Related to this, we have attempted to explain the complexities of the many theories and phenomena unique to international business so the student might fully comprehend the statements of a theory or the reasons a phenomenon is the way it is. These theories and phenomena typically are explained in more depth in *Global Business Today* than they are in competing textbooks.

FOCUS ON BUSINESS IMPLICATIONS AND ACCESSIBLE PRESENTATION

The Canadian edition of *Global Business Today* offers many opportunities for students to engage with and apply the material to their lives and their future careers. The features listed below are explained in greater detail in the Learning Features section beginning on page xviii.

- NEW to the Canadian edition, each chapter concludes with an **Implications for Business** section that explains the managerial implications of the chapter material. This feature helps business students to understand the linkage between practice and theory.
- Each chapter begins with an **Opening Case** and concludes with a **Closing Case** that illustrates the

relevance of chapter material for the practice of international business. Ten Closing Cases are new to the Canadian edition. The opening case in Chapter 4, "Imagine No Metal," looks at mining and how "big business" in northern Ontario is also an important and growing sector worldwide. Chapter 12 opens with the ING Group case and its rapid expansion of ING Direct Canada to serve over one million clients. The closing case to Chapter 2, "Delivering Electricity in Canada," looks at the challenges of ensuring energy supplies through the electrical grid in Canada. The case accentuates the regulatory aspects of companies delivering electricity within Canada, in the context of Canada being the fifth largest electricity producer in the world.

- Each chapter also contains two types of focus boxes. **Management Focus** boxes, like the cases, illustrate the relevance of the chapter material for the practice of international business; eleven are new to the Canadian edition. Examples include: "Bringing Gambling to Your Home" in Chapter 2, "Four Seasons Hotels and Resorts" in Chapter 7, "NAFTA–Friend or Foe of Canadian Business" in Chapter 8, "Barrick Gold" in Chapter 9, and "The 'Reel' Threat to the Canadian Film Industry" in Chapter 10. **Country Focus** boxes provide background on the political, economic, social, or cultural aspects of countries grappling with an international business issue. For example, "40 Years of Corruption in Nigeria" in Chapter 2, "Foreign Direct Investment in China" in Chapter 7, "Team Canada, A Vital Part of the Canadian Government's Global Business Strategy" in Chapter 11, and "Countries Want to Hold on to Their Jobs" in Chapter 16. Seven Country Focus boxes are new to the Canadian edition.
- **Another Perspective** sidebars help students to think critically about adjacent text material.
- **NEW Sustainability in Practice Part-Ending Cases** help students to understand how businesses are engaging in the solutions to sustainable development challenges.
- **NEW GlobalEdge™ Research Tasks** allow students to practise using real business data.
- **"Could You Do This?" Entrepreneurial Peer Profiles** featuring real students' experiences with starting their own global businesses are available at the text's Online Learning Centre Web site at www.mcgrawhill.ca/college/hill.

THE STRUCTURE OF *GLOBAL BUSINESS TODAY*, CANADIAN EDITION

Global Business Today, Canadian Edition, offers a tight, integrated flow of topics from chapter to chapter.

Part One: Globalization

Chapter 1 provides an overview of the key issues to be addressed and explains the plan of the book.

Part Two: Country Differences

Chapters 2, 3, and 4 focus on national differences in political economy and culture and the implications of these differences for ethical decision making. Most international business textbooks place this material later, but we believe it is vital to discuss national differences first. After all, many of the central issues in international trade and investment, the global monetary system, international business strategy and structure, and international business operations arise out of national differences in political economy and culture. To understand these issues, students must first appreciate the differences in countries and cultures.

Part Three: Cross-Border Trade and Investment

Chapters 5 through 8 investigate the political economy of international trade and investment, fostering understanding of the trade and investment environment in which international business occurs.

Part Four: Global Money System

Chapters 9 and 10 detail the global monetary system, while detailing the monetary framework in which international business transactions are carried out.

Part Five: Competing in a Global Marketplace

Chapters 11 through 16 move away from the macro environment of the international business realities into the workings of companies within this framework. How do companies adapt their strategies in order to compete beyond their own borders? How does manufacturing on a global scale proceed? These chapters explain how firms can perform their key functions—manufacturing, marketing, R&D, and human resource management—to compete and succeed in the international business environment.

WHAT'S NEW IN THE CANADIAN EDITION?

As stated above, the Canadian edition integrates the Canadian perspective with regard to current events, statistics, and examples in addition to providing up-to-date global examples and statistics.

This book attempts to not only explain theoretical aspects of international trade, but more importantly, attempts to connect the practical applications involving international trade, into a framework of helpful understanding for those exporters, both new and experienced in this field.

In addition to offering fully integrated Canadian content, the Canadian edition offers three significant changes to meet student and instructor needs:

- NEW Chapter 4, "Ethics in International Business," adapted by Tim Richardson, was added in response to feedback for more expansive coverage of the important role that ethics plays. Ethical dilemmas arise frequently in international business because of the many cultural differences among countries. This chapter discusses the challenges Canadian and international companies face when dealing with human rights issues, environmental pollution, and corruption.
- At the end of every part, we have added a NEW feature called "Sustainability in Practice," originally compiled for the U.S. edition by Debra Rowe, professor or Environmental Systems and Behavioral Sciences at Oakland Community College. Dr. Rowe is also the Senior Fellow of University Leaders for a Sustainable Future. By offering this new feature on business and sustainable development, global business educators have a unique opportunity to help students understand how businesses are engaging in the solutions to sustainable development challenges.
- This edition also welcomes the addition of new GlobalEdge™ Research Tasks. By using the text and the GlobalEdge Web site, globaledge.msu.edu, students solve realistic international business problems related to each chapter. These exercises expose students to the types of tools and data sources international managers use to make informed business decisions.

CHAPTER-BY-CHAPTER CHANGES

Chapter 1: Globalization. All of the statistics have been updated to the most recent available at the time of this book going to production. This chapter includes an introductory concept of global manufacturing as seen from a Canadian perspective, and provides current examples of Canadian companies succeeding at doing business abroad. The emergence of global institutions is detailed along with the latest round of World Trade Organization talks (WTO) aimed at further liberalizing global trade. Likewise, in Canada, the role of the Internet sheds an insight into the broader picture of how the Internet has changed the way people and enterprises communicate in Canada and beyond.

Also, the latest outcry by some high profile pro-Canada crusaders, such as Maude Barlow, in the sensitive area of job losses in Canada due to outsourcing to companies in developing countries, such as India and Mexico, is detailed.

Chapter 2: Country Differences in Political Economy. The section on economic development includes a review of the work of Nobel prize-winning economist Amartya Sen. Sen has argued that development should be assessed less by material output measures such as GNP per capita and more by the capabilities and opportunities that people enjoy. The discussion of differences in legal systems provides insight into the linkage between corruption and negative economics within a country. Intellectual property is discussed in the framework of inroads being made into allowing the sale of cheaper generic versions of patented medicines–including a powerful new drug for AIDS, without permission from the patent owner.

Chapter 3: The Cultural Environment. The Implications for Business section covers a broad cross-section ranging from cross-cultural literacy to culture and competitive advantage to culture and business ethics. These themes pose problems for Canadians doing business abroad. In many cases, countries now have legal frameworks in place to regulate and interpret what constitutes proper ethics in doing business, internationally. Bill S- 21, passed into law in the late 1990s, lays out ethical business standards to be adhered to by Canadian businesspeople when dealing abroad. Some areas of contravention allow for criminal prosecutions of those Canadian individuals and/or corporations in breech of this law. Other areas of cultural differences are described within this chapter. Various religions and their significance within the world are discussed.

Chapter 4: Ethics in International Business. New Chapter 4 features Canadian examples such as the Talisman company in Sudan, SARS in Toronto, Ivanhoe Mines in Myanmar, and the Gomery Inquiry, while maintaining a global focus.

Chapter 5: International Trade Theories. Over the past few years, numerous empirical studies have been published that look at the relationship between a country's "openness" to international trade and its economic growth. This work is discussed in this chapter. The work gives empirical support to the theory of comparative advantage.

Chapter 6: The Political Economy of International Trade. The contentious bi-lateral trade issues that have periodically soured Canadian trade relations with the United States over the past couple of decades are dealt with in the context of the World Trade Organization and the North American Free Trade Agreement.

Chapter 7: Foreign Direct Investment. Both up-to-date international Foreign Direct Investment (FDI) Flows and FDI figures show the importance of FDI, in its different forms, including mergers and acquisitions, in the economies of Canada and other countries, around the world.

Chapter 8: Regional Economic Integration. On May 1, 2004, 10 new member states joined the European Union. This chapter covers the post-World War II levels of economic integration within Europe, leading to the European Union and its monetary union, while covering lesser initiatives, including the

Free Trade Agreement, now NAFTA, including Mexico, Canada, and the United States. Other efforts of regional economic integration are also discussed and these include customs unions in South America such as Mercosur and the Andean Pact countries, along with similar undertakings in Asia (Association of Southeast Asian Nations–ASEAN and the Asia Pacific Economic Cooperation–APEC) and Africa.

Chapter 9: The Foreign Exchange Market. Even if the Canadian dollar does not figure onto the stage of major international currencies, it still plays a vital role in Canada's export industries. Also, economic theories of Exchange Rate Determination are explained that are all vital to businesspeople conducting business abroad.

Chapter 10: The Global Monetary System. One of the more interesting phases of the development and growth of the Canadian economy came during the period of time in which Canada was under the gold standard from 1854–1914 and 1914–1926. Internationally, many policies and institutions have influenced and shaped the value of currencies.

Chapter 11: Global Strategy. Multinational corporations have long ago recognized the importance of leveraging skills, strategic alliances, and competencies in their foreign locations for improved business practices at home and abroad. How Canadian companies apply their know-how in foreign situations is discussed in several sections within this chapter, including the Canadian Managers Abroad component on "Team Canada."

Chapter 12: Entering Foreign Markets. The ways through which companies enter foreign markets is covered through a look at the pros and cons of Green-Field investments and other forms of alternative strategies for entering foreign markets. The Management Focus features Globalive, Canada's fastest growing company, according to the June 2004 issue of *Profit Magazine*.

Chapter 13: Exporting, Importing, and Countertrade. Export assistance to Canadian companies provides a detailed look at the institutional means and mechanisms through which many Canadian companies engage in export, for example, Export Development Canada and the Canadian Commercial Corporation.

Chapter 14: Global Marketing and R&D. Global marketing and R&D are what makes or breaks a company. The Management Focus "The Jean Coutu Group," depicts one successful Canadian company's foray into markets beyond our borders. Distribution and communication strategies are also discussed within this chapter.

Chapter 15: Global Manufacturing and Materials Management. Web-based IT systems now play a vital role in materials management around the world. Global tracking systems enable goods to be located within a 45-metre (50-yard) radius, as they travel to their destination. Cashier entries in the local supermarket are also tied into inventory data signaling when certain goods should be replenished by the manufacturer.

Chapter 16: Global Human Resource Management. Employment legislation can have both positive and negative impacts for foreign businesses operating abroad and it impinges upon each company to be aware of rules and guidelines, accordingly. This chapter discusses the complete range of factors affecting human resource management in other countries.

SUPERIOR SERVICE

Your **Integrated Learning Sales Specialist** is a McGraw-Hill Ryerson representative who has the experience, product knowledge, training, and support to help you assess and integrate any of the below-noted products, technology, and services into your course for optimum teaching and learning performance. Whether it's using our test bank software, helping your students improve their grades, or putting your entire course online, your *i*Learning Sales Specialist is there to help you do it. Contact your local *i*Learning Sales Specialist today to learn how to maximize all of McGraw-Hill Ryerson's resources!

*i*Learning Services Program

McGraw-Hill Ryerson offers a unique *i*Services package designed for Canadian faculty. Our mission is to equip providers of higher education with superior tools and resources required for excellence in teaching. For additional information visit http://www.mcgrawhill.ca/highereducation/iservices.

INSTRUCTOR'S SUPPLEMENTS

Instructor's Online Learning Centre (OLC)

The OLC at www.mcgrawhill.ca/college/hill includes a password-protected Web site for instructors. The site offers downloadable supplements, including an Instructor's Manual and Microsoft® PowerPoint® slides.

Instructor's CD-ROM contains the Instructor's Manual, Test Bank in Rich Text Format, Computerized Test Bank, and Microsoft® PowerPoint® slides:

Instructor's Manual The Instructor's Manual contains lecture notes and teaching suggestions for each chapter.

Test Bank in Rich Text Format The test bank contains approximately 100 questions per chapter.

Computerized Test Bank. This flexible and easy-to-use electronic testing program allows instructors to create tests from book-specific items. It accommodates a wide range of question types and instructors may add their own questions. Multiple versions of the test can be created and printed.

Microsoft® PowerPoint® Slides These presentations offer approximately 15 to 20 slides per chapter.

Video Collection

This edition includes a video collection, consisting of news footage and original business documentaries for each chapter.

Course Management

Visit www.mhhe.com/pageout to create a Web page for your course using our resources. PageOut is the McGraw-Hill Ryerson Web site development centre. This Web page-generation software is free to adopters and is designed to help faculty create an online course, complete with assignments, quizzes, links to relevant Web sites, and more—all in a matter of minutes.

In addition, content cartridges are available for the course management systems **WebCT and Blackboard**. These platforms provide instructors with user-friendly, flexible teaching tools. Please contact your local McGraw-Hill Ryerson *i*Learning Sales Specialist for details.

STUDENT SUPPLEMENTS

Student Online Learning Centre The OLC at www.mcgrawhill.ca/college/hill includes learning and study tools such as quizzes, a searchable glossary, streaming video, *Globe and Mail* headlines, interactive exercises, web links, and more!

ACKNOWLEDGEMENTS

Numerous people deserve recognition for their assistance in preparing this book.

First and foremost, I would like to thank my parents, Dorothy and Russell McKaig, for always being my greatest supporters. Their zest for life and endless energy has proven to me that age is a state of mind. Many thanks also to my sister, Janet McKaig and brother Woody McKaig for their support and advice.

I couldn't have been more fortunate to have my Research Directors, Susanna Boehm and Jim Helik. They were able to handle my endless requests for massive amounts of required research information, and synthesizing it to meet my demanding time lines and exceed my expectations in the quality of their input. They knew *exactly* what I wanted and made this massive mission of creating a Canadian focused textbook on global business a "Mission Possible." Their dedication, "can-do" attitude, patience, intelligence, and sense of humour is humbling to me and I can only say that I have found the best researchers possible.

I would like to thank Charles W.L. Hill, for creating an excellent textbook and strong base from which this Canadian edition was made possible.

I felt that it was important to capture the spirit of young entrepreneurs, where possible, with either Canadian or those foreign students studying in Canada. In several instances, they accepted my invitation to contribute their real story to the book in the "Entrepreneurial Peer Profiles" located on the Online Learning Centre.

Thank you to Stephen Gill, Robert Duxter, and my Research Director, Jim Helik. Trevor Buss also epitomizes the spirit of entrepreneurship. As a young adult student, his business travels to China formed the basis for his insightful article "Doing Business in China" in the Management Focus box in Chapter 3. Anthony Lacavera, owner of Globalive Communications, which was named as Canada's fastest growing company in the June 2004 issue of *Profit Magazine*, has duplicated his stellar Canadian successes on the international stage. His greatly appreciated assistance, along with that of other Globalive individuals who helped in the interview process—Amanda Alvaro, Leslie Mitchell, and Tricia Soltys— was crucial in helping me piece together the rapid fire successes of this new company.

Joe Janthur, president of DEPAG, and his son, Charles, vice-president of DEPAG and teaching colleague, have over the years provided me with invaluable support, guidance, and assistance that was once again generously extended to me for book-related enquiries. Other mentors through the years and to whom I owe a deep debt of gratitude are my wonderful cousin, Susan Duxter, for her great moral support and Elaine Strang for her incisive perspective. Colleagues who have endlessly stood by me, such as Kirk Bailey, Program Director for the School of Business Management at Ryerson University; University of Guelph colleagues, Dr. Paulette Padanyi, Chair–Marketing and Consumer Studies, Dr. Marion Joppe, Director, School of Hospitality and Tourism Management, and Dr. John Pratschke, Jean Monnet Chair in European Integration Studies. All were instrumental in helping me achieve this milestone in my evolving personal, academic, and business goals. Jack Speake, Dr. John Vardalas, Robert Warren, Jaime Rozinsky, Sallie Storey, Dr. Viggo von Wietersheim, and Claudia Lang have encouraged me to go that extra mile to reach excellence. Also, I would like to thank Hazel Cake for her lifelong belief in me and the wonderful adventurous times we have when together. Dr. Ulricke Dambmann, Munich-based author of many books, has provided me with deep moral support over the decades. Finally, I would like to thank Dr. Ernest Moser, Dean of the College of Business & Public Affairs at the University of Tennessee and his team of amazing academics who made my brief stay, as Executive in Residence, such a rewarding experience.

Market feedback indicated that more expansive coverage of the important role that ethics plays in the international business arena was necessary. We called upon Tim Richardson, who teaches at Seneca College of Applied Arts and Technology and the University of Toronto, Department of Management, www.witiger.com. Tim enthusiastically and ably responded to this request, providing a chapter rich in Canadian content and current research. We thank him for his invaluable contribution to this text.

As for my Developmental Editor, Sarah Dann, her clarity and project leadership skills kept me on the straight and narrow as she worked with me through thick and thin, always in the best of spirits, and fostering enthusiasm for this daunting task.

The team at McGraw-Hill Ryerson was also superb:

- Nicole Lukach, Publisher
- Kim Brewster, Sponsoring Editor
- Jennifer DiDomenico, Managing Editor, Development
- Kelly Dickson, Manager, Editorial Services
- Erin Moore, Copy Editor

Finally, I extend sincere thanks to the reviewers of the Canadian edition, who provided insightful feedback that helped shape this book:

Preet S. Aulakh, *York University, Schulich School of Business*
Neil Beattie, *Sheridan College, Davis Campus*
Shengliang Deng, *Brock University*
Dorothee Feils, *University of Alberta, School of Business*
Keith Fleming, *University of Western Ontario*
Diane Gauvin, *Dawson College* and *McGill University*
Laurie Grant, *British Columbia Institute of Technology*
Algis Juzukonis, *Seneca College of Applied Arts and Technology*
Henry Klaise, *Durham College*
Xiaohua Lin, *University of Windsor, Odette School of Business*
Douglas Peterson, *Grant MacEwan College* and *University of Alberta*
J. Barrie Reid, *Nova Scotia Community College*
Tim G. Richardson, *Seneca College* and *University of Toronto*
Linda Stockton, *McMaster University*
Surinder K. Suri, *University of Toronto*
Leslie Wilder, *Red River College*

Thomas McKaig

LEARNING FEATURES

Global Business Today, Canadian Edition, has a rich selection of learning features that highlight companies' ups and downs in the international business arena, stimulate learning and understanding, and challenge students to respond.

Learning Objectives

Learning Objectives tell students what they will know after completing the chapter.

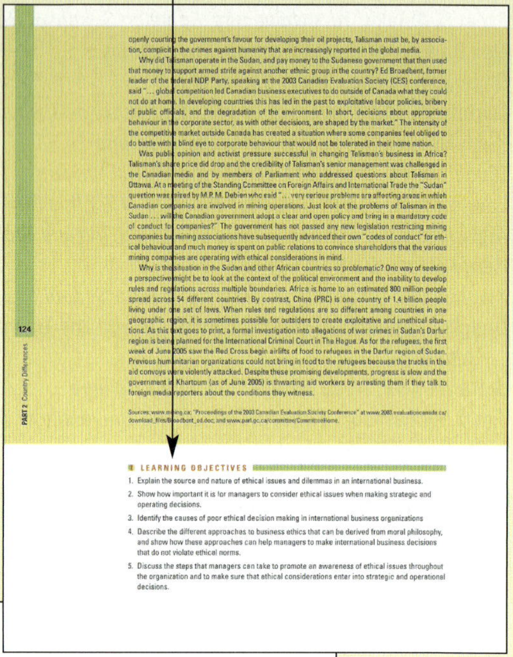

Opening Case

Each chapter begins with an engaging opening case that sets the stage for the chapter. These brief case studies introduce students to critical issues and often challenge their preconceptions. For actual countries/organizations providing rich, introductory examples, look to each chapter's opening case.

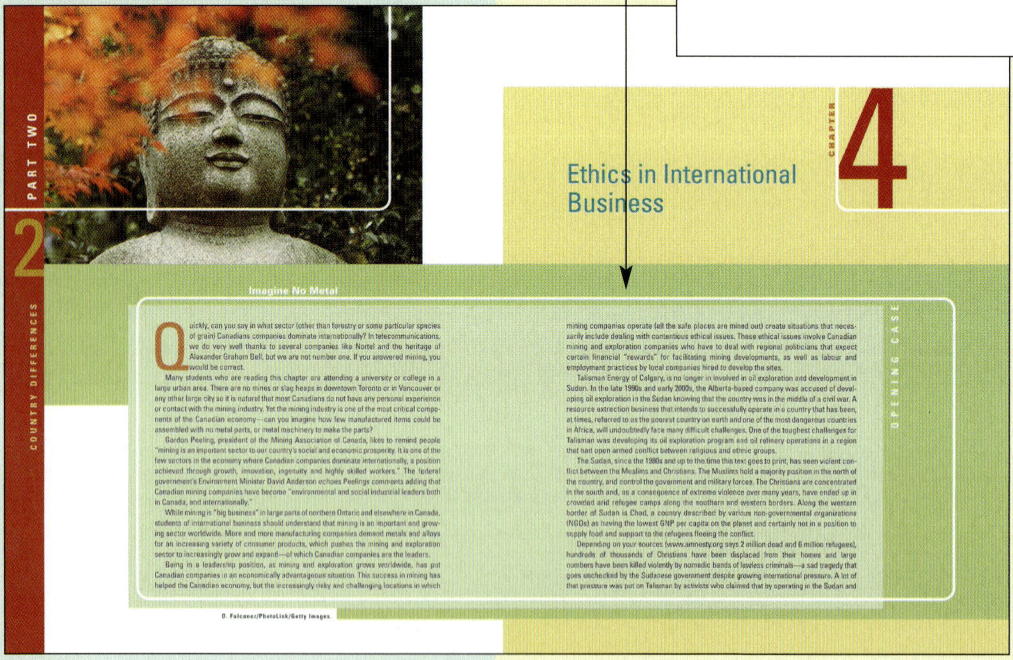

ANOTHER PERSPECTIVE

Maple Leaf Life Savers?

In 2002, Life Savers, a Michigan company, announced it was moving production from Michigan to Canada. Why would such a move make business sense, you might wonder. Not because of lower labour costs, lower tax rates, or colder winters.

Here's why Life Savers moved. The United States protects sugar along with other agricultural products. The domestic sugar price is considerably higher than the world market price. Sugar is the main ingredient of Life Savers, and the company will be able to purchase sugar at a much lower world market price in Canada.

Another Perspective

With three examples per chapter, Another Perspective boxes provide students with an alternate way of thinking about important global issues presented in the text. These not only hone students' critical thinking skills but also give a deeper understanding of chapter topics.

Country Focus

Country Focus boxes provide real-world examples of how different countries grapple with political, economic, social, or cultural issues. Seven are **new** to the Canadian Edition.

COUNTRY FOCUS

LUMBERJACKS OR ROBBER BARONS

Canada has always been an exporter of resources and there is no resource issue to date that has created so many trade irritants as has the Canada–U.S. softwood lumber dispute. The Canadian lumber industry annually exports over $10 billion per year to feed the hungry U.S. housing industry. According to some sources, the Canadian lumber industry accounts for approximately one third of the U.S. demand. And more specifically, it is softwood lumber, used in the home construction industry, which has become a headline grabber on both sides of the border. Canadian lumber companies make Canada the world's second largest producer of plywood standing at 2002 figures of 2475 cubic metres far behind the U.S. production of 15 494 cubic metres, yet ahead of Russian production, which stands at 1808 million cubic metres.

Historically speaking, Canada's logging companies in most provinces cut trees from Crown leased land. In the Maritimes, however, lumber is cut from private lands. When viewed from south of the border, this practice is seen as a form of Canadian government subsidy. The American government contests this "Canadian state intervention" as dumping, or selling the product cheaper in the U.S. than in Canada, giving rise to unfair competitive advantage of Canadian softwood lumber products being sold within the U.S. market to the detriment of American lumber companies. The first step in formalizing this complaint dates back to the early 1980s when the Canadian lumber industry (not the government, which has since become involved) vigorously defended itself against the heavy-hitting U.S. lumber industry lobby group. The initial ruling on this was that the Canadian lumber industry did not breech standard business practices, and thus, the Americans lost the battle to impose countervailing (antidumping) penalties on the Canadian lumber industry.

Since then, this has become more of a government issue that has reached fever pitch from the halls of Parliament Hill to the U.S. Congress and beyond. The Canadian Lumber Trade Alliance, which is the primary association for the Canadian lumber industry, voices its trade protests to the Canadian government, which is met with counter complaints from the U.S. Coalition for Fair Lumber Imports (a voice to over 50 percent of the U.S. lumber industry) through the American government. NAFTA and the WTO panels (the NAFTA panel includes three Americans and two Canadians) have ruled that although much of Canada's lumber industry is subsidized, the 18 to 27 percent American punitive duties imposed on Canadian lumber imports are too high. In spite of NAFTA and WTO rulings that the imposition of the American countervailing duty on Canadian softwood lumber is illegal, the United States won't let go and even the United States International Trade Commission (ITC) insists that Canadian imports threaten the U.S. lumber industry.

The 1996–2001 Bilateral Softwood Lumber Agreement between Canada and the United States appeared to have placated the aggressive U.S. lumber groups. During the course of this agreement, which expired on March 31, 2001, Canadian softwood lumber exporters were largely assured market access to the U.S., free of U.S. trade action during the five-year accord. In a sense, Canada agreed to a kind of voluntary export restraint, free of U.S. customs duties, as long as Canadian lumber exports from Crown lands and thus, primarily from British Columbia, Alberta, Ontario, and Quebec, did not exceed 14.7 billion board feet per year. Above that limit, the onus was on the Government of Canada to collect fees that varied according to the 1996–2001 Softwood Lumber Agreement. The agreement seemed to bring about commercial peace and stability to the thorny issue of Canadian softwood lumber exports.

However, the problems flared up again upon expiry of this agreement. Somewhere in the twilight zone of the post 1996–2001 U.S.–Canada bilateral lumber agreement, U.S. Customs began to take a public stand on the issue by posting its concerns on electronic bulletin boards and the U.S. even required cash deposits on lumber imported from Canada that to date amount to $4.1 billion.

With 2003 and more recent NAFTA and WTO rulings clearly in Canada's favour, the increasingly frustrated Canadian government has requested permission from the WTO to slap the equivalent amount of duties collected ($4.1 billion) on American goods imported into Canada, if its first option of diplomatic negotiations fails. Although the current United States administration prides itself on broadening and deepening free trade ties and principles within the Americas, it tends to have developed a version of acute selective vision in justifying its anti-free trade stance within the lumber-specific dispute and subsequent NAFTA rulings against it.

465

MANAGEMENT FOCUS

THE "REEL" THREAT TO THE CANADIAN FILM INDUSTRY

As avid moviegoers, many Canadians might not realize the magnitude of the film business, both foreign and domestic, operating within Canada. Movie trailers and film lights are a common sight in Canada's major cities to small towns. Many major American television series and movies, such as the *X-Files*, have been filmed in Canada. However, this industry has been put at risk with the recent rise of the Canadian dollar, which makes filming in Canada, compared to the United States, far less attractive than it has been.

In 2002 and 2003, the Canadian film industry grew by 4 percent for a total volume of nearly $5 billion in foreign location production, and brought in an excess of $4 billion to Canadian coffers. The cultural industry makes up almost 3 percent of GDP, employing over 500 000 Canadians. Nearly one quarter of all Hollywood films are now shot in Canada, with many Canadians showing front stage in this lucrative industry—James Cameron, Ivan Reitman, and Norman Jewison, with the latter having founded the Canadian Film Centre. Canadians also make movies outside the Hollywood system including such renowned directors as Rock Demers, Deepa Mehta, David Cronenberg, Denys Arcand, and Atom Egoyan.

Provincial and federal film tax credits do their share of the work in keeping the business of filming in Canada. Over the years, governments in Canada have come to power on pledges to protect and to bolster the Canadian film and cultural industries. The Liberal's now famous "1993 handbook" and accompanying pledge to strengthen and protect the Canadian cultural industries against incursions by the American cultural juggernaut—claimed by some to be all talk and no action—is a well-known moniker of Liberal party cultural heritage policy. Sheila Copps, the former Minister of Canadian Heritage, became associated with shining the beacon on Canadian culture, even if some pro-Canada culture interests, such as the CBC, seemed to weaken during her time in power.

The Canadian government's "intervention" or intention to intervene in the business of Canadian culture has met with culture shock in American media circles, where culture is not viewed as a national heritage, but as a profit-making industry. Labour unrest in the Hollywood film industry has frequently been a byproduct of the actors union, up in arms about lost jobs to cheaper and perhaps, friendlier climes, particularly in the great White North. Ed Asner, as head of the Screen Actors Guild and union activist, has spoken out over the decades about the outflow of Hollywood movie productions to Canada.

The latest to join this chorus is Arnold Schwarzenegger, Governor of California, who has threatened the Hollywood movie industry with punitive measures for those companies filming in Canada, and elsewhere. It is clear that government intervention or lack thereof can play a determining role in the future of this lucrative Canadian industry. To those American studios filming in Canada, there are many attractive features built into the equation. One of the major factors is the currency question. The Canadian dollar has been rising relative to the U.S. dollar since early 2004, making filming in Canada far more expensive than it used to be. Canadian concerns for a higher dollar intermittently send shivers through the Canadian film industry as the thought of losing productions to a more expensive Canadian dollar, subconsciously resonate.

The fact that the Canadian film industry and the government have been able to make huge gains in spite of the American cultural giants over the past century lends a degree of expectation about the continuation of highly successful Canadian cultural industries. However, no industry is immune to competitive threats. A strong Canadian dollar, and a weak U.S. dollar, may be enough to reverse the trend of the past several decades.

Sources: CBC at www.cbc.ca/arts/stories/arnold091003; ITC at www.dfait-maeci.gc.ca_new-delhi_film-en.asp and www.dfait-maeci.gc.ca/tna-nac/stories94-en.asp#max; OANDA at www.oanda.com/convert/classic.

345

Management Focus

Management Focus boxes illustrate the relevance of chapter concepts for the practice of international business. Eleven are **new** to the Canadian Edition.

explore how countries differ from each other with regard to their political, economic, legal, and cultural institutions. Chapter 4 examines the role of ethics in international business. Chapters 5 to 8 look at the international trade and investment environment within which international businesses must operate. Chapters 9 and 10 review the international monetary system. These chapters focus on the nature of the foreign exchange market and the emerging global monetary system. Chapters 11 and 12 explore the strategy of international businesses. Chapters 13 to 16 look at the management of various functional operations within an international business, including production, marketing, and human relations. By the time you complete this book, you should have a good grasp of the issues that managers working within international business have to grapple with on a daily basis, and you should be familiar with the range of strategies and operating policies available to compete more effectively in today's rapidly emerging global economy.

IMPLICATIONS FOR BUSINESS

As we will see throughout this book, the international business arena is becoming an increasingly open environment for goods and services to be bought and sold. For example, Canadian businesses can no longer operate in an insular manner, according to their own rules and regulations. Business managers need to see the world of strengths, weaknesses, opportunities, and threats in a global sense. What once were viable business survival and expansion strategies no longer work. Businesses are now forced to address the broader scope of commercial realities brought forth over the years through the General Agreement on Trade and Tariffs, and evolved through the World Trade Organization. Other synchronous tools of the globalization wave, as cited at the beginning of this chapter, are the United Nations, the World Bank, and others. Foreign direct investment, a crucial strategy in the globalization process, will be discussed in later chapters.

As of June 2004, the World Trade Organization (WTO) consisted of 148 members. The WTO is the host to new negotiations, under the "Doha Development Agenda" launched in 2001. In some circumstances, WTO rules support maintaining trade barriers, for example, to protect consumers or prevent the spread of disease. Membership requires that ground rules for international commerce, including contracts, be followed thus binding governments to keep their trade policies within agreed limits.

Since 1948, the General Agreement on Tariffs and Trade (GATT) had provided the rules for the system. Over the years, GATT evolved through several rounds of negotiations. The last and largest GATT round was the Uruguay Round, which lasted from 1986 to 1994 and led to the WTO's creation. Whereas GATT had mainly dealt with trade in goods, the WTO and its agreements now cover trade in services, and in traded inventions, creations, and intellectual property.[65]

Membership comes with responsibilities, but also with benefits. Adhering to the World Trade Organization, initiatives on a plethora of trade-related issues are paramount to a country's accession to inclusion into the "WTO club." Poorer countries might benefit from easier access to financing through international funding agencies. In South America, commercial and customs unions such as Mercosur and the Andean Pact are opening new doors for South American companies within these intra-markets. The Caribbean nations, through CARICOM, are benefiting through the same less restrictive commercial markets.

Other similar types of initiatives include: ASEAN, Association of Southeast Nations; AU, African Union; CAFTA, Central American Free Trade Agreement; CARICOM, Caribbean Community; CEMAC, Communauté Economique et Monétaire de l'Afrique Centrale; EAC, East African Community; EU, External Trade; GCC, Gulf Co-operation Council; JSEPA, Japan/Singapore Economic Partnership Agreement; MERCOSUR, Mercado Comun del Sur; and NAFTA, North American Free Trade Agreement.[66]

The European Union in 2005 will be very close to the WTO's concept of how free trade areas should appear. Mercosur, the Andean Pact, and other existing commercial unions, will cease to exist due to a growing NAFTA.

33

CHAPTER 1 Globalization

Implications for Business

At the end of every chapter, this section spotlights the managerial implications of the chapter material.

Key Terms and Summary

These resources help students review key concepts.

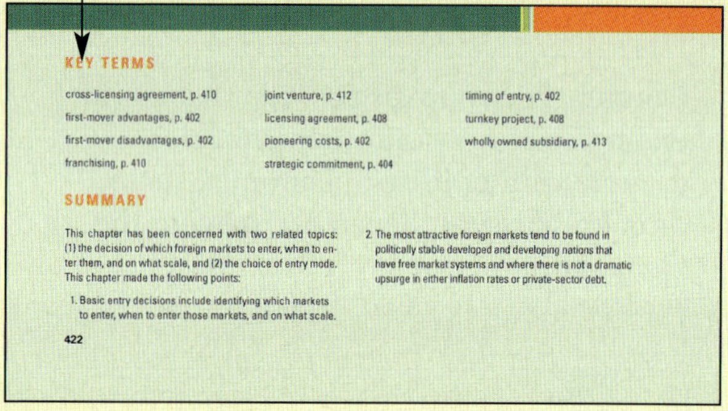

KEY TERMS

cross-licensing agreement, p. 410
first-mover advantages, p. 402
first-mover disadvantages, p. 402
franchising, p. 410
joint venture, p. 412
licensing agreement, p. 408
pioneering costs, p. 402
strategic commitment, p. 404
timing of entry, p. 402
turnkey project, p. 408
wholly owned subsidiary, p. 413

SUMMARY

This chapter has been concerned with two related topics: (1) the decision of which foreign markets to enter, when to enter them, and on what scale, and (2) the choice of entry mode. This chapter made the following points:

1. Basic entry decisions include identifying which markets to enter, when to enter those markets, and on what scale.
2. The most attractive foreign markets tend to be found in politically stable developed and developing nations that have free market systems and where there is not a dramatic upsurge in either inflation rates or private-sector debt.

422

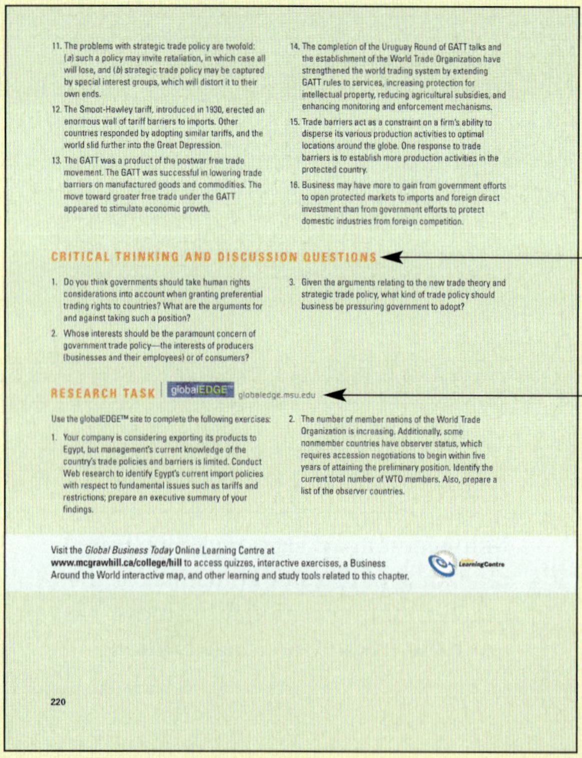

11. The problems with strategic trade policy are twofold: (*a*) such a policy may invite retaliation, in which case all will lose, and (*b*) strategic trade policy may be captured by special interest groups, which will distort it to their own ends.
12. The Smoot-Hawley tariff, introduced in 1930, erected an enormous wall of tariff barriers to imports. Other countries responded by adopting similar tariffs, and the world slid further into the Great Depression.
13. The GATT was a product of the postwar free trade movement. The GATT was successful in lowering trade barriers on manufactured goods and commodities. The move toward greater free trade under the GATT appeared to stimulate economic growth.
14. The completion of the Uruguay Round of GATT talks and the establishment of the World Trade Organization have strengthened the world trading system by extending GATT rules to services, increasing protection for intellectual property, reducing agricultural subsidies, and enhancing monitoring and enforcement mechanisms.
15. Trade barriers act as a constraint on a firm's ability to disperse its various production activities to optimal locations around the globe. One response to trade barriers is to establish more production activities in the protected country.
16. Business may have more to gain from government efforts to open protected markets to imports and foreign direct investment than from government efforts to protect domestic industries from foreign competition.

CRITICAL THINKING AND DISCUSSION QUESTIONS

1. Do you think governments should take human rights considerations into account when granting preferential trading rights to countries? What are the arguments for and against taking such a position?
2. Whose interests should be the paramount concern of government trade policy—the interests of producers (businesses and their employees) or of consumers?
3. Given the arguments relating to the new trade theory and strategic trade policy, what kind of trade policy should business be pressuring government to adopt?

RESEARCH TASK | globalEDGE™ globaledge.msu.edu

Use the globalEDGE™ site to complete the following exercises:

1. Your company is considering exporting its products to Egypt, but management's current knowledge of the country's trade policies and barriers is limited. Conduct Web research to identify Egypt's current import policies with respect to fundamental issues such as tariffs and restrictions; prepare an executive summary of your findings.
2. The number of member nations of the World Trade Organization is increasing. Additionally, some nonmember countries have observer status, which requires accession negotiations to begin within five years of attaining the preliminary position. Identify the current total number of WTO members. Also, prepare a list of the observer countries.

Visit the *Global Business Today* Online Learning Centre at **www.mcgrawhill.ca/college/hill** to access quizzes, interactive exercises, a Business Around the World interactive map, and other learning and study tools related to this chapter.

220

Critical Thinking and Discussion Questions

These questions are suited for in-class discussion or personal reflection.

NEW! GlobalEDGE/CIBER™ Research Task

Using the text and the GlobalEDGE™ Web site, http://globaledge.msu.edu, students solve realistic international business problems related to each chapter. These exercises expose students to the types of tools and data sources international managers use to make informed business decisions.

CLOSING CASE

WHEN DO GOVERNMENT TAX INCENTIVES BECOME EXPORT SUBSIDIES?

Historically speaking, when countries embarked on tit-for-tat responses for real and/or perceived economic injustices against one another, political instability, economic protectionism and often war followed. Since WWII many institutions have been founded to stave off potential recurrent irritants that had until that time, ravaged Europe's history.

Consequently, government subsidies are increasingly becoming a thing of the past, and with new free trade rulings being heralded on an ongoing basis by the World Trade Organization, member countries are required to comply. When out of line, the trade dispute mechanisms of the WTO intervene and deliberate on a case by case basis. Canada and Brazil have been engaged in several trade disputes over the past two decades, but none is as high profile and high stakes as the Bombardier–Embraer dilemma. Each company accuses the other of being in breach of WTO government subsidies practices.

Government subsidies come in different shapes and forms, and often boil down to pure semantics, the art of language, which attempts to circumvent the WTO interpretations on the matter. This could be said to be the source of the decade plus Brazil–Canada trade dispute over Embraer. Although mostly focused on the aircraft industry, it, like many trade irritants over time, has occasionally spilled out of that realm and into other areas. As usually is the case with country to country trade disputes, sub disputes frequently will spin off. Such was the case with the epic Bombardier–Embraer saga. In early 2001, Canada imposed a three-week ban on Brazilian beef, claiming its concern that Brazilian beef might be contaminated with Bovine Spongiform Encephalopathy or mad cow disease. This created an uproar in Brazil, which in turn threatened trade retaliation against Canada. The Canadian government lifted the ban after three weeks.

Ever since WWII, nations around the world have at one time or another, attempted to aid domestic industries through tax breaks and other types of incentives. Many countries, in the year 2005, owe their current state of wealth to strong government policies that bolstered, sometimes fledgling industries.

The Bombardier–Embraer dispute began in the 1990s when Canada complained to the WTO that Brazil was providing unfair state aid to Embraer. According to Bombardier—Embraer's Canadian rival—the subsidies amounted to US$3.7 billion for the nearly 900 aircraft on order but not yet delivered by the 1999 WTO deadline for removing them. Though the arbitrators slashed by more than half the annual Cdn$700 million Canada claimed in retaliation, the Cdn$344.2 million (US$233.4 million) authorized was the largest in any WTO dispute to date.

When one country subsidizes an industry to the tune of hundreds of millions of dollars per year, as Brazil had been doing, this raises the spectrum that it will damage a competitor firm elsewhere on the planet. As then Canadian Industry Minister Brian Tobin pointed out, if global competition is based purely on product, this is fair trade. In January 2001, the Canadian government stated its concerns that as many as 24 000 workers could lose their jobs in Canada if Brazil continued their support of Embraer. The Canadian government was not going to wait and see if this would happen. Bombardier had already lost significant market share to Embraer in the last five years, solely because of the preferential financing Embraer was getting.

That wasn't the end of the protracted dispute. Dissatisfied with the WTO ruling against Embraer, Brazil launched a counter complaint to the WTO against Bombardier. On January 29, 2003, the WTO ruled that a $1.7-billion low-interest loan the federal government made to Bombardier broke international trade rules. The loan was to help Bombardier land a 75-plane order from Air Wisconsin. Canadian government officials had argued the low-interest loans were similar to loans offered by Brazil to help Brazilian regional jetmaker Embraer land similar aircraft contracts. Yet, as of March 2003, Canada had still not imposed retaliatory measures despite authorization to do so by the WTO.

Fast forward to Tuesday, March 18, 2003, the WTO granted Brazil the right to impose almost US$250 million per year in trade sanctions against Canada, far short of the US$3.3 billion that had been requested. Based on this WTO ruling, Brazil can immediately impose 100-percent duties on a wide range of imports from Canada, including chickpeas, waffles, newsprint, coal, and radioactive isotopes.

While Canada has stated that its objective is to ensure that Brazil adheres to WTO rules, Brazil makes the same claim. Slow progress towards agreement is still being made, yet more work has to be done.

221

Closing Case

The closing case wraps up the material in the chapter by relating the experience of a company to the practice of international business. Ten are **new** to the Canadian Edition.

NEW! Sustainability in Practice

Located at the end of each part, these vignettes illustrate how business are engaging in the solutions to sustainable development challenges.

SUSTAINABILITY IN PRACTICE

B.C. HYDRO'S ABORIGINAL RELATIONS PROGRAMS

According to Canada's First Nations 2001 Census data, there are 1 319 890 Aboriginal people in Canada (or 4.4 percent of Canada's total population). They are often identified as being from Inuit or Métis descent. (Métis are Aboriginal people with an original mixture of French and Aboriginal ancestry. They live primarily in the western provinces of Canada.) Aboriginal peoples are members of a large number of distinctly different and well-defined cultures and societies. This case study explains the cultural challenges and opportunities faced by a corporation conducting business in Aboriginal areas.

B.C. Hydro, one of the largest electric utilities in Canada, is a Crown corporation owned by the province of British Columbia, which is home to 197 First Nations bands. B.C. Hydro has facilities on at least 168 of these band's reserve lands. Consequently, building sustainable, mutually beneficial relationships with Aboriginal peoples is critical for B.C. Hydro.

In 1993, B.C. Hydro developed a comprehensive approach to managing Aboriginal issues. The main elements of B.C. Hydro's approach are addressing the past, building for the future, and effectively managing its Aboriginal relations initiatives. Key components of the relationship-building strategy are facilitating participation in resource management and development decisions, fostering economic development, supporting education for Aboriginal peoples, and contributing to community projects and events.

To increase economic development opportunities for First Nations, B.C. Hydro negotiates contracts for work on reserve lands and assists Aboriginal-owned businesses to improve their tendering practices. The utility provides start-up and expansion grants to Aboriginal-owned businesses and in some cases explores joint ventures. B.C. Hydro also has developed an Aboriginal Business Directory that is used throughout the corporation and is available to government and private-sector companies as a source for products and services.

Within B.C. Hydro, education is a key component of the strategy. Cross-cultural training programs address historical facts, court decisions, and cultural issues. More than 4700 B.C. Hydro employees have taken at least one half-day cross-cultural training course. Those who frequently interact with First Nations have taken more rigorous training. B.C. Hydro's cross-cultural training, which has also been delivered to more than 100 outside organizations, received the 1999 Province of British Columbia Multiculturalism Award. Aboriginal education is also a priority, with education scholarships, Aboriginal language and culture preservation programs, and stay-in-school programs forming a part of the strategy.

The biggest challenges faced by B.C. Hydro in this field flow from the prevailing legal and political uncertainty both as to the outcomes of treaty negotiations and the nature and extent of Aboriginal rights and titles. B.C. Hydro addresses these uncertainties by seeking "interest-based" rather than "rights-based" solutions to problems, and by providing input into the treaty process. Open dialogue with First Nations is a key component of the strategy for managing this uncertainty.

In November 1997, B.C. Hydro commissioned the Ipsos Reid Group to conduct interviews with Aboriginal leaders across British Columbia. The First Nations opinion leaders told B.C. Hydro representatives that the company's principles that guide its relationship-building activities are the right ones. The findings revealed that while relationships have improved over the past ten years, the company still has a long way to go. First Nations identified the following goals as most important in contributing to improved relationships:

- Consulting with Aboriginal communities in the early stages of a project.
- Cooperating with Aboriginal peoples and education institutions to develop initiatives and programs.
- Encouraging Aboriginal people to take advantage of any economic social or other opportunities from B.C. Hydro projects.
- Developing employment equity programs.

Those who thought that relations with Hydro were still poor cited a lack of respect toward Aboriginal peoples and insufficient communication as the main reasons.

Perhaps the most critical lesson that B.C. Hydro has learned is that problems cannot be solved overnight or with simple, one-size-fits-all solutions. First Nations share the need for better business relationships, and they will work with B.C. Hydro when they see that the company's commitment is real and sustained.

Source: Reprinted with permission from the World Business Council for Sustainable Development's Web site at www.wbcsd.org.

PART ONE

1

GLOBALIZATION

The Global Grocer

Food retailers are going global. The leaders in this trend include Wal-Mart of the United States, Carrefour of France, Ahold of Holland, and Tesco from the United Kingdom. Carrefour, the world's second largest retailer, is perhaps the most global of the lot. In 2004, Carrefour, the pioneer of the hypermarket concept, was operating in 29 countries while generating most of its sales outside France. By December 2004, Carrefour had 6546 stores worldwide.

By 2004, Wal-Mart, the world's biggest retailer had more than 3200 stores in the United States with 1506 Wal-Mart units in nine non-U.S. countries (Mexico, Brazil, Argentina, United Kingdom, China, South Korea, Germany, Puerto Rico, and Canada with 231 stores). Wal-Mart has 1.3 million sales associates in the U.S., and over 330 000 worldwide with more than 138 million customers visiting its stores each week. Unlike Carrefour, which generates most of its sales outside France, Wal-Mart receives the majority of its revenues from within the U.S. Wal-Mart sells general merchandise in addition to food, but food retailing is an increasingly important part of its business, particularly internationally. Acquisitions are driving expansion. Wal-Mart built new stores in Mexico, entered the German market through acquisitions, and acquired Asda, a nationwide food retailer, in Britain.

By 2004, Ahold had 1322 stores operating under six different names in the United States, and was selling almost 70 percent of its products outside Holland. In 2003, it had started selling off most of its Central and South American operations with restructuring and downsizing also evident in many of its European locations. In 2004, Tesco had 2318 stores of which 261 were in other European countries, with 179 locations in Asia and employing 326 000 people. Carrefour does not yet have a U.S. presence, but is said to be looking at potential acquisitions in the United States, including Kmart and Target. Britain's Tesco, a latecomer to the global game, is now expanding rapidly, particularly in Southeast Asia and Eastern Europe, where a combination of acquisitions and expansions have helped Tesco pass Carrefour and become the largest foreign retailer in Thailand and Poland.

Photo by NASA.

CHAPTER 1

Globalization

OPENING CASE

The world's top 25 retailers in 2002 ranged in sales from number one Wal-Mart at $229.6 billion to CVS Corporation of Woonsocket Rhode Island at $24.1 billion. Carrefour placed second with sales of $64.7 billion, with Ahold in sixth place at $47.1 billion, and Tesco showing in eighth place with sales of $39.5 billion. Forecasts suggest the figure could reach 40 percent by 2009, with Latin America, Southeast Asia, and Eastern Europe being the main battlegrounds. A number of factors are driving this development. First, as barriers to cross-border investment fell during the 1990s, it became possible for retailers to enter foreign nations on a significant scale. Second, many of these retailers faced market saturation and slow growth in their domestic markets. Expanding internationally seemed an obvious way to boost sales growth, particularly by entering developing nations in Southeast Asia and Latin America where rapid economic growth was raising living standards and making these markets more attractive to retailers. Third, once Carrefour started to blaze the trail, other large retailers such as Tesco and Wal-Mart began to follow suit lest they arrive too late and find a country already dominated by other foreign retailers.

Fourth, these retailers believed that by expanding internationally, they could reap significant economies of scale from their global buying power. Many of their key suppliers had long been international companies; for example, Unilever, Procter & Gamble, and Kellogg all sell products globally. If the retailers also built global reach, they could use their size to demand deeper discounts from their suppliers, which would increase the retailers' profit margins.

Fifth, all these retailers held a strong position in their domestic markets, primarily because they were very efficient operations. Carrefour's chief executive officer, for example, believes his company's greatest advantage is its sophisticated understanding of supply chains, beginning with electronic links that tie sales rung up at a checkout register to inventory in the store to production schedules at suppliers. By keeping inventory to a minimum, Carrefour can devote more of a store's floor space to selling products, increasing sales per square foot. Retailers such as Carrefour believe they can gain market share and create significant value by transferring the operating skills they developed in their home markets to nations where indigenous retailers lack the same level of sophistication. Wal-Mart believes it can gain share in markets ranging from Mexico and Brazil to Britain and Germany by applying its skills in supply chain management, information systems, and employee management—skills that propelled Wal-Mart to U.S. dominance. If Wal-Mart, Carrefour, and others execute their plans successfully, they may come to dominate global retailing.

However, these grand strategic designs have run headlong into difficult realities. National differences in tastes and preferences may mean that what sells in Britain may not sell in Brazil. This reduces retailers' ability to centralize their purchasing, buying the same product from the same global suppliers and selling that product worldwide. In a concession to local tastes, the aisles in Tesco's Thai stores carry many food products not found in the aisles in British stores. Wal-Mart tried to sell cheap Colombian coffee in Brazil, only to find that Brazilians insisted on drinking their own, more expensive brands. If retailers cannot sell the same products worldwide, they cannot realize the economies of scale that they sought. Local tastes crucially affect the way retailers sell their goods too. In 1996 Wal-Mart set up efficient, clean superstores in Indonesia, only to find that Indonesians preferred Matahari, a chain of shabbier local stores that reminded shoppers of traditional street markets where they can haggle and buy the freshest fruit and vegetables. Two years later, Wal-Mart pulled out of Indonesia.

Retailing models aren't always easy to transfer from one location to another. Differences in labour costs, the supply of desirable locations, and the sophistication of the local supply base may make it difficult to transfer a retailing model across borders. In developing nations, Carrefour has found it difficult to implement the sophisticated supply chain management system it uses in France. Suppliers in developing nations lack the required computer-based infrastructure and are hesitant to invest in it. It took Wal-Mart a decade to introduce its electronic supply chain management system into Mexico, primarily because of resistance from local suppliers and confusion on the part of local employees.

Despite these difficulties, most retailers are pushing ahead in their attempts to build a global brand. In this vision of the future, Wal-Mart, Carrefour, and Tesco stores one day will blanket the world. In contrast, Holland's Ahold has adopted a different strategy for going global. Believing that brand loyalty is local and consumer tastes, preferences, and shopping habits all vary from nation to nation, Ahold varies its retailing formula and brand name from nation to nation. In the United States, it still operates under the names of acquired companies, such as Giant and Stop & Shop, because these names and their associated retailing models resonate with locals. Ahold adds value by improving the operating efficiency of the retailers it acquires and transferring valuable skills and practices between countries. In the long run, there may be room for both Ahold's "going global with a local face" strategy and Wal-Mart's "global retail brand" strategy. Despite the impediments, the globalization of retailing likely will continue—the potential payoffs are too great for this not to occur.

Sources: M. N. Hamilton, "Global Food Fight," *Washington Post,* November 19, 2000, p. H1; A. Stewart, "Easier Access to World Markets," *Financial Times,* December 3, 1997, p. 8; "Global Strategy—Why Tesco Will Beat Carrefour," *Retail Week,* April 6, 2001, p. 14; "Shopping All over the World," *The Economist,* June 19, 1999, pp. 59–61; and M. Flagg, "In Asia, Going to the Grocery Increasingly Means Heading for a European Retail Chain," *Wall Street Journal,* April 24, 2001, p. A21; Wal-Mart at www.walmart.com; Ahold at www.ahold.com/operatingcompanies/; Carrefour at www.carrefour.com/English/groupcarrefour/ouverturesMagasins.jsp; and Tesco at www.tesco.com/corporateinfo/.

LEARNING OBJECTIVES

1. Understand what is meant by the term *globalization.*
2. Be familiar with the main causes of globalization.
3. Understand why globalization and innovation are now proceeding at a rapid rate.
4. Appreciate how changing international trade patterns, foreign direct investment flows, differences in economic growth rates among countries, and the rise of new multinational corporations are all changing the nature of the world economy.
5. Have a good grasp of the main arguments in the debate over the impact of globalization on job security, income levels, labour and environmental policies, and national sovereignty.
6. Appreciate that the process of globalization is giving rise to numerous opportunities and challenges that business managers must confront in Canada and beyond.

INTRODUCTION

A fundamental shift is occurring in the world economy. We are moving away from a world in which national economies were relatively self-contained entities, isolated from each other by barriers to cross-border trade and investment; by distance, time zones, and language; and by national differences in government regulation, culture, and business systems. And we are moving toward a world in which barriers to cross-border trade and investment are tumbling; perceived distance is shrinking due to advances in transportation and telecommunications technology; material culture is starting to look similar the world over; and national economies are merging into an interdependent global economic system. The process by which this is occurring is commonly referred to as globalization.

In this interdependent global economy, a Canadian might drive to work in a car designed in Germany that was assembled in Canada by DaimlerChrysler from components made in the United Kingdom and Japan, and that were fabricated from Korean steel and Malaysian rubber. She may have filled the car with gasoline at a service centre owned by a Dutch multinational company that changed its name to Shell Canada in order to hide its national origins. The gasoline could have been made from oil pumped out of a well in the Hibernia fields off the coast of Newfoundland "owned jointly by Exxon Mobil Canada (33.125 percent), Chevron Canada Resources (26.875 percent), Petro-Canada (20 percent), Canada Hibernia Holding Corporation (8.5 percent), Murphy Oil (6.5 percent), and Norsk Hydro (5 percent)."[1]

While driving to work, the Canadian might talk to her investment adviser on a Finnish manufactured, but Texas assembled, Nokia cellphone that is linked through a Nortel PBX system in Toronto. Afterwards, she might turn on her car radio, which was made in Malaysia by a Japanese firm, to hear a popular song composed by an Italian and sung by a group of Quebecers residing in France. After the song ends, a news announcer might announce that there has been more anti-globalization demonstrations at the latest round of World Trade Organization talks.

This is the world we live in. It is a world where the volume of goods, services, and investment crossing national borders expanded faster than world output every year during the last two decades of the twentieth century. It is a world where more than $1.2 billion in foreign exchange transactions are made every day. It is a world in which international institutions such as the World Trade Organization and gatherings of leaders from the world's most powerful economies have called for even lower barriers to cross-border trade and investment. It is a world where the symbols of material and popular culture are increasingly global: from Coca-Cola and McDonald's to Sony PlayStations, Nokia cellphones, MTV shows, and Disney films. It is a world in which products are made from inputs that come from all over the world. It is a world in which an economic crisis in Asia can cause a recession in Canada, and a slowdown in the United States really did help drive Japan's Nikkei index in 2001 to lows not seen since 1985. It is also a world in which a vigorous and vocal minority is protesting against globalization, which they blame for a list of ills, from unemployment in developed nations to environmental degradation and the Americanization of popular culture. And yes, these protests really have turned violent.

For businesses, this is in many ways the best of times. Globalization has increased the opportunities for a firm to expand its revenues by selling around the world and reduce its costs by producing in nations where key inputs are cheap. Since the collapse of communism at the end of the 1980s, the pendulum of public policy in nation after nation has swung toward the free market end of the economic spectrum. Regulatory and administrative barriers to doing business in foreign nations have come down, while those nations have often transformed their economies, privatizing state-owned enterprises,

Estimates from the World Trade Organization (WTO) suggest that the price for international telephone calls should fall by 80 percent over 3–5 years as competition increases. Soon it will cost no more to place a call halfway around the world than it does to call next door. What do you think will be the effect on the price of cellphones, such as these on sale in Tokyo? CORBIS. All rights reserved.

deregulating markets, increasing competition, and welcoming investment by foreign businesses. This has allowed businesses both large and small, from both advanced nations and developing nations, to expand internationally.

The global retailing industry, profiled in the opening case, is a late mover in this development. Some industries, such as commercial jet aircraft, automobiles, petroleum, semiconductor chips, and computers, have been global for decades. Retailing has been primarily local in orientation, but in a testament to the scope and pace of globalization, this too is now changing. Falling barriers to cross-border investment have made this possible. Rapid economic growth in developing nations and market saturation at home have made globalization a strategic imperative for established retailers seeking to expand their business. Many, such as Wal-Mart and Tesco, believe they must move aggressively now lest they lose the initiative to early movers like Carrefour. They see their strategic advantage in terms of building a global brand, realizing economies of scale, and leveraging skills across national borders. In this, they are no different from companies in other industries that have already gone global.

Going global is not without problems. This too was evident in the opening case. The grand strategic vision of retailers such as Wal-Mart and Carrefour has often run up against the hard reality that for all the superficial similarities in material and popular culture and in business systems, doing business in foreign nations still has unique challenges. Because of different tastes and preferences, what sells in Britain may not sell in Thailand, business processes that give a retailer a competitive advantage in the United States may be difficult to implement in Mexico, and a brand that means something in Kansas may mean little in Indonesia.

The tension evident in the opening case between the economic opportunities associated with going global and the challenges associated with doing business across borders is an important one in international business. We shall consider this tension repeatedly in this book. To begin with, however, we need to look more closely at the process of globalization. We need to understand what is driving this process, appreciate how it is changing the face of international businesses, and better comprehend why globalization has become a flash point for debate, demonstration, and conflict over the future direction of our civilization.

WHAT IS GLOBALIZATION?

As used in this book, **globalization** refers to the shift toward a more integrated and interdependent world economy. Globalization has several different facets, including the globalization of markets, the globalization of production, and the globalization of consumers. The developments in communications technology and a homogenization of economies have resulted in the concept of a worldwide consumer.

GLOBALIZATION
Trend away from distinct national economic units and toward one huge global market.

THE GLOBALIZATION OF MARKETS

The **globalization of markets** refers to the merging of historically distinct and separate national markets into one huge global marketplace. Falling barriers to cross-border trade have made it easier to sell internationally. It has been argued for some time that the tastes and preferences of consumers in different nations are beginning to converge on some global norm, thereby helping to create a global market.[2] Consumer products such as Citicorp credit cards, Coca-Cola soft drinks, Sony PlayStation, and McDonald's hamburgers are frequently held up as prototypical examples of this trend. Firms such as Citicorp, Coca-Cola, McDonald's, and Sony are more than just benefactors of this trend; they are also facilitators of it. By offering a standardized product worldwide, they help to create a global market.

GLOBALIZATION OF MARKETS
Moving away from an economic system in which national markets are distinct entities, isolated by trade barriers and barriers of distance, time, and culture, and toward a system in which national markets are merging into one global market.

For example, Matrex Company of Locust Hill, Ontario, manufactures road emulsions that are used in pothole repairs and generates "40 percent of its \$2.9 million sales to five continents."[3] Supply Chain Alliance Inc. of Unionville, Ontario, derives 35 percent of its \$3.4 million annual revenues, from exports."[4]

Despite the global prevalence of Citicorp credit cards and McDonald's hamburgers, it is important not to push too far the view that national markets are giving way to the global market. As we shall see in later chapters, very significant differences still exist between national markets along many relevant dimensions, including consumer tastes and preferences, distribution channels, culturally embedded value systems, business systems, and legal regulations. These differences frequently require that marketing strategies, product features, and operating practices be customized to best match conditions in a country. For example, automobile companies will promote different car models depending on a range of factors such as local fuel costs, income levels, traffic congestion, and cultural values. Similarly, as we saw in the opening case, global retailers may still need to vary their product mix from country to country depending on local tastes and preferences.

Most global markets currently are not markets for consumer products–where national differences in tastes and preferences are still often important enough to act as a brake on globalization–but markets for industrial goods and materials that serve a universal need the world over. These include the markets for commodities such as aluminum, oil, and wheat; the markets for industrial products such as microprocessors, DRAMs (computer memory chips), and commercial jet aircraft; the markets for computer software; and the markets for financial assets from Canadian Treasury bills to eurobonds and futures on the Nikkei index or the Mexican peso.

In many global markets, the same firms frequently confront each other as competitors in nation after nation. Coca-Cola's rivalry with Pepsi is a global one, as are the rivalries between Ford and Toyota, Bombardier and Embraer, Caterpillar and Komatsu, and Nintendo and Sega. If one firm moves into a nation that is not currently served by its rivals, those rivals are sure to follow to prevent their competitor from gaining an advantage.[5] The opening case revealed that retailers such as Wal-Mart, Carrefour, and Tesco are starting to engage in a global rivalry. As firms follow each other around the world, they bring with them many of the assets that served them well in other national markets–including their products, operating strategies, marketing strategies, and brand names–creating some homogeneity across markets. Thus, greater uniformity replaces diversity. Due to such developments, in an increasing number of industries it is no longer meaningful to talk about "the German market," "the American market," "the Brazilian market," or "the Canadian market"; for many firms there is only the global market.

THE GLOBALIZATION OF PRODUCTION

GLOBALIZATION OF PRODUCTION Trend by individual firms to disperse parts of their productive processes to different locations around the globe to take advantage of differences in cost and quality of factors of production.

The **globalization of production** refers to the sourcing of goods and services from locations around the globe to take advantage of national differences in the cost and quality of factors of production (such as labour, energy, land, and capital). By doing this, companies hope to lower their overall cost structure and/or improve the quality or functionality of their product offering, thereby allowing them to compete more effectively. Consider Bombardier's ongoing expansion in manufacturing its CRJ series regional jet aircraft. On December 9, 2003, CRJ had 1289 firm aircraft orders with 1000 orders already delivered. Depending on market conditions, these figures could increase by another 1000 over the next ten years. [6]

The global dispersal of productive activities is not limited to giants such as Boeing. Smaller firms are also tapping into the global marketplace. Matrikon, based in Edmonton, Alberta, had 2003 year-end sales totalling $48.86 million. Matrikon specializes in industrial information technology with clients in different industry sectors. Foreign direct investment along with diversification of its manufacturing, design, and distributor channels, enable Matrikon to build a global competitive advantage for process-improvement software.[7]

As a consequence of the trend exemplified by Bombardier and Matrikon, in many industries it is becoming irrelevant to talk about American products, Japanese products, German products, or Korean products. Given the growth of international outsourcing, manufactured goods are increasingly being described as global products. But as with the globalization of markets, one must be careful not to push the globalization of production too far. As we will see in later chapters, substantial impediments still make it difficult for firms to achieve the optimal dispersion of their productive activities to locations around the globe. These impediments include formal and informal barriers to trade between countries, barriers to foreign direct investment, transportation costs, and issues associated with economic and political risk.

Nevertheless, we are travelling down the road toward a future characterized by the increased globalization of markets and production. Modern firms are important actors in this drama, by their very actions fostering increased globalization. These firms, however, are merely responding in an efficient manner to changing conditions in their operating environment–as they should. In the next section, we look at the main drivers of globalization.

THE EMERGENCE OF GLOBAL INSTITUTIONS

GENERAL AGREEMENT ON TARIFFS AND TRADE (GATT) International treaty that committed signatories to lowering barriers to the free flow of goods across national borders and led to the WTO.

As markets globalize and an increasing proportion of business activity transcends national borders, institutions need to help manage, regulate, and police the global marketplace, and to promote the establishment of multinational treaties to govern the global business system. During the past 50 years, a number of important global institutions have been created to help perform these functions. These institutions include the **General Agreement on Tariffs and Trade (GATT)** and its successor, the World Trade Organization (WTO); the International Monetary Fund (IMF) and its sister institution, the World Bank; and the United Nations (UN). All these institutions were created by voluntary agreement between individual nation-states, and their functions are enshrined in international treaties.

The **World Trade Organization** (like the GATT before it) is primarily responsible for policing the world trading system and making sure nation-states adhere to the rules laid down in trade treaties signed by WTO member states. As of January 1, 2002, 148 nations were members of the WTO, including all significant trading nations, which gives the WTO enormous scope and influence. The WTO is also responsible for facilitating the establishment of additional multinational agreements between WTO member states. Over its entire history, and that of the GATT before it, the WTO has promoted the lowering of barriers to cross-border trade and investment. In doing so, the WTO has been the instrument of its member states, which have sought to create a more open global business system unencumbered by barriers to trade and investment between countries. Without an institution such as the WTO, it is unlikely that globalization would have proceeded as far as it has. However, as we shall see in this chapter and in Chapter 6 when we take a close look at the WTO, critics charge that the WTO is usurping the national sovereignty of individual nation-states.

WORLD TRADE ORGANIZATION (WTO) The organization that succeeded the General Agreement on Tariffs and Trade (GATT) as a result of the successful completion of the Uruguay Round of GATT negotiations.

The **International Monetary Fund** and the **World Bank** were both created in 1944 by 44 nations that met at Bretton Woods, New Hampshire. The task of the IMF was to maintain order in the international monetary system, and that of the World Bank was to promote economic development. In the nearly 60 years since their creation, both institutions have emerged as significant players in the global economy. The World Bank is the less controversial of the two sister institutions. It has focused on making low interest rate loans to cash-strapped governments in poor nations that wish to undertake significant infrastructure investments (such as building dams or road systems).

INTERNATIONAL MONETARY FUND (IMF) International institution set up to maintain order in the international monetary system.

WORLD BANK International institution set up to promote general economic development in the world's poorer nations.

The IMF is often seen as the lender of last resort to nation-states whose economies are in turmoil and currencies are losing value against those of other nations. Repeatedly during the last decade, for example, the IMF has lent money to the governments of troubled states including Argentina, Indonesia, Mexico, Russia, South Korea, Thailand, and Turkey to name a few of the more high-profile cases. The IMF loans come with strings attached; in return for loans, the IMF requires nation-states to adopt specific policies aimed at returning their troubled economies to stability and growth. These "strings" have generated the most debate; some critics charge that the IMF's policy recommendations are often inappropriate, while others maintain that, like the WTO, by telling national governments what economic policies they must adopt, the IMF is usurping their sovereignty. We shall look at the debate over the role of the IMF in Chapter 10.

The **United Nations** was established October 24, 1945, by 51 countries committed to preserving peace through international cooperation and collective security. Today nearly every nation in the world belongs to the United Nations; membership now totals 189 countries. When states become members of the United Nations, they agree to accept the obligations of the UN Charter, an international treaty that sets out basic principles of international relations. According to the charter, the UN has four purposes: to maintain international peace and security, to develop friendly relations among nations, to cooperate in solving international problems and in promoting respect for human rights, and to be a centre for harmonizing the actions of nations. Although the UN is perhaps best known for its peacekeeping role, one of the UN's central mandates is the promotion of higher standards of living, full employment, and conditions of economic and social progress and development–all issues that are central to the creation of a vibrant global economy. As much as 70 percent of the work of the UN system is devoted to accomplishing this mandate. To do so, the UN works closely with other international institutions such as the World Bank. Guiding the work is the belief that eradicating poverty and improving the well-being of people everywhere are necessary steps in creating conditions for lasting world peace.[8]

UNITED NATIONS An international organization made up of 189 countries headquartered in New York City, formed in 1945 to promote peace, security, and cooperation.

DRIVERS OF GLOBALIZATION

Two macro factors seem to underlie the trend toward greater globalization.[9] The first is the decline in barriers to the free flow of goods, services, and capital that has occurred since the end of World War II. The second factor is technological change, particularly the dramatic developments in recent years in communication, information processing, and transportation technologies.

DECLINING TRADE AND INVESTMENT BARRIERS

INTERNATIONAL TRADE Occurs when a firm exports goods or services to consumers in another country.

FOREIGN DIRECT INVESTMENT (FDI) Direct investment in business operations in a foreign country.

During the 1920s and 30s, many nations erected formidable barriers to international trade and foreign direct investment. **International trade** occurs when a firm exports goods or services to consumers in another country. **Foreign direct investment** occurs when a firm invests resources in business activities outside its home country. Many of the barriers to international trade took the form of high tariffs on imports of manufactured goods. The typical aim of such tariffs was to protect domestic industries from foreign competition. One consequence, however, was "beggar thy neighbour" retaliatory trade policies with countries progressively raising trade barriers against each other. Ultimately, this depressed world demand and contributed to the Great Depression of the 1930s.

Having learned from this experience, the advanced industrial nations of the West committed themselves after World War II to removing barriers to the free flow of goods, services, and capital between nations.[10] This goal was enshrined in the General Agreement on Tariffs and Trade (GATT). Under the umbrella of GATT, eight rounds of negotiations among member states, which now number 148, have worked to lower barriers to the free flow of goods and services. The most recent round of negotiations, known as the Uruguay Round, was completed in December 1993. The Uruguay Round further reduced trade barriers; extended GATT to cover services as well as manufactured goods; provided enhanced protection for patents, trademarks, and copyrights; and established the World Trade Organization (WTO) to police the international trading system.[11] Table 1.1 summarizes the impact of GATT agreements on average tariff rates for manufactured goods. As can be seen, average tariff rates have fallen significantly since 1950 and now stand at 3.9 percent.

In late 2003, the WTO launched a new round of talks between member states aimed at further liberalizing global trade, investment, and agricultural subsidies that wealthy countries pay to their farmers. For this meeting, it picked the remote location of Doha, Qatar. Scheduled talks are expected to last over a period of three years or more. In September 2003, the talks continued in Cancun, and all but broke down due to the strong anti-global movement participants from the world's poorer countries. These protesters fail to see the advantage in continually reducing tariff barriers worldwide, in spite of the WTO's assurances to the contrary that points out that wealthy countries subsidize their farm sectors to the tune of $300 billion a year and that agricultural tariff rates are still around 40 percent. While reducing trade barriers, many

TABLE 1.1

Average Tariff Rates on Manufactured Products as Percent of Value

Source: 1913–1990 data from "Who Wants to Be a Giant?" *The Economist: A Survey of the Multinationals,* June 24, 1995, pp. 3–4.

	1913	1950	1990	2000
France	21%	18%	5.9%	3.9%
Germany	20	26	5.9	3.9
Italy	18	25	5.9	3.9
Japan	30	—	5.3	3.9
Holland	5	11	5.9	3.9
Sweden	20	9	4.4	3.9
Britain	—	23	5.9	3.9
United States	44	14	4.8	3.9

countries have also been progressively removing restrictions to foreign direct investment, which "since 1959, the year of the first bilateral investment treaty, has grown to 2181 treaties in 2002, encompassing 176 countries."[12]

In the early 1960s, the United States was still by far the world's dominant industrial power. In 1963, for example, the United States accounted for 40.3 percent of world output. By 2000, the United States accounted for 27 percent of world output, still by far the world's largest industrial power, but down significantly in relative size since the 1960s. Nor was the United States the only developed nation to see its relative standard slip. The same occurred to Germany, France, and the United Kingdom, all nations that were among the first to industrialize. This decline in the U.S. position was not an absolute decline, since the U.S. economy grew at a robust average annual rate of over 3 percent from 1963 to 2000 (the economies of Germany, France, and the United Kingdom also grew over this time period). Rather it was a relative decline, reflecting the faster economic growth of several other economies, particularly in Asia.

Such trends facilitate both the globalization of markets and the globalization of production. The lowering of barriers to international trade enables firms to view the world, rather than a single country, as their market. The lowering of trade and investment barriers also allows firms to base production at the optimal location for that activity, serving the world market from that location. Thus, a firm might design a product in one country, produce component parts in two other countries, assemble the product in yet another country, and then export the finished product around the world.

The lowering of trade barriers has facilitated the globalization of production. According to data from the World Trade Organization, the volume of world trade has grown consistently faster than the volume of world output since 1950.[13] From 1950 to 2000, world trade expanded almost 20-fold, far outstripping world output, which grew by six and a half times. As suggested by Table 1.2, the growth in world trade seems to have accelerated in recent years. However, 2001 brought a sudden slowdown to this long-term trend. Between 2000 and 2001, the volume of world trade fell by 1 percent, the first decline in two decades, while world output grew by a sluggish 1 percent. The primary reason for this was the global economic slowdown that occurred in 2001 brought on by the economic aftermath of the September 11 terrorist attacks on the United States. This contraction was short lived. Table 1.2 shows the dramatic increase in world trade in merchandise after 2001.

The data summarized in Table 1.2 imply two things. First, more firms are doing what Bombardier does, to a degree, with its aircraft manufacturing: dispersing parts of its production process to different locations around the globe to drive down production costs and increase product quality. The economies of the world's nation-states are becoming more intertwined. As trade expands, nations are becoming increasingly dependent on each other for important goods and services.

The evidence also suggests that foreign direct investment is playing an increasing role in the global economy as firms ranging in size from Boeing to Matrikon increase their cross-border investments. The average yearly outflow of FDI increased from about $14 billion in 1970 to a record $1.3 trillion in 2000. However, like world trade, the flow of FDI also fell over 40 percent in 2002 to $647 billion.[14] Notwithstanding the slowdown in 2001, the flow of FDI not only accelerated over the last quarter century, but it also accelerated faster than the growth in world trade. For example, between 1990 and 2000, the total flow of FDI from all countries increased about five-fold, while world trade grew by some 82 percent and world output by 23 percent.[15] As a result of the strong FDI flow, by 2000 the global stock of FDI exceeded $6 trillion. In total, by 2000, 60 000 parent companies had 820 000 affiliates in foreign markets that collectively produced an estimated $14 trillion in global sales, nearly twice as high as the value of global exports.[16]

TABLE 1.2

Global Outlook in Summary, 2002–2006

Source: © World Bank, "Global Development Finance, Harnessing Cyclical Gains for Development," 2004 Analysis Summary Tables, p. 14.

	2002	2003[c]	2004[f]	2005[f]	2006[f]	GEP 2004 FORECASTS 2003	2004
Global Conditions							
World trade volume[a]	3.5	4.6	8.7	7.9	7.1	4.6	7.9
Consumer prices							
G-7 countries [b, c]	1.3	2.0	1.4	1.7	1.9	1.4	0.9
United States	1.6	2.3	1.5	2.3	2.7	1.9	1.2
Commodity prices ($ terms)							
Non-oil commodities	5.1	10.0	10.4	-2.9	-2.8	6.9	1.0
Oil price (OPEC average)	24.9	28.9	26.0	23.0	20.0	26.5	22.0
Oil price (% change)	2.4	16.0	-10.0	-11.5	-13.0	6.3	-17.0
Manufactures unit export value[d]	-1.3	6.5	4.3	-1.7	-0.8	4.0	-0.4
Interest rates							
$, 6-month (%)	1.8	1.2	1.5	3.5	3.7	1.0	2.0
€, 6-month (%)	3.3	2.3	2.0	2.4	3.4	2.1	2.1
Real GDP growth[e]							
World	1.8	2.6	3.7	3.1	3.0	2.0	3.0
Memo item: World (PPP weights)[f]	2.9	3.7	4.6	4.1	3.9	3.1	3.9
High Income	1.4	2.1	3.3	2.6	2.5	1.5	2.5
OECD countries	1.4	2.0	3.1	2.6	2.4	1.5	2.5
Euro area	0.9	0.4	1.7	2.3	2.3	0.7	1.7
Japan	-0.3	2.7	3.1	1.4	1.2	0.8	1.3
United States	2.2	3.2	4.6	3.2	2.9	2.2	3.4
Non-OECD countries	2.3	2.6	5.0	4.5	4.2	2.1	4.1
Developing Countries	3.4	4.8	5.4	5.2	5.0	4.0	4.9
East Asia and Pacific[g]	6.7	7.7	7.4	6.7	6.3	6.1	6.7
Europe and Central Asia	4.6	5.5	4.9	4.8	4.7	4.3	4.5
Latin America and the Caribbean	-0.6	1.3	3.8	3.7	3.5	1.8	3.7
Middle East and N. Africa	3.3	5.1	3.7	3.9	4.0	3.3	3.9
South Asia	4.3	6.5	7.2	6.7	6.5	5.4	5.4
Sub-Saharan Africa	3.3	2.4	3.4	4.2	3.9	2.8	3.5
Memo Items:							
Developing countries							
Excluding transition	3.3	4.6	5.5	5.2	5.0	3.9	4.9
Excluding China and India	2.1	3.4	4.4	4.5	4.2	3.0	4.1

Note: PPP = purchasing power parity; GEP 2004 = *Global Economic Prospects and the Developing Countries*, World Bank, January 2004; e = estimate; f = forecasts.

a. Goods and non-factor services.

b. Canada, France, Germany, Italy, Japan, the United Kingdom, and the United States.

c. In local currency, aggregated using 1995 GDP weights.

d. Unit value index of manufactured exports from major economies, expressed in U.S dollars.

e. GDP in 1995 constant dollars; 1995 prices and market exchange rates.

f. GDP measured at 1995 PPP weights.

g. Now excludes the Republic of Korea, which has been reclassified as high-income OCED.

The globalization of markets and production and the resulting growth of world trade, foreign direct investment, and imports all imply that firms are finding their home markets under attack from foreign competitors. This is true in Japan, where U.S. companies such as Kodak, Procter & Gamble, and Merrill Lynch are expanding their presence. It is true in Canada, where Japanese automobile firms have taken market share away from General Motors and Ford. And it is true in Europe, where the once-dominant Dutch company Philips has seen its market share in the consumer electronics industry taken by Japan's JVC, Matsushita, and Sony. The growing integration of the world economy into a single, huge marketplace is increasing the intensity of competition in a range of manufacturing and service industries.

Having said all this, declining trade barriers can't be taken for granted. As we shall see in the following chapters, demands for "protection" from foreign competitors are still often heard in countries around the world, including Canada. Although a return to the restrictive trade policies of the 1920s and 30s is unlikely, it is not clear whether the political majority in the industrialized world favours further reductions in trade barriers. If trade barriers decline no further, at least for the time being, a temporary limit may have been reached in the globalization of both markets and production.

THE ROLE OF TECHNOLOGICAL CHANGE

The lowering of trade barriers made globalization of markets and production a theoretical possibility. Technological change has made it a tangible reality. Since the end of World War II, the world has seen major advances in communication, information processing, and transportation technology, including the explosive emergence of the Internet and World Wide Web. In the words of Renato Ruggiero, the former director general of the World Trade Organization,

> Telecommunications is creating a global audience. Transport is creating a global village. From Buenos Aires to Boston to Beijing, ordinary people are watching MTV, they're wearing Levi's jeans, and they're listening to Sony Walkmans as they commute to work.[17]

Microprocessors and Telecommunications

Perhaps the single most important innovation has been development of the microprocessor, which enabled the explosive growth of high-power, low-cost computing, vastly increasing the amount of information that can be processed by individuals and firms. The microprocessor also underlies many recent advances in telecommunications technology. Over the past 30 years, global communications have been revolutionized by developments in satellite, optical fibre, and wireless technologies, and now the Internet and the World Wide Web. These technologies rely on the microprocessor to encode, transmit, and decode the vast amount of information that flows along these electronic highways. The cost of microprocessors continues to fall, while their power increases (a phenomenon known as **Moore's Law,** which predicts that the power of microprocessor technology doubles and its cost of production falls in half every 18 months).[18] As this happens, the costs of global communications are plummeting, which lowers the costs of coordinating and controlling a global organization. Thus, between 1930 and 1990, the cost of a three-minute phone call between New York and London fell from $244.65 to $3.32 in inflation adjusted dollars.[19]

MOORE'S LAW
The power of microprocessor technology doubles and its costs of production fall in half every 18 months.

The Internet and World Wide Web

The phenomenal recent growth of the Internet and the associated World Wide Web (which utilizes the Internet to communicate between World Wide Web sites) is the latest expression of this development. In 1990, fewer than 1 million users were connected to the Internet. By 1995, the figure had risen to 50 million. In 2001, it grew to 490 million. By the year 2005, forecasts suggest that the Internet may have over 1.12 billion users, or about 18 percent of the world's population.[20] The Internet has changed the way people communicate. A 2003 United Nations e-commerce study reported that there were 591 567 000 Internet users in 2003.[21] In Canada, for example, Statistics Canada reported that the number of Internet household users in 2004 reached 64 percent of 12.3 million households. E-commerce is also experiencing similar growth patterns, and in Canada, private and public sector online sales soared to $19.1 billion last year. Private sector sales accounted for the majority of these figures.[22] The 2004 U.S. B2B e-commerce revenues reached US$1.01 trillion. The 2004 world e-commerce revenues are expected to exceed US$2.7 trillion.[23]

The Internet and World Wide Web (WWW) promise to develop into the information backbone of tomorrow's global economy. According to Forrester Research, the value of Web-based transactions hit $657 billion in 2000, from virtually nothing in 1994, and

ANOTHER PERSPECTIVE

Technological change as a driver of globalization in the classroom

Your team members are from Germany, Austria, Japan, and, in Canada, NWT and New Brunswick; and your team assignment in your international business class is to conduct a global market analysis for a product your team has devised. To meet at one time and one place, your team has set up an Internet chat room and designated meeting times. Yesterday you had to get up at 3 A.M. for the meeting. Your team also maintains a Listserv so that team members can keep in touch and make decisions between meetings. Team rules include checking email twice a day; responding to all emails, even if you have nothing to add; and being at all scheduled meetings. Such a virtual team assignment in your international classes is solid practice for the international business world.

could grow to $6.8 trillion by 2004, with the United States accounting for 47 percent of all Web-based transactions.[24] Many of these transactions are not business-to-consumer transactions, but business-to-business transactions. The greatest current potential of the Web seems to be in the business-to-business arena.

Included in the expanding volume of Web-based traffic is a growing percentage of cross-border trade. Viewed globally, the Web is emerging as an equalizer. It rolls back some of the constraints of location, scale, and time zones.[25] The Web allows businesses, both small and large, to expand their global presence at a lower cost than ever before. The Web makes it much easier for buyers and sellers to find each other, wherever they may be located and whatever their size.

Transportation Technology

In addition to developments in communication technology, several major innovations in transportation technology have occurred since World War II. In economic terms, the most important are probably the development of commercial jet aircraft and superfreighters and the introduction of containerization, which simplifies transshipment from one mode of transport to another. The advent of commercial jet travel, by reducing the time needed to get from one location to another, has effectively shrunk the globe (see Figure 1.1). In terms of travel time, Toronto is now "closer" to Tokyo than it was to Montreal in the Colonial days.

Containerization has revolutionized the transportation business, significantly lowering the costs of shipping goods over long distances. Before the advent of containerization, moving goods from one mode of transport to another was very labour intensive, lengthy, and costly. It could take days and several hundred longshoremen to unload a ship and reload goods onto trucks and trains. With the advent of widespread containerization in the 1970s and 1980s, the whole process can be executed by a handful of longshoremen in a couple of days. Since 1980, the world's containership fleet has more than quadrupled, reflecting in part the growing volume of international trade and in part the switch to this mode of transportation. As a result of the efficiency gains associated with containerization, transportation costs have plummeted, making it much more economical to ship goods around the globe, thereby helping to drive the globalization of markets and production. Between 1920 and 1990, the average ocean freight and port charges per tonne of U.S. export and import cargo fell from $95 to $29 (in 1990 dollars).[26] The cost of shipping freight per tonne-mile on railroads in the United States fell from 3.04 cents in 1985 to 2.3 cents in 2000, largely as a result of efficiency gains from the widespread use of containers.[27] An increased share of cargo now goes by air, due to the falling costs of air transportation. Between 1930 and 1990, average air transportation revenue per passenger mile fell from $0.68 to $0.11.[28]

The Globalization of Production

As transportation costs associated with the globalization of production declined, dispersal of production to geographically widespread locations became more economical. As a result of the technological innovations discussed above, the real costs of information processing and communication have fallen dramatically in the past two decades. These developments make it possible for a firm to create and then manage a globally dispersed production system, further facilitating the globalization of production.

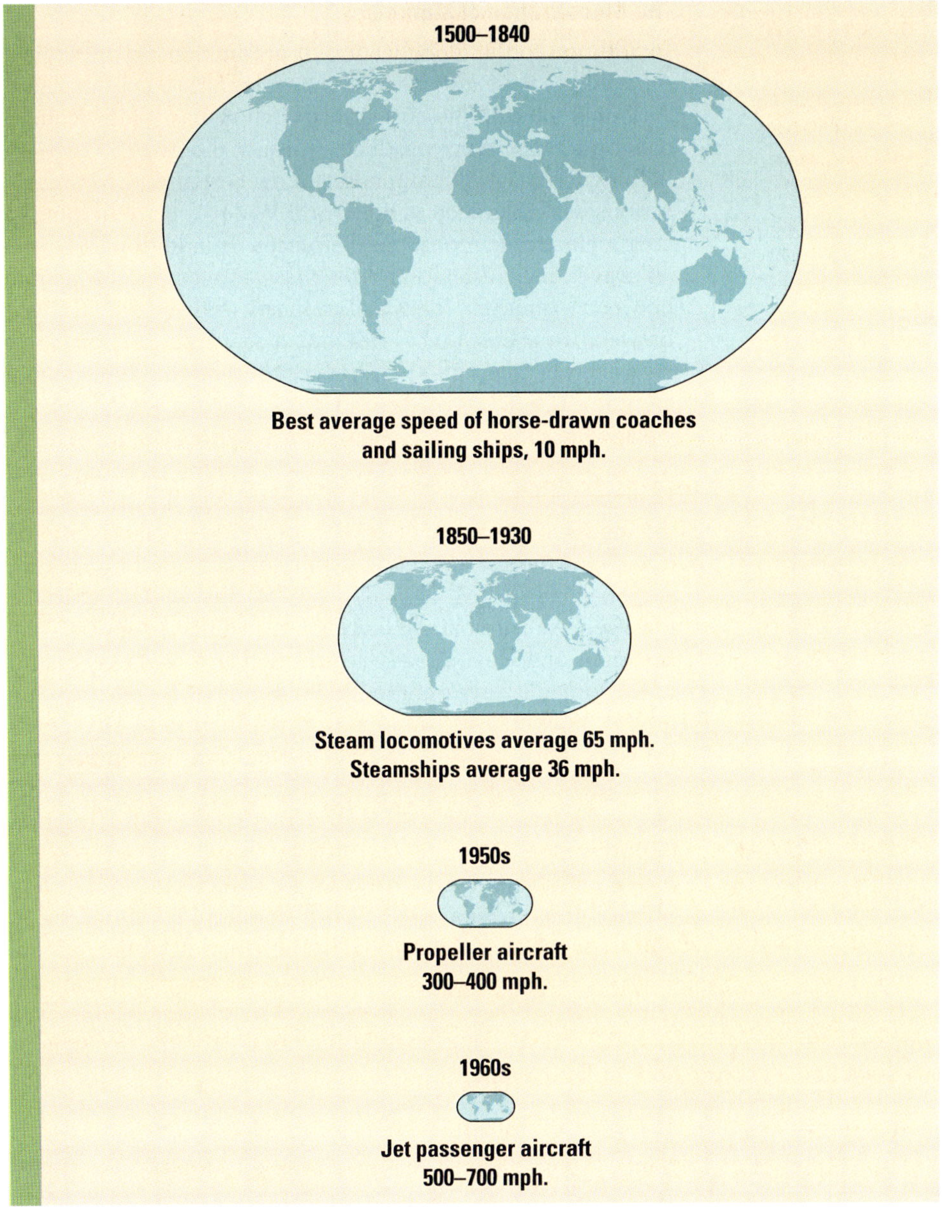

FIGURE 1.1

The Shrinking Globe

Source: P. Dicken, *Global Shift* (New York: Guilford Press, 1992), p. 104.

A worldwide communications network has become essential for many international businesses. For example, Hewlett-Packard uses satellite communications and information processing technologies to link its worldwide operations. Hewlett-Packard's product development teams consist of individuals based in different countries (e.g., Japan, the United States, Great Britain, and Germany). When developing new products, these individuals use videoconferencing to "meet" on a weekly basis. They also communicate with each other daily via telephone, electronic mail, and fax. Communication technologies have enabled Hewlett-Packard to integrate its globally dispersed operations and to reduce the time needed for developing new products.[29]

The development of commercial jet aircraft has also helped knit together the worldwide operations of many international businesses. Using jet travel, a North American manager need spend a day at most travelling to her firm's European or Asian operations. This enables her to oversee a globally dispersed production system.

ANOTHER PERSPECTIVE

Small companies benefit from globalization, too

Junko Watanabe, a Japanese student studying management at a major U.S. university, had a project for her Internet business class: to design a commercial Web page. She set up a Web site for her father's small, local PVC pipe manufacturing company located in the suburbs of Tokyo. To please her father, she used his actual product and pricing lists and guessed at shipping costs. To ensure a good evaluation on her product from her professor, she researched tariff rates and other trade barriers, calculating the additional costs of the product by country. Rather than present these data in terms of export from Japan, she organized her exhibits from a consumer's point of view, including estimated delivery time, shipping, and insurance costs. The potential consumer could then easily compare delivery, price, and product quality. Her exhibit for these additional charges drew on what she'd learned in her graphics and trade and finance classes.

Much to her surprise, a few weeks after she went public with her site, she received an inquiry from a branch of the Saudi Arabian government, which resulted in a visit to her father's company in Tokyo and a large, multi-year order.

The Globalization of Markets

In addition to the globalization of production, technological innovations have also facilitated the globalization of markets. As noted above, low-cost transportation has made it more economical to ship products around the world, thereby helping to create global markets. Low-cost global communications networks such as the World Wide Web are helping to create electronic global marketplaces. In addition, low-cost jet travel has resulted in the mass movement of people between countries. This has reduced the cultural distance between countries and is bringing about some convergence of consumer tastes and preferences. At the same time, global communication networks and global media are creating a worldwide culture. U.S. television networks such as CNN, MTV, and HBO are now received in many countries, and Hollywood films are shown the world over. In any society, the media are primary conveyors of culture; as global media develop, we must expect the evolution of something akin to a global culture. A logical result of this evolution is the emergence of global markets for consumer products. The first signs of this are already apparent. It is now as easy to find a McDonald's restaurant in Tokyo as it is in Toronto, to buy a Sony Walkman in Rio as it is in Berlin, and to buy Levi's jeans in Paris as it is in Vancouver. The accompanying Management Focus, "Homer Simpson–A Global Brand!" illustrates the power of the media to create global market opportunities.

Despite these trends, we must be careful not to overemphasize their importance. While modern communication and transportation technologies are ushering in the "global village," very significant national differences remain in culture, consumer preferences, and business practices. A firm that ignores differences between countries does so at its peril. We shall stress this point repeatedly throughout this book and elaborate on it in later chapters.

THE CHANGING DEMOGRAPHICS OF THE GLOBAL ECONOMY

Hand in hand with the trend toward globalization has been a fairly dramatic change in the demographics of the global economy over the past 30 years. As late as the 1960s, four stylized facts described the demographics of the global economy. The first was U.S. dominance in the world economy and world trade picture. The second was U.S. dominance in world foreign direct investment. Related to this, the third fact was the dominance of large, multinational U.S. firms on the international business scene. The fourth was that roughly half the globe–the centrally planned economies of the Communist world–was off-limits to Western international businesses. As will be explained below, all four of these qualities either have changed or are now changing rapidly.

THE CHANGING WORLD OUTPUT AND WORLD TRADE PICTURE

In the early 1960s, the United States was still by far the world's dominant industrial power. In 1963 the United States accounted for 40.3 percent of world output. By 2000, the United States accounted for 27 percent of world output, still by far the world's

MANAGEMENT FOCUS

HOMER SIMPSON—A GLOBAL BRAND!

If a poll were held to identify the world's favourite dysfunctional family, the Simpsons would probably win hands down. The Fox Broadcasting Company production that documents the life and times of Homer and his irreverent clan is the most decorated and longest running animated TV show in history. Some 60 million viewers in more than 70 countries tune in to watch the weekly antics of the Simpsons. The show seems to have universal appeal, with the audience split 50/50 between adults and children, and with audience ratings running high in countries as diverse as Spain and Japan. *Time* magazine named "The Simpsons" the 20th century's best TV show, and the chair of the philosophy department at the University of Manitoba wrote an article claiming "The Simpsons" is the deepest show on television.

Whatever the sources of the show's appeal, there is no question that Homer and his family have become a powerful global brand. Not only do Fox and its parent News Corporation benefit from the huge syndication rights of the show, but they also have made a significant sum from licensing the characters. Since the inception of the show in 1990, "The Simpsons" has generated more than $1 billion in retail sales from tie-in merchandise, much of it outside the United States. In 2000, about 50 large brand and marketing partners around the world used the Simpsons to sell everything from toilet paper in Germany, Kit Kat bars and potato chips in the United Kingdom, El Cortes Bart Simpson dolls in Spain, and Intel microprocessors in the United States. Clinton Cards, a British greeting card retailer, used Father's Day in 2000 as the perfect opportunity to find the British father whose behaviour most resembles that of Homer Simpson. The competition was rolled out across all the company's 692 stores and supported by TV advertising.

So what's next for the Simpsons? Fox has been careful to manage the licensing deals so that Homer and clan don't suffer from overexposure or aren't used in inappropriate ways. According to Matt Groening, the show's creator, " 'The Simpsons' is a commercial enterprise and we embrace the capitalistic nature of this project. What we try to do with 'The Simpsons' is not do a label slap—that is, we don't just slap their drawings on the side of a product. We try to make each item witty, and sometimes we comment on the absurdity of the item itself." In short, Fox tries to make sure that "The Simpsons" characters are used in a way that is consistent with the irreverent nature of the show itself. "If we didn't do this," notes a Fox spokesman, "we would lose credibility with the fans, and we have to make sure that doesn't happen."

Sources: D. Finnigan, "Homer Improvement," *Brandweek,* November 27, 2000, pp. 22–25, and "The Simpsons—Picking a Winner," *Marketing,* June 29, 2000, pp. 28–29.

largest industrial power but down significantly in relative size since the 1960s (see Table 1.3). Nor was the United States the only developed nation to see its relative standing slip. The same occurred to Germany, France, and the United Kingdom, all nations that were among the first to industrialize. This decline in the U.S. position was not an absolute decline, since the U.S. economy grew at a robust average annual rate of more than 3 percent from 1963 to 2003 (the economies of Germany, France, and the United Kingdom also grew during this time). Rather, it was a relative decline, reflecting the faster economic growth of several other economies, particularly in Asia.

TABLE 1.3

The Changing Pattern of World Output and Trade

COUNTRY	SHARE OF WORLD OUTPUT, 1963	SHARE OF WORLD OUTPUT, 2003	SHARE OF WORLD EXPORTS, 2003
United States	40.3%	21.1%	11%
Germany	9.7	4.5	9.6
France	6.3	3.2	5.7
Italy	3.4	3.0	4.1
United Kingdom	6.5	3.2	4.7
Canada	3.0	1.9	3.6
Japan	5.5	7.0	5.7
China	NA	12.6	5.0

Source: IMF World Economic Outlook, April 2004; Data for 1963 from N. Hood and J. Young, *The Economics of the Multinational Enterprise* (New York: Longman, 1973).

Fido travels well and communicates in all languages. What phone plan do you have and why do you have it? Is it portable in other countries? Courtesy of Fido.

For example, as can be seen from Table 1.3, from 1963 to 2003, China's share of world output increased from a trivial amount to 12.6 percent. Other countries that markedly increased their share of world output included Japan, Thailand, Malaysia, Taiwan, and South Korea.

By the end of the 1980s, the U.S. position as the world's leading exporter was threatened. Over the past 30 years, U.S. dominance in export markets has waned as Japan, Germany, and a number of newly industrialized countries such as South Korea and China have taken a larger share of world exports. During the 1960s, the United States routinely accounted for 20 percent of world exports of manufactured goods. But as Table 1.3 shows, the U.S. share of world exports of goods and services had slipped to 11 percent by 2003. Despite the fall, the United States still remained the world's largest exporter, ahead of Germany, Japan, France, and the fast-rising economic power, China.

In 1997 and 1998, the dynamic economies of the Asian Pacific region were hit by a serious financial crisis that threatened to slow their economic growth rates for several years. Despite this, their powerful growth may continue over the long run, as will that of several other important emerging economies in Latin America (e.g., Brazil) and Eastern Europe (e.g., Poland). Thus, a further relative decline in the share of world output and world exports accounted for by the United States and other long-established developed nations seems likely. By itself, this is not bad. The relative decline of the United States reflects the growing economic development and industrialization of the world economy, as opposed to any absolute decline in the health of the U.S. economy, which entered the new millennium stronger than ever.

Canada is by far the United States' largest trading partner–the U.S. exported over $169 billion of goods to Canada in 2003, up from approximately $150 billion in 1997. Mexico followed with U.S.-bound exports worth over $97 billion (see Table 1.4a). The United States imported over $210 billion of merchandise from Canada in 2003, followed by a distant second place China from which the United States imported approximately $152 million (see Table 1.4b). Canada exports and imports to and from the United States more than with any of its other key trading partners (see Figures 1.2a

TABLE 1.4a

Exports of Harmonized System (HS) Total—Total All Merchandise (in $thousands)

Source: www.tse.export.gov/. Presented by the Office of Trade and Industry Information (OTII), Manufacturing and Services, International Trade Administration, U.S. Department of Commerce.

PARTNER	1997	1998	1999	2000	2001	2002	2003
World Total	**$687,597,999**	**$680,474,248**	**$692,820,620**	**$780,418,628**	**$731,025,906**	**$693,257,300**	**$723,743,177**
Canada	150,124,378	154,152,162	163,912,764	176,429,632	163,724,462	160,799,214	169,480,937
Mexico	71,378,310	79,010,087	87,044,038	111,720,878	101,509,075	97,530,613	97,457,420
Japan	65,672,594	57,887,875	57,483,535	65,254,366	57,639,072	51,439,625	52,063,765
United Kingdom	36,435,090	39,070,195	38,337,793	41,579,356	40,797,923	33,253,090	33,895,379
Germany	24,466,907	26,641,872	26,788,867	29,243,960	30,113,948	26,628,438	28,847,948
China	12,805,416	14,257,953	13,117,677	16,253,029	19,234,827	22,052,679	28,418,493
South Korea	25,066,765	16,538,271	22,953,951	27,901,881	22,196,592	22,595,871	24,088,587
Netherlands	19,821,580	19,003,800	19,412,130	21,973,675	19,524,685	18,334,472	20,702,905
Taiwan	20,387,909	18,157,132	19,121,126	24,380,278	18,151,574	18,394,301	17,487,899
France	15,981,589	17,727,954	18,838,451	20,252,812	19,895,664	19,018,869	17,068,157

PARTNER	1997	1998	1999	2000	2001	2002	2003
World Total	**$870,212,682**	**$913,884,886**	**$1,024,765,969**	**$1,216,887,535**	**$1,141,959,125**	**$1,163,548,552**	**$1,259,395,643**
Canada	168,050,511	174,843,763	198,323,974	229,209,119	216,968,815	210,589,632	224,166,070
China	62,551,934	71,155,860	81,785,930	100,062,958	102,280,484	125,167,886	152,379,236
Mexico	85,872,345	94,708,666	109,706,486	135,910,534	131,432,957	134,732,185	138,073,297
Japan	121,359,200	121,981,583	131,403,584	146,576,578	126,601,729	121,494,231	118,028,982
Germany	43,069,159	49,823,932	55,093,519	58,736,615	59,151,323	62,480,446	68,046,988
Unite Kingdom	32,688,870	34,792,479	39,190,769	43,458,946	41,396,933	40,869,712	42,666,934
South Korea	23,159,041	23,936,461	31,261,995	40,300,349	35,184,728	35,575,187	36,963,336
Taiwan	32,623,992	33,122,902	35,198,495	40,514,187	33,391,321	32,199,347	31,599,871
France	20,724,930	24,077,254	25,909,645	29,782,444	30,295,508	28,408,008	29,221,178
Ireland	5,873,560	8,384,886	11,002,403	16,409,790	18,539,490	22,387,868	25,840,773

TABLE 1.4b

Imports of Harmonized System (HS) Total—Total All Merchandise (in $thousands)

Source: www.tse.export.gov/. Presented by the Office of Trade and Industry Information (OTII), Manufacturing and Services, International Trade Administration, U.S. Department of Commerce.

and 1.2b). In 2003, Canada exported over $300 billion of goods to the U.S. and imported over $200 billion of goods from the U.S.

If we look 20 years into the future, most forecasts now predict a rapid rise in the share of world output accounted for by developing nations such as China, India, Indonesia, Thailand, South Korea, Mexico, and Brazil, and a commensurate decline in the share enjoyed by rich industrialized countries such as Great Britain, Germany, Japan, and the United States. The World Bank, for example, has estimated that if current trends continue, by 2020 the Chinese economy could be larger than that of the United States, while the economy of India will approach that of Germany. The World Bank also estimates that today's developing nations may account for more than 60 percent of world economic activity by 2020, while today's rich nations, which currently account for over 55 percent of world economic activity, may account

FIGURE 1.2a

Canadian Total Exports for All Industries

Source: Adapted in part from the Statistics Canada Web site, www.statcan.ca/trade/scripts/trade_search.cgi.

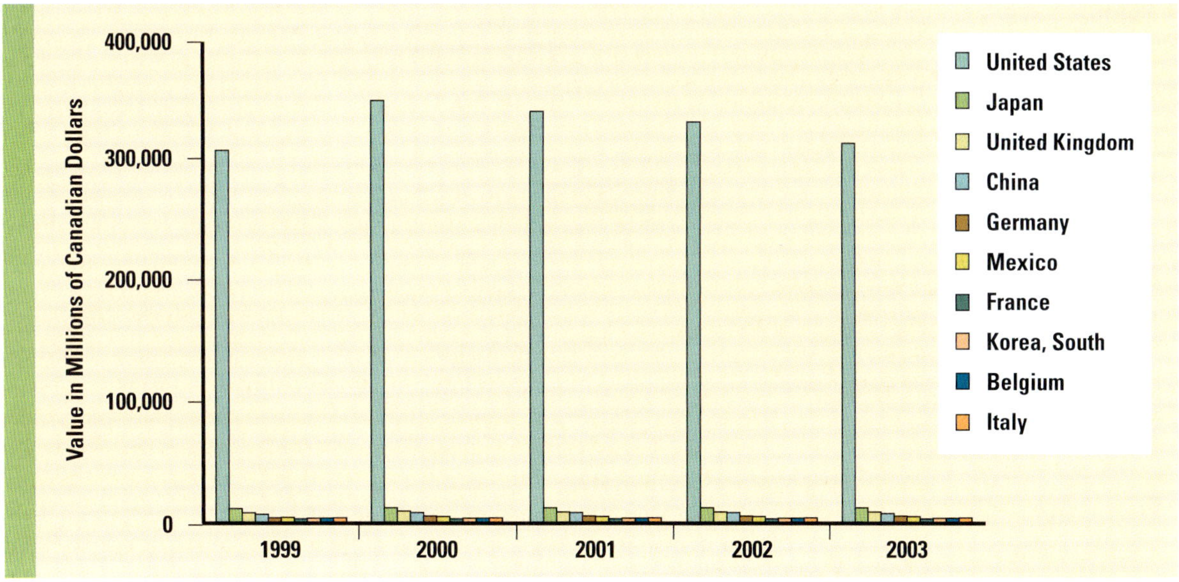

FIGURE 1.2b

Canadian Total Imports for All Industries

Source: Adapted in part from the Statistics Canada Web site, www.statcan.ca/trade/scripts/trade_search.cgi.

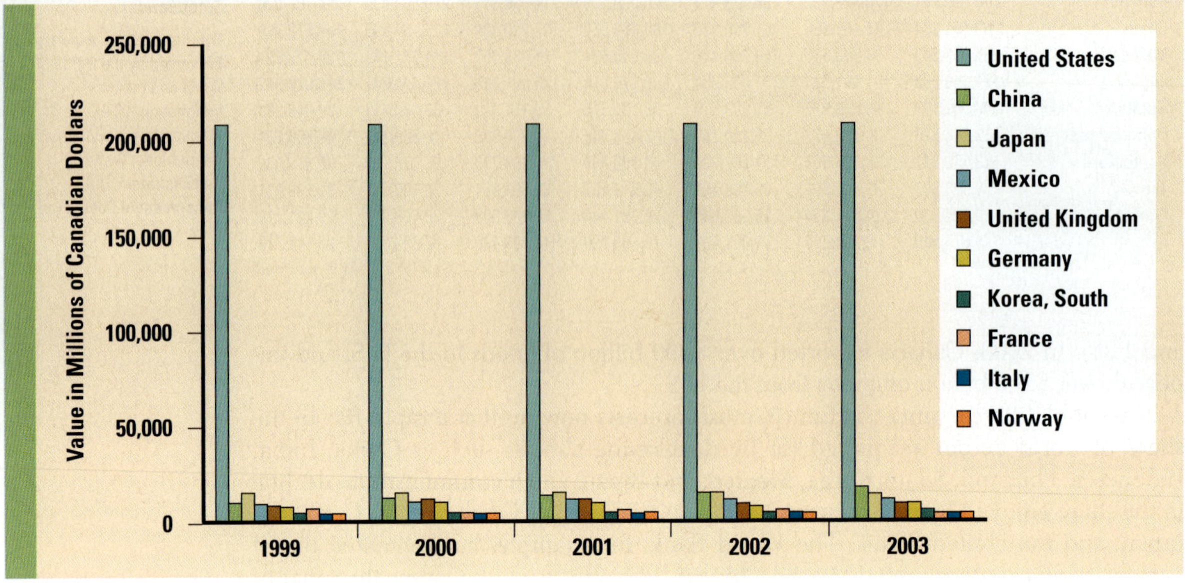

for only about 38 percent by 2020.[30] Forecasts are not always correct, but these suggest that a shift in the economic geography of the world is now under way, although the magnitude of that shift is still not totally evident. For international businesses, the implications of this changing economic geography are clear: Many of tomorrow's economic opportunities may be found in the developing nations of the world, and many of tomorrow's most capable competitors will probably also emerge from these regions.

> **ANOTHER PERSPECTIVE**
>
> **Opposition to globalization: They just don't see what it's really about**
>
> The antiglobalization concerns about the effects of globalization on developing countries are reasonable ones. Yet the Vancouver-based Fraser Institute's Economic Freedom of the World report, which measures relative economic freedom in 123 countries, suggests that globalization can be a positive force. This report offers evidence that economic freedom correlates with prosperity and economic growth. What might surprise the protesters is that on this index, the African country Botswana ranks as economically free as France. The most economically free countries are Hong Kong (it is counted as a country by the Fraser Institute), Singapore, and the United States. See www.freetheworld.com/ for more details. (*The Economist*, June 22, 2002, p. 78)

THE CHANGING FOREIGN DIRECT INVESTMENT PICTURE

Reflecting the dominance of the United States in the global economy, U.S. firms accounted for 66.3 percent of worldwide foreign direct investment flows in the 1960s. British firms were second, accounting for 10.5 percent, while Japanese firms were a distant eighth, with only 2 percent. The dominance of U.S. firms was so great that books were written about the economic threat posed to Europe by U.S. corporations.[31] Several European governments, most notably that of France, talked of limiting inward investment by U.S. firms.

However, as the barriers to the free flow of goods, services, and capital fell, and as other countries increased their shares of world output, non-U.S. firms increasingly began to invest across national borders. The motivation for much of this foreign direct investment by non-U.S. firms was the desire to disperse production activities to optimal locations and to build a direct presence in major foreign markets. Thus, beginning in the 1970s, European and Japanese firms began to shift labour-intensive manufacturing operations from their home markets to developing nations where labour costs were lower. In addition,

FIGURE 1.3a

Foreign Direct Investment of Stock—Inward

Source: United Nations Conference on Trade and Development, *2004 Facts and Figures*, p. 35.

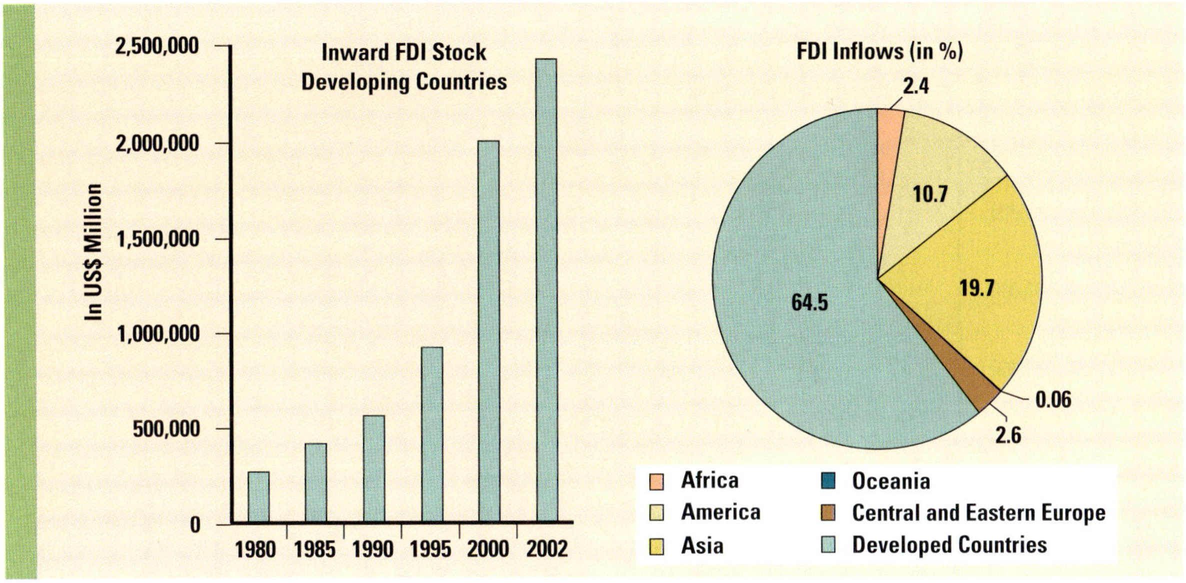

FIGURE 1.3b

Foreign Direct Investment of Stock—Outward

Source: United Nations Conference on Trade and Development, *2004 Facts and Figures*, p. 35.

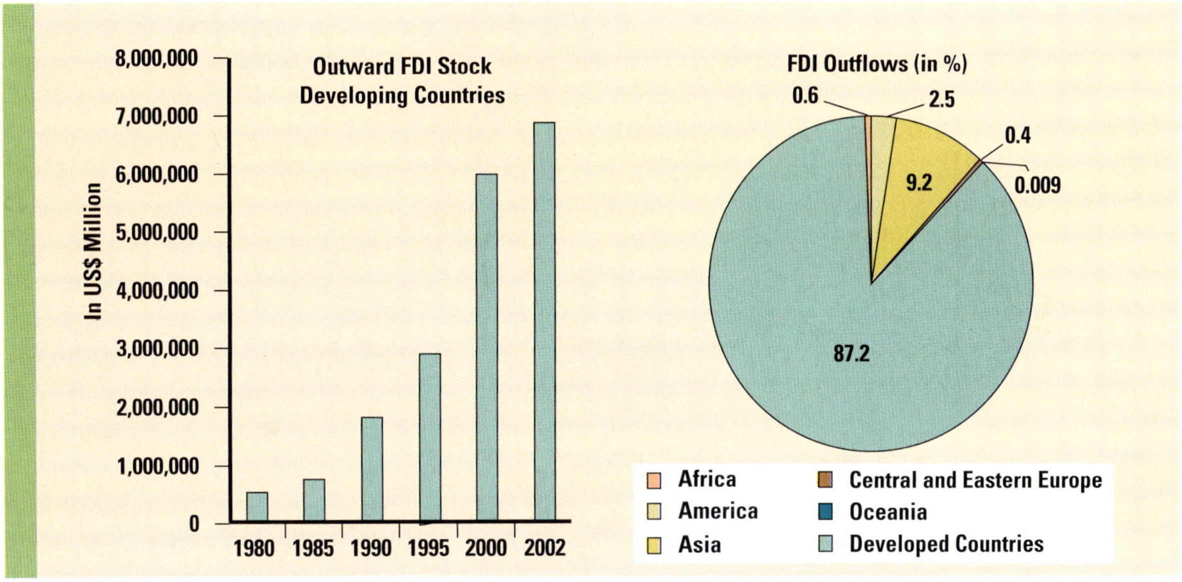

many Japanese firms invested in North America and Europe–often as a hedge against unfavourable currency movements and the possible imposition of trade barriers. For example, Toyota, the Japanese automobile company, rapidly increased its investment in automobile production facilities in the United States and Great Britain during the late 1980s and early 1990s. Toyota executives believed that an increasingly strong Japanese yen would price Japanese automobile exports out of foreign markets; therefore, production in the most important foreign markets, as opposed to exports

FIGURE 1.4a

Foreign Direct Investment Inflows

Source: United Nations Conference on Trade and Development, *2004 Facts and Figures*, p. 33.

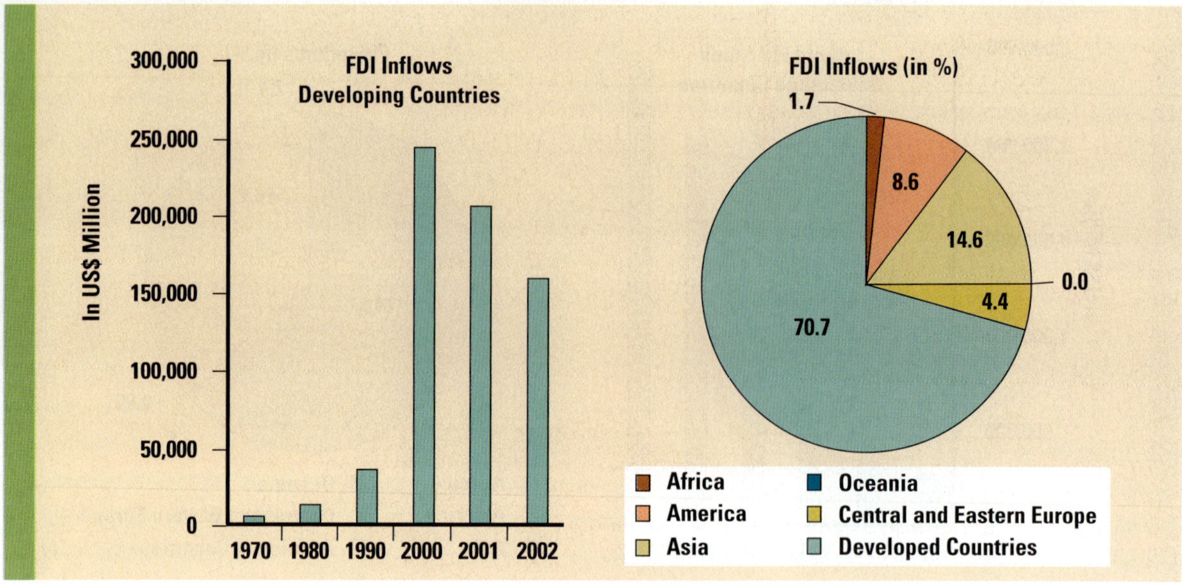

FIGURE 1.4b

Foreign Direct Investment Outflows

Source: United Nations Conference on Trade and Development, *2004 Facts and Figures*, p. 33.

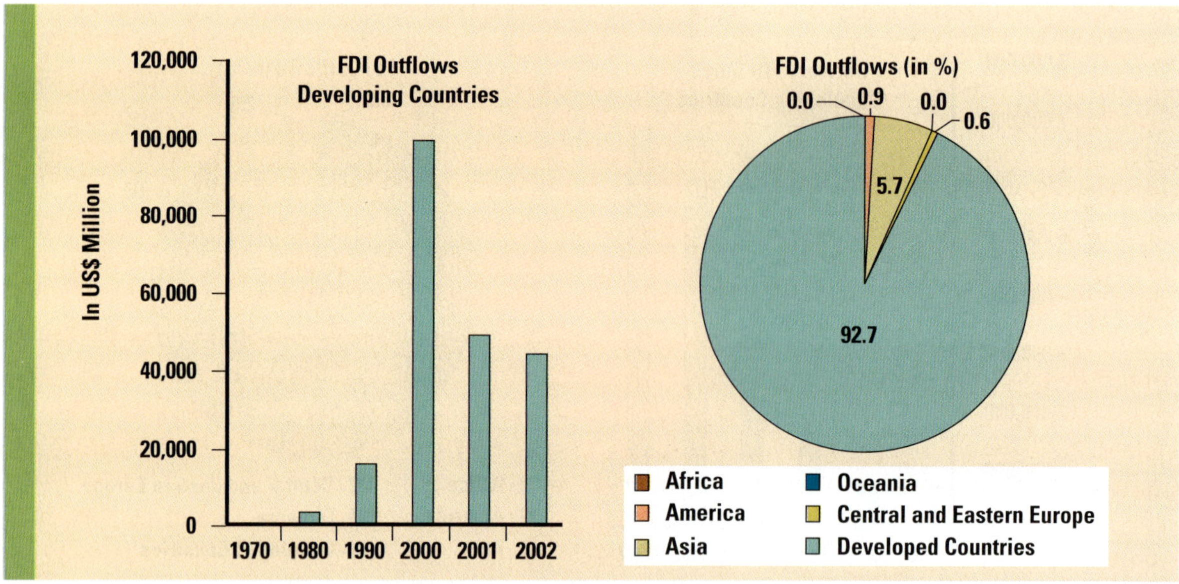

STOCK OF FOREIGN DIRECT INVESTMENT The total accumulated value of foreign-owned assets at a given time.

from Japan, made sense. Toyota also undertook these investments to head off growing political pressures in the United States and Europe to restrict Japanese automobile exports into those markets.

One consequence of these developments is illustrated in Figures 1.3a and 1.3b, which show how the world stock of foreign direct investment changed between 1980 and 2002. (The **stock of foreign direct investment** refers to the total cumulative value of foreign investments.) Figure 1.3a also shows the inward FDI stock by firms from developed and developing economies. From 1980 to 2002, this world total grew from $699,415 billion to over US$7.1 billion. The value of total inward FDI stock accounted for by North American firms rose dramatically tenfold from $137.2 billion in 1980 (about 20 percent of the world total) to over $1.5 trillion in 2002 (about 22 percent of the world total), yet in percentage terms, only increased marginally. As Figure 1.3b also shows, the outward flow of FDI stock by firms from developed and developing economies is similar to those of inward flows of stock of foreign direct investment.[32]

Figures 1.4a and 1.4b illustrate two other important trends–the continued rapid growth in cross-border flows of foreign direct investment (Figure 1.4a) and the emerging importance of developing nations as the destination of foreign direct investment (Figure 1.4b). From the 1990s, the amount of investment directed at both developed and developing nations increased dramatically, a trend that reflects the increasing internationalization of business corporations. Until 2000, developing nations were taking an increasingly large percentage share of this flow. However, the Asian economic crisis of 1997 had a worldwide effect that lasted until 2000.[33]

THE CHANGING NATURE OF THE MULTINATIONAL ENTERPRISE

A **multinational enterprise (MNE)** is any business that has productive activities in two or more countries. Since the 1960s, there have been two notable trends in the demographics of the multinational enterprise: (1) the rise of non-U.S. multinationals, particularly Japanese multinationals, and (2) the growth of mini-multinationals.

MULTINATIONAL ENTERPRISE (MNE) A firm that owns business operations in more than one country.

Non-U.S. Multinationals

In the 1960s, global business activity was dominated by large U.S. multinational corporations. With U.S. firms accounting for about two-thirds of foreign direct investment during the 1960s, one would expect most multinationals to be U.S. enterprises. The second largest source country was the United Kingdom, with 18.8 percent of the largest multinationals. Japan accounted for only 3.5 percent of the world's largest multinationals at the time. The large number of U.S. multinationals reflected U.S. economic dominance in the three decades after World War II, while the large number of British multinationals reflected that country's industrial dominance in the early decades of the twentieth century. The globalization of the world economy together with Japan's rise to the top rank of economic powers has resulted in a relative decline in the dominance of U.S. (and, to a lesser extent, British) firms in the global marketplace. If we look at smaller firms, we see significant growth in the number of multinationals from developing economies.

The Rise of Mini-Multinationals

Another trend in international business has been the growth of medium-sized and small multinationals (mini-multinationals). When people think of international businesses, they tend to think of firms such as Exxon, General Motors, Ford, Fuji, Bombardier, Matsushita, Procter & Gamble, Sony, and Unilever–large, complex multinational corporations with operations that span the globe. Although it is certainly true that most international trade and investment is still conducted by large firms, it is also true that many medium-sized and small businesses are becoming increasingly involved in international trade and investment. For another example, consider Sterner Automation Ltd. of Toronto, Ontario. Sterner Automation provides engineering solutions for customizing machinery and automated control systems. It employs a staff of 38 and generates 64 percent of its total revenue of $7.6 million from export sales.[34] Their clients are located around the globe; including the United States, Mexico, Korea, Germany, and the U.K.[35] Although a tiny player, they are making increasingly larger inroads internationally.

Or consider the case of Toronto-based Bravado! Designs Inc., a small manufacturer and design firm of chic maternity apparel. About 85 percent of its $4.5 million in revenues comes from export sales. Bravado! exports to 15 countries and currently has an office in the U.K., where they are working to expand the company's product line into France and Germany.[36]

Finally, look at Carmanah Technologies Inc. of Victoria, B.C., a manufacturer of solar-powered light-emitting LED lighting fixtures utilizing a patented, proprietary solar-powered technology. Employing just 81 people, and accessing a distributor network in over 80 countries, this small company is the only supplier of LED aviation lights for airports.[37]

THE CHANGING WORLD ORDER

Between 1989 and 1991 a series of remarkable democratic revolutions swept the Communist world. For reasons that are explored in more detail in Chapter 2, in country after country throughout Eastern Europe and eventually in the Soviet Union itself, Communist governments collapsed like the shells of rotten eggs. The Soviet Union is now history, having been replaced by 15 independent republics. Czechoslovakia divided itself into two states, while Yugoslavia dissolved into a bloody civil war among its five successor states.

Many of the former Communist nations of Europe and Asia seem to share a commitment to democratic politics and free market economics. If this continues, the opportunities for international businesses may be enormous. For nearly half a century, these countries were essentially closed to Western international businesses. Now they present a host of export and investment opportunities. Just how this will play out over the next ten to 20 years is difficult to say. The economies of most of the former Communist states are in very poor condition, and their continued commitment to democracy and free market economics cannot be taken for granted. Disturbing signs of growing unrest and totalitarian tendencies continue to be seen in many Eastern

Amazon.com takes advantage of Internet sales by providing a section entitled "Amazon International," which allows customers to shop by region. Visuals Unlimited.

European states. Thus, the risks involved in doing business in such countries are very high, but then, so may be the returns.

In addition to these changes, more quiet revolutions have been occurring in China and Latin America. Their implications for international businesses may be just as profound as the collapse of communism in Eastern Europe. China suppressed its own prodemocracy movement in the bloody Tiananmen Square massacre of 1989. Despite this, China continues to move progressively toward greater free market reforms. If what is occurring in China continues for two more decades, China may move from Third World to industrial superpower status even more rapidly than Japan did. If China's gross domestic product (GDP) per capita grows by an average of 6 percent to 7 percent, which is slower than the 8 percent growth rate achieved during the last decade, then by 2020, this nation of 1.273 billion people could boast an average income per capita of about $13,000, roughly equivalent to that of Spain's today.

The potential consequences for international business are enormous. With 1.3 billion people, China represents a huge and largely untapped market. China's new firms are proving to be very capable competitors, and they could take global market share away from Western and Japanese enterprises. Thus, the changes in China are creating both opportunities and threats for established international businesses.

As for Latin America, both democracy and free market reforms also seem to have taken hold. For decades, most Latin American countries were ruled by dictators, many of whom seemed to view Western international businesses as instruments of imperialist domination. Accordingly, they restricted direct investment by foreign firms. In addition, the poorly managed economies of Latin America were characterized by low growth, high debt, and hyperinflation–all of which discouraged investment by international businesses. Now much of this seems to be changing. Throughout most of Latin America, debt and inflation are down, governments are selling state-owned enterprises to private investors, foreign investment is welcomed, and the region's economies are growing rapidly. These changes have increased the attractiveness of Latin America, both as a market for exports and as a site for foreign direct investment. At the same time, given the long history of economic mismanagement in Latin America, there is no guarantee that these favourable trends will continue. As in the case of Eastern Europe, substantial opportunities are accompanied by substantial risks.

THE GLOBAL ECONOMY OF THE TWENTY-FIRST CENTURY

The last quarter century has seen rapid changes in the global economy. Barriers to the free flow of goods, services, and capital have been coming down. The volume of cross-border trade and investment has been growing more rapidly than global output, indicating that national economies are becoming more closely integrated into a single, interdependent, global economic system. As their economies advance, more nations are joining the ranks of the developed world. A generation ago, South Korea and Taiwan were viewed as second-tier developing nations. Now they boast large economies, and their firms are major players in many global industries from shipbuilding and steel to electronics and chemicals. The move toward a global economy has been further strengthened by the widespread adoption of liberal economic policies by countries that for two generations or more were firmly opposed to them. Thus, following the normative prescriptions of liberal economic ideology, in country after country we are seeing privatization of state-owned businesses, widespread deregulation, markets being opened to more competition, and increased commitment to removing barriers to cross-border trade and investment. This suggests that over the next few decades, countries such as the Czech Republic, Poland, Brazil, China, and South Africa may build powerful market-oriented economies. In short, current trends indicate the world is moving rapidly toward an economic system that is more favourable for the practice of international business.

On the other hand, it is always hazardous to take established trends and use them to predict the future. The world may be moving toward a more global economic system, but globalization is not inevitable. Countries may pull back from the recent commitment to liberal economic ideology if their experiences do not match their expectations. There are signs, for example, of a retreat from liberal economic ideology in Russia. Russia has experienced considerable economic pain as it tries to shift from a centrally planned economy to a market economy. If Russia's hesitation were to become more permanent and widespread, the liberal vision of a more prosperous global economy based on free market principles might not come to pass as quickly as many hope. Clearly, this would be a tougher world for international businesses to compete in.

Moreover, greater globalization brings with it risks of its own. This was starkly demonstrated in 1997 and 1998 when a financial crisis in Thailand spread first to other East Asian nations and then in 1998 to Russia and Brazil. Ultimately the crisis threatened to plunge the economies of the developed world, including the United States, into a recession. We explore the causes and consequences of this and other similar global financial crises in Chapters 9 and 10. For now it is simply worth noting that even from a purely economic perspective, globalization is not all good. The opportunities for doing business in a global economy may be significantly enhanced, but as we saw in 1997–98, the risks associated with global financial contagion are also greater. Still, as explained later in this book, there are ways for firms to exploit the opportunities associated with globalization, while at the same time reducing the risks through appropriate hedging strategies.

THE GLOBALIZATION DEBATE

Is the shift toward a more integrated and interdependent global economy a good thing? Many influential economists, politicians, and business leaders seem to think so. They argue that falling barriers to international trade and investment are the twin engines driving the global economy toward greater prosperity. They say increased international trade and cross-border investment will result in lower prices for goods and services. They believe that globalization stimulates economic growth, raises the incomes of consumers, and helps to create jobs in all countries that participate in the global trading system. However, despite the existence of a compelling body of theory and evidence, globalization has its critics.[38] Some of these critics have become increasingly vocal and active, taking to the streets to demonstrate their opposition to globalization.

ANTIGLOBALIZATION PROTESTS

Street demonstrations against globalization date to December 1999, when more than 40 000 protesters blocked the streets of Seattle in an attempt to shut down a World Trade Organization meeting being held in the city. The demonstrators were protesting against a wide range of issues, including job losses in industries under attack from foreign competitors, downward pressure on the wage rates of unskilled workers, environmental degradation, and the cultural imperialism of global media and multinational enterprises, which was seen as being dominated by what some protesters called the "culturally impoverished" interests and values of the United States. All these ills, the demonstrators claimed, could be laid at the feet of globalization. Meanwhile, the World Trade Organization meeting failed to reach agreement, and although the protests outside the meeting halls had little to do with that failure, the impression took hold that the demonstrators had derailed the meetings.

Emboldened by the experience in Seattle, antiglobalization protesters have turned up at almost every major meeting of a global institution. (see the accompanying Country Focus for details).

COUNTRY FOCUS

ANTIGLOBALIZATION PROTESTS IN FRANCE

One night in August 1999, ten men under the leadership of local sheep farmer and rural activist Jose Bove crept into the town of Millau in central France and vandalized a McDonald's restaurant under construction, causing an estimated $150,000 worth of damage. These were no ordinary vandals, however, at least according to their supporters, for the "symbolic dismantling" of the McDonald's outlet had noble aims, or so it was claimed. The attack was initially presented as a protest against unfair American trade policies. The European Union had banned imports of hormone-treated beef from the United States, primarily because of fears that hormone-treated beef might lead to health problems (although EU scientists had concluded there was no evidence of this). After a careful review, the World Trade Organization stated the EU ban was not allowed under trading rules that the EU and United States were party to, and that the EU would have to lift it or face retaliation. The EU refused to comply, so the U.S. government imposed a 100-percent tariff on imports of certain EU products, including French staples such as foie gras, mustard, and Roquefort cheese. On farms near Millau, Bove and others raised sheep whose milk was used to make Roquefort. They felt incensed by the American tariff and decided to vent their frustrations on McDonald's.

Bove and his compatriots were arrested and charged. They quickly became a focus of the emerging antiglobalization movement in France that was protesting everything from a loss of national sovereignty and "unfair" trade policies that were trying to force hormone-treated beef on French consumers, to the invasion of French culture by alien American values, so aptly symbolized by McDonald's. Lionel Jospin, France's prime minister, called the cause of Jose Bove "just." Allowed to remain free pending his trial, Bove travelled to Seattle in December to protest against the World Trade Organization, where he was feted as a hero of the antiglobalization movement. Back in France, Bove's July 2000 trial drew some 40 000 supporters to the small town of Millau, where they camped outside the courthouse and waited for the verdict. Bove was found guilty and sentenced to three months in jail, far less than the maximum possible sentence of five years. His supporters wore T-shirts claiming, "The world is not merchandise, and neither am I."

About the same time in the Languedoc region of France, California winemaker Robert Mondavi had reached agreement with the mayor and council of the village of Aniane and regional authorities to turn 125 acres of wooded hillside belonging to the village into a vineyard. Mondavi planned to invest $7 million in the project and hoped to produce top quality wine that would sell in Europe and the United States for $60 a bottle. However, local environmentalists objected to the plan, which they claimed would destroy the area's unique ecological heritage. Jose Bove, basking in sudden fame, offered his support to the opponents, and the protests started. In May 2001, the Socialist mayor who had approved the project was defeated in local elections in which the Mondavi project had become the major issue. He was replaced by a Communist, Manuel Diaz, who denounced the project as a capitalist plot designed to enrich wealthy U.S. shareholders at the cost of his villagers and the environment. Following Diaz's victory, Mondavi announced he would pull out of the project. A spokesman noted, "It's a huge waste, but there are clearly personal and political interests at play here that go way beyond us."

So are the French opposed to foreign investment? The experience of McDonald's and Mondavi seems to suggest so, as does the associated news coverage, but look closer and a different reality seems to emerge. McDonald's has more than 800 restaurants in France and continues to do well there. The level of foreign investment in France reached record levels in the late 1990s and 2000. In 2000, France recorded 563 major inward investment deals, a record, and American companies accounted for the largest number, some 178. French enterprises are also investing across borders at record levels. Given all the talk about American cultural imperialism, it is striking that a French company, Vivendi, now owns two of the propagators of American cultural values: Universal Pictures and publisher Houghton Mifflin. And French politicians seem set on removing domestic barriers that make it difficult for French companies to compete effectively in the global economy.

Sources: "Behind the Bluster," *The Economist,* May 26, 2001; "The French Farmers' Anti-global Hero," *The Economist,* July 8, 2000; C. Trueheart, "France's Golden Arch Enemy?" *Toronto Star,* July 1, 2000; and J. Henley, "Grapes of Wrath Scare off U.S. Firm," *The Economist,* May 18, 2001, p. 11.

On July 29, 2003, protesters make themselves known for a second day in a row at a World Trade Organization session in Montreal. Fewer arrests were made on this day than on the first day, but the protesters were still loud and clear. Was this behaviour necessary and did these protesting initiatives result in any changes? CP/Paul Chiasson.

ANOTHER PERSPECTIVE

Antiglobalization movement as a global protest
We can think about globalization as a complex collection of increasingly networked relationships and logistic systems. Although protesters object to this networked international trading system based on open borders, free flow of information, free movement, and free trade, in a sense the protest movement is exactly that: a tightly networked communication system that delivers protesters to the meeting sites of global organizations.

While violent protests may give the antiglobalization effort a bad name, the scale of the demonstrations shows that support for the cause goes beyond a core of protesters. Large sections of the population in many countries believe that globalization harms living standards and the environment. Both theory and evidence suggest that many of these fears are exaggerated, but this may not be communicated clearly. Both politicians and businesspeople need to do more to counter these fears. Many protests against globalization are tapping into a general sense of loss at the passing of a world in which barriers of time and distance, and vast differences in economic institutions, political institutions, and the level of development of different nations, produced a world rich in the diversity of human cultures.

GLOBALIZATION, JOBS, AND INCOME

There has been evidence of outsourcing of Canadian jobs to developing countries, with fears that this process will have long-term harmful effects on Canada's well being as a whole. Many Canadian nationalists, including Maude Barlow and Mel Hurtig, echo these concerns in relation to NAFTA and the WTO. As evidence of this outsourcing trend, GreenBud Manufacturing Ltd., a Toronto clothing manufacturer and former supplier to Roots Canada Ltd., closed its operations in 2004, costing 200 workers their jobs.[39]

Outsourcing is extending to Canada's IT industry. David Ticoll, an IT strategist at PricewaterhouseCoopers and co-author of the report, "A Fine Balance, The Impact of Offshore IT Services on Canada's IT Landscape" predicts that as many as 75 000 Canadian IT jobs would be lost to outsourcing to by 2010.[40] For example, as of December 31, 2003, a total of 18 510 employees have been released from Celestica with approximately another 620 employer positions still to be eliminated. Almost 70 percent of the employee terminations were in the Americas and 30 percent in Europe.[41] Company downsizing and outsourcing is done in the name of remaining competitive.

Supporters of globalization do concede that the wage rate enjoyed by unskilled workers in many advanced economies may have declined in recent years.[42] For example, data for the Organization for Economic Cooperation and Development suggest that since 1980 the lowest 10 percent of American workers have seen a drop in their real wages (adjusted for inflation) of about 20 percent, while the top 10 percent have enjoyed a real pay increase of around 10 percent.[43] In the same vein, a U.S. Federal Reserve study found that in the seven years preceding 1996, the earnings of the best paid 10 percent of U.S. workers rose in real terms by 0.6 percent annually while the earnings of the 10 percent at the bottom of the heap fell by 8 percent. In some areas, the fall was much greater.[44] Similar trends can be seen in many other countries.

However, while globalization critics argue that the decline in unskilled wage rates is due to the migration of low-wage manufacturing jobs offshore and a corresponding reduction in demand for unskilled workers, supporters of globalization see a more complex picture. They maintain that the declining real wage rates of unskilled workers owes far more to a technology-induced shift within advanced economies away from jobs where the only qualification was a willingness to turn up for work every day and toward jobs that require significant education and skills. They point out that many advanced economies report a shortage of highly skilled workers and an excess supply of unskilled workers. Thus, growing income inequality is a result of the wages for skilled workers being bid up by the labour market, and the wages for unskilled workers being discounted. If one agrees with this logic, a solution to the problem of declining incomes is to be found not in limiting free trade and globalization, but in increasing society's investment in education to reduce the supply of unskilled workers.[45]

Some research also suggests that the evidence of growing income inequality may be suspect. Robert Lerman of the Urban Institute believes that the finding of inequality is based on inappropriate calculations of wage rates. Reviewing the data using a different methodology, Lerman has found that far from income inequality increasing, an index of wage rate inequality for all workers actually fell by 5.5 percent between 1987 and 1994.[46] If future research supports this finding–and it may not–the argument that globalization leads to growing income inequality may lose much of its punch. During the last few years of the 1990s, the income of the worst paid 10 percent of the population actually rose twice as fast as that of the average worker, suggesting that the high employment levels of these years have triggered a rise in the income of the lowest paid.[47]

GLOBALIZATION, LABOUR POLICIES, AND THE ENVIRONMENT

A second source of concern is that free trade encourages firms from advanced nations to move manufacturing facilities to less developed countries that lack adequate regulations to protect labour and the environment from abuse by the unscrupulous.[48] Globalization critics often argue that adhering to labour and environmental regulations significantly increases the costs of manufacturing enterprises and puts them at a competitive disadvantage in the global marketplace vis-à-vis firms based in developing nations that do not have to comply with such regulations. Firms deal with this cost disadvantage, the theory goes, by moving their production facilities to nations that do not have such burdensome regulations or that fail to enforce the regulations they have.

If this is the case, one might expect free trade to lead to an increase in pollution and result in firms from advanced nations exploiting the labour of less developed nations.[49] This argument was used repeatedly by those who opposed the 1994 formation of the North American Free Trade Agreement (NAFTA) between Canada, Mexico, and the United States. They painted a picture of U.S. manufacturing firms moving to Mexico in droves so that they would be free to pollute the environment, employ child labour, and ignore workplace safety and health issues, all in the name of higher profits.[50]

Supporters of free trade and greater globalization express doubts about this scenario. They argue that tougher environmental regulations and stricter labour standards go hand in hand with economic progress.[51] In general, as countries get richer, they enact tougher environmental and labour regulations.[52] Because free trade enables developing countries to increase their economic growth rates and become richer, this should lead to tougher environmental and labour laws. In this view, the critics of free trade have got it backward–free trade does not lead to more pollution and labour exploitation, it leads to less. By creating wealth and incentives for enterprises to produce technological innovations, the free market system and free trade could make it easier for the world to cope with problems of pollution and population growth. Indeed, while pollution levels are rising in the world's poorer countries, they have been falling in developed nations. In Canada, for example, the concentration of carbon monoxide and sulphur dioxide emissions has decreased at a steady rate of 20 percent from 1980 to 2000, while total suspended particulates has decreased 60 percent–and these reductions occurred against a background of sustained economic expansion.[53] Drawn from a study undertaken for the Organization for Economic Cooperation and Development (OECD), it appears that the better a country performs economically, the more it does to protect the environment.[54]

Supporters of free trade also point out that it is possible to tie free trade agreements to the implementation of tougher environmental and labour laws in less developed countries. NAFTA, for example, was passed only after side agreements had been negotiated that committed Mexico to tougher enforcement of environmental protection regulations. Thus, supporters of free trade argue that factories based in Mexico are now cleaner than they would have been without the passage of NAFTA.[55]

They also argue that business firms are not the amoral organizations that critics suggest. While there may be some rotten apples, most business enterprises are staffed by managers who are committed to behave in an ethical manner and would be unlikely to move production offshore just so they could pump more pollution into the atmosphere or exploit labour. Furthermore, the relationship between pollution, labour exploitation, and production costs may not be that suggested by critics. In general, a well-treated labour force is productive, and it is productivity rather than base wage rates that often has the greatest influence on costs. The vision of greedy managers who shift production to low-wage countries to exploit their labour force may be misplaced.

GLOBALIZATION AND NATIONAL SOVEREIGNTY

Another concern voiced by critics of globalization is that today's increasingly interdependent global economy shifts economic power away from national governments and toward supranational organizations such as the World Trade Organization, the European Union, and the United Nations. As perceived by critics, unelected bureaucrats now impose policies on the democratically elected governments of nation-states, thereby undermining the sovereignty of those states and limiting the nation-state's ability to control its own destiny.[56]

The World Trade Organization is a favorite target of those who attack the headlong rush toward a global economy. As noted earlier, the WTO was founded in 1994 to police the world trading system established by the General Agreement on Tariffs and Trade. The WTO arbitrates trade disputes between the 148 states that are signatories to the GATT. The arbitration panel can issue a ruling instructing a member state to change trade policies that violate GATT regulations. If the violator refuses to comply with the ruling, the WTO allows other states to impose appropriate trade sanctions on the transgressor. Speaking at the Seattle IFG Teach-In on November 26, 1999, the prominent Canadian critic, activist writer, and policy critic, Maude Barlow stated:

At the heart of the WTO is an assault on everything left standing in the commons, in the public realm. Everything is now for sale. Even those areas of life that we once considered sacred like health and education, food and water and air and seeds and genes and a heritage. It is all now for sale. Economic freedom–not democracy, and not ecological stewardship–is the defining metaphor of the WTO and its central goal is humanity's mastery of the natural world through its total commodification." [57]

"There is a common assumption that the world's water supply is huge and infinite," Barlow has said. "This assumption of an unlimited water supply is false. At some time in the near future, water bankruptcy will result."[58]

In contrast to Barlow's rhetoric, many economists and politicians maintain that the power of supranational organizations such as the WTO is limited to that which nation-states collectively agree to grant. They argue that bodies such as the United Nations and the WTO exist to serve the collective interests of member states, not to subvert those interests. Supporters of supranational organizations point out that the power of these bodies rests largely on their ability to persuade member states to follow a certain action. If these bodies fail to serve the collective interests of member states, those states will withdraw their support and the supranational organization will quickly collapse. In this view, real power still resides with individual nation-states, not supranational organizations.

GLOBALIZATION AND THE WORLD'S POOR

Critics of globalization argue that despite the supposed benefits associated with free trade and investment, over the last hundred years or so the gap between the rich and poor nations of the world has gotten wider. In 1870 the average income per capita in the world's 17 richest nations was 2.4 times that of all other countries. In 1990 the same group was 4.5 times as rich as the rest.[59] While recent history has shown that some of the world's poorer nations are capable of rapid periods of economic growth–witness the transformation that has occurred in some Southeast Asian nations such as South Korea, Thailand, and Malaysia–there appear to be strong forces for stagnation among the world's poorest nations. A quarter of the countries with a GDP per capita of less than $1,000 in 1960 had growth rates of less than zero from 1960 to 1995, and a third had growth rates of less than 0.05 percent.[60] Critics argue that if globalization is such a positive development, this divergence between the rich and poor should not have occurred.

Although the reasons for economic stagnation vary, several factors stand out, none of which have anything to do with free trade or globalization. Many of the world's poorest countries have suffered from totalitarian governments, economic policies that destroyed wealth rather than facilitated its creation, scant protection for property rights, and war. Such factors help explain why countries such as Afghanistan, Cambodia, Cuba, Haiti, Iraq, Libya, Nigeria, Sudan, Vietnam, and Zaire have failed to improve the economic lot of their citizens during recent decades. A complicating factor is the rapidly expanding populations in many of these countries. Without a major change in government, population growth may exacerbate their problems. Promoters of free trade argue that the best way for these countries to improve their lot is to lower their barriers to free trade and investment and to implement economic policies based on free market economics.[61]

On the other hand, it is also true that many of the world's poorer nations are being held back by large debt burdens. Of particular concern are the 40 or so highly indebted poorer countries (HIPCs), which are home to some 700 million people. Among these countries, on average the government debt burden is equivalent to 85 percent of the value of the economy, as measured by gross domestic product, and the annual costs of serving government debt consumes 15 percent of the country's export earnings.[62] Servicing such a heavy debt load leaves the governments of these countries with little left to invest in important public infrastructure projects, such as high indebted poor countries

education, health care, roads, and power. The result: The HIPCs are trapped in a cycle of poverty and debt that inhibits economic development. Free trade alone, some argue, is not sufficient to help these countries bootstrap themselves out of poverty. What is needed is large-scale debt relief for the world's poorest nations to give them the opportunity to restructure their economies and start the long climb toward prosperity. Supporters of debt relief also argue that new democratic governments in poor nations should not be forced to honour debts that were incurred and mismanaged long ago by their corrupt and dictatorial predecessors.

In the late 1990s, a debt relief movement began to gain ground among the political establishment in the world's richer nations.[63] Fuelled by high-profile endorsements ranging from Irish rock star Bono (who has been a tireless and increasingly effective advocate for debt relief), to Pope John Paul II, the Dalai Lama, and influential Harvard economist Jeffry Sachs, the debt relief movement was instrumental in persuading the United States to enact legislation in 2000 that provided $435 million in debt relief for HIPCs. More importantly perhaps, the United States also backed an IMF plan to sell some gold reserves and use the proceeds to help with debt relief. The IMF and World Bank have now picked up the banner and are actively embarked on a systematic debt relief program.

For such a program to have a lasting effect, however, debt relief must be matched by wise investment in public projects that boost economic growth (such as education) and by the adoption of economic policies that facilitate investment and trade. The rich nations of the world can also help by reducing barriers to the importation of products from the world's poorer nations, particularly tariffs on imports of agricultural products and textiles. Debt relief is not new–it has been tried before.[64] Too often in the past, however, the short-term benefits were squandered by corrupt governments who used their newfound financial freedom to make unproductive investments in military infrastructure or grandiose projects that did little to foster long-run economic development. Developed nations, too, contributed to past failures by refusing to open their markets to the products of poor nations. If such a scenario can be avoided this time, the entire world will benefit.

MANAGING IN THE GLOBAL MARKETPLACE

INTERNATIONAL BUSINESS Any firm that engages in international trade or investment.

As their organizations increasingly engage in cross-border trade and investment, managers need to recognize that the task of managing an **international business**, one that engages in international trade or investment, differs from that of managing a purely domestic business in many ways. At the most fundamental level, the differences arise from the simple fact that countries are different. Countries differ in their cultures, political systems, economic systems, legal systems, and levels of economic development.

Differences between countries require that an international business vary its practices country by country. Managers within international businesses must develop strategies and policies for dealing with cross-border government interventions.

Cross-border transactions also require that money be converted from the firm's home currency into a foreign currency and vice versa. Since currency exchange rates vary in response to changing economic conditions, an international business must develop policies for dealing with exchange rate movements. A firm that adopts a wrong policy can lose large amounts of money, while a firm that adopts the right policy can increase the profitability of its international transactions.

In this book we examine all these issues in depth, paying close attention to the different strategies and policies that managers pursue to deal with the various challenges created when a firm becomes an international business. Chapters 2 and 3 explore how countries differ from each other with regard to their political, economic, legal, and cultural institutions. Chapter 4 examines the role of ethics in international business. Chapters 5 to 8 look at the international trade and investment environment within which international businesses must operate. Chapters 9 and 10 review the international monetary system. These chapters focus on the nature of the foreign exchange market and the emerging global monetary system. Chapters 11 and 12 explore the strategy of international businesses. Chapters 13 to 16 look at the management of various functional operations within an international business, including production, marketing, and human relations. By the time you complete this book, you should have a good grasp of the issues that managers working within international business have to grapple with on a daily basis, and you should be familiar with the range of strategies and operating policies available to compete more effectively in today's rapidly emerging global economy.

IMPLICATIONS FOR BUSINESS

As we will see throughout this book, the international business arena is becoming an increasingly open environment for goods and services to be bought and sold. For example, Canadian businesses can no longer operate in an insular manner, according to their own rules and regulations. Business managers need to see the world of strengths, weaknesses, opportunities, and threats in a global sense. What once were viable business survival and expansion strategies no longer work. Businesses are now forced to address the broader scope of commercial realities brought forth over the years through the General Agreement on Trade and Tariffs, and evolved through the World Trade Organization. Other synchronous tools of the globalization wave, as cited at the beginning of this chapter, are the United Nations, the World Bank, and others. Foreign direct investment, a crucial strategy in the globalization process, will be discussed in later chapters.

As of June 2004, the World Trade Organization (WTO) consisted of 148 members. The WTO is the host to new negotiations, under the "Doha Development Agenda" launched in 2001. In some circumstances, WTO rules support maintaining trade barriers, for example, to protect consumers or prevent the spread of disease. Membership requires that ground rules for international commerce, including contracts, be followed thus binding governments to keep their trade policies within agreed limits.

Since 1948, the General Agreement on Tariffs and Trade (GATT) had provided the rules for the system. Over the years, GATT evolved through several rounds of negotiations. The last and largest GATT round was the Uruguay Round, which lasted from 1986 to 1994 and led to the WTO's creation. Whereas GATT had mainly dealt with trade in goods, the WTO and its agreements now cover trade in services, and in traded inventions, creations, and intellectual property.[65]

Membership comes with responsibilities, but also with benefits. Adhering to the World Trade Organization, initiatives on a plethora of trade-related issues are paramount to a country's accession to inclusion into the "WTO club." Poorer countries might benefit from easier access to financing through international funding agencies. In South America, commercial and customs unions such as Mercosur and the Andean Pact are opening new doors for South American companies within these intra-markets. The Caribbean nations, through CARICOM, are benefiting through the same less restrictive commercial markets.

Other similar types of initiatives include: ASEAN, Association of Southeast Nations; AU, African Union; CAFTA, Central American Free Trade Agreement; CARICOM, Caribbean Community; CEMAC, Communauté Economique et Monétaire de l'Afrique Centrale; EAC, East African Community; EU, External Trade; GCC, Gulf Co-operation Council; JSEPA, Japan/Singapore Economic Partnership Agreement; MERCOSUR, Mercado Comun del Sur; and NAFTA, North American Free Trade Agreement.[66]

The European Union in 2005 will be very close to the WTO's concept of how free trade areas should appear. Mercosur, the Andean Pact, and other existing commercial unions, will cease to exist due to a growing NAFTA.

THE NORTH–SOUTH DIVIDE

The World Trade Organization is aiming for a world free of customs duties and trade barriers. Whether that goal will be attained is still to be determined. The transformations have not been, and will not be, smooth. Many of the world's wealthier nations appear to be pitted against the poor. In this north (wealthy)–south (developing countries) divide, there is continual divergence of views on the benefits of a "WTO world," frequently played out in much publicized WTO anti-globalization protests. Developing countries fear that they do not have the means and know-how to compete against the significantly more efficient industries of wealthy nations. In theory, as developing countries "subscribe" to WTO trade practices, standards of living, and social and political stabilities will increase and the economic gap between rich and poor nations will narrow.

THE ROLE OF TECHNOLOGY IN INTERNATIONAL TRADE

Without technology, the degree of globalization as we know it in 2005 would be less dominant. According to proponents of global free trade, the sheer volume of the world's business lends to decreased costs, contributing to increased purchasing power and rising standards of living. The World Wide Web has resulted in rapid border clearance of shipments of foods, internationally, while reducing costs in communications. After the September 11, 2001 terrorist attacks, technology has become core to the secure growth of international trade proving that technology benefits both rich and poor nations.

KEY TERMS

foreign direct investment (FDI), p. 10

General Agreement on Tariffs and Trade (GATT), p. 8

globalization, p. 7

globalization of markets, p. 7

globalization of production, p. 8

international business, p. 32

International Monetary Fund (IMF), p. 9

international trade, p. 10

Moore's Law, p. 13

multinational enterprise (MNE), p. 23

stock of foreign direct investment, p. 22

United Nations, p. 9

World Bank, p. 9

World Trade Organization (WTO), p. 9

SUMMARY

This chapter sets the scene for the rest of the book. We have seen how the world economy is becoming more global, and we have reviewed the main drivers of globalization and argued that they seem to be thrusting nation-states toward a more tightly integrated global economy. We have looked at how the nature of international business is changing in response to the changing global economy; we have discussed some concerns raised by rapid globalization; and we have reviewed implications of rapid globalization for individual managers. These major points were made in the chapter:

1. Over the past two decades, we have witnessed the globalization of markets and production.
2. The globalization of markets implies that national markets are merging into one huge marketplace. However, it is important not to push this view too far.
3. The globalization of production implies that firms are basing individual productive activities at the optimal world locations for the particular activities. As a consequence, it is increasingly irrelevant to talk about North American products, Japanese products, or German products, since these are being replaced by "global" products.
4. Two factors seem to underlie the trend toward globalization: declining trade barriers and changes in communication, information, and transportation technologies.

5. Since the end of World War II, there has been a significant lowering of barriers to the free flow of goods, services, and capital. More than anything else, this has facilitated the trend toward the globalization of production and has enabled firms to view the world as a single market.
6. As a consequence of the globalization of production and markets, in the last decade world trade has grown faster than world output, foreign direct investment has surged, imports have penetrated more deeply into the world's industrial nations, and competitive pressures have increased in industry after industry.
7. The development of the microprocessor and related developments in communication and information processing technology have helped firms link their worldwide operations into sophisticated information networks. Jet air travel, by shrinking travel time, has also helped to link the worldwide operations of international businesses. These changes have enabled firms to achieve tight coordination of their worldwide operations and to view the world as a single market.
8. The most dramatic environmental trend has been the collapse of Communist power in Eastern Europe, which has created enormous long-run opportunities for international businesses. In addition, the move toward free market economies in China and Latin America is creating opportunities (and threats) for Western international businesses.
9. The benefits and costs of the emerging global economy are being hotly debated among businesspeople, economists, and politicians. The debate focuses on the impact of globalization on jobs, wages, the environment, working conditions, and national sovereignty.
10. Managing an international business is different from managing a domestic business for at least four reasons: *(i)* countries are different, *(ii)* the range of problems confronted by a manager in an international business is wider and the problems themselves more complex than those confronted by a manager in a domestic business, *(iii)* managers in an international business must find ways to work within the limits imposed by governments' intervention in the international trade and investment system, and *(iv)* international transactions involve converting money into different currencies.

CRITICAL THINKING AND DISCUSSION QUESTIONS

1. Describe the shifts in the world economy over the past 30 years. What are the implications of these shifts for international businesses based in Great Britain? North America? Hong Kong?
2. The study of international business is fine if you are going to work in a large multinational enterprise, but it has no relevance for individuals who are going to work in small firms. Evaluate this statement.
3. How have changes in technology contributed to the globalization of markets and production? Would the globalization of production and markets have been possible without these technological changes?
4. Ultimately, the study of international business is no different from the study of domestic business. Thus, there is no point in having a separate course on international business. Evaluate this statement.
5. How might the Internet and the associated World Wide Web affect international business activity and the globalization of the world economy?
6. If current trends continue, China may be the world's largest economy by 2050. Discuss the possible implications for such a development for
   a. The world trading system.
   b. The world monetary system.
   c. The business strategy of today's European and U.S.-based global corporations.

RESEARCH TASK | globalEDGE™ globaledge.msu.edu

Use the globalEDGE™ site to complete the following exercises:

1. Your company has developed a new product that is expected to achieve high penetration rates in all the countries in which it is introduced, regardless of the average income status of the local populace. Considering the costs of the product launch, the management team has decided to initially introduce the product only in countries that have a sizeable population base. You are required to prepare a preliminary report with the top ten countries of the world in terms of population size. Since growth opportunities are another major concern, the average population growth rates also should be listed for management's consideration.
2. You are working for a company that is considering investing in a foreign country. Management has requested a report regarding the attractiveness of alternative countries based on the potential return of FDI. Accordingly, the ranking of the top 25 countries in terms of FDI attractiveness is a crucial ingredient for your report. A colleague mentioned a potentially useful tool called the "FDI Confidence Index," which is updated periodically. Find this index, and provide additional information regarding how the index is constructed.

Visit the *Global Business Today* Online Learning Centre at **www.mcgrawhill.ca/college/hill** to access quizzes, interactive exercises, a Business Around the World interactive map, and other learning and study tools related to this chapter.

Online LearningCentre

CLOSING CASE

THE CANADIAN BEEF INDUSTRY AND MAD COW DISEASE

Globalization results in an interconnected world where goods and ideas flow across national borders. Unfortunately for North Americans in 2003, a disease affecting the beef industry was also able to jump between countries, drastically affecting beef imports to almost 50 countries.

The technical name for mad cow disease is Bovine Spongiform Encephalopathy (BSE), which is the type of Transmissible Spongiform Encephalopathy (TSE) found in cattle. TSE is a family of progressive, incurable, and fatal diseases caused by prions. Prions are not a virus or a bacterium, but rather an infectious protein that can set off a chain reaction that destroys nerve cells. TSE can be transmitted between mammals when one mammal eats parts of the nervous system, such as the brain or spinal cord, of another mammal.

After two years of investigation into cattle that developed strange symptoms and soon after died, BSE was first diagnosed in Great Britain in 1986. Eventually, almost 5 million cattle were slaughtered, but not before nearly 1 million had made it into the food chain.

The origins of BSE remain unknown. Initially, it was thought that this disease posed no harm to people. However, the first case of transmission to humans emerged in 1995 when two teens in the U.K. were diagnosed with a variant of Creutzfeldt-Jakob disease, an otherwise rare disease known to affect the elderly. Eventually, there were 140 cases of BSE, all of them fatal.

For many years, Canada was thought to be free of mad cow disease. However, in May 2003, officials in Alberta confirmed that a sick cow had been inspected and a single case of mad cow disease had been confirmed. On May 20, 2003, Japan, the United States, and Mexico banned imports of beef and cattle from Canada.

The results were dramatic to Canada's $7.8-billion a year cattle industry. After Australia and the United States, Canada is the third largest beef exporter in the world. Beef exports from

Canada total about $2.2 billion annually. The ban was estimated to cost beef producers in Canada about $11 million a day.

Though 1400 cows were tested for the disease, only the single case was ever found.

Three months later, the United States eased a ban on most types of processed Canadian beef, which accounted for about 40 percent of the total value of Canadian beef and cattle sales to the U.S.; live cattle were still banned.

In December 2003, as the U.S. was considering reopening the border to Canadian live cattle, it was announced that the first apparent case of BSE was found in a cow in Washington State. The effects of this finding were even more dramatic. Many countries, eventually totalling 50, banned beef from the U.S.

Cattle prices quickly plunged by more than 20 percent, affecting a range of industries. In Canada, there was a surplus of milk because dairy cows could not be exported. This surplus resulted in downward pressure on Canadian milk prices. In the U.S., prices for corn, which is a staple in the cattle diet, dropped on fears that a large scale slaughter of U.S. cattle might be necessary, which would reduce the need for corn feed. Prices for beef alternatives, such as pork and poultry, rose. The stock prices of meat processors and packaging plants, such as Swift, Tyson Foods, and Cargill Inc. fell. Companies that manufactured farm machinery also saw their stock fall in value. However, companies that processed poultry, or that sold diagnostic tests to detect BSE, saw a rise in their stock prices.

The shares of restaurants that had beef as a main component of their menus, such as McDonald's, also dropped in price.

Since December 2003, such initial impacts have become more muted as consumers have maintained their strong consumption of U.S. and Canadian beef as continued assurances have been made that the product is safe for humans. Nonetheless, both governments are reviewing their beef tracking systems, slaughterhouse rules, feed restrictions, and testing of animals.

As the beef industry in both Canada and the U.S. total their losses in 2004 it is unknown when, and if, the disease will re-emerge in either country as well as the scope that any outbreak will ultimately take.

The story continues in 2005 as yet another case is found in Canada, but no widespread outbreak has emerged.

Sources: Commodity Research Bureau, *CRB Commodity Yearbook, 2004, Guide to World Commodity Markets*, 6th ed, (New York, Probus Publishing, 2004); CBC News at www.cbc.ca/news/background/madcow; Organic Consumers Association at www.organicconsumers.org/madcow.htm.

CASE DISCUSSION QUESTIONS

1. How isolated is one industry from another in today's globalized world? What are the positive and negative implications of this?
2. Currently, fewer then 1/10 of 1 percent of cattle are tested for BSE, at a cost of about $50 a cow. Is testing the best way to spend money to battle BSE?
3. Should ranchers and beef producers be compensated for their losses? Who should pay this compensation?

ADIDAS-SALOMON: SUPPLY-CHAIN MANAGEMENT

SITUATION

The Adidas sporting goods brand is famous across the world and, like any household name, it could potentially become the target of protests and media pressure if its parent company's policies and practices fail to win public approval.

Using an external supply chain has allowed Adidas-Salomon to keep its costs down and remain competitive. However, the company's supply chain is long and complex, relying on about 570 factories around the world. In Asia alone, its suppliers operate in 18 countries. Its cost-saving use of external suppliers is not without risks—in particular, the company has less control over workplace conditions at its suppliers' factories than it would have at company-owned sites.

Outsourcing raises a broad range of issues and concerns. The company must evaluate employment standards throughout the supply chain to ensure fairness and legal compliance on such matters as wages and benefits, working hours, freedom of association, and disciplinary practices as well as on the even more serious issues of forced labour, child labour, and discrimination. Health and safety issues, environmental requirements, and community involvement also need to be considered.

TARGETS

Outsourcing supply should not mean outsourcing moral responsibility. Recognizing this along with the risks and responsibilities associated with managing a global supply chain, Adidas-Salomon designed and implemented a comprehensive supply-chain management strategy.

That strategy is to source the company's supplies from the cheapest *acceptable* sources rather than from the cheapest possible. The company has its own so-called standards of engagement (SOE), and the level of acceptability is based on the values of the company itself. Contractors, subcontractors, suppliers, and others are expected to conduct themselves in line with Adidas-Salomon's SOE.

The strategy is based on a long-term vision of self-governance for suppliers—Adidas does not wish to be forever in the position of looking over the shoulders of its suppliers.

ACTIONS

The SOE team's 30 members, most of whom are based in the countries where suppliers are located (Asia, Europe, and the United States), know the labour laws and safety regulations in their countries and often can conduct interviews in the workers' language.

Before forming a relationship with any new supplier, the company conducts an internal audit to ensure working conditions in that supplier meet Adidas-Salomon's SOE criteria. All business partners sign an agreement to comply with the SOE and to take responsibility for their subcontractors' performance on workplace conditions. Suppliers are audited at least once a year, and more often if serious problems are detected.

Training is an even more important part of the process than monitoring because it goes beyond the policing role to one that will have a long-term impact. As of October 2001, some 200 SOE training sessions had been held for business partners during the year—a significant increase from the 150 courses held the year before.

RESULTS

About 800 audits were conducted at different levels in the supply chain during 2000. This involved interviewing managers and workers, reviewing documentation, and inspecting facilities. Since then, the audit process has continued.

Using the information gained from these audits, the SOE team makes presentations to the management of the supplier, outlining any problems found and the consequential action points. Site managers then agree upon clearly defined responsibilities and timelines. Where serious problems are detected, a follow-up visit may be conducted within one to three months. If the supplier is unwilling to make the necessary improvements, Adidas-Salomon may withdraw its business. This course of action is a last resort; the company prefers to stay in partnership and to work from the inside to help encourage improvements.

In 2000, Adidas-Salomon adopted a system of scoring and reporting on its suppliers' performance. This system gave an overview of the supply chain and highlighted the main issues and problem areas on a country-by-country basis, but an improved and extended system is now being developed. This will allow the company to publish even more detailed reports about the progress that it, as a company that manages large and complex supply chains, has been able to make in the important areas of social and environmental performance.

Source: Case study reprinted with permission from the Web site of the World Business Council for Sustainable Development (www.wbcsd.org).

PART TWO

2

COUNTRY DIFFERENCES

The Changing Political Economy of India

After gaining independence from Britain in 1947, India adopted a democratic system of government. The economic system that developed in India after 1947 was a mixed economy characterized by many state-owned enterprises, central planning, and subsidies. This system constrained the growth of the private sector. Private companies could expand only with government permission. Under this system, dubbed the "License Raj," private companies often had to wait for months for government approval of routine business activities such as expanding production or hiring a new director. It could take years to get permission to diversify into a new product. Much of heavy industry, such as auto, chemical, and steel production, was reserved for state-owned enterprises. Production quotas and high tariffs on imports also stunted the development of a healthy private sector, as did restrictive labour laws that made it difficult to fire employees. Access to foreign exchange was limited, investment by foreign firms was severely restricted, land use was strictly controlled, and the government routinely managed prices as opposed to letting them be set by market forces.

By the early 1990s, it was clear that after 40 years of near stagnation, this system was incapable of delivering the kind of economic progress that many Southeastern Asian nations had started to enjoy. In 1994, India's economy was still smaller than Belgium's, despite having a population of 950 million. Its gross domestic product (GDP) per capita was a paltry \$310; less than half the population could read; only 6 million had access to telephones; only 14 percent had access to clean sanitation; the World Bank estimated that some 40 percent of the world's desperately poor lived in India; and only 23 percent of the population had a household income in excess of \$2,484.

In 1991, the lack of progress led the government of Prime Minister P. V. Narasimha Rao, a member of the Congress Party, to embark on an ambitious economic reform program. Much of

CHAPTER 2

Country Differences in Political Economy

OPENING CASE

the industrial licensing system was dismantled, and several areas once closed to the private sector were opened, including electricity generation, parts of the oil industry, steelmaking, air transport, and some areas of the telecommunications industry. Foreign investment, formerly allowed only grudgingly and subject to arbitrary ceilings, was suddenly welcomed. Approval was made automatic for foreign equity stakes of up to 51 percent in an Indian enterprise, and 100 percent foreign ownership was allowed under certain circumstances. The government announced plans to privatize many of India's state-owned businesses. Raw materials and many industrial goods could be freely imported, and the maximum tariff that could be levied on imports was reduced from 400 percent to 65 percent in 1994, and then to 35 percent in 1997.

Judged by some measures, the response to these economic reforms was impressive. The economy expanded at an annual rate of about 6.1 percent throughout the 1990s, exports began to grow at a respectable pace, and corporate profits jumped. Foreign investment surged from $150 million in 1991 to an estimated $3.5 billion in 1997.

However, by the late 1990s, economic reform had stalled. While economic growth remained reasonably strong, driven in part by a boom in certain sectors, such as India's computer software industry, the Indian government was running a budget deficit equivalent to 9.6 percent of GDP.

Moreover, a decade of reform had done little to solve India's crippling poverty problem. Although the Indian middle class had grown richer during the 1990s, by 2000 some 40 percent of India's nearly 1 billion people still lived in abject poverty, earning less than $1 a day, a figure little changed from 1990. At the start of the new century, 44 percent of the adult population was illiterate, 19 percent had no access to safe water supplies, 25 percent had no access to health services, 71 percent had no access to sanitation, and 16 percent of the population was not expected to survive to age 40.

Against this background, in October 1999, the nationalist BJP Party was elected to power in India. There were fears that the BJP would withdraw from economic reform. The BJP has close ties to Hindu nationalist organizations that emphasize economic self-sufficiency, protectionism, and "Hindu first" policies, which are potentially socially divisive in a country with a large Muslim minority. Far from pulling back from economic reform, BJP Prime Minister Atal Behari Vajpayee, initiated a second wave of reforms aimed at increasing privatization, reducing subsidies and import barriers, and dismantling the bureaucratic mishmash of laws that interfere with private business.

By 2003, the BJP party continued to defend privatization, pointing out the increases in production in sectors that had been privatized, as well as rising wages. Yet, the party recognized that rural poor were being left behind by many of these reforms. At the party's National Executive meeting, they demanded that states be given substantial incentives for completing irrigation works, and that the government must pursue accelerated development of all infrastructure. Farmers, they added, should be provided with adequate security against market uncertainty.

The 2004 elections saw the victory of the Congress Party, riding a wave of discontentment among the unemployed and rural voters. As the election was announced, India's stock market declined by 6 percent in one day. While the party has announced that reforms will continue, as it points out that they were the party that initiated the process of dismantling the old socialist economy in 1991, it has said that priorities will be different from those of the BJP. The Congress Party will be attempting to stimulate the agricultural sector, and increase jobs for the poor by bringing development to the countryside. These actions, combined with an increase in infrastructure spending, can be good for the people and good for the economy.

The jury is still out as to whether all of these goals can be met. Economists are projecting that India's economy will grow by 6 percent annually; down from the remarkable 10.4 percent growth in the last quarter of 2003, but far ahead of other countries.

Sources: "A Survey of India: The Tiger Steps Out," *The Economist*, January 21, 1995; "Tarnished Silver," *The Economist*, September 6, 1997, pp. 64–65; P. Moore, "Three Steps Forward," *Euromoney*, September 1997, pp. 190–195; "India's Breakthrough Budget?" *The Economist*, March 3, 2001; Shankar Aiyar, "Reforms: Time to Just Do It," *India Today*, January 24, 2000, p. 47; United Nations Development Program, *Human Development Report* 2000 (New York Oxford University Press, 2000); and "India's Economy, Shining Less Brightly," *Time Asia Magazine*, May 17, 2004, at www.time.com/time/searchresults?query=india%27s%20economy%20shining%20less%20brightly&venue=timeasia&search_date_range=all.

LEARNING OBJECTIVES

1. Understand how the political systems of countries differ.
2. Understand how the economic systems of countries differ.
3. Understand how the legal systems of countries differ.
4. Understand how political, economic, and legal systems collectively influence a country's ability to achieve meaningful economic progress.
5. Be familiar with the main changes that are currently reshaping the political, economic, and legal systems of many nation-states.
6. Appreciate how a country's political, economic, and legal systems influence the benefits, costs, and risks associated with doing business in that country.
7. Be conversant with the ethical issues that can arise when doing business in a nation in which the political and legal systems do not support basic human rights.

INTRODUCTION

As noted in Chapter 1, international business is much more complicated than domestic business because countries differ in many ways. Countries have different political, economic, and legal systems. Cultural practices can vary dramatically from country to country, as can the education and skill level of the population, and countries are at different stages of economic development. All these differences can and do have major implications for the practice of international business. They have a profound impact on the benefits, costs, and risks associated with doing business in different countries; the way in which operations in different countries should be managed; and the strategy international firms should pursue in different countries. A main function of this chapter and the next is to develop an awareness of and appreciation for the significance of country differences in political systems, economic systems, legal systems, and national culture. Another function of this chapter and the next is to describe how the political, economic, legal, and cultural systems of many of the world's nation-states are evolving and to draw out the implications of these changes for the practice of international business.

The opening case illustrates the changes occurring in the political and economic systems of one nation, India. As in many other countries, since the early 1990s, political and economic ideology in India has shifted away from state planning and toward a free market orientation. One consequence of this shift in ideology has been adoption of an economic reform program that includes as its main elements the privatization of state-owned enterprises, the removal of subsidies, the repeal of laws that hamstring private business practice, and the removal of barriers to foreign investment and trade. This program has made India a more attractive location in which international businesses can operate, thus increasing foreign investment in India during the 1990s.

However, as the opening case makes clear, while the Indian program has had some success, it has also run into significant roadblocks and it has yet to alleviate the poverty that afflicts so much of the nation's population. Advocates of economic reform will claim that India's economic reform program achieved only partial success because political opposition has significantly slowed the pace of reform. There is probably much truth to this claim. At the same time, the combination of political and cultural legacies and current realities in India is such that rapid reform would be difficult even under the most pro-reform government. This is not unique to India. The pace of reform in many countries is determined by the interplay between the economic goals of the reformers and the political and cultural realities of the country.

The Indian example suggests that the economic, political, legal, and cultural systems of a country are not independent of each other. After all, it is politicians who write the laws that help to shape economic activity in a nation-state, and politicians, like all of us, are influenced by the prevailing culture or cultures of their nation. To understand the economic prospects of a nation such as India and to appreciate its importance to international business, we must also understand the interplay between the political, economic, legal, and cultural systems prevailing in that country.

This chapter focuses on how the political, economic, and legal systems of countries differ. Collectively we refer to these systems as constituting the political economy of a country. We use the term **political economy** to stress that the political, economic, and legal systems of a country are not independent of each other. They interact and influence each other, and in doing so they affect the level of economic well-being in a country. In addition to reviewing these systems, we also explore how differences in political economy influence the benefits, costs, and risks associated with doing business in different countries, and how they affect management practice and strategy. In the next chapter, we will look at how differences in culture influence the practice of international business. The political economy and culture of a nation are not independent of each other. As will become apparent in Chapter 3, culture can affect political economy–political, economic, and legal systems in a nation–and the converse can also hold true.

POLITICAL ECONOMY The political, economic, and legal systems of a country.

POLITICAL SYSTEMS

The economic and legal systems of a country are shaped by its political system.[1] As such, it is important that we understand the nature of different political systems before discussing economic and legal systems. By **political system** we mean the system of government in a nation. Political systems can be assessed according to two related dimensions. The first is the degree to which they emphasize collectivism as opposed to individualism. The second dimension is the degree to which they are democratic or totalitarian. These dimensions are interrelated; systems that emphasize collectivism tend toward totalitarian, while systems that place a high value on individualism tend to be democratic. However, a large grey area exists in the middle. It is possible to have democratic societies that emphasize a mix of collectivism and individualism. Similarly, it is possible to have totalitarian societies that are not collectivist.

POLITICAL SYSTEM System of government in a nation.

COLLECTIVISM AND INDIVIDUALISM

The term **collectivism** refers to a political system that stresses the primacy of collective goals over individual goals.[2] When collectivism is emphasized, the needs of society as a whole are generally viewed as being more important than individual freedoms. In such circumstances, an individual's right to do something may be restricted on the grounds that it runs counter to "the good of society" or to "the common good." Advocacy of collectivism can be traced to the ancient Greek philosopher Plato (427–347 B.C.), who in the *Republic* argued that individual rights should be sacrificed for the good of the majority and that property should be owned in common. It should be noted that Plato did not equate collectivism with equality–he believed that society should be stratified into classes, with those best suited to rule (which for Plato, naturally, were philosophers and soldiers) administering society for the benefit of all. In modern times, the collectivist mantle has been picked up by socialists.

COLLECTIVISM A political system that emphasizes collective goals as opposed to individual goals.

Socialism

Modern socialists trace their intellectual roots to Karl Marx (1818–1883), although socialist thought clearly predates Marx (elements of it can be traced back to Plato). Marx argued that the few benefit at the expense of the many in a capitalist society where individual freedoms are not restricted. According to Marx, the pay of workers does not reflect the full value of their labour. To correct this perceived wrong, Marx advocated state ownership of the basic means of production, distribution, and exchange (i.e., businesses). His logic was that if the state owned the means of production, the state could ensure that workers were fully compensated for their labour. Thus, the idea is to manage state-owned enterprise to benefit society as a whole, rather than individual capitalists.[3]

In the early twentieth century, the socialist ideology split into two broad camps. The **communists** believed that socialism could be achieved only through violent revolution and totalitarian dictatorship, while the **social democrats** committed themselves to achieving socialism by democratic means and turned their backs on violent revolution and dictatorship. Both versions of socialism waxed and waned during the twentieth century. The communist version of socialism reached its high point in the late 1970s, when the majority of the world's population lived in communist states. The countries under Communist Party rule at that time included the former Soviet Union; its Eastern European client nations (e.g., Poland, Czechoslovakia, Hungary); China; the Southeast Asian nations of Cambodia, Laos, and Vietnam; various African nations (e.g., Angola, Mozambique); and the Latin American nations of Cuba and Nicaragua. By the mid-1990s, however, communism was in retreat worldwide. The Soviet Union had collapsed and had been replaced by a collection of 15 republics, most of which were at least nominally structured as democracies. Communism was swept out of Eastern Europe by the largely bloodless revolutions of 1989. Apart from China, communism hangs on only in some small states, such as North Korea and Cuba.

COMMUNISTS Those who believe socialism can be achieved only through revolution and totalitarian dictatorship.

SOCIAL DEMOCRATS Those committed to achieving socialism by democratic means.

Social democracy also seems to have passed a high-water mark, although the ideology may prove to be more enduring than communism. Social democracy has had perhaps its greatest influence in a number of democratic Western nations including Australia, Great Britain, France, Germany, Norway, Spain, and Sweden, where Social Democratic parties have from time to time held political power. Other countries where social democracy has had an important influence include India and Brazil. Consistent with their Marxists roots, many social democratic governments nationalized private companies in certain industries, transforming them into state-owned enterprises to be run for the "public good rather than private profit." Protected from significant competition by their monopoly position and guaranteed government financial support, many state-owned companies became increasingly inefficient. In the end, individuals found themselves paying for the luxury of state ownership through higher prices and higher taxes. Many Social Democratic parties were voted out of office during the 1970s and 1980s.

Individualism

Individualism is the opposite of collectivism. In a political sense, individualism refers to a philosophy that an individual should have freedom in his or her economic and political pursuits. In contrast to collectivism, individualism stresses that the interests of the individual should take precedence over the interests of the state. Like collectivism, individualism can be traced to an ancient Greek philosopher, in this case Plato's disciple Aristotle (384–322 B.C.). In contrast to Plato, Aristotle argued that individual diversity and private ownership are desirable. In a passage that might have been taken from a speech by contemporary politicians who adhere to a free market ideology, he argued that private property is more highly productive than communal property and will thus stimulate progress. According to Aristotle, communal property receives little care, whereas property that is owned by an individual will receive the greatest care and therefore be most productive.

INDIVIDUALISM
An emphasis on the importance of guaranteeing individual freedom and self-expression.

Individualism was reborn as an influential political philosophy in the Protestant trading nations of England and the Netherlands during the sixteenth century. The philosophy was refined in the work of a number of British philosophers including David Hume (1711–1776), Adam Smith (1723–1790), and John Stuart Mill (1806–1873). The philosophy of individualism exercised a profound influence on those in the American colonies who sought independence from Great Britain. Individualism underlies the ideas expressed in the Declaration of Independence.

Individualism is built on two central tenets. The first is an emphasis on the importance of guaranteeing individual freedom and self-expression. As John Stuart Mill put it,

> The sole end for which mankind are warranted, individually or collectively, in interfering with the liberty of action of any of their number is self-protection . . . The only purpose for which power can be rightfully exercised over any member of a civilized community, against his will, is to prevent harm to others. His own good, either physical or moral, is not a sufficient warrant . . . The only part of the conduct of any one, for which he is amenable to society, is that which concerns others. In the part which merely concerns himself, his independence is, of right, absolute. Over himself, over his own body and mind, the individual is sovereign.[4]

ANOTHER PERSPECTIVE

Marx on globalization

Karl Marx, the originator of communist political and economic doctrines, wrote in the mid-1800s and predated the concept of globalization by some 115 years, his writings indicate a concern with issues directly related to the effects of globalization. In the following excerpt, he summarizes his concern for the alienation of labour. His understanding of possible effects of economies of scale and market size relative to production is interesting. He thought there was a connection between mass production, materialism, and a spiritual void. What do you think of Marx's argument?

We shall begin from a contemporary economic fact. The worker becomes poorer the more wealth he produces and the more his production increases in power and extent. The worker becomes an ever cheaper commodity the more goods he creates. The *devaluation* of the human world increases in direct relation with the *increase in value* of the world of things. Source: *Karl Marx: Early Writings, The Economic and Philosophic Manuscripts of 1844,* trans. T. B. Bottomore (New York: McGraw-Hill, 1963).

The second tenet of individualism is that the welfare of society is best served by letting people pursue their own economic self-interest, as opposed to some collective body (such as government) dictating what is in society's best interest. Or as Adam Smith put it in a famous passage from *The Wealth of Nations,* an individual who intends his own gain is

any good you do for yourself, will ultimately benefit the public

> led by an invisible hand to promote an end which was no part of his intention. Nor is it always worse for the society that it was no part of it. By pursuing his own interest he frequently promotes that of the society more effectually than when he really intends to promote it. I have never known much good done by those who effect to trade for the public good.[5]

The central message of individualism, therefore, is that individual economic and political freedoms are the ground rules on which a society should be based. This puts individualism in conflict with collectivism. Collectivism asserts the primacy of the collective over the individual, while individualism asserts the opposite. This underlying ideological conflict has shaped much of the recent history of the world. The Cold War, for example, was essentially a war between collectivism, championed by the now-defunct Soviet Union, and individualism, championed by the United States. In practical terms, individualism translates into an advocacy for democratic political systems and free market economics.

DEMOCRACY AND TOTALITARIANISM

DEMOCRACY Political system in which government is by the people, exercised either directly or through elected representatives.

TOTALITARIANISM Form of government in which one person or political party exercises absolute control over all spheres of human life and opposing political parties are prohibited.

REPRESENTATIVE DEMOCRACY A political system in which citizens periodically elect individuals to represent them in government.

Democracy and totalitarianism are at different ends of a political dimension. **Democracy** refers to a political system in which government is by the people, exercised either directly or through elected representatives. **Totalitarianism** is a form of government in which one person or political party exercises absolute control over all spheres of human life and opposing political parties are prohibited. The democratic–totalitarian dimension is not independent of the collectivism–individualism dimension. Democracy and individualism go hand in hand, as do the communist version of collectivism and totalitarianism.

Democracy

The pure form of democracy, as originally practised by several city-states in ancient Greece, is based on a belief that citizens should be directly involved in decision making. In complex, advanced societies with populations in the tens or hundreds of millions this is impractical. Most modern democratic states practise what is commonly referred to as **representative democracy.** In a representative democracy, citizens periodically elect individuals to represent them. These elected representatives then form a government, whose function is to make decisions on behalf of the electorate. A representative democracy rests on the assumption that if elected representatives fail to perform this job adequately, they will be voted down at the next election.

To guarantee that elected representatives can be held accountable for their actions by the electorate, an ideal representative democracy has a number of safeguards that are typically enshrined in constitutional law. These include (1) an individual's right to freedom of expression, opinion, and organization; (2) a free media; (3) regular elections in which all eligible citizens are allowed to vote; (4) universal adult suffrage; (5) limited terms for elected representatives; (6) a fair court system that is independent from the political system; (7) a nonpolitical state bureaucracy; (8) a nonpolitical police force and armed service; and (9) relatively free access to state information.[6]

Totalitarianism

In a totalitarian country, all the constitutional guarantees on which representative democracies are built–such as an individual's right to freedom of expression and organization,

Democratic ideals and free market economics have swept away socialism and communism in many countries, as evidenced by this McDonald's in Moscow. AP Photo/Victor Yurchenko.

a free media, and regular elections–are denied to the citizens. In most totalitarian states, political repression is widespread and those who question the right of the rulers to rule find themselves imprisoned, or worse.

Four major forms of totalitarianism exist in the world today. Until recently the most widespread was **communist totalitarianism.** As discussed earlier, communism is a version of collectivism that advocates that socialism can be achieved only through totalitarian dictatorship. Communism, however, is in decline worldwide and many of the old Communist Party dictatorships have collapsed since 1989. The major exceptions to this trend (so far) are China, Vietnam, Laos, North Korea, and Cuba, although all of these states exhibit clear signs that the Communist Party's monopoly on political power is under attack.

A second form of totalitarianism might be labelled **theocratic totalitarianism.** Theocratic totalitarianism is found in states where political power is monopolized by a party, group, or individual that governs according to religious principles. The most common form of theocratic totalitarianism is based on Islam and is exemplified by states such as Iran and Saudi Arabia. These states limit freedom of political and religious expression while the laws of the state are based on Islamic principles.

A third form of totalitarianism might be referred to as **tribal totalitarianism.** Tribal totalitarianism has arisen from time to time in African countries such as Zimbabwe, Tanzania, Uganda, and Kenya. The borders of most African states reflect the administrative boundaries drawn by the old European colonial powers, rather than tribal realities. Consequently, the typical African country contains a number of different tribes. Tribal totalitarianism occurs when a political party that represents the interests of a particular tribe (and not always the majority tribe) monopolizes power. Such one-party states still exist in Africa.

A fourth major form of totalitarianism might be described as **right-wing totalitarianism.** Right-wing totalitarianism generally permits some individual economic freedom but restricts individual political freedom on the grounds that it would lead to the rise of communism. One common feature of most right-wing

COMMUNIST TOTALITARIANISM
A version of collectivism advocating that socialism can be achieved only through a totalitarian dictatorship.

THEOCRATIC TOTALITARIANISM
A political system in which political power is monopolized by a party, group, or individual that governs according to religious principles.

TRIBAL TOTALITARIANISM
A political system in which a party, group, or individual that represents the interests of a particular tribe (ethnic group) monopolizes political power.

RIGHT-WING TOTALITARIANISM
A political system in which political power is monopolized by a party, group, or individual that generally permits individual economic freedom but restricts individual political freedom, including free speech, often on the grounds that it would lead to the rise of communism.

dictatorships is an overt hostility to socialist or communist ideas. Many right-wing totalitarian governments are backed by the military, and in some cases the government may be made up of military officers. The fascist regimes that ruled Germany and Italy in the 1930s and 1940s were right-wing totalitarian states. Until the early 1980s, right-wing dictatorships, many of which were military dictatorships, were common throughout Latin America. They were also found in several Asian countries, particularly South Korea, Taiwan, Singapore, Indonesia, and the Philippines.

ECONOMIC SYSTEMS

It should be clear from the previous section that there is a connection between political ideology and economic systems. In countries where individual goals are given primacy over collective goals, we are more likely to find free market economic systems. In contrast, in countries where collective goals are given preeminence, the state may have taken control over many enterprises, while markets in such countries are likely to be restricted rather than free. We can identify three broad types of economic systems–a market economy, a command economy, and a mixed economy.

MARKET ECONOMY

MARKET ECONOMY An economic system in which the interaction of supply and demand determines the quantity in which goods and services are produced.

In a pure **market economy,** all productive activities are privately owned, as opposed to being owned by the state. The goods and services that a country produces, and the quantity in which they are produced, are not planned by anyone. Rather, production is determined by the interaction of supply and demand and signalled to producers through the price system. If demand for a product exceeds supply, prices will rise, signalling producers to produce more. If supply exceeds demand, prices will fall, signalling producers to produce less. In this system consumers are sovereign. The purchasing patterns of consumers, as signalled to producers through the mechanism of the price system, determine what is produced and in what quantity.

For a market to work in this manner there must be no restrictions on supply. A restriction on supply occurs when a market is monopolized by a single firm. In such circumstances, rather than increase output in response to increased demand, a monopolist might restrict output and let prices rise. This allows the monopolist to take a greater profit margin on each unit it sells. Although this is good for the monopolist, it is bad for the consumer, who has to pay higher prices. It also is probably bad for the welfare of society. Since a monopolist has no competitors, it has no incentive to search for ways to lower production costs. Rather, it can simply pass on cost increases to consumers in the form of higher prices. The net result is that the monopolist is likely to become increasingly inefficient, producing high-priced, low-quality goods, while society suffers as a consequence.

Given the dangers inherent in monopoly, the role of government in a market economy is to encourage vigorous competition between private producers. Governments do this by outlawing monopolies and restrictive business practices designed to monopolize a market (antitrust laws serve this function in the United States). Private ownership also encourages vigorous competition and economic efficiency. Private ownership ensures that entrepreneurs have a right to the profits generated by their own efforts. This gives entrepreneurs an incentive to search for better ways of serving consumer needs. That may be through introducing new products, by developing more efficient production processes, by better marketing and after-sale service, or simply through managing their businesses more efficiently than their competitors. In turn, the constant improvement in product and process that results from such an incentive has been argued to have a major positive impact on economic growth and development.[7]

COMMAND ECONOMY

In a pure **command economy,** the goods and services that a country produces, the quantity in which they are produced, and the prices at which they are sold are all planned by the government. Consistent with the collectivist ideology, the objective of a command economy is for government to allocate resources for "the good of society." In addition, in a pure command economy, all businesses are state owned, the rationale being that the government can then direct them to make investments that are in the best interests of the nation as a whole, rather than in the interests of private individuals. Historically, command economies were found in communist countries where collectivist goals were given priority over individual goals. Since the demise of communism in the late 1980s, the number of command economies has fallen dramatically. Some elements of a command economy were also evident in a number of democratic nations led by socialist-inclined governments. France and India both experimented with extensive government planning and state ownership, although government planning has fallen into disfavour in both countries.

COMMAND ECONOMY An economic system where the allocation of resources, including determination of what goods and services should be produced, and in what quantity, is planned by the government.

While the objective of a command economy is to mobilize economic resources for the public good, the opposite seems to have occurred. In a command economy, state-owned enterprises have little incentive to control costs and be efficient, because they cannot go out of business. Also, the abolition of private ownership means there is no incentive for individuals to look for better ways to serve consumer needs; hence, dynamism and innovation are absent from command economies. Instead of growing and becoming more prosperous, such economies tend to be characterized by stagnation.

MIXED ECONOMY

Between market economies and command economies can be found mixed economies. In a **mixed economy,** certain sectors of the economy are left to private ownership and free market mechanisms while other sectors have significant state ownership and government planning. India, which was profiled in the opening case, has a mixed economy. Mixed economies were once very common throughout much of the world, although they are becoming much less so. Not long ago, Great Britain, France, and Sweden were mixed economies, but extensive privatization has reduced state ownership of businesses in all three countries. As we saw in the opening case, a similar trend can be observed in India and in many other countries where there was once a large state sector, such as Brazil and Italy.

MIXED ECONOMY Certain sectors of the economy are left to private ownership and free market mechanisms, while other sectors have significant government ownership and government planning.

In mixed economies, governments also tend to take into state ownership troubled firms whose continued operation is thought to be vital to national interests. The French automobile company Renault was state owned until recently. The government took over the company when it ran into serious financial problems. The French government reasoned that the social costs of the unemployment that might result if Renault collapsed were unacceptable, so it nationalized the company to save it from bankruptcy. Renault's competitors weren't thrilled by this move, since they had to compete with a company whose costs were subsidized by the state.

LEGAL SYSTEMS

The **legal system** of a country refers to the rules, or laws, that regulate behaviour along with the processes by which the laws are enforced and through which redress for grievances is obtained. The legal system of a country is of immense importance to international business. A country's laws regulate business practice, define the manner in which business transactions are to be executed, and set down the rights and

LEGAL SYSTEM System of rules that regulate behaviour and the processes by which the laws of a country are enforced and through which redress of grievances is obtained.

obligations of those involved in business transactions. The legal environments of countries differ in significant ways. As we shall see, differences in legal systems can affect the attractiveness of a country as an investment site and/or market.

Like the economic system of a country, the legal system is influenced by the prevailing political system (although it is also strongly influenced by historical tradition). The government of a country defines the legal framework within which firms do business–and often the laws that regulate business reflect the rulers' dominant political ideology. For example, collectivist-inclined totalitarian states tend to enact laws that severely restrict private enterprise, while the laws enacted by governments in democratic states where individualism is the dominant political philosophy tend to be pro-private enterprise and pro-consumer.

Here we focus on several issues that illustrate how legal systems can vary–and how such variations can affect international business. First, we look at some basic differences in legal systems. Next we look at contract law. Third, we look at the laws governing property rights with particular reference to patents, copyrights, and trademarks. Fourth, we look at laws covering product safety and product liability.

DIFFERENT LEGAL SYSTEMS

There are three main types of legal systems–or legal tradition–in use around the world: common law, civil law, and theocratic law.

Common Law

COMMON LAW A system of law based on tradition, precedent, and custom. When law courts interpret common law, they do so with regard to these characteristics.

The common law system evolved in England over hundreds of years. It is now found in most of Great Britain's former colonies. **Common law** is based on tradition, precedent, and custom. *Tradition* refers to a country's legal history, *precedent* to cases that have come before the courts in the past, and *custom* to the ways in which laws are applied in specific situations. When law courts interpret common law, they do so with regard to these characteristics. This gives a common law system a degree of flexibility that other systems lack. Judges in a common law system have the power to *interpret* the law so that it applies to the unique circumstances of an individual case. In turn, each new interpretation sets a precedent that may be followed in future cases. As new precedents arise, laws may be altered, clarified, or amended to deal with new situations.

Civil Law

CIVIL LAW A system of law based on a very detailed set of written laws and codes.

A **civil law** system is based on a very detailed set of laws organized into codes. When law courts interpret civil law, they do so with regard to these codes. More than 80 countries, including Germany, France, Japan, Canada (Quebec), and Russia, operate with a civil law system. A civil law system tends to be less adversarial than a common law system, since the judges rely upon detailed legal codes rather than tradition, precedent, and custom, which they interpret. Judges under a civil law system have less *flexibility* than those under a common law system. Judges in a common law system have the power to *interpret* the law, while judges in a civil law system have the power only to *apply* the law.

Theocratic Law

THEOCRATIC LAW A system of law based on religious teachings.

A **theocratic law** system is one in which the law is based on religious teachings. Islamic law is the most widely practised theocratic legal system in the modern world, although usage of both Hindu and Jewish law persisted into the twentieth century. Islamic law is primarily a moral rather than a commercial law and is intended to govern all aspects of life.[8] The foundation for Islamic law is the holy book of Islam, the Koran, along with the Sunnah, or decisions and sayings of the Prophet Muhammad, and the writings of Islamic scholars who have derived rules by analogy from the principles established in the Koran and the Sunnah. Since the Koran and Sunnah are holy documents, this means the basic foundations of Islamic law cannot be changed. However, in practice, Islamic jurists and scholars are constantly debating the application of Islamic law to the modern world. Moreover, many Muslim countries have legal systems that are a blend of Islamic law and a common or civil law system. Moreover, in the province of Ontario, the use of Sharia law, or Islamic law, has been instituted for those Muslims wishing to resolve marital agreements and other civil disputes, and make decisions. Muslims cannot be excluded from Ontario's 1991 Arbitration Act, which allows religious groups to resolve family disputes. Hassidic Jews have been running their own Beit Din arbitrations based on Jewish law for years, as well as Catholics and even Ismaili Muslims. Rulings are to be binding, but must be consistent with Canadian laws and the Charter of Rights.[9]

Although Islamic law is primarily concerned with moral behaviour, it has been extended to cover certain commercial activities. An example is the payment or receipt of interest, which is considered usury and outlawed by the Koran. To the devout Muslim, acceptance of interest payments is seen as a very grave sin; the giver and the taker are equally damned. This is not just a matter of theology; in several Islamic states it has also become a matter of law. In 1992, for example, Pakistan's Federal Shariat Court, the highest Islamic law-making body in the country, pronounced interest to be un-Islamic and therefore illegal and demanded that the government amend all financial laws accordingly. In 1999, Pakistan's Supreme Court ruled that Islamic banking methods should be used in the country after July 1, 2001.[10]

DIFFERENCES IN CONTRACT LAW

The difference between common law and civil law system can be illustrated by the approach of each to contract law (remember, most theocratic legal systems also have elements of common or civil law). A **contract** is a document that specifies the conditions under which an exchange is to occur and details the rights and obligations of the parties involved. Many business transactions are regulated by some form of contract. **Contract law** is the body of law that governs contract enforcement. The parties to an agreement normally resort to contract law when one party believes the other has violated either the letter or the spirit of an agreement.

Since common law tends to be relatively ill specified, contracts drafted under a common law framework tend to be very detailed with all contingencies spelled out. In civil law systems, however, contracts tend to be much shorter and less specific because many of the issues typically covered in a common law contract are already covered in a civil code. This implies that it is more expensive to draw up contracts in a common law jurisdiction, and that resolving contract disputes can be a very adversarial process in common law systems. On the other hand, common law systems have the advantage of greater flexibility and allow for judges to interpret a contract dispute in light of the prevailing situation. International businesses need to be sensitive to these differences since approaching a contract dispute in a state with a civil law system as if it had a common law system may backfire (and vice versa).

When contract disputes arise in international trade, there is always the question of which country's laws apply. To try to resolve this issue, a number of countries including Canada have ratified the **United Nations Convention on Contracts for the International Sale of Goods (CIGS).** CIGS establishes a uniform set of rules governing certain aspects of the making and performance of everyday commercial contracts between sellers and buyers who have their places of business in different nations. By adopting CIGS, a nation signifies to the other nations that have adopted it that it will treat the convention's rules as part of its law. CIGS applies automatically to all contracts for the sale of goods between different firms based in countries that have ratified the convention, unless the parties to the contract explicitly opt out. One problem with CIGS,

CONTRACT A document that specifies the conditions under which an exchange is to occur and details the rights and obligations of the parties involved.

CONTRACT LAW The body of law that governs contract enforcement.

UNITED NATIONS CONVENTION ON CONTRACTS FOR THE INTERNATIONAL SALE OF GOODS (CIGS) A set of rules governing certain aspects of the making and performance of commercial contracts between sellers and buyers who have their places of businesses in different nations.

however, is that only 61 nations have ratified the convention as of 2002 (CIGS went into effect in 1988).[11] Many of the world's larger trading nations, including Japan and the United Kingdom, have not ratified it.

When firms do not wish to accept CIGS, they often opt for arbitration by a recognized arbitration court to settle contract disputes. Most well known of these is the International Court of Arbitration of the International Chamber of Commerce in Paris. In 2001, this court handled 566 requests for arbitration involving 1492 parties from 116 countries.[12] The size of the disputes ranged from $50,000 to more than $1 billion.

PROPERTY RIGHTS

In a legal sense, the term *property* refers to a resource over which an individual or business holds a legal title; that is, a resource that it owns. Resources include land, buildings, equipment, capital, mineral rights, businesses, and intellectual property (such as patents, copyrights, and trademarks). **Property rights** refer to the bundle of legal rights over the use to which a resource is put and over the use made of any income that may be derived from that resource.[13] Countries differ significantly in the extent to which their legal system protects property rights. Although almost all countries have laws on their books that protect property rights, the reality is that in many countries these laws are not well enforced by the authorities and property rights are violated. Property rights can be violated in two ways–through private action and through public action.

PROPERTY RIGHTS
Bundle of legal rights over the use to which a resource is put and over the use made of any income that may be derived from that resource.

Private Action

Private action refers to theft, piracy, blackmail, and the like by private individuals or groups. While theft occurs in all countries, a weak legal system allows for a much higher level of criminal activity in some than in others. One example was Russia, in the chaotic period following the collapse of communism. An outdated legal system, coupled with a weak police force and judicial system, offered both domestic and foreign businesses scant protection from blackmail by the "Russian Mafia." Successful business owners in Russia often had to pay "protection money" to the Mafia or face violent retribution, including bombings and assassinations (about 500 contract killings of businessmen occurred in 1995 and again in 1996).[14] In one example, Ivan Kivelidi, a banker and founder of the Russian Business Roundtable, was murdered by poison applied to the rim of his coffee cup. In another, Vladislav Listiev, the head of Channel 1, Russia's largest nationwide TV network, announced in 1996 that he was going to remove unsavoury elements (i.e., Mafia) from the network. Soon afterward he was gunned down by professional assassins outside his apartment building.[15] In another example, Norex Petroleum, a Calgary-based company operating its Russian subsidiary, Yugraneft, in Western Siberia lost US$40 million when it was taken over at gunpoint by the Tyumen Oil Company (TNK) in 2001. TNK is owned by the Russian corporate giant Alfa Group with close ties to the Kremlin, and Russian emigrés living in America, working in unison with the Alfa Group.[16]

In another instance, in 2002, Acres International, a Canadian engineering firm that operates internationally was convicted of bribing an official in the southern African country of Lesotho. The case arose after Acres hired a Lesotho engineer, Zalisiwonga Bam, to be its local representative as it sought and won contracts for a massive electrical project. Bam, whose pay was deposited by Acres in a Swiss bank account, secretly relayed part of his fees

PRIVATE ACTION
The theft, piracy, blackmail, and the like by private individuals or groups.

ex. Mafia

ANOTHER PERSPECTIVE

No interest? How can that work?
In Islam, charging interest is forbidden. One reason for this is that Islam recognizes that business is all about risks. The successful businessperson figures out which risks are the right ones to take. Interest on a collateralized loan has little or no risk; the return is guaranteed. When a competent banker lends money with a legal contract and collateral, she has minimal risk, regardless of what results the business achieves. In Islam, the banker accepts some of the risk of the business venture, sharing it along with the business owner. If the business does well, the banker shares in the profit. If it doesn't do so well, neither does the banker. There are no guaranteed returns in Islamic banking.

to the director of the project, Masupha Ephraim Sole. Sole is appealing an 18-year sentence for accepting the equivalent of more than Cdn$1.6 million from intermediaries for a dozen international companies, including $320,000 from Bam.[17]

Of course, Russia, as discussed in the first three examples, is not alone in having Mafia problems (the situation in Russia has improved significantly since the mid-1990s). The Mafia has a long history in the United States (Chicago in the 1930s was similar to Moscow in the 1990s). In Japan, the local version of the Mafia, known as the *yakuza,* runs protection rackets, particularly in the food and entertainment industries.[18] However, there was (and perhaps still is) a big difference today between the magnitude of such activity in Russia and its limited impact in Japan and the United States. This difference arose because of the weak legal enforcement apparatus, such as the police and court system, in Russia following the collapse of communism. Many other countries have from time to time had problems similar to or even greater than those experienced by Russia. In Somalia from 1993 to 1994, for example, the breakdown of law and order was so complete that even U.N. food relief convoys proceeding to famine areas under armed guard were held up by bandits.

Public Action and Corruption

PUBLIC ACTION The extortion of income or resources from property holders by public officials, such as politicians and government bureaucrats.

Public action to violate property rights occurs when public officials, such as politicians and government bureaucrats, extort income or resources from property holders. This can be done through a number of legal mechanisms such as levying excessive taxation, requiring expensive licences or permits from property holders, or taking assets into state ownership without compensating the owners. It can also be done by illegal means, or corruption, by demanding bribes from businesses in return for the rights to operate in a country, industry, or location.[19] For example, the government of the late Ferdinand Marcos in the Philippines was famous for demanding bribes from foreign businesses wishing to set up operations in that country.[20] The same was true of government officials in Indonesia under the rule of ex-President Suharto.

Corruption has been well documented in every society, from the banks of the Congo River to the palace of the Dutch royal family, from Japanese politicians to Brazilian bankers, and from Indonesian government officials to the New York City Police Department. No society is immune to corruption. However, there are systematic differences in the extent of corruption across countries. In some countries, the rule of law is such that corruption is kept to a minimum. Corruption is seen and treated as illegal, and, when discovered, violators are punished by the full force of the law. Unfortunately, in other countries the rule of law is weak and corruption by bureaucrats and politicians is rife. Corruption is so endemic in some countries that politicians and bureaucrats regard it as a perk of office and openly flout laws against corruption. On May 13, 2004, John Sewell, former Mayor of Toronto, said in a speech to the Schulich School of Business that:

> The most well known recent incident of bad behaviour at Toronto City Hall is the MFP Scandal. City Council signed a contract with MFP Financial Services for the purchase and leasing of computers for a price it thought to be $43 million. The actual cost to the city was more like $110 million. .... It is now known that Mr. Domi withdrew 27–$1,000 bills from his bank, shortly thereafter he telephoned a key lobbyist for MFP, Jeff Lyons, and a few minutes later Tom Jakobek. He then visited City Hall for about 15 minutes and the next day, Mr. Jakobek deposited about $21,000 in his bank account. Whether the withdrawal by Mr. Domi and the deposits by Mr. Jakobek are directly linked is still unclear [21]

Table 2.1 presents data concerning the degree of corruption as seen by business people, academics, and risk analysts in different countries.

TABLE 2.1

Country Rankings of Corruption in 2003

Source: Transparency International, *Corruption Perceptions* Index 2003, www.transparency.org.

COUNTRY RANK	COUNTRY	CPI 2003 SCORE	SURVEYS USED	STANDARD DEVIATION	HIGH–LOW RANGE
1	Finland	9.7	8	0.3	9.2–10.0
2	Iceland	9.6	7	0.3	9.2–10.0
3	Denmark	9.5	9	0.4	8.8–9.9
	New Zealand	9.5	8	0.2	9.2–9.6
5	Singapore	9.4	12	0.1	9.2–9.5
6	Sweden	9.3	11	0.2	8.8–9.6
7	Netherlands	8.9	9	0.3	8.5–9.3
8	Australia	8.8	12	0.9	6.7–9.5
	Norway	8.8	8	0.5	8.0–9. 3
	Switzerland	8.8	9	0.8	6.9–9.4
11	Canada	8.7	12	0.9	6.5–9.4
	Luxembourg	8.7	6	0.4	8.0–9.2
	United Kingdom	8.7	13	0.5	7.8–9.2
124	Azerbaijan	1.8	7	0.3	1.4–2.3
	Cameroon	1.8	5	0.2	1.4–2.0
	Georgia	1.8	6	0.7	0.9–2.8
	Tajikistan	1.8	3	0.3	1.5–2.0
129	Myanmar	1.6	3	0.3	1.4–2.0
	Paraguay	1.6	6	0.3	1.2–2.0
131	Haiti	1.5	5	0.6	0.7–2.3
132	Nigeria	1.4	9	0.4	0.9–2.0
133	Bangladesh	1.3	8	0.7	0.3–22

CPI 2003 Score relates to the perceptions of the degree of corruption as seen by business people, academics, and risk analysts, and ranges between 10—highly clean and 0—highly corrupt. The least corrupt countries are in the top 11 grouping, stopping with Canada, Luxembourg, and the UK. The most corrupt countries ran from 129 to the absolute bottom of 133.

Surveys Used refers to the number of surveys that assessed a country's performance. A total of 17 surveys were used from 13 independent institutions, and at least three surveys were required for a country to be included in the CPI.

Standard Deviation indicates differences in the values of the sources: the greater the standard deviation, the greater the differences of perceptions of a country among the sources.

High–Low Range provides the highest and lowest values of the different sources.

Economic evidence suggests that high levels of corruption significantly reduce the economic growth rate in a country.[22] By siphoning off profits, corrupt politicians and bureaucrats reduce the returns to business investment and, hence, reduce the incentive for both domestic and foreign businesses to invest in that country. The lower level of investment that results has a negative impact on economic growth. Thus, we would expect countries such as Nigeria and Bangladesh to have a much lower rate of economic growth than might otherwise have been the case. A detailed example of the negative effect that corruption can have on economic progress is given in the accompanying Country Focus, which looks at the impact of corruption on economic growth in Nigeria.

The American Foreign Corrupt Practices Act and Canadian Bill S-21

FOREIGN CORRUPT PRACTICES ACT
U.S. law regulating behaviour regarding the conduct of international business in the taking of bribes and other unethical actions.

In the United States, the **Foreign Corrupt Practices Act** was passed during the 1970s following revelations that U.S. companies had bribed government officials in foreign countries in an attempt to win lucrative contracts. This law makes it a violation of U.S. law to bribe a foreign government official to obtain or maintain business over which that foreign official has authority, and it requires all publicly traded companies (whether or not they are involved in international trade) to keep detailed records to allow someone to determine whether a violation of the act has occurred.

In May 1997, the Organization for Economic Cooperation and Development called for the negotiation of a binding convention to address the bribery of foreign public officials by the end of 1997, and recommended that member states submit legislative proposals to their national legislatures to criminalize such bribery and seek their enactment by the end of 1998. On June 21, 1997, leaders of the G-7 countries (including Prime Minister Chrétien) issued a statement in Denver endorsing this approach and timetable for the OECD. Negotiations of the Convention on Combating Bribery of Foreign Public Officials in International Business Transactions (the OECD Convention) concluded on November 21, 1997, and Canada signed the Convention in Paris on December 17, 1997. In the Final Communiqué of the G-8 Birmingham Summit, dated May 17, 1998, heads of state or government pledged to make every effort to ratify the OECD Convention by the end of 1998.

Out of these initiatives, grew Canada's **Bill S-21**, an Act regarding the Corruption of Foreign Public Officials and the Implementation of the Convention on Combating Bribery of Foreign Public Officials in International Business Transactions was introduced in the Senate on December 1, 1998, and received Royal Assent on December 10 (S.C. 1998, c. 34). Canada ratified the OECD Convention on December 17, 1998, and the Corruption of Foreign Public Officials Act entered into force on February 14, 1999.[23]

BILL S-21 Otherwise known as the Corruption of Foreign Officials Act that entered into force on February 14, 1999. It is Canadian legislation that makes the bribery, or other business corruption "tool" of a foreign official by a Canadian business person, a criminal offence.

As with the U.S. Foreign Corrupt Practices Act, the Canadian Bill S-21 does have "loophole" provisions to cover for those instances in which a bribe might be solely a perception, due to cultural considerations of gift giving, in other countries. Paragraph 3(3)(a) of Bill S-21, sets out a lawful exception that an accused could use as a defence, namely, that the payment was lawful in the foreign state or public international organization for which the foreign public official performs duties or functions. If successful, this would be a full defence to the offence in subsection 3(1). Paragraph 3(3)(b) sets out an additional defence. To use this defence, the accused must show that the loan, reward, advantage, or benefit was:

- a reasonable expense,
- incurred in good faith,
- made by or on behalf of the foreign public official, and *directly related* to the promotion, demonstration or explanation of the person's products and services or to the execution or performance of a contract between the person and the foreign state for which the official performs duties or functions.[24]

This defence is virtually identical to a defence in the U.S. Foreign Corrupt Practices Act.

THE PROTECTION OF INTELLECTUAL PROPERTY

Intellectual property refers to property that is the product of intellectual activity, such as computer software, a screenplay, a music score, or the chemical formula for a new drug. Ownership rights over intellectual property are established through patents, copyrights, and trademarks. A **patent** grants the inventor of a new product or process exclusive rights for a defined period to the manufacture, use, or sale of that invention. **Copyrights** are the exclusive legal rights of authors, composers, playwrights, artists, and publishers to publish and disperse their work as they see fit. **Trademarks** are designs and names, often officially registered, by which merchants or manufacturers designate and differentiate their products (e.g., Christian Dior clothes). In the high-technology "knowledge" economy of the twenty-first century, intellectual property has become an increasingly important source of economic value for businesses. Protecting intellectual property has also become increasingly problematic, particularly if it can be rendered in a digital form and then copied and distributed at very low cost via pirated CDs or over the Internet (e.g., computer software, music and video recordings).[25]

PATENT Grants the inventor of a new product or process exclusive rights to the manufacture, use, or sale of that invention.

COPYRIGHTS Exclusive legal rights of authors, composers, playwrights, artists, and publishers to publish and dispose of their work as they see fit.

TRADEMARKS Designs and names, often officially registered, by which merchants or manufacturers designate and differentiate their products.

The philosophy behind intellectual property laws is to reward the originator of a new invention, book, musical record, clothes design, restaurant chain, and

COUNTRY FOCUS

40 YEARS OF CORRUPTION IN NIGERIA

When Nigeria gained independence from Great Britain in 1960, there were hopes that the country might emerge as an economic heavyweight in Africa. Not only was Nigeria Africa's most populous country, but it was also blessed with abundant natural resources, particularly oil, which rose sharply in value in the 1970s after two rounds of increases in oil prices engineered by the Organization of Petroleum Exporting Countries (OPEC). Between 1970 and 2000, Nigeria earned more than $300 billion from the sale of oil, but at the end of this period it remained one of the poorest countries in the world. In 2000, gross national product per capita was just $300, 40 percent of the adult population was illiterate, life expectancy at birth was only 50 years, and the country was begging for relief on $30 billion in debt. The Human Development Index compiled by the United Nations ranked Nigeria 151 out of 174 countries covered.

What went wrong? Although there is no simple answer, a number of factors seem to have conspired to damage economic activity in Nigeria. The country is composed of several competing ethnic, tribal, and religious groups, and the conflict between them has limited political stability and led to political strife, including a brutal civil war in the 1970s. With the legitimacy of the government always in question, political leaders often purchased support by legitimizing bribes and by raiding the national treasury to reward allies. Civilian rule after independence was followed by a series of military dictatorships, each of which seemed more corrupt and inept than the last (the country returned to civilian rule in 1999).

The most recent military dictator, Sani Abacha, openly and systematically plundered the state treasury for his own personal gain. His most blatant scam was the Petroleum Trust Fund, which he set up in the mid-1990s ostensibly to channel extra revenue from an increase in fuel prices into much-needed infrastructure projects and other investments. The fund was not independently audited and almost none of the money that passed through it was properly accounted for. It was, in fact, a vehicle for Abacha and his supporters to spend a sum that in 1996 was equivalent to some 25 percent of the total federal budget. Abacha, aware of his position as an unpopular and unelected leader, lavished money on personal security and handed out bribes to those whose support he coveted. With examples like this at the very top of the government, it is not surprising that corruption could be found throughout the political and bureaucratic apparatus.

Some of the excesses were astounding. In the 1980s, an aluminum smelter was built on the orders of the government, which wanted to industrialize Nigeria. The cost of the smelter was $2.4 billion, some 60 to 100 percent higher than the cost of comparable plants elsewhere in the developed world. This high cost was widely interpreted to reflect the bribes that had to be paid to local politicians by the international contractors that built the plant. The smelter has never operated at more than a fraction of its intended capacity. Another example of corruption in Nigeria was the cement scandal of the early 1980s. At that time, the president announced a grand public housing project. Public officials promptly ordered vast quantities of cement from foreign contractors, taking a percentage of each contract in the form of a kickback. They ordered far more cement than was needed and more than Nigerian ports could cope with. Soon ships loaded with cement formed a line that stretched for several miles outside of Lagos harbor and that took months to unload. Meanwhile, the officials responsible were making a fortune from selling cement import licences.

Sources: "A Tale of Two Giants," *The Economist, Nigeria: a Survey,* January 15, 2000, p. 5; J. Coolidge and S. Rose Ackerman, "High Level Rent Seeking and Corruption in African Regimes," World Bank policy research working paper #1780, June 1997; and D. L. Bevan, P. Collier, and J. W. Gunning, *Nigeria and Indonesia: The Political Economy of Poverty, Equity and Growth* (Oxford: Oxford University Press, 1999).

the like, for his or her idea and effort. Such laws are a very important stimulus to innovation and creative work. They provide an incentive for people to search for novel ways of doing things, and they reward creativity. For example, consider innovation in the pharmaceutical industry. A patent will grant the inventor of a new drug a 20-year monopoly in production of that drug. This gives pharmaceutical firms an incentive to undertake the expensive, difficult, and time-consuming basic research required to generate new drugs (it can cost $500 million in R&D and take 12 years to get a new drug on the market). Without the guarantees provided by patents, it is unlikely that companies would commit themselves to extensive basic research.[26]

The protection of intellectual property rights differs greatly from country to country. While many countries have stringent intellectual property regulations on their books, the enforcement of these regulations has often been lax. This has been the case even among some of the 96 countries that have signed the **Paris Convention for the Protection of Industrial Property,** an important international agreement to protect intellectual property. Weak enforcement encourages the piracy of intellectual property. China and Thailand have recently been among the worst offenders in Asia. Pirated computer software is widely available in China. Similarly, the streets of Bangkok, the capital of Thailand, are lined with stands selling pirated copies of Rolex watches, Levi blue jeans, videotapes, and computer software.

PARIS CONVENTION FOR THE PROTECTION OF INDUSTRIAL PROPERTY International agreement to protect intellectual property; signed by 96 countries.

Piracy in music recordings is rampant. In Canada, music swapping aficionados were beginning to feel the chill of impending American-style clampdowns on Internet file-swapping-music lovers, since the 2002 demise of U.S.-owned Napster. American recording studios were vigorously pursuing and suing everyone in their paths from 12-year-olds to grandparents.

Recording artists, wherever they are, normally feel that the music they create is to be paid for by their fans and so too they assumed the courts of Canada would agree during an April 2004 ruling brought down by Canadian Federal Court Judge, Konrad von Finkelstein. He essentially ruled that song-swapping in the Great White North is legal. The decision throws a curve ball at the music business, which has been ramping up its international efforts to thwart online music piracy. The most notable example is the International Federation of the Phonographic Industry, which started taking legal action against hundreds of suspected European file-sharers. The Recording Industry Association of America (RIAA) also has been on a lawsuit binge since 2004.[27] See Table 2.2 for a summary of domestic music piracy levels around the world.

International businesses have a number of possible responses to violations of their intellectual property. Firms can lobby their respective governments to push for international agreements to ensure that intellectual property rights are protected and that the law is enforced. Partly as a result of such actions, international laws are being strengthened. As we shall see in Chapter 6, the most recent world trade agreement, which was signed in 1994, for the first time extends the scope of the General Agreement on Tariffs and Trade (GATT) to cover intellectual property. Under the new agreement, known as the **Trade Related Aspects of Intellectual Property Rights (TRIPS),** as of 1995 a World Trade Organization council is overseeing enforcement of much stricter intellectual property regulations. These regulations oblige WTO members to grant and enforce patents lasting at least 20 years and copyrights lasting 50 years. Rich countries had to comply with the rules within a year. Poor countries, in which such protection generally was much weaker, had five years' grace, and the very poorest have ten years.[28] (For further details of the TRIPS agreement, see Chapter 6.)

TRADE RELATED ASPECTS OF INTELLECTUAL PROPERTY RIGHTS (TRIPS) An agreement among members of the WTO to enforce stricter intellectual property regulations, including granting and enforcing patents lasting at least 20 years and copyrights lasting 50 years.

While many governments are increasing their enforcement of intellectual property rights and abiding by international agreements such as the WTO's TRIPS agreement, some have recently taken a counterposition and seem to support the selective violation of intellectual property rights within their borders. In the late 1990s, the government of South Africa passed a law that allowed the country to import cheap generic versions of patented medicines, including powerful new drugs for treating AIDS, without permission from the patent owner. In 2001, this law became the focus of a legal battle between

TABLE 2.2
Domestic Music Piracy Levels Around the World in 2002 (units)

Source: IFPI, *The 2003 Recording Industry Commercial Piracy Report,*, p. 7.

TERRITORY	OVER 50%	25–50%	10–25%	0–10%
North America				Canada USA
Western Europe	Greece	Cyprus Italy Portugal Spain	Belgium Finland Netherlands	Austria Denmark France Germany Iceland Ireland Norway Sweden Switzerland UK
Eastern Europe	Bulgaria Estonia Latvia Lithuania Romania Russia Ukraine	Croatia Czech Republic Hungary Poland Slovakia	Turkey Slovenia	
Asia	China Indonesia Malaysia Pakistan	Hong Kong India Philippines Taiwan Thailand	Singapore South Korea	Japan
Latin America	Argentina Bolivia Brazil Colombia Ecuador Mexico Paraguay Peru Uruguay Venezuela	Chile Costa Rica		
Middle East	Egypt Israel Lebanon	Kuwait Saudi Arabia	Bahrain Oman Qatar	UAE
Australasia				Australia New Zealand
Africa		South Africa	Zimbabwe	

multinational drug companies seeking to protect their intellectual property rights, AIDS activists demanding access to inexpensive treatments for the poor, and the government of South Africa.

In addition to lobbying governments, firms may want to file lawsuits on their own behalf, as the drug companies are doing in South Africa. They may also choose to stay out of countries where intellectual property laws are lax, rather than risk having their ideas stolen by local entrepreneurs (such reasoning partly underlay decisions by Coca-Cola Co. and IBM to pull out of India in the early 1970s). Firms also need to be on the alert to ensure that pirated copies of their products produced in countries where intellectual property laws are lax do not turn up in their home market or in third countries. U.S. computer software giant Microsoft, for example, discovered that pirated Microsoft software, produced illegally in Thailand, was being sold worldwide as the real thing (including in the United States). In addition, Microsoft has encountered significant problems with pirated software in China. See the accompanying Management Focus on the legal challenges of online gambling.

MANAGEMENT FOCUS

BRINGING GAMBLING TO YOUR HOME

The 1980s and 1990s saw casino gambling spread across North America, as governments were attracted to the tax revenue that gambling can produce, and as cities sought to keep up with the growing number of jurisdictions that allowed casino gambling in at least some format.

Internet growth in the late 1990s spread the reach of gambling to a broader market than had previously been known. It also brought up an interesting legal question: if an online casino gets a gambling licence in an offshore jurisdiction, does that make it legal? Can it offer services to Canadians? Just as important, players want to know who regulates such gambling. Players know that a casino in Las Vegas will pay out if they win, but who will make sure that an online casino will do the same.

In this rapidly emerging field, there has been no single government response. Some jurisdictions, like Australia, have legalized online gambling and granted licences. Others, like the United Kingdom, are considering doing so. In the United States, some states have enacted an outright ban on online gambling. Oregon, for example, prevents the collection of online gambling debts.

In Canada, provincial governments are not permitted to issue licences to run online gambling operations. The operation of an unlicensed gambling facility is an offence. However, while it is easier to apply the Canadian Criminal Code to traditional gambling operations that have a physical location in Canada, it is far more difficult to apply the law where the casino is a virtual one. Canadian laws only operate within this country's borders. No part of an online operation has to be located in Canada for Canadians to have access to casino gambling over the Internet. The question therefore becomes one of determining whether there is enough connection between the gambling operation and the Canadian jurisdiction.

Into this legal quagmire comes the Canadian firm CryptoLogic Inc. The company, founded in 1996, produces software for the Internet gambling industry. Since 1996, CryptoLogic states that its systems have securely processed over US$16 billion in wagers for 1.7 million players in 240 countries. According to Lewis Rose, the company's president and CEO, "Online gaming is about trust—trusted brand name customers, trusted software solutions, and transparent, credible service providers."

To that end, CryptoLogic extended agreements with two companies well known in the U.K.: William Hill and Littlewoods Gaming. CryptoLogic sees international markets as providing further, though selective opportunities. While Asia, for example, offers a large potential market, fragmented legislation as well as the lack of any single popular form of online payment, means that entering the market will be costly and time consuming.

Challenges remain for the entire industry, as new legislation emerges, and as competitors become attracted to the field. For example, in 2002, some U.S. banks disallowed their credit cards from being used for online gambling due to the uncertain regulatory climate in the U.S. The result was that the entire online gambling industry was hit by a decline in card payments, which was one of the reasons for CryptoLogic's lower revenues in 2002. Internally, the company installed a new management team in the same year, including Lewis Rose as the new president, who had previously served as president of Alliance Atlantis Communications, and before that as president of Maple Leaf Foods' Grocery Products Division. These management changes may not be over, as in the summer of 2004, the company's CFO abruptly left and was "in employment talks with a rival."

Sources: CryptoLogic, *Annual Report*, 2003, 2002; CryptoLogic at www.cryptologic.com; Fasken Martineau, *Is Internet Gaming Legal In Canada: A Look At Starnet*, at www.fasken.com.

Piracy in countries like China and Thailand can be the result of weak enforcement of the protection of intellectual property rights. In this photo, a man in Thailand destroys thousands of counterfeit Winnie-the-Poohs. Why do you think the demand for these goods in these countries is so high as to make pirating a lucrative business? AFP/CORBIS.

PRODUCT SAFETY AND PRODUCT LIABILITY

Product safety laws set certain safety standards to which a product must adhere. **Product liability** involves holding a firm and its officers responsible when a product causes injury, death, or damage. Product liability can be much greater if a product does not conform to required safety standards. There are both civil and criminal product liability laws. Civil laws call for payment and monetary damages. Criminal liability laws result in fines or imprisonment. Both civil and criminal liability laws are probably more extensive in the United States than in any other country, although many other Western nations also have comprehensive liability laws. Liability laws are typically least extensive in less developed nations. A boom in product liability suits and awards in the United States resulted in a dramatic increase in the cost of liability insurance. Many business executives argue that the high costs of liability insurance make American businesses less competitive in the global marketplace.

In addition to the competitiveness issue, country differences in product safety and liability laws raise an important ethical issue for firms doing business abroad. When product safety laws are tougher in a firm's home country than in a foreign country and/or when liability laws are more lax, should a firm doing business in that foreign country follow the more relaxed local standards or should it adhere to the standards of its home country? While the ethical thing to do is undoubtedly to adhere to home-country standards, firms have been known to take advantage of lax safety and liability laws to do business in a manner that would not be allowed back home.

PRODUCT SAFETY LAWS Set certain safety standards to which a product must adhere.

PRODUCT LIABILITY Involves holding a firm and its officers responsible when a product causes injury, death, or damage.

THE DETERMINANTS OF ECONOMIC DEVELOPMENT

The political, economic, and legal systems of a country can have a profound impact on the level of economic development and hence on the attractiveness of a country as a possible market and/or production location for a firm. Here we look first at how countries differ in their level of development. Then we look at how political economy affects economic progress.

DIFFERENCES IN ECONOMIC DEVELOPMENT

Different countries have dramatically different levels of economic development. One common measure of economic development is a country's gross national product per head of population. Prior to 2001, the term GNP (gross national product) was commonly used by the World Bank as a yardstick for economic activity of a country; it measures the total value of the goods and services produced annually. Since 2001 the replacement term for GNP is **GNI (gross national income)**. The GNP was seen as the value (in US$) of a country's final output of goods and services in a year. The value of GNP could be calculated by adding up the amount of money spent on a country's final output of foods and services, or by totalling the income of all citizens of a country including the income from factors of production used abroad (now applied to GNI).

GROSS NATIONAL INCOME (GNI) Since 2001, the World Bank has used this term instead of the previously used GNP.

Different countries have different levels of development. Table 2.3 summarizes the GNP (GNI) per capita of the world's ten wealthiest and two poorest nations in 2003 (the right column). On the left column, the World Bank Atlas method is used. It calculates gross national income (GNI–formerly referred to as GNP) and GNI per capita in U.S. dollars for certain operational purposes. The World Bank uses the Atlas conversion factor to reduce the impact of exchange rate fluctuations in the cross-country comparison of national incomes. The Atlas conversion factor for any year is the average of a country's exchange rate (or alternative conversion factor) for that year and its exchange rates for the two preceding years, adjusted for the difference between the rate of inflation in the country.[29]

However, GNI per capita figures can be misleading because they don't consider differences in the cost of living. For example, although the 2003 GNI per capita of Norway at $37,300, exceeded that of Switzerland which was $32,030, the higher cost of living in Norway meant that a Swiss could actually afford more goods and services than a Norwegian. To account for differences in the cost of living, one can adjust GNI per capita by purchasing power. Referred to as **purchasing power parity** (PPP) adjustment, it allows for a more direct comparison of living standards in different countries. The base for the adjustment is the cost of living in the United States. The PPP for different countries is then adjusted up (or down) depending upon whether the cost of living is lower (or higher) than in the United States, For example, in 2003, while the GNI per capita in China was $1,100 (Atlas Method), the PPP per capita was $4,990 suggesting that the cost of living was lower in China and that $1100 in China would buy as much as $4,990 in the United States. Table 2.3 gives the GNI per capita measured at PPP in 2003 for a selection of countries, along with their GNI per capita.[30]

PURCHASING POWER PARITY (PPP) An adjustment in gross domestic product per capita to reflect differences in the cost of living.

TABLE 2.3

GNI per capita in 2003, Atlas

Source: © World Bank, "GNI per Capita 2003, Atlas Mehtod and PPP," excerpt from pages 1-4 of *World Development Indicators Database 2003.* This work is protected by copyright and the making of this copy was with the permission of *Access Copyright.* Any alteration of its content or further copying in any form whatsoever is strictly prohibited.

COUNTRY	ATLAS METHODOLOGY—US$	RANK	COUNTRY	2003 PURCHASING POINT PARITY—US$
Bermuda	(ranking available without figure)	1	Luxembourg	$54,430
Luxembourg	$43,940	2	Bermuda	(ranking available without figure)
Norway	$43,350	3	United States	$37,500
Switzerland	$39,880	4	Norway	$37,300
United States	$37,610	5	Lichtenstein	(ranking available without figure)
Lichtenstein	(ranking available without figure)	6	Channel Islands	(ranking available without figure)
Japan	$34,510	7	Switzerland	$32,030
Denmark	$33,750	8	Denmark	$31,210
Channel Islands	(ranking available without figure)	9	Ireland	$30,450
Iceland	$30,810	10	Iceland	$30,140
Sweden	$28,840	11	Canada	$29,740
Canada	$23,930	23	Germany	$27,460
Ecuador	$1790	118	China	$4990
China	$1100	133	Jamaica	$3790
DR—Congo	$100	207	Malawi	$600
Ethiopia	$90	208	Sierra Leone	$530

BROADER CONCEPTIONS OF DEVELOPMENT: AMARTYA SEN

The Nobel prize-winning economist Amartya Sen has argued that development should be assessed less by material output measures such as GNP per capita and more by the capabilities and opportunities that people enjoy.[31] According to Sen, development should be seen as a process of expanding the real freedoms that people experience. Hence, development requires the removal of major impediments to freedom: poverty as well as tyranny, poor economic opportunities as well as systematic social deprivation, neglect of public facilities as well as the intolerance of repressive states. In Sen's view, development is not just an economic process, but it is a political one too, and to succeed requires the "democratization" of political communities to give citizens a voice in the important decisions made for the community. This perspective leads Sen to emphasize basic health care, especially for children, and basic education, especially for women. Not only are these factors desirable for their instrumental value in helping to achieve higher income levels, but they are also beneficial in their own right. People cannot develop their capabilities if they are chronically ill or woefully ignorant.

HUMAN DEVELOPMENT INDEX (HDI) An attempt by the United Nations to assess the impact of a number of factors on the quality of human life in a country.

Sen's influential thesis has been picked up by the United Nations, which has developed the **Human Development Index (HDI)** to measure the quality of human life in different nations. The HDI is based on three measures: life expectancy at birth (which is a function of health care), educational attainment (which is measured by a combination of the adult literacy rate and enrolment in primary, secondary, and tertiary education), and whether average incomes, based on PPP estimates, are sufficient to meet the basic needs of life in a country (adequate food, shelter, and health care). As such, the HDI comes much closer to Sen's conception of how development should be measured than narrow economic measures such as GNP per capita–although Sen's thesis suggests that political freedoms should also be included in the index, and they are not. The Human Development Index is scaled from 0 to 1. Countries scoring less than 0.5 are classified as having low human development (the quality of life is poor), those scoring from 0.5 to 0.8 are classified as having medium human development, while those countries that score above 0.8 are classified as having high human development. Map 2.1 summarizes the Human Development Index scores for 2001, the most recent year for which data are available.

POLITICAL ECONOMY AND ECONOMIC PROGRESS

It is often argued that a country's economic development is a function of its economic and political systems. What then is the nature of the relationship between political economy and economic progress? This question has been the subject of vigorous debate among academics and policy makers for some time. Despite the long debate, this remains a question for which it is not possible to give an unambiguous answer. However, it is possible to untangle the main threads of the academic arguments and make a few broad generalizations as to the nature of the relationship between political economy and economic progress.

Innovation and Entrepreneurship Are the Engines of Growth

INNOVATION Development of new products, processes, organizations, management practices, and strategies.

Agreement is fairly wide that innovation and entrepreneurial activity are the engines of long-run economic growth.[32] Those who make this argument define **innovation** broadly to include not just new products, but also new processes, new organizations, new management practices, and new strategies. Thus, the Toys "R" Us strategy of establishing large warehouse-style toy stores and then engaging in heavy advertising and price discounting to sell the merchandise can be classified as an innovation because Toys "R" Us was the first company to pursue this strategy. Innovation is also seen as the product of entrepreneurial activity. Often, entrepreneurs first commercialize innovative new products and processes, and entrepreneurial activity provides much of the dynamism

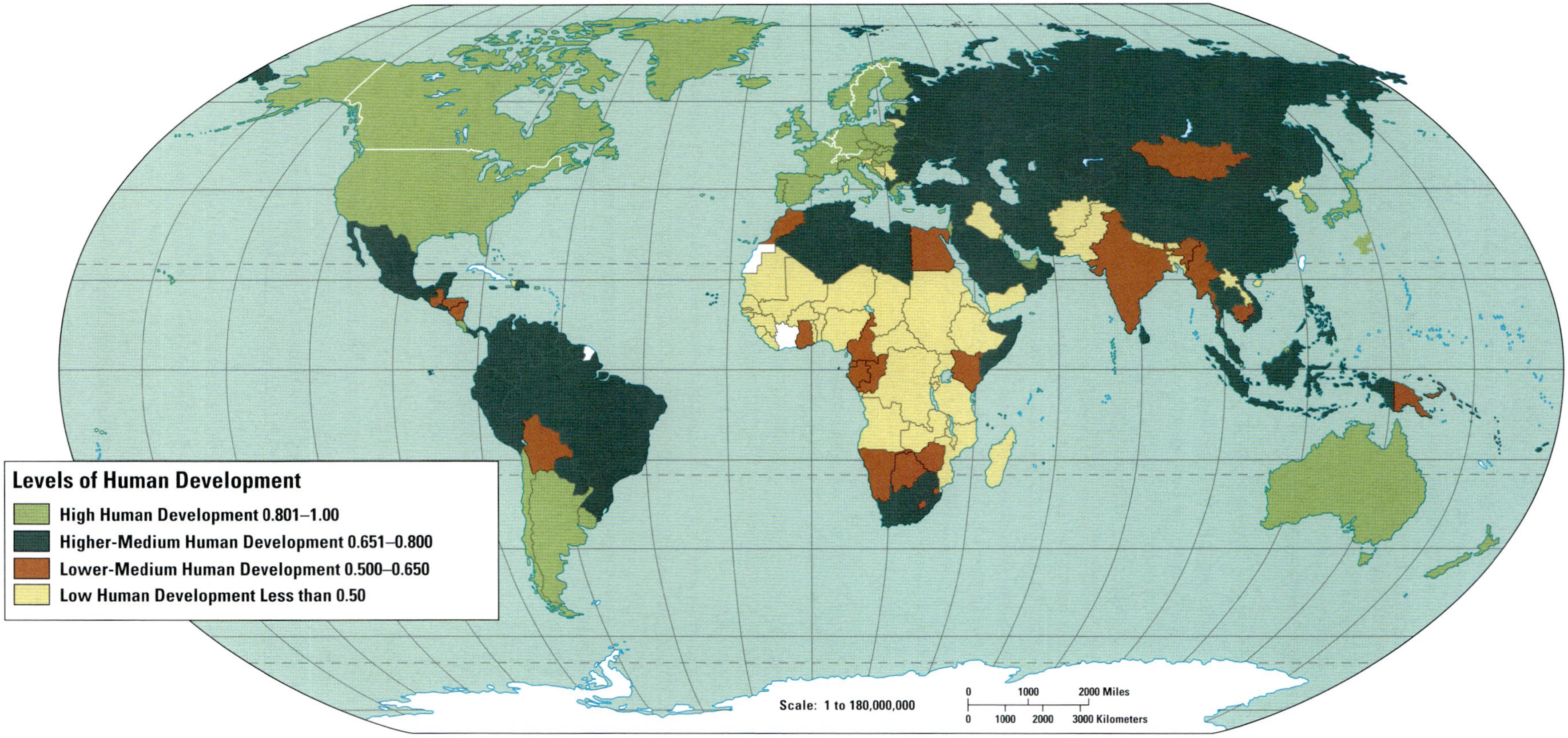

MAP 2.1

The Human Development Index, 2001

Source: United Nations, *Human Development Report, 2003,* Human Development Index.

in an economy. For example, the economy of the United States has benefited greatly from a high level of entrepreneurial activity, which has resulted in rapid innovation in products and process. Firms such as Cisco Systems, Dell Computer Corp., Microsoft, and Oracle were all founded by entrepreneurial individuals to exploit advances in technology, and all these firms created significant economic value by helping to commercialize innovations in products and processes. Thus, one can conclude that if a country's economy is to sustain long-run economic growth, the business environment must be conducive to the consistent production of product and process innovations and to entrepreneurial activity.

Innovation and Entrepreneurship Require a Market Economy

This leads logically to a further question–What is required for the business environment of a country to be conducive to innovation and entrepreneurial activity? Those who have considered this issue highlight the advantages of a market economy.[33] It has been argued that the economic freedom associated with a market economy creates greater incentives for innovation and entrepreneurship than either a planned or a mixed economy. In a market economy, any individual who has an innovative idea is free to try to make money out of that idea by starting a business (by engaging in entrepreneurial activity). Similarly, existing businesses are free to improve their operations through innovation. To the extent that they are successful, both individual entrepreneurs and established businesses can reap rewards in the form of high profits. Thus, market economies contain enormous incentives to develop innovations.

In a planned economy, the state owns all means of production. Consequently, entrepreneurial individuals have little economic incentive to develop valuable new innovations, since it is the state, rather than the individual, that captures most of the gains. The lack of economic freedom and incentives for innovation was probably a main factor in the economic stagnation of so many former Communist states and led ultimately to their collapse at the end of the 1980s. Similar stagnation occurred in many mixed economies in those sectors where the state had a monopoly (such as health care and telecommunications in Great Britain). This stagnation provided the impetus for the widespread privatization of state-owned enterprises that we witnessed in many mixed economies during the mid-1980s and is still going on today (privatization refers to the process of selling state-owned enterprises to private investors).

A study of 102 countries over a 20-year period provided evidence of a strong relationship between economic freedom (as provided by a market economy) and economic growth.[34] The study found that the more economic freedom a country had between 1975 and 1995, the more economic growth it achieved and the richer its citizens became. The three countries that had persistently high ratings of economic freedom from 1975 to 1995 (Hong Kong, Switzerland, and Singapore) were also all in the top ten in terms of economic growth rates. In contrast, no country with persistently low economic freedom achieved a respectable growth rate. For the 16 countries for which the index of economic freedom declined the most during the 1975–95 period, gross domestic product fell at an annual rate of 0.6 percent.

ANOTHER PERSPECTIVE

Purchasing power parity and Big Macs

The Economist, a British weekly magazine worth taking a look at, compares currency valuations across countries by examining the prices of Big Macs sold at McDonald's. The Big Mac index applies the idea of purchasing power parity by assuming that across national-level economies, the Big Mac price should be at parity. By comparing exchange rates using the Big Mac price as a basis, the index describes the over- or undervaluation of the country's currency. This index is published in April and October. You can find the most recent one at www.economist.com.

Innovation and Entrepreneurship Require Strong Property Rights

Strong legal protection of property rights is another requirement for a business environment to be conducive to innovation, entrepreneurial activity, and hence economic growth.[35] Both individuals and businesses must be given the opportunity to profit from innovative ideas. Without strong property rights protection, businesses and individuals run the risk that the profits from their innovative efforts will be expropriated, either by criminal elements or by the state. The state can expropriate the profits from innovation through legal means, such as excessive taxation, or through illegal means, such as demands from state bureaucrats for kickbacks in return for granting an individual or firm a license to do business in a certain area (i.e., corruption). According to the Nobel prize-winning economist Douglass North, throughout history many governments have displayed a tendency to engage in such behaviour. Inadequately enforced property rights reduce the incentives for innovation and entrepreneurial activity–since the profits from such activity are "stolen"–and hence reduce the rate of economic growth.

The Required Political System

There is a great deal of debate as to the kind of political system that best achieves a functioning market economy with strong protection for property rights.[36] We in the West tend to associate a representative democracy with a market economic system, strong property rights protection, and economic progress. Building on this, we tend to argue that democracy is good for growth.[37] However, some totalitarian regimes have fostered a market economy and strong property rights protection and have experienced rapid economic growth. Four of the fastest-growing economies of the past 30 years–South Korea, Taiwan, Singapore, and Hong Kong–had one thing in common at the start of their economic growth: undemocratic governments! At the same time, countries with stable democratic governments, such as India, experienced sluggish economic growth for long periods. In 1992, Lee Kuan Yew, Singapore's leader for many years, told an audience, "I do not believe that democracy necessarily leads to development. I believe that a country needs to develop discipline more than democracy. The exuberance of democracy leads to undisciplined and disorderly conduct which is inimical to development."[38] Others have argued that many of the current problems in Eastern Europe and the states of the former Soviet Union arose because democracy arrived before economic reform, making it more difficult for elected governments to introduce the policies that, while painful in the short run, were needed to promote rapid economic growth. China, which maintains a totalitarian government, has moved rapidly toward a market economy.

However, those who argue for the value of a totalitarian regime miss an important point: if dictators made countries rich, then much of Africa, Asia, and Latin America should have been growing rapidly from 1960 to 1990, and this was not the case. Only a certain kind of totalitarian regime is capable of promoting economic growth. It must be a dictatorship that is committed to a free market system and strong protection of property rights. Also, there is no guarantee that a dictatorship will continue to pursue such progressive policies. Dictators are rarely so benevolent. Many are tempted to use the apparatus of the state to further their own private ends, violating property rights and stalling economic growth. Given this, it seems likely democratic regimes are far more conducive to long-term economic growth than are dictatorships, even benevolent ones. Only in a well-functioning, mature democracy are property rights truly secure.[39] We should not forget Amartya Sen's arguments that we reviewed earlier. Totalitarian states, by limiting human freedom, also suppress human development and therefore are detrimental to progress.

Economic Progress Begets Democracy

While it is possible to argue that democracy is not a necessary precondition for a free market economy in which property rights are protected, subsequent economic growth often leads to establishment of a democratic regime. Several of the fastest-growing Asian economies adopted more democratic governments during the past two decades, including South Korea and Taiwan. Thus, while democracy may not always be the cause of initial economic progress, it seems to be one consequence of that progress.

A strong belief that economic progress leads to adoption of a democratic regime underlies the fairly permissive attitude that many Western governments have adopted toward human rights violations in China. Although China has a totalitarian government in which human rights are abused, many Western countries have been hesitant to criticize the country too much for fear that this might hamper the country's march toward a free market system. The belief is that once China has a free market system, democracy will follow. Whether this optimistic vision comes to pass remains to be seen.

GEOGRAPHY, EDUCATION, AND ECONOMIC DEVELOPMENT

While a country's political and economic system is probably the big locomotive driving its rate of economic development, other factors are also important. One that has received attention recently is geography.[40] But the belief that geography can influence economic policy, and hence economic growth rates, goes back to Adam Smith. The influential Harvard University economist Jeffrey Sachs argues

> that throughout history, coastal states, with their long engagements in international trade, have been more supportive of market institutions than landlocked states, which have tended to organize themselves as hierarchical (and often military) societies. Mountainous states, as a result of physical isolation, have often neglected market-based trade. Temperate climes have generally supported higher densities of population and thus a more extensive division of labour than tropical regions.[41]

Sachs's point is that by virtue of favourable geography, certain societies were more likely to engage in trade than others and were thus more likely to be open to and to develop market-based economic systems, which in turn would promote faster economic growth. He also argues that, irrespective of the economic and political institutions a country adopts, adverse geographical conditions, such as the high rate of disease, poor soils, and hostile climate that afflict many tropical countries, can have a negative impact on development. Together with colleagues at Harvard's Institute for International Development, Sachs tested for the impact of geography on a country's economic growth rate between 1965 and 1990. He found that landlocked countries grew more slowly than coastal economies and that being entirely landlocked reduced a country's growth rate by roughly 0.7 percent per year. He also found that tropical countries grew 1.3 percent more slowly each year than countries in the temperate zone.

Education emerges as another important determinant of economic development (a point that Amartya Sen emphasizes). The general assertion is that nations that invest more in education will have higher growth rates because an educated population is a more productive population. Some rather striking anecdotal evidence suggests this is true. In 1960, Pakistanis and South Koreans were on equal footing economically. However, just 30 percent of Pakistani children were enrolled in primary schools, while 94 percent of South Koreans were. By the mid-1980s, South Korea's GNP per person was three times that of Pakistan's.[42] A survey of 14 statistical studies that looked at the relationship between a country's investment in education and its subsequent growth rates concluded investment in education had a positive and statistically significant impact on a country's rate of economic growth.[43] Similarly, the work by Sachs discussed above suggests that investments in education help explain why some countries in Southeast Asia, such as Indonesia, Malaysia, and Singapore, have been able to overcome the disadvantages associated with their tropical geography and grow far more rapidly than tropical nations in Africa and Latin America.

STATES IN TRANSITION

The political economy of many of the world's nation-states has changed radically since the late 1980s. Two trends have been evident. First, during the late 1980s and early 1990s, a wave of democratic revolutions swept the world. Totalitarian governments collapsed and were replaced by democratically elected governments that were typically more committed to free market capitalism than their predecessors had been. The change was most dramatic in Eastern Europe, where the collapse of communism brought an end to the Cold War and led to the breakup of the Soviet Union, but similar changes were occurring throughout the world during the same period. Across much of Asia, Latin America, and Africa, there was a marked shift toward greater democracy. Second, there has been a strong move away from centrally planned and mixed economies and toward a more free market economic model. We shall look first at the spread of democracy and then turn our attention to the spread of free market economics.

THE SPREAD OF DEMOCRACY

Between 1993 and 2003, the number of not free countries grew from 43 to 48 nations. The Map of Political Freedom, 2003 (Map 2.2) also shows that there were less free countries in 2003 than there were in 1993 (55 in 2003 and 73 nations in 1993) while the number of free countries grew from 75 to 89. On a scale of 1, for the highest degree of political freedom to 7 for the lowest, Freedom House uses the following criteria for determining the ratings for political freedom:

- Free and fair elections of the head of state and legislative representatives.
- Fair electoral laws, equal campaigning opportunities, and fair polling.

Although Hong Kong switched from a British colony to Chinese sovereignty in 1997, its economy still displays democratic influence. This shopping district street in Hong Kong could be mistaken for a big city street in the United States. What do you think are some of the reasons that places like Hong Kong, Singapore, and Taiwan have flourished, while others in Eastern Europe, the former Soviet Union, and India have not? CORBIS. All rights reserved.

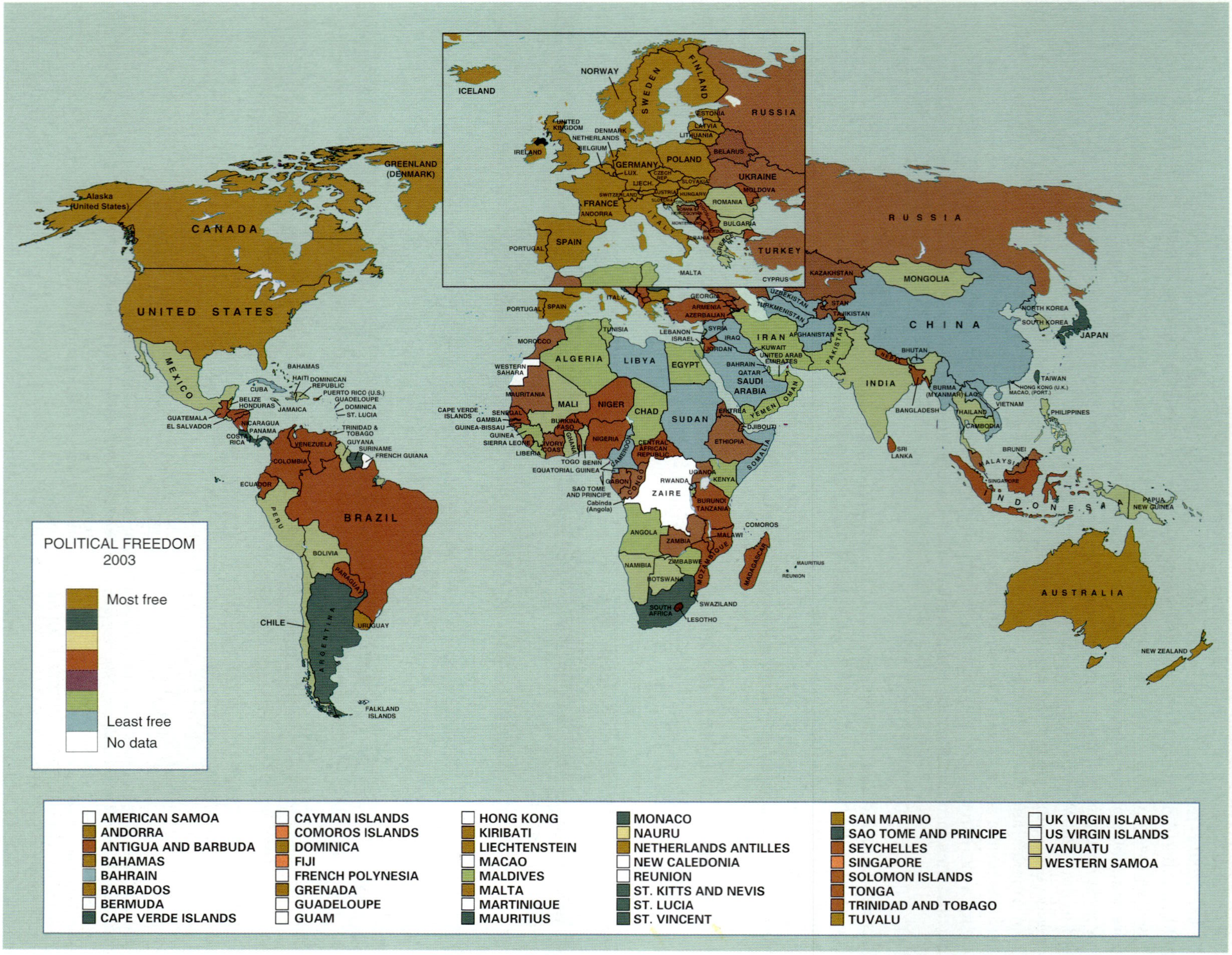

MAP 2.2

Political Freedom in 2003

Source: Freedom House, www.freedomhouse.org. Reprinted with permission.

- The right to organize into different political parties.
- A parliament with effective power.
- A significant opposition that has a realistic chance of gaining power.
- Freedom from domination by the military, foreign powers, totalitarian parties, religious hierarchies, or any other powerful group.
- A reasonable amount of self-determination for cultural, ethnic, and religious minorities.

Factors contributing to a low rating (i.e., to totalitarianism) include military or foreign control, the denial of self-determination to major population groups, a lack of decentralized political power, and an absence of democratic elections.

As of January 2003, Freedom House classified some 89 democracies as free while 55 countries were partly free and 48 countries were not free. There were 121 electoral democracies in the world at the end of 2002, which represent over 60 percent of the world's 192 countries. This represents a significant increase over the 40 percent of countries considered to be elected democracies in 1987. However, only 89 of today's 121 elected democracies are considered to be free, maintaining an environment in which there is broad respect for human rights and stable rule of law. Democracy is associated with prosperity. In 2002, the GDP of free countries stood at $26.8 trillion, while the GDP of not free countries was $1.7 trillion.[44]

Three main reasons account for the spread of democracy.[45] First, many totalitarian regimes failed to deliver economic progress to the vast bulk of their populations.

Second, new information and communication technologies, including shortwave radio, satellite television, fax machines, desktop publishing, and now the Internet, have broken down the ability of the state to control access to uncensored information. These technologies have created new conduits for the spread of democratic ideals and information from free societies.

Third, in many countries the economic advances of the last quarter century have led to the emergence of increasingly prosperous middle and working classes who have pushed for democratic reforms. This was certainly a factor in the democratic transformation of South Korea. Entrepreneurs and other business leaders, eager to protect their property rights and ensure the dispassionate enforcement of contracts, are another force pressing for more accountable and open government.

Also, democracy is still rare in large parts of the world. In Africa, just 20 nations, one-third of those on the continent, are electoral democracies. Among the 12 countries that are full or associated members of the Commonwealth of Independent States (i.e., the republics of the former Soviet Union minus the Baltic states) only four are electoral democracies. And there are no democracies among the 16 Arabic states of the Middle East and North Africa.

THE NEW WORLD ORDER?

The end of the Cold War and the "new world order" that followed the collapse of communism in Eastern Europe and the former Soviet Union, taken together with the collapse of many authoritarian regimes in Latin America, have given rise to intense speculation about the future shape of global geopolitics. Author Francis Fukuyama has argued that "we may be witnessing . . . the end of history as such: that is, the end point of mankind's ideological evolution and the universalization of Western liberal democracy as the final form of human government."[46] Fukuyama goes on to say that the war of ideas may be at an end and that liberal democracy has triumphed.

Others have questioned Fukuyama's vision of a more harmonious world dominated by a universal civilization characterized by democratic regimes and free market capitalism. In a controversial book, the influential political scientist Samuel Huntington argues that there is no "universal" civilization based on widespread acceptance of Western liberal democratic ideals.[47] Huntington maintains that while many societies may be modernizing–they are adopting the material paraphernalia of the modern world, from automobiles to Coca-Cola and MTV–they are not becoming more Western. On the contrary, Huntington theorizes that modernization in non-Western societies can result in a retreat toward the traditional, such as the resurgence of Islam in many traditionally Muslim societies:

> The Islamic resurgence is both a product of and an effort to come to grips with modernization. Its underlying causes are those generally responsible for indigenization trends in non-Western societies: urbanization, social mobilization, higher levels of literacy and education, intensified communication and media consumption, and expanded interaction with Western and other cultures. These developments undermine traditional village and clan ties and create alienation and an identity crisis. Islamist symbols, commitments, and beliefs meet these psychological needs, and Islamist welfare organizations, the social, cultural and economic needs of Muslims caught in the process of modernization. Muslims feel a need to return to Islamic ideas, practices, and institutions to provide the compass and the motor of modernization.[48]

Thus, the rise of Islamic fundamentalism is portrayed as a response to the alienation produced by modernization.

In contrast to Fukuyama, Huntington sees a world that is split into different civilizations, each of which has its own value systems and ideology. In addition to Western civilization, Huntington predicts the emergence of strong Islamic and Sinic (Chinese) civilizations, as well as civilizations based on Japan, Africa, Latin America, Eastern Orthodox Christianity (Russian), and Hinduism (Indian). Huntington also sees the civilizations as headed for conflict, particularly along the "fault lines" that separate them, such as Bosnia (where Muslims and Orthodox Christians have clashed), Kashmir (where Muslims and Hindus clash), and the Sudan (where a bloody war between Christians and Muslims has persisted for decades). Huntington predicts conflict between the West and Islam and between the West and China. He bases his predictions on an analysis of the different value systems and ideology of these civilizations, which in his view tend to bring them into conflict with each other. While some commentators originally dismissed Huntington's thesis, in the aftermath of the terrorist attacks on the United States on September 11, 2001, Huntington's thesis received new attention.

If Huntington's views are even partly correct–the events of September 11 added weight to his thesis–they have important implications for international business. They suggest many countries may be increasingly difficult places in which to do business, either because they are shot through with violent conflicts or because they are part of a civilization that is in conflict with an enterprise's home country. Huntington's views are speculative and controversial. It is not clear that his predictions will come to pass. More likely is the evolution of a global political system that is positioned somewhere between Fukuyama's universal global civilization based on liberal democratic ideals and Huntington's vision of a fractured world. That would still be a world, however, in which geopolitical forces periodically limit the ability of business enterprises to operate in certain foreign countries.

THE SPREAD OF MARKET-BASED SYSTEMS

Paralleling the spread of democracy since the 1980s has been the transformation from centrally planned command economies to market-based economies. More than 30 countries that were in the former Soviet Union or the Eastern European Communist bloc are now changing their economic systems. A complete list of countries would also include Asian states such as China and Vietnam, as well as African countries such as Angola, Ethiopia, and Mozambique.[49] There has been a similar shift away from a mixed economy. Many states in Asia, Latin America, and Western Europe have sold state-owned businesses to private investors (privatization) and deregulated their economies to promote greater competition.

The underlying rationale for economic transformation has been the same the world over. In general, command and mixed economies failed to deliver the kind of sustained economic performance that was achieved by countries adopting market-based systems, such as the United States, Switzerland, Hong Kong, and Taiwan. The Heritage Foundation's index of economic freedom is based on ten indicators, such as the extent to which the government intervenes in the economy, trade policy, the degree to which property rights are protected, foreign investment regulations, and taxation rules. A country can score between 1 (most free) and 5 (least free) on each of these indicators. The lower a country's average score across all ten indicators, the more closely its economy represents the pure market model. According to the 2004 index, which is summarized in Map 2.3, the world's freest economies are (in rank order) Hong Kong, Singapore, New Zealand, Luxembourg, Estonia, United Kingdom, Ireland, Denmark, Switzerland, and the United States. Japan is ranked at 38; France at 44; Mexico, 63; Brazil, 72; Russia, 114; India, 121; China, 128; while the command economies of Cuba, Laos, Iraq, and North Korea are to be found at the bottom of the rankings.[50]

Economic freedom does not necessarily equate with political freedom, as detailed in Map 2.3. For example, three of the top 16 countries in the Heritage Foundation index, Hong Kong, Singapore, and Bahrain, cannot be classified as politically free. Hong Kong was reabsorbed into Communist China in 1997, and the first thing Beijing did was shut down Hong Kong's freely elected legislature. Singapore is ranked as only partly free on Freedom House's index of political freedom due to practices such as widespread press censorship, while Bahrain is classified as least free due to the monopolization of political power by a hereditary monarchy.

THE NATURE OF ECONOMIC TRANSFORMATION

The shift toward a market-based economic system often entails a number of steps: deregulation, privatization, and creation of a legal system to safeguard property rights.[51] We shall review each before looking at the track record of states engaged in economic transformation.

Deregulation

Deregulation involves removing legal restrictions to the free play of markets, the establishment of private enterprises, and the manner in which private enterprises operate. Before the collapse of communism, the governments in most command economies exercised tight control over prices and output, setting both through detailed state planning. They also prohibited private enterprises from operating in most sectors of the economy, severely restricted direct investment by foreign enterprises, and limited international trade. Deregulation in these cases involved removing price controls, thereby allowing prices to be set by the interplay between demand and supply; abolishing laws regulating the establishment and operation of private enterprises; and relaxing or removing restrictions on direct investment by foreign enterprises and international trade.

DEREGULATION
Removal of government restrictions concerning the conduct of a business.

In mixed economies, the role of the state was more limited, but here too, in certain sectors the state set prices, owned businesses, limited private enterprise, restricted investment by foreigners, and restricted international trade. For these countries, deregulation has involved the same kind of initiatives that we have seen in former command economies, although the transformation has been easier because there was always a vibrant private sector in these countries. India is a good example of a mixed

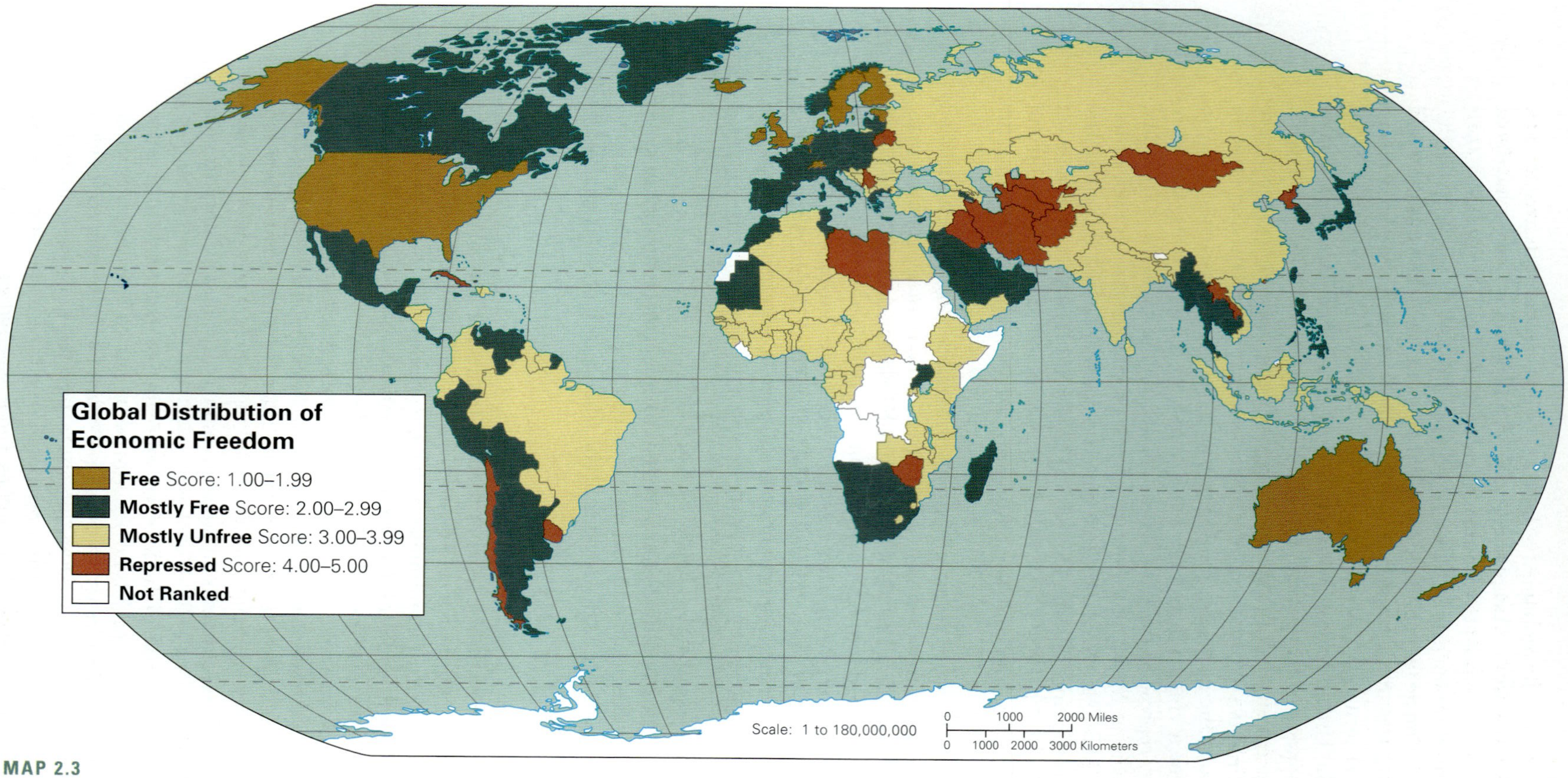

MAP 2.3

Distribution of Economic Freedom

Source: Heritage Foundation, *2004 Index of Economic Freedom,* www.heritage.org. Reprinted with permission.

economy that is currently deregulating large areas of its economy. Deregulation has involved reforming the industrial licensing system that made it difficult to establish private enterprises and opening areas that were once closed to the private sector (including electricity generation, parts of the oil industry, steelmaking, air transport, and some areas of the telecommunications industry). It has also involved the removal of limits on foreign ownership of Indian assets and the lowering of barriers to international trade.

Privatization

Hand in hand with deregulation has come a sharp increase in privatization. **Privatization** transfers the ownership of state property into the hands of private individuals, frequently by the sale of state assets through an auction.[52] Privatization is seen as a way to unlock gains in economic efficiency by giving new private owners a powerful incentive–the reward of greater profits–to search for increases in productivity, to enter new markets, and to exit losing ones.[53]

PRIVATIZATION
The sale of state-owned enterprises to private investors.

The privatization movement started in Great Britain in the early 1980s when then Prime Minister Margaret Thatcher started to sell state-owned assets such as the British telephone company, British Telecom (BT). In a pattern that has been repeated around the world, this sale was linked with the deregulation of the British telecommunications industry. By allowing other firms to compete head to head with BT, deregulation ensured that privatization did not simply replace a state-owned monopoly with a private monopoly. The opening case discussed privatization in India. As this example suggests, privatization has become a worldwide movement. In Africa, for example, Mozambique and Zambia are leading the way with very ambitious privatization plans. Zambia put more than 145 state-owned companies up for sale, while Mozambique has already sold scores of enterprises, ranging from tea plantations to a chocolate factory. The most dramatic privatization programs, however, have occurred in the economies of the former Soviet Union and its Eastern European satellite states. In the Czech Republic, three-quarters of all state-owned enterprises were privatized between 1989 and 1996, helping to push the share of gross domestic product accounted for by the private sector up from 11 percent in 1989 to 60 percent in 1995. In Russia, where the private sector had been almost completely repressed before 1989, 50 percent of GDP was in private hands by 1995, again much as a result of privatization. And in Poland, the private sector accounted for 59 percent of GDP in 1995, up from 20 percent in 1989.[54] However, Poland also illustrates how far some of these countries still have to travel. Despite an aggressive privatization program, Poland still had 4000 state-owned enterprises that dominate the heavy industry, mining, and transportation sectors.

The ownership structure of newly privatized firms also is important.[55] Many former command economies, for example, lack the legal regulations regarding corporate governance that are found in advanced Western economies. In advanced market economies, boards of directors are appointed by shareholders to make sure managers consider the interests of shareholders when making decisions and try to manage the firm in a manner that is consistent with maximizing the wealth of shareholders. However, some former Communist states lack laws requiring corporations to establish effective boards. In such cases, managers with a small ownership stake can often gain control over the newly privatized entity and run it for their own benefit, while ignoring the interests of other shareholders. Sometimes these managers are the same Communist bureaucrats who ran the enterprise before privatization. Because they have been schooled in the old ways of doing things, they often hesitate to take drastic action to increase the efficiency of the enterprise. Instead, they continue to run the firm as a private fiefdom, seeking to extract whatever economic value they can for their own betterment (in the form of perks that are not reported) while doing little to increase the economic efficiency of the enterprise so that shareholders benefit.

Legal Systems

As noted earlier in this chapter, laws protecting private property rights and providing mechanisms for contract enforcement are required for a well-functioning market economy. Without a legal system that protects property rights, and without the machinery to enforce that system, the incentive to engage in economic activity can be reduced substantially by private and public entities, including organized crime, that expropriate the profits generated by the efforts of private-sector entrepreneurs. As noted earlier, this has become a problem in many former Communist states. When communism collapsed, many of these countries lacked the legal structure required to protect property rights, all property having been held by the state. Although many states have made big strides toward instituting the required system, it will be many more years before the legal system is functioning as smoothly as it does in the West. For example, in most Eastern European nations, the title to urban and agricultural property is often uncertain because of incomplete and inaccurate records, multiple pledges on the same property, and unsettled claims resulting from demands for restitution from owners in the pre-Communist era. Also, while most countries have improved their commercial codes, institutional weaknesses still undermine contract enforcement. Court capacity is often inadequate, and procedures for resolving contract disputes out of court are often inadequate or poorly developed.[56]

The Rocky Road

In practice, the road that must be travelled to reach a market-based economic system has often been rocky.[57] This has been particularly true for the states of Eastern Europe in the post-Communist era. In this region, the move toward greater political and economic freedom has sometimes been accompanied by economic and political chaos.[58] Most Eastern European states began to liberalize their economies in the heady days of the early 1990s. They dismantled decades of price controls, allowed widespread private ownership of businesses, and permitted much greater competition. Most also planned to sell state-owned enterprises to private investors. However, given the vast number of such enterprises and how inefficient many were, making them unappealing to private investors, most privatization efforts moved forward slowly. In this new environment, many inefficient state-owned enterprises found that they could not survive without a guaranteed market. The newly democratic governments often continued to support these money-losing enterprises to stave off massive unemployment. The resulting subsidies to state-owned enterprises led to ballooning budget deficits that were typically financed by printing money. Printing money, along with the lack of price controls, often led to hyperinflation. In 1993, the inflation rate was 21 percent in Hungary, 38 percent in Poland, 841 percent in Russia, and a staggering 10 000 percent in the Ukraine. Since then, however, many governments have instituted tight monetary policies and reduced their inflation rates.

Another consequence of the shift toward a market economy was collapsing output as inefficient state-owned enterprises failed to find buyers for their goods. Real gross domestic product fell dramatically in many post-Communist states between 1990 and 1994. However, the corner has been turned in several countries. Poland, the Czech Republic, and Hungary now all boast growing economies and relatively low inflation. But some countries, such as Russia and the Ukraine, still find themselves grappling with major economic problems.

A study by the World Bank suggests that the post-Communist states that have been most successful at transforming their economies were those that followed an economic policy best described as "shock therapy." In these countries–which include the Czech Republic, Hungary, and Poland–prices and trade were liberated quickly, inflation was held in check by tight monetary policy, and the privatization of state-owned industries was implemented rapidly. Among the 26 economies of Eastern Europe and the former Soviet Union, the World Bank found a strong positive correlation between the imposition of such shock therapy and subsequent economic growth. Speedy reformers suffered smaller falls in output and returned to growth more quickly than those such as Russia and the Ukraine that moved more slowly.[59]

Despite variations within the group, in general, the transformation of former command economies has progressed significantly.

IMPLICATIONS

The global changes in political and economic systems discussed above have several implications for international business. The ideological conflict between collectivism and individualism that so defined the twentieth century is less in evidence today. The West won the Cold War, and Western ideology has never been more widespread than it was at the beginning of the millennium. Although command economies still remain and totalitarian dictatorships can still be found around the world, the tide has been running in favour of free markets and democracy.

The implications for business are enormous. For the best part of 50 years, half of the world was off-limits to Western businesses. Now all that is changing. Many of the national markets of Eastern Europe, Latin America, Africa, and Asia may still be undeveloped and impoverished, but they are potentially enormous. With a population of 1.2 billion, the Chinese market alone is potentially bigger than that of the United States, the European Union, and Japan combined! Similarly India, with its 1 billion people, is a potentially huge future market. Latin America has another 400 million potential consumers. It is unlikely that China, Russia, Poland, or any of the other states now moving toward a free market system will attain the living standards of the West anytime soon. Nevertheless, the upside potential is so large that companies need to consider making inroads now.

However, just as the potential gains are large, so are the risks. There is no guarantee that democracy will thrive in the newly democratic states of Eastern Europe, particularly if these states have to grapple with severe economic setbacks. Totalitarian dictatorships could return, although they are unlikely to be of the communist variety. Although the bipolar world of the Cold War era has vanished, it may be replaced by a multipolar world dominated by a number of civilizations. In such a world, much of the economic promise inherent in the global shift toward market-based economic systems may evaporate in the face of conflicts between civilizations. While the long-term potential for economic gain from investment in the world's new market economies is large, the risks associated with any such investment are also substantial. It would be foolish to ignore these.

IMPLICATIONS FOR BUSINESS

The implications for international business of the material discussed in this chapter fall into two broad categories. First, the political, economic, and legal environment of a country clearly influences the attractiveness of that country as a market and/or investment site. The benefits, costs, and risks associated with doing business in a country are a function of that country's political, economic, and legal systems. Second, the political, economic, and legal systems of a country can raise important ethical issues that have implications for the practice of international business. Here we consider each of these issues.

ATTRACTIVENESS

The overall attractiveness of a country as a market and/or investment site depends on balancing the likely long-term benefits of doing business in that country against the likely costs and risks. Below we consider the determinants of benefits, costs, and risks.

Benefits

In the most general sense, the long-run monetary benefits of doing business in a country are a function of the size of the market, the present wealth (purchasing power) of consumers in that market, and the likely future wealth of consumers. While some markets are very large when measured by number of consumers (e.g., China and India), low living standards may imply limited purchasing power and, therefore, a relatively small market when measured in economic terms. While international businesses need to be aware of this distinction, they also need to keep in mind the likely future prospects of a country. In 1960, for example, South Korea was viewed as just another impoverished Third World nation. By 2000 it was the world's 12th largest economy, measured in terms of GDP. International firms that recognized South Korea's potential in 1960 and began to do business in that country may have reaped greater benefits than those that wrote off South Korea.

By identifying and investing early in a potential future economic star, international firms may build brand loyalty and gain experience in that country's business practices. These will pay back substantial dividends if that country achieves sustained high economic growth rates. In contrast, late entrants may find that they lack the brand loyalty and experience necessary to achieve a significant presence in the market. In the language of business strategy, early entrants into potential future economic stars may be able to reap substantial first-mover advantages, while late entrants may fall victim to late-mover disadvantages.[60] (**First-mover advantages** are the advantages that accrue to early entrants into a market. **Late-mover disadvantages** are the handicap that late entrants might suffer.)

FIRST-MOVER ADVANTAGES
Advantages accruing to the first to enter a market.

LATE-MOVER DISADVANTAGES
Handicap experienced by being a late entrant in a market.

A country's economic system and property rights regime are reasonably good predictors of economic prospects. Countries with free market economies in which property rights are well protected tend to achieve greater economic growth rates than command economies and/or economies where property rights are poorly protected. It follows that a country's economic system and property rights regime, when taken together with market size (in terms of population), probably constitute reasonably good indicators of the potential long-run benefits of doing business in a country.

Costs

A number of political, economic, and legal factors determine the costs of doing business in a country. With regard to political factors, the costs of doing business in a country can be increased by a need to pay off the politically powerful to be allowed by the government to do business. The need to pay what are essentially bribes is greater in closed totalitarian states than in open democratic societies where politicians are held accountable by the electorate (although this is not a hard-and-fast distinction). Whether a company should actually pay bribes in return for market access should be determined on the basis of the legal and ethical implications of such action. We discuss this consideration below.

With regard to economic factors, one of the most important variables is the sophistication of a country's economy. It may be more costly to do business in relatively primitive or undeveloped economies because of the lack of infrastructure and supporting businesses. At the extreme, an international firm may have to provide its own infrastructure and supporting business, which obviously raises costs. When McDonald's decided to open its first restaurant in Moscow, it found that to serve food and drink indistinguishable from that served in McDonald's restaurants elsewhere, it had to vertically integrate backward to supply its own needs. The quality of Russian-grown potatoes and meat was too poor. Thus, to protect the quality of its product, McDonald's set up its own dairy farms, cattle ranches, vegetable plots, and food processing plants within Russia. This raised the cost of doing business in Russia, relative to the cost in more sophisticated economies where high-quality inputs could be purchased on the open market.

As for legal factors, it can be more costly to do business in a country where local laws and regulations set strict standards with regard to product safety, safety in the workplace, environmental pollution, and the like (since adhering to such regulations is costly). It can also be more costly to do business in a country like the United States, where the absence of a cap on damage awards has meant spiralling liability insurance rates. It can be more costly to do business in a country that lacks well-established laws for regulating business practice (as is the case in many of the former Communist nations). In the absence of a well-developed body of business contract law, international firms may find no satisfactory way to resolve contract disputes and, consequently, routinely face large losses from contract violations. Similarly, local laws that fail to adequately protect intellectual property can lead to the "theft" of an international business's intellectual property, and lost income.

Risks

As with costs, the risks of doing business in a country are determined by a number of political, economic, and legal factors. **Political risk** has been defined as the likelihood that political forces will cause drastic changes in a country's business environment that adversely affect the profit and other goals of a particular business enterprise.[61] So defined, political risk tends to be greater in countries experiencing social unrest and disorder or in countries where the underlying nature of a society increases the likelihood of social unrest. Social unrest typically finds expression in strikes, demonstrations, terrorism, and violent conflict. Such unrest is more likely to be found in countries that contain more than one ethnic nationality, in countries where competing ideologies are battling for political control, in countries where economic mismanagement has created high inflation and falling living standards, or in countries that straddle the "fault lines" between civilizations, such as Bosnia.

POLITICAL RISK The likelihood that political forces will cause drastic changes in a country's business environment that will adversely affect the profit and other goals of a particular business enterprise.

Social unrest can result in abrupt changes in government and government policy or, in some cases, in protracted civil strife. Such strife tends to have negative economic implications for the profit goals of business enterprises. For example, in the aftermath of the 1979 Islamic revolution in Iran, the Iranian assets of numerous U.S. companies were seized by the new Iranian government without compensation. Similarly, the violent disintegration of the Yugoslavian federation into warring states, including Bosnia, Croatia, and Serbia, precipitated a collapse in the local economies and in the profitability of investments in those countries.

Although likely never at risk from a violent Yugoslav-type disintegration, the perception of Canada as a unified and politically stable country has, over the past four decades been intermittently tested in the eyes of the world. The FLQ crisis of the 1960s brought bombings, violence, and political kidnappings to Montreal. Since then, however, the flare-ups have been, for the most part, peaceful. Quebec separatism, still on the Parti Quebecois agenda as an achievable reality, has taken a back seat over the past few years to economic concerns.

On the economic front, economic risks arise from economic mismanagement by the government of a country. **Economic risk** can be defined as the likelihood that economic mismanagement will cause drastic changes in a country's business environment that adversely affect the profit and other goals of a particular business enterprise. Economic risks are not independent of political risk. Economic mismanagement may give rise to significant social unrest and hence political risk. Nevertheless, economic risks are worth emphasizing as a separate category because there is not always a one-to-one relationship between economic mismanagement and social unrest. One visible indicator of economic mismanagement tends to be a country's inflation rate. Another tends to be the level of business and government debt in the country.

ECONOMIC RISK The likelihood that events, including economic mismanagement, will cause drastic changes in a country's business environment that adversely affect the profit and other goals of a particular business enterprise.

In Asian states such as Indonesia, Thailand, and South Korea, businesses increased their debt rapidly during the 1990s, often at the bequest of the government, which was encouraging them to invest in industries deemed to be of "strategic importance" to the country. The result was overinvestment, with more industrial (factories) and commercial capacity (office space) being built than could be justified by demand conditions. Many of these investments turned out to be uneconomic. The borrowers failed to generate the profits required to meet their debt payment. In turn, the banks that had lent money to these businesses suddenly found that they had rapid increases in nonperforming loans on their books. Foreign investors, believing that many local companies and banks might go bankrupt, pulled their money out of these countries, selling local stock, bonds, and currency. This action precipitated the 1997–1998 financial crisis in Southeast Asia. The crisis included a precipitous decline in the value of Asian stock markets, which in some cases exceeded 70 percent; a similar collapse in the value of many Asian currencies against the U.S. dollar; an implosion of local demand; and a severe economic recession that will affect many Asian countries for years to come. In short, economic risks were rising throughout Southeast Asia during the 1990s. Astute foreign businesses and investors, seeing this situation, limited their exposure in this part of the world. More naive businesses and investors lost their shirts!

On the legal front, risks arise when a country's legal system fails to provide adequate safeguards in the case of contract violations or to protect property rights. When legal safeguards are weak, firms are more likely to break contracts and/or steal intellectual property if they perceive it as being in their interests to do so. Thus, **legal risk** might be defined as the likelihood that a trading partner will opportunistically break a contract or expropriate property rights. When legal risks in a country are high, an international business might hesitate entering into a long-term contract or joint-venture agreement with a firm in that country. For example, in the 1970s when the Indian government passed a law

LEGAL RISK The likelihood that a trading partner will opportunistically break a contract or expropriate intellectual property rights.

requiring all foreign investors to enter into joint ventures with Indian companies, U.S. companies such as IBM and Coca-Cola closed their investments in India. They believed that the Indian legal system did not provide for adequate protection of intellectual property rights, creating the very real danger that their Indian partners might expropriate the intellectual property of the American companies—which for IBM and Coca-Cola amounted to the core of their competitive advantage.

Overall Attractiveness

The overall attractiveness of a country as a potential market and/or investment site for an international business depends on balancing the benefits, costs, and risks associated with doing business in that country. Generally, the costs and risks associated with doing business in a foreign country are typically lower in economically advanced and politically stable democratic nations and greater in less developed and politically unstable nations. The calculus is complicated, however, by the fact that the potential long-run benefits are not dependent only upon a nation's current stage of economic development or political stability. Rather, the benefits depend on likely future economic growth rates. Economic growth appears to be a function of a free market system and a country's capacity for growth (which may be greater in less developed nations). This leads one to conclude that, other things being equal, the benefit–cost–risk trade-off is likely to be most favourable in politically stable developed and developing nations that have free market systems and no dramatic upsurge in either inflation rates or private-sector debt. It is likely to be least favourable in politically unstable developing nations that operate with a mixed or command economy or in developing nations where speculative financial bubbles have led to excess borrowing.

ETHICS AND REGULATIONS

Country differences give rise to some important and contentious ethical issues. Three important issues that have been the focus of much debate in recent years are (1) the ethics of doing business in nations that violate human rights, (2) the ethics of doing business in countries with very lax labour and environmental regulations, and (3) the ethics of corruption.

Ethics and Human Rights

One major ethical dilemma facing firms from democratic nations is whether they should do business in totalitarian countries, such as China, that routinely violate the human rights of their citizens. There are two sides to this issue. Some argue that investing in totalitarian countries provides comfort to dictators and can help prop up repressive regimes that abuse basic human rights. For instance, Human Rights Watch, an organization that promotes the protection of basic human rights around the world, has argued that the progressive trade policies adopted by Western nations toward China has done little to deter human rights abuses.[62] According to Human Rights Watch, the Chinese government stepped up its repression of political dissidents in 1996 after the Clinton administration removed human rights as a factor in determining China's trade status with the United States. Without investment by Western firms and the support of Western governments, many repressive regimes would collapse and be replaced by more democratically inclined governments, critics such as Human Rights Watch argue. Firms that have invested in Chile, China, Iraq, and South Africa have all been the direct targets of such criticisms. The 1994 dismantling of the apartheid system in South Africa has been credited to economic sanctions by Western nations, including a lack of investment by Western firms. This, say those who argue against investment in totalitarian countries, is proof that investment boycotts can work (although decades of U.S.-led investment boycotts against Cuba and Iran, among other countries, have failed to have a similar impact).

In contrast, some argue that Western investment, by raising the level of economic development of a totalitarian country, can help change it from within. They note that economic well-being and political freedoms often go hand in hand. Thus, when arguing against attempts to apply trade sanctions to China in the wake of the violent 1989 government crackdown on pro-democracy demonstrators, the U.S. government claimed that U.S. firms should continue to be allowed to invest in mainland China because greater political freedoms would follow the resulting economic growth. The Clinton administration used similar logic as the basis for its 1996 decision decoupling human rights issues from trade policy considerations.

Since both positions have some merit, it is difficult to arrive at a general statement of what firms should do. Unless mandated by government (as in the case of investment in South Africa) each firm must make its own judgments about the ethical implications of investing in totalitarian states on a case-by-case basis. The more repressive the regime, however, and the less amenable it seems to be to change, the greater the case for not investing.

Ethics and Regulations

A second important ethical issue is whether an international firm should adhere to the same standards of product safety, work safety, and environmental protection that are required in its home country. This is of particular concern to many firms based in Western nations, where product safety, worker safety, and environmental protection laws are among the toughest in the world. Should Western firms investing in less developed countries adhere to tough Western standards, even though local regulations don't require them to do so? This issue has taken on added importance in recent years following revelations that Western enterprises have been using child labour or very poorly paid "sweatshop" labour in developing nations. Companies criticized for using sweatshop labour include the Gap, Disney, Wal-Mart, and Nike.[63]

Again there is no easy answer. While the argument for adhering to Western standards might seem strong, on closer examination the issue becomes more complicated. What if adhering to Western standards would make the foreign investment unprofitable, thereby denying the foreign country much-needed jobs? What is the ethical thing to do? To adhere to Western standards and not invest, thereby denying people jobs, or to adhere to local standards and invest, thereby providing jobs and income? As with many ethical dilemmas, there is no easy answer. Each case needs to be assessed on its own merits.

Ethics and Corruption

A final ethical issue concerns bribes and corruption. Should an international business pay bribes to corrupt government officials to gain market access to a foreign country? To most Westerners, bribery seems to be a corrupt and morally repugnant way of doing business, so the answer might initially be no. Some countries have laws on their books that prohibit their citizens from paying bribes to foreign government officials in return for economic favours. As noted earlier, in the United States the Foreign Corrupt Practices Act prohibits U.S. companies from making "corrupt" payments to foreign officials to obtain or retain business, although many other developed nations lack similar laws. Similarly, the Canadian Bill S-21 encompasses the same spirit of checks and balances against corrupt business practices on the international stage. Trade and finance ministers from the member states of the Organization for Economic Cooperation and Development (OECD), an association of the world's 20 or so most powerful economies, are working on a convention that would oblige member states to make the bribery of foreign public officials a criminal offence.

However, in many parts of the world, payoffs to government officials are a part of life. One can argue that not investing ignores the fact that such investment can bring substantial benefits to the local populace in terms of income and jobs. From a pragmatic standpoint, the practice of giving bribes, although a little evil, might be the price that must be paid to do a greater good (assuming the investment creates jobs where none existed before and assuming the practice is not illegal). Several economists advocate this reasoning, suggesting that in the context of pervasive and cumbersome regulations in developing countries, corruption may actually improve efficiency and help growth! These economists theorize that in a country where preexisting political structures distort or limit the workings of the market mechanism, corruption in the form of black-marketeering, smuggling, and side payments to government bureaucrats to "speed up" approval for business investments may actually enhance welfare.[64] Arguments like this persuaded the U.S. congress to exempt certain "grease payments" from the Foreign Corrupt Practices Act. Similarly, Bill S-21 allows for exemptions under such circumstances.

However, other economists have argued that corruption reduces the returns on business investment.[65] In a country where corruption is common, the profits from a business activity may be siphoned off by unproductive bureaucrats who demand side payments for granting the enterprise permission to operate. This reduces the incentive that businesses have to invest and may hurt a country's economic growth rate. One economist's study of the connection between corruption and growth in 70 countries found that corruption had a significant negative impact on a country's economic growth rate.[66] Given the debate and the complexity of this issue, one again might conclude that generalization is difficult. Yes, corruption is bad, and yes, it may harm a country's economic development, but yes, there are also cases where side payments to government officials can remove the bureaucratic barriers to investments that create jobs. This pragmatic stance ignores, however, that corruption tends to "corrupt" both the bribe giver and the bribe taker. Corruption feeds on itself, and once an individual has started to walk down the road of corruption, pulling back may be difficult if not impossible. This strengthens the moral case for never engaging in corruption, no matter how compelling the benefits might seem.

KEY TERMS

Bill S-21, p. 55
civil law, p. 50
collectivism, p. 44
command economy, p. 49
common law, p. 50
communist totalitarianism, p. 47
communists, p. 44
contract, p. 51
contract law, p. 51
copyrights, p. 55
democracy, p. 46
deregulation, p. 71
economic risk, p. 77
first-mover advantages, p. 76
Foreign Corrupt Practices Act, p. 54
gross national income (GNI), p. 61
Human Development Index (HDI), p. 62
individualism, p. 45
innovation, p. 62
late-mover disadvantages, p. 76
legal risk, p. 77
legal system, p. 49
market economy, p. 48
mixed economy, p. 49
Paris Convention for the Protection of Industrial Property, p. 57
patent, p. 55
political economy, p. 43
political risk, p. 77
political system, p. 44
private action, p. 52
privatization, p. 73
product liability, p. 60
product safety laws, p. 60
property rights, p. 52
public action p. 53
purchasing power parity (PPP), p. 61
representative democracy, p. 46
right-wing totalitarianism, p. 47
social democrats, p. 44
theocratic law, p. 50
theocratic totalitarianism, p. 47
totalitarianism, p. 46
Trade Related Aspects of Intellectual Property Rights (TRIPS), p. 57
trademarks, p. 55
tribal totalitarianism, p. 47
United Nations Convention on Contracts for the International Sale of Goods (CIGS), p. 51

SUMMARY

This chapter has reviewed how the political, economic, and legal systems of different countries vary. The potential benefits, costs, and risks of doing business in a country are a function of its political, economic, and legal systems. These major points were made in the chapter:

1. Political systems can be assessed according to two dimensions: the degree to which they emphasize collectivism as opposed to individualism, and the degree to which they are democratic or totalitarian.
2. Collectivism is an ideology that views the needs of society as being more important than the needs of the individual. Collectivism translates into an advocacy for state intervention in economic activity and, in the case of communism, a totalitarian dictatorship.
3. Individualism is an ideology built on an emphasis of the primacy of individual's freedoms in the political, economic, and cultural realms. Individualism translates into an advocacy for democratic ideals and free market economics.
4. Democracy and totalitarianism are at different ends of the political spectrum. In a representative democracy, citizens periodically elect individuals to represent them and political freedoms are guaranteed by a constitution. In a totalitarian state, political power is monopolized by a party, group, or individual, and basic political freedoms are denied to citizens of the state.
5. There are three broad types of economic systems: a market economy, a command economy, and a mixed economy. In a market economy, prices are free of controls and private ownership is predominant. In a command economy, prices are set by central planners, productive assets are owned by the state, and private ownership is forbidden. A mixed economy has elements of both a market economy and a command economy.
6. Differences in the structure of law between countries can have important implications for the practice of international business. The degree to which property rights are protected can vary dramatically from country

to country, as can product safety and product liability legislation and the nature of contract law.

7. The rate of economic progress in a country seems to depend on the extent to which that country has a well-functioning market economy in which property rights are protected.
8. Many countries are now in a state of transition. There is a marked shift away from totalitarian governments and command or mixed economic systems and toward democratic political institutions and free market economic systems.
9. The attractiveness of a country as a market and/or investment site depends on balancing the likely long-run benefits of doing business in that country against the likely costs and risks.
10. The benefits of doing business in a country are a function of the size of the market (population), its present wealth (purchasing power), and its future growth prospects. By investing early in countries that are currently poor but are nevertheless growing rapidly, firms can gain first-mover advantages that may pay back substantial dividends in the future.
11. The costs of doing business in a country tend to be greater where political payoffs are required to gain market access, where supporting infrastructure is lacking or underdeveloped, and where adhering to local laws and regulations is costly.
12. The risks of doing business in a country tend to be greater in countries that are (*i*) politically unstable, (*ii*) subject to economic mismanagement, and (*iii*) lacking a legal system to provide adequate safeguards in the case of contract or property rights violations.
13. Country differences give rise to several ethical dilemmas, including (i) should a firm do business in a repressive totalitarian state, (ii) should a firm conform to its home product, workplace, and environmental standards when they are not required by the host country, and (iii) should a firm pay bribes to government officials to gain market access?

CRITICAL THINKING AND DISCUSSION QUESTIONS

1. Free market economies stimulate greater economic growth, whereas state-directed economies stifle growth! Discuss.
2. A democratic political system is an essential condition for sustained economic progress. Discuss.
3. What is the relationship between corruption in a country (i.e., bribe taking by government officials) and economic growth? Is corruption always bad?
4. The Nobel Prize-winning economist Amartya Sen argues that the concept of development should be broadened to include more than just economic development. What other factors does Sen think should be included in an assessment of development? How might adoption of Sen's views influence government policy? Do you think Sen is correct that development is about more than just economic development? Explain.
5. During the late 1980s and early 1990s, China was routinely cited by various international organizations such as Amnesty International and Freedom Watch for major human rights violations, including torture, beatings, imprisonment, and executions of political dissidents. Despite this, in the late 1990s, China received record levels of foreign direct investment, mainly from firms based in democratic societies such as the United States, Japan, and Germany. Evaluate this trend from an ethical perspective. If you were the CEO of a firm that had the option of making a potentially very profitable investment in China, what would you do?
6. You are the CEO of a company that has to choose between making a $100-million investment in Russia or the Czech Republic. Both investments promise the same long-run return, so your choice is driven by risk considerations. Assess the various risks of doing business in each of these nations. Which investment would you favour and why?

RESEARCH TASK | globalEDGE™ globaledge.msu.edu

Use the globalEDGE™ site to complete the following exercises:

1. The "Freedom in the World" survey evaluates the state of political rights and civil liberties around the world. Provide a description of this survey and a ranking, in terms of "freedom," of the leaders and laggards. What factors are considered in this survey when forming the rankings?
2. Market Potential Indicators (MPI) is an indexing study conducted by the Michigan State University Center for International Business Education and Research (MSU-CIBER) to compare emerging markets on a variety of dimensions. Provide a description of the indicators used in the indexing procedure. Which of the indicators would have greater importance for a company that markets laptop computers? Considering the MPI rankings, which developing countries would you advise this company to enter first?

Visit the *Global Business Today* Online Learning Centre at **www.mcgrawhill.ca/college/hill** to access quizzes, interactive exercises, a Business Around the World interactive map, and other learning and study tools related to this chapter.

Online Learning Centre

CLOSING CASE

DELIVERING ELECTRICITY IN CANADA

Electricity is a unique raw material in the world, and its methods of delivery show how interconnected our globe has become. The way electricity is traded also shows how the notion of the role that government should play in the Canadian economy is influenced by events in other jurisdictions.

Canada is the fifth largest electricity producer in the world—only the United States, China, Russia, and Japan produce more. Electricity is a unique product in that it cannot easily be stored in the same way that other commodities, such as oil and natural gas, can be. Since electricity must be used as it is produced, trade of electricity across provincial and country borders becomes very important. For example, while the Province of Ontario is a net exporter of electricity, it also imports power from Quebec, Manitoba, and the United States.

For much of the 1900s, electricity in Canada and in other industrialized nations was highly monopolized and regulated. Electricity was thought of as being too important to be left in the hands of the private sector. However, starting in the 1980s, it was becoming clear that public monopolies were introducing unnecessary, costly, and often unsafe practices to the delivery of a wide range of essential services. As governments watched market forces wring efficiencies from regulated monopolies such as airlines and telecommunications, there was the inevitable look to see if the same price mechanism could create efficiencies in the electricity market.

These forces impacted the Canadian electricity industry. While the electrical and regulatory situation across the country varied widely by province, some provinces, such as Alberta and Ontario undertook major changes in their regulatory environment. Alberta, for example, was the first province to introduce privatization legislation in 1995, with later amendments allowing retail customers to choose their suppliers of electricity from the beginning of 2001. Ontario introduced its own privatization legislation in 1998 and retail access was to be provided in Ontario in May 2002.

However, other forces in the United States were emerging to cast great suspicion on deregulated electricity markets. California deregulated its markets in 1998, and for its first two years the system worked very well. However, beginning in May 2000, electricity prices increased dramatically. This was due to a combination of factors, including natural gas prices that had increased by 400 percent in one year, a dry year that affected the demand for hydroelectric power, hot summer weather and cold winter temperatures, both of which increased demand, and lack of new supply. During the 1990s no major power plants were built in California, as utilities and other private companies were unwilling to make such large investments in an uncertain regulatory environment. The result was a series of rolling blackouts, the bankruptcy of some utilities, and questioning of the role of private companies.

This situation was made worse as information came forward about the role of Enron in California's power crisis. The name Enron has now entered the public realm as a synonym for greed, corruption, and everything that is seemingly wrong with capitalism.

Enron and other power companies abused the system that was in place, sometimes by giving false information to electricity price reporting agencies. None of these findings have added any credibility to the increasingly fragile electricity marketplace throughout North America.

In Ontario, in 2002 and 2003, events including changing political leaders, shifting public sentiment, and political expediency combined to present an erratic landscape for electricity. In December 2001, it was announced that the province would sell the former Ontario Hydro's electricity delivery business, to become the largest privatization in Canadian history. In 2002, a judge ruled that the government did not have the authority to sell the business. By the end of 2002, new Premier Ernie Eves announced a freezing of power rates, effectively ending the experiment with market forces determining the price of power.

In August 2003, the downside of having an interconnected marketplace was shown as 50 million North Americans suffered through a power blackout. A power failure that began in Ohio quickly cascaded through eight U.S. states and into Canada. Some parts of Ontario suffered rolling blackouts for more than a week before electricity was fully restored. It is estimated that in Canada 18.9 million work hours were lost due to the blackout. An aging power grid was one culprit, as were the actions of FirstEnergy Corp, a power utility based in Akron, Ohio, which failed to contain what should have been a routine interruption of local service.

In place of market mechanisms, government struggled with the issues of electricity lows. By the end of 2004, Ontario did not have a policy on the long-term future of nuclear energy, and consumers did not know how much they would be paying for electricity in the coming year, or how the price would be determined.

Sources: Canadian Securities Institute, *Energy Markets-Risk Management*, 2003; A. Lindgren, "Ontario to Get U.S.-Style Power Authority," *National Post*, June 16, 2004; CBC at www.cbc.ca/national/news/electricity.

CASE DISCUSSION QUESTIONS

1. In a switch from government regulated monopolies to competitive markets, who wins, and who loses?
2. Is electricity too important to be left in private hands?
3. How can political and policy changes in one country impact another?

2

Guanxi—Ties That Bind

In 1992, McDonald's Corporation opened its first restaurant in Beijing, China, after a decade of market research. The restaurant, then the largest McDonald's in the world, was located on the corner of Wangfujing Street and the Avenue of Eternal Peace, just two blocks from Tiananmen Square, the very heart of China's capital. The location choice seemed auspicious, and within two years, sales at the restaurant were surpassing expectations. Then the Beijing city government dropped a bombshell; officials abruptly informed McDonald's that it would have to make way for a commercial, residential, and office complex planned by Hong Kong developer Li Ka-shing. At the time, McDonald's still had 18 years left on its 20-year lease. A stunned McDonald's did what any good Western company would do—it took the Beijing city government to court to try to enforce the lease. The court refused to enforce the lease, and McDonald's had to move. Chinese observers had a simple explanation for the outcome. McDonald's, they said, lacked the *guanxi* of Li Ka-shing. Given this, how could the company expect to prevail? Company executives should have accepted the decision in good grace and moved on, but instead, McDonald's filed a lawsuit—a move that would further reduce what *guanxi* McDonald's might have with the city government!

This example illustrates a basic difference between doing business in the West and doing business in China. In the advanced economies of the West, business transactions are conducted and regulated by the centuries-old framework of contract law, which specifies the rights and obligations of parties to a business contract and provides mechanisms for seeking to redress grievances if one party in the exchange fails to live up to the legal agreement. In the West, McDonald's could have relied on the courts to enforce its legal contract with the Beijing government. In China, this approach didn't work. China does not have the same legal infrastructure. Personal power and relationships or connections, rather than the rule of law, have always been the key to getting things done in China. Decades of Communist rule stripped away the basic legal infrastructure that did exist to regulate business transactions.

CHAPTER 3

The Cultural Environment

OPENING CASE

Power, relationships, and connections are an important, and some say necessary, influence on getting things done and enforcing business agreements in China. The key to understanding this process is the concept of *guanxi*.

Guanxi literally means relationships, although in business settings it can be better understood as "connections." McDonald's lost its lease in central Beijing because it lacked the *guanxi* enjoyed by the powerful Li Ka-shing. The concept of *guanxi* is deeply rooted in Chinese culture, particularly the Confucian philosophy of valuing social hierarchy and reciprocal obligations. Confucian ideology has a 2000-year history in China, and half a century of Communist rule has done little to dent its influence on everyday culture in China. Confucianism stresses the importance of relationships, both within the family and between master and servant. Confucian ideology teaches that people are not created equal. In Confucian thought, loyalty and obligations to one's superiors (or to family) is regarded as a sacred duty, but at the same time, this loyalty has its price. Social superiors are obligated to reward the loyalty of their social inferiors by bestowing "blessings" upon them; thus, the obligations are reciprocal.

Today, Chinese will often cultivate a *guanxiwang,* or "relationship network," for help. Reciprocal obligations are the glue that holds such networks together. If those obligations are not met—if favours done are not paid back or reciprocated—the reputation of the transgressor is tarnished and he or she will be less able to draw on *guanxiwang* for help in the future. Thus, the implicit threat of social sanctions is often sufficient to ensure that favours are repaid, that obligations are met, and that relationships are honoured. In a society that lacks a rule-based legal tradition, and thus legal ways of redressing wrongs such as violations of business agreements, *guanxi* is an important mechanism for building long-term business relationships and getting business done in China. There is a tacit acknowledgment that if you have the right *guanxi,* legal rules can be broken, or at least bent. Li Ka-shing had the right *guanxi;* McDonald's apparently did not. Li Ka-shing's empire spans 40 countries, including Canada (initially through a purchase of a block of Husky Oil in 1987). His eldest son, Victor Li, a Canadian citizen, recently put in a bid for the bankrupt Air Canada.

As they have come to understand this, many Western businesses have tried to build *guanxi* to grease the wheels required to do business in China. Increasingly, *guanxi* has become a commodity that is for sale to foreigners. Many of the sons and daughters of high-ranking government officials have set up "consulting" firms and offered to mobilize their *guanxiwang* or those of their parents to help Western companies navigate their way through Chinese bureaucracy. Taking advantage of such services, however, requires good ethical judgment. There is a fine line between relationship building, which may require doing favours to meet obligations, and bribery. Consider the case of a lucrative business contract that was under consideration for more than a year between a large Chinese state-owned enterprise and two competing multinational firms. After months of negotiations, the Chinese elected to continue discussions with just one of the competitors—the one that had recently hired the son of the principal Chinese negotiator at a significant salary. This occurred even though the favoured firm's equipment was less compatible with Chinese equipment already in place than that offered by the rejected multinational. The clear implication is that the son of the negotiator had mobilized his *guanxiwang* to help his new employer gain an advantage in the contract negotiations. While hiring the son of the principal negotiator may be viewed as good business practice by some in the context of Chinese culture, others might argue that this action was ethically suspect and could be viewed as a thinly concealed bribe.

Sources: S. D. Seligman, "Guanxi: Grease for the Wheels of China," *China Business Review,* September/October 1999, pp. 34–38; L. Dana, "Culture Is the Essence of Asia," *Financial Times,* November 27, 2000, p. 12; L. Minder, "McDonald's to Close Original Beijing Store," *USA Today,* December 2, 1996, p. 1A; and M. W. Peng, *Business Strategies in Transition Economies* (Thousand Oaks, CA: Sage Publications, 2000).

LEARNING OBJECTIVES

1. Understand that substantial differences between societies arise from cultural differences.
2. Know what is meant by the term *culture.*
3. Appreciate that cultures vary because of differences in social structure, religion, language, education, economic philosophy, and political philosophy.
4. Understand the relationship between culture and the values found in the workplace.
5. Appreciate that culture is not a constant, but changes over time.
6. Appreciate that much of the change in contemporary social culture is being driven by economic advancement, technological change, and globalization.
7. Understand the implications for international business management of differences among cultures.

INTRODUCTION

International business is different from domestic business because countries are different. In Chapter 2 we saw how national differences in political, economic, and legal systems influence the benefits, costs, and risks associated with doing business in different countries. In this chapter, we will explore how differences in culture across and within countries can affect international business. Several themes run through this chapter.

The first theme is that business success in a variety of countries requires cross-cultural literacy. By cross-cultural literacy, we mean an understanding of how cultural differences across and within nations can affect the way business is practised. In these days of global communications, rapid transportation, and global markets, when the era of the global village seems just around the corner, it is easy to forget just how different various cultures really are. Underneath the veneer of modernism, deep cultural differences often remain. Westerners in general, and Americans in particular, are quick to conclude that because people from other parts of the world also wear blue jeans, listen to Western popular music, eat at McDonald's, and drink Coca-Cola, they also accept the basic tenets of Western (or American) culture. But this is not true. Increasingly, the Chinese are embracing the material products of modern society. Anyone who has visited Shanghai, for example, cannot fail to be struck by how modern the city seems, with its skyscrapers, department stores, and freeways. But as the opening case demonstrates, beneath the veneer of Western modernism, long-standing cultural traditions rooted in a 2000-year-old ideology continue to influence business transactions in China. In China, *guanxi,* or relationships backed by reciprocal obligations, are central to getting business done. As the opening case demonstrates, firms that lack sufficient *guanxi,* as McDonald's apparently did, may find themselves at a disadvantage when doing business in China. In this chapter, we shall argue that it is important for foreign businesses to gain an understanding of the culture, or cultures, that prevail in countries where they do business.

The opening case also illustrates another important theme that we shall develop further in this chapter: The old adage of "when in Rome do as the Romans do" may have ethical ramifications. Prevailing cultural mores in a country may put a foreign business in a difficult ethical position. For example, while it is important to build *guanxi* in China, there is a thin line between giving gifts to support the establishment of relationships, which is culturally normal behaviour, and bribery or corruption, which is viewed dimly in the West and is against the law in some nations such as the United States, where the Foreign Corrupt Practices Act makes it illegal for a U.S. company to bribe government officials to gain business in a foreign nation. In the late 1990s, Canada enacted a similar law, Bill S-21.

Another theme developed in this chapter is that a relationship may exist between culture and the cost of doing business in a country or region. Different cultures are more or less supportive of the capitalist mode of production and may increase or lower the costs of doing business. For example, some observers have argued that cultural factors lowered the costs of doing business in Japan and helped to explain Japan's rapid economic assent during the 1960s, 70s, and 80s.[1] By the same token, cultural factors can sometimes raise the costs of doing business. Historically, class divisions were an important aspect of British culture, and for a long time, firms operating in Great Britain found it difficult to achieve cooperation between management and labor. Class divisions led to a high level of industrial disputes in that country during the 1960s and 1970s and raised the costs of doing business in Great Britain relative to the costs in countries such as Switzerland, Norway, Germany, or Japan, where class conflict was historically less prevalent.

The British example, however, brings us to the final theme we will explore in this chapter: Culture is not static. It can and does evolve, although the rate at which culture can change is disputed. Important aspects of British culture have changed significantly over the past 20 years, and this is reflected in weaker class distinctions and a lower level of industrial disputes. Between 1993 and 2002, the number of days lost per 1000 workers due to strikes in the United Kingdom was on average 23 each year, significantly less than in the United States (where the figure was 45), Australia (where 75 days were lost), and Canada (where 187 were lost).[2] Similarly, there is evidence of cultural change in Japan, with the traditional Japanese emphasis on group identification giving way to greater emphasis on individualism.

We open this chapter with a general discussion of what culture is. Then we focus on how differences in social structure, religion, language, and education influence the culture of a country. We then discuss the process of cultural change. The implications

Cultural differences can often affect management expectations and styles. Loren Santow/ Tony Stone Images.

for business practice will be highlighted throughout the chapter and summarized in a section at the end.

WHAT IS CULTURE?

Scholars have never been able to agree on a simple definition of culture. In the 1870s, the anthropologist Edward Tylor defined culture as "that complex whole which includes knowledge, belief, art, morals, law, custom, and other capabilities acquired by man as a member of society."[3] Since then hundreds of other definitions have been offered. Geert Hofstede, an expert on cross-cultural differences and management, defined culture as "the collective programming of the mind which distinguishes the members of one human group from another . . . Culture, in this sense, includes systems of values; and values are among the building blocks of culture."[4] Another definition of culture comes from sociologists Zvi Namenwirth and Robert Weber who see culture as a system of ideas and argue that these ideas constitute a design for living.[5]

VALUES Abstract ideas about what a society believes to be good, right, and desirable.

Here we follow both Hofstede and Namenwirth and Weber by viewing culture as a system of values and norms that are shared among a group of people and that when taken together constitute a design for living. By **values** we mean abstract ideas about what a group believes to be good, right, and desirable. Put differently, values are shared assumptions about how things ought to be.[6] By **norms** we mean the social rules and guidelines that prescribe appropriate behaviour in particular situations. We shall use the term **society** to refer to a group of people who share a common set of values and norms. While a society may be equivalent to a country, some countries harbor several "societies" (i.e., they support multiple cultures) and some societies embrace more than one country.

NORMS Social rules and guidelines that prescribe appropriate behaviour in particular situations.

VALUES AND NORMS

SOCIETY Group of people who share a common set of values and norms.

Values form the bedrock of a culture. They provide the context within which a society's norms are established and justified. They may include a society's attitudes toward such concepts as individual freedom, democracy, truth, justice, honesty, loyalty, social obligations, collective responsibility, the role of women, love, sex, marriage, and so on. Values are not just abstract concepts; they are invested with considerable emotional significance. People argue, fight, and even die over values such as freedom. Values also often are reflected in the political and economic systems of a society. As we saw in Chapter 2, democratic free market capitalism is a reflection of a philosophical value system that emphasizes individual freedom.

Norms are the social rules that govern people's actions toward one another. Norms can be subdivided further into two major categories: folkways and mores. **Folkways** are the routine conventions of everyday life. Generally, folkways are actions of little moral significance. Rather, folkways are social conventions concerning things such as the appropriate dress code in a particular situation, good social manners, neighbourly behaviour, and the like. While folkways define the way people are expected to behave, violation of folkways is not normally a serious matter. People who violate folkways may be thought of as eccentric or ill-mannered, but they are not usually considered to be evil or bad. In many countries, foreigners may initially be excused for violating folkways.

FOLKWAYS Routine conventions of everyday life.

A good example of folkways concerns attitudes toward time in different countries. People are very time conscious in Canada. Canadians tend to arrive a few minutes early for business appointments. When invited for dinner to someone's home, it is considered polite to arrive on time or just a few minutes late. The concept of time can be very different in other countries. It is not necessarily a breach of etiquette to arrive a little late for a business appointment; it might even be considered more impolite to arrive early. Arriving on time for a dinner engagement can be very bad manners. In Great Britain, for example, when someone says, "Come for dinner at 7:00 P.M.," what he means is "come for dinner at 7:30 to 8:00 P.M." The guest who arrives at 7:00 P.M. is likely to find an unprepared and embarrassed host. Similarly, when an Argentinean says, "Come for dinner anytime after 8:00 P.M." what she means is don't come at 8:00 P.M.–it's far too early!

Mores are norms that are seen as central to the functioning of a society and to its social life. They have much greater significance than folkways. Accordingly, violating mores can bring serious retribution. Mores include such factors as indictments against theft, adultery, incest, and cannibalism. In many societies, certain mores have been enacted into law. Thus, all advanced societies have laws against theft, incest, and cannibalism. However, there are also many differences between cultures as to what is perceived as mores. In America, for example, drinking alcohol is widely accepted, whereas in Saudi Arabia the consumption of alcohol is viewed as violating important social mores and is punishable by imprisonment (as some Western citizens working in Saudi Arabia have discovered).

MORES Norms seen as central to the functioning of a society and to its social life.

CULTURE, SOCIETY, AND THE NATION-STATE

We have defined a society as a group of people that share a common set of values and norms; that is, people who are bound together by a common culture. However, there is not a strict one-to-one correspondence between a society and a nation-state. Nation-states are political creations. They may contain a single culture or several cultures. While the French nation can be thought of as the political embodiment of French culture, the nation of Canada has at least three cultures–an Anglo culture, a French-speaking "Quebecois" culture, and a Native American culture. Similarly, many African nations have important cultural differences between tribal groups, as exhibited in the early 1990s when Rwanda dissolved into a bloody civil war between two tribes, the Tutsis and Hutus. Africa is not alone in this regard. India is composed of many distinct cultural groups. During the Gulf War, the prevailing view presented to Western audiences was that Iraq was a homogenous Arab nation. But the chaos that followed the war revealed several different societies within Iraq, each with its own culture. The Kurds in the north do not view themselves as Arabs and have their own distinct history and traditions. There are two Arab societies: the Shiites in the South and the Sunnis who populate the middle of the country and who rule Iraq (the terms *Shiites* and *Sunnis* refer to different sects within the religion of Islam). Among the southern Sunni is another distinct society of 500 000 "Marsh Arabs" who live at the confluence of the Tigris and Euphrates rivers, pursuing a way of life that dates back 5000 years.[7]

At the other end of the scale, we can speak of cultures that embrace several nations. Several scholars argue that we can speak of an Islamic society or culture that is shared by the citizens of many nations in the Middle East, Asia, and Africa. As you will recall from the last chapter, this view of expansive cultures that embrace several nations underpins Samuel Huntington's view of a world that is fragmented into different civilizations including Western, Islamic, and Sinic (Chinese).[8]

To complicate things further, it is also possible to talk about culture at different levels. It is reasonable to talk about "Canadian society" and "Canadian culture," but there are several societies within Canada, each with its own culture. One can talk about Afro-Canadian culture, Cajun culture, Chinese-Canadian culture, Hispanic culture, Native-Canadian culture, Irish-Canadian culture, and Western culture. Although Canada is a multicultural country with many vibrant and new communities, particularly settling in major centres across Canada, its historical early founding cultures still carry clout in today's society. English Canadians view their culture as unique and different from that of its counterparts in the U.S. The Aboriginal cultures have their own culture. Similarly, the Quebec culture, entwined in its own unique Quebecois language, culture, cuisine, and joie de vivre, has survived and flourished over the centuries. The point is that the relationship between culture and country is often ambiguous. One cannot always characterize a country as having a single homogenous culture, and even when one can, one must also often recognize that the national culture is a mosaic of subcultures.

ANOTHER PERSPECTIVE

Sticky problems in culture research

Conducting research across cultures is difficult. The travel and the building of collaborative relationships in other countries is time-consuming, sometimes difficult, and always full of surprises. But one of the most interesting challenges is how to be certain that the concept on which you are working or about which you want to communicate has a similar meaning across the culture border. This challenge is far more than language translation; it is *concept* translation, or what researchers call *concept equivalence.* Take the complicated concept of bribery, for example. Does it mean the same thing in Manitoba as it does in an undeveloped, centralized economy such as North Korea? What do you think?

THE DETERMINANTS OF CULTURE

The values and norms of a culture do not emerge fully formed. They are the evolutionary product of a number of factors, including the prevailing political and economic philosophy, the social structure of a society, and the dominant religion, language, and education (see Figure 3.1). We discussed political and economic philosophy at length in Chapter 2. Such philosophy clearly influences the value systems of a society. For example, the values found in the former Soviet Union toward freedom, justice, and individual achievement were clearly different from the values found in Canada, precisely because each society operated according to a different political and economic philosophy. Below we will discuss the influence of social structure, religion, language, and education. Remember that the chain of causation runs both ways. While factors such as social structure and religion clearly influence the values and norms of a society, the values and norms of a society can influence social structure and religion.

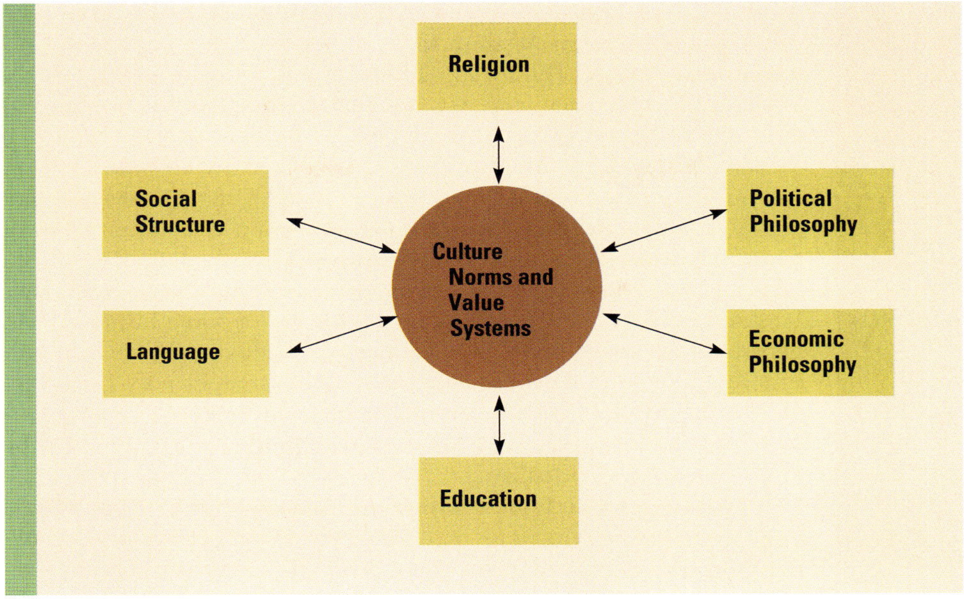

FIGURE 3.1
The Determinants of Culture

SOCIAL STRUCTURE

A society's "social structure" refers to its basic social organization. Although social structure consists of many different aspects, two dimensions are particularly important when explaining differences between cultures. The first is the degree to which the basic unit of social organization is the individual, as opposed to the group. Western societies tend to emphasize the primacy of the individual, while groups tend to figure much larger in many other societies. The second dimension is the degree to which a society is stratified into classes or castes. Some societies are characterized by a relatively high degree of social stratification and relatively low mobility between strata (e.g., Indian), while other societies are characterized by a low degree of social stratification and high mobility between strata (e.g., Canadian).

INDIVIDUALS AND GROUPS

A **group** is an association of two or more individuals who have a shared sense of identity and who interact with each other in structured ways on the basis of a common set of expectations about each other's behaviour.[9] Human social life is group life. Individuals are involved in families, work groups, social groups, recreational groups, and so on. However, while groups are found in all societies, societies differ according to the degree to which the group is viewed as the primary means of social organization.[10] In some societies, individual attributes and achievements are viewed as being more important than group membership, while in other societies the reverse is true.

GROUP An association of two or more individuals who have a shared sense of identity and who interact with each other in structured ways on the basis of a common set of expectations about each other's behaviour.

The Individual

In Chapter 2, we discussed individualism as a political philosophy. However, individualism is more than just an abstract political philosophy. In many Western societies, the individual is the basic building block of social organization. This is reflected not just in the political and economic organization of society, but also in the way people perceive

Avon has long been the queen of direct selling, with its omnipresent "Avon ladies." Avon has been selling in international markets since the 1950s and today does business in 56 different currencies. The entrepreneurial spirit among Chinese women, for example, has proven to fit well with Avon's sales-rep model. The same is true for Latin America's family-oriented culture—which Avon's president and chief operating officer, Susan Kropf calls "a dream environment for direct selling." Carolina Salguero/Getty Images.

themselves and relate to each other in social and business settings. The value systems of many Western societies, for example, emphasize individual achievement. The social standing of individuals is not so much a function of whom they work for, as of their individual performance in whatever work setting they choose.

The emphasis on individual performance in many Western societies has both beneficial and harmful aspects. In the United States, the emphasis on individual performance finds expression in an admiration of "rugged individualism" and entrepreneurship. One benefit of this is the high level of entrepreneurial activity in the United States and other Western societies. New products and new ways of doing business (e.g., personal computers, photocopiers, computer software, biotechnology, supermarkets, and discount retail stores) have repeatedly been created in the United States by entrepreneurial individuals. One can argue that the dynamism of the U.S. economy owes much to the philosophy of individualism.

Individualism also finds expression in a high degree of managerial mobility between companies, and this is not always good. While moving from company to company may be good for individual managers, who are trying to build impressive résumés, it is not necessarily beneficial for American companies. The lack of loyalty and commitment to an individual company, and the tendency to move on when a better offer comes along, can result in managers that have good general skills but lack the knowledge, experience, and network of interpersonal contacts that come from years of working within the same company. An effective manager draws on company-specific experience, knowledge, and a network of contacts to find solutions to current problems, and American companies may suffer if their managers lack these attributes.

One positive aspect of high managerial mobility is that executives are exposed to different ways of doing business. The ability to compare business practices helps U.S. executives identify how good practices and techniques developed in one firm might be profitably applied to other firms.

The emphasis on individualism may also make it difficult to build teams within an organization to perform collective tasks. If individuals are always competing with each other on the basis of individual performance, it may be difficult for them to cooperate. One study of U.S. competitiveness by the Massachusetts Institute of Technology concluded that U.S. firms are being hurt in the global economy by a failure to achieve cooperation both within a company (e.g., between functions; between management and labour) and between companies (e.g., between a firm and its suppliers). Given the emphasis on individualism in the American value system, this failure is not surprising.[11] The emphasis on individualism in the United States, while helping to create a dynamic entrepreneurial economy, may raise the costs of doing business due to its adverse impact on managerial stability and cooperation.

The high level of appreciated individualism is not seen to be as prevalent in Canada as in the U.S. In the U.S., neither of the two political parties espouse the great degree of government interference in the daily lives of Americans that we tend to see happening to Canadians, through high taxes, group social programs, and government-sanctioned (perceived and real) interference in business. Forecasts, however, shed a more optimistic light on Canada's state of competitive well-being, which inevitably encourages the development of a spirit of entrepreneurship.

The Economist projects Canada to be the second most competitive economy globally through 2007. Table 3.1 shows the levels of economic competitiveness as set out by the Centre for Research and Information on Canada for 2002 and 2003.

TABLE 3.1

Economic Competitiveness Group I—Population greater than 20 million

Source: IMD World Competitiveness Centre, IMD International, Switzerland.

	2003		2002	
USA	100.000	1	100.000	1
Australia	86.547	2	77.777	3
Canada	84.123	3	81.691	2
Malaysia	72.872	4	63.249	6
Germany	69.768	5	71.446	4
Taiwan	69.283	6	62.614	7
United Kingdom	66.489	7	70.789	5
France	66.407	8	58.479	9
Spain	59.758	9	59.986	8
Thailand	58.416	10	49.560	13
Japan	56.303	11	52.070	11
China Mainland	50.813	12	50.252	12
Sao Paulo	47.787	13	0.000	
Zhejiang	47.354	14	0.000	
Korea	46.476	15	55.643	10
Columbia	44.499	16	36.653	20
Italy	44.310	17	46.557	14
South Africa	43.877	18	41.845	16
Maharashtra	42.507	19	0.00	
India	42.181	20	39.990	17
Brazil	40.667	21	45.768	15
Philippines	37.851	22	39.318	18
Romania	33.636	23	0.00	
Mexico	33.337	24	37.205	19
Turkey	29.803	25	23.773	23
Russia	24.584	26	33.162	21
Poland	21.526	27	24.141	22
Indonesia	13.213	28	21.157	25
Argentina	12.464	29	19.010	26
Venezuela	9.811	30	22.017	24

The Group

In contrast to the Western emphasis on the individual, the group is the primary unit of social organization in many other societies. For example, in Japan, the social status of an individual is determined as much by the standing of the group to which he or she belongs as by his or her individual performance.[12] In traditional Japanese society, the group was the family or village to which an individual belonged. Today the group has frequently come to be associated with the work team or business organization to which an individual belongs. In a now classic study of Japanese society, Nakane has noted how this expresses itself in everyday life:

> When a Japanese faces the outside (confronts another person) and affixes some position to himself socially he is inclined to give precedence to institution over kind of occupation. Rather than saying, "I am a typesetter" or "I am a filing clerk," he is likely to say, "I am from B Publishing Group" or "I belong to S company."[13]

Nakane goes on to observe that the primacy of the group to which an individual belongs often evolves into a deeply emotional attachment in which identification with the group becomes all important in one's life. One central value of Japanese culture is the importance attached to group membership. This may have beneficial implications for business firms. Strong identification with the group is argued to create pressures for mutual self-help and collective action. If the worth of an individual is closely linked to the achievements of the group (e.g., firm), as Nakane maintains is the case in Japan, this creates a strong incentive for individual members of the group to work together for the common good. In Japan, a nation known for its strict work ethic, the Japanese language even has a word for dying from overwork–**karoshi**. Some argue that the success of Japanese enterprises in the global economy during the 1970s and 1980s was based partly on their ability to achieve close cooperation between individuals within a company and

KAROSHI Japanese term meaning to die from overwork.

between companies. This found expression in the widespread diffusion of self-managing work teams within Japanese organizations, the close cooperation between different functions within Japanese companies (e.g., between manufacturing, marketing, and R&D), and the cooperation between a company and its suppliers on issues such as design, quality control, and inventory reduction.[14] In all these cases, cooperation is driven by the need to improve the performance of the group (i.e., the business firm).

The primacy of the value of group identification also discourages managers and workers from moving from company to company. Lifetime employment in a particular company was long the norm in certain sectors of the Japanese economy (estimates suggest that between 20 and 40 percent of all Japanese employees have formal or informal lifetime employment guarantees). Over the years, managers and workers build up knowledge, experience, and a network of interpersonal business contacts. All these things can help managers perform their jobs more effectively and achieve cooperation with others.

However, the primacy of the group is not always beneficial. Just as U.S. society is characterized by a great deal of dynamism and entrepreneurship, reflecting the primacy of values associated with individualism, some argue that Japanese society is characterized by a corresponding lack of dynamism and entrepreneurship. Although it is not clear how this will play out in the long run, the United States could continue to create more new industries than Japan and continue to be more successful at pioneering radically new products and new ways of doing business.

SOCIAL STRATA
Hierarchical social categories often based on family background, occupation, and income.

SOCIAL STRATIFICATION

All societies are stratified on a hierarchical basis into social categories–that is, into **social strata.** These strata are typically defined on the basis of characteristics such as family background, occupation, and income. Individuals are born into a particular stratum. They become a member of the social category to which their parents belong. Individuals born into a stratum toward the top of the social hierarchy tend to have better life chances than individuals born into a stratum toward the bottom of the hierarchy. They are likely to have better education, health, standard of living, and work opportunities. Although all societies are stratified to some degree, they differ in two related ways of interest to us here. First, they differ from each other with regard to the degree of mobility between social strata, and second, they differ with regard to the significance attached to social strata in business contexts.

SOCIAL MOBILITY
The extent to which individuals can move out of the social strata into which they are born.

Social Mobility

The term **social mobility** refers to the extent to which individuals can move out of the strata into which they are born. Social mobility varies significantly among societies. The most rigid system of stratification is a caste system. A **caste system** is a closed system of stratification in which social position is determined by the family into which a person is born, and change in that position is usually not possible during an individual's lifetime. Often a caste position carries with it a specific occupation. Members of one caste might be shoemakers, members of another caste might be butchers, and so on. These occupations are embedded in the caste and passed down through the family to succeeding generations. Although the number of societies with caste systems has diminished rapidly during the twentieth century, one partial example still remains. India has four main castes and several thousand subcastes. Even though the caste system was officially abolished in 1949, two years after India became independent, it is still a powerful force in rural Indian society where occupation and marital opportunities are still partly related to caste.

CASTE SYSTEM
A system of social stratification in which social position is determined by the family into which a person is born, and change in that position is usually not possible during an individual's lifetime.

A **class system** is a less rigid form of social stratification in which social mobility is possible. A class system is a form of open stratification in which the position a person

CLASS SYSTEM
A system of social stratification in which social status is determined by the family into which a person is born and by subsequent socioeconomic achievements. Mobility between classes is possible.

has by birth can be changed through his or her own achievements and/or luck. Individuals born into a class at the bottom of the hierarchy can work their way up, while individuals born into a class at the top of the hierarchy can slip down.

While many societies have class systems, social mobility within a class system varies from society to society. For example, some sociologists have argued that Britain has a more rigid class structure than certain other Western societies, such as the United States.[15] Historically, British society was divided into three main classes: the upper class, which was made up of individuals whose families for generations had wealth, prestige, and occasionally power; the middle class, whose members were involved in professional, managerial, and clerical occupations; and the working class, whose members earned their living from manual occupations. The middle class was further subdivided into the upper-middle class, whose members were involved in important managerial occupations and the prestigious professions (e.g., lawyers, accountants, doctors), and the lower-middle class, whose members were involved in clerical work (e.g., bank tellers) and the less prestigious professions (e.g., schoolteachers). Although Canada is steeped in British tradition, to this day there are nonetheless fewer signs of class difference within this country, as Canada has evolved in a more egalitarian light under the shadow of its U.S. neighbour.

Historically, the British class system exhibited significant divergence between the life chances of members of different classes. The upper and upper-middle classes typically sent their children to a select group of private schools, where they wouldn't mix with lower-class children, and where they picked up many of the speech accents and social norms that marked them as being from the higher strata of society. These same private schools also had close ties with the most prestigious universities, such as Oxford and Cambridge. Until recently, Oxford and Cambridge guaranteed to reserve a certain number of places for the graduates of these private schools. Having been to a prestigious university, the offspring of the upper and upper-middle classes then had an excellent chance of being offered a prestigious job in companies, banks, brokerage firms, and law firms run by members of the upper and upper-middle classes.

In contrast, the members of the British working and lower-middle classes typically went to state schools. The majority left at age 16, and those that went on to higher education found it more difficult to get accepted at the best universities. When they did, they found that their lower-class accent and lack of social skills marked them as being from a lower social stratum, which made it more difficult for them to get access to the most prestigious jobs.

As a result of these factors, the class system in Britain perpetuated itself from generation to generation, and mobility was limited. Although upward mobility was possible, it could not normally be achieved in one generation. While an individual from a working-class background may have established an income level that was consistent with membership in the upper-middle class, he or she may not have been accepted as such by others of that class due to accent and background. However, by sending his or her offspring to the "right kind of school," the individual could ensure that his or her children were accepted.

According to many commentators, modern British society is now rapidly leaving this class structure behind and moving toward a classless society. However, sociologists continue to dispute this finding and present evidence that this is not the case. For example, a study reported that in 1994, state schools in the London suburb of Islington, which has a population of 175 000, had only 79 candidates for university, while one prestigious private school alone, Eton, sent more than that number to Oxford and Cambridge.[16] This, according to the study's authors, implies that "money still begets money." They argue that a good school means a good university, a good university means a good job, and "merit" has only a limited chance of elbowing its way into this tight little circle.

The class system in the United States is less extreme than in Britain and mobility is greater. Like Britain, the United States has its own upper, middle, and working classes. However, class membership is determined principally by individual economic achievements, as opposed to background and schooling. Thus, an individual can, by his or her own economic achievement, move smoothly from the working class to the upper class in a lifetime. Successful individuals from humble origins are highly respected in American society.

Significance

From a business perspective, the stratification of a society is significant if it affects the operation of business organizations. In American society, the high degree of social mobility and the extreme emphasis on individualism limits the impact of class background on business operations. The same is true in Japan, where most of the population perceives itself to be middle class. In a country such as Great Britain, however, the relative lack of class mobility and the differences between classes have resulted in the emergence of class consciousness. **Class consciousness** refers to people perceiving themselves in terms of their class background, which shapes their relationships with members of other classes.

CLASS CONSCIOUSNESS A tendency for individuals to perceive themselves in terms of their class background.

This has been played out in British society in the traditional hostility between upper-middle-class managers and their working-class employees. Mutual antagonism and lack of respect historically made it difficult to achieve cooperation between management and labour in many British companies and resulted in a relatively high level of industrial disputes. However, as noted earlier, the last two decades have seen a dramatic reduction in industrial disputes (the level of industrial disputes in the United Kingdom is now lower than in the United States), which bolsters the arguments of those who claim that the country is moving toward a classless society. An antagonistic relationship between management and labour, and the resulting lack of cooperation and high level of industrial disruption, tends to raise the costs of production in countries characterized by significant class divisions. In turn, this can make it more difficult for companies based in such countries to establish a competitive advantage in the global economy.

RELIGIOUS AND ETHICAL SYSTEMS

Religion may be defined as a system of shared beliefs and rituals that are concerned with the realm of the sacred.[17] **Ethical systems** refer to a set of moral principles, or values, that are used to guide and shape behaviour. Most of the world's ethical systems are the product of religions. Thus, we can talk about Christian ethics and Islamic ethics. However, there is a major exception to the principle that ethical systems are grounded in religion. Confucianism and Confucian ethics influence behaviour and shape culture in parts of Asia, yet it is incorrect to characterize Confucianism as a religion.

RELIGION A system of shared beliefs and rituals concerned with the realm of the sacred.

ETHICAL SYSTEMS Cultural beliefs about what is proper behaviour and conduct.

The relationship among religion, ethics, and society is subtle and complex. There are thousands of religions in the world today, but in terms of number of adherents, four dominate–Christianity with nearly 2 billion, Islam with 1.2 billion, Hinduism with 750 million, and Buddhism with 500 million. Two lesser dominant, yet very important religions, are Sikhism with 20 million adherents and Judaism with 12 million followers around the world.[18] (See Map 3.1.)

Table 3.2 presents the most recent religious statistics available and compares them to the statistics gleaned from the 1991 Census. Although many other religions have an important influence in certain parts of the modern world (for example, Judaism, which has 18 million adherents) their numbers pale in comparison with these dominant religions

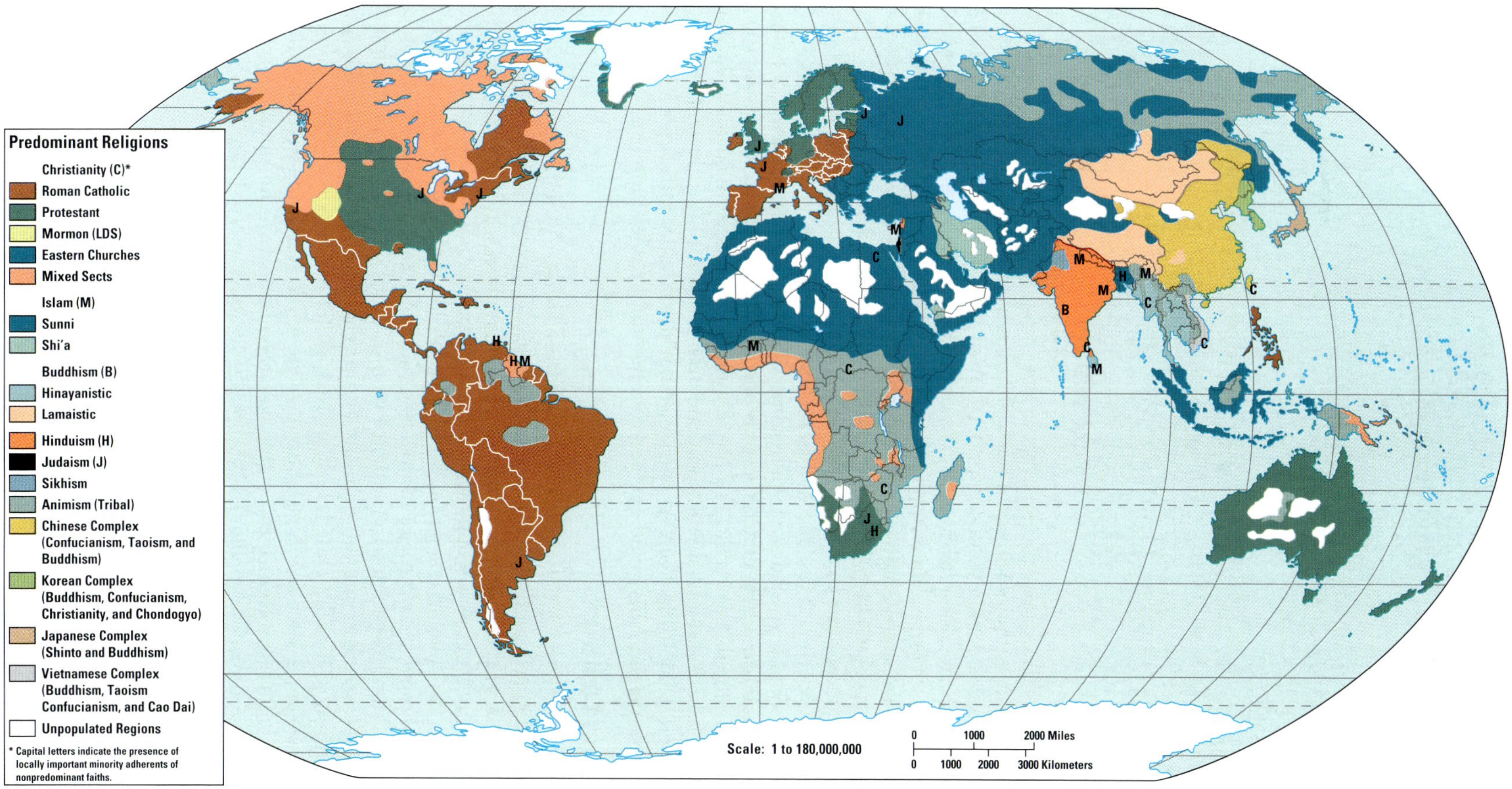

MAP 3.1

World Religions

Source: From *Student Atlas of World Geography,* Second Edition, by John L. Allen. Copyright © 2001 by McGraw-Hill Companies, Inc. Reprinted by permission of McGraw-Hill/Dushkin, a division of the McGraw-Hill Companies, Guilford, CT 06437.

TABLE 3.2

Major Religious Denominations, Canada, 1991[1] and 2001

Source: Statistics Canada, *Religions in Canada*, 2001 Census, Analysis series, 2001 Census, Catalogue 96F0030, May 13, 2003, p. 18.

	2001		1991		PERCENTAGE CHANGE
	NUMBER	%	NUMBER	%	1991–2001
Roman Catholic	12,793,125	43.2	12,203,625	45.2	4.8
Protestant	8,654,845	29.2	9,427,675	34.9	-8.2
Christian Orthodox	479,620	1.6	387,395	1.4	23.8
Christian, not included elsewhere[2]	780,450	2.6	353,040	1.3	121.1
Muslim	579,640	2.0	253,265	0.9	128.9
Jewish	329,995	1.1	318,185	1.2	3.7
Buddhist	300,345	1.0	163,415	0.6	83.8
Hindu	297,200	1.0	157,015	0.6	89.3
Sikh	278,415	0.9	147,440	0.5	88.8
No religion	4,796,325	16.2	3,333,245	12.3	43.9

1 For comparability purposes, 1991 data are presented according to 2001 boundaries.
2 Includes persons who report "Christian," as well as those who report "Apostolic," "Born-again Christian," and "Evangelical."

(however, as the precursor of both Christianity and Islam, Judaism has an indirect influence that goes beyond its numbers). We review these four religions, along with Confucianism, focusing on their business implications. Some scholars have argued that the most important business implications of religion center on the extent to which different religions shape attitudes toward work and entrepreneurship and the degree to which the religious ethics affect the costs of doing business in a country.

It is hazardous to make sweeping generalizations about the nature of the relationship between religion and ethical systems on the one hand and business practice on the other. As we shall see, while some scholars argue that there is a relationship between religious and ethical systems and business practice, in a world where nations with Catholic, Protestant, Muslim, Hindu, and Buddhist majorities all show entrepreneurial activity and sustainable economic growth, it is important to view such proposed relationships with skepticism. While the proposed relationships may exist, their impact is probably small compared to the impact of economic policy.

CHRISTIANITY

Christianity is widely practised around the world. About 20 percent of the world's population identify themselves as Christians. The vast majority of Christians live in Europe and the Americas, although their numbers are growing rapidly in Africa. Christianity grew out of Judaism. Like Judaism, it is a monotheistic religion (monotheism is the belief in one god). A religious division in the eleventh century led to the establishment of two major Christian organizations–the Roman Catholic church and the Orthodox church. Today the Roman Catholic church accounts for more than half of all Christians, most of whom are found in Southern Europe and Latin America. The Orthodox church, while less influential, is still of major importance in several countries (e.g., Greece and Russia). In the sixteenth century, the Reformation led to a further split with Rome; the result was Protestantism. The nonconformist nature of Protestantism has facilitated the emergence of numerous denominations under the Protestant umbrella (e.g., Baptist, Methodist, Calvinist).

Economic Implications of Christianity: The Protestant Work Ethic

Some sociologists have argued that of the main branches of Christianity–Roman Catholic, Orthodox, and Protestant–the latter has the most important economic implications. In 1904, German sociologist Max Weber made a connection, which has since become famous, between Protestant ethics and "the spirit of capitalism."[19]

Weber noted that capitalism emerged in Western Europe. He also noted that in Western Europe,

> Business leaders and owners of capital, as well as the higher grades of skilled labor, and even more the higher technically and commercially trained personnel of modern enterprises, are overwhelmingly Protestant.[20]

According to Weber, there was a relationship between Protestantism and the emergence of modern capitalism. Weber argued that Protestant ethics emphasize the importance of hard work and wealth creation (for the glory of God) and frugality (abstinence from worldly pleasures). According to Weber, this value system was needed to facilitate the development of capitalism. Protestants worked hard and systematically to accumulate wealth. However, their ascetic beliefs suggested that rather than consuming this wealth by indulging in worldly pleasures, they should invest it in the expansion of capitalist enterprises. Thus, the combination of hard work and the accumulation of capital, which could be used to finance investment and expansion, paved the way for the development of capitalism in Western Europe and subsequently in the United States. In contrast, Weber argued that the Catholic promise of salvation in the next world, rather than this world, did not foster the same kind of work ethic.

Protestantism also may have encouraged capitalism's development in another way. By breaking away from the hierarchical domination of religious and social life that characterized the Catholic church for much of its history, Protestantism gave individuals significantly more freedom to develop their own relationship with God. The right to freedom of form of worship was central to the nonconformist nature of early Protestantism. This emphasis on individual religious freedom may have paved the way for the subsequent emphasis on individual economic and political freedoms and the development of individualism as an economic and political philosophy. As we saw in Chapter 2, such a philosophy forms the bedrock on which entrepreneurial free market capitalism is based. Building on this, some scholars claim there is a connection between individualism, as inspired by Protestantism, and the extent of entrepreneurial activity in a nation.[21] Again, one must be careful not to generalize too much from this historical sociological view. While nations with a strong Protestant tradition such as Britain, Germany, and the United States were early leaders in the industrial revolution, in the modern world there is clearly significant and sustained entrepreneurial activity and economic growth in nations with Catholic or Orthodox majorities.

ISLAM

With some estimates placing Islam with approximately 2 billion adherents, Islam is one of the fastest growing and one of the largest of the world's major religions. Islam dates back to 610 A.D. when the prophet Muhammad began spreading the word, although the Muslim calendar begins in 622 A.D. when Muhammad left Mecca to escape growing opposition for the oasis settlement of Yathrib, later known as Madina. Adherents of Islam are referred to as Muslims. Muslims constitute a majority in more than 35 countries and inhabit a nearly contiguous stretch of land from the northwest coast of Africa, through the Middle East, to China and Malaysia in the Far East.

Islam has roots in both Judaism and Christianity (Islam views Jesus Christ as one of God's prophets). Like Christianity and Judaism, Islam is a monotheistic religion. The central principle of Islam is that there is but the one true omnipotent God. Islam requires unconditional acceptance of the uniqueness, power, and authority of God and the understanding that the objective of life is to fulfill the dictates of his will in the hope of admission to paradise. According to Islam, worldly gain and temporal power are an illusion. Those who pursue riches on Earth may gain them, but those who forgo worldly ambitions to seek the favour of Allah may gain the greater treasure–entry into paradise.

Other major principles of Islam include: (1) honouring and respecting parents, (2) respecting the rights of others, (3) being generous but not a squanderer, (4) avoiding killing except for justifiable causes, (5) not committing adultery, (6) dealing justly and equitably with others, (7) being of pure heart and mind, (8) safeguarding the possessions of orphans, and (9) being humble and unpretentious.[22] There are obvious parallels here with many of the central principles of both Judaism and Christianity.

Islam is an all-embracing way of life governing the totality of a Muslim's being.[23] As God's surrogate in this world, a Muslim is circumscribed by religious principles–by a code of conduct for interpersonal relations–in social and economic activities. Religion is paramount in all areas of life. The Muslim lives in a social structure that is shaped by Islamic values and norms of moral conduct. The ritual nature of everyday life in a Muslim country is striking to a Western visitor. Among other things, orthodox Muslim ritual requires prayer five times a day (it is not unusual for business meetings to be put on hold while the Muslim participants engage in their daily prayer ritual), requires that women should be dressed in a certain manner, and forbids the consumption of either pig meat or alcohol.

Islamic Fundamentalism

The past two decades have witnessed the growth of a social movement often referred to as "Islamic fundamentalism."[24] In the West, Islamic fundamentalism is associated in the media with militants, terrorists, and violent upheavals, such as the September 11, 2001 attacks on the World Trade Center and Pentagon in the United States, the bloody conflict occurring in Algeria, or the killing of foreign tourists in Egypt. This characterization is very misleading. Just as "Christian fundamentalists" in the West are motivated by sincere and deeply held religious values firmly rooted in their faith, so are "Islamic fundamentalists." The violence that the Western media associates with Islamic fundamentalism is perpetrated by a very small minority of radical "fundamentalists" who have hijacked the religion to further their own political and violent ends (some Christian "fundamentalists" have done exactly the same, including Jim Jones and David Koresh). The vast majority of Muslims point out that Islam teaches peace, justice, and tolerance, not violence and intolerance, and that Islam explicitly repudiates the violence that a radical minority practises.

The rise of fundamentalism has no one cause. In part, it is a response to the social pressures created in traditional Islamic societies by the move toward modernization and by the influence of Western ideas, such as liberal democracy, materialism, equal rights for women, and by Western attitudes toward sex, marriage, and alcohol. In many Muslim countries, modernization has been accompanied by a growing gap between a rich urban minority and an impoverished urban and rural majority. For the impoverished majority, modernization has offered little in the way of tangible economic progress, while threatening the traditional value system. Thus, for a Muslim who cherishes his traditions and feels that his identity is jeopardized by the encroachment of alien Western values, Islamic fundamentalism has become a cultural anchor.

Fundamentalists demand a rigid commitment to traditional religious beliefs and rituals. The result has been a marked increase in the use of symbolic gestures that confirm Islamic values. In areas where fundamentalism is strong, women once again are wearing floor-length, long-sleeved dresses and covering their hair; religious studies have expanded in universities; the publication of religious tracts has increased; and more religious orations are heard in public.[25] Also, the sentiments of some fundamentalist groups are increasingly anti-Western. Rightly or wrongly, Western influence is blamed for a range of social ills, and many fundamentalists' actions are directed against Western governments, cultural symbols, businesses, and even individuals.

In several Muslim countries, fundamentalists have gained political power and tried to make Islamic law (as set down in the Koran, the bible of Islam) the law of the land.

There are good grounds for this in Islam. Islam makes no distinction between church and state. It is not just a religion; Islam is also the source of law, a guide to statecraft, and an arbiter of social behaviour. Muslims believe that every human endeavour is within the purview of the faith–and this includes political activity–because the only purpose of any activity is to do God's will.[26] (Muslims are not unique in this view; it is also shared by some Christian fundamentalists.) The fundamentalists have been most successful in Iran, where a fundamentalist party has held power since 1979, but they also have had an influence in many other countries, such as Algeria, Afghanistan (where the Taliban established an extreme fundamentalist state), Egypt, Pakistan, the Sudan, and Saudi Arabia.

Economic Implications of Islam

Some explicit economic principles are set down in the Koran.[27] Many of the economic principles of Islam favour free enterprise. The Koran speaks approvingly of free enterprise and of earning legitimate profit through trade and commerce (the prophet Muhammad was once a trader). The protection of the right to private property is also embedded within Islam, although Islam asserts that all property is a favour from Allah (God), who created and so owns everything. Those who hold property are regarded as trustees who are entitled to receive profits from it, rather than owners in the Western sense of the word, and they are admonished to use it in a righteous, socially beneficial, and prudent manner. This reflects Islam's concern with social justice. Islam is critical of those who earn profit through the exploitation of others. In the Islamic view of the world, humans are part of a collective in which the wealthy and successful have obligations to help the disadvantaged. Put simply, in Muslim countries, it is fine to earn a profit, so long as that profit is justly earned and not based on the exploitation of others for one's own advantage. It also helps if those making profits undertake charitable acts to help the poor. Furthermore, Islam stresses the importance of living up to contractual obligations, of keeping one's word, and of abstaining from deception.

Given the Islamic proclivity to favour market-based systems, Muslim countries are likely to be receptive to international businesses as long as those businesses behave in a manner that is consistent with Islamic ethics. Businesses that are perceived as making an unjust profit through the exploitation of others, by deception, or by breaking contractual obligations are unlikely to be welcomed in an Islamic country. In addition, in Islamic countries where fundamentalism is on the rise, hostility toward Western-owned businesses is likely to increase.

In the previous chapter, we noted that one economic principle of Islam prohibits the payment or receipt of interest, which is considered usury. This is not just a matter of theology; in several Islamic states, it is also a matter of law. In 1992, for example, Pakistan's Federal Shariat Court, the highest Islamic law-making body in the country, pronounced interest to be un-Islamic and therefore illegal and demanded that the government amend all financial laws accordingly. In 1999, Pakistan's Supreme Court ruled that Islamic banking methods should be used in the country after July 1, 2001.[28] The accompanying Country Focus looks at how Pakistan's banks are dealing with this issue.

HINDUISM

Hinduism has approximately 750 million adherents, most of who are on the Indian subcontinent. Hinduism began in the Indus Valley in India more than 4000 years ago, making it the world's oldest major religion. Unlike Christianity and Islam, its founding is not linked to a particular person. Nor does it have an officially sanctioned sacred book such as the Bible or the Koran. Hindus believe that a moral force in society requires the acceptance of certain responsibilities, called *dharma*. Hindus believe in reincarnation, or rebirth into a different body after death. Hindus also believe in

COUNTRY FOCUS

ISLAMIC BANKING IN PAKISTAN

The Koran clearly condemns interest, which is called *riba* in Arabic, as exploitative and unjust. For many years, banks operating in Islamic countries conveniently ignored this condemnation, but about 25 years ago, with the establishment of an Islamic bank in Egypt, Islamic banks started to open in predominantly Muslim countries. Now some 170 Islamic financial institutions worldwide manage more than $150 billion in assets and make an average return on capital of over 16 percent. Even conventional banks are entering the market—both Citigroup and HSBC, two of the world's largest financial institutions, now offer Islamic financial services. Until mid-2001, only Iran and the Sudan enforced Islamic banking conventions, but in many other countries, customers could choose between conventional banks and Islamic banks.

In July 2001, Pakistan became the third country to require its banks to adopt Islamic methods. The transition to Islamic banking in Pakistan may determine the fate of Islamic banking elsewhere in the world. Conventional banks make a profit on the spread between the interest rate they have to pay to depositors and the higher interest rate they charge borrowers. Because Islamic banks cannot pay or charge interest, they must find a different way to make money. Pakistan's banks are set to experiment with two different Islamic banking methods—the *mudarabah* and the *murabaha.*

A *mudarabah* contract is similar to a profit-sharing scheme. Under *mudarabah,* when an Islamic bank lends money to a business, rather than charging that business interest on the loan, it takes a share in the profits that are derived from the investment. Similarly, when a business (or individual) deposits money at an Islamic bank in a savings account, the deposit is treated as an equity investment in whatever activity the bank uses the capital for. Thus, the depositor receives a share in the profit from the bank's investment (as opposed to interest payments) according to an agreed-on ratio. Some Muslims claim this is a more efficient system than the Western banking system because it encourages long-term savings and investment. However, there is no hard evidence of this, and many believe that a *mudarabah* system is less efficient than a conventional Western banking system.

The second Islamic banking method, the *murabaha* contract, is the most widely used among the world's Islamic banks. It seems set to become the most popular method in Pakistan, primarily because it is the easiest to implement. In a *murabaha* contract, when a firm wishes to purchase something using a loan—say a piece of equipment that costs $1,000—the firm tells the bank after having negotiated the price with the equipment manufacturer. The bank then buys the equipment for $1,000, and the borrower buys it from the bank at some later date for, say, $1,100, a price that includes a $100 markup for the bank. A cynic might point out that such a markup is functionally equivalent to an interest payment, and it is the similarity between this method and conventional banking that makes it so much easier to adopt.

Whichever method is most widely used, observers expect the transition from traditional to Islamic banking to be challenging. One fear is that there could be large-scale withdrawals by depositors, driven by worries that they could suffer without fixed interest rates. Another concern is that the country needs to have a tight regulatory regime to ensure that unscrupulous borrowers using a *mudarabah* contract do not declare themselves bankrupt, even when their businesses are running a profit. A third concern is that the uncertainty created by the transition will scare off foreign investors, leaving Pakistan starved of capital.

Sources: "Forced Devotion," *The Economist,* February 17, 2001, pp. 76–77; "Islamic Banking Marches On," *The Banker,* February 1, 2000; and F. Bokhari, "Bankers Fear Introduction of Islamic System Will Prompt Big Withdrawals," *Financial Times,* March 6, 2001, p. 4.

karma, the spiritual progression of each person's soul. A person's karma is affected by the way he or she lives. The moral state of an individual's karma determines the challenges he or she will face in their next life. By perfecting the soul in each new life, Hindus believe that an individual can eventually achieve *nirvana,* a state of complete spiritual perfection that renders reincarnation no longer necessary. Many Hindus believe that the way to achieve nirvana is to lead a severe ascetic lifestyle of material and physical self-denial, devoting life to a spiritual rather than material quest.

Economic Implications of Hinduism

Max Weber, who is famous for expounding on the Protestant work ethic, also argued that the ascetic principles embedded in Hinduism do not encourage the kind of entrepreneurial activity in pursuit of wealth creation that we find in Protestantism.[29] According to Weber, traditional Hindu values emphasize that individuals should be judged not by their material achievements, but by their spiritual achievements. Hindus perceive the pursuit of material well-being as making the attainment of nirvana more difficult. Given the emphasis on an ascetic lifestyle, Weber thought that devout Hindus would be less likely to engage in entrepreneurial activity than devout Protestants.

Mahatma Gandhi, the famous Indian nationalist and spiritual leader, was certainly the embodiment of Hindu asceticism. It has been argued that the values of Hindu asceticism and self-reliance that Gandhi advocated had a negative impact on the economic development of post-independence India.[30] But one must be careful not to read too much into Weber's arguments. Modern India is a very entrepreneurial society, and millions of hardworking entrepreneurs form the economic backbone of India's rapidly growing economy.

Historically, Hinduism also supported India's caste system. The concept of mobility between castes within an individual's lifetime makes no sense to traditional Hindus. Hindus see mobility between castes as something that is achieved through spiritual progression and reincarnation. An individual can be reborn into a higher caste in his next life if he achieves spiritual development in this life. In so far as the caste system limits individuals' opportunities to adopt positions of responsibility and influence in society, the economic consequences of this religious belief are somewhat negative. For example, within a business organization, the most able individuals may find their route to the organization's higher levels blocked simply because they come from a lower caste. By the same token, individuals may get promoted to higher positions within a firm as much because of their caste background as because of their ability. But the caste system has been abolished in India, and its influence is now fading.

BUDDHISM

Buddhism was founded in India in the sixth century B.C. by Siddhartha Gautama, an Indian prince who renounced his wealth to pursue an ascetic lifestyle and spiritual perfection. Siddhartha achieved *nirvana* but decided to remain on Earth to teach his followers how they too could achieve this state of spiritual enlightenment. Siddhartha became known as the Buddha (which means "the awakened one"). Today Buddhism has 350 million followers, most of whom are found in Central and Southeast Asia, China, Korea, and Japan. According to Buddhism, suffering originates in people's desires for pleasure. Cessation of suffering can be achieved by following a path for transformation. Siddhartha offered the Noble Eightfold Path as a route for transformation. This emphasizes right seeing, thinking, speech, action, living, effort, mindfulness, and meditation. Unlike Hinduism, Buddhism does not support the caste system. Nor does Buddhism advocate the kind of extreme ascetic behaviour that is encouraged by Hinduism. Nevertheless, like Hindus, Buddhists stress the afterlife and spiritual achievement rather than involvement in this world.

Because of this, the emphasis on wealth creation that is embedded in Protestantism is not found in Buddhism. Thus, in Buddhist societies, we do not see the same kind of historical cultural stress on entrepreneurial behaviour that Weber claimed could be found in the Protestant West. But unlike Hinduism, the lack of support for the caste system and extreme ascetic behaviour suggests that a Buddhist society may represent a more fertile ground for entrepreneurial activity than a Hindu culture.

CONFUCIANISM

Confucianism was founded in the fifth century B.C. by K'ung-Fu-tzu, more generally known as Confucius. For more than 2000 years until the 1949 Communist revolution, Confucianism was the official ethical system of China. While observance of Confucian ethics has been weakened in China since 1949, more than 200 million people still follow the teachings of Confucius, principally in China, Korea, and Japan. Confucianism teaches the importance of attaining personal salvation through right action. Although not a religion, Confucian ideology has become deeply embedded in the culture of these countries over the centuries and through that affects the lives of many millions more. Confucianism is built around a comprehensive ethical code that sets down guidelines for relationships with others. The need for high moral and ethical conduct and loyalty to others are central to Confucianism. Unlike religions, Confucianism is not concerned with the supernatural and has little to say about the concept of a supreme being or an afterlife.

Economic Implications of Confucianism

Some scholars maintain that Confucianism may have economic implications as profound as those Weber argued were to be found in Protestantism, although they are of a different nature.[31] Their basic thesis is that the influence of Confucian ethics on the cultures of China, Japan, South Korea, and Taiwan, by lowering the costs of doing business in those countries, may help explain their economic success. In this regard, three values central to the Confucian system of ethics are of particular interest–loyalty, reciprocal obligations, and honesty.

In Confucian thought, loyalty to one's superiors is regarded as a sacred duty, an absolute obligation. In modern organizations based in Confucian cultures, the loyalty that binds employees to the heads of their organization can reduce the conflict between management and labour that we find in more class-conscious societies. Cooperation between management and labour can be achieved at a lower cost in a culture where the value systems emphasize loyalty.

However, in a Confucian culture, loyalty to one's superiors, such as a worker's loyalty to management, is not blind loyalty. The concept of reciprocal obligations also comes into play. Confucian ethics stress that superiors are obliged to reward the loyalty of their subordinates by bestowing blessings on them. If these "blessings" are not forthcoming, then neither will be the loyalty. As we saw in the opening case, in China this Confucian ethic is central to the concept of *guanxi,* which refers to relationship networks supported by reciprocal obligations. Similarly, in Japan this ethic finds expression in the concept of lifetime employment. The employees of a Japanese company are loyal to the leaders of the organization, and in return the leaders bestow on them the "blessing" of lifetime employment. The lack of mobility between companies implied by the lifetime employment system suggests that managers and workers build up knowledge, experience, and a network of interpersonal business contacts over the years. All these can help managers and workers perform their jobs more effectively and cooperate with others in the organization. One result is improved economic performance for the company.

A third concept found in Confucian ethics is the importance attached to honesty. Confucian thinkers emphasize that, although dishonest behaviour may yield short-term benefits for the transgressor, dishonesty does not pay in the long run. The importance attached to honesty has major economic implications. When companies can trust each other not to break contractual obligations, the costs of doing business are lowered. Expensive lawyers are not needed to resolve contract disputes. In a Confucian society, there may be less hesitation to commit substantial resources to cooperative ventures than in a society where honesty is less pervasive. When companies adhere to Confucian ethics, they can trust each other not to violate the terms of cooperative agreements. Thus, the costs of achieving cooperation between companies may be lowered in societies such as Japan relative to societies where trust is less pervasive.

For example, it has been argued that the close ties between the automobile companies and their component parts suppliers in Japan are facilitated by a combination of trust and reciprocal obligations. These close ties allow the auto companies and their suppliers to work together on a range of issues, including inventory reduction, quality control, and design. The competitive advantage of Japanese auto companies such as Toyota may in part be explained by such factors.[32] Similarly, the opening case showed how the combination of trust and reciprocal obligations is central to the workings and persistence of *guanxi* networks in China. Someone seeking and receiving help through a *guanxi* network is then obligated to return the favour and faces social sanctions if that obligation is not reciprocated when it is called upon. If the person does not return the favour, his reputation will be tarnished and he will be unable to draw on the resources of the network in the future. It is claimed that these relationship-based networks can be more important in helping to enforce agreements between businesses than the Chinese legal system. Some claim that *guanxi* networks are a substitute for the legal system.[33]

LANGUAGE

One obvious way in which countries differ is language. By language, we mean both spoken and unspoken means of communication. Language is a defining characteristic of a culture.

SPOKEN LANGUAGE

Language does far more than just enable people to communicate with each other. The nature of a language also structures the way we perceive the world. The language of a society can direct the attention of its members to certain features of the world rather than others. The classic illustration of this phenomenon is that whereas the English language has but one word for snow, the language of the Inuit (Eskimos) lacks a general term for it. Instead, because distinguishing different forms of snow is so important in the lives of the Inuit, they have 24 words that describe different types of snow (e.g., powder snow, falling snow, wet snow, drifting snow).[34]

Because language shapes the way people perceive the world, it also helps define culture. In countries with more than one language, one also often finds more than one culture. Canada has an English-speaking culture and a French-speaking culture. The early phases of official bilingualism in Canada were often met with suspicion and cries of "I only want to read English on my cornflakes box." Canadian bilingualism in the year 2006 has changed significantly. French is a valuable asset to Canadians' international trade and often synchronous diplomatic interests. In the world of diplomacy, French resonates strongly from the Caribbean to Africa and across Europe. While Canadians can make their voices heard at Commonwealth conferences, so too can they be heard at Francophone meetings around the world. Often on the tails of diplomacy, business deals can follow. Belgium is divided into Flemish and French speakers, and tensions between the two groups exist; in Spain, a Basque-speaking minority with its own distinctive culture has been agitating for independence from the Spanish-speaking majority for decades; on the Mediterranean island of Cyprus, the culturally diverse Greek- and Turkish-speaking populations of the island engaged in open conflict in the 1970s, and the island is now partitioned into two parts. While it does not necessarily follow that language differences create differences in culture and, therefore, separatist pressures (e.g., witness the harmony in Switzerland, where four languages are spoken), there seems to be a tendency in this direction.[35]

Chinese is the "mother tongue" of the largest number of people, followed by English and Hindi, which is spoken in India (see Figure 3.2). However, the most widely spoken language in the world is English, followed by French, Spanish, and Chinese (i.e., many people speak English as a second language). English is increasingly becoming the language of international business. When a Japanese and a German businessperson get together to do business, it is almost certain that they will communicate in English. However, while English is widely used, learning the local language yields considerable advantages in business. Most people prefer to converse in their own language, so speaking the local language can build rapport, which may be very important for a business deal. International businesses that do not understand the local language can make major blunders through improper translation. For example, the Sunbeam Corporation used the English words for its "Mist-Stick" mist-producing hair-curling iron when it entered the German market, only to discover after an expensive advertising campaign that *mist* means excrement in German. General Motors was troubled by the lack of enthusiasm among Puerto Rican dealers for its new Chevrolet Nova. When literally translated into Spanish, *Nova* means star. However, when spoken it sounded like "no va," which in Spanish means "it doesn't go." General Motors changed the name of the car to Caribe.[36]

UNSPOKEN LANGUAGE

Unspoken language refers to nonverbal communication. We all communicate with each other by a host of nonverbal cues. The raising of eyebrows, for example, is a sign of recognition in most cultures, while a smile is a sign of joy. Many nonverbal cues, however, are culturally bound. A failure to understand the nonverbal cues of another culture can lead to a failure of communication. For example, making a circle with the thumb and the forefinger is a friendly gesture in Canada, but it is a vulgar sexual invitation in Greece and Turkey. Similarly, while most Canadians and Europeans use the thumbs-up gesture to indicate that "it's all right," in Greece the gesture is obscene.

Another aspect of nonverbal communication is personal space, which is the comfortable amount of distance between people. In Canada, the customary distance apart adopted by parties in a business discussion is 1.5 to 2.5 metres (5 to 8 feet). In Latin America, it is 1 to 1.5 metres (3 to 5 feet). Consequently, many North Americans unconsciously feel that Latin Americans are invading their personal space and can be

FIGURE 3.2

Percentage of the World's Population for Whom This Is a First Language

Source: *The Economist Atlas* (London: The Economist Books, 1991), p. 116. Copyright © 1989 and © 1991 The Economist Books, Ltd.

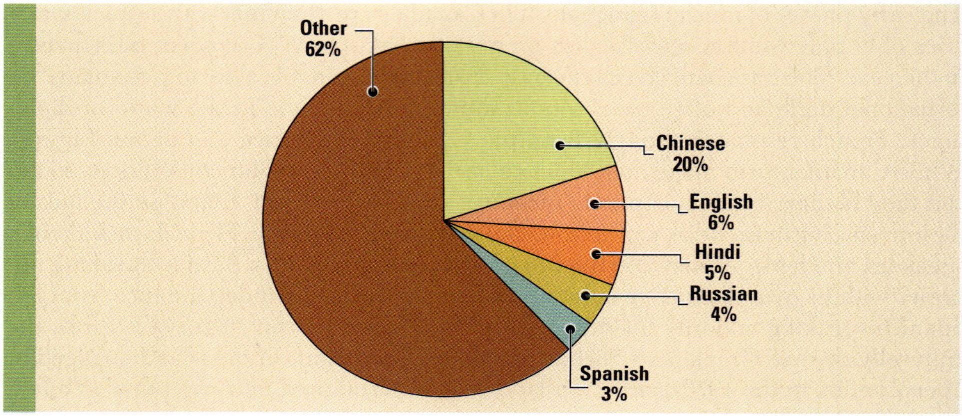

seen backing away from them during a conversation. In turn, the Latin American may interpret such backing away as aloofness. The result can be a regrettable lack of rapport between two businesspeople from different cultures.

EDUCATION

From an international business perspective, one important aspect of education is its role as a determinant of national competitive advantage.[37] The availability of skilled and educated workers seems to be a major determinant of the likely economic success of a country. In analyzing the competitive success of Japan since 1945, for example, Michael Porter notes that after the war, Japan had almost nothing except for a pool of skilled and educated human resources.

> With a long tradition of respect for education that borders on reverence, Japan possessed a large pool of literate, educated, and increasingly skilled human resources . . . Japan has benefited from a large pool of trained engineers. Japanese universities graduate many more engineers per capita than in the United States . . . A first-rate primary and secondary education system in Japan operates based on high standards and emphasizes math and science. Primary and secondary education is highly competitive . . . Japanese education provides most students all over Japan with a sound education for later education and training. A Japanese high school graduate knows as much about math as most American college graduates.[38]

Porter's point is that Japan's excellent education system was an important factor explaining the country's postwar economic success. It would make little sense to base production facilities that require highly skilled labour in a country where the education system was so poor that a skilled labour pool wasn't available, no matter how attractive the country might seem on other dimensions. It might make sense to base production operations that require only unskilled labour in such a country.

The general education level of a country is also a good index of the kind of products that might sell in a country and of the type of promotional material that should be used. For example, in a country such as Pakistan where the illiteracy rate is higher than 50 percent (Map 3.2), there is unlikely to be a good market for popular books. In Figure 3.3, taken from a 2004 report from the United Nations Conference on Trade and Development (UNCTAD), there have been slow, but definite strides in enrolment in the primary and secondary school systems in developing and developed nations between 1960 and 2000. Literacy among adult men and women has grown from roughly 70 percent in 1980 to 80 percent in 2000. Still, among the estimated 862 million illiterate people in 2000, two-thirds are women, 99 percent of whom live in developing countries.[39] As such, promotional material containing written descriptions of mass-marketed products is unlikely to have an effect in a country where almost three-quarters of the population cannot read. It is far better to use pictorial promotions in such circumstances.

Figures 3.3 and 3.4, and Map 3.2 provide important data on education worldwide. Map 3.2 shows illiteracy rates. Figure 3.3 shows world education primary and secondary school enrolment while Figure 3.4 shows the money that nations spend on education, per capita. Although there is not a perfect one-to-one correspondence between the percentage of GNI devoted to education and the quality of education, the overall level of spending indicates a country's commitment to education. Note that the United States spends more of its GNI on education than many other advanced industrialized nations, including Germany and Japan. Despite this, the quality of U.S. education is often argued to be inferior to that offered in many other industrialized countries.

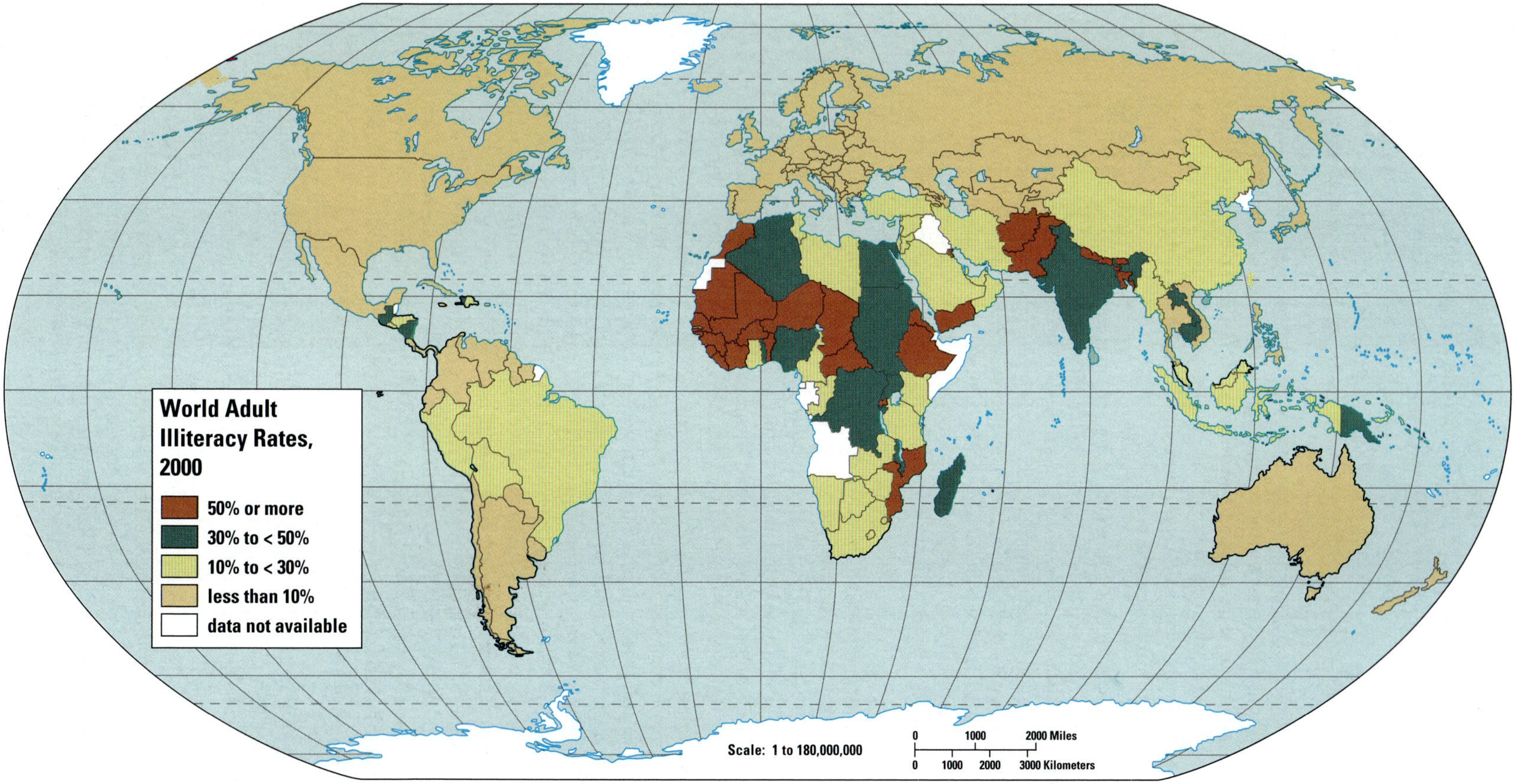

MAP 3.2

World Adult Illiteracy Rates, 2000

Source: The UNESCO Institute for Statistics (UIS) 2002 at www.uis.unesco.org/en/stats/statistics/ed/map_illit_monde2000.jpg.

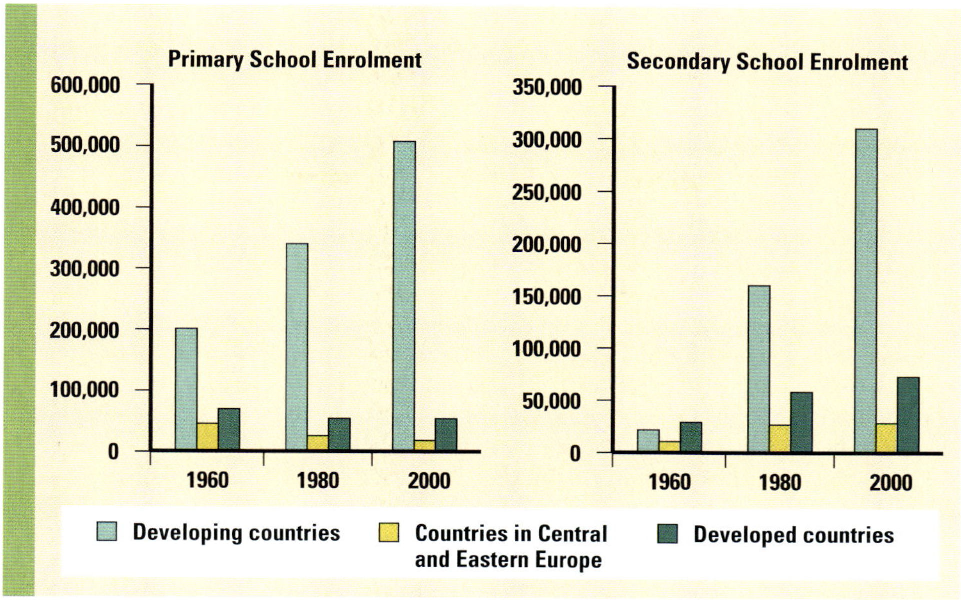

FIGURE 3.3

Education and Literacy

Source: United Nations Conference on Trade and Development, *2004 Development Facts and Figures,* p.13.

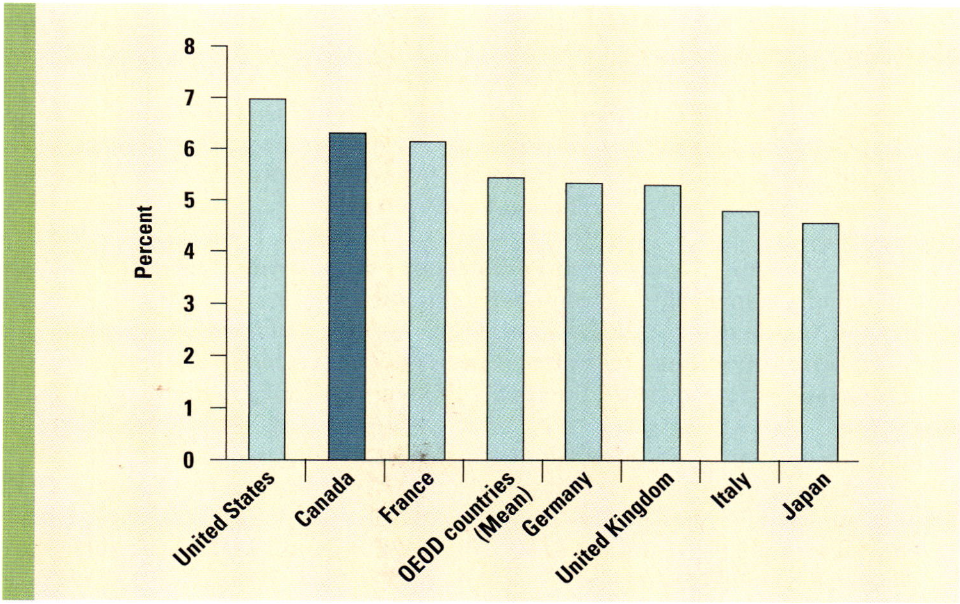

FIGURE 3.4

National Spending on Education Per Capita

Source: Figure B1.6: "Combined public and private expenditures on educational institutions per student, university level, G-7 countries and OECD mean, 2000" from the Statistics Canada Web site, www.statcan.ca/english/freepub/81-582-XIE/2003001/excel/updates/chapB1.xls.

CULTURE AND THE WORKPLACE

How a society's culture affects the values found in the workplace is of considerable importance to an international business with operations in different countries. Management process and practices may need to vary according to culturally determined work-related values. For example, if the cultures of the United States and France result in different work-related values, an international business with operations in both countries should vary its management process and practices to account for these differences.

Probably the most famous study of how culture relates to values in the workplace was undertaken by Geert Hofstede.[40] As part of his job as a psychologist working for IBM, Hofstede collected data on employee attitudes and values for more than 100 000 individuals from 1967 to 1973. This data enabled him to compare dimensions of culture across 40 countries. Hofstede isolated five dimensions that he claimed summarized different cultures–power distance, individualism versus collectivism, uncertainty avoidance, masculinity versus femininity, and long-term versus short-term orientation.

POWER DISTANCE Theory of how a society deals with the fact that people are unequal in physical and intellectual capabilities. High power distance cultures are found in countries that let inequalities grow over time into inequalities of power and wealth. Low power distance cultures are found in societies that try to play down such inequalities as much as possible.

Hofstede's **power distance** dimension focused on how a society deals with the fact that people are unequal in physical and intellectual capabilities. According to Hofstede, high power distance cultures were found in countries that let inequalities grow over time into inequalities of power and wealth. Low power distance cultures were found in societies that tried to play down such inequalities as much as possible.

INDIVIDUALISM VERSUS COLLECTIVISM Theory focusing on the relationship between the individual and his or her fellows. In individualistic societies, the ties between individuals are loose and individual achievement is highly valued. In societies where collectivism is emphasized, ties between individuals are tight, people are born into collectives, such as extended families, and everyone is supposed to look after the interests of his or her collective.

The **individualism versus collectivism** dimension focused on the relationship between the individual and his or her fellows. In individualistic societies, the ties between individuals were loose and individual achievement and freedom were highly valued. In societies where collectivism was emphasized, the ties between individuals were tight. In such societies, people were born into collectives, such as extended families, and everyone was supposed to look after the interest of his or her collective.

UNCERTAINTY AVOIDANCE Extent to which cultures socialize members to accept ambiguous situations and to tolerate uncertainty.

Hofstede's **uncertainty avoidance** dimension measured the extent to which different cultures socialized their members into accepting ambiguous situations and tolerating uncertainty. Members of high uncertainty avoidance cultures placed a premium on job security, career patterns, retirement benefits, and so on. They also had a strong need for rules and regulations; the manager was expected to issue clear instructions, and subordinates' initiatives were tightly controlled. Lower uncertainty avoidance cultures were characterized by a greater readiness to take risks and less emotional resistance to change.

Hofstede's **masculinity versus femininity** dimension looked at the relationship between gender and work roles. In masculine cultures, sex roles were sharply differentiated and traditional "masculine values," such as achievement and the effective exercise of power, determined cultural ideals. In feminine cultures, sex roles were less sharply distinguished, and little differentiation was made between men and women in the same job.

The fifth dimension, **long-term versus short-term orientation**, was found in a study among students in 23 countries around the world using a questionnaire designed by Chinese scholars. It deals with virtue regardless of truth. Values associated with long-term orientation are thrift and perseverance; values associated with short-term orientation are respect for tradition, fulfilling social obligations, and protecting one's "face."

Hofstede created an index score for each of these five dimensions that ranged from 0 to 100 and scored high for high individualism, high power distance, high uncertainty avoidance, and high masculinity. He averaged the score for all employees from a given country. Table 3.3 summarizes this data for 20 countries. Western nations such as Canada, the United States, and Great Britain score high on the individualism scale and low on the power distance scale. At the other extreme are a group of Latin American and Asian countries that emphasize collectivism over individualism and score high on the power distance scale. Table 3.3 also reveals that Japan's culture has strong uncertainty avoidance and high masculinity. This characterization fits the standard stereotype of Japan as a country that is male dominant and where uncertainty avoidance exhibits itself in the institution of lifetime employment. Sweden and Denmark stand out as countries that have both low uncertainty avoidance and low masculinity (high emphasis on "feminine" values).

Hofstede's results are interesting for what they tell us in a very general way about differences between cultures. Many of Hofstede's findings are consistent with standard Western stereotypes about cultural differences. For example, many people believe Americans are more individualistic and egalitarian (they have a lower power

	POWER DISTANCE	UNCERTAINTY AVOIDANCE	INDIVIDUALISM	MASCULINITY
Argentina	49	86	46	56
Australia	36	51	90	61
Brazil	69	76	38	49
Canada	39	48	80	52
Denmark	18	23	74	16
France	68	86	71	43
Germany (F.R.)	35	65	67	66
Great Britain	35	35	89	66
Indonesia	78	48	14	46
India	77	40	48	56
Israel	13	81	54	47
Japan	54	92	46	95
Mexico	81	82	30	69
Netherlands	38	53	80	14
Panama	95	86	11	44
Spain	57	86	51	42
Sweden	31	29	71	5
Thailand	64	64	20	34
Turkey	66	85	37	45
United States	40	46	91	62

TABLE 3.3

Work-Related Values for 20 Selected Countries

Source: From Geert Hofstede, "The Cultural Relativity of Organizational Practices and Theories," *Journal of International Business Studies,* 14, Fall 1983, pp. 75–89. Reprinted with permission.

distance) than the Japanese, who in turn are more individualistic and egalitarian than Mexicans. Similarly, many might agree that Latin countries such as Mexico place a higher emphasis on masculine value–they are machismo cultures–than the Nordic countries of Denmark and Sweden.

However, one should be careful about reading too much into Hofstede's research. It has been criticized on a number of points.[41] First, Hofstede assumes there is a one-to-one correspondence between culture and the nation-state, but as we saw earlier, many countries have more than one culture. Hofstede's results do not capture this distinction. Second, the research may have been culturally bound. The research team was composed of Europeans and Americans. The questions they asked of IBM employees and their analysis of the answers may have been shaped by their own cultural biases and concerns. So it is not surprising that Hofstede's results confirm Western stereotypes, since it was Westerners who undertook the research!

Third, Hofstede's informants worked not only within a single industry, the computer industry, but also within one company, IBM. At the time, IBM was renowned for its own strong corporate culture and employee selection procedures, making it possible that the employees' values were different in important respects from the values of the cultures from which those employees came. Also, certain social classes (such as unskilled manual workers) were excluded from Hofstede's sample. A final caution is that Hofstede's work is now beginning to look dated. Cultures do not stand still; they evolve, albeit slowly. What was a reasonable characterization in the 1960s and 1970s may not be so today.

Still, just as it should not be accepted without question, Hofstede's work should not be dismissed entirely either. It represents a starting point for managers trying to figure out how cultures differ and what that might mean for management practices. Also, several other scholars have found strong evidence that differences in culture affect values and practices in the workplace, and Hofdstede's basic results have been replicated using more diverse samples of individuals in different settings.[42] Still, managers should use the results with caution, for they are not necessarily accurate.

Hofstede subsequently expanded his original research to include a fifth dimension that he argued captured additional cultural differences not brought out in his earlier work.[43] He referred to this dimension as "Confucian dynamism" (sometimes

MASCULINITY VERSUS FEMININITY
Theory of the relationship between gender and work roles. In masculine cultures, sex roles are sharply differentiated and traditional "masculine values" such as achievement and the effective exercise of power determine cultural ideals. In feminine cultures, sex roles are less sharply distinguished, and little differentiation is made between men and women in the same job.

LONG-TERM VERSUS SHORT-TERM ORIENTATION
Theory that deals with virtue regardless of truth; values associated with long-term orientation are thrift and perseverance; values associated with short-term orientation are respect for tradition, fulfilling social obligations, and protecting one's "face."

CONFUCIAN DYNAMISM
Theory that Confucian teachings affect attitudes toward time, persistence, ordering by status, protection of face, respect for tradition, and reciprocation of gifts and favours.

called long-term orientation). According to Hofstede, **Confucian dynamism** captures attitudes toward time, persistence, ordering by status, protection of face, respect for tradition, and reciprocation of gifts and favours. The label refers to these "values" being derived from Confucian teachings. As might be expected, East Asian countries such as Japan, Hong Kong, and Thailand scored high on Confucian dynamism, while nations like Canada and the United States scored low. Hofstede and his associates went on to argue that their evidence suggested that nations with higher economic growth rates scored high on Confucian dynamism and low on individualism–the implication being Confucianism is good for growth. However, subsequent studies have shown that this finding does not hold up under more sophisticated statistical analysis.[44] During the past decade, countries with high individualism and low Confucian dynamics such as the United States have attained high growth rates, while some Confucian cultures such as Japan have had stagnant economic growth. In reality, while culture might influence the economic success of a nation, it is just one of many factors, and while its importance should not be ignored, it should not be overstated either. The factors discussed in Chapter 2–economic, political, and legal systems–are probably more important than culture in explaining economic growth rates over time.

CULTURAL CHANGE

Culture is not a constant; it evolves over time. Changes in value systems can be slow and painful for a society. In the 1960s, for example, American values toward the role of women, love, sex, and marriage changed significantly.

Much of the social turmoil of that time reflected these changes. Change can often be quite profound. For example, at the beginning of the 1960s, the idea that women might hold senior management positions in major corporations was not widely accepted. Many scoffed at the idea. Today, it is a reality and few in the mainstream of American society question the development or the capability of women in the business world. American culture has changed (although it is still more difficult for women to gain senior management positions than men). Similarly, the value systems of many ex-Communist states, such as Russia, are undergoing significant changes as those countries move away from values that emphasize collectivism and toward those that emphasize individualism. While social turmoil is an inevitable outcome of such a shift, the shift will still probably occur. The accompanying Management Focus offers guidelines for working and travelling in China from a Canadian perspective.

Some claim that a major cultural shift is occurring in Japan, with a move toward greater individualism.[45] The model Japanese office worker, or "salaryman," is pictured as being loyal to his boss and the organization to the point of giving up evenings, weekends, and vacations to serve the organization, which is the collective of which he is a member. However, a new generation of office workers does not seem to fit this model. An individual from the new generation is more direct than the traditional Japanese. He acts more like a Westerner, a *gaijian*. He does not live for the company and will move on if he is offered a better job. He is not keen on overtime, especially if he has a date. He has his own plans for his free time, and they may not include drinking or playing golf with the boss.[46]

Several studies have suggested that economic advancement and globalization may be important factors in societal change.[47] For example, evidence shows that economic progress is accompanied by a shift in values away from collectivism and toward individualism.[48] Thus, as Japan has become richer, the cultural emphasis on collectivism has declined and greater individualism is being witnessed. One reason for this shift may be that richer societies exhibit less need for social and material support structures built on collectives, whether the collective is the extended family or the paternalistic company.

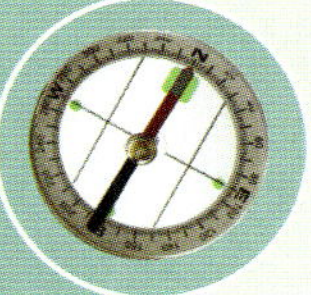

WORKING IN CHINA

Trevor Buss juggles his university studies in Toronto with a full-time career that frequently takes him to China. During his many trips to China, he has learned how to be successful while adhering to age-old customs and traditions. Demonstrating some knowledge of the local customs allows for enhanced business contacts, as local businesspeople appreciate the extra effort made to be sensitive to their culture.

When travelling in China, Trevor makes certain that if he is going to a business lunch or dinner in a rural area he has left the remainder of his day open. There are many customs and rituals, particularly in rural areas, where much socializing is expected. Trevor offers some good advice on doing business in China. The hierarchy of seniority, even in small companies, is paramount. Never make anyone lose face. Have a proper title on your business card and ensure that you present yourself in a professional manner. A good translator is a must.

As he is frequently invited for dinner, customs as basic as seating arrangements can have a bearing on the outcome of business negotiations. For example, the guest of honour is always seated on the right facing towards the door. The host will try to establish the order of command, and seating may change based simply on the title on your business card or how the guest perceives your position in the company.

As for smoking, Trevor has noticed that cigarettes are offered throughout meetings, even for non-smokers. He has found that by the end of some meetings he has 20 or 30 cigarettes lined up in front of his plate. Expectancies are that men smoke, while it is frowned on for women to smoke.

Unlike in Canada, toasting (and drinking) in China is more customary. If not willing to imbibe, it is best to tell the host that one's inability to drink is due to medical reasons.

Foreigners are normally expected to drink two shots of bai jiu, a Chinese rice wine (between 35 and 65 percent alcohol), with each guest. Two drinks are the norm. The drinks go up in counts of two, not one, so if toasting be certain to have two drinks per toast. Through rotating toasts, it is possible to acquaint oneself with everybody at the reception.

As a sign of respect when toasting or drinking, make sure the lip of your glass remains lower than the glass of the person toasting. Trevor has found this quite funny to watch, since the host will often try to get their glass lower than yours. He has even found himself tipping his glass on an angle to try and get the lip of the glass lower. When drinking across the table from somebody it is also customary to tap the table with the glass. *Gan bei* means "bottoms up" and if this is met with silence, then the glass must be emptied. It is customary to demonstrate this by tipping the emptied glass towards the centre of the table to show everyone that it is empty.

When eating, meals are served to the centre of the table. The guest is expected to try most dishes first, though a guest may be excused from this if the host knows that the guest is not too familiar with Chinese customs.

In summary, here are a few guidelines:

- Travel with some basic knowledge of the host's business. Learn some basic Mandarin, but be prepared for some potential embarrassments. For example, the word used for "colleague" in China is also the slang word for mistress or lover used by Malaysian Mandarin-speaking people.
- Go with an open mind and don't expect business to be done quickly. You need to build a relationship before any business transaction will occur.
- To avoid potential embarrassment, get a good translator/business partner who can help with translation, local customs, and colloquial terms.
- Have business cards with proper titles that translate to the proper position. A title like manager does not carry the same weight in China as director or vice-president, even if the actual roles being performed are the same.

Source: Interview with Trevor Buss, student at Ryerson University in Toronto.

Some have argued that the rise of global corporations, whose products can be found around the world, has created the conditions for the merging of cultures and a reduction in cultural variation. Do you think that this is so? Or could globalization of companies and products foster a shift towards and a re-emphasis of a culture's roots and customs? Paul Chelsey/Tony Stone Images.

People are better able to take care of their own needs. As a result, the importance attached to collectivism declines, while greater economic freedoms lead to an increase in opportunities for expressing individualism.

The culture of societies may also change as they become richer because economic progress affects a number of other factors, which in turn influence culture. For example, increased urbanization and improvements in the quality and availability of education are both a function of economic progress, and both can lead to declining emphasis on the traditional values associated with poor rural societies.

As for globalization, some have argued that advances in transportation and communication technologies, the dramatic increase in trade that we have witnessed since World War II, and the rise of global corporations such as Hitachi, Disney, Microsoft, and Levi Strauss, whose products and operations can be found around the globe, are creating the conditions for the merging of cultures.[49] With McDonald's hamburgers in China, Levi's in India, Sony Walkmans in South Africa, and MTV everywhere helping to foster a ubiquitous youth culture, some argue that the conditions for less cultural variation have been created. But culture is not a one-way street, with the large necessarily dominating the small. For example, in 2004, Tim Hortons, that dominant Canadian icon of "culture," expanded into 42 locations in Rhode Island, Connecticut, and Massachusetts. At the same time, one must not ignore important countertrends, such as the shift toward Islamic fundamentalism in several countries; the separatist movement in Quebec; or the continuing ethnic strains and separatist movements in Russia. Such countertrends in many ways are a reaction to the pressures for cultural convergence. In an increasingly modern and materialistic world, some societies are trying to reemphasize their cultural roots and uniqueness. Cultural change is not therefore unidirectional, with national cultures converging toward some homogenous global entity. Also, while some elements of culture change quite rapidly–particularly the use of material symbols–other elements change only slowly if at all. Thus, just because people the world over wear blue jeans and eat at McDonald's, one should not assume they have also adopted North American values–for more often than not, they have not.

IMPLICATIONS FOR BUSINESS

International business is different from national business because countries and societies are different. In this chapter, we have seen just how different societies can be. Societies differ because their cultures vary. Their cultures vary because of profound differences in social structure, religion, language, education, economic philosophy, and political philosophy. Three important implications for international business flow from these differences. The first is the need to develop cross-cultural literacy. There is a need not only to appreciate that cultural differences exist, but also to appreciate what such differences mean for international business. A second implication looks at the connection between culture and ethics in decision making. A third implication for international business centers on the connection between culture and national competitive advantage. Making the matter even more complex is that new "types" of customers are grouping, in ways that do not mirror national borders. For example, some firms may target the "Asian" customer, rather than the Chinese customer or the Korean customer. Still other firms might target "North America seniors," seeing it as one type of demographic, rather than one with Canadian, American, and Mexican distinctions.

CROSS-CULTURAL LITERACY

One of the biggest dangers confronting a company that goes abroad for the first time is the danger of being ill-informed. International businesses that are ill-informed about the practices of another culture are likely to fail. Doing business in different cultures requires adaptation to conform with the value systems and norms of that culture. Adaptation can embrace all aspects of an international firm's operations in a foreign country. The way deals are negotiated, the appropriate incentive pay systems for salespeople, the structure of the organization, the name of a product, the tenor of relations between management and labour, the manner in which the product is promoted, and so on, are all sensitive to cultural differences. What works in one culture might not work in another.

To combat the danger of being ill-informed, international businesses should consider employing local citizens. They must also ensure that home-country executives are cosmopolitan enough to understand how differences in culture affect the practice of international business. Transferring executives overseas at regular intervals to expose them to different cultures will help build a cadre of cosmopolitan executives. An international business must also be constantly on guard against the dangers of **ethnocentric behaviour.** Ethnocentrism is a belief in the superiority of one's own ethnic group or culture. Hand in hand with ethnocentrism goes a disregard or contempt for the culture of other countries. Unfortunately, ethnocentrism is prevalent; many Americans are guilty of it, as are many Canadians, Japanese people, British people, and so on. Ugly as it is, ethnocentrism is a fact of life, one that international businesses must be on continual guard against.

ETHNOCENTRIC BEHAVIOUR
Behaviour that is based on the belief in the superiority of one's own ethnic group or culture; often shows disregard or contempt for the culture of other countries.

CULTURE AND COMPETITIVE ADVANTAGE

One theme that repeatedly surfaced in this chapter is the relationship between culture and national competitive advantage. Put simply, the value systems and norms of a country influence the costs of doing business. The costs of doing business in a country influence the ability of firms to establish a competitive advantage in the global marketplace. We have seen how attitudes toward cooperation between management and labour, toward work, and toward the payment of interest are influenced by social structure and religion. It can be argued that the class-based conflict between workers and management in class-conscious societies, when it leads to industrial disruption, raises the costs of doing business in that society. Similarly, we have seen how some sociologists have argued that the ascetic "other-worldly" ethics of Hinduism may not be as supportive of capitalism as the ethics embedded in Protestantism and Confucianism. Also, Islamic laws banning interest payments may raise the costs of doing business by constraining a country's banking system.

Japan presents an interesting example of how culture can influence competitive advantage. Some scholars have argued that the culture of modern Japan lowers the costs of doing business relative to the costs in most Western nations. Japan's emphasis on group affiliation, loyalty, reciprocal obligations, honesty, and education all boost the competitiveness of Japanese companies. The emphasis on group affiliation and loyalty encourages individuals to identify strongly with the companies in which they work. This fosters an ethic of hard work and cooperation between management and labour "for the good of the company." Similarly, reciprocal obligations and honesty help build an atmosphere of trust between companies

ANOTHER PERSPECTIVE

A hierarchy of concepts?

Perhaps culture is a deeper level concept, one upon which the values of the economic, political, and legal systems rest. For example, Canada adopts legislation whose goal is to maintain fairness and a level playing field. These values are consistent with a culture that has a low power distance and values the individual. The high levels of competition in the Canadian economy, both among companies and among individuals, can be seen to support the high levels of individualism that are central to Canadian culture. Contrast the focus on the individual in Canada with the Chinese value of *guanxi*. The Canadian notion of fairness, the level playing field, can be seen as the basis for prohibiting insider trading in Canada. Yet for the Chinese, *guanxi* suggests that the holder of privileged information relevant to the market would have an obligation to share this information with friends. Such an obligation supports networked, close relationships and obligation to the group.

and their suppliers. This encourages them to enter into long-term relationships with each other to work on inventory reduction, quality control, and joint design—all of which have been shown to improve an organization's competitiveness. This level of cooperation has often been lacking in the West, where the relationship between a company and its suppliers tends to be a short-term one structured around competitive bidding, rather than one based on long-term mutual commitments. In addition, the availability of a pool of highly skilled labour, particularly engineers, has helped Japanese enterprises develop cost-reducing process innovations that have boosted their productivity.[50] Thus, cultural factors may help explain the competitive advantage enjoyed by many Japanese businesses in the global marketplace. The rise of Japan as an economic power during the second half of the twentieth century may be attributed in part to the economic consequences of its culture.

It has also been argued that the Japanese culture is less supportive of entrepreneurial activity than, say, American society. In many ways, entrepreneurial activity is a product of an individualistic mind-set, not a classic characteristic of the Japanese. This may explain why American enterprises, rather than Japanese corporations, dominate industries where entrepreneurship and innovation are highly valued, such as computer software and biotechnology. Of course, there are obvious and significant exceptions to this generalization. Masayoshi Son recognized the potential of software far faster than any of Japan's corporate giants; set up his company, Softbank, in 1981; and has since built it into Japan's top software distributor. Similarly, dynamic entrepreneurial individuals established major Japanese companies such as Sony and Matsushita. But these examples may be the exceptions that prove the rule, for there has been no surge in entrepreneurial high-technology enterprises in Japan equivalent to what has occurred in Canada and the United States.

For the international business, the connection between culture and competitive advantage is important for two reasons. First, the connection suggests which countries are likely to produce the most viable competitors. For example, one might argue that Canadian enterprises are likely to see continued growth in aggressive, cost-efficient competitors from those Pacific Rim nations where a combination of free market economics, Confucian ideology, group-oriented social structures, and advanced education systems can all be found (e.g., South Korea, Taiwan, Japan, and increasingly China).

Second, the connection between culture and competitive advantage has important implications for the choice of countries in which to locate production facilities and do business. Consider a hypothetical case when a company has to choose between two countries, A and B, for locating a production facility. Both countries are characterized by low labour costs and good access to world markets. Both countries are of roughly the same size (in terms of population) and both are at a similar stage of economic development. In country A, the education system is undeveloped, the society is characterized by a marked stratification between the upper and lower classes, and there are six major linguistic groups. In country B, the education system is well developed, there is a lack of social stratification, group identification is valued by the culture, and there is only one linguistic group. Which country makes the best investment site?

Country B probably does. In country A, conflict between management and labour, and between different language groups, can be expected to lead to social and industrial disruption, thereby raising the costs of doing business.[51] The lack of a good education system can also be expected to work against the attainment of business goals.

The same kind of comparison could be made for an international business trying to decide where to push its products, country A or B. Again, country B would be the logical choice because cultural factors suggest that in the long run, country B is the nation most likely to achieve the greatest level of economic growth.

But as important as culture is, it is probably far less important than economic, political, and legal systems in explaining differential economic growth between nations. Cultural differences are significant, but their importance in the economic sphere should not be overemphasized. For example, earlier we noted that Max Weber argued that the ascetic principles embedded in Hinduism do not encourage entrepreneurial activity. While this is an interesting academic thesis, recent years have seen an increase in entrepreneurial activity in India, particularly in information technology where India is rapidly becoming an important global player. The ascetic principles of Hinduism and caste-based social stratification have apparently not held back entrepreneurial activity in this sector!

CULTURE AND BUSINESS ETHICS

Many ethical principles are universally held across cultures. For example, basic moral principles such as don't kill or don't steal apply everywhere, despite differences in local culture. Similarly, in all cultures it is regarded as unethical to unilaterally and without reason break a business agreement. As Adam Smith pointed out more than 200 years ago, if people cannot trust each other to honour agreements, business activity will not take place, and economic growth will not occur. A certain level of faith that agreements will be honoured—that parties to a transaction will do the ethical thing—is required to encourage economic activity no matter what the culture. In the West, the legal system, particularly the system of contract law, evolved to help assure people that agreements will be honoured, but the legal system is designed to deal only with the exceptions to the general principle (which is embedded in our culture) that one should honour agreements. In nations that lack a similar legal tradition, other institutions have emerged to help assure people that business agreements will be honoured.

As we pointed out earlier, *guanxi* networks may fulfill that role in China (see the opening case). Individuals who break agreements will have their reputation tarnished and will be unable to draw on the *guanxi* network in the future. Whether we are talking about China or the West, however, the basic principle remains the same—it is unethical to break business agreements without good reason, and those that do will face sanctions (either legal or cultural). Earlier in the chapter we saw that Japanese have a word for dying from overwork—*karoshi*, which also implies loyalty. Traditionally, it was perceived to be ethical for Japanese workers to die of overwork for the company and, unethical for them to have more than one job in one's lifetime. In Canada, it is not unusual for an individual to have many jobs within one's lifetime.

Although many ethical principles are universal, some are culturally bound.[52] When this is the case, international businesses may be confronted with difficult ethical dilemmas. For example, *guanxi* networks are often supported by the idea of reciprocal gift giving. But if a Western company gives a "gift" to a government official, as an attempt to build a relationship that may be useful in the future, that company may subsequently be accused of bribery and supporting corruption. What then is the ethical thing to do?

One response to such a dilemma is to argue that because customs vary from country to country, businesses should adopt the customs (and by extension, ethical practices) of the country in which they are currently doing business. This is the *relativist* or "when in Rome" approach to business ethics. It is also a dangerously flawed approach.[53] It would suggest, for example, that if slavery is practised in a country, it is OK to practise slavery when doing business in that nation! Obviously, this is not the case. Similarly, as several Western businesses have discovered, just because local sweatshops in parts of Asia employ child labour and pay them below subsistence wages, it doesn't follow that one should adopt the same practices. Ethical values are not like a coat that one puts on in certain seasons and certain places and takes off elsewhere. You cannot leave your ethics behind as you venture around the globe. This suggests that one answer to the question "Whose ethics do you use in international business?" is "Your ethics."[54]

But what should "your ethics" be? The answer is somewhat clearer than it used to be. Organizations such as the United Nations have pushed hard to get countries to ratify agreements that have clear ethical implications. An important example is the Universal Declaration of Human Rights, which has been ratified by almost every country and lays down basic principles that should always be adhered to irrespective of the culture in which one is doing business. For example, Article 23 of this declaration states that

1. Everyone has the right to work, to free choice of employment, to just and favourable conditions of work, and to protection against unemployment.
2. Everyone, without any discrimination, has the right to equal pay for equal work.
3. Everyone who works has the right to just and favourable remuneration ensuring for himself and his family an existence worthy of human dignity and supplemented, if necessary, by other means of social protection.
4. Everyone has the right to form and to join trade unions for the protection of his interests.

ANOTHER PERSPECTIVE

Online view of a new culture

Visit the online versions of some English-language daily newspapers in major foreign cities to get a sense of their cultures and their markets. Look at the ads and business names. Check out the classifieds. A good list link is at: http://www.geocities.com/Hollywood/Boulevard/1529/ newspapers.html. In addition, check out the Nation (Nairobi, Kenya) at: http://www.nationaudio.com/News/DailyNation/Today.

Clearly, the rights to "just and favourable work conditions," "equal pay for equal work," and remuneration that ensures an "existence worthy of human dignity" embodied in Article 23 imply that it is unethical to employ child labour in sweatshop settings and pay less than subsistence wages, even if that happens to be common in some countries. But does that mean one should not employ children or buy from suppliers who employ children, even if that is common in a certain country? Here the ethical thing to do becomes less clear. If the choice for the child is between living on the streets and begging for food or working in an apparel factory for subsistence wages, what should a firm do? Should it continue to sanction the employment of child labour as a lesser evil? Again probably not, but neither should the firm simply wash its hands of the situation. If a firm already has a relationship with a supplier that is employing child labour and that fact is suddenly uncovered, walking away from that relationship because of moral outrage may do more harm than good to the children whose interests the firm wishes to protect. In such circumstances, the ethical thing to do may be to find a way to improve life for the children.

For example, when Levi Strauss found that one of its suppliers employed child labour, it did not terminate the relationship. Instead, it looked into the situation. It discovered that many of the women who worked in the factory brought their children to work with them because there was no local school and because the pittance that the children earned kept the family's income above subsistence level. So Levi Strauss built a school for the children under 14, and it paid the parents the additional money that their children would otherwise have earned. This was a small price for Levi Strauss to pay, but it made a big difference in the lives of the affected children.

Grey areas will always exist that require managers to use their own moral judgment to solve ethical dilemmas, but those judgments should be made with regard to a high ethical code. Consider again the example of giving gifts to support relationships. What is the ethical thing to do? Should one respond to the cultural expectation that a gift should be given, and do so to try to build a relationship that might pay dividends in the future? In nations such as China, where reciprocal gift giving is common and helps to cement *guanxi* relationships, this is a reasonable approach, although it may conflict with Western notions of fair play.[55] For example, consider a situation where two Western companies are competing to win a supply contract from a Chinese firm. Imagine that the firm that wins the contract is not the lowest bidder but is the firm that employed the son of the CEO of the Chinese firm as a consultant to advise it on the negotiations. The losing company might believe that principles of fair play have been violated here, but this is not necessarily so. Rather, the winning firm has simply recognized that relationships matter in China and employed an individual with connections to help it win the contract. By employing the son of the CEO, the firm that won the bid helped someone in the CEO's *guanxiwang,* which increased the probability that this "gift" or gesture would be reciprocated.

The practice becomes obviously problematic, however, when government officials are the recipients of the gifts, either directly or indirectly, for then the gifts can be construed as bribery. There is a dividing line between corruption and legitimate gift giving to support business transactions. It is a line that a manager with a strong moral compass should be able to recognize.

Reflecting on such dilemmas, the ethicist Thomas Donaldson has argued that when thinking through ethical problems in international business, firms should be guided by three principles.[56]

1. Respect for core human values (human rights), which determine the absolute moral threshold for all business activities.
2. Respect for local tradition.
3. The belief that context matters when deciding what is right and what is wrong.

Donaldson's point is that respect of core human values must be the starting point for all ethical decisions. Once those are assured, businesses must also respect local cultural differences, which he defines as traditions and context. Thus, Donaldson argues that "gift giving" is not unethical, even though some Western businesses might feel that it is wrong. Gift giving does not violate core human values and is important in the context of some cultures such as China and Japan. By the same token, Donaldson would condemn as unethical decisions that clearly violate core human values. Employing child labor at less than subsistence wages would fall into that category.

KEY TERMS

caste system, p. 94
class consciousness, p. 96
class system, p. 94
Confucian dynamism, p. 112
ethical systems, p. 96
ethnocentric behaviour, p. 115
folkways, p. 89
group, p. 91
individualism versus collectivism, p. 110
karoshi, p. 93
long-term vs. short-term orientation, p. 111
masculinity versus femininity, p. 111
mores, p. 89
norms, p. 88
power distance, p. 110
religion, p. 96
social mobility, p. 94
social strata, p. 94
society, p. 88
uncertainty avoidance, p. 110
values, p. 88

SUMMARY

We have looked at the nature of social culture and studied some implications for business practice. The following points have been made:

1. Culture is a complex whole that includes knowledge, beliefs, art, morals, law, customs, and other capabilities acquired by people as members of society.
2. Values and norms are the central components of a culture. Values are abstract ideals about what a society believes to be good, right, and desirable. Norms are social rules and guidelines that prescribe appropriate behaviour in particular situations.
3. Values and norms are influenced by political and economic philosophy, social structure, religion, language, and education.
4. The social structure of a society refers to its basic social organization. Two main dimensions along which social structures differ are the individual–group dimension and the stratification dimension.
5. In some societies, the individual is the basic building block of social organization. These societies emphasize individual achievements above all else. In other societies, the group is the basic building block of social organization. These societies emphasize group membership and group achievements above all else.
6. All societies are stratified into different classes. Class-conscious societies are characterized by low social mobility and a high degree of stratification. Less class-conscious societies are characterized by high social mobility and a low degree of stratification.
7. Religion may be defined as a system of shared beliefs and rituals that is concerned with the realm of the sacred. Ethical systems refer to a set of moral principles, or values, that are used to guide and shape behavior. The world's major religions are Christianity, Islam, Hinduism, and Buddhism. Although not a religion, Confucianism has an impact on behaviour that is as profound as that of many religions. The value systems of different religious and ethical systems have different implications for business practice.
8. Language is one defining characteristic of a culture. It has both a spoken and an unspoken dimension. In countries with more than one spoken language, we tend to find more than one culture.
9. Formal education is the medium through which individuals learn skills and are socialized into the values and norms of a society. Education plays an important role in the determination of national competitive advantage.
10. Geert Hofstede studied how culture relates to values in the workplace. Hofstede isolated four dimensions that he claimed summarized different cultures: power distance, uncertainty avoidance, individualism versus collectivism, and masculinity versus femininity.
11. Culture is not a constant; it evolves over time. Economic progress and globalization seem to be two important engines of cultural change.
12. One danger confronting a company that goes abroad for the first time is being ill-informed. To develop cross-cultural literacy, international businesses need to employ host-country nationals, build a cadre of cosmopolitan executives, and guard against the dangers of ethnocentric behaviour.
13. The value systems and norms of a country can affect the costs of doing business in that country.
14. Although many ethical principles are universal, some are culturally bounded. What is not ethical in one country might be common in another. Despite this, the "when in Rome" approach to business ethics is dangerous. International businesses need to adhere to a consistent set of ethics derived from a high moral code.

CRITICAL THINKING AND DISCUSSION QUESTIONS

1. Outline why the culture of a country might influence the costs of doing business in that country. Illustrate your answer with examples.
2. Do you think that business practices in an Islamic country are likely to differ from business practices in Canada, and if so how?
3. What are the implications for international business of differences in the dominant religion and/or ethical system of a country?
4. Choose two countries that appear to be culturally diverse. Compare the cultures of those countries and then indicate how cultural differences influence *(a)* the costs of doing business in each country, *(b)* the likely future economic development of that country, *(c)* business practices, and *(d)* business ethics.
5. It is unreasonable to expect Western businesses active in developing nations to adhere to the same ethical standards that they use at home. Discuss!
6. A Western firm is trying to get a licence from the government of a developing nation to set up a factory in that country. The firm knows the factory will bring many benefits to the country. It will provide jobs in an area where unemployment is high and it will produce exports for the country, allowing that nation to earn valuable foreign exchange. So far, the government official with whom the firm is negotiating has been noncommittal, neither rejecting nor approving the request, but simply asking for more and more information. The firm has been told that relationships are important in this country, and that if it hired the daughter of the government official as a consultant, she could use her influence to get the licence application approved, to everyone's betterment. What should the firm do?

RESEARCH TASK | globalEDGE™ globaledge.msu.edu

Use the globalEDGE™ site to complete the following exercises:

1. You are preparing for a business trip to Venezuela where you will need to interact extensively with local professionals. Therefore, you consider collecting information regarding local culture and business habits before your departure. Prepare a short description of the most striking cultural characteristics that may affect business interactions in this country.
2. Asian cultures exhibit significant differences in business etiquette when compared to Western cultures. For example, in Thailand it is considered offensive to show the sole of the shoe or foot to another. Find five additional tips regarding the business etiquette of a specific Asian country of your choice.

Visit the *Global Business Today* Online Learning Centre at **www.mcgrawhill.ca/college/hill** to access quizzes, interactive exercises, a Business Around the World interactive map, and other learning and study tools related to this chapter.

Online LearningCentre

CLOSING CASE

DISNEY IN FRANCE

Until 1992, the Walt Disney Company had experienced nothing but success in the theme park business. Its first park, Disneyland, opened in Anaheim, California, in 1955. Its theme song, "It's a Small World After All," promoted "an idealized vision of America spiced with reassuring glimpses of exotic cultures all calculated to promote heartwarming feelings about living together as one happy family. There were dark tunnels and bumpy rides to scare the children a little but none of the terrors of the real world . . . The Disney characters that everyone knew from the cartoons and comic books were on hand to shepherd the guests and to direct them to the Mickey Mouse watches and Little Mermaid records."[57] The Anaheim park was an instant success.

In the 1970s, the triumph was repeated in Florida, and in 1983, Disney proved the Japanese also have an affinity for Mickey

Mouse with the successful opening of Tokyo Disneyland. Having wooed the Japanese, Disney executives in 1986 turned their attention to France and, more specifically, to Paris, the self-proclaimed capital of European high culture and style. "Why did they pick France?" many asked. When word first got out that Disney wanted to build another international theme park, officials from more than 200 locations all over the world descended on Disney with pleas and cash inducements to work the Disney magic in their hometowns. But Paris was chosen because of demographics and subsidies. About 17 million Europeans live less than a two-hour drive from Paris. Another 310 million can fly there in the same time or less. Also, the French government was so eager to attract Disney that it offered the company more than $1 billion in various incentives, all in the expectation that the project would create 30 000 French jobs.

From the beginning, cultural gaffes by Disney set the tone for the project. By late 1986, Disney was deep in negotiations with the French government. To the exasperation of the Disney team, headed by Joe Shapiro, the talks were taking far longer than expected. Jean-Rene Bernard, the chief French negotiator, said he was astonished when Mr. Shapiro, his patience depleted, ran to the door of the room and, in a very un-Gallic gesture, began kicking it repeatedly, shouting, "Get me something to break!" There was also snipping from Parisian intellectuals who attacked the transplantation of Disney's dream world as an assault on French culture; "a cultural Chernobyl," one prominent intellectual called it. The minister of culture announced he would boycott the opening, proclaiming it to be an unwelcome symbol of American clichés and a consumer society. Unperturbed, Disney pushed ahead with the planned summer 1992 opening of the $5-billion park. Shortly after Euro-Disneyland opened, French farmers drove their tractors to the entrance and blocked it. This globally televised act of protest was aimed not at Disney but at the U.S. government, which had been demanding that French agricultural subsidies be cut. Still, it focused world attention on the loveless marriage of Disney and Paris.

Then there were the operational errors. Disney's policy of serving no alcohol in the park, since reversed, caused astonishment in a country where a glass of wine for lunch is a given. Disney thought that Monday would be a light day for visitors and Friday a heavy one and allocated staff accordingly, but the reality was the reverse. Another unpleasant surprise was the hotel breakfast debacle. "We were told that Europeans 'don't take breakfast,' so we downsized the restaurants," recalled one Disney executive. "And guess what? Everybody showed up for breakfast. We were trying to serve 2500 breakfasts in a 350-seat restaurant at some of the hotels. The lines were horrendous. Moreover, they didn't want the typical French breakfast of croissants and coffee, which was our assumption. They wanted bacon and eggs." Lunch turned out to be another problem. "Everybody wanted lunch at 12:30. The crowds were huge. Our smiling cast members had to calm down surly patrons and engage in some 'behaviour modification' to teach them that they could eat lunch at 11:00 A.M. or 2:00 P.M."

There were major staffing problems too. Disney tried to use the same teamwork model with its staff that had worked so well in America and Japan, but it ran into trouble in France. In the first nine weeks of Euro-Disneyland's operation, roughly 1000 employees, 10 percent of the total, left. One former employee was a 22-year-old medical student from a nearby town who signed up for a weekend job. After two days of "brainwashing," as he called Disney's training, he left following a dispute with his supervisor over the timing of his lunch hour. Another former employee noted, "I don't think that they realize what Europeans are like . . . that we ask questions and don't think all the same way."

One of the biggest problems, however, was that Europeans didn't stay at the park as long as Disney expected. While Disney succeeded in getting close to 9 million visitors a year through the park gates, in line with its plans, most stayed only a day or two. Few stayed the four to five days that Disney had hoped for. It seems that most Europeans regard theme parks as places for day excursions. A theme park is not seen as a destination for an extended vacation. This was a big shock for Disney. The company had invested billions in building luxury hotels next to the park—hotels that the day-trippers didn't need and that stood half empty most of the time. To make matters worse, the French didn't show up in the expected numbers. In 1994, only 40 percent of the park's visitors were French. One puzzled executive noted that many visitors were Americans living in Europe or, stranger still, Japanese on a European vacation! As a result, by the end of 1994 Euro-Disney had cumulative losses of $2 billion. At this point, Euro-Disney changed its strategy. First, the company changed the name to Disneyland Paris in an attempt to strengthen the park's identity. Second, food and fashion offerings changed. To quote one manager, "We opened with restaurants providing French-style food service, but we found that customers wanted self-service like in the U.S. parks. Similarly, products in the boutiques were initially toned down for the French market, but since then the range has changed to give it a more definite Disney image." Third, the prices for day tickets and hotel rooms were cut by one-third. The result was an attendance of 11.7 million in 1996, up from a low of 8.8 million in 1994.

Sources: P. Gumble and R. Turner, "Mouse Trap: Fans Like Euro Disney But Its Parent's Goofs Weigh the Park Down," *Wall Street Journal,* March 10, 1994, p. A1; R. J. Barnet and J. Cavanagh, *Global Dreams* (New York: Touchstone Books, 1994), pp. 33–34; J. Huey, "Eisner Explains Everything," *Fortune,* April 17, 1995, pp. 45–68; R. Anthony, "Euro-Disney: The First 100 Days," Harvard Business School Case #9-693-013; and Charles Masters, "French Fall for the Charms of Disney," *Sunday Telegraph,* April 13, 1997, p. 21.

CASE DISCUSSION QUESTIONS

1. What assumptions did Disney make about the tastes and preferences of French consumers? Which of these assumptions were correct? Which were not?
2. How might Disney have had a more favourable initial experience in France? What steps might it have taken to reduce the mistakes associated with the launch of Euro-Disney?
3. In retrospect, was France the best choice for the location of Euro-Disney?

PART TWO

2

COUNTRY DIFFERENCES

Imagine No Metal

Quickly, can you say in what sector (other than forestry or some particular species of grain) Canadians companies dominate internationally? In telecommunications, we do very well thanks to several companies like Nortel and the heritage of Alexander Graham Bell, but we are not number one. If you answered mining, you would be correct.

Many students who are reading this chapter are attending a university or college in a large urban area. There are no mines or slag heaps in downtown Toronto or in Vancouver or any other large city so it is natural that most Canadians do not have any personal experience or contact with the mining industry. Yet the mining industry is one of the most critical components of the Canadian economy—can you imagine how few manufactured items could be assembled with no metal parts, or metal machinery to make the parts?

Gordon Peeling, president of the Mining Association of Canada, likes to remind people "mining is an important sector to our country's social and economic prosperity. It is one of the few sectors in the economy where Canadian companies dominate internationally, a position achieved through growth, innovation, ingenuity and highly skilled workers." The federal government's Environment Minister David Anderson echoes Peelings comments adding that Canadian mining companies have become "environmental and social industrial leaders both in Canada, and internationally."

While mining is "big business" in large parts of northern Ontario and elsewhere in Canada, students of international business should understand that mining is an important and growing sector worldwide. More and more manufacturing companies demand metals and alloys for an increasing variety of consumer products, which pushes the mining and exploration sector to increasingly grow and expand—of which Canadian companies are the leaders.

Being in a leadership position, as mining and exploration grows worldwide, has put Canadian companies in an economically advantageous situation. This success in mining has helped the Canadian economy, but the increasingly risky and challenging locations in which

D. Falconer/PhotoLink/Getty Images.

CHAPTER 4

Ethics in International Business

OPENING CASE

mining companies operate (all the safe places are mined out) create situations that necessarily include dealing with contentious ethical issues. These ethical issues involve Canadian mining and exploration companies who have to deal with regional politicians that expect certain financial "rewards" for facilitating mining developments, as well as labour and employment practices by local companies hired to develop the sites.

Talisman Energy of Calgary, is no longer in involved in oil exploration and development in Sudan. In the late 1990s and early 2000s, the Alberta-based company was accused of developing oil exploration in the Sudan knowing that the country was in the middle of a civil war. A resource extraction business that intends to successfully operate in a country that has been, at times, referred to as the poorest country on earth and one of the most dangerous countries in Africa, will undoubtedly face many difficult challenges. One of the toughest challenges for Talisman was developing its oil exploration program and oil refinery operations in a region that had open armed conflict between religious and ethnic groups.

The Sudan, since the 1980s and up to the time this text goes to print, has seen violent conflict between the Muslims and Christians. The Muslims hold a majority position in the north of the country, and control the government and military forces. The Christians are concentrated in the south and, as a consequence of extreme violence over many years, have ended up in crowded arid refugee camps along the southern and western borders. Along the western border of Sudan is Chad, a country described by various non-governmental organizations (NGOs) as having the lowest GNP per capita on the planet and certainly not in a position to supply food and support to the refugees fleeing the conflict.

Depending on your sources (www.amnesty.org says 2 million dead and 6 million refugees), hundreds of thousands of Christians have been displaced from their homes and large numbers have been killed violently by nomadic bands of lawless criminals—a sad tragedy that goes unchecked by the Sudanese government despite growing international pressure. A lot of that pressure was put on Talisman by activists who claimed that by operating in the Sudan and openly courting the government's favour for developing their oil projects, Talisman must be, by association, complicit in the crimes against humanity that are increasingly reported in the global media.

Why did Talisman operate in the Sudan, and pay money to the Sudanese government that then used that money to support armed strife against another ethnic group in the country? Ed Broadbent, former leader of the federal NDP Party, speaking at the 2003 Canadian Evaluation Society (CES) conference, said "... global competition led Canadian business executives to do outside of Canada what they could not do at home. In developing countries this has led in the past to exploitative labour policies, bribery of public officials, and the degradation of the environment. In short, decisions about appropriate behaviour in the corporate sector, as with other decisions, are shaped by the market." The intensity of the competitive market outside Canada has created a situation where some companies feel obliged to do battle with a blind eye to corporate behaviour that would not be tolerated in their home nation.

Was public opinion and activist pressure successful in changing Talisman's business in Africa? Talisman's share price did drop and the credibility of Talisman's senior management was challenged in the Canadian media and by members of Parliament who addressed questions about Talisman in Ottawa. At a meeting of the Standing Committee on Foreign Affairs and International Trade the "Sudan" question was raised by M.P. M. Debien who said "... very serious problems are affecting areas in which Canadian companies are involved in mining operations. Just look at the problems of Talisman in the Sudan ... will the Canadian government adopt a clear and open policy and bring in a mandatory code of conduct for companies?" The government has not passed any new legislation restricting mining companies but mining associations have subsequently advanced their own "codes of conduct" for ethical behaviour and much money is spent on public relations to convince shareholders that the various mining companies are operating with ethical considerations in mind.

Why is the situation in the Sudan and other African countries so problematic? One way of seeking a perspective might be to look at the context of the political environment and the inability to develop rules and regulations across multiple boundaries. Africa is home to an estimated 800 million people spread across 54 different countries. By contrast, China (PRC) is one country of 1.4 billion people living under one set of laws. When rules and regulations are so different among countries in one geographic region, it is sometimes possible for outsiders to create exploitative and unethical situations. As this text goes to print, a formal investigation into allegations of war crimes in Sudan's Darfur region is being planned for the International Criminal Court in The Hague. As for the refugees, the first week of June 2005 saw the Red Cross begin airlifts of food to refugees in the Darfur region of Sudan. Previous humanitarian organizations could not bring in food to the refugees because the trucks in the aid convoys were violently attacked. Despite these promising developments, progress is slow and the government in Khartoum (as of June 2005) is thwarting aid workers by arresting them if they talk to foreign media reporters about the conditions they witness.

Sources: www.mining.ca; "Proceedings of the 2003 Canadian Evaluation Society Conference" at www.2003.evaluationcanada.ca/download_files/Broadbent_ed.doc; and www.parl.gc.ca/committee/CommitteeHome.

LEARNING OBJECTIVES

1. Explain the source and nature of ethical issues and dilemmas in an international business.
2. Show how important it is for managers to consider ethical issues when making strategic and operating decisions.
3. Identify the causes of poor ethical decision making in international business organizations
4. Describe the different approaches to business ethics that can be derived from moral philosophy, and show how these approaches can help managers to make international business decisions that do not violate ethical norms.
5. Discuss the steps that managers can take to promote an awareness of ethical issues throughout the organization and to make sure that ethical considerations enter into strategic and operational decisions.

INTRODUCTION

The previous two chapters detail how societies differ in terms of their economic, political, and legal systems, and their culture. We also mapped out some of these implications for the practice of international business. This chapter focuses on the ethical issues that arise when companies do business in different nations. Many of these ethical issues arise precisely because of differences in economic development, politics, legal systems, and culture.

ETHICS, AS EFFECTED BY THE "ENVIRONMENTS"

The circumstances that effect ethical considerations in the new millennium are circumstances caused by drastic changes in the

- Political environment (regional, national and international) and the consequent laws and regulations that are established (discussed in Chapter 2 noting the new Canadian law (Bill S-21)).
- Social-cultural environment that has been influenced by immigration patterns worldwide and a continued movement of populations from rural to urban areas.
- Technological environment that has effected communications regionally and globally and also effected the work environment and productivity.
- Economic environment that sees currency fluctuations and international NGOs like the IMF and World Bank playing a more significant role in national and regional economies. Need for corporations to remain economically competitive also influences corporate objectives and has consequences for consumer priorities.
- Competitive environment that is causing companies to make decisions in a global context and resulting in actions that sometimes negatively effect their employees or customers

There has always been pressure on companies to behave ethically, but in years past this pressure was not so intense as it is in the new millennium where the mistakes of a corporate executive can have international repercussions such as when CNN makes it a headline story or it is posted on Yahoo!'s news site, thereby making it possible for millions of people to know about a company's violation.

Let's consider how politics has an effect on ethics. In the new millennium, the people you elect to run the city government cannot just attend to municipal affairs but must also take into account national and even international influences–recent examples that Canadians will be aware of are SARS and Toronto's bid for the 2008 Olympics:

- Combating the fast spread of SARS challenged traditional concepts of privacy and government regulations of health records that caused awkward situations for Toronto authorities communicating with some of the international NGOs such as the World Health Organization.
- In the period when several cities were competing aggressively to host the 2008 Olympics, newspaper stories worldwide noted some countries using unethical practices to incur favourable reviews from IOC committee members. Canadian regulations on bribery and corporate ethics forbade the types of behaviour that some countries participated in, leading some Canadians to claim that our strong ethical rules put us at a disadvantage when competing against nations that did not follow such ethical practices.

Rules, regulations, laws, and guidelines which may be created to serve the local citizens are now being influenced by events and circumstances far away from the municipality. Politics at the local and national level is also strongly effected by a worldwide shift in the social-cultural environment such that many groups of *identified cultures* use technology and economic influence to exert pressure on governments to change rules and regulations, such as allowing gay marriage, or permitting Shari'a law, or changing the age of retirement, or banning smoking in public restaurants, etc.

The term *ethics* refers to accepted principles of right or wrong that govern the conduct of a person, the members of a profession, or the actions of an organization. **Business ethics** are the accepted principles of right or wrong governing the conduct of businesspeople, and an **ethical strategy** is a strategy, or course of action, that does not violate these accepted principles.

BUSINESS ETHICS Accepted principles of right or wrong governing the conduct of businesspeople.

ETHICAL STRATEGY A course of action that does not violate a company's business ethics.

In our society and others, many ethical principles are codified into law–prohibitions against murder, stealing, and incest, for example–but many others are not, such as the principle that an author should not plagiarize another's work. As long as it does not involve word-for-word copying, plagiarism does not technically violate copyright law, but it surely is unethical. Similarly, the history of science is replete with examples of researchers who claim their idea was "stolen" by an unscrupulous colleague for his own personal gain before the originator had the chance to file for a patent or publish the idea himself. Such behaviour is not illegal, but it is obviously unethical.

This chapter looks at how ethical issues can and should be incorporated into decision making in an international business. We start by looking at the source and nature of ethical issues and dilemmas in an international business. Next, we review the reasons for poor ethical decision making in international businesses. Then we discuss the different philosophical approaches to business ethics. We close the chapter by reviewing the different processes that managers can adopt to make sure that ethical considerations are incorporated into decision making in an international business firm.

ETHICAL ISSUES IN INTERNATIONAL BUSINESS

Many of the ethical issues and dilemmas in international business are rooted in the fact that political systems, law, economic development, and culture vary significantly from nation to nation. Consequently, what is considered normal practice in one nation may be considered unethical in others. Because they work for an institution that transcends national borders and cultures, managers in a multinational firm need to be particularly sensitive to these differences and able to choose the ethical action in those circumstances where variation across societies creates the potential for ethical problems. In the international business setting, the most common ethical issues involve employment practices, human rights, environmental regulations, corruption, and the moral obligation of multinational corporations. The challenge in 2006 and beyond is that these ethical issues and challenges are intensified by fast moving developments facilitated by the "technological environment."

ETHICS, AS EFFECTED BY THE "TECHNOLOGICAL ENVIRONMENTS"

The competitive nature of the national and global broadcast networks (e.g., CNN and the BBC) and the ease with which individuals can post content on the Internet, allow corporations and individuals to bring stories to the forefront at a startling speed, and consequently regional ethical issues can gain international exposure in a short time. In the summer of 2004, a small story out of New Brunswick came to prominence at such speed in July, that within a matter of 24 hours, millions of people worldwide had heard about the blind French-speaking student who was barred from speaking French to his seeing-eye dog from various online news sites and portals. UNB student Yvan Tessier, who wanted to be in the English language immersion program at the University of New Brunswick, wanted to have his seeing-eye dog accompany him to his English classes but was told he could not speak French to the dog–Tessier responded by saying "the dog is not bilingual!" As reported by several media outlets, UNB responded by threatening to restrict Tessier from the ESL classes. Tessier spoke to the Canadian Press, which in turn ran the story on the international wire. Due to the sensational nature of the story (facilitated by postings on numerous Web sites), the CP piece was picked up as a "human interest story" by media outlets globally in a matter of hours and used by news directors who are always looking for a story about "good guy gets restricted by red tape."

EMPLOYMENT PRACTICES

As we saw in the opening case, ethical issues may be associated with employment practices in other nations. When work conditions in a host nation are clearly inferior to those in a multinational's home nation, what standards should be applied? Those of the home nation, those of the host nation, or something in between? While few would suggest that pay and work conditions should be the same across nations, how much divergence is acceptable? For example, while 12-hour workdays, extremely low pay, and a failure to protect workers against toxic chemicals may be common in some developing nations, does this mean that it is OK for a multinational to tolerate such working conditions in its subsidiaries there, or to condone it by using local subcontractors?

A strong argument can be made that such behaviour is not appropriate. But this still leaves unanswered the question of what standards should be applied. We shall return to and consider this issue in more detail later in the chapter. For now, establishing minimal acceptable standards that safeguard the basic rights and dignity of employees, auditing foreign subsidiaries and subcontractors on a regular basis to make sure those standards are met, and taking corrective action if they are not, is a good way to guard against ethical abuses. Apparel company, Levi Strauss, has long taken such an approach. In the early 1990s, the company terminated a long-term contract with one of its large suppliers, the Tan family. The Tans were allegedly forcing 1200 Chinese and Filipino women to work 74 hours per week in guarded compounds on the Mariana Islands.[1]

HUMAN RIGHTS

Beyond employment issues, questions of human rights can arise in international business. Basic human rights still are not respected in many nations. Rights that we take for granted in developed nations, such as freedom of association, freedom of speech, freedom of assembly, freedom of movement, freedom from political repression, and so on, are by no means universally accepted (see Chapter 2 for details). One of the most obvious examples was South Africa during the days of white rule and apartheid, which did not end until 1994. Among other things, the apartheid system denied basic political rights to the majority nonwhite population of South Africa, mandated segregation between whites and nonwhites, reserved certain occupations exclusively for

> **ANOTHER PERSPECTIVE**
>
> **The issue of giving meaning across cultures**
>
> One difficulty in making ethical decisions across cultural borders is that expatriate managers may interpret a local cultural practice in the way such behaviour would be understood in their home culture. If the manager does not attempt to understand the practice's meaning in the local culture, the manager may miss a huge step in ethical analysis. For example, Western standards would fail to properly interpret Muslim women's practice of covering their heads and faces in conservative Muslim cultures. Remember to consider context when conducting an ethical analysis. In such a process, a local informant can be helpful. At the same time, be aware of the ethical trap of cultural relativism captured in the adage, "When in Rome, do as the Romans do."
>
> (Example from H. Lane, M. Maznevski, M. Mendenhall, and J. McNett, *The Blackwell Handbook of Global Management: A Guide to Managing Complexity,* 2004.)

Mandela, shown receiving the Order of Canada, was embraced by Canadians from all walks of life for his heroic struggle to end apartheid in South Africa. CP/Jonathan Hayward.

whites, and prohibited blacks from being placed in positions where they would manage whites. Despite the odious nature of this system, Western businesses operated in South Africa. By the 1980s, however, many questioned the ethics of doing so. They argued that inward investment by foreign multinationals, by boosting the South African economy, supported the repressive apartheid regime.

Canada, as an influential member of the British Commonwealth, played a role in contributing to worldwide pressure on the South African government to abolish apartheid. Canadian politicians used their influence to affect political and economic sanctions on the government of South Africa. Canadian Foreign Affairs Minister Don Jamieson established in 1977 measures which ended "… government support for commercial activities in South Africa, establishing a voluntary 'code of ethics' for Canadian companies active in South Africa, and required visas for South African visitors."[2]

Through the 1980s and early 1990s Canadian government officials at the highest levels, businesspeople, and senior Canadian clergy of several denominations, continued to advocate loudly for the end of apartheid and played a role in facilitating the all-race elections in 1994. Direct support for South Africans included special circumstances allowing mixed race couples (who were in danger for their lives since inter-racial relationships were outlawed in South Africa) to immigrate to Canada, along with other Black Africans and Indian-South Africans who were at risk by virtue of their political activities. South African politicians were angered at Canada's growing influence and countered with allegations that Canada should look at the condition of Native tribes on the reserve system in Canada before moralizing about other country's circumstances. In the end, apartheid was crushed, and just four months after Nelson Mandela's release from prison he visited Canada in 1990 and made several speeches in which he thanked Canadians for their role. In a speech to the Canadian parliament, Mandela expressed appreciation, and encouraged Canadians to maintain economic sanctions against South Africa, which was enforced until Mandela was elected president in May 1994. In 1998, on his second visit to Canada, Nelson Mandela became the first foreign leader to be awarded the Order of Canada–a distinguished honour that has never been repeated.

Although change has come in South Africa, many repressive regimes still exist in the world. Is it ethical for multinationals to do business in them? It is often argued that inward investment by a multinational can be a force for economic, political, and social progress that ultimately improves the rights of people in repressive regimes. This position was first discussed in Chapter 2, when we noted that economic progress in a nation can create pressure for democratization. In general, this belief suggests it is ethical for a multinational to do business in nations that lack the democratic structures and human rights records of developed nations. Investment in China, for example, is frequently justified on the grounds that although China's human rights record is often questioned by human rights groups, and although the country is not a democracy, continuing inward investment will help boost economic growth and raise living standards. These developments will ultimately create pressures from the Chinese people for more participative government, political pluralism, and freedom of expression and speech.

But there is a limit to this argument. As in the case of South Africa, some regimes are so repressive that investment cannot be justified on ethical grounds. A current example would be Myanmar (formally known as Burma). Ruled by a military dictatorship for more than 40 years, Myanmar has one of the worst human rights records in the world. Beginning in the mid-1990s, many Western companies exited Myanmar, judging the human rights violations to be so extreme that doing business there cannot be justified on ethical grounds.

Canada and Myanmar and Ivanhoe Mines Ltd. of Vancouver

Canada's objection to the way the Myanmar regime had been treating dissidents reached its peak in 2003 when Ottawa looked for a way to leverage pressure on the country formerly called Burma. Foreign Affairs Minister Bill Graham was reported as saying that he would seek the help of one of the Canadian mining companies that has a $60-million joint-venture copper mine in Myanmar. Minister Graham explained that the purpose of soliciting Vancouver-based Ivanhoe Mines Ltd. was to "put pressure on the country's military junta to release the jailed opposition leader Aung San Suu Kyi." Ivanhoe Mines is one of the largest foreign investors in Myanmar and very active in many aspects of the country, as would be appropriate to a large mining project.[3] Following the same position as when the Canadian government directly challenged specific Canadian companies that intended to do business with South Africa during apartheid, the government of Prime Minister Chretien publicly challenged Ivanhoe that it should not invest any further money in Myanmar under "present conditions." Why was Ivanhoe so interested in exploring and mining in a region that would make investors and Canadian politicians anxious? Ivanhoe is in the copper-mining business. As of early 2005, there is a worldwide deficit in copper and the prices have risen as China and other economies surge ahead in manufacturing products that require copper (mostly used in wiring). All the "safe places" to mine and extract copper are fully exploited, therefore the only places left on the planet are in regions that are climatically and topographically extreme, or inside the borders of a regime that has a poor human rights record. Throughout much of the 1990s copper prices were at 60 cents a pound; at the time of writing, copper averaged $1.48 per pound on the London Metal Exchange (LME), thereby providing a strong economic incentive for mining companies to withstand political pressure.

More generally, the question remains, What is the responsibility of a foreign multinational when operating in a country where basic human rights are trampled on? Should the company be there at all, and if it is there, what actions should it take to avoid the situation Ivanhoe found itself in?

ENVIRONMENTAL POLLUTION

Ethical issues arise when environmental regulations in host nations are far inferior to those in the home nation. Many developed nations have substantial regulations governing the emission of pollutants, the dumping of toxic chemicals, the use of toxic materials in the workplace, and so on. Those regulations are often lacking in developing nations, and according to critics, the result can be higher levels of pollution from the operations of multinationals than would be allowed at home. For example, consider the case of foreign oil companies in Nigeria. According to a 1992 report prepared by environmental activists in Nigeria, in the Niger Delta region,

> Apart from air pollution from the oil industry's emissions and flares day and night, producing poisonous gases that are silently and systematically wiping out vulnerable airborne biota and endangering the life of plants, game, and man himself, we have widespread water pollution and soil/land pollution that results in the death of most aquatic eggs and juvenile stages of the life of fin fish and shell fish on the one hand, whilst, on the other hand, agricultural land contaminated with oil spills becomes dangerous for farming, even where they continue to produce significant yields."[4]

The implication inherent in this description is that pollution controls applied by foreign companies in Nigeria were much laxer than those in developed nations.

Should a multinational feel free to pollute in a developing nation? (To do so hardly seems ethical.) Is there a danger that amoral management might move production to a developing nation precisely because costly pollution controls are not required, and the company is therefore free to despoil the environment and perhaps endanger local people in its quest to lower production costs and gain a competitive advantage? What is the right and moral thing to do in such circumstances? Pollute to gain an economic advantage, or make sure that foreign subsidiaries adhere to common standards regarding pollution controls?

A Corporate Right to Pollute?

Asarco is a U.S.-based subsidiary of the giant Mexican mining conglomerate Grupo Mexico. Asarco has copper mining operations near the towns of Hayden and Winkelman in Arizona. According to some documents dating back to 1912, the original operator of the property was granted special considerations to discharge a "limitless amount of smoke, dust and fumes" without the threat of being responsible for the consequences. Moving forward to May 2005, the powerful American United Steelworkers union is backing residents of Hayden and Winkelman as they fight a legal battle with the Mexican owner. Asarco has gone to court in Arizona to assert that it is obvious pollution would be evident in the immediate area surrounding the mine, and anybody who lives in the region is willfully exposing themselves to a risky situation and therefore has no claim against the operators producing any harm or effects.

These questions take on added importance because some parts of the environment are a public good that no one owns, but anyone can despoil. No one owns the atmosphere or the oceans, but polluting both, no matter where the pollution originates, harms all.[5] The atmosphere and oceans can be viewed as a global commons from which everyone benefits but for which no one is specifically responsible. In such cases, a phenomenon known as the *tragedy of the commons* becomes applicable. The tragedy of the commons occurs when a resource held in common by all, but owned by no one, is overused by individuals, resulting in its degradation.

In the modern world, corporations can contribute to the global tragedy of the commons by moving production to locations where they are free to pump pollutants into the atmosphere or dump them in oceans or rivers, thereby harming these valuable global commons. While such action may be legal, is it ethical? Again, such actions seem to violate basic societal notions of ethics and social responsibility.

Even though some developing countries have fewer restrictions on pollution, does that give companies the right to pollute there? Digital Vision/Getty Images.

CORRUPTION

As noted in Chapter 2, corruption has been a problem in almost every society in history, and it continues to be one today. There always have been and always will be corrupt government officials. International businesses can and have gained economic advantages by making payments to those officials. The Accompanying Country Focus looks at the controversy surrounding Acres International.

In 1997, the trade and finance ministers from the member states of the Organization for Economic Cooperation and Development (OECD) followed the U.S. lead and adopted the **Convention on Combating Bribery of Foreign Public Officials in International Business Transactions.**[6] The convention, which went into force in 1999, obliges member states to make the bribery of foreign public officials a criminal offence. The convention excludes facilitating payments made to expedite routine government action from the convention. To be truly effective, however, the convention must be translated into domestic law by each signatory nation, and that is still in process.

CONVENTION ON COMBATING BRIBERY OF FOREIGN PUBLIC OFFICIALS IN INTERNATIONAL BUSINESS TRANSACTIONS The convention obliges member states to make the bribery of foreign public officials a criminal offence.

While facilitating payments, or speed money, are excluded from both the Foreign Corrupt Practices Act and the OECD convention on bribery, the ethical implications of making such payments are unclear. In many countries, payoffs to government officials in the form of speed money are a part of life. One can argue that not investing because government officials demand speed money ignores the fact that such investment can bring substantial benefits to the local populace in terms of income and jobs. From a pragmatic standpoint, giving bribes, although a little evil, might be the price that must be paid to do a greater good (assuming the investment creates jobs where none existed and assuming the practice is not illegal). Several economists advocate this reasoning, suggesting that in the context of pervasive and cumbersome regulations in developing countries, corruption may improve efficiency and help growth! These economists theorize that in a country where preexisting political structures distort or limit the workings of the market mechanism, corruption in the form of black-marketeering, smuggling, and side payments to government bureaucrats to "speed up" approval for business investments may enhance welfare.[7]

In contrast, other economists have argued that corruption reduces the returns on business investment and leads to low economic growth.[8] In a country where corruption is common, unproductive bureaucrats who demand side payments for granting the enterprise permission to operate may siphon off the profits from a business activity. This reduces businesses' incentive to invest and may retard a country's economic growth rate.

COUNTRY FOCUS

ACRES INTERNATIONAL IN LESOTHO

In July 2004, after an investigation reaching back to events in the late 1980s, the World Bank publicly announced that they were officially laying sanctions against Acres International Limited. Acres, a Canadian engineering consulting firm based in Mississauga, Ontario, was found guilty of paying bribes to win contracts on a multibillion-dollar dam project in the tiny African country of Lesotho. The Lesotho High Court convicted Acres of bribery for paying nearly US$266,000 to Mr. Masupha Sole, the former chief executive of the Lesotho Highlands Water Project. Acres had mounted a defence that they were not responsible for the payments to Sole because Sole was bribed through an intermediary Acres had hired. Which begs the questions that not only do international companies have to behave ethically and according to the rules and regulations in the jurisdictions they operate, but they must also assure that any persons acting on their behalf as contract consultants or advisers, also behave ethically since the consequences may impinge on the parent firm. Sole, a Canadian-trained engineer (who was later sentenced to 18 years in prison) was the person Acres cast in the role of overseeing the $6-billion Lesotho Highlands Water Project. Publicly released court documents noted that Sole was reported as having passed the bribe money through Zalisiwonga Bam, a local engineer hired by Acres—a situation that the Lesotho Court later ruled was a ploy to disguise the bribe. Acres was not alone in being challenged as to its ethical practices—the French company Spie Batignolles and the Italian firm Impregilo also face disbarment from World Bank contracts. Germany's Lahmeyer International is also scheduled to go to trial over circumstances involving as many as 12 large foreign firms in a highly competitive bid for a project in which hundreds of millions of dollars was at stake to the winners.

What did it cost Acres, other than the obvious bad press throughout Canada and the international community? The World Bank imposed a three-year ineligibility period within which Acres would not be allowed to compete for contracts financed by the World Bank. Keeping in mind that this institution is actually five banks, including the International Bank for Reconstruction and Development, the International Development Association and the International Finance Corporation, such a penalty could be considered severe since Acres is the type of company that is specifically oriented to working on large development aid projects that are predominantly structured by NGOs like the World Bank. As this text goes to print, Acres is involved in the Bujagali Dam in Uganda and Nam Theun 2 Dam in Laos, both projects are scheduled to receive World Bank funding. Acres also participated in the large Three Gorges Dam Project in China.

Perceptions of "Corrupt Politicians" Effecting Exporters?

In the spring of 2005, daily headlines in every Canadian newspaper, Web site, and magazine were recounting events of the Gomery Inquiry, headed by Mr. Justice John H. Gomery (www.gomery.ca). The Gomery Inquiry is investigating the events surrounding the spending of an estimated $100 million on ad campaigns and events in Quebec. The "sponsorship scandal" as it is now called, broke in 2002 when federal Auditor General Sheila Fraser recommended that the RCMP should investigate how $1.6 million in federal government advertising contracts were distributed to Quebec-based agencies and consulting firms, which were supposed to use that money to convince voters to reject separatism and support federalism. When former Prime Minister Chretien appeared before the Gomery Inquiry in 2005, the CBC reported he ". . . vigorously defended the federal sponsorship as an important part of the battle against Quebec sovereigntists in the wake of the 1995 referendum." Despite Chretien's nobly expressed intentions, the media in June 2005 focused on events such as advertising executives pleading guilty to fraud charges and courtroom tales of how certain agencies pocketed millions for doing very little work Various Canadian taxpayer groups sought public forums to explain how outraged they were that government money was wasted. Why would students of international business be worried about these revelations being recounted in the media in Canada and throughout the world?

First, Canada is an exporting nation. As you learned from the first three chapters, exporting leads our economy. Our ability to be competitive exporters depends on several perceptions held by international customers, and certain influences in the economic environment. As a country that is highly regarded by many nations for the activities of our Armed Forces as peacekeepers, coupled with the comparatively polite way that Canadian tourists behave abroad, Canada has enjoyed favourable and confident opinions by nations around the globe. Political scandals based on unethical dealings and played out daily in the Gomery hearings, raise the concern of international business-people dealing with Canada.

If the government appears to have difficulty passing legislation (as we saw in the spring of 2005 when an alliance of the Conservatives and the Bloc forced a tie in the House of Commons on an important budget bill), it causes international currency traders to be concerned. And if currency traders are concerned, they will sell their Canadian dollars, causing the value of the Canadian dollar to fall, as it did in May 2005. On announcement that the budget was passed at the end of May (the Speaker of the House broke the tie by voting for the government), the Canadian dollar rose on world currency markets the next day.

While it may be irritating to some nationalistic Canadians that the value of our currency rises and falls on the opinions held by non-Canadians, it is a reality of international business and the consequences are challenging to deal with. A low Canadian dollar, which we had for most of 2002 and 2003 (before it began rising in 2004) has always been considered good for the Canadian economy in respect of the many companies that earn their income exporting products derived from our abundant resources. A low dollar is also good for our tourism industry and makes Canada an attractive destination compared to more expensive tourist attractions in the U.S. There are thousands of communities and hundreds of thousands of Canadians who depend on tourist dollars from Newfoundland to the Northwest Territories and every spot in between.

A high Canadian dollar, which we have had in 2004 and parts of 2005 has been challenging for exporters and tough for government bond raising (as will be explained below) but good for Canadians who make their business importing products and component parts that are then manufactured and sold for a higher profit because their importing costs have been lower. If the high dollar is eroded due to political ethical scandals, the decline in the purchasing power of our currency could effect thousands of small to medium-sized enterprises (SMEs) that import products worldwide, and we should remember that most business is indeed carried out by SMEs.

Another reason for concern about how the dollar could be effected by an ethics scandal lies with the bond market. Canada, like many large economies, raises money for the federal government by floating bonds on the foreign debt markets. This money has a significant role to play in how the government budget can be forecast, and determines to what extent the government spends money on education, health care, etc. If foreign investors lose confidence in the ability of the Canadian government to govern, which in turn effects the chance the bonds might not be payable on maturity, then the price of the bonds falls and this negatively effects the ability of the government to count on these amounts when they are planning national revenue.

Given the debate and the complexity of this issue, one again might conclude that generalization is difficult and the demand for speed money creates a genuine ethical dilemma. Yes, corruption is bad, and yes, it may harm a country's economic development, but yes, there are also cases where side payments to government officials can remove the bureaucratic barriers to investments that create jobs. However, this pragmatic stance ignores the fact that corruption tends to corrupt both the bribe giver and the bribe taker. Corruption feeds on itself, and once an individual starts down the road of corruption, pulling back may be difficult if not impossible. This argument strengthens the ethical case for never engaging in corruption, no matter how compelling the benefits might seem.

MORAL OBLIGATIONS

Multinational corporations have power that comes from their control over resources and their ability to move production from country to country. Although that power is constrained not only by laws and regulations, but also by the discipline of the market and the competitive process, it is nevertheless substantial. Some moral philosophers argue that with power comes the social responsibility for multinationals to give something back to the societies that enable them to prosper and grow. The concept of **social responsibility** refers to the idea that businesspeople should consider the social consequences of economic actions when making business decisions, and that there should be a presumption in favour of decisions that have both good economic and social consequences.[9] In its purest form, social responsibility can be supported for its own sake simply because it is the right way for a business to behave. Advocates of this approach argue that businesses, particularly large successful businesses, need to recognize their *noblesse oblige* and give something back to the societies that have made their success possible. *Noblesse oblige* is a French term that refers to honourable and benevolent behavior considered the responsibility of people of high (noble) birth. In a business setting, it is taken to mean benevolent behaviour that is the responsibility of *successful* enterprises. This has long been recognized by many businesspeople, resulting in a substantial and venerable history of corporate giving to society and in businesses making social investments designed to enhance the welfare of the communities in which they operate.

SOCIAL RESPONSIBILITY
The idea that businesspeople should consider the social consequences of economic actions when making business decisions.

However, there are examples of multinationals that have abused their power for private gain. The most famous historic example relates to one of the earliest multinationals, the British East India Company. Established in 1600, the East India Company grew to dominate the entire Indian subcontinent in the nineteenth century. At the height of its power, the company deployed over 40 warships, possessed the largest standing army in the world, was the de facto ruler of India's 240 million people, and even hired its own church bishops, extending its dominance into the spiritual realm.[10]

Power itself is morally neutral. It is how power is used that matters. It can be used in a positive way to increase social welfare, which is ethical, or it can be used in a manner that is ethically and morally suspect. Consider the case of News Corporation, one of the largest media conglomerates in the world. The power of media companies derives from their ability to shape public perceptions by the material they choose to publish. News Corporation founder and CEO Rupert Murdoch has long considered China to be one of the most promising media markets in the world and has sought permission to expand News Corporation's operations in China, particularly the satellite broadcasting operations of Star TV. Some critics believe that Murdoch used the power of News Corporation in an unethical way to attain this objective.

Some multinationals have acknowledged a moral obligation to use their power to enhance social welfare in the communities where they do business. BP, one of the world's largest oil companies, has made it part of the company policy to undertake "social investments" in the countries where it does business.[11] In Algeria, BP has been investing in a major project to develop gas fields near the desert town of Salah. When the company noticed the lack of clean water in Salah, it built two desalination plants to provide drinking water for the local community and distributed containers to residents so they could take water from the plants to their homes. There was no economic reason for BP to make this social investment, but the company believes it is morally obligated to use its power in constructive ways. The action, while a small thing for BP, is a very important thing for the local community.

ETHICAL DILEMMAS

The ethical obligations of a multinational corporation toward employment conditions, human rights, corruption, environmental pollution, and the use of power are not always clear cut. There may be no agreement about accepted ethical principles. From an international business perspective, some argue that what is ethical depends upon one's cultural perspective.[12] In the United States, it is considered acceptable to execute murderers, but in many cultures this is not acceptable–execution is viewed as an affront to human dignity and the death penalty is outlawed. Many Americans find this attitude very strange, but many Europeans and a significant percentage of Canadians find the American approach barbaric. For a more business-oriented example, consider the practice of "gift giving" between the parties to a business negotiation. While this is considered right and proper behaviour in many Asian cultures, some Westerners view the practice as a form of bribery, and therefore unethical, particularly if the gifts are substantial. However Canadian businesspeople, who are very multiculturally oriented, are sometimes quite understanding of the role of gift-giving in various cultures and will replicate those customs when they meet and greet people from around the globe. Some people humorously accuse Canadians of going too far in handing out Inuit stone carvings and candy gifts made from maple syrup, which was a trend initiated by many participants of the "Team Canada" trade missions in the 1990s.

Managers must confront very real ethical dilemmas. For example, imagine that a visiting American executive finds that a foreign subsidiary in a poor nation has hired a 12-year-old girl to work on a factory floor. Appalled to find that the subsidiary is using child labour in direct violation of the company's own ethical code, the American instructs the local manager to replace the child with an adult. The local manager dutifully complies. The girl, an orphan, who is the only breadwinner for herself and her 6-year-old brother, is unable to find another job, so in desperation she turns to prostitution. Two years later she dies of AIDS. Meanwhile, her brother takes up begging. He encounters the American while begging outside the local McDonald's. Oblivious that this was the man responsible for his fate, the boy begs him for money. The American quickens his pace and walks rapidly past the outstretched hand into the McDonald's, where he orders a quarter-pound cheeseburger with fries and cold milk shake. A year later the boy contracts tuberculosis and dies.

Had the visiting American understood the gravity of the girl's situation, would he still have requested her replacement? Perhaps not! Would it have been better, therefore, to stick with the status quo and allow the girl to continue working? Probably not, because that would have violated the reasonable prohibition against child labour found in the company's own ethical code. What then would have been the right thing to do? What was the obligation of the executive given this ethical dilemma?

There is no easy answer to these questions. That is the nature of **ethical dilemmas**–they are situations in which none of the available alternatives seems ethically acceptable.[13] In this case, employing child labour was not acceptable, but given that she was employed, neither was denying the child her only source of income. What the American executive needed, what all managers need, was a moral compass, or perhaps an ethical algorithm, that would guide him through such an ethical dilemma to find an acceptable solution. Later in this chapter we will outline what such a moral compass, or ethical algorithm, might look like. For now, it is enough to note that ethical dilemmas exist

ETHICAL DILEMMA
A situation in which there is no ethically acceptable solution.

because many real-world decisions are complex, difficult to frame, and involve first-, second-, and third-order consequences that are hard to quantify. Doing the right thing, or even knowing what the right thing might be, is often far from easy.

THE ROOTS OF UNETHICAL BEHAVIOUR

Examples abound of managers behaving in a manner that might be judged unethical in an international business setting. A group of American investors became interested in restoring the SS United States, at one time a luxurious ocean liner.[14] The first step in the restoration project involved stripping the ship of its asbestos lining. Asbestos is a highly toxic material that produces a fine dust that when inhaled can cause scarring and result in lung disease, cancer, and death. Accordingly, very tight standards in developed countries govern the removal of asbestos. A bid from a U.S. company, based on the standards established in the United States, priced the job at more than $100 million. A company in the Ukraine offered to do the job for $2 million, so the ship was towed to the Ukrainian port of Sevastopol. By agreeing to do the work for $2 million, it is implied that the Ukrainian company could not have adopted standards even remotely close to those required in the United States. As a consequence, its employees were at a significant risk of developing asbestos-related disease. If this was the case, the desire to limit costs had resulted in the American investors acting in an unethical manner, for they were knowingly rewarding a company that exposed its workers to a significant health risk.

Why do managers behave in a manner that is unethical? There is no simple answer to this question, for the causes are complex, but a few generalizations can be made (see Figure 4.1).[15] First, business ethics are not divorced from *personal ethics,* which are the generally accepted principles of right and wrong governing the conduct of individuals. As individuals, we are typically taught that it is wrong to lie and cheat–it is unethical–and that it is right to behave with integrity and honour, and to stand up for what we believe to be right and true. This is generally true across societies. The personal ethical code that guides our behaviour comes from a number of sources, including our parents, our schools, our religion, and the media. Our personal ethical code exerts a profound influence on the way we behave as businesspeople. An individual with a strong sense of personal ethics is less likely to behave in an unethical manner in a business setting. It follows that the first step to establishing a strong sense of business ethics is for a society to emphasize strong personal ethics.

FIGURE 4.1
Determinants of Ethical Behaviour

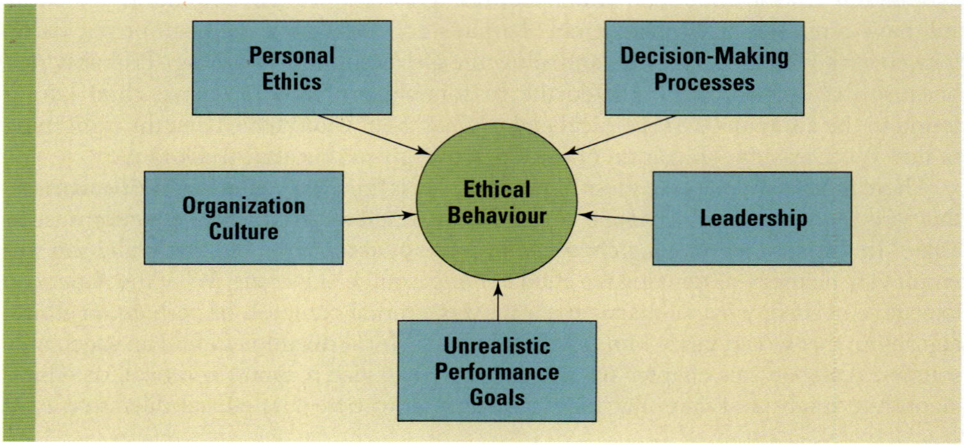

Home-country managers working abroad in multinational firms (expatriate managers) may experience more than the usual degree of pressure to violate their personal ethics. They are away from their ordinary social context and supporting culture, and they are psychologically and geographically distant from the parent company. They may be based in a culture that does not place the same value on ethical norms important in the manager's home country, and they may be surrounded by local employees who have less rigorous ethical standards. The parent company may pressure expatriate managers to meet unrealistic goals that can only be fulfilled by cutting corners or acting unethically. For example, to meet centrally mandated performance goals, expatriate managers might give bribes to win contracts or might implement working conditions and environmental controls that are below minimal acceptable standards. Local managers might encourage the expatriate to adopt such behaviour. And due to its geographical distance, the parent company may be unable to see how expatriate managers are meeting goals, or may choose not to see how they are doing so, allowing such behaviour to flourish and persist.

Also, many studies of unethical behaviour in a business setting have concluded that businesspeople sometimes do not realize they are behaving unethically, primarily because they simply fail to ask, Is this decision or action ethical?[16] Instead, they apply a straightforward business calculus to what they perceive to be a business decision, forgetting that the decision may also have an important ethical dimension. The fault lies in processes that do not incorporate ethical considerations into business decision making. Those decisions were probably made on the basis of good economic logic. Subcontractors were probably chosen on the basis of business variables such as cost, delivery, and product quality, and the key managers simply failed to ask, How does this subcontractor treat its workforce? If they thought about the question at all, they probably reasoned that it was the subcontractor's concern, not theirs. (For an example of a business decision that may have been unethical, see the Management Focus describing Pfizer's decision to test an experimental drug on children suffering from meningitis in Nigeria.)

Unfortunately, the climate in some businesses does not encourage people to think through the ethical consequences of business decisions. This brings us to the third cause of unethical behaviour in businesses–an organizational culture that deemphasizes business ethics, reducing all decisions to the purely economic. The term **organization culture** refers to the values and norms that are shared among employees of an organization. You will recall from Chapter 3 that values are abstract ideas about what a group believes to be good, right, and desirable, while norms are the social rules and guidelines that prescribe appropriate behaviour in particular situations. Just as societies have cultures, so do business organizations. Together, values and norms shape the culture of a business organization, and that culture has an important influence on the ethics of business decision making.

ORGANIZATION CULTURE The values and norms shared among an organization's employees.

Author Robert Bryce has explained how the organization culture at now-bankrupt multinational energy company Enron was built on values that emphasized greed and deception.[17] According to Bryce, the tone was set by top managers who engaged in self-dealing to enrich themselves and their own families. Bryce tells how former Enron CEO Kenneth Lay made sure his own family benefitted handsomely from Enron. Much of Enron's corporate travel business was handled by a travel agency part owned by Lay's sister. When an internal auditor recommended that the company could do better by using another travel agency, he soon found himself out of a job. In 1997, Enron acquired a company owned by Kenneth Lay's son, Mark Lay, which was trying to establish a business trading paper and pulp products. At the time, Mark Lay and another company he controlled were targets of a federal criminal investigation of bankruptcy fraud and embezzlement. As part of the deal, Enron hired

MANAGEMENT FOCUS

TESTING DRUGS IN THE DEVELOPING WORLD

The drug development process is long, risky, and expensive. It can take ten years and cost in excess of $500 million to develop a new drug. Moreover, between 80 and 90 percent of drug candidates fail in clinical trials. Pharmaceutical companies rely upon a handful of successes to pay for their failures. Among the most successful of the world's pharmaceutical companies is New York-based Pfizer. Given the risks and costs of developing a new drug, pharmaceutical companies will jump at opportunities to reduce them, and in 1996 Pfizer thought it saw one.

Pfizer had been developing a novel antibiotic, Trovan, that was proving to be useful in treating a wide range of bacterial infections. Wall Street analysts were predicting that Trovan could be a blockbuster, one of a handful of drugs capable of generating sales of more than $1 billion a year. In 1996, Pfizer was pushing to submit data on Trovan's efficacy to the Food and Drug Administration (FDA) for review. A favourable review would allow Pfizer to sell the drug in the United States, the world's largest market. Pfizer wanted the drug to be approved for both adults and children, but it was having trouble finding sufficient numbers of sick children in the United States to test the drug on. Then in early 1996, a researcher at Pfizer read about an emerging epidemic of bacterial meningitis in Kano, Nigeria. This seemed like a quick way to test the drug on a large number of sick children.

Within weeks, a team of six doctors had flown to Kano and were administering the drug, in oral form, to children with meningitis. Desperate for help, Nigerian authorities had given the go-ahead for Pfizer to give the drug to children (the epidemic would ultimately kill nearly 16 000 people). Over the next few weeks, Pfizer treated 198 children. The protocol called for half the patients to get Trovan and half to get a comparison antibiotic already approved for the treatment of children. After a few weeks, the Pfizer team left, the experiment complete. Trovan seemed to be about as effective and safe as the already approved antibiotic. The data from the trial were put into a package with data from other trials of Trovan and delivered to the FDA.

Questions were soon raised about the nature of Pfizer's experiment. Allegations charged that the Pfizer team kept children on Trovan, even after they failed to show a response to the drug, instead of switching them quickly to another drug. The result, according to critics, was that some children died who might have been saved had they been taken off Trovan sooner. Questions were also raised about the safety of the oral formulation of Trovan, which some doctors feared might lead to arthritis in children. Fifteen children who took Trovan showed signs of joint pain during the experiment, three times the rate of children taking the other antibiotic. Then there were questions about consent. The FDA requires that patient (or parent) consent be given before patients are enrolled in clinical trials, no matter where in the world the trials are conducted. Critics argue that in the rush to get the trial established in Nigeria, Pfizer did not follow proper procedures, and that many parents of the infected children did not know their children were participating in a trial for an experimental drug. Many of the parents were illiterate, could not read the consent forms, and had to rely upon the questionable translation of the Nigerian nursing staff. Pfizer rejected these charges and contends that it did nothing wrong.

Trovan was approved by the FDA for use in adults in 1997, but it was never approved for use in children. Launched in 1998, by 1999 there were reports that up to 140 patients in Europe had suffered liver damage after taking Trovan. The FDA subsequently restricted the use of Trovan to those cases where the benefits of treatment outweighed the risk of liver damage. European regulators banned sales of the drug. In 2003, two dozen Nigerian families sued Pfizer in a federal court in New York. The families claim their children either died or were injured because Pfizer did not adequately inform them of the risks and alternatives for treatment with Trovan. The case is still ongoing.

Did Pfizer behave unethically by rushing to take advantage of an epidemic in Nigeria to test an experimental drug on children? Should it have been less opportunistic and proceeded more carefully? Were corners cut with regard to patient consent in the rush to establish a trial? And did doctors keep patients on Trovan too long, when they should have switched them to another medication? Is it ethical to test an experimental drug on children in a crisis setting in the developing world, where the overall standard of health care is so much lower than in the developed world and proper protocols might not be followed? These questions are all raised by the Pfizer case, and they remain unanswered, by the company at least.

Source: Joe Stephens, "Where Profits and Lives Hang in the Balance," *Washington Post,* December 17, 2000, p. A1; Andra Brichacek, "What Price Corruption?" *Pharmaceutical Executive* 21, no. 11 (November 2001), p. 94; and Scott Hensley, "Court Revives Suit against Pfizer on Nigeria Study," *The Wall Street Journal,* October 13, 2004, p. B4.

Conrad Black, who renounced his Canadian citizenship to become "Lord Black of Crossharbour," has gone from being a media baron to a media target. CP/Toronto Globe and Mail (Deborah Baic).

Mark Lay as an executive with a three-year contract that guaranteed him at least $1 million in pay over that period, plus options to purchase about 20 000 shares of Enron. Bryce also details how Lay's grown daughter used an Enron jet to transport her king-sized bed to France. With Kenneth Lay as an example, it is perhaps not surprising that self-dealing soon became endemic at Enron. The most notable example was Chief Financial Officer Andrew Fastow, who set up "off balance sheet" partnerships that not only hid Enron's true financial condition from investors, but also paid tens of millions of dollars directly to Fastow. (Fastow was subsequently indicted by the government for criminal fraud and went to jail.)

With the Enron case in the U.S. now a few years old, persons studying examples of corruption at the highest levels of a large company have lots of material in the current situation being played out in the Canadian newspapers about the challenges facing media baron Conrad Black. Famous for his personal excesses in entertainment, houses, lavish events, and self-aggrandizing portraits of himself and his wife, Black, or as he became known in England, Lord Black of Crossharbour, has most recently been accused of removing boxes from the offices of a company of which he is no longer a director. After security tapes were played in court, Black said he would bring back the boxes, claiming in his defence that they contained personal items and their removal did not violate a court order forbidding him to remove items without the approval of a court-appointed inspector. Such a "fall from grace" has been recounted throughout the months in late 2004 and early 2005 as the story of Black's crumbling empire crosses courtrooms in Canada, the U.S., and Europe.

In 1999, Conrad Black (born and educated as a Canadian) saw his influence and business in the U.K. rewarded with a nomination to be appointed a peer of the realm, essentially, the British government intended to make him Lord Black. Prime Minister Jean Chretien, who had, over the years, been often criticized in Black's many newspapers, sought to thwart Black's appointment. Citing a decades old Canadian regulation, Chretien said regulations forbade foreign governments from granting

ANOTHER PERSPECTIVE

Ethical questions of foreign drug testing

Increasingly, U.S. drug companies are testing their drugs overseas. Popular sites are Russia, Poland, and Hungary. This is largely because they can find trial participants easily and the process is cheaper than in the United States because there are fewer governmental restrictions on protocols, the medical standards are high, and well-trained clinical trial investigators earn as little as a few hundred dollars a month. Thus, the testing goes more quickly and costs less. The company's goal is to determine if the drug is effective, and if so, get it to the market. When the trials are successful and the drug is marketed in developed countries, what if any obligation does the drug company have to the people who participated in the trials? Often the drug company won't market the drug in their country. Should drug companies do "parachute research," where they drop in, do their testing, and then leave? Or do they have a moral responsibility to continue treatment? Is there a difference if the drug in question is life-sustaining, such as an AIDS drug, or life-improving but not life-prolonging?

honours to Canadians that carry a title or privilege. Black unsuccessfully challenged the ruling in Canadian courts and responded by renouncing his citizenship and accepted the British title in 2001.

What precipitated the downfall of the newspaper mogul? In 2003, Black announced he would agree to resign as CEO of U.S.-based newspaper conglomerate Hollinger International–a very large company with much influence in the newspaper and magazine business. Black's resignation followed findings of a special committee that he and other senior Hollinger executives received millions in payments that were not authorized according to regulations of the various companies he held, and the regulations for corporate governance within the jurisdiction his companies operated. In 2004 Black was sued by investor groups, and others, claiming that Black and some of his senior managers participated in highly inappropriate financial dealings and audit fraud regarding circumstances at the papers owned by his closely held parent company. In terms of corporate ethics, most countries have rules and regulations saying you can't just take money out of a publicly incorporated company, even if you are the CEO. Black's argument, explained in a more complicated way in court, was "its my money, I can do with it what I want," to which the courts essentially said, "no, it is also the money of the people who buy shares in your company, and you stole from them." Black, who is also under criminal investigations from U.S. regulators, is presently (June 2005) fighting in Ontario courts to deflect further restrictions that may require him to surrender documents and grant access to inspectors from an accounting firm that has been given the task of doing a forensic audit.

The fourth cause of unethical behaviour has already been hinted at–it is pressure from the parent company to meet unrealistic performance goals that can be attained only by cutting corners or acting in an unethical manner. Again, Bryce discusses how this may have occurred at Enron. Lay's successor as CEO, Jeff Skilling, put a performance evaluation system in place that weeded out 15 percent of underperformers every six months. This created a pressure-cooker culture with a myopic focus on short-run performance, and some executives and energy traders responded to that pressure by falsifying their performance–inflating the value of trades, for example–to make it look as if they were performing better than was actually the case.

The lesson from the Enron debacle is that an organizational culture can legitimize behaviour that society would judge as unethical, particularly when this is mixed with a focus on unrealistic performance goals, such as maximizing short-term economic performance, no matter what the costs. In such circumstances, there is a greater than average probability that managers will violate their own personal ethics and engage in unethical behaviour. By the same token, an organization culture can do just the opposite and reinforce the need for ethical behaviour. At Conrad Black's companies, for example, Black, propagated a set of values contrary to accepted Canadian corporate culture. These values, which shape the way business is conducted both within and by the corporation, have an important ethical component. Among other things, they stress the need for confidence in and respect for people, open communication, and concern for the individual employee.

The Enron and Black examples suggest a fifth root cause of unethical behaviour—leadership. Leaders help to establish the culture of an organization, and they set the example that others follow. Other employees in a business often take their cue from business leaders, and if those leaders do not behave in an ethical manner, they might not either. It is not what leaders say that matters, but what they do. Enron, for example, had a code of ethics that Kenneth Lay himself often referred to, but Lay's own actions to enrich family members spoke louder than any words.

PHILOSOPHICAL APPROACHES TO ETHICS

We shall look at several different approaches to business ethics here, beginning with some that can best be described as straw men, which either deny the value of business ethics or apply the concept in a very unsatisfactory way. Having discussed, and dismissed, the straw men, we then move on to consider approaches that are favoured by most moral philosophers and form the basis for current models of ethical behaviour in international businesses.

STRAW MEN

Straw men approaches to business ethics are raised by business ethics scholars primarily to demonstrate that they offer inappropriate guidelines for ethical decision making in a multinational enterprise. Four such approaches to business ethics are commonly discussed in the literature. These approaches can be characterized as the Friedman doctrine, cultural relativism, the righteous moralist, and the naive immoralist. All of these approaches have some inherent value, but all are unsatisfactory in important ways. Nevertheless, sometimes companies adopt these approaches.

The Friedman Doctrine Nobel Prize-winning economist Milton Friedman wrote an article in 1970 that has since become a classic straw man that business ethics scholars outline only to then tear down.[18] Friedman's basic position is that the only social responsibility of business is to increase profits, so long as the company stays within the rules of law. He explicitly rejects the idea that businesses should undertake social expenditures beyond those mandated by the law and required for the efficient running of a business. For example, his arguments suggest that improving working conditions beyond the level required by the law *and* necessary to maximize employee productivity will reduce profits and are therefore not appropriate. His belief is that a firm should maximize its profits because that is the way to maximize the returns that accrue to the owners of the firm, its stockholders. If stockholders then wish to use the proceeds to make social investments, that is their right, according to Friedman, but managers of the firm should not make that decision for them.

Although Friedman is talking about social responsibility, rather than business ethics per se, most business ethics scholars equate social responsibility with ethical behaviour, and thus believe Friedman is also arguing against business ethics. However, the assumption that Friedman is arguing against ethics is not quite true, for Friedman does state,

> There is one and only one social responsibility of business—to use its resources and engage in activities designed to increase its profits so long as it stays within the rules of the game, which is to say that it engages in open and free competition without deception or fraud.[19]

In other words, Friedman states that businesses should behave in an ethical manner and not engage in deception and fraud.

Nevertheless, Friedman's arguments do break down under examination. This is particularly true in the realm of international business where the "rules of the game" are not well-established or differ substantially from country to county. Consider again the case of sweatshop labour. Child labour may not be against the law in a developing nation, and maximizing productivity may not require that a multinational firm stop using child labour in that country, but it is still immoral to use child labour because the practice conflicts with widely held views about what is the right and proper thing to do. Similarly, there may be no rules against pollution in a developed nation and spending money on pollution control may reduce the profit rate of the firm, but generalized notions of morality would hold that it is still unethical to dump toxic pollutants into rivers or foul the air with gas releases. In addition to the local consequences of such pollution, which may have serious health effects for the surrounding population, there is also a global consequence as pollutants degrade those two global commons so important to us all–the atmosphere and the oceans.

CULTURAL RELATIVISM The belief that ethics are culturally determined and that firms should adopt the ethics of the cultures in which they operate.

Cultural Relativism Another straw man often raised by business ethics scholars is **cultural relativism,** which is the belief that ethics are nothing more than the reflection of a culture–all ethics are culturally determined–and that accordingly, a firm should adopt the ethics of the culture in which it is operating.[20] This approach is often summarized by the maxim *when in Rome do as the Romans do*. As with Friedman's approach, cultural relativism does not stand up to a closer look. At its extreme, cultural relativism suggests that if a culture supports slavery, it is OK to use slave labour in a country. Clearly it is not. Cultural relativism implicitly rejects the idea that universal notions of morality transcend different cultures, but, as we shall argue later in the chapter, some universal notions of morality are found across cultures.

While dismissing cultural relativism in its most sweeping form, some ethicists argue there is residual value in this approach.[21] As we noted in Chapter 3, societal values and norms do vary from culture to culture, customs do differ, so it might follow that certain business practices are ethical in one country, but not another. Indeed, the facilitating payments allowed in the U.S. Foreign Corrupt Practices Act can be seen as an acknowledgment that in some countries, the payment of speed money to government officials is necessary to get business done, and if not ethically desirable, it is at least ethically acceptable.

However, not all ethicists or companies agree with this pragmatic view. As noted earlier, oil company BP explicitly states it will not make facilitating payments, no matter what the prevailing cultural norms are. In 2002, BP enacted a zero-tolerance policy for facilitation payments, primarily on the basis that such payments are a low-level form of corruption, and thus cannot be justified because corruption corrupts both the bribe giver and the bribe taker, and perpetuates the corrupt system. As BP notes on its Web site, as a result of its zero-tolerance policy:

> Some oil product sales in Vietnam involved inappropriate commission payments to the managers of customers in return for placing orders with BP. These were stopped during 2002 with the result that BP failed to win certain tenders with potential profit totalling $300k. In addition, two sales managers resigned over the issue. The business, however, has recovered using more traditional sales methods and has exceeded its targets at year-end.
>
> BP in India has been working in an environment where facilitation payments are commonplace. The business unit took measures not only to eliminate direct facilitation payments but also extended the policy application to agents, consultants, sales distributors, and suppliers. Workshops covering suppliers, distributors, and agents were held and key third parties provided signed statements confirming their compliance with our ethics policy. Contracts with three distributors and one freight agent were terminated for unethical

behaviour. The main lesson learnt was that perseverance is eventually rewarded despite delays. A plant was connected to the national grid, an office co-location project was approved, and a major income tax refund was received–all without making the facilitation payments that would have been required in the past.[22]

BP's experience suggests that companies should not use cultural relativism as an argument for justifying behaviour that is clearly based upon suspect ethical grounds, even if that behaviour is both legal and routinely accepted in the country where the company is doing business.

The Righteous Moralist A **righteous moralist** claims that a multinational's home-country standards of ethics are the appropriate ones for companies to follow in foreign countries. This approach is typically associated with managers from developed nations. While this seems reasonable at first blush, the approach can create problems. Consider the following example: A North American bank manager was sent to Italy and was appalled to learn that the local branch's accounting department recommended grossly underreporting the bank's profits for income tax purposes.[23] The manager insisted that the bank report its earnings accurately, North American style. When he was called by the Italian tax department to the firm's tax hearing, he was told the firm owed three times as much tax as it had paid, reflecting the department's standard assumption that each firm underreports its earnings by two-thirds. Despite his protests, the new assessment stood. In this case, the righteous moralist has run into a problem caused by the prevailing cultural norms in the country where he is doing business. How should he respond? The righteous moralist would argue for maintaining the position, while a more pragmatic view might be that in this case, the right thing to do is to follow the prevailing cultural norms, since there is a big penalty for not doing so.

RIGHTEOUS MORALIST claims that a multinational's home-country standards of ethics are the appropriate ones to follow in foreign countries.

The main criticism of the righteous moralist approach is that its proponents go too far. While there are some universal moral principles that should not be violated, it does not always follow that the appropriate thing to do is adopt home-country standards. For example, Canadian laws set down strict guidelines with regard to minimum wage and working conditions. Does this mean it is ethical to apply the same guidelines in a foreign country, paying people the same as they are paid in Canada, providing the same benefits and working conditions? Probably not, because doing so might nullify the reason for investing in that country and therefore deny locals the benefits of inward investment by the multinational. Clearly, a more nuanced approach is needed.

The Naive Immoralist A **naive immoralist** asserts that if a manager of a multinational sees that firms from other nations are not following ethical norms in a host nation, that manager should not either. The classic example to illustrate the approach is known as the drug lord problem. In one variant of this problem, a Canadian mine manager in Congo routinely pays off the local tribal chief to guarantee that his plant will not be sabotaged and that none of his employees will be kidnapped. The manager argues that such payments are ethically defensible because everyone is doing it.

NAIVE IMMORALIST asserts that if a manager of a multinational sees that firms from other nations are not following ethical norms in a host nation, that manager should not either.

The objection is twofold. First, to simply say that an action is ethically justified if everyone is doing it is not sufficient. If firms in a country routinely employ 12-year-olds and makes them work ten-hour days, is it therefore ethically defensible to do the same? Obviously not, and the company does have a clear choice. It does not have to abide by local practices, and it can decide not to invest in a country where the practices are particularly odious. Second, the multinational must recognize that it does have the ability to change the prevailing practice in a country. It can use its power for a positive moral purpose. This is what BP is doing by adopting a zero-tolerance policy with regard to facilitating payments. BP is stating that the prevailing practice of making facilitating payments in countries such as India is ethically wrong, and it is incumbent upon the company to use its power to try to change the standard. While some might argue that such an approach smells of moral imperialism and a lack of cultural sensitivity, if it is consistent with widely accepted moral standards in the global community, it may be ethically justified.

To return to the mine in Congo problem, an argument can be made that it is ethically defensible to make such payments, not because everyone else is doing so but because not doing so would cause greater harm (i.e., the tribal chief might seek retribution and engage in killings and kidnappings). Another solution to the problem is to refuse to invest in a country where the rule of law is so weak that tribal chiefs can demand protection money. This solution, however, is also imperfect, for it might mean denying the law-abiding citizens of that country the benefits associated with inward investment by the multinational (i.e., jobs, income, greater economic growth and welfare). Clearly, the tribal chief problem constitutes one of those intractable ethical dilemmas where there is no obvious right solution, and managers need a moral compass to help them find an acceptable solution to the dilemma.

UTILITARIAN AND KANTIAN ETHICS

UTILITARIAN APPROACHES to ethics hold that the moral worth of actions or practices is determined by their consequences.

The utilitarian approach to business ethics dates to philosophers such as David Hume (1771–1776), Jeremy Bentham (1784–1832), and John Stuart Mill (1806–1873). **Utilitarian approaches** to ethics hold that the moral worth of actions or practices is determined by their consequences.[24] An action is judged to be desirable if it leads to the best possible balance of good consequences over bad consequences. Utilitarianism is committed to the maximization of good and the minimization of harm. Utilitarianism recognizes that actions have multiple consequences, some of which are good in a social sense and some of which are harmful. As a philosophy for business ethics, it focuses attention on the need to carefully weigh all of the social benefits and costs of a business action and to pursue only those actions where the benefits outweigh the costs. The best decisions, from a utilitarian perspective, are those that produce the greatest good for the greatest number of people.

Many businesses have adopted specific tools such as cost-benefit analysis and risk assessment that are firmly rooted in a utilitarian philosophy. Managers often weigh the benefits and costs of an action before deciding whether to pursue it. A diamond exploration company considering drilling in the NWT wildlife preserve must weigh the economic benefits of increased oil production and the creation of jobs against the costs of environmental degradation in a fragile ecosystem. An agricultural biotechnology company such as Saskatchewan Wheat Pool (SWP) must decide whether the benefits of genetically modified crops that produce natural pesticides outweigh the risks. The benefits include increased crop yields and reduced need for chemical fertilizers. The risks include the possibility that SWP's insect-resistant crops might make matters worse over time if insects evolve a resistance to the natural pesticides engineered into SWP's plants, rendering the plants vulnerable to a new generation of super bugs.

For all of its appeal, utilitarian philosophy does have some serious drawbacks as an approach to business ethics. One problem is measuring the benefits, costs, and risks of a course of action. In the case of a diamond exploration company considering drilling in NWT, how does one measure the potential harm done to the region's ecosystem? In the SWP example, how can one quantify the risk that genetically engineered crops might ultimately result in the evolution of super bugs that are resistant to the natural pesticide engineered into the crops? In general, utilitarian philosophers recognize that the measurement of benefits, costs, and risks is often not possible due to limited knowledge.

The second problem with utilitarianism is that the philosophy omits the consideration of justice. The action that produces the greatest good for the greatest number of people may result in the unjustified treatment of a minority. Such action cannot be ethical, precisely because it is unjust. For example, suppose that in the interests of keeping down health insurance costs, the government decides to screen people for the HIV virus and deny insurance coverage to those who are HIV positive. By reducing health costs, such action might produce significant benefits for a large number of people, but the action is unjust because it discriminates unfairly against a minority.

Kantian ethics are based on the philosophy of Immanuel Kant (1724–1804). **Kantian ethics** hold that people should be treated as ends and never purely as *means* to the ends of others. People are not instruments, like a machine. People have dignity and need to be respected as such. Employing people in sweatshops, making them work long hours for low pay in poor work conditions, is a violation of ethics, according to Kantian philosophy, because it treats people as mere cogs in a machine and not as conscious moral beings that have dignity. Although contemporary moral philosophers tend to view Kant's ethical philosophy as incomplete—for example, his system has no place for moral emotions or sentiments such as sympathy or caring—the notion that people should be respected and treated with dignity still resonates in the modern world.

Large grain elevators like the one shown here used to be called "Sentinels of the Prairies." These imposing structures are less common as transportation technology developments and international marketing practices change the way grain is marketed globally. CP /Regina Leader-Post (Roy Antal).

RIGHTS THEORIES

Developed in the twentieth century, **rights theories** recognize that human beings have fundamental rights and privileges that transcend national boundaries and cultures. Rights establish a minimum level of morally acceptable behaviour. One well-known definition of a fundamental right construes it as something that takes precedence over or "trumps" a collective good. Thus, we might say that the right to free speech is a fundamental right that takes precedence over all but the most compelling collective goals and overrides, for example, the interest of the state in civil harmony or moral consensus.[25] Moral theorists argue that fundamental human rights form the basis for the *moral compass* that managers should navigate by when making decisions that have an ethical component. More precisely, they should not pursue actions that violate these rights.

The notion that there are fundamental rights that transcend national borders and cultures was the underlying motivation for the United Nations **Universal Declaration of Human Rights,** which has been ratified by almost every country on the planet and lays down basic principles that should always be adhered to irrespective of the culture in which one is doing business.[26] Echoing Kantian ethics, Article 1 of this declaration states:

> Article 1: All human beings are born free and equal in dignity and rights. They are endowed with reason and conscience and should act towards one another in a spirit of brotherhood.

Article 23 of this declaration, which relates directly to employment, states:

1. Everyone has the right to work, to free choice of employment, to just and favourable conditions of work, and to protection against unemployment.

KANTIAN ETHICS hold that people should be treated as ends, and never purely as means to the ends of others.

RIGHTS THEORIES A twentieth century theory that recognizes that human beings have fundamental rights and privileges that transcend national boundaries and cultures.

THE UNIVERSAL DECLARATION OF HUMAN RIGHTS is a United Nations document that lays down the basic principles of human rights that should be adhered to.

2. Everyone, without any discrimination, has the right to equal pay for equal work.
3. Everyone who works has the right to just and favourable remuneration ensuring for himself and his family an existence worthy of human dignity, and supplemented, if necessary, by other means of social protection.
4. Everyone has the right to form and to join trade unions for the protection of his interests.

Clearly, the rights to "just and favourable work conditions," "equal pay for equal work," and remuneration that ensures an "existence worthy of human dignity" embodied in Article 23 imply that it is unethical to employ child labour in sweatshop settings and pay less than subsistence wages, even if that happens to be common practice in some countries. These are fundamental human rights that transcend national borders.

It is important to note that along with *rights* come *obligations*. Because we have the right to free speech, we are also obligated to make sure that we respect the free speech of others. The notion that people have obligations is stated in Article 29 of the Universal Declaration of Human Rights:

> Article 29: Everyone has duties to the community in which alone the free and full development of his personality is possible.

Within the framework of a theory of rights, certain people or institutions are obligated to provide benefits or services that secure the rights of others. Such obligations also fall upon more than one class of moral agent (a moral agent is any person or institution that is capable of moral action such as a government or corporation).

For example, to escape the high costs of toxic waste disposal in the West, in the late 1980s several firms shipped their waste in bulk to African nations, where it was disposed of at a much lower cost. In 1987, five European ships unloaded toxic waste containing dangerous poisons in Nigeria. Workers wearing sandals and shorts unloaded the barrels for $2.50 a day and placed them in a dirt lot in a residential area. They were not told about the contents of the barrels.[27] Who bears the obligation for protecting the rights of workers and residents to safety in a case like this? According to rights theorists, the obligation rests not on the shoulders of one moral agent, but on the shoulders of all moral agents whose actions might harm or contribute to the harm of the workers and residents. Thus, it was the obligation not just of the Nigerian government but also of the multinational firms that shipped the toxic waste to make sure it did no harm to residents and workers. In this case, both the government and the multinationals apparently failed to recognize their basic obligation to protect the fundamental human rights of others.

JUSTICE THEORIES

Justice theories focus on the attainment of a just distribution of economic goods and services. A **just distribution** is one that is considered fair and equitable. There is no one theory of justice, and several theories of justice conflict with each other in important ways.[28] Here we shall focus on one particular theory of justice that is both very influential and has important ethical implications. The theory is attributed to philosopher John Rawls.[29] Rawls argues that all economic goods and services should be distributed equally except when an unequal distribution would work to everyone's advantage.

JUST DISTRIBUTION
A distribution that is considered fair and equitable.

According to Rawls, valid principles of justice are those with which all persons would agree if they could freely and impartially consider the situation. Impartiality is guaranteed by a conceptual device that Rawls calls the *veil of ignorance*. Under the veil of ignorance, everyone is imagined to be ignorant of all of his or her particular characteristics, for example, race, sex, intelligence, nationality, family background, and special talents. Rawls then asks what system people would design under a veil of ignorance. Under these conditions, people would unanimously agree on two fundamental principles of justice.

The first principle is that each person be permitted the maximum amount of basic liberty compatible with a similar liberty for others. Rawls takes these to be political liberty (e.g., the right to vote), freedom of speech and assembly, liberty of conscience and freedom of thought, the freedom and right to hold personal property, and freedom from arbitrary arrest and seizure.

The second principle is that once equal basic liberty is assured, inequality in basic social goods–such as income and wealth distribution, and opportunities–is to be allowed *only* if such inequalities benefit everyone. Rawls accepts that inequalities can be just if the system that produces inequalities is to the advantage of everyone. More precisely, he formulates what he calls the *difference principle,* which is that inequalities are justified if they benefit the position of the least-advantaged person. So, for example, wide variations in income and wealth can be considered just if the market-based system that produces this unequal distribution also benefits the least-advantaged members of society. One can argue that a well-regulated, market-based economy and free trade, by promoting economic growth, benefit the least-advantaged members of society. In principle at least, the inequalities inherent in such systems are therefore just (in other words, the rising tide of wealth created by a market-based economy and free trade lifts all boats, even those of the most disadvantaged).

In the context of international business ethics, Rawls's theory creates an interesting perspective. Managers could ask themselves whether the policies they adopt in foreign operations would be considered just under Rawls's veil of ignorance. Is it just, for example, to pay foreign workers less than workers in the firm's home country? Rawls's theory would suggest it is, so long as the inequality benefits the least-advantaged members of the global society (which is what economic theory suggests). Alternatively, it is difficult to imagine that managers operating under a veil of ignorance would design a system where foreign employees were paid subsistence wages to work long hours in sweatshop conditions and where they were exposed to toxic materials. Such working conditions are clearly unjust in Rawls's framework, and therefore, it is unethical to adopt them. Similarly, operating under a veil of ignorance, most people would probably design a system that imparts some protection from environmental degradation to important global commons, such as the oceans, atmosphere, and tropical rain forests. To the extent that this is the case, it follows that it is unjust, and by extension unethical, for companies to pursue actions that contribute toward extensive degradation of these commons. Thus, Rawls's veil of ignorance is a conceptual tool that contributes to the moral compass that managers can use to help them navigate through difficult ethical dilemmas.

ANOTHER PERSPECTIVE

Ethical analysis: *In a Different Voice*
In addition to utilitarian, Kantian, rights, and justice approaches to business ethics, Carol Gilligan offers another way to think about our moral actions, as a series of caring relationships that evolve over time, focused first on the self, then on dependent others, and finally, on establishing equality of needs between self and others so that dynamic relationships can replace dependent ones. Such an approach (self, dependent other, dynamic equality) may be a helpful way of thinking about a multinational's evolving corporate involvement in a developing country. (Carol Gilligan, 1982, *In a Different Voice*)

ETHICAL DECISION MAKING

What then is the best way for managers in a multinational firm to make sure that ethical considerations figure into international business decisions? How do managers decide upon an ethical course of action when confronted with decisions pertaining to working conditions, human rights, corruption, and environmental pollution?

From an ethical perspective, how do managers determine the moral obligations that flow from the power of a multinational? In many cases, there are no easy answers to these questions, for many of the most vexing ethical problems arise because there are very real dilemmas inherent in them and no obvious correct action. Nevertheless, managers can and should do many things to make sure that basic ethical principles are adhered to and that ethical issues are routinely inserted into international business decisions.

Here we focus on five things that an international business and its managers can do to make sure ethical issues are considered in business decisions. These are (1) favour hiring and promoting people with a well-grounded sense of personal ethics; (2) build an organizational culture that places a high value on ethical behaviour; (3) make sure that leaders within the business not only articulate the rhetoric of ethical behaviour, but also act in a manner that is consistent with that rhetoric; (4) put decision-making processes in place that require people to consider the ethical dimension of business decisions; and (5) develop moral courage.

HIRING AND PROMOTION

It seems obvious that businesses should strive to hire people who have a strong sense of personal ethics and would not engage in unethical or illegal behaviour. Similarly, you would rightly expect a business to not promote people, and perhaps to fire people, whose behaviour does not match generally accepted ethical standards. But actually doing so is very difficult. How do you know that someone has a poor sense of personal ethics? In our society, we have an incentive to hide a lack of personal ethics from public view. Once people realize that you are unethical, they will no longer trust you.

Is there anything that businesses can do to make sure they do not hire people who subsequently turn out to have poor personal ethics, particularly given that people have an incentive to hide this from public view (indeed, the unethical person may lie about his or her nature)? Businesses can give potential employees psychological tests to try to discern their ethical predisposition, and they can check with prior employees regarding someone's reputation (e.g., by asking for letters of reference and talking to people who have worked with the prospective employee). The latter is common and does influence the hiring process. Promoting people who have displayed poor ethics should not occur in a company where the organization culture values the need for ethical behaviour and where leaders act accordingly.

Not only should businesses strive to identify and hire people with a strong sense of personal ethics, but it also is in the interests of prospective employees to find out as much as they can about the ethical climate in an organization. Who wants to work at a multinational such as Enron, which ultimately entered bankruptcy because unethical executives had established risky partnerships that were hidden from public view and that existed in part to enrich those same executives? Table 4.1 lists some questions job seekers might want to ask a prospective employer.

ORGANIZATION CULTURE AND LEADERSHIP

To foster ethical behaviour, businesses need to build an organization culture that values ethical behaviour. Three things are particularly important in building an organization culture that emphasizes ethical behaviour. First, the businesses must explicitly articulate values that emphasize ethical behaviour. Many companies now do this by drafting a **code of ethics,** which is a formal statement of the ethical priorities a business adheres to. Often, the code of ethics draws heavily upon documents such as the UN Universal Declaration of Human Rights, which itself is grounded in Kantian and rights-based theories of moral philosophy. Others have incorporated ethical statements into documents that articulate the values or mission of

CODE OF ETHICS A business's formal statement of ethical priorities

TABLE 4.1

A Job Seeker's Ethics Audit

Source: Linda K. Trevino, chair of the Department of Management and Organization, Smeal College of Business, Pennsylvania State University. Reported in K. Maher, "Career Journal. Wanted: Ethical Employer," *The Wall Street Journal*, July 9, 2002, p. B1.

Some probing questions to ask about a prospective employer:

1. Is there a formal code of ethics? How widely is it distributed? Is it reinforced in other formal ways such as through decision-making systems?
2. Are workers at all levels trained in ethical decision making? Are they also encouraged to take responsibility for their behaviour or to question authority when asked to do something they consider wrong?
3. Do employees have formal channels available to make their concerns known confidentially? Is there a formal committee high in the organization that considers ethical issues?
4. Is misconduct disciplined swiftly and justly within the organization?
5. Is integrity emphasized to new employees?
6. How are senior managers perceived by subordinates in terms of their integrity? How do such leaders model ethical behaviour?

the business. For example, the Canadian Marketing Association has a code of ethics to which all association members must adhere to. The Code of Ethics, prominently displayed on the CMA Web site at www.the-cma.org, is written in language that adheres to existing provincial and federal regulations governing human rights, privacy, and ethics. For example:

> **A2.4** No marketer shall participate in any campaign involving the disparagement of any person or group on the grounds of race, colour, religion, national origin, gender, sexual orientation, marital status.
>
> **E3.3 Privacy:** No marketer shall knowingly call any person who has an unlisted or unpublished telephone number, except where the telephone number was furnished by the customer to that marketer.

Note the CMA's refusal to disparage any person or group, a statement that is grounded in Kantian ethics. The CMA's principles send a very clear message about appropriate ethics to managers and employees.

Having articulated values in a code of ethics or some other document, leaders in the business must give life and meaning to those words by repeatedly emphasizing their importance *and then acting on them.* This means using every relevant opportunity to stress the importance of business ethics and making sure that key business decisions not only make good economic sense but also are ethical. Many companies have gone a step further, hiring independent auditors to make sure they are behaving in a manner consistent with their ethical codes. Nortel, for example, has hired independent auditors to make sure that subcontractors used by the company are living up to Nortel's code of conduct.

DECISION-MAKING PROCESSES

In addition to establishing the right kind of ethical culture in an organization, businesspeople must be able to think through the ethical implications of decisions in a systematic way. To do this, they need a moral compass, and both rights theories and Rawls's theory of justice help to provide such a compass. Beyond these theories, some experts on ethics have proposed a straightforward practical guide—or ethical algorithm—to determine whether a decision is ethical.[30] According to these experts, a decision is acceptable on ethical grounds if a businessperson can answer yes to each of these questions:

1. Does my decision fall within the accepted values or standards that typically apply in the organizational environment (as articulated in a code of ethics or some other corporate statement)?
2. Am I willing to see the decision communicated to all stakeholders affected by it—for example, by having it reported in newspapers or on television?

3. Would the people with whom I have a significant personal relationship, such as family members, friends, or even managers in other businesses, approve of the decision?

Others have recommended a five-step process to think through ethical problems (this is another example of an ethical algorithm).[31] In step 1, businesspeople should identify which stakeholders a decision would affect and in what ways. A firm's **stakeholders** are individuals or groups that have an interest, claim, or stake in the company, in what it does, and in how well it performs.[32] They can be divided into internal stakeholders and external stakeholders. **Internal stakeholders** are individuals or groups who work for or own the business. They include all employees, the board of directors, and stockholders. **External stakeholders** are all other individuals and groups that have some claim on the firm. Typically, this group comprises customers, suppliers, lenders, governments, unions, local communities, and the general public.

STAKEHOLDERS The individuals or groups who have an interest, stake, or claim in the actions and overall performance of a company.

INTERNAL STAKEHOLDERS People who work for or who own the business such as employees, the board of directors, and stockholders.

EXTERNAL STAKEHOLDERS The individuals or groups who have some claim on a firm, such as customers, suppliers, and unions.

All stakeholders are in an exchange relationship with the company. Each stakeholder group supplies the organization with important resources (or contributions), and in exchange each expects its interests to be satisfied (by inducements).[33] For example, employees provide labour, skills, knowledge, and time and in exchange expect commensurate income, job satisfaction, job security, and good working conditions. Customers provide a company with its revenues and in exchange they want quality products that represent value for money. Communities provide businesses with local infrastructure and in exchange they want businesses that are responsible citizens and seek some assurance that the quality of life will be improved as a result of the business firm's existence.

Stakeholder analysis involves a certain amount of what has been called *moral imagination*.[34] This means standing in the shoes of a stakeholder and asking how a proposed decision might impact that stakeholder. For example, when considering outsourcing to subcontractors, managers might need to ask themselves how it might feel to be working under substandard health conditions for long hours.

Step 2 involves judging the ethics of the proposed strategic decision, given the information gained in step 1. Managers need to determine whether a proposed decision would violate the *fundamental rights* of any stakeholders. For example, we might argue that the right to information about health risks in the workplace is a fundamental entitlement of employees. Similarly, the right to know about potentially dangerous features of a product is a fundamental entitlement of customers (something tobacco companies violated when they did not reveal to their customers what they knew about the health risks of smoking). Managers might also want to ask themselves whether they would allow the proposed strategic decision if they were designing a system under Rawls's veil of ignorance. For example, if the issue under consideration was whether to outsource work to a subcontractor with low pay and poor working conditions, managers might want to ask themselves whether they would allow for such action if they were considering it under a veil of ignorance, where they themselves might ultimately be the ones to work for the subcontractor.

The judgment at this stage should be guided by various moral principles that should not be violated. The principles might be those articulated in a corporate code of ethics or other company documents. In addition, certain moral principles that we have adopted as members of society–for instance, the prohibition on stealing–should not be violated. The judgment at this stage will also be guided by the decision rule that is chosen to assess the proposed strategic decision. Although maximizing long-run profitability is the decision rule that most businesses stress, it should be applied subject to the constraint that no moral principles are violated–that the business behaves in an ethical manner.

Step 3 requires managers to establish moral intent. This means the business must resolve to place moral concerns ahead of other concerns in cases where either the fundamental rights of stakeholders or key moral principles have been violated. At this stage, input from top management might be particularly valuable. Without the proactive encouragement of top managers, middle-level managers might tend to place the narrow economic interests of the company before the interests of stakeholders. They might do so in the (usually erroneous) belief that top managers favour such an approach.

Step 4 requires the company to engage in ethical behaviour. Step 5 requires the business to audit its decisions, reviewing them to make sure they were consistent with ethical principles, such as those stated in the company's code of ethics. This final step is critical and often overlooked. Without auditing past decisions, businesspeople may not know if their decision process is working and if changes should be made to ensure greater compliance with a code of ethics.

ANOTHER PERSPECTIVE

Stages of ethical development in global managers

An adaptation of William Perry's stages of ethical development (*Forms of Intellectual and Ethical Development in the College Years: A Scheme,* 1970) suggests that the novice global manager can develop ethical decision-making abilities as he or she gains experience.

(J. McNett, "Ethical Decision-Making for Global Managers," in H. Lane, et al., *The Blackwell Handbook of Global Management: A Guide to Managing Complexity,* 2004)

APPROACH	LEVEL	DESCRIPTION	LIKELY OUTCOMES
Commitment in Relativism	Advanced; coincident with expert global managers	Relativist understanding of the world is combined with a commitment to a set of values and principles within an expanded worldview.	Manager assumes responsibility for actions and decisions based on analysis and reasoning.
Relativism	More developed; frequently found in stage 2 and 3 global managers	Dualistic view is moderated by an awareness of context: knowledge and values are relative.	May lead to a *When in Rome do as the Romans do* approach, a problematic basis for ethical judgment.
Dualism	Least developed; often found in novice global managers	Bipolar model for ethical judgments. Assumption is there is a clear differentiation between right and wrong approaches; the manager's way is the right way.	Leads to empire style approach to ethical differences.

ETHICS OFFICERS

To make sure that a business behaves in an ethical manner, a number of firms now have ethics officers. These individuals are responsible for making sure that all employees are trained to be ethically aware, that ethical considerations enter the business decision-making process, and that the company's code of ethics is adhered to. Ethics officers may also be responsible for auditing decisions to make sure they are consistent with this code. In many businesses, ethics officers act as an internal ombudsperson with responsibility for handling confidential inquiries from employees, investigating complaints from employees or others, reporting findings, and making recommendations for change.

For example, United Technologies, a multinational aerospace company with worldwide revenues of more than $28 billion, has had a formal code of ethics since 1990.[35] There are now some 160 business practice officers within United Technologies (this is the company's name for ethics officers) who are responsible for making sure the code is followed. United Technologies also established an ombudsperson program in 1986 that lets employees inquire anonymously about ethics issues. The program has received some 56 000 inquiries since 1986, and 8000 cases have been handled by an ombudsperson.

MORAL COURAGE

Finally, it is important to recognize that employees in an international business may need significant *moral courage*. Moral courage enables managers to walk away from a decision that is profitable, but unethical. Moral courage gives an employee the strength to say no to a superior who instructs her to pursue actions that are unethical. And moral courage gives employees the integrity to go public to the media and blow the whistle on persistent unethical behaviour in a company. This moral courage does not come easily; there are well-known cases where individuals have lost their jobs because they blew the whistle on corporate behaviours they thought unethical, telling the media about what was occurring.[36]

However, companies can strengthen the moral courage of employees by committing themselves to not retaliate against employees who exercise moral courage, say no to superiors, or otherwise complain about unethical actions. For example, consider the following extract from Unilever's code of ethics:

> **Telling the Truth** Employees should evaluate all communications for which they are responsible, including sales representations and advertising, and ensure information is true and does not mislead the public, either directly or indirectly.[37]

Clearly this statement gives permission to employees to exercise moral courage. Companies can also set up ethics hotlines, which allow employees to anonymously register a complaint with a corporate ethics officer.

SUMMARY OF DECISION-MAKING STEPS

All of the steps discussed here—hiring and promoting people based upon ethical considerations as well as more traditional metrics of performance, establishing an ethical culture in the organization, instituting ethical decision-making processes, appointing ethics officers, and creating an environment that facilitates moral courage—can help to make sure that when making business decisions, managers are cognizant of the ethical implications and do not violate basic ethical prescripts. At the same time, it must be recognized that not all ethical dilemmas have a clean and obvious solution—that is why they are dilemmas. There are clearly things that international businesses should not do and there are things that they should do but there are also actions that present managers with true dilemmas. In these cases, a premium is placed on managers' ability to make sense out of complex situations and make balanced decisions that are as just as possible.

IMPLICATIONS FOR BUSINESS

The material in this chapter has implications for how managers operate internationally in a globalized economy where advances in Internet-enabled communications and mass media allow worldwide audiences to be instantly aware of events anywhere and anytime. In addition to the "threat" that the technological environment can speedily broadcast news of an unethical situation, companies also have to deal with the consequences of an intensified competitive environment that both creates and worsens situations in which ethics is compromised to produce products and services at lower costs and sold at higher margins. Framing the background is a volatile political environment in which regional and national politicians have to create compromise from increasingly "blended cultures" and the stress that comes from having to accommodate different values and beliefs in a more diverse society.

The managerial implications for attending to ethical considerations put the burden on company executives to not only "do the right thing" but also appear to be doing the right thing and make sure the media report the circumstances in a favourable way that will hold investor confidence and keep share prices sustainable.

BENEFITS

One of the benefits of a company behaving in an ethical way is the confidence of knowing that when the increasingly sophisticated consumer discovers some unethical circumstances within your competition, your product and your firm can withstand any subsequent scrutiny that may come with the global media seeking out other instances within the sector.

COSTS

It is being said these days that to succeed in business is not necessarily a matter of doing things well, but rather being in a position to handle the consequences when things do not go well—as they inevitably do. Having a clear conscience regarding the way your company has been handling a sensitive ethical situation, in a region of conflict, may serve you well when the CBC *National News* does an expose on the circumstances, and all your competitors are implicated—except your company that handled things ethically from the beginning. It may have cost you more to have proper effluent pollution controls in place, or it may have been more expensive to provide special services to workers when other companies didn't, but your company will more than make up for these costs by selling product while your competitors are spending money on high priced publicity to recover public opinion.

RISKS

Operating in a way that appears to be ethical is not an exact science; sometimes it is a matter of opinion. While bribery of government officials may not be tolerated, or illegal, in the home country, bribery of government officials may be a natural way that services are rendered in the host country. In circumstances where a national government has a limited corporate tax base, certain government services might be considered on a "user pay" basis. So if somebody wanted special concessions from a regional administrator to allow permits for some activity to take place, it might be considered perfectly acceptable to directly pay that administrator a "bonus" for handling the required paperwork in a timely fashion. The risk you take is proportionate to the nature of the activity and unfortunately, there is no "manual" that can be referenced to see if certain activities are ethically acceptable in the broader scheme of things. There is also the risk that media interpretation (should they find out there was a "bonus") might be broadcast in a way that does not include an understanding of the cultural or political environment, so perceptions might be twisted out of context.

KEY TERMS

business ethics, p. 126

code of ethics, p. 148

Convention on Combating Bribery of Foreign Public Officials in International Business Transactions, p. 131

cultural relativism, p. 142

ethical dilemma, p. 135

ethical strategy, p. 126

external stakeholders, p. 150

internal stakeholders, p. 150

just distribution, p. 146

Kantian ethics, p. 145

naive immoralist, p. 143

organization culture, p. 137

righteous moralist, p. 143

rights theories, p. 145

social responsibility, p. 134

stakeholder, p. 150

Universal Declaration of Human Rights, p. 145

utilitarian approaches, p. 144

SUMMARY

This chapter has discussed the source and nature of ethical issues in international businesses, the different philosophical approaches to business ethics, and the steps managers can take to ensure that ethical issues are respected in international business decisions. The chapter made these points:

1. The term *ethics* refers to accepted principles of right or wrong that govern the conduct of a person, the members of a profession, or the actions of an organization. Business ethics are the accepted principles of right or wrong governing the conduct of businesspeople, and an ethical strategy is one that does not violate these accepted principles.
2. Ethical issues and dilemmas in international business are rooted in the variations among political systems, law, economic development, and culture from country to country.
3. The most common ethical issues in international business involve employment practices, human rights, environmental regulations, corruption, and the moral obligation of multinational corporations.
4. Ethical dilemmas are situations in which none of the available alternatives seems ethically acceptable.
5. Unethical behaviour is rooted in poor personal ethics, the psychological and geographical distances of a foreign subsidiary from the home office, a failure to incorporate ethical issues into strategic and operational decision making, a dysfunctional culture, and failure of leaders to act in an ethical manner.
6. Moral philosophers contend that approaches to business ethics such as the Friedman doctrine, cultural relativism, the righteous moralist, and the naive immoralist are unsatisfactory in important ways.
7. The Friedman doctrine states that the only social responsibility of business is to increase profits, as long as the company stays within the rules of law. Cultural relativism contends that one should adopt the ethics of the culture in which one is doing business. The righteous moralist monolithically applies home-country ethics to a foreign situation, while the naive immoralist believes that if a manager of a multinational sees that firms from other nations are not following ethical norms in a host nation, that manager should not either.
8. Utilitarian approaches to ethics hold that the moral worth of actions or practices is determined by their consequences, and the best decisions are those that produce the greatest good for the greatest number of people.
9. Kantian ethics state that people should be treated as ends and never purely as *means* to the ends of others. People are not instruments, like a machine. People have dignity and need to be respected as such.
10. Rights theories recognize that human beings have fundamental rights and privileges that transcend national boundaries and cultures. These rights establish a minimum level of morally acceptable behaviour.

11. The concept of justice developed by John Rawls suggests that a decision is just and ethical if people would allow for it when designing a social system under a veil of ignorance.
12. To make sure that ethical issues are considered in international business decisions, managers should (*a*) favour hiring and promoting people with a well-grounded sense of personal ethics; (*b*) build an organization culture that places a high value on ethical behaviour; (*c*) make sure that leaders within the business not only articulate the rhetoric of ethical behaviour, but also act in a manner that is consistent with that rhetoric; (*d*) put decision-making processes in place that require people to consider the ethical dimension of business decisions; and (*e*) be morally courageous and encourage others to do the same.

CRITICAL THINKING AND DISCUSSION QUESTIONS

1. Review the Management Focus on testing drugs in the developing world and discuss the following questions:
   a. Did Pfizer behave unethically by rushing to take advantage of a Nigerian epidemic to test an experimental drug on sick children? Should the company have proceeded more carefully?
   b. Is it ethical to test an experimental drug on children in emergency settings in the developing world where the overall standard of health care is much lower than in the developed world, and where proper protocols might not be followed?
2. A visiting North American executive finds that a foreign subsidiary in a poor nation has hired a 12-year-old girl to work on a factory floor, in violation of the company's prohibition on child labour. He tells the local manager to replace the child and tell her to go back to school. The local manager tells the North American executive that the child is an orphan with no other means of support, and she will probably become a street child if she is denied work. What should the North American executive do?
3. Drawing upon John Rawls's concept of the veil of ignorance, develop an ethical code that will (*a*) guide the decisions of a large oil multinational toward environmental protection, and (*b*) influence the policies of a clothing company to outsourcing of manufacturing process.
4. Under what conditions is it ethically defensible to outsource production to the developing world where labour costs are lower when such actions also involve laying off long-term employees in the firm's home country?
5. Are facilitating payments ethical?

RESEARCH TASK | globalEDGE™ globaledge.msu.edu

Use the globalEDGE™ site to complete the following exercises:

1. Promoting respect for universal human rights is a central dimension of all countries' foreign policy. As history has repeatedly shown, human rights abuses are everybody's concern. Begun in 1977, the annual Country Reports on Human Rights Practices are designed to assess the state of democracy and human rights around the world, and call attention to violations. Find the annual Country Reports on Human Right Practices, and provide information on how the reports are prepared.
2. The Corruption Perceptions Index (CPI) is a comparative assessment of a country's integrity performance, along with related academic research on corruption. Provide a description of this index and its ranking. Identify the five countries with the lowest and five with the highest CPI scores according to this index.

Visit the *Global Business Today* Online Learning Centre at **www.mcgrawhill.ca/college/hill** to access quizzes, interactive exercises, a Business Around the World interactive map, and other learning and study tools related to this chapter.

Online LearningCentre

CLOSING CASE

ETCH-A-SKETCH ETHICS

The Ohio Art Company is perhaps best known as the producer of one of the top selling toys of all time, the venerable Etch-A-Sketch. More than 100 million of the familiar red rectangular drawing toys have been sold since 1960 when it was invented. The late 1990s, however, became a troubled time for the toy's maker. Confronted with sluggish toy sales, the Ohio Art Company lost money for two years. In December 2000, it made the strategic decision to outsource production of the Etch-A-Sketch toys to Kin Ki Industrial, a leading Chinese toy maker, laying off 100 U.S. workers in the process.

The closure of the Etch-A-Sketch line was not unexpected among employees. The company had already moved the production of other toy lines to China, and most employees knew it was just a matter of time before Etch-A-Sketch went too. Still, the decision was a tough one for the company, which did most of its manufacturing in its home base, the small Ohio town of Bryan (population 8000). As William Killgallon, the CEO of the Ohio Art Company, noted, the employees who made the product "were like family. It was a necessary financial decision we saw coming for some time, and we did it gradually, product by product. But that doesn't mean it's emotionally easy."

In a small town such as Bryan, the cumulative effect of outsourcing to China has been significant. The tax base is eroding from a loss of manufacturing and a population decline. The local paper is full of notices of home foreclosures and auctions. According to former employees, the biggest hole in their lives after Etch-A-Sketch moved came from the death of a community. For many workers, the company was their family, and now that family was gone.

The rational for the outsourcing was simple enough. Pressured to keep the cost of Etch-A-Sketch under $10 by big retailers such as Wal-Mart and Toys "R" Us, the Ohio Art Company had to get its costs down or lose money. In this case, unionized workers making $1,500 a month were replaced by Chinese factory workers who made $75 a month. However, according to Killgallon, the main savings came not from lower wages, but from lower overhead costs for plant, maintenance, electricity, and payroll, and the ability to get out from the soaring costs of providing health benefits to U.S. manufacturing employees.

The choice of Kin Ki as manufacturer for Etch-A-Sketch was easy—the company had been making pocket-sized Etch-A-Sketch toys for nearly a decade and always delivered on cost. To help Kin Ki, the Ohio Art Company shipped some of its best equipment to the company, and it continues to send crucial raw materials, such as aluminum powder, which is hard to get in China.

The story would have ended there had it not been for an exposé in *The New York Times* in December 2003. The *Times* reporter painted a dismal picture of working conditions at the Kin Ki factory that manufactured the Etch-A-Sketch. According to official Kin Ki publications:

> Workers at Kin Ki make a decent salary, rarely work nights or weekends, and often "hang out along the streets, playing Ping Pong and watching TV." They all have work contracts, pensions, and medical benefits. The factory canteen offers tasty food. The dormitories are comfortable.

Not so, according to Joseph Kahn, the *Times* reporter. He alleged that real-world Kin Ki employees, mostly teenage migrants from internal Chinese provinces, work long hours for 40 percent less than the company claims. They are paid 24 cents per hour, below the legal minimum wage of 33 cents an hour in Shenzhen province where Kin Ki is located. Most do not have pensions, medical benefits, or employment contracts. Production starts at 7:30 A.M. and continues until 10 P.M., with breaks only for lunch and dinner. Saturdays and Sundays are treated as normal workdays. This translates into a work week of seven 12-hour days, or 84 hours a week, well above the standard 40-hour week set by authorities in Shenzhen. Local rules also allow for no more than 32 hours of overtime and stipulate that the employees must be paid 1.5 times the standard hourly wage, but Kin Ki's overtime rate is just 1.3 times base pay.

As for the "comfortable dormitories," the workers sleep head to toe in tiny rooms with windows that are covered with chicken wire. To get into and out of the factories, which are surrounded by high walls, workers must enter and leave through a guarded gate. As for the tasty food, it is apparently a mix of boiled vegetables, beans, and rice, with meat or fish served only twice a month.

The workers at Kin Ki have apparently become restless. They went on strike twice in 2003, demanding higher wages and better working conditions. The company responded by raising wages a few cents and allotting an extra dish of food to each worker per day (but still no more meat)! However, Kin Ki simultaneously made "fried squid" of two workers who were ring leaders of the strike ("fried squid" is apparently a popular term for dismissal). Johnson Tao, a senior executive at the company, denies that the two ring leaders were dismissed for organizing the strikes. Rather, he noted that they were well-known troublemakers who left the factory of their own accord. Mr. Tao acknowledges the low wages at the company, stating, "I know that I need to increase wages to comply with the law. I have the intention of doing this and will raise all wages in 2004."

Meanwhile, in Ohio, William Killgallon, Ohio Art Company's CEO, stated to the *Times* reporter that he considered Kin Ki's executives to be honest and that he had no knowledge of labour problems there. But he said he intended to visit China soon to make sure "they understand what we expect."

Joseph Kahn, "Ruse in Toyland: Chinese Worker's Hidden Woe," *The New York Times,* December 7, 2003, pp. A1, A8; Joseph Kahn, "An Ohio Town Is Hard Hit as Leading Industry Moves to China," *The New York Times,* December 7, 2003, p. A8; Carol Hymowitz, "Toy Maker Survives by Moving an Icon from Ohio to China," *The Wall Street Journal,* October 21, 2003, p. B1; and John Seewer, "Etch A Sketch Enters Fourth Decade," *Columbian,* November 22, 2001, p. E3.

CASE DISCUSSION QUESTIONS

1. Was it ethical of the Ohio Art Company to move production to China? What were the economic *and* social costs and benefits of this decision? What would have happened if production had not been moved?
2. Assuming that the description of working conditions given in *The New York Times* is correct, is it ethical for the Ohio Art Company to continue using Kin Ki to manufacture Etch-A-Sketch toys?
3. Is it possible, as Mr. Killgallon claims, that the Ohio Art Company had no knowledge of labour problems at Kin Ki? Do you think company executives had any knowledge of the working conditions?
4. What steps can executives at the Ohio Art Company take to make sure they do not find the company profiled in *The New York Times* again as an enterprise that benefits from sweatshop labour?

B.C. HYDRO'S ABORIGINAL RELATIONS PROGRAMS

According to Canada's First Nations 2001 Census data, there are 1 319 890 Aboriginal people in Canada (or 4.4 percent of Canada's total population). They are often identified as being from Inuit or Métis descent. (Métis are Aboriginal people with an original mixture of French and Aboriginal ancestry. They live primarily in the western provinces of Canada.) Aboriginal peoples are members of a large number of distinctly different and well-defined cultures and societies. This case study explains the cultural challenges and opportunities faced by a corporation conducting business in Aboriginal areas.

B.C. Hydro, one of the largest electric utilities in Canada, is a Crown corporation owned by the province of British Columbia, which is home to 197 First Nations bands. B.C. Hydro has facilities on at least 168 of these band's reserve lands. Consequently, building sustainable, mutually beneficial relationships with Aboriginal peoples is critical for B.C. Hydro.

In 1993, B.C. Hydro developed a comprehensive approach to managing Aboriginal issues. The main elements of B.C. Hydro's approach are addressing the past, building for the future, and effectively managing its Aboriginal relations initiatives. Key components of the relationship-building strategy are facilitating participation in resource management and development decisions, fostering economic development, supporting education for Aboriginal peoples, and contributing to community projects and events.

To increase economic development opportunities for First Nations, B.C. Hydro negotiates contracts for work on reserve lands and assists Aboriginal-owned businesses to improve their tendering practices. The utility provides start-up and expansion grants to Aboriginal-owned businesses and in some cases explores joint ventures. B.C. Hydro also has developed an Aboriginal Business Directory that is used throughout the corporation and is available to government and private-sector companies as a source for products and services.

Within B.C. Hydro, education is a key component of the strategy. Cross-cultural training programs address historical facts, court decisions, and cultural issues. More than 4700 B.C. Hydro employees have taken at least one half-day cross-cultural training course. Those who frequently interact with First Nations have taken more rigorous training. B.C. Hydro's cross-cultural training, which has also been delivered to more than 100 outside organizations, received the 1999 Province of British Columbia Multiculturalism Award. Aboriginal education is also a priority, with education scholarships, Aboriginal language and culture preservation programs, and stay-in-school programs forming a part of the strategy.

The biggest challenges faced by B.C. Hydro in this field flow from the prevailing legal and political uncertainty both as to the outcomes of treaty negotiations and the nature and extent of Aboriginal rights and titles. B.C. Hydro addresses these uncertainties by seeking "interest-based" rather than "rights-based" solutions to problems, and by providing input into the treaty process. Open dialogue with First Nations is a key component of the strategy for managing this uncertainty.

In November 1997, B.C. Hydro commissioned the Ipsos Reid Group to conduct interviews with Aboriginal leaders across British Columbia. The First Nations opinion leaders told B.C. Hydro representatives that the company's principles that guide its relationship-building activities are the right ones. The findings revealed that while relationships have improved over the past ten years, the company still has a long way to go. First Nations identified the following goals as most important in contributing to improved relationships:

- Consulting with Aboriginal communities in the early stages of a project.
- Cooperating with Aboriginal peoples and education institutions to develop initiatives and programs.
- Encouraging Aboriginal people to take advantage of any economic social or other opportunities from B.C. Hydro projects.
- Developing employment equity programs.

Those who thought that relations with Hydro were still poor cited a lack of respect toward Aboriginal peoples and insufficient communication as the main reasons.

Perhaps the most critical lesson that B.C. Hydro has learned is that problems cannot be solved overnight or with simple, one-size-fits-all solutions. First Nations share the need for better business relationships, and they will work with B.C. Hydro when they see that the company's commitment is real and sustained.

Source: Reprinted with permission from the World Business Council for Sustainable Development's Web site at www.wbcsd.org.

PART THREE

3

CROSS-BORDER TRADE AND INVESTMENT

RF/Corbis.

The Gains from Trade: Ghana and South Korea

Living standards in Ghana and South Korea were roughly comparable in 1970. Ghana's 1970 gross national product (GNP) per capita was $250, and South Korea's was $260. By 1998 the situation had changed dramatically. South Korea had a GNP per head of $8,600 and boasted the world's 12th largest economy. Ghana's GNP per capita in 1998 was only $390, while its economy ranked 96 in the world. These differences in economic circumstances were due to vastly different economic growth rates since 1970. Between 1968 and 1998, the average annual growth rate in Ghana's GNP was less than 1.5 percent. In contrast, South Korea achieved a rate of more than 8 percent annually between 1968 and 1998.

While no simple explanation addresses the difference in growth rates between Ghana and South Korea, part of the answer may be found in the countries' attitudes toward international trade. A now classic study by the World Bank suggests that while the South Korean government implemented policies that encouraged companies to engage in international trade, the actions of the Ghanaian government discouraged domestic producers from becoming involved in international trade. As a consequence, in 1980 trade accounted for 18 percent of Ghana's GNP by value compared to 74 percent of South Korea's GNP.

In 1957, Ghana became the first of Great Britain's West African colonies to gain independence. Its first president, Kwame Nkrumah, influenced the rest of the continent with his theories of pan-African socialism. For Ghana this meant the imposition of high tariffs on many imports, an import substitution policy aimed at fostering Ghana self-sufficiency in certain manufactured goods, and the adoption of policies that discouraged Ghana's enterprises from engaging in exports. The results were an unmitigated disaster that transformed one of Africa's most prosperous nations into one of the world's poorest. As an illustration of how Ghana's antitrade policies destroyed the Ghanaian economy, consider the Ghanaian government's involvement in the cocoa trade. A combination of favourable climate, good soils, and ready access to world shipping routes has given Ghana an absolute advantage in cocoa

CHAPTER 5

International Trade Theories

OPENING CASE

production. Quite simply, it is one of the best places in the world to grow cocoa. As a consequence, Ghana was the world's largest producer and exporter of cocoa in 1957. Then the government of the newly independent nation created a state-controlled cocoa marketing board. The board was given the authority to fix prices for cocoa and was designated the sole buyer of all cocoa grown in Ghana. The board held down the prices that it paid farmers for cocoa, while selling the cocoa on the world market at world prices. Thus, it might buy cocoa from farmers at 25 cents a pound and sell it on the world market for 50 cents a pound. In effect, the board was taxing exports by paying farmers considerably less for their cocoa than it was worth on the world market and putting the difference into government coffers. This money was used to fund the government policy of nationalization and industrialization.

One result of the cocoa policy was that between 1963 and 1979 the price paid by the cocoa marketing board to Ghana's farmers increased by a factor of 6, while the price of consumer goods in Ghana increased by a factor of 22 and the price of cocoa in neighbouring countries increased by a factor of 36! In real terms, the Ghanaian farmers were paid less every year for their cocoa by the cocoa marketing board, while the world price increased significantly. As of 2003, the Ivory Coast produces about 43 percent of the world's cocoa, with Ghana being far behind at the number two spot with 14 percent of the world's output. At the same time, the Ghanaian government's attempt to build an industrial base through state-run enterprises failed. The resulting drop in Ghana's export earnings plunged the country into recession, led to a decline in its foreign currency reserves, and limited its ability to pay for necessary imports.

The inward-oriented trade policy of the Ghanaian government resulted in a shift of that country's resources away from the profitable activity of growing cocoa. While Ghana's cocoa production has been hindered by factors outside its control, such as battling black pod disease and smuggling of the crop into neighbouring Ivory Coast, the fact remains that inefficient use of the country's resources severely damaged the Ghanaian economy and held back the country's economic development.

The international trade policies for Ghana and South Korea offer strikingly contrasting results. What factors could have motivated Ghana's first president, Kwame Nkrumah, to make the decisions he did? How could two countries with similar living standards change so dramatically in 25 years?

In contrast, consider the trade policy adopted by the South Korean government. The World Bank has characterized the trade policy of South Korea as "strongly outward-oriented." Unlike in Ghana, the policies of the South Korean government emphasized low import barriers on manufactured goods (but not on agricultural goods) and incentives to encourage South Korean firms to export. Beginning in the late 1950s, the South Korean government progressively reduced import tariffs from an average of 60 percent of the price of an imported good to less than 20 percent in the mid-1980s. On most nonagricultural goods, import tariffs were reduced to zero. In addition, the number of imported goods subject to quotas was reduced from more than 90 percent in the late 1950s to zero by the early 1980s. Over the same period, South Korea progressively reduced the subsidies given to South Korean exporters from an average of 80 percent of their sales price in the late 1950s to an average of less than 20 percent in 1965 and down to zero in 1984. With the exception of the agricultural sector (where a strong farm lobby maintained import controls), South Korea moved progressively toward a free trade stance.

South Korea's outward-looking orientation has been rewarded by a dramatic transformation of its economy. Initially, South Korea's resources shifted from agriculture to the manufacture of labour-intensive goods, especially textiles, clothing, and footwear. An abundant supply of cheap but well-educated labour helped form the basis of South Korea's comparative advantage in labour-intensive manufacturing. More recently, as labour costs have risen, the growth areas in the economy have been in the more capital-intensive manufacturing sectors, especially motor vehicles, semiconductors, consumer electronics, and advanced materials. As a result of these developments, South Korea has changed dramatically. In the late 1950s, 77 percent of the country's employment was in the agricultural sector; today the figure is less than 20 percent. Over the same period the percentage of its GNP accounted for by manufacturing increased from less than 10 percent to more than 30 percent, while the overall GNP grew at an annual rate of more than 9 percent.

Sources: "Poor Man's Burden: A Survey of the Third World," *The Economist,* September 23, 1989; World Bank, *World Development Report, 2000* (Oxford: Oxford University Press, 2000), Table 1; J. Wha-Lee, "International Trade, Distortions, and Long-Run Economic Growth," *International Monetary Fund Staff Papers* 40, no. 2 (June 1993), p. 299.

LEARNING OBJECTIVES

1. Understand why nations trade with each other.
2. Be aware of the different theories that explain trade flows between nations.
3. Understand why many economists believe that unrestricted (free) trade between nations will raise the economic welfare of all countries that participate in a free trade system.
4. Be familiar with the arguments of those who maintain that government can play a proactive role in promoting national competitive advantage in certain industries.
5. Understand the important implications that international trade theory holds for business practice.

INTRODUCTION

The opening case illustrates the gains that come from international trade. For a long time, the economic policies of the Ghanaian government discouraged trade with other nations. The result was a shift in Ghana's resources away from productive uses (growing cocoa) and toward unproductive uses (subsistence agriculture). The economic policies of the South Korean government encouraged trade with other nations. The result was a shift in South Korea's resources away from uses where it had no comparative advantage in the world economy (agriculture) and toward more productive uses (labour-intensive manufacturing). As a direct result of their policies toward international trade, Ghana's economy declined while South Korea's grew.

This chapter has two goals that are related to the story of Ghana and South Korea. The first is to review a number of theories that explain why it is beneficial for a country to engage in international trade. The second goal is to explain the pattern of international trade that we observe in the world economy. With regard to the pattern of trade, we will be primarily concerned with explaining the pattern of exports and imports of products between countries. We will not be concerned with the pattern of foreign direct investment between countries; that is discussed in Chapter 7.

AN OVERVIEW OF TRADE THEORY

We open this chapter with a discussion of mercantilism. Propagated in the sixteenth and seventeenth centuries, mercantilism advocated that countries should simultaneously encourage exports and discourage imports. Although mercantilism is an old and largely discredited doctrine, its echoes remain in modern political debate and in the trade policies of many countries. Next we will look at Adam Smith's theory of absolute advantage. Proposed in 1776, Smith's theory was the first to explain why unrestricted free trade is beneficial to a country. **Free trade** refers to a situation where a government does not attempt to influence through quotas or duties what its citizens can buy from another country, or what they can produce and sell to another country. Smith argued that the invisible hand of the market mechanism, rather than government policy, should determine what a country imports and what it exports. His arguments imply that such a laissez-faire stance toward trade was in the best interests of a country. Building on Smith's work are two additional theories that we shall review. One is the theory of comparative advantage, advanced by the nineteenth century English economist David Ricardo. This theory is the intellectual basis of the modern argument for unrestricted free trade. In the twentieth century, Ricardo's work was refined by two Swedish economists, Eli Heckscher and Bertil Ohlin, whose theory is known as the Heckscher–Ohlin theory.

FREE TRADE The absence of barriers to the free flow of goods and services between countries.

THE BENEFITS OF TRADE

The great strength of the theories of Smith, Ricardo, and Heckscher–Ohlin is that they identify with precision the specific benefits of international trade. Common sense suggests that some international trade is beneficial. For example, nobody would suggest that Iceland should grow its own oranges. Iceland can benefit from trade by exchanging some of the products it can produce at a low cost (fish) for some products it cannot produce at all (oranges). Thus, by engaging in international trade, Icelanders are able to add oranges to their diet of fish.

The theories of Smith, Ricardo, and Heckscher–Ohlin go beyond this commonsense notion, however, to show why it is beneficial for a country to engage in international trade *even for products it is able to produce for itself.* This is a difficult concept for people to grasp. For example, many Canadians believe that to help save Canadian jobs from foreign competition, Canadian consumers should buy products produced in Canada by Canadian companies whenever possible. Similar thinking apparently influenced a 1997 decision by the International Trade Commission to protect the Louisiana crawfish industry from inexpensive Chinese imports (see the accompanying Country Focus).

The same kind of nationalistic sentiments can be observed in many other countries. However, the theories of Smith, Ricardo, and Heckscher–Ohlin tell us that a country's economy may gain if its citizens buy certain products from other nations that could be produced at home. The gains arise because international trade allows a country to specialize in the manufacture and export of products that can be produced most efficiently in that country, while importing products that can be produced more efficiently in other countries. Since we are recognized as pioneers in the mining industry, it may make sense for Canada to specialize in the production of heavy mining equipment, and export our expertise to Chile, Papua New Guinea, and beyond. On the other hand, it may make sense for Canada to import textiles from India, since the efficient production of textiles requires a relatively cheap labour force–and cheap labour is not abundant in Canada.

This economic argument is often difficult for segments of a country's population to accept. With their future threatened by imports, Canadian textile companies and their employees have, in the past, tried to persuade the federal government to limit the importation of textiles by demanding quotas and tariffs. Recent World Trade Organization decisions have overruled independent country wishes to keep tariff barriers in place. As of January 2005, tariffs on textiles will be abolished for member WTO countries. Similarly, as the Country Focus illustrates, with their future threatened by imports, the Louisiana crawfish industry persuaded the government to limit imports of crawfish from China. Although such import controls may benefit particular groups, such as American textile businesses and their employees or Louisiana crawfish farmers, the theories of Smith, Ricardo, and Heckscher–Ohlin suggest that the economy as a whole is hurt by this action. Limits on imports are often in the interests of domestic producers, but not domestic consumers.

THE PATTERN OF INTERNATIONAL TRADE

The theories of Smith, Ricardo, and Heckscher–Ohlin also help to explain the pattern of international trade that we observe in the world economy. Some aspects of the pattern are easy to understand. Climate and natural-resource endowments explain why Ghana exports cocoa, Brazil exports coffee, Saudi Arabia exports oil, and China exports crawfish. But much of the observed pattern of international trade is more difficult to explain. For example, why does Japan export automobiles, consumer electronics, and machine tools? Why does Switzerland export chemicals, watches, and jewellery? David Ricardo's theory of comparative advantage offers an explanation in terms of international differences in labour productivity. The more sophisticated Heckscher–Ohlin theory emphasizes the interplay between the proportions in which the factors of production (such as land, labour, and capital) are available in different countries and the proportions in which they are needed for producing particular

COUNTRY FOCUS

CRAWFISH WARS

Once upon a time, Louisiana was owned by the French. Napoleon sold the territory to the United States when Thomas Jefferson was president, but many of the French stayed on. Over time, their descendants developed the distinctive Cajun culture that today is celebrated in the United States for its cuisine and music. At the heart of that cuisine can be found the venerable crawfish, as Louisianians call the crayfish. The crawfish is a fresh-water crustacean native to the bayous of Louisiana. A central ingredient of crawfish pie, bisque, étouffée, and gumbo, the crawfish is to Cajun Louisiana what wine is to France: a culinary symbol of its culture. It is also a major industry that generates $300 million per year in revenues for Louisiana crawfish farmers—or at least it did until the Chinese appeared.

In the early 1990s, development of the Chinese industry was encouraged by Louisiana importers to meet the growing demand for crawfish. In China, the crawfish industry attracted entrepreneurial farmers. Chinese crawfish started to appear on the Louisiana scene in 1991. Although old-time Cajuns were quick to claim that the Chinese crawfish had an inferior taste, consumers didn't seem to notice the difference. More importantly perhaps, they liked the price, which ran between $2 and $3 per pound depending on the season, compared to $5 to $8 per pound for native Louisiana crawfish. With the significant price advantage, sales of Chinese imports skyrocketed from 353,000 pounds in 1992 to 5.5 million pounds in 1996. By 1996, Louisiana state officials estimated that 3,000 jobs had been lost in the local industry, mostly minimum-wage crawfish peelers, due to market share gains made by the Chinese.

This was too much for the Louisiana industry to stomach. In 1996, Louisiana's Crawfish Promotion and Research Board filed a petition with the International Trade Commission, an arm of the U.S. government, requesting an antidumping action. The petition claimed that Chinese crawfish producers were dumping their product, selling at below cost to drive Louisiana producers out of business. The industry requested that a 200 percent to 300 percent import tax be placed on Chinese crawfish. The State of Louisiana appropriated $350,000 from state funds to support the action.

Lawyers representing the Chinese crawfish industry claimed that lower production costs in China were the reason for the low prices—not dumping. One Louisiana-based importer of Chinese crawfish pointed out that 27 processing plants in China supplied his company. Workers at these plants were given housing and other amenities and paid 15 cents per hour, or $9 for a 60-hour week. The lawyers also said Chinese crawfish have been good for American consumers, who have saved money and benefited from a steadier supply, and good for Louisiana cuisine, because it is has become less expensive to cook. The lawyers pointed out that the action was not in the interests of American consumers, since it was nothing more than an attempt by Louisiana producers to reestablish their lucrative monopoly on the production of crawfish, a monopoly that would enable them to extract higher prices from consumers.

However, the International Trade Commission was deaf to such arguments. The commission deemed that China was a "nonmarket economy" since it was not yet a member of the World Trade Organization (something that changed in 2001). The commission then used prices in a "market economy," Spain, to establish a benchmark for a "fair market value" for crawfish. Since Spanish crawfish sell for approximately twice the price of Chinese crawfish and about the same as Louisiana crawfish, the commission concluded that the Chinese were dumping (selling below costs of production). In August 1997, the commission levied a 110 to 123 percent duty on imports of Chinese crawfish, effective October 1997, negating the price advantage enjoyed by Chinese producers. In the interests of protecting American jobs, the commission sided with Louisiana producers and against American consumers, who would now have to pay higher prices for crawfish. Under commission regulations, the ruling would stay in place for five years, after which the legitimacy of the import duty must be reevaluated.

Sources: Donna St. George, "Crawfish Wars: Cajun Country vs China," *New York Times,* May 7, 1997, pp. B1, B10; P. Passell, "Protecting America's Shores from Those Chinese Crawfish," *New York Times,* August 28, 1997, p. D2; N. Dunne, "Shellfish Imports Stick in the Cajun Craw," *Financial Times,* August 21, 1997, p. 16; and B. Thevenot, "Getting Pinched," *Times Picayune,* March 11, 2000, p. C1.

goods. This explanation rests on the assumption that countries have varying endowments of the factors of production. Tests of this theory, however, suggest it is a less powerful explanation of real-world trade patterns than once thought.

One early response to the failure of the Heckscher–Ohlin theory to explain the observed pattern of international trade was the *product life-cycle theory.* Proposed by Raymond Vernon, this theory suggests that early in their life cycle, most new products are produced in and exported from the country in which they were developed. As a new product becomes widely accepted internationally, however, production starts in other countries. As a result, the theory suggests, the product may ultimately be exported back to the country of its original innovation.

In a similar vein, during the 1980s, economists such as Paul Krugman of the Massachusetts Institute of Technology developed what has come to be known as the *new trade theory.* New trade theory stresses that in some cases countries specialize in the production and export of particular products not because of underlying differences in factor endowments, but because in certain industries the world market can support only a limited number of firms. (This is argued to be the case for the commercial aircraft industry.) In such industries, firms that enter the market first build a competitive advantage that is difficult to challenge. Thus, the observed pattern of trade between nations may be due in part to the ability of firms within a given nation to capture first-mover advantages. The United States dominates in the export of commercial jet aircraft because American firms such as Boeing were first movers in the world market. Boeing built a competitive advantage that has subsequently been difficult for firms from countries with equally favourable factor endowments to challenge.

In a work related to the new trade theory, Michael Porter of the Harvard Business School developed a theory, referred to as the theory of national competitive advantage, that attempts to explain why particular nations achieve international success in certain industries. Like the new trade theorists, in addition to factor endowments, Porter points out the importance of country factors such as domestic demand and domestic rivalry in explaining a nation's dominance in the production and export of particular products.

TRADE THEORY AND GOVERNMENT POLICY

Although all these theories agree that international trade is beneficial to a country, they lack agreement in their recommendations for government policy. Mercantilism makes a case for government involvement in promoting exports and limiting imports. The theories of Smith, Ricardo, and Heckscher–Ohlin form part of the case for unrestricted free trade. The argument for unrestricted free trade is that both import controls and export incentives (such as subsidies) are self-defeating and result in wasted resources. Both the new trade theory and Porter's theory of national competitive advantage can be interpreted as justifying some limited government intervention to support the development of certain export-oriented industries. We will discuss the pros and cons of this argument, known as strategic trade policy, as well as the pros and cons of the argument for unrestricted free trade in Chapter 6.

MERCANTILISM

MERCANTILISM An economic philosophy advocating that countries should simultaneously encourage exports and discourage imports.

The first theory of international trade emerged in England in the mid-sixteenth century. Referred to as *mercantilism,* its principal assertion was that gold and silver were the mainstays of national wealth and essential to vigorous commerce. The main tenet of **mercantilism** was that it was in a country's best interests to maintain a trade surplus, to export more than it imported. By doing so, a country would accumulate gold and silver and, consequently, increase its national wealth and prestige. As the English mercantilist writer Thomas Mun put it in 1630:

> The ordinary means therefore to increase our wealth and treasure is by foreign trade, wherein we must ever observe this rule: to sell more to strangers yearly than we consume of theirs in value.[1]

Consistent with this belief, the mercantilist doctrine advocated government intervention to achieve a surplus in the balance of trade. The mercantilists saw no virtue in a large volume of trade per se. Rather, they recommended policies to maximize exports and minimize imports. To achieve this, imports were limited by tariffs and quotas, while exports were subsidized.

The classical economist David Hume pointed out an inherent inconsistency in the mercantilist doctrine in 1752. According to Hume, if England had a balance-of-trade surplus with France (it exported more than it imported) the resulting inflow of gold and silver would swell the domestic money supply and generate inflation in England. In France, however, the outflow of gold and silver would have the opposite effect. France's money supply would contract, and its prices would fall. This change in relative prices between France and England would encourage the French to buy fewer English goods (because they were becoming more expensive) and the English to buy more French goods (because they were becoming cheaper). The result would be a deterioration in the English balance of trade and an improvement in France's trade balance, until the English surplus was eliminated. Hence, according to Hume, in the long run no country could sustain a surplus on the balance of trade and so accumulate gold and silver as the mercantilists had envisaged.

The flaw with mercantilism was that it viewed trade as a zero-sum game. (A **zero-sum game** is one in which a gain by one country results in a loss by another.) It was left to Adam Smith and David Ricardo to show the shortsightedness of this approach and to demonstrate that trade is a **positive-sum game,** or a situation in which all countries can benefit. The mercantilist doctrine is by no means dead.[2] For example, Jarl Hagelstam, a director at the Finnish Ministry of Finance, has observed that in most trade negotiations:

ZERO-SUM GAME A situation in which an economic gain by one country results in an economic loss by another.

POSITIVE-SUM GAME A situation in which all countries can benefit even if some benefit more than others.

> The approach of individual negotiating countries, both industrialized and developing, has been to press for trade liberalization in areas where their own comparative competitive advantages are the strongest, and to resist liberalization in areas where they are less competitive and fear that imports would replace domestic production.[3]

Hagelstam attributes this strategy by negotiating countries to a neomercantilist belief held by the politicians of many nations. This belief equates political power with economic power and economic power with a balance-of-trade surplus. Thus, the trade strategy of many nations is designed to simultaneously boost exports and limit imports.

ABSOLUTE ADVANTAGE

In his 1776 landmark book *The Wealth of Nations,* Adam Smith attacked the mercantilist assumption that trade is a zero-sum game. Smith argued that countries differ in their ability to produce goods efficiently. In his time, the English, by virtue of their superior manufacturing processes, were the world's most efficient textile manufacturers. Due to the combination of favourable climate, good soils, and accumulated expertise, the French had the world's most efficient wine industry. The English had an *absolute advantage* in the production of textiles, while the French had an *absolute advantage* in the production of wine. Thus, a country has an **absolute advantage** in the production of a product when it is more efficient than any other country in producing it.

ABSOLUTE ADVANTAGE A country has an absolute advantage in the production of a product when it is more efficient than any other country at producing it.

According to Smith, countries should specialize in the production of goods for which they have an absolute advantage and then trade these for goods produced by other countries. Smith's basic argument, therefore, is that a country should never produce goods at home that it can buy at a lower cost from other countries. According to Smith, by specializing in the production of goods in which each has an absolute advantage, both countries benefit by engaging in trade.

Consider the effects of trade between Ghana and South Korea. The production of any good (output) requires resources (inputs) such as land, labour, and capital. Assume that Ghana and South Korea both have the same amount of resources and that these resources can be used to produce either rice or cocoa. Assume further that 200 units of resources are available in each country. Imagine that in Ghana it takes 10 resources to produce 1 tonne of cocoa and 20 resources to produce 1 tonne of rice. Thus, Ghana could produce 20 tonnes of cocoa and no rice, 10 tonnes of rice and no cocoa, or some combination of rice and cocoa between these two extremes. The different combinations that Ghana could produce are represented by the line GG′ in Figure 5.1. This is referred to as Ghana's production possibility frontier (PPF). Similarly, imagine that in South Korea it takes 40 resources to produce 1 tonne of cocoa and 10 resources to produce 1 tonne of rice. Thus, South Korea could produce 5 tonnes of cocoa and no rice, 20 tonnes of rice and no cocoa, or some combination between these two extremes. The different combinations available to South Korea are represented by the line KK′ in Figure 5.1, which is South Korea's PPF. Clearly, Ghana has an absolute advantage in the production of cocoa. (More resources are needed to produce a tonne of cocoa in South Korea than in Ghana.) By the same token, South Korea has an absolute advantage in the production of rice.

Now consider a situation in which neither country trades with any other. Each country devotes half of its resources to the production of rice and half to the production of cocoa. Each country must also consume what it produces. Ghana would be able to produce 10 tonnes of cocoa and 5 tonnes of rice (point A in Figure 5.1), while South Korea would be able to produce 10 tonnes of rice and 2.5 tonnes of cocoa. Without trade, the combined production of both countries would be 12.5 tonnes of cocoa (10 tonnes in Ghana plus 2.5 tonnes in South Korea) and 15 tonnes of rice (5 tonnes in Ghana and 10 tonnes in South Korea). If each country were to specialize in producing the good for which it had an absolute advantage and then trade with the other for the good it lacks, Ghana could produce 20 tonnes of cocoa, and South Korea could produce 20 tonnes of rice. Thus, specializing could increase the production of both goods. Production of cocoa would increase from 12.5 tonnes to 20 tonnes, while production of rice would increase from 15 tonnes to 20 tonnes. The increase in production that would result from specialization is therefore 7.5 tonnes of cocoa and 5 tonnes of rice. Table 5.1 summarizes these figures.

By engaging in trade and swapping 1 tonne of cocoa for 1 tonne of rice, producers in both countries could consume more of both cocoa and rice. Imagine that Ghana and South Korea swap cocoa and rice on a one-to-one basis; that is, the price of 1 tonne of cocoa is equal to the price of 1 tonne of rice. If Ghana decided to export 6 tonnes of cocoa to South Korea and import 6 tonnes of rice in return, its final consumption after trade would be 14 tonnes of cocoa and 6 tonnes of rice. This is 4 tonnes more cocoa than it could have consumed before specialization and trade and 1 tonne more rice. Similarly, South Korea's final consumption after trade would be 6 tonnes of cocoa and 14 tonnes of rice. This is 3.5 tonnes more cocoa than it could have consumed before specialization and trade and 4 tonnes more rice. Thus, as a result of specialization and trade, output of both cocoa and rice would be increased, and consumers in both nations would be able to consume more. Thus, we can see that trade is a positive-sum game; it produces net gains for all involved.

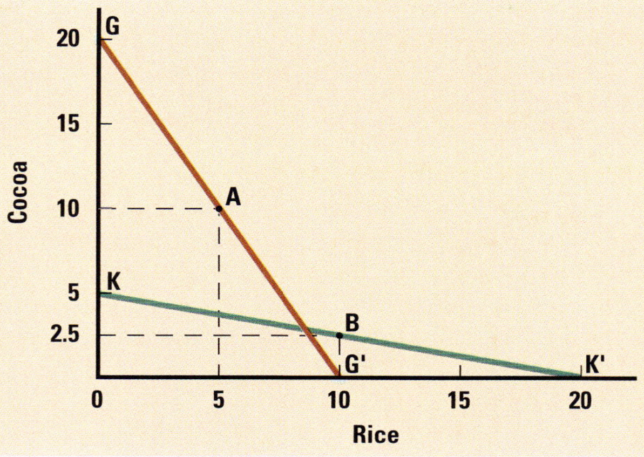

FIGURE 5.1

The Theory of Absolute Advantage

TABLE 5.1

Absolute Advantage and the Gains from Trade

	COCOA	RICE
Resources Required to Produce 1 Tonne of Cocoa and Rice		
Ghana	10	20
South Korea	40	10
Production and Consumption without Trade		
Ghana	10.0	5.0
South Korea	2.5	10.0
Total production	12.5	15.0
Production with Specialization		
Ghana	20.0	0.0
South Korea	0.0	20.0
Total production	20.0	20.0
Consumption after Ghana Trades 6 Tonnes of Cocoa for 6 Tonnes of South Korean Rice		
Ghana	14.0	6.0
South Korea	6.0	14.0
Increase in Consumption as a Result of Specialization and Trade		
Ghana	4.0	1.0
South Korea	3.5	4.0

COMPARATIVE ADVANTAGE

David Ricardo took Adam Smith's theory one step further by exploring what might happen when one country has an absolute advantage in the production of all goods.[4] Smith's theory of absolute advantage suggests that such a country might derive no benefits from international trade. In his 1817 book *Principles of Political Economy,* Ricardo showed this was not the case. According to Ricardo's theory of **comparative advantage,** it makes sense for a country to specialize in the production of those goods that it produces most efficiently and to buy the goods that it produces less efficiently from other countries, even if this means buying goods from other countries that it could

COMPARATIVE ADVANTAGE The theory that countries should specialize in the production of goods and services they can produce most efficiently. A country is said to have a comparative advantage in the production of such goods and services.

produce more efficiently itself.[5] While this may seem counterintuitive, the logic can be explained with a simple example.

Assume that Ghana is more efficient in the production of both cocoa and rice; that is, Ghana has an absolute advantage in the production of both products. In Ghana it takes 10 resources to produce 1 tonne of cocoa and 13 1/3 resources to produce 1 tonne of rice. Thus, given its 200 units of resources, Ghana can produce 20 tonnes of cocoa and no rice, 15 tonnes of rice and no cocoa, or any combination in between on its PPF (the line GG′ in Figure 5.2). In South Korea it takes 40 resources to produce 1 tonne of cocoa and 20 resources to produce 1 tonne of rice. Thus, South Korea can produce 5 tonnes of cocoa and no rice, 10 tonnes of rice and no cocoa, or any combination on its PPF (the line KK′ in Figure 5.2). Again assume that without trade, each country uses half of its resources to produce rice and half to produce cocoa. Thus, without trade, Ghana will produce 10 tonnes of cocoa and 7.5 tonnes of rice (point A in Figure 5.2), while South Korea will produce 2.5 tonnes of cocoa and 5 tonnes of rice (point B in Figure 5.2).

In light of Ghana's absolute advantage in the production of both goods, why should it trade with South Korea? Although Ghana has an absolute advantage in the production of both cocoa and rice, it has a comparative advantage only in the production of cocoa: Ghana can produce 4 times as much cocoa as South Korea, but only 1.5 times as much rice. Ghana is *comparatively* more efficient at producing cocoa than it is at producing rice.

Without trade, the combined production of cocoa will be 12.5 tonnes (10 tonnes in Ghana and 2.5 in South Korea), and the combined production of rice will also be 12.5 tonnes (7.5 tonnes in Ghana and 5 tonnes in South Korea). Without trade, each country must consume what it produces. By engaging in trade, the two countries can increase their combined production of rice and cocoa, and consumers in both nations can consume more of both goods.

THE GAINS FROM TRADE

Imagine that Ghana exploits its comparative advantage in the production of cocoa to increase its output from 10 tonnes to 15 tonnes. This uses up 150 units of resources, leaving the remaining 50 units of resources to use in producing 3.75 tonnes of rice (point C in Figure 5.2). Meanwhile, South Korea specializes in the production of rice, producing 10 tonnes. The combined output of both cocoa and rice has now increased. Before specialization, the combined output was 12.5 tonnes of cocoa and 12.5 tonnes of rice. Now

FIGURE 5.2
The Theory of Comparative Advantage

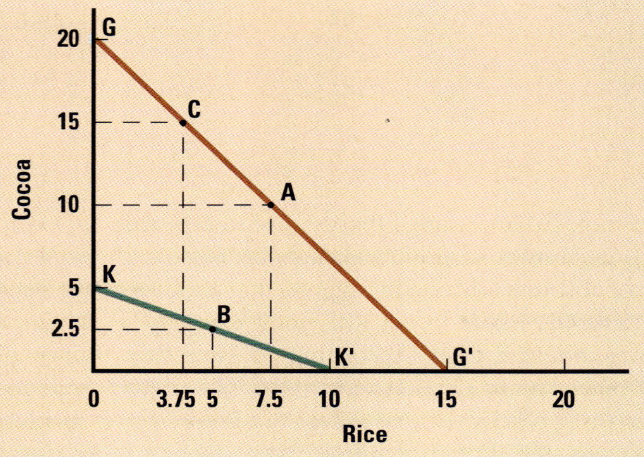

it is 15 tonnes of cocoa and 13.75 tonnes of rice (3.75 tonnes in Ghana and 10 tonnes in South Korea). The source of the increase in production is summarized in Table 5.2.

Not only is output higher, but also both countries can now benefit from trade. If Ghana and South Korea swap cocoa and rice on a one-to-one basis, with both countries choosing to exchange 4 tonnes of their export for 4 tonnes of the import, both countries are able to consume more cocoa and rice than they could before specialization and trade (see Table 5.2). Thus, if Ghana exchanges 4 tonnes of cocoa with South Korea for 4 tonnes of rice, it is still left with 11 tonnes of rice, which is 1 tonne more than it had before trade. The 4 tonnes of rice it gets from South Korea in exchange for its 4 tonnes of cocoa, when added to the 3.75 tonnes it now produces domestically, leaves it with a total of 7.75 tonnes of rice, which is one-fourth of a tonne more than it had before specialization. Similarly, after swapping 4 tonnes of rice with Ghana, South Korea still ends up with 6 tonnes of rice, which is more than it had before specialization. In addition, the 4 tonnes of cocoa it receives in exchange is 1.5 tonnes more than it produced before trade. Thus, consumption of cocoa and rice can increase in both countries as a result of specialization and trade.

The basic message of the theory of comparative advantage is that *potential world production is greater with unrestricted free trade than it is with restricted trade*. Ricardo's theory suggests that consumers in all nations can consume more if there are no trade restrictions. This occurs even in countries that lack an absolute advantage in the

ANOTHER PERSPECTIVE

Maple Leaf Life Savers?

In 2002, Life Savers, a Michigan company, announced it was moving production from Michigan to Canada. Why would such a move make business sense, you might wonder. Not because of lower labour costs, lower tax rates, or colder winters.

Here's why Life Savers moved. The United States protects sugar along with other agricultural products. The domestic sugar price is considerably higher than the world market price. Sugar is the main ingredient of Life Savers, and the company will be able to purchase sugar at a much lower world market price in Canada.

TABLE 5.2

Comparative Advantage and the Gains from Trade

Resources Required to Produce 1 Tonne of Cocoa and Rice		
	COCOA	**RICE**
Ghana	10	13.33
South Korea	40	20
Production and Consumption without Trade		
	COCOA	**RICE**
Ghana	10.0	7.5
South Korea	2.5	5.0
Total production	12.5	12.5
Production with Specialization		
	COCOA	**RICE**
Ghana	15.0	3.75
South Korea	0.0	10.0
Total production	15.0	13.75
Consumption after Ghana Trades 4 Tonnes of Cocoa for 4 Tonnes of South Korean Rice		
	COCOA	**RICE**
Ghana	11.0	7.75
South Korea	4.0	6.0
Increase in Consumption as a Result of Specialization and Trade		
	COCOA	**RICE**
Ghana	1.0	0.25
South Korea	1.5	1.0

production of any good. In other words, to an even greater degree than the theory of absolute advantage, *the theory of comparative advantage suggests that trade is a positive-sum game in which all countries that participate realize economic gains.* As such, this theory provides a strong rationale for encouraging free trade. So powerful is Ricardo's theory that it remains a major intellectual weapon for those who argue for free trade.

QUALIFICATIONS AND ASSUMPTIONS

The conclusion that free trade is universally beneficial is a rather bold one to draw from such a simple model. Our simple model includes many unrealistic assumptions:

1. We have assumed a simple world in which there are only two countries and two goods. In the real world, there are many countries and many goods.
2. We have assumed away transportation costs between countries.
3. We have assumed away differences in the prices of resources in different countries. We have said nothing about exchange rates, simply assuming that cocoa and rice could be swapped on a one-to-one basis.
4. We have assumed that resources can move freely from the production of one good to another within a country. In reality, this is not always the case.
5. We have assumed constant returns to scale; that is, that specialization by Ghana or South Korea has no effect on the amount of resources required to produce one ton of cocoa or rice. In reality, both diminishing and increasing returns to specialization exist. The amount of resources required to produce a good might decrease or increase as a nation specializes in production of that good.
6. We have assumed that each country has a fixed stock of resources and that free trade does not change the efficiency with which a country uses its resources. This static assumption makes no allowances for the dynamic changes in a country's stock of resources and in the efficiency with which the country uses its resources that might result from free trade.
7. We have assumed away the effects of trade on income distribution within a country.

Given these assumptions, can the conclusion that free trade is mutually beneficial be extended to the real world of many countries, many goods, transportation costs, volatile exchange rates, immobile domestic resources, nonconstant returns to specialization, and dynamic changes? Although a detailed extension of the theory of comparative advantage is beyond the scope of this book, economists have shown that the basic result derived from our simple model can be generalized to a world composed of many countries producing many different goods.[6] Despite the shortcomings of the Ricardian model, research suggests that the basic proposition that countries will export the goods that they are most efficient at producing is supported by the data.[7] However, once all the assumptions are dropped, the case for unrestricted free trade, while still positive, has been argued by some economists associated with the "new trade theory" to lose some of its strength.[8] We return to this issue later in this chapter and in the next.

TRADE AND SIMPLE EXTENSIONS OF THE RICARDIAN MODEL

Let us explore the effect of relaxing two of the assumptions identified above in the simple comparative advantage model. Below we relax the assumption that resources move freely from the production of one good to another within a country, and the assumption that trade does not change a country's stock of resources or the efficiency with which those resources are utilized.

Immobile Resources

In our simple comparative model of Ghana and South Korea, we assumed that producers (farmers) could easily convert land from the production of cocoa to rice, and vice versa. While this assumption may hold for some agricultural products, resources do not always shift quite so easily from producing one good to another. A certain amount of friction is involved. For example, embracing a free trade regime for an advanced economy such as Canada often implies that the country will produce less of some labour-intensive goods, such as textiles, and more of some knowledge-intensive goods, such as computer software or biotechnology products. Although the country as a whole will gain from such a shift, textile producers will lose. A textile worker in Quebec is probably not qualified to write software for Microsoft. Thus, the shift to free trade may mean that she becomes unemployed or has to accept another less attractive job, such as working at a fast-food restaurant.

Resources do not always move easily from one economic activity to another. The process creates friction and human suffering too. While the theory predicts that the benefits of free trade outweigh the costs by a significant margin, this is little comfort to those who bear the costs. Accordingly, political opposition to a free trade regime typically comes from those whose jobs are most at risk. In Canada, for example, textile workers and their unions have long opposed the move toward free trade precisely because this group has much to lose. Governments often ease the transition toward free trade by helping to retrain those who lose their jobs as a result. The pain caused by the movement toward a free trade regime is a short-term phenomenon, while the gains from trade once the transition has been made are both significant and enduring.

Dynamic Effects and Economic Growth

Our simple comparative advantage model assumed that trade does not change a country's stock of resources or the efficiency with which it utilizes those resources. This static assumption makes no allowances for the dynamic changes that might result from trade. If we relax this assumption, it becomes apparent that opening an economy to trade is likely to generate dynamic gains of two sorts.[9] First, free trade might increase a country's stock of resources as increased supplies of labour and capital from abroad become available for use within the country. This is occurring now in Eastern Europe, where many Western businesses are investing large amounts of capital in the former Communist countries.

Second, free trade might also increase the efficiency with which a country uses its resources. Gains in the efficiency of resource utilization could arise from a number of factors. For example, economies of large-scale production might become available as trade expands the size of the total market available to domestic firms. Trade might make better technology from abroad available to domestic firms; better technology can increase labour productivity or the productivity of land. (The so-called green revolution had this effect on agricultural outputs in developing countries.) Also, opening an economy to foreign competition might stimulate domestic producers to look for ways to increase their efficiency. Again, this phenomenon is arguably occurring in the once-

Team Canada mission leader Prime Minister Paul Martin waves from a bus during a January 21, 2005, visit to Beijing. Martin was visiting a Beijing depot that uses Canadian-made fuel cell technology in their buses. CP/Tom Hanson.

protected markets of Eastern Europe, where many former state monopolies are increasing their efficiency to survive in the competitive world market. The theory suggests that opening an economy to free trade not only results in static gains of the type discussed earlier, but also results in dynamic gains that stimulate economic growth. If this is so, the case for free trade becomes stronger.

Evidence for the Link between Trade and Growth

Many economic studies have looked at the relationship between trade and economic growth. In general, these studies suggest that, as predicted by the theory, countries that adopt a more open stance toward international trade enjoy higher growth rates than those that close their economies to trade. Jeffrey Sachs and Andrew Warner created a measure of how "open" to international trade an economy was and then looked at the relationship between "openness" and economic growth for a sample of more than 100 countries from 1970 to 1990.[10] Among other findings, they reported:

> We find a strong association between openness and growth, both within the group of developing and the group of developed countries. Within the group of developing countries, the open economies grew at 4.49 percent per year, and the closed economies grew at 0.69 percent per year. Within the group of developed economies, the open economies grew at 2.29 percent per year, and the closed economies grew at 0.74 percent per year.[11]

The message of this study seems clear: Adopt an open economy and embrace free trade, and over time your nation will be rewarded with higher economic growth rates. Higher growth will raise income levels and living standards. This last point has recently been confirmed by a study that looked at the relationship between trade and growth in incomes. The study, undertaken by Jeffrey Frankel and David Romer, found that on average, a one percentage point increase in the ratio of a country's trade to its gross domestic product increases income per person by at least one-half percent.[12] For every 10 percent increase in the importance of international trade in an economy, average income levels will rise by at least 5 percent. Despite the short-term adjustment costs associated with adopting a free trade regime, trade would seem to produce greater economic growth and higher living standards in the long run, just as the theory of Ricardo would lead us to expect.[13]

HECKSCHER–OHLIN THEORY

Ricardo's theory stresses that comparative advantage arises from differences in productivity. Thus, whether Ghana is more efficient than South Korea in the production of cocoa depends on how productively it uses its resources. Ricardo stressed labour productivity and argued that differences in labour productivity between nations underlie the notion of comparative advantage. Swedish economists Eli Heckscher (in 1919) and Bertil Ohlin (in 1933) put forward a different explanation of comparative advantage. They argued that comparative advantage arises from differences in national factor endowments.[14] By factor endowments they meant the extent to which a country is endowed with such resources as land, labour, and capital. Nations have varying factor endowments, and different factor endowments explain differences in factor costs. The more abundant a factor, the lower its cost. The Heckscher–Ohlin theory predicts that countries will export those goods that make intensive use of factors that are locally abundant, while importing goods that make intensive use of factors that are locally scarce. Thus, the Heckscher–Ohlin theory attempts to explain the pattern of international trade that we observe in the world economy. Like Ricardo's theory, the Heckscher–Ohlin theory argues that free trade is beneficial. Unlike Ricardo's theory, however, the

Heckscher–Ohlin theory argues that the pattern of international trade is determined by differences in factor endowments, rather than differences in productivity.

The Heckscher–Ohlin theory also has commonsense appeal. For example, the United States has long been a substantial exporter of agricultural goods, reflecting in part its unusual abundance of arable land. In contrast, China excels in the export of goods produced in labour-intensive manufacturing industries, such as textiles and footwear. This reflects China's relative abundance of low-cost labour. The United States, which lacks abundant low-cost labour, has been a primary importer of these goods. Note that it is relative, not absolute, endowments that are important; a country may have larger absolute amounts of land and labour than another country, but be relatively abundant in one of them.

THE LEONTIEF PARADOX

The Heckscher–Ohlin theory has been one of the most influential theoretical ideas in international economics. Most economists prefer the Heckscher–Ohlin theory to Ricardo's theory because it makes fewer simplifying assumptions. Because of its influence, the theory has been subjected to many empirical tests. Beginning with a famous study published in 1953 by Wassily Leontief (winner of the Nobel Prize in economics in 1973), many of these tests have raised questions about the validity of the Heckscher–Ohlin theory.[15] Using the Heckscher–Ohlin theory, Leontief postulated that since the United States was relatively abundant in capital compared to other nations, the United States would be an exporter of capital-intensive goods and an importer of labour-intensive goods. To his surprise, however, he found that U.S. exports were less capital intensive than U.S. imports. Since this result was at variance with the predictions of the theory, it has become known as the Leontief paradox.

No one is quite sure why we observe the Leontief paradox. One possible explanation is that the United States has a special advantage in producing new products or goods made with innovative technologies. Such products may be less capital intensive than products whose technology has had time to mature and become suitable for mass production. Thus, the United States may be exporting goods that heavily use skilled labour and innovative entrepreneurship, such as computer software, while importing heavy manufacturing products that use large amounts of capital. Some more recent empirical studies tend to confirm this.[16] Further tests of the Heckscher–Ohlin theory using data for many countries tend to confirm the existence of the Leontief paradox.[17]

This leaves economists with a difficult dilemma. They prefer Heckscher–Ohlin on theoretical grounds, but it is a relatively poor predictor of real-world international trade patterns. On the other hand, the theory they regard as being too limited, Ricardo's theory of comparative advantage, predicts trade patterns with greater accuracy. The best solution to this dilemma may be to return to the Ricardian idea that trade patterns are largely driven by international differences in productivity. Thus, one might argue that the United States exports commercial aircraft and imports automobiles not because its factor endowments are especially suited to aircraft manufacture and not suited to automobile manufacture, but because the United States is more efficient at producing aircraft than automobiles. A key assumption in the Heckscher–Ohlin theory is that technologies are the same across countries. This may not be the case, and differences in technology may lead to differences in productivity, which in turn, drives international trade patterns.[18] Thus, Japan's success in exporting automobiles in the 1970s and 1980s was based not just on the relative abundance of capital, but also on its development of innovative manufacturing technology that enabled it to achieve higher productivity levels in automobile production than other countries that also had abundant capital.

THE PRODUCT LIFE-CYCLE THEORY

Raymond Vernon proposed the product life-cycle theory in the mid-1960s.[19] Vernon's theory was based on the observation that for most of the twentieth century a very large proportion of the world's new products had been developed by U.S. firms and sold first in the U.S. market (e.g., mass-produced automobiles, televisions, instant cameras, photocopiers, personal computers, and semiconductor chips). To explain this, Vernon argued that the wealth and size of the U.S. market gave U.S. firms a strong incentive to develop new consumer products. In addition, the high cost of U.S. labour gave U.S. firms an incentive to develop cost-saving process innovations.

Just because a new product is developed by a U.S. firm and first sold in the U.S. market, it does not follow that the product must be produced in the United States. It could be produced abroad at some low-cost location and then exported back into the United States. However, Vernon argued that most new products were initially produced in America.

Vernon went on to argue that early in the life cycle of a typical new product, while demand is starting to grow rapidly in the United States, demand in other advanced countries is limited to high-income groups. The limited initial demand in other advanced countries does not make it worthwhile for firms in those countries to start producing the new product, but it does necessitate some exports from the United States to those countries.

Over time, demand for the new product starts to grow in other advanced countries (e.g., Great Britain, France, Germany, and Japan). As it does, it becomes worthwhile for foreign companies to begin producing for their home markets. In addition, U.S. firms might set up production facilities in those advanced countries where demand is growing. Consequently, production within other advanced countries begins to limit the potential for exports from the United States.

As the market in the United States and other advanced nations matures, the product becomes more standardized, and price becomes the main competitive weapon. As this occurs, cost considerations start to play a greater role in the competitive process. Producers based in advanced countries where labour costs are lower than in the United States (e.g., Italy, Spain) might now be able to export to the United States.

If cost pressures become intense, the process might not stop there. The cycle by which the United States lost its advantage to other advanced countries might be repeated once more, as developing countries (e.g., Thailand) begin to acquire a production advantage over advanced countries. Thus, the locus of global production initially switches from the United States to other advanced nations and then from those nations to developing countries.

The consequence of these trends for the pattern of world trade is that over time the United States switches from being an exporter of the product to an importer of the product as production becomes concentrated in lower-cost foreign locations. Figure 5.3 shows the growth of production and consumption over time in the United States, other advanced countries, and developing countries.

THE NEW TRADE THEORY

The new trade theory began to emerge in the 1970s when a number of economists were arguing that increasing returns to specialization might exist in some industries.[20] Economies of scale represent one particularly important source of increasing returns.

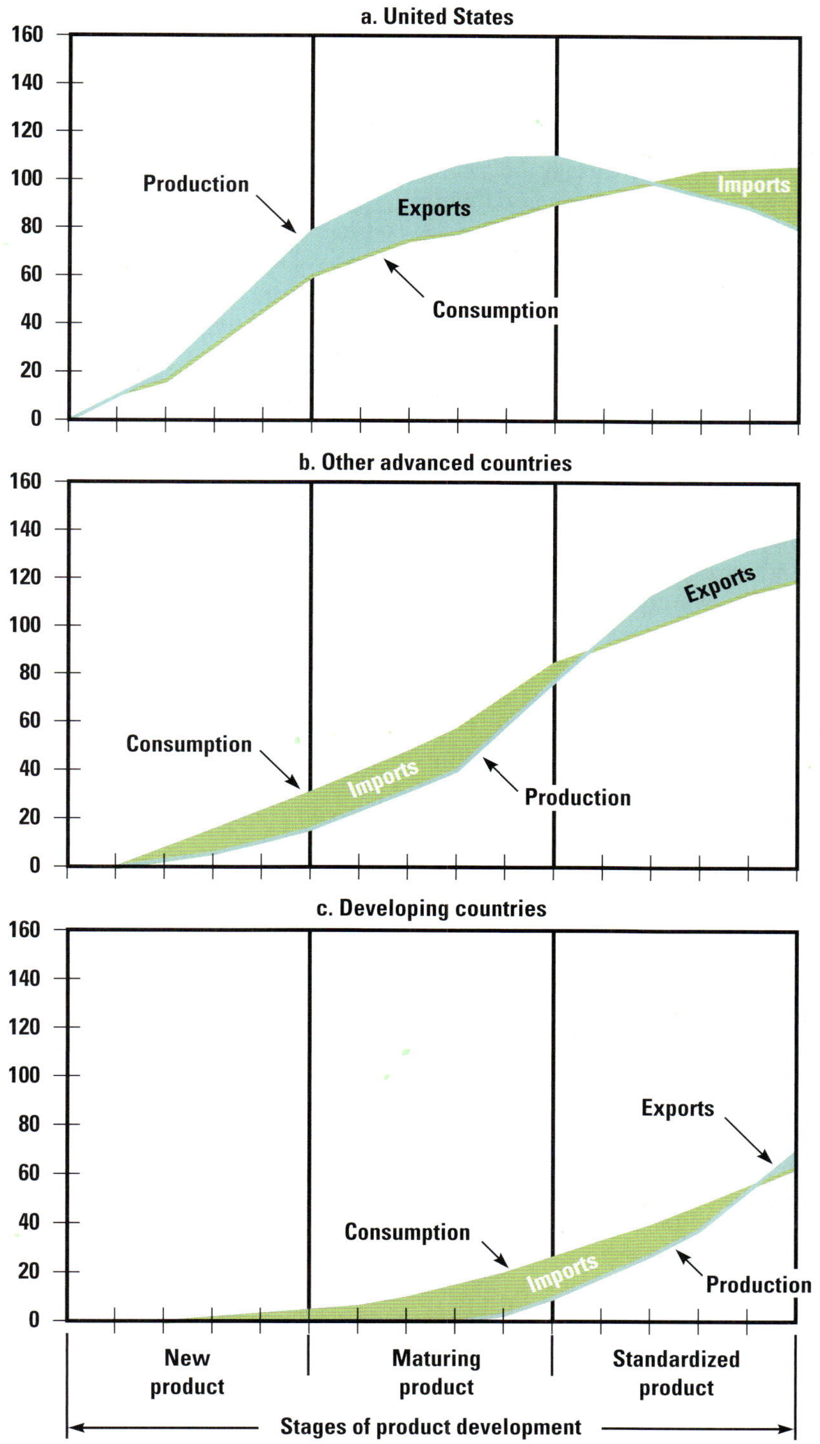

FIGURE 5.3

The Product Life-Cycle Theory

ECONOMIES OF SCALE Cost advantages associated with large-scale production.

Economies of scale are unit cost reductions associated with a large scale of output. If international trade results in a country specializing in the production of a certain good, and if there are economies of scale in producing that good, then as output of that good expands, unit costs will fall. In such a case, there will be increasing returns to specialization, not diminishing returns! Put differently, as a country produces more of the good, due to the realization of economies of scale, productivity will increase and the unit costs of producing the good will fall.

New trade theory also argues that if the output required to realize significant scale economies represents a substantial proportion of total world demand for that product, the world market may be able to support only a limited number of firms producing that product. Those firms that enter the world market first may gain an advantage that may be difficult for other firms to match. Thus, a country may dominate in the export of a particular product where scale economies are important, and where the volume of output required to gain scale economies represents a significant proportion of world output, because it is home to a firm that was an early mover in this industry.

THE AEROSPACE EXAMPLE

The commercial aerospace industry, which is currently dominated by just two firms, Boeing and Airbus (although there are several niche players, including Bombardier and Embraer), is a good example of this theory. Economies of scale in this industry come from the ability to spread fixed costs over a large output. The fixed costs of developing a new commercial jet airliner are astronomical. Boeing spent an estimated $5 billion to develop its Boeing 777 jetliner. If Boeing makes only 100 of the Boeing 777, its fixed costs will amount to $50 million per unit (i.e., $5 billion divided by 100). If the variable costs such as labour, equipment, and parts equal $80 million per aircraft, the total cost of each aircraft would be $130 million (i.e., $80 million in per unit variable costs plus $50 million in per unit fixed costs). If Boeing makes 500 of these aircraft, the fixed costs fall to $10 million per unit (i.e., $5 billion divided by 500), bringing the total cost of each aircraft to just $90 million (i.e., $80 million plus $10 million). The economies of scale here are significant, with average unit costs falling by $40 million as output expands from 100 units to 500 units.

LEARNING EFFECTS Cost savings from learning by doing.

In addition to economies of scale, learning effects also exist in this industry. These too may result in increasing returns to specialization. **Learning effects** are cost savings that come from learning by doing. Labour, for example, learns by repetition how best to carry out a task. Labour productivity increases over time and variable unit costs fall as individuals learn the most efficient way to perform a particular task. Learning effects tend to be more significant when a complex task is repeated because there is more to learn. Thus, learning effects will be more significant in an assembly process involving 1000 complex steps than in a process involving 100 simple steps–and assembling a commercial jetliner involves more complex steps than perhaps any other product. Learning effects were first documented in the aerospace industry where it was found that each time accumulated output of airframes was doubled, unit costs declined to 80 percent of their previous level.[21] Thus, the fourth airframe typically cost only 80 percent of the second airframe to produce, the eighth airframe only 80 percent of the fourth, the 16th only 80 percent of the eighth, and so on. This observation implies that the $80 million in per unit variable costs required to build a 777 will decline over time as output expands, primarily because of gains in labour productivity. Thus, while variable costs per unit might be $80 million by the time 100 aircraft have been manufactured, by the time 500 aircraft have been manufactured, they may have fallen to $60 million per unit.

Combine learning effects with our earlier calculation of the decline in unit fixed costs, and our analysis suggests that as output of 777s expands from 100 to 500 units, unit costs will fall from $130 million ($80 million variable costs and $50 million fixed costs per unit) to $70 million ($60 million variable costs plus $10 million fixed costs per unit). Obviously, increasing returns to specialization are very important in this industry. Just how important they are can be appreciated by the fact that the list price for a new Boeing 777 is about $120 million. Thus, if Boeing sells only 100 aircraft, it will not make any money on this product. If it sells 500 aircraft, due to scale economies and learning effects, it will make acceptable profits.

World demand is large enough to support only a limited number of aircraft producers at high output levels. Forecasts suggest that the global market for long-range aircraft with a seating capacity of about 300, such as the 777, will be about 1500 aircraft between 1997 and 2008. If we assume that Boeing has to sell about 500 aircraft to make a decent return on its investment, this suggests the world market is large enough to support only three producers profitably!

IMPLICATIONS

New trade theory has important implications. The theory suggests that a country may predominate in the export of a good simply because it was lucky enough to have one or more firms among the first to produce that good. Underpinning this argument is the notion of first-mover advantages, which are the economic and strategic advantages that accrue to early entrants into an industry.[22] Because they are able to gain economies of scale and learning effects, the early entrants in an industry may get a lock on the world market, discouraging subsequent entries. First movers' ability to benefit from increasing returns creates a barrier to entry. In the commercial aircraft industry, for example, the fact that Boeing and Airbus are already in the industry and have the benefits of economies of scale and learning effects render it more difficult, but not impossible, for new entrants such as Bombardier and Embraer to enter into the commercial manufacturing of jet aircraft. Still, Airbus and Boeing remain the largest players in the commercial aircraft business. This dominance can be further reenforced because global demand may not be sufficient to profitably support another producer in the industry. So although Japanese firms might be able to compete in the market, they have decided not to enter the industry but to ally themselves as major subcontractors with primary producers (e.g., Mitsubishi Heavy Industries is a major subcontractor for Boeing on the 767 and 777 programs).

New trade theory is at variance with the Heckscher–Ohlin theory, which suggests that a country will predominate in the export of a product when it is particularly well endowed with those factors used intensively in its manufacture. New trade theorists argue that the United States leads in exports of commercial jet aircraft not because it is better endowed with the factors of production required to manufacture aircraft, but because one of the first movers in the industry, Boeing, was a U.S. firm. The new trade theory is not at variance with the theory of comparative advantage. Economies of scale and learning effects both increase the efficiency of resource utilization, and hence increase productivity. Thus, the new trade theory identifies an important source of comparative advantage.

It is perhaps too early to say how useful this theory is in explaining trade patterns. The theory is still relatively new and little supporting empirical work has been done. Consistent with the theory, however, a study by Harvard business historian Alfred Chandler suggests the existence of first-mover advantages is an important factor in explaining the dominance of firms from certain nations in certain industries.[23] The number of firms is very limited in many global industries, including the chemical industry, the heavy construction-equipment industry, the heavy truck industry, the tire industry, the consumer electronics industry, the jet engine industry, and the computer software industry.

Even though de Havilland built the world's first jet airliner, the Comet had many technological flaws when it was introduced. It is widely believed that Boeing was "lucky" and able to exploit its technological know-how with the 707 to become the world's leading jet airliner manufacturer. Pictured here is a de Havilland plane on display Sept. 6, 1949, at the Society of British Aircraft Constructors Display at Farnborough. Tim Matsui/Getty Images.

Perhaps the most contentious implication of the new trade theory is the argument that it generates for government intervention and strategic trade policy.[24] New trade theorists stress the role of luck, entrepreneurship, and innovation in giving a firm first-mover advantages. According to this argument, the reason Boeing was the first mover in commercial jet aircraft manufacture–rather than firms such as Great Britain's DeHavilland and Hawker Siddely, or Holland's Fokker, all of which could have been–was that Boeing was both lucky and innovative. One way Boeing was lucky is that DeHavilland shot itself in the foot when its Comet jet airliner, introduced two years earlier than Boeing's first jet airliner, the 707, was full of serious technological flaws. Had DeHavilland not made some serious technological mistakes, Great Britain might now be the world's leading exporter of commercial jet aircraft! Boeing's innovativeness was demonstrated by its independent development of the technological know-how required to build a commercial jet airliner. Several new trade theorists have pointed out, however, that Boeing's R&D was largely paid for by the U.S. government; the 707 was a spinoff from a government-funded military program. Herein lies a rationale for government intervention. By the sophisticated and judicious use of subsidies, could a government increase the chances of its domestic firms becoming first movers in newly emerging industries, as the U.S. government apparently did with Boeing? If this is possible, and the new trade theory suggests it might be, then we have an economic rationale for a proactive trade policy that is at variance with the free trade prescriptions of the trade theories we have reviewed so far. We will consider the policy implications of this issue in Chapter 6.

NATIONAL COMPETITIVE ADVANTAGE: PORTER'S DIAMOND

In 1990, Michael Porter of the Harvard Business School published the results of intensive research that attempted to determine why some nations succeed and others fail in international competition.[25] Porter and his team looked at 100 industries in ten nations. The book that contains the results of this work, *The Competitive Advantage of Nations,* has made an important contribution to thinking about trade. Like the work of the new trade theorists, Porter's work was driven by a belief that existing theories of international trade told only part of the story. For Porter, the essential task was to explain why a nation achieves international success in a particular industry. Why does Canada do so well in the manufacturing of heavy mining equipment? Canada has developed a competitive advantage in the mining industry because it has a vast wealth of natural resources and has learned how to extract them in relation to meeting local and international demands. Why does Switzerland excel in the production and export of precision instruments and pharmaceuticals? Why do Germany and the United States do so well in the chemical industry? These questions cannot be answered easily by the Heckscher–Ohlin theory, and the theory of comparative advantage offers only a partial explanation. The theory of comparative advantage would say that Switzerland excels in the production and export of precision instruments because it uses its resources very productively in these industries. Although this may be correct, this does not explain why Switzerland is more productive in this industry than Great Britain, Germany, or Spain. Porter tries to solve this puzzle.

Porter theorizes that four broad attributes of a nation shape the environment in which local firms compete and these attributes promote or impede the creation of competitive advantage (see Figure 5.4). These attributes are

- *Factor endowments*–a nation's position in factors of production such as skilled labour or the infrastructure necessary to compete in a given industry.
- *Demand conditions*–the nature of home demand for the industry's product or service.

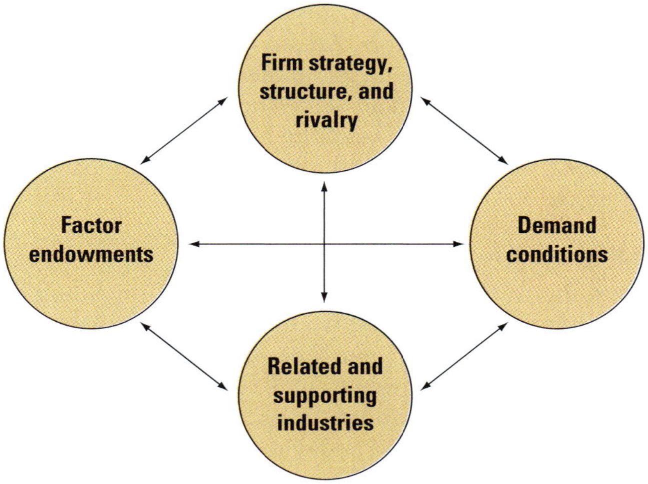

FIGURE 5.4

Determinants of National Competitive Advantage: Porter's Diamond

Source: Reprinted by permission of *Harvard Business Review.* From "The Competitive Advantage of Nations," by Michael E. Porter, March/April 1990. © Copyright 1990 by the Harvard Business School Publishing Corporation; all rights reserved.

- *Relating and supporting industries*–the presence or absence of supplier industries and related industries that are internationally competitive.
- *Firm strategy, structure, and rivalry*–the conditions governing how companies are created, organized, and managed and the nature of domestic rivalry.

Porter speaks of these four attributes as constituting the *diamond*. He argues that firms are most likely to succeed in industries or industry segments where the diamond is most favourable. He also argues that the diamond is a mutually reinforcing system. The effect of one attribute is contingent on the state of others. For example, Porter argues favourable demand conditions will not result in competitive advantage unless the state of rivalry is sufficient to cause firms to respond to them.

Porter maintains that two additional variables can influence the national diamond in important ways: chance and government. Chance events, such as major innovations, can reshape industry structure and provide the opportunity for one nation's firms to supplant another's. Government, by its choice of policies, can detract from or improve national advantage. For example, regulation can alter home demand conditions, antitrust policies can influence the intensity of rivalry within an industry, and government investments in education can change factor endowments.

FACTOR ENDOWMENTS

Factor endowments lie at the centre of the Heckscher–Ohlin theory. While Porter does not propose anything radically new, he does analyze the characteristics of factors of production. He recognizes hierarchies among factors, distinguishing between basic factors (e.g., natural resources, climate, location, and demographics) and advanced factors (e.g., communication infrastructure, sophisticated and skilled labour, research facilities, and technological know-how). He argues that advanced factors are the most significant for competitive advantage. Unlike the naturally endowed basic factors, advanced factors are a product of investment by individuals, companies, and governments. Thus, government investments in basic and higher education, by improving the general skill and knowledge level of the population and by stimulating research at higher education institutions, can upgrade a nation's advanced factors.

The relationship between advanced and basic factors is complex. Basic factors can provide an initial advantage that is subsequently reinforced and extended by investment in advanced factors. Conversely, disadvantages in basic factors can create pressures to invest in advanced factors. An obvious example of this phenomenon is Japan, a country that lacks arable land and mineral deposits and yet through investment has built a substantial endowment of advanced factors. Porter notes that Japan's large pool of engineers (reflecting a much higher number of engineering graduates per capita than almost any other nation) has been vital to Japan's success in many manufacturing industries.

DEMAND CONDITIONS

Porter emphasizes the role domestic demand plays in upgrading competitive advantage. Firms are typically most sensitive to the needs of their closest customers. Thus, the characteristics of home demand are particularly important in shaping the attributes of domestically made products and in creating pressures for innovation and quality. Porter argues that a nation's firms gain competitive advantage if their domestic consumers are sophisticated and demanding. Such consumers pressure local firms to meet high standards of product quality and to produce innovative products. Porter notes that Japan's sophisticated and knowledgeable camera buyers helped stimulate the Japanese camera industry to improve product quality and to introduce innovative models. A similar example can be found in the wireless telephone equipment industry, where sophisticated and demanding local customers in Scandinavia helped push Nokia of Finland and Ericsson of Sweden to invest in cellular phone technology long before demand for cellular phones took off in other developed nations. As a result, Nokia and Ericsson, together with Motorola, today are dominant players in the global cellular telephone equipment industry. Finland has the highest penetration rate for mobile phones in the world with more than 70 percent of Finns owning a wireless handset. The case of Nokia is reviewed in more depth in the accompanying Management Focus.

RELATED AND SUPPORTING INDUSTRIES

The third broad attribute of national advantage in an industry is the presence of suppliers or related industries that are internationally competitive. The benefits of investments in advanced factors of production by related and supporting industries can spill over into an industry, thereby helping it achieve a strong competitive position internationally. Swedish strength in fabricated steel products (e.g., ball bearings and cutting tools) has drawn on strengths in Sweden's specialty steel industry. Technological leadership in the U.S. semiconductor industry until the mid-1980s provided the basis for U.S. success in personal computers and several other technically advanced electronic products. Similarly, Switzerland's success in pharmaceuticals is closely related to its previous international success in the technologically related dye industry.

One consequence of this process is that successful industries within a country tend to be grouped into clusters of related industries. This was one of the most pervasive findings of Porter's study. One such cluster is the German textile and apparel sector, which includes high-quality cotton, wool, synthetic fibres, sewing machine needles, and a wide range of textile machinery. Such clusters are important because valuable knowledge can flow between the firms within a geographic cluster, benefiting all within that cluster. Knowledge flows occur when employees move between firms within a region and when national industry associations bring employees from different companies together for conferences or workshops.[26]

FIRM STRATEGY, STRUCTURE, AND RIVALRY

The fourth broad attribute of national competitive advantage in Porter's model is the strategy, structure, and rivalry of firms within a nation. Porter makes two important points here. First, different nations are characterized by different management ideologies, which either help them or do not help them to build national competitive advantage. For example, Porter notes the predominance of engineers in top management at German and Japanese firms. He attributes this to these firms' emphasis on improving manufacturing processes and product design. In contrast, Porter notes a predominance of people with finance backgrounds leading many U.S. firms. He links this to U.S. firms' lack of attention to improving manufacturing processes and product design, particularly during the 1970s and 80s. He also argues that the dominance of finance has led to a corresponding overemphasis on maximizing short-term financial returns. According to Porter, one consequence of these different management ideologies has been a relative loss of U.S. competitiveness in those engineering-based industries where manufacturing processes and product design issues are all-important (e.g., the automobile industry).

Porter's second point is that there is a strong association between vigorous domestic rivalry and the creation and persistence of competitive advantage in an industry. Vigorous domestic rivalry induces firms to look for ways to improve efficiency, which makes them better international competitors. Domestic rivalry creates pressures to innovate, to improve quality, to reduce costs, and to invest in

MANAGEMENT FOCUS

THE RISE OF FINLAND'S NOKIA

The mobile telephone equipment industry is one of the great growth stories of recent years. The number of wireless subscribers has been expanding rapidly. By the end of 2000, there were more than 550 million wireless subscribers worldwide, up from less than 10 million in 1990. Forecasts suggested that by 2004, the number would reach 1.4 billion. Three firms currently dominate the global market for wireless equipment (e.g., wireless phones, base-station equipment, digital switches): Motorola, Nokia, and Ericsson. Nokia leads the market in mobile telephone sales and is gaining rapidly on Motorola in the network equipment segment.

Nokia's roots are in Finland, not normally a country that comes to mind when one talks about leading-edge technology companies. In the 1980s, Nokia was a rambling Finnish conglomerate with activities that embraced tire manufacturing, paper production, consumer electronics, and telecommunication equipment. By 2000 it had transformed itself into a focused telecommunications equipment manufacturer with a global reach, sales of $24 billion, and earnings of $4.5 billion. How has this former conglomerate emerged to take a global leadership position in wireless telecommunication equipment? Much of the answer lies in the history, geography, and political economy of Finland and its Nordic neighbors.

The story starts in 1981 when the Nordic nations got together to create the world's first international mobile telephone network. They had good reason to become pioneers; in the sparsely populated and inhospitably cold areas, it cost far too much to lay a traditional wireline telephone service. Yet those same geographic features make telecommunications all the more valuable; people driving through the Arctic winter and owners of remote northern houses need a telephone to summon help if things go wrong. As a result, Sweden, Norway, and Finland became the first nations to take wireless telecommunications seriously. They found, for example, that while it cost up to $800 per subscriber to bring a traditional wireline service to remote locations in the far north, the same locations could be linked by wireless telephones for only $500 per person. As a consequence, by 1994, 12 percent of people in Scandinavia owned wireless phones, compared with less than 6 percent in the United States, the world's second most developed market. This leadership has continued. In mid-2000, some 70 percent of the population in Finland owned a wireless phone, compared with 30 percent in the United States.

Nokia, as a longtime telecommunication equipment supplier, was well positioned to take advantage of this development. Other forces were also at work in Finland that helped Nokia develop its competitive edge. Unlike virtually every other developed nation, Finland has never had a national telephone monopoly. Instead, the country's telephone services have long been provided by about 50 autonomous local telephone companies, whose elected boards set prices by referendum (which naturally means low prices). This army of independent and cost-conscious telephone service providers prevented Nokia from taking anything for granted in its home country. With typical Finnish pragmatism, they were willing to buy from the lowest-cost supplier, whether that was Nokia, Ericsson, Motorola, or someone else. This situation contrasted sharply with that prevailing in most developed nations until the late 1980s and early 1990s; domestic telephone monopolies typically purchased equipment from a dominant local supplier or made it themselves.

Nokia responded to this competitive pressure by doing everything possible to drive down its manufacturing costs while still staying at the leading edge of wireless technology.

The consequences of these forces are clear. Nokia is now the leader in digital wireless technology, which is the wave of the future. Many now regard Finland as the lead market for wireless telephone services. If you want to see the future of wireless, you don't go to New York or San Francisco, you go to Helsinki, where Finns use their wireless handsets not just to talk to each other, but also to browse the Web, execute e-commerce transactions, control household heating and lighting systems, or purchase Coke from a wireless-enabled vending machine. Nokia has gained this lead because Scandinavia started switching to digital technology five years before the rest of the world. Spurred on by its cost-conscious Finnish customers, Nokia now has the lowest cost structure of any cellular phone equipment manufacturer in the world, making it a more profitable enterprise than Motorola, its leading global rival. Nokia's operating margins in 2000 were 20 percent, compared with 6.4 percent at Motorola.

Sources: "Lessons from the Frozen North," *The Economist,* October 8, 1994, pp. 76–77; G. Edmondson, "Grabbing Markets from the Giants," *Business Week, Special Issue: 21st Century Capitalism,* 1995, p. 156; company news releases; "A Finnish Fable," *The Economist,* October 14, 2000; "To the Finland Base Station," *The Economist,* October 9, 1999, pp. 23–27; and "A Survey of Telecommunications," *The Economist,* October 9, 1999.

upgrading advanced factors. All this helps to create world-class competitors. Porter cites the case of Japan.

Nowhere is the role of domestic rivalry more evident than in Japan, where it is all-out warfare in which many companies fail to achieve profitability. With goals that stress market share, Japanese companies engage in a continuing struggle to outdo each other. Shares fluctuate markedly. The process is prominently covered in the business press. Elaborate rankings measure which companies are most popular with university graduates. The rate of new product and process development is breathtaking.[27]

A similar point about the stimulating effects of strong domestic competition can be made with regard to the rise of Nokia to global preeminence in the market for cellular telephone equipment. For details, see the Management Focus.

ANOTHER PERSPECTIVE

Business clusters and trade theory

Business clusters are everywhere. Fast-food restaurants tend to cluster, as do department stores. We have heavy manufacturing areas in and around Hamilton, Ontario. That similar businesses set up in the same geographic area might seem illogical at first, especially if they are sales organizations (if they were alone, they would face less competition). Modern trade theory suggests that businesses cluster to draw on resources they have created by clustering. These resources form a comparative advantage for the area.

Think about the Markham/Newmarket, Ontario, corridor and the comparative advantage it offers high-tech firms that decide to locate there: many innovative people developing new ideas, a labour market that is educated and experienced and knows how to manage knowledge innovation. Informal networking among similarly focused people while at the health club or in a restaurant or bar creates additional stimulation, which drives further innovation. This explanation works for fast food, too, albeit with different drivers. Clusters create a pool of trained labour and an area that functions as a magnet for the hungry consumer who chooses a quick-service restaurant. Plus the robust competition such clusters create pushes innovation. Clustered companies learn from each other.

EVALUATING PORTER'S THEORY

Porter contends that the degree to which a nation is likely to achieve international success in a certain industry is a function of the combined impact of factor endowments, domestic demand conditions, related and supporting industries, and domestic rivalry. He argues that the presence of all four components is usually required for this diamond to boost competitive performance (although there are exceptions). Porter also contends that government can influence each of the four components of the diamond—either positively or negatively. Factor endowments can be affected by subsidies, policies toward capital markets, policies toward education, and so on. Government can shape domestic demand through local product standards or with regulations that mandate or influence buyer needs. Government policy can influence supporting and related industries through regulation and affect firm rivalry through such devices as capital market regulation, tax policy, and antitrust laws.

If Porter is correct, we would expect his model to predict the pattern of international trade that we observe in the real world. Countries should be exporting products from those industries where all four components of the diamond are favourable, while importing in those areas where the components are not favourable. Is he correct? We simply do not know. Porter's theory has not yet been subjected to independent empirical testing. Much about the theory rings true, but the same can be said for the new trade theory, the theory of comparative advantage, and the Heckscher–Ohlin theory. It may be that each of these theories, which complement each other, explains something about the pattern of international trade.

IMPLICATIONS FOR BUSINESS

Why does all this matter for business? There are at least three main implications for international businesses of the material discussed in this chapter: location implications, first-mover implications, and policy implications.

LOCATION IMPLICATIONS

Underlying most of the theories we have discussed is the notion that different countries have particular advantages in different productive activities. Thus, from a profit perspective, it makes sense for a firm to disperse its productive activities to those countries where, according to the theory of international trade, they can be performed most efficiently (transportation costs and tariffs permitting). If design can be performed most efficiently in France, that is where design facilities should be located; if the manufacture of basic components can be performed most efficiently in Singapore, that is where they should be manufactured; and if final assembly can be performed most efficiently in China, that is where final assembly should be performed. The result is a global web of productive activities, with different activities being performed in different locations around the globe depending on considerations of comparative advantage, factor endowments, and the like. If the firm does not do this, it may find itself at a competitive disadvantage relative to firms that do.

Consider the production of a laptop computer, a process with four major stages: (1) basic research and development of the product design, (2) manufacture of standard electronic components (e.g., memory chips), (3) manufacture of advanced components (e.g., flat-top color display screens and microprocessors), and (4) final assembly. Basic R&D requires a pool of highly skilled and educated workers with good backgrounds in microelectronics. The two countries with a comparative advantage in basic microelectronics R&D and design are Japan and the United States, so most producers of laptop computers locate their R&D facilities in one, or both, of these countries. (Apple, IBM, Motorola, Texas Instruments, Toshiba, and Sony all have major R&D facilities in both Japan and the United States.)

The manufacture of standard electronic components is a capital-intensive process requiring semiskilled labour, and cost pressures are intense. The best locations for such activities today are places such as Singapore, Taiwan, and Malaysia. These countries have pools of relatively skilled, low-cost labour. Thus, many producers of laptop computers have standard components, such as memory chips, produced at these locations.

The manufacture of advanced components such as microprocessors and display screens is a capital-intensive process requiring skilled labour. Because cost pressures are not so intense at this stage, these components can be—and are—manufactured in countries with high labour costs that also have pools of highly skilled labour (primarily Japan, South Korea, and the United States).

Finally, assembly is a relatively labour-intensive process requiring only low-skilled labour, and cost pressures are intense. As a result, final assembly may be carried out in a country such as Mexico, which has an abundance of low-cost, low-skilled labour. A laptop computer produced by a U.S. manufacturer may be designed in California, have its standard components produced in Taiwan and Singapore, have its advanced components produced in Japan and the United States, have its final assembly in Mexico, and be sold in the United States or elsewhere in the world. By dispersing production activities to different locations around the globe, the U.S. manufacturer is taking advantage of the differences between countries identified by the various theories of international trade.

ANOTHER PERSPECTIVE

Steel and citrus

The European Union (EU) was hit hard by the U.S. steel tariff in 2002. It had already taken the difficult path to make steel producers more efficient by upgrading production technology and rationalizing the workforce by paying off redundant employees. Then, quite unexpectedly, robust European exports to the United States fell off considerably when they cost the U.S. importer an additional 30 percent.

The EU retaliated by increasing tariffs on citrus, an important export to Europe from Florida, a key Republican state.

FIRST-MOVER IMPLICATIONS

According to the new trade theory, firms that establish a first-mover advantage with regard to the production of a particular new product may subsequently dominate global trade in that product. This is particularly true in industries where the global market can profitably support only a limited number of firms, such as the aerospace market, but early commitments also seem to be important in less concentrated industries such as the market for cellular telephone equipment (see the Management Focus on Nokia). For the individual firm, the clear message is that it pays to invest substantial financial resources in trying to build a first-mover, or early-mover, advantage, even if that means several years of substantial losses before a new venture becomes profitable. Although the details of how to achieve this are beyond the scope of this book, many publications offer strategies for exploiting first-mover advantages.[28]

POLICY IMPLICATIONS

The theories of international trade also matter to international businesses because firms are major players on the international trade scene. Business firms produce exports, and business firms import the products of other countries. Because of their pivotal role in international trade, businesses can influence government trade policy, lobbying to promote free trade or trade restrictions. The theories of international trade claim that promoting free trade is generally in the best interests of a country, although it may not always be in the best interest of an individual firm or its employees. Many firms recognize this and lobby for open markets (although those adversely affected often lobby for greater protectionism).

For example, when the U.S. government announced in the early 1990s its intention to place a tariff on Japanese imports of liquid crystal display (LCD) screens, IBM and Apple Computer protested strongly. Both IBM and Apple pointed out that (1) Japan was the lowest-cost source of LCD screens, (2) they used these screens in their own laptop computers, and (3) the proposed tariff, by increasing the cost of LCD screens, would increase the cost of laptop computers produced by IBM and Apple, thus making them less competitive in the world market. In other words, the tariff, designed to protect U.S. firms, would be self-defeating. In response to these pressures, the U.S. government reversed its posture.

Unlike IBM and Apple, however, businesses do not always lobby for free trade. In the United States, for example, restrictions on imports of automobiles, machine tools, textiles, and steel are the result of direct pressure by U.S. firms on the government. In some cases, the government responded by getting foreign companies to agree to "voluntary" restrictions on their imports, using the implicit threat of more comprehensive formal trade barriers to get them to adhere to these agreements. In other cases, such as steel, the government has used what are called "antidumping" actions to justify tariffs on imports from other nations (these mechanisms will be discussed in detail in the next chapter).

As predicted by international trade theory, many of these agreements have been self-defeating, such as the voluntary restriction on machine tool imports agreed to in 1985. Due to limited import competition from more efficient foreign suppliers, the prices of machine tools in the United States rose to higher levels than would have prevailed under free trade. Because machine tools are used throughout the manufacturing industry, the costs of U.S. manufacturing in general increased, creating a corresponding loss in world market competitiveness. Shielded from international competition by import barriers, the U.S. machine tool industry had no incentive to increase its efficiency, and it lost many of its export markets to more efficient foreign competitors. As a consequence of this action, the U.S. machine tool industry shrunk during the period when the agreement was in force. For anyone schooled in international trade theory, this was not surprising.[29]

Finally, Porter's theory of national competitive advantage also contains policy implications. Porter's theory suggests that it is in the best interest of business for a firm to invest in upgrading advanced factors of production; for example, to invest in better training for its employees and to increase its commitment to research and development. It is also in the best interests of business to lobby the government to adopt policies that have a favourable impact on each component of the national diamond. Thus, according to Porter, businesses should urge government to increase investment in education, infrastructure, and basic research (since all these enhance advanced factors) and to adopt policies that promote strong competition within domestic markets (since this makes firms stronger international competitors, according to Porter's findings).

KEY TERMS

absolute advantage, p. 167
comparative advantage, p. 169
economies of scale, p. 178
free trade, p. 163
learning effects, p. 178
mercantilism, p. 166
positive-sum game, p. 167
zero-sum game, p. 167

SUMMARY

This chapter has reviewed a number of theories that explain why it is beneficial for a country to engage in international trade and has explained the pattern of international trade that we observe in the world economy. We have seen how the theories of Smith, Ricardo, and Heckscher–Ohlin all make strong cases for unrestricted free trade. In contrast, the mercantilist doctrine and, to a lesser extent, the new trade theory can be interpreted to support government intervention to promote exports through subsidies and to limit imports through tariffs and quotas.

In explaining the pattern of international trade, the second objective of this chapter, we have seen that with the exception of mercantilism, which is silent on this issue, the different theories offer largely complementary explanations. Although no one theory may explain the apparent pattern of international trade, taken together, the theory of comparative advantage, the Heckscher–Ohlin theory, the product life-cycle theory, the new trade theory, and Porter's theory of national competitive advantage do suggest which factors are important. Comparative advantage tells us that productivity differences are important; Heckscher–Ohlin tells us that factor endowments matter; the product life-cycle theory tells us that where a new product is introduced is important; the new trade theory tells us that increasing returns to specialization and first-mover advantages matter; and Porter tells us that all these factors may be important insofar as they affect the four components of the national diamond.

The following points have been made in this chapter:

1. Mercantilists argued that it was in a country's best interests to run a balance-of-trade surplus. They viewed trade as a zero-sum game, in which one country's gains cause losses for other countries.
2. The theory of absolute advantage suggests that countries differ in their ability to produce goods efficiently. The theory suggests that a country should specialize in producing goods in areas where it has an absolute advantage and import goods in areas where other countries have absolute advantages.
3. The theory of comparative advantage suggests that it makes sense for a country to specialize in producing those goods that it can produce most efficiently, while buying goods that it can produce relatively less efficiently from other countries—even if that means buying goods from other countries that it could produce more efficiently itself.
4. The theory of comparative advantage suggests that unrestricted free trade brings about increased world production; that is, that trade is a positive-sum game.
5. The theory of comparative advantage also suggests that opening a country to free trade stimulates economic growth, which creates dynamic gains from trade. The empirical evidence seems to be consistent with this claim.
6. The Heckscher–Ohlin theory argues that the pattern of international trade is determined by differences in factor endowments. It predicts that countries will export those goods that make intensive use of locally abundant factors and will import goods that make intensive use of factors that are locally scarce.
7. The product life-cycle theory suggests that trade patterns are influenced by where a new product is introduced. In an increasingly integrated global economy, the product life-cycle theory may be less predictive than it was between 1945 and 1975.
8. The new trade theory argues that in those industries where substantial economies of scale imply that the world market will profitably support only a few firms, countries may predominate in the export of certain products simply because they had a firm that was a first mover in that industry.
9. Some new trade theorists have promoted the idea of strategic trade policy. The argument is that government, by the sophisticated and judicious use of subsidies, might be able to increase the chances of domestic firms becoming first movers in newly emerging industries.
10. Porter's theory of national competitive advantage suggests that the pattern of trade is influenced by four attributes of a nation: *(a)* factor endowments, *(b)* domestic demand conditions, *(c)* relating and supporting industries, and *(d)* firm strategy, structure, and rivalry.
11. Theories of international trade are important to an individual business firm primarily because they can help the firm decide where to locate its various production activities.
12. Firms involved in international trade can and do influence government policy toward trade. By lobbying government, business firms can promote free trade or trade restrictions.

CRITICAL THINKING AND DISCUSSION QUESTIONS

1. Mercantilism is a bankrupt theory that has no place in the modern world. Discuss.
2. China is a neomercantilist nation. It protects industries where it has no competitive advantage in the world economy, while demanding that other countries open up those markets where Chinese producers have a competitive advantage. Discuss this statement.
3. Unions in developed nations often oppose imports from low-wage countries and advocate trade barriers to protect jobs from what they often characterize as "unfair" import competition. Is such competition

"unfair"? Do you think this argument is in the best interests of (*a*) the unions, (*b*) the people they represent, and/or (*c*) the country as a whole?

4. Drawing on the theory of comparative advantage to support your arguments, outline the case for free trade.
5. What are the potential costs of adopting a free trade regime? Do you think governments should do anything to reduce these costs? What?
6. Using the new trade theory and Porter's theory of national competitive advantage, outline the case for government policies that would build national competitive advantage in a particular industry. What kinds of policies would you recommend that the government adopt? Are these policies at variance with the basic free trade philosophy?
7. The world's poorest countries are at a competitive disadvantage in every sector of their economies. They have nothing to export. They have no capital; their land is of poor quality; they often have too many people given available work opportunities; and they are poorly educated. Free trade cannot possibly be in the interests of such nations! Discuss.
8. In general, policies designed to limit competition from low-cost foreign competitors do not help a country to achieve greater economic growth. Discuss this statement.

RESEARCH TASK | globalEDGE™ globaledge.msu.edu

Use the globalEDGE™ site to complete the following exercises:

1. WTO's International Trade Statistics is an annual report that provides comprehensive, comparable, and up-to-date statistics on trade in merchandise and commercial services. This report allows for an assessment of world trade flows by country, region, and main product groups or service categories. Using the most recent statistics available, identify the top five countries that lead in the export and import of merchandise, respectively.
2. Your company is interested in importing Australian wine to Canada. As part of the initial analysis, you want to identify the strengths of the Australian wine industry. Provide a short description of the current status of Australian wine exports by variety, and a list of the top importing countries of Australian wines.

Visit the *Global Business Today* Online Learning Centre at **www.mcgrawhill.ca/college/hill** to access quizzes, interactive exercises, a Business Around the World interactive map, and other learning and study tools related to this chapter.

Online LearningCentre

CLOSING CASE

THE RISE OF THE INDIAN SOFTWARE INDUSTRY

As a relatively poor country, India is not normally thought of as a nation capable of building a major presence in a high-technology industry, such as computer software. In little more than a decade, however, the Indian software industry has astounded its skeptics and emerged from obscurity to become an important force in the global software industry. Between 1991–1992 and 1999–2000, sales of Indian software companies grew at a compound rate in excess of 60 percent annually. In 1991–1992, the industry had sales totalling $388 million. By 2000, they were about $6 billion. By the late 1990s, more than 900 software companies in India employed 200 000 software engineers, the third largest concentration of such talent in the world.

Much of this growth was powered by exports. In 1985, Indian software exports were worth less than $10 million. They surged to $1.8 billion in 1997 and hit a record $4 billion in 2000. The future looks very bright. Powered by continued export-led growth, India's National Association of Software and Service Companies projects that total software revenues generated by Indian companies will hit $28 billion by 2004–2005 and $87 billion by 2007–2008. As a testament to this growth, many foreign software companies are now investing heavily in Indian software development operations including Microsoft, IBM, Oracle, and Computer Associates, the four largest U.S.-based software houses. Equally significantly, two out of every five global companies now source their software services from India.

Most of the current growth of the Indian software industry has been based on contract or project-based work for foreign clients. Many Indian companies, for example, maintain applications for their clients, convert code, or migrate software from one platform to another. Increasingly, Indian companies are also involved in important development projects for foreign clients. For example, TCS, India's largest software company, has an alliance with Ernst & Young under which TCS will develop and maintain customized software for Ernst & Young's global clients. TCS also has a development alliance with Microsoft under which the company developed a paperless National Share Depositary system for the Indian stock market based on Microsoft's Windows NT operating system and SQL server database technology. Indian companies are also moving aggressively into e-commerce projects. From almost zero in 1997, e-commerce projects now account for about 10 percent of all software development and service work in India and are projected to reach 20 percent within two years.

The Indian software industry has emerged despite a poor information technology infrastructure. The installed base of personal computers in India stood at just 3 million in 1999, and this in a nation of nearly 1 billion people. With just 22 telephone lines per 1000 people, India has one of the lowest penetration rates for fixed telephone lines in Asia, if not the world. Internet connections numbered less than 100 000 in 1998, compared to 60 million in the United States. But sales of personal computers are starting to take off, and the rapid growth of mobile telephones in India's main cities is to some extent compensating for the lack of fixed telephone lines.

In explaining the success of their industry, India's software entrepreneurs point to a number of factors. Although the general level of education in India is low, India's important middle class is highly educated and its top educational institutions are world class. Also, India has always emphasized engineering. Another great plus from an international perspective is that English is the working language throughout much of middle-class India—a remnant from the days of the British raja. Then there is the wage rate. American software engineers are increasingly scarce, and the basic salary has been driven up to one of the highest for any occupational group in the country, with entry-level programmers earning $70,000 per year. An entry-level programmer in India, in contrast, starts at around $5,000 per year, which is very low by international standards but high by Indian standards. Salaries for programmers are rising rapidly in India, but so is productivity. In 1992, productivity was about $21,000 per software engineer. By 1997, the figure had risen to $45,000. As a consequence of these factors, by 2000 work done in India for U.S. software companies amounted to $25 to $35 an hour, compared to $75 to $100 per hour for software development done in the United States.

Another factor helping India is that satellite communications have removed distance as an obstacle to doing business for foreign clients. Because software is nothing more than a stream of zeros and ones, it can be transported at the speed of light and at negligible cost to any point in the world. In a world of instant communication, India's geographical position between Europe and the United States has given it a time zone advantage. Indian companies have been able to exploit the rapidly expanding international market for outsourced software services, including the expanding market for remote maintenance. Indian engineers can fix software bugs, upgrade systems, or process data overnight while their users in Western companies are asleep.

To maintain their competitive position, Indian software companies are now investing heavily in training and leading-edge programming skills. They have also been enthusiastic adopters of international quality standards, particularly ISO 9000 certification. Indian companies are also starting to make forays into the application and shrink-wrapped software business, primarily with applications aimed at the domestic market. It may only be a matter of time, however, before Indian companies start to compete head to head with companies such as Microsoft, Oracle, PeopleSoft, and SAP in the applications business.

Sources: P. Taylor, "Poised for Global Growth," *Financial Times: India's Software Industry,* December 3, 1997, pp. 1, 8; P. Taylor, "An Industry on the Up and Up," *Financial Times: India's Software Industry,* December 3, 1997, p. 3; Krishna Guha, "Strategic Alliances with Global Partners," *Financial Times: India's Software Industry,* December 3, 1997, p. 6; "Indian SW Industry to Touch $13 Billion in 2001–02," *Computers Today,* December 15, 2000, pp. 14–17; United Nations, *Human Development Report* (New York: Oxford University Press, 2000); and Table 12, *The Economist,* October 12, 1991, p. 71.

CASE DISCUSSION QUESTIONS

1. To what extent does the theory of comparative advantage explain the rise of the Indian software industry?
2. To what extent does the Heckscher–Ohlin theory explain the rise of the Indian software industry?
3. Use Michael Porter's diamond to analyze the rise of the Indian software industry. Does this analysis help explain the rise of this industry?
4. Which of the above theories—comparative advantage, Heckscher–Ohlin, or Porter's—gives the best explanation of the rise of the Indian software industry? Why?

PART THREE

3

CROSS-BORDER TRADE AND INVESTMENT

The Great Banana Wars

Under the terms of a long-standing agreement, banana producers from 71 countries in Africa, the Caribbean, and the Pacific have been granted preferential access to the European Union (EU) market. Most of the countries are former colonies of either Great Britain or France, both members of the EU. The original goal of the agreement was to help these developing nations by making it easier for them to sell bananas in the EU. Some of the developing nations that have benefited from this arrangement are highly dependent on banana exports and claim their economies would be devastated without the agreement, which requires the EU to erect trade barriers against imports from other nations, particularly those in Latin America. Under the agreement, up to 875 000 tonnes of Caribbean, African, and Pacific bananas can enter the EU each year duty free. In contrast, the EU has imposed tariffs of 15 to 20 percent by value on the first 2.5 million tonnes of banana imports from Latin America. The EU has also placed prohibitive tariffs on any imports from Latin America in excess of 2.5 million tonnes, in effect capping imports at that amount. These tariffs result in consumers within the EU paying higher prices for bananas. According to a study by one French economist, banana import restrictions cost European consumers up to $2 billion a year, or 55 cents per kilogram of bananas, some two-thirds of which ends up as bigger profits for European fruit distributors.

Two leading U.S.-based growers and marketers of bananas, Chiquita Brands and Dole Food Co., complained to the U.S. government in 1995 that the EU's preferential banana agreement violated World Trade Organization rules and shut them out of the lucrative EU market. The U.S. government agreed to appeal to the WTO on behalf of the banana industry. The United States was joined in its complaint by four banana-producing nations in Latin America—Ecuador, Guatemala, Honduras, and Mexico. Under the terms of the 1995 global trade agreement that established the World Trade Organization, the WTO has the right to review complaints brought by one member state against another. If a WTO arbitration panel

CHAPTER 6

The Political Economy of International Trade

OPENING CASE

finds that a nation's trade policies violate WTO rules, it can recommend changes in those policies. If those recommendations are not adopted, the injured party has the right to impose punitive tariffs on imports from the violating nation or, in this case, trade bloc. This dispute was the first to involve the United States and the EU. It was widely seen as a test of the WTO's credibility. Would the WTO issue an unbiased ruling? More importantly, would it be able to make the ruling stick?

Defenders of the agreement claimed the EU was helping impoverished developing nations. They painted the dispute as a confrontation that unjustly pitted the interests of U.S. banana multinationals against the interests of these developing nations (ignoring the fact that European consumers are also hurt by these restrictions). The WTO arbitration panel was not convinced by these arguments. It issued its first ruling on the banana issue in late 1997. The EU banana agreement was found to violate WTO rules and would have to be changed. The EU was given until January 1, 1999, to bring its regime in line with WTO rules. Although the EU did make some changes, neither the United States nor several of its Latin American partners saw these as going far enough. Nor did most independent observers. In February 1999, the United States sought WTO permission to use retaliatory trade measures against the EU, hoping to put economic pressure on the EU to change the banana agreement. When the EU failed to move on the issue, the WTO authorized the United States to impose sanctions of $191.4 million annually on European imports into the United States. These took the form of import tariffs amounting to 100 percent of the value of a range of European goods including salt, cashmere clothing items, packaging products, and lead acid batteries.

A year later the sanctions were still in force. While the EU made some effort to change its banana agreement to bring it in line with WTO rules, internal political conflicts within the EU had stalled progress. In the meantime, developing nations allied with the EU continued to be given preferential access to the EU market, while Latin American banana producers are facing the same hurdles they did in 1995. And tariffs are not the only barriers that companies face. As tariffs have disappeared around the globe, there has been a rise in non-tariff barriers that regional governments have put in force to protect their own industries. This can include labelling laws (for example, Canadian labels have to include both official languages) or a new inspection process that only applies to foreign-made goods. The result of these actions is the imposition of a new "invisible" barrier to foreign goods.

Sources: L. Kemeny, "Banana War Slips into the Courts," *Sunday Times,* November 5, 2000; E. Drew, "Deadlock Continues in Banana Wars," *African Business,* June 2000; "The Beef over Bananas," *The Economist,* March 6, 1999, pp. 65–67; "Stealing from the Poor," *The Economist,* April 24, 1999, pp. 70–71; and "Europe's Burden," *The Economist,* May 22, 1999, pp. 84–85.

LEARNING OBJECTIVES

1. Discuss the various policy instruments that governments use to restrict imports and promote exports.
2. Understand why some governments intervene in international trade to restrict imports and promote exports.
3. Appreciate the position of those who argue that government intervention in international trade can be self-defeating and typically fails to produce the gains that advocates of intervention claim.
4. Be familiar with the evolution, purpose, current status, and future prospects of the global trading system as embodied in the General Agreement on Tariffs and Trade and the World Trade Organization.
5. Understand the important implications for business practice of government intervention in international trade and of the current global trading system.

INTRODUCTION

Our review of the classical trade theories of Smith, Ricardo, and Heckscher–Ohlin in Chapter 5 showed us that, in a world without trade barriers, trade patterns are determined by the relative productivity of different factors of production in different countries. Countries will specialize in products that they can make most efficiently, while importing products that they can produce less efficiently. Chapter 5 also laid out the intellectual case for free trade. Remember, **free trade** refers to a situation where a government does not attempt to restrict what its citizens can buy from another country or what they can sell to another country. As we saw in Chapter 5, the theories of Smith, Ricardo, and Heckscher–Ohlin predict that the consequences of free trade include both static economic gains (because free trade supports a higher level of domestic consumption and more efficient utilization of resources) and dynamic economic gains (because free trade stimulates economic growth and the creation of wealth).

FREE TRADE The absence of barriers to the free flow of goods and services between countries.

In this chapter, we look at the political reality of international trade. The political reality is that while many nations are nominally committed to free trade, they tend to intervene in international trade to protect the interests of politically important groups. The opening case illustrates the nature of such political realities. The case describes how the European Union (EU) erected trade barriers against the importation of bananas from Latin America, most of which are marketed by U.S. multinational enterprises. The EU erected these barriers for political reasons. It wanted to help a number of developing countries that were once former colonies of two prominent members of the EU: Great Britain and France. However, the EU is also a member of the World Trade Organization and has to abide by its rules if it wants to enjoy the benefits of membership. Unfortunately for the EU, the WTO ruled that the banana tariff is illegal. This decision placed the EU between a rock and a hard place. On the one hand, the EU is under considerable pressure from powerful political interests within Europe to maintain the ban. On the other hand, the EU would like to abide by the rules of the WTO–rules that have brought significant benefits to the EU (as we shall discuss later in this chapter). For now, the EU has chosen to live with this dilemma and bear the costs in terms of the punitive retaliatory tariffs on EU imports into the United States that have been authorized by the WTO. This decision undermines the authority of the World Trade Organization and raises trade tensions between the United States and the EU, tensions that some fear might lead to a trade war between the two entities.

In this chapter, we explore the political and economic reasons that governments have for intervening in international trade. When governments intervene, they often do so by restricting imports of goods and services into their nation, while adopting policies that promote exports. Normally their motives are to protect domestic producers and jobs from foreign competition while increasing the foreign market for products of domestic producers. However, in recent years, "social" issues have intruded into the decision-making calculus. In the United States, for example, there is a movement to try to ban imports of goods from countries that do not abide by the same labor, health, and environmental regulations as the United States.

We start this chapter by describing the range of policy instruments that governments use to intervene in international trade. This is followed by a detailed review of the various political and economic motives that governments have for intervention. In the third section of this chapter we consider how the case for free trade stands up in view of the various justifications given for government intervention in international trade. Then we look at the emergence of the modern international trading system, which is based on the General Agreement on Tariffs and Trade (GATT) and its successor, the World Trade Organization (WTO). The GATT and WTO are the creations of a series of multinational treaties. The most recent was completed in 1995, involved more than 120 countries, and resulted in the creation of the WTO. The purpose of these treaties has been to lower barriers to the free flow of goods and services between nations. Like the GATT before it, the WTO promotes free trade by limiting the ability of national governments to adopt policies that restrict imports into their nations. In the final section of this chapter, we discuss the implications of this material for business practice.

INSTRUMENTS OF TRADE POLICY

Trade policy uses seven main instruments: tariffs, subsidies, import quotas, voluntary export restraints, local content requirements, administrative policies, and antidumping duties. Tariffs are the oldest and simplest instrument of trade policy. As we shall see later in this chapter, they are also the instrument that GATT and WTO have been most successful in limiting. A fall in tariff barriers in recent decades has been accompanied by a rise in nontariff barriers, such as subsidies, quotas, voluntary export restraints, and antidumping duties.

TARIFF A tax levied on imports.

TARIFFS

A **tariff** is a tax levied on imports. Tariffs fall into two categories. **Specific tariffs** are levied as a fixed charge for each unit of a good imported (for example, $3 per barrel of oil). **Ad valorem tariffs** are levied as a proportion of the value of the imported good. The European Union has imposed such a tariff on imports of bananas from Latin America; the tariff amounts to 15 to 20 percent by value on the first 2.5 million tonnes of imports of bananas from Latin America (see the opening case).

SPECIFIC TARIFF Tariff levied as a fixed charge for each unit of good imported.

AD VALOREM TARIFF A tariff levied as a proportion of the value of an imported good.

A tariff raises the cost of imported products. In most cases, tariffs are put in place to protect domestic producers from foreign competition. In early 2003, both the U.S.

In 1989 the European Union (EU) responded to concerns about hormone-treated beef by banning the use of growth-promoting hormones in the production of livestock, and also on the importation of hormone-treated meat essentially for political reasons. The ban was controversial because a reasonable consensus existed among scientists that the hormones posed no health risk. After the United States and Canada filed formal complaints with the World Trade Organization (WTO), the EU kept the ban. On July 29, 1999, the U.S. responded with retaliatory trade sanctions equal to about $116.8 million.

Senate and the House of Representatives considered bills that could raise U.S. duties on Canadian softwood lumber from 27 percent to 45 percent and reports from Washington say they will have wide support from both Democrats and Republicans.[1]

The important thing to understand about a tariff is who suffers and who gains. The government gains, because the tariff increases government revenues. Domestic producers gain, because the tariff affords them some protection against foreign competitors by increasing the cost of imported foreign goods. Consumers lose because they must pay more for certain imports. The already high U.S.-imposed tariff on Canadian softwood lumber is hurting the U.S. home buyers. Susan Petunias, spokesperson for American Consumers for Affordable Homes, indicated that the duties imposed by the U.S. federal government could add $1,000 to the cost of a house.[2] Whether the gains to the government and domestic producers exceed the loss to consumers depends on various factors such as the amount of the tariff, the importance of the imported good to domestic consumers, the number of jobs saved in the protected industry, and so on.

Although detailed consideration of these issues is beyond the scope of this book, two conclusions can be derived from a more advanced analysis.[3] First, tariffs are unambiguously pro-producer and anticonsumer. While they protect producers from foreign competitors, this restriction of supply also raises domestic prices. Thus, as noted in the opening case, the tariff on banana imports into the European Union has raised prices for bananas in the EU and cost consumers some $2 billion a year. Another study by Japanese economists

ANOTHER PERSPECTIVE

Check out Canadian import tariffs

You can find an updated list of Government of Canada imposed tariffs at www.cbsa-asfc.gc.ca%2Fgeneral%2Fpublications%2Fcustoms_tariff-e.html and www.ccra-adrc.gc.ca/tax/business/smallbusiness/c124-e.html.

You will be required to consult many of the links on the page in order to better judge the detail associated with import tariffs. If you were the manager of a company in Australia and wanted to export to Canada, how might these tariffs affect your export strategy strategy? How might they affect your relationship with your own Australian Government? See www.ccra-adrc.gc.ca/tax/business/smallbusiness/c124-e.html.

COUNTRY FOCUS

THE COSTS OF PROTECTIONISM IN THE UNITED STATES

The United States likes to think of itself as a nation committed to unrestricted free trade. In their negotiations with trading partners such as China, the European Union, and Japan, U.S. trade representatives can often be heard claiming that the U.S. economy is an open one with few import tariffs. However, while U.S. tariffs on the importation of goods are low when compared to those found in many other nations, they still exist. One study concluded that these tariffs cost U.S. consumers about $32 billion per year during the 1980s. A more recent study suggested that in 1996, import protection cost U.S. consumers $223.4 billion in higher prices.

Gary Hufbauer and Kim Elliott of the Institute for International Economics undertook the first study. They looked at the effect of import tariffs on economic activity in 21 industries with annual sales of $1 billion or more that the U.S. protected most heavily from foreign competition. The industries included apparel, ceramic tiles, luggage, and sugar. In most of these industries, import tariffs had originally been imposed to protect U.S. firms and employees from the effects of low-cost foreign competitors. The typical reasoning behind the tariffs was that without such protection, U.S. firms in these industries would go out of business and substantial unemployment would result. So the tariffs were presented as having positive effects for the U.S. economy, not to mention the U.S. Treasury, which benefited from the associated revenues.

The study found, however, that while these import tariffs saved about 200 000 jobs in the protected industries that would otherwise have been lost to foreign competition, they also cost American consumers about $32 billion per year in the form of higher prices. Even when the proceeds from the tariff that accrued to the U.S. Treasury were added into the equation, the total cost to the nation of this protectionism still amounted to $10.2 billion per year, or over $50,000 per job saved.

The two economists argued that these figures understated the tariffs' true cost to the nation. They maintained that by making imports less competitive with American-made products, tariffs allowed domestic producers to charge more than they might otherwise because they did not have to compete with low-priced imports. By dampening competition, these tariffs removed an incentive for firms in the protected industries to become more efficient, thereby retarding economic progress. Further, the study's authors noted that if the tariffs had not been imposed, some of the $32 billion freed up every year would have been spent on other goods and services, and growth in these areas would have created additional jobs, thereby offsetting the loss of 200 000 jobs in the protected industries.

In a 1999 study, Howard Wall used a different methodology to provide updated estimates on the impact of protectionism on trade volume and prices. Wall found that while the United States imported more than $723 billion in merchandise from countries outside of NAFTA in 1996, it would have imported over $111 billion more if it had a policy of pure free trade. (NAFTA is the North American Free Trade Agreement signed by Canada, Mexico, and the United States.) Wall concluded that the higher prices resulting from import protection cost U.S. consumers some $223.4 billion in 1996, or 3.4 percent of GDP. However, Wall's estimates also suggest that the United States suffered from trade barriers in other countries. While the United States exported $499 billion of goods in 1996, according to Wall, it would have exported an additional $130 billion of goods to non-NAFTA countries had those countries not had trade barriers.

Sources: G. Hufbauer and K. A. Elliott, *Measuring the Costs of Protectionism in the United States* (Washington, DC: Institute for International Economics, 1993), and H. J. Wall, "Using the Gravity Model to Estimate the Costs of Protectionism," *Federal Reserve Bank of St. Louis Review*, January–February 1999, pp. 33–40.

calculated that tariffs on imports of foodstuffs, cosmetics, and chemicals into Japan in 1989 cost the average Japanese consumer about $890 per year in the form of higher prices.[4] Almost all studies that have looked at this issue find that import tariffs impose significant costs on domestic consumers in the form of higher prices.[5] For another example, see the accompanying Country Focus, which looks at the cost to U.S. consumers of tariffs on imports into the United States.

Second, tariffs reduce the overall efficiency of the world economy. They reduce efficiency because a protective tariff encourages domestic firms to produce products at home that, in theory, could be produced more efficiently abroad. The consequence is an inefficient utilization of resources. For example, tariffs on the importation of rice into South Korea have caused the land of South Korean rice farmers to be used in an unproductive manner. It would make more sense for the South Koreans to purchase their rice from lower-cost foreign producers and to utilize the land now employed in rice production in some other way, such as growing foodstuffs that cannot be produced more efficiently elsewhere or for residential and industrial purposes.

SUBSIDIES

SUBSIDY
Government financial assistance to a domestic producer.

A **subsidy** is a government payment to a domestic producer. Subsidies take many forms including cash grants, low-interest loans, tax breaks, and government equity participation in domestic firms. By lowering production costs, subsidies help domestic producers in two ways: they help them compete against foreign imports and they help them gain export markets.

Agriculture tends to be one of the largest beneficiaries of subsidies in most countries. In 1998, for example, developed countries paid some $360 billion in support to farmers. In Japan, agricultural subsidies amounted to a staggering 62 percent of the value of gross farm receipts, or $21,000 per farmer. In the European Union, where the Common Agricultural Policy (CAP) has long provided subsidies to help farmers stay in business, subsidies amounted to 43 percent of the value of gross farm receipts, or $19,000 per farmer. In the United States, subsidies were 22 percent of gross farm receipts, which again amounts to $19,000 per farmer. In Canada, subsidies were 18 percent of gross farm receipts, or $8,000 per farmer.[6] In 2002, the European Union was paying $43 billion annually in farm subsidies. Not to be outdone, in May 2002, President Bush signed a bill that contained subsidies of over $180 billion for U.S. farmers spread over a number of years.

Outside of agriculture, subsidies are much lower, but they are still significant. One study found that government subsidies to manufacturing industries in most industrialized countries amounted to between 2 and 3.5 percent of the value of industrial output. The average rate of subsidy in the United States was 0.5 percent; in Japan it was 1 percent, and in Europe it ranged from just below 2 percent in Great Britain and Germany to as much as 6 to 7 percent in Sweden and Ireland.[7] These figures, however, almost certainly underestimate the true value of subsidies, since they are based only on cash grants and ignore other kinds of subsidies (e.g., equity participation or low-interest loans).

The main gains from subsidies accrue to domestic producers, whose international competitiveness is increased as a result of them. Advocates of strategic trade policy (which, as you will recall from Chapter 5, is an outgrowth of the new trade theory) favour subsidies to help domestic firms achieve a dominant position in those industries where economies of scale are important and the world market is not large enough to profitably support more than a few firms (e.g., aerospace). According to this argument, subsidies can help a firm achieve

ANOTHER PERSPECTIVE

Canadian government subsidies to foreign companies

Is this reasonable? Increasingly, there is pressure exerted by the WTO on governments that seek to offer "sweeteners" to entice foreign companies to come and set up shop. Before the era of free trade, Canada and the U.S. signed the historic Auto Pact in 1965 whereby U.S. carmakers, in exchange for tariff-free access, had to assemble in Canada at least one vehicle for every one sold in the country. This exclusive relationship ended in 1999 when the World Trade Organization overruled parts of the Auto Pact.

Still we have seen other types of incentives offered by the Canadian government to foreign car manufacturers, such as Honda in Alliston, Ontario, and Toyota in Cambridge, Ontario, where jobs are created, communities prosper, and cars are built.

The WTO is gradually seeking to phase out member country government incentives, including tax breaks and other fiscal motivators. Canada is not immune. Do you think that the WTO is overstepping its bounds? There are many Web sites expressing opinions on this topic. Check out the WTO's Web site at www.wto.org and briefly search for their rulings on these matters.

a first-mover advantage in an emerging industry (just as Canadian government subsidies, in the form of substantial interest-free loans, allegedly helped Bombardier). If this is achieved, further gains to the domestic economy arise from the employment and tax revenues that a major global company can generate.

Subsidies must be paid for. Governments typically pay for subsidies by taxing individuals. Therefore, whether subsidies generate national benefits that exceed their national costs is debatable. In practice, many subsidies are not successful at increasing the international competitiveness of domestic producers. Rather, they tend to protect the inefficient and promote excess production. Agricultural subsidies (1) allow inefficient farmers to stay in business, (2) encourage countries to overproduce heavily subsidized agricultural products, (3) encourage countries to produce products that could be grown more cheaply elsewhere and imported, and, therefore, (4) reduce international trade in agricultural products. One recent study estimated that if advanced countries abandoned subsidies to farmers, global trade in agricultural products would be 50 percent higher and the world as a whole would be better off to the tune of $160 billion.[8] This increase in wealth arises from the more efficient use of agricultural land.

IMPORT QUOTAS AND VOLUNTARY EXPORT RESTRAINTS

An **import quota** is a direct restriction on the quantity of some good that may be imported into a country. The restriction is usually enforced by issuing import licences to a group of individuals or firms. For example, the United States has a quota on cheese imports. The only firms allowed to import cheese are certain trading companies, each of which is allocated the right to import a maximum number of kilograms of cheese each year. In some cases, the right to sell is given directly to the governments of exporting countries. This is the case for sugar and textile imports in the United States.

IMPORT QUOTA A direct restriction on the quantity of a good that can be imported into a country.

A variant on the import quota is the voluntary export restraint (VER). A **voluntary export restraint** is a quota on trade imposed by the exporting country, typically at the request of the importing country's government. One of the most famous examples is the limitation on auto exports to the United States enforced by Japanese automobile producers in 1981. A response to direct pressure from the U.S. government, this VER limited Japanese imports to no more than 1.68 million vehicles per year. The agreement was revised in 1984 to allow 1.85 million Japanese vehicles per year. The agreement was allowed to lapse in 1985, but the Japanese government indicated its intentions at that time to continue to restrict exports to the United States to 1.85 million vehicles per year.[9] Foreign producers agree to VERs because they fear far more damaging punitive tariffs or import quotas might follow if they do not. Agreeing to a VER is seen as a way of making the best of a bad situation by appeasing protectionist pressures in a country.

VOLUNTARY EXPORT RESTRAINT A quota on trade imposed from the exporting country's side, instead of the importer's; usually imposed at the request of the importing country's government.

As with tariffs and subsidies, both import quotas and VERs benefit domestic producers by limiting import competition. As with all restrictions on trade, quotas do not benefit consumers. An import quota or VER always raises the domestic price of an imported good. When imports are limited to a low percentage of the market by a quota or VER, the price is bid up for that limited foreign supply. In the case of the automobile industry, for example, the VER increased the price of the limited supply of Japanese imports. According to a study by the U.S. Federal Trade Commission, the automobile industry VER cost U.S. consumers about $1 billion per year between 1981 and 1985. That $1 billion per year went to Japanese producers in the form of higher prices.[10] The extra profit that producers make when supply is artificially limited by an import quota is referred to as a quota rent.

If a domestic industry lacks the capacity to meet demand, an import quota can raise prices for *both* the domestically produced and imported good. This happened in the U.S. sugar industry, where an import quota has long limited the amount foreign producers can sell in the U.S. market. According to one study, as a result of import quotas the price of sugar in the United States has been as much as 40 percent greater than the world price.[11] These higher prices have translated into greater profits for U.S. sugar producers, who have lobbied politicians to keep the lucrative agreement in place. They argue that U.S. jobs in the sugar industry will be lost to foreign producers if the quota system is scrapped.

Another industry that has long operated with import quotas is the textile industry, which has a complex set of multinational agreements that govern the amount one country can export to others. In this industry, quotas on imports into the United States have restricted the supply of certain apparel products and increased their price by as much as 70 percent.[12] Quotas also encourage firms to engage in strategic actions designed to circumvent quotas. The United States is not alone in imposing quotas on textile imports. Most other developed nations have similar quotas. Under a World Trade Organization agreement struck in 1995, many quotas on textile products are scheduled to be phased out by 2005. See the accompanying Management Focus to understand how Nova Scotia-based Clearwater Seafoods has brought a global perspective to fishing quotas.

LOCAL CONTENT REQUIREMENTS

LOCAL CONTENT REQUIREMENT A requirement that some specific fraction of a good be produced domestically.

A **local content requirement** demands that some specific fraction of a good be produced domestically. The requirement can be expressed either in physical terms (e.g., 75 percent of component parts for this product must be produced locally) or in value terms (e.g., 75 percent of the value of this product must be produced locally). Local content regulations have been widely used by developing countries to shift their manufacturing base from the simple assembly of products whose parts are manufactured elsewhere into the local manufacture of component parts. They have also been used in developed countries to try to protect local jobs and industry from foreign competition. For example, a little-known law in the United States, the Buy America Act, specifies that government agencies must give preference to American products when putting contracts for equipment out to bid unless the foreign products have a significant price advantage. The law specifies a product as "American" if 51 percent of the materials by value are produced domestically. This amounts to a local content requirement. If a foreign company, or an American one, wishes to win a contract from a U.S. government agency to provide some equipment, it must ensure that at least 51 percent of the product by value is manufactured in the United States.

For a domestic producer of parts, local content regulations provide protection in the same way an import quota does: by limiting foreign competition. The aggregate economic effects are also the same; domestic producers benefit, but the restrictions on imports raise the prices of imported components. In turn, higher prices for imported components are passed on to consumers of the final product in the form of higher final prices. So as with all trade policies, local content regulations tend to benefit producers and not consumers.

ADMINISTRATIVE POLICIES

ADMINISTRATIVE TRADE POLICIES Administrative policies, typically adopted by government bureaucracies, that can be used to restrict imports or boost exports.

In addition to the formal instruments of trade policy, governments of all types sometimes use informal or administrative policies to restrict imports and boost exports. **Administrative trade policies** are bureaucratic rules designed to make it difficult for imports to enter a country. Some would argue that the Japanese are the masters of this kind of trade barrier. In recent years, Japan's formal tariff and nontariff barriers have been among the lowest in the world. However, critics charge that the country's informal administrative barriers to imports more than compensate for this. For example, the Netherlands exports tulip bulbs to almost every country in the world except Japan. In Japan, customs inspectors insist on checking every tulip bulb by

MANAGEMENT FOCUS

CLEARWATER SEAFOODS

John Risley, a co-founder and now the chairman of Clearwater Seafoods, and Colin Macdonald the other co-founder and now chief executive officer, have brought a global perspective to the fishing business they began in Nova Scotia in 1976.

Once a low-tech industry, things have changed. Captain's logbooks have been replaced by notebook computers while Global Positioning Systems (GPS) track both the vessels and map the ocean bottom. It also operates the first and only dryland lobster storage facility that can store up to 1 million kilograms of lobster in top condition for up to six months. Clearwater has actively integrated technology and is the largest shellfish company in North America, harvesting, processing, and selling over 36 million kilograms of seafood a year.

Clearwater provides a wide variety of premium seafoods, such as scallops, lobster, Arctic surf clams, cold water shrimp, Argentine scallops, and crab. It is truly a global company. Argentine scallops accounted for $33 million of sales in 2003, or 10 percent of Clearwater's worldwide sales. The principal markets for the scallops is Europe and the United States. Clams, which are harvested in the Atlantic ocean, are sold in Japan, China, and North America. Cold water shrimp, harvested off the coast of Newfoundland, are marketed in Asia, Europe and the United States. In total, North America accounts for just over one-half of the company's sales, Europe being another 25 percent, and Asia about 20 percent.

Aside from the integration of technology and the diversity of products and markets, Clearwater also benefits from vertical integration. The company controls the process from harvesting to processing, to marketing and delivery, which produces price efficiencies for both the company and its customers.

Fishing is subject to quotas, and thus the right of being allowed to harvest a certain amount of fish becomes a valuable property. For example, in 2003, Clearwater acquired the right to certain scallop quotas from High Liner Foods Inc. This increased Clearwater's share of the Canadian sea scallop supply—called the Total Allowable Catch, or TAC, from 36 percent to 50 percent. Quota ownership is a very important part of Clearwater's competitive advantage. It owns between 50 to 100 percent of the supply (TAC) for sea scallops, offshore lobster, cold water shrimps, arctic surf clams, Jonah crab, and Argentine scallops. Owning such a high percentage of the fish quota allows the company to "control its own destiny" and ensures a consistent supply of product to customers.

The other component to fish supply is ensuring sustainability of the resource. In Canada, Clearwater works with the Canadian Department of Fisheries and Oceans and the equivalent agency in Argentina, the INIDEP, to create a sustainable resource management system. The result, in both cases, has been a stable and even rising total allowable catch.

On the customer side, Clearwater is seeking new markets for its products. Currently it has over 1100 customers around the world, including Sobeys, Marks & Spencer, and The Keg. Colin Macdonald has noted the potential in China, as a slowly growing middle class will lead to increased consumption of seafood. Currently, China is a net exporter of seafood, but the growing wealth of the population is forecast to turn China into a net importer of seafood in the coming years. However, while Clearwater is a top-end producer of seafood, China is the world's low-cost seafood producer, due to a combination of state-owned enterprises and workers' pay near subsistence levels. Thus China may be a current competitor to Clearwater, but can serve as a large potential consumer in the future.

Sources: Clearwater, *Annual Report*, 2004; Clearwater at www.clearwater.ca; K. Cox, "Clearwater Trawls For Fresh Opportunities," *The Globe and Mail*, May 22, 2004.

cutting it vertically down the middle, and even Japanese ingenuity cannot put them back together again! Federal Express has had a tough time expanding its global express shipping services into Japan because Japanese customs inspectors insist on opening a large proportion of express packages to check for pornography, a process that can delay an "express" package for days. Japan is not the only country that engages in such

DUMPING Selling goods in a foreign market for less than their cost of production or below their "fair" market value.

policies. France required that all imported videotape recorders arrive through a small customs entry point that was both remote and poorly staffed. The resulting delays kept Japanese VCRs out of the French market until a VER agreement was negotiated.[13] As with all instruments of trade policy, administrative instruments benefit producers and hurt consumers, who are denied access to possibly superior foreign products.

ANTIDUMPING POLICIES

In the context of international trade, **dumping** is variously defined as selling goods in a foreign market at below their costs of production, or as selling goods in a foreign market at below their "fair" market value. There is a difference between these two definitions; the "fair" market value of a good is normally judged to be greater than the costs of producing that good because the former includes a "fair" profit margin. Dumping is viewed as a method by which firms unload excess production in foreign markets. Some dumping may be the result of predatory behaviour, with producers using substantial profits from their home markets to subsidize prices in a foreign market with a view to driving indigenous competitors out of that market. Once this has been achieved, so the argument goes, the predatory firm can raise prices and earn substantial profits.

An alleged example of dumping occurred in 1997, when two South Korean manufacturers of semiconductors, LG Semicon and Hyundai Electronics, were accused of selling dynamic random access memory chips (DRAMs) in the U.S. market at below their costs of production. This action occurred in the middle of a worldwide glut of chip-making capacity. It was alleged that the firms were trying to unload their excess production in the United States.

Antidumping policies are designed to punish foreign firms that engage in dumping. The ultimate objective is to protect domestic producers from "unfair" foreign competition. Although antidumping policies vary somewhat from country to country, the majority are similar to U.S. policies. If a domestic producer believes that a foreign firm is dumping production in the U.S. market, it can file a petition with two government agencies, the Commerce Department and the International Trade Commission. In the Korean DRAM case, Micron Technology, a U.S. manufacturer of DRAMs, filed the petition. The government agencies then investigate the complaint. If they find it has merit, the Commerce Department may impose an antidumping duty on the offending foreign imports (antidumping duties are often called **countervailing duties**). These duties, which represent a special tariff, can be fairly substantial and stay in place for up to five years. For example, after reviewing Micron's complaint, the Commerce Department imposed 9 percent and 4 percent countervailing duties on LG Semicon and Hyundai DRAM chips, respectively.

ANOTHER PERSPECTIVE

Kodak's case against Fujifilm: Those tricky invisible trade barriers

In late 1997, the World Trade Organization ruled against the United States in the Kodak–Fuji case, in which Kodak, through the U.S. Trade Representative, had charged that Japanese distribution systems and anticompetitive practices by Fujifilm restricted Kodak film and photographic paper imports into the Japanese market. The WTO report concluded that no government regulations, administrative guidance, or other measures in the Japanese film market either restrain competition or limit sales of imported film.

The reason Kodak had only 10 percent of the market in Japan was largely because Japanese retailers chose not to carry Kodak products. The Japanese distribution system has long, vertical distribution chains. At the retailer level, there are frequent deliveries, little local inventory, and small shelf space. The Fujifilm dealers had long-term, committed relationships with their retailers, a situation that takes an outsider a strong desire and a commitment to build. Fujifilm argued successfully that Kodak expected its product to sell itself; Kodak did not manage the process well, from a management, marketing, or investment perspective. This is a good example of an invisible barrier to trade. Do you think Kodak's case is one of poor management?

ANTIDUMPING POLICIES Policies designed to punish foreign firms that engage in dumping and thus protect domestic producers from unfair foreign competition.

COUNTERVAILING DUTIES Antidumping duties.

THE CASE FOR GOVERNMENT INTERVENTION

Now that we have reviewed the various instruments of trade policy that governments can use, it is time to take a more detailed look at the case for government intervention in international trade. Arguments for government intervention take two paths–political and economic. Political arguments for intervention are concerned with protecting the interests of certain groups within a nation (normally producers), often at the expense of other groups (normally consumers). Economic arguments for intervention are typically concerned with boosting the overall wealth of a nation (to the benefit of all, both producers and consumers).

POLITICAL ARGUMENTS FOR INTERVENTION

Political arguments for government intervention cover a range of issues including protecting jobs, protecting industries deemed important for national security, retaliating to unfair foreign competition, protecting consumers from "dangerous" products, furthering the goals of foreign policy, and protecting the human rights of individuals in exporting countries.

Protecting Jobs and Industries

Perhaps the most common political argument for government intervention is that it is needed to protect jobs, culture, and industries from foreign competition.

Over the past three decades, Canadian cultural content policies were implemented and amended, in order to buffer Canadian cultural "institutions" from American print media, radio, and television advertisements and programming, much to the chagrin of big U.S. business interests that view culture as an industry, not an "off limits" abstract heritage concept. The perceived need to protect all Canadian cultural pillars from encroachment by American media industries and values, has, in some circles done Canada well.

In 1973, the Canadian Foreign Investment Review Act (FIRA) came into existence as a means to monitor and control foreign corporate acquisitions of Canadian companies. An unforeseen offshoot of this Act was that, in fact, it slowed growth in the oil patch sector and other Canadian industry sectors by categorically turning away investment. A second more insidious side effect is still being felt to this day. FIRA drove a political wedge between Eastern and Western Canada. Many potential oil-related acquisitions of Albertan firms by foreign firms were overturned due to this policy, restraining economic growth and expansion in Alberta.

The unpopularity of FIRA reached its peak during the early 1980s and evolved to a gentler version of protecting jobs and industries from foreign encroachment with the signing of the 1985 Investment Act. It, in part, paved the way for the 1988 Free Trade Agreement.

The following Web sites from the CRTC also offer interesting perspectives on this subject at www.crtc.gc.ca/eng/info_sht/g11.htm and www.crtc.gc.ca/eng/info_sht/r1.htm.

National Security

Countries sometimes argue that it is necessary to protect certain industries because they are important for national security. Defence-related industries often get this kind of attention (e.g., aerospace, advanced electronics, semiconductors, etc.). Although not as common as it used to be, this argument is still made. Those in favour of protecting the U.S. semiconductor industry from foreign competition, for example, argue that semiconductors are now such important components of defence products that it would be dangerous to rely primarily on foreign producers for them. In 1986, this argument helped persuade the U.S. federal government to support Sematech, a consortium of 14 U.S. semiconductor companies that accounted for 90 percent of the U.S. industry's revenues. Sematech's mission was to conduct joint research into manufacturing techniques that can be parcelled out to members. The government saw the venture as so critical that Sematech was specially protected from antitrust laws. Initially, the U.S. government provided Sematech with $100 million per year in subsidies. By the mid-1990s, however, the U.S. semiconductor industry had regained its leading market position, largely through the personal computer boom and demand for microprocessor chips made by Intel. In 1994, the consortium's board voted to seek an end to U.S. federal funding, and since 1996 the consortium has been funded entirely by private money.[14]

Retaliation

Some argue that governments should use the threat to intervene in trade policy as a bargaining tool to help open foreign markets and force trading partners to "play by the rules of the game." The U.S. government has used the threat of punitive trade sanctions to try to get the Chinese government to enforce intellectual property laws. Lax enforcement of these laws had given rise to massive copyright infringements in China that have been costing U.S. companies such as Microsoft hundreds of millions of dollars per year in lost sales revenues. After the United States threatened to impose 100 percent tariffs on a range of Chinese imports, and after harsh words between officials from the two countries, the Chinese agreed to tighter enforcement of intellectual property regulations.[15]

If it works, such a politically motivated rationale for government intervention may liberalize trade and bring with it resulting economic gains. It is a risky strategy, however. A country that is being pressured may not back down and instead may respond to the imposition of punitive tariffs by raising trade barriers of its own. This is exactly what the Chinese government threatened to do when pressured by the United States, although it ultimately backed down. If a government does not back down, however, the results could be higher trade barriers all around and an economic loss to all involved.

Protecting Consumers

Many governments have long had regulations in place to protect consumers from "unsafe" products. The indirect effect of such regulations often is to limit or ban the importation of such products. Since 1989, a reported 1700 toddlers have been injured in baby walkers–either from falling down the stairs or pulling dangerous objects onto themselves.[16] Injuries suffered by young children included burns, concussions, fractures, brain hemorrhages, and even death. In April 2004, the Canadian government imposed a permanent ban on the sale and import of baby walkers, making Canada the first country to ban such devices.

The conflict over the ban on the sale of importation of hormone-treated beef into the European Union may be a taste of things to come. In addition to the use of hormones to promote animal growth and meat production, the science of biotechnology has made it possible to genetically alter many crops so that they are resistant to common herbicides, produce proteins that are natural insecticides, have dramatically improved yields, or can withstand inclement weather. A new breed of genetically modified tomatoes has an antifreeze gene inserted into its genome and can thus be grown in colder climates than hitherto possible. Another example is a genetically engineered cotton seed produced by Monsanto. The seed has been engineered to express a protein that provides protection against three common insect pests: the cotton bollworm, tobacco budworm, and pink bollworm. Use of this seed reduces or eliminates the need for traditional pesticide applications for these pests. As enticing as such innovations sound, they have met with intense resistance from consumer groups, particularly in Europe. The fear is that the widespread use of genetically altered seed corn could have unanticipated and harmful effects on human health and may result in "genetic pollution." (An example of genetic pollution would be when the widespread use of crops that produce "natural pesticides" stimulates the evolution of "super-bugs" that are resistant to those pesticides.) Such concerns have led Austria and Luxembourg to outlaw the importation, sale, or use of genetically altered organisms. Sentiment against genetically altered organisms also runs strongly in several other European countries, most notably Germany and Switzerland. It seems likely, therefore, that the World Trade Organization will be drawn into the conflict between those that want to expand the global market for genetically altered organisms, such as Monsanto, and those that want to limit it, such as Austria and Luxembourg.[17]

Furthering Foreign Policy Objectives

Governments sometimes use trade policy to support their foreign policy objectives.[18] A government may grant preferential trade terms to a country it wants to build strong relations with. Trade policy has also been used several times to pressure or punish "rogue states" that do not abide by international law or norms. Iraq has laboured under extensive trade sanctions since the UN coalition defeated the country in the 1991 Gulf War. Once again, in early 2003, Iraq was front and centre in the world's news as Saddam Hussein's government was overthrown by the U.S. government. Since the 1991 U.S. invasion, Iraq had persistently ignored international calls to open its doors to United Nations' weapons inspectors. Iraq had been accused of being in a state of readiness to deploy an arsenal of WMD (weapons of mass destruction). Other than hurting the poor, trade sanctions seemed to have little effect in Iraq. The wealthier Iraqis procured products through the inflated black market controlled by Saddam Hussein, who pocketed huge profits. Therefore, economic punishment of "rogue states" does not always have its desired effect. The theory is that such pressure might persuade the "rogue state" to mend its ways or it might hasten a change of government. In the case of Iraq, the sanctions are seen as a way of forcing that country to comply with several UN resolutions. In another example, the United States has maintained long-running trade sanctions against Cuba. Their principal function is to impoverish Cuba in the hope that the resulting economic hardship will lead to the downfall of Cuba's Communist government and its replacement with a more democratically inclined (and pro-U.S.) regime. The United States also has trade sanctions in place against Libya and Iran, both of which it accuses of supporting terrorist action against U.S. interests.

Other countries can undermine any unilateral trade sanctions. The U.S. sanctions against Cuba, for example, have not stopped other Western countries from trading with Cuba. The U.S. sanctions have done little more than help create a vacuum into which other trading nations, such as Canada and Germany, have stepped. In an attempt to halt this and further tighten the screws on Cuba, in 1996 the U.S. Congress passed the **Helms–Burton Act.** This act allows Americans to sue foreign firms that use property in Cuba confiscated from them after the 1959 revolution. A similar act, the **D'Amato Act,** aimed at Libya and Iran was also passed that year.

The passage of Helms-Burton elicited protests from America's trading partners, including the European Union, Canada, and Mexico, all of which claim the law violates their sovereignty and is illegal under World Trade Organization rules. For example, Canadian companies that have been doing business in Cuba for years see no reason they should suddenly be sued in U.S. courts when Canada does not restrict trade with Cuba. They are not violating Canadian law and they are not U.S. companies, so why should they be subject to U.S. law? Despite such protests, the law is still on the books in the United States, although the U.S. government has been less than enthusiastic about enforcing it–probably because it is unenforceable.

HELMS–BURTON ACT Act passed in 1996 that allowed Americans to sue foreign firms that use Cuban property confiscated from them after the 1959 revolution.

D'AMATO ACT Act passed in 1996, similar to the Helms–Burton Act, aimed at Libya and Iran.

Hudson's Bay Canada president and CEO George Heller and Du Yu Zhou, president of the China National Textile and Apparel Council, share a joke during a Toronto luncheon in 2004. When the trade quotes of a 30-year-old treaty ended, many thought that the international flow of textiles would remain similar to the historical volume and flow of the textile trade. However, some have since claimed that North American markets have been flooded by cheap Chinese textiles. CP/Dick Loek.

Protecting Human Rights

Protecting and promoting human rights in other countries is an important element of foreign policy for many democracies. Governments sometimes use trade policy to try to improve the human rights policies of trading partners. For years the most obvious example of this was the annual debate in the United States over whether to grant most-favoured-nation (MFN) status to China. MFN status allows countries to export goods to the United Status under favourable terms. Under MFN rules, the average tariff on Chinese goods imported into the United States is 8 percent. If China's MFN status were rescinded, tariffs would probably rise to about 40 percent. Trading partners who are signatories of the World Trade Organization, as most are, automatically receive MFN status. However, China did not join the WTO until 2001, so historically the decision of whether to grant MFN status to China was a real one. The decision was made more difficult by the perception that China had a poor human rights record. As indications of the country's disregard for human rights, critics of China often point to the 1989 Tiananmen Square massacre, China's continuing subjugation of Tibet (which China occupied in the 1950s), and the squashing of political dissent in China (there are an estimated 1700 political prisoners in China).[19] These critics argued that it was wrong for the United States to grant MFN status to China, and that instead, the United States should withhold MFN status until China showed measurable improvement in its human rights record. Put differently, the critics argued that trade policy should be used as a political weapon to force China to change its internal policies toward human rights.

But others contend that limiting trade with such countries would make matters worse, not better. They argue that the best way to change the internal human rights stance of a country is to engage it through international trade. At its core, the argument is simple: Growing bilateral trade raises the income levels of both countries, and as a state becomes richer, its people begin to demand–and generally receive–better treatment with regard to their human rights. This is a variant of the argument in Chapter 2 that economic progress begets political progress (if political progress is measured by the adoption of a democratic government that respects human rights). This argument ultimately won the day in 1999 when the Clinton administration blessed China's application to join the WTO and announced that trade and human rights issues should be decoupled.

ECONOMIC ARGUMENTS FOR INTERVENTION

With the development of the new trade theory and strategic trade policy (see Chapter 5), the economic arguments for government intervention have undergone a renaissance in recent years. Until the early 1980s, most economists saw little benefit in government intervention and strongly advocated a free trade policy. This position has changed at the margins with the development of strategic trade policy, although as we will see in the next section, there are still strong economic arguments for sticking to a free trade stance.

The Infant Industry Argument

The infant industry argument is by far the oldest economic argument for government intervention. Alexander Hamilton proposed it in 1792. According to this argument, many developing countries have a potential comparative advantage in manufacturing, but new manufacturing industries cannot initially compete with well-established industries in developed countries. To allow manufacturing to get a toehold, the argument is that governments should temporarily support new industries (with tariffs, import quotas, and subsidies) until they have grown strong enough to meet international competition.

This argument has had substantial appeal for the governments of developing nations during the past 50 years, and the GATT has recognized the infant industry argument as a legitimate reason for protectionism. Nevertheless, many economists remain very critical of this argument. They make two main points. First, protection of manufacturing from foreign competition does no good unless the protection helps make the industry efficient. In case after case, however, protection seems to have done little more than foster the development of inefficient industries that have little hope of ever competing in the world market. Brazil, for example, built the world's 10th largest auto industry behind tariff barriers and quotas. Once those barriers were removed in the late 1980s, however, foreign imports soared and the industry was forced to admit that after 30 years of protection, the Brazilian industry was one of the world's most inefficient.[20]

Second, the infant industry argument relies on an assumption that firms are unable to make efficient long-term investments by borrowing money from the domestic or international capital market. Consequently, governments have been required to subsidize long-term investments. Given the development of global capital markets over the past 20 years, this assumption no longer looks as valid as it once did. Today, if a developing country really does have a potential comparative advantage in a manufacturing industry, firms in that country should be able to borrow money from the capital markets to finance the required investments. Given financial support, firms based in countries with a potential comparative advantage have an incentive to go through the necessary period of initial losses to make long-run gains without requiring government protection. Many Taiwanese and South Korean firms did this in industries such as textiles, semiconductors, machine tools, steel, and shipping. Thus, given efficient global capital markets, the only industries that would require government protection would be those that are not worthwhile.

Strategic Trade Policy

Some new trade theorists have proposed the strategic trade policy argument.[21] We reviewed the basic argument in Chapter 5 when we considered the new trade theory. The new trade theory argues that in industries where the existence of substantial scale economies implies that the world market will profitably support only a few firms, countries may predominate in the export of certain products simply because they had firms that were able to capture first-mover advantages. The dominance of Boeing in the commercial aircraft industry is attributed to such factors.

The strategic trade policy argument consists of two components. First, it is argued that by appropriate actions, a government can help raise national income if it can somehow ensure that the firm or firms to gain first-mover advantages in such an industry are domestic rather than foreign enterprises. Thus, according to the strategic trade policy argument, a government should use subsidies to support promising firms that are active in newly emerging industries. Advocates of this argument point out that the substantial R&D grants the U.S. government gave Boeing in the 1950s and 60s probably helped tilt the field of competition in the newly emerging market for jet passenger planes in Boeing's favour. (Boeing's 707 jet airliner was derived from a military plane.) Similar arguments are now made with regard to Japan's dominance in the production of liquid crystal display screens (used in laptop computers). Although these screens were invented in the United States, the Japanese government, in cooperation with major electronics companies, targeted this industry for research support in the late 1970s and early 80s. The result was that Japanese firms, not U.S. firms, subsequently captured the first-mover advantages in this market.

The second component of the strategic trade policy argument is that it might pay government to intervene in an industry if it helps domestic firms overcome the barriers to entry created by foreign firms that have already reaped first-mover advantages. This argument underlies government support of Airbus Industrie, Boeing's major competitor. Formed in 1966 as a consortium of four companies from Great Britain, France, Germany, and Spain, Airbus had less than 5 percent of the world commercial aircraft market when it began production in the mid-1970s. By 2000, it had increased its share to about 45 percent and was threatening Boeing's dominance. How did Airbus achieve this? According to the U.S. government, the answer is a $13.5 billion subsidy from the governments of Great Britain, France, Germany, and Spain.[22] Without this subsidy, Airbus would have never been able to break into the world market. In another example, the rise to dominance of the Japanese semiconductor industry, despite the first-mover advantages enjoyed by U.S. firms, is attributed to intervention by the Japanese government. In this case, the government did not subsidize the costs of domestic manufacturers. Rather, it protected the Japanese home market while pursuing policies that ensured Japanese companies got access to the necessary manufacturing and product know-how.

If these arguments are correct, they clearly suggest a rationale for government intervention in international trade. Governments should target technologies that may be important in the future and use subsidies to support development work aimed at commercializing those technologies. Furthermore, government should provide export subsidies until the domestic firms have established first-mover advantages in the world market. Government support may also be justified if it can help domestic firms overcome the first-mover advantages enjoyed by foreign competitors and emerge as viable competitors in the world market (as in the Airbus and semiconductor examples). In this case, a combination of home-market protection and export-promoting subsidies may be called for.

THE REVISED CASE FOR FREE TRADE

The strategic trade policy arguments of the new trade theorists suggest an economic justification for government intervention in international trade. This justification challenges the rationale for unrestricted free trade found in the work of classic trade theorists such as Adam Smith and David Ricardo. In response to this challenge to economic orthodoxy, a number of economists–including some of those responsible for the development of the new trade theory, such as Paul Krugman of MIT–have been quick to point out that although strategic trade policy looks nice in theory, in practice it may be unworkable. This response to the strategic trade policy argument constitutes the revised case for free trade.[23]

RETALIATION AND TRADE WAR

Krugman argues that a strategic trade policy aimed at establishing domestic firms in a dominant position in a global industry is a beggar-thy-neighbour policy that boosts national income at the expense of other countries. A country that attempts to use such policies will probably provoke retaliation. In many cases, the resulting trade war between two or more interventionist governments will leave all countries involved worse off than if a hands-off approach had been adopted in the first place. If the U.S. government were to respond to the Airbus subsidy by increasing its own subsidies to Boeing, for example, the result might be that the subsidies would cancel each other out. In the process, both European and U.S. taxpayers would end up supporting an expensive and pointless trade war, and both Europe and the United States would be worse off.

Krugman may be right about the danger of a strategic trade policy leading to a trade war. The problem, however, is how to respond when one's competitors are already being supported by government subsidies; that is, how should Boeing and the United States respond to the subsidization of Airbus? According to Krugman, the answer is probably not to engage in retaliatory action, but to help establish rules that minimize the use of trade-distorting subsidies. This is what the World Trade Organization seeks to do.

DOMESTIC POLITICS

Governments do not always act in the national interest when they intervene in the economy; politically important interest groups often influence them. The European Union's support for the Common Agricultural Policy (CAP), which arose because of the political power of French and German farmers, is an example. The CAP benefited inefficient farmers and the politicians who relied on the farm vote, but not consumers in the EU, who pay more for their foodstuffs. Thus, a further reason for not embracing strategic trade policy, according to Krugman, is that such a policy is almost certain to be captured by special interest groups within the economy, who will distort it to their own ends. Krugman concludes that in the United States:

> To ask the Commerce Department to ignore special-interest politics while formulating detailed policy for many industries is not realistic: to establish a blanket policy of free trade, with exceptions granted only under extreme pressure, may not be the optimal policy according to the theory but may be the best policy that the country is likely to get.[24]

DEVELOPMENT OF THE WORLD TRADING SYSTEM

There are strong economic arguments for supporting unrestricted free trade. While many governments have recognized the value of these arguments, they have been unwilling to unilaterally lower their trade barriers for fear that other nations might not follow suit. Consider the problem that two neighboring countries, say Brazil and Argentina, face when considering whether to lower barriers to trade between them. In principle, the government of Brazil might be in favour of lowering trade barriers, but it might be unwilling to do so for fear that Argentina will not do the same. Instead, the government might fear that the Argentineans will take advantage of Brazil's low barriers to enter the Brazilian market, while at the same time continuing to shut Brazilian products out of their market through high trade barriers. The Argentinean government might believe that it faces the same dilemma. The essence of the problem is a lack of trust. Both governments recognize that their respective nations will benefit from lower trade barriers between them, but neither government is willing to lower barriers for fear that the other might not follow.[25]

Such a deadlock can be resolved if both countries negotiate a set of rules to govern cross-border trade and lower trade barriers. But who is to monitor the governments to make sure they play by the trade rules? And who is to impose sanctions on a government that cheats? Both governments could set up an independent body whose function is to act as a referee. This referee could monitor trade between the countries, make sure that no side cheats, and impose sanctions on a country if it does cheat in the trade game.

While it might sound unlikely that any government would compromise its national sovereignty by submitting to such an arrangement, since World War II an international trading framework has evolved that has exactly these features. For its first 50 years, this framework was known as the General Agreement on Tariffs and Trade (the

GATT). Since 1995, it has been known as the World Trade Organization (WTO). Here we look at the evolution and workings of the GATT and WTO. We set the scene with a brief discussion of the pre-GATT history of world trade.

FROM SMITH TO THE GREAT DEPRESSION

As we saw in Chapter 5, the theoretical case for free trade dates to the late eighteenth century and the work of Adam Smith and David Ricardo. Free trade as a government policy was first officially embraced by Great Britain in 1846, when the British Parliament repealed the Corn Laws. The Corn Laws placed a high tariff on imports of foreign corn. The objectives of the Corn Laws tariff were to raise government revenues and to protect British corn producers. There had been annual motions in Parliament in favour of free trade since the 1820s when David Ricardo was a member. However, agricultural protection was withdrawn only as a result of a protracted debate when the effects of a harvest failure in Great Britain were compounded by the imminent threat of famine in Ireland. Faced with considerable hardship and suffering among the populace, Parliament narrowly reversed its long-held position.

During the next 80 years or so, Great Britain, as one of the world's dominant trading powers, pushed the case for trade liberalization; but the British government was a voice in the wilderness. Its major trading partners did not reciprocate the British policy of unilateral free trade. The only reason Britain kept this policy for so long was that, as the world's largest exporting nation, it had far more to lose from a trade war than did any other country.

By the 1930s, however, the British attempt to stimulate free trade was buried under the economic rubble of the Great Depression. The Great Depression had roots in the failure of the world economy to mount a sustained economic recovery after the end of World War I in 1918. Things got worse in 1929 with the U.S. stock market collapse and the subsequent run on the U.S. banking system. Economic problems were compounded in 1930 when the U.S. Congress passed the Smoot-Hawley tariff. Aimed at avoiding rising unemployment by protecting domestic industries and diverting consumer demand away from foreign products, the Smoot-Hawley tariff erected an enormous wall of tariff barriers. Almost every industry was rewarded with its "made-to-order" tariff. A particularly odd aspect of the Smoot-Hawley tariff-raising binge was that the United States was running a balance-of-payment surplus at the time and it was the world's largest creditor nation. The Smoot-Hawley tariff had a damaging effect on employment abroad. Other countries reacted to the U.S. action by raising their own tariff barriers. U.S. exports tumbled in response, and the world slid further into the Great Depression.[26]

1947–1979: GATT, TRADE LIBERALIZATION, AND ECONOMIC GROWTH

The economic damage caused by the beggar-thy-neighbour trade policies that the Smoot-Hawley Act ushered in exerted a profound influence on the economic institutions and ideology of the post-World War II world. The United States emerged from the war both victorious and economically dominant. After the debacle of the Great Depression, opinion in the U.S. Congress had swung strongly in favour of free trade. Under U.S. leadership, GATT was established in 1947.

The GATT was a multilateral agreement whose objective was to liberalize trade by eliminating tariffs, subsidies, import quotas, and the like. From its foundation in 1947 until it was superseded by the WTO, the GATT's membership grew from 19 to more than 120 nations. The GATT did not attempt to liberalize trade restrictions in one fell swoop; that would have been impossible. Rather, tariff reduction was spread over eight rounds. The most recent, the Uruguay Round, was launched in 1986 and completed in December 1993. In these rounds, mutual tariff reductions were negotiated among all members, who then committed themselves not to raise import tariffs above negotiated rates. GATT regulations were enforced by a mutual monitoring mechanism. If a country thought that one of its trading partners was violating a GATT regulation, it could ask the Geneva-based bureaucracy that administered the GATT to investigate. If GATT investigators found the complaints to be valid, member countries could be asked to pressure the offending party to change its policies. In general, such pressure was sufficient to get an offending country to change its policies. If it were not, the offending country could have been expelled from the GATT.

In its early years, the GATT was by most measures very successful. For example, the average tariff declined by nearly 92 percent in the United States between the Geneva Round of 1947 and the Tokyo Round of 1973–79. Consistent with the theoretical arguments first advanced by Ricardo and reviewed in Chapter 5, the move toward free trade under the GATT appeared to stimulate economic growth. From 1953 to 1963, world trade grew at an annual rate of 6.1 percent, and world income grew at an annual rate of 4.3 percent. Performance from 1963 to 1973 was even better; world trade grew at 8.9 percent annually, and world income grew at 5.1 percent annually.[27]

1980–1993: DISTURBING TRENDS

During the 1980s and early 1990s, the world trading system erected by the GATT came under strain as pressures for greater protectionism increased around the world. Three reasons caused the rise in such pressures during the 1980s. First, the economic success of Japan strained the world trading system. Japan was in ruins when the GATT was created. By the early 1980s, however, it had become the world's second largest economy and its largest exporter. Japan's success in such industries as automobiles and semiconductors by itself might have been enough to strain the world trading system. Things were made worse, however, by the widespread perception in the West that despite low tariff rates and subsidies, Japanese markets were closed to imports and foreign investment by administrative trade barriers.

Second, the world trading system was strained by the persistent trade deficit in the world's largest economy, the United States. Although the deficit peaked in 1987 at more than $170 billion, by the end of 1992 the annual rate was still running about $80 billion. From a political perspective, the matter was worsened in 1992 by the United States' $45 billion trade deficit with Japan, a country perceived as not playing by the rules. The consequences of the U.S. deficit included painful adjustments in industries such as automobiles, machine tools, semiconductors, steel, and textiles, where domestic producers steadily lost market share to foreign competitors. The resulting unemployment gave rise to renewed demands in the U.S. Congress for protection against imports.

A third reason for the trend toward greater protectionism was that many countries found ways to get around GATT regulations. Bilateral voluntary export restraints (VERs) circumvent GATT agreements, because neither the importing country nor the exporting country complain to the GATT bureaucracy in Geneva–and without a complaint, the GATT bureaucracy can do nothing. Exporting countries agreed to VERs to avoid more damaging punitive tariffs. One of the best-known examples is the VER between Japan and the United States, under which Japanese producers promised to limit their auto imports into the United States to defuse growing trade tensions. According to a World Bank study, 13 percent of the imports of industrialized countries in 1981 were subjected to nontariff trade barriers such as VERs. By 1986, this figure had increased to 16 percent. The most rapid rise was in the United States, where the value of imports affected by nontariff barriers (primarily VERs) increased by 23 percent between 1981 and 1986.[28]

THE URUGUAY ROUND AND THE WORLD TRADE ORGANIZATION

Against the background of rising pressures for protectionism, in 1986 the GATT members embarked on their eighth round of negotiations to reduce tariffs, the Uruguay Round (so named because it occurred in Uruguay). This was the most difficult round of negotiations yet, primarily because it was also the most ambitious. Until then, GATT rules had applied only to trade in manufactured goods and commodities. In the Uruguay Round, member countries sought to extend GATT rules to cover trade in services. They also sought to write rules governing the protection of intellectual property, to reduce agricultural subsidies, and to strengthen the GATT's monitoring and enforcement mechanisms.

The Uruguay Round dragged on for seven years before an agreement was reached December 15, 1993. The agreement was formally signed by member states at a meeting in Marrakech, Morocco, on April 15, 1994. It went into effect July 1, 1995. The Uruguay Round contained the following provisions: (1) tariffs on industrial goods were to be reduced by more than one-third, and tariffs were to be scrapped on over 40 percent of manufactured goods; (2) average tariff rates imposed by developed nations on manufactured goods were to be reduced to less than 4 percent of value, the lowest level in modern history; (3) there was to be a substantial reduction in agricultural subsidies; (4) for the first time GATT fair trade and market access rules were to be extended to cover a wide range of services; (5) GATT rules were also to be extended to provide enhanced protection for patents, copyrights, and trademarks (intellectual property); (6) barriers on trade in textiles were to be significantly reduced over 10 years; and (7) a World Trade Organization (WTO) was to be created to implement the GATT agreement.

Services and Intellectual Property

In the long run, the extension of GATT rules to cover services and intellectual property may be particularly significant. Until 1995, GATT rules applied only to industrial goods (i.e., manufactured goods and commodities). In 2003, world trade in services accounted for US$1,743 billion compared to world trade in goods of US$7,557 billion.[29] Extension of GATT rules to this important trading arena could significantly increase both the total share of world trade accounted for by services and the overall volume of world trade. The extension of GATT rules to cover intellectual property will make it much easier for high-technology companies to do business in developing nations where intellectual property rules have historically been poorly enforced (see Chapter 2 for details). High-technology companies now have a mechanism to force countries to prohibit the piracy of intellectual property.

The World Trade Organization

The clarification and strengthening of GATT rules and the creation of the World Trade Organization also hold out the promise of more effective policing and enforcement of GATT rules. The WTO acts as an umbrella organization that encompasses the GATT along with two new sister bodies, one on services and the other on intellectual property. The WTO's General Agreement on Trade in Services (GATS) has taken the lead to extending free trade agreements to services. The WTO's Agreement on Trade Related Aspects of Intellectual Property Rights (TRIPS) is an attempt to narrow the gaps in the way intellectual property rights are protected around the world, and to bring them under common international rules. WTO has taken over responsibility for arbitrating trade disputes and monitoring the trade policies of member countries. While the WTO operates on the basis of consensus as the GATT did, in the area of dispute settlement, member countries will no longer be able to block adoption of arbitration reports. Arbitration panel reports on trade disputes between member countries will be automatically adopted by the WTO unless there is a consensus to reject them. Countries that have been found by the arbitration panel to violate GATT rules may appeal to a permanent appellate body, but its verdict is binding. If offenders fail to comply with the recommendations of the arbitration panel, trading partners have the right to compensation or, in the last resort, to impose (commensurate) trade sanctions (for an example, see the opening case on the banana wars). Every stage of the procedure is subject to strict time limits. Thus, the WTO has something that the GATT never had–teeth.[30]

Expanding Trade Agreements

The WTO was given the role of brokering future agreements to open global trade in services. The WTO was also encouraged to extend its reach to encompass regulations governing foreign direct investment, something the GATT had never done. Two of the first industries targeted for reform were the global telecommunication and financial services industries.

The WTO tackled telecommunications first. The goal of the WTO was to get countries to agree to open their telecommunication markets to competition, allowing foreign operators to purchase ownership stakes in domestic telecommunication providers and establishing a set of common rules for fair competition. The benefits claimed for such agreements were threefold.

First, advocates argued that inward investment and increased competition would stimulate the modernization of telephone networks around the world and lead to higher-quality service. Second, supporters maintained that the increased competition would benefit customers through lower prices. Estimates suggested that a deal would soon reduce the average cost of international telephone calls by 80 percent and save users $1,000 billion over three years.[31] Third, the WTO argued that trade in other goods and services invariably depends on flows of information matching buyers to sellers. As telecommunication services improve in quality and decline in price, international trade increases in volume and becomes less costly for traders. Telecommunication reform, therefore, should promote cross-border trade in other goods and services.

A deal was reached February 15, 1997. Under the pact, 68 countries accounting for more than 90 percent of world telecommunication revenues pledged to start opening their markets to foreign competition and to abide by common rules for fair competition in telecommunications. Most of the world's biggest markets, including the United States, European Union, and Japan, were fully liberalized by January 1, 1998, when the pact went into effect. All forms of basic telecommunication service are covered, including voice telephony, data and fax transmissions, and satellite and radio communications. Many telecommunication companies responded positively to the deal, pointing out that it would give them a much greater ability to offer their business customers "one-stop shopping"–a global, seamless service for all their corporate needs and a single bill.[32]

Fresh from success in brokering a telecommunication agreement, in 1997 the WTO embarked on a series of negotiations to liberalize the global financial services industry. The financial services industry includes banking, securities businesses, insurance, asset management services, and the like. The global financial services industry is enormous. The sector executes $1.2 trillion a day in foreign exchange transactions. International financing extended by banks around the world reporting to the Bank for International Settlements is estimated at $6.4 trillion, including $4.6 trillion net international lending. Total world banking assets are put at more than $20 trillion, insurance premiums at $2 trillion, stock market capitalization at over $10 trillion, and market value of listed bonds at around $10 trillion. In addition, practically every international trade in goods or services requires credit, capital, foreign exchange, and insurance.[33]

Negotiation participants wanted to see more competition in the sector, both to allow firms greater opportunities abroad and to encourage greater efficiency. Developing countries need the capital and financial infrastructure for their development. But governments also have to ensure that the system is sound and stable because of the economic shocks that can be caused if exchange rates, interest rates, or other market conditions fluctuate excessively. They also have to avoid economic crises caused by bank failures. Therefore, government intervention in prudential safeguards is an important condition underpinning financial market liberalization.

An agreement was reached December 14, 1997.[34] The deal covers more than 95 percent of the world's financial services market. Under the agreement, which took effect at the beginning of March 1999, 102 countries pledged to open to varying degrees their banking, securities, and insurance sectors to foreign competition. In common with the telecommunication deal, the accord covers not just cross-border trade but also foreign direct investment. Seventy countries agreed to dramatically lower or eradicate barriers to foreign direct investment in their financial services sector. The United States and the European Union, with minor exceptions, are fully open to inward investment by foreign banks, insurance, and securities companies. As part of the deal, many Asian countries made important concessions that allow significant foreign participation in their financial services sectors for the first time.

THE FUTURE OF THE WTO: UNRESOLVED ISSUES AND THE DOHA ROUND

Much remains to be done on the international trade front. Three issues at the forefront of the current WTO agenda are the rise of antidumping policies, the high level of protectionism in agriculture, and the lack of strong protection for intellectual property rights in many nations. We shall look at each in turn before discussing the latest attempt to launch a round of talks between WTO members aimed at reducing trade barriers, the Doha Round.

Antidumping Actions

Antidumping actions have proliferated in recent years. WTO rules allow countries to impose antidumping duties on foreign goods that are being sold cheaper than at home, or below their cost of production, when domestic producers can show that they are being harmed. Unfortunately, the rather vague definition of what constitutes "dumping" has proved to be a loophole, which many countries are exploiting to pursue protectionism. Figure 6.1 shows the incidence of antidumping measures initiated by various countries over a ten-year period from 1995 to 2004. The WTO is clearly worried by this trend, suggesting it reflects persistent protectionist tendencies, and is pushing members to strengthen the regulations governing the imposition of antidumping duties.

Protectionism in Agriculture

Another recent focus of the WTO has been the high level of tariffs and subsidies in the agricultural sector of many economies. Tariff rates on agricultural products are generally much higher than tariff rates on manufactured products or services. In 2000, for example, the average tariff rates on nonagricultural products was 4.4 percent for Canada, 4.5 percent for the European Union, 4.0 percent for Japan, and 4.7 percent for the United States. On agricultural products, however, the average tariffs rates were 22.9 percent for Canada, 17.3 percent for the European Union, 18.2 percent for Japan, and 11 percent for the United States.[35] The implication is that consumers in these countries are paying significantly higher prices than necessary for agricultural products imported from abroad, which leaves them with less money to spend on other goods and services.

FIGURE 6.1

Antidumping Measures, 1995–2004

Source: World Trade Organization. Data from spreadsheet at www.wto.org/english/tratop_e/adp_e/adp_stattab2_e.xls.

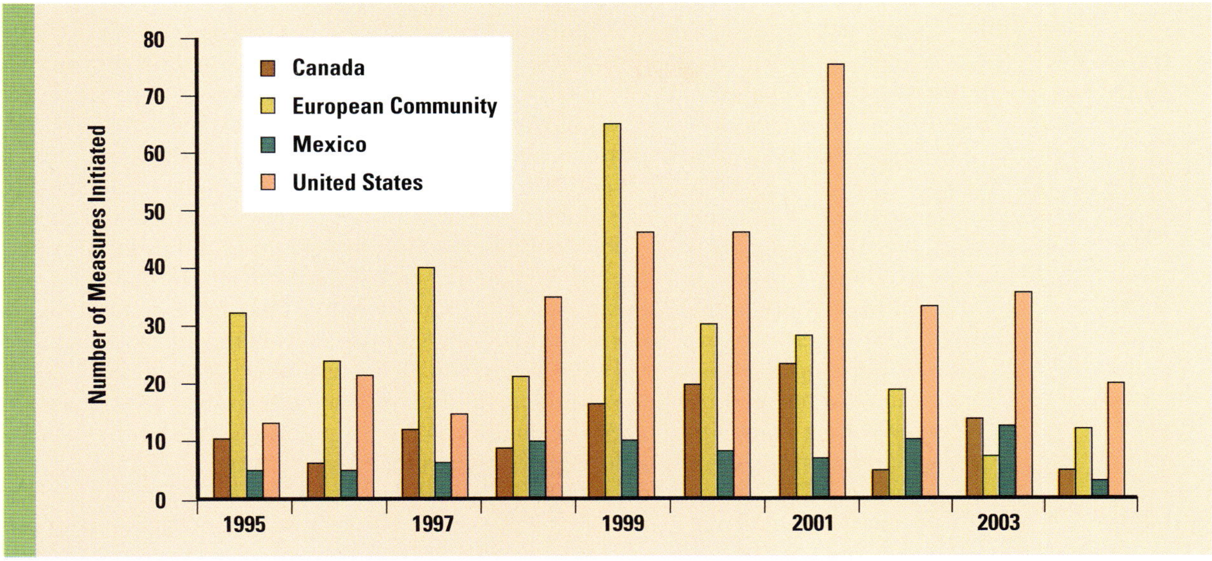

The historically high tariff rates on agricultural products reflect a desire to protect domestic agriculture and traditional farming communities from foreign competition. In addition to high tariffs, agricultural producers also benefit from substantial subsidies as noted earlier. According to estimates from the Organization for Economic Cooperation and Development (OECD), on average government subsidies account for some 20 percent of the cost of agricultural production in Canada, 24 percent in the United States, 49 percent in the European Union, and 64 percent in Japan.[36] In total, OECD countries spend more than $300 billion a year in subsidies to agricultural producers.

The combination of high tariff barriers and significant subsidies distort the production of agricultural products and international trade of those products. The net effect is to raise prices to consumers, reduce the volume of agricultural trade, and encourage the overproduction of products that are heavily subsidized (with the government typically buying the surplus). Because global trade in agriculture currently amounts to 10.5 percent of total merchandised trade, or about $700 billion per annum, the WTO argues that removing tariff barriers and subsidies could significantly boost the overall level of trade, lower prices to consumers, and raise global economic growth by freeing consumption and investment resources for more productive uses. The biggest defenders of the existing system have been the advanced nations of the world, who want to protect their agricultural sectors from competition by low-cost producers in developing nations. In contrast, developing nations have been pushing hard for reforms that would allow their producers greater access to the protected markets of the developed nations.

Protecting Intellectual Property

Another issue that has become increasingly important to the WTO has been protecting intellectual property. As noted earlier, the 1995 Uruguay agreement that established the WTO also contained an agreement to protect intellectual property. The basis for this agreement was a strong belief among signatory nations that the protection of intellectual property through patents, trademarks, and copyrights must be an essential element of the international trading system. Without adequate protections for intellectual property, the incentive for innovation is reduced. Since innovation is a central engine of economic growth and, therefore, rising living standards, the argument has been that a multilateral agreement is needed to protect intellectual property.

Without such an agreement, there has been a fear that producers in a country, say India, might produce imitations of patented innovations pioneered in a different country, say the United States. This can affect international trade in two ways. First, it reduces the export opportunities in India for the original innovator in the United States. Second, to the extent that the Indian producer exports its pirated imitation to third countries, it also reduces the export opportunities for the U.S. inventor in those countries. One also can argue that because the size of the total world market for the innovator is reduced, its incentive to pursue risky and expensive innovations is also reduced. The net effect would be less innovation in the world economy and less economic growth.

This is not a hypothetical example; something very like this has been occurring in the pharmaceutical industry, with Indian drug companies making copies of patented drugs developed elsewhere. In 1970, the Indian government stopped recognizing product patents on drugs but elected to continue respecting process patents. This permitted Indian companies to reverse-engineer Western pharmaceuticals without paying licensing fees. As a result, foreigners' share of the Indian drug market fell from 75 percent in 1970 to 30 percent in 2000. In a typical example, an Indian company sells its version of Byers' patented antibiotic Cipro for $0.12 a pill, versus the $5.50 it costs in the United States. Under a WTO agreement, India has agreed to adopt and enforce the international drug patent regime by 2005.[37]

Launching a New Round of Talks: Doha

Antidumping actions, trade in agricultural products, and better enforcement of intellectual property laws were three issues the WTO wanted to tackle at the 1999 meetings in Seattle, but, as noted earlier, those meetings were derailed. In late 2001, the WTO tried again to launch a new round of talks between member states aimed at further liberalizing the global trade and investment framework. For this meeting, it picked the remote location of Doha in the Gulf state of Qatar, no doubt with an eye on the difficulties that antiglobalization protesters would have making their way to that state. At Doha, the member states agreed to launch a new round of talks and staked out an agenda. The talks are scheduled to last three years, although if history is any guide, they could last much longer. The November 2001 declaration of the Fourth Ministerial Conference in Doha, Qatar, provided the mandate for negotiations on a range of subjects and other work, including the implementation of the present agreements. The negotiations included those on agriculture and services, which began in early 2000. The date for completing most of the negotiations was set as January 1, 2005.

Progress was reviewed at the Fifth Ministerial Conference in Cancun, Mexico, in September 2003. This meeting ended in deadlock. WTO members in Geneva then began efforts to put the negotiations back on track. A new target date of July 30, 2004 was set for reaching agreement on a package of framework agreements. This "July package" was agreed to on August 1, 2004. Although these frameworks are not final agreements they do include significant commitments. For the first time, member governments agreed to abolish all forms of agricultural export subsidies by a certain date. Governments also agreed to launch negotiations to set new rules streamlining trade and customs procedures, and also set guidelines for opening trade in manufactured products. The agreement also set a new deferred deadline beyond the original deadline of January 1, 2005, and set the date and location for the next ministerial conference (December 2005 in Hong Kong).

The agenda agreed upon at Doha should be seen as a game plan for negotiations over the next few years. It includes cutting tariffs on industrial goods and services, phasing out subsidies to agricultural producers, reducing barriers to cross-border investment (FDI), and limiting the use of antidumping laws. Some difficult compromises were made to reach agreement on this agenda. The EU and Japan had to give significant ground on agricultural subsidies, which they use extensively to support politically powerful farmers. The United States bowed to pressure from virtually every other nation to negotiate revisions of antidumping rules, which the United States has used to protect its steel producers from foreign competition. Europe had to scale back its efforts to include environmental policy in the trade talks, primarily because of pressure from developing nations that see environmental protection policies as trade barriers by another name. Excluded from the agenda was any language pertaining to attempts to tie trade to labour standards in a country.

Countries with big pharmaceutical sectors acquiesced to demands from Africa, Asia, and Latin American nations on the issue of drug patents. Specifically, the language in the agreement declares that WTO intellectual property regulation "does not and should not prevent members from taking measures to protect public health." This language was meant to assure the world's poorer nations, which cannot afford patented drugs, that they can make or buy generic equivalents to fight such killers as AIDS and malaria.

If the talks are successful, agricultural producers in these nations will ultimately see the global markets for their goods expand. Developing nations also gain from the lack of language on labour standards, which many saw as simply an attempt by rich nations to erect trade barriers. The sick and poor of the world also benefit from guaranteed access to cheaper medicines. There are also clear losers in this agreement, including EU and Japanese farmers, U.S. steelmakers, environmental activists, and pharmaceutical firms in the developed world. These losers can be expected to lobby their government hard during the ensuing year to make sure the final agreement is more in their favour.[38]

IMPLICATIONS FOR BUSINESS

What are the implications of all this for business practice? Why should the international manager care about the political economy of free trade or about the relative merits of arguments for free trade and protectionism? There are two answers to this question. The first concerns the impact of trade barriers on a firm's strategy. The second concerns the role that business firms can play in promoting free trade and/or trade barriers.

TRADE BARRIERS AND FIRM STRATEGY

To understand how trade barriers affect a firm's strategy, consider first the material we covered in Chapter 5. Drawing on the theories of international trade, we discussed how it makes sense for the firm to disperse its production activities to those countries where they can be performed most efficiently. Thus, it may make sense for a firm to design and engineer its product in one country, to manufacture components in another, to perform final assembly operations in yet another country, and then to export the finished product to the rest of the world.

Clearly, trade barriers constrain a firm's ability to disperse its productive activities in such a manner. First, and most obviously, tariff barriers raise the costs of exporting products to a country (or of exporting partly finished products between countries). This may put the firm at a competitive disadvantage vis-à-vis indigenous competitors in that country. In response, the firm may then find it economical to locate production facilities in that country so that it can compete on an even footing with indigenous competitors. Second, quotas and voluntary export restraints may limit a firm's ability to serve a country from locations outside of that country. Again, the response by the firm might be to set up production facilities in that country—even though it may result in higher production costs. Such reasoning was one factor behind the rapid expansion of Japanese automaking capacity in the United States during the 1980s and 1990s. This followed the establishment of a VER agreement between the United States and Japan that limited U.S. imports of Japanese automobiles.

Third, to conform to local content regulations, a firm may have to locate more production activities in a given market than it would otherwise. Again, from the firm's perspective, the consequence might be to raise costs above the level that could be achieved if each production activity was dispersed to the optimal location for that activity. And finally, even when trade barriers do not exist, the firm may still want to locate some production activities in a given country to reduce the threat of trade barriers being imposed in the future.

All the above effects are likely to raise the firm's costs above the level that could be achieved in a world without trade barriers. The higher costs that result need not translate into a significant competitive disadvantage relative to other foreign firms, however, if the countries imposing trade barriers do so to the imported products of all foreign firms, irrespective of their national origin. But when trade barriers are targeted at exports from a particular nation, firms based in that nation are at a competitive disadvantage to firms of other nations. The firm may deal with such targeted trade barriers by moving production into the country imposing barriers. Another strategy may be to move production to countries whose exports are not targeted by the specific trade barrier.

Finally, the threat of antidumping action limits the ability of a firm to use aggressive pricing to gain market share in a country. Firms in a country can also use antidumping measures to limit aggressive competition from low-cost foreign producers.

POLICY IMPLICATIONS

As noted in Chapter 5, business firms are major players on the international trade scene. Because of their pivotal role in international trade, firms exert a strong influence on government policy toward trade. This influence can encourage protectionism or it can encourage the government to support the WTO and push for open markets and freer trade among all nations. Government policies with regard to international trade can have a direct impact on business.

Consistent with strategic trade policy, examples can be found of government intervention in the form of tariffs, quotas, antidumping actions, and subsidies helping firms and industries establish a competitive advantage in the world economy. In general, however, the arguments contained in this chapter and in Chapter 5 suggest that government intervention has three drawbacks. Intervention can be self-defeating, since it tends to protect the inefficient rather than help firms become efficient global competitors. Intervention is dangerous; it may invite retaliation and trigger a trade war. Finally, intervention is unlikely to be well-executed, given the opportunity for such a policy to be captured by special interest groups. Does this mean that business should simply encourage government to adopt a laissez-faire free trade policy?

Most economists would probably argue that the best interests of international business are served by a free trade stance, but not a laissez-faire stance. It is probably in the best long-run interests of the business community to encourage the government to aggressively promote greater free trade by, for example, strengthening the WTO. Business probably has much more to gain from government efforts to open protected markets to imports and foreign direct investment than from government efforts to support certain domestic industries in a manner consistent with the recommendations of strategic trade policy.

This conclusion is reinforced by a phenomenon we touched on in Chapter 1—the increasing integration of the world economy and internationalization of production that has occurred over the past two decades. We live in a world where many firms of all national origins increasingly depend for their competitive advantage on globally dispersed production systems. Such systems are the result of freer trade. Freer trade has brought great advantages to firms that have exploited it and to consumers who benefit from the resulting lower prices. Given the danger of retaliatory action, business firms that lobby their governments to engage in protectionism must realize that by doing so they may be denying themselves the opportunity to build a competitive advantage by constructing a globally dispersed production system. By encouraging their governments to engage in protectionism, their own activities and sales overseas may be jeopardized if other governments retaliate. This does not mean a firm should never seek protection in the form of antidumping actions and the like, but it should review its options carefully and think through the larger consequences.

KEY TERMS

ad valorem tariff, p. 195
administrative trade policies, p. 200
antidumping policies, p. 202
countervailing duties, p. 202
D'Amato Act, p. 205
dumping, p. 202
free trade, p. 194
Helms–Burton Act, p. 205
import quota, p. 199
local content requirement, p. 200
specific tariff, p. 195
subsidy, p. 198
tariff, p. 195
voluntary export restraint (VER), p. 199

SUMMARY

The objective of this chapter was to describe how the reality of international trade deviates from the theoretical ideal of unrestricted free trade reviewed in Chapter 5. Consistent with this objective, in this chapter we have reported the various instruments of trade policy, reviewed the political and economic arguments for government intervention in international trade, reexamined the economic case for free trade in light of the strategic trade policy argument, and looked at the evolution of the world trading framework. While a policy of free trade may not always be the theoretically optimal policy (given the arguments of the new trade theorists), in practice it is probably the best policy for a government to pursue. In particular, the long-run interests of business and consumers may be best served by strengthening international institutions such as the WTO. Given the danger that isolated protectionism might escalate into a trade war, business probably has far more to gain from government efforts to open protected markets to imports and foreign direct investment (through the WTO) than from government efforts to protect domestic industries from foreign competition.

In this chapter the following points have been made:

1. The effect of a tariff is to raise the cost of imported products. Gains accrue to the government (from revenues) and to producers (who are protected from foreign competitors). Consumers lose because they must pay more for imports.
2. By lowering costs, subsidies help domestic producers to compete against low-cost foreign imports and to gain export markets. However, subsidies must be paid for by taxpayers. They also tend to be captured by special interests that use them to protect the inefficient.
3. An import quota is a direct restriction imposed by an importing country on the quantity of some good that may be imported. A voluntary export restraint (VER) is a quota on trade imposed from the exporting country's side. Both import quotas and VERs benefit domestic producers by limiting import competition, but they result in higher prices, which hurts consumers.
4. An administrative policy is an informal instrument or bureaucratic rule that can be used to restrict imports and boost exports. Such policies benefit producers but hurt consumers, who are denied access to possibly superior foreign products.
5. There are two types of arguments for government intervention in international trade: political and economic. Political arguments for intervention are concerned with protecting the interests of certain groups, often at the expense of other groups, or with promoting goals with regard to foreign policy, human rights, consumer protection, and the like. Economic arguments for intervention are about boosting the overall wealth of a nation.
6. The most common political argument for intervention is that it is necessary to protect jobs. However, political intervention often hurts consumers and it can be self-defeating.
7. Countries sometimes argue that it is important to protect certain industries for reasons of national security.
8. Some argue that government should use the threat to intervene in trade policy as a bargaining tool to open up foreign markets. This can be a risky policy; if it fails, the result can be higher trade barriers.
9. The infant industry argument for government intervention contends that to let manufacturing get a toehold, governments should temporarily support new industries. In practice, however, governments often end up protecting the inefficient.
10. Strategic trade policy suggests that with subsidies, government can help domestic firms gain first-mover advantages in global industries where economies of scale are important. Government subsidies may also help domestic firms overcome barriers to entry into such industries.

11. The problems with strategic trade policy are twofold: (*a*) such a policy may invite retaliation, in which case all will lose, and (*b*) strategic trade policy may be captured by special interest groups, which will distort it to their own ends.
12. The Smoot-Hawley tariff, introduced in 1930, erected an enormous wall of tariff barriers to imports. Other countries responded by adopting similar tariffs, and the world slid further into the Great Depression.
13. The GATT was a product of the postwar free trade movement. The GATT was successful in lowering trade barriers on manufactured goods and commodities. The move toward greater free trade under the GATT appeared to stimulate economic growth.
14. The completion of the Uruguay Round of GATT talks and the establishment of the World Trade Organization have strengthened the world trading system by extending GATT rules to services, increasing protection for intellectual property, reducing agricultural subsidies, and enhancing monitoring and enforcement mechanisms.
15. Trade barriers act as a constraint on a firm's ability to disperse its various production activities to optimal locations around the globe. One response to trade barriers is to establish more production activities in the protected country.
16. Business may have more to gain from government efforts to open protected markets to imports and foreign direct investment than from government efforts to protect domestic industries from foreign competition.

CRITICAL THINKING AND DISCUSSION QUESTIONS

1. Do you think governments should take human rights considerations into account when granting preferential trading rights to countries? What are the arguments for and against taking such a position?
2. Whose interests should be the paramount concern of government trade policy—the interests of producers (businesses and their employees) or of consumers?
3. Given the arguments relating to the new trade theory and strategic trade policy, what kind of trade policy should business be pressuring government to adopt?

RESEARCH TASK | globalEDGE™ globaledge.msu.edu

Use the globalEDGE™ site to complete the following exercises:

1. Your company is considering exporting its products to Egypt, but management's current knowledge of the country's trade policies and barriers is limited. Conduct Web research to identify Egypt's current import policies with respect to fundamental issues such as tariffs and restrictions; prepare an executive summary of your findings.
2. The number of member nations of the World Trade Organization is increasing. Additionally, some nonmember countries have observer status, which requires accession negotiations to begin within five years of attaining the preliminary position. Identify the current total number of WTO members. Also, prepare a list of the observer countries.

Visit the *Global Business Today* Online Learning Centre at **www.mcgrawhill.ca/college/hill** to access quizzes, interactive exercises, a Business Around the World interactive map, and other learning and study tools related to this chapter.

Online LearningCentre

CLOSING CASE

WHEN DO GOVERNMENT TAX INCENTIVES BECOME EXPORT SUBSIDIES?

Historically speaking, when countries embarked on tit-for-tat responses for real and/or perceived economic injustices against one another, political instability, economic protectionism and often war followed. Since WWII many institutions have been founded to stave off potential recurrent irritants that had until that time, ravaged Europe's history.

Consequently, government subsidies are increasingly becoming a thing of the past, and with new free trade rulings being heralded on an ongoing basis by the World Trade Organization, member countries are required to comply. When out of line, the trade dispute mechanisms of the WTO intervene and deliberate on a case by case basis. Canada and Brazil have been engaged in several trade disputes over the past two decades, but none is as high profile and high stakes as the Bombardier–Embraer dilemma. Each company accuses the other of being in breach of WTO government subsidies practices.

Government subsidies come in different shapes and forms, and often boil down to pure semantics, the art of language, which attempts to circumvent the WTO interpretations on the matter. This could be said to be the source of the decade plus Brazil–Canada trade dispute over Embraer. Although mostly focused on the aircraft industry, it, like many trade irritants over time, has occasionally spilled out of that realm and into other areas. As usually is the case with country to country trade disputes, sub disputes frequently will spin off. Such was the case with the epic Bombardier–Embraer saga. In early 2001, Canada imposed a three-week ban on Brazilian beef, claiming its concern that Brazilian beef might be contaminated with Bovine Spongiform Encephalopathy or mad cow disease. This created an uproar in Brazil, which in turn threatened trade retaliation against Canada. The Canadian government lifted the ban after three weeks.

Ever since WWII, nations around the world have at one time or another, attempted to aid domestic industries through tax breaks and other types of incentives. Many countries, in the year 2005, owe their current state of wealth to strong government policies that bolstered, sometimes fledgling industries.

The Bombardier–Embraer dispute began in the 1990s when Canada complained to the WTO that Brazil was providing unfair state aid to Embraer. According to Bombardier—Embraer's Canadian rival—the subsidies amounted to US$3.7 billion for the nearly 900 aircraft on order but not yet delivered by the 1999 WTO deadline for removing them. Though the arbitrators slashed by more than half the annual Cdn$700 million Canada claimed in retaliation, the Cdn$344.2 million (US$233.4 million) authorized was the largest in any WTO dispute to date.

When one country subsidizes an industry to the tune of hundreds of millions of dollars per year, as Brazil had been doing, this raises the spectrum that it will damage a competitor firm elsewhere on the planet. As then Canadian Industry Minister Brian Tobin pointed out, if global competition is based purely on product, this is fair trade. In January 2001, the Canadian government stated its concerns that as many as 24 000 workers could lose their jobs in Canada if Brazil continued their support of Embraer. The Canadian government was not going to wait and see if this would happen. Bombardier had already lost significant market share to Embraer in the last five years, solely because of the preferential financing Embraer was getting.

That wasn't the end of the protracted dispute. Dissatisfied with the WTO ruling against Embraer, Brazil launched a counter complaint to the WTO against Bombardier. On January 29, 2003, the WTO ruled that a $1.7-billion low-interest loan the federal government made to Bombardier broke international trade rules. The loan was to help Bombardier land a 75-plane order from Air Wisconsin. Canadian government officials had argued the low-interest loans were similar to loans offered by Brazil to help Brazilian regional jetmaker Embraer land similar aircraft contracts. Yet, as of March 2003, Canada had still not imposed retaliatory measures despite authorization to do so by the WTO.

Fast forward to Tuesday, March 18, 2003, the WTO granted Brazil the right to impose almost US$250 million per year in trade sanctions against Canada, far short of the US$3.3 billion that had been requested. Based on this WTO ruling, Brazil can immediately impose 100-percent duties on a wide range of imports from Canada, including chickpeas, waffles, newsprint, coal, and radioactive isotopes.

While Canada has stated that its objective is to ensure that Brazil adheres to WTO rules, Brazil makes the same claim. Slow progress towards agreement is still being made, yet more work has to be done.

The irony of it is that if Bombardier and Embraer continue to be so thoroughly ensconced in their lengthy dispute, they might not see newcomer competitors arriving on the horizon, leaving both at odds with the world's rapidly changing aircraft industries. The key lesson (and there are many) to be learned is that there is a fine line between tax incentives and export subsidies in the land of international trade.

CASE DISCUSSION QUESTIONS

1. Do you think that Bombardier and Embraer are guilty as charged? Please explain your answer.
2. Do you think that such matters should be considered internal and therefore not fall within the jurisdiction of the WTO?
3. Why do you believe that the Canadian and Brazilian governments are still so willing to subsidize export industries?
4. Can you see a solution to this trade dispute?

Sources: CBC, "Canada Retaliates for Brazilian Jet Subsidies," at www.cbc.ca/stories/2001/01/10/business/bombardier010110; "Canada Won't Appeal WTO Ruling on Bombardier Loans," at www.cbc.ca/stories/2002/02/19/business/bombardier_020219; "Brazil Can Impose Trade Sanctions on Canada in Subsidy Fight: WTO," at www.cbc.ca/stories/2003/03/18/wto_030318.

PART THREE

3

CROSS-BORDER TRADE AND INVESTMENT

Starbucks' Foreign Direct Investment

Thirty years ago Starbucks was a single store in Seattle's Pike Place Market selling premium roasted coffee. In 1995, with almost 700 stores across the United States, Starbucks began exploring foreign opportunities. By 2004, Starbucks had over 2000 stores spanning the globe, in countries from Australia and Austria, to Turkey and the United Kingdom. Its first target market was Japan. Although Starbucks had resisted a franchising strategy in North America, where its stores are company owned, Starbucks initially decided to license its format in Japan. However, the company also realized that a pure licensing agreement would not give Starbucks the control needed to ensure that the Japanese licensees closely followed Starbucks' successful formula. So the company established a joint venture with a local retailer, Sazaby Inc. Each company held a 50-percent stake in the venture, Starbucks Coffee of Japan. Starbucks initially invested $10 million in this venture, its first foreign direct investment. The Starbucks' format was then licensed to the venture, which was charged with taking over responsibility for expanding Starbucks' presence in Japan.

To make sure the Japanese operations replicated the "Starbucks experience" in North America, Starbucks transferred some employees to the Japanese operation. The licensing agreement required all Japanese store managers and employees to attend training classes similar to those given to U.S. employees. The agreement also required that stores adhere to the design parameters established in the United States. In 2001, the company introduced a stock option plan for all Japanese employees, making it the first company in Japan to do so. Skeptics doubted that Starbucks would be able to replicate its North American success overseas, but by 2001, Starbucks had more than 150 stores in Japan and plans to continue opening them at a brisk pace.

AP/World Wide Photos.

CHAPTER 7

Foreign Direct Investment

OPENING CASE

After getting its feet wet in Japan, the company embarked on an aggressive foreign investment program. In 1998, it purchased Seattle Coffee, a British coffee chain with 60 retail stores, for $84 million. An American couple, originally from Seattle, had started Seattle Coffee with the intention of establishing a Starbucks-like chain in Britain. In the late 1990s, Starbucks opened stores in Taiwan, China, Singapore, Thailand, New Zealand, South Korea, and Malaysia.

In Asia, Starbucks' most common strategy was to license its format to a local operator in return for initial licensing fees and royalties on store revenues. Starbucks also sold coffee and related products to the local licensees, who then resold them to customers. As in Japan, Starbucks insisted on an intensive employee training program and strict specifications regarding the format and layout of the store. However, Starbucks became disenchanted with some of the straight licensing arrangements and converted several into joint-venture arrangements or wholly owned subsidiaries. As its first entry point on the European mainland (Starbucks had 150 stores in Great Britain), Starbucks chose Switzerland. Drawing on its experience in Asia, the company entered into a joint venture with a Swiss company, Bon Appetit Group, Switzerland's largest food-service company. Bon Appetit was to hold a majority stake in the venture, and Starbucks would license its format to the Swiss company using a similar agreement to those it had used successfully in Asia.

Sources: Starbucks 10K, various years; C. McLean, "Starbucks Set to Invade Coffee-Loving Continent," *Seattle Times,* October 4, 2000, p. E1; and J. Ordonez, "Starbucks to Start Major Expansion in Overseas Market," *Wall Street Journal,* October 27, 2000, p. B10.

LEARNING OBJECTIVES

1. Identify the forces underpinning the rising tide of foreign direct investment in the world economy.
2. Understand why firms often prefer direct investment as a strategy for entering a foreign market over alternatives such as exporting and granting foreign entities the right to produce the firm's product under licence.
3. Appreciate why firms based in the same industry often undertake foreign direct investment at the same time.
4. Understand why certain locations are favoured as the target of foreign direct investment.
5. Appreciate how political ideology influences government policy toward foreign direct investment.
6. Be conversant with the costs and benefits of foreign direct investment for receiving and source countries.
7. Understand the policy instruments governments can use to restrict and to encourage foreign direct investment.

FOREIGN DIRECT INVESTMENT (FDI) Direct investment in business operations in a foreign country.

MULTINATIONAL ENTERPRISE (MNE) A firm that owns business operations in more than one country.

GREEN-FIELD INVESTMENT Establishing a new operation in a foreign country.

FLOW OF FOREIGN DIRECT INVESTMENT (FDI) The amount of foreign direct investment undertaken over a given time period (normally one year).

STOCK OF FDI The total accumulated value of foreign-owned assets at a given time.

OUTFLOWS OF FDI Flow of foreign direct investment out of a country.

INFLOWS OF FDI Flow of foreign direct investment into a country.

INTRODUCTION

This chapter is concerned with foreign direct investment (FDI). **Foreign direct investment** occurs when a firm invests directly in facilities to produce and/or market a product in a foreign country. When Starbucks invested $10 million in Starbucks Coffee of Japan in 1996, it was engaging in its first foreign direct investment. By the end of 2000, the company had made cumulative foreign investments of some $150 million, including its $84-million purchase of British retailer Seattle Coffee, its $12-million purchase of Coffee Partners in Thailand, and cumulative investments of $52 million in various joint ventures. According to the U.S. Department of Commerce, FDI occurs whenever a U.S. citizen, organization, or affiliated group takes an interest of 10 percent or more in a foreign business entity (all of Starbucks' foreign investments were for more than 10 percent of the equity of a business). Once a firm undertakes FDI, it becomes a **multinational enterprise** (the meaning of multinational being "more than one country"). The term transnational is used interchangeably with multinational.

FDI takes on two main forms; the first is a **green-field investment,** which involves the establishment of a wholly new operation in a foreign country. The second involves acquiring or merging with an existing firm in the foreign country. Acquisitions can be a minority (where the foreign firm takes a 10 percent to 49 percent interest in the firm's voting stock), majority (foreign interest of 50 percent to 99 percent), or full outright stake (foreign interest of 100 percent).[1]

We begin this chapter by looking at the importance of foreign direct investment in the world economy. Next, we review the theories that have been used to explain foreign direct investment. The chapter then looks at government policy toward foreign direct investment. The chapter closes with a section on implications for business.

FOREIGN DIRECT INVESTMENT IN THE WORLD ECONOMY

When discussing foreign direct investment, it is important to distinguish between the flow of FDI and the stock of FDI. The **flow of FDI** refers to the amount of FDI undertaken over a given time period (normally a year). The **stock of FDI** refers to the total accumulated value of foreign-owned assets at a given time. We also talk of **outflows of FDI,** meaning the flow of FDI out of a country, and **inflows of FDI,** meaning the flow of FDI into a country.

THE GROWTH OF FDI

The globalization of the world economy, a phenomenon discussed in Chapter 1, is also having a positive impact on the volume of FDI. Firms such as Starbucks, discussed in the opening case, now see the world as their whole market and are undertaking FDI in an attempt to ensure that they have a significant presence in many regions of the world. For reasons that we shall explore later on in the book, many firms now believe it is important to have production facilities based close to their major customers. This, too, is creating pressures for greater FDI.

Since World War II, the United States has been the largest source country for FDI outflows, followed by the United Kingdom. U.S. firms have traditionally dominated the growth of FDI to the degree that the words American and multinational/transnational (two words frequently used interchangeably) became almost synonymous.

The high level of FDI outflows from the United States has been driven by a combination of factors including a strong U.S. economy, increasing corporate profits and cash flow that have given firms the capital to invest abroad, and a relatively strong currency since 1995. Similar factors explain the growth of FDI outflows from the United Kingdom during the 1990s.

For the most part, FDI flows have grown since the 1980s (see Figure 7.1). The 1990–2000 upward spike in investments stands in sharp contrast with the decline in the post September 11, 2001 period.

The ensuing weak economic growth and falling stock markets had a negative impact on cross-border mergers and acquisitions. The number of cross-border mergers and acquisitions transactions dropped from 7894 in 2000 to 4493 in 2002. The average value per transaction also slid from $145 million in 2000 to only $82 million in 2002–as the number of hyper deals (worth over $1 billion) fell from 175 in 2000 to only 81 in 2002, the lowest level since 1998.[2] (see Figure 7.2).

FDI inflows to developed countries totalled over 70 percent in 2002. The share of inflows to developing countries increased to 25 percent in 2002, which was up from 18 percent during the 1986–1990 period. Inflows to least developed countries (LDC)

FIGURE 7.1

Foreign Direct Investment Flows

Source: United Nations Conference on Trade and Development, *2004 Development Facts and Figures*, p. 33.

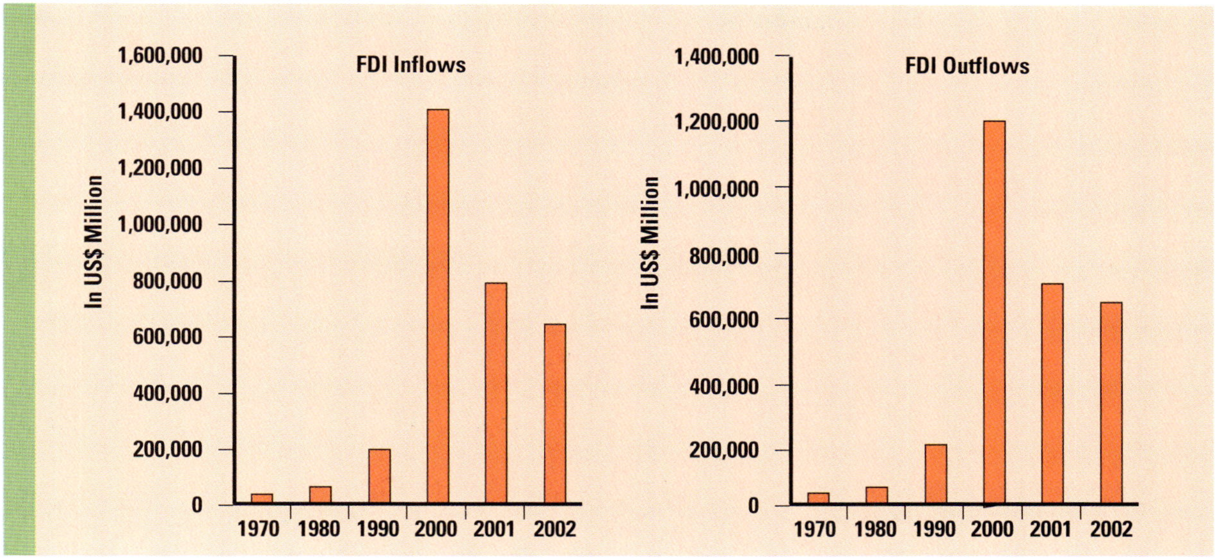

FIGURE 7.2

The Share of Cross-Border M&As Worldwide, 1987–2002 (in %)

Source: United Nations Conference on Trade and Development, *2004 Development Facts and Figures*, p. 17.

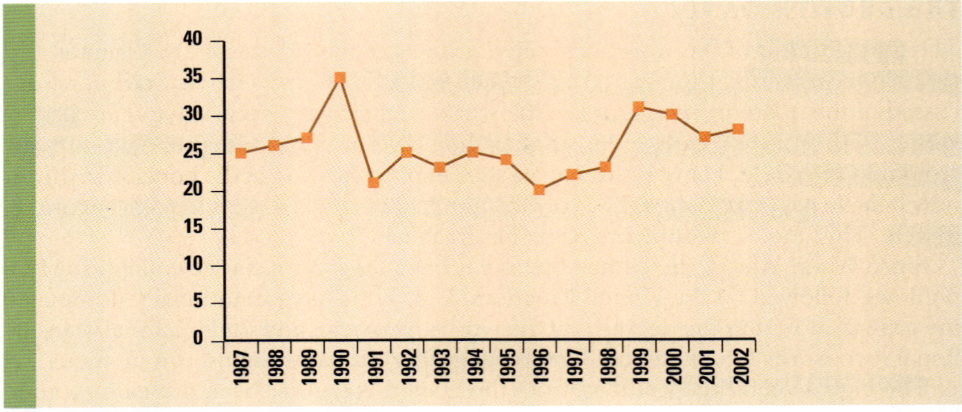

amounted to $5 billion, and represented a small, yet growing portion (3 percent) of developing countries' inflows, compared to just 2 percent in 1997.

Another way of looking at the importance of FDI inflows is to express them as a percentage of gross fixed capital formation. **Gross fixed capital formation** summarizes the total amount of capital invested in factories, stores, office buildings, etc. Other things being equal, the greater the capital investment in an economy, the more favourable is its future growth prospects.

GROSS FIXED CAPITAL FORMATION
Summarizes the total amount of capital invested in factories, stores, office buildings, and the like.

According to the United Nations 2003 World Investment Report on FDI Policies for Development: National and International Perspectives, the trend towards liberalization is continuing to increase. After the record number of FDI friendly changes in national FDI legislation in 2001, 2002 reached another record: 248 changes in legislation, of which 236 were favourable to FDI (Table 7.1), with a third related to promotional measures. These policy developments have helped sustain FDI flows to developing countries during the downturn. Looking at the period from 1991 to 2002, 1551 (95 percent) out of the 1641 changes introduced by 165 countries in their FDI laws served to enhance greater liberalization. All of this has served to create a more favourable environment for FDI.[3]

The desire to create FDI has also been reflected in a dramatic increase in the number of bilateral investment treaties designed to protect and promote investment between two countries. In 2002, there were 82 bilateral investment treaties (BIT), concluded by 76 countries, and 68 double taxation treaties (DTT) concluded by 64 countries. There has been a significant increase in the number of related regulatory changes recently as well[4] (see Figure 7.3).

TABLE 7.1

Changes in National Regulations of FDI 1991–2002

Sources: UNCTAD, *World Investment Report, 2003 FDI Policies for Development: National and International Perspectives*, Chapter 1, p. 21.

ITEM	1991	1992	1993	1994	1995	1996	1997	1998	1999	2000	2001	2002
Number of countries that introduced changes in their investment regimes	35	43	57	49	64	65	76	60	63	69	71	70
Number of regulatory changes	82	79	102	110	112	114	151	145	140	150	208	248
of which:												
More favourable to FDI [a]	80	79	101	108	106	98	135	136	131	147	194	236
Less favourable to FDI [b]	2	—	1	2	6	16	16	9	9	3	14	12

a. Including liberalizing changes or changes aimed at strengthening market functioning, as well as increased incentives.
b. Including changes aimed at increasing control as well as reducing incentives.

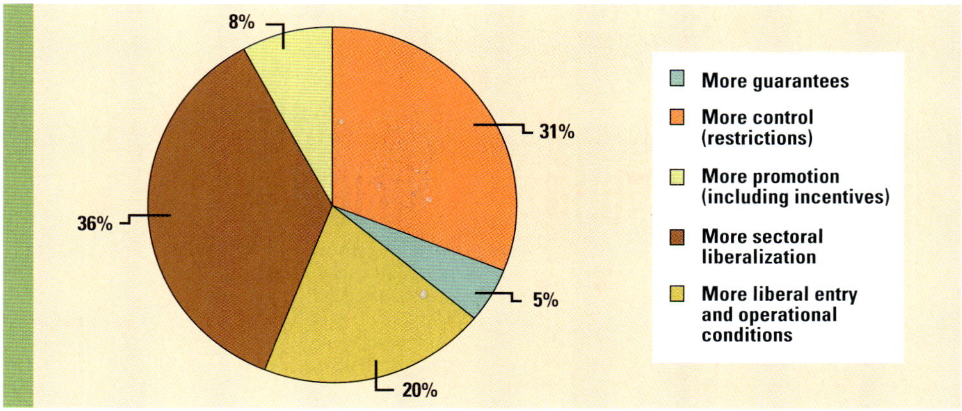

FIGURE 7.3

Types of Changes in FDI Laws and Regulations in 2002

Sources: UNCTAD, *World Investment Report, 2003 FDI Policies for Development: National and International Perspectives*, Chapter 1, p. 20.

FDI has grown more rapidly than world trade and world output for several reasons. Despite the general decline in trade barriers that we have witnessed over the past 30 years, business firms still fear protectionist pressures. Executives see FDI as a way of circumventing future trade barriers. Much of the Japanese automobile companies' investment in the United States during the 1980s and early 1990s was driven by a desire to reduce exports from Japan, thereby alleviating trade tensions between the two nations. Also, much of the recent increase in FDI is being driven by the dramatic political and economic changes that have been occurring in many of the world's developing nations. The general shift toward democratic political institutions and free market economies that we discussed in Chapter 2 has encouraged FDI. Across much of Asia, Eastern Europe, and Latin America, economic growth combined with deregulation and privatization programs that are open to foreign investors, and the removal of many restrictions on FDI have made all these countries more attractive to foreign investors. According to AT Kearney, Canada has slipped out of the top ten ranking as a destination for receiving foreign direct investment. Canada fell from 8th to 14th place, with China retaining its number one ranking.[5] China registered actual FDI of US$25.91 billion in the first five months of 2004.[6] Surprisingly, Luxembourg attracted more notional FDI than did China, but the Organization for Economic Cooperation and Development said most of this was money passing through holding companies.[7] The reasons for the strong flow of investment into China are discussed in the accompanying Country Focus on page 231.

In 2002, the actual world FDI stock had risen to $7.1 trillion, almost tenfold since 1980. That stock forms the basis of international production. Approximately 64 000 transnational (multinational) corporations control about 870 000 foreign affiliates (Table 7.2). Only three Canadian firms were ranked in this category–Thomson Corporation, Nortel Corporation, and Bell Canada Enterprises. They placed 55th, 56th, and 97th, respectively. It remains to be seen if Nortel will maintain this ranking, given its well-publicized financial problems.

The source of FDI remains highly concentrated. U.S. corporations hold the lead, followed by the United Kingdom, France, Germany, Japan, and Switzerland. Fluctuations in the yearly value of FDI increase the stock of FDI. Consequently, FDI stocks are more important than FDI flows, in terms of deepening global integration through production networks and generating the benefits associated with FDI and international production. It is also important that new FDI capital flow through the reinvestment of earnings and subsequent flows to FDI.[8]

TABLE 7.2

The World's Top 100 Non-Financial TNCs, Ranked by Foreign Assets, 2001[a] (in $ millions)

Source: UNCTAD/Erasmus University database; *World Investment Report 2003 FDI Policies for Development; National and International*, pp. 187 and 188.

RANKING				ASSETS	
FOREIGN ASSETS	CORPORATION	HOME ECONOMY	INDUSTRY[c]	FOREIGN	TOTAL
1	Vodafone	United Kingdom	Telecommunications	187 792	207 458
2	General Electric	United States	Electrical & electrical equipment	180 031	495 210
3	BP	United Kingdom	Petroleum expl./ref/.distr.	111 207	141 158
4	Vivendl Universal	France	Diversified	91 120[d]	123 156
5	Deutsche Telekom AG	Germany	Telecommunications	90 657[d]	145 802
6	Exxonmobil Corporation	United States	Petroleum expl./ref/.distr.	89 426	143 174
7	Ford Motor Company	United States	Motor vehicles	81 169	276 543
8	General Motors	United States	Motor vehicles	75 379	323 969
9	Royal Dutch/Sheel Group [h]	United Kingdom/ Netherlands	Petroleum expl./ref/.distr.	73 492[f]	111 543
10	TotalFinaElf	France	Petroleum expl./ref/.distr.	70 030[d]	78 500
50	National Grid Transco [h]	United Kingdom	Electricity, gas and water	19 080	24 839
51	Pinault–Printemps Redoute SA	France	Retail	18 285[d]	30 991
52	Pfizer Inc	United States	Pharmaceuticals	18 160	39 153
53	Motorola Inc	United States	Telecommunications	18 116	33 398
54	Texas Utilities Company	United States	Electricity, gas and water	17 966[d]	42 275
55	Thompson Corporation	Canada	Printing & publishing	17 815	18 402
56	Nortel Networks	Canada	Telecommunications	17 474[d]	21 137
57	Alcatel	France	Machinery and equipment	17 356	32 382
58	Procter & Gamble	United States	Diversified	17 342[d]	40 776
59	Coca-Cola Company	United States	Food and beverage	17 058[k]	22 417
60	Hewlett-Packard	United States	Electrical and electrical equipment	17 007	32 584
90	Merck & Co	United States	Pharmaceuticals	10 750[d]	44 007
91	Amerada Hess Corporation	United States	Petroleum expl./ref/.distr.	10 721[d]	15 369
92	British American Tobacco Plc	United Kingdom	Tobacco	10 355[d]	16 403
93	Abbott Laboratories	United States	Pharmaceuticals	10 286[d]	23 296
94	LVHM Moët-Hennessy Louis Vuitton SA	France	Luxury goods	10 208	21 115
95	Verizon Commuincations	United States	Telecommunications	10 159	170 795
96	Alcoa	United States	Metal and metal products	9 966	28 355
97	Bell Canada Enterprises	Canada	Telecommunications	9 900	34 160
98	Ericsson LM	Sweden	Telecommunications	9 742	24 130
99	Mirant Corp.	United States	Electricity, gas and water	9 730	22 754
100	International Paper Company	United States	Paper	9 536	37 158

a. All data are based on the companies' annual report unless otherwise stated.

c. Industry Classification for the companies follows the United States Standard Industrial Classification as used by the United States Securities and Exchange Commission (SEC).

d. In a number of cases companies reported only partial foreign assets. In these cases the ratio of the partial foreign assets to the partial (total) assets was applied to total assets to calculate the foreign assets. In all cases the resulting figures have been sent for confirmation to the companies.

f. Data were derived from the company as a response to an UNCTAD survey.

h. Data for outside Europe

k. Data for outside North America

THE FORM OF FDI: ACQUISITIONS VERSUS GREEN-FIELD INVESTMENTS

As noted earlier, FDI can take the form of a green-field investment in a new facility or an acquisition of or a merger with an existing local firm. The data suggest the majority of cross-border investment is in the form of mergers and acquisitions rather than green-field investments. In Latin America and the Caribbean, FDI flows declined for the third consecutive year, from $84 billion in 2001 to $56 billion, affecting all sub-regions and

COUNTRY FOCUS

FOREIGN DIRECT INVESTMENT IN CHINA

Beginning in late 1978, China's leadership decided to move the economy away from a centrally planned system to one that was more market driven, while still maintaining the rigid political framework of Communist Party control. The strategy had a number of key elements, including a switch to household responsibility in agriculture instead of the old collectivization, increases in the authority of local officials and plant managers in industry, establishment of small- to medium-scale private enterprises in services and light manufacturing, and increased foreign trade and investment. The result has been two decades of sustained high economic growth rates of between 10 and 11 percent annually compounded.

Starting from a tiny base, foreign investment surged to an annual average rate of $2.7 billion between 1985 and 1990 and then exploded to reach a record $64 billion in 2000, making China the second biggest recipient of FDI inflows in the world after the United States. Over the past 20 years, this inflow has resulted in establishment of 170 000 foreign-funded enterprises in China. The total stock of FDI in China had grown to $346 billion in 2000 ($470 billion in Hong Kong is added to this figure), amounting to 28 percent of China's total GDP and more than 14 percent of annualized gross fixed capital formation between 1994 and 2000. FDI inflows have been a major source of investment and economic growth in China since liberalization began, accounting for perhaps as much as 30 percent of the country's growth.

The reasons for the rise in investment are fairly obvious. With a population of 1 billion people, China represents the largest potential market in the world. Import tariffs have made it difficult to serve this market via exports, so FDI was required if a company wanted to tap into the huge potential of the country. Although China joined the World Trade Organization in 2001, which will ultimately mean a reduction in import tariffs, this will occur only slowly, so this motive for investing in China will persist. Also, many foreign firms believe that doing business in China requires a substantial presence in the country to build *guanxi,* the crucial relationship networks (see Chapter 3 for details). Furthermore, a combination of cheap labour and tax incentives, particularly for enterprises that establish themselves in special economic zones, makes China an attractive base from which to serve Asian or world markets with exports.

Less obvious, at least to begin with, was how difficult it would be for foreign firms to do business in China. Blinded by the size and potential of China's market, many firms have paid scant attention to the complexities of operating a business in this country until after the investment has been made. China may have a huge population, but despite two decades of rapid growth, it is still a poor country where the average income is little more than $750 per year. This lack of purchasing power translates into a weak market for many Western consumer goods from automobiles to household appliances. Another problem is the lack of a well-developed transportation infrastructure or distribution system. PepsiCo discovered this problem at its subsidiary in Chongqing. Perched above the Yangtze River in southwest Sichuan province, Chongqing lies at the heart of China's massive hinterland. The Chongqing municipality, which includes the city and its surrounding regions, contains over 30 million people, but according to Steve Chen, the manager of the Pepsi subsidiary, the lack of well-developed road and distribution systems means he can reach only about half of this population with his product.

Other problems include a highly regulated environment that can make it problematic to conduct business transactions and shifting tax and regulatory regimes. For example, in 1997, the Chinese government suddenly scrapped a tax credit scheme that had made it attractive to import capital equipment into China. This immediately made it more expensive to set up operations in the country. There are also difficulties finding qualified personnel to staff operations. The cultural revolution produced a generation of people who lack the basic educational background that is taken for granted in the West. Because of the country's past, few local people understand the complexities of managing a modern industrial enterprise. Then there are problems with local joint-venture partners who are inexperienced, opportunistic, or simply operate according to different goals. One U.S. manager explained that when he laid off 200 people to reduce costs, his Chinese partner hired them all back the next day. When he inquired why they had been hired back, the Chinese partner, which was government owned, explained that as an agency of the government, it had an "obligation" to reduce unemployment.

To continue to attract foreign investment, the Chinese government has committed itself to invest more than $800 billion in infrastructure projects over the next ten years. This should improve the nation's poor highway system. By giving preferential tax breaks to companies that invest in special regions, such as that around Chongqing, the Chinese have created incentives for foreign companies to invest in China's vast interior where markets are underserved. They have been pursuing a macroeconomic policy that includes an emphasis on maintaining steady economic growth, low inflation, and a stable currency, all of which are attractive to foreign investors. And to deal with the lack of qualified personnel, in 1997 the government instructed universities to establish 30 business schools to train Chinese in basic skills such as accounting, finance, and human resource management. Given these developments, it seems likely that the country will continue to be an important magnet for foreign investors well into the future.

Source: Interviews by the author while in China, March 1998; L. Sly, "China Losing Its Golden Glow," Chicago Tribune, September 15, 1997, p. 1; M. Miller, "Search for Fresh Capital Widens," South China Morning Post, April 9, 1998, p. 1; S. Mufson, "China Says Asian Crisis Will Have an Impact," Washington Post, March 8, 1998, p. A27; and United Nations, World Investment Report, 2000 (New York and Geneva: United Nations, 2001).

28 of the region's 40 economies. The Argentine economic crisis had a sweeping negative effect on the economic and political situations in Argentina and in neighbouring countries such as Uruguay, Paraguay, Brazil, and Chile.[9] Yet overall, FDI forecasts between now and the year 2007 appear positive for all regions (see Figure 7.4).

CANADA'S CASE

Canada's flows of FDI mirror those of other developed countries from 1998–2002 (Table 7.3). At the end of 2002, the U.S. accounted for 47 percent of Canada's foreign direct investment stock, compared with almost 60 percent ten years ago. FDI inflows and outflows peaked in 2000 (Figure 7.5). This situation is constantly shifting, with the announced Coors/Molsons merger representing an increase of foreign FDI in the Canadian beer market.

FIGURE 7.4

Prospects for FDI Flows are Positive in All Regions

Sources: UNCTAD-DITE, *Global Investments Prospects Assessment (GIPA)*, 2004 Figure 1.

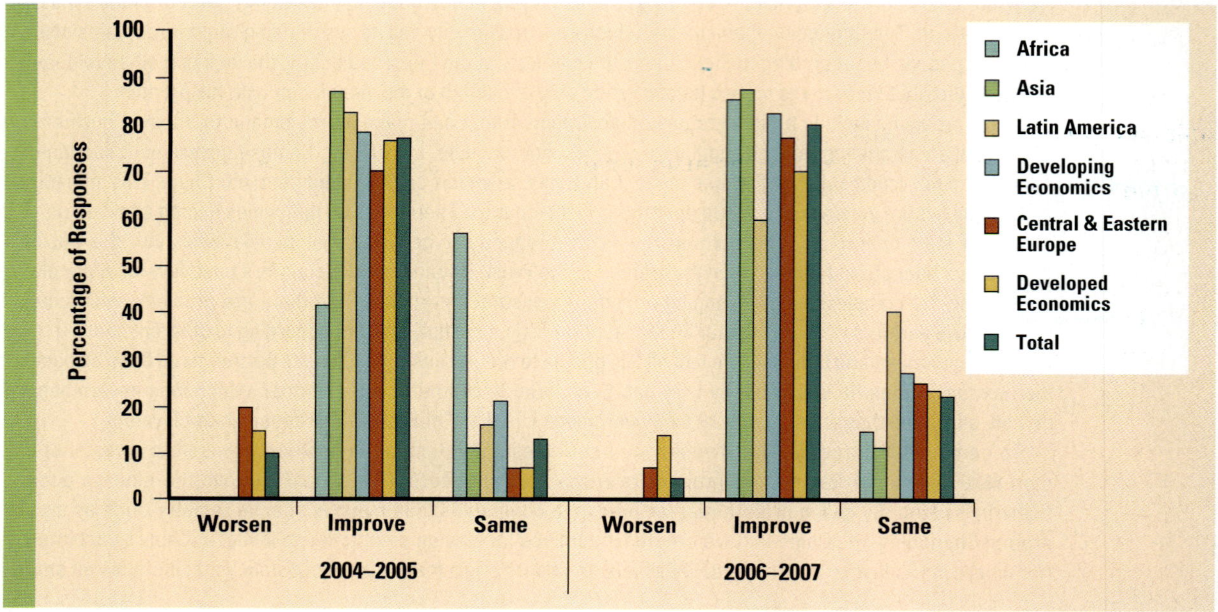

	FDI INFLOW	FDI OUTFLOW	BALANCE (OUT-IN)
1998	33.8	51.0	17.2
1999	36.8	25.6	-11.2
2000	99.1	69.2	-29.9
2001	44.6	56.7	12.1
2002	32.3	45.2	2.9

TABLE 7.3

1998–2002 Canadian Foreign Direct Investment Flows (in Cdn$ billions)

Source: Data adapted from Statistics Canada, www.cansim2.statcan.ca, Table 376-0015.

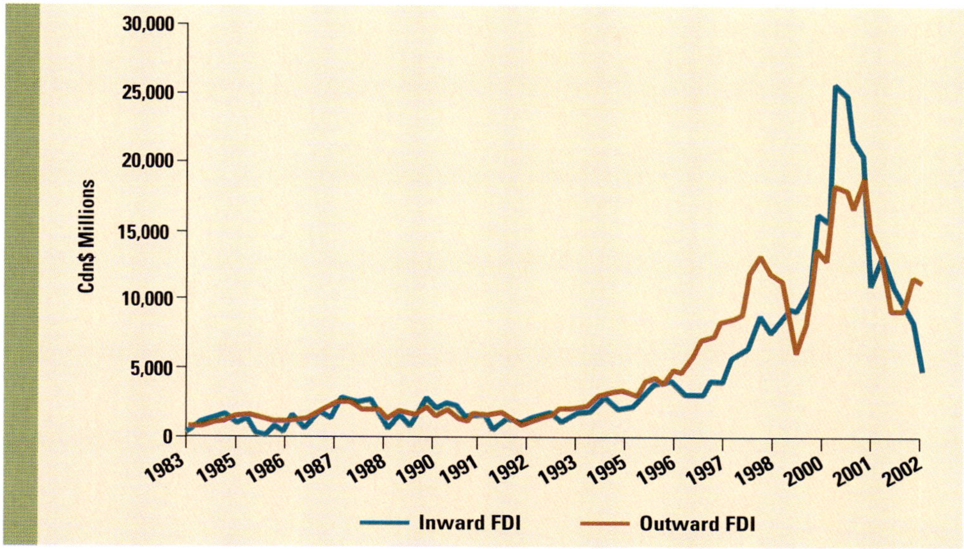

FIGURE 7.5

Canadian FDI Flows 1983–2002 (4-quarter moving average)

Sources: Data adapted from Statistics Canada publication "Canada's balance of international payments," Catalogue 67-001, various years.

Outbound FDI from Canada increased to $16.2 billion in the fourth quarter of 2002, twice the $8-billion average registered from late 2001 to June 2002. First quarter 2003 experienced a slowdown as Canadian direct investment abroad fell by $5.6 billion, the lowest quarterly outflow in almost three years.

For the most part, Canada's FDI outflow in the past few quartiles went to Canadian affiliates and subsidiaries in the United States. Statistics Canada reported that most overseas investments made by Canadian companies in 2002 went to existing affiliates and subsidiaries for working capital purposes. This investment, which bolsters the Canadian corporate presence abroad, might also be a good sign that Canadian companies are strengthening their global supply and production networks. The acquisition of foreign assets and companies was the main driver of Canadian FDI outflows from 1999 to 2001.

Canadian direct investment in the United States jumped ahead $11.3 billion in the fourth quarter of 2002 but slumped again in the first quarter to just under $3 billion. Canadian FDI flows to the U.S. dropped to $168 million during the third quarter of 2002. Recent strengthening in the Canadian dollar also gives more buying power to Canadian firms looking to expand south of the border.[10] See the accompanying Management Focus feature.

When contemplating FDI, why do firms apparently prefer to acquire existing assets rather than undertake green-field investments? We shall return to this and consider it in greater depth in Chapter 12, so for now we will make only a few basic observations. First, mergers and acquisitions are quicker to execute than green-field investments. This is an important consideration in the modern business world where markets evolve very rapidly. Many firms apparently believe that if they do not acquire a desirable target firm, then their global rivals will.

MANAGEMENT FOCUS

FOUR SEASONS HOTELS AND RESORTS

Few large companies can boast of continuity of management over a 40-year period, and Four Seasons Hotels and Resorts, is one of the few corporations that is able to do just that. Often the entrepreneurial flair exhibited by a company founder, turns to a more bureaucratic style of management as the company grows.

Isadore Sharp, chairman and Chief Executive Officer, founded the first Four Seasons hotel in 1960, as a mid-priced inn on the fringes of downtown Toronto. In keeping with his entrepreneurial flair, and after a decade of being in business, he developed the formula of creating the Four Seasons brand as a luxury group of hotels and resorts. Aside from being properties of exceptional design and finish, the company is well known for its personal service, catering to the needs of the discriminating traveller.

The service component has become such a feature of the company that Four Seasons has shifted its focus in the past decades. Once a major owner of the hotel properties, today it is mostly engaged in the management of the hotels that have the Four Seasons name. Under the terms of a typical management agreement, Four Seasons supervises all aspects of the day-to-day operations of the hotel on behalf of the property owner. This includes hiring, training, and supervising staff, providing sales and marketing services, undertaking purchasing and budgeting, as well as providing for the repair and maintenance of the physical structure of the hotel. Four Seasons manages a total of 65 hotels and resorts. The properties are operated in 29 countries in North America, the Caribbean, Europe, Asia, Australia, the Middle East, and South America. In 2004, the company opened its first European resort at Terre Blanche in Provence.

In return for managing a property, Four Seasons earns a number of fees, including a base fee, an incentive fee based on the profits of the hotel or the resort, a sales and marketing fee, as well as additional fees if the company provided pre-opening design and consulting work. These fees provide an ongoing, relatively steady stream of revenue for the company.

Four Seasons also develops the sales and marketing strategies for its entire portfolio of hotels and resorts. The company's marketing efforts are conducted by its headquarters in Toronto. Four Seasons also operates a smaller number of properties under the Regent brand name. Marketing services for the Regent hotels is provided by Carlson Hospitality Group of Minneapolis.

For many years now, the company has become focused on hotel management, not hotel ownership. In 2004, it sold its holdings in the Four Seasons Hotel Berlin.

A key component of the company is to provide a high level of standardized service throughout the world, as well as centralized purchasing and reservation systems, while at the same time ensuring that each property is unique. A Four Seasons Hotel should not look, or feel, like a cookie-cutter Holiday Inn, which is mostly the same whether you are in Atlanta or Calgary. One of the company's latest properties, Four Seasons Hotel Budapest, which opened in June 2004, is a good example of this individualization depending on the local environment. The hotel was already a nearly 100-year-old prominent landmark in the city, and was renovated with a $110-million facelift. The hotel also includes a spa and fitness centre, appropriate "in a country renowned for its rich spa heritage," says the company. The restaurant makes purchases from local food producers and wineries to ensure the availability of traditional Hungarian dishes, as well as other cuisines.

Sources: www.fourseasons.com and www.cbc.ca. Reprinted with permission of Four Seasons Hotels Limited.

Second, foreign firms are acquired because those firms have valuable strategic assets, such as brand loyalty, customer relationships, trademarks or patents, distribution systems, production systems, and the like. It is easier and perhaps less risky for a firm to acquire those assets than to build them from the ground up through a green-field investment.

Third, firms make acquisitions because they believe they can increase the efficiency of the acquired unit by transferring capital, technology, or management skills. Thus, there are some fairly compelling arguments for favouring mergers and acquisitions over green-field investments. But many mergers and acquisitions fail to realize their anticipated gains.[11] Chapter 12 further studies this issue.

THE THEORY OF FOREIGN DIRECT INVESTMENT

In this section we review several theories of foreign direct investment. These theories approach the phenomenon of foreign direct investment from three complementary perspectives. One set of theories seeks to explain why a firm will favour direct investment as a means of entering a foreign market when two other alternatives are open to it, exporting and licensing. Another set of theories seeks to explain why firms in the same industry often undertake foreign direct investment at the same time, and why certain locations are favoured over others as targets for foreign direct investment. These theories attempt to explain the observed *pattern* of foreign direct investment flows. A third theoretical perspective, known as the **eclectic paradigm,** attempts to combine the two other perspectives into a single holistic explanation of foreign direct investment (the term *eclectic* means picking the best aspects of other theories and combining them into a single explanation).

ECLECTIC PARADIGM Argument that combining location-specific assets or resource endowments and the firm's own unique assets often requires FDI; it requires the firm to establish production facilities where those foreign assets or resource endowments are located.

WHY FOREIGN DIRECT INVESTMENT?

Why do firms go to all the trouble of establishing operations abroad through foreign direct investment when two alternatives are available for exploiting the profit opportunities in a foreign market: exporting and licensing? **Exporting** involves producing goods at home and then shipping them to the receiving country for sale. **Licensing** involves granting a foreign entity (the licensee) the right to produce and sell the firm's product in return for a royalty fee on every unit the foreign entity sells. The question is an important one given that foreign direct investment can be both expensive and risky when compared to exporting and licensing. FDI is expensive because a firm must bear the costs of establishing production facilities in a foreign country or of acquiring a foreign enterprise. FDI is risky because of the problems associated with doing business in a different culture where the "rules of the game" may be very different. Relative to indigenous firms, there is a greater probability that a foreign firm undertaking FDI in a country for the first time will make costly mistakes due to its ignorance. When a firm exports, it need not bear the costs associated with foreign direct investment, and the risks associated with selling abroad can be reduced by using a native sales agent. Similarly, when a firm allows another enterprise to produce its products under licence, it need not bear the costs or risks of FDI, since these are born by the licensee. So why do so many firms apparently prefer FDI over either exporting or licensing? A deeper examination of the issue reveals that the answer can be found in the limitations of exporting and licensing as means for capitalizing on foreign market opportunities.

EXPORTING Sale of products produced in one country to residents of another country.

LICENSING Occurs when a firm (the licensor) licenses the right to produce its product, use its production processes, or use its brand name or trademark to another firm (the licensee). In return for giving the licensee these rights, the licensor collects a royalty fee on every unit the licensee sells.

Limitations of Exporting

The viability of an exporting strategy is often constrained by transportation costs and trade barriers. When transportation costs are added to production costs, it becomes unprofitable to ship some products over a large distance. This is particularly

A Coors Light mini-van is parked in the lot at the Molson brewery in Montreal in 2005, prior to shareholders voting on a merger with Adolph Coors Co. during a special shareholders' meeting. CP/Paul Chiasson.

true of products that have a low value-to-weight ratio and can be produced in almost any location (e.g., cement, soft drinks, etc.). For such products, relative to either FDI or licensing, the attractiveness of exporting decreases. For products with a high value-to-weight ratio, however, transport costs are normally a very minor component of total landed cost (e.g., electronic components, personal computers, medical equipment, computer software, etc.) and have little impact on the relative attractiveness of exporting, licensing, and FDI.

Transportation costs aside, much FDI is undertaken as a response to actual or threatened trade barriers such as import tariffs or quotas. By placing tariffs on imported goods, governments can increase the cost of exporting relative to foreign direct investment and licensing. Similarly, by limiting imports through quotas, governments increase the attractiveness of FDI and licensing. For example, the wave of FDI by Japanese auto companies in the United States during the 1980s and 1990s was partly driven by protectionist threats from Congress and by quotas on the importation of Japanese cars. For Japanese auto companies, these factors decreased the profitability of exporting and increased that of foreign direct investment. Trade barriers do not have to be in place for foreign direct investment to be favoured over exporting. Often, the desire to reduce the "threat" that trade barriers might be imposed is enough to justify foreign direct investment as an alternative to exporting.

Limitations of Licensing

INTERNALIZATION THEORY Marketing imperfection approach to foreign direct investment.

A branch of economic theory known as **internalization theory** seeks to explain why firms often prefer foreign direct investment over licensing as a strategy for entering foreign markets.[12] According to internalization theory, licensing has three major drawbacks as a strategy for exploiting foreign market opportunities. First, *licensing may result in a firm giving away valuable technological know-how to a potential foreign competitor.* For example, in the 1960s, RCA licensed its leading-edge colour television technology to a number of Japanese companies, including Matsushita and Sony. At the time, RCA saw licensing as a way to earn a good return from its technological know-how in the Japanese market without the costs and risks associated with foreign direct investment. However, Matsushita and Sony quickly assimilated RCA's technology and used it to enter the U.S. market to compete directly against RCA. As a result, RCA is now a minor player in its home market, while Matsushita and Sony have a much bigger market share.

A second problem is that *licensing does not give a firm the tight control over manufacturing, marketing, and strategy in a foreign country that may be required to maximize its profitability.* With licensing, control over manufacturing, marketing, and strategy is granted to a licensee in return for a royalty fee. However, for *both* strategic and operational reasons, a firm may want to retain control over these functions. The rationale for wanting control over the *strategy* of a foreign entity is that a firm might want its foreign subsidiary to price and market very aggressively to keep a foreign competitor in check. Kodak has pursued this strategy in Japan. The competitive attacks launched by Kodak's Japanese subsidiary are keeping its major global competitor, Fuji, busy defending its competitive position in Japan. Consequently, Fuji has had to pull back from its earlier strategy of attacking Kodak aggressively in the United States. Unlike a wholly owned subsidiary, a licensee would be unlikely to accept such an imposition, since such a strategy implies the licensee would be allowed to make only a low profit, or might have to take a loss.

The rationale for wanting control over the *operations* of a foreign entity is that the firm might wish to take advantage of differences in factor costs across countries, producing only part of its final product in a given country, while importing other parts from where they can be produced at lower cost. Again, a licensee would be unlikely to accept such an arrangement, since it would limit the licensee's autonomy. Thus, for these reasons, when tight control over a foreign entity is desirable, foreign direct investment is preferable to licensing.

A third problem with licensing arises when the firm's competitive advantage is based not so much on its products, as on the management, marketing, and manufacturing capabilities that produce those products. However, *such capabilities are often not amenable to licensing*. While a foreign licensee may be able to physically reproduce the firm's product under licence, it often may not be able to do so as efficiently as the firm could itself. As a result, the licensee may not be able to fully exploit the profit potential inherent in a foreign market.

For example, consider Toyota, a company whose competitive advantage in the global auto industry is acknowledged to come from its superior ability to manage the overall process of designing, engineering, manufacturing, and selling automobiles, that is, from its management and organizational capabilities. Toyota is credited with pioneering the development of a new production process, known as lean production, that enables it to produce higher-quality automobiles at a lower cost than its global rivals.[13]

Although Toyota has certain products that could be licensed, its real competitive advantage comes from its management and process capabilities. These kinds of skills are difficult to articulate or codify; they certainly cannot be written down in a simple licensing contract. They are organizationwide, and they have been developed over the years. They are not embodied in any one individual, but instead are widely dispersed throughout the company. Toyota's skills are embedded in its organizational culture, and culture is something that cannot be licensed. Thus, if Toyota were to allow a foreign entity to produce its cars under licence, chances are the entity could not do so nearly as efficiently as could Toyota. In turn, this would limit the ability of the foreign entity to fully develop the market potential of that product.

Such reasoning underlies Toyota's preference for direct investment in foreign markets, as opposed to allowing foreign automobile companies to produce its cars under licence. Starbucks may also have found it difficult to transfer its management and marketing know-how via a licensing strategy, hence its recent preference for FDI in the form of acquisitions or joint ventures over straight licensing deals (see the opening case).

All this suggests that when one or more of the following conditions holds, markets fail as a mechanism for selling know-how and FDI is more profitable than licensing: (1) when the firm has valuable know-how that cannot be adequately protected by a licensing contract, (2) when the firm needs tight control over a foreign entity to maximize its market share and earnings in that country, and (3) when a firm's skills and know-how are not amenable to licensing.

Advantages of Foreign Direct Investment

It follows from the above discussion that a firm will favour foreign direct investment over exporting as an entry strategy when transportation costs or trade barriers make exporting unattractive. Furthermore, the firm will favour foreign direct investment over licensing (or franchising) when it wishes to maintain control over its technological know-how, or over its operations and business strategy, or when the firm's capabilities are simply not amenable to licensing.

THE PATTERN OF FOREIGN DIRECT INVESTMENT

Observation suggests that firms in the same industry often undertake foreign direct investment about the same time. Also, there is a clear tendency for firms to direct their investment activities toward certain locations. The two theories we consider in this section attempt to explain the patterns that we observe in FDI flows.

Strategic Behaviour

OLIGOPOLY An industry composed of a limited number of large firms.

One theory used to explain foreign direct investment patterns is based on the idea that FDI flows are a reflection of strategic rivalry between firms in the global marketplace. An early variant of this argument was expounded by F. T. Knickerbocker, who looked at the relationship between FDI and rivalry in oligopolistic industries.[14] An **oligopoly** is an industry composed of a limited number of large firms (an industry in which four firms control 80 percent of a domestic market is considered an oligopoly). A critical competitive feature of such industries is interdependence of the major players: What one firm does can have an immediate impact on the major competitors, forcing a response in kind. Thus, if one firm in an oligopoly cuts prices, this can take market share away from its competitors, forcing them to respond with similar price cuts to retain their market share.

Such imitative behaviour can take many forms in an oligopoly. One firm raises prices, the others follow; someone expands capacity, and the rivals imitate lest they be left at a disadvantage in the future. Building on this, Knickerbocker argued that the same kind of imitative behaviour characterizes foreign direct investment. Consider an oligopoly in the United States in which three firms–A, B, and C–dominate the market. Firm A establishes a subsidiary in France. Firms B and C reflect that if this investment is successful, it may knock out their export business to France and give firm A a first-mover advantage. Furthermore, firm A might discover some competitive asset in France that it could repatriate to the United States to torment firms B and C on their native soil. Given these possibilities, firms B and C decide to follow firm A and establish operations in France.

Imitative behaviour does lead to foreign direct investment. Several studies of U.S. enterprises suggest that firms based in oliogopolistic industries do tend to imitate each other's FDI.[15] The same phenomenon has been observed among Japanese firms.[16] For example, Toyota and Nissan responded to investments by Honda in the United States and Europe by undertaking their own FDI in the United States and Europe.

MULTIPOINT COMPETITION Arises when two or more enterprises encounter each other in different regional markets, national markets, or industries.

Knickerbocker's theory can be extended to embrace the concept of multipoint competition. **Multipoint competition** arises when two or more enterprises encounter each other in different regional markets, national markets, or industries. Economic theory suggests that, like chess players jockeying for advantage, firms will try to match each other's moves in different markets to try to hold each other in check. The idea is to ensure that a rival does not gain a commanding position in one market and then use the profits generated there to subsidize competitive attacks in other markets. Kodak and Fuji Photo Film Co., for example, compete against each other around the world. If Kodak enters a particular foreign market, Fuji will not be far behind. Fuji feels compelled to follow Kodak to ensure that Kodak does not gain a dominant position that it could leverage to gain a competitive advantage elsewhere. The converse also holds, with Kodak following Fuji when the Japanese firm is the first to enter a foreign market.

The Product Life Cycle

We considered Raymond Vernon's product life-cycle theory in Chapter 5. However, we did not dwell on Vernon's contention that his theory also explains the pattern of

FDI over time. Vernon argued that the same firm or firms that pioneered the product and introduced it in their home market often establish facilities abroad to produce a product for consumption in that market or for export to other markets. Thus, Xerox originally introduced the photocopier into the U.S. market, and it was Xerox that originally set up production facilities in Japan (Fuji-Xerox) and Great Britain (Rank-Xerox) to serve those markets.

Vernon's view is that firms undertake FDI at particular stages in the life cycle of a product they have pioneered. They invest in other advanced countries when local demand in those countries grows large enough to support local production (as Xerox did). They subsequently shift production to developing countries when product standardization and market saturation give rise to price competition and cost pressures. Investment in developing countries, where labour costs are lower, is seen as the best way to reduce costs.

There is merit to Vernon's theory; firms do invest in a foreign country when demand in that country will support local production, and they do invest in low-cost regions when cost pressures become intense.[17] But Vernon's theory fails to explain why it is profitable for a firm to undertake FDI at such times, rather than continuing to export from its home base, and rather than licensing a foreign firm to produce its product. Just because demand in a foreign country is large enough to support local production, it does not necessarily follow that local production is the most profitable option. It may still be more profitable to produce at home and export to that country (to realize the scale economies that arise from serving the global market from one location). Alternatively, it may be more profitable for the firm to license a foreign firm to produce its product for sale in that country. The product life-cycle theory ignores these options and, instead, simply argues that once a foreign market is large enough to support local production, FDI will occur. This limits its explanatory power and its usefulness to business (in that it fails to identify when it is profitable to invest abroad).

The Eclectic Paradigm

The eclectic paradigm has been championed by the British economist John Dunning.[18] Dunning argues that in addition to the various factors discussed above, location-specific advantages are also important in explaining both the rationale for, and the direction of foreign direct investment. By **location-specific advantages,** Dunning means the advantages that arise from utilizing resource endowments or assets that are tied to a particular foreign location and that a firm finds valuable to combine with its own unique assets (such as the firm's technological, marketing, or management capabilities). Dunning accepts the argument of internalization theory that it is difficult for a firm to license its own unique capabilities and know-how. Therefore, he argues that combining location-specific assets or resource endowments *and* the firm's own unique capabilities often requires foreign direct investment. That is, it requires the firm to establish production facilities where those foreign assets or resource endowments are located.

LOCATION-SPECIFIC ADVANTAGES
Advantages that arise from using resource endowments or assets that are tied to a particular foreign location and that a firm finds valuable to combine with its own unique assets (such as the firm's technological, marketing, or management know-how).

An obvious example of Dunning's arguments are natural resources, such as oil and other minerals, which are by their character specific to certain locations. Dunning suggests that to exploit such foreign resources a firm must undertake FDI. Clearly this explains the FDI undertaken by many of the world's oil companies, which have to invest where oil is located to combine their technological and managerial capabilities with this valuable location-specific resource. Another obvious example are valuable human resources, such as low-cost, high-skilled labour. The cost and skill of labour varies from country to country. Since labour is not internationally mobile, according to Dunning it makes sense for a firm to locate production facilities where the cost and skills of local labour are most suited to its particular production processes.

However, Dunning's theory has implications that go beyond basic resources such as minerals and labour. Consider Silicon Valley, which is the world centre for the computer and semiconductor industry. Many of the world's major computer and semi-conductor companies, such as Apple Computer, Hewlett-Packard, and Intel, are located close to each other in the Silicon Valley region of California. As a result, much of the cutting-edge research and product development in computers and semiconductors takes place here. According to Dunning's arguments, knowledge being generated in Silicon Valley with regard to the design and manufacture of computers and semiconductors is available nowhere else in the world. As it is commercialized, that knowledge diffuses throughout the world, but the leading edge of knowledge generation in the computer and semiconductor industries is to be found in Silicon Valley. In Dunning's language, this means that Silicon Valley has a *location-specific advantage* in the generation of knowledge related to the computer and semiconductor industries. In part, this advantage comes from the sheer concentration of intellectual talent in this area, and in part it arises from a network of informal contacts that allow firms to benefit from each others' knowledge generation. Economists refer to such knowledge "spill-overs" as **externalities,** and a well-established theory suggests that firms can benefit from such externalities by locating close to their source.[19]

EXTERNALITIES
Knowledge spillovers.

Given this, it may make sense for foreign computer and semiconductor firms to invest in research and (perhaps) production facilities so that they can benefit from being in the location where the knowledge is first generated. Externalities may allow firms based there to learn about and utilize valuable new knowledge before those based elsewhere, thereby giving them a competitive advantage in the global marketplace. If this argument is correct, one would expect to see significant evidence of FDI by European, Japanese, South Korean, Canadian, and Taiwanese computer and semiconductor firms in the Silicon Valley region. In fact, evidence seems to show that firms from these countries are investing in the Silicon Valley region, precisely because they wish to benefit from the externalities that arise there.[20] In a similar vein, others have argued that direct investment by foreign firms in the U.S. biotechnology industry has been motivated by desires to gain access to the unique location-specific technological knowledge of U.S. biotechnology firms.[21] Dunning's theory, therefore, seems to be a useful addition to those outlined above, for it helps explain like no other how location factors affect the direction of FDI.

POLITICAL IDEOLOGY AND FOREIGN DIRECT INVESTMENT

Government policy toward FDI has typically been driven by political ideology. Historically, ideology toward FDI has ranged from a radical stance that is hostile to all FDI to the noninterventionist principle of free market economics. In between these two extremes is an approach that might be called pragmatic nationalism.

THE RADICAL VIEW

The radical view traces its roots to Marxist political and economic theory. Radical writers argue that the multinational enterprise (MNE) is an instrument of imperialist domination. They see the MNE as a tool for exploiting host countries to the exclusive benefit of their capitalist-imperialist home countries. They argue that MNEs extract profits from the host country and take them to their home country, giving nothing of value to the host country. They note, for example, that key technology is tightly controlled by the MNE, and that important jobs in the foreign subsidiaries of MNEs go to home-country nationals rather than to citizens of the host country. Because of this, according to the radical view, FDI by the MNEs of advanced capitalist nations keeps the developing countries of the world relatively backward and dependent on advanced capitalist nations for investment, jobs, and technology. Thus, according to the extreme version of this view, no country should ever permit foreign corporations to undertake FDI, since they can never be instruments of economic development, only of economic domination. Moreover, where MNEs already exist in a country, they should be immediately nationalized.[22]

By the end of the 1980s, however, the radical position was in retreat almost everywhere. There seem to be three reasons for this: (1) the collapse of communism in Eastern Europe; (2) the generally abysmal economic performance of those countries that embraced the radical position, and a growing belief by many of these countries that FDI can be an important source of technology and jobs and can stimulate economic growth; and (3) the strong economic performance of those developing countries that embraced capitalism rather than radical ideology (e.g., Singapore, Hong Kong, and Taiwan). For example, even though the governing African National Congress party in South Africa contains many former Communists, the government has not adopted a radical stance and is encouraging foreign firms to undertake FDI. Twenty years ago this would not have occurred, but in the new world order ushered in by the collapse of communism it is a common position.

THE FREE MARKET VIEW

The free market view has its roots in classical economics and the international trade theories of Adam Smith and David Ricardo (see Chapter 5). The free market view argues that international production should be distributed among countries according to the theory of comparative advantage. That is, countries should specialize in the production of those goods and services that they can produce most efficiently. Within this framework, the MNE is seen as an instrument for dispersing the production of goods and services to those locations where they can be produced most efficiently. Viewed this way, FDI by the MNE is a way to increase the overall efficiency of the world economy.

Consequently, there has been a global move toward the removal of restrictions on inward and outward foreign direct investment. According to the United Nations Conference on Trade and Development between 1991 and 2002, some 94 percent of the total 1641 changes worldwide in laws governing foreign direct investment created a more favourable environment for FDI. The desire of governments to facilitate FDI has also been reflected in a dramatic increase in the number of bilateral investment treaties designed to protect and promote investment between two countries. As of 2002, there were 2181 bilateral investment treaties (BIT) in the world involving 722 countries, a significant increase from the 180 treaties that existed in 1981.[23] However, in practice, no country has adopted the free market view in its pure form (just as no country has adopted the radical view in its pure form). Countries such as Great Britain, the United States, and Canada are among the most open to FDI, but governments of these three countries intervene. Great Britain does so by reserving the right to block foreign takeovers of domestic firms if the takeovers are seen as "contrary to national security interests" or if they have the potential for reducing competition. (In practice this right is rarely exercised.) U.S. controls on FDI are more limited and largely informal. For political reasons, the United States will occasionally restrict U.S. firms from undertaking FDI in certain countries (e.g., Cuba, North Korea, and Iran). In addition, there are some limited restrictions on FDI. For example, foreigners are prohibited from purchasing more than 25 percent of any U.S. airline or from acquiring a controlling interest in a U.S. television broadcast network. Since 1989, the government has had the right to review foreign investment on the grounds of national security. Canada's approach to FDI was seen as

ANOTHER PERSPECTIVE

New encouragement for FDI in Africa
Bernie de Haldevang, director of the new African Trade Insurance Agency, suggests that what Africa needs is not aid but investment. He is directing this new export credit and investment insurance agency, a collaborative established by a group of African nations to reduce the perceived risk of FDI into Africa.

A Lloyds of London political risk broker recently categorized all but five countries in Africa at the highest risk level. Whether real or imagined, perception matters when it comes to risk, so the African Trade Insurance Agency, backed by the World Bank, is now there to insure export credit and investment risk in Burundi, Kenya, Malawi, Rwanda, Tanzania, Uganda, and Zambia. Haldevang expects that the availability of insurance will also increase trade among African nations. Currently, much of the trade in Africa moves to developed nations, with goods then shipped back to Africa. Given that Africa holds the bulk of the world's mineral deposits, with insurance available, we can expect its share of global FDI, which is now at less than half of 1 percent, to increase. (*International Herald Tribune,* June 28, 2002, p. A6.)

socialist by many during the initial stages of the Foreign Investment Review Agency (FIRA). In 1985, it changed its name to Investment Canada, which was far more appealing to foreign investment than its predecessor. Part of Canada's reticence to FDI has traditionally been part and parcel of Canada's insecurity about increased American dominance of Canada's economy and lurking fears of outright political and territorial takeover of the country. This first was felt during the 1840s, during which the notion of Manifest Destiny was born. American politicians and businesspeople began expressing an interest in expanding its territories to the North Pole.

Still, Canada is not entirely open for business to foreign entities. For example, foreign ownership within the Canadian airline industry cannot exceed 25 percent, in spite of repeated calls to raise it to 49 percent.[24]

In the Canadian broadcasting industry, regulated by the Canadian Radio-Television and Telecommunications Commission, similar restrictions apply. In a speech given by CRTC Chairperson Charles Dalfen on December 12, 2002 to the Standing Committee on Canadian Heritage in Ottawa, he stated "The Commission is instructed under the Broadcasting Act to give effect to certain directions of the Governor-in-Council. One of the most important of these is the direction dealing with the ineligibility of non-Canadians to hold broadcasting licences, which was originally issued in 1969, and was last amended in 1998. Under this direction, the Commission can neither issue broadcasting licences nor grant amendments or renewals to applicants that are non-Canadian. The direction spells out the criteria that applicants must satisfy in order to qualify as Canadian. In the case of a corporation, these include the following: a minimum of 80 percent of the issued and outstanding voting shares of a licensee corporation and 80 percent of its voting rights must be owned and controlled by Canadians; the chief executive officer and a minimum of 80 percent of the corporation's directors must be Canadians who normally reside in Canada; and where the licensee is a subsidiary, 66 2/3 percent of the parent corporation's issued and outstanding voting shares and voting rights must be owned by Canadians. Where the foreign ownership of a parent corporation is over 20 percent, the parent corporation or its directors cannot influence the programming decisions of the licensee."[25]

PRAGMATIC NATIONALISM

In practice, many countries have adopted neither a radical policy nor a free market policy toward FDI, but instead a policy that can best be described as pragmatic nationalism. The pragmatic nationalist view is that FDI has both benefits and costs. FDI can benefit a host country by bringing capital, skills, technology, and jobs, but those benefits often come at a cost. When products resulting from an investment are sold by a foreign company rather than a domestic company, the profits from that investment go abroad. Many countries are also concerned that a foreign-owned manufacturing plant may import many components from its home country, which has negative implications for the host country's balance-of-payments position.

Recognizing this, countries adopting a pragmatic stance pursue policies designed to maximize the national benefits and minimize the national costs. According to this view, FDI should be allowed only if the benefits outweigh the costs.

Another aspect of pragmatic nationalism is the tendency to aggressively court FDI seen to be in the national interest by, for example, offering subsidies to foreign MNEs in the form of tax breaks or grants. Countries often compete with each other to attract foreign investment, offering large tax breaks and subsidies to enterprises considering investment. For example, in Europe, Britain has been the most successful at attracting Japanese investment in the automobile industry, often in the face of major competition from other European nations. Nissan, Toyota, and Honda have major assembly plants in Britain. All three now use this country as their base for serving the rest of Europe—with obvious employment and balance-of-payments benefits for Britain.

SHIFTING IDEOLOGY

Recent years have seen a marked decline in the number of countries that adhere to a radical ideology. Moreover, although no countries have adopted a *pure* free market policy stance, an increasing number of countries are gravitating toward the free market end of the spectrum and have liberalized their foreign investment regime. One result has been the surge in the volume of FDI worldwide, which as we noted earlier, has been growing twice as fast as the growth in world trade. Another result has been a dramatic increase in the volume of FDI directed at countries that have recently liberalized their FDI regimes, such as China, India, and Vietnam.

COSTS AND BENEFITS OF FDI TO THE NATION-STATE

To a greater or lesser degree, many governments can be considered pragmatic nationalists when it comes to FDI. Accordingly, their policy is shaped by a consideration of the costs and benefits of FDI. Here we explore the benefits and costs of FDI, first from the perspective of a host country, and then from the perspective of the home country. Later, we look at the policy instruments governments use to manage FDI.

HOST-COUNTRY EFFECTS: BENEFITS

There are three main benefits of inward FDI for a host country: the resource-transfer effect, the employment effect, and the balance-of-payments effect. In the following section we will explore the costs of FDI to host countries.

Resource-Transfer Effects

Foreign direct investment can make a positive contribution to a host economy by supplying capital, technology, and management resources that would otherwise not be available. If capital, technology, or management skills are scarce in a country, the provision of these skills by an MNE (through FDI) may boost that country's economic growth rate.

The argument with regard to capital is that many MNEs, by virtue of their large size and financial strength, have access to financial resources not available to host-country firms. These funds may be available from internal company sources, or, because of their reputation, large MNEs may find it easier to borrow money from capital markets than host-country firms would.

As for technology, you will recall from Chapter 2 that technology can stimulate a country's economic growth and industrialization.[26] Technology can take two forms, both of which are valuable. It can be incorporated in a production process (e.g., the technology for discovering, extracting, and refining oil) or it can be incorporated in a product (e.g., personal computers). However, many countries lack the research and development resources and skills required to develop their own indigenous product and process technology. This is particularly true of the world's less developed nations. Such countries must rely on advanced industrialized nations for much of the technology required to stimulate economic growth, and FDI can provide it.

The foreign management skills provided through FDI may also produce important benefits for the host country. Beneficial spin-off effects arise when local personnel who are trained to occupy managerial, financial, and technical posts in the subsidiary of a foreign MNE subsequently leave the firm and establish indigenous firms. Similar benefits may arise if the superior management skills of a foreign MNE stimulate local suppliers, distributors, and competitors to improve their own management skills.

The beneficial effects may be reduced if most management and highly skilled jobs in the subsidiaries of foreign firms are reserved for home-country nationals. In such cases, citizens of the host country do not receive the benefits of training by the MNE. This may limit the spin-off effect. Consequently, the percentage of management and skilled jobs that go to citizens of the host country can be a major negotiating point between an MNE wishing to undertake FDI and a potential host government. In recent years, most MNEs have responded to host-government pressures on this issue by agreeing to reserve a large proportion of management and highly skilled jobs for citizens of the host country.

Employment Effects

Another beneficial effect of FDI is that it brings jobs to a host country that would otherwise not be created there. The effects of FDI on employment are both direct and indirect. Direct effects arise when a foreign MNE employs a number of host-country citizens. Indirect effects arise when jobs are created in local suppliers as a result of the investment and when jobs are created because of increased local spending by employees of the MNE. The indirect employment effects are often as large as, if not larger than, the direct effects. Over the years, the Toyota factory in Cambridge, Ontario, has grown to employ 3900 workers. This example of FDI increasing employment within its host country is what makes FDI a favourable investment to its recipients, while also being of value to Toyota to have a plant closer to its eastern North American markets.[27]

Cynics argue that not all the "new jobs" created by FDI represent net additions in employment. In the case of FDI by Japanese auto companies in the United States, some argue that the jobs created by this investment have been more than offset by the jobs lost in U.S.-owned auto companies, which have lost market share to their Japanese competitors. Because of such substitution effects, the net number of new jobs created by FDI may not be as great as initially claimed by an MNE. The issue of the likely net gain in employment may be a major negotiating point between an MNE wishing to undertake FDI and the host government.

When FDI takes the form of an acquisition of an established enterprise in the host economy, as opposed to a green-field investment, the immediate effect may be to reduce employment as the multinational tries to improve operating efficiency. However, even in such cases, research suggests that after the initial restructuring, enterprises acquired by foreign firms tend to grow their employment base at a faster rate than domestic rivals. For example, an OECD study found that between 1989 and 1996, foreign firms created new jobs at a faster rate than their domestic counterparts.[28] The same study found that foreign firms tended to pay higher wage rates than domestic firms, suggesting that the quality of employment was better. Another study looking at FDI in Eastern European transition economies found that although employment fell after acquisition of an enterprise by a foreign firm, often those enterprises were in competitive difficulties and would not have survived if they had not been acquired. After an initial period of adjustment and retrenchment, employment downsizing was often followed by new investments, and employment either remained stable or increased.[29]

Balance-of-Payments Effects

The effect of FDI on a country's balance-of-payments accounts is an important policy issue for most host governments. A country's **balance-of-payments accounts** keep track of both its payments to and its receipts from other countries. Governments normally are concerned when their country is running a deficit on the current account of their balance of payments. The **current account** tracks the export and import of goods and services. A current account deficit, or trade deficit as it is often called, arises when a country is importing more goods and services than it is exporting. Governments typically prefer to see a current account surplus rather than a deficit. The only way a current account deficit can be supported in the long run is by selling assets to foreigners (for a detailed explanation of why this is the case, see Krugman and Obstfeld).[30] For example, the persistent U.S. current account deficit of the 1980s and 1990s was financed by a steady sale of U.S. assets (stocks, bonds, real estate, and whole corporations) to foreigners. Because national governments invariably dislike seeing the assets of their country fall into foreign hands, they prefer their nation to run a current account surplus. FDI can help a country achieve this goal in two ways.

BALANCE-OF-PAYMENTS ACCOUNTS National accounts that track both payments to and receipts from foreigners.

CURRENT ACCOUNT In the balance of payments, records transactions involving the export or import of goods and services.

First, if the FDI is a substitute for imports of goods or services, the effect can be to improve the current account of the host country's balance of payments. Much of the FDI by Japanese automobile companies in Canada and the United Kingdom, for example, substitutes for imports from Japan. Thus, the current account of Canadian balance of payments has improved somewhat because many Japanese companies are now supplying the U.S. market from production facilities in Canada, as opposed to facilities in Japan. Insofar as this has reduced the need to finance a current-account deficit by asset sales to foreigners, Canada has clearly benefited from this. A second potential benefit arises when the MNE uses a foreign subsidiary to export goods and services to other countries.

HOST-COUNTRY EFFECTS: COSTS

Three main costs of inward FDI concern host countries: (1) the possible adverse effects of FDI on competition within the host nation, (2) adverse effects on the balance of payments, and (3) the perceived loss of national sovereignty and autonomy.

Adverse Effects on Competition

Host governments sometimes worry that the subsidiaries of foreign MNEs operating in their country may have greater economic power than indigenous competitors. Because they may be part of a large international organization, the foreign MNE may be able to draw on funds generated elsewhere to subsidize its costs in the host market, which could drive indigenous companies out of business and allow the firm to monopolize the market. Once the market was monopolized, the foreign MNE could raise prices above those that would prevail in competitive markets, with harmful effects on the economic welfare of the host nation. This concern tends to be greater in countries that have few large firms of their own that are able to compete effectively with the subsidiaries of foreign MNEs (generally less developed countries). It tends to be a relatively minor concern in most advanced industrialized nations.

Another variant of the competition argument is related to the infant industry c oncern we discussed in Chapter 6. Import controls may be motivated by a desire to let a local industry develop to a stage where it is capable of competing in world markets. The same logic suggests that FDI should be restricted. If a country with a potential comparative advantage in a particular industry allows FDI in that industry, indigenous firms may never have a chance to develop.

ANOTHER PERSPECTIVE

FDI—modern day colonialism

FDI is seen by many as a boon to the expansion and equalization of world trade. Its critics tell a darker tale of exploitation, doom, and infringement on human rights. To them it is colonialism with a new face. FDI is not just about major retail or fast food chains setting up shop in other countries. FDI can be carried out by an industry wishing to take advantage of a business situation in a potential host country.

For example, Placer Dome Mines, a Canadian-based mining operation has operations in Porgera Papua New Guinea where large gold deposits are being mined. Critics of this facility have stated that during the 1990s the company had shown negative cultural and environmental examples towards area Aboriginals.

Yet Placer Dome works with local communities to develop plans compatible with host Aboriginal cultural and spiritual sites and traditions. It also provides significant employment opportunities. The company has set up formal and informal networks with government and social communities in and around the mining community. It also enables local Aboriginals to upgrade their work skills through training programs at educational institutions.

Though these are just some of the initiatives that Placer Dome has put in place, there are many who stand firm that this is yet another example of FDI producing a new form of paternalism

Is such form of FDI acceptable in today's world? (www.placerdome.com/sustainability/social/aboriginal.html.)

In practice, the above arguments are often used by inefficient indigenous competitors when lobbying their government to restrict direct investment by foreign MNEs. Although a host government may state publicly in such cases that its restrictions on inward FDI are designed to protect indigenous competitors from the market power of foreign MNEs, they may have been enacted to protect inefficient but politically powerful indigenous competitors from foreign competition.

Adverse Effects on the Balance of Payments

The possible adverse effects of FDI on a host country's balance-of-payments position are twofold. First, set against the initial capital inflow that comes with FDI must be the subsequent outflow of income as the foreign subsidiary repatriates earnings to its parent company. Such outflows show up as a debit on the current account of the balance of payments. A second concern arises when a foreign subsidiary imports a substantial number of its inputs from abroad, which also results in a debit on the current account of the host country's balance of payments.

National Sovereignty and Autonomy

Many host governments worry that FDI is accompanied by some loss of economic independence. The concern is that key decisions that can affect the host country's economy will be made by a foreign parent that has no real commitment to the host country and over which the host country's government has no real control. A quarter of a century ago this concern was expressed by several European countries, which feared that FDI by U.S. MNEs was threatening their national sovereignty. The same concerns have surfaced in the United States with regard to European and Japanese FDI. The main fear seems to be that if foreigners own assets in the United States, they can somehow "hold the country to economic ransom." Twenty-five years ago when officials in the French government were making similar complaints about U.S. investments in France, many U.S. politicians dismissed the charge as silly. Now that the shoe is on the other foot, some U.S. politicians no longer think the notion is silly. However, most economists dismiss such concerns as groundless and irrational. Political scientist Robert Reich has noted that such concerns are the product of outmoded thinking because they fail to account for the growing interdependence of the world economy.[31] In a world where firms from all advanced nations are increasingly investing in each other's markets, it is not possible for one country to hold another to "economic ransom" without hurting itself.

HOME-COUNTRY EFFECTS: BENEFITS

Although the cost and benefits of FDI for a host country have received the most attention, there are also costs and benefits to the home (or source) country. For example, does the U.S. economy benefit or lose from investments by a firm such as Starbucks in foreign markets? Some would argue that FDI is not always in the home country's national interest and should, therefore, be restricted. Others argue that the benefits far outweigh the costs, and that any restrictions would be contrary to national interests. To understand why people take these positions, let us look at the benefits and costs of FDI to the home (source) country.[32]

When a Canadian textile company shuts down its plants and moves production to Mexico, as some have, imports into Canada rise and the trade position deteriorates. One objection raised by Canadian labour leaders to the NAFTA free trade pact between the United States, Mexico, and Canada is that Canada will lose hundreds of thousands of jobs as Canadian firms invest in Mexico to take advantage of cheaper labour and then export back to the Canadian market.

The benefits of FDI to the home country arise from three sources. First, the current account of the home country's balance of payments benefits from the inward flow of foreign earnings. Thus, Starbucks' investments in Asia directly benefit the U.S. economy because it repatriates profits earned in Asia to the United States. FDI can also boost the current account of the home country's balance of payments if the foreign subsidiary creates demands for home-country exports of capital equipment, intermediate goods, complementary products, and the like.

Second, benefits to the home country from outward FDI arise from employment effects. As with the balance of payments, positive employment effects arise when the foreign subsidiary creates demand for home-country exports of capital equipment, intermediate goods, complementary products, and the like. Third, benefits arise when the home-country MNE learns valuable skills from its exposure to foreign markets that can subsequently be transferred back to the home country. This amounts to a reverse resource-transfer effect. Through its exposure to a foreign market, an MNE can learn about superior management techniques and superior product and process technologies. These resources can then be transferred back to the home country, with a commensurate beneficial effect on the home country's economic growth rate.[33] For example, one purpose behind the investment by General Motors and Ford in Japanese automobile companies (GM owns part of Isuzu, and Ford owns part of Mazda) has been for GM and Ford to learn about the apparently superior Japanese management techniques and production processes. If GM and Ford are successful in transferring this know-how back to their U.S. operations, the result may be a net gain for the U.S. economy.

HOME-COUNTRY EFFECTS: COSTS

Against these benefits must be set the apparent costs of FDI for the home (source) country. The most important concerns center around the balance of payments and employment effects of outward FDI. The home country's trade position (its current account) may deteriorate if the purpose of the foreign investment is to serve the home market from a low-cost production location. For example, when a Canadian textile company closes its plants in Quebec and moves production to Mexico, as many have, imports into Canada rise and the trade position deteriorates. The current account of the balance of payments also suffers if the FDI is a substitute for direct exports. Thus, insofar as Toyota's assembly operations in Canada are intended to substitute for direct exports from Japan, the current-account position of Japan will deteriorate.

With regard to employment effects, the most serious concerns arise when FDI is seen as a substitute for domestic production. If the labour market in the home country is already very tight, this concern may not be great. However, if the home country is suffering from high unemployment, concern about the export of jobs may rise to the fore. For example, one objection frequently raised by Canadian labour leaders to the NAFTA free trade pact between the United States, Mexico, and Canada (see the next chapter) is that Canada may lose thousands of jobs as Canadian firms invest in Mexico to take advantage of cheaper labour and then export back to the Canadian market.[34]

INTERNATIONAL TRADE THEORY AND FOREIGN DIRECT INVESTMENT

When assessing the costs and benefits of FDI to the home country, keep in mind the lessons of international trade theory (see Chapter 5). International trade theory tells us that home-country concerns about the negative economic effects of offshore production may be misplaced. The term *offshore production* refers to FDI undertaken to serve the home market. Far from reducing home-country employment, such FDI may actually stimulate economic growth (and hence employment) in the home country by freeing home-country resources to concentrate on activities where the home country has a comparative advantage. In addition, home-country consumers benefit if the price of the particular product falls as a result of the FDI. Also, if a company were prohibited from making such investments on the grounds of negative employment effects while its international competitors reaped the benefits of low-cost production locations, it would undoubtedly lose market share to its international competitors. Under such a scenario, the adverse long-run economic effects for a country would probably outweigh the relatively minor balance-of-payments and employment effects associated with offshore production.

GOVERNMENT POLICY INSTRUMENTS AND FDI

We have now reviewed the costs and benefits of FDI from the perspective of both home country and host country. Before tackling the important issue of bargaining between the MNE and the host government, we need to discuss the policy instruments governments use to regulate FDI activity by MNEs. Both home (source) countries and host countries have a range of policy instruments available. We will look at each in turn.

HOME-COUNTRY POLICIES

Through their choice of policies, home countries can both encourage and restrict FDI by local firms. We look at policies designed to encourage outward FDI first. These include foreign risk insurance, capital assistance, tax incentives, and political pressure. Then we will look at policies designed to restrict outward FDI.

Encouraging Outward FDI

Many investor nations now have government-backed insurance programs to cover major types of foreign investment risk. The types of risks insurable through these programs include expropriation (nationalization), war losses, and the inability to transfer profits home. Such programs are particularly useful in encouraging firms to undertake investments in politically unstable countries.[35] In addition, several advanced countries also have special funds or banks that make government loans to firms wishing to invest in developing countries. As a further incentive to encourage domestic firms to undertake FDI, many countries have eliminated double taxation of foreign income (i.e., taxation of income in both the host country and the home country). Last, and perhaps most significant, a number of investor countries (including the United States) have used their political influence to persuade host countries to relax their restrictions on inbound FDI. For example, in response to direct U.S. pressure, Japan relaxed many of its formal restrictions on inward FDI in the 1980s. Now, in response to further U.S. pressure, Japan moved toward relaxing its informal barriers to inward FDI. One beneficiary of this trend has been Toys "R" Us, which, after five years of intensive lobbying by company and U.S. government officials, opened its first retail stores in Japan in December 1991. By 2004, Toys "R" Us had more than 135 stores in Japan, and its Japanese operation, in which the company retained a controlling stake, had a listing on the Japanese stock exchange.

Restricting Outward FDI

Virtually all investor countries, including Canada, have exercised some control over outward FDI from time to time. One common policy has been to limit capital outflows out of concern for the country's balance of payments. From the early 1960s until 1979, for example, Great Britain had exchange-control regulations that limited the amount of capital a firm could take out of the country. Although the main intent of such policies was to improve the British balance of payments, an important secondary intent was to make it more difficult for British firms to undertake FDI.

In addition, countries have occasionally manipulated tax rules to try to encourage their firms to invest at home. The objective behind such policies is to create jobs at home rather than in other nations. At one time these policies were also adopted by Great Britain. The British advanced corporation tax system taxed British companies' foreign earnings at a higher rate than their domestic earnings. This tax code created an incentive for British companies to invest at home.

Finally, countries sometimes prohibit firms from investing in certain countries for political reasons. Such restrictions can be formal or informal. For example, formal rules prohibited U.S. firms from investing in countries such as Cuba, Libya, and Iran, whose political ideology and actions are judged to be contrary to U.S. interests. Similarly, during the 1980s, informal pressure was applied to dissuade U.S. firms from investing in South Africa. In this case, the objective was to pressure South Africa to change its apartheid laws, which occurred during the early 1990s. Thus, this policy was successful.

HOST-COUNTRY POLICIES

Host countries adopt policies designed both to restrict and to encourage inward FDI. As noted earlier in this chapter, political ideology has determined the type and scope of these policies in the past. In the last decade of the twentieth century, many countries moved quickly away from adhering to some version of the radical stance and prohibiting much FDI and toward a combination of free market objectives and pragmatic nationalism.

Encouraging Inward FDI

It is increasingly common for governments to offer incentives to foreign firms to invest in their countries. Such incentives take many forms, but the most common are tax concessions, low-interest loans, and grants or subsidies. Incentives are motivated by a desire to gain from the resource-transfer and employment effects of FDI. They are also motivated by a desire to capture FDI away from other potential host countries.

Over the past two decades, the Hollywood movie industry, including the governor of California, Arnold Schwarzenegger, has blamed Canada for the loss of jobs within its film industry. Movies and television shows have filmed in and around Vancouver and Toronto, which offer a large talent pool at a lower cost than can be found in California. Most recently, calls for investigation of Canadian government film subsidies have been raised by some high level Hollywood film industry individuals citing that the subsidies put forth by the Government of Canada amount to unfair trading practices under NAFTA. Yet there are signs this tide may be turning. The recent rise in the Canadian dollar has shifted some productions back to the United States. For example, the film version of *The Producers* was shifted from Toronto to New York, due to the rising Canadian dollar and attractive incentives offered by the City of New York.

In the mid-1990s the governments of Great Britain and France competed with each other on the incentives they offered Toyota to invest in their respective countries. In Canada, provincial governments can even compete with each other to attract FDI. For example, Ontario offered Toyota an incentive package to persuade it to build its Canadian automobile assembly plant in Cambridge.

Restricting Inward FDI

Host governments use a wide range of controls to restrict FDI in one way or another. The two most common are ownership restraints and performance requirements. Ownership restraints can take several forms. In some countries, foreign companies are excluded from specific fields. For example, they are excluded from tobacco and mining in Sweden and from the development of certain natural resources in Brazil, Finland, and Morocco. In other industries, foreign ownership may be permitted although a significant proportion of the equity of the subsidiary must be owned by local investors. For example, foreign ownership is restricted to 25 percent or less of an airline in Canada.

Foreign firms are often excluded from certain sectors on the grounds of national security or competition. Particularly in less developed countries, the belief seems to be that local firms might not be able to develop unless foreign competition is restricted by a combination of import tariffs and FDI controls. This is really a variant of the infant industry argument discussed in Chapter 6.

Also, ownership restraints seem to be based on a belief that local owners can help to maximize the resource-transfer and employment benefits of FDI for the host country. Until the early 1980s, the Japanese government prohibited most FDI but allowed joint ventures between Japanese firms and foreign MNEs if the MNE had a valuable technology. The Japanese government clearly believed such an arrangement would speed up the subsequent diffusion of the MNE's valuable technology throughout the Japanese economy.

Performance requirements can also take several forms. Performance requirements are controls over the behaviour of the MNE's local subsidiary. The most common performance requirements are related to local content, exports, technology transfer, and local participation in top management. As with certain ownership restrictions, the logic underlying performance requirements is that such rules help to maximize the benefits and minimize the costs of FDI for the host country. Virtually all countries employ some form of performance requirements when it suits their objectives. However, performance requirements tend to be more common in less developed countries than in advanced industrialized nations. For example, one study found that some 30 percent of the affiliates of U.S. MNEs in less developed countries were subject to performance requirements, while only 6 percent of the affiliates in advanced countries were faced with such requirements.[36]

ORGANIZATION FOR ECONOMIC COOPERATION AND DEVELOPMENT (OECD) A Paris-based intergovernmental organization of "wealthy" nations whose purpose is to provide its 29 member states with a forum in which governments can compare their experiences, discuss the problems they share, and seek solutions that can then be applied within their own national contexts.

INTERNATIONAL INSTITUTIONS AND THE LIBERALIZATION OF FDI

Until the 1990s, there was no consistent involvement by multinational institutions in the governing of FDI. This changed with the formation of the World Trade Organization in 1995. As noted in Chapter 6, the role of the WTO embraces the promotion of international trade in services. Because many services have to be produced where they are sold, exporting is not an option (for example, one cannot export McDonald's hamburgers or consumer banking services). Given this, the WTO has become involved in regulations governing FDI. As might be expected for an institution created to promote free trade, the thrust of the WTO's efforts has been to push for the liberalization of regulations governing FDI, particularly in services. Under the auspices of the WTO, two extensive multinational agreements were reached in 1997 to liberalize trade in telecommunications and financial services. Both these agreements contained detailed clauses that require signatories to liberalize their regulations governing inward FDI, essentially opening their markets to foreign telecommunication and financial services companies.

However, the WTO has had less success trying to initiate talks aimed at establishing a universal set of rules designed to promote the liberalization of FDI. Led by Malaysia and India, developing nations have so far rejected any attempts by the WTO to start such discussions. In an attempt to make progress on this issue, the **Organization for Economic Cooperation and Development (OECD)** in 1995 initiated talks between its members. (The OECD is a Paris-based intergovernmental organization of "wealthy" nations whose purpose is to provide its 29 member states with a forum in which governments can compare their experiences, discuss the problems they share, and seek solutions that can then be applied within their own national contexts. The members include most European Union countries, the United States, Canada, Japan, and South Korea.) The aim of the talks was to draft a **Multilateral Agreement on Investment (MAI)** that would make it illegal for signatory states to discriminate against foreign investors. This would liberalize rules governing FDI between OECD states. Unfortunately for those promoting the agreement, the talks broke down in early 1998, primarily because the United States refused to sign the agreement. According to the United States, the proposed agreement contained too many exceptions that would weaken its powers. For example, the proposed agreement would not have barred discriminatory taxation of foreign-owned companies, and it would have allowed countries to restrict foreign television programs and music in the name of preserving culture. Also campaigning against the MAI were environmental and labour groups, who criticized the proposed agreement on the grounds that it contained no binding environmental or labour agreements. Despite these problems, negotiations on a revised MAI treaty may be restarted. Also, as noted earlier, individual nations have continued to unilaterally remove restrictions to inward FDI as a wide range of countries from South Korea to South Africa try to encourage foreign firms to invest in their economies.[37]

MULTILATERAL AGREEMENT ON INVESTMENT (MAI) An agreement that would make it illegal for signatory states to discriminate against foreign investors; would have liberalized rules governing FDI between OECD states.

IMPLICATIONS FOR BUSINESS

Several implications for business are inherent in the material discussed in this chapter. We deal first with the implications of the theory, and then turn our attention to the implications of government policy.

THE THEORY OF FDI

The implications of the theories of FDI for business practice are straightforward. The location-specific-advantages argument associated with John Dunning does help explain the *direction* of FDI. However, this argument does not explain *why* firms prefer FDI to licensing, or to exporting. In this regard, from both an explanatory and a business perspective, perhaps the most useful theories are those that focus on the limitations of exporting and licensing. These theories are useful because they identify with some precision how the relative profitability of foreign direct investment, exporting, and licensing vary with circumstances. The theories suggest that exporting is preferable to licensing and foreign direct investment as long as transport costs are minor and trade barriers are trivial. As transport costs and/or trade barriers increase, exporting becomes unprofitable, and the choice is between FDI and licensing. Because FDI is more costly and more risky than licensing, other things being equal, the theories argue that licensing is preferable to FDI. Other things are seldom equal, however. Although licensing may work, it is not an attractive option when one or more of the following conditions exist: (*a*) the firm has valuable know-how that cannot be adequately protected by a licensing contract, (*b*) the firm needs tight control over a foreign entity to maximize its market share and earnings in that country, and (*c*) a firm's skills and capabilities are not amenable to licensing. Figure 7.6 presents these considerations as a decision tree.

FIGURE 7.6

A Decision Framework

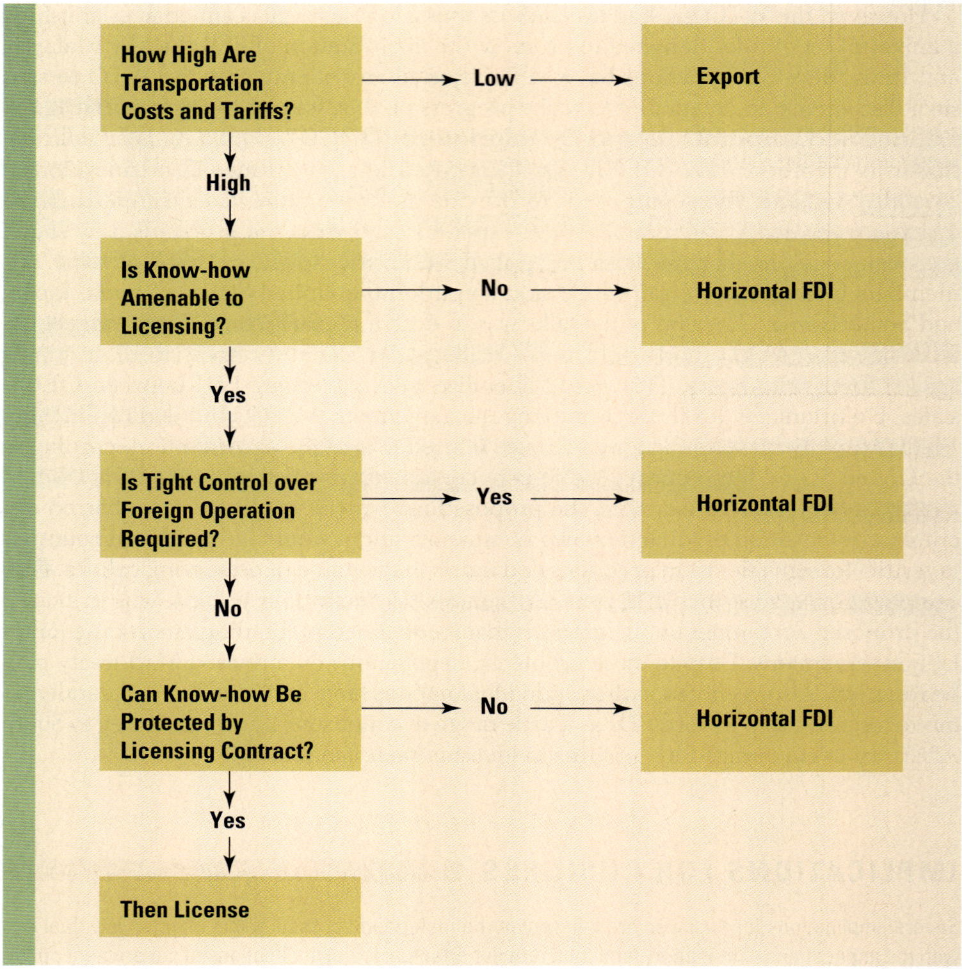

Firms for which licensing is not a good option tend to be clustered in three types of industries:

1. High-technology industries where protecting firm-specific expertise is of paramount importance and licensing is hazardous.
2. Global oligopolies, where competitive interdependence requires that multinational firms maintain tight control over foreign operations so that they can launch coordinated attacks against their global competitors (as Kodak has done with Fuji).
3. Industries where intense cost pressures require that multinational firms maintain tight control over foreign operations (so that they can disperse manufacturing to locations around the globe where factor costs are most favourable in order to minimize costs).

Although empirical evidence is limited, the majority of the evidence seems to support these conjectures.[38]

Firms for which licensing is a good option tend to be in industries whose conditions are opposite to those specified above. That is, licensing tends to be more common (and more profitable) in fragmented, low-technology industries in which globally dispersed manufacturing is not an option. A good example is the fast-food industry. McDonald's has expanded globally by using a franchising strategy. Franchising is essentially the service-industry version of licensing, although it normally involves much longer-term commitments than licensing. With franchising, the firm licenses its brand name to a foreign firm in return for a percentage of the franchisee's profits. The franchising contract specifies the conditions that the franchisee must fulfill if it is to use the franchisor's brand name. Thus, McDonald's allows foreign firms to use its brand name so long as they agree to run their restaurants on exactly the same lines as McDonald's restaurants elsewhere in the world. This strategy makes sense for McDonald's because (*a*) like many services, fast food cannot be exported, (*b*) franchising economizes the costs and risks associated with opening up foreign markets, (*c*) unlike technological know-how, brand names are relatively easy to protect using a contract, (*d*) there is no compelling reason for McDonald's to have tight control over franchisees, and (*e*) McDonald's know-how, in terms of how to run a fast-food restaurant, is amenable to being specified in a written contract (e.g., the contract specifies the details of how to run a McDonald's restaurant). As another example, Tim Hortons has expanded aggressively beyond Canada's borders by using a franchising strategy that has seen the opening of its 228th U.S. location in Rhode Island. [39]

By using a franchising strategy, McDonald's has expanded globally, but can continue to guarantee (relatively) that a Big Mac anywhere in Asia is the same as a Big Mac in Canada or the United States. Ric Ergenbright/CORBIS.

Finally, it should be noted that the product life-cycle theory and Knickerbocker's theory of FDI tend to be less useful from a business perspective. These two theories are descriptive rather than analytical. They do a good job of describing the historical evolution of FDI, but they do a relatively poor job of identifying the factors that influence the relative profitability of FDI, licensing, and exporting. The issue of licensing as an alternative to FDI is ignored by both of these theories.

GOVERNMENT POLICY

A host government's attitude toward FDI should be an important variable in decisions about where to locate foreign production facilities and where to make a foreign direct investment. Other things being equal, investing in countries that have permissive policies toward FDI is clearly preferable to investing in countries that restrict FDI. Canada's investment policies and tolerance towards FDI have evolved considerably since the early days of Pierre Elliot Trudeau's government of the 1970s, and no better indicator of this is Canada's willingness (even if not unanimous) to sign the FTA of 1988 and the subsequent 1994 NAFTA. This same recognition of the importance of international trade expansion is also evidenced in Canada's active role within the World Trade Organization.

However, often the issue is not this straightforward. Despite the move toward a free market stance in recent years, many countries still have a rather pragmatic stance toward FDI. In such cases, a firm considering FDI must often negotiate the specific terms of the investment with the country's government. Such negotiations center on two broad issues. If the host government is trying to attract FDI, the central issue is likely to be the kind of incentives the host government is prepared to offer to the MNE and what the firm will commit in exchange. If the host government is uncertain about the benefits of FDI and might restrict access, the central issue is likely to be the concessions that the firm must make to be allowed to go forward with a proposed investment.

To a large degree, the outcome of any negotiated agreement depends on the relative bargaining power of both parties. Each side's bargaining power depends on three factors:

- The value each side places on what the other has to offer.
- The number of comparable alternatives available to each side.
- Each party's time horizon.

From the perspective of a firm negotiating the terms of an investment with a host government, the firm's bargaining power is high when the host government places a high value on what the firm has to offer, the number of comparable alternatives open to the firm is greater, and the firm has a long time in which to complete the negotiations. The converse also holds. The firm's bargaining power is low when the host government places a low value on what the firm has to offer, the number of comparable alternatives open to the firm is fewer, and the firm has a short time in which to complete the negotiations.[40]

KEY TERMS

balance-of-payments accounts, p. 245

current account, p. 245

eclectic paradigm, p. 235

exporting, p. 235

externalities, p. 240

flow of FDI, p. 226

foreign direct investment (FDI), p. 226

green-field investment, p. 226

gross fixed capital formation, p. 228

inflows of FDI, p. 226

internalization theory, p. 236

licensing, p. 235

location-specific advantages, p. 239

Multilateral Agreement on Investment (MAI), p. 251

multinational enterprise (MNE), p. 226

multipoint competition, p. 238

oligopoly, p. 238

Organization for Economic Cooperation and Development (OECD), p. 251

outflows of FDI, p. 226

stock of FDI, p. 226

SUMMARY

The objectives of this chapter were to review theories that attempt to explain the pattern of FDI between countries and to examine the influence of governments on firms' decisions to invest in foreign countries. The following points have been made:

1. Any theory seeking to explain FDI must explain why firms go to the trouble of acquiring or establishing operations abroad, when the alternatives of exporting and licensing are available.
2. High transportation costs and/or tariffs imposed on imports help explain why many firms prefer FDI or licensing over exporting.
3. Firms often prefer FDI to licensing when: *(i)* a firm has valuable know-how that cannot be adequately protected by a licensing contract, *(ii)* a firm needs tight control over a foreign entity to maximize its market share and earnings in that country, and *(iii)* a firm's skills and capabilities are not amenable to licensing.
4. Knickerbocker's theory suggests that much FDI is explained by imitative behaviour by rival firms in an oligopolistic industry.
5. Vernon's product life-cycle theory suggests that firms undertake FDI at particular stages in the life cycle of products they have pioneered. However, Vernon's theory does not address the issue of whether FDI is more efficient than exporting or licensing for expanding abroad.
6. Dunning has argued that location-specific advantages are of considerable importance in explaining the nature and direction of FDI. According to Dunning, firms undertake FDI to exploit resource endowments or assets that are location specific.
7. Political ideology is an important determinant of government policy toward FDI. Ideology ranges from a radical stance that is hostile to FDI to a noninterventionist, free market stance. Between the two extremes is an approach best described as pragmatic nationalism.
8. Benefits of FDI to a host country arise from resource-transfer effects, employment effects, and balance-of-payments effects.
9. The costs of FDI to a host country include adverse effects on competition and balance of payments and a perceived loss of national sovereignty.
10. The benefits of FDI to the home (source) country include improvement in the balance of payments as a result of the inward flow of foreign earnings, positive employment effects when the foreign subsidiary creates demand for home-country exports, and benefits from a reverse resource-transfer effect. A reverse resource-transfer effect arises when the foreign subsidiary learns valuable skills abroad that can be transferred back to the home country.
11. The costs of FDI to the home country include adverse balance-of-payments effects that arise from the initial capital outflow and from the export substitution effects of FDI. Costs also arise when FDI exports jobs abroad.
12. Home countries can adopt policies designed to both encourage and restrict FDI. Host countries try to attract FDI by offering incentives and try to restrict FDI by dictating ownership restraints and requiring that foreign MNEs meet specific performance requirements.

CRITICAL THINKING AND DISCUSSION QUESTIONS

1. In the 1990s, Japanese FDI in the United States grew more rapidly than U.S. FDI in Japan. Why do you think this is the case? What are the implications of this trend?
2. Compare and contrast these explanations of FDI: internalization theory, Vernon's product life-cycle theory, and Knickerbocker's theory of FDI. Which theory do you think offers the best explanation of the historical pattern of FDI? Why?
3. Read the opening case on Starbucks. Using the market imperfections approach to FDI, explain Starbucks' approach to expanding its presence in Thailand, Canada, Great Britain, and Japan.
4. You are the international manager of a Canadian business that has just developed a revolutionary new personal computer that can perform the same functions as IBM and Apple computers and their clones but costs only half as much to manufacture. Your CEO has asked you to formulate a recommendation for how to expand into Western Europe. Your options are *(i)* to export from Canada, *(ii)* to license a European firm to manufacture and market the computer in Europe, and *(iii)* to set up a wholly owned subsidiary in Europe. Evaluate the pros and cons of each alternative and suggest a course of action to your CEO.
5. Explain how the political ideology of a host government might influence the process of negotiating access between the host government and a foreign MNE.

RESEARCH TASK | globalEDGE™ globaledge.msu.edu

Use the globalEDGE™ site to complete the following exercises:

1. The UNCTAD World Investment Report and World Investment Directory provide quick electronic access to comprehensive statistics on foreign direct investment (FDI) and the operations of transnational corporations. Gather a list of the largest transnational corporations in terms of their foreign direct investment; also, identify their home country (i.e., headquarters country). Provide a commentary about the characteristics of countries that have the greatest number of transnational firms.
2. Your company is considering opening a new factory in Latin America, and management is evaluating the specific country locations for this direct investment. The pool of candidate countries has been narrowed to Argentina, Mexico, and Brazil. Prepare a short report comparing the foreign direct investment environment and regulations of these three countries.

Visit the *Global Business Today* Online Learning Centre at **www.mcgrawhill.ca/college/hill** to access quizzes, interactive exercises, a Business Around the World interactive map, and other learning and study tools related to this chapter.

Online Learning Centre

CLOSING CASE

MANULIFE FINANCIAL BUYS JOHN HANCOCK

The normally quiet insurance industry has been going through upheavals recently due to both internal and external pressures. The most recent example of this has been Manulife Financial's purchase of John Hancock Financial Services, the largest cross-border transaction in Canadian history.

Both Manulife and John Hancock demutualized in 1999 and 2000, which is a process by which a mutual insurance company converts to being a publicly traded stock insurance company. Life insurance companies in North America, and especially in Canada, were demutualizing as a way of improving their competitive position as the financial industry underwent changes in the 1980s and 1990s. Globalization, competition from banks and other financial service providers, a weak stock market, and historically low interest rates, all effected the insurance industry.

Manulife Financial's approach was to "get big," to both benefit from economies of scale and to diversify risk by being in different markets in different countries. It already offered insurance, pension products, annuities, and mutual funds to institutional and retail customers in Canada, the United States, and Japan. It was the second largest life insurer in Canada, with revenues of over $16.5 billion (Sun Life Financial was Canada's largest insurer, with revenues of over $22 billion). However, in 2003, Manulife made a bid to acquire John Hancock Financial Services. This Boston-based company provided insurance and investment products within North America, and had Maritime Life as its Canadian subsidiary. When the merger received all of its regulatory approvals on April 28, 2004, Manulife became the largest public company, as well as the largest life insurance company, in Canada. It also became the second largest life insurer in North America, and the fifth largest in the world.

The reorganization of the company is taking place. Maritime Life is being integrated into Manulife's Canadian operations. John Hancock's president and chief executive will retire by the end of 2004, with his position being divided into a senior executive vice-president of the life insurance products and a senior executive vice-president of financial services. Both will report to president and chief executive of Manulife Financial, Dominic D'Alessandro.

The merger is thought to offer many advantages to Manulife. John Hancock's competitive position had slid for some years before it was acquired by Manulife. The company was hurt by the bankruptcy of some major bond issuers, like Enron, that Hancock held in its investment portfolio. Sales growth in its institutional investment products had slowed from 10 to 15 percent annually to zero. Finally, the company's former CEO and its board received criticism for its extensive pay packages for top managers, as the company's share price declined in value.

In 2003, Manulife, by comparison had several years of strong growth, increasing its 2002 earnings by 15 percent. The company experienced strong new sales growth while keeping a sharp eye on its expenses. The combined company is expected to have some useful synergies and benefit from economies of scale, as well as Manulife's discipline over expenses. The John Hancock name is also well known, and the company has a wide range of investment products that will benefit the newly merged company. However any corporate merger involves change, and thus some risk that the forecast benefits will not come about as quickly as may be thought.

The insurance industry still faces many challenges for this new company. Interest rates for the company's investments remain low, but are forecast to slowly improve. Fewer company bankruptcies, negatively affecting the insurance company's bond portfolio, are forecast for 2004 and 2005. Manulife's competitors in both Canada and the United States are unlikely to stand still, and will be exploring new markets and possible mergers themselves.

Sources: Standard and Poor's, "Industry Report Card: North American Life Insurance Companies," *Credit Week*, May 26, 2004; Morningstar, "John Hancock Financial Services," *Morningstar Stocks 500*; Yahoo, Corporate Profile Manulife Financial, at www.yahoo.com.

CASE DISCUSSION QUESTIONS

1. What are some competitive advantages a large company can have over a small company?
2. Can a company ever become too big to be effective? Could this happen to Manulife?
3. Is insurance a product that can be easily managed from a distance across borders? Could a smaller, local insurance company offer any meaningful advantages to customers?

PART THREE

3

CROSS-BORDER TRADE AND INVESTMENT

Changes in the European Insurance Market

During the late 1990s, a wave of mergers swept through the insurance industry in the European Union. The mergers were the result of a process begun January 1, 1993, when the Single European Act became law among the member states of the European Union. The goal of the Single European Act was to remove barriers to cross-border trade and investment within the confines of the EU, thereby creating a single market instead of a collection of distinct national markets.

Under the act, the EU insurance industry was deregulated and liberalized in mid-1994. Before that, wide variations in competitive conditions, regulations, and prices existed among the different national insurance markets. For example, in early 1994, a simple ten-year life insurance policy in Portugal cost three times more than the same policy in France, while automobile insurance for an experienced driver cost twice as much in Ireland as in Italy and four times as much as in Great Britain. The new rules did two main things. First, they made cross-border trade possible by allowing insurance companies to sell their products anywhere in the EU on the basis of regulations in their home state, the so-called single licence. Second, insurers throughout the EU were allowed to set their own rates for all classes of insurance policies. They no longer needed to submit policy wordings to local officials for approval, thereby dismantling the highly regulated regime behind which much of the industry had sheltered. Among the expected outcomes of these changes were an increase in competition and downward pressure on prices.

In 1999, the move toward a single market in the EU was given a further push by the adoption of a common currency, the euro, among a majority of the EU's member states. On January 1, 1999, 11 of the EU's 15 member states locked in their currency exchange rates against each other and began handing over responsibility for monetary policy to the newly created European Central Bank. On January 1, 2002, the currencies of the participating states were formally abolished and replaced by a common monetary unit, the euro. The introduction of the euro has made it easier for consumers to compare the insurance products offered by companies based

Annie Reynolds/PhotoLink/Getty Images.

CHAPTER 8

Regional Economic Integration

OPENING CASE

in different EU states. This should increase competition and lower prices. Also, the spread of the Internet has made it much easier for consumers to comparison shop. Insurance policies are well suited to being sold over the Internet, and the spread of this communication technology has now made it practical for a French citizen, for example, to use the Internet to buy an insurance policy from a Dutch company and pay for that policy in euros.

The initial response to the actual and impending changes in the competitive environment of the insurance industry was muted. However, by mid-1996, insurance companies were beginning to realize they needed to reposition themselves to compete more effectively in a single market dominated by a single currency. This realization resulted in a wave of mergers between firms within nations as they tried to attain the scale economies necessary to compete on a larger European playing field. In 1996, Axa and UAP, two French insurance companies, merged to create the largest European insurance company. As part of the deal, Axa gained control over several subsidiary companies that UAP had acquired in Germany in 1994, allowing Axa to increase its presence in this important market. Two large British insurance companies, Royal Insurance and Sun Alliance, also joined forces in 1996. This was followed in 1997 and early 1998 by a number of cross-border mergers, the most notable of which was between Germany's Allianz and AGF, a large French insurance company. The merger between Allianz and AGF was prompted by a takeover bid for AGF launched by the large Italian insurance company Generali. Generali wanted to acquire AGF to expand its presence in France. The bid spurred Allianz into action. Allianz, which dominates the German insurance market, had been feeling threatened by increased competition in its home market arising in part from a merger between Munich-based Hamburg–Mannheimer and Britain's Victoria Insurance and in part from the increased strength of the Axa–UAP combination. Displaying a sensitivity for French sentiments that Generali lacked, Allianz promised that AGF's management would remain French and that Allianz executives would be in the minority on the board of the merged company. Unwilling to make such concessions, Generali eventually withdrew its counterbid for AGF, but not before it had won a significant concession from Allianz and AGF. In return for withdrawing its bid, the German and French companies agreed to sell several important subsidiaries to the Italian insurer, boosting Generali's premiums by more than half and giving it a sizeable presence in both Germany and Italy.

As a result of these developments, the shape of the EU insurance industry had been substantially altered by early 2000. Allianz had emerged as the largest pan-European insurer, with $64 billion in total premium income. In addition to its leading position in Germany, Allianz had become one of the top five insurers in Belgium, Spain, and France. The Axa–UAP combination had become the second largest European insurer with significant activities in France and Germany, while Italy's Generali with premium income of $31 billion was now the third largest pan-European insurance company. The insurance market in the EU had become much more concentrated. According to one study, the seven largest insurance companies in Europe had increased their share of the EU insurance market from less than 20 percent in 1990 to more than 40 percent by 2000, with much of the increase in concentration coming about due to mergers and acquisitions. Meanwhile, companies that have remained focused on individual national markets within Europe have seen their market share decline.

Despite these changes, the EU is still some way off from having a truly single European insurance market. According to the European Commission, onerous obligations laid on by regulators in individual member states continue to make it difficult for insurance companies to market the same policy across the region. For example, various EU member states still have different policies for taxing insurance premiums, making the use of a single policy complex. As a result, while the EU insurance industry has consolidated, and pan-European companies have emerged, most policies that are written are still local. In an effort to change this, the European Commission is now pushing member states to harmonize regulations, thereby removing the last legal impediment to the emergence of a truly pan-European insurance market.

Sources: R. Lapper, "Hard Work to Be Free and Single," *Financial Times,* July 1, 1994, p. 19; "A Singular Market. In the European Union: A Survey," *The Economist,* October 22, 1994, pp. 10–16; "Insurance: Can the Empire Strike Back?" *The Economist,* April 25, 1998, p. 76; C. Adams, A. Jack, and A. Fisher, "Allianz Bid Mirrors Its Global Ambitions," *Financial Times,* November 11, 1997, p. 20; S. Shapiro, "Cross-Border Freedom Upheld," *Business Insurance,* February 21, 2000, pp. 39–41; and J. Croft, "Big Push for More Growth in Europe," *Financial Times,* April 27, 2001, p. 4.

LEARNING OBJECTIVES

1. Appreciate all the possible different levels of economic integration between nations.
2. Understand the economic and political arguments for regional economic integration.
3. Understand the economic and political arguments against regional economic integration.
4. Be familiar with the history, current scope, and future prospects of the world's most important regional economic agreements including the European Union, the North American Free Trade Agreement, MERCOSUR, and Asla-Pacific Economic Cooperation.
5. Understand the implications for business that are inherent in regional economic integration agreements.

REGIONAL ECONOMIC INTEGRATION Agreements among countries in a geographic region to reduce and ultimately remove tariff and nontariff barriers to the free flow of goods, services, and factors of production between each other.

INTRODUCTION

One notable trend in the global economy in recent years has been the accelerated movement toward regional economic integration. By **regional economic integration,** we mean agreements among countries in a geographic region to reduce, and ultimately remove, tariff and nontariff barriers to the free flow of goods, services, and factors of production between each other. The last few years have witnessed an unprecedented proliferation of regional trade arrangements. World Trade Organization members are required to notify the WTO of any regional trade agreements in which they participate. By 2004, nearly all of the WTO's 148 members had notified the organization of participation in one or more regional trade agreements. From 1948 to 1994, there were 124 notifications to the GATT of regional trade agreements. Since the creation of the WTO in 1995, more than 100 additional arrangements covering trade in goods or services have been created. Not all regional trade agreements reached in the past half century are still in force. Most of the discontinued agreements, however, have been superseded by redesigned agreements among the same signatories. Out of the more than 200 agreements or enlargements so far notified to the GATT and the WTO, some 150 are deemed to be currently in force.[1]

Nowhere has the movement toward regional economic integration been more successful than in Europe. As noted in the opening case, on January 1, 1993, the European Union effectively became a single market with 340 million consumers. Its member states launched the single currency, known as the euro in 2002 and accepted ten new members on May 1, 2004, bringing its membership ranks to 25 countries.[2] There are four candidate countries, Bulgaria, Romania, Croatia and Turkey, with Macedonia's application pending. The EUs expansion is not without its detractors, some complaining that the Europe of 15 was already fraught with difficulties before expansion. Claims that larger membership will only serve to dilute an already over-extended European budget and spirit of cohesive unity within the populous, are frequently reported by the mainstream European press.[3]

Similar moves toward regional integration are being pursued elsewhere in the world. Canada, Mexico, and the United States have implemented the North American Free Trade Agreement (NAFTA). While promises to ultimately remove all barriers to the free flow of goods and services between the three countries bode well for industry and pundits of NAFTA, these same commitments alarm NAFTA detractors who blame NAFTA for Canadian and American job losses to Mexico. Anti-free traders have also cited glaring examples of unenforced NAFTA regulations on labour laws and environmental practices. Argentina, Brazil, Paraguay, and Uruguay have implemented a 1991 agreement to start reducing barriers to trade between themselves. Known as MERCOSUR, this free trade area is viewed by some as the first step in a move toward creation of a South American Free Trade Area (SAFTA). There is also talk of establishing a hemispherewide Free Trade Agreement of the Americas (FTAA). Negotiations between 34 countries in the Americas to establish the FTAA began in 2001 and are currently scheduled to conclude in 2005. Along similar lines, 18 Pacific Rim countries, including the NAFTA member states, Japan, and China, have been discussing a possible pan-Pacific free trade area under the auspices of the Asia-Pacific Economic Cooperation forum (APEC). There are also active attempts at regional economic integration in Central America, the Andean region of South America, Southeast Asia, and parts of Africa.

As the opening case on the European insurance industry demonstrates, a move toward greater regional economic integration can potentially deliver important benefits to consumers and present firms with new challenges. In the European insurance industry, creation of a single EU insurance market opened formerly protected national markets to increased competition, which should result in lower prices for insurance products. This will benefit consumers, who will have more money to spend on other goods and services. As for insurance companies, the increase in competition and greater price pressure that has followed the creation of a single market has forced them to look for cost savings from economies of scale. They have also sought to increase their presence in different nations. The mergers occurring in the European insurance industry are seen as a way of achieving both these goals. As the opening case makes clear, however, the promise of a single market has yet to be fully attained due to the lingering persistence of regulatory differences between member states of the EU. The European Commission is tackling this issue.

The euro—the common currency for the EU member states—replaced all the different currencies across the European Union in January 2002. As you read about in the opening case, for the insurance industry, the coming of the euro helps consumers to compare insurance products, not to mention other products, offered by companies in different EU states.
AP Photo/Joerg Sarbach.

The rapid spread of regional trade agreements raises the fear among some of a world in which regional trade blocs compete against each other. In this scenario of the future, free trade will exist within each bloc, but each bloc will protect its market from outside competition with high tariffs. The specter of the EU and NAFTA turning into "economic fortresses" that shut out foreign producers with high tariff barriers is worrisome to those who believe in unrestricted free trade. If such a scenario were to materialize, the resulting decline in trade between blocs could more than offset the gains from free trade within blocs.

With these issues in mind, the main objectives of this chapter are (1) to explore the economic and political debate surrounding regional economic integration, paying particular attention to the economic and political benefits and costs of integration; (2) to review progress toward regional economic integration around the world; and (3) to map the important implications of regional economic integration for the practice of international business. Before tackling these objectives, however, we first need to examine the levels of integration that are theoretically possible.

LEVELS OF ECONOMIC INTEGRATION

Several levels of economic integration are possible in theory (see Figure 8.1). From least integrated to most integrated, they are a free trade area, a customs union, a common market, an economic union, and, finally, a full political union.

In a free trade area, all barriers to the trade of goods and services among member countries are removed. In the theoretically ideal free trade area, no discriminatory tariffs, quotas, subsidies, or administrative impediments are allowed to distort trade between members. Each country, however, is allowed to determine its own trade policies with regard to nonmembers. Thus, for example, the tariffs placed on the products of nonmember countries may vary from member to member. Free trade agreements are the most popular form of regional economic integration, accounting for almost 90 percent of regional agreements.[4]

The most enduring free trade area in the world is the European Free Trade Association (EFTA). Established in January 1960, EFTA currently joins four countries–Norway, Iceland, Liechtenstein, and Switzerland–down from seven in 1995 (three EFTA members, Austria, Finland, and Sweden, joined the EU on January 1, 1996). EFTA was founded by those Western European countries that initially decided not to be part of the European Community (the forerunner of the EU). Its original members included

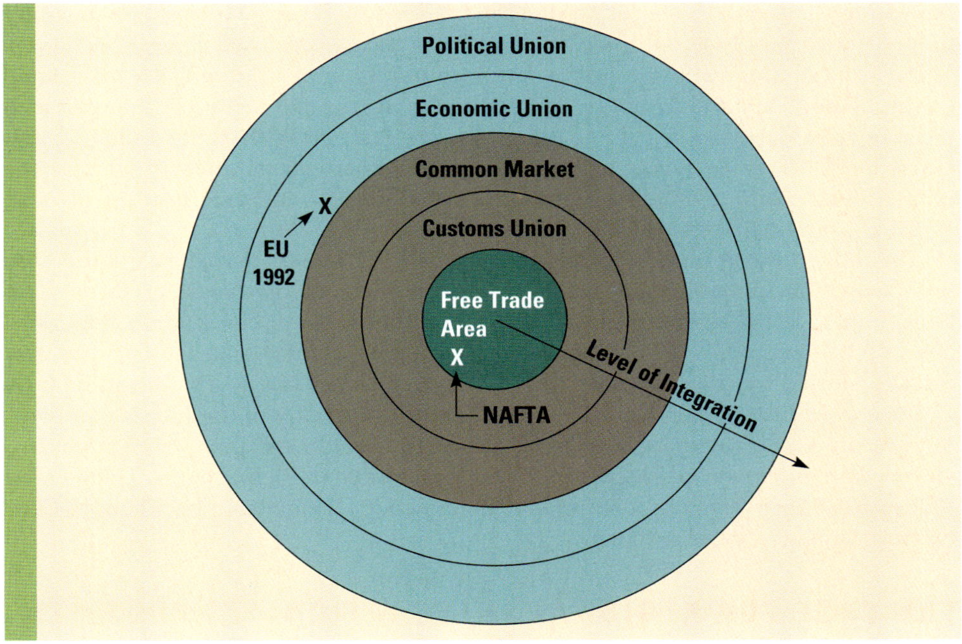

FIGURE 8.1
Levels of Economic Integration

Austria, Great Britain, Denmark, Finland, and Sweden, all of which are now members of the EU. The emphasis of EFTA has been on free trade in industrial goods. Agriculture was left out of the arrangement, each member being allowed to determine its own level of support. Members are also free to determine the level of protection applied to goods coming from outside EFTA. Other free trade areas include the North American Free Trade Agreement (NAFTA), which we shall discuss in depth later in the chapter.

The customs union is one step further along the road to full economic and political integration. A customs union eliminates trade barriers between member countries and adopts a common external trade policy. Establishment of a common external trade policy necessitates significant administrative machinery to oversee trade relations with nonmembers. Most countries that enter into a customs union desire even greater economic integration down the road. The EU began as a customs union and has moved beyond this stage. Other customs unions around the world include the current version of the Andean Pact (between Bolivia, Colombia, Ecuador, and Peru). The Andean Pact established free trade between member countries and imposes a common tariff, of 5 to 20 percent, on products imported from outside.[5]

Like a customs union, the theoretically ideal common market has no barriers to trade between member countries and a common external trade policy. Unlike a customs union, a common market also allows factors of production to move freely between members. Labour and capital are free to move because there are no restrictions on immigration, emigration, or cross-border flows of capital between member countries. Establishing a common market demands a significant degree of harmony and cooperation on fiscal, monetary, and employment policies. Achieving this degree of cooperation has proven very difficult. For years the European Union functioned as a common market, although it has now moved beyond this stage. MERCOSUR, the South America grouping of Argentina, Brazil, Paraguay, and Uruguay, hopes to eventually establish itself as a common market.

An economic union entails even closer economic integration and cooperation than a common market. Like the common market, an economic union involves the free flow of products and factors of production between member countries and the adoption of a common external trade policy. Unlike a common market, a full economic union also requires a common currency, harmonization of members' tax rates, and a common monetary and fiscal policy. Such a high degree of integration demands a coordinating bureaucracy and the sacrifice of some national sovereignty to that bureaucracy. The EU is an economic union, although an imperfect one since not all members of the EU have adopted the euro, the currency of the EU, and differences in tax rates across countries still remain.

The move toward economic union raises the issue of how to make a coordinating bureaucracy accountable to the citizens of member nations. The answer is through political union. The EU is on the road toward at least partial political union. The European Parliament, which is playing an ever more important role in the EU, has been directly elected by citizens of the EU countries since the late 1970s. In addition, the Council of Ministers (the controlling, decision-making body of the EU) is composed of government ministers from each EU member. Canada and the United States provide examples of even closer degrees of political union; in each country, independent states were effectively combined into a single nation. Ultimately, the EU may move toward a similar federal structure.

THE CASE FOR REGIONAL INTEGRATION

The case for regional integration is both economic and political but is typically not accepted by many groups within a country, which explains why most attempts to achieve regional economic integration have been contentious and halting. In this section, we examine the economic and political cases for integration and two impediments to integration. In the next section, we look at the case against integration.

THE ECONOMIC CASE FOR INTEGRATION

The economic case for regional integration is straightforward. We saw in Chapter 5 how economic theories of international trade predict that unrestricted free trade will allow countries to specialize in the production of goods and services that they can produce most efficiently. The result is greater world production than would be possible with trade restrictions. We also saw in that chapter how opening a country to free trade stimulates economic growth in the country, which creates dynamic gains from trade. Further, we saw in Chapter 7 how foreign direct investment (FDI) can transfer technological, marketing, and managerial know-how to host nations. Given the central role of knowledge in stimulating economic growth, opening a country to FDI also is likely to stimulate economic growth. In sum, economic theories suggest that free trade and investment is a positive-sum game, in which all participating countries stand to gain.

Given this, the theoretical ideal is a total absence of barriers to the free flow of goods, services, and factors of production among nations. However, as we saw in Chapters 6 and 7, a case can be made for government intervention in international trade and FDI. Because many governments have accepted part or all of the case for intervention, unrestricted free trade and FDI have proved to be only an ideal. Although international institutions such as GATT and the WTO have been moving the world toward a free trade regime, success has been less than total. In a world of many nations and many political ideologies, it is very difficult to get all countries to agree to a common set of rules.

Against this background, regional economic integration can be seen as an attempt to achieve additional gains from the free flow of trade and investment between countries beyond those attainable under international agreements such as the WTO. It is easier to establish a free trade and investment regime among a limited number of adjacent countries than among the world community. Problems of coordination and policy harmonization are largely a function of the number of countries that seek agreement. The greater the number of countries involved, the greater the number of perspectives that must be reconciled, and the harder it will be to reach agreement. Thus, attempts at regional economic integration are motivated by a desire to exploit the gains from free trade and investment.

THE POLITICAL CASE FOR INTEGRATION

The political case for regional economic integration has also loomed large in most attempts to establish free trade areas, customs unions, and the like. Linking neighbouring economies and making them increasingly dependent on each other creates incentives for political cooperation between the neighbouring states. This reduces the potential for violent conflict between the states. In addition, by grouping their economies, the countries can enhance their political weight in the world.

These considerations underlay establishment of the European Community (EC) in 1957 (the EC was the forerunner of the EU). Europe had suffered two devastating wars in the first half of the century, both arising out of the unbridled ambitions of nation-states. Those who have sought a united Europe have always had a desire to make another war in Europe unthinkable. Many Europeans also believed that after World War II the European nation-states were no longer large enough to hold their own in world markets and world politics. The need for a united Europe to deal with the United States and the politically alien Soviet Union loomed large in the minds of many of the EC's founders.[6] A long-standing joke in Europe is that the European Commission should erect a statue to Joseph Stalin, for without the aggressive policies of the former dictator of the old Soviet Union, the countries of Western Europe may have lacked the incentive to cooperate and form the EC.

IMPEDIMENTS TO INTEGRATION

Despite the strong economic and political arguments for integration, it has never been easy to achieve or sustain for two main reasons. First, although economic integration benefits the majority, it has its costs. While a nation as a whole may benefit significantly from a regional free trade agreement, certain groups may lose. Moving to a free trade regime involves some painful adjustments. For example, because of the 1994 establishment of NAFTA, some Canadian and U.S. workers in such industries as textiles, which employ low-cost, low-skilled labour, lost their jobs as Canadian and U.S. firms moved production to Mexico. The promise of significant net benefits to the Canadian and U.S. economies as a whole is little comfort to those who lose as a result of NAFTA. It is understandable then, that such groups have been at the forefront of opposition to NAFTA and will continue to oppose any widening of the agreement (see the accompanying Country Focus).

A second impediment to integration arises from concerns over national sovereignty. For example, Mexico's concerns about maintaining control of its oil interests resulted in an agreement with Canada and the United States to exempt the Mexican oil industry from any liberalization of foreign investment regulations achieved under NAFTA. Concerns about national sovereignty arise because close economic integration demands that countries give up some degree of control over such key policy issues as monetary policy, fiscal policy (e.g., tax policy), and trade policy. This has been a major stumbling block in the EU. To achieve full economic union, the EU introduced a common currency to be controlled by a central EU bank. Although most member states have signed on to such a deal, Great Britain remains an important holdout. A politically important segment of public opinion in that country opposes a common currency on the grounds that it would require relinquishing control of the country's

COUNTRY FOCUS

NAFTA AND THE U.S. TEXTILE INDUSTRY

When the North American Free Trade Agreement went into effect in 1994, many expressed fears that one consequence would be large job losses in the U.S. textile industry as companies moved production from the United States to Mexico. NAFTA opponents argued passionately, but unsuccessfully, that the treaty should not be adopted because of the negative impact it would have on employment in the United States.

A quick glance at the data available seven years after the passage of NAFTA suggests the critics had a point. Between 1993 and 2000, employment in the U.S. textile industry fell from about 1 million to 560,000, a 45 percent reduction. Over the same period, exports of garments from Mexico to the United States surged from $1.6 billion to $8.3 billion (see Figure 8.2). Such data seem to indicate that the job losses have been due to apparel production migrating from the United States to Mexico. Examples are plentiful. In 1995, Fruit of the Loom Inc., the largest manufacturer of underwear in the United States, said it would close six of its domestic plants and cut back operations at two others, laying off about 3200 workers, or 12 percent of its U.S. workforce. The company announced the closures were part of its drive to move its operations to cheaper plants abroad, particularly in Mexico. Before the closures, less than 30 percent of its sewing was done outside the United States, but Fruit of the Loom planned to move the majority of that work to Mexico. Similarly, fabric makers have been moving production to Mexico. Cone Mills of South Carolina, one of the country's largest producers of denim fabric, has reduced its U.S. employment by one-third since 1994, while investing $200 million in two new factories in Mexico. Similarly, Burlington Industries in 1999 eliminated 2900 jobs in its North Carolina fabric plants, or 17 percent of its total workforce, while investing heavily in Mexican manufacturing capability.

For textile manufacturers, Mexico's advantages include cheap labour and cheap inputs. Labour rates in Mexico average between $10 and $20 a day, compared to $10 to $12 an hour for U.S. textile workers. Another advantage for denim makers such as Cone Mills is cheap water (water is essential for dyeing cotton yarn with indigo). In Mexico, Cone Mills pays about 30 cents per cubic metre for water, about one-fifth of the rate in South Carolina. In addition, Cone Mills and other fabric makers have been locating in Mexico because many of their customers—garment makers—have already located there and being in the same region reduces transportation costs.

However, job losses in the U.S. textile industry do not mean that the overall effects of NAFTA have been negative. Clothing prices in the United States have also fallen since 1994 as textile production shifted from high-cost U.S. producers to lower-cost Mexican producers. This benefits consumers, who now have more money to spend on other items. Denim fabric, which used to sell for $3.20 per metre, now sells for $2.40 per metre. The cost of a typical pair of designer jeans, for example, fell from US$55 in 1994 to around US$48 today. In 1994, blank T-shirts wholesaled for $24 a dozen. Now they sell for $14 a dozen. Nor is the fall in prices simply a result of the movement of production from the United States to Mexico. NAFTA has also resulted in textile production being moved from Asia to Mexico. In 1980, 83 percent of all U.S. textile imports came from Asia. By 1997, Asia accounted for 41 percent of U.S. textile imports as companies switched their source of textiles from Asia to Mexico.

In addition to lower prices, the textile production shift to Mexico has also benefited the U.S. economy in other ways. First, despite the shift of fabric and apparel production to Mexico, there has been a surge in exports from U.S. fabric and yarn makers, many of which are in the chemical industry. Before the passage of NAFTA, U.S. yarn producers, such as E.I. du Pont, supplied only small amounts of fabric and yarn to Asian producers. However, as apparel production has moved from Asia to Mexico, exports of fabric and yarn to that country have surged. U.S. producers supply 70 percent of the raw material going to Mexican sewing shops. Between 1994 and 2000, U.S. fabric and yarn exports to Mexico, mostly in the form of cut pieces ready for sewing, grew from US$760 million to US$3 billion. In addition, U.S. manufacturers of textile equipment have also seen an increase in their sales as apparel factories in Mexico order textile equipment. Exports of textile equipment to Mexico nearly doubled in 2000 over the 1994 level, to US$35.5 million.

Although there have been job losses in the U.S. textile industry, advocates of NAFTA argue that there have been benefits to the U.S. economy in the form of lower clothing prices and an increase in exports from fabric and yarn producers and from producers of textile machinery, to say nothing of the gains in other sectors of the U.S. economy. Trade has been created as a result of NAFTA. The gains from trade are being captured by U.S. consumers and by producers in certain sectors. As always, the establishment of a free trade area creates winners and losers—and the losers have been employees in the textile industry—but advocates argue that the gains outweigh the losses.

Sources: C. Burritt, "Seven Years into NAFTA, Textile Makers Seek a Payoff in Mexico," *Atlanta Journal-Constitution,* December 17, 2000, p. Q1; I. McAllister, "Trade Agreements: How They Affect U.S. Textile," *Textile World,* March 2000, pp. 50–54; and J. Millman, "Mexico Weaves More Ties," *Wall Street Journal,* August 21, 2000, p. A12.

FIGURE 8.2

Canada/Mexico Textile Trade

Source: Strategis Canada Web site www.strategis.ic.gc.ca/sc_mrkti/tdst/tdo/tdo.php#tag. Reproduced with the permission of the minister of Public Works and Government Services, 2005.

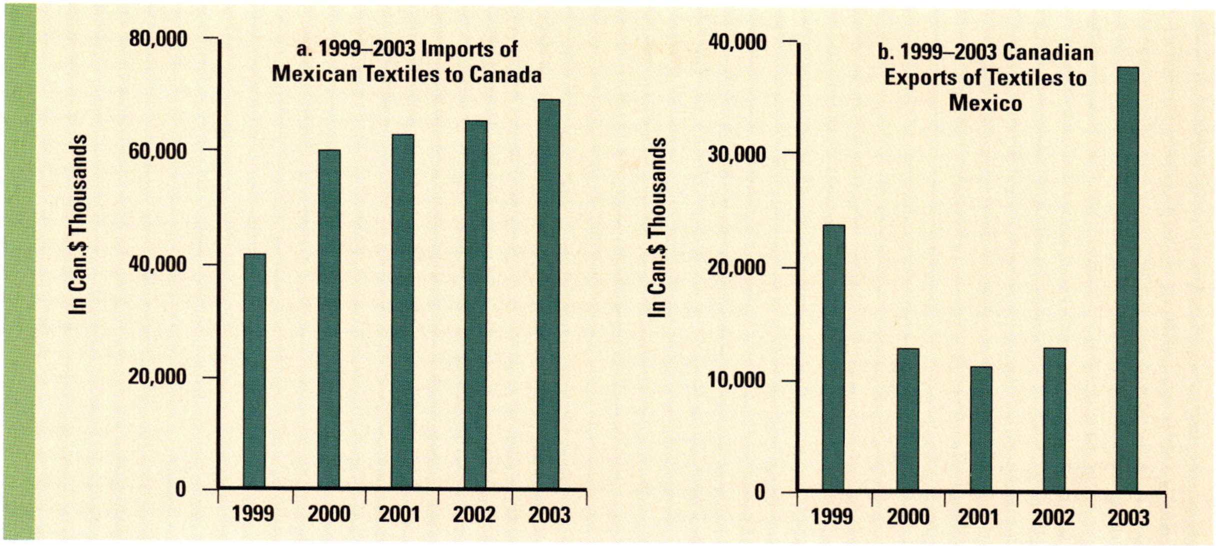

monetary policy to the EU, which many British perceive as a bureaucracy run by foreigners. In 1992, the British won the right to opt out of any single currency agreement, and as of 2002, the British government had yet to reverse its decision.

THE CASE AGAINST REGIONAL INTEGRATION

Although the tide has been running strongly in favour of regional free trade agreements in recent years, some economists have expressed concern that the benefits of regional integration have been oversold, while the costs have often been ignored.[7] They point out that the benefits of regional integration are determined by the extent of trade creation, as opposed to trade diversion. **Trade creation** occurs when high-cost domestic producers are replaced by low-cost producers within the free trade area. It may also occur when higher-cost external producers are replaced by lower-cost external producers within the free trade area (see the accompanying Country Focus for an example). **Trade diversion** occurs when lower-cost external suppliers are replaced by higher-cost suppliers within the free trade area. A regional free trade agreement will benefit the world only if the amount of trade it creates exceeds the amount it diverts.

TRADE CREATION
Trade created due to regional economic integration; occurs when high-cost domestic producers are replaced by low-cost foreign producers in a free trade area.

Suppose Canada and Mexico imposed tariffs on imports from all countries, and then they set up a free trade area, scrapping all trade barriers between themselves but maintaining tariffs on imports from the rest of the world. If Canada began to import textiles from Mexico, would this change be for the better? If Canada previously produced all its own textiles at a higher cost than Mexico, then the free trade agreement has shifted production to the cheaper source. According to the theory of comparative advantage, trade has been created within the regional grouping, and there would be no decrease in trade with the rest of the world. Clearly, the change would be for the better. If, however, Canada previously imported textiles from Costa Rica, which produced them more cheaply than either Mexico or Canada, then trade has been diverted from a low-cost source–a change for the worse. The Management Focus discusses NAFTA after ten years.

TRADE DIVERSION
Trade diverted due to regional economic integration; occurs when low-cost foreign suppliers outside a free trade area are replaced by higher-cost foreign suppliers in a free trade area.

In theory, WTO rules should ensure that a free trade agreement does not result in trade diversion. These rules allow free trade areas to be formed only if the members

MANAGEMENT FOCUS

NAFTA—FRIEND OR FOE OF CANADIAN BUSINESS?

January 1, 2004 heralded a significant milestone in trade and economic relations among Canada, the United States, and Mexico. NAFTA turned ten. NAFTA forms the world's largest trading bloc with a gross domestic product (GDP) of US$11.4 trillion, or one third of the world's total GDP.

The North American Free Trade Agreement (NAFTA), like all free trade entities, has seen its share of critics and fans, individual, corporate, and government alike. On the one hand, it is viewed to be the root cause of job exoduses from Canada to Mexico. Yet on the other hand, it is seen to be a vehicle for universal prosperity for all within its realm. These same types of pro and con feelings permeate the worlds of free trade negotiations. The negotiations among the 34 member nations in the western hemisphere of the Free Trade Agreement of the Americas are expected to conclude in January 2005, and these have not been without drama. The stakes are equally high for countries, individuals, and companies.

Canada's anti-free trade crusaders, including Maude Barlow have lambasted NAFTA's alleged poor track record on a multitude of issues ranging from worsening environmental standards to job losses to Mexico's **maquilladoras** while Canadian government officials have praised the merits of the agreement.

Small and large businesses have and will continue to fail indirectly or directly as a result of NAFTA. Then again, before NAFTA businesses either succeeded or failed. Competitive advantage makes a business survive and succeed and an inability to adapt makes it stall and end.

For consumers in all three countries, NAFTA increasingly provides more choices at competitive prices. Lower tariffs mean that families pay less for the products they buy and have a greater selection of goods and services, which increases their standard of living.

Snapshots of the success stories of NAFTA abound and two Canadian companies' success stories unfold.

Baultar Inc., www.baultar.com/, of Windsor, Quebec, manufactures and designs flooring and related products for two markets: passenger transportation (such as subways and commuter rail) and commercial buildings (loading docks, entrance ways, and stairwells). Mexico has been a major market for the company. In order to strengthen its competitive position, Baultar transferred its manufacturing and installation expertise to a Mexican company. Thanks to this partnership, the company landed a major contract with the STC (Sistema de Transporte Colectivo). Baultar's activities in Mexico were supported by Export Development Canada (EDC) and Canada's Trade Commissioner Service. Baultar's foray into the Mexican market was assisted by a team of Canadian government officials, assisting the company through the labyrinth of export details for setting up a green-field operation in Mexico.

Outside of Mexico, Baultar has supplied flooring to transit systems in Vancouver, Toronto, Cleveland, Philadelphia, New York, Baltimore, Singapore, Johannesburg, and Paris. It has also undertaken a study to extend the life of the commuter cars in Capetown. "The cars are (were) 40 years old and severely corroded from the use of dissimilar metals on the structure, from water ingress at missing doors and windows, and from the lack of adequate protection from wash water and acid rain." The suggested repairs and new flooring would extend car life by at least 25 years.

Another "star" is Eggplant Interactive, www.eggplantinteractive.com/, of Regina, Saskatchewan, is yet another Canadian company that has increased its business within the NAFTA framework. In many ways, the digital world makes going global that much easier.

For Eggplant Interactive, the digital division of the Phoenix Group—one of the largest full-service communications agencies in Saskatchewan—offering its services to the United States is a natural progression. The company, which specializes in digital strategy, programming, and online design currently services clients across Canada and in local markets across the United States. The company hopes to use these first forays into the U.S. market as a base to expand across the continent.

Like many companies, much of Eggplant Interactive's growth has come through word of mouth. "With the help of our contacts at the Department of Foreign Affairs and International Trade, new networking opportunities have arisen, and they will be key to more business wins south of the border," says Pam Klein, vice-president of Eggplant Interactive.

Ability combined with willingness to adjust to new competitive situations is paramount to staying afloat in today's dynamic business world. Coupled with the abundance of readily available Canadian government export advisory and financial services, Canadian companies are testing their mettle in new markets.

Sources: International Trade Canada, "Why Trade Matters," at www.dfait-maeci.gc.ca/tna-nac/stories74-en.asp; SBA Online Women's Business Centre at www.onlinewbc.gov/docs/market/Expanding_Your_Reach.html; Baulter Inc. at www.baultar.com/eng/achievements/Achievements_Detail.aspx?sID=5; Eggplant Interactive at www.eggplantinteractive.com/.

set tariffs that are not higher or more restrictive to outsiders than the ones previously in effect. However, as we saw in Chapter 6, GATT and the WTO do not cover some nontariff barriers. As a result, regional trade blocs could emerge whose markets are protected from outside competition by high nontariff barriers. In such cases, the trade diversion effects might outweigh the trade creation effects. The only way to guard against this possibility, according to those concerned about this potential, is to increase the scope of the WTO so it covers nontariff barriers to trade. There is no sign that this is going to occur anytime soon, however; so the risk remains that regional economic integration will result in trade diversion.

MAQUILLADORAS
NAFTA-related Mexican work zones of cheap labour that are commonly found along the Texas-Mexico border.

REGIONAL ECONOMIC INTEGRATION IN EUROPE

Europe has two trade blocs–the European Union and the European Free Trade Association. Of the two, the EU is by far the more significant, not just in terms of membership (the EU has 25 members, and EFTA has four), but also in terms of economic and political influence in the world economy. Many now see the EU as an emerging economic and political superpower of the same order as the United States and Japan. Accordingly, we will concentrate our attention on the EU.[8]

EVOLUTION OF THE EUROPEAN UNION

The EU is the product of two political factors: (1) the devastation of two world wars on Western Europe and the desire for a lasting peace, and (2) the European nations' desire to hold their own on the world's political and economic stage.

The original forerunner of the EU, the European Coal and Steel Community, was formed in 1951 by Belgium, France, West Germany, Italy, Luxembourg, and the Netherlands. Its objective was to remove barriers to intragroup shipments of coal, iron, steel, and scrap metal. With the signing of the Treaty of Rome in 1957, the European Community was established. The name changed again in 1994 when the European Community became the European Union following the ratification of the Maastricht Treaty (discussed later).

The Treaty of Rome provided for the creation of a common market. Article 3 of the treaty laid down the key objectives of the new community, calling for the elimination of internal trade barriers and the creation of a common external tariff and requiring member states to abolish obstacles to the free movement of factors of production among the members. To facilitate the free movement of goods, services, and factors of production, the treaty provided for any necessary harmonization of the member states' laws. Furthermore, the treaty committed the EC to establish common policies in agriculture and transportation.

The EU is composed of 15 member states representing 374 million people (year of entry in brackets): Belgium (1950); Germany (1950); France (1950); Italy (1950); Luxembourg (1950); the Netherlands (1950); Denmark (1973); Ireland (1973); United Kingdom (1973); Greece (1981); Spain (1986); Portugal (1986); Austria (1995); Finland (1995) and Sweden (1995).

The ten nations that joined on May 1, 2004, were the Greek sector of Cyprus, the Czech Republic, Estonia, Hungary, Latvia, Lithuania, Malta, Poland, Slovakia, and Slovenia. On April 24, 2004, Greek Cypriots in the south of the country rejected reunification with the Turkish north, meaning only the Greek sector will be eligible for entry into the EU. Turkish Cypriots, with a population of 450 million in 2005, backed the proposal.

Bulgaria and Romania are expected to join in 2007. The European Council was to decide by the end of 2004 whether to begin membership negotiations with Turkey.

Croatia applied for EU membership in February 2003, and the former Yugoslav republic of Macedonia applied in March 2004.[9] (See Map 8.1.)

POLITICAL STRUCTURE OF THE EUROPEAN UNION

The economic policies of the EU are formulated and implemented by a complex and still-evolving political structure. The five main institutions in this structure are the European Council, the Council of Ministers, the European Commission, the European Parliament, and the Court of Justice.[10]

The European Council is composed of the heads of state of the EU's member nations and the president of the European Commission. Each head of state is normally accompanied by a foreign minister to these meetings. The European Council meets at least twice a year and often resolves major policy issues and sets policy directions.

The European Commission is responsible for proposing EU legislation, implementing it, and monitoring compliance with EU laws by member states. Headquartered in Brussels, Belgium, the commission has more than 10 000 employees. It is run by a group of 20 commissioners appointed by each member country for four-year renewable terms. Most countries appoint only one commissioner, although the most populated states–Great Britain, France, Germany, Italy, and Spain–appoint two each. A president and six vice-presidents are chosen from among these commissioners for two-year renewable terms. The commission has a monopoly in proposing European Union legislation. The

MAP 8.1
European Union Countries
Source: Reproduced with permission of the European Communities from www.eurunion.org/legislat/agd2000/agd2000.htm.

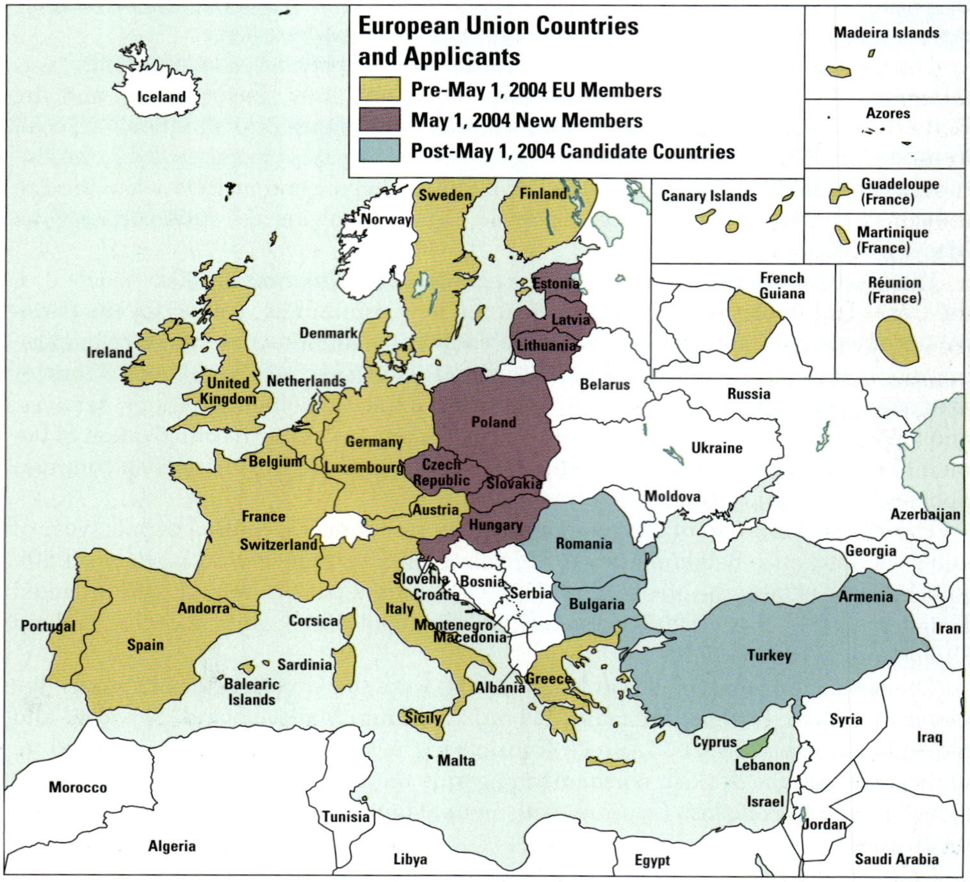

commission starts the legislative ball rolling by making a proposal, which goes to the Council of Ministers and then to the European Parliament. The Council of Ministers cannot legislate without a commission proposal in front of it. The commission is also responsible for implementing aspects of EU law, although in practice much of this must be delegated to member states. Another responsibility of the commission is to monitor member states to make sure they are complying with EU laws. In this policing role, the commission will normally ask a state to comply with any EU laws that are being broken. If this persuasion is not sufficient, the commission can refer a case to the Court of Justice.

The European Commission's role in competition policy has become increasingly important to business in recent years. Since 1990 when the office was formally assigned a role in competition policy, the EU's competition commissioner has been steadily gaining influence as the chief regulator of competition policy in the 15 member nations of the EU. As with the Canadian Competition Tribunal (Competition Act, R.S. 1985, c. C-34), which includes the Canadian Department of Justice, the role of the European Competition Commissioner is to ensure that no one enterprise uses its market power to drive out competitors and monopolize markets.[11] The Commissioner also reviews proposed mergers and acquisitions to make sure they do not create a dominant enterprise with substantial market power. Between 1990 and 2004, the commission reviewed over 2500 cases. During this time, 18 cases were rejected.[12] For example, in 2000 a proposed merger between Time Warner of the United States and EMI of the United Kingdom, both music recording companies, was withdrawn after the commission expressed concerns that the merger would reduce the number of major record companies from five to four and create a dominant player in the $40-billion global music industry. Similarly, the commission blocked a proposed merger between two U.S. telecommunication companies, WorldCom and Sprint, because their combined holdings of Internet infrastructure in Europe would give the merged companies so much market power that the commission argued the combined company would dominate that market.

The Council of Ministers represents the interests of member states. It is clearly the ultimate controlling authority within the EU since draft legislation from the commission can become EU law only if the council agrees. The council is composed of one representative from the government of each member state. The membership, however, varies depending on the topic being discussed. When agricultural issues are being discussed, the agriculture ministers from each state attend council meetings; when transportation is being discussed transportation ministers attend, and so on. Before 1993, all council issues had to be decided by unanimous agreement between member states. This often led to marathon council sessions and a failure to make progress or reach agreement on proposals submitted from the commission. In an attempt to clear the resulting logjams, the Single European Act formalized the use of majority voting rules on issues "which have as their object the establishment and functioning of a single market." Most other issues, however, such as tax regulations and immigration policy, still require unanimity among council members if they are to become law.

The European Parliament, which now has about 700 members, is directly elected by the populations of the member states. The parliament, which meets in Strasbourg, France, is primarily a consultative rather than legislative body. It debates legislation proposed by the commission and forwarded to it by the council. It can propose amendments to that legislation, which the commission and ultimately the council are not obliged to take up but often will. The power of the parliament recently has been increasing, although not by as much as parliamentarians would like. The European Parliament now has the right to vote on the appointment of commissioners and has veto power over some laws (such as the EU budget and single-market legislation).

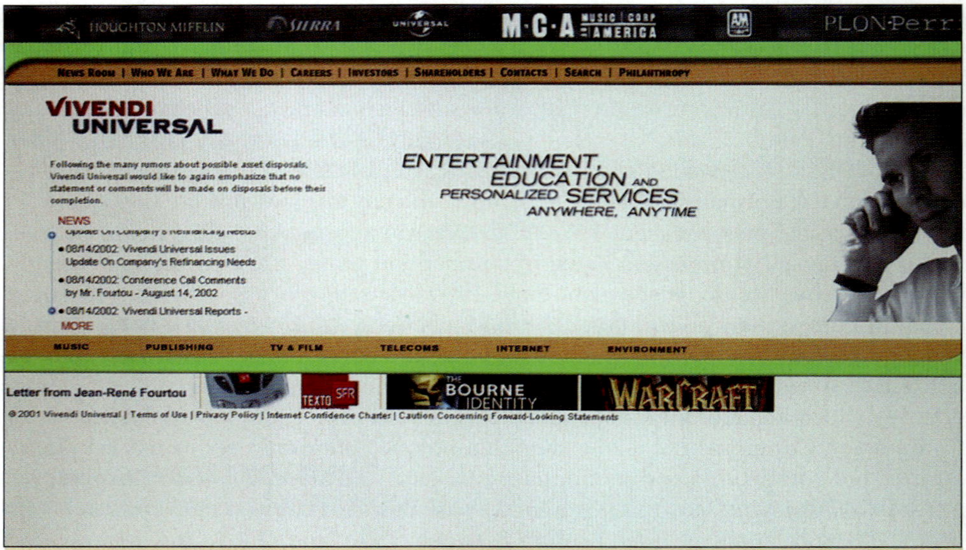

Although the Vivendi/Seagram deal came to fruition, by August of 2002, there was talk of the media giant selling off some of its pieces. Note the paragraph here on Vivendi's website: "Following the many rumors about possible asset disposals, Vivendi Universal would like to again emphasize that no statement or comments will be made on disposals before their completion." Visuals Unlimited.

The Court of Justice, which is comprised of one judge from each country, is the supreme appeals court for EU law. Like commissioners, the judges are required to act as independent officials, rather than as representatives of national interests. The commission or a member country can bring other members to the court for failing to meet treaty obligations. Similarly, member countries, companies, or institutions can bring the commission or council to the court for failure to act according to an EU treaty.

THE SINGLE EUROPEAN ACT

Two revolutions occurred in Europe in the late 1980s. The first was the collapse of communism in Eastern Europe. The second revolution was much quieter, but its impact on Europe and the world may have been just as profound as the first. It was the 1987 adoption of the Single European Act by the EC member nations. This act committed the EC countries to work toward establishment of a single market by December 31, 1992.

The Stimulus for the Single European Act

The Single European Act was born of a frustration among EC members that the community was not living up to its promise. By the early 1980s, it was clear that the EC had fallen short of its objectives to remove barriers to the free flow of trade and investment between member countries and to harmonize the wide range of technical and legal standards for doing business.

Against this background, many of the EC's prominent businesspeople mounted an energetic campaign in the early 1980s to end the EC's economic divisions. The EC responded by creating the Delors Commission. Under the chairmanship of Jacques Delors, the former French finance minister and president of the EC Commission, the Delors Commission produced a discussion paper in 1985 proposing that all impediments to the formation of a single market be eliminated by December 31, 1992. The result was the Single European Act, which was independently ratified by the parliaments of each member country and became EC law in 1987.

The Objectives of the Act

The purpose of the Single European Act was to have a single market in place by December 31, 1992. The act proposed the following changes:[13]

- Remove all frontier controls between EC countries, thereby abolishing delays and reducing the resources required for complying with trade bureaucracy.
- Apply the principle of "mutual recognition" to product standards. A standard developed in one EC country should be accepted in another, provided it meets basic requirements in such matters as health and safety.
- Open public procurement to nonnational suppliers, reducing costs directly by allowing lower-cost suppliers into national economies and indirectly by forcing national suppliers to compete.
- Lift barriers to competition in the retail banking and insurance businesses, which should drive down the costs of financial services, including borrowing, throughout the EC.
- Remove all restrictions on foreign exchange transactions between member countries by the end of 1992.
- Abolish restrictions on cabotage–the right of foreign truckers to pick up and deliver goods within another member state's borders–by the end of 1992. Estimates suggested this would reduce the cost of haulage within the EC by 10 to 15 percent.

All those changes were predicted to lower the costs of doing business in the EC, but the single-market program was also expected to have more complicated supply-side effects. To signify the importance of the Single European Act, the European Community also decided to change its name to the European Union once the act took effect. If the EU is successful in establishing a single market, the member countries can expect significant gains from the free flow of trade and investment.

THE ESTABLISHMENT OF THE EURO

In December 1991, leaders of the EC member states met in Maastricht, the Netherlands, to discuss the next steps for the EC. The results of the Maastricht meeting surprised both Europe and the rest of the world. For months the EC countries had been fighting over the issue of a common currency. Although many economists believed a common currency was required to cement a closer economic union, deadlock had been predicted. The British in particular had opposed any attempt to establish a common currency. Instead, the 12 members signed a treaty that committed them to adopting a common currency by January 1, 1999, and paved the way for closer political cooperation.

The treaty laid down the main elements, if only in embryo, of a future European government: a single currency–the euro–a common foreign and defence policy, a common citizenship, and an EU parliament with teeth. It is now just a matter of waiting, some believe, for history to take its course and a "United States of Europe" to emerge. Of more immediate interest are the implications for business of the establishment of a single currency.[14]

The euro currency unit is now used by 12 of the 15 member states of the European Union; these 12 states are now members of what is often referred to as the euro zone. The establishment of the euro has rightly been described as an amazing political feat. There are few precedents for what the Europeans are doing. Establishing the euro required the participating national governments not only to give up their own currencies, but also to give up control over monetary policy. Governments do not routinely sacrifice national sovereignty for the greater good, indicating the importance that the Europeans attach to the euro. By adopting the euro, the EU has created the second largest currency zone in the world after that of the U.S. dollar. Some believe that ultimately the euro could come to rival the dollar as the most important currency in the world.

For now three EU countries, Britain, Denmark, and Sweden, are still sitting on the sidelines, although there is speculation that Great Britain and Sweden may join. The 12 countries agreeing to the euro locked their exchange rates against each other January 1, 1999. Euro notes and coins were not actually issued until January 1, 2002. In the interim, national currencies circulated in each of the 12 countries. However, in each participating state the national currency stood for a defined amount of euros. After January 1, 2002, euro notes and coins were issued and the national currencies were taken out of circulation. By mid-2002, all prices and routine economic transactions within the euro zone were in euros.

Benefits of the Euro

Europeans decided to establish a single currency in the EU for a number of reasons. First, they believe that business and individuals will realize significant savings from having to handle one currency, rather than many. These savings come from lower foreign exchange and hedging costs.

Second, and perhaps more importantly, the adoption of a common currency will make it easier to compare prices across Europe. This should increase competition because it will be much easier for consumers to shop around.

Third, faced with lower prices, European producers will be forced to look for ways to reduce their production costs to maintain their profit margins. The introduction of a common currency, by increasing competition, should ultimately produce long-run gains in the economic efficiency of European companies.

Fourth, the introduction of a common currency should give a strong boost to the development of a highly liquid pan-European capital market. Such a capital market should lower the cost of capital and lead to an increase in both the level of investment and the efficiency with which investment funds are allocated. This could be especially helpful to smaller companies that have historically had difficulty borrowing money from domestic banks. For example, the capital market of Portugal is very small and illiquid, which makes it extremely difficult for bright Portuguese entrepreneurs with a good idea to borrow money at a reasonable price. However, in theory, such companies should soon be able to tap a much more liquid pan-European capital market. Now Europe has no continentwide capital market, such as the NASDAQ market in the United States, that funnels investment capital to dynamic young growth companies. The euro's introduction could facilitate establishment of such a market. The long-run benefits of such a development should not be underestimated.

Finally, the development of a pan-European euro-denominated capital market will increase the range of investment options open to both individuals and institutions. For example, it will now be much easier for individuals and institutions based in, let's say, Holland to invest in Italian or French companies. This will enable European investors

ANOTHER PERSPECTIVE

The Euro conversion and tipping the taxi driver

Twelve countries of the European Union (EU) have now converted to a single currency, the euro (€). This common currency makes trade and travel across national borders much easier. The conversion to a single currency market has had unexpected effects. With the Greek drachma, it used to be that an acceptable tip on a taxi fare of 10,000 drachma (about US$25.00) would be about 100 drachma (about US$.25). Yet in today's euro world, leaving a tip of €.25 (also around US$.25) would be insulting. In fact, the acceptable tip is €1.00, which makes taxi drivers quite happy. Their tip has increased by 300 percent.

to better diversify their risk, which again lowers the cost of capital and should also increase the efficiency with which capital resources are allocated.[15]

Costs of the Euro

The drawback, for some, of a single currency is that national authorities have lost control over monetary policy. Thus, it is crucial to ensure that the EU's monetary policy is well managed. The Maastricht Treaty called for establishment of an independent European Central Bank (ECB), similar in some respects to the U.S. Federal Reserve, with a clear mandate to manage monetary policy so as to ensure price stability. The ECB, based in Frankfurt, is meant to be independent from political pressure, although critics question this. Among other things, the ECB sets interest rates and determines monetary policy across the euro zone. The implied loss of national sovereignty to the ECB underlies the decision by Great Britain, Denmark, and Sweden to stay out of the euro zone for now. In these countries, many are suspicious of the ECB's ability to remain free from political pressure and to keep inflation under control. In theory, the design of the ECB should ensure that it remains free of political pressure. The ECB is modelled on the German Bundesbank, which historically has been the most independent and successful central bank in Europe. The Maastricht Treaty prohibits the ECB from taking orders from politicians. The executive board of the bank, which consists of a president, vice-president, and four other members, carries out policy by issuing instructions to national central banks. The policy itself is determined by the governing council, which consists of the executive board plus the central bank governors from the 12 euro zone countries. The governing council votes on interest rate changes. Members of the executive board are appointed for eight-year nonrenewable terms, insulating them from political pressures to get reappointed. Nevertheless, the jury is still out on the issue of the ECB's independence, and it will take some time for the bank to establish its inflation-fighting credentials.

According to critics, another drawback of the euro is that the EU is not what economists would call an optimal currency area. In an optimal currency area, similarities in the underlying structure of economic activity make it feasible to adopt a single currency and use a single exchange rate as an instrument of macroeconomic policy. Many of the European economies in the euro zone, however, are very dissimilar. For example, Finland and Portugal are very dissimilar economies. The structure of economic activity within each country is very different. They have different wage rates and tax regimes, different business cycles, and may react very differently to external economic shocks. A change in the euro exchange rate that helps Finland may hurt Portugal. Obviously, such differences complicate macroeconomic policy. For example, when euro economies are not growing in unison, a common monetary policy may mean that interest rates are too high for depressed regions and too low for booming regions. It will be interesting to see how the EU copes with the strains caused by such divergent economic performance.

One way of dealing with such divergent effects within the euro zone might be for the EU to engage in fiscal transfers, taking money from prosperous regions and pumping it into depressed regions. Such a move, however, would open a political can of worms. Would the citizens of Germany forgo their "fair share" of EU funds to create jobs for underemployed Portuguese workers?

Several critics believe that the euro puts the economic cart before the political horse. In their view, a single currency should follow, not precede, political union. They argue that the euro will unleash enormous pressures for tax harmonization and fiscal transfers from the center, both policies that cannot be pursued without the appropriate political structure. The most apocalyptic vision that flows from these negative views is that far from stimulating economic growth, as its advocates claim, the euro will lead to lower economic growth and higher inflation within Europe. To quote one critic:

> Imposing a single exchange rate and an inflexible exchange rate on countries that are characterized by different economic shocks, inflexible wages, low labor mobility, and separate national fiscal systems without significant cross-border fiscal transfers will raise the overall level of cyclical unemployment among EMU members. The shift from national monetary policies dominated by the (German) Bundesbank within the European Monetary System to a European Central Bank governed by majority voting with a politically determined exchange rate policy will almost certainly raise the average future rate of inflation.[16]

The Early Experience

In the first 30 months of its existence, the euro did not live up to expectations of all its supporters. In January 1999, the euro was trading at 1 euro = $1.17. By late November of that year, the value of the euro had slumped to 1 euro = $1. Although it recovered slightly in December, by the end of the year the euro had still lost 15 percent of its value against the U.S. dollar and was also down significantly against the Japanese yen. The slide continued in 2000, and by fall 2000 the euro was trading at 0.885 = $1, representing a decline against the dollar of more than 20 percent. It stayed in that range during much of 2001 before recovering to around 1 euro = $1 in mid-2002.

Critics were quick to claim that the fall in the euro demonstrated the foreign exchange market's lack of confidence in the ability of the ECB to effectively manage monetary policy. However, there are no signs that the ECB is mismanaging monetary policy in the euro zone.[17] Inflationary pressures seem to be under control, the ECB seems to have managed interest rates with some skill, and there is no sign that the ECB is bowing to political pressure. Initially the decline in the value of the euro was attributed to two factors: the growth differential and the interest rate differential between the United States and the European Union.[18] During 1999 and 2000, U.S. economic growth was higher than growth in the euro zone, while U.S. interest rates were higher than interest rates on euros. Given the growth and interest rate differential, internationally mobile capital flowed out of Europe and toward the United States in anticipation of higher returns. This increased demand for dollars, decreased demand for euros, and resulted in a depreciation of the euro against the dollar.

However, by mid-2001, these factors were no longer relevant. Economic growth in the United States had slowed to less than that in Europe, and the Federal Reserve had aggressively reduced U.S. interest rates, and yet the dollar remained strong relative to the euro. Why? One explanation is that in times of economic uncertainty, the dollar retains its role as a "safe haven" currency, and 2001 was a time of significant economic uncertainty with some predicting the world was entering a recession. Another explanation is that investors still expect the U.S. economy to emerge from the 2001 economic slowdown ahead of Europe, and so they continue to hold dollars.[19] Whatever the reason for the decline in the value of the euro, one thing remains clear–it is still too early to judge whether the ECB is doing a good job, and whether the euro is a success. That will take several more years. Indeed, by mid-2002, the dollar was starting to weaken against the euro as turmoil in U.S. financial markets drove foreign investors out of dollars and into other currencies, such as the Japanese yen and the euro.

FORTRESS EUROPE?

One concern often voiced by commentators in the United States and Asian countries is that the EU at some point will impose new barriers on imports from outside the EU.

The fear is that the EU might increase external protection as weaker member states attempt to offset their loss of protection against other EU countries by arguing for limitations on outside competition.

In theory, given the free market philosophy that underpins the Single European Act, this should not occur. In October 1988, the European Commission debated external trading policy and published a detailed statement of the EC's trading intentions in the post-1992 era.[20] The commission stressed the EC's interests in vigorous external trade. In 2001, exports by EU countries to non-European countries amounted to 19 percent of world trade in goods and 24 percent of world trade in services.[21] It is not in the EU's interests to adopt a protectionist stance, given the reliance on external trade. The commission has also promised loyalty to GATT and WTO rules on international trade. As for the types of trade not covered by the WTO, the EU states it will push for reciprocal access. The EU has stated that in certain cases it might replace individual national trade barriers with EU protection against imports, but it also has promised that the overall level of protection would not rise.

Despite such reassurances, there is no guarantee that the EU will not adopt a protectionist stance toward external trade. However, in a published report on the issue, the WTO stated that the growth of regional trade groups such as the EU has not impeded the growth of freer world trade, as some fear, and may have helped to promote it.[22]

REGIONAL ECONOMIC INTEGRATION IN THE AMERICAS

No other attempt at regional economic integration comes close to the EU in its boldness or its potential implications for the world economy, but regional economic integration is on the rise in the Americas. The most significant attempt is the North American Free Trade Agreement. In addition to NAFTA, several other trade blocs are in the offing in the Americas (see Map 8.2), the most significant of which appear to be the Andean Group and MERCOSUR. There are also plans to establish a hemispherewide Free Trade Area of the Americas (FTAA) by late 2005.

THE NORTH AMERICAN FREE TRADE AGREEMENT

The governments of the United States and Canada in 1988 agreed to enter into a free trade agreement, which took effect January 1, 1989. The agreement's goal was to eliminate all tariffs on bilateral trade between Canada and the United States by 1998. This was followed in 1991 by talks among the United States, Canada, and Mexico aimed at establishing a North American Free Trade Agreement for the three countries. The talks concluded in August 1992 with an agreement in principle, and by late 1993, the agreement had been ratified by the governments of all three countries.

NAFTA's Contents

The agreement became law January 1, 1994.[23] The contents of NAFTA include the following:

- Abolition within ten years of tariffs on 99 percent of the goods traded between Mexico, Canada, and the United States.
- Removal of most barriers on the cross-border flow of services, allowing financial institutions, for example, unrestricted access to the Mexican market by 2000.
- Protection of intellectual property rights.

MAP 8.2

Economic Integration in the Americas

Source: From "All in the Family," *The Economist,* April 21, 2001. Copyright © 2001 The Economist Newspaper Ltd. All rights reserved. Reprinted with permission. Further reproduction prohibited. www.economist.com.

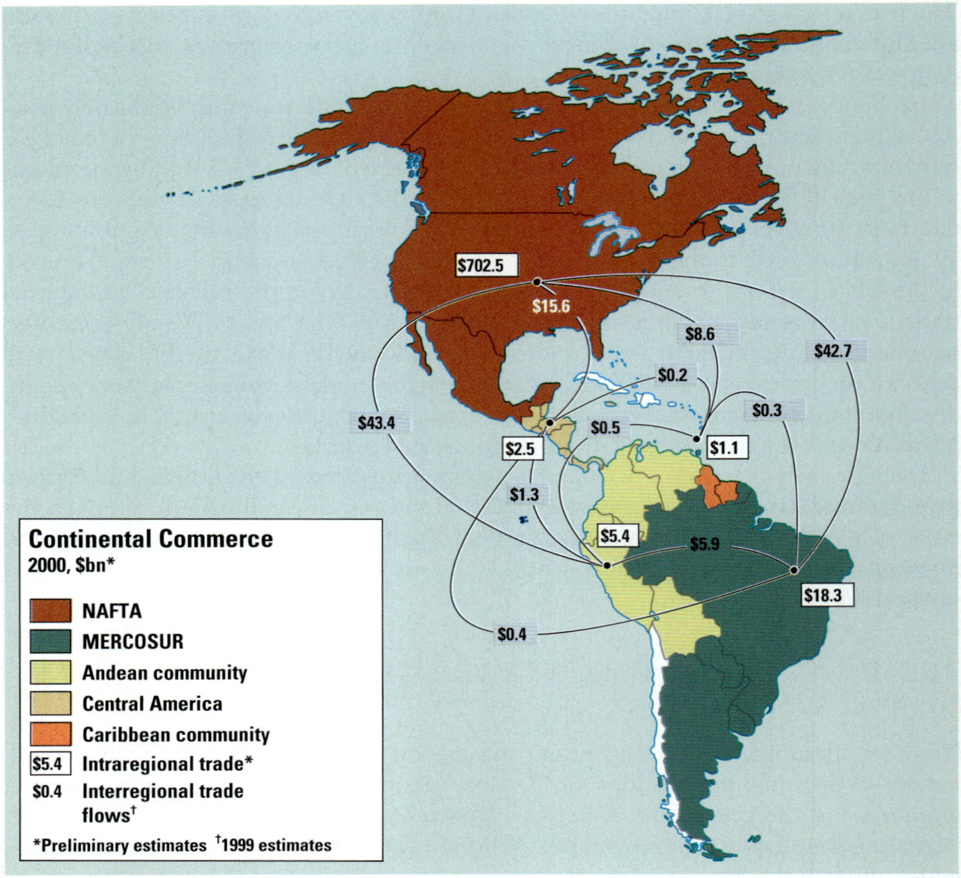

- Removal of most restrictions on foreign direct investment between the three member countries, although special treatment (protection) will be given to Mexican energy and railway industries, American airline and radio communications industries, and Canadian culture.
- Application of national environmental standards, provided such standards have a scientific basis. Lowering of standards to lure investment is described as being inappropriate.
- Establishment of two commissions with the power to impose fines and remove trade privileges when environmental standards or legislation involving health and safety, minimum wages, or child labour are ignored.

The Case for NAFTA

Opinions remain divided as to the consequences of NAFTA. Proponents argue that NAFTA should be viewed as an opportunity to create an enlarged and more efficient productive base for the entire region. One likely effect of NAFTA will be that many U.S. and Canadian firms will move some production to Mexico to take advantage of lower labour costs. In 2003, the average Mexican wage was $1.47 per hour[24] and in Canada, the average wage ranged between $13.14 and $21.59.[25] Movement of production to Mexico is most likely to occur in low-skilled, labour-intensive manufacturing industries where Mexico might have a comparative advantage, such as in textiles (see the Country Focus). Many will benefit from such a trend. Mexico benefits because it gets much-needed investment and employment. The United States and Canada should benefit because the increased incomes of the Mexicans will allow them to import more U.S. and Canadian goods, thereby increasing demand and making up for the jobs lost in industries that moved production to Mexico. U.S. and Canadian consumers will benefit from the lower prices of products produced in Mexico. In addition, the international competitiveness of U.S. and Canadian firms that move production to Mexico to take advantage of lower labour costs will be enhanced, enabling them to better compete with Asian and European rivals.

The Case against NAFTA

Those who opposed NAFTA claimed that ratification would be followed by a mass exodus of jobs from the United States and Canada into Mexico as employers sought to profit from Mexico's lower wages and less strict environmental and labour laws. According to one extreme opponent, Ross Perot, up to 5.9 million U.S. jobs would be lost to Mexico after NAFTA. Most economists, however, dismissed these numbers as being absurd and alarmist. They argued that Mexico would have to run a bilateral trade surplus with the United States of close to $300 billion for job loss on such a scale to occur–and $300 billion is about the size of Mexico's present GDP. In other words, such a scenario is implausible.

More sobre estimates of the impact of NAFTA ranged from a net creation of 170 000 jobs in the United States (due to increased Mexican demand for U.S. goods and services) and an increase of $15 billion per year to the U.S. and Mexican GDP, to a net loss of 490 000 U.S. jobs. To put these numbers in perspective, employment in the U.S. economy was predicted to grow by 18 million from 1993 to 2003. As most economists repeatedly stressed, NAFTA would have a small impact on both Canada and the United States. It could hardly be any other way, since the Mexican economy is only 5 percent of the size of the U.S. economy. Signing NAFTA required the largest leap of economic faith from Mexico rather than Canada or the United States. Falling trade barriers are exposing Mexican firms to highly efficient U.S. and Canadian competitors that, when compared to the average Mexican firm, have far greater capital resources, access to highly educated and skilled workforces, and much greater technological sophistication. The short-run outcome is bound to be painful economic restructuring and unemployment in Mexico. But if economic theory is any guide, there should be dynamic gains in the long run in the efficiency of Mexican firms as they adjust to the rigours of a more competitive marketplace. To the extent that this happens, an acceleration of Mexico's long-run rate of economic growth will follow, and Mexico might yet become a major market for Canadian and U.S. firms.[26]

Environmentalists have also voiced concerns about NAFTA. They point to the sludge in the Rio Grande River and the smog in the air over Mexico City and warn that Mexico could degrade clean air and toxic waste standards across the continent. They claim the lower Rio Grande is the most polluted river in the United States, increasing in chemical waste and sewage along its course from El Paso, Texas, to the Gulf of Mexico.

There is also continued opposition in Mexico to NAFTA from those who fear a loss of national sovereignty. Mexican critics argue that their country will be dominated by U.S. firms that will not really contribute to Mexico's economic growth, but instead will use Mexico as a low-cost assembly site, while keeping their high-paying, high-skilled jobs north of the border.

A recurring theme in the pro- and anti-NAFTA dialogue centres on differing views as to its influence on Canadian sovereignty.
CP/Chuck Stoody

Experience So Far

The first year after NAFTA turned out to be a largely positive experience for all three countries. U.S. trade with Canada and Mexico expanded at about twice the rate of trade with non-NAFTA countries in the first nine months of 1994, compared with the same period in 1993. U.S. exports to Mexico grew by 22 percent, while Mexican exports to the United States grew by 23 percent. Anti-NAFTA campaigners had warned of doom for the U.S. auto industry, but exports of autos to Mexico increased by nearly 500 percent in the first nine months of 1993. The U.S. Commerce Department estimated that the surge in exports to Mexico secured about 130 000 U.S. jobs, while only 13 000 people applied for aid under a program designed to help workers displaced by the movement of jobs to Mexico, suggesting that job losses from NAFTA had been small.[27]

However, the early euphoria over NAFTA was snuffed out in December 1994 when the Mexican economy was shaken by a financial crisis. Through 1993 and 1994, Mexico's trade deficit with the rest of the world had grown sharply, while Mexico's inflation rate had started to accelerate. This put increasing pressure on the Mexican currency, the peso. Traders in the foreign exchange markets, betting that there would be a large decline in the value of the peso against the dollar, began to sell pesos and buy dollars. As a result, in December 1994, the Mexican government was forced to devalue the peso by about 35 percent against the dollar. This effectively increased the cost of imports from the United States by 35 percent. The devaluation of the peso was followed quickly by a collapse in the value of the Mexican stock market, and the country suddenly and unexpectedly appeared to be in the midst of a major economic crisis. Soon afterward, the Mexican government introduced an austerity program designed to rebuild confidence in the country's financial institutions and rein in growth and inflation. The program was backed by a $20-billion loan guarantee from the U.S. government.[28]

One result of this turmoil was a sharp decline in Canadian and U.S. exports to Mexico. Many companies also reduced or postponed their plans to expand into Mexico. NAFTA critics seized on Mexico's financial crisis to crow that they had been right. But in reality, just as the celebrations of NAFTA's success were premature, so were claims of its sudden demise. By the late 1990s, Mexico had recovered from its crisis, its economy was growing again, and the volume of trade with its NAFTA partners was once more expanding.

Early studies of NAFTA's impact suggest that so far at least, its effects have been at best muted.[29] The most comprehensive study to date was undertaken by researchers at the University of California, Los Angeles, and funded by various departments of the U.S. government.[30] Their findings are enlightening. First, they conclude that the growth in trade between Mexico and the United States began to change nearly a decade before the implementation of NAFTA when Mexico unilaterally started to liberalize its own trade regime to conform with GATT standards. The period since NAFTA took effect has had little impact on trends already in place. The study found that trade growth in those sectors that underwent tariff liberalization in the first two and a half years of NAFTA was only marginally higher than trade growth in sectors not yet liberalized. For example, between 1993 and 1996, U.S. exports to Mexico in sectors liberalized under NAFTA grew by 5.83 percent annually, while exports in sectors not liberalized under NAFTA grew by 5.35 percent. In short, the authors argue that NAFTA has so far had only a marginal impact on the level of trade between the United States and Mexico.

As for NAFTA's much-debated impact on jobs in the United States, the study concluded the impact was positive but very small. The study found that while NAFTA created 31 158 new jobs in the United States, 28 168 jobs were also lost due to imports from Mexico, for a net job gain of around 3000 in the first two years of the NAFTA regime.

However, as the authors of the report point out, trade flows and employment in 1995 and 1996 were significantly affected by the peso devaluation and subsequent economic crisis that gripped Mexico in early 1995. Given this, it is probably too early to draw conclusions about the true impact of NAFTA on trade flows and employment. It will be some time before any meaningful conclusions can be stated. The most that can be said at this juncture is that while the optimistic picture of job creation painted by NAFTA's advocates has not yet come to pass, neither has the apocalyptic vision of widespread job losses in the United States and Canada propagated by NAFTA's opponents.

Enlargement

One big issue now confronting NAFTA is that of enlargement. A number of other Latin American countries have indicated their desire to eventually join NAFTA. The governments of both Canada and the United States are adopting a wait-and-see attitude with regard to most countries. Getting NAFTA approved was a bruising political experience, and neither government is eager to repeat the process soon. Nevertheless, the Canadian, Mexican, and U.S. governments began talks in 1995 regarding Chile's possible entry into NAFTA. As of 2001, however, these talks have yielded little progress, primarily because of political opposition in the U.S. Congress to expanding NAFTA.

THE ANDEAN PACT

The Andean Pact was formed in 1969 when Bolivia, Chile, Ecuador, Colombia, and Peru signed the Cartagena Agreement. The Andean Pact was largely based on the EU model, but it has been far less successful at achieving its stated goals. The integration steps begun in 1969 included an internal tariff reduction program, a common external tariff, a transportation policy, a common industrial policy, and special concessions for the smallest members, Bolivia and Ecuador.

By the mid-1980s, the Andean Pact had all but collapsed and had failed to achieve any of its stated objectives. There was no tariff-free trade between member countries, no common external tariff, and no harmonization of economic policies. Political and economic problems seem to have hindered cooperation between member countries. The countries of the Andean Pact have had to deal with low economic growth, hyperinflation, high unemployment, political unrest, and crushing debt burdens. In addition, the dominant political ideology in many of the Andean countries during this period tended toward the radical/socialist end of the political spectrum. Since such an ideology is hostile to the free market economic principles on which the Andean Pact was based, progress toward closer integration could not be expected.

The tide began to turn in the late 1980s when, after years of economic decline, the governments of Latin America began to adopt free market economic policies. In 1990, the heads of the five current members of the Andean Pact–Bolivia, Ecuador, Peru, Colombia, and Venezuela–met in the Galápagos Islands. The resulting Galápagos Declaration effectively relaunched the Andean Pact. The declaration's objectives included the establishment of a free trade area by 1992, a customs union by 1994, and a common market by 1995.

This last milestone has not been reached. However, there are some grounds for cautious optimism. For the first time, the controlling political ideology of the Andean countries is at least consistent with the free market principles underlying a common market. In addition, since the Galápagos Declaration, internal tariff levels have been reduced by all five members, and a customs union with a common external tariff was established in mid-1994, six months behind schedule.

Significant differences between member countries still exist that may make harmonization of policies and close integration difficult. For example, Venezuela's GNP per person is four times that of Bolivia's, and Ecuador's tiny production-line industries cannot compete with Colombia's and Venezuela's more advanced industries. Such differences are a recipe for disagreement and suggest that many of the adjustments required to achieve a true common market will be painful, even though the net benefits will probably outweigh the costs.[31] To complicate matters even further, in recent years Peru and Ecuador have fought a border war, Venezuela has remained aloof during a banking crisis, and Colombia has suffered from domestic political turmoil and problems related to its drug trade. This has led some to argue that the pact is more "formal than real."[32] The outlook for the Andean Pact started to change in 1998 when the group entered into negotiations with MERCOSUR to establish a South American free trade area. However, these negotiations broke down in 1999, and there has been no progress since.

MERCOSUR

MERCOSUR originated in 1988 as a free trade pact between Brazil and Argentina. The modest reductions in tariffs and quotas accompanying this pact reportedly helped bring about an 80 percent increase in trade between the two countries in the late 1980s.[33] Encouraged by this success, the pact was expanded in March 1990 to include Paraguay and Uruguay. The initial aim was to establish a full free trade area by the end of 1994 and a common market sometime thereafter. The four countries of MERCOSUR have a combined population of 200 million. With a market of this size, MERCOSUR could have a significant impact on the economic growth rate of the four economies. In December 1995, MERCOSUR's members agreed to a five-year program under which they hoped to perfect their free trade area and move toward a full customs union.[34]

For its first eight years or so, MERCOSUR seemed to be making a positive contribution to the economic growth rates of its member states. Trade between MERCOSUR's four core members quadrupled between 1990 and 1998. The combined GDP of the four member states grew at an annual average rate of 3.5 percent between 1990 and 1996, a performance that is significantly better than the four attained during the 1980s.[35]

However, MERCOSUR has its critics, including Alexander Yeats, a senior economist at the World Bank, who wrote a stinging critique of MERCOSUR that was "leaked" to the press in October 1996.[36] According to Yeats, the trade diversion effects of MERCOSUR outweigh its trade creation effects. Yeats points out that the fastest-growing items in intra-MERCOSUR trade are cars, buses, agricultural equipment, and other capital-intensive goods that are produced relatively inefficiently in the four member countries. In other words, MERCOSUR countries, insulated from outside competition by tariffs that run as high as 70 percent of value on motor vehicles, are investing in factories that build products that are too expensive to sell to anyone but themselves. The result, according to Yeats, is that MERCOSUR countries might not be able to compete globally once the group's external trade barriers come down. In the meantime, capital is being drawn away from more efficient enterprises. In the near term, countries with more efficient manufacturing enterprises lose because MERCOSUR's external trade barriers keep them out of the market.

The leak of Yeats's report caused a storm at the World Bank, which typically does not release reports that are critical of member states (the MERCOSUR countries are members of the World Bank). It also drew strong protests from Brazil, one of the primary targets of the critique. Still, in tacit admission that at least some of Yeats's arguments have merit, a senior MERCOSUR diplomat let it be known that external trade barriers will gradually be reduced, forcing member countries to compete globally. Many external MERCOSUR tariffs, which average 14 percent, are lower than they were before the group's creation, and there are plans for a hemispheric Free Trade Area of the Americas to be established by 2005 (which will combine MERCOSUR, NAFTA, and other American nations). If that occurs, MERCOSUR will have no choice but to reduce its external tariffs further.

MERCOSUR hit a significant roadblock in 1998, when its member states slipped into recession and intrabloc trade slumped. Trade fell further in 1999 following a financial crisis in Brazil that led to the devaluation of the Brazilian real, which immediately made the goods of other MERCOSUR members 40 percent more expensive in Brazil, their largest export market. At this point, progress toward establishing a customs union all but came to a halt. Things deteriorated further in 2001 when Argentina, beset by economic stresses, suggested that the customs union be "temporarily suspended." Argentina wanted to suspend MERCOSUR's tariff so that it could abolish duties on imports of capital equipment, while raising those on consumer goods to 35 percent (MERCOSUR had established a 14 percent import tariff on both sets of goods). Brazil agreed to this request, effectively putting an end for now to MERCOSUR's quest to become a fully functioning customs union.[37]

CENTRAL AMERICAN COMMON MARKET AND CARICOM

Two other trade pacts in the Americas have not made much progress. In the early 1960s, Costa Rica, El Salvador, Guatemala, Honduras, and Nicaragua attempted to set up a Central American common market. It collapsed in 1969 when war broke out between Honduras and El Salvador after a riot at a soccer match between teams from the two countries. Now the five countries are trying to revive their agreement, although no definite progress has been made.

A customs union was to have been created in 1991 between the English-speaking Caribbean countries under the auspices of the Caribbean Community. Referred to as CARICOM, it was established in 1973. However, it has repeatedly failed to progress toward economic integration. A formal commitment to economic and monetary union was adopted by CARICOM's member states in 1984, but since then little progress has been made. In October 1991, the CARICOM governments failed, for the third consecutive time, to meet a deadline for establishing a common external tariff.

FREE TRADE AREA OF THE AMERICAS

At a hemispherewide "Summit of the Americas" in December 1994, a Free Trade Area of the Americas (FTAA) was proposed. It took more than three years for talks to begin, but in April 1998, 34 heads of state travelled to Santiago, Chile, for the second Summit of the Americas where they formally inaugurated talks to establish an FTAA by 2005. The continuing talks will address a wide range of economic, political, and environmental issues related to cross-border trade and investment. Although the United States was an early advocate of an FTAA, support from the United States seems to be mixed at this point. Since the United States has by far the largest economy in the region, strong U.S. support is a precondition for establishment of an FTAA. Canada is chairing the crucial first stage of negotiations and hosted the second Summit of the Americas in early 2001. If an FTAA is established, it will have major implications for cross-border trade and investment flows within the hemisphere. The FTAA would open a free trade umbrella over nearly 800 million people who accounted for more than $11 trillion in GDP in 2000. At this point, however, any definitive agreement is still several years away.

REGIONAL ECONOMIC INTEGRATION ELSEWHERE

There have been numerous attempts at regional economic integration throughout Asia and Africa. However, few exist in anything other than name. Perhaps the most significant is the Association of Southeast Asian Nations (ASEAN). In addition, the Asia-Pacific Economic Cooperation (APEC) forum has recently emerged as the seed of a potential free trade region.

ASSOCIATION OF SOUTHEAST ASIAN NATIONS

Formed in 1967, ASEAN includes Brunei, Indonesia, Laos, Malaysia, Myanmar, Philippines, Singapore, Thailand, and Vietnam. Laos, Myanmar, and Vietnam have all joined recently, and their inclusion complicates matters because their economies are a long way behind those of the original members. China, Japan, India, and the Republic of Korea are also becoming more closely associated with ASEAN. ASEAN's basic objectives are to foster freer trade between member countries and to achieve cooperation in their industrial policies. Progress has been very limited, however. For example, only 5 percent of intra-ASEAN trade currently consists of goods whose tariffs have been reduced through an ASEAN preferential trade arrangement. Future progress seems limited because the financial crisis that swept through Southeast Asia in 1997 hit several ASEAN countries particularly hard, most notably Indonesia, Malaysia, and Thailand. Until these countries can get back on their economic feet, it is unlikely that much progress will be made.

ASIA-PACIFIC ECONOMIC COOPERATION

Asia-Pacific Economic Cooperation (APEC) was founded in 1990 at the suggestion of Australia. APEC currently has 18 member states including such economic powerhouses as the United States, Japan, and China (see Map 8.3). Collectively the 18 member states account for half of the world's GNP, 40 percent of world trade, and most of the growth in the world economy. The stated aim of APEC is to increase multilateral cooperation in view of the economic rise of the Pacific nations and the growing interdependence within the region. U.S. support for APEC was also based on the belief that it might prove a viable strategy for heading off any moves to create Asian groupings from which it would be excluded.

Interest in APEC was heightened considerably in November 1993 when the heads of APEC member states met for the first time at a two-day conference in Seattle. Debate before the meeting speculated on the likely future role of APEC. One view was that APEC should commit itself to the ultimate formation of a free trade area. Such a move would transform the Pacific Rim from a geographical expression into the world's largest free trade area. Another view was that APEC would produce no more than hot air and lots of photo opportunities for the leaders involved. As it turned out, the APEC meeting produced little more than some vague commitments from mem-

MAP 8.3
Asia-Pacific Economic Cooperation
Source: APEC.

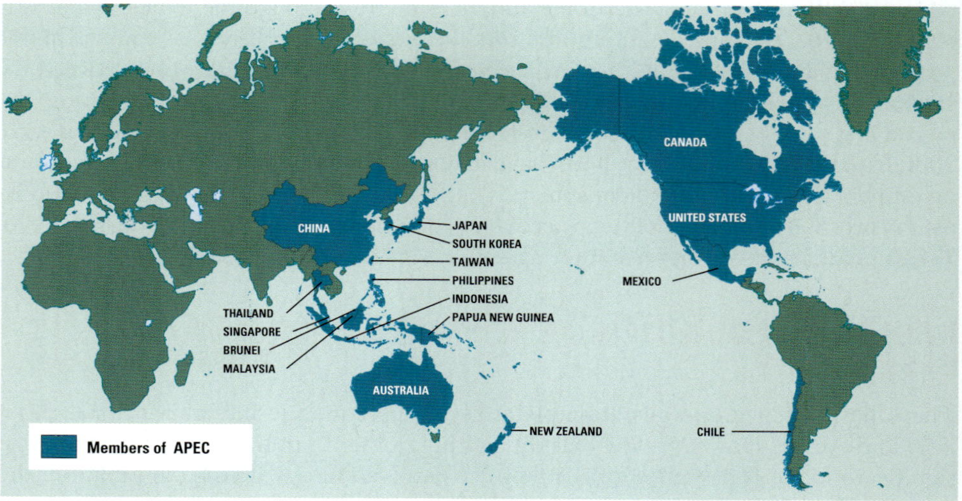

ber states to work together for greater economic integration and a general lowering of trade barriers. However, significantly, member states did not rule out the possibility of closer economic cooperation in the future.[38]

The heads of state met again in November 1994 in Jakarta, Indonesia. This time they agreed to take more concrete steps, and the joint statement at the end of the meeting formally committed APEC's industrialized members to remove their trade and investment barriers by 2010 and for developing economies to do so by 2020. They also called for a detailed blueprint charting how this might be achieved. This blueprint was presented and discussed at the next APEC summit, held in Osaka, Japan, in November 1995.[39] This was followed by further annual meetings. At the 1997 meeting, member states formally endorsed proposals designed to remove trade barriers in 15 sectors, ranging from fish to toys. However, the plan is vague and commits APEC to doing no more than holding further talks. Commenting on the vagueness of APEC pronouncements, the influential Brookings Institution, a U.S.-based economic policy institution, noted that APEC "is in grave danger of shrinking into irrelevance as a serious forum." Despite the slow progress, APEC is worth watching. If it eventually does transform itself into a free trade area, it will probably be the world's largest.[40]

REGIONAL TRADE BLOCS IN AFRICA

African countries have been experimenting with regional trade blocs for half a century. There are now nine trade blocs on the African continent (see Map 8.4). Many countries are members of more than one group. Although the number of trade groups is impressive, progress toward the establishment of meaningful trade blocs has been slow.

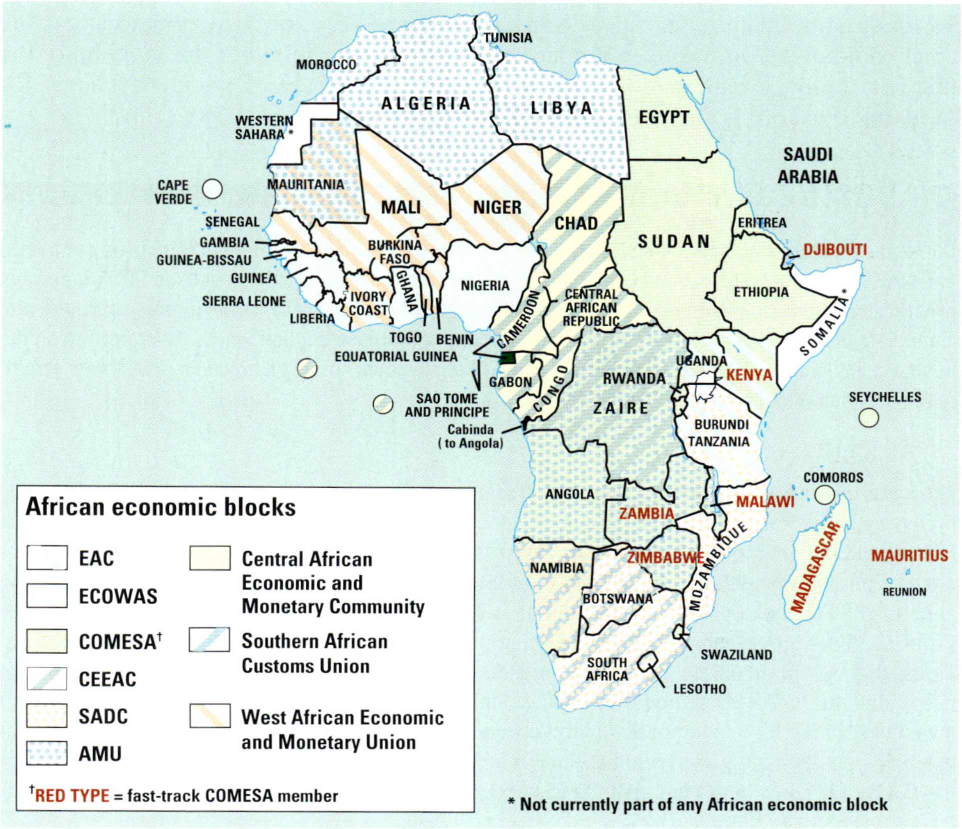

MAP 8.4

Trade Blocs in Africa

Source: From "Afrabet Soup," *The Economist,* February 10, 2001. Copyright © 2001 The Economist Newspaper Ltd. All rights reserved. Reprinted with permission. Further reproduction prohibited. www.economist.com.

ANOTHER PERSPECTIVE

In the EU but not with the euro
Britain is one of the three EU members whose populations voted to not join the currency union. Holding out along with them, largely because their populations thought that governmental monetary control was important, were Denmark and Sweden. Now, a visitor can travel from Spain, Italy, and Greece, through France, Germany, Holland, all in the same currency. But crossing the English Channel requires a trip to the bank for currency exchange. Imagine that you were deciding to set up headquarters in Europe, either for your Asian-based or American-based company. How might Britain's decision to remain outside the common currency affect your location choice for your European base?

Many of these groups have been dormant for years. Significant political turmoil in several African nations has been a persistent impediment to any meaningful progress. Also, deep suspicion of free trade exists in several African countries. The argument most frequently heard is that since these countries have less developed and less diversified economies, they need to be "protected" by tariff barriers from unfair foreign competition. Given the prevalence of this argument, it has been hard to establish free trade areas or customs unions.

The most recent attempt to reenergize the free trade movement in Africa occurred in early 2001, when Kenya, Uganda, and Tanzania, member states of the East African Community (EAC), committed themselves to relaunching their bloc, 24 years after it collapsed. The three countries, with 80 million inhabitants, intend to establish a customs union, regional court, legislative assembly, and, eventually, a political federation. Their program includes cooperation on immigration, road and telecommunication networks, investment, and capital markets. However, while local business leaders welcomed the relaunch as a positive step, they were critical of the EAC's failure in practice to make progress on free trade. At the EAC treaty's signature in November 1999, members gave themselves four years to negotiate a customs union, with a draft slated for the end of 2001. But that fell far short of earlier plans for an immediate free trade zone, shelved after Tanzania and Uganda, fearful of Kenyan competition, expressed concerns that the zone could create imbalances similar to those that contributed to the breakup of the first community.[41] It remains to be seen if these countries can have great success this time, but if history is any guide, it will be an uphill road.

IMPLICATIONS FOR BUSINESS

Currently the most significant developments in regional economic integration are occurring in the EU and NAFTA. Although some of the Latin American trade blocs, APEC and the proposed FTAA, may have greater economic significance in the future, at present the EU and NAFTA have more profound and immediate implications for business practice. Accordingly, in this section we will concentrate on the business implications of those two groups. Similar conclusions, however, could be drawn with regard to the creation of a single market anywhere in the world.

OPPORTUNITIES

The creation of a single market offers significant opportunities because markets that were formerly protected from foreign competition are opened. For example, in Europe before 1992 the large French and Italian markets were among the most protected. These markets are now much more open to foreign competition in the form of both exports and direct investment. Nonetheless, the specter of "Fortress Europe" suggests that to fully exploit such opportunities, it may pay non-EU firms to set up EU subsidiaries. Many major U.S. firms have long had subsidiaries in Europe. Those that do not would be advised to consider establishing them now, lest they run the risk of being shut out of the EU by nontariff barriers. In fact, non-EU firms rapidly increased their direct investment in the EU in anticipation of the creation of a single market. Between 1985 and 1989, for example, approximately 37 percent of the FDI inflows into industrialized countries was directed at the EC. By 1991, this figure had risen to 66 percent, and FDI inflows into the EU has been substantial ever since (see Chapter 7).[42]

Additional opportunities arise from the inherent lower costs of doing business in a single market—as opposed to 15 national markets in the case of the EU or three national markets in the case of NAFTA. Free movement of goods across borders, harmonized product standards, and simplified tax regimes make it possible for firms based in the EU and the NAFTA countries to realize potentially significant cost economies by centralizing production in those EU and NAFTA locations where the mix of factor costs and skills is optimal. Rather than producing a product in each of the 15 EU countries or the three NAFTA countries, a firm may be able to serve the whole EU or North American market from a single location. This location must be chosen carefully, of course, with an eye on local factor costs and skills.

Over the past century, companies have seen the value in being close to their markets and one such company, 3M, has been in business in Canada for over 50 years, since creating its first subsidiary operation in London, Ontario.[43]

The growth of free markets since that time, has, in some ways heightened the need for companies to centralize locations closest to their biggest markets. In response to changes created by the EU after 1992, the St. Paul-based 3M Company has been consolidating its European manufacturing and distribution facilities to take advantage of economies of scale.[44] Thus, a plant in Great Britain now produces 3M's printing products and a German factory its reflective traffic control materials for all of the EU. In each case, 3M chose a location for centralized production after carefully considering the likely production costs in alternative locations within the EU. The ultimate goal of 3M is to dispense with all national distinctions, directing R&D, manufacturing, distribution, and marketing for each product group from an EU headquarters.[45] Similarly, Unilever, one of Europe's largest companies, began rationalizing its production in advance of 1992 to attain scale economies. Unilever concentrated its production of dishwashing powder for the EU in one plant, bath soap in another, and so on.[46]

ANOTHER PERSPECTIVE

Economic integration in Africa

Many efforts are pushing regional economic integration in Africa, and they tend to fall into geographic groupings. One huge benefit of economic integration would be a reduction in the perceived political risk for trade among African countries and a development of African-based distribution channels. Now, largely because of this perceived risk, companies that manufacture for export tend to ship their finished goods to industrialized countries, which then export their imports. A manufactured good from Kenya, say a solar panel, might be shipped to London to be then sent to Nigeria. Integration would lead to a more direct alternative, across the continent. Political scientists suggest that integrated political and economic unions need a shared national hardship to push the collaboration. For the EU it was the devastation of World War II. Craig Jackson, a legal scholar of integration forces, suggests that the devastation in Africa due to poverty and underdevelopment is the kind of force that might push toward the development of the African Union.

Source: www.law.cam.ac.uk/rcil/jackson.rtf +African+economic+integration&hl=en&ie=UTF-8/.

Even after the removal of barriers to trade and investment, enduring differences in culture and competitive practices often limit the ability of companies to realize cost economies by centralizing production in key locations and producing a standardized product for a single multicountry market.

THREATS

The emergence of single markets in the EU and America creates opportunities for business, but it also presents threats. For one thing, the business environment within each grouping will become more competitive. The lowering of barriers to trade and investment between countries is likely to lead to increased price competition throughout the EU and NAFTA. For example, before 1992 a Volkswagen Golf cost 55 percent more in Great Britain than in Denmark and 29 percent more in Ireland than in Greece.[47] Over time, such price differentials will vanish in a single market. This is a direct threat to any firm doing business in EU or NAFTA countries. To survive in the tougher single-market environment, firms must take advantage of the opportunities offered by the creation of a single market to rationalize their production and reduce their costs. Otherwise, they will be severely disadvantaged.

A further threat to firms outside these trading blocs arises from the likely long-term improvement in the competitive position of many firms within the areas. This is particularly relevant in the EU, where many firms are currently limited by a high cost structure in their ability to compete globally with North American and Asian firms. The creation of a single market and the resulting increased competition in the EU is beginning to produce serious attempts by many EU firms to reduce their cost structure by rationalizing production. This could transform many EU companies into efficient global competitors. The message for non-EU businesses is that they need to prepare for the emergence of more capable European competitors by reducing their own cost structures.

Another threat to firms outside of trading areas is the threat of being shut out of the single market by the creation of a "trade fortress." The charge that regional economic integration might lead to a fortress mentality is most often leveled at the EU. As noted earlier in the chapter, although the free trade philosophy underpinning the EU theoretically argues against the creation of any fortress in Europe, there are signs that the EU may raise barriers to imports and investment in certain "politically sensitive" areas, such as autos. Non-EU firms might be well advised, therefore, to set up their own EU operations as quickly as possible. This could also occur in the NAFTA countries, but it seems less likely.

Finally, the emerging role of the European Commission in competition policy suggests the EU is increasingly willing and able to intervene and impose conditions on companies proposing mergers and acquisitions. This is a threat insofar as it limits the ability of firms to pursue the corporate strategy of their choice. While this constrains the strategic options for firms, in taking such action, the commission is trying to maintain the level of competition in Europe's single market, which should benefit consumers.

KEY TERMS

maquilladoras, p. 269

regional economic integration, p. 260

trade creation, p. 267

trade diversion, p. 267

SUMMARY

This chapter pursued three main objectives: to examine the economic and political debate surrounding regional economic integration; to review the progress toward regional economic integration in Europe, the Americas, and elsewhere; and to distinguish the important implications of regional economic integration for the practice of international business. This chapter made the following points:

1. A number of levels of economic integration are possible in theory. In order of increasing integration, they include a free trade area, a customs union, a common market, an economic union, and full political union.
2. In a free trade area, barriers to trade between member countries are removed, but each country determines its own external trade policy. In a customs union, internal barriers to trade are removed and a common external trade policy is adopted. A common market is similar to a customs union, except that a common market also allows factors of production to move freely between countries. An economic union involves even closer integration, including the establishment of a common currency and the harmonization of tax rates. A political union is the logical culmination of attempts to achieve ever-closer economic integration.
3. Regional economic integration is an attempt to achieve economic gains from the free flow of trade and investment between neighboring countries.
4. Integration is not easily achieved or sustained. Although integration brings benefits to the majority, it is never without costs for the minority. Concerns over national sovereignty often slow or stop integration attempts.
5. Regional integration will not increase economic welfare if the trade creation effects in the free trade area are outweighed by the trade diversion effects.
6. The Single European Act sought to create a true single market by abolishing administrative barriers to the free flow of trade and investment between EU countries.
7. The Maastricht Treaty aims to take the EU even further along the road to economic union by establishing a common currency. The economic gains from a common currency come from reduced exchange costs, reduced risk associated with currency fluctuations, and increased price competition within the EU.
8. Increasingly, the European Commission is taking an activist stance with regard to competition policy, intervening to restrict mergers and acquisitions that it believes will reduce competition in the EU.

9. Although no other attempt at regional economic integration comes close to the EU in terms of potential economic and political significance, various other attempts are being made in the world. The most notable include NAFTA in North America, the Andean Pact and MERCOSUR in Latin America, ASEAN in Southeast Asia, and perhaps APEC.
10. The creation of single markets in the EU and North America means that many markets that were formerly protected from foreign competition are now more open. This creates major investment and export opportunities for firms within and outside these regions.
11. The free movement of goods across borders, the harmonization of product standards, and the simplification of tax regimes make it possible for firms based in a free trade area to realize potentially enormous cost economies by centralizing production in those locations within the area where the mix of factor costs and skills is optimal.
12. The lowering of barriers to trade and investment between countries within a trade group will probably be followed by increased price competition.

CRITICAL THINKING AND DISCUSSION QUESTIONS

1. NAFTA is likely to produce net benefits for the Canadian, Mexican, and U.S. economies. Discuss.
2. What are the economic and political arguments for regional economic integration? Given these arguments, why don't we see more integration in the world economy?
3. What effect is creation of a single market and a single currency within the EU likely to have on competition within the EU? Why?
4. How should a U.S. firm that currently exports only to Western Europe respond to the creation of a single market?
5. How should a firm with self-sufficient production facilities in several EU countries respond to the creation of a single market? What are the constraints on its ability to respond in a manner that minimizes production costs?
6. After a promising start, in the last few years MERCOSUR, the major Latin American trade agreement, has faltered and by 2001 seemed to be in trouble. What problems are hurting MERCOSUR? What can be done to solve these problems?
7. Would establishment of a Free Trade Area of the Americas (FTAA) in 2005 be good for the two most advanced economies in the hemisphere, the United States and Canada? How might the establishment of the FTAA impact the strategy of North American firms?

RESEARCH TASK | globalEDGE™ globaledge.msu.edu

Use the globalEDGE™ site to complete the following exercises:

1. Your company is considering expanding its market by placing new representatives in the European Union. The size of the investment is significant, and top management wishes to have a clearer picture of the current and probable future economic status of the EU. Prepare an executive summary describing the features you consider as crucial in making such a decision.
2. The establishment of the Free Trade Area of the Americas can be a threat, as well as an opportunity, for your company. Identify the countries participating in the negotiations for the FTAA. What are the main themes of the negotiation process?

Visit the *Global Business Today* Online Learning Centre at **www.mcgrawhill.ca/college/hill** to access quizzes, interactive exercises, a Business Around the World interactive map, and other learning and study tools related to this chapter.

Online LearningCentre

DEUTSCHE BANK'S PAN-EUROPEAN RETAIL BANKING STRATEGY

In March 2000, Deutsche Bank, Germany's largest bank, announced it would merge with Dresdner Bank, Germany's third largest bank. The stated strategic goal of the merger was to create a European investment and asset management institution that would have the economies of scale required to compete with the top global investment banks, including Citicorp and Merrill Lynch. An important component of the proposed merger was a plan by Deutsche Bank and Dresdner to combine their retail bank operations into Deutsche Bank's retail banking division, Bank 24, and then spin off Bank 24 as an independent entity in which the merged company would have no more than a 10 percent ownership stake. At the time, Bank 24 had some 11 million customers, the majority in Germany but 1.5 million in Italy and another 600 000 in Spain. In addition to its 2000 retail branches, Bank 24 had also been a pioneer in using the Internet to sell banking services, and by 2000 some 20 percent of all transactions were online. The plan to spin off Bank 24 indicated the two banks had decided to withdraw from retail banking, instead concentrating on the wholesale side of the business (investment banking and money management). Most analysts applauded the proposed deal, noting that retail banking in Germany was a low-margin business that held few attractions, while investment banking was a high-margin business.

By April 2000, however, the proposed deal had collapsed following significant disagreements between management teams at the two companies. Initially, few thought that this would lead to a change in strategy at Deutsche Bank, but six months later the bank announced it had rethought its retail strategy. Suddenly, Bank 24 was at the heart of a new strategy by Deutsche Bank to build a pan-European retail channel. The change of strategy stemmed from a growing realization that Deutsche Bank's branch and online banking platform provided a powerful sales channel to a rapidly growing "money class"—Europe's highly educated and prosperous 30- and 40-year-olds. Deutsche Bank estimated the EU has more than 60 million people in this demographic. Increasingly, this group is switching their savings from deposit accounts into equities and investment funds as they begin to plan for their retirement. Deutsche Bank realized it could use its retail branch network to sell the investment products churned out by its investment banking and asset management operations. Deutsche Bank also realized that with the advent of the euro, the impediments to the cross-border sale of money management products had been significantly reduced, at least within the euro zone.

To implement the strategy, Deutsche Bank plans to weld Bank 24's operations, which are scattered across seven European countries, into a coherent whole. The model in each country will be the same. The basic idea will be to offer a full range of financial services via branch offices, telephones, and increasingly the Internet. But in an effort to curb costs, the emphasis is likely to be the Internet. Thus, the company wants to grow its retail customer base to 14 million by 2004, while keeping the number of branches constant at 2000 and reducing total employment by about 10 percent. The geographical distribution of branches will change, however, with some branches in Germany being consolidated or closed, while retail branches are opened in other European countries. The initial plans call for further expansion in Italy, Spain, France, and Belgium, where Bank 24 already has a presence. The company, however, also states that if the concept works, it will move into the Netherlands and the United Kingdom, as well as some non-EU countries, such as Poland and the Czech Republic (both of which have applied to enter the EU). Deutsche Bank also indicated that Bank 24 might make selected acquisitions to establish a larger retail presence in other EU nations.

Another element of the strategy calls for Deutsche Bank to expand the reach of its online brokerage unit, Maxblue, into a pan-European discount broker. Bank 24 will be used to market Maxblue. In late 2000, Maxblue had some 300 000 client accounts, the majority in Germany. The plan calls for this number to grow to 1.5 million by 2004, many of whom would be outside of Germany. If attained, this would give Deutsche Bank a 30 percent share of the online market that is expected to exist by 2004.

Implementing this strategy will require heavy investments, particularly in information technology. Before the change in strategy, Deutsche Bank had budgeted some $110 million for building up Bank 24, including redesigning branches abroad, unifying information technology, and marketing the new look.

Now estimates suggest it will take some $250 million of marketing expenditure just to achieve brand recognition across Europe, and significant additional investments will be required in information technology. Despite this investment, Deutsche Bank claims the shift in strategy will boost Bank 24's profits from euro 400 million in 2000 to euro 1 billion by 2004.

Sources: "German Banking," *The Economist,* April 8, 2000; M. Walker, "Deutsche Bank Plans to Make Its Retail Unit a Stock Outlet," *Wall Street Journal,* October 23, 2000, p. A25; and T. Major, "DB24 Reprived to Target Europe's Forty Somethings," *Financial Times,* November 17, 2000, p. 33.

CASE DISCUSSION QUESTIONS

1. What are the main elements of Deutsche Bank's strategy for Bank 24? Does this strategy hold appeal given *(a)* the creation of a single market in the European Union and *(b)* the introduction of the euro?
2. What potential impediments do you think might get in the way of Deutsche Bank's aspirations to establish a pan-European retail presence and a pan-European discount brokerage?
3. How easy do you think it might be for other European banks to adopt a similar strategy and for American banks to enter Europe and go after the same "money class"? Given this, how competitive do you think this market is likely to be?
4. Deutsche Bank estimates it can more than double the profits of Bank 24 by 2004, while holding the number of branches roughly constant and increasing its customer base from 11 million to 14 million. How realistic do you think this profit goal is given your answers to questions 2 and 3 and the investments apparently required to implement the strategy?

FOREIGN INVESTMENT FOR SUSTAINABLE COMMUNITY DEVELOPMENT

MULTINATIONALS LEARNING FROM THE GRAMEEN EXAMPLE

The following case studies describe the micro-credit programs at the Grameen Bank and at the world banking group ABN AMRO. The first case study explains how the Grameen Bank uses micro-credit within Bangladesh as a sustainable development tool to help build local economies and reduce poverty. The second case study describes how ABN AMRO partnered with a nongovernmental organization to build upon the successful micro-credit model at the Grameen Bank. ANB AMRO created an innovative program of foreign investment in local economic development.

The Grameen Bank has shown that innovative business models can deliver services in novel ways that create business profit as well as opportunities for the poor. Set up in 1976 to overturn conventional banking mentality, Grameen Bank provides services to the rural poor through micro-credit.

The bank demonstrates how a traditional service can be repackaged to reach new customers in the segment that has been called the "market at the bottom of the pyramid." Nontraditional business models need to be innovative and based on lower margins from larger markets. But if successful, they can begin to overcome many of the barriers to meeting the needs of these markets—such as a lack of electricity, poor educational systems, limited infrastructure, and finance for large-scale products and services.

In many countries, including Bangladesh, poor people lack access to institutional credit because the rural banking system operates on "no collateral, no credit." The Grameen scheme provides credit to the poorest of the poor in rural Bangladesh without any collateral. Instead, it relies on supervision, accountability, participation, and creativity.

Since formally becoming a bank in 1983, Grameen has made nearly 16 million micro-loans, and now collects $1.5 million a week in instalments—at a profit. The bank works with more than 2.4 million borrowers and has proved to be an effective instrument in the fight against poverty by giving access to capital, helping to increase incomes, and building the capacity of rural Bangladesh.

As a result of its success, Grameen has diversified, creating additional products and services that conventional business does not provide, such as renewable energy schemes, telecommunications services, and information technology development.

Grameen Bank simultaneously provides credit to a new market while contributing to sustainable development. The needs of the rural poor are far from satisfied, but this market holds considerable promise. Services that are better tailored to the need of clients lead to better performance and sustainability among clients, which in turn can lead to better performance and sustainability for the company.

On a broader scale, these management structures contribute to sustainable development by building the capacity of the poor to govern themselves and the organizations to which they belong.

FOREIGN INVESTMENT IN MICRO-CREDIT: THE ABN AMRO EXAMPLE

The success of micro-credit in Bangladesh intrigued ABN AMRO. ACCION International was replicating the Grameen Bank success in other countries. ABN AMRO chose to partner with ACCION to make a positive difference and a profit in Brazil, as described in the following case study.

An estimated 15.7 million people in Brazil work in the informal economy as micro-entrepreneurs, outnumbering formal-sector entrepreneurs by more than three to one. Of these informal micro-entrepreneurs 93 percent run profitable business, but 84 percent of them do not have access to credit. An estimated 50 percent of these micro-entrepreneurs would apply for a micro-credit loan if they had access to banking services, a potential $3.7 billion per year in loans.

Recognizing a potential market and seeing a service that could both help the community and be self-sustaining, ABN AMRO's Brazilian subsidiary Banco ABN AMRO Real launched Real Microcredito in July 2002, in partnership with ACCION (www.accion.org), a nongovernmental organization specializing in micro-credit worldwide. ACCION provides the technical expertise in micro-lending while ABN AMRO provides its strong financial background, infrastructure, and banking network in Brazil. Its first branch office opened in 2002 in Favela Heliopolis, one of Sao Paulo's crowded shantytowns. With approximately 100 000 inhabitants and 3000 low-income micro-entrepreneurs, and its proximity to ABN AMRO Real headquarters, this was a logical location choice.

Real Microcredito offers small loans at a monthly interest to growing businesses that lack access to conventional forms of credit. The majority of Real Microcredito's loans (86 percent) are used for working capital. The remaining 14 percent are used for either home improvements or equipment purchases. While there is clearly a social component to the Real Microcredito initiative, ABN AMRO has made it clear that this is not a philanthropic initiative.

Real Microcredito uses a door-to-door sales technique to communicate its product offerings to potential customers. The turnaround time from the time a customer applies for a loan and the time he/she receives the loan (if approved) is 48 hours. Even with this short turnaround, Real Microcredito performs an extensive check to verify the customers' creditworthiness.

By spring 2004, Real Microcredito had 1000 clients. Typical loan sizes range from $176 to $1,760. As of July 2003, the maximum loan size allowed was $3,521 and the average repayment time was seven months. The on-time repayment rate was 92.36 percent.

While it is too early to firmly identify the social impact of the Real Microcredito program, evidence of improved living conditions, especially home improvements, can be seen among Real Microcredito clients. Additional time will be needed to assess the full social and economic impact on the community. Real Microcredito has opted not to include specific social measures as part of its measure of success. Real Microcredito has determined that its social impact is too difficult to measure and has therefore chosen to remain focused on the financial results of this venture.

In the meantime, ABN AMRO has expanded operations to India, and ACCION International is working on micro-credit in more than 30 countries.

Source: Both the Grameen Bank and ABN AMCO case studies were adapted by Dr. Debra Rowe and used with the permission of the World Business Council for Sustainable Development at www.wbcsd.org.

PART FOUR

4

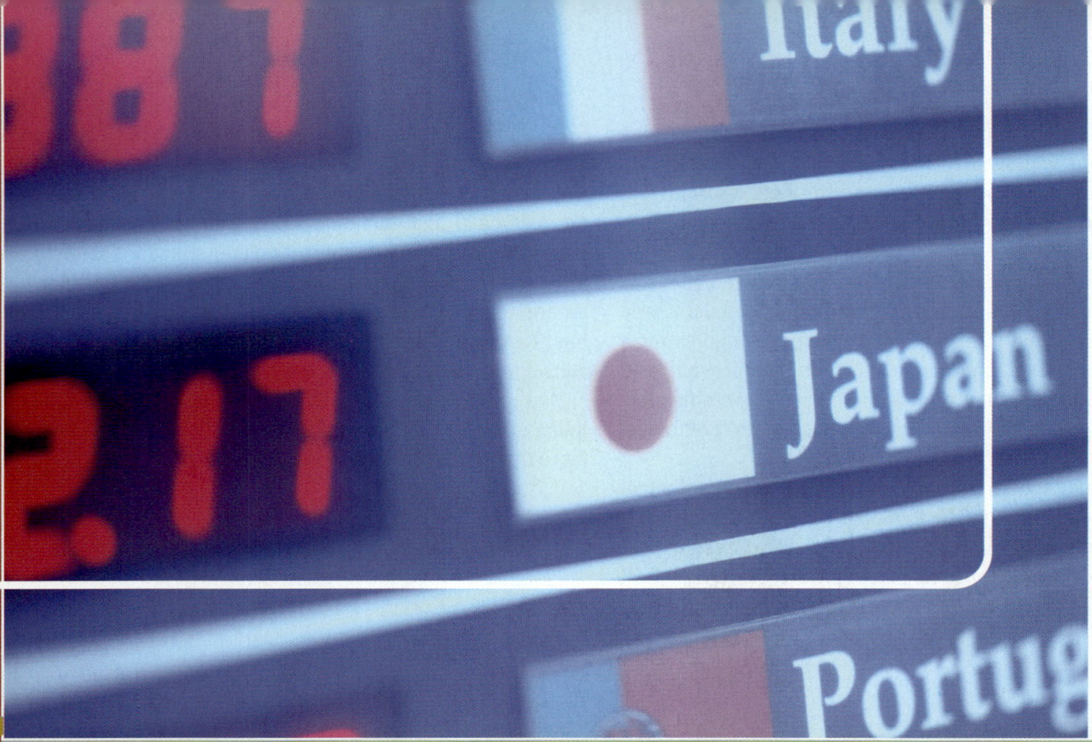

Foreign Exchange Losses at JAL

One of the world's largest airlines, Japan Airlines (JAL), is also one of the best customers of Boeing, the world's biggest manufacturer of commercial airplanes. Every year JAL needs to raise about $800 million to purchase aircraft from Boeing. Boeing aircraft are priced in U.S. dollars, with prices ranging from about $35 million for a 737 to $160 million for a top-of-the-line 747–400. JAL orders an aircraft two to six years before the plane is actually needed and normally pays Boeing a 10 percent deposit when ordering. The bulk of the payment is made when the aircraft is delivered.

The long lag between placing an order and making a final payment presents a conundrum for JAL. Most of JAL's revenues are in Japanese yen, not U.S. dollars (which is not surprising for a Japanese airline). When purchasing Boeing aircraft, JAL must change its yen into dollars to pay Boeing. In the interval between placing an order and making final payment, the value of the yen against the dollar may change. This can increase or decrease the cost of an aircraft. Consider an order placed for a 747 aircraft that was to be delivered in five years. The dollar value of this order was $100 million. Suppose the prevailing exchange rate at the time of ordering was US$1 = ¥240 (i.e., one dollar was worth 240 yen), making the price of the 747 ¥2.4 billion. When final payment is due, however, the U.S. dollar/yen exchange rate might have changed. The yen might have declined in value against the dollar. For example, the U.S. dollar/yen exchange rate might be US$1 = ¥300. If this occurs, the price of the 747 would go from ¥2.4 billion to ¥3.0 billion, a 25-percent increase. Another (more favourable) scenario is that the yen might rise in value against the U.S. dollar to US$1 = ¥200. If this occurs, the yen price of the 747 would fall 16.7 percent to ¥2.0 billion.

JAL has no way of knowing what the value of the yen will be against the dollar in five years. However, JAL can enter into a contract with foreign exchange traders to purchase dollars five years hence based on the assessment of those traders as to what they think the

Daisuke Morita/Getty Images.

CHAPTER 9

The Foreign Exchange Market

OPENING CASE

dollar/yen exchange rate will be then. This is called entering into a forward exchange contract. The advantage of entering into a forward exchange contract is that JAL knows now what it will have to pay for the 747 in five years. For example, if the value of the yen is expected to increase against the dollar, foreign exchange traders might offer a forward exchange contract that allows JAL to purchase dollars at a rate of US$1 = ¥185 in five years, instead of the US$1 = ¥240 rate that prevailed at the time of ordering. At this forward exchange rate, the 747 would cost only ¥1.85 billion, a 23 percent saving over the yen price implied at time of ordering.

JAL was confronted with just this scenario in 1985 when it entered into a ten-year forward exchange contract with a total value of about $3.6 billion. This contract gave JAL the right to buy U.S. dollars from a consortium of foreign exchange traders at various points during the next ten years for an average exchange rate of US$1 = ¥185. This looked like a great deal to JAL given the 1985 exchange rate of US$1 = ¥240. However, by September 1994 when the bulk of the contract had been executed, it no longer looked like a good deal. To everyone's surprise, the value of the yen had surged against the dollar. By 1992, the exchange rate stood at US$1 = ¥120, and by 1994, it was US $1 = ¥99. Unfortunately, JAL could not take advantage of this more favourable exchange rate. Instead, JAL was bound by the terms of the contract to purchase dollars at the contract rate of US$1 = ¥185, a rate that by 1994 looked outrageously expensive. This misjudgment cost JAL dearly. In 1994, JAL was paying 86 percent more than it needed to for each Boeing aircraft bought with dollars purchased via the forward exchange contract! In October 1994, JAL admitted publicly that the loss in its most recent financial year from this misjudgment amounted to US$450 million, or ¥45 billion. Furthermore, foreign exchange traders speculated that JAL had probably lost ¥155 billion (US$1.5 billion) on this contract since 1988.

Source: W. Dawkins, "JAL to Disclose Huge Currency Hedge Loss," *Financial Times,* October 4, 1994, p. 19, and W. Dawkins, "Tokyo to Lift Veil on Currency Risks," *Financial Times,* October 5, 1994, p. 23.

LEARNING OBJECTIVES

1. Be familiar with the form and function of the foreign exchange market.
2. Understand the difference between spot and forward exchange rates.
3. Understand how currency exchange rates are determined.
4. Appreciate the role of the foreign exchange market in insuring against foreign exchange risk.
5. Be familiar with the merits of different approaches toward exchange rate forecasting.
6. Appreciate why some currencies cannot always be converted into other currencies.
7. Understand how countertrade is used to mitigate problems associated with an inability to convert currencies.

INTRODUCTION

This chapter has three main objectives. The first is to explain how the foreign exchange market works. The second is to examine the forces that determine exchange rates and to discuss the degree to which it is possible to predict future exchange rate movements. The third objective is to map the implications for international business of exchange rate movements and the foreign exchange market. This chapter is the first of two that deal with the international monetary system and its relationship to international business. In the next chapter, we will explore the institutional structure of the international monetary system. The institutional structure is the context within which the foreign exchange market functions. As we shall see, changes in the institutional structure of the international monetary system can exert a profound influence on the development of foreign exchange markets.

FOREIGN EXCHANGE MARKET A market for converting the currency of one country into that of another country.

EXCHANGE RATE The rate at which one currency is converted into another.

The **foreign exchange market** is a market for converting the currency of one country into that of another country. An **exchange rate** is simply the rate at which one currency is converted into another. We saw in the opening case how JAL used the foreign exchange market to convert Japanese yen into U.S. dollars. Without the foreign exchange market, international trade and international investment on the scale that we see today would be impossible; companies would have to resort to barter. The foreign exchange market is the lubricant that enables companies based in countries that use different currencies to trade with each other. On August 29, 2002, the exchange rate between the U.S. dollar and the Japanese yen was US$1 = ¥118.8, meaning that US$1 bought ¥118.8.

We know from earlier chapters that international trade and investment have their risks. As the opening case illustrates, some of these risks exist because future exchange rates cannot be perfectly predicted. The rate at which one currency is converted into another can change over time. One function of the foreign exchange market is to provide some insurance against the risks that arise from changes in exchange rates, commonly referred to as foreign exchange risk. Although the foreign exchange market offers some insurance against foreign exchange risk, it cannot provide complete insurance. JAL's loss of US$1.5 billion on foreign exchange transactions is an extreme example of what can happen, but it is not unusual for international businesses to suffer losses because of unpredicted changes in exchange rates. Currency fluctuations can make seemingly profitable trade and investment deals unprofitable, and vice versa. The opening case contains an example.

In addition to altering the value of trade deals and foreign investments, currency movements can also open or close export opportunities and alter the attractiveness of imports. While the existence of foreign exchange markets is a necessary precondition for large-scale international trade and investment, as suggested by this example and the opening case, the movement of exchange rates introduces many risks into international trade and investment. Some of these risks can be insured against by using instruments offered by the foreign exchange market, such as the forward exchange contracts discussed in the opening case; others cannot be.

We begin this chapter by looking at the functions and the form of the foreign exchange market. This includes distinguishing among spot exchanges, forward exchanges, and currency swaps. Then we will consider the factors that determine exchange rates. We will also look at how foreign trade is conducted when a country's currency cannot be exchanged for other currencies; that is, when its currency is not convertible. The chapter closes with a discussion of these things in terms of their implications for business.

The foreign exchange market enables companies based in countries that use different currencies to trade with each other. However, it can be difficult and risky in the interim between when an order is placed and when a final payment is made for an item, as was illustrated by the value change of the Japanese yen against the U.S. dollar for JAL. Why do you suppose companies would not negotiate to purchase at an established price according to currency value at the time of the initial deposit? AP Photo/Tsugufumi Matsumoto.

THE FUNCTIONS OF THE FOREIGN EXCHANGE MARKET

The foreign exchange market serves two main functions. The first is to convert the currency of one country into the currency of another. The second is to provide some insurance against **foreign exchange risk,** by which we mean the adverse consequences of unpredictable changes in exchange rates.[1]

CURRENCY CONVERSION

Each country has a currency in which the prices of goods and services are quoted. In the United States, it is the dollar ($); in Great Britain, the pound (£); in the rest of Europe, the euro (€); in Canada, the (Cdn$); and so on. In general, within the borders of a particular country, one must use the national currency. A Candian tourist cannot walk into a store in Edinburgh, Scotland, and use Canadian dollars to buy a bottle of Scotch whisky. Dollars are not recognized as legal tender in Scotland; the tourist must use British pounds. Fortunately, the tourist can go to a bank and exchange her dollars for pounds. Then she can buy the whisky.

FOREIGN EXCHANGE RISK
The risk that changes in exchange rates will hurt the profitability of a business deal.

When a tourist changes one currency into another, she is participating in the foreign exchange market. Exchange rates allow us to compare the relative price of goods and services in different countries. A Canadian tourist wishing to buy a bottle of Scotch whisky in Glasgow learns that she must pay £30 for the bottle, knowing that the same bottle costs $50 in Canada. Is this a good deal? The July 1, 2004 £ /Cdn$ is 2.42. Upon calculation of this exchange rate, the tourist calculates the exchange rate for the £30 bottle of whisky. (The calculation is 2.42 × £30). She finds that the bottle of Scotch costs the equivalent of Cdn$72.60. She is surprised that a bottle of Scotch whisky could cost less in Canada than in Scotland. (This is true; alcohol is heavily taxed in Great Britain.)

Tourists are minor participants in the foreign exchange market; companies engaged in international trade and investment are major ones. International businesses have four main uses of foreign exchange markets. First, the payments a company receives for its exports, the income it receives from foreign investments, or the income it receives from licensing agreements with foreign firms may be in foreign currencies. To use those funds in its home country, the company must convert them to its home country's currency. Consider the Scotch distillery that exports its whisky to Canada. The distillery is paid in dollars (most likely in U.S. dollars) but since those dollars cannot be spent in Great Britain, they must be converted to British pounds. (The Canadian firm would have first converted Canadian dollars to U.S. dollars on the foreign exchange markets and paid the U.S./Canadian dollar exchange rate at the time of the conversion.)

Second, international businesses use foreign exchange markets when they must pay a foreign company for its products or services in its country's currency. For example, Dell Computer buys many components for its computers from Malaysian firms. The Malaysian companies are required to be paid in Malaysia's currency, the ringgit, so Dell must convert money from dollars into ringgit.

Third, international businesses use foreign exchange markets when they have spare cash that they wish to invest for short terms in money markets. Imagine that Barrick Gold, (see Management Focus) has $10 million it wants to invest for three months in its U.S. dollar account. The best rate it might earn on this amount in its U.S. dollar account is 2 percent. Investing in an Australian money market account, however, may earn it 10 percent. Thus, for example, the company may change its $10 million in Australian dollars and invest it into its existing Australian operations. Note, however, that the rate of return it earns on this investment depends not only on the Australian dollar interest rate, but also on the changes in the value of the Australian dollar against the U.S. dollar, in the intervening period. Large Canadian companies normally have huge U.S. dollar reserves and thus do not always have to convert back to the "home currency"–the Canadian dollar.

ANOTHER PERSPECTIVE

Exchange rates and the lucky traveller

You are taking a trip to Japan, and you convert $1,000 to Japanese yen to cover expenses while there. Your bank gives you ¥140,000 for your $1,000. During your two weeks in Japan, the dollar weakens against the yen, to ¥110 to the dollar. Meanwhile, your Japanese friends were so hospitable you have spent only ¥30,000. After you land in Vancouver, you take ¥110,000 to the bank in the airport to convert to dollars. How much have you spent for your trip? Will you list these expenses on your expense report?

CURRENCY SPECULATION Involves short-term movement of funds from one currency to another in hopes of profiting from shifts in exchange rates.

Finally, **currency speculation** is another use of foreign exchange markets. Currency speculation typically involves the short-term movement of funds from one currency to another in the hope of profiting from shifts in exchange rates. Consider again the Canadian company with US$10 million to invest for three months. Suppose the company suspects that the U.S. dollar will be overvalued against the Japanese yen. That is, it expects the U.S. dollar to depreciate (fall) against that of the yen. Imagine the current dollar/yen exchange rate is US$1 = 120 yen. The company exchanges $10 million into yen receiving 1.2 billion yen ($10 million × 120 = 1.2 billion yen). Over the next three months, the value of the dollar depreciates against the yen until $1 = 100 yen. Now the company exchanges its 1.2 billion yen back into dollars and finds that it has $12 million. The company has made a $2-million profit on currency speculation in three months on an initial investment of $10 million. However, currency speculation does not always yield gains. Had the currencies moved in the other direction in this example, then the Canadian company could have lost US$2 million.

THE WORLD AND THE CANADIAN DOLLAR

As for the Canadian dollar, the reality is that it is a secondary currency, of little international business use in the world of the yen, euro, U.S. dollar, pound sterling, and even the Swiss franc. The Canadian dollar is not immune to speculation as it does rise and fall, accordingly. Money market traders will take advantage of such moves irrespective of the nationality of the currency. More people around the world relate to the U.S. dollar, Swiss franc, yen, pound sterling, and euro, than to the Canadian dollar.

Canadian businesses normally all but forget about using the Canadian dollar in most international business deals, be they with Australia or other countries. Commercial payments usually occur in universally accepted U.S. dollars. Although less frequent than U.S. dollar international payments, yen, euros, and Swiss francs are also used. The foreign use of the Canadian dollar is common among Canadian tourists, but when they venture outside of traditional southern vacation and European vacation havens, they will frequently convert to U.S. dollars due to host-country unfamiliarity with the Canadian dollar. When doing business abroad, smaller Canadian companies likely will settle in U.S. dollars, but only on a transaction per transaction basis. Large Canadian companies operate internationally through established U.S. dollar accounts or other major currency accounts, less concerned about the Canadian dollar and its fluctuations than small Canadian businesses. Although larger firms may have to make an initial one-time currency conversion from Canadian dollars into U.S. dollars or other major currency accounts, once done, the state of the Canadian dollar is of little or no concern to the execution of foreign business transactions.

On the contrary, small Canadian businesses can be highly susceptible to exchange rate fluctuations when exporting to the U.S. and fear that a rise in the Canadian dollar will increase the cost to the U.S. consumer and damage export related profits. If an American were to purchase a Canadian product for Cdn$100 at the July 1, 2004 exchange rate of .75 (Cdn$1 = US$0.75) the product would cost the American US$75.[2] If the Canadian dollar were to rise to US$0.85, then the American would purchase the same product for US$85. Such a move could stand to erode Canadian exports to the United States and increase the unemployment rate in Canada.

However, many Canadian businesspeople do not "buy into" this "story line" that plays with the idea of increasing value of Canadian dollar = loss exports = loss of jobs. During the twentieth century, before the onset of the euro, several countries had very expensive currencies, such as Germany with the deutschemark. Yet, in spite of the highly unfavourable German deutschemark exchange rate, thereby making the acquisition of German products very expensive in relation to similar domestic products in other countries, the Germans still managed to capture huge market share of the automobile market, heavy machinery market, and so on.

This German success was achieved through efficient manufacturing processes, the execution of aggressive international sales and marketing strategies, and continuous quality improvement practices that made and make foreign buyers flock to German products. Quality and an understanding of the needs of foreign buyers all but cancelled out unfavourable deutschemark foreign exchange rate concerns. German manufacturers were not oblivious to the risk of losing business due to high exchange rates. They worked with that knowledge and created a competitive advantage through higher quality products than those of other foreign companies competing for the same market share.

The "mean and lean" argument when applied to Canadian businesses doing business abroad is not always well received in Canadian government circles, often in denial of quality + lean = success principles. Nonetheless in 2003, Canadian exports totalled $260,500,000,000 and ranked eighth in the world.[3]

As indicated, if the operations of major companies are grounded in the U.S. dollar, pound sterling, Swiss franc or yen payments, they will all but ignore the Canada-major currency exchange rates. For small Canadian businesses, it remains to be seen if a more expensive Canadian dollar would hamper small business exports.

INSURING AGAINST FOREIGN EXCHANGE RISK

A second function of the foreign exchange market is to provide insurance to protect against the possible adverse consequences of unpredictable changes in exchange rates (foreign exchange risk). To explain how the market performs this function, we must first distinguish among spot exchange rates, forward exchange rates, and currency swaps.

MANAGEMENT FOCUS

BARRICK GOLD

Canada is the world's fifth largest producer of gold, behind South Africa, the United States, Australia, and China. Canadian-based gold explorers and producers have taken a global approach to precious metals mining, growing in a field once characterized by South African and Australian firms. Barrick Gold, with its head offices in Toronto, is the world's third largest gold producer, and operates mines and development projects on four continents.

The fortunes of any mining company are tied closely to the price of its product—in this case the price of gold. During 2003 and 2004, the price of gold rallied on several occasions on geopolitical concerns caused by the war with Iraq. In each case gold prices eventually returned to around the US$400 per ounce level. The factors that affect the price of gold bullion include supply/demand imbalances, the readiness of major gold holders such as central banks to sell some of their holdings, speculative interest, long-term investment interest, as well as seasonal changes in demand. Speculative and long-term interest comes from the view that gold is an alternative to traditional investments. It is seen as a hedge against disaster, inflation, weak stock markets, and volatile currency markets.

The other major factor in a mining company's health are the number of years left in production from existing mines. A mine is a wasting asset so, all other things being equal, a company will tend to lose value over time unless it can constantly find and develop new properties. Barrick Gold, for example, has around 20 years left in its mines throughout the world. Such a level is necessary due to regulatory concerns. In North America a new mine can take from five to seven years to go from discovery to production. Controversial projects can take even longer. Even in other countries, the average time to get a mine up and running is three to five years. Thus, companies with between five and seven years of reserves can face considerable pressure as time starts running out.

Mining companies, like all companies, are also affected by the state and health of the overall industry, the economy, and the stock market generally. Barrick Gold expects to produce about 6 million ounces of gold annually, at a total cost of about US$195 an ounce. Between 2005 and 2008, the company has four mines that are scheduled to come online that will add a further 2 million ounces of annual gold production.

Because of Barrick's hedging strategy the company's stock price has been far less volatile than other gold producers such as Freeport McMoran Copper and Gold, and Placer Dome. Hedging is the sale of gold at a fixed price in the future. This reduces any loss that can occur if the price of gold falls dramatically after Barrick has entered into an agreement to sell the gold at a fixed (higher) price. However, if gold prices were to rise dramatically, Barrick would not benefit from such price increases, as it had already entered into agreements to sell its gold. Thus, hedging reduces the impact of price volatility on a company. Approximately 19 percent of the firm's 86 million ounces of gold reserves are hedged.

With the price of gold being flat or declining throughout the last decade, this hedging strategy paid off well for Barrick. Barrick was able to sell its gold at amounts that were above the market price for 15 years from 1988 to 2002, which netted the company about $2 billion.

Barrick has announced that it is scrapping its hedging program. This will result in the company being more able to benefit from a rise in gold prices. At the same time, it is more vulnerable to any decline in the price of the base metal.

Sources: F. Freeman, "Gold," *Handbook of Canadian Security Analysis*, Volume 1 (Toronto: John Wiley, 1997); Morningstar, "Barrick Gold," *Morningstar Stocks 500*; Barrick Gold at www.barrick.com/1_Global_Operations.

Spot Exchange Rates

When two parties agree to exchange currency and execute the deal immediately, the transaction is referred to as a spot exchange. Exchange rates governing such "on the spot" trades are referred to as spot exchange rates. The **spot exchange rate** is the rate at which a foreign exchange dealer converts one currency into another currency on a particular day. Thus, when our Canadian tourist in Edinburgh goes to a bank to convert her Canadian dollars into pounds, the exchange rate is the spot rate for that day.

SPOT EXCHANGE RATE The exchange rate at which a foreign exchange dealer will convert one currency into another that particular day.

Spot exchange rates are reported daily in the financial pages of newspapers. Table 9.1 shows the dollar exchange rates for currencies traded in the New York Foreign Exchange market as of March 2, 2004. Spot exchange rates can also be found on the Web (for example, at www.finance.yahoo.com). An exchange rate can be quoted in two ways: as the price of the foreign currency in terms of dollars (for example, $0.008095 per yen; $0.8808 per euro) or as the price of dollars in terms of the foreign currency (for example, ¥123.54 per dollar; €1.1353 per dollar). The first of these exchange rate quotations (dollar per foreign currency) is said to be in *direct* (or American) terms, the second (foreign currency units per dollar) in *indirect* terms.

Spot rates change continually, often on a day-by-day basis (although the magnitude of the changes over such short time periods is small). The value of a currency is determined by the interaction between the demand and supply of that currency relative to the demand and supply of other currencies. For example, if lots of people want U.S. dollars and dollars are in short supply, and few people want British pounds and pounds are in plentiful supply, the spot exchange rate for converting dollars into pounds will change. The dollar is likely to appreciate against the pound (or, conversely, the pound will depreciate against the dollar). Imagine the spot exchange rate is £1 = US$1.50 when the market opens. As the day progresses, dealers demand more dollars and fewer pounds. By the end of the day, the spot exchange rate might be £1 = US$1.48. The dollar has appreciated, and the pound has depreciated.

Forward Exchange Rates

The fact that spot exchange rates change continually as determined by the relative demand and supply for different currencies can be problematic for an international business. A large Canadian company with an active U.S. dollar account that imports laptop computers from Japan knows that in 30 days it must pay yen to a Japanese supplier when a shipment arrives. The company will pay the Japanese supplier ¥200,000 for each laptop computer, and the current dollar/yen spot exchange rate is $1 = ¥120. At this rate, each computer costs the importer $1,667 (i.e., 1,667 = 200,000/120). The importer knows she can sell the computers the day they arrive for $2,000 each, which yields a gross profit of $333 on each computer ($2,000 − $1,667). However, the importer will not have the funds to pay the Japanese supplier until the computers have been sold. If over the next 30 days the dollar unexpectedly depreciates against the yen, say to $1 = ¥95, the importer will still have to pay the Japanese company ¥200,000 per computer, but in dollar terms that would be equivalent to $2,105 per computer, which is more than she can sell the computers for. A depreciation in the value of the dollar against the yen from $1 = ¥120 to $1 = ¥95 would transform a profitable deal into an unprofitable one.

FORWARD EXCHANGE When two parties agree to exchange currency and execute a deal at some specific date in the future.

To avoid this risk, the Canadian importer might want to engage in a forward exchange in U.S. dollars. A **forward exchange** occurs when two parties agree to exchange currency and execute the deal at some specific date in the future. Exchange rates governing such future transactions are referred to as **forward exchange rates.** For most major currencies, forward exchange rates are quoted for 30 days, 90 days, and 180 days into the future. (Forward exchange rate quotations appear in Table 9.1.) In some cases, it is possible to get forward exchange rates for several years into the future. The opening case,

FORWARD EXCHANGE RATES The exchange rates governing forward exchange transactions.

TABLE 9.1

Foreign Exchange Quotations, March 2, 2004

Source: www.x-rates.com/d/USD/table.html.

	UNITS OF FOREIGN CURRENCY ONE U.S. DOLLAR BUYS	U.S. DOLLARS ONE UNIT OF FOREIGN CURRENCY BUYS
Australian dollar	1.31406	0.761
Botswana pula	4.82044	0.20745
Brazilian real	2.907	0.343997
British pound	0.543892	1.8386
Canadian dollar	1.3437	0.744214
Chinese yuan	8.2768	0.12082
Danish krone	6.1045	0.163814
Euro	0.818867	1.2212
Hong Kong dollar	7.7858	0.128439
Hungarian forint	206.66	0.00483887
Indian rupee	45.25	0.0220994
Japanese yen	110.27	0.00906865
Malaysian ringgit	3.8	0.263158
Mexican peso	10.962	0.0912242
New Zealand dollar	1.46864	0.680902
Norwegian kroner	7.1325	0.140203
Singapore dollar	1.7087	0.58524
South African rand	6.715	0.14892
South Korean won	1174	0.000851789
Sri Lanka rupee	97.65	0.0102407
Swedish krona	7.5925	0.131709
Swiss franc	1.2963	0.771426
Taiwan dollar	33.3	0.03003
Thai baht	39.35	0.025413
Venezuelan bolivar	1920	0.000520833

for example, reported how JAL entered into a contract that predicted forward exchange rates up to ten years in the future. Returning to our computer importer example, let us assume the 30-day forward exchange rate for converting dollars into yen is \$1 = ¥110. The importer enters into a 30-day forward exchange transaction with a foreign exchange dealer at this rate and is guaranteed that she will have to pay no more than \$1,818 for each computer (1,818 = 200,000/110). This guarantees her a profit of \$182 per computer (\$2,000 − \$1,818). She also insures herself against the possibility that an unanticipated change in the dollar/yen exchange rate will turn a profitable deal into an unprofitable one. In this example, the spot exchange rate (\$1 = ¥120) and the 30-day forward rate (\$1 = ¥110) differ. Such differences are normal; they reflect the expectations of the foreign exchange market about future currency movements. In our example, the fact that \$1 bought more yen with a spot exchange than with a 30-day forward exchange indicates foreign exchange dealers expected the dollar to depreciate against the yen in the next 30 days. When this occurs, we say the dollar is selling at a *discount* on the 30-day forward market (i.e., it is worth less than on the spot market). Of course, the opposite can also occur. If the 30-day forward exchange rate were \$1 = ¥130, for example, \$1 would buy more yen with a forward exchange than with a spot exchange. In such a case, we say the dollar is selling at a *premium* on the 30-day forward market. This reflects the foreign exchange dealers' expectations that the dollar will appreciate against the yen over the next 30 days.

Currency Swaps

The above discussion of spot and forward exchange rates might lead you to conclude that the option to buy forward is very important to companies engaged in international trade–and you would be right. By 2001, the last year for which international data are available, forward instruments accounted for some 67 percent of all foreign exchange transactions, while spot exchanges accounted for 33 percent.[4] However, the vast majority of these forward exchanges were not forward exchanges of the type we have been discussing, but rather a more sophisticated instrument known as currency swaps.

A **currency swap** is the simultaneous purchase and sale of a given amount of foreign exchange for two different value dates. Swaps are transacted between international businesses and their banks, between banks, and between governments when it is desirable to move out of one currency into another for a limited period without incurring foreign exchange risk. A common kind of swap is spot against forward. Consider a company such as Apple Computer. Apple assembles laptop computers in the United States, but the screens are made in Japan. Apple also sells some of the finished laptops in Japan. So, like many companies, Apple both buys from and sells to Japan. Imagine Apple needs to change $1 million into yen to pay its supplier of laptop screens today. Apple knows that in 90 days it will be paid ¥120 million by the Japanese importer that buys its finished laptops. It will want to convert these yen into dollars for use in the United States. Let us say today's spot exchange rate is $1 = ¥120 and the 90-day forward exchange rate is $1 = ¥110. Apple sells $1 million to its bank in return for ¥120 million. Now Apple can pay its Japanese supplier. At the same time, Apple enters into a 90-day forward exchange deal with its bank for converting ¥120 million into dollars. Thus, in 90 days Apple will receive $1.09 million (¥120 million/110 = $1.09 million). Since the yen is trading at a premium on the 90-day forward market, Apple ends up with more dollars than it started with (although the opposite could also occur). The swap deal is just like a conventional forward deal in one important respect: It enables Apple to insure itself against foreign exchange risk. By engaging in a swap, Apple knows today that the ¥120 million payment it will receive in 90 days will yield $1.09 million.

CURRENCY SWAP
Simultaneous purchase and sale of a given amount of foreign exchange for two different value dates.

THE NATURE OF THE FOREIGN EXCHANGE MARKET

So far we have dealt with the foreign exchange market only as an abstract concept. It is now time to take a closer look at the nature of this market. The foreign exchange market is not located in any one place. It is a global network of banks, brokers, and foreign exchange dealers connected by electronic communications systems. When companies wish to convert currencies, they typically go through their own banks rather than entering the market directly. The foreign exchange market has been growing at a rapid

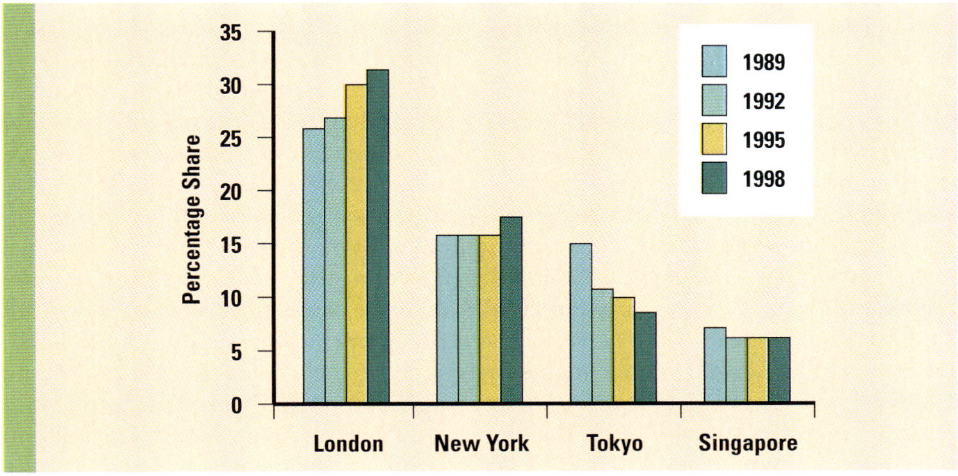

FIGURE 9.1
Geographical Distribution of Global Foreign Exchange Activity (percentage share of total average daily turnover)

Source: Bank for International Settlements, *Central Bank Survey of Foreign Exchange and Derivatives Market Activity, April 2001* (Basle, Switzerland: BIS, 2001).

London's central position between Tokyo and Singapore to the east and New York to the west has made it the critical link between the East Asian and New York markets.
AP Photo/Sang Tan.

pace, reflecting a general growth in the volume of cross-border trade and investment (see Chapter 1). In March 1986, the average total value of global foreign exchange trading was about $200 billion per day. By April 1995, it was over $1.200 billion per day, and by April 1998 it reached $1.490 billion per day. However, it fell back to $1.200 billion per day in April 2001, largely due to the introduction of the euro, which reduced the number of major trading currencies in the world.[5] The world's key money trading centres are London, New York, Tokyo, and Singapore. Major secondary trading centres include Zurich, Frankfurt, Paris, Hong Kong, San Francisco, and Sydney. Much to the dismay of pundits' claim of Toronto's status as a world class city, Toronto does not figure on the map as a second-tier global financial city.

As seen earlier in this chapter, the Canadian dollar is not widely used in cross-border trade, investment, and payments. In exchange traded currencies, if an individual or a company wants to trade large quantities of the Canadian dollar, they cannot even do this within Canada. Instead, they would have to trade it through the Chicago Mercantile Exchange. To put this in perspective, if we take all of the futures contracts traded on every commodity, in every American Futures Exchange, the Canadian dollar ranked 29th in trading 4.2 million contracts.[6]

London's dominance in the foreign exchange market is due to both history and geography. As the capital of the world's first major industrial trading nation, London had become the world's largest centre for international banking by the end of the nineteenth century, a position it has retained. Today London's central position between Tokyo and Singapore to the east and New York to the west has made it the critical link between the East Asian and New York markets. Due to time zone differences, London opens soon after Tokyo closes for the night and is still open for the first few hours of trading in New York.

Two features of the foreign exchange market are of particular note. The first is that the market never sleeps. Tokyo, London, and New York are all shut for only three hours out of every 24. During these three hours, trading continues in a number of minor centres, particularly San Francisco and Sydney, Australia. The second feature of the market is the extent of integration of the various trading centres. High-speed computer links between trading centres around the globe have effectively created a single market. The integration of financial centres implies there can be no significant difference in exchange rates quoted in the trading centres. For example, if the yen/dollar exchange rate quoted in London at 3 P.M. is ¥120 = $1, the yen/dollar exchange rate quoted in New York at the same time (10 A.M. New York time) will be identical. If the New York yen/dollar exchange rate were ¥125 = $1, a dealer could make a profit through **arbitrage,** buying a currency low and selling it high. For example, if the prices differed in London and New York as given, a dealer in New York could take $1 million and use that to purchase ¥125 million. She could then immediately sell the ¥125 million for dollars in London, where the

ARBITRAGE The purchase of securities in one market for immediate resale in another to profit from a price discrepancy.

transaction would yield $1.046666 million, allowing the trader to book a profit of $46,666 on the transaction. If all dealers tried to cash in on the opportunity, however, the demand for yen in New York would rise, resulting in an appreciation of the yen against the dollar such that the price differential between New York and London would quickly disappear. Since foreign exchange dealers are continually watching their computer screens for arbitrage opportunities, the few that arise tend to be small, and they disappear in minutes.

Another feature of the foreign exchange market is the important role played by the U.S. dollar. Although a foreign exchange transaction can in theory involve any two currencies, most transactions involve dollars on one side. This is true even when a dealer wants to sell a non-dollar currency and buy another. A dealer wishing to sell the Korean won for Canadian dollars, for example, will usually sell the won for U.S. dollars, and then use the U.S. dollars to buy the Canadian dollars. Although this may seem a roundabout way of doing things, it is actually cheaper than trying to find a holder of Canadian dollars who wants to buy won. Because the volume of international transactions involving U.S. dollars is so great, it is not hard to find dealers who wish to trade U.S. dollars for won or Canadian dollars.

Due to its central role in so many foreign exchange deals, the dollar is a vehicle currency. In April 2001, 90 percent of all foreign exchange transactions involved dollars on one side of the transaction. After the dollar, the most important vehicle currencies were the euro and the British pound–reflecting the importance of these trading entities in the world economy. Since the implementation of the euro, it has replaced the German mark as the world's second most important vehicle currency. The British pound used to be second in importance to the dollar as a vehicle currency, but its importance has diminished in recent years. Despite this, London has retained its leading position in the global foreign exchange market.

ECONOMIC THEORIES OF EXCHANGE RATE DETERMINATION

At the most basic level, exchange rates are determined by the demand and supply of one currency relative to the demand and supply of another. For example, if the demand for dollars outstrips the supply of them and if the supply of Japanese yen is greater than the demand for them, the dollar/yen exchange rate will change. The dollar will appreciate against the yen (or the yen will depreciate against the dollar). However, differences in relative demand and supply explain the determination of exchange rates only in a superficial sense. This simple explanation does not tell us what factors underlie the demand for and supply of a currency. Nor does it tell us when the demand for dollars will exceed the supply (and vice versa) or when the supply of Japanese yen will exceed demand for them (and vice versa). Neither does it tell us under what conditions a currency is in demand or under what conditions it is not demanded. In this section, we will review economic theory's answers to these questions. This will give us a deeper understanding of how exchange rates are determined.

If we understand how exchange rates are determined, we may be able to forecast exchange rate movements. Since future exchange rate movements influence export opportunities, the profitability of international trade and investment deals, and the price competitiveness of foreign imports, this is valuable information for an international business. Unfortunately, there is no simple explanation. The forces that determine exchange rates are complex, and no theoretical consensus exists, even among academic economists who study the phenomenon every day. Nonetheless, most economic theories of exchange rate movements seem to agree that three factors have an important impact on future exchange rate movements in a country's currency: the country's price inflation, its interest rate, and market psychology.[7]

PRICES AND EXCHANGE RATES

To understand how prices are related to exchange rate movements, we first need to discuss an economic proposition known as the law of one price. Then we will discuss the theory of purchasing power parity (PPP), which links changes in the exchange rate between two countries' currencies to changes in the countries' price levels.

The Law of One Price

LAW OF ONE PRICE In competitive markets free of transportation costs and barriers to trade, identical products sold in different countries must sell for the same price when their price is expressed in the same currency.

The **law of one price** states that in competitive markets free of transportation costs and barriers to trade (such as tariffs), identical products sold in different countries must sell for the same price when their price is expressed in terms of the same currency.[8] For example, if the exchange rate between the British pound and the U.S. dollar is £1=US$1.50, a jacket that retails for US$75 in New York should sell for £50 in London (since $75/1.50 = £50). Consider what would happen if the jacket cost £40 in London ($60 in U.S. currency). At this price, it would pay a trader to buy jackets in London and sell them in New York (an example of arbitrage). The company initially could make a profit of $15 on each jacket by purchasing it for £40 ($60) in London and selling it for $75 in New York (we are assuming away transportation costs and trade barriers). However, the increased demand for jackets in London would raise their price in London, and the increased supply of jackets in New York would lower their price there. This would continue until prices were equalized. Thus, prices might equalize when the jacket cost £44 ($66) in London and $66 in New York (assuming no change in the exchange rate of £1=US$1.50).

ANOTHER PERSPECTIVE

The Internet and the law of one price

The law of one price applies to Internet buying across national borders because Internet research can provide accurate pricing information across markets. Many Americans are trying to invoke the law of one price with pharmaceuticals, which, they have discovered, sell at lower costs in Canada than in the United States. There are several barriers, though—transportation costs and a U.S. law, designed to protect U.S. consumers, that forbids the import of pharmaceuticals. As these barriers fall, we should see the law of one price force down U.S. prescription drug costs.

Purchasing Power Parity

If the law of one price were true for all goods and services, the purchasing power parity (PPP) exchange rate could be found from any individual set of prices. By comparing the prices of identical products in different currencies, it would be possible to determine the "real" or PPP exchange rate that would exist if markets were efficient. (An **efficient market** has no impediments to the free flow of goods and services, such as trade barriers.)

EFFICIENT MARKET A market where prices reflect all available information.

RELATIVELY EFFICIENT MARKETS One in which few impediments to international trade and investment exist.

A less extreme version of the PPP theory states that given **relatively efficient markets**–that is, markets in which few impediments to international trade exist–the price of a "basket of goods" should be roughly equivalent in each country. To express the PPP theory in symbols, let $P_\$$ be the U.S. dollar price of a basket of particular goods and $P_¥$ be the price of the same basket of goods in Japanese yen. The PPP theory predicts that the dollar/yen exchange rate, $E_{\$/¥}$, should be equivalent to:

$$E_{\$/¥} = P_\$/P_¥$$

Thus, if a basket of goods costs $200 in the United States and ¥20,000 in Japan, PPP theory predicts that the dollar/yen exchange rate should be US$200/¥20,000 or $0.01 per Japanese yen (i.e., US$1=¥100).

Every year, the newsmagazine *The Economist* publishes its own version of the PPP theorem, which it refers to as the "Big Mac Index." *The Economist* has selected McDonald's "Big Mac" as a proxy for a "basket of goods" because it is produced according to more or less the same recipe in about 120 countries. The Big Mac PPP is the exchange rate that would leave hamburgers costing the same in each country. According to *The Economist,* comparing a country's actual exchange rate with the one predicted by the PPP theorem based on relative prices of Big Macs is a test on whether a currency is undervalued or not. This is not a totally serious exercise, as *The Economist* admits, but it does illustrate the PPP theorem.

Table 9.2 reproduces the Big Mac index for May 2004. The first column of the table shows the price of a Big Mac, converted into U.S. dollars at current exchange rates. The average price of a Big Mac in Canada is $2.33, in Russia it is $1.45, and in the

TABLE 9.2

The Hamburger Standard

Source: "Big Mac Index," *The Economist,* May 27, 2004. www.economist.com.

	BIG MAC PRICE IN DOLLARS*	IMPLIED PPP† OF THE DOLLAR	UNDER (−)/ OVER(+) VALUATION AGAINST THE DOLLAR, %		BIG MAC PRICE IN DOLLARS*	IMPLIED PPP† OF THE DOLLAR	UNDER (−)/ OVER(+) VALUATION AGAINST THE DOLLAR, %
United States‡	2.90	–	–	Aruba	2.29	1.41	-21
Argentina	1.48	1.50	-49	Belarus	1.37	1021	-53
Australia	2.27	1.12	-22	Bulgaria	1.85	1.03	-36
Brazil	1.70	1.86	-41	Columbia	2.35	2241	-19
Britain	3.37	1.54§	+16	Costa Rica	2.61	390	-10
Canada	2.33	1.10	-20	Croatia	2.42	5.14	-17
Chile	2.18	483	-25	Dom. Rep.	1.32	20.7	-54
China	1.26	3.59	-57	Estonia	2.27	10.2	-22
Czech Rep.	2.13	19.5	-27	Fuji	2.35	1.47	-19
Denmark	4.46	9.57	+54	Georgia	1.90	1.26	-34
Egypt	1.62	3.45	-44	Guatemala	2.01	5.52	-31
Euro area	3.28**	1.06††	+13	Honduras	1.98	12.4	-32
Hong Kong	1.54	4.14	-47	Iceland	6.01	151	107
Hungary	2.52	183	-13	Jamaica	1.88	39.0	-35
Indonesia	1.77	5,552	-39	Jordan	3.65	0.89	26
Japan	2.33	90.3	-20	Kuwait	7.33	0.74	153
Malaysia	1.33	1.74	-54	Latvia	2.00	0.38	-31
Mexico	2.08	8.28	-28	Lebanon	2.84	1483	-2
New Zealand	2.65	1.50	-8	Lithuania	2.26	2.24	-22
Peru	2.57	3.10	-11	Macau	1.40	3.86	-52
Philippines	1.23	23.8	-57	Macedonia	1.84	32.8	-36
Poland	1.63	2.17	-44	Moldova	1.93	7.93	-33
Russia	1.45	14.5	-50	Morocco	0.26	0.82	-91
Singapore	1.92	1.14	-34	Nicaragua	2.19	11.9	-25
South Africa	1.86	4.28	-36	Norway	5.18	12.2	79
South Korea	2.72	1,103	-6	Pakistan	1.90	37.9	-34
Sweden	3.94	10.3	+36	Qatar	0.68	0.85	-77
Switzerland	4.90	2.17	+69	Saudi Arabia	0.64	0.83	-78
Taiwan	2.24	25.9	-23	Slovakia	1.98	22.8	-32
Thailand	1.45	20.3	-50	Slovenia	2.42	166	-17
Turkey	2.58	1,362,069	-11	Sri Lanka	1.41	48.3	-51
Venezuela	1.48	1,517	-49	Ukraine	1.36	2.50	-53
				UAE	0.67	0.84	-77
				Uruguay	1.00	10.3	-65

*At current exchange rates

†Purchasing-power parity

‡Average of New York, Chicago, San Francisco and Atlanta

§Dollars per pound

**Weighted average of member countries

††Dollars per euro

United States it is \$2.90. The next column shows the PPP exchange rate implied by these different prices. Thus, the PPP exchange rate for the Canadian dollar to the U.S. dollar is 1.10. The PPP of the Russian ruble to the U.S. dollar is 14.5. Column three shows the actual exchange rate compared to the exchange rate predicted by PPP. This tells us that the Canadian dollar is 20 percent undervalued against the U.S. dollar and should appreciate against the U.S. dollar by that amount, according to the PPP theorem. If the Big Mac index were an accurate indicator of PPPs, which it is not, a glance down column three suggests that the U.S. dollar was significantly overvalued against the majority of currencies in early 2004 and would be expected to depreciate in value over the next few months.

The next step in the PPP theory is to argue that the exchange rate will change if relative prices change. For example, imagine there is no price inflation in the United States, while prices in Japan are increasing by 10 percent a year. At the beginning of the year, a basket of goods costs \$200 in the United States and ¥20,000 in Japan, so the dollar/yen exchange rate, according to PPP theory, should be US\$1 = ¥100. At the end of the year, the basket of goods still costs \$200 in the United States, but it costs ¥22,000 in Japan. PPP theory predicts that the exchange rate should change as a result. More precisely, by the end of the year:

$$E_{\$/¥} = \text{US\$200/¥22,000}$$

Thus, ¥1 = US\$0.0091 (or US\$1 = ¥110). Because of 10 percent price inflation, the Japanese yen has *depreciated* by 10 percent against the dollar. One U.S. dollar will buy 10 percent more yen at the end of the year than at the beginning.

Money Supply and Price Inflation

In essence, PPP theory predicts that changes in relative prices will result in a change in exchange rates. Theoretically, a country in which price inflation is running wild should expect to see its currency depreciate against that of countries in which inflation rates are lower. If we can predict what a country's future inflation rate is likely to be, we can also predict how the value of its currency relative to other currencies–its exchange rate–is likely to change. The growth rate of a country's money supply determines its likely future inflation rate.[9] Thus, in theory at least, we can use information about the growth in money supply to forecast exchange rate movements.

Inflation is a monetary phenomenon. It occurs when the quantity of money in circulation rises faster than the stock of goods and services; that is, when the money supply increases faster than output increases. Imagine what would happen if everyone in the country was suddenly given \$10,000 by the government. Many people would rush out to spend their extra money on those things they had always wanted–new cars, new furniture, better clothes, and so on. There would be a surge in demand for goods and services. Car dealers, department stores, and other providers of goods and services would respond to this upsurge in demand by raising prices. The result would be price inflation.

A government increasing the money supply is analogous to giving people more money. An increase in the money supply makes it easier for banks to borrow from the government and for individuals and companies to borrow from banks. The resulting increase in credit causes increases in demand for goods and services. Unless the output of goods and services is growing at a rate similar to that of the money supply, the result will be inflation. This relationship has been observed time after time in country after country.

So now we have a connection between the growth in a country's money supply, price inflation, and exchange rate movements. Put simply, when the growth in a country's money supply is faster than the growth in its output, price inflation is fuelled. The PPP theory tells us that a country with a high inflation rate will see a depreciation in its currency exchange rate. In one of the clearest historical examples, in the mid-1980s, Bolivia experienced hyperinflation–an explosive and seemingly uncontrollable price inflation in which money loses value very rapidly. Table 9.3 presents data on Bolivia's money supply, inflation rate, and its peso's exchange rate with the U.S. dollar during the period of hyperinflation. The exchange rate is actually the "black market" exchange rate; the Bolivian government prohibited converting the peso to other currencies during the period. The data show that the growth in money supply, the rate of price inflation, and the depreciation of the peso against the dollar all moved in step with each other. This is just what PPP theory and monetary economics predict. Between April 1984 and July 1985, Bolivia's money supply increased by 17 433 percent, prices increased by 22 908 percent, and the value of the peso against the U.S. dollar fell by 24 662 percent! In October 1985, the Bolivian government instituted a dramatic stabilization plan–which included the introduction of a new currency and tight control of the money supply–and by 1987 the country's annual inflation rate was down to 16 percent.[10]

Another way of looking at the same phenomenon is that an increase in a country's money supply, which increases the amount of currency available, changes the relative demand and supply conditions in the foreign exchange market. If the U.S. money supply is growing more rapidly than U.S. output, dollars will be relatively more plentiful than the currencies of countries where monetary growth is closer to output growth. As a result of this relative increase in the supply of dollars, the dollar will depreciate on the foreign exchange market against the currencies of countries with slower monetary growth.

Government policy determines whether the rate of growth in a country's money supply is greater than the rate of growth in output. A government can increase the money supply simply by telling the country's central bank to print more money. Governments tend to do this to finance public expenditure (building roads, paying government workers, paying for defence, etc.). A government could finance public expenditure by raising taxes, but because nobody likes paying more taxes and politicians do not like to

MONTH	MONEY SUPPLY (BILLIONS OF PESOS)	PRICE LEVEL RELATIVE TO 1982 (AVERAGE = 1)	EXCHANGE RATE (PESOS PER DOLLAR)
1984			
April	270	21.1	3,576
May	330	31.1	3.512
June	440	32.3	3,342
July	599	34.0	3,570
August	718	39.1	7,038
September	889	53.7	13,685
October	1,194	85.5	15,205
November	1,495	112.4	18,469
December	3,296	180.9	24,515
1985			
January	4,630	305.3	73,016
February	6,455	863.3	141,101
March	9,089	1,078.6	128,137
April	12,885	1,205.7	167,428
May	21,309	1,635.7	272,375
June	27,778	2,919.1	481,756
July	47,341	4,854.6	885,476
August	74,306	8,081.0	1,182,300
September	103,272	12,647.6	1,087,440
October	132,550	12,411.8	1,120,210

TABLE 9.3

Macroeconomic Data for Bolivia, April 1984–October 1985

Source: From Juan-Antino Morales, "Inflation Stabilization in Bolivia," in *Inflation Stabilization: The Experience of Israel, Argentina, Brazil, Bolivia, and Mexico,* ed. Michael Bruno et al. MIT Press, 1998. Reprinted with permission.

be unpopular, they have a natural preference for printing money. Unfortunately, there is no magic money tree. The inevitable result of excessive growth in money supply is price inflation. However, this has not stopped governments around the world from printing money, with predictable results. If an international business is attempting to predict future movements in the value of a country's currency on the foreign exchange market, it should examine that country's policy toward monetary growth. If the government seems committed to controlling the rate of growth in money supply, the country's future inflation rate may be low (even if the current rate is high) and its currency should not depreciate too much on the foreign exchange market. If the government seems to lack the political will to control the rate of growth in money supply, the future inflation rate may be high, which is likely to cause its currency to depreciate. Historically, many Latin American governments have fallen into this latter category, including Argentina, Bolivia, and Brazil. More recently, many of the newly democratic states of Eastern Europe made the same mistake.

Empirical Tests of PPP Theory

PPP theory predicts that exchange rates are determined by relative prices, and that changes in relative prices will result in a change in exchange rates. A country in which price inflation is running wild should expect to see its currency depreciate against that of countries with lower inflation rates. This is intuitively appealing, but is it true? There are several good examples of the connection between a country's price inflation and exchange rate position (such as Bolivia). However, extensive empirical testing of PPP theory has yielded mixed results.[11] While PPP theory seems to yield relatively accurate predictions in the long run, it does not appear to be a strong predictor of short-run movements in exchange rates covering time spans of five years or less.[12] In addition, the theory seems to best predict exchange rate changes for countries with high rates of inflation and underdeveloped capital markets. The theory is less useful for predicting short-term exchange rate movements between the currencies of advanced industrialized nations that have relatively small differentials in inflation rates.

The failure to find a strong link between relative inflation rates and exchange rate movements has been referred to as the purchasing power parity puzzle. Several factors may explain the failure of PPP theory to predict exchange rates more accurately.[13] PPP theory assumes away transportation costs and barriers to trade. In practice, these factors are significant and they tend to create significant price differentials between countries. Transportation costs are certainly not trivial for many goods. Moreover, as we saw in Chapter 6, governments routinely intervene in international trade, creating tariff and nontariff barriers to cross-border trade. Barriers to trade limit the ability of traders to use arbitrage to equalize prices for the same product in different countries, which is required for the law of one price to hold. Government intervention in cross-border trade, by violating the assumption of efficient markets, weakens the link between relative price changes and changes in exchange rates predicted by PPP theory.

In addition, the PPP theory may not hold if many national markets are dominated by a handful of multinational enterprises that have sufficient market power to influence prices, control distribution channels, and differentiate their product offerings between nations.[14] In fact, this situation seems to prevail in a number of industries. In the detergent industry, two companies, Unilever and Procter & Gamble, dominate the market in nation after nation. In heavy earthmoving equipment, Caterpillar Inc. and Komatsu are global market leaders. In the market for semiconductor equipment, Applied Materials has a commanding market share lead in almost every important national market. Microsoft dominates the market for personal computer operating systems and applications systems around the world, and so on. In such cases, dominant enterprises may be able to exercise a degree of pricing power, setting different prices in different markets to reflect varying demand conditions. This is referred to as price discrimination (we consider the topic from a strategic perspective in Chapter 14).

For price discrimination to work, arbitrage must be limited. According to this argument, enterprises with some market power may be able to control distribution channels and therefore limit the unauthorized resale (arbitrage) of products purchased in another national market. They may also be able to limit resale (arbitrage) by differentiating otherwise identical products among nations along some line, such as design or packaging. For example, even though the version of Microsoft Office sold in China may be less expensive than the version sold in the United States, the use of arbitrage to equalize prices may be limited because few Americans would want a version that was based on Chinese characters. The design differentiation between Microsoft Office for China and for the United States means that the law of one price would not work for Microsoft Office, even if transportation costs were trivial and tariff barriers between the United States and China did not exist. If the inability to practice arbitrage were widespread enough, it would break the connection between changes in relative prices and exchange rates predicted by the PPP theorem and help explain the limited empirical support for this theory.

Another factor of some importance is that governments also intervene in the foreign exchange market in attempting to influence the value of their currencies. We will look at why and how they do this in Chapter 10. For now, the important thing to note is that governments regularly intervene in the foreign exchange market, and this further weakens the link between price changes and changes in exchange rates. One more factor explaining the failure of PPP theory to predict short-term movements in foreign exchange rates is the impact of investor psychology and other factors on currency purchasing decisions and exchange rate movements. We will discuss this issue in more detail later in this chapter.

INTEREST RATES AND EXCHANGE RATES

Economic theory tells us that interest rates reflect expectations about likely future inflation rates. In countries where inflation is expected to be high, interest rates also will be high, because investors want compensation for the decline in the value of their money. This relationship was first formalized by economist Irvin Fisher and is referred to as the Fisher Effect. The Fisher Effect states that a country's "nominal" interest rate (i) is the sum of the required "real" rate of interest (r) and the expected rate of inflation over the period for which the funds are to be lent (I). More formally,

$$i = r + I$$

For example, if the real rate of interest in a country is 5 percent and annual inflation is expected to be 10 percent, the nominal interest rate will be 15 percent. As predicted by the Fisher Effect, a strong relationship seems to exist between inflation rates and interest rates.[15]

We can take this one step further and consider how it applies in a world of many countries and unrestricted capital flows. When investors are free to transfer capital between countries, real interest rates will be the same in every country. If differences in real interest rates did emerge between countries, arbitrage would soon equalize them. For example, if the real interest rate in Canada was 10 percent and only 6 percent in the United States, it would pay investors to borrow money in the United States and invest it in Canada. The resulting increase in the demand for money in the United States would raise the real interest rate there, while the increase in the supply of foreign money in Canada would lower the real interest rate there. This would continue until the two sets of real interest rates were equalized. (In practice, differences in real interest rates may persist due to government controls on capital flows; investors are not always free to transfer capital between countries.)

It follows from the Fisher Effect that if the real interest rate is the same worldwide, any difference in interest rates between countries reflects differing expectations about inflation rates. Thus, if the expected rate of inflation in the United States is greater than that in Canada, U.S. nominal interest rates will be greater than Canadian nominal interest rates.

INTERNATIONAL FISHER EFFECT
For any two countries, the spot exchange rate should change in an equal amount but in the opposite direction to the difference in nominal interest rates between countries.

Since we know from PPP theory that there is a link (in theory at least) between inflation and exchange rates, and since interest rates reflect expectations about inflation, it follows that there must also be a link between interest rates and exchange rates. This link is known as the **International Fisher Effect** (IFE). The International Fisher Effect states that for any two countries, the spot exchange rate should change in an equal amount but in the opposite direction to the difference in nominal interest rates between the two countries. The change in the spot exchange rate between the United States and Canada, for example, can be modelled as follows:

$$(S_1 - S_2)/S_2 \times 100 = i_{\$} - i_{CAD}$$

where $i_{\$}$ and i_{CAD} are the respective nominal interest rates in the United States and Canada, S_1 is the spot exchange rate at the beginning of the period, and S_2 is the spot exchange rate at the end of the period. If the U.S. nominal interest rate is higher than Canada's, reflecting greater expected inflation rates, the value of the dollar against the yen should fall by that interest rate differential in the future. So if the interest rate in the United States is 10 percent and in Canada it is 6 percent, we would expect the value of the dollar to depreciate by 4 percent against the Canadian dollar.

Do interest rate differentials help predict future currency movements? The evidence is mixed; as in the case of PPP theory, in the long run, there seems to be a relationship between interest rate differentials and subsequent changes in spot exchange rates. However, considerable short-run deviations occur. Like PPP, the International Fisher Effect is not a good predictor of short-run changes in spot exchange rates.[16]

INVESTOR PSYCHOLOGY AND BANDWAGON EFFECTS

Empirical evidence suggests that neither PPP theory nor the International Fisher Effect are particularly good at explaining short-term movements in exchange rates. One reason may be the impact of investor psychology on short-run exchange rate movements. Increasing evidence reveals that psychological factors play an important role in determining the expectations of market traders as to likely future exchange rates.[17] In turn, expectations have a tendency to become self-fulfilling prophecies.

According to a number of studies, investor psychology and bandwagon effects play a major role in determining short-run exchange rate movements.[18] However, these effects can be hard to predict. Investor psychology can be influenced by political factors and by microeconomic events, such as the investment decisions of individual firms, many of which are only loosely linked to macroeconomic fundamentals, such as relative inflation rates. Also, bandwagon effects can be both triggered and exacerbated by the idiosyncratic behaviour of politicians. Something like this seems to have occurred in Southeast Asia during 1997 when one after another, the currencies of Thailand, Malaysia, South Korea, and Indonesia lost between 50 percent and 70 percent of their value against the U.S. dollar in a few months. For a detailed look at what occurred in South Korea, see the accompanying Country Focus. The collapse in the value of the Korean currency did not occur because South Korea had a higher inflation rate than the United States. It occurred because of an excessive buildup of dollar-denominated debt among South Korean firms. By mid-1997, it was clear that these companies were having trouble servicing this debt. Foreign investors, fearing a wave of corporate bankruptcies, took their money out of the country, exchanging won for U.S. dollars. As this began to depress the exchange rate, currency traders jumped on the bandwagon and speculated against the won (selling it short).

SUMMARY

Relative monetary growth, relative inflation rates, and nominal interest rate differentials are all moderately good predictors of long-run changes in exchange rates. They are poor predictors of short-run changes in exchange rates, however, perhaps because of the impact of psychological factors, investor expectations, and bandwagon effects on short-term currency movements. This information is useful for an international business. Insofar as the long-term profitability of foreign investments, export opportunities, and the price competitiveness of foreign imports are all influenced by long-term movements in exchange rates, international businesses would be advised to pay attention to countries' differing monetary growth, inflation, and interest rates. International businesses that engage in foreign exchange transactions on a day-to-day basis could benefit by knowing some predictors of short-term foreign exchange rate movements. Unfortunately, short-term exchange rate movements are difficult to predict.

EXCHANGE RATE FORECASTING

A company's need to predict future exchange rate variations raises the issue of whether it is worthwhile for the company to invest in exchange rate forecasting services to aid decision making. Two schools of thought address this issue. The efficient market school argues that forward exchange rates do the best possible job of forecasting future spot exchange rates, and, therefore, investing in forecasting services would be a waste of money. The other school of thought, the inefficient market school, argues that companies can improve the foreign exchange market's estimate of future exchange rates (as contained in the forward rate) by investing in forecasting services. In other words, this school of thought does not believe the forward exchange rates are the best possible predictors of future spot exchange rates.

THE EFFICIENT MARKET SCHOOL

Forward exchange rates represent market participants' collective predictions of likely spot exchange rates at specified future dates. If forward exchange rates are the best possible predictor of future spot rates, it would make no sense for companies to spend additional money trying to forecast short-run exchange rate movements. Many economists believe the foreign exchange market is efficient at setting forward rates.[19] An efficient market is one in which prices reflect all available public information. (If forward rates reflect all available information about likely future changes in exchange rates, there is no way a company can beat the market by investing in forecasting services.)

If the foreign exchange market is efficient, forward exchange rates should be unbiased predictors of future spot rates. This does not mean the predictions will be accurate in any specific situation. It means inaccuracies will not be consistently above or below future spot rates; they will be random. Many empirical tests have addressed the efficient market hypothesis. Although most of the early work seems to confirm the hypothesis (suggesting that companies should not waste their money on forecasting services), more recent studies have challenged it.[20] There is some evidence that forward rates are not unbiased predictors of future spot rates, and that more accurate predictions of future spot rates can be calculated from publicly available information.[21]

THE INEFFICIENT MARKET SCHOOL

Citing evidence against the efficient market hypothesis, some economists believe the foreign exchange market is inefficient. An **inefficient market** is one in which

INEFFICIENT MARKET One in which prices do not reflect all available information.

COUNTRY FOCUS

WHY DID THE KOREAN WON COLLAPSE?

In early 1997, South Korea could look back with pride on a 30-year "economic miracle" that had raised the country from the ranks of the poor and given it the world's 11th largest economy. By the end of 1997, the Korean currency, the won, had lost a staggering 67 percent of its value against the U.S. dollar, the South Korean economy lay in tatters, and the International Monetary Fund was overseeing a $55-billion rescue package. This sudden turn of events had its roots in investments made by South Korea's large industrial conglomerates, or *chaebol,* during the 1990s, often at the bequest of politicians. In 1993, Kim Young-Sam, a populist politician, became president of South Korea. Mr. Kim took office during a mild recession and promised to boost economic growth by encouraging investment in export-oriented industries. He urged the *chaebol* to invest in new factories. South Korea enjoyed an investment-led economic boom in 1994–95, but at a cost. The *chaebol,* always reliant on heavy borrowing, built massive debts that were equivalent, on average, to four times their equity.

As might be expected, as the volume of investments ballooned during the 1990s, the quality of many of these investments declined significantly. The investments often were made on the basis of unrealistic projections about future demand conditions. This resulted in significant excess capacity and falling prices. An example is investments made by South Korean *chaebol* in semiconductor factories. Investments in such facilities surged in 1994 and 1995 when a temporary global shortage of dynamic random access memory chips (DRAMs) led to sharp price increases for this product. However, supply shortages had disappeared by 1996 and excess capacity was beginning to make itself felt, just as the South Koreans started to bring new DRAM factories on stream. The results were predictable; prices for DRAMs plunged and the earnings of South Korean DRAM manufacturers fell by 90 percent, which meant it was difficult for them to make scheduled payments on the debt they had taken on to build the extra capacity. The risk of corporate bankruptcy increased significantly, and not just in the semiconductor industry. South Korean companies were also investing heavily in a wide range of other industries, including automobiles and steel.

Matters were complicated further because much of the borrowing had been in U.S. dollars, as opposed to Korean won. This had seemed like a smart move at the time. The dollar/won exchange rate had been stable at around US$1 = won 850. Interest rates on dollar borrowings were two to three percentage points lower than rates on borrowings in Korean won. Much of this borrowing was in the form of short-term, dollar-denominated debt that had to be paid back to the lending institution within one year. While the borrowing strategy seemed to make sense, there was a risk. If the won were to depreciate against the dollar, this would increase the size of the debt burden that South Korean companies would have to service, when measured in the local currency. Currency depreciation would raise borrowing costs, depress corporate earnings, and increase the risk of bankruptcy. This is exactly what happened.

By mid-1997, foreign investors had become alarmed at the rising debt levels of South Korean companies, particularly given the emergence of excess capacity and plunging prices in several areas where the

prices do not reflect all available information. In an inefficient market, forward exchange rates will not be the best possible predictors of future spot exchange rates.

If this is true, it may be worthwhile for international businesses to invest in forecasting services (as many do). The belief is that professional exchange rate forecasts might provide better predictions of future spot rates than forward exchange rates do. However, the track record of professional forecasting services is not that good. An analysis of the forecasts of 12 major forecasting services between 1978 and 1982 concluded the forecasters in general did not provide better forecasts than the forward exchange rates.[22] Also, forecasting services did not predict the 1997 currency crisis that swept through Southeast Asia.

APPROACHES TO FORECASTING

Assuming the inefficient market school is correct that the foreign exchange market's estimate of future spot rates can be improved, on what basis should forecasts be prepared?

companies had made huge investments, including semiconductors, automobiles, and steel. Given increasing speculation that many South Korean companies would not be able to service their debt payments, foreign investors began to withdraw their money from the Korean stock and bond markets. In the process, they sold Korean won and purchased U.S. dollars. The selling of won accelerated in mid-1997 when two of the smaller *chaebol* filed for bankruptcy, citing their inability to meet scheduled debt payments. The increased supply of won and the increased demand for U.S. dollars pushed down the price of won in dollar terms from around won 840 = US$1 to won 900 = US$1.

At this point, the South Korean central bank entered the foreign exchange market to try to keep the exchange rate above won 1,000 = US$1. It used dollars that it held in reserve to purchase won. The idea was to try to push up the price of the won in dollar terms and restore investor confidence in the stability of the exchange rate. This action, however, did not address the underlying debt problem faced by South Korean companies. Against a backdrop of more corporate bankruptcies in South Korea, and the government's stated intentions to take some troubled companies into state ownership, Standard & Poor's, the U.S. credit rating agency, downgraded South Korea's sovereign debt. This caused the Korean stock market to plunge 5.5 percent, and the Korean won to fall to won 930 = US$1. According to S&P, "The downgrade of . . . ratings reflects the escalating cost to the government of supporting the country's ailing corporate and financial sectors."

The S&P downgrade triggered a sharp sale of the Korean won. In an attempt to protect the won against what was fast becoming a classic bandwagon effect, the South Korean central bank raised short-term interest rates to over 12 percent, more than double the inflation rate. The bank also stepped up its intervention in the currency exchange markets, selling dollars and purchasing won in an attempt to keep the exchange rate above won 1,000 = US$1. The main effect of this action, however, was to rapidly deplete South Korea's foreign exchange reserves. These stood at $30 billion on November 1, but fell to only $15 billion two weeks later. With its foreign exchange reserves almost exhausted, the South Korean central bank gave up its defence of the won November 17. Immediately, the price of won in dollars plunged to around won 1,500 = US$1, effectively increasing by 60 to 70 percent the amount of won heavily indebted Korean companies had to pay to meet scheduled payments on their dollar-denominated debt. These losses, due to adverse changes in foreign exchange rates, depressed the profits of many firms. South Korean firms suffered foreign exchange losses of more than $15 billion in 1997.

Sources: J. Burton and G. Baker, "The Country That Invested Its Way into Trouble," *Financial Times,* January 15, 1998, p. 8; J. Burton, "South Korea's Credit Rating is Lowered," *Financial Times,* October 25, 1997, p. 3; J. Burton, "Currency Losses Hit Samsung Electronics," *Financial Times,* March 20, 1998, p. 24; and "Korean Firms' Foreign Exchange Losses Exceed US $15 Billion," *Business Korea,* February 1998, p. 55.

Here again, there are two schools of thought. One adheres to fundamental analysis, while the other uses technical analysis.

Fundamental Analysis

Fundamental analysis draws on economic theory to construct sophisticated econometric models for predicting exchange rate movements. The variables contained in these models typically include those we have discussed, such as relative money supply growth rates, inflation rates, and interest rates. In addition, they may include variables related to balance-of-payments positions.

FUNDAMENTAL ANALYSIS Draws on economic theory to construct sophisticated econometric models for predicting exchange rate movements.

Running a deficit on a balance-of-payments current account (a country is importing more goods and services than it is exporting) creates pressures that result in the depreciation of the country's currency on the foreign exchange market.[23] (For background on the balance of payments, see Chapter 7.) Consider what might happen if the United States was running a persistent current account balance-of-payments deficit. Since the United States would be importing more than it was exporting, people in other countries would be increasing their holdings of U.S. dollars. If these people were willing to hold their dollars, the dollar's exchange rate would not be influenced. However, if these people converted their dollars into other currencies, the supply of dollars in the foreign exchange market would increase (as would demand for the other currencies). This shift in demand and supply would create pressures that could lead to the depreciation of the dollar against other currencies.

This argument hinges on whether people in other countries are willing to hold dollars. This depends on such factors as U.S. interest rates and inflation rates. So, in a sense, the balance-of-payments position is not a fundamental predictor of future exchange rate movements. As shown in this chapter's closing case, from mid 2002 and into 2004, the U.S. dollar fell 25 percent against a basket of foreign currencies. Relatively high real interest rates in the United States made the dollar attractive to foreigners, so they did not convert their dollars into other currencies. Given this, we are back to the argument that the fundamental determinants of exchange rates are monetary growth, inflation rates, and interest rates.

TECHNICAL ANALYSIS Uses price and volume data to determine past trends, which are expected to continue into the future.

Technical Analysis

Technical analysis uses price and volume data to determine past trends, which are expected to continue into the future. This approach does not rely on a consideration of economic fundamentals. Technical analysis is based on the premise that there are analyzable market trends and waves and that previous trends and waves can be used to predict future trends and waves. Since there is no theoretical rationale for this assumption of predictability, many economists compare technical analysis to fortune-telling. Despite this skepticism, technical analysis has gained favour in recent years.[24]

FREELY CONVERTIBLE CURRENCY A country's currency is freely convertible when the government of that country allows both residents and nonresidents to purchase unlimited amounts of foreign currency with the domestic currency.

CURRENCY CONVERTIBILITY

Until this point, we have assumed that the currencies of various countries are freely convertible into other currencies. This assumption is invalid. Many countries restrict the ability of residents and nonresidents to convert the local currency into a foreign currency, making international trade and investment more difficult. Many international businesses have used "countertrade" practices to circumvent problems that arise when a currency is not freely convertible.

EXTERNALLY CONVERTIBLE CURRENCY Nonresidents can convert their holdings of domestic currency into foreign currency, but the ability of residents to convert the currency is limited in some way.

CONVERTIBILITY AND GOVERNMENT POLICY

Due to government restrictions, a significant number of currencies are not freely convertible into other currencies. A country's currency is said to be **freely convertible** when the country's government allows both residents and nonresidents to purchase unlimited amounts of a foreign currency with it. A currency is said to be **externally convertible** when only nonresidents may convert it into a foreign currency without any limitations. A currency is **nonconvertible** when neither residents nor nonresidents are allowed to convert it into a foreign currency.

NONCONVERTIBLE CURRENCY A currency is not convertible when both residents and nonresidents are prohibited from converting their holdings of that currency into another currency.

Free convertibility is the exception rather than the rule. Many countries restrict residents' ability to convert the domestic currency into a foreign currency (a policy of external convertibility). Restrictions range from the relatively minor (such as restricting the amount of foreign currency they may take with them out of the country on trips) to the major (such as restricting domestic businesses' ability to take foreign currency out of the country). External convertibility restrictions can limit domestic companies' ability to invest abroad, but they present few problems for foreign companies wishing to do business in that country. For example, even if the Japanese government tightly controlled the ability of its residents to convert the yen into U.S. dollars, all U.S. businesses with deposits in Japanese banks may at any time convert all their yen into dollars and take them out of the country. Thus, a U.S. company with a subsidiary in Japan is assured that it will be able to convert the profits from its Japanese operation into dollars and take them out of the country.

Serious problems arise, however, under a policy of nonconvertibility. This was the practice of the former Soviet Union, and it continued to be the practice in Russia until recently. When strictly applied, nonconvertibility means that although a U.S. company doing business in a country such as Russia may be able to generate significant ruble profits, it may not convert those rubles into dollars and take them out of the country. Obviously this is not desirable for international business.

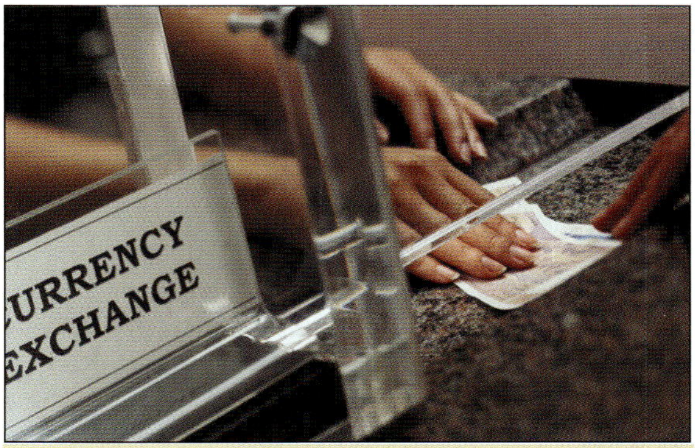

In many countries, the ability of residents and nonresidents to convert local currency into a foreign currency is restricted by government policy. A government restricts the convertibility of its currency in an attempt to protect the country's foreign exchange reserves and to halt any capital flight. Photo Disc.

Governments limit convertibility to preserve their foreign exchange reserves. A country needs an adequate supply of these reserves to service its international debt commitments and to purchase imports. Governments typically impose convertibility restrictions on their currency when they fear that free convertibility will lead to a run on their foreign exchange reserves. This occurs when residents and nonresidents rush to convert their holdings of domestic currency into a foreign currency–a phenomenon generally referred to as **capital flight.** Capital flight is most likely to occur when the value of the domestic currency is depreciating rapidly because of hyperinflation, or when a country's economic prospects are shaky in other respects. Under such circumstances, both residents and nonresidents tend to believe that their money is more likely to hold its value if it is converted into a foreign currency and invested abroad. Not only will a run on foreign exchange reserves limit the country's ability to service its international debt and pay for imports, but it will also lead to a precipitous depreciation in the exchange rate as residents and nonresidents unload their holdings of domestic currency on the foreign exchange markets (thereby increasing the market supply of the country's currency). Governments fear that the rise in import prices resulting from currency depreciation will lead to further increases in inflation. This fear provides another rationale for limiting convertibility.

CAPITAL FLIGHT
Residents convert domestic currency into a foreign currency.

ANOTHER PERSPECTIVE

Exchange rate language: mirror images

The language used to describe exchange rate movements can be confusing. Here's why: One observation describes a changing relationship (the movement in the currencies) that itself describes two relationships (the exchange rates for the two currencies). The important aspect to remember is that an exchange rate is described in terms of other exchange rates.

The language of exchange rates works this same, dual way: The euro gains against the U.S. dollar, so the euro is strengthening, or becoming dearer, from a U.S. dollar perspective. Meanwhile, the same observation indicates that the U.S. dollar is becoming cheaper, or weaker against the euro, from a euro perspective.

COUNTERTRADE

Companies can deal with the nonconvertibility problem by engaging in countertrade. Countertrade is discussed in detail in Chapter 13, so we will merely introduce the concept here. **Countertrade** refers to a range of barterlike agreements by which goods and services can be traded for other goods and services. Countertrade can make sense when a country's currency is nonconvertible. For example, consider the deal that General Electric struck with the Romanian government in 1984, when that country's currency was nonconvertible. When General Electric won a contract for a $150-million generator project in Romania, it agreed to take payment in the form of Romanian goods that could be sold for $150 million on international markets. In a similar case, the Venezuelan government negotiated a contract with Caterpillar in 1986 under which Venezuela would trade 350 000 tonnes of iron ore for Caterpillar heavy construction equipment. Caterpillar subsequently traded the iron ore to Romania in exchange for Romanian farm products, which it then sold on international markets for dollars.[25]

COUNTERTRADE
The trade of goods and services for other goods and services.

How important is countertrade? One estimate is that 20 to 30 percent of world trade in 1985 involved some form of countertrade agreements. Since then, however, more currencies have become freely convertible, and the percentage of world trade that involves countertrade has fallen to between 10 and 20 percent.[26]

IMPLICATIONS FOR BUSINESS

This chapter contains a number of clear implications for business. First, it is critical that international businesses understand the influence of exchange rates on the profitability of trade and investment deals. Adverse changes in exchange rates can make apparently profitable deals unprofitable. The risk introduced into international business transactions by changes in exchange rates is referred to as foreign exchange risk. Means of hedging against foreign exchange risk are available. Forward exchange rates and currency swaps allow companies to insure against this risk.

International businesses must also understand the forces that determine exchange rates. This is particularly true in light of the increasing evidence that forward exchange rates are not unbiased predictors. If a company wants to know how the value of a particular currency is likely to change over the long term on the foreign exchange market, it should look closely at those economic fundamentals that appear to predict long-run exchange rate movements (i.e., the growth in a country's money supply, its inflation rate, and its nominal interest rates). For example, an international business should be very cautious about trading with or investing in a country with a recent history of rapid growth in its domestic money supply. The upsurge in inflation that is likely to follow such rapid monetary growth could lead to a sharp drop in the value of the country's currency on the foreign exchange market, which could transform a profitable deal into an unprofitable one. This is not to say that an international business should not trade with or invest in such a country. Rather, it means an international business should take some precautions before doing so, such as buying currency forward on the foreign exchange market or structuring the deal around a countertrade arrangement.

Complicating this picture is the issue of currency convertibility. The proclivity that many governments seem to have to restrict currency convertibility suggests that the foreign exchange market does not always provide the lubricant necessary to make international trade and investment possible. Given this, international businesses need to explore alternative mechanisms for facilitating international trade and investment that do not involve currency conversion. Countertrade seems the obvious mechanism. We return to the topic of countertrade and discuss it in depth in Chapter 13.

KEY TERMS

arbitrage, p. 304
capital flight, p. 317
countertrade, p. 317
currency speculation, p. 298
currency swap, p. 303
efficient market, p. 306
exchange rate, p. 296
externally convertible currency, p. 316
foreign exchange market, p. 296
foreign exchange risk, p. 297
forward exchange, p. 301
forward exchange rates, p. 301
freely convertible currency, p. 316
fundamental analysis, p. 315
inefficient market, p. 313
International Fisher Effect, p. 312
law of one price, p. 306
nonconvertible currency, p. 316
relatively efficient markets, p. 306
spot exchange rate, p. 301
technical analysis, p. 316

SUMMARY

This chapter explained how the foreign exchange market works, examined the forces that determine exchange rates, and then discussed the implications of these factors for international business. Given that changes in exchange rates can dramatically alter the profitability of foreign trade and investment deals, this is an area of major interest to international business. This chapter made the following points:

1. One function of the foreign exchange market is to convert the currency of one country into the currency of another.
2. International businesses participate in the foreign exchange market to facilitate international trade and investment, to invest spare cash in short-term money market accounts abroad, and to engage in currency speculation.
3. A second function of the foreign exchange market is to provide insurance against foreign exchange risk.
4. The spot exchange rate is the exchange rate at which a dealer converts one currency into another currency on a particular day.
5. Foreign exchange risk can be reduced by using forward exchange rates. A forward exchange rate is an exchange rate governing future transactions.
6. Foreign exchange risk can also be reduced by engaging in currency swaps. A swap is the simultaneous purchase and sale of a given amount of foreign exchange for two different value dates.
7. The law of one price holds that in competitive markets that are free of transportation costs and barriers to trade, identical products sold in different countries must sell for the same price when their price is expressed in the same currency.
8. Purchasing power parity (PPP) theory states the price of a basket of particular goods should be roughly equivalent in each country. PPP theory predicts that the exchange rate will change if relative prices change.
9. The rate of change in countries' relative prices depends on their relative inflation rates. A country's inflation rate seems to be a function of the growth in its money supply.
10. The PPP theory of exchange rate changes yields relatively accurate predictions of long-term trends in exchange rates, but not of short-term movements. The failure of PPP theory to predict exchange rate changes more accurately may be due to the existence of transportation costs, barriers to trade and investment, and the impact of psychological factors such as bandwagon effects on market movements and short-run exchange rates.
11. Interest rates reflect expectations about inflation. In countries where inflation is expected to be high, interest rates also will be high.
12. The International Fisher Effect states that for any two countries, the spot exchange rate should change in an equal amount but in the opposite direction to the difference in nominal interest rates.
13. The most common approach to exchange rate forecasting is fundamental analysis. This relies on variables such as money supply growth, inflation rates, nominal interest rates, and balance-of-payments positions to predict future changes in exchange rates.
14. In many countries, the ability of residents and nonresidents to convert local currency into a foreign currency is restricted by government policy. A government restricts the convertibility of its currency to protect the country's foreign exchange reserves and to halt any capital flight.
15. Particularly bothersome for international business is a policy of nonconvertibility, which prohibits residents and nonresidents from exchanging local currency for foreign currency. A policy of nonconvertibility makes it very difficult to engage in international trade and investment in the country.
16. One way of coping with the nonconvertibility problem is to engage in countertrade—to trade goods and services for other goods and services.

CRITICAL THINKING AND DISCUSSION QUESTIONS

As shown in this chapter's closing case, from mid 2002 and into 2004, the U.S. dollar fell 25 percent against a basket of foreign currencies.

1. The interest rate on one-year Canadian government securities is 6 percent and expected inflation rate for the coming year is 2 percent. The U.S. one-year government security instrument interest rate is 4 percent with expected inflation for this coming year of 1 percent. The exchange rate for the US$/Cdn$ as of July 2, 2004 is US$1 = Cdn$1.32300 (US$100 = Cdn$132.3). What is the spot exchange rate a year from now? What is the forward exchange rate a year from now? Explain the logic of your answers.
2. Two countries, Canada and the U.S., produce just one good: beef. Suppose the price of beef in the United States is $3 per kilogram and in Canada it is $4 per kilogram.
   a. According to the PPP theory, what should the spot exchange rate be?

b. Suppose the price of beef is expected to rise to $3.50 per kilogram in the U.S. and to $4.75 per kilogram in Canada. What should the one-year forward US$/Cdn$ exchange rate be?

c. Given your answers to parts a and b, if the current interest rate in the United States is 10 percent, what would you expect the current interest rate to be in Canada?

RESEARCH TASK | globalEDGE™ globaledge.msu.edu

Use the globalEDGE™ site to complete the following exercises:

1. You are assigned the duty of ensuring the availability of 100,000 yen for the payment that is scheduled for next month. Your company possesses only U.S. dollars, so identify the spot and forward exchange rates. What factors affect your decision of utilizing spot versus forward exchange rates? Which one would you choose? How many dollars do you have to spend to acquire the amount of yen required?
2. As an entrepreneur, you are interested in expanding your business to Bulgaria. As part of your initial analysis, you would like to know if it is too risky. PRS Group provides country risk analysis. While a majority of its reports are available only for purchase, the site provides sample data for free (under International Country Risk Guide). Using this sample data, provide a short report of the current status of Bulgaria's country risk based on economical risk, external conflicts, and exchange rate stability.

Visit the *Global Business Today* Online Learning Centre at **www.mcgrawhill.ca/college/hill** to access quizzes, interactive exercises, a Business Around the World interactive map, and other learning and study tools related to this chapter.

Online LearningCentre

CLOSING CASE

IS BIGGER ALWAYS BETTER?

The years 2003 and 2004 were volatile ones in the foreign exchange business. For the benchmark U.S. dollar, the slide that began during the last part of 2002 extended through 2003 and into 2004. One index, which showed the value of the U.S. dollar against a basket of foreign currencies, showed a decline of over 25 percent in the two-year period. The Canadian dollar, as did most worldwide currencies, rose against the U.S. dollar. In Canada's case, the dollar rose to levels last seen in January 1997.

There have been many explanations put forward to explain the weakness of the U.S. dollar. The first was an easy monetary policy that kept the federal funds rate at a 40-year low and aggressively pumped reserves and dollars into the U.S. banking system. The second was the massive U.S. account deficit, which is roughly equal to 5 percent of the country's GDP. This means that the U.S. has to import more than $1.5 billion of capital every day in order to cover its trade and services deficit.

While these reasons are apparent after the fact, it is important to note that very few economists predicted such a drop before it happened. Certainly on the Canadian side, the rise of the Canadian dollar was a fate that caught most people off-guard.

These sudden movements in currencies brought currency hedging to the minds of many companies that deal in cross-border trade. Clearly, the old model of a strong U.S. dollar would not always apply, and firms that based their trading on this approach felt some losses in 2003 and 2004. Foreign exchange was suddenly much more important to firms.

Banks have long dominated the foreign exchange market. This is natural, as they have the technology, the international relationships, the money and access to clients through pre-existing relationships (i.e., as a small business it seems "natural" to let the bank that has given you a business loan also handle your foreign exchange needs). In the past decade, some smaller firms such as Custom House and Travelex (which incorporated Thomas Cook) have been making headway in the Canadian marketplace. Much of this has to do with the wider availability, and lower costs, of the technology necessary to process and follow foreign exchange transactions.

Cambridge Mercantile Corp. is another example of a foreign exchange firm that goes head-to-head against the large Canadian banks. In under a decade, the firm's client base has grown from 100 clients to about 4000. The company's head office is in Toronto and it has grown to include offices in Montreal, Vancouver, and Cambridge. In the United States its head office is in Princeton, New Jersey (which is the location of a number of hedge funds and institutional money management firms) along with offices in Dallas, Coral Gables, Chicago, and San Francisco.

Cambridge sees its competitive advantage in two areas: better prices than those available through bank foreign exchange rates, and more personalized service than that offered by the banks. The service is extended through individual account representatives for even the smallest commercial account. This account representative, who is directly responsible for the foreign exchange requirements, is available when there are orders to be executed or, which Cambridge sees as more valuable to its clients, when something goes wrong. Despite the technology and automation, mistakes can occur—ranging from unexpected changes in currency exchange rates, to lost payments and delayed confirmation of payments and receivables. It is through the relationship of an account representative and his client—with a client having to make only one call, as opposed to having to make several if dealing with a larger institution, that Cambridge hopes to continue building its business.

Sources: Cambridge Mercantile Corp at www.cambridgefx.com; CRB, Commodity Yearbook 2004; RBC Investments at www.rbcfunds.com/archives/canadian_dollar.html; TD Commercial Banking at www.tdcommercialbanking.com/foreignx/products/participating.jsp.

CASE DISCUSSION QUESTIONS

1. If currency exchange rates settle down, what do you think will happen to firms such as Cambridge? What would happen to the foreign exchange desks of the major Canadian banks?
2. In a globalized world, is it important to have your foreign exchange bank or dealer close to your firm?
3. Which do you think is more important to Cambridge's prospects—beating the major banks on price, or on service?

PART FOUR

4

PART FOUR GLOBAL MONEY SYSTEM

Turkey's 18th IMF Program

In May 2001, the International Monetary Fund (IMF) agreed to lend $8 billion to Turkey to help the country stabilize its economy and halt a sharp slide in the value of its currency. This was the third time in two years that the international lending institution had assembled a loan program for Turkey, and it was the 18th program since Turkey became a member of the IMF in 1958.

Many of Turkey's problems stemmed from a large and inefficient state sector and heavy subsidies to various private sectors of the economy such as agriculture. Although the Turkish government started to privatize state-owned companies in the late 1980s, it proceeded at a glacial pace, hamstrung by political opposition within Turkey. Instead of selling state-owned assets to private investors, successive governments increased support to unprofitable state-owned industries and raised the wage rates of state employees. Nor did the government cut subsidies to politically powerful private sectors of the economy, such as agriculture. To support state industries and finance subsidies, Turkey issued significant amounts of government debt. To limit the amount of debt, the government simply printed money to finance spending. The result, predictably, was rampant inflation and high interest rates. During the 1990s, inflation averaged more than 80 percent a year while real interest rates rose to more than 50 percent several times. Despite this, the Turkish economy continued to grow at a healthy pace of 6 percent annually in real terms, a remarkable achievement given the high inflation rates and interest rates.

By the late 1990s, however, the "Turkish miracle" of sustained growth in the face of high inflation and interest rates was running out of steam. Government debt had risen to 60 percent of gross domestic product, government borrowing was leaving little capital for private enterprises, and the cost of financing government debt was spiraling out of control. Rampant inflation was putting pressure on the Turkish currency, the lira, which at the time was pegged in value to a basket of other currencies. Realizing that it needed to drastically reform its economy, the

CHAPTER 10

The Global Monetary System

OPENING CASE

Turkish government sat down with the IMF in late 1999 to work out a recovery program, adopted in January 2000.

As with most IMF programs, the focus was on bringing down the inflation rate, stabilizing the value of the Turkish currency, and restructuring the economy to reduce government debt. The Turkish government committed itself to reducing government debt by taking a number of steps. These included an accelerated privatization program, using the proceeds to pay down debt; the reduction of agricultural subsidies; reform to make it more difficult for people to qualify for public pension programs; and tax increases. The government also agreed to rein in the growth in the money supply to better control inflation. To limit the possibility of speculative attacks on the Turkish currency in the foreign exchange markets, the Turkish government and IMF announced that Turkey would peg the value of the lira against a basket of currencies and devalue the lira by a predetermined amount each month throughout 2000, bringing the total devaluation for the year to 25 percent. To ease the pain, the IMF agreed to provide the Turkish government with $5 billion in loans that could be used to support the value of the lira.

Initially the program seemed to be working. Inflation fell to 35 percent in 2000, while the economy grew by 6 percent. By the end of 2000, however, the program was in trouble. Burdened with nonperforming loans, a number of Turkish banks faced default and had been taken into public ownership by the government. When a criminal fraud investigation uncovered evidence that several of these banks had been pressured by politicians into providing loans at below-market interest rates, foreign investors, worried that more banks might be involved, started to pull their money out of Turkey. This sent the Turkish stock market into a tailspin and put enormous pressure on the Turkish lira. Sensing that the government might be forced to devalue the lira at a faster rate than planned, traders in the foreign exchange market started to sell the lira short, while the flow of foreign capital out of Turkey increased to a flood, which put even more pressure on the lira. The government raised Turkish overnight interbank lending rates to as high as 1950 percent to try to stem the outflow of capital, but it was clear that Turkey alone could not halt the flow.

The IMF stepped once more into the breach December 6, 2000, announcing a quickly arranged $7.5-billion loan program for the country. In return for the loan, the IMF required the Turkish government to close ten insolvent banks, speed up its privatization plans (which had once more stalled), and cap any pay increases for government workers. The IMF also reportedly urged the Turkish government to let its currency float freely in the foreign exchange markets, but the government refused, arguing that the result would be a rapid devaluation in the lira, which would raise import prices and fuel price inflation. The government insisted that reducing inflation should be its first priority.

This plan started to come apart in February 2001. A surge in inflation and a rapid slowdown in economic growth once more spooked foreign investors. Into this explosive mix waded Turkey's prime minister and president, who engaged in a highly public argument about economic policy and political corruption. This triggered a rapid outflow of capital. The government raised the overnight interbank lending rate to 7500 percent to try to persuade foreigners to leave their money in the country, but to no avail. Realizing that it would be unable to keep the lira within its planned monthly devaluation range without raising interest rates to absurd levels or seriously depleting the country's foreign exchange reserves, on February 23, 2001, the Turkish government decided to let the lira float freely. The lira immediately dropped 50 percent in value against the U.S. dollar, but ended the day down some 28 percent.

Over the next two months, the Turkish economy continued to weaken as a global economic slowdown affected the nation. Inflation stayed high, and progress at reforming the country's economy remained bogged down by political considerations. By early April 2001, the lira had fallen 40 percent against the dollar since February 23, and the country was teetering on the brink of an economic meltdown. For the third time in 18 months, the IMF stepped in, arranging for another $8 billion in loans. Once more, the IMF insisted the Turkish government accelerate privatization, close insolvent banks, deregulate its market, and cut government spending. Critics of the IMF, however, claimed this "austerity program" would only slow the Turkish economy and make matters worse, not better. These critics advocated a mix of sound monetary policy and tax cuts to boost Turkey's economic growth.

Sources: P. Blustein, "Turkish Crisis Weakens the Case for Intervention," *Washington Post,* March 2, 2001, p. E1; H. Pope, "Can Turkey Finally Mend Its Economy?" *Wall Street Journal,* May 22, 2001, p. A18; "Turkish Bath," *Wall Street Journal,* February 23, 2001, p. A14; E. McBride, "Turkey—Fingers Crossed," *The Economist,* June 10, 2000, pp. SS16–SS17; and "Turkey and the IMF," *The Economist,* December 9, 2000, pp. 81–82.

LEARNING OBJECTIVES

1. Understand the role played by the global monetary system in determining exchange rates.
2. Be familiar with the historical development of the modern global monetary system.
3. Appreciate the differences between a fixed and a floating exchange rate system.
4. Understand why the world's fixed exchange rate regime collapsed in the 1970s.
5. Understand the arguments for and against fixed and floating exchange systems.
6. Be familiar with the role played by the International Monetary Fund and the World Bank in the global monetary system.
7. Understand the implications of the global monetary system for currency management and business strategy.

INTRODUCTION

INTERNATIONAL MONETARY SYSTEM Institutional arrangements countries adopt to govern exchange rates.

The **international monetary system** refers to the institutional arrangements that countries adopt to govern exchange rates. In Chapter 9, we assumed the foreign exchange market was the primary institution for determining exchange rates and the impersonal market forces of demand and supply determined the relative value of any two currencies (i.e., their exchange rate). Furthermore, we explained that the demand and supply of currencies is influenced by their respective countries' relative inflation rates and interest rates. When the foreign exchange market determines the relative value of a currency, we say that the country is adhering to a **floating exchange rate** regime. The world's four major trading currencies—the U.S. dollar, the European Union's euro, the Japanese yen, and the British pound—are all free to float against each other. Thus, their exchange rates are determined by market forces and fluctuate against each other on a day-to-day, if not minute-to-minute, basis. However, the exchange rates of many currencies are not determined by the free play of market forces; other institutional arrangements are adopted.

FLOATING EXCHANGE RATES A system under which the exchange rate for converting one currency into another is continuously adjusted depending on the laws of supply and demand.

In the opening case, for example, we learned that until recently, the value of the Turkish lira was pegged to a basket of currencies. Many of the world's smaller nations peg their currencies, primarily to the dollar or the euro. A **pegged exchange rate** means the value of the currency is fixed relative to a reference currency, such as the U.S. dollar, and then the exchange rate between that currency and other currencies is determined by the reference currency exchange rate. Thus, Belize pegs its currency to the dollar, and the exchange rate between the Belizean currency and the euro is determined by the U.S. dollar/euro exchange rate.

PEGGED EXCHANGE RATE Currency value is fixed relative to a reference currency.

Other countries, while not adopting a formal pegged rate, try to hold the value of their currency within some range against an important reference currency such as the U.S. dollar. This is often referred to as a **dirty-float system.** It is a float because in theory, the value of the currency is determined by market forces, but it is a dirty float (as opposed to a clean float) because the central bank of a country will intervene in the foreign exchange market to try to maintain the value of its currency if it depreciates too rapidly against an important reference currency.

DIRTY-FLOAT SYSTEM A system under which a country's currency is nominally allowed to float freely against other currencies, but in which the government will intervene, buying and selling currency, if it believes that the currency has deviated too far from its fair value.

Still other countries have operated with a **fixed exchange rate** system, in which the values of a set of currencies are fixed against each other at some mutually agreed on exchange rate. Before the introduction of the euro in 2000, several member states of the European Union operated with fixed exchange rates within the context of the European Monetary System (EMS). For a quarter of a century after World War II, the world's major industrial nations participated in a fixed exchange rate system. Although this system collapsed in 1973, some still argue that the world should attempt to reimpose it.

FIXED EXCHANGE RATES A system under which the exchange rate for converting one currency into another is fixed.

Pegged exchange rate, dirty-float, and fixed exchange rate systems all require some degree of government intervention in the foreign exchange market to maintain the value of a currency. A currency may come under pressure when the nation experiences significant economic problems. In the case of Turkey, for example, these included high inflation, excessive government debt, and a crisis in the banking system (see the opening case). A government can try to maintain the value of its currency by using foreign currency held in reserve (foreign exchange reserves) to buy its currency in the market, thereby increasing demand for the currency and raising its price. Thus, as the Turkish lira began to depreciate rapidly in late 2000, the Turkish central bank entered the foreign exchange market, using foreign currency it held in reserve, such as U.S. dollars, Japanese yen, and euros, to purchase lira in an attempt to halt the depreciation in the exchange rate. However, since governments may not have sufficient foreign exchange reserves to defend the value of their currency, they sometimes call on a powerful multinational institution, the International Monetary Fund (IMF), for loans to help them do this. The IMF is another important player in the international monetary system. As we saw in the opening case, the IMF does not simply lend money to a country in trouble. In exchange for the loan, it requires that the government adopt policies designed to correct whatever economic problems caused the depreciation in the nation's currency. Thus, the IMF insisted that Turkey take steps to reduce its inflation rate and government debt and to resolve problems in the country's banking system.

In this chapter, we will explain how the international monetary system works and point out its implications for international business. To understand how the international monetary system works, we must review the system's evolution. We will begin with a discussion of the gold standard and its breakup during the 1930s. Then we will discuss the 1944 Bretton Woods conference. This established the basic framework for the post-World War II international monetary system. The Bretton Woods system called for fixed exchange rates against the U.S. dollar. Under this fixed exchange rate system, the value of most currencies in terms of U.S. dollars was fixed for long periods and allowed to change only under a specific set of circumstances. The Bretton Woods conference also created two major international institutions that play a role in the international monetary system–the International Monetary Fund (IMF) and the World Bank. The IMF was given the task of maintaining order in the international monetary system; the World Bank's role was to promote development.

Today, both these institutions continue to play major roles in the world economy. In 1997 and 1998, for example, the IMF helped several Asian countries deal with the dramatic decline in the value of their currencies that occurred during the Asian financial crisis that started in 1997. By 2001, the IMF had programs in more than 70 countries. There is, however, a growing debate about the role of the IMF and to a lesser extent the World Bank and the appropriateness of their policies for many developing nations. In the case of Turkey, several prominent critics claim that IMF policy might make things worse, not better, and they point out that despite successive IMF-sponsored "austerity programs" over the years, the country still has serious economic problems. The debate over the role of the IMF took on new urgency given the institution's extensive involvement in the economies of Asia and Eastern Europe during the latter part of the 1990s. We shall discuss the issue in some depth.

The Bretton Woods system of fixed exchange rates collapsed in 1973. Since then, the world has operated with a mixed system in which some currencies are allowed to float freely, but many are either managed by government intervention or pegged to another currency. We will explain the reasons for the failure of the Bretton Woods system as well as the nature of the present system. We will also discuss how pegged exchange rate systems work. Two decades after the breakdown of the Bretton Woods system, the debate continues over what kind of exchange rate regime is best for the world. Some economists advocate a system in which major currencies are allowed to float against each other. Others argue for a return to a fixed exchange rate regime similar to the one established at Bretton Woods. This debate is intense and important, and we will examine the arguments of both sides.

Finally, we will discuss the implications of all this material for international business. We will see how the exchange rate policy adopted by a government can have an important impact on the outlook for business operations in a given country. If government exchange rate policies result in currency devaluation, for example, exporters based in that country may benefit as their products become more price competitive in foreign markets. Alternatively, importers will suffer from an increase in the price of their products. We will also look at how the policies adopted by the IMF can affect the economic outlook for a country and, accordingly, the costs and benefits of doing business in that country.

THE GOLD STANDARD

The gold standard had its origin in the use of gold coins as a medium of exchange, unit of account, and store of value–a practice that dates to ancient times. When international trade was limited in volume, payment for goods purchased from another country was typically made in gold or silver. However, as the volume of international trade expanded in the wake of the Industrial Revolution, a more convenient means was needed. The solution adopted was to arrange for payment in paper currency and for governments to agree to convert the paper currency into gold on demand at a fixed rate.

MECHANICS OF THE GOLD STANDARD

Pegging currencies to gold and guaranteeing convertibility is known as the **gold standard.** By 1880, most of the world's major trading nations, including Great Britain, Germany, Japan, and the United States, had adopted the gold standard.

GOLD STANDARD The practice of pegging currencies to gold and guaranteeing convertibility.

STRENGTH OF THE GOLD STANDARD

The great strength claimed for the gold standard was that it contained a powerful mechanism for achieving balance-of-trade equilibrium by all countries.[1] A country is said to be in balance-of-trade equilibrium when the income its residents earn from exports is equal to the money its residents pay to people in other countries for imports (the current account of its balance of payments is in balance). Suppose there are only two countries in the world, Japan and the United States. Imagine Japan's trade balance is in surplus because it exports more to the United States than it imports from the United States. Japanese exporters are paid in U.S. dollars, which they exchange for Japanese yen at a Japanese bank. The Japanese bank submits the dollars to the U.S. government and demands payment of gold in return. (This is a simplification of what would occur, but it will make our point.)

Under the gold standard, when Japan has a trade surplus, there will be a net flow of gold from the United States to Japan. These gold flows automatically reduce the U.S. money supply and swell Japan's money supply. As we saw in Chapter 9, there is a close connection between money supply growth and price inflation. An increase in money supply will raise prices in Japan, while a decrease in the U.S. money supply will push U.S. prices downward. The rise in the price of Japanese goods will decrease demand for these goods, while the fall in the price of U.S. goods will increase demand for these goods. Thus, Japan will start to buy more from the United States, and the United States will buy less from Japan, until a balance-of-trade equilibrium is achieved.

This adjustment mechanism seems so simple and attractive that even today, more than 60 years after the final collapse of the gold standard, some people believe the world should return to a gold standard.

THE PERIOD BETWEEN THE WARS: 1918–1939

The gold standard worked reasonably well from the 1870s until the start of World War I. During the war, several governments financed part of their massive military expenditures by printing money.

Great Britain which abandoned the gold standard at the beginning of World War I returned to the gold standard by pegging the pound to gold at the prewar gold parity level of £4.25 per ounce, despite substantial inflation between 1914 and 1925. This priced British goods out of foreign markets, which pushed the country into a deep depression. When foreign holders of pounds lost confidence in Great Britain's commitment to maintaining its currency's value, they began converting their holdings of pounds into gold. The British government saw that it could not satisfy the demand for gold without seriously depleting its gold reserves, so it suspended convertibility in 1931.

The United States followed suit and left the gold standard in 1933 but returned to it in 1934, raising the dollar price of gold from $20.67 per ounce to $35 per ounce. Since more dollars were needed to buy an ounce of gold than before, the implication was that the dollar was worth less. This effectively amounted to a devaluation of the dollar relative to other currencies. A number of other countries adopted a similar tactic, and in the cycle of competitive devaluations that soon emerged, no country could win.

The Canadian dollar was under the gold standard from 1854 to1914. With the beginning of World War I, it went off the gold standard from 1914 to1926 and temporarily went back on from 1926 to1931.

In 1944, at the height of World War II, representatives from 44 countries met at Bretton Woods, New Hampshire, to design a new international monetary system. Pictured here is Henry Morgenthau, then Secretary of the Treasury, addressing the opening meeting of the conference where the IMF and the World Bank were established. Bettmann/CORBIS.

The Currency Act was first proclaimed on August 1, 1854 and until World War I, Canada remained on the gold standard whereby the value of the Canadian dollar was fixed in terms of gold. It was also valued at par with the U.S. dollar, with a British sovereign valued at Cdn$4.8666, and both U.S. and British gold coins were legal tender in Canada. Paper money was freely convertible into gold without restriction and there were no controls on the export or import of gold.[2]

The start of World War I marked the end of the gold standard era. Most countries suspended the convertibility of domestic bank notes into gold and the free movement of gold between countries. As fear mounted in the days immediately before the declaration of war on August 4, 1914, there were heavy withdrawals of gold from Canadian banks. In an "atmosphere of incipient financial panic" (Macmillan Report 1933, 22), there were concerns about the possibility of bank runs from bank customers rushing to redeem their paper money in gold. Since there was not enough gold to cover for paper money, an emergency meeting was held in Ottawa, on August 3, 1914 between the federal government and the Canadian Bankers Association to discuss the crisis. Later that day, an Order-in-Council was issued to provide protection for banks, which were threatened by insolvency, by giving bank notes issued by banks legal tender status. This allowed the banks to meet their depositor demands with their own bank notes rather than with dominion notes or gold. The government also increased the amount of notes that banks were legally permitted to issue. The government was also empowered to make advances to banks by issuing dominion notes against securities deposited with the minister of finance. This provision enabled banks to increase the amount of their bank notes in circulation. A second Order-in-Council, issued on August 10, 1914, suspended the redemption of dominion notes into gold.[3]

With Canada's return to the gold standard, from 1926 to 1931, currency supplied by the chartered banks lost its legal tender status, although the government, in the event of an emergency, could restore this status under the Finance Act. Consequently, legal tender in Canada once again consisted of British gold sovereigns and other current British gold coins, U.S. gold eagles ($10), double eagles, and half eagles, Canadian gold coins (denominations of $5 and $10), and dominion notes. To a lesser degree, legal tender status was also accorded silver, nickel, and bronze coins minted in Canada.[4]

On April 10, 1933 an Order-in-Council officially suspended the redemption of dominion notes for gold thus ending Canada's relationship with the gold standard.[5]

The net result was the shattering of any remaining confidence in the system. With countries devaluing their currencies at will, one could no longer be certain how much gold a currency could buy. By the start of World War II in 1939, the gold standard was dead.

THE BRETTON WOODS SYSTEM

In 1944, at the height of World War II, representatives from 44 countries met at Bretton Woods, New Hampshire, to design a new international monetary system. With the collapse of the gold standard and the Great Depression of the 1930s fresh in their minds, these statesmen were determined to build an enduring economic order that would facilitate postwar economic growth. There was general consensus that fixed exchange rates were desirable.

The agreement reached at Bretton Woods established two multinational institutions–the International Monetary Fund (IMF) and the World Bank. The task of the IMF would be to maintain order in the international monetary system and that of the World Bank would be to promote general economic development. The Bretton Woods agreement also called for a system of fixed exchange rates that would be policed by the IMF. Under the agreement, all countries were to fix the value of their currency in terms of gold but were not required to exchange their currencies for gold. Only the dollar remained convertible into gold–at a price of $35 per ounce. Each country decided what it wanted its exchange rate to be vis-à-vis the dollar and then calculated the gold par value of the currency based on that selected dollar exchange rate.

Another aspect of the Bretton Woods agreement was a commitment not to use devaluation as a weapon of competitive trade policy. However, if a currency became too weak to defend, a devaluation of up to 10 percent would be allowed without any formal approval by the IMF. Larger devaluations required IMF approval.

> **ANOTHER PERSPECTIVE**
>
> **The IMF conspiracy theory**
>
> In Kuala Lumpur just after the Malaysian ringgit had begun building up from its lows of 1997, two Chinese-Malay bankers met American friends for dinner. They had been together in business school in London and had kept their friendships going over the 15 ensuing years through mutual visits, letters, and email. Imagine the Americans' disbelief when their good, loved, and trusted friends confided that the real problem with the currency crisis was a conspiracy between Wall Street and the CEOs of American corporations to take over Malay industry. The Malaysians were not dissuaded by the Americans' counterpoint that such a diverse group of people could never orchestrate such a clandestine operation in the United States, even if they wanted to.

THE ROLE OF THE IMF

The IMF Articles of Agreement were heavily influenced by the worldwide financial collapse, competitive devaluations, trade wars, high unemployment, hyperinflation in Germany and elsewhere, and general economic disintegration that occurred between the two world wars. The aim of the Bretton Woods agreement, of which the IMF was the main custodian, was to try to avoid a repetition of that chaos through a combination of discipline and flexibility.

Discipline

A fixed exchange rate regime imposes discipline in two ways. First, the need to maintain a fixed exchange rate puts a brake on competitive devaluations and brings stability to the world trade environment. Second, a fixed exchange rate regime imposes monetary discipline on countries, thereby curtailing price inflation. For example, consider what would happen under a fixed exchange rate regime if Great Britain rapidly increased its money supply by printing pounds. As explained in Chapter 9, the increase in money supply would lead to price inflation. Given fixed exchange rates, inflation would make British goods uncompetitive in world markets, while the prices of imports would become more attractive in Great Britain. The result would be a widening trade deficit in Great Britain, with the country importing more than it exports. To correct this trade imbalance under a fixed exchange rate regime, Great Britain would be required to restrict the rate of growth in its money supply to bring price inflation back under control. Thus, fixed exchange rates are seen as a mechanism for controlling inflation and imposing economic discipline on countries.

Flexibility

Although monetary discipline was a central objective of the Bretton Woods agreement, it was recognized that a rigid policy of fixed exchange rates would be too inflexible. It would probably break down just as the gold standard had. In some cases, a country's attempts to reduce its money supply growth and correct a persistent balance-of-payments deficit could force the country into recession and create high unemployment. The architects of the Bretton Woods agreement wanted to avoid high unemployment, so they built limited flexibility into the system. Two major features of the IMF Articles of Agreement fostered this flexibility: IMF lending facilities and adjustable parities.

The IMF stood ready to lend foreign currencies to members to tide them over during short periods of balance-of-payments deficits, when a rapid tightening of monetary or fiscal policy would hurt domestic employment. A pool of gold and currencies contributed by IMF members provided the resources for these lending operations. A persistent balance-of-payments deficit can lead to a depletion of a country's reserves of foreign currency, forcing it to devalue its currency. By providing deficit-laden countries with short-term foreign currency loans, IMF funds would buy time for countries to bring down their inflation rates and reduce their balance-of-payments deficits. The belief was that such loans would reduce pressures for devaluation and allow for a more orderly and less painful adjustment.

THE ROLE OF THE WORLD BANK

The official name for the World Bank is the International Bank for Reconstruction and Development (IBRD). When the Bretton Woods participants established the World Bank, the need to reconstruct the war-torn economies of Europe was foremost in their minds. The bank's initial mission was to help finance the building of Europe's economy by providing low-interest loans. As it turned out, the World Bank was overshadowed in this role by the Marshall Plan, under which the United States lent money directly to European nations to help them rebuild. So the bank turned its attention to "development" and began lending money to Third World nations. In the 1950s, the bank concentrated on public-sector projects. Power stations, road building, and other transportation investments were much in favour. During the 1960s, the bank also began to lend heavily in support of agriculture, education, population control, and urban development.

The bank lends money under two schemes. Under the IBRD scheme, money is raised through bond sales in the international capital market. Borrowers pay what the bank calls a market rate of interest–the bank's cost of funds plus a margin for expenses. This "market" rate is lower than commercial banks' market rate. Under the IBRD scheme, the bank offers low-interest loans to risky customers whose credit rating is often poor.

A second scheme is overseen by the International Development Agency (IDA), an arm of the bank created in 1960. Resources to fund IDA loans are raised through subscriptions from wealthy members such as the United States, Japan, and Germany. IDA loans go only to the poorest countries. Borrowers have 50 years to repay at an interest rate of 1 percent a year.

THE COLLAPSE OF THE FIXED EXCHANGE RATE SYSTEM

The system of fixed exchange rates established at Bretton Woods worked well until the late 1960s, when it began to show signs of strain. The system finally collapsed in 1973, and since then we have had a managed-float system. To understand why the system collapsed, one must appreciate the special role of the U.S. dollar in the system. As the only currency that could be converted into gold, and as the currency that served as the reference point for all others, the dollar occupied a central place in the system. Any pressure on the dollar to devalue could wreak havoc with the system, and that is what occurred.

Most economists trace the breakup of the fixed exchange rate system to the U.S. macroeconomic policy package of 1965–1968.[6] To finance both the Vietnam conflict and his welfare programs, U.S. President Lyndon Johnson backed an increase in U.S. government spending that was not financed by an increase in taxes. Instead, it was financed by an increase in the money supply, which led to a rise in price inflation from less than 4 percent in 1966 to close to 9 percent by 1968. At the same time, the rise in government spending stimulated the economy. With more money in their pockets, people spent more–particularly on imports–and the U.S. trade balance began to deteriorate.

The increase in inflation and the worsening of the U.S. foreign trade position gave rise to speculation in the foreign exchange market that the dollar would be devalued. Things came to a head in spring 1971 when U.S. trade figures showed that for the first time since 1945, the United States was importing more than it was exporting. This set off massive purchases of German deutschemarks in the foreign exchange market by speculators who guessed that the mark would be revalued against the dollar. On a single day, May 4, 1971, the Bundesbank (Germany's central bank) had to buy $1 billion to hold the dollar/deutschemark exchange rate at its fixed exchange rate given the great demand for deutschemarks. On the morning of May 5, the Bundesbank purchased another $1 billion during the first hour of foreign exchange trading! At that point, the Bundesbank faced the inevitable and allowed its currency to float.

In the weeks following the decision to float the deutschemark, the foreign exchange market became increasingly convinced that the dollar would have to be devalued. However, devaluation of the dollar was no easy matter. Under the Bretton Woods provisions, any other country could change its exchange rates against all currencies simply by fixing its dollar rate at a new level. But as the key currency in the system, the dollar could be devalued only if all countries agreed to simultaneously revalue against the dollar. And many countries did not want this, because it would make their products more expensive relative to U.S. products.

To force the issue, President Nixon announced in August 1971 that the dollar was no longer convertible into gold. He also announced that a new 10 percent tax on imports would remain in effect until U.S. trading partners agreed to revalue their currencies against the dollar. This brought the trading partners to the bargaining table, and in December 1971 an agreement was reached to devalue the dollar by about 8 percent against foreign currencies. The import tax was then removed.

The problem was not solved, however. The U.S. balance-of-payments position continued to deteriorate throughout 1972, while the nation's money supply continued to expand at an inflationary rate. Speculation continued to grow that the dollar was still overvalued and that a second devaluation would be necessary. In anticipation, foreign exchange dealers began converting dollars to deutschemarks and other currencies. After a massive wave of speculation in February 1972, which culminated with European central banks spending \$3.6 billion on March 1 to try to prevent their currencies from appreciating against the dollar, the foreign exchange market was closed. When the foreign exchange market reopened March 19, the currencies of Japan and most European countries were floating against the dollar, although many developing countries continued to peg their currency to the dollar, and many do to this day. At that time, the switch to a floating system was viewed as a temporary response to unmanageable speculation in the foreign exchange market. But it is now 30 years since the Bretton Woods system of fixed exchange rates collapsed, and the temporary solution looks permanent.

The Bretton Woods system had an Achilles' heel: The system could not work if its key currency, the U.S. dollar, was under speculative attack. The Bretton Woods system could work only as long as the U.S. inflation rate remained low and the United States did not run a balance-of-payments deficit. Once these things occurred, the system soon became strained to the breaking point.

THE FLOATING EXCHANGE RATE REGIME

The floating exchange rate regime that followed the collapse of the fixed exchange rate system was formalized in January 1976 when IMF members met in Jamaica and agreed to the rules for the international monetary system that are in place today.

THE JAMAICA AGREEMENT

The Jamaica meeting revised the IMF's Articles of Agreement to reflect the new reality of floating exchange rates. The main elements of the Jamaica agreement include the following:

1. Floating rates were declared acceptable. IMF members were permitted to enter the foreign exchange market to even out "unwarranted" speculative fluctuations.
2. Gold was abandoned as a reserve asset. The IMF returned its gold reserves to members at the current market price, placing the proceeds in a trust fund to help poor nations. IMF members were permitted to sell their own gold reserves at the market price.
3. Total annual IMF quotas–the amount member countries contribute to the IMF–were increased to \$41 billion. (Since then they have been increased to \$300 billion while the membership of the IMF has been expanded to include 183 countries.) Non-oil-exporting, less developed countries were given greater access to IMF funds.

After Jamaica, the IMF continued its role of helping countries cope with macroeconomic and exchange rate problems, albeit within the context of a radically different exchange rate regime.

EXCHANGE RATES SINCE 1973

Since March 1973, exchange rates have become much more volatile and less predictable than they were between 1945 and 1973.[7] This volatility has been partly due to a number of unexpected shocks to the world monetary system, including:

1. The oil crisis in 1971, when the Organization of Petroleum Exporting Countries (OPEC) quadrupled the price of oil. The harmful effect of this on the U.S. inflation rate and trade position resulted in a further decline in the value of the dollar.
2. The loss of confidence in the dollar that followed the rise of U.S. inflation in 1977 and 1978.
3. The oil crisis of 1979, when OPEC once again increased the price of oil dramatically–this time it was doubled.
4. The unexpected rise in the dollar between 1980 and 1985, despite a deteriorating balance-of-payments picture.
5. The rapid fall of the U.S. dollar against the Japanese yen and German deutschemark between 1985 and 1987, and against the yen between 1993 and 1995.
6. The partial collapse of the European Monetary System in 1992.
7. The 1997 Asian currency crisis, when the Asian currencies of several countries, including South Korea, Indonesia, Malaysia, and Thailand, lost between 50 percent and 80 percent of their value against the U.S. dollar in a few months.

Figure 10.1 summarizes the volatility of the U.S. dollar (USD), British pound (GBP), a basket of Euro currencies (EUR12), and the Japanese yen (JPY) from 1970 to 2002. The chart depicts a volatility inherent in these currencies. Note the rapid rise of the U.S. dollar from 1979 to 1985 and its subsequent fall and stabilization from 1986 to 1996. The Japanese yen rose sharply from 1992 to 1996.

The rise in the value of the U.S. dollar is particularly interesting because it occurred when the United States was running a large and growing trade deficit, importing substantially more than it exported. Conventional wisdom would suggest that the increased supply of dollars in the foreign exchange market as a result of the deficit should lead to a reduction in the value of the dollar, but it increased in value.

The fall in the value of the dollar between 1985 and 1988 was caused by a combination of government intervention and market forces. The rise in the dollar, which priced U.S. goods out of foreign markets and made imports relatively cheap, had contributed to a dismal trade picture. In 1985, the United States posted a record-high trade deficit of more than $160 billion. This led to growth in demands for protectionism in the

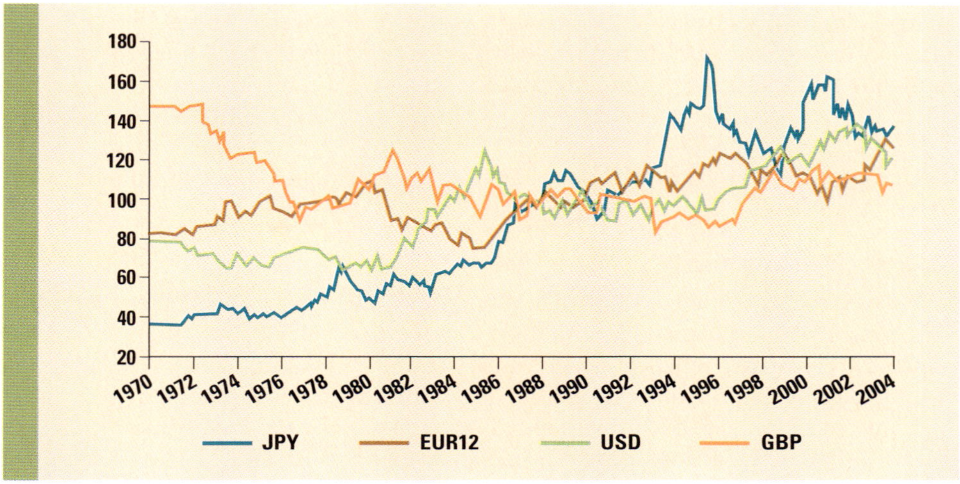

FIGURE 10.1

Nominal Effective Exchange Rates Since 1970 (average 1980-2002 = 100).

Source: From the "Third Quarter Price-Cost-Competitiveness Report," 2003, Economic and Financial Affairs Directorate of the European Commission. Courtesy of the European Communities.

United States. In September 1985, the finance ministers and central bank governors of the so-called Group of Five major industrial countries (Great Britain, France, Japan, Germany, and the United States) met at the Plaza Hotel in New York and reached what was later referred to as the Plaza Accord. They announced that it would be desirable for most major currencies to appreciate vis-à-vis the U.S. dollar and pledged to intervene in the foreign exchange markets, selling dollars, to encourage this objective. The dollar had already begun to weaken in the summer of 1985, and this announcement further accelerated the decline.

The dollar continued to decline until early 1987. The governments of the Group of Five even began to worry that the dollar might decline too far, so the finance ministers of the Group of Five met in Paris in February 1987 and reached a new agreement known as the Louvre Accord. They agreed that exchange rates had been realigned sufficiently and pledged to support the stability of exchange rates around their current levels by intervening in the foreign exchange markets when necessary to buy and sell currency. Although the dollar continued to decline for a few months after the Louvre Accord, the rate of decline slowed, and by early 1988 the decline had ended. Except for a brief speculative flurry around the Persian Gulf War in 1991, the dollar was relatively stable for most of the 1990s against most major currencies with the notable exception of the Japanese yen. However, in 2000 and 2001, the dollar began to appreciate against most major currencies, including the euro, even though the United States was once more running a record balance-of-payments deficit.

Thus, we see that in recent history, the value of the dollar has been determined by both market forces and government intervention. Under a floating exchange rate regime, market forces have produced a volatile dollar exchange rate. Governments have responded by intervening in the market–buying and selling dollars–in an attempt to limit the market's volatility and to correct what they see as overvaluation (in 1985) or potential undervaluation (in 1987) of the dollar. The frequency of government intervention in the foreign exchange markets explains why the current system is often referred to as a managed-float system or a dirty-float system.

FIXED VERSUS FLOATING EXCHANGE RATES

The breakdown of the Bretton Woods system has not stopped the debate about the relative merits of fixed versus floating exchange rate regimes. Disappointment with the system of floating rates in recent years has led to renewed debate about the merits of fixed exchange rates. In this section, we review the arguments for fixed and floating exchange rate regimes.[8] We will discuss the case for floating rates before discussing why many commentators are disappointed with the experience under floating exchange rates and yearn for a system of fixed rates.

THE CASE FOR FLOATING EXCHANGE RATES

The case for floating exchange rates has two main elements: monetary policy autonomy and automatic trade balance adjustments.

Monetary Policy Autonomy

It is argued that under a fixed system, a country's ability to expand or contract its money supply as it sees fit is limited by the need to maintain exchange rate parity. Monetary expansion can lead to inflation, which puts downward pressure on a fixed exchange rate (as predicted by the PPP theory; see Chapter 9). Similarly, monetary contraction requires high interest rates (to reduce the demand for money). Higher interest rates lead to an inflow of money from abroad, which puts upward pressure on a fixed exchange rate.

Thus, to maintain exchange rate parity under a fixed system, countries were limited in their ability to use monetary policy to expand or contract their economies.

Advocates of a floating exchange rate regime argue that removing the obligation to maintain exchange rate parity would restore monetary control to a government. If a government faced with unemployment wanted to increase its money supply to stimulate domestic demand and reduce unemployment, it could do so unencumbered by the need to maintain its exchange rate. While monetary expansion might lead to inflation, this would lead to a depreciation in the country's currency. If PPP theory is correct, the resulting currency depreciation on the foreign exchange markets should offset the effects of inflation. Although domestic inflation would have an impact on the exchange rate under a floating exchange rate regime, it should have no impact on businesses' international cost competitiveness due to exchange rate depreciation. The rise in domestic costs should be exactly offset by the fall in the value of the country's currency on the foreign exchange markets. Similarly, a government could use monetary policy to contract the economy without worrying about the need to maintain parity.

Trade Balance Adjustments

Under the Bretton Woods system, if a country developed a permanent deficit in its balance of trade (importing more than it exported) that could not be corrected by domestic policy, this would require the IMF to agree to a currency devaluation. Critics of this system argue that the adjustment mechanism works much more smoothly under a floating exchange rate regime. They argue that if a country is running a trade deficit, the imbalance between the supply and demand of that country's currency in the foreign exchange markets (supply exceeding demand) will lead to depreciation in its exchange rate. In turn, by making its exports cheaper and its imports more expensive, an exchange rate depreciation should correct the trade deficit.

THE CASE FOR FIXED EXCHANGE RATES

The case for fixed exchange rates rests on arguments about monetary discipline, speculation, uncertainty, and the lack of connection between the trade balance and exchange rates.

Monetary Discipline

We have already discussed the nature of monetary discipline inherent in a fixed exchange rate system when we discussed the Bretton Woods system. The need to maintain a fixed exchange rate parity ensures that governments do not expand their money supplies at inflationary rates. While advocates of floating rates argue that each country should be allowed to choose its own inflation rate (the monetary autonomy argument), advocates of fixed rates argue that governments all too often give in to political pressures and expand the monetary supply far too rapidly, causing unacceptably high price inflation. A fixed exchange rate regime will ensure that this does not occur.

Speculation

Critics of a floating exchange rate regime also argue that speculation can cause fluctuations in exchange rates. They point to the dollar's rapid rise and fall during the 1980s, which they claim had nothing to do with comparative inflation rates and the U.S. trade deficit, but everything to do with speculation. They argue that when foreign exchange dealers see a currency depreciating, they tend to sell the currency in the expectation of future depreciation regardless of the currency's longer-term prospects. As more traders jump on the bandwagon, the expectations of depreciation are realized. Such destabilizing speculation tends to accentuate the fluctuations around the exchange rate's long-run value. It can damage a country's economy by distorting export and import prices. Thus, advocates of a fixed exchange rate regime argue that such a system will limit the destabilizing effects of speculation.

Uncertainty

Speculation also adds to the uncertainty surrounding future currency movements that characterizes floating exchange rate regimes. The unpredictability of exchange rate movements in the post-Bretton Woods era has made business planning difficult, and it makes exporting, importing, and foreign investment risky activities. Given a volatile exchange rate, international businesses do not know how to react to the changes–and often they do not react. Why change plans for exporting, importing, or foreign investment after a 6 percent fall in the dollar this month, when the dollar may rise 6 percent next month? This uncertainty, according to the critics, dampens the growth of international trade and investment. They argue that a fixed exchange rate, by eliminating such uncertainty, promotes the growth of international trade and investment. Advocates of a floating system reply that the forward exchange market insures against the risks associated with exchange rate fluctuations (see Chapter 9), so the adverse impact of uncertainty on the growth of international trade and investment has been overstated.

Trade Balance Adjustments

Those in favour of floating exchange rates argue that floating rates help adjust trade imbalances. Critics question the closeness of the link between the exchange rate and the trade balance. They claim trade deficits are determined by the balance between savings and investment in a country, not by the external value of its currency.[9] They argue that depreciation in a currency will lead to inflation (due to the resulting increase in import prices). This inflation will wipe out any apparent gains in cost competitiveness that come from currency depreciation. In other words, a depreciating exchange rate will not boost exports and reduce imports, as advocates of floating rates claim; it will simply boost price inflation. In support of this argument, those who favour fixed rates point out that the 40 percent drop in the value of the dollar between 1985 and 1988 did not correct the U.S. trade deficit. In reply, advocates of a floating exchange rate regime argue that between 1985 and 1992, the U.S. trade deficit fell from over $160 billion to about $70 billion, and they attribute this in part to the decline in the value of the dollar.

WHO IS RIGHT?

Which side is right in the vigorous debate between those who favour a fixed exchange rate and those who favour a floating exchange rate? Economists cannot agree on this issue. From a business perspective, this is unfortunate because business, as a major player on the international trade and investment scene, has a large stake in the resolution of the debate. Would international business be better off under a fixed regime, or are flexible rates better? The evidence is not clear.

We do, however, know that a fixed exchange rate regime modeled along the lines of the Bretton Woods system will not work. Speculation ultimately broke the system, a phenomenon that advocates of fixed rate regimes claim is associated with floating exchange rates! Nevertheless, a different kind of fixed exchange rate system might be more enduring and might foster the stability that would facilitate more rapid growth in international trade and investment. In the next section, we look at potential models for such a system and the problems with such systems.

EXCHANGE RATE REGIMES IN PRACTICE

A number of different exchange rate policies are pursued by governments around the world. These range from a pure "free float," where the exchange rate is determined by market forces, to a pegged system that has some aspects of the pre-1973 Bretton Woods system of fixed exchange rates. Figure 10.2 summarizes the exchange rate regime categories adopted by member states of the IMF in 2003. Some 27 percent of the IMF's 183 members allow their currency to float freely. Another 15 percent intervene in only a limited way (the so-called managed float). Some 20 percent of IMF members now have no separate legal tender of their own. These include the 12 European Union countries that have adopted the euro, and effectively given up their own currencies, along with some 26 smaller states mostly in Africa or the Caribbean that have no domestic currency and have adopted a foreign currency as legal tender within their borders, typically the U.S. dollar or the euro. The remaining countries use more inflexible systems, including a fixed peg arrangement (24 percent) under which they peg their currencies to other currencies, such as the U.S. dollar or the euro, or to a basket of currencies. Other countries have adopted a somewhat more flexible system under which their exchange rate is allowed to fluctuate against other currencies within a target zone (an adjustable peg system). In this section, we will look more closely at the mechanics and implications of exchange rate regimes that rely on a currency peg or target zone.

PEGGED EXCHANGE RATES

Under a pegged exchange rate regime, a country will peg the value of its currency to that of a major currency so that, for example, as the U.S. dollar rises in value, its own

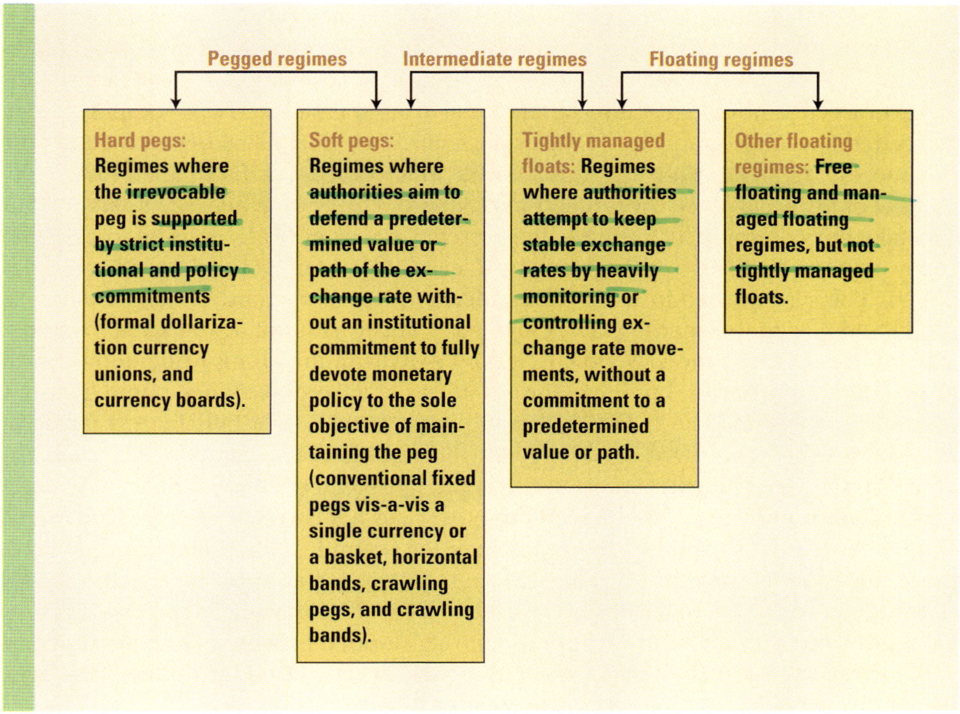

FIGURE 10.2

The Current Spectrum of Exchange Rate Regime Categories.

Source: International Monetary Fund and the World Bank, A. Babula and I. Otker-Robe, "The Continuing Bipolar Conundrum," *Finance and Development* 24, March 2004, p. 32. Accessed via IMF Web site at www.imf.org/external/pubs/ft/fandd/2004/pdf/babula.pdf. This work is protected by copyright and the making of this copy was with the permission of *Access Copyright*. Any alteration of its content or further copying in any form whatsoever is strictly prohibited.

currency rises too. Pegged exchange rates are popular among many of the world's smaller nations. As with a full fixed exchange rate regime, the great virtue claimed for a pegged exchange rate is that it imposes monetary discipline on a country and leads to low inflation. For example, if Belize pegs the value of the Belizean dollar to that of the U.S. dollar so that US\$1=B\$1.97 (the peg as of 2001), then the Belizean government must make sure the inflation rate in Belize is similar to that in the United States. If the Belizean inflation rate is greater than the U.S. inflation rate, this will lead to pressure to devalue the Belizean dollar (i.e., to alter the peg). To maintain the peg, the Belizean government would be required to rein in inflation. Of course, for a pegged exchange rate to impose monetary discipline on a country, the country whose currency is chosen for the peg must also pursue sound monetary policy.

Evidence shows that adopting a pegged exchange rate regime does moderate inflationary pressures in a country. An IMF study concluded that countries with pegged exchange rates had an average annual inflation rate of 8 percent, compared with 14 percent for intermediate regimes and 16 percent for floating regimes.[10] However, many countries operate with only a nominal peg and in practice are willing to devalue their currency rather than pursue a tight monetary policy. It can be very difficult for a smaller country to maintain a peg against another currency if capital is flowing out of the country and foreign exchange traders are speculating against the currency. Something like this occurred in 1997 when a combination of adverse capital flows and currency speculation forced several Asian countries, including Thailand and Malaysia, to abandon pegs against the U.S. dollar and let their currencies float freely. Malaysia and Thailand would not have been in this position had they dealt with a number of problems that began to arise in their economies during the 1990s, including excessive private-sector debt and expanding current account trade deficits.

CURRENCY BOARDS

Hong Kong's experience during the 1997 Asian currency crisis, however, has added a new dimension to the debate over how to manage a pegged exchange rate. During late 1997 when other Asian currencies were collapsing, Hong Kong maintained the value of its currency against the U.S. dollar at around US\$1=HK\$7.8 despite several concerted speculative attacks. Hong Kong's currency board has been credited with this success. A country that introduces a **currency board** commits itself to converting its domestic currency on demand into another currency at a fixed exchange rate. To make this commitment credible, the currency board holds reserves of foreign currency equal at the fixed exchange rate to at least 100 percent of the domestic currency issued. The system used in Hong Kong means its currency must be fully backed by the U.S. dollar at the specified exchange rate. This is still not a true fixed exchange rate regime, because the U.S. dollar, and by extension the Hong Kong dollar, floats against other currencies, but it has some features of a fixed exchange rate regime.

CURRENCY BOARD
Means of controlling a country's currency.

Under this arrangement, the currency board can issue additional domestic notes and coins only when there are foreign exchange reserves to back it. This limits the ability of the government to print money and, thereby, create inflationary pressures. Under a strict currency board system, interest rates adjust automatically. If investors want to switch out of domestic currency into, for example, U.S. dollars, the supply of domestic currency will shrink. This will cause interest rates to rise until it eventually becomes attractive for investors to hold the local currency again. In the case of Hong Kong, the interest rate on three-month deposits climbed as high as 20 percent in late 1997, as investors switched out of Hong Kong dollars and into U.S. dollars. However, the dollar peg held, and interest rates declined again.

Since its establishment in 1983, the Hong Kong currency board has weathered several storms, including the latest. This success seems to be persuading other countries in the developing world to consider a similar system. Argentina introduced a currency board in 1991, and Bulgaria, Estonia, and Lithuania have all gone down this road in recent years (eight IMF members had currency boards in 2000). Despite growing interest in the arrangement, however, critics are quick to point out that currency boards have their drawbacks.[11] If local inflation rates remain higher than the inflation rate in the country to which the currency is pegged, the currencies of countries with currency boards can become uncompetitive and overvalued. Also, under a currency board system, government lacks the ability to set interest rates. Interest rates in Hong Kong, for example, are effectively set by the U.S. Federal Reserve. Despite these drawbacks, Hong Kong's success in avoiding the currency collapse that afflicted its Asian neighbours suggests that other developing countries may adopt a similar system.

CRISIS MANAGEMENT BY THE IMF

Many observers initially believed that the collapse of the Bretton Woods system in 1973 would diminish the role of the IMF within the international monetary system. The IMF's original function was to provide a pool of money from which members could borrow, short term, to adjust their balance-of-payments position and maintain their exchange rate. Some believed the demand for short-term loans would be considerably diminished under a floating exchange rate regime. A trade deficit would presumably lead to a decline in a country's exchange rate, which would help reduce imports and boost exports. No temporary IMF adjustment loan would be needed. Consistent with this, after 1973, most industrialized countries tended to let the foreign exchange market determine exchange rates in response to demand and supply. No major industrial country has borrowed funds from the IMF since the mid-1970s, when Great Britain and Italy did. Since the early 1970s, the rapid development of global capital markets has allowed developed countries such as Great Britain and the United States to finance their deficits by borrowing private money, as opposed to drawing on IMF funds.

Despite these developments, the activities of the IMF have expanded over the past 30 years. By 2002, the IMF had 184 members, 88 of which had some kind of IMF program in place in June 2002. In 1997, the institution implemented its largest rescue packages, committing more than $110 billion in short-term loans to three troubled Asian countries–South Korea, Indonesia, and Thailand. The IMF's activities have expanded because periodic financial crises have continued to hit many economies in the post-Bretton Woods era, particularly among the world's developing nations. The IMF has repeatedly lent money to nations experiencing financial crises, requesting in return that the governments enact certain macroeconomic policies. IMF critics claim these policies have not always been as beneficial as the IMF might have hoped and in some cases may have made things worse (for example, review the Country Focus on the IMF's involvement in the Congo). With the recent IMF loans to several Asian economies, these criticisms reached new levels and a vigorous debate is under way as to the appropriate role of the IMF. In this section, we shall discuss some of the main challenges the IMF has had to deal with over the last quarter of a century and review the ongoing debate over the role of the IMF.

FINANCIAL CRISES IN THE POST-BRETTON WOODS ERA

A number of broad types of financial crises have occurred over the past quarter century, many of which have required IMF involvement. A **currency crisis** occurs when a speculative attack on the exchange value of a currency results in a sharp depreciation in the value of the currency or forces authorities to expend large volumes of international currency reserves and sharply increase interest rates to defend the prevailing exchange rate. A **banking crisis** refers to a loss of confidence in the banking system that leads to a run on banks, as individuals and companies withdraw their

CURRENCY CRISIS
Occurs when a speculative attack on the exchange value of a currency results in a sharp depreciation in the value of the currency or forces authorities to expend large volumes of international currency reserves and sharply increase interest rates to defend the prevailing exchange rate.

BANKING CRISIS
A loss of confidence in the banking system that leads to a run on banks, as individuals and companies withdraw their deposits.

COUNTRY FOCUS

THE TRAGEDY OF THE CONGO (ZAIRE)

The Democratic Republic of the Congo, formerly known as Zaire, gained its independence from Belgium in 1960. The central African nation, rich in natural resources such as copper, seemed to have a promising future. If the country had simply sustained its preindependence economic growth rate, its gross national product (GNP) would have been $1,400 per capita by 1997, making it one of the richest countries in Africa. Instead, by 1997, the country was a wreck. Battered by a brutal civil war that led to the ousting of the country's longtime dictator, Mobutu Sese Seko, the economy had shrunk to its 1958 level with a GNP per capita below $100. The annual inflation rate exceeded 750 percent, an improvement from the 9800 percent rate recorded in 1994. Consequently, the local currency was almost worthless. Most transactions were made by barter or, for the lucky few, with U.S. dollars. Infant mortality stood at a dismal 106 per 1000 live births, and life expectancy stood at 47 years, roughly comparable to that of Europe in the Middle Ages.

What were the underlying causes of the economic, political, and social collapse of Zaire? While the story is a complex one, according to several influential critics, some of the blame must be placed at the feet of two multinational lending institutions, the International Monetary Fund and the World Bank. Both institutions were established in 1944 at the famous Bretton Woods conference, which paved the way for the post-World War II international monetary system. The IMF was given the task of maintaining order in the international monetary system, while the role of the World Bank was to promote general economic development, particularly among the world's poorer nations. The IMF typically provides loans to countries whose currencies are losing value due to economic mismanagement. In return for these loans, the IMF imposes on debtor countries strict financial policies that are designed to rein in inflation and stabilize their economies. The World Bank has historically provided low interest rate loans to help countries build basic infrastructure. Both institutions are funded by subscriptions from member states, including significant contributions from the world's developed nations.

The IMF and the World Bank were major donors to postindependence Zaire. The IMF's involvement with Zaire dates to 1967, when the IMF approved Zaire's first economic stabilization plan, backed by a $27-million line of credit. About the same time, the World Bank began to make low interest rate infrastructure loans to the government of Mobutu Sese Seko. This was followed by a series of further plans and loans between 1976 and 1981. At the urging of the IMF, Zaire's currency was devalued five times during this period to help boost exports and reduce imports, while taxes were raised in an effort to balance Zaire's budget. IMF and other Western officials were also placed in key positions at the Zairian central bank, finance ministry, and office of debt management.

Despite all this help, Zaire's economy continued to deteriorate. By 1982, after 15 years of IMF assistance, Zaire had a lower GNP than in 1967 and faced default on its debt. Some critics, including Jeffrey Sachs, the noted development economist from Harvard University, claim that this poor performance could in part be attributed to the policies imposed by the IMF, which included tax hikes, cuts in government subsidies, and periodic competitive currency devaluations. These policies, claim critics, were ill suited to such a poor country and created a vicious cycle of economic decline. The tax hikes simply drove work into the "underground economy" or created a disincentive to work. As a consequence, government tax revenues dwindled and the budget deficit expanded, making it difficult for the government to service its debt obligations. By raising import prices, the devaluations helped fuel the phenomenon the IMF was trying to control: inflation. In turn, high inflation of both prices and wages soon brought ordinary Zairians into high tax brackets, which drove even more work into the underground economy and further shrank government tax revenues.

When explaining Zaire's malaise, others point to corruption. In 1982, a senior IMF official in Zaire reported that President Mobutu Sese Seko and his cronies were systematically stealing IMF and World Bank loans. Later news reports suggest that Mobutu accumulated a personal fortune of $4 billion by the mid-1980s, making him one of the richest men in the world at that time.

In 1982, Zaire was initially suspended from further use of its IMF credit line. However, the position was reversed in 1983 when a new agreement was negotiated that included an additional $356 million in IMF loans. The loans were linked to a further devaluation of the Zairian currency, more tax hikes, and cuts in government subsidies. The IMF's decision to turn a blind eye to the corruption problem and extend new loans was influenced by pressure from Western politicians who saw Mobutu's pro-Western regime as a bulwark against the spread of Marxism in Africa. By ignoring the corruption, the IMF could claim it was abiding by IMF rules, which stated the institution should offer only economic advice and stay out of internal political issues. The IMF's decision lent credence to Mobutu Sese Seko's government and enabled Zaire to attract more foreign loans. As a consequence, the country's overall foreign debt increased to $5 billion by the mid-1980s, up from $3 billion in 1978.

Unfortunately, the new loans and IMF policies did little to improve Zaire's economic performance, which continued to deteriorate. In 1987, Zaire was forced to abandon its agreement with the IMF due to food riots. The IMF negotiated another agreement for the 1989–1991 period, which included further currency devaluation. This also failed to produce any tangible progress. The Zairian economy continued to implode while the country's civil war flared. In 1993, Zaire suspended its debt repayments, effectively going into default. In 1994, the World Bank announced it would shut down its operations in the country. About the same time, the IMF suspended Zaire's membership in the institution, making Zaire ineligible for further loans.

In 1997, after a long civil war, Mobutu Sese Seko was deposed. The new government inherited $14.6 billion of external debt, including debt arrears exceeding $1 billion. At a formal meeting chaired by the World Bank to discuss rescheduling of the country's debt, delegates from the new government claimed that the World Bank, IMF, and other institutions acted irresponsibly by lending money to Mobutu's regime despite evidence of both substantial corruption and Zaire's inability to service such a high level of debt. In an implicit acknowledgment that this may have been the case, the IMF and World Bank began telling debtor countries to stamp out corruption or lose access to IMF and World Bank loans.

Sources: G. Fossedal, "The IMF's Role in Zaire's Decline," *Wall Street Journal,* May 15, 1997, p. 22; J. Burns and M. Holman, "Mobutu Built a Fortune of $4 Billion from Looted Aid," *Financial Times,* May 12, 1997, p. 1; J. D. Sachs and R. I. Rotberg, "Help Congo Now," *New York Times,* May 29, 1997, p. 21; H. Dunphy, "IMF, World Bank Now Make Political Judgements," *Journal of Commerce,* August 21, 1997, p. 3A; and *CIA World Factbook* (Washington, DC: CIA, 1998).

The economic, political, and social collapse of the Democratic Republic of Congo (formerly Zaire) led several prominent critics to claim that IMF policy actually contributed to the economic misery of the country, rather than curing it. Liba Taylor/CORBIS.

FOREIGN DEBT CRISIS Situation in which a country cannot service its foreign debt obligations, whether private-sector or government debt.

deposits. A **foreign debt crisis** is a situation in which a country cannot service its foreign debt obligations, whether private or government debt. These crises tend to have common underlying macroeconomic causes: high relative price inflation rates, a widening current account deficit, excessive expansion of domestic borrowing, and asset price inflation (such as sharp increases in stock and property prices).[12] At times, elements of currency, banking, and debt crises may be present simultaneously, as in the 1997 Asian crisis or in the 1999–2001 Turkish crisis (see the opening case).

To assess the frequency of financial crises, the IMF looked at the macroeconomic performance of a group of 53 countries from 1975 to 1997 (22 of these countries were developed nations, and 31 were developing countries).[13] The IMF found there were 158 currency crises, including 55 episodes in which a country's currency declined by more than 25 percent. There were also 54 banking crises. The IMF's data, which are summarized in Figure 10.3, suggest that developing nations were more than twice as likely to experience currency and banking crises than developed nations. It is not surprising, therefore, that most of the IMF's loan activities since the mid-1970s have been targeted toward developing nations.

Four crises have been of particular significance in terms of IMF involvement: the Third World debt crisis of the 1980s, the crisis experienced by Russia as it moved toward a market-based economic system, the 1995 Mexican currency crisis, and the 1997 Asian financial crisis. All four were the result of excessive foreign borrowing, a weak or poorly regulated banking system, and high inflation rates. These factors came together to trigger simultaneous debt and currency crises. Checking the resulting crises required IMF involvement.

FIGURE 10.3

Incidence of Currency and Banking Crises, 1975–1997

Source: From International Monetary Fund, *World Economic Outlook, 1998,* May 1998, p. 77. Reprinted with permission.

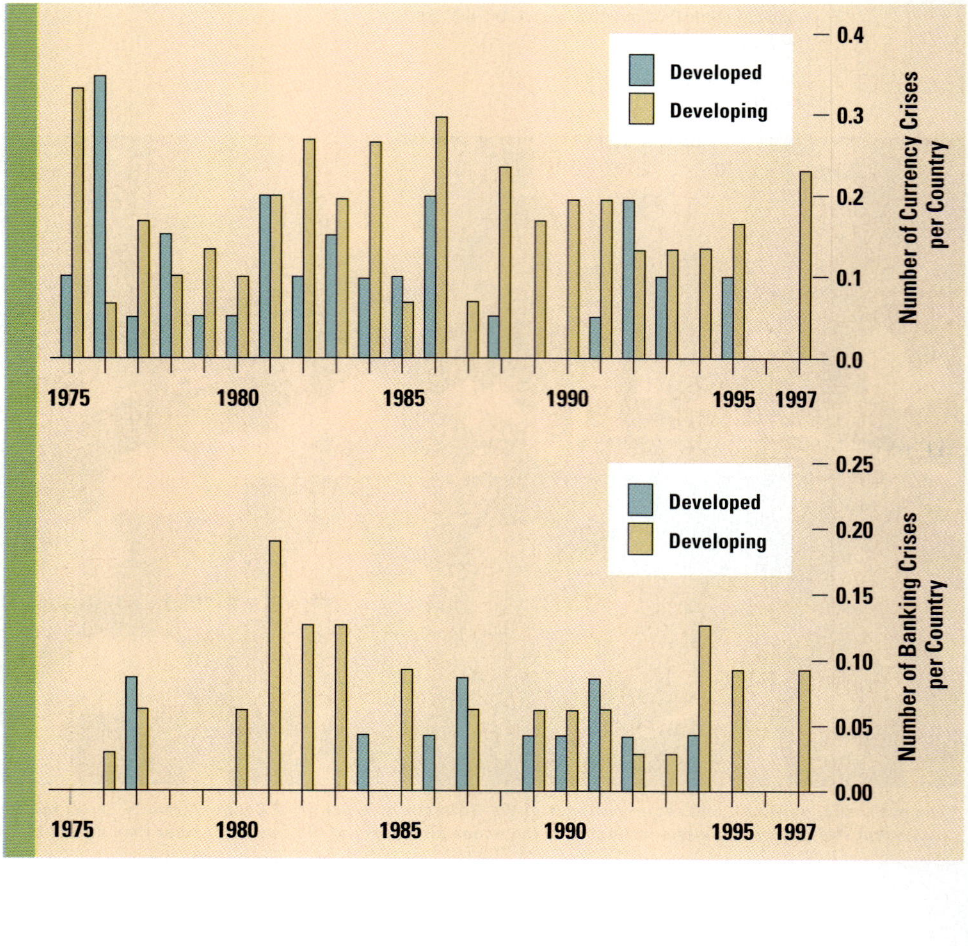

THIRD WORLD DEBT CRISIS

The Third World debt crisis had its roots in the OPEC oil price hikes of 1973 and 1979. These resulted in massive flows of funds from the major oil-importing nations (Germany, Japan, and the United States) to the oil-producing nations of OPEC. Commercial banks stepped in to recycle this money, borrowing from OPEC countries and lending to governments and businesses around the world. Much of the recycled money ended up in the form of loans to the governments of various Latin American and African nations. The loans were made on the basis of optimistic assessments about these nations' growth prospects, which did not materialize. Instead, Third World economic growth was choked in the early 1980s by a combination of factors, including high inflation, rising short-term interest rates (which increased the costs of servicing the debt), and recession conditions in many industrialized nations (which were the markets for Third World goods).

The consequence was a Third World debt crisis of huge proportions. At one point, commercial banks had more than $1 trillion of bad debts on their books which the debtor nations had no hope of paying off. Against this background, Mexico announced in 1982 that it could no longer service its $80 billion in international debt without an immediate new loan of $3 billion. Brazil quickly followed, revealing it could not meet the required payments on its borrowed $87 billion. Then Argentina and several dozen other countries of lesser credit standings followed suit. The international monetary system faced a crisis of enormous dimensions.

The call to forgive debt and contribute funds to fight AIDS in developing countries has been repeated by both Bono and governments around the world. In 2004, Prime Minister Paul Martin announced $100 million for an international initiative aimed at AIDS treatments. CP/Tom Hanson.

Into the breach stepped the IMF. Together with several Western governments, particularly that of the United States, the IMF emerged as the key player in resolving the debt crisis. The deal with Mexico involved three elements: (1) rescheduling of Mexico's old debt, (2) new loans to Mexico from the IMF, the World Bank, and commercial banks, and (3) the Mexican government's agreement to abide by a set of IMF-dictated macroeconomic prescriptions for its economy, including tight control over the growth of the money supply and major cuts in government spending.

However, the IMF's solution to the debt crisis contained a major weakness: It depended on the rapid resumption of growth in the debtor nations. If this occurred, their capacity to repay debt would grow faster than their debt itself, and the crisis would be resolved. By the mid-1980s, it was clear this was not going to happen. The IMF-imposed macroeconomic policies did bring the trade deficits and inflation rates of many debtor nations under control, but it created sharp contractions in their economic growth rates.

It was apparent by 1989 that the debt problem was not going to be solved merely by rescheduling debt. In April of that year, the IMF endorsed a new approach that had been proposed by Nicholas Brady, the U.S. Treasury secretary. The Brady Plan, as it became known, stated that debt reduction, as distinguished from debt rescheduling, was a necessary part of the solution and the IMF and World Bank would assume roles in financing it. The essence of the plan was that the IMF, the World Bank, and the Japanese government would each contribute $10 billion toward debt reduction. To gain access to these funds, a debtor nation would once again have to submit to imposed conditions for macroeconomic policy management and debt repayment. The first application of the Brady Plan was the Mexican debt reduction of 1989. The deal reduced Mexico's 1989 debt of $107 billion by about $15 billion and until 1995 was widely regarded as a success.[14]

MEXICAN CURRENCY CRISIS OF 1995

The Mexican peso had been pegged to the dollar since the early 1980s when the International Monetary Fund had made it a condition for lending money to help bail the country out of a 1982 financial crisis. Under the IMF-brokered arrangement, the peso had been allowed to trade within a tolerance band of plus or minus 3 percent against the dollar. The band was also permitted to "crawl" down daily, allowing for an annual peso depreciation of about 4 percent against the dollar. The IMF believed that the need to maintain the exchange rate within a fairly narrow trading band would force the Mexican government to adopt stringent financial policies to limit the growth in the money supply and contain inflation.

Until the early 1990s, it looked as if the IMF policy had worked. However, the strains were beginning to show by 1994. Since the mid-1980s, Mexican producer prices had risen 45 percent more than prices in the United States, and yet there had not been a corresponding adjustment in the exchange rate. By late 1994, Mexico was running a $17-billion trade deficit, which amounted to some 6 percent of the country's gross domestic product, and there had been an uncomfortably rapid expansion in the country's public and private-sector debt. Despite these strains, Mexican government officials had been stating publicly that they would support the peso's dollar peg at around US$1 = 3.5 pesos by adopting appropriate monetary policies and by intervening in the currency markets if necessary. Encouraged by such public statements, $64 billion of foreign investment money poured into Mexico between 1990 and 1994 as corporations and mutual fund money managers sought to take advantage of the booming economy.

However, many currency traders concluded that the peso would have to be devalued, and they began to dump pesos on the foreign exchange market. The government tried to hold the line by buying pesos and selling dollars, but it lacked the foreign currency reserves required to halt the speculative tide (Mexico's foreign exchange reserves fell from $6 billion at the beginning of 1994 to less than $3.5 billion at the end of the year). In mid-December 1994, the Mexican government abruptly announced a devaluation. Immediately, much of the short-term investment money that had flowed into Mexican stocks and bonds over the previous year reversed its course, as foreign investors bailed out of peso-denominated financial assets. This exacerbated the sale of the peso and contributed to the rapid 40 percent drop in its value.

The IMF stepped in again, this time with the U.S. government and the Bank for International Settlements. Together the three institutions pledged close to $50 billion to help Mexico stabilize the peso and to redeem $47 billion of public and private-sector debt that was set to mature in 1995. Of this amount, $20 billion came from the U.S. government and another $18 billion came from the IMF (which made Mexico the largest recipient of IMF aid to that point). Without the aid package, Mexico would probably have defaulted on its debt obligations, and the peso would have gone into free fall. As is normal in such cases, the IMF insisted on tight monetary policies and further cuts in public spending, both of which helped push the country into a deep recession. However, the recession was relatively short-lived, and by 1997 the country was once more on a growth path, had pared down its debt, and had paid back the $20 billion borrowed from the U.S. government ahead of schedule.[15] (The accompanying Management Focus details how the rise in the Canadian dollar has affected the Canadian film industry.)

RUSSIAN RUBLE CRISIS

The IMF's involvement in Russia came about as the result of a persistent decline in the value of the Russian ruble, which was the product of high inflation rates and growing public-sector debt. Between January 1992 and April 1995, the value of the ruble against the U.S. dollar fell from US$1=R125 to US$1=R5,130. This fall occurred while Russia

MANAGEMENT FOCUS

THE "REEL" THREAT TO THE CANADIAN FILM INDUSTRY

As avid moviegoers, many Canadians might not realize the magnitude of the film business, both foreign and domestic, operating within Canada. Movie trailers and film lights are a common sight in Canada's major cities to small towns. Many major American television series and movies, such as the *X-Files*, have been filmed in Canada. However, this industry has been put at risk with the recent rise of the Canadian dollar, which makes filming in Canada, compared to the United States, far less attractive than it has been.

In 2002 and 2003, the Canadian film industry grew by 4 percent for a total volume of nearly $5 billion in foreign location production, and brought in an excess of $4 billion to Canadian coffers. The cultural industry makes up almost 3 percent of GDP, employing over 500 000 Canadians. Nearly one quarter of all Hollywood films are now shot in Canada, with many Canadians showing front stage in this lucrative industry—James Cameron, Ivan Reitman, and Norman Jewison, with the latter having founded the Canadian Film Centre. Canadians also make movies outside the Hollywood system including such renowned directors as Rock Demers, Deepa Mehta, David Cronenberg, Denys Arcand, and Atom Egoyan.

Provincial and federal film tax credits do their share of the work in keeping the business of filming in Canada. Over the years, governments in Canada have come to power on pledges to protect and to bolster the Canadian film and cultural industries. The Liberal's now famous "1993 handbook" and accompanying pledge to strengthen and protect the Canadian cultural industries against incursions by the American cultural juggernaut—claimed by some to be all talk and no action—is a well-known moniker of Liberal party cultural heritage policy. Sheila Copps, the former Minister of Canadian Heritage, became associated with shining the beacon on Canadian culture, even if some pro-Canada culture interests, such as the CBC, seemed to weaken during her time in power.

The Canadian government's "intervention" or intention to intervene in the business of Canadian culture has met with culture shock in American media circles, where culture is not viewed as a national heritage, but as a profit-making industry. Labour unrest in the Hollywood film industry has frequently been a byproduct of the actors union, up in arms about lost jobs to cheaper and perhaps, friendlier climes, particularly in the great White North. Ed Asner, as head of the Screen Actors Guild and union activist, has spoken out over the decades about the outflow of Hollywood movie productions to Canada.

The latest to join this chorus is Arnold Schwarzenegger, Governor of California, who has threatened the Hollywood movie industry with punitive measures for those companies filming in Canada, and elsewhere. It is clear that government intervention or lack thereof can play a determining role in the future of this lucrative Canadian industry. To those American studios filming in Canada, there are many attractive features built into the equation. One of the major factors is the currency question. The Canadian dollar has been rising relative to the U.S. dollar since early 2004, making filming in Canada far more expensive than it used to be. Canadian concerns for a higher dollar intermittently send shivers through the Canadian film industry as the thought of losing productions to a more expensive Canadian dollar, subconsciously resonate.

The fact that the Canadian film industry and the government have been able to make huge gains in spite of the American cultural giants over the past century lends a degree of expectation about the continuation of highly successful Canadian cultural industries. However, no industry is immune to competitive threats. A strong Canadian dollar, and a weak U.S. dollar, may be enough to reverse the trend of the past several decades.

Sources: CBC at www.cbc.ca/arts/stories/arnold091003; ITC at www.dfait-maeci.gc.ca_new-delhi_film-en.asp and www.dfait-maeci.gc.ca/tna-nac/stories94-en.asp#imax; OANDA at www.oanda.com/convert/classic.

was implementing an economic reform program designed to transform the country's crumbling centrally planned economy into a dynamic market economy. The reform program involved a number of steps, including the removal of price controls on January 1, 1992. Prices surged immediately and inflation was soon running at a monthly rate of about 30 percent. For the whole of 1992, the inflation rate in Russia was 3000 percent. The annual rate for 1993 was approximately 900 percent.

Several factors contributed to Russia's high inflation. Prices had been held at artificially low levels by state planners during the Communist era. At the same time, many basic goods were in short supply, so with nothing to spend their money on, many Russians simply hoarded rubles. After the liberalization of price controls, the country was suddenly awash in rubles chasing a still limited supply of goods. The result was to rapidly bid up prices. The inflationary fires that followed price liberalization were stoked by the Russian government itself. Unwilling to face the social consequences of the massive unemployment that would follow if many state-owned enterprises quickly were privatized, the government continued to subsidize the operations of many money-losing establishments. The result was a surge in the government's budget deficit. In the first quarter of 1992, the budget deficit amounted to 1.5 percent of the country's GDP. By the end of 1992, it had risen to 17 percent. Unable or unwilling to finance this deficit by raising taxes, the government found another solution–it printed money, which added fuel to the inflation fire.

With inflation rising, the ruble tumbled. By the end of 1992, the exchange rate was US$1=R480. By the end of 1993, it was US$1=R1,500. As 1994 progressed, it became increasingly evident that due to vigorous political opposition, the government would not be able to bring down its budget deficit as quickly as had been thought. By September the monthly inflation rate was accelerating. October started badly, with the ruble sliding more than 10 percent in value against the U.S. dollar in the first ten days of the month. On October 11, the ruble plunged 21.5 percent against the dollar, reaching a value of US$15=R3,926 by the time the foreign exchange market closed!

Despite the announcement of a tough budget plan that placed tight controls on the money supply, the ruble continued to slide and by April 1995 the exchange rate stood at US$1=R5,120. However, by mid-1995, inflation was again on the way down. In June 1995, the monthly inflation rate was at a yearly low of 6.7 percent. Also, the ruble had recovered to stand at US$1=R4,559 by July 6. On that day the Russian government announced it would intervene in the currency market to keep the ruble in a trading range of R4,300 to R4,900 against the U.S. dollar. The Russian government believed it was essential to maintain a relatively stable currency. Government officials announced that the central bank would be able to draw on US$10 billion in foreign exchange reserves to defend the ruble against any speculative selling in Russia's relatively small foreign exchange market.

In the world of international finance, US$10 billion is small change and it wasn't long before Russia found that its foreign exchange reserves were being depleted. At this point the Russian government requested IMF loans. In February 1996, the IMF obliged with its second largest rescue effort after Mexico, a loan of US$10 billion. In return for the loan, Russia agreed to limit the growth in its money supply, reduce public-sector debt, increase government tax revenues, and peg the ruble to the dollar.

Initially the package seemed to have the desired effect. Inflation declined from nearly 50 percent in 1996 to about 15 percent in 1997; the exchange rate stayed within its predetermined band; and the balance-of-payments situation remained broadly favourable. In 1997, the Russian economy grew for the first time since the breakup of the former Soviet Union, if only by a modest half of 1 percent of GDP. However, the public-sector debt situation did not improve. The Russian government continued to spend more than it agreed to under IMF targets, while government tax revenues were much lower than projected. Low tax revenues were in part due to falling oil prices (the government collected tax on oil sales), in part due to the difficulties of collecting tax where so much activity was in the "underground economy," and partly due to a complex tax system that was peppered with loopholes. Currently available estimates indicate that in 1997, Russian federal government spending amounted to 18.3 percent of GDP, while revenues were only 10.8 percent of GDP, implying a deficit of 7.5 percent of GDP, which was financed by an expansion in public debt.

The IMF responded by suspending its scheduled payment to Russia in early 1998, pending reform of Russia's complex tax system and a sustained attempt by the Russian government to cut public spending. This put further pressure on the Russian ruble, forcing the Russian central bank to raise interest rates on overnight loans to 150 percent. In June 1998, the U.S. government indicated it would support a new IMF bailout. The IMF was more circumspect, insisting instead that the Russian government push through a package of corporate tax increases and public spending cuts to balance the budget. The Russian government indicated it would do so, and the IMF released a tranche of US$640 million that had been suspended. The IMF followed this with an additional US$11.2 billion loan designed to preserve the ruble's stability.

Almost as soon as the funding was announced, however, it began to unravel. The IMF loan required the Russian government to take concrete steps to raise personal tax rates, improve tax collections, and cut government spending. A bill containing the required legislative changes was sent to the Russian parliament, where it was emasculated by antigovernment forces. The IMF responded by withholding US$800 million of its first $5.6 billion tranche, undermining the credibility of its own program. The Russian stock market plummeted on the news, closing down 6.5 percent. Selling of rubles accelerated. The central bank began hemorrhaging foreign exchange reserves as it tried to maintain the value of the ruble. Foreign exchange reserves fell by $1.4 billion in the first week of August alone, to US$17 billion, while interest rates surged again.

Against this background, on the weekend of August 15–16, top Russian officials huddled to develop a response to the most recent crisis. Their options were limited. The patience of the IMF had been exhausted. Foreign currency reserves were being rapidly depleted. Social tensions in the country were running high. The government faced upcoming redemptions on US$18 billion of domestic bonds, with no idea of where the money would come from.

On Monday, August 17, Prime Minister Sergei Kiriyenko announced the results of the weekend's conclave. He said Russia would restructure the domestic debt market, unilaterally transforming short-term debt into long-term debt. In other words, the government had decided to default on its debt commitments. The government also announced a 90-day moratorium on the repayment of private foreign debt and stated it would allow the ruble to decline by 34 percent against the U.S. dollar. In short, Russia had turned its back on the IMF plan. The effect was immediate. Overnight, shops marked up the price of goods by 20 percent. As the ruble plummeted, currency exchange points were only prepared to sell dollars at a rate of 9 rubles per dollar, rather than the new official exchange rate of 6.43 rubles to the dollar. As for Russian government debt, it lost 85 percent of its value in a matter of hours, leaving foreign and Russian holders of debt alike suddenly gaping at a huge black hole in their financial assets.[16]

The Russian banking system has had its share of woes, but the banking business (Figure 10.4) is rapidly maturing. Nonetheless, in July 2004, problems arising from too much growth too quickly came to a head. Moody's Investors Service Inc. placed 18 banks under review for possible downgrades. To help boost liquidity in the market, the central bank slashed the funds commercial banks must offset from 7 percent to 3.5 percent. According to the Association of Russian Banks, this measure should inject 130 billion rubles (US$4.47 billion) into the banking system.

FIGURE 10.4

Russian Banks Are Here To Stay—Total Assets%, 2002 (*2001*)

Source: *The Banker*, "Sberbank Enjoys the Lion's Share," December 2, 2003, www.thebanker.com/news/fullstory.php/aid/938/Sberbank_enjoys_the_lion%92s_share.html. Reprinted with permission.

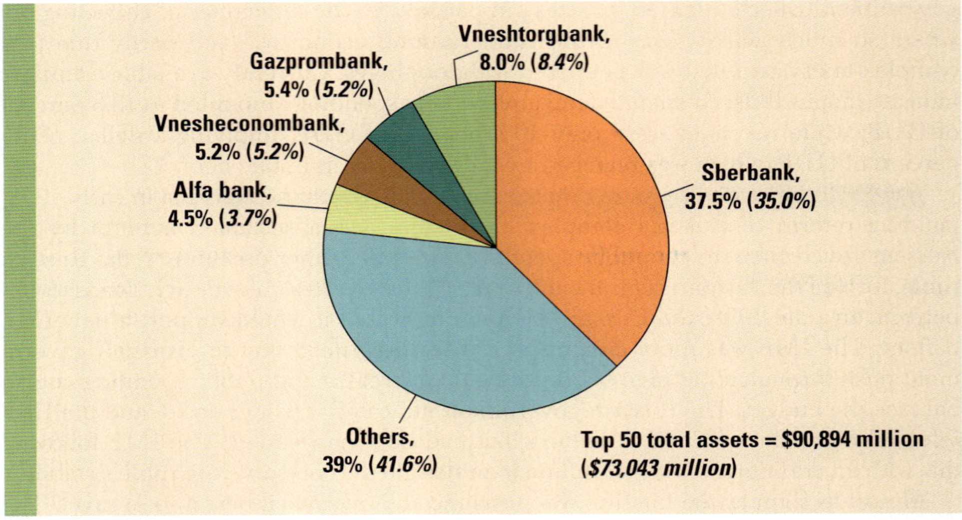

THE ASIAN CRISIS

The financial crisis that erupted across Southeast Asia during the fall of 1997 has emerged as the biggest challenge ever. Holding the crisis in check required IMF loans to help the shattered economies of Indonesia, Thailand, and South Korea stabilize their currencies. In addition, although they did not request IMF loans, the economies of Japan, Malaysia, Singapore, and the Philippines were also badly hurt by the crisis.

The seeds of this crisis were sown during the previous decade when these countries were experiencing unprecedented economic growth. Although there were and remain important differences between the individual countries, a number of elements were common to most. Exports had long been the engine of economic growth in these countries. From 1990 to 1996, the value of exports from Malaysia had grown by 18 percent annually, Thai exports had grown by 16 percent per year, Singapore's by 15 percent, Hong Kong's by 14 percent, and those of South Korea and Indonesia by 12 percent annually.[17] The nature of these exports had also shifted in recent years from basic materials and products such as textiles to complex and increasingly high-technology products, such as automobiles, semiconductors, and consumer electronics.

To many, the Sydney Opera House epitomizes the land "down under." Sydney, like most major urban centres, is experiencing an ever spiraling cost of living. McDaniel Woolf/Getty Images.

The Investment Boom

The wealth created by export-led growth helped fuel an investment boom in commercial and residential property, industrial assets, and infrastructure. The value of commercial and residential real estate in cities such as Hong Kong and Bangkok soared. This fed a building boom the likes of which had never been seen in Asia. Heavy borrowing from banks financed much of this construction. As for industrial assets, the success of Asian exporters encouraged them to make bolder investments in industrial capacity.

By the mid-1990s, Southeast Asia was in the grips of an unprecedented investment boom, much of it financed with borrowed money. Between 1990 and 1995, gross domestic investment grew by 16.3

percent annually in Indonesia, 16 percent inMalaysia, 15.3 percent in Thailand, and 7.2 percent in South Korea. By comparison, investment grew by 4.1 percent annually over the same period in the United States and 0.8 percent in all high-income economies.[18] And the rate of investment accelerated in 1996. In Malaysia, for example, spending on investment accounted for a remarkable 43 percent of GDP in 1996.[19]

Excess Capacity

As the volume of investments ballooned during the 1990s, often at the bequest of national governments, the quality of many of these investments declined significantly. The investments often were made on the basis of unrealistic projections about future demand conditions. The result was significant excess capacity. For example, South Korean *chaebol* investments in semiconductor factories surged in 1994 and 1995 when a temporary global shortage of dynamic random access memory chips (DRAMs) led to sharp price increases for this product. However, supply shortages had disappeared by 1996, and excess capacity was beginning to make itself felt, just as the South Koreans started to bring new DRAM factories on stream. The results were predictable; prices for DRAMs plunged, and the earnings of South Korean DRAM manufacturers fell by 90 percent, which meant it was difficult for them to make scheduled payments on the debt they had taken on to build the extra capacity.[20]

The Debt Bomb

By early 1997, what was happening in the South Korean semiconductor industry and the Bangkok property market was being played out elsewhere in the region. Massive investments in industrial assets and property had created excess capacity and plunging prices, while leaving the companies that had made the investments groaning under huge debt burdens that they were now finding it difficult to service.

To make matters worse, much of the borrowing had been in U.S. dollars, as opposed to local currencies. This had originally seemed like a smart move. Throughout the region, local currencies were pegged to the dollar, and interest rates on dollar borrowings were generally lower than rates on borrowings in domestic currency. Thus, it often made economic sense to borrow in dollars if the option was available. However, if the governments could not maintain the dollar peg and their currencies started to depreciate against the dollar, this would increase the size of the debt burden, when measured in the local currency. Currency depreciation would raise borrowing costs and could result in companies defaulting on their debt obligations.

Expanding Imports

A final complicating factor was that by the mid-1990s, although exports were still expanding across the region, imports were too. The investments in infrastructure, industrial capacity, and commercial real estate were sucking in foreign goods at unprecedented rates. To build infrastructure, factories, and office buildings, Southeast Asian countries were purchasing capital equipment and materials from America, Europe, and Japan. Many Southeast Asian states saw the current accounts of their balance of payments shift strongly into the red during the mid-1990s. By 1995, Indonesia was running a current account deficit that was equivalent to 3.5 percent of its GDP, Malaysia's was 5.9 percent, and Thailand's was 8.1 percent.[21] With deficits like these, it was increasingly

ANOTHER PERSPECTIVE

Procter & Gamble and the meltdown in Thailand

In 1988 in Thailand, Procter & Gamble (P&G) produced globally branded personal care products targetted to the growing Thai middle class. To sustain its product quality, P&G used imported ingredients. Then came the crisis. Used Mercedes-Benz cars began selling at the Thai baht equivalent of pennies on the dollar. P&G's supplies overnight doubled in cost. All of a sudden, customers could not afford P&G's premium pricing. Meanwhile, locally produced soaps and shampoos, made from local ingredients, were not affected by this currency crisis. P&G couldn't lower its selling price unless it sold below cost. What would you do?

difficult for the governments of these countries to maintain their currencies against the U.S. dollar. If that peg could not be held, the local currency value of dollar-denominated debt would increase, raising the specter of large-scale default on debt service payments. The scene was now set for a potentially rapid economic meltdown.

The Crisis

The Asian meltdown began in mid-1997 in Thailand when it became clear that several key Thai financial institutions were on the verge of default. These institutions had been borrowing dollars from international banks at low interest rates and lending Thai baht at higher interest rates to local property developers. However, due to speculative overbuilding, these developers could not sell their commercial and residential property, forcing them to default on their debt obligations. In turn, the Thai financial institutions seemed increasingly likely to default on their dollar-denominated debt obligations to international banks. Sensing the beginning of the crisis, foreign investors fled the Thai stock market, selling their positions and converting them into U.S. dollars. The increased demand for dollars and increased supply of Thai baht, pushed down the dollar/baht exchange rate, while the stock market plunged.

Seeing these developments, foreign exchange dealers and hedge funds started speculating against the baht, selling it short. For the previous 13 years, the Thai baht had been pegged to the U.S. dollar at an exchange rate of about US$1=Bt25. The Thai government tried to defend the peg, but only succeeded in depleting its foreign exchange reserves. On July 2, 1997, the Thai government abandoned its defence and announced it would allow the baht to float freely against the dollar. The baht started a slide that would bring the exchange rate down to $1=Bt55 by January 1998. As the baht declined, the Thai debt bomb exploded. The 55 percent decline in the value of the baht against the dollar doubled the amount of baht required to serve the dollar-denominated debt commitments taken on by Thai financial institutions and businesses. This increased the probability of corporate bankruptcies and further pushed down the battered Thai stock market. The Thailand Set stock market index ultimately declined from 787 in January 1997 to a low of 337 in December of that year, on top of a 45 percent decline in 1996.

On July 28, the Thai government called in the International Monetary Fund. With its foreign exchange reserves depleted, Thailand lacked the foreign currency needed to finance its international trade and service debt commitments and desperately needed the capital the IMF could provide. It also needed to restore international confidence in its currency and needed the credibility associated with gaining access to IMF funds. Without IMF loans, the baht likely would increase its free fall against the U.S. dollar, and the whole country might go into default. The IMF agreed to provide the Thai government with $17.2 billion in loans, but the conditions were restrictive.[22] The IMF required the Thai government to increase taxes, cut public spending, privatize several state-owned businesses, and raise interest rates—all steps designed to cool Thailand's overheated economy. The IMF also required Thailand to close illiquid financial institutions. In December 1997, the government shut 56 financial institutions, laying off 16 000 people, and further deepening the recession that now gripped the country.

Following the devaluation of the Thai baht, wave after wave of speculation hit other Asian currencies. One after another in a period of weeks, the Malaysian ringgit, Indonesian rupiah, and the Singapore dollar were all marked sharply lower. With its foreign exchange reserves down to $28 billion, Malaysia let the ringgit float on July 14, 1997. Before the devaluation, the ringgit was trading at $1=2.525 ringgit. Six months later it had declined to $1=4.15 ringgit. Singapore followed on July 17, and the Singapore dollar quickly dropped in value from $1=S$1.495 before the devaluation to $1=S$2.68 a few days later. Next up was Indonesia, whose rupiah was allowed to float August 14. For Indonesia, this was the beginning of a precipitous decline in the value of its currency, which was to fall from \$1=2,400 rupiah in August 1997 to \$1=10,000 rupiah on January 6, 1998, a loss of 75 percent.

With the exception of Singapore, whose economy is probably the most stable in the region, these devaluations were driven by factors similar to those behind the earlier devaluation of the Thai baht–a combination of excess investment; high borrowings, much of it in dollar-denominated debt; and a deteriorating balance-of-payments position. Although both Malaysia and Singapore were able to halt the slide in their currencies and stock markets without the help of the IMF, Indonesia was not. Indonesia was struggling with a private-sector, dollar-denominated debt of close to \$80 billion. With the rupiah sliding precipitously almost every day, the cost of servicing this debt was exploding, pushing more Indonesian companies into technical default.

On October 31, 1997, the IMF announced it had put together a \$37-billion rescue deal for Indonesia in conjunction with the World Bank and the Asian Development Bank. In return, the Indonesian government agreed to close a number of troubled banks, reduce public spending, remove government subsidies on basic foodstuffs and energy, balance the budget, and unravel the crony capitalism that was so widespread in Indonesia. But the government of President Suharto appeared to backtrack several times on commitments made to the IMF. This precipitated further declines in the Indonesian currency and stock markets. Ultimately, Suharto caved in and removed costly government subsidies, only to see the country dissolve into chaos as the populace took to the streets to protest the resulting price increases. This unleashed a chain of events that led to Suharto's removal from power in May 1998.

The final domino to fall was South Korea (for further details, see the Country Focus in Chapter 9). During the 1990s, South Korean companies had built up huge debt loads as they invested heavily in new industrial capacity. Now they found they had too much industrial capacity and could not generate the income required to service their debt. South Korean banks and companies had also made the mistake of borrowing in dollars, much of it in the form of short-term loans that would come due within a year. Thus, when the Korean won started to decline in the fall of 1997 in sympathy with the problems elsewhere in Asia, South Korean companies saw their debt obligations balloon. Several large companies were forced to file for bankruptcy. This triggered a decline in the South Korean currency and stock market that was difficult to halt. The South Korean central bank tried to keep the U.S. dollar/won exchange rate above US\$1=W1,000 but found that this only depleted its foreign exchange reserves. On November 17, the South Korean central bank gave up the defense of the won, which quickly fell to US\$1=W1,500.

With its economy on the verge of collapse, the South Korean government on November 21 requested \$20 billion in standby loans from the IMF. As the negotiations progressed, it became apparent that South Korea was going to need far more than \$20 billion. Among other problems, the country's short-term foreign debt was found to be twice as large as previously thought at close to \$100 billion, while the country's foreign exchange reserves were down to less than \$6 billion. On December 3, the IMF and South Korean government reached a deal to lend \$55 billion to the country. The agreement with the IMF called for the South Koreans to open their economy and banking system to foreign investors. South Korea also pledged to restrain the *chaebol* by reducing their share of bank financing and requiring them to publish consolidated financial statements and undergo annual independent external audits. On trade liberalization, the IMF said South Korea would comply with its commitments to the World Trade Organization to eliminate trade-related subsidies and restrictive import licensing and would streamline its import certification procedures, all of which should open the South Korean economy to greater foreign competition.[23]

EVALUATING THE IMF'S POLICY PRESCRIPTIONS

By 2004, the IMF had 184 member countries, with a staff of 2700 in 141 countries and loans outstanding amounting to $97 billion to 84 countries.[24]

Inappropriate Policies

One criticism is that the IMF's "one-size-fits-all" approach to macroeconomic policy is inappropriate for many countries. This point was made in the Country Focus that looked at how the IMF's policies toward Zaire may have made things worse rather than better. In the recent Asian crisis, critics argue that the tight macroeconomic policies imposed by the IMF are not well suited to countries that are suffering not from excessive government spending and inflation, but from a private-sector debt crisis with deflationary undertones.[25] In South Korea, for example, the government has been running a budget surplus for years (it was 4 percent of South Korea's GDP in the 1994–1996 period) and inflation is low at about 5 percent. South Korea has the second strongest financial position of any country in the Organization for Economic Cooperation and Development. Despite this, critics say, the IMF is insisting on applying the same policies that it applies to countries suffering from high inflation. The IMF is requiring South Korea to maintain an inflation rate of 5 percent. However, given the collapse in the value of its currency and the subsequent rise in price for imports such as oil, inflationary pressures will inevitably increase in South Korea. So to hit a 5 percent inflation rate, the South Koreans are being forced to apply an unnecessarily tight monetary policy. Short-term interest rates in South Korea jumped from 12.5 percent to 21 percent immediately after the country signed its initial deal with the IMF. Increasing interest rates make it even more difficult for companies to service their already excessive short-term debt obligations, so the cure prescribed by the IMF may actually increase the probability of widespread corporate defaults, not reduce them.

The IMF rejects this criticism. According to the IMF, the critical task is to rebuild confidence in the won. Once this has been achieved, the won will recover from its oversold levels. This will reduce the size of South Korea's dollar-denominated debt burden when expressed in won, making it easier for companies to service their dollar-denominated debt. The IMF also argues that by requiring South Korea to remove restrictions on foreign direct investment, foreign capital will flow into the country to take advantage of cheap assets. This, too, will increase demand for the Korean currency and help to improve the dollar/won exchange rate.

The South East Asian currency crisis shook the region and the world, yet the gross domestic product growth for the years 2002 and 2003 shows a clear return to stability for most of the nations of the region, when compared to 1997, the year of the crisis and the 1998 hangover.

The dust has settled and the economies of the region are slowly rebuilding at a healthy rate of GDP growth in the years 2002 and 2003 (see Table 10.1).

Inflation rates still have to come down, but for the most part they are low and within internationally accepted standards, with the exception of Laos at 12.8 percent in 2003 and Myanmar at 57.2 percent inflation in 2002 (see Table 10.2).

One area of concern for economic recovery in the Far East lies with Japan, one of the world's leading economic powerhouses that was also shaken by the South East Asian currency crisis. Its economy is growing steadily in 2004, but there are lingering doubts about the sustainability of this most recent in a series of upturns that Japan has experienced since ridding itself of the initial shock of the 1997 and 1998 South East Asian currency crisis. Actually, the Japanese economy has been gaining momentum since 2002 and in the year 2004, financial growth projections indicate economic growth in the range of 3.5 to 4.0 percent. However, due to an increasing inflow of imported products

TABLE 10.1

GDP Growth in South East Asia (%, year over year)

Source: ASEAN Finance and Macroeconomic Surveillance Unit (FMSU) Database, Table 2.1.

COUNTRY	1996	1997	1998	1999	2000	2001	2002	2003
Brunei	1.01	3.60	-3.99	2.56	2.82	3.05	2.83	3.20
Cambodia	4.60	6.82	3.70	10.78	7.03	5.67	5.48	5.00
Indonesia	7.82	4.70	-13.13	0.79	4.92	3.45	3.69	4.10
Lao, PDR	6.89	6.91	3.99	7.28	5.81	5.76	5.70	5.90
Malaysia	10.00	7.32	-7.36	6.14	8.55	0.32	4.12	5.20
Myanmar [1]	6.44	5.74	5.77	10.92	13.70	10.50	5.00	5.10
Philippines	5.85	5.19	-0.59	3.41	4.38	4.52	4.43	4.52
Singapore	7.71	8.51	-0.86	6.42	9.41	-2.37	3.29	1.09
Thailand	5.90	-1.37	-10.51	4.45	4.76	2.14	5.41	6.75
Viet Nam	9.34	8.15	5.83	4.71	6.76	6.93	7.04	7.24
ASEAN	7.30	4.16	-7.14	3.58	5.88	3.26	4.52	4.97
ASEAN 5[2]	7.23	3.76	-8.93	3.11	5.50	2.59	4.26	4.76
BCLMV[3]	7.85	7.23	5.21	6.71	8.36	7.57	6.20	6.34

1 Fiscal year beginning in April and ending in March of the following year
2 ASEAN 5: Indonesia, Malaysia, Philippines, Singapore, and Thailand
3 BCLMV: Brunei Darussalam, Cambodia, Lao PDR, Myanmar, and Vietnam

TABLE 10.2

Inflation Rates in South East Asia (%, year over year)

Source: ASEAN Finance and Macroeconomic Surveillance Unit (FMSU) Database, Table 3.2.

COUNTRY	BASE PERIOD	1996	1997	1998	1999	2000	2001	2002	2003
Brunei		2.1	1.4	-0.7	0.0	1.6	-3.1	-0.3	-14.7
Cambodia	1,994.0	10.0	9.2	11.1	0.2	0.3	3.0	1.7	0.3
Indonesia	1,996.0	7.9	10.3	77.5	2.0	9.3	12.5	10.0	5.1
Lao, PDR	36,495.0	13.0	39.0	141.9	89.5	10.6	7.5	15.2	12.6
Malaysia	2,000.0	3.3	2.3	5.4	2.1	2.1	1.2	1.7	1.2
Myanmar[1]	1,995.0	20.0	31.7	46.8	8.6	-6.3	51.0	57.2	
Philippines	1,994.0	7.1	7.2	10.4	4.3	6.6	4.1	2.6	3.1
Singapore	97-98[1]	2.0	2.0	-1.4	0.7	2.1	-0.6	0.4	0.8
Thailand	1,994.0	4.8	7.6	4.3	0.7	1.4	0.8	1.6	1.8
Viet Nam	1,995.0	4.9	3.6	8.6	-0.2	-0.6	0.5	4.1	
ASEAN[2]		6.5	8.3	33.6	2.4	4.7	7.1	6.8	
ASEAN 5[3]		6.2	7.8	35.3	2.0	5.6	6.1	5.1	3.2
BCLMV[4]		9.1	11.8	21.9	4.9	-1.6	13.7	17.6	

1 November to October
2 Average of the country figure weighted by PPP-GDP
3 ASEAN: Indonesia, Malaysia, Philippines, Singapore, and Thailand
4 BCLMV: Brunei, Darussalam, Lao PDR, Myanmar, and Vietnam

and an outsourcing of manufacturing jobs to countries such as China, where cheaper labour prevails, the impact on Japan's corporate headquarters is still unclear.[26] It is not certain if this growth will solidify Japan, or lead the way to yet another recession.

Moral Hazard

A second criticism of the IMF is that its rescue efforts are exacerbating a problem known to economists as moral hazard. **Moral hazard** arises when people behave recklessly because they know they will be saved if things go wrong. Critics point out that many Japanese and Western banks were far too willing to lend large amounts of capital to overleveraged Asian companies during the boom years of the 1990s. These critics argue that the banks should now be forced to pay the price for their rash lending policies, even if that means some banks must close.[27] Only by taking such drastic action, the argument goes, will banks learn the error of their ways and not engage in

MORAL HAZARD
Arises when people behave recklessly because they know they will be saved if things go wrong.

rash lending in the future. By providing support to these countries, the IMF is reducing the probability of debt default and in effect bailing out the banks whose loans gave rise to this situation.

This argument ignores two critical points. First, if some Japanese or Western banks with heavy exposure to the troubled Asian economies were forced to write off their loans due to widespread debt default, the impact would be difficult to contain. The failure of large Japanese banks, for example, could trigger a meltdown in the Japanese financial markets. This would almost inevitably lead to a serious decline in stock markets around the world. That is the very risk the IMF was trying to avoid by stepping in with financial support. Second, it is incorrect to imply that some banks have not had to pay the price for rash lending policies. The IMF has insisted on the closure of banks in South Korea, Thailand, and Indonesia. Foreign banks with short-term loans outstanding to South Korean enterprises have been forced by circumstances to reschedule those loans at interest rates that do not compensate for the extension of the loan maturity.

Lack of Accountability

The final criticism of the IMF is that it has become too powerful for an institution that lacks any real mechanism for accountability.[28] The IMF was determining macroeconomic policies in those countries, yet according to critics such as noted Harvard economist Jeffrey Sachs, the IMF, with a staff of less than 1000, lacks the expertise required to do a good job. Evidence of this, according to Sachs, can be found in the fact that the IMF was singing the praises of the Thai and South Korean governments only months before both countries lurched into crisis. Then the IMF put together a draconian program for South Korea without having deep knowledge of the country. Sachs's solution to this problem is to reform the IMF so it makes greater use of outside experts and its operations are open to outside scrutiny.

Observations

As with many debates about international economics, it is not clear which side has the winning hand about the appropriateness of IMF policies. There are cases where one can argue that IMF policies have been counterproductive, such as Zaire, which we discussed in the Country Focus. In addition, one might question the success of the IMF's involvement in Turkey, given that the country has had to implement 18 IMF programs since 1958! But the IMF can also point to some notable accomplishments, including its success in containing the Asian crisis, which could have rocked the global international monetary system to its core. Similarly, many observers give the IMF credit for its deft handling of politically difficult situations, such as the Russian ruble crisis and Mexican peso crisis, and for successfully promoting a free market philosophy.

Several years after the IMF's intervention, the economies of Asia, Russia, and Mexico had all recovered to some extent. Certainly they had all averted the kind of catastrophic implosion that might have occurred had the IMF not stepped in, and although some countries still faced considerable problems, it is not clear that the IMF should take much blame for this. At the end of the day, the IMF cannot force countries to adopt the policies required to correct economic mismanagement. As the opening case on Turkey illustrates, while a government may commit to taking corrective action in return for an IMF loan, internal political problems may make it difficult for a government to act on that commitment. In such cases, the IMF is caught between a rock and hard place, for if it decided to withhold money, it might trigger financial collapse and the kind of contagion that it seeks to avoid.

IMPLICATIONS FOR BUSINESS

The implications for international businesses of the material discussed in this chapter fall into three main areas: currency management, business strategy, and corporate–government relations.

CURRENCY MANAGEMENT

An obvious implication with regard to currency management is that companies must recognize that the foreign exchange market does not work quite as depicted in Chapter 9. The current system is a mixed system in which a combination of government intervention and speculative activity can drive the foreign exchange market. Companies engaged in significant foreign exchange activities need to be aware of this and to adjust their foreign exchange transactions accordingly. For example, the currency management unit of Caterpillar claims it made millions of dollars in the hours following the announcement of the Plaza Accord by selling dollars and buying currencies that it expected to appreciate on the foreign exchange market following government intervention.

We have seen how speculative buying and selling of currencies can create very volatile movements in exchange rates (as exhibited by the rise and fall of the dollar during the 1980s) under the present system. Contrary to the predictions of the purchasing power parity theory (see Chapter 9), we have seen that exchange rate movements during the 1980s, at least with regard to the dollar, did not seem to be strongly influenced by relative inflation rates. Insofar as volatile exchange rates increase foreign exchange risk, this is not good news for business. On the other hand, as we saw in Chapter 9, the foreign exchange market has developed a number of instruments, such as the forward market and swaps, that can help to insure against foreign exchange risk. Not surprisingly, use of these instruments has increased markedly since the breakdown of the Bretton Woods system in 1973.

ANOTHER PERSPECTIVE

The euro (€) and exchange rate volatility

The euro is used now in 12 of the 15 EU countries. Denmark, Sweden, and Britain chose not to participate. By eliminating exchange rates among these 12 countries, the common currency also does away with one of the more difficult to manage risks of international business—exchange rate volatility. Whether you sell from Spain to Germany or from Greece to Holland, now exchange rate movements will not concern you. What do you think the impact on trade flows of the euro might be?

BUSINESS STRATEGY

The volatility of the present global exchange rate regime presents a conundrum for international businesses. Exchange rate movements are difficult to predict, and yet their movement can have a major impact on a business's competitive position. Faced with uncertainty about the future value of currencies, firms can utilize the forward exchange market. However, the forward exchange market is far from perfect as a predictor of future exchange rates (see Chapter 9). It is also difficult if not impossible to get adequate insurance coverage for exchange rate changes that might occur several years in the future. The forward market tends to offer coverage for exchange rate changes a few months—not years—ahead. Given this, it makes sense to pursue strategies that will increase the company's strategic flexibility in the face of unpredictable exchange rate movements.

Maintaining strategic flexibility can take the form of dispersing production to different locations around the globe as a real hedge against currency fluctuations. Consider the case of Daimler-Benz (now Daimler/Chrysler), Germany's export-oriented automobile and aerospace company. In June 1995, the company stunned the German business community when it announced it expected to post a severe loss in 1995 of about $720 million. The cause was Germany's strong currency, which had appreciated by 4 percent against a basket of major currencies since the beginning of 1995 and had risen by more than 30 percent against the U.S. dollar since late 1994. By mid-1995, the exchange rate against the U.S. dollar stood at $1=DM1.38. Daimler's management believed it could not make money with an exchange rate under $1=DM1.60. Daimler's senior managers concluded that the appreciation of the mark against the dollar was probably permanent, so they decided to move substantial production outside of Germany and increase purchasing of foreign components. The idea was to reduce the vulnerability of the company to future exchange rate movements. The Mercedes-Benz division has begun to implement this move. Even before its acquisition of Chrysler Corporation in 1998, Mercedes planned to produce 10 percent of its cars outside of Germany by 2000, mostly in the United States.[29] Similarly, the move by Japanese automotive companies to expand their production capacity in Canada, beginning in 1986 in Cambridge, Ontario (Toyota) and Alliston, Ontario (Honda) and throughout Europe can be seen in the context of the increase in the value of the yen between 1985 and 1995, which raised the price of Japanese exports. For the Japanese companies, building production capacity overseas is a hedge against continued appreciation of the yen (as well as against trade barriers).

Another way of building strategic flexibility involves contracting out manufacturing. This allows a company to shift suppliers from country to country in response to changes in relative costs brought about by exchange rate movements. However, this kind of strategy works only for low-value-added manufacturing (e.g., textiles), in which the individual manufacturers have few if any firm-specific skills that contribute to the value of the product. It is inappropriate for high-value-added manufacturing, in which firm-specific technology and skills add significant value to the product (e.g., the heavy equipment industry) and in which switching costs are correspondingly high. For high-value-added manufacturing, switching suppliers will lead to a reduction in the value that is added, which may offset any cost gains arising from exchange rate fluctuations.

The roles of the IMF and the World Bank in the present international monetary system also have implications for business strategy. Increasingly, the IMF has been acting as the macroeconomic police of the world economy, insisting that countries seeking significant borrowings adopt IMF-mandated macroeconomic policies. These policies typically include anti-inflationary monetary policies and reductions in government spending. In the short run, such policies usually result in a sharp contraction of demand. International businesses selling or producing in such countries need to be aware of this and plan accordingly. In the long run, the kind of policies imposed by the IMF can promote economic growth and an expansion of demand, which create opportunities for international business.

CORPORATE–GOVERNMENT RELATIONS

As major players in the international trade and investment environment, businesses can influence government policy toward the international monetary system. For example, intense government lobbying by U.S. exporters helped convince the U.S. government that intervention in the foreign exchange market was necessary. Similarly, much of the impetus behind establishment of the exchange rate mechanism of the European monetary system came from European businesspeople, who understood the costs of volatile exchange rates.

With this in mind, business can and should use its influence to promote an international monetary system that facilitates the growth of international trade and investment. Whether a fixed or floating regime is optimal is a subject for debate. However, exchange rate volatility such as the world experienced during the 1980s and 1990s creates an environment less conducive to international trade and investment than one with more stable exchange rates. Therefore, it would seem to be in the interests of international business to promote an international monetary system that minimizes volatile exchange rate movements, particularly when those movements are unrelated to long-run economic fundamentals.

KEY TERMS

banking crisis, p. 339

currency board, p. 338

currency crisis, p. 339

dirty-float system, p. 325

fixed exchange rates, p. 325

floating exchange rates, p. 325

foreign debt crisis, p. 342

gold standard, p. 327

international monetary system, p. 324

moral hazard, p. 353

pegged exchange rate, p. 325

SUMMARY

This chapter explained the workings of the international monetary system and pointed out its implications for international business. This chapter made the following points:

1. The gold standard is a monetary standard that pegs currencies to gold and guarantees convertibility to gold.
2. It was thought that the gold standard contained an automatic mechanism that contributed to the simultaneous achievement of a balance-of-payments equilibrium by all countries.
3. The gold standard broke down during the 1930s as countries engaged in competitive devaluations.
4. The Bretton Woods system of fixed exchange rates was established in 1944. The U.S. dollar was the central currency of this system; the value of every other currency was pegged to its value. Significant exchange rate devaluations were allowed only with the permission of the IMF.
5. The role of the IMF was to maintain order in the international monetary system *(i)* to avoid a repetition of the competitive devaluations of the 1930s and *(ii)* to control price inflation by imposing monetary discipline on countries.
6. To build flexibility into the system, the IMF stood ready to lend countries funds to help protect their currency on the foreign exchange market in the face of speculative pressure and to assist countries in correcting a fundamental disequilibrium in their balance-of-payments position.
7. The fixed exchange rate system collapsed in 1973, primarily due to speculative pressure on the dollar following a rise in U.S. inflation and a growing U.S. balance-of-trade deficit.
8. Since 1973 the world has operated with a floating exchange rate regime, and exchange rates have become more volatile and far less predictable. Volatile exchange rate movements have helped reopen the debate over the merits of fixed and floating systems.
9. The case for a floating exchange rate regime claims: *(i)* such a system gives countries autonomy regarding their monetary policy and *(ii)* floating exchange rates facilitate smooth adjustment of trade imbalances.
10. The case for a fixed exchange rate regime claims: *(i)* the need to maintain a fixed exchange rate imposes monetary discipline on a country, *(ii)* floating exchange rate regimes are vulnerable to speculative pressure, *(iii)* the uncertainty that accompanies floating exchange rates dampens the growth of international trade and investment, and *(iv)* far from correcting trade imbalances, depreciating a currency on the foreign exchange market tends to cause price inflation.
11. In today's international monetary system, some countries have adopted floating exchange rates, some have pegged their currency to another currency, such as the U.S. dollar, and some have pegged their currency to a basket of other currencies, allowing their currency to fluctuate within a zone around the basket.
12. In the post-Bretton Woods era, the IMF has continued to play an important role in helping countries navigate their way through financial crises by lending significant capital to embattled governments and by requiring them to adopt certain macroeconomic policies.
13. An important debate is occuring over the appropriateness of IMF-mandated macroeconomic policies. Critics charge that the IMF often imposes inappropriate conditions on developing nations that are the recipients of its loans.
14. The present managed-float system of exchange rate determination has increased the importance of currency management in international businesses.
15. The volatility of exchange rates under the present managed-float system creates both opportunities and threats. One way of responding to this volatility is for companies to build strategic flexibility by dispersing production to different locations around the globe by contracting out manufacturing (in the case of low-value-added manufacturing) and other means.

CRITICAL THINKING AND DISCUSSION QUESTIONS

1. Why did the gold standard collapse? Is there a case for returning to some type of gold standard? What is it?
2. What opportunities might current IMF lending policies to developing nations create for international businesses? What threats might they create?
3. Do you think the standard IMF policy prescriptions of tight monetary policy and reduced government spending are always appropriate for developing nations experiencing a currency crisis? How might the IMF change its approach? What would the implications be for international businesses?
4. Debate the relative merits of fixed and floating exchange rate regimes. From the perspective of an international business, what are the most important criteria in a choice between the systems? Which system is the more desirable for an international business?

5. Imagine that Canada, the United States, and Mexico decide to adopt a fixed exchange rate system similar to the ERM of the European Monetary System. What would be the likely consequences of such a system for *(a)* international businesses and *(b)* the flow of trade and investment among the three countries?

RESEARCH TASK | globalEDGE™ globaledge.msu.edu

Use the globalEDGE™ site to complete the following exercises:

1. Until recently, the U.S. Department of State provided annual country reports on economic policy and trade practices. Locate the archives of these reports and prepare a description of the exchange rate and debt management policies of an emerging market of your choice based on the latest report available.

2. The Biz/ed Web site presents a "Trade Balance and Exchange Rate Simulation" that explains how a change in exchange rate influences the trade balance. Locate the online simulator (check under the Academy section of globalEDGE) and identify what the trade balance is assumed to be a function of. Run the simulation to identify how exchange rate changes affect exports, imports, and trade balance.

Visit the *Global Business Today* Online Learning Centre at **www.mcgrawhill.ca/college/hill** to access quizzes, interactive exercises, a Business Around the World interactive map, and other learning and study tools related to this chapter.

CLOSING CASE

CATERPILLAR INC.

Caterpillar Inc. (Cat) is the world's largest manufacturer of heavy earthmoving equipment. Earthmoving equipment typically represents about 70 percent of the annual dollar sales of construction equipment worldwide. In 1980, Cat held 53.3 percent of the global market for earthmoving equipment. Its closest competitor was Komatsu of Japan, with 60 percent of the Japanese market but only 15.2 percent worldwide.

In 1980, Caterpillar was widely considered one of the premier manufacturing and exporting companies in the United States. The company had enjoyed 50 consecutive years of profits and returns on shareholder equity as high as 27 percent. In 1981, 57 percent of its sales were outside the United States, and roughly two-thirds of these orders were filled by exports. Cat was the third largest U.S. exporter. Reflecting this underlying strength, Cat recorded record pretax profits of $579 million in 1981. However, the next three years were disastrous. Caterpillar lost a total of $1 billion and saw its market share slip to as low as 40 percent in 1985, while Komatsu increased its share to 25 percent. Three factors explain this startling turn of events: the higher productivity of Komatsu, the rise in the value of the dollar, and the Third World debt crisis.

Komatsu had been creeping up on Cat for a long time. In the 1960s, the company had a minuscule presence outside of Japan. By 1974, it had increased its global market share of heavy earthmoving equipment to 9 percent, and by 1980 it was more than 15 percent. Part of Komatsu's growth was due to its superior labour productivity; throughout the 1970s, it had been able to price its machines 10 to 15 percent below Caterpillar's. However, Komatsu lacked an extensive dealer network outside of Japan, and Cat's worldwide dealer network and superior after-sale service and support functions were seen as justifying a price premium for Cat machines. For these reasons, many industry observers believed Komatsu would not increase its share much beyond its 1980 level.

An unprecedented rise in the value of the dollar against most major world currencies changed the picture. Between 1980 and 1987, the dollar rose an average of 87 percent against the currencies of ten other industrialized countries. The dollar was driven up by strong economic growth in the United States, which attracted heavy inflows of capital from foreign investors seeking high returns on capital assets. High real interest rates attracted foreign investors seeking high returns on financial assets. At the same time, political turmoil in other parts of the world and relatively slow economic growth in Europe helped create the view that the United States was a good place in which to invest. These inflows of capital increased the demand for dollars in the foreign exchange market, which pushed the value of the dollar upward against other currencies.

The strong dollar substantially increased the dollar price of Cat's machines. At the same time, the dollar price of Komatsu products imported into the United States fell. Because of the shift in the relative values of the dollar and the yen, Komatsu priced its machines as much as 40 percent below Caterpillar's prices by 1985. Because of this enormous price difference, many consumers chose to forgo Caterpillar's superior after-sale service and support and bought Komatsu machines.

The third factor, the Third World debt crisis, became apparent in 1982. During the early 1970s, the nations of OPEC quadrupled the price of oil, which resulted in a massive flow of funds into these nations. Commercial banks borrowed this money from the OPEC countries and lent it to the governments of many Third World nations to finance massive construction projects, which led to a global boom in demand for heavy earthmoving equipment. Caterpillar benefited from this development. By 1982, however, it became apparent that the commercial banks had lent too much money to risky and unproductive investments, and the governments of several countries (including Mexico, Brazil, and Argentina) threatened to suspend debt payments. The International Monetary Fund stepped in and arranged for new loans to indebted Third World countries, on the condition that they adopt deflationary macroeconomic policies. For Cat, the party was over; orders for heavy earthmoving equipment dried up almost overnight, and those that were placed went to the lowest bidder, which often was Komatsu.

As a result of these factors, Caterpillar was in deep trouble by late 1982. The company responded quickly and between 1982 and 1985 cut costs by more than 20 percent. This was achieved by a 40 percent reduction in the workforce, the closure of nine plants, and a $1.8 billion investment in flexible manufacturing technologies designed to boost quality and lower cost. The company also pressed the government to lower the value of the dollar on foreign exchange markets. By 1984, Cat was a leading voice among U.S. exporters trying to get the Reagan administration to intervene in the foreign exchange market.

Things began to go Caterpillar's way in early 1985. Prompted by Cat and other exporters, representatives of the U.S. government met with representatives of Japan, Germany, France, and Great Britain at the Plaza Hotel in New York. In the resulting communiqué—known as the Plaza Accord—the five governments acknowledged that the dollar was overvalued and pledged to take actions that would drive down its price on the foreign exchange market. The central bank of each country intervened in the foreign exchange market, selling dollars and buying other currencies (including its own). The dollar had already begun to fall in early 1985 in response to a string of record U.S. trade deficits. The Plaza Accord accelerated this trend, and over the next three years the dollar fell back to its 1980 level.

The effect for Caterpillar was almost immediate. Like any major exporter, Caterpillar had its own foreign exchange unit. Suspecting that an adjustment in the dollar would come soon, Cat had increased its holdings of foreign currencies in early 1985, using the strong dollar to purchase them. As the dollar fell, the company converted these currencies back into dollars for a healthy profit. In 1985, Cat had pretax profits of $32 million; without foreign exchange gains of $89 million, it would have lost money. In 1986, foreign exchange gains of $100 million accounted for nearly two-thirds of its pretax profits of $159 million.

More significant for Cat's long-term position, the fall in the dollar against the yen and Caterpillar's cost-cutting efforts by 1988 had helped to eradicate the 40 percent cost advantage that Komatsu had enjoyed over Caterpillar four years earlier. After trying to hold its prices down, Komatsu had to raise its prices that year by 18 percent, while Cat was able to hold its price increase to 3 percent. With the terms of trade no longer handicapping Caterpillar, the company regained some of its lost market share. By 1989, it reportedly held 47 percent of the world market for heavy earthmoving equipment, up from a low of 40 percent three years earlier, while Komatsu's share had slipped to below 20 percent.

Sources: R. S. Eckley, "Caterpillar's Ordeal: Foreign Competition in Capital Goods," *Business Horizons,* March–April 1989, pp. 80–86; H. S. Byrne, "Track of the Cat: Caterpillar Is Bulldozing Its Way Back to Higher Profits," *Barron's,* April 6, 1987, pp. 13, 70–71; R. Henkoff, "This Cat Is Acting like a Tiger," *Fortune,* December 19, 1988, pp. 71–76; and "Caterpillar and Komatsu," in *Transnational Management: Text, Cases, and Readings in Cross-Border Management,* ed. C. A. Bartlett and S. Ghoshal (Homewood, IL: Richard D. Irwin, 1992).

CASE DISCUSSION QUESTIONS

1. To what extent is the competitive position of Caterpillar against Komatsu dependent on the U.S. dollar/yen exchange rate? Between mid-1996 and early 1998, the U.S. dollar appreciated by more than 40 percent against the yen. How do you think this affected the relatively competitive position of Caterpillar and Komatsu?
2. If you were the CEO of Caterpillar, what actions would you take now to make sure there is no repeat of the early 1980s experience?
3. What potential impact can the actions of the IMF and World Bank have on Caterpillar's business? Is there anything Cat can do to influence the actions of the IMF and the World Bank?
4. As the CEO of Caterpillar, would you prefer a fixed exchange rate regime or a continuation of the current managed-float regime? Why?

A TAX ON CURRENCY SPECULATION TO FINANCE SUSTAINABLE DEVELOPMENT AND OTHER SUGGESTIONS FOR A SUSTAINABLE GLOBAL ECONOMY

THE TOBIN TAX

James Tobin, a Nobel Prize-winning American economist, in 1972 and 1978 proposed a very small tax on foreign exchange transactions to reduce short-term currency speculation. Such speculation increases the volatility and decreases the stability of national budgets and international markets. Short-term currency speculation also hampers economic planning and the efficient allocation of resources. Tobin suggested the funds collected from such a tax be dedicated to peace and sustainable development.

Many NGOs (nongovernmental organizations) and citizen action groups around the world have advocated the passage of a Tobin tax to fund sustainable development. Hundreds of NGOs signed the Copenhagen Alternative Declaration, which supported the Tobin tax, at the World Summit for Sustainable Development. Groups from Africa, Asia, Europe, Latin America, and North America have declared active support for passage of a Tobin tax (for a list of organizations, see www.ceedweb.org/iirp/camnet.htm).

A number of economists, including David Felix, Rodney Schmidt, and Paul Bernd Spahn, have examined the possible effects of charging a tax on international currency transactions, delineating the possible strengths and weaknesses of such a tax. Annual currency trading is very large (approximately ten times global GNP). Even with a very small tax of one-quarter of 1 percent, the revenue from the tax would be tremendous, with estimates that the annual amount would be greater than 20 times the United Nations' annual budget for sustainable development.

Some economists object that little evidence supports a reduction in market volatility from such taxes. They wonder whether such a tax could even increase volatility, and express concern about the increased transaction costs with such a tax. Some argue this could hinder the operation of financial markets. Other economists refute these arguments. In addition, some economists have written that implementing such a tax would cause enormous administrative difficulties, while other articles have said administration of the tax easily could be addressed.

Other suggestions for a sustainable global economy

Herman Daly, a professor at the Maryland School of Public Affairs, was previously senior economist in the Environment Department at the World Bank, helping to develop policy guidelines related to sustainable development. To foster a global sustainable economy where human suffering is decreased; local, global, and national economies are healthier; and the environment is protected for present and future generations, Daly suggests changes in the way we structure the economy and tax policies. Three of these suggestions are:

1. Stop counting the consumption of natural capital as income.
2. Shift taxes from labour and income to resource consumption, thereby encouraging more income and discouraging overconsumption of natural resources.
3. Face the lurking inconsistency. Daly suggests that many economists suggest less regulation is better and advocate a "pure science" of economics. He argues against this, saying the global economic system is a human creation—it will always be affected by regulations and laws—and suggesting we need to consciously create a modified economic system that both supports the reduction of poverty and reduces the destruction of our biosphere. (Juliet Schor and Betsy Taylor ed., *Sustainable Planet—Solutions for the Twenty-first Century* [Boston: Beacon Press, 2002])

The impacts of both currency speculation and national tax policies affect how resources are distributed and consumed in our world. Economists will continue to explore and will probably disagree on the best policies to build healthy local and global economies. When looking at the global economic system in a context of measuring poverty and related human suffering worldwide, the World Bank uses a reference poverty line expressed in a common unit across countries. The World Bank uses reference lines set at $1 and $2 per day in 1993 purchasing power parity (PPP) terms. PPPs measure the relative purchasing power of currencies across countries.

> It has been estimated that in 1999 1.2 billion people worldwide had consumption levels below $1 a day—23 percent of the population of the developing world—and 2.8 billion lived on less than $2 a day. These figures are lower than earlier estimates, indicating that some progress has taken place, but they still remain too high in terms of human suffering, and much more remains to be done. And it should be emphasized that for analysis of poverty in a particular country, the World Bank always uses poverty line(s) based on norms for that society. (www.worldbank.org/poverty/mission/up2.htm)

As citizens, we have the right, the opportunity, and the responsibility to educate ourselves about the issues of environmental sustainability and human suffering as they relate to the created structures of our national and global economic systems, and engage in producing a more positive future.

Source: Printed with permission of Dr. Debra Rowe, Senior Fellow, Association of University Leaders for a Sustainable Future.

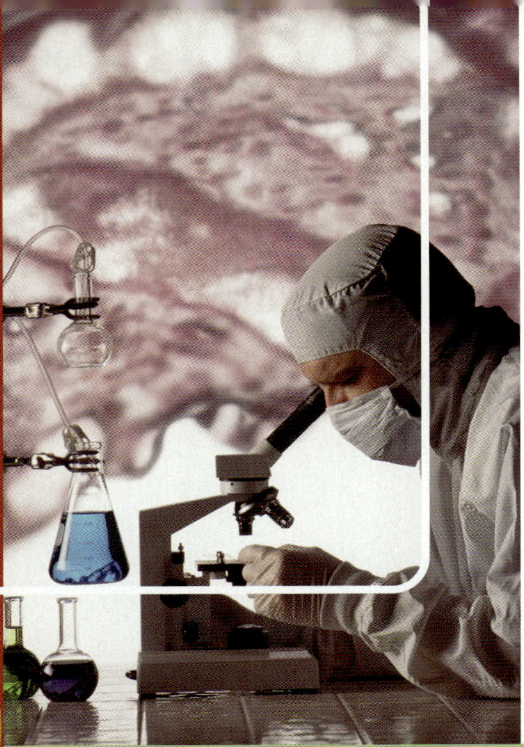

PART FIVE

5

COMPETING IN A GLOBAL MARKETPLACE

Global Strategy at MTV Networks

MTV Networks has become a symbol of globalization. Established in 1981, the U.S.-based music TV network has been expanding outside of its North American base since 1987 when it opened MTV Europe. Now owned by media conglomerate Viacom, MTV Networks, which includes siblings Nickelodeon and VH1, the music station for the aging baby boomers, generates more than $1 billion in operating profit per year on annual revenues nearing $3 billion. Since 1987, MTV has become the most ubiquitous cable programmer in the world. By early 2001, the network had 29 channels, or distinct feeds, that reached a combined total of 330 million households in 140 countries.

While the United States still leads in number of households, with 70 million, the most rapid growth is elsewhere, particularly in Asia, where nearly two-thirds of the region's 3 billion people are under 35, the middle class is expanding quickly, and TV ownership is spreading rapidly. MTV Networks figures that every second of every day almost 2 million people are watching MTV around the world, the majority outside the United States.

Despite its international success, MTV's global expansion got off to a weak start. In 1987, it piped a single feed across Europe almost entirely composed of American programming with English-speaking veejays. Naively, the network's U.S. managers thought Europeans would flock to the American programming. But while viewers in Europe shared a common interest in a handful of global superstars, who at the time included Madonna and Michael Jackson, their tastes turned out to be surprisingly local. What was popular in Germany might not be popular in Great Britain. Many staples of the American music scene left Europeans cold. MTV suffered as a result. Soon local copycat stations were springing up in Europe that focused on the music scene in individual countries. They took viewers and advertisers away from MTV. As explained by Tom Freston, chairman of MTV Networks, "We were going for the most shallow layer of what united viewers and brought them together. It didn't go over too well."

Photo by © Photodisc/Getty Images.

CHAPTER 11

Global Strategy

OPENING CASE

In 1995, MTV changed its strategy and broke Europe into regional feeds, of which there are now eight: one for the United Kingdom and Ireland; another for Germany, Austria, and Switzerland; one for Scandinavia; one for Italy; one for France; one for Spain; one for Holland; and a feed for other European nations including Belgium and Greece. The network adopted the same localization strategy elsewhere in the world. For example, in Asia it has an English-Hindi channel for India, separate Mandarine feeds for China and Taiwan, a Korean feed for South Korea, a Bahasa-language feed for Indonesia, Japanese feed for Japan, and so on. Digital and satellite technology have made the localization of programming cheaper and easier. MTV Networks can now beam half a dozen feeds off one satellite transponder.

While MTV Networks exercises creative control over these different feeds, and while all the channels have the same familiar frenetic look and feel of MTV in the United States, an increasing share of the programming and content is now local. When MTV opens a local station now, it begins with expatriates from elsewhere in the world to do a "gene transfer" of company culture and operating principles. Canada's MuchMusic has also branched into regional feeds. MuchBogota serves the Columbian market and MuchArgentina serves the Argentine market. Each of these network feeds have adapted to the local cultures of these countries. But once these are established, the network switches to local employees and the expatriates move on. The idea is to "get inside the heads" of the local population and produce programming that matches their tastes. Although as much as 60 percent of the programming still originates in the United States, with staples such as "The Real World" having equivalents in different countries, an increasing share of programming is local in conception. In Italy, "MTV Kitchen" combines cooking with a music countdown. "Erotica" airs in Brazil and features a panel of youngsters discussing sex. The Indian channel produces 21 homegrown shows hosted by local veejays who speak "Hinglish," a city-bred cross of Hindi and English. Hit shows include "MTV Cricket in Control," appropriate for a land where cricket is a national

After local imitators threatened MTV profits by taking away local viewers and advertisers, MTV changed its strategy and created regional feeds to accommodate the tastes of viewers. AP Photo/Ng Han Guan.

obsession, "MTV Housefull," which hones in on Hindi film stars (India has the biggest film industry outside of Hollywood), and "MTV Bakra," which is modelled after "Candid Camera."

The same local variation is evident in the music videos aired by the different feeds. While some music stars still have global appeal, in most markets 70 percent of the video content is now local. In a direct countertrend to the notion that popular culture is becoming more global and homogenous, William Roedy, the president of MTV's international networks, observes, "People root for the home team, both culturally and musically. Local repertoire is a worldwide trend. There are fewer global megastars." When music tastes do transcend borders, MTV has found that it is often in ways that would have been difficult to predict. Currently, Japanese pop music is all the rage in Taiwan, while soul and hip-hop are big in South Korea.

This localization push has reaped big benefits for MTV, capturing viewers back from local imitators. In India, ratings increased by more than 700 percent between 1996 when the localization push began and 2000. In turn, localization helps MTV to capture more of those all-important advertising revenues, even from other multinationals such as Coca-Cola, whose own advertising budgets are often locally determined. In Europe, MTV's advertising revenues increased by 50 percent between 1995 and 2000. While the total market for pan-European advertising is valued at just $200 million, the total market for local advertising across Europe is a much bigger pie, valued at $12 billion. MTV now gets 70 percent of its European advertising revenue from local spots, up from 15 percent in 1995. Similar trends are evident elsewhere in the world.

Sources: B. Pulley and A. Tanzer, "Sumner's Gemstone," *Forbes,* February 21, 2000, pp. 107–11; K. Hoffman, "Youth TV's Old Hand Prepares for the Digital Challenge," *Financial Times,* February 18, 2000, p. 8; presentation by Sumner M. Redstone, chairman and CEO, Viacom Inc., delivered to Salomon Smith Barney 11th Annual Global Entertainment Media, Telecommunications Conference, Scottsdale, AZ, January 8, 2001. Archived at www.viacom.com. Citytv at www.citytv.com.co/mucha_musica/index.html.

LEARNING OBJECTIVES

1. Be conversant with the concept of strategy.
2. Understand how firms can profit from expanding their activities globally.

3. Be familiar with the different strategies for competing globally.
4. Understand how cost pressures influence a firm's choice of global strategy.
5. Understand how country differences can influence a firm's choice of global strategy.
6. Understand how firms can use strategic alliances to support their global strategies.

INTRODUCTION

Our primary concern thus far has been with aspects of the larger environment in which international businesses compete. As we have described it in the preceding chapters, this environment has included the different political, economic, and cultural institutions found in nations, the international trade and investment framework, and the international monetary system. Now our focus shifts from the environment to the firm itself and, in particular, to the actions managers can take to compete more effectively as an international business. In this chapter, we look at how firms can increase their profitability by expanding their operations in foreign markets. We discuss the different strategies that firms pursue when competing internationally. We consider the pros and cons of these strategies. We discuss the various factors that affect a firm's choice of strategy. We also look at why firms often enter into strategic alliances with their global competitors, and we discuss the benefits, costs, and risks of strategic alliances. In subsequent chapters we shall build on the framework established here to discuss a variety of topics including the design of organization structures and control systems for international businesses, strategies for entering foreign markets, the use and misuse of strategic alliances, strategies for exporting, and the various manufacturing, marketing, R&D, human resource, accounting, and financial strategies pursued by international businesses.

MTV Networks, profiled in the opening case, gives us a preview of some issues that we will explore in this chapter. When MTV began its global expansion in 1987, its strategy was to transfer its programming and content wholesale from the successful U.S. network. This strategy, which treated the world as a homogenous cultural entity with little variation in local tastes and preferences, was a failure. MTV soon found itself outmaneuvered by local imitators, which captured viewers and advertising revenues from the network by tailoring programming and content to local tastes and preferences. Realizing that it had made a serious error, MTV changed its strategy in 1995 and emphasized localization. At MTV, localization means local programming and local video content hosted by local veejays and aimed at local markets. At the same time, MTV has been careful to ensure that its local channels still have the look and feel of MTV, and that its local operations share a common "genetic code" or set of operating principles. This strategy has enabled MTV to capture more viewers and to increase its advertising revenues at a double-digit rate. Thus, at MTV, the strategy has shifted from one that emphasized global standardization to one that emphasized local responsiveness. As we shall see, finding the correct balance between global standardization and local responsiveness is a major strategic challenge for many multinational enterprises. It is one that MTV appears to have solved, at least for now.

STRATEGY AND THE FIRM

Before we discuss the strategies that multinational enterprises can pursue, we need to review basic principles of strategy. A firm's **strategy** can be defined as the actions that managers take to attain the goals of the firm. For most firms, the preeminent goal is to maximize long-term profitability. A firm makes a profit if the price it can charge

STRATEGY Actions managers take to attain the firm's goals.

PROFIT Difference between total revenues and total costs.

for its output is greater than its costs of producing that output. **Profit** (Π) is thus defined as the difference between total revenues (TR) and total costs (TC), or

$$\Pi = TR - TC$$

Total revenues (TR) are equal to price (Π) times the number of units sold by the firm (Q) or $TR = \Pi \times Q$. Total costs (TC) are equal to cost per unit (C) times the number of units sold or $TC = C \times Q$. Total profit (Π) is equal to profit per unit (π) times the number of units sold, or $\Pi = \pi \times Q$.

PROFITABILITY A ratio or rate of return concept.

Profitability is a ratio or rate of return concept. A simple example would be the rate of return on sales (ROS), which is defined as profit (Π) over total revenues, or

$$ROS = \Pi / TR$$

Thus, a firm might operate with the goal of maximizing its profitability, as defined by its return on sales (ROS), and its strategy would be the actions that its managers take to attain that goal. (A more common goal is to maximize the firm's return on investment, or ROI, which is defined as $ROI = \Pi / I$ where I represents the total capital, including both equity and debt, that has been invested in the firm.)

VALUE CREATION

Two basic conditions determine a firm's profits (Π): the amount of value customers place on the firm's goods or services (sometimes referred to as perceived value) and the firm's costs of production. In general, the more value customers place on a firm's products, the higher the price the firm can charge for those products. Note, however, that the price a firm charges for a good or service is typically less than the value placed on that good or service by the customer. This is so because the customer captures some of that value in the form of what economists call a consumer surplus.[1] The customer is able to do this because the firm is competing with other firms for the customer's business, so the firm must charge a lower price than it could were it a monopoly supplier. Also, it is normally impossible to segment the market to such a degree that the firm can charge each customer a price that reflects that individual's assessment of the value of a product, which economists refer to as a customer's reservation price. For these reasons, the price that gets charged tends to be less than the value placed on the product by many customers.

Figure 11.1 illustrates these concepts. The value of a product to a consumer is V; the price that the firm can charge for that product given competitive pressures and its

FIGURE 11.1
Value Creation

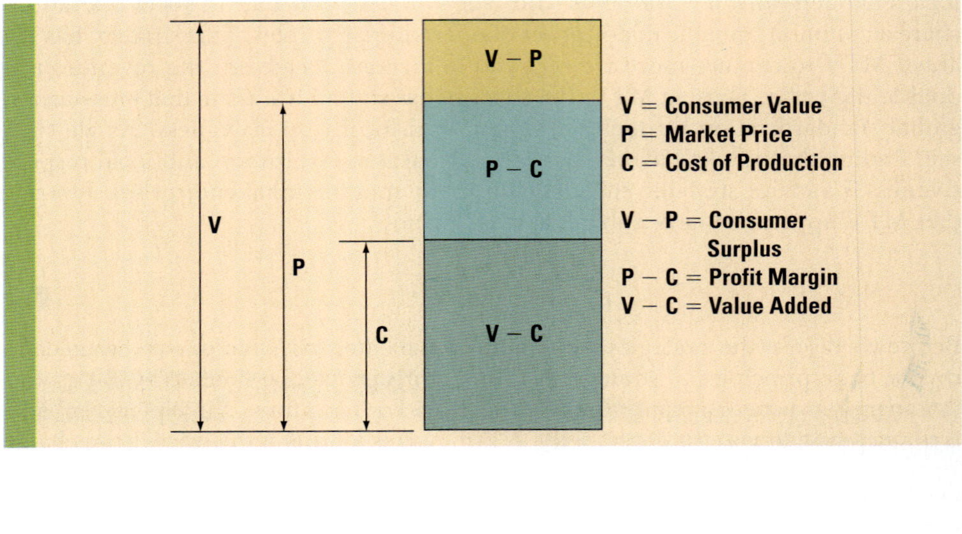

ability to segment the market is P; and the costs of producing that product are C. The firm's profit per unit sold (π) is equal to $P-C$, while the consumer surplus is equal to $V-P$. The firm makes a profit so long as P is greater than C, and its profit will be greater the lower C is *relative* to P. The difference between V and P is in part determined by the intensity of competitive pressure in the marketplace. The lower the intensity of competitive pressure, the higher the price that can be charged relative to V.[2]

The **value creation** of a firm is measured by the difference between V and C ($V-C$); a company creates value by converting inputs that cost C into a product on which consumers place a value of V. A company can create more value for its customers either by lowering production costs, C, or by making the product more attractive through superior design, functionality, quality, and the like, so that consumers place a greater value on it (V increases) and, consequently, are willing to pay a higher price (P increases). This discussion suggests that a firm has high profits when it creates more value for its customers and does so at a lower cost. We refer to a strategy that focuses on lowering production costs as a *low cost strategy*. We refer to a strategy that focuses on increasing the attractiveness of a product as a *differentiation strategy*.[3] Michael Porter has argued that *low cost* and *differentiation* are two basic strategies for creating value and attaining a competitive advantage in an industry.[4] According to Porter, superior profitability goes to those firms that can create superior value, and the way to create superior value is to drive down the cost structure of the business and/or differentiate the product in some way so that consumers value it more and are prepared to pay a premium price. Superior value creation relative to rivals does not necessarily require a firm to have the lowest cost structure in an industry, or to create the most valuable product in the eyes of consumers. However, it does require that the gap between value (V) and cost of production (C) is greater than the gap attained by competitors.

VALUE CREATION
Activities performed that increase the value of goods or services to consumers.

THE FIRM AS A VALUE CHAIN

It is useful to think of the firm as a value chain composed of a series of distinct value creation activities including production, marketing and sales, materials management, R&D, human resources, information systems, and the firm infrastructure. We can categorize these value creation activities as primary activities and support activities (see Figure 11.2).[5]

Primary Activities

Primary activities have to do with the design, creation, and delivery of the product; its marketing; and its support and after-sale service. In the value chain illustrated in

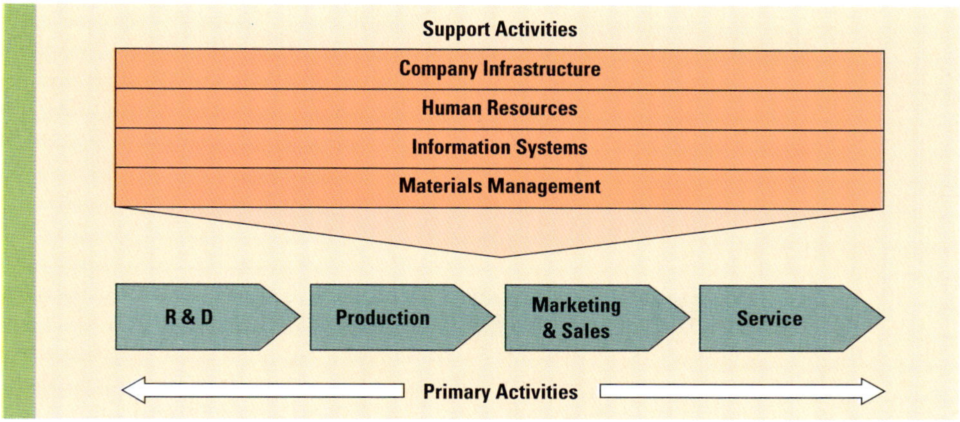

FIGURE 11.2
The Firm as a Value Chain

Figure 11.2, the primary activities are broken into four functions: research and development, production, marketing and sales, and service.

Research and development (R&D) is concerned with the design of products and production processes. Although we think of R&D as being associated with the design of physical products and production processes in manufacturing enterprises, many service companies also undertake R&D. For example, banks compete with each other by developing new financial products and new ways of delivering those products to customers. Online banking and smart debit cards are two recent examples of new product development in the banking industry. Earlier examples of innovation in the banking industry include automated teller machines, credit cards, and debit cards. Through superior product design, R&D can increase the functionality of products, which makes them more attractive to consumers (raising V). Alternatively, R&D may result in more efficient production processes, thereby lowering production costs (lowering C). Either way, the R&D function can create value.

Production is concerned with the creation of a good or service. For physical products, when we talk about production we generally mean manufacturing. For services such as banking or retail operations, "production" typically occurs when the service is delivered to the customer (for example, when a bank originates a loan for a customer it is engaged in "production" of the loan). For a media company such as MTV, production involves the creation and delivery of content (programming). The production activity of a firm creates value by performing its activities efficiently so lower costs result (lower C) or by performing them in such a way that a more reliable and higher-quality product is produced (which results in higher V).

The marketing and sales functions of a firm can help to create value in several ways. Through brand positioning and advertising, the marketing function can increase the value (V) that consumers perceive to be contained in a firm's product. If these create a favourable impression of the firm's product in the minds of consumers, they increase the price that can be charged for the firm's product. For example, in the 1980s the French company Perrier did a wonderful job of convincing U.S. consumers that slightly carbonated bottled water was worth $1.50 per bottle, rather than a price closer to the $0.50 that it cost to physically collect, bottle, and distribute the water. Perrier's marketing function essentially increased the perception of value (V) that consumers ascribed to the product. Marketing and sales can also create value by discovering consumer needs and communicating them back to the R&D function of the company, which can then design products that better match those needs.

The role of the enterprise's service activity is to provide after-sale service and support. This function can create a perception of superior value (V) in the minds of consumers by solving customer problems and supporting customers after they have purchased the product. For example, Caterpillar, the U.S.-based manufacturer of heavy earthmoving equipment, can get spare parts to any point in the world within 24 hours, thereby minimizing the amount of downtime customers have to suffer if their Caterpillar equipment malfunctions. This is an extremely valuable capability in an industry where downtime is very expensive. It has helped to increase the value that customers associate with Caterpillar products and thus the price that Caterpillar can charge for its products.

Support Activities

The support activities of the value chain provide inputs that allow the primary activities to take place (see Figure 11.2). The materials management (or logistics) function controls the transmission of physical materials through the value chain, from procurement through production and into distribution. The efficiency with which this is carried out can significantly lower cost (lower C), thereby creating more value.

Similarly, the human resource function can help create more value in a number of ways. It ensures that the company has the right mix of skilled people to perform its value creation activities effectively. Recall from the opening case how MTV staffs its foreign operations with local nationals–the idea being that local nationals will have a better feel for the tastes and preferences of local viewers than expatriate managers from the United States. MTV believes that better programming results from this staffing choice. In so far as this improves the fit between MTV's programming and local tastes, and drives viewer ratings, it raises the value (V) to advertisers of a slot on MTV. In turn, this increases the price that MTV can charge for those advertising slots. The human resource function also ensures that people are adequately trained, motivated, and compensated to perform their value creation tasks.

ANOTHER PERSPECTIVE

Education as a part of your value chain

The concept of value chain can be used to examine the role your undergraduate education plays in your life plans. If you examine your personal development plans (education, internship, physical and emotional/spiritual fitness, extracurricular activities) and think about them in terms of primary and support activities, how does your choice of major fit into your personal development strategy? How do your choices of how you spend your time fit into your value chain? Do you ever spend time doing things that don't support the strategic goals of your "personal value chain"?

Information systems refer to the normally electronic systems for managing inventory, tracking sales, pricing products, selling products, dealing with customer service inquiries, and so on. Information systems, when coupled with the communications features of the Internet, can alter the efficiency and effectiveness with which a firm manages its other value creation activities. As we shall see, good information systems are very important in the global arena.

The final support activity is the company infrastructure. By infrastructure we mean the context within which all the other value creation activities occur. The infrastructure includes the organizational structure, control systems, and culture of the firm. Because top management can exert considerable influence in shaping these aspects of a firm, top management should also be viewed as part of the firm's infrastructure. Through strong leadership, top management can consciously shape the infrastructure of a firm and through that the performance of all other value creation activities within it.

THE ROLE OF STRATEGY

Many international markets are now extremely competitive due to the liberalization of the world trade and investment environment. In industry after industry, capable competitors confront each other around the globe. To be profitable in such an environment, a firm must both reduce the costs of value creation (lower C) and differentiate its product offering so that consumers value that product more (raise V) and are willing to pay more for the product than it costs to produce it. Thus, strategy is often concerned with identifying and taking actions that will *lower the costs* of value creation and/or will *differentiate* the firm's product offering through superior design, quality, service, functionality, and so on.

There have been many developments in the growth of the Canadian economy since Confederation. One of the most significant phases of Canadian economic prosperity can be attributed to the post-World War II period during which Canada became a branch plant of the United States. Until that time, Canada was an exporter of raw materials and an importer of finished products. In its shift to a branch plant economy, Canada suffered from weak research and development initiatives, both in the government and private sectors. This made Canada less competitive in international markets, while at the same time, making it more dependent on American trade. Today, with the exception of British Columbia, the rest of Canada exports over 80 percent of its goods and services to the United States. British Columbia exports less than this, in part due to its proximity to Asia.

Along with a shift in immigration, more business-friendly policies have been implemented by the federal government since the dismantlement of the Trudeau-initiated Foreign Investment in Canada Act (FICA) and the passing in 1985 of the more foreign-takeover friendly Investment Canada Act (ICA) (see Chapter 7).

For an example of how this works, consider Brockville, Ontario-based Canarm Ltd., a manufacturer and marketer of ceiling fans and lighting products. Canarm began as a small sheet metal shop and was originally known as Danor Manufacturing Co. Ltd. By 1963 they had moved their operations to Brockville, the location of their present operations. In 2002, this privately owned company generated estimated revenues of $48 million. Not exactly small, but no corporate giant either, Canarm is a multinational firm with production facilities in China and Taiwan and retailers in North America and Europe.

With the energy crisis in the early 1970s, there was a pressing need to conserve energy. Slow-moving fans pushed spent hot air, gathered at ceiling levels to floor level. By using this low-energy solution, warm air could be salvaged in the winter and, in the summer, could circulate to cool the air. Danor imported these industrial three-metal blade 140-cm (56-inch) ceiling fans from Hong Kong manufacturers in 1975.

By 1981, Canadian prime interest soared to 22 percent, and commercial businesses were being forced to reduce their spending budget. Also, Asian manufacturers had an excess supply of ceiling fans with barely any international buyers. The metal-blade industrial ceiling fan was being replaced by more decorative wooden blades, thus opening up the market for ceiling fans. After extensive market research, Danor targetted restaurants and residential homeowners, with these imported fans, as they redesigned their retail chains and lighting showrooms to attract this expanding market niche.

In 1980, the merger of Danor and Canadian Armature Works created Canarm Ltd. Today, Canarm's residential lighting and ceiling fans are imported from China and Taiwan where several facilities in these countries are dedicated to manufacturing Canarm products.

The choice of the Asian manufacturers was influenced by its combination of low labour costs and skilled work force. The firm's objective at this point was to lower production costs (lower C) by locating value creation activities at an appropriate location. Canarm currently employs 800 people in facilities in China and Taiwan.[6]

PROFITING FROM GLOBAL EXPANSION

As suggested by the Canarm example, expanding globally allows firms to increase their profitability in ways not available to purely domestic enterprises. Firms that operate internationally are able to:

1. Realize location economies by dispersing individual value creation activities to those locations around the globe where they can be performed most efficiently and effectively.
2. Realize greater cost economies from experience effects by serving an expanded global market from a central location thereby reducing the costs of value creation.
3. Earn a greater return from the firm's distinctive skills or core competencies by leveraging those skills and applying them to other entities within the firm's global network of operations.

As we will see, however, a firm's ability to increase its profitability by pursuing these strategies is to some extent constrained by the need to customize its product offering, marketing strategy, and business strategy to differing national conditions by the imperative of localization.

LOCATION ECONOMIES

We know from earlier chapters that countries differ along a range of dimensions including social, technological, economic, political, and legal, and that these differences can either raise or lower costs of doing business in a country. The theory of international trade also teaches us that due to differences in factor costs, certain countries have a comparative advantage in the production of certain products. Japan might excel in the production of automobiles and consumer electronics; Canada in the production of forestry products the United States in the production of computer software, pharmaceuticals, biotechnology products, and financial services; Switzerland in the production of precision instruments and pharmaceuticals; and South Korea in the production of steel.

What does all this mean for a firm trying to survive in a competitive global market? It means that, *trade barriers and transportation costs* permitting, the firm will benefit by basing each value creation activity it performs at that location where economic, political, and cultural conditions, including relative factor costs, are most conducive to the performance of that activity. Thus, if the best designers for a product live in France, then a firm should base its design operations there. If the most productive labour force for assembly operation is in Mexico, assembly operations should be based in Mexico. If the best marketers are in the United States, the marketing strategy should be formulated in the United States. If the best film animation production facilities are in Canada, the film animation strategy should be formulated in Canada. And so on.

> **ANOTHER PERSPECTIVE**
>
> **Location economies at work in ways we may not realize**
>
> When we call a company's customer service, we expect that call centre to be in Canada, especially when someone who sounds middle-Atlantic answers the call. This isn't always the case. Call centres train employees in achieving middle-Atlantic accents so they sound as if they are in Canada, but they may actually be located in India or, more recently, in Ghana. In addition, much of the programming support work for the Canadian corporate world is done in Asia, especially in India. Think about having a job as an Indian pretending to be from P.E.I. What do you think of the ethics of such intentional misleading?

Firms that pursue such a strategy can realize what we refer to as **location economies**, the economies that arise from performing a value creation activity in the optimal location for that activity, wherever in the world that might be (transportation costs and trade barriers permitting). Locating a value creation activity in the optimal location for that activity can have one of two effects. *It can lower the costs of value creation and help the firm to achieve a low cost position, and/or it can enable a firm to differentiate its product offering from those of competitors.* In terms of Figure 11.1, it can lower C or increase V, which in general supports higher pricing (P). We can apply these considerations to Canarm, discussed earlier. Canarm moved its manufacturing operations out of Canada to China and Taiwan to take advantage of low labour costs, thereby lowering the costs of value creation (C). Canarm thinks that the optimal location for performing manufacturing operations is Asia. The firm has configured its value chain accordingly. By doing so, Canarm hopes to be able to simultaneously lower its cost structure and differentiate its product offering. In turn, differentiation should allow Canarm to charge a premium price for its product offering.

> **LOCATION ECONOMIES** Cost advantages from performing a value creation activity at the optimal location for that activity.

Creating a Global Web

Generalizing from the Canarm example, one result of this kind of thinking is the creation of a **global web** of value creation activities, with different stages of the value chain being dispersed to those locations around the globe where perceived value is maximized or where the cost of value creation are minimized.

> **GLOBAL WEB** When different stages of value chain are dispersed to those locations around the globe where value added is maximized or where costs of value creation are minimized.

In theory, a firm that realizes location economies by dispersing each of its value creation activities to its optimal location should have a competitive advantage vis-à-vis a firm that bases all its value creation activities at a single location. It should be able to better differentiate its product offering (thereby raising perceived value, V) and lower its cost structure (C) than its single-location competitor. In a world where competitive pressures are increasing, such a strategy may become an imperative for survival (as it seems to have been for Canarm).

Some Caveats

Introducing transportation costs and trade barriers complicates this picture somewhat. Due to favourable factor endowments, New Zealand may have a comparative advantage for automobile assembly operations, but high transportation costs would make it an uneconomical location from which to serve global markets. A consideration of transportation costs and trade barriers helps explain why many U.S. firms are now shifting their production from Asia to Mexico. Mexico has three distinct advantages over many Asian countries as a location for value creation activities. First, low labour costs make it a good location for labour-intensive production processes. In recent years, wage rates have increased significantly in Japan, Taiwan, and Hong Kong, but they have remained low in Mexico. Second, Mexico's proximity to the large U.S. market reduces transportation costs. This is particularly important in the case of products with high weight-to-value ratios (e.g., automobiles). And third, the North American Free Trade Agreement (see Chapter 8) has removed many trade barriers between Mexico, the United States, and Canada, increasing Mexico's attractiveness as a production site for the North American market. Although value added and the costs of value creation are important, transportation costs and trade barriers also must be considered in location decisions.

Another caveat concerns the importance of assessing political and economic risks when making location decisions. Even if a country looks very attractive as a production location when measured against all the standard criteria, if its government is unstable or totalitarian, the firm might be advised not to base production there. (Political risk is discussed in Chapter 2.) Similarly, if the government appears to be pursuing inappropriate economic policies, that might be another reason for not basing production in that location, even if other factors look favourable.

EXPERIENCE EFFECTS

EXPERIENCE CURVE Systematic production cost reductions that occur over the life of a product.

The **experience curve** refers to systematic reductions in production costs that have been observed to occur over the life of a product.[7] A number of studies have observed that a product's production costs decline by some characteristic about each time accumulated output doubles. The relationship was first observed in the aircraft industry, where each time accumulated output of airframes was doubled, unit costs typically declined to 80 percent of their previous level.[8] Thus, production cost for the fourth airframe would be 80 percent of production cost for the second airframe, the eighth airframe's production costs 80 percent of the fourth's, the 16th's 80 percent of the eighth's, and so on. Figure 11.3 illustrates this experience curve relationship between production costs and output. Two things explain this: learning effects and economies of scale.

Learning Effects

LEARNING EFFECTS Cost savings from learning by doing.

Learning effects refer to cost savings that come from learning by doing. Labour, for example, learns by repetition how to carry out a task such as assembling airframes most efficiently. Labour productivity increases over time as individuals learn the most efficient ways to perform particular tasks. Equally important, in new production facilities, management typically learns how to manage the new operation more efficiently over time. Hence, production costs eventually decline due to increasing labour productivity and management efficiency.

Learning effects tend to be more significant when a technologically complex task is repeated, since there is more that can be learned about the task. Thus, learning effects will be more significant in an assembly process involving 1000 complex steps

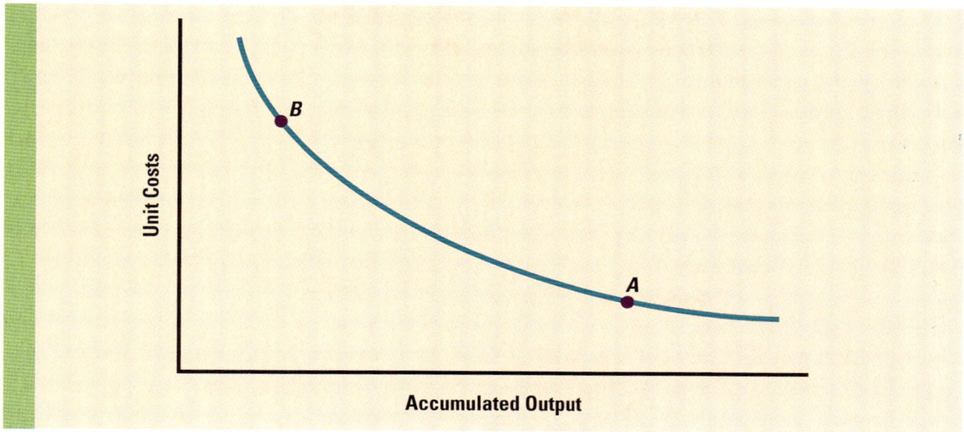

FIGURE 11.3
The Experience Curve

than in one of only 100 simple steps. No matter how complex the task, however, learning effects typically disappear after a while. It has been suggested that they are really important only during the start-up period of a new process and that they cease after two or three years.[9] Any decline in the experience curve after such a point is due to economies of scale.

Economies of Scale

Economies of scale refer to the reductions in unit cost achieved by producing a large volume of a product. Economies of scale have a number of sources. One of the most important seems to be the ability to spread fixed costs over a large volume.[10] Fixed costs are the costs required to set up a production facility, develop a new product, and the like, and they can be substantial. For example, establishing a new production line to manufacture semiconductor chips costs about $1 billion. According to one estimate, developing a new drug costs about $500 million and takes about ten years.[11] The only way to recoup such high fixed costs is to sell the product worldwide, which reduces unit costs by spreading them over a larger volume. The more rapidly that cumulative sales volume is built up, the more rapidly fixed costs can be amortized, and the more rapidly unit costs fall.

ECONOMIES OF SCALE Cost advantages associated with large-scale production.

Another source of scale economies arises from the ability of large firms to employ increasingly specialized equipment or personnel. This theory goes back more than 200 years to Adam Smith, who argued that the division of labour is limited by the extent of the market. As a firm's output expands, it is better able to fully utilize specialized equipment and can justify hiring specialized personnel. For example, consider a metal stamping machine that is used in the production of body parts for automobiles. The machine can be purchased in a customized form, which is optimized for the production of a particular type of body part—say door panels—or a general-purpose form that will produce any kind of body part. The general-purpose form is less efficient and costs more to purchase than the customized form, but it

Manufacturers of pharmaceuticals use economies of scale, or a production of a high volume of product, to overcome the high fixed cost of developing a new drug. CORBIS. All Rights Reserved.

is more flexible. Since these machines are very expensive, costing millions of dollars each, they have to be used continually to recoup a return on their costs. Fully utilized, a machine can turn out about 200 000 units a year. If an automobile company sells only 100 000 cars per year, it will not be worthwhile to purchase the specialized equipment, and it will have to purchase general-purpose machines. This will give it a higher cost structure than a firm that sells 200 000 cars per year, and for which it is economical to purchase a specialized stamping machine. Thus, because a firm with a large output can more fully utilize specialized equipment (and personnel), it should have a lower unit cost than a generalized firm.

Strategic Significance

The strategic significance of the experience curve is clear. Moving down the experience curve allows a firm to reduce its cost of creating value (to lower C in Figure 11.1). The firm that moves down the experience curve most rapidly will have a cost advantage vis-à-vis its competitors. Thus, firm A in Figure 11.3, because it is farther down the experience curve, has a clear cost advantage over firm B.

Many of the underlying sources of experience-based cost economies are plant based. This is true for most learning effects as well as for the economies of scale derived by spreading the fixed costs of building productive capacity over a large output. Thus, one key to progressing downward on the experience curve as rapidly as possible is to increase the volume produced by a single plant as rapidly as possible. Because global markets are larger than domestic markets, a firm that serves a global market from a single location is likely to build accumulated volume more quickly than a firm that serves only its home market or that serves multiple markets from multiple production locations. Thus, serving a global market from a single location is consistent with moving down the experience curve and establishing a low cost position (i.e., lowering the costs of value creation, C). In addition, to get down the experience curve rapidly, a firm may need to price and market aggressively so demand will expand rapidly. It will also need to build sufficient production capacity for serving a global market. Also, the cost advantages of serving the world market from a single location will be even more significant if that location is the optimal one for performing the particular value creation activity.

Once a firm has established a low cost position, it can act as a barrier to new competition. Specifically, an established firm that is well down the experience curve, such as firm A in Figure 11.3, can price so that it is still making a profit while new entrants, which are farther up the curve such as firm B in the figure, are suffering losses.

The classic example of the successful pursuit of such a strategy concerns the Japanese consumer electronics company Matsushita. Along with Sony and Philips, Matsushita was in the race to develop a commercially viable videocassette recorder in the 1970s. Although Matsushita initially lagged behind Philips and Sony, it was able to get its VHS format accepted as the world standard and to reap enormous experience-curve-based cost economies in the process. This cost advantage subsequently constituted a formidable barrier to new competition. Matsushita's strategy was to build global volume as rapidly as possible. To ensure it could accommodate worldwide demand, the firm increased its production capacity 33-fold from 205 000 units in 1977 to 6.8 million units by 1984. By serving the world market from a single location in Japan, Matsushita was able to realize significant learning effects and economies of scale. These allowed Matsushita to drop its prices 50 percent within five years of selling its first VHS-formatted VCR. As a result, Matsushita was the world's major VCR producer by 1983, accounting for about 45 percent of world production and enjoying a significant cost advantage over its competitors. The next largest firm, Hitachi, accounted for only 11.1 percent of world production in 1983.[12] Today, firms such as Intel are the masters of this kind of strategy.

The costs of building a state-of-the-art facility to manufacture microprocessors are so great (easily in excess of $1 billion), that to make this investment profitable, Intel *must* pursue experience curve effects, serving world markets from a limited number of plants to maximize the cost economies that derive from scale and learning effects.

LEVERAGING CORE COMPETENCIES

The term **core competence** refers to skills within the firm that competitors cannot easily match or imitate.[13] These skills may exist in any of the firm's value creation activities–production, marketing, R&D, human resources, general management, and so on. Such skills are typically expressed in product offerings that other firms find difficult to match or imitate, and thus the core competencies are the bedrock of a firm's competitive advantage. They enable a firm to reduce the costs of value creation (C) and/or to create perceived value (V) in such a way that premium pricing is possible. For example, Toyota has a core competence in the production of cars. It is able to produce high-quality, well-designed cars at a lower delivered cost than any other firm in the world. The skills that enable Toyota to do this seem to reside primarily in the firm's production and materials management functions.[14] McDonald's has a core competence in managing fast-food operations (it seems to be one of the most skilled firms in the world in this industry); Canadian Tire opened a Shanghai office in the fall of 2004 and Canadian Tire has a core competence in developing and marketing discount hardware tools;[15] Procter & Gamble has a core competence in developing and marketing name brand consumer products (it is one of the most skilled firms in the world in this business); Wal-Mart has a core competence in information systems and logistics; MTV has a core competence in managing the programming and delivery of cable TV music and related offerings.

CORE COMPETENCE
Firm skills that competitors cannot easily match or imitate.

For such firms, global expansion is a way of further exploiting the value creation potential of their skills and product offerings by applying those skills and products in a larger market. The potential for creating value from such a strategy is greatest when the skills and products of the firm are most unique, when the value placed on them by consumers is great, and when there are very few capable competitors with similar skills and/or products in foreign markets. Firms with unique and valuable skills can often realize enormous returns by applying those skills, and the products they produce, to foreign markets where indigenous competitors lack similar skills and products. MTV has built a vibrant global business by leveraging its skills in the programming and delivery of music and related content and applying those skills to local markets where indigenous competitors lacked equivalent skills. The network's success has raised the value (V) that viewers ascribe to MTV and, by extension, the value that advertisers ascribe to an advertising slot on an MTV channel. In turn, this has enabled MTV to command a higher price for advertising slots than competitors.

In earlier eras, U.S. firms such as Kellogg, Coca-Cola, H. J. Heinz, and Procter & Gamble expanded overseas to exploit their skills in developing and marketing name brand consumer products. These skills and the resulting products, which were developed in the U.S. market during the 1950s and 60s, yielded enormous returns when applied to European markets, where most indigenous competitors lacked similar marketing skills and products. Their near-monopoly on consumer marketing skills allowed these U.S. firms to dominate many European consumer product markets during the 1960s and 70s. Similarly, in the 1970s and 80s, many Japanese firms expanded globally to exploit their skills in production, materials management, and new product development–skills that many of their indigenous North American and European competitors seemed to lack at the time. Today, retail companies such as Wal-Mart and financial companies such as Citicorp, Merrill Lynch, and American Express are transferring the valuable skills they developed in their core home market to other developed and emerging markets where indigenous competitors lack those skills. The same can be said of MTV, profiled in the opening case. For example, SNC-Lavalin, with revenues of over $3 billion, is working in over 100 countries. It is active in such traditional engineering fields as chemicals, petroleum, and mining, but also in more service-oriented fields as project financing, investment, and facilities management.

LEVERAGING SUBSIDIARY SKILLS

Implicit in the discussion of leveraging core competencies is the idea that skills are developed first at home and then transferred to foreign operations. Thus, MTV developed its programming skills in the United States and McDonald's its skills in managing fast-food restaurants before each enterprise decided to transfer them to foreign locations. However, for more mature multinationals that have already established a network of subsidiary operations in foreign markets, the development of valuable skills can just as well occur in foreign subsidiaries.[16] Skills can be created anywhere within a multinational's global network of operations, wherever people have the opportunity and incentive to try new ways of doing things. The creation of skills that help to lower the costs of production or to enhance perceived value and support higher product pricing, are not the monopoly of the corporate centre.

Leveraging the skills created within subsidiaries and applying them to other operations within the firm's global network may create value. For example, Hewlett-Packard has decentralized the authority for the design and production of many of its leading-edge ink-jet printers to its operation in Singapore. Hewlett-Packard made this decision after employees in Singapore distinguished themselves by finding ways to reduce production costs through better product design. Hewlett-Packard now views its Singapore subsidiary as an important source for valuable new knowledge about production and product design that can be applied to other activities within the firm's global network of operations.[17]

For the managers of the multinational enterprise, this phenomenon creates important new challenges. First, they must have the humility to recognize that valuable skills can arise anywhere within the firm's global network, not just at the corporate centre. Second, they must establish an incentive system that encourages local employees to acquire new skills. This is not as easy as it sounds. Creating new skills involves a degree of risk. Not all new skills add value. For every valuable idea created by a McDonald's subsidiary in a foreign country, there may be several failures. The management of the multinational must install incentives that encourage employees to take the necessary risks. They must reward people for successes and not sanction them unnecessarily for taking risks that did not pan out. Third, managers must have a process for identifying when valuable new skills have been created in a subsidiary, and finally, they need to act as facilitators, helping to transfer valuable skills within the firm.

PRESSURES FOR COST REDUCTIONS AND LOCAL RESPONSIVENESS

Firms that compete in the global marketplace typically face two types of competitive pressure. They face *pressures for cost reductions* and *pressures to be locally responsive* (see Figure 11.4). These competitive pressures place conflicting demands on a firm. Responding to pressures for cost reductions requires that a firm try to minimize its unit costs. Attaining such a goal may necessitate that a firm base its productive activities at the most favourable low-cost location, wherever in the world that might be. It may also necessitate that a firm offer a standardized product to the global marketplace. This helps the firm spread the fixed costs of developing a product offering over as large a volume as possible, thereby lowering its average unit costs. Offering a standardized

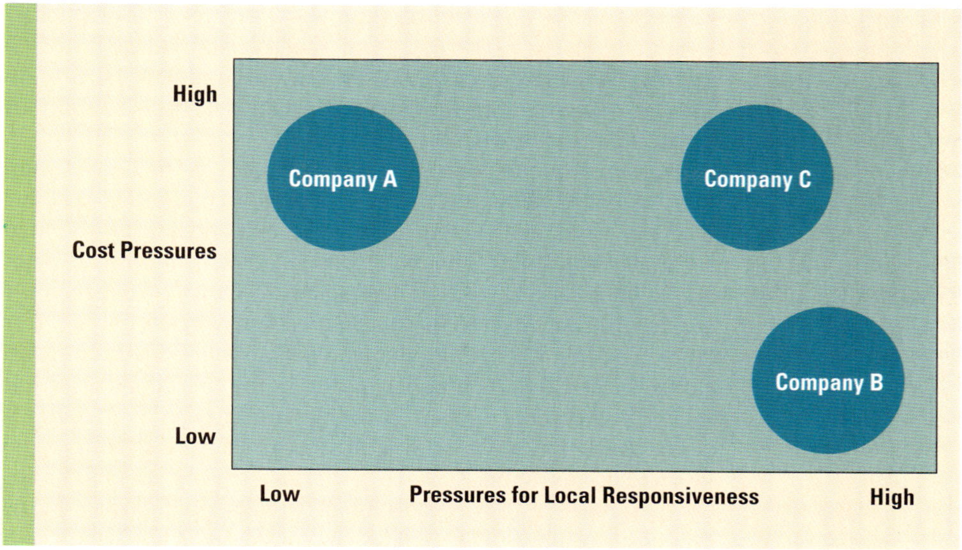

FIGURE 11.4

Pressures for Cost Reduction and Local Responsiveness

product also enables the firm to attain other scale economies and ride down the experience curve as quickly as possible. In contrast, responding to pressures to be locally responsive requires that a firm differentiate its product offering and marketing strategy from country to country in an attempt to accommodate the diverse demands that arise from national differences in consumer tastes and preferences, business practices, distribution channels, competitive conditions, and government policies. Because customizing product offerings to different national requirements can involve significant duplication and a lack of product standardization, the result may be to raise costs.

Some firms, such as firm A in Figure 11.4, face high pressures for cost reductions and low pressures for local responsiveness. Others, such as firm B, face low pressures for cost reductions and high pressures for local responsiveness. Many others are in the position of firm C in Figure 11.4. They face high pressures for cost reductions and high pressures for local responsiveness. Dealing with these conflicting and contradictory pressures is a difficult strategic challenge for a firm, primarily because being locally responsive tends to raise costs. In the remainder of this section, we shall look at the source of pressures for cost reductions and local responsiveness. In the next section, we look at the strategies that firms adopt to deal with these pressures.

PRESSURES FOR COST REDUCTIONS

Increasingly, international businesses are facing pressures for cost reductions. Responding to pressures for cost reduction requires a firm to try to lower the costs of value creation by mass producing a standardized product at the optimal location in the world to realize location and experience curve economies. Cost reduction pressures can be particularly intense in industries producing commodity-type products where meaningful differentiation on nonprice factors is difficult and price is the main competitive weapon. This tends to be the case for products that serve universal needs. Universal needs exist when the tastes and preferences of consumers in different nations are similar if not identical. This is the case for conventional commodity products such as bulk chemicals, petroleum, steel, sugar, and the like. It also tends to be the case for many industrial and consumer products; for example, handheld calculators, semiconductor chips, personal computers, and liquid crystal display screens. Pressures for cost reductions are also intense in industries where major competitors are based in low-cost locations, where there is persistent excess capacity, and where

Because tires are a commodity product, price is usually the differentiating point among competitors for auto manufacturers' business. In the early 1990s, a decline in the global demand for automobiles created a surplus of tires, which resulted in a worldwide price war. Considering what your text has said about price wars among competitors for the attention of automobile manufacturers, why do you think tire manufacturers try to distinguish themselves with consumers on the basis of such things as safety features, rather than price? Rachel Epstein/PhotoEdit.

consumers are powerful and face low switching costs. Many commentators have also argued that the liberalization of the world trade and investment environment in recent decades, by facilitating greater international competition, has generally increased cost pressures.[18]

Pressures for cost reductions have been intense in the global tire industry in recent years. Tires are essentially a commodity product where meaningful differentiation is difficult and price is the main competitive weapon. The major buyers of tires, automobile firms, are powerful and face low switching costs, so they have been playing tire firms against each other in an attempt to get lower prices. And the decline in global demand for automobiles in the early 1990s created serious excess capacity in the tire industry, with as much as 25 percent of world capacity standing idle. The result was a worldwide price war with almost all tire firms suffering heavy losses in the 1990s. In response to the resulting cost pressures, most tire firms are now trying to rationalize their operations to attain a low cost position. This includes moving production facilities to low-cost facilities and offering globally standardized products to try to realize experience curve economies.[19]

PRESSURES FOR LOCAL RESPONSIVENESS

Pressures for local responsiveness arise from a number of sources including (*i*) differences in consumer tastes and preferences, (*ii*) differences in infrastructure and traditional practices, (*iii*) differences in distribution channels, and (*iv*) host government demands.

Differences in Consumer Tastes and Preferences

Strong pressures for local responsiveness emerge when consumer tastes and preferences differ significantly between countries, as they may for historic or cultural reasons. In such cases, product and/or marketing messages have to be customized to appeal to the tastes and preferences of local consumers. This typically creates pressure to delegate production and marketing functions to national subsidiaries.

The opening case provided a good example of this. Other things being equal, MTV would probably have preferred to centralize as much programming and content in the United States as possible. Offering standardized programming and content around the world would have allowed MTV to realize scale economies by leveraging its fixed costs of programming and content development over a global viewer base. However, this strategy essentially failed. Instead, to gain viewers in different countries, MTV found that it needs to respond to local tastes and preferences, customizing its programming and content accordingly. Thus, while "MTV Cricket in Control" would be unlikely to whet the appetite of Canadian viewers, it is an important program in India.

The automobile industry in the 1980s and early 1990s moved toward the creation of "world cars." The idea was that global companies such as General Motors, Ford, and Toyota would be able to sell the same basic vehicle the world over, sourcing it from centralized production locations. If successful, the strategy would have enabled automobile companies to reap significant gains from global scale economies. However, this strategy has frequently run aground upon the hard rocks of consumer reality. Consumers in different automobile markets seem to have different tastes and preferences, and these require different types of vehicles. For example, North American consumers show a strong demand for pickup trucks. This is particularly true in the South and West where many families have a pickup truck as a second or third car. But in European countries, pickup trucks are seen purely as utility vehicles and are purchased primarily by firms rather than individuals. As a consequence, the marketing message needs to be tailored to the different nature of demand in North America and Europe.

As a counterpoint, in a now classic article, Harvard Business School Professor Theodore Levitt argued that consumer demands for local customization are on the decline worldwide.[20] According to Levitt, modern communication and transportation technologies have created the conditions for a convergence of the tastes and preferences of consumers from different nations. The result is the emergence of enormous global markets for standardized consumer products. Levitt cites worldwide acceptance of McDonald's hamburgers, Coca-Cola, Levi Strauss jeans, and Sony television sets, all of which are sold as standardized products, as evidence of the increasing homogeneity of the global marketplace.

Levitt's argument, however, has been characterized as extreme by many commentators. For example, Christopher Bartlett and Sumantra Ghoshal have observed that, in the consumer electronics industry, consumers reacted to an overdose of standardized global products by showing a renewed preference for products that are differentiated to local conditions.[21] They note that Amstrad, the British computer and electronics firm, got its start by recognizing and responding to local consumer needs. Amstrad captured a major share of the British audio player market by moving away from the standardized inexpensive music centres marketed by global firms such as Sony and Matsushita. Amstrad's product was encased in teak rather than metal cabinets and had a control panel tailor-made to appeal to British consumers' preferences. In response, Matsushita reversed its earlier bias toward standardized global design and placed more emphasis on local customization. Similarly, as we saw in the opening case, to fight off competitive threats from local competitors, MTV customized its programming and content to tastes and preferences in local markets. In direct counterpoint to Levitt's thesis, the music industry seems to have moved away from global megastars and toward more local tastes.

Differences in Infrastructure and Traditional Practices

Pressures for local responsiveness emerge when there are differences in infrastructure and/or traditional practices between countries. In such circumstances, the product may need to be customized to the distinctive infrastructure and practices of different nations. This may necessitate the delegation of manufacturing and production functions to foreign subsidiaries. For example, in North America, consumer electrical systems are based on 110 volts, while in some European countries 240-volt systems are standard. Thus, domestic electrical appliances have to be customized for this difference in infrastructure. Traditional practices also often vary across nations. For example, in Great Britain, people drive on the left side of the road, thus creating a demand for right-hand drive cars, whereas in neighbouring France, people drive on the right side of the road, thus creating a demand for left-hand drive cars. Obviously automobiles have to be customized for this difference in traditional practices.

While many of the country differences in infrastructure are rooted in history, some are quite recent. For example, in the wireless telecommunication industry, technical standards vary around the world. A technical standard known as GSM is common in Europe, while an alternative standard, referred to as CDMA, is more common in Canada, the United States, and parts of Asia. Equipment designed for GSM will not work on a CDMA network, and vice versa. Thus, companies such as Nokia, Motorola, and Ericsson, which manufacture wireless handsets and infrastructure such as switches, need to customize their product offering according to the technical standard prevailing in a given country.

ANOTHER PERSPECTIVE

Cellphone service packaging: a strategic difference

In Canada, cellular phone service comes with a long-term service contract tied to a particular provider, with a usual minimum of one year. In Europe, cellphone service is packaged in smaller units. Users can buy service in tiny units, for as little as 7 euro, about Cdn$11. If you choose this approach, you don't have a contract with the service provider and are not in the phone company's records. Rather, you buy the service in increments at the local kiosk, the grocery store, and the cellphone store. What forces and conditions might explain these different business strategies followed by Canadian and European cellular phone companies?

Differences in Distribution Channels

A firm's marketing strategies may have to be responsive to differences in distribution channels between countries. This may necessitate the delegation of marketing functions to national subsidiaries. In Germany, for example, a handful of food retailers dominate the market, but the market is very fragmented in neighbouring Italy. Thus, retail chains have considerable buying power in Germany but relatively little in Italy. Dealing with these differences requires varying marketing approaches for detergent firms. Similarly, in the pharmaceutical industry, the British and Japanese distribution systems are radically different from the U.S. system. British and Japanese doctors will not accept or respond favourably to an American-style high-pressure sales force. Thus, pharmaceutical firms have to adopt different marketing practices in Great Britain and Japan compared to the United States (soft sell versus hard sell).

Host-Government Demands

Economic and political demands imposed by host-country governments may necessitate a degree of local responsiveness. For example, the politics of health care around the world requires that pharmaceutical firms manufacture in multiple locations. Pharmaceutical firms are subject to local clinical testing, registration procedures, and pricing restrictions, all of which require that the manufacturing and marketing of a drug should meet local requirements. Because governments and government agencies control a significant proportion of the health care budget in most countries, they can demand a high level of local responsiveness. Yet at the same time, outsiders attempt to benefit from changes in local conditions. For several years now, patients in the United States have used online pharmacies to purchase Canadian drugs at a lower price than in the U.S.

Threats of protectionism, economic nationalism, and local content rules (which require that a certain percentage of a product be manufactured locally), all dictate that international businesses manufacture locally. Consider Bombardier, the Canadian-based manufacturer of railcars, aircraft, jet boats, and snowmobiles. Bombardier has 12 railcar factories across Europe. Critics of the firm argue that the resulting duplication of manufacturing facilities leads to high costs and explains why Bombardier makes lower profit margins on its railcar operations than on its other business lines. Managers at Bombardier argue that in Europe, informal rules with regard to local content favour people who use local workers. To sell railcars in Germany, they claim, you must manufacture in Germany. The same goes for Belgium, Austria, and France. To address its cost structure in Europe, Bombardier has centralized its engineering and purchasing functions, but it has no plans to centralize manufacturing.[22]

STRATEGIC CHOICES

Firms use four basic strategies to enter and compete in the international environment: an international strategy, a multidomestic strategy, a global strategy, and a transnational strategy.[23] Each of these strategies has its advantages and disadvantages. The appropriateness of each strategy varies with the extent of pressures for cost reductions and local responsiveness. Figure 11.5 illustrates when each of these strategies is most appropriate.

In this section we describe each strategy, identify when it is appropriate, and discuss the pros and cons of each. See the Country Focus for Canada'a global business strategy.

IKEA, realizing that it could not sell a "typically Swedish" product line in North America, redesigned and customized its products to fit North American consumers' tastes. Spencer Grant/PhotoEdit.

INTERNATIONAL STRATEGY

Firms that pursue an international strategy try to create value by transferring valuable skills and products to foreign markets where indigenous competitors lack those skills and products. Most international firms have created value by transferring differentiated product offerings developed at home to new markets overseas. Accordingly, they tend to centralize product development functions at home (e.g., R&D). However, they also tend to establish manufacturing and marketing functions in each major country in which they do business. But while they may undertake some local customization of product offering and marketing strategy, this tends to be limited. In most international firms, the head office retains tight control over marketing and product strategy.

International firms include McDonald's, IBM, Kellogg, Procter & Gamble, Wal-Mart, and Microsoft. Microsoft, for example, develops the core architecture underlying its products at its Redmond campus in Washington state and also writes the bulk of the computer code there. However, the company does allow national subsidiaries to develop their own marketing and distribution strategy and to customize aspects of the product to account for such basic local differences as language and alphabet. The accompanying Management Focus profiles IKEA, a Swedish retailer that has traditionally pursued an international strategy, transferring its retailing formula developed in Sweden wholesale into other markets. As the feature makes clear, however, this strategy did not work for IKEA once it opened stores in the United States.

FIGURE 11.5
Four Basic Strategies

TEAM CANADA: A VITAL PART OF THE CANADIAN GOVERNMENT'S GLOBAL BUSINESS STRATEGY

Governments around the world go about promoting their countries' industries through various ways and means. The promotion list of attributes can include hotel & tourism and its many offshoots; its favourable corporate tax system; its skilled labour markets; or its perfect climate. Some "pitches" are made through the media, while others are more "hands on." But what can Canada use as its strategic difference?

Take for example the role that Team Canada plays within the strategy of expanding Canadian exports. Other governments use business tactics to bolster exports. Princess Diana was at the forefront of promoting the British fashion industry. A picture with Princess Diana wearing a gown, with the heading "made by rising British designer" translated into huge sales of other British products. Although less glamorous, a photo opportunity of foreign business leaders speaking with, for example, the prime minister of Canada on a foreign visit, can speak volumes. Team Canada provides this opportunity.

Team Canada trade missions have been around since the 1980s. These venues have grown into huge potential business opportunities for Canadian businesspeople seeking new markets. Sometimes, the mission might be led by a minister of Finance, or, the minister of Industry Trade and Commerce, while at other times, the prime minister might jump in. Interested businesses can participate in the trade mission, at costs varying according to the destination, and sometimes exceeding $20,000.

"Exports, which account for more than 43 percent of all goods and services in Canada, are vital to the Canadian economy. Every one in three jobs in Canada is tied to exports and every $1 billion in exports creates or sustains 11 000 jobs in Canada. Team Canada missions have helped more than 2800 representatives of Canadian businesses and organizations gain access to senior government and private-sector leaders in international markets, directly contributing to some $30.6 billion in new business. Business that creates or sustains jobs in Canada."

Participants are diverse and representative of Canada's multicultural business environment. Entrepreneurs, established exporters, university presidents, cultural and arts leaders, small businesspeople, and major corporate executives along with those doing exploratory export research for business expansion, Aboriginals, and so on form the face of Team Canada. All are jockeying to make a lucrative business deal for their own institutions or businesses.

For Team Canada delegates, trade missions provide a cost-effective means for becoming familiar with new markets. Also, Team Canada members benefit from access to foreign political and business leaders and enhanced visibility in foreign markets. Working at high levels can facilitate and accelerate the making of contacts, and the closing of contracts for Canadian companies.

As soon as they set foot on the plane, and in many cases, a government of Canada plane, the networking begins. Normally, a dozen or so industry sectors will be selected for a trip, which can be geared to visit several countries over the course of three weeks, and corporate leaders from within these industries will make up the bulk of the trip's participants, along with an entourage of ministerial advisors, Department of Foreign Affairs industry specialists. Once in the host country, local Canadian embassy staff will have scheduled, well in advance of the team's arrival, meetings with leading executives of that country's corporations.

Over the years, Team Canada missions, to name a few, have been to Pakistan, Indonesia, Latin America, South Korea, the Philippines, Thailand, China, the Ukraine, and Russia.

Companies need all the support and help they can muster when competing in the international business arena and Team Canada is one way to break through the international trade wall.

As an outcome of the 2002 Team Canada trade mission to Germany, Warnex of Laval, Quebec, was able to explore new business opportunities for its new technology known as Genevision that will analyze components and enable food products to be traced. The technology will also be capable of testing for "the presence of bacteria" and genetically modified organisms (GMOs) in foods.

In 1998, Genesis Organic Inc. of Corner Brook, Newfoundland, participated in a Team Canada mission to Chile. Genesis Organic Inc., "uses aerobic composting technology to transform pure organic waste, like wood bark and fish, into high-grade organic soil conditioners." On other occasions, Genesis, has participated in other Team Canada missions to other destinations in South America. When on site, many Team Canada participants are guided through the maze of foreign business culture by on site Canadian trade commissioners.

Former Prime Minister Jean Chretien and members of the Team Canada trade mission gathered in Berlin, Germany in 2002. From left to right, Alberta Premier Ralph Klein, PEI Premier Pat Binns, former Prime Minister Jean Chretien, Manitoba Premier Gary Doer, Nova Scotia Premier John Hamm, former Yukon leader Pat Duncan, Nunavut leader Paul Okalik, and Saskatchewan Premier Lorne Calvert. CP/Fred Chartrand

Sources: ITC at www.tcm-mec.gc.ca/what-en.asp; www.tcm-mec.gc.ca/success/new/warnex-en.asp; www.tcm-mec.gc.ca/success/new/genesis-en.asp.

An international strategy makes sense if a firm has a valuable core competence that indigenous competitors in foreign markets lack and if the firm faces relatively weak pressures for local responsiveness and cost reductions (as is the case for Microsoft). In such circumstances, an international strategy can be very profitable. However, when pressures for local responsiveness are high, firms pursuing this strategy lose to firms that emphasize customizing the product offering and market strategy to local conditions. IKEA experienced this problem in the United States and subsequently shifted its strategy to accommodate local differences in tastes and preferences (see the Management Focus). Similarly, when MTV expanded into Europe, it pursued an international strategy, but as we saw from the opening case, this strategy failed. In addition, due to the duplication of manufacturing facilities, firms that pursue an international strategy tend to suffer from high operating costs. This makes the strategy inappropriate in manufacturing industries where cost pressures are high.

MULTIDOMESTIC STRATEGY

Firms pursuing a multidomestic strategy orient themselves toward achieving maximum local responsiveness. The key distinguishing feature of multidomestic firms is that they extensively customize both their product offering and their marketing strategy to match different national conditions. Consistent with this, they also tend to establish a complete set of value creation activities, including production, marketing, and R&D, in each major national market in which they do business. As a consequence, they are generally unable to realize value from experience curve effects and location economies. Accordingly, many multidomestic firms have a high cost structure. They also tend to do a poor job of leveraging core competencies within the firm.

A multidomestic strategy makes most sense when there are high pressures for local responsiveness and low pressures for cost reductions. The high cost structure associated with the duplication of production facilities makes this strategy inappropriate in industries where cost pressures are intense. Another weakness associated with this strategy is that many multidomestic firms have developed into decentralized federations in which each national subsidiary functions in a largely autonomous manner.

MANAGEMENT FOCUS

IKEA

Established in the 1940s in Sweden by Ingvar Kamprad, IKEA has grown rapidly in recent years to become one of the world's largest retailers of home furnishings. In its initial push to expand globally, IKEA largely ignored the retailing rule that international success involves tailoring product lines closely to national tastes and preferences. Instead, IKEA stuck with the vision, articulated by founder Kamprad, that the company should sell a basic product range that is "typically Swedish" wherever it ventures in the world. The company also remained primarily production oriented; that is, the Swedish management and design group decided what it was going to sell and then presented it to the worldwide public—often with little research as to what the public actually wanted. The company also emphasized its Swedish roots in its international advertising, even insisting on a blue-and-gold colour scheme for its stores.

Despite breaking some key rules of international retailing, the formula of selling Swedish-designed products in the same manner everywhere seemed to work. Between 1974 and 2000, IKEA expanded from a company with ten stores, only one of which was outside Scandinavia, and annual revenues of $210 million to a group with 159 stores in 30 countries and sales of $8.6 billion. It now has 186 stores worldwide, in 34 countries, and growing. In 2003, IKEA sold over 12.37 billion euros (almost $20 billion Canadian) worth of goods. Almost 350 million customers visited its stores in 2003. There are now 11 stores in Canada. In 2003, Asia accounted for 3 percent of IKEA's sales, North America, 15 percent, and Europe, accounted for 82 percent.

The foundation of IKEA's success has been to offer consumers good value. IKEA's approach starts with a global network of suppliers, which now numbers 1960 firms in 53 countries. An IKEA supplier gains long-term contracts, technical advice, and leased equipment from the company. In return, IKEA demands an exclusive contract and low prices. IKEA's designers work closely with suppliers to build savings into the products from the outset by designing products that can be produced at a low cost. IKEA displays its enormous range of more than 10 000 products in cheap out-of-town stores. It sells most of its furniture as kits for customers to take home and assemble themselves. The firm reaps huge economies of scale from the size of each store and the big production runs made possible by selling the same products all over the world. This strategy allows IKEA to match its rivals on quality, while undercutting them by up to 30 percent on price and still maintaining a healthy after-tax return on sales of about 7 percent.

This strategy worked well until IKEA entered the North American market. Between 1985 and 1996, IKEA opened six stores in North America, but unlike the company's experience across Europe, the stores did not quickly become profitable. As early as 1990, it was clear that IKEA's North American operations were in trouble. Part of the problem was adverse movement in exchange rates. In 1985, the exchange rate was

This was exemplified by the failure of Philips NV to establish its V2000 VCR format as the standard in the industry during the late 1970s. Its U.S. subsidiary refused to adopt the V2000 format; instead, it bought VHS-format VCRs produced by Matsushita and put its own label on them!

GLOBAL STRATEGY

From a different perspective, the Country Focus on "Team Canada" provides a good example of one of the many types of tools available to Canadian companies seeking to expand internationally. This Government of Canada sponsored initiative has created jobs in Canada while connecting Canadian companies to many interesting international business opportunities.

Firms that pursue a global strategy focus on increasing profitability by reaping the cost reductions that come from experience curve effects and location economies. That is, they are pursuing a low cost strategy. The production, marketing, and R&D activities of firms pursuing a global strategy are concentrated in a few favourable locations.

US$1 = 8.6 Swedish kronor; by 1990 it was US$1 = SKr5.8. At this exchange rate, many products imported from Sweden did not look inexpensive to American consumers.

But there was more to IKEA's problems than adverse exchange rates. IKEA's unapologetically Swedish products, which had sold so well across Europe, jarred with American tastes and sometimes physiques. Swedish beds were narrow and measured in centimetres. IKEA did not sell the matching bedroom suites that Americans liked. Its kitchen cupboards were too narrow for large dinner plates. Its glasses were too small for a nation that added ice to everything. The drawers in IKEA's bedroom chests were too shallow for Canadian and American consumers, who tend to store sweaters in them. And the company made the mistake of selling European-size curtains that did not fit North American windows. As one senior IKEA manager joked later, "Americans just wouldn't lower their ceilings to fit our curtains."

By 1991, the company's top management realized that if it was going to succeed in North America, it would have to customize its product offering to North American tastes. The company set about redesigning its product range. The drawers on bedroom chests were designed to be 5 cm (2 inches) deeper, and sales immediately increased by 30 to 40 percent. IKEA now sells American-style king- and queen-size beds, measured in centimetres and inches, and it sells them as part of complete bedroom suites. It redesigned its kitchen furniture and kitchenware to better appeal to American tastes. The company also boosted the amount of products sourced locally from 15 percent in 1990 to 45 percent in 1997, which makes the company far less vulnerable to adverse exchange rate movements. By 2000, about one-third of IKEA's total product offerings were designed exclusively for the U.S. market.

This break with IKEA's traditional strategy seems to be paying off. Between 1990 and 1994, IKEA's North American sales tripled to $480 million, and they nearly doubled again to about $900 million in 1997 and reached $1.38 billion in 2000. Sales in North America have improved since 2000. The stores provide a complete shopping experience for consumers, including a restaurant with inexpensive meals, a children's play area, and complete feeding and changing stations for customers' infants. The company claims it has been making a profit in North America since early 1993, although it does not release precise figures and does admit that its profit rate is lower in America than in Europe. Still, the company is pushing ahead with plans for further expansions in North America, including a goal of opening 15 new stores between 2000 and 2005, which will bring its total to 35.

Sources: "Furnishing the World," *The Economist,* November 19, 1994, pp. 79–80; H. Carnegy, "Struggle to Save the Soul of IKEA," *Financial Times,* March 27, 1995, p. 12; J. Flynn and L. Bongiorno, "IKEA's New Game Plan," *Business Week,* October 6, 1997, pp. 99–102; and IKEA's website at www.ikea.com, www.franchisor.ikea.com/showContent.asp?swfld=facts1, and www.ikea.ca.

Global firms tend not to customize their product offering and marketing strategy to local conditions because customization raises costs (it involves shorter production runs and the duplication of functions). Instead, global firms prefer to market a standardized product worldwide so they can reap the maximum benefits from the economies of scale that underlie the experience curve. They may also use their cost advantage to support aggressive pricing in world markets.

This strategy makes most sense where there are strong pressures for cost reductions and where demands for local responsiveness are minimal. Increasingly, these conditions prevail in many industrial goods industries. In the semiconductor industry, for example, global standards have created enormous demands for standardized global products. Accordingly, firms such as Intel, Texas Instruments, and Motorola all pursue a global strategy. However, as we noted earlier, these conditions are not found in many consumer goods markets, where demands for local responsiveness remain high (e.g., processed food products). The strategy is inappropriate when demands for local responsiveness are high.

TRANSNATIONAL STRATEGY

Christopher Bartlett and Sumantra Ghoshal have argued that in today's environment, competitive conditions are so intense that to survive in the global marketplace, firms *must exploit experience-based cost economies and location economies, they must transfer core competencies within the firm, and they must do all of this while paying attention to pressures for local responsiveness.*[24] They note that in the modern multinational enterprise, core competencies do not just reside in the home country. Valuable skills can develop in any of the firm's worldwide operations. Thus, Bartlett and Ghoshal maintain that the flow of skills and product offerings should not be all one way, from home firm to foreign subsidiary, as in the case of firms pursuing an international strategy. Rather, the flow should also be from foreign subsidiary to home country, and from foreign subsidiary to foreign subsidiary—a process they refer to as **global learning.**[25] Bartlett and Ghoshal refer to the strategy pursued by firms that are trying to simultaneously create value in these different ways as a **transnational strategy.**

GLOBAL LEARNING The flow of skills and product offerings from foreign subsidiary to home country and from foreign subsidiary to foreign subsidiary.

TRANSNATIONAL STRATEGY Plan to exploit experience-based cost and location economies, transfer core competencies with the firm, and pay attention to local responsiveness.

A transnational strategy makes sense when a firm faces high pressures for cost reductions, high pressures for local responsiveness, and significant opportunities for leveraging valuable skills within a multinational's global network of operations. In some ways, firms that pursue a transnational strategy are trying to simultaneously achieve cost and differentiation advantages. In terms of the framework summarized in Figure 11.1, they are trying to simultaneously lower C and increase V. As attractive as this may sound, the strategy is not easy to pursue. Pressures for local responsiveness and cost reductions place conflicting demands on a firm. Being locally responsive raises costs. How can a firm effectively pursue a transnational strategy? Some clues can be derived from the case of Caterpillar. In the 1980s, the need to compete with low cost competitors such as Komatsu and Hitachi of Japan forced Caterpillar to look for greater cost economies. At the same time, variations in construction practices and government regulations across countries meant that Caterpillar had to remain responsive to local demands. Therefore, as illustrated in Figure 11.6, Caterpillar was confronted with significant pressures for cost reductions and for local responsiveness.

To deal with cost pressures, Caterpillar redesigned its products to use many identical components and invested in a few large-scale component-manufacturing facilities,

FIGURE 11.6

Cost Pressures and Pressures for Local Responsiveness Facing Caterpillar

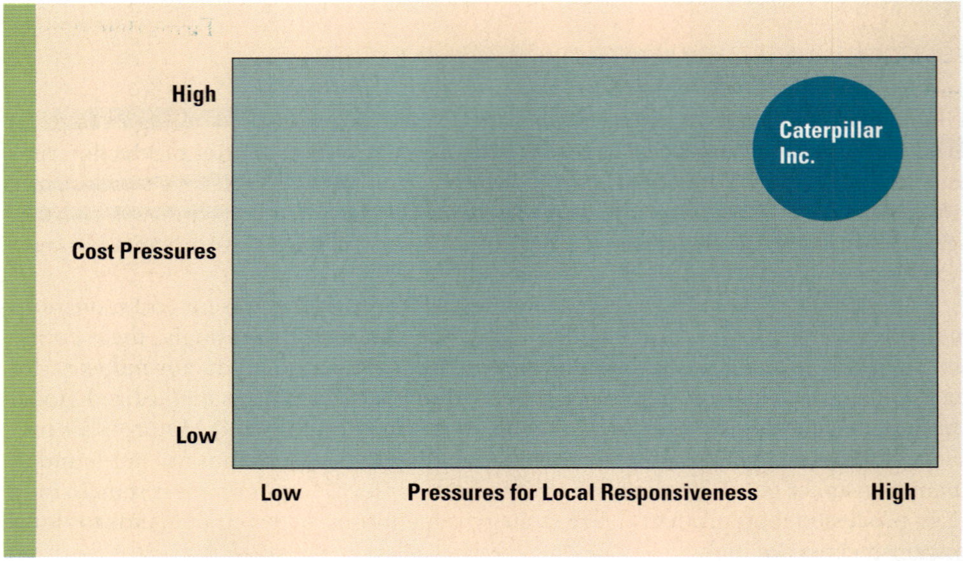

sited at favourable locations, to fill global demand and realize scale economics. The firm also augmented the centralized manufacturing of components with assembly plants in each of its major global markets. At these plants, Caterpillar added local product features, tailoring the finished product to local needs. By pursuing this strategy, Caterpillar realized many of the benefits of global manufacturing while also responding to pressures for local responsiveness by differentiating its product among national markets.[26] Caterpillar started to pursue this strategy in the early 1980s and by 1997 had doubled output per employee, significantly reducing its overall cost structure. Meanwhile, Komatsu and Hitachi, which are still wedded to a Japan-centric global strategy, have seen their cost advantages evaporate and have been steadily losing market share to Caterpillar.

Unilever, once a classic multidomestic firm, has had to shift toward more of a transnational strategy. A rise in competition that increased cost pressures forced Unilever to look for ways of rationalizing its detergent business. During the 1980s, Unilever had 17 largely self-contained detergent operations in Europe alone. The duplication of assets and marketing was enormous. Because Unilever was so fragmented, it could take as long as four years for the firm to introduce a new product across Europe. Now Unilever has integrated its European operations into a single entity, with detergents manufactured in a handful of cost-efficient plants, and standard packaging and advertising used across Europe. According to the firm, the result was an annual cost saving of more than $200 million. At the same time, due to national differences in distribution channels and brand awareness, Unilever recognizes that it must still remain locally responsive, even while it tries to realize economies from consolidating production and marketing at the optimal locations.[27] One might also argue that the MTV Networks shifted from an international to a transnational strategy in the 1990s (see the opening case). Rather than creating everything in the United States, MTV now tries to strike a balance between the need to maintain uniformity in operating principles and the "frenetic look" of MTV programming across its global operations and the need to customize programming and content to local tastes and preferences.

Bartlett and Ghoshal admit that building an organization that is capable of supporting a transnational strategic posture is complex and difficult. Simultaneously trying to achieve cost efficiencies, global learning (the leveraging of skills), and local responsiveness places contradictory demands on an organization. The organizational problems associated with pursuing what are essentially conflicting objectives constitute a major impediment to the pursuit of a transnational strategy. Firms that attempt to pursue a transnational strategy can become bogged down in an organizational morass that leads only to inefficiencies.

Also, Bartlett and Ghoshal may be overstating the case for the transnational strategy. They present the transnational strategy as the only viable strategy. While no one doubts that in some industries the firm that can adopt a transnational strategy will have a competitive advantage, in other industries, global, multidomestic, and international strategies remain viable. In the semiconductor industry, for example, pressures for local customization are minimal and competition is purely a cost game, in which case a global strategy, not a transnational strategy, is optimal. This is the case in many industrial goods markets where the product serves universal needs. On the other hand, the argument can be made that to compete in certain consumer goods markets, such as the automobile and consumer electronics industry, a firm has to try to adopt a transnational strategy.

SUMMARY

The advantages and disadvantages of each of the four strategies discussed above are summarized in Table 11.1. While a transnational strategy appears to offer the most

TABLE 11.1

The Advantages and Disadvantages of the Four Strategies

STRATEGY	ADVANTAGES	DISADVANTAGES
Global	Exploit experience curve effects Exploit location economies	Lack of local responsiveness
International	Transfer core competencies to foreign markets	Lack of local responsiveness Inability to realize location economies Failure to exploit experience curve effects
Multidomestic	Customize product offerings and marketing in accordance with local responsiveness	Inability to realize location economies Failure to exploit experience curve effects Failure to transfer core competencies to foreign markets
Transnational	Exploit experience curve effects Exploit location economies Customize product offerings and marketing in accordance with local responsiveness Reap benefits of global learning	Difficult to implement due to organizational problems

advantages, implementing a transnational strategy raises difficult organizational issues. As shown in Figure 11.5, the appropriateness of each strategy depends on the relative strength of pressures for cost reductions and for local responsiveness.

STRATEGIC ALLIANCES

STRATEGIC ALLIANCES Cooperative agreements between two or more firms.

Strategic alliances refer to cooperative agreements between potential or actual competitors. In this section, we are concerned specifically with strategic alliances between firms from different countries. Strategic alliances run the range from formal joint ventures, in which two or more firms have equity stakes (e.g., Fuji–Xerox), to short-term contractual agreements, in which two companies agree to cooperate on a particular task (such as developing a new product). Collaboration between competitors is fashionable; the 1980s and 1990s saw an explosion in the number of strategic alliances, and this seems to have continued into the new century.

THE ADVANTAGES OF STRATEGIC ALLIANCES

Firms ally themselves with actual or potential competitors for various strategic purposes.[28] First, as noted earlier in the chapter, strategic alliances may facilitate entry into a foreign market. For example, Cinram, a Toronto-based manufacturer of pre-recorded DVD, VHS videos, audio CDs, and CD-ROMs, found access to the lucrative European Union market. Up until 1995, Cinram had an established presence in Canada, the U.S., and Mexico. In 1995, the company took the steps to enter Europe. They purchased Duplication France, S.A., a leading French videocassette duplication company.

In 1997, Cinram continued to grow in Europe. Cinram purchased shares in the PolyGram Manufacturing and Distribution Centres B.V., which owned a manufacturing operation that produced music cassettes and VHS tapes in Amersfoort, The Netherlands. Cinram UK Limited, a subsidiary of Cinram, then forged an agreement with Sony Music Entertainment (UK) Limited of London, England, to acquire the manufacturing assets of Sony's UK videocassette operation facilities.

In 2004, Cinram purchased British multimedia distributor The Entertainment Network Ltd., known as TEN. A year earlier, the company acquired AOL Time Warner's CD and DVD manufacturing operations.[29]

Aside from growing through acquisitions, Cinram has also entered into strategic alliances. In the fall of 2004, Cinram signed an exclusive, multi-year agreement with Twentieth Century Fox Home Entertainment Inc. to manufacture and distribute DVDs and VHS videocassettes in the United Kingdom, Ireland, France, Germany, Austria and the Benelux. Earlier in that same year, the company signed a multi-year agreement with Metro-Goldwyn-Mayer Studios Inc. for DVD and VHS manufacturing and distribution in the United States and Canada.

Motorola initially found it very difficult to gain access to the Japanese cellular telephone market. In the mid-1980s, the firm complained loudly about formal and informal Japanese trade barriers. The turning point for Motorola came in 1987 when it allied itself with Toshiba to build microprocessors. As part of the deal, Toshiba provided Motorola with marketing help, including some of its best managers. This helped Motorola in the political game of securing government approval to enter the Japanese market and getting radio frequencies assigned for its mobile communications systems. Motorola no longer complains about Japan's trade barriers. Although privately the company admits they still exist, with Toshiba's help Motorola has become skilled at getting around them.[30]

Strategic alliances also allow firms to share the fixed costs (and associated risks) of developing new products or processes. Motorola's alliance with Toshiba also was partly motivated by a desire to share the high fixed costs of setting up an operation to manufacture microprocessors. The microprocessor business is so capital intensive–Motorola and Toshiba each contributed close to $1 billion to set up their facility–that few firms can afford the costs and risks by themselves. Similarly, an alliance between Boeing and a number of Japanese companies to build the 767 was motivated by Boeing's desire to share the estimated $2 billion investment required to develop the aircraft.

Third, an alliance is a way to bring together complementary skills and assets that neither company could easily develop on its own. An example is the alliance between France's Thomson and Japan's JVC to manufacture videocassette recorders. JVC and Thomson traded core competencies; Thomson needed product technology and manufacturing skills, while JVC needed to learn how to succeed in the fragmented European market. Both sides believed there was an equitable chance for gain. Similarly, AT&T struck a deal in 1990 with NEC Corporation of Japan to trade technological skills. AT&T gave NEC some of its computer-aided design technology, and NEC gave AT&T access to the technology underlying its advanced logic computer chips. Such trading of core competencies seems to underlie many of the most successful strategic alliances.

Fourth, it can make sense to form an alliance that will help the firm establish technological standards for the industry that will benefit the firm. For example, in 1992, Philips NV allied with its global competitor Matsushita to manufacture and market the digital compact cassette (DCC) system Philips had developed. This linking with Matsushita was expected to help Philips establish the DCC system as a new technological standard in the recording and consumer electronics industries. The issue was important because Sony had developed a competing "mini compact disc" technology that it hoped to establish as the new technical standard. Since the two technologies did very similar things, there was room for only one new standard. Philips saw its alliance with Matsushita as a tactic for winning the race.[31]

THE DISADVANTAGES OF STRATEGIC ALLIANCES

The advantages we have discussed can be very significant. Despite this, some commentators have criticized strategic alliances on the grounds that they give competitors a low-cost route to new technology and markets.[32] For example, Robert Reich and Eric Mankin argued that in the 1980s many strategic alliances between U.S. and Japanese firms were part of an implicit Japanese strategy to keep higher-paying, higher-value-added jobs in Japan while gaining the project engineering and production process skills that underlie the competitive success of many U.S. companies.[33] They argued that Japanese success in the machine tool and semiconductor industries was built on U.S. technology acquired through strategic alliances. And they argued that U.S. managers were aiding the Japanese in achieving their goals by entering alliances that channel new inventions to Japan and provide a U.S. sales and distribution network for the resulting products. Although such deals may generate short-term profits, Reich and Mankin argue, in the long run the result is to "hollow out" U.S. firms, leaving them with no competitive advantage in the global marketplace.

Reich and Mankin have a point. Alliances have risks. Unless a firm is careful, it can give away more than it receives. But there are so many examples of apparently successful alliances between firms–including alliances between U.S. and Japanese firms–that Reich and Mankin's position seems extreme. It is difficult to see how the Motorola–Toshiba alliance or the Fuji–Xerox alliance fit Reich and Mankin's thesis. In these cases, both partners seem to have gained from the alliance. Why do some alliances benefit both firms while others benefit one firm and hurt the other? The next section answers this question.

MAKING ALLIANCES WORK

The failure rate for international strategic alliances seems to be high. One study of 49 international strategic alliances found that two-thirds run into serious managerial and financial troubles within two years of their formation, and that although many of these problems are solved, 33 percent are ultimately rated as failures by the parties involved.[34] The success of an alliance seems to be a function of three main factors: partner selection, alliance structure, and the manner in which the alliance is managed.

PARTNER SELECTION

One key to making a strategic alliance work is to select the right ally. A good ally, or partner, has three characteristics. First, a good partner helps the firm achieve its strategic goals, whether they are market access, sharing the costs and risks of product development, or gaining access to critical core competencies. The partner must have capabilities that the firm lacks and that it values. Second, a good partner shares the firm's vision for the purpose of the alliance. If two firms approach an alliance with radically different agendas, the chances are great that the relationship will not be harmonious, will not flourish, and will end in divorce. Third, a good partner is unlikely to try to opportunistically exploit the alliance for its own ends; that is, to expropriate the firm's technological know-how while giving away little in return. In this respect, firms with reputations for "fair play" probably make the best allies. For example, IBM is involved in so many strategic alliances that it would not pay the company to trample over individual alliance partners. This would tarnish IBM's reputation of being a good ally and would make it more difficult for IBM to attract alliance partners. Since IBM attaches great importance to its alliances, it is unlikely to engage in the kind of opportunistic behaviour that Reich and Mankin highlight. Similarly, their reputations make it less likely (but by no means impossible) that such Japanese firms as Sony, Toshiba, and Fuji, which have histories of alliances with non-Japanese firms, would opportunistically exploit an alliance partner.

To select a partner with these three characteristics, a firm needs to conduct comprehensive research on potential alliance candidates. To increase the probability of selecting a good partner, the firm should:

1. Collect as much pertinent, publicly available information on potential allies as possible.

2. Collect data from informed third parties. These include firms that have had alliances with the potential partners, investment bankers who have had dealings with them, and former employees.
3. Get to know the potential partner as well as possible before committing to an alliance. This should include face-to-face meetings between senior managers (and perhaps middle-level managers) to ensure that the chemistry is right.

ALLIANCE STRUCTURE

Having selected a partner, the alliance should be structured so that the firm's risks of giving too much away to the partner are reduced to an acceptable level. Figure 11.7 depicts four safeguards against opportunism by alliance partners. (Opportunism includes the theft of technology and/or markets that Reich and Mankin describe.) First, alliances can be designed to make it difficult (if not impossible) to transfer technology not meant to be transferred. The design, development, manufacture, and service of a product manufactured by an alliance can be structured so as to wall off sensitive technologies to prevent their leakage to the other participant. In the alliance between General Electric and Snecma to build commercial aircraft engines, for example, GE reduced the risk of excess transfer by walling off certain sections of the production process. The modularization effectively cut off the transfer of what GE regarded as key competitive technology, while permitting Snecma access to final assembly. Similarly, in the alliance between Boeing and the Japanese to build the 767, Boeing walled off research, design, and marketing functions considered central to its competitive position, while allowing the Japanese to share in production technology. Boeing also walled off new technologies not required for 767 production.[35]

Second, contractual safeguards can be written into an alliance agreement to guard against the risk of opportunism by a partner. For example, TRW, Inc., has three strategic alliances with large Japanese auto component suppliers to produce seat belts, engine valves, and steering gears for sale to Japanese-owned auto assembly plants in the United States. TRW has clauses in each of its alliance contracts that bar the Japanese firms from competing with TRW to supply U.S.-owned auto companies with component parts. By doing this, TRW protects itself against the possibility that the Japanese companies are entering into the alliances merely to gain access to TRW's home market.

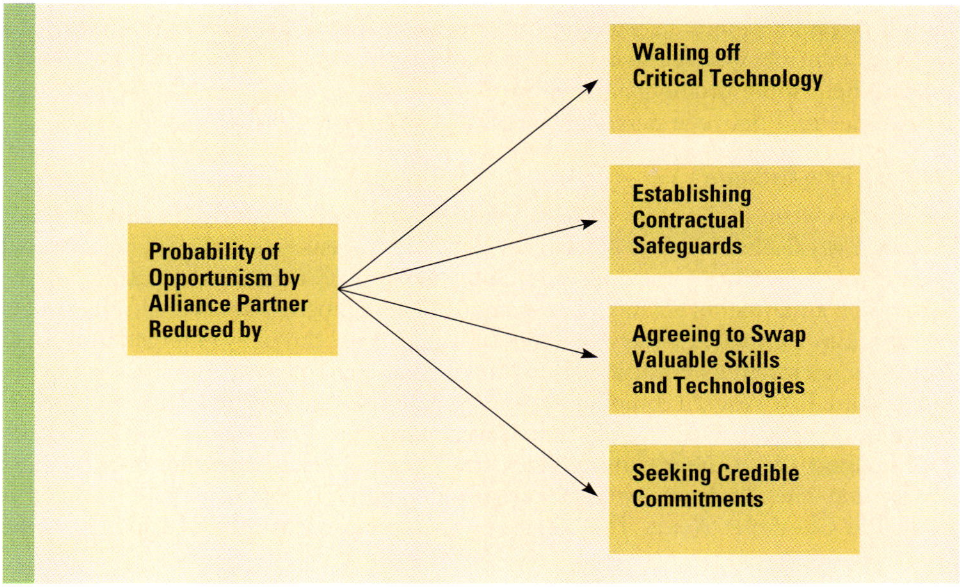

FIGURE 11.7
Structuring Alliances to Reduce Opportunism

Third, both parties to an alliance can agree in advance to swap skills and technologies that the other covets, thereby ensuring a chance for equitable gain. Cross-licensing agreements are one way to achieve this goal. For example, in the alliance between Motorola and Toshiba, Motorola has licensed some of its microprocessor technology to Toshiba, and in return, Toshiba has licensed some of its memory chip technology to Motorola.

Fourth, the risk of opportunism by an alliance partner can be reduced if the firm extracts a significant credible commitment from its partner in advance. The long-term alliance between Xerox and Fuji to build photocopiers for the Asian market perhaps best illustrates this. Rather than enter into an informal agreement or a licensing arrangement (which Fuji Photo initially wanted), Xerox insisted that Fuji invest in a 50/50 joint venture to serve Japan and East Asia. This venture constituted such a significant investment in people, equipment, and facilities that Fuji Photo was committed from the outset to making the alliance work in order to earn a return on its investment. By agreeing to the joint venture, Fuji essentially made a credible commitment to the alliance. Given this, Xerox felt secure in transferring its photocopier technology to Fuji.[36]

MANAGING THE ALLIANCE

Once a partner has been selected and an appropriate alliance structure has been agreed on, the task facing the firm is to maximize its benefits from the alliance. As in all international business deals, an important factor is sensitivity to cultural differences (see Chapter 3). Many differences in management style are attributable to cultural differences, and managers need to make allowances for these in dealing with their partner. Beyond this, maximizing the benefits from an alliance seems to involve building trust between partners and learning from partners.[37]

Building Trust

Managing an alliance successfully requires building interpersonal relationships between the firms' managers, or what is sometimes referred to as *relational capital*.[38] This is one lesson that can be drawn from the successful strategic alliance between Ford and Mazda. Ford and Mazda have set up a framework of meetings within which their managers not only discuss matters pertaining to the alliance but also have time to get to know each other better. The belief is that the resulting friendships help build trust and facilitate harmonious relations between the two firms. Personal relationships also foster an informal management network between the firms. This network can then be used to help solve problems arising in more formal contexts (such as in joint committee meetings between personnel from the two firms).

Learning from Partners

After a five-year study of 15 strategic alliances between major multinationals, Gary Hamel, Yves Doz, and C. K. Prahalad concluded that a major determinant of how much a company gains from an alliance is its ability to learn from its alliance partner.[39] They focused on a number of alliances between Japanese companies and Western (European or American) partners. In every case in which a Japanese company emerged from an alliance stronger than its Western partner, the Japanese company had made a greater effort to learn. Few Western companies studied seemed to want to learn from their Japanese partners. They tended to regard the alliance purely as a cost-sharing or risk-sharing device, rather than as an opportunity to learn how a potential competitor does business.

Consider the alliance between General Motors and Toyota constituted in 1985 to build the Chevrolet Nova. This alliance was structured as a formal joint venture, called New United Motor Manufacturing, Inc., and each party had a 50 percent equity stake. The venture owned an auto plant in Fremont, California. According to one Japanese manager, Toyota quickly achieved most of its objectives from the alliance: "We learned about U.S. supply and transportation. And we got the confidence to manage U.S. workers."[40] All that knowledge was then transferred to Georgetown, Kentucky, where Toyota opened its own plant in 1988. On the other hand, possibly all GM got was a new product, the Chevrolet Nova. Some GM managers complained that the knowledge they gained through the alliance with Toyota has never been put to good use inside GM. They believe they should have been kept together as a team to educate GM's engineers and workers about the Japanese system. Instead, they were dispersed to various GM subsidiaries.

To maximize the learning benefits of an alliance, a firm must try to learn from its partner and then apply the knowledge within its own organization. It has been suggested that all operating employees should be well briefed on the partner's strengths and weaknesses and should understand how acquiring particular skills will bolster their firm's competitive position. Hamel, Doz, and Prahalad note that this is already standard practice among Japanese companies. They made this observation:

> We accompanied a Japanese development engineer on a tour through a partner's factory. This engineer dutifully took notes on plant layout, the number of production stages, the rate at which the line was running, and the number of employees. He recorded all this despite the fact that he had no manufacturing responsibility in his own company, and that the alliance did not encompass joint manufacturing. Such dedication greatly enhances learning.[41]

For such learning to be of value, it must be diffused throughout the organization (as was seemingly not the case at GM after the GM–Toyota joint venture). To achieve this, the managers involved in the alliance should educate their colleagues about the skills of the alliance partner.

IMPLICATIONS FOR BUSINESS

There are many layers of business strategy required for succeeding. Corporate success hinges on efficiency; effectiveness; communication; management; technologies; strategy, goals and vision; people; operations management; finances; product or service, and more. When benchmarked against domestic and international competitors, the picture becomes clearer. Companies who adapt, innovate, and make sacrifices are more likely to survive and expand than those who do not. Take for example the case of Air Canada that has undergone a decade-long flirtation with bankruptcy. After making huge concessions and changes, which include employee wage reductions, it appears geared for a journey into the black.

INTERNATIONAL BUSINESS REQUIREMENTS

Many Canadian companies have made the tactical error of using Canadian marketing companies to lay the groundwork for foreign product launches. Failure to understand the strategic significance of speaking to foreign consumers from their culture base is a frequent recipe for disappointing results. For example, in spite of certain breweries' initiatives to market their beer to other countries, local tastes and loyalties to existing brands prevail. Foreign brewers have difficulty accessing this market, in spite of best efforts.

However, Molson Brewers went head to head with the Brazilian beer industry by acquiring the Bavaria Brewery of Brazil in 2000 and the Kaiser Breweries in 2002. Molson now brews more beer in Brazil than it makes in Canada.

KEY TERMS

core competence, p. 375

economies of scale, p. 373

experience curve, p. 372

global learning, p. 386

global web, p. 371

learning effects, p. 372

location economies, p. 371

profit, p. 366

profitability, p. 366

strategic alliances, p. 388

strategy, p. 365

transnational strategy, p. 386

value creation, p. 367

SUMMARY

In this chapter, we reviewed basic principles of strategy and the various ways in which firms can profit from global expansion, and we looked at the strategies that firms that compete globally can adopt. The following points have been made in this chapter:

1. A firm's strategy can be defined as the actions that managers take to attain the goals of the firm. For most firms, the preeminent goal is to maximize long-term profitability. Maximizing profitability requires firms to focus on value creation.
2. Due to national differences, it may pay a firm to base each value creation activity it performs at that location where factor conditions are most conducive to the performance of that activity. We refer to this strategy as focusing on the attainment of location economies.
3. By rapidly building sales volume for a standardized product, international expansion can assist a firm in moving down the experience curve.
4. International expansion may enable a firm to earn greater returns by transferring the skills and product offerings derived from its core competencies to markets where indigenous competitors lack those skills and product offerings.
5. A multinational firm can create additional value by identifying valuable skills created within its foreign subsidiaries and leveraging those skills within its global network of operations.
6. The best strategy for a firm to pursue often depends on a consideration of the pressures for cost reductions and for local responsiveness.
7. Pressures for cost reductions are greatest in industries producing commodity-type products where price is the main competitive weapon.
8. Pressures for local responsiveness arise from differences in consumer tastes and preferences, national infrastructure and traditional practices, distribution channels, and host-government demands.
9. Firms pursuing an international strategy transfer the skills and products derived from distinctive competencies to foreign markets, while undertaking some limited local customization.
10. Firms pursuing a multidomestic strategy customize their product offering, marketing strategy, and business strategy to national conditions.
11. Firms pursuing a global strategy focus on reaping the cost reductions that come from experience curve effects and location economies.
12. Many industries are now so competitive that firms must adopt a transnational strategy. This involves a simultaneous focus on reducing costs, transferring skills and products, and boosting local responsiveness. Implementing such a strategy may not be easy.
13. Strategic alliances are cooperative agreements between actual or potential competitors.
14. The advantage of alliances are that they facilitate entry into foreign markets, enable partners to share the fixed costs and risks associated with new products and processes, facilitate the transfer of complementary skills between companies, and help firms establish technical standards.
15. The disadvantage of a strategic alliance is that the firm risks giving away technological know-how and market access to its alliance partner in return for very little.

16. The disadvantages associated with alliances can be reduced if the firm selects partners carefully, paying close attention to the firm's reputation and the structure of the alliance so as to avoid unintended transfers of know-how.

17. Two keys to making alliances work seem to be building trust and informal communications networks between partners and taking proactive steps to learn from alliance partners.

CRITICAL THINKING AND DISCUSSION QUESTIONS

1. In a world of zero transportation costs, no trade barriers, and nontrivial differences between nations with regard to factor conditions, firms must expand internationally if they are to survive. Discuss.
2. Are the following global industries or multidomestic industries: bulk chemicals, pharmaceuticals, branded food products, moviemaking, television manufacturing, personal computers, airline travel?
3. Discuss how the need for control over foreign operations varies with the strategy and core competencies of a firm. What are the implications of this for the choice of entry mode?
4. What do you see as the main organizational problems likely to be associated with implementation of a transnational strategy?
5. A small Canadian firm that has developed some valuable new medical products using its unique biotechnology know-how is trying to decide how best to serve the European Community market. Its choices are:
   a. Manufacture the product at home and let foreign sales agents handle marketing.
   b. Manufacture the products at home and set up a wholly owned subsidiary in Europe to handle marketing.
   c. Enter into a strategic alliance with a large European pharmaceutical firm. The product would be manufactured in Europe by the 50/50 joint venture and marketed by the European firm.

   The cost of investment in manufacturing facilities will be a major one for the Canadian firm, but it is not outside its reach. If these are the firm's only options, which one would you advise it to choose? Why?

RESEARCH TASK | globalEDGE™ globaledge.msu.edu

Use the globalEDGE™ site to complete the following exercises:

1. Several classifications and rankings of multinational corporations are prepared by a variety of sources. Find one such ranking system and identify the criteria that are used in ranking the top global companies. Extract the list of the highest ranked 25 companies, paying particular attention to the home countries of the companies.
2. The top management of your company, a manufacturer and marketer of laptop computers, has decided to pursue international expansion opportunities in Eastern Europe. To achieve some economies of scale, your management is aiming toward a strategy of minimum local adaptation. Focusing on an Eastern European country of your choice, prepare an executive summary that features those aspects of the product where standardization will simply not work, and adaptation to local conditions will be essential.

Visit the *Global Business Today* Online Learning Centre at **www.mcgrawhill.ca/college/hill** to access quizzes, interactive exercises, a Business Around the World interactive map, and other learning and study tools related to this chapter.

CLOSING CASE

GENERAL MOTORS' GLOBAL STRATEGY INCLUDES CANADA

Incentive funding is nothing new when it comes to governments jockeying to attract big business and economic, job-creating machines. Governments vie to curry favour from big transnational corporations interested in manufacturing, researching, both of which are great employment boosters.

Governments in Canada are no different. In mid-2004, the General Motors Corporation of Canada entered into discussions with Ottawa and Ontario in which it tabled its strategy for further expansion within Canada if it received funding assistance from both the federal and Ontario governments. The stakes are high and so is the amount requested by GM if renovations to two assembly plants are to take place and R&D activities are to be increased. In these talks, the $2-billion price tag is what is required to move forward with these plans and Ottawa and Ontario's requested contributions have not yet proven to be a major stumbling block to discussions. GM asked both levels of government to contribute $400 million to the GM projects. These figures are guesstimates as the real numbers will remain hidden in veils of secrecy, until further along in the negotiations. However, by early 2004, Ontario had announced that it was creating a $500-million fund designed to attract new or replacement assembly plant investments. It did, however, stipulate that it intends to limit the amount it will provide to 10 percent of a project's total cost.

This welcome initiative is in contrast to much recently publicized Canadian automotive factory closures, shifting of operations, and investment flows to other countries. Nowadays, even job preservation makes the headlines. This cash influx would preserve thousands of well paid jobs at two GM car assembly plants in Oshawa, and create hundreds of new R&D jobs, as well as other layers of jobs in the auto parts sector and elsewhere.

Research has its benefactors and in this instance, the General Motors conglomerate is hinting at increasing its financing to the University of Windsor, in Windsor, Ontario, the automotive capital of Canada.

Canada has traditionally been seen to be low on the scale of R&D funding in industry and in academia and any sign of R&D funds, especially at the level of a possible GM inducement, would be a major score for R&D, particularly within the halls of academia. The lag in Canada's research and development initiatives can be attributed to Canada's branch plant economy that took shape after World War II whereby an increasing number of corporations operating in Canada were headquartered in the United States. Therefore, when R&D cost outlays by American firms were under consideration, the American firms would execute R&D measures at home, not in Canada.

The significance of this possible venture is not lost on the federal and Ontario governments. Instead of viewing this as a "loan," they see it as a partnership for the long term, aimed at creating stability in the automotive job market. The manufacturing side of the investment would target the automaker's two Oshawa car assembly plants that currently manufacture the Chevrolet Impala and Monte Carlo models as well as the Buick Regal and Century sedans. The possibilities being discussed range from the creation of an assembly line, which would be far more flexible and capable of dealing with market demands to the manufacture of rear wheel drive cars, and perhaps front wheel drive vehicles. Not to be unnoticed by the Motor City (Detroit), Oshawa has earned its stripes as a gem within GM factories scoring consistently high on quality and productivity studies.

These plans at the GM production facilities sight forward to 2007. The new capital (if approved) would mean that the two Oshawa facilities might run as many as two extra shifts per workday. These assembly plants employ 11 000 workers while the Regional Engineering Centre in Oshawa employs 300 engineers.

Hot on the tails of the GM–federal–Ontario government discussions is a similar request from the Ford Motor Company. Situated in Oakville, Ontario, Ford is seeking about $200 million for its facility in order to compete at a higher level.

Provincial and federal governments alike recognize the importance of the Canadian automotive industry as a mainstay of jobs, employment, and prosperity for southern Ontarians and Canadians as a whole. Ever since the 1965

Free Trade Auto pact created a North American market for Canadian produced vehicles, the importance in sustaining and expanding the automotive industry's presence within Canada has been a major strategy of all Canadian (and Ontario) governments in power since that time.

Partnership and strategic alliances abound in the world of business, and the Canadian automotive industry is yet another solid example of these vital business–government linkages.

Sources: CBC, "GM Expands in St. Catharines," at www.cbc.ca/story/business/national/2000/10/11/GM_engine001011.html.

CASE DISCUSSION QUESTIONS

1. How would you characterize the state of the automotive industry in Canada?
2. What do you think are the competitive effects of government involvement in the Canadian automotive industry?
3. How would you characterize this strategy used by GM in Canada, and what strategy do you think that GM might utilize internationally?

PART FIVE

5

COMPETING IN A GLOBAL MARKETPLACE

ING Group

ING Group was formed in 1991 from the merger between the third largest bank in the Netherlands and the country's largest insurance company. Since then, the company has grown rapidly to become one of the top ten financial services firms in the world, with operations in 65 countries and a wide range of products in banking, insurance, and asset management. ING's strategy has been to expand rapidly across national borders, primarily through a series of careful acquisitions. Its formula has been to pick a target that has good managers and a strong local presence, take a small stake in the company, win the trust of managers, and then propose a takeover. The management and products of the acquired companies have been left largely intact, but ING has required them to sell ING products alongside their own. ING's big push has been the selling of insurance, banking, and investment products, something it has been doing in Holland since the original 1991 merger (in Holland, some 20 percent of ING's insurance products are sold through banks).

Two changes in the regulatory environment have helped ING pursue this strategy. One has been a trend to remove regulatory barriers that traditionally kept different parts of the financial services industry separate. In the United States, for example, a Depression-era law known as the Glass Steagall Act forbid insurance companies, banks, and asset managers such as mutual fund companies from selling each other's products. The U.S. Congress repealed this act in 1999, opening the way for the consolidation of the U.S. financial services industry. Many other countries that had similar regulations removed them in the 1990s. ING's native Holland was one of the first countries to remove barriers between different areas of the financial services industry. ING took advantage of this to become a pioneer of banking and insurance combinations in Europe. Another significant regulatory development occurred in 1997 when the World Trade Organization struck a deal between its member nations that effectively removed barriers to cross-border investment in financial services. This made it much easier for a company such as ING to build a global financial services business.

Barry Iverson/Time Life Pictures/Getty Images.

CHAPTER 12

Entering Foreign Markets

OPENING CASE

ING's expansion was initially centred on Europe where its largest acquisitions have included banks in Germany and Belgium. However, in recent years, the centrepiece of ING's strategy has been its aggressive moves into the United States. While ING's Dutch insurance predecessor, Nationale-Nederlanden, had owned several small, regional U.S. insurance companies since the 1970s, the big push into the United States began with the 1997 acquisition of Equitable Life Insurance Company of Iowa. This was followed by the acquisitions of Furman Selz, a New York investment bank, whose activities complement those of Barings, a British-based investment bank with significant U.S. activities that ING acquired in 1995. In 2000, ING acquired ReliaStar Financial Services and the nonhealth insurance units of Aetna Financial Services. These acquisitions combined to make ING one of the top ten financial services companies in the United States.

ING was attracted to the United States by several factors. The United States is by far the world's largest financial services market, so any company aspiring to be a global player must have a significant presence there. Deregulation made ING's strategy of cross-selling financial service products feasible in the United States. Despite some state-by-state regulation of insurance, ING says it is easier to do business in America than in the European Union, where the patchwork of languages and cultures makes it difficult to build a pan-European business with a single identity. Another lure is that with more and more Americans responsible for managing their own retirement with 401k plans and the like rather than traditional pensions, the personal investment business in the United States is booming, which has increased ING's appetite for U.S. financial services firms. In contrast, pensions are still primarily administered by national governments in Europe. Furthermore, in recent years American insurance companies have traded at relatively low price-earnings ratios, making them seem like bargains compared to their European counterparts, which trade at higher valuations. Building a substantial U.S. presence also brings with it the benefits of geographic diversification, allowing ING to offset any revenue or profit shortfalls in one region with earnings elsewhere in the world.

Finally, ING has found it somewhat easier to make acquisitions in the United States than in Europe, where despite the rise of the European Union, national pride has made it difficult for ING to acquire local companies. ING's initial attempt to acquire a Belgium bank in 1992 was rebuffed, primarily due to nationalistic concerns, and it took ING until 1997 to make the acquisition. Similarly, a 1999 attempt to acquire a major French bank, Credit Commercial de France, in which it already held a 19 percent stake, was turned down. According to news reports, French regulators had expressed concerns over what would have been the first foreign acquisition of a French bank, and the board of CCF believed the acquisition should not proceed without the regulators' blessing.

Having established a major U.S. presence, ING's strategy now is to push forward with the cross-selling of its various insurance, banking, and asset management products. In mid-2000, the company announced the establishment of ING Direct, an online banking concept the company introduced in Canada, Australia, Spain, and France, where it has performed well. For example, ING Direct Canada began in 1997 and as of 2004 has grown to over 1 million customers and Cdn$14.5 billion in assets. Worldwide, ING Direct also continues to grow, most recently through the purchase of Zurich Insurance. Today it serves over 8 million customers. The online bank features a savings account that pays an interest rate about triple that found at traditional banks but in line with other virtual banks, which have a much lower cost structure. Although ING Direct does not offer chequing accounts, which are money losers for traditional banks, it can electronically link an ING account to chequing accounts that customers have at other banks, allowing them to easily transfer money. In addition to a savings account, ING Direct also offers consumer loans, mortgages, life insurance, and mutual funds. Instead of bank branches, the company is setting up a scattering of cyber-cafes where customers can drop in, buy a cup of coffee and a muffin, browse the Web, and access their online account.

Sources: J. Carreyrou, "Dutch Financial Giant Maps Its U.S. Invasion," *Wall Street Journal,* June 22, 2000, p. A17; J. B. Treaster, "ING Group Makes Its Move in Virtual Banking and Insurance," *New York Times,* August 26, 2000, p. C1; "The Lion's Friendly Approach," *The Economist,* December 18, 2000; and Canadian News Wire at www.cnw.ca/fr/releases/archive/July2004/22/c5191.html.

LEARNING OBJECTIVES

1. Explore the three basic decisions that a firm contemplating foreign expansion must make: which markets to enter, when to enter those markets, and on what scale.
2. Review the different modes that firms use to enter a foreign market.
3. Understand the advantages and disadvantages of each entry mode.
4. Appreciate the relationship between strategy and a firm's choice of entry mode.
5. Appreciate some pitfalls of exporting.
6. Be familiar with the steps a firm can take to improve its export performance.
7. Understand the mechanics of export and import financing.

INTRODUCTION

This chapter is concerned with two closely related topics: (1) the decision of which foreign markets to enter, when to enter them, and on what scale, and (2) the choice of entry mode. Any firm contemplating foreign expansion must first struggle with the issue of which foreign markets to enter and the timing and scale of entry. The choice of which markets to enter should be driven by an assessment of relative long-run growth and profit potential. The opening case reported ING's rapid expansion into the United States through several major acquisitions. This significant commitment on ING's part was made in response to an assessment that the U.S. financial services market was not only the world's largest, but also was growing rapidly. ING decided it needed to move with haste to build a U.S. presence in advance of slower moving competitors, thereby serving notice that it intended to be one of the top ten financial services companies in both the United States and the world. The timing of entry was also driven by deregulation, which changed the nature of the financial services industry in the United States, allowing insurance companies and banks to enter each other's markets. ING already had experience cross-selling in Europe, and it wanted to be among the first to exploit a similar opportunity in the United States.

The choice of mode for entering a foreign market is another major issue with which international businesses must wrestle. The various modes for serving foreign markets are exporting, licensing or franchising to host-country firms, establishing joint ventures with a host-country firm, setting up a new wholly owned subsidiary in a host country to serve its market, or acquiring an established enterprise in the host nation to serve that market. Each of these options has advantages and disadvantages. The magnitude of the advantages and disadvantages associated with each entry mode is determined by a number of factors, including transport costs, trade barriers, political risks, economic risks, costs, and firm strategy. The optimal entry mode varies by situation, depending on these factors. Thus, whereas some firms may best serve a given market by exporting, other firms may better serve the market by setting up a new wholly owned subsidiary or by acquiring an established enterprise. As we saw in the opening case, ING has primarily entered foreign markets through acquisitions of established players in those markets. ING wanted to be one of the first companies to take advantage of changes in the national regulatory environments that allowed insurance companies and banks to enter each other's markets. Acquisitions enabled the company to attain this goal more rapidly than establishing new ventures.

BASIC ENTRY DECISIONS

In this section, we look at three basic decisions that a firm contemplating foreign expansion must make: which markets to enter, when to enter those markets, and on what scale.[1]

WHICH FOREIGN MARKETS?

There are more than 180 nation-states in the world, but they do not all hold the same profit potential for a firm contemplating foreign expansion. Ultimately, the choice must be based on an assessment of a nation's long-run profit potential. This potential is a function of several factors, many of which we have already studied in earlier chapters. In Chapter 2, we looked in detail at the economic and political factors that influence the potential attractiveness of a foreign market. There we noted that the attractiveness of a country as a potential market for an international business depends on balancing the benefits, costs, and risks associated with doing business in that country.

Chapter 2 also noted that the long-run economic benefits of doing business in a country are a function of factors such as the size of the market (in terms of demographics), the present wealth (purchasing power) of consumers in that market, and the likely future wealth of consumers. While some markets are very large when measured by number of consumers (e.g., China and India), low living standards may imply limited purchasing power and a relatively small market when measured in economic terms. We also argued that the costs and risks associated with doing business in a foreign country are typically lower in economically advanced and politically stable democratic nations, and they are greater in less developed and politically unstable nations.

However, this calculus is complicated by the fact that the potential long-run benefits bear little relationship to a nation's current stage of economic development or political stability. Long-run benefits depend on likely future economic growth rates, and economic growth appears to be a function of a free market system and a country's capacity for growth (which may be greater in less developed nations). This leads to the conclusion that, other things being equal, the benefit–cost–risk trade-off is likely to be most favourable in politically stable developed and developing nations that have free market systems, and where there is not a dramatic upsurge in either inflation rates or private-sector debt. The trade-off is likely to be least favourable in politically unstable developing nations that operate with a mixed or command economy or in developing nations where speculative financial bubbles have led to excess borrowing (see Chapter 2 for further details).

By applying the reasoning processes alluded to above and discussed in more detail in Chapter 2, a firm can rank countries in terms of their attractiveness and long-run profit potential. Preference is then given to entering markets that rank highly. In the case of ING, its recent international ventures in the financial services business have been focused on Europe and North America (see the opening case). These regions have large financial services markets and exhibit relatively low political and economic risks, so it makes sense that they would be attractive to ING. The company should be able to capture a large enough share of the market in each country to justify its investment.

One other fact we have not yet discussed is the value an international business can create in a foreign market. This depends on the suitability of its product offering to that market and the nature of indigenous competition.[2] If the international business can offer a product that has not been widely available in that market and that satisfies an unmet need, the value of that product to consumers is likely to be much greater than if the international business simply offers the same type of product that indigenous competitors and other foreign entrants are already offering. Greater value translates into an ability to charge higher prices and/or to build sales volume more rapidly. Because ING already had substantial experience in cross-selling insurance and banking products in Holland, it was relatively well positioned to exploit the opportunities in the United States, where cross-selling had been limited by regulatory constraints until 1999.

TIMING OF ENTRY Entry is early when a firm enters a foreign market before other foreign firms and late when a firm enters after other international businesses have established themselves.

TIMING OF ENTRY

FIRST-MOVER ADVANTAGES Advantages accruing to the first to enter a market.

FIRST-MOVER DISADVANTAGES Disadvantages associated with entering a foreign market before other international businesses.

PIONEERING COSTS Costs an early entrant bears that later entrants avoid, such as the time and effort in learning the rules, failure due to ignorance, and the liability of being a foreigner.

Once attractive markets have been identified, it is important to consider the **timing of entry.** We say that entry is early when an international business enters a foreign market before other foreign firms and late when it enters after other international businesses have established themselves. The advantages frequently associated with entering a market early are commonly known as **first-mover advantages.**[3] One first-mover advantage is the ability to preempt rivals and capture demand by establishing a strong brand name. A second advantage is the ability to build sales volume in that country and ride down the experience curve ahead of rivals, giving the early entrant a cost advantage over later entrants. This cost advantage may enable the early entrant to cut prices below that of later entrants, thereby driving them out of the market. A third advantage is the ability of early entrants to create switching costs that tie customers into their products or services. Such switching costs make it difficult for later entrants to win business.

Entering a foreign market before other international businesses also has disadvantages. These are often referred to as **first-mover disadvantages.**[4] These disadvantages may give rise to pioneering costs. **Pioneering costs** are costs that an early entrant has to bear that a later entrant can avoid. Pioneering costs arise when the business system in a foreign country is so different from that in a firm's home market that the enterprise has to devote considerable effort, time, and expense to learning the rules of the game. Pioneering costs include the costs of business failure if the firm, due to its ignorance of the foreign environment, makes major mistakes. A certain liability is associated with being a foreigner, and this liability is greater for foreign firms that enter

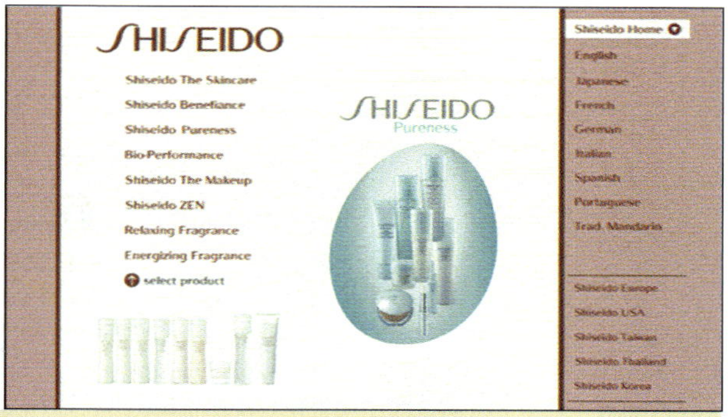

L'Oreal's 2003 sales amounted to 14 billion euro. It employs 50 500 worldwide and is number one in the worldwide sales of cosmetics. The Shiseido Group, including affiliates, employs approximately 24 500 people around the globe. Of the 5500 persons employed by Shiseido overseas, less than 2 percent are Japanese nationals demonstrating Shiseido's firm belief in and actualization of assimilation with the host country. Most of the sales for these two corporations emanate from outside their home-country operations (France for L'Oreal and Japan for Shiseido). Courtesy of L'Oreal. Courtesy of Shiseido.

a national market early.[5] Recent research seems to confirm that the probability of survival increases if an international business enters a national market after several other foreign firms have already done so.[6] The late entrant may benefit by observing and learning from the mistakes made by early entrants.

Pioneering costs also include the costs of promoting and establishing a product offering, including the costs of educating customers. These costs can be particularly significant when the product being promoted is unfamiliar to local consumers. In contrast, later entrants may be able to ride on an early entrant's investments in learning and customer education by watching how the early entrant proceeded in the market, by avoiding costly mistakes made by the early entrant, and by exploiting the market potential created by the early entrant's investments in customer education. For example, KFC introduced the Chinese to American-style fast food, but a later entrant, McDonald's, has capitalized on the market in China. See the accompanying Management Focus on entering foreign markets the Globalive way.

An early entrant may be at a severe disadvantage, relative to a later entrant, if regulations change in a way that diminishes the value of an early entrant's investments. This is a serious risk in many developing nations where the rules that govern business practices are still evolving. Early entrants can find themselves at a disadvantage if a subsequent change in regulations invalidates prior assumptions about the best business model for operating in that country.

SCALE OF ENTRY AND STRATEGIC COMMITMENTS

Another issue that an international business needs to consider when contemplating market entry is the scale of entry. Entering a market on a large scale involves the commitment of significant resources. For example, ING had to spend several billion dollars to acquire its U.S. operations. Not all firms have the resources necessary to enter on a large scale, and even some large firms prefer to

ANOTHER PERSPECTIVE

Ben and Jerry's French market entry cancellation

In the mid-1990s, Ben & Jerry's Homemade was still privately owned (it is now owned by Unilever) and was successful beyond the wildest dreams of its founders, who had not entered the international premium ice cream markets served by corporate-owned rival Haagen Dazs and various small, local competitors. But Ben & Jerry's new leader, Robert Holland, who had been recruited through a writing contest (his entry was an epic-length prose poem about corporate strategy development), planned to change that by entering France, the top gourmet market in Europe. A national-level distribution channel had been developed and product rollout was imminent. Then France decided to test a nuclear device in French territory in the South Pacific. That was it! France had gone too far; this was social responsibility at its worst for Messieurs Ben and Jerry. They nixed the market entry, despite incurring substantial losses. Holland decided to leave soon after. Ben & Jerry's also operates in Canada and has recently opened a store in Toronto.

MANAGEMENT FOCUS

ENTERING FOREIGN MARKETS THE GLOBALIVE WAY

When Tony Lacavera graduated from the University of Toronto School of Engineering in 1997, few people realized the stir he would create. Beginning with the kick off of his company in 1998, the Globalive group of companies has turned the Canadian telecommunications industry on its ear. In the June 2004 issue of *Profit Magazine*, Globalive ranked first among Canada's fastest growing companies.

Globalive takes new products and services, develops and adapts them through the innovative use of technology, and markets them throughout the world. The list of companies grown from the original company is impressive: Assemble Conferencing; One Connect (Internet-based phone service) to Freefone, Lucky Call, and Interclear. An open mind, hard work, and know-how, keep this business on a stellar growth pattern. Initially formed to service the hotel and hospitality industries, Globalive's scope of business has remained true to its core, while expanding and capturing market share on the international business stage.

In 1998, the company's revenues totalled $278,713 and by 2003, they had grown to $35,058,420. The company's initial focus was on business-to-business marketing. Through expansion of its proprietary technology, its scope of business has broadened to reach out to consumers.

Thinking outside the box works for president and CEO Tony Lacavera. His approach is "whatever works for the market, works for us." Without flexibility, there is little room for breakthroughs. Another strategy is to look for business that other larger companies might not necessarily want. Tony's philosophy to "go where the big guys aren't going" is paying off.

Where the Canadian tourist goes, Globalive is hot on their trail.

The company is present at major European airports from Charles de Gaulle to London's Heathrow Airport. Public phones are a part of the company's international initiative. These public phones lines invite tourists to make local calls. No detail is left uncovered. For example, separate contracts are in place with facilities' cleaning staff in various European locations to guarantee that the company's phone logos and phones will remain unblemished and clean.

Tony believes that through a network of workable joint venture and marketing solutions "various levels of granularity" can be achieved. Recognizing the decline in the North American payphone industry, Globalive has introduced "Freefones" in North America. As the world's first advertising driven courtesy phone, these strategically placed phones, increasingly visible within a growing number of Canadian and American airports, hotels and hospitals, succeed in capturing the attention of change strapped passersby in need of placing a local call.

enter foreign markets on a small scale and then build slowly as they become more familiar with the market.

STRATEGIC COMMITMENT A decision that has a long-term impact and is difficult to reverse, such as entering a foreign market on a large scale.

The consequences of entering on a significant scale are associated with the value of the resulting strategic commitments.[7] A **strategic commitment** has a long-term impact and is difficult to reverse. Deciding to enter a foreign market on a significant scale is a major strategic commitment. Strategic commitments, such as large-scale market entry, can have an important influence on the nature of competition in a market. For example, by entering the U.S. financial services market on a significant scale, ING has signalled its commitment to the market. This will have several effects. On the positive side, it will make it easier for the company to attract customers and distributors (such as insurance agents). The scale of entry gives both customers and distributors reasons for believing that ING will remain in the market for the long run. The scale of entry may also give other foreign institutions considering entry into the United States pause; now they will have to compete not only against indigenous institutions in the United States, but also against an aggressive and successful European institution. On the negative side, by committing itself heavily to the United States,

While talking, they receive digitally clear advertisements on the phone screens. True to Globalive's belief in making strategic alliances work, they teamed up with Bell Canada for the Canadian end of their Freefone strategy. Similar alliances already exist and are being developed with American telecommunications carriers.

Getting into foreign markets works best if the Canadian company works within the host country or region's norms, as different as they might be from the Canadian way. Getting the product to the markets as quickly as possible, through the right channels, and while it is hot, combine for a winning success strategy for Globalive. The South American model is similar to the North American model yet different from the Central American, European, and Asian models. In Argentina, Peru, Colombia and Venezuela, Globalive goes for the direct marketing channel method, utilizing existent phone carrier companies. In North America, particularly in the United States, some ventures, in addition to the direct marketing method, also have capital funding provided by large carriers. In Central America, where "pay in advance" is the norm, and where hierarchical chains of companies are established, a small co-investment with the hotel property, for example, can facilitate market penetration. In Asia, Globalive's business functions predominate through wholesale partners in the Philippines, Taiwan, Hong Kong, South Korea, and Vietnam. These wholesale partners concentrate on selling to hotel chains in the region.

Breaking into markets requires know-how and know-who, along with all the help that is available. One avenue for host country market research is the Trade Commissioners at Canadian embassies around the world who provide vital resource information and connections to Canadian companies expanding abroad. Other equally useful avenues that bolster Canadian firms going international include the Canadian International Development Agency (CIDA) and Export Development Canada. Globalive seeks out countries where host business practices are as compatible as possible with those in Canada. Once a market region is penetrated, the Globalive group of companies is there to stay and grow. Globalive has found an interesting and unlikely ally in using the United States embassy services, in the same manner it draws upon the expertise of the Canadian embassies around the world. Large parts of technology related business are made in the U.S.A. and the American embassies are more than happy to connect Globalive to the right places.

Globalive does what it takes to navigate the foreign markets and its plans for the upcoming years point to further innovation, leadership, and expansion.

Sources: Andy Holloway, "Master of All Niches," *Profit Magazine*, June 2004.

ING may have fewer resources available to support expansion in other desirable markets, such as Japan. The commitment to the United States limits the company's strategic flexibility.

As suggested by this example, significant strategic commitments are neither unambiguously good nor bad. Rather, they affect the competitive playing field and unleash a number of changes, some of which may be desirable and some of which will not be. It is important for a firm to think through the implications of large-scale entry into a market and act accordingly. Of particular relevance is trying to identify how actual and potential competitors might react to large-scale entry into a market. Also, the large-scale entrant is more likely than the small-scale entrant to be able to capture first-mover advantages associated with demand preemption, scale economies, and switching costs.

ANOTHER PERSPECTIVE

What's the market entry logic here?

Often the initial market entry decision is greatly influenced by culture. The assumption at work here is that the more similar the culture (and this means language often, too) the easier the entry and the more assured the results. We see companies based in Canada enter Australia and New Zealand while they ignore Mexico. Looking at rough population figures, Australia has about 19.7 million people; New Zealand, 3.9 million; and Mexico, 91 million. What do you think?

The value of the commitments that flow from large-scale entry into a foreign market must be balanced against the resulting risks and lack of flexibility associated with significant commitments. But strategic inflexibility can also have value. A famous example from military history illustrates the value of inflexibility. When Hernán Cortés landed in Mexico, he ordered his men to burn all but one of his ships. Cortés reasoned that by eliminating their only method of retreat, his men had no choice but to fight hard to win against the Aztecs–and ultimately they did.[8]

Balanced against the value and risks of the commitments associated with large-scale entry are the benefits of a small-scale entry. Small-scale entry allows a firm to learn about a foreign market while limiting the firm's exposure to that market. Small-scale entry is a way to gather information about a foreign market before deciding whether to enter on a significant scale and how best to enter. By giving the firm time to collect information, small-scale entry reduces the risks associated with a subsequent large-scale entry. But the lack of commitment associated with small-scale entry may make it more difficult for the small-scale entrant to build market share and to capture first-mover or early-mover advantages. The risk-averse firm that enters a foreign market on a small scale may limit its potential losses, but it may also miss the chance to capture first-mover advantages.

SUMMARY

There are no "right" decisions here, just decisions that are associated with different levels of risk and reward. Entering a large developing nation such as China or India before most other international businesses in the firm's industry, and entering on a large scale, will be associated with high levels of risk. In such cases, the liability of being foreign is increased by the absence of prior foreign entrants whose experience can be a useful guide. At the same time, the potential long-term rewards associated with such a strategy are great. The early large-scale entrant into a major developing nation may be able to capture significant first-mover advantages that will bolster its long-run position in that market.[9] In contrast, entering developed nations such as Australia or Canada after other international businesses in the firm's industry, and entering on a small scale to first learn more about those markets, will be associated with much lower levels of risk. However, the potential long-term rewards are also likely to be lower because the firm is essentially forgoing the opportunity to capture first-mover advantages and because the lack of commitment signalled by small-scale entry may limit its future growth potential.

This section has been written largely from the perspective of a business based in a developing country considering entry into foreign markets. In a recent article, Christopher Bartlett and Sumantra Ghoshal pointed out the ability that businesses based in developing nations have to enter foreign markets and become global players.[10] Although such firms tend to be late entrants into foreign markets, and although their resources may be limited, Bartlett and Ghoshal argue that such late movers can still succeed against well-established global competitors by pursuing appropriate strategies. In particular, Bartlett and Ghoshal argue that companies based in developing nations should benchmark their operations and performance against competing foreign multinationals. They suggest that the local company may be able to differentiate itself from a foreign multinational, for example, by focusing on market niches that the multinational ignores or is unable to serve effectively if it has a standardized global product offering. Having improved its performance through learning and differentiating its product offering, the firm from a developing nation may then be able to pursue its own international expansion strategy. Even though the firm may be a late entrant into many countries, by benchmarking and then differentiating itself from early movers in global markets, the firm from the developing nation may build a strong international business presence.

ENTRY MODES

Once a firm decides to enter a foreign market, the question arises as to the best mode of entry. Firms can use six different modes to enter foreign markets: exporting, turnkey projects, licensing, franchising, establishing joint ventures with a host-country firm, or setting up a new wholly owned subsidiary in the host country. Each entry mode has advantages and disadvantages. Managers need to consider these carefully when deciding which to use.[11]

EXPORTING

Many manufacturing firms begin their global expansion as exporters and later switch to another mode for serving a foreign market. We take a close look at the mechanics of exporting in the next chapter. Here we focus on the advantages and disadvantages of exporting as an entry mode.

Advantages

Exporting has two distinct advantages. First, it avoids the often-substantial costs of establishing manufacturing operations in the host country. Second, exporting may help a firm achieve experience curve and location economies (see Chapter 11). By manufacturing the product in a centralized location and exporting it to other national markets, the firm may realize substantial scale economies from its global sales volume. This is how Sony came to dominate the global TV market, how Matsushita came to dominate the VCR market, how many Japanese automakers made inroads into the U.S. market, and how South Korean firms such as Samsung gained market share in computer memory chips.

Disadvantages

Exporting has a number of drawbacks. First, exporting from the firm's home base may not be appropriate if there are lower-cost locations for manufacturing the product abroad (i.e., if the firm can realize location economies by moving production elsewhere). Thus, particularly for firms pursuing global or transnational strategies, it may be preferable to manufacture where the mix of factor conditions is most favourable from a value creation perspective and to export to the rest of the world from that location. This is not so much an argument against exporting as an argument against exporting from the firm's home country. Many U.S. electronics firms have moved some of their manufacturing to the Far East because of the availability of low-cost, highly skilled labour there. They then export from that location to the rest of the world, including the United States.

A second drawback to exporting is that high transport costs can make exporting uneconomical, particularly for bulk products. One way of getting around this is to manufacture bulk products regionally. This strategy enables the firm to realize some economies from large-scale production and at the same time to limit its transport costs. For example, many multinational chemical firms manufacture their products regionally, serving several countries from one facility.

Another drawback is that tariff barriers can make exporting uneconomical. Similarly, the threat of tariff barriers can make exporting very risky. An implicit threat by the U.S. Congress to impose tariffs on imported Japanese autos led many Japanese auto firms to set up manufacturing plants in the United States. By 1990, almost 50 percent of all Japanese cars sold in the United States were manufactured locally–up from none in 1985.

A fourth drawback to exporting arises when a firm delegates its marketing in each country where it does business to a local agent. (This is common for firms that are just beginning to export.) Foreign agents often carry the products of competing firms and so have divided loyalties. In such cases, the foreign agent may not do as good a job as the firm would if it managed its marketing itself. One way around this is to set up a wholly owned subsidiary in the country to handle local marketing. By doing this, the firm can exercise tight control over marketing in the country while reaping the cost advantages of manufacturing the product in a single location.

TURNKEY PROJECTS

TURNKEY PROJECT
A project in which a firm agrees to set up an operating plant for a foreign client and hand over the "key" when the plant is fully operational.

Firms that specialize in the design, construction, and start-up of turnkey plants are common in some industries. In a **turnkey project,** the contractor agrees to handle every detail of the project for a foreign client, including the training of operating personnel. At completion of the contract, the foreign client is handed the "key" to a plant that is ready for full operation–hence, the term *turnkey.* This is a means of exporting process technology to other countries. Turnkey projects are most common in the chemical, pharmaceutical, petroleum refining, and metal refining industries, all of which use complex, expensive production technologies.

Advantages

The know-how required to assemble and run a technologically complex process, such as refining petroleum or steel, is a valuable asset. Turnkey projects are a way of earning great economic returns from that asset. The strategy is particularly useful where FDI is limited by host-government regulations. For example, the governments of many oil-rich countries have set out to build their own petroleum refining industry, so they restrict FDI in their oil and refining sectors. But because many of these countries lacked petroleum refining technology, they gained it by entering into turnkey projects with foreign firms that had the technology. Such deals are often attractive to the selling firm because without them, the firm would have no way to earn a return on its valuable know-how in that country. A turnkey strategy can also be less risky than conventional FDI. In a country with unstable political and economic environments, a longer-term investment might expose the firm to unacceptable political and/or economic risks (e.g., the risk of nationalization or of economic collapse).

Disadvantages

Three main drawbacks are associated with a turnkey strategy. First, the firm that enters into a turnkey deal will have no long-term interest in the foreign country. This can be a disadvantage if that country subsequently proves to be a major market for the output of the process that has been exported. One way around this is to take a minority equity interest in the operation.

Second, the firm that enters into a turnkey project with a foreign enterprise may inadvertently create a competitor. For example, many of the Western firms that sold oil refining technology to firms in Saudi Arabia, Kuwait, and other Gulf states now find themselves competing with these firms in the world oil market. Third, if the firm's process technology is a source of competitive advantage, then selling this technology through a turnkey project is also selling competitive advantage to potential and/or actual competitors.

LICENSING

LICENSING AGREEMENT
Arrangement in which a licensor grants the rights to intangible property to the licensee for a specified period and receives a royalty fee in return.

A **licensing agreement** is an arrangement whereby a licensor grants the rights to intangible property to another entity (the licensee) for a specified period, and in return, the licensor receives a royalty fee from the licensee.[12] Intangible property includes patents, inventions, formulas, processes, designs, copyrights, and trademarks. For example, to enter the Japanese market, Xerox, inventor of the photocopier, established a joint venture with Fuji Photo that is known as Fuji–Xerox. Xerox then licensed its xerographic know-how to Fuji–Xerox. In return, Fuji–Xerox paid Xerox a royalty fee equal to 5 percent of the net sales revenue that Fuji–Xerox earned from the sales of photocopiers based on Xerox's patented know-how. In the Fuji–Xerox case, the licence was originally granted for ten years, and it has been renegotiated and extended several times since. The licensing agreement between Xerox and Fuji–Xerox also limited Fuji–Xerox's direct sales to the Asian Pacific region (although Fuji–Xerox does supply Xerox with photocopiers that are sold in North America under the Xerox label).[13]

Advantages

In the typical international licensing deal, the licensee puts up most of the capital necessary to get the overseas operation going. Thus, a primary advantage of licensing is that the firm does not have to bear the development costs and risks associated with opening a foreign market. Licensing is very attractive for firms lacking the capital to develop operations overseas. In addition, licensing can be attractive when a firm is unwilling to commit substantial financial resources to an unfamiliar or politically volatile foreign market. Licensing is also often used when a firm wishes to participate in a foreign market but is prohibited from doing so by barriers to investment. This was one of the original reasons for the formation of the Fuji–Xerox joint venture. Xerox wanted to participate in the Japanese market but was prohibited from setting up a wholly owned subsidiary by the Japanese government. So Xerox set up the joint venture with Fuji and then licensed its know-how to the joint venture.

Finally, licensing is frequently used when a firm possesses some intangible property that might have business applications, but it does not want to develop those applications itself. For example, Bell Laboratories at AT&T originally invented the transistor circuit in the 1950s, but AT&T decided it did not want to produce transistors, so it licensed the technology to a number of other companies, such as Texas Instruments. Similarly, Coca-Cola has licensed its famous trademark to clothing manufacturers, which have incorporated the design into their clothing.

Disadvantages

Licensing has three serious drawbacks. First, it does not give a firm the tight control over manufacturing, marketing, and strategy that is required for realizing experience curve and location economies (as global and transnational firms must do; see Chapter 11). Licensing typically involves each licensee setting up its own production operations. This severely limits the firm's ability to realize experience curve and location economies by producing its product in a centralized location. When these economies are important, licensing may not be the best way to expand overseas.

Second, competing in a global market may require a firm to coordinate strategic moves across countries by using profits earned in one country to support competitive attacks in another (see Chapter 11). Licensing limits a firm's ability to do this. A licensee is unlikely to allow a multinational firm to use its profits (beyond those due in the form of royalty payments) to support a different licensee operating in another country.

A third problem with licensing is one that we encountered in Chapter 7 when we reviewed the economic theory of FDI. This is the risk associated with licensing technological know-how to foreign companies. Technological know-how constitutes the basis of many multinational firms' competitive advantage. Most firms wish to maintain control over how their know-how is used, and a firm can quickly lose control over its technology by licensing it. Many firms have made the mistake of thinking they could maintain control within the framework of a licensing agreement. RCA Corporation, for example, once licensed its colour TV technology to Japanese firms including Matsushita and Sony. The Japanese firms quickly assimilated the technology, improved on it, and used it to enter the U.S. market. Now the Japanese firms have a bigger share of the U.S. market than the RCA brand.

CROSS-LICENSING AGREEMENT An arrangement in which a company licenses valuable intangible property to a foreign partner and receives a licence for the partner's valuable knowledge; reduces risk of licensing.

There are ways of reducing the risks of this occurring. One way is by entering into a **cross-licensing agreement** with a foreign firm. Under a cross-licensing agreement, a firm might license some valuable intangible property to a foreign partner, but in addition to a royalty payment, the firm might also request that the foreign partner license some of its valuable know-how to the firm. Such agreements are believed to reduce the risks associated with licensing technological know-how, since the licensee realizes that if it violates the licensing contract (by using the knowledge obtained to compete directly with the licensor), the licensor can do the same to it. Cross-licensing agreements enable firms to hold each other hostage, which reduces the probability that they will behave opportunistically toward each other.[14] Such cross-licensing agreements are increasingly common in high-technology industries. For example, the U.S. biotechnology firm Amgen has licensed one of its key drugs, Nuprogene, to Kirin, the Japanese pharmaceutical company. The licence gives Kirin the right to sell Nuprogene in Japan. In return, Amgen receives a royalty payment and, through a licensing agreement, gained the right to sell some of Kirin's products in the United States.

Another way of reducing the risk associated with licensing is to follow the Fuji–Xerox model and link an agreement to license know-how with the formation of a joint venture in which the licensor and licensee take important equity stakes. Such an approach aligns the interests of licensor and licensee, since both have a stake in ensuring that the venture is successful. Thus, the risk that Fuji Photo might appropriate Xerox's technological know-how, and then compete directly against Xerox in the global photocopier market, was reduced by the establishment of a joint venture in which both Xerox and Fuji Photo had an important stake.

FRANCHISING

FRANCHISING A specialized form of licensing in which the franchiser sells intangible property to the franchisee and insists on rules to conduct the business.

Franchising is similar to licensing, although franchising tends to involve longer-term commitments than licensing. **Franchising** is a specialized form of licensing in which the franchiser not only sells intangible property (normally a trademark) to the franchisee, but also insists that the franchisee agree to abide by strict rules as to how it does business. The franchiser will also often assist the franchisee to run the business on an ongoing basis. As with licensing, the franchiser typically receives a royalty payment, which amounts to some percentage of the franchisee's revenues. Whereas licensing is pursued primarily by manufacturing firms, franchising is employed primarily by service firms.[15] McDonald's is a good example of a firm that has grown by using a franchising strategy. McDonald's has strict rules as to how franchisees should operate a restaurant. These rules extend to control over the menu, cooking methods, staffing policies, and design and location of a restaurant. McDonald's also organizes the supply chain for its franchisees and provides management training and financial assistance.[16]

Boston Pizza has come a long way from its 1964 Edmonton foundation to become one of Canada's premier franchises combining both a sports bar and family restaurant under the same roof. Registered trademarks of Boston Pizza Royalties Limited Partnership, used under licence. © Boston Pizza International Inc. 2005.

Advantages

The advantages of franchising as an entry mode are very similar to those of licensing. The firm is relieved of many of the costs and risks of opening a foreign market on its own. Instead, the franchisee typically assumes those costs and risks. This creates a good incentive for the franchisee to build a profitable operation as quickly as possible. Thus, using a franchising strategy, a service firm can build a global presence quickly and at a relatively low cost and risk, as McDonald's has.

Disadvantages

The disadvantages are less pronounced than in the case of licensing. Since franchising is often used by service companies, there is no reason to consider the need for coordination of manufacturing to achieve experience curve and location economies. But franchising may inhibit the firm's ability to take profits out of one country to support competitive attacks in another.

A more significant disadvantage of franchising is quality control. The foundation of franchising arrangements is that the firm's brand name conveys a message to consumers about the quality of the firm's product. Thus, a business traveller checking in at a Hilton hotel in Hong Kong can reasonably expect the same quality of room, food, and service that she would receive in New York. The Hilton name is supposed to guarantee consistent product quality. This presents a problem in that foreign franchisees may not be as concerned about quality as they are supposed to be, and the result of poor quality can extend beyond lost sales in a particular foreign market to a decline in the firm's worldwide reputation. For example, if the business traveller has a bad experience at the Hilton in Hong Kong, she may never go to another Hilton hotel and may urge her colleagues to do likewise. The geographical distance of the firm from its foreign franchisees can make poor quality difficult to detect. In addition, the sheer numbers of franchisees–in the case of McDonald's, tens of thousands–can make quality control difficult. Due to these factors, quality problems may persist.

One way around this disadvantage is to set up a subsidiary in each country in which the firm expands. The subsidiary might be wholly owned by the company or a joint venture with a foreign company. The subsidiary assumes the rights and obligations to establish franchises throughout the particular country or region. McDonald's, for example, establishes a master franchisee in many countries. Typically, this master franchisee is a joint venture between McDonald's and a local firm. The proximity and the smaller number of franchises to oversee reduce the quality control challenge. In addition, because the subsidiary (or master franchisee) is at least partly owned by the firm, the firm can place its own managers in the subsidiary to help ensure that it is doing a good job of monitoring the franchises. This organizational arrangement has proven very satisfactory for McDonald's, KFC, Hilton Hotel Corp., Four Seasons Hotels and Resorts, and others.

ANOTHER PERSPECTIVE

Technology and knowledge transfer: a benefit and a danger

A joint venture is like a party where everyone brings something and takes something. In a joint venture located in a developing country, the company with the business brings knowledge about the business and its processes, while often the local partner brings knowledge about the market and long-standing relationships, along with personnel. In its early preparation for entry into South Korea, KFC (then known as Kentucky Fried Chicken) selected a joint-venture partner, began training the partner, and began to bring in its systems and layout, including the pressure-cooked process, special equipment, and the 11 herbs and spices, to share with its new Korean partner. Imagine the Americans' surprise when they found hundreds of Kentucky Fried Chicken stores already up and running in and around Seoul. They were tiny mom-and-pop shops, a result of a family's U.S. vacation, and although they didn't prepare chicken the same way or offer the same product line, they did confuse the public about the KFC concept for a while. Even today, you can find little Kentucky Fried Chicken stalls in the middle of Seoul.

A business traveller may have certain expectations about a hotel, or others in that hotel chain based on the impressions he or she gained from visits to other locations. Is this always valid? Can a customer checking into a Hilton in Hong Kong reasonably expect the same quality as a Hilton in Cleveland? Have you ever made reservations with a hotel chain in one city based on your favourable experiences with that chain in another city, only to find one inferior to the other you had visited? Mark Richards/PhotoEdit.

JOINT VENTURES

JOINT VENTURE A cooperative undertaking between two or more firms.

A **joint venture** entails establishing a firm that is jointly owned by two or more otherwise independent firms. Fuji–Xerox, for example, was set up as a joint venture between Xerox and Fuji Photo. Establishing a joint venture with a foreign firm has long been a popular mode for entering a new market. The most typical joint venture is a 50/50 arrangement in which there are two parties, each of which holds a 50 percent ownership stake (as is the case with the Fuji–Xerox joint venture) and contributes a team of managers to share operating control. Some firms, however, have sought joint ventures in which they have a majority share and thus tighter control.[17]

Advantages

Joint ventures have a number of advantages. First, a firm benefits from a local partner's knowledge of the host country's competitive conditions, culture, language, political systems, and business systems. Thus, for many U.S. firms, joint ventures have involved the U.S. company providing technological know-how and products and the local partner providing the marketing expertise and the local knowledge necessary for competing in that country. This was the case with the Fuji–Xerox joint venture. Second, when the development costs and/or risks of opening a foreign market are high, a firm might gain by sharing these costs and/or risks with a local partner. Third, in many countries, political considerations make joint ventures the only feasible entry mode. Again, this was a consideration in the establishment of the Fuji–Xerox venture. Research suggests joint ventures with local partners face a low risk of being subject to nationalization or other forms of adverse government interference.[18] This appears to be because local equity partners, who may have some influence on host-government policy, have a vested interest in speaking out against nationalization or government interference.

Disadvantages

Despite these advantages, there are major disadvantages with joint ventures. First, as with licensing, a firm that enters into a joint venture risks giving control of its technology to its partner. Thus, a proposed joint venture between Boeing and Mitsubishi Heavy Industries to build a new version of the 747, the 747-X, raised fears that Boeing might unwittingly give away its commercial airline technology to the Japanese. However, joint-venture agreements can be constructed to minimize this risk. One option is to hold majority ownership in the venture. This allows the dominant partner to exercise greater control over its technology. The drawback with this is that it can be difficult to find a foreign partner who is willing to settle for minority ownership. Another option is to "wall off" technology that is central to the core competence of the firm, while sharing other technology.

A second disadvantage is that a joint venture does not give a firm the tight control over subsidiaries that it might need to realize experience curve or location economies. Nor does it give a firm the tight control over a foreign subsidiary that it might need for engaging in coordinated global attacks against its rivals. Consider the entry of Texas Instruments (TI) into the Japanese semiconductor market. When TI established semiconductor facilities in Japan, it did so for the dual purpose of checking Japanese manufacturers' market share and limiting their cash available for invading TI's global market. In other words, TI was engaging in global strategic coordination. To implement this strategy, TI's subsidiary in Japan had to be prepared to take instructions from corporate headquarters regarding competitive strategy. The strategy also required the Japanese subsidiary to run at a loss if necessary. Few if any potential joint-venture partners would have been willing to accept such conditions because it would have necessitated a willingness to accept a negative return on investment. Thus, to implement this strategy, TI set up a wholly owned subsidiary in Japan.

A third disadvantage with joint ventures is that the shared ownership arrangement can lead to conflicts and battles for control between the investing firms if their goals and objectives change or if they take different views as to what the strategy should be. This has apparently not been a problem with the Fuji–Xerox joint venture. According to Tony Kobayashi, the former CEO of Fuji–Xerox, a primary reason is that both Xerox and Fuji Photo adopted an arm's-length relationship with Fuji–Xerox, giving the venture's management considerable freedom to determine its own strategy.[19] However, much research indicates that conflicts of interest over strategy and goals often arise in joint ventures. These conflicts tend to be greater when the venture is between firms of different nationalities, and they often end in the dissolution of the venture.[20] Such conflicts tend to be triggered by shifts in the relative bargaining power of venture partners. For example, in the case of ventures between a foreign firm and a local firm, as a foreign partner's knowledge about local market conditions increases, it depends less on the expertise of a local partner. This increases the bargaining power of the foreign partner and ultimately leads to conflicts over control of the venture's strategy and goals.[21]

WHOLLY OWNED SUBSIDIARIES

In a **wholly owned subsidiary,** the firm owns 100 percent of the stock. Establishing a wholly owned subsidiary in a foreign market can be done two ways. The firm can either set up a new operation in that country, often referred to as a green-field venture, or it can acquire an established firm in that host nation and use that firm to promote its products.[22] For example, as we saw in the opening case, ING's strategy for entering the U.S. market was to acquire established U.S. enterprises, rather than try to build an operation from the ground floor.

WHOLLY OWNED SUBSIDIARY A subsidiary in which the firm owns 100 percent of the stock.

Advantages

There are three clear advantages of wholly owned subsidiaries. First, when a firm's competitive advantage is based on technological competence, a wholly owned subsidiary will often be the preferred entry mode because it reduces the risk of losing control over that competence. (See Chapter 7 for more details.) Many high-tech firms prefer this entry mode for overseas expansion (e.g., firms in the semiconductor, electronics, and pharmaceutical industries). Second, a wholly owned subsidiary gives a firm tight control over operations in different countries. This is necessary for engaging in global strategic coordination (i.e., using profits from one country to support competitive attacks in another). Third, a wholly owned subsidiary may be required if a firm is trying to realize location and experience curve economies (as firms pursuing global and transnational strategies try to do). As we saw in Chapter 11, when cost pressures are intense, it may pay a firm to configure its value chain in such a way that the value added at each stage is maximized. Thus, a national subsidiary may specialize in manufacturing only part of the product line or certain components of the end product, exchanging parts and products with other subsidiaries in the firm's global system. Establishing such a global production system requires a high degree of control over the operations of each affiliate. The various operations must be prepared to accept centrally determined decisions as to how they will produce, how much they will produce, and how their output will be priced for transfer to the next operation. Since licensees or joint-venture partners are unlikely to accept such a subservient role, establishment of wholly owned subsidiaries may be necessary.

Disadvantages

Establishing a wholly owned subsidiary is generally the most costly method of serving a foreign market. Firms doing this must bear the full costs and risks of setting up overseas operations. The risks associated with learning to do business in a new culture are less if the firm acquires an established host-country enterprise. However, acquisitions raise additional problems, including those associated with trying to marry divergent corporate cultures. These problems may more than offset any benefits derived by acquiring an established operation. Because the choice between greenfield ventures and acquisition is such an important one, we shall discuss it in more detail later in the chapter.

SELECTING AN ENTRY MODE

As the preceding discussion demonstrated, advantages and disadvantages are associated with all the entry modes; they are summarized in Table 12.1. Due to these advantages and disadvantages, trade-offs are inevitable when selecting an entry mode. For example, when considering entry into an unfamiliar country with a track record for nationalizing foreign-owned enterprises, a firm might favour a joint venture with a local enterprise. Its rationale might be that the local partner will help it establish operations in an unfamiliar environment and will speak out against nationalization should the possibility arise. However, if the firm's core competence is based on proprietary technology, entering a joint venture might risk losing control of that technology to the joint-venture partner, in which case the strategy may seem unattractive. Despite the existence of such trade-offs, it is possible to make some generalizations about the optimal choice of entry mode.[23]

CORE COMPETENCIES AND ENTRY MODE

We saw in Chapter 11 that firms often expand internationally to earn greater returns from their core competencies, transferring the skills and products derived from their core competencies to foreign markets where indigenous competitors lack those skills. We say that such firms are pursuing an international strategy. The optimal entry mode for these firms depends to some degree on the nature of their core competencies. A distinction can be drawn between firms whose core competency is in technological know-how and those whose core competency is in management know-how.

Technological Know-How

As was observed in Chapter 7, if a firm's competitive advantage (its core competence) is based on control over proprietary technological know-how, licensing and joint-venture arrangements should be avoided if possible to minimize the risk of losing control over that technology. Thus, if a high-tech firm sets up operations in a foreign country to profit from a core competency in technological know-how, it will probably do so through a wholly owned subsidiary.

This rule should not be viewed as hard and fast, however. One exception is when a licensing or joint-venture arrangement can be structured so as to reduce the risks of a firm's technological knowledge being expropriated by licensees or joint-venture partners. We will see how this might be achieved later in the chapter when we examine the structuring of strategic alliances. Another exception exists when a firm perceives its technological advantage to be only transitory, when it expects rapid imitation of its core technology by competitors. In such cases, the firm might want to license its technology as rapidly as possible to foreign firms to gain global acceptance for its technology before the imitation occurs.[24] Such a strategy has some advantages. By licensing its technology to competitors, the firm may deter them from developing

TABLE 12.1

Advantages and Disadvantages of Entry Modes

ENTRY MODE	ADVANTAGES	DISADVANTAGES
Exporting	Ability to realize location and experience curve economies	High transport costs Trade barriers Problems with local marketing agents
Turnkey contracts	Ability to earn returns from process technology skills in countries where FDI is restricted	Creating efficient competitors Lack of long-term market presence
Licensing	Low development costs and risks	Lack of control over technology Inability to realize location and experience curve economies Inability to engage in global strategic coordination
Franchising	Low development costs and risks	Lack of control over quality Inability to engage in global strategic coordination
Joint ventures	Access to local partner's knowledge Sharing development costs and risks Politically acceptable	Lack of control over technology Inability to engage in global strategic coordination Inability to realize location and experience economies
Wholly owned subsidiaries	Protection of technology Ability to engage in global strategic coordination Ability to realize location and experience economies	High costs and risks

their own, possibly superior, technology. Further, by licensing its technology, the firm may establish its technology as the dominant design in the industry (as Matsushita did with its VHS format for VCRs). This may ensure a steady stream of royalty payments. However, the attractions of licensing are probably outweighed by the risks of losing control over technology, and thus licensing should be avoided.

Management Know-How

The competitive advantage of many service firms is based on management know-how (e.g., McDonald's). For such firms, the risk of losing control over the management skills to franchisees or joint-venture partners is not that great. These firms' valuable asset is their brand name, and brand names are generally well protected by international laws pertaining to trademarks. Given this, many of the issues arising in the case of technological know-how are of less concern here. As a result, many service firms favor a combination of franchising and subsidiaries to control the franchises within particular countries or regions. The subsidiaries may be wholly owned or joint ventures, but most service firms have found that joint ventures with local partners work best for the controlling subsidiaries. A joint venture is often politically more acceptable and brings a degree of local knowledge to the subsidiary.

PRESSURES FOR COST REDUCTIONS AND ENTRY MODE

The greater the pressures for cost reductions are, the more likely a firm will want to pursue some combination of exporting and wholly owned subsidiaries. By manufacturing in those locations where factor conditions are optimal and then exporting to the rest of the world, a firm may be able to realize substantial location and experience curve economies. The firm might then want to export the finished product to marketing subsidiaries based in various countries. These subsidiaries will typically be wholly owned and have the responsibility for overseeing distribution in their particular countries. Setting up wholly owned marketing subsidiaries is preferable to joint-venture arrangements and to using foreign marketing agents because it gives the firm the tight control over marketing that might be required for coordinating a globally dispersed value chain. It also gives the firm the ability to use the profits generated in one market to improve its competitive position in another market. In other words, firms pursuing global or transnational strategies tend to prefer establishing wholly owned subsidiaries. See the accompanying Country Focus on Bolivia and its concerns over privatization.

ESTABLISHING A WHOLLY OWNED SUBSIDIARY: GREEN-FIELD VENTURE OR ACQUISITION?

A firm can establish a wholly owned subsidiary in a country by building a subsidiary from the ground up, the so-called green-field strategy, or by acquiring an established enterprise in the target market. The volume of cross-border acquisitions has been growing at a rapid rate for two decades. Some 80 percent of the world's FDI flows is now in the form of mergers and acquisitions (see Chapter 7 for details).[25] The value of cross-border acquisitions grew at an average annual rate of 42 percent a year compounded between 1980 and 1999 and exceeded $2.3 trillion in 1999 when more than 24 000 cross-border acquisitions occurred. By the end of the 1990s, some 31 percent of all acquisitions worldwide were cross-border acquisitions.[26]

PROS AND CONS OF ACQUISITIONS

Benefits of Acquisitions

Acquisitions have three major points in their favour. First, they are quick to execute. By acquiring an established enterprise, a firm can rapidly build its presence in the target foreign market. ING's rapid rise in the U.S. financial services market was primarily due to a number of acquisitions (see the opening case). When the German automobile company Daimler-Benz decided it needed a bigger presence in the U.S. automobile market, it did not increase that presence by building new factories to serve the United States, a process that would have taken years. Instead, it acquired the number three U.S. automobile company, Chrysler, and merged the two operations to form DaimlerChrysler. When the Spanish telecommunications service provider Telefonica wanted to build a service presence in Latin America, it did so through a series of acquisitions, purchasing telecommunications companies in Brazil and Argentina. In all these cases, the acquiring firms made acquisitions because that was the quickest way to establish a sizeable presence in the target market.

Second, in many cases firms make acquisitions to preempt their competitors. The need for preemption is particularly great in markets that are rapidly globalizing, such as telecommunications, where a combination of deregulation within nations and liberalization of regulations governing cross-border foreign direct investment has made it much easier for enterprises to enter foreign markets through acquisitions. In such markets, there can be concentrated waves of acquisitions as firms race each other to attain global scale. In the telecommunications industry, for example, regulatory changes triggered what can be called a feeding frenzy, with firms entering each other's markets via acquisitions to establish a global presence. These acquisitions included the $60-billion purchase of Air Touch Communications in the United States by the British company Vodafone, which was the largest acquisition ever; the $13-billion acquisition of One 2 One in Britain by the German company Deutsche Telekom; and the $6.4-billion acquisition of Excel Communications in the United States by Teleglobe of Canada, all of which occurred in 1998 and 1999.[27] A similar wave of cross-border acquisitions occurred in the global automobile industry over the same time period, with Daimler acquiring Chrysler, Ford acquiring Volvo, and Renault acquiring Nissan.

COUNTRY FOCUS

WHAT PRIVATIZATION MEANS TO THE RESIDENTS OF BOLIVIA

La Paz, one of the highest major cities on earth with an estimated population of 1 million, is situated at an altitude of up to 4100 metres. Its high altitude means that fires are truly difficult to ignite. The same lack of incendiary possibilities cannot be said of the city-wide strife that flared in June 2005, in protest over the Bolivian government's pro-privatization stance.

The juggernaut of sweeping privatization landed on the doorstep of Bolivia with the enactment of the privatization law of 1992, which was implemented in three core "waves" of action. First, 50 percent-ownership of money-losing corporations (SOE or state-owned enterprises) were listed for sale while the state retained the other 50 percent-ownership. There were just over 30 of these corporations up for partial sale. Second, privatization would allow for an outright sake of 100 percent-ownership to private investors. Finally, the initiative was to rid the government of a further dozen corporations with total buyouts by the private sector. Despite studies that point to the fact that the Bolivian privatization initiative, first born in 1992, has been helpful in improving Bolivia's standard of living, there remain many dissenting voices.

Since its cessation from Spain in 1825, Bolivia's history is filled with foreign incursions into its territories, thus honing an acute sense of exploitation of the country's sovereignty by the outside world. First in a long line of incursions into Bolivia's sovereignty was a lengthy battle with Chile that began in the late 1870s. As a result of Bolivia's defeat, it lost access to the Pacific. In the 1930s, yet another territorial war erupted with Paraguay assuming territorial control over Bolivia's oil wealth in the southeast.

Since the 1950s, a series of endless coups have afflicted this very poor country. To this day, for example, Bolivia's demise of its Boliviano currency during the 1980s remains a world-class example of extreme inflation (up to 35 000 percent during some years). In terms of GDP growth rate for 2004, Bolivia's economy grew at a pace of 2.1 percent or in a ranking of 134th out of 184 economies showing positive economic growth. Still, many Bolivians earn only $1 per day.

It is clear that Bolivia is a poor country in need of a long-term social and economic vision with dramatically improved living standards. One of the many contentious issues surrounding this most recent outbreak of pandemonium in La Paz stems from the actions by citizens over the privatization of water agreement from the late 1990s. In this agreement, the privatizing parties agreed to make vast investments in improving the water supplies of neighbouring El Alto and the city of La Paz. As this initial privatization initiative was funded by the World Bank, and from the contract tendering stage until contract signature and beyond, the agreement has not lived up to its opening promise to inclusively allow for improved water for some 80 000 inhabitants. Sources and statistics vary, but the populist opinion disagrees with the "benefits" claimed by pro-privatization sources and claims that this "for the people" initiative is yet one more slap in the face for those Bolivians subjected to acute poverty.

In the new millennium, other irritants have continued. In 2003, Bolivians angered over the exploitation and exportation of Bolivian gas by foreign gas companies in order to keep North Americans warm, while people in the cold high altitudes were freezing without gas connections.

Other circumstances have exacerbated the over-riding anti-privatization protests. A regression to a state-controlled economy seems to be the direction sought by the public. In recognition of this, the pro-privatization government of Carlos Mesa recently stepped down. The anti-privatization movement is so strong that there is a vocal cry to enshrine ownership of natural gas and oil ownership into a new constitution. This has been accompanied by a strong dose of anti-Americanism, which may play well in Bolivia but not so well in the Washington corridors of international aid agencies.

It remains to be seen if interim President Eduardo Rodriguez and the surviving Congress can cultivate a more moderate intermediating tone between pro-privatization groups and nationalization groups. The real opposition (nationalization) party led by Evo Morales, who also rose to become the head of Bolivia's coco-growing association will merit attention if an election is in fact called to replace the interim Congress and President Eduardo Rodriguez. Only time will tell.

Sources: "Indepth: Bolivia, Land-locked and Struggling," CBC News Online, June 10, 2005, www.cbc.ca/news/background/bolivia/ ; Index Mundi GDP Growth Rates, www.indexmundi.com/g/r.aspx?c=bl&v=66 ; "Comments on the Revised Bolivian Poverty Reduction Strategy 2004-2007", 07/11/2003 *Eurodad*, www.eurodad.org/articles/default.aspx?id=506 ; Hayden, Tom "Bolivia's Indian Revolt, *Agence Global*, June 4, 2004, www.agenceglobal.com/article.asp?id=152 ; "Letter to the World Bank, Inter-American Development Bank, and KFW calling on them to stop promoting the privatization of water," Choike.org, April 5, 2005 www.choike.org/nuevo_eng/informes/2837.html; Ruiz-Mier, F; Garrón, M. B.; Machicado, C.G.; Capra, K. / Unidad de Analisis de Políticas Sociales y Económicas (UDAPE), Bolivia , 2002 "Management of privatized firms is the key to efficiency" 2002, www.eldis.org/static/DOC10704.htm .

Third, managers may believe acquisitions to be less risky than green-field ventures. When a firm makes an acquisition, it buys a set of assets that are producing a known revenue and profit stream. In contrast, the revenue and profit stream that a green-field venture might generate is uncertain because it does not yet exist. When a firm makes an acquisition in a foreign market, it not only acquires a set of tangible assets, such as factories, logistics systems, customer service systems, and so on, but it also acquires valuable intangible assets including a local brand name and managers' knowledge of the business environment. Such knowledge can reduce the risk of mistakes caused by ignorance of the national culture.

Despite the arguments for making acquisitions, acquisitions often produce disappointing results.[28] For example, a study by Mercer Management Consulting looked at 150 acquisitions worth more than $500 million each that were undertaken between January 1990 and July 1995.[29] The Mercer study concluded that 50 percent of these acquisitions ended up eroding, or substantially eroding, shareholder value, while another 33 percent created only marginal returns. Only 17 percent were judged to be successful. In a major study of the postacquisition performance of acquired companies, David Ravenscraft and Mike Scherer concluded that many good companies were acquired during this period and, on average, their profits and market shares declined following acquisition.[30] They also noted that a smaller but substantial subset of those good companies experienced traumatic difficulties, which ultimately led to their being sold by the acquiring company. Ravenscraft and Scherer's evidence suggests that many acquisitions destroy rather than create value. While most of this research has looked at domestic acquisitions, the findings probably also apply to cross-border acquisitions.[31]

Why Do Acquisitions Fail?

Acquisitions fail for several reasons. First, the acquiring firms often overpay for the assets of the acquired firm. The price of the target firm can get bid up if more than one firm is interested in its purchase, as is often the case. In addition, the management of the acquiring firm is often too optimistic about the value that can be created via an acquisition and is thus willing to pay a significant premium over a target firm's market capitalization. This is called the "hubris hypothesis" of why acquisitions fail. The hubris hypothesis postulates that top managers typically overestimate their ability to create value from an acquisition, primarily because they have an exaggerated sense of their own capabilities.[32] For example, Daimler paid $40 billion for Chrysler in 1998, a premium of 40 percent over the market value of Chrysler before the takeover bid. Daimler paid this much because it thought it could use Chrysler to help it grow market share in the United States. At the time, Daimler's management issued bold announcements about the "synergies" that would be created from combining the operations of the two companies. Executives believed they could attain greater scale economies from the global presence, take costs out of the German and American operations, and boost the profitability of the combined entity. However, within a year of the acquisition, Daimler's German management was faced with a crisis at Chrysler, which was suddenly losing money due to weak sales in the United States. In retrospect, Daimler's management had been far too optimistic about the potential for future demand in the U.S. auto market and about the opportunities for creating value from "synergies." Daimler acquired Chrysler at the end of a multi-year boom in U.S. auto sales and paid a large premium over Chrysler's market value just before demand slumped.[33]

Second, many acquisitions fail because there is a clash between the cultures of the acquiring and acquired firm. After an acquisition, many acquired companies experience high management turnover, possibly because their employees do not like the acquiring company's way of doing things.[34] This happened at DaimlerChrysler; many senior managers left Chrysler in the first year after the merger. Apparently, Chrysler executives disliked the dominance in decision making by Daimler's German managers, while the Germans resented that Chrysler's American managers were paid two to three times as much as their German counterparts. These cultural differences created tensions, which ultimately exhibited themselves in high management turnover at Chrysler.[35] The loss of management talent and expertise can materially harm the performance of the acquired unit.[36] This may be particularly problematic in an international business, where managers of the acquired unit may have valuable local knowledge that may be difficult to replace.

Third, many acquisitions fail because attempts to realize synergies by integrating the operations of the acquired and acquiring entities often run into roadblocks and take much longer than forecast. Differences in management philosophy and company culture can slow the integration of operations. These problems are likely to be exacerbated by differences in national culture. Bureaucratic haggling between managers also complicates the process. Again, this reportedly occurred at DaimlerChrysler, where grand plans to integrate the operations of the two companies were bogged down by endless committee meetings and by simple logistical considerations such as the six-hour time difference between Detroit and Germany. By the time an integration plan had been worked out, Chrysler was losing money, and Daimler's German managers suddenly had a crisis on their hands.

Finally, many acquisitions fail due to inadequate preacquisition screening.[37] Many firms decide to acquire other firms without thoroughly analyzing the potential benefits and costs. They often move with undue haste to execute the acquisition, perhaps because they fear another competitor may preempt them. After the acquisition, however, many acquiring firms discover that instead of buying a well-run business, they have purchased a troubled organization. This may be a particular problem in cross-border acquisitions because the acquiring firm may not fully understand the target firm's different national culture and business system.

Reducing the Risks of Failure

These problems can all be overcome if the firm is careful about its acquisition strategy.[38] Screening of the foreign enterprise to be acquired, including a detailed auditing of operations, financial position, and management culture, can help to make sure the firm (1) does not pay too much for the acquired unit, (2) does not uncover any nasty surprises after the acquisition, and (3) acquires a firm whose organization culture is not antagonistic to that of the acquiring enterprise. It is also important for the acquirer to allay any concerns that management in the acquired enterprise might have. The objective should be to reduce unwanted management attrition after the acquisition. Finally, managers must move rapidly after an acquisition to put an integration plan in place and to act on that plan. Some people in both the acquiring and acquired units will try to erect roadblocks to slow or stop any integration efforts, particularly when losses of employment or management power are involved, and managers should have a plan for dealing with such impediments before they arise.

PROS AND CONS OF GREEN-FIELD VENTURES

The big advantage of establishing a green-field venture in a foreign country is that it gives the firm a much greater ability to build the kind of subsidiary company that it wants. For example, it is much easier to build an organization culture from scratch than it is to change the culture of an acquired unit. Similarly, it is much easier to establish a set of operating routines in a new subsidiary than it is to convert the operating routines of an acquired unit. This is a very important advantage for many international businesses, where transferring products, competencies, skills, and know-how from the established operations of the firm to the new subsidiary are principal ways of creating value. For example, when McCain Foods Ltd., "the world leader of producing French fries," first ventured into the Chinese market in 1996, they did so by establishing a sales office for importing French fries and vegetables. In mature markets, where in developed countries demand for low-carbohydrate foods is the craze, McCain Foods are expanding aggressively into developing countries. McCain invested $43.3-million to construct a potato processing plant in the northeast city of Harbin, China in August 2004. Commercial production is scheduled for September 2005.

Whether to proceed or not with green-field investments in China proved to be a challenge for McCain. The New Brunswick-based company completed a six-year agronomy program to guarantee that the quality of Chinese potatoes would meet McCain's high standards. Potatoes need to be a specific size and shape to be processed at the McCain plant, and the levels of sugar and moisture must be consistent.

This intensive groundwork and research proved worthwhile in reaching an investment decision to build a processing plant in China. Fast-food outlets such as McDonald's and KFC are opening and McCain hopes to supply this growing market.[39]

Set against this significant advantage are the disadvantages of establishing a green-field venture. Green-field ventures are slower to establish. They are also risky. As with any new venture, a degree of uncertainty is associated with future revenue and profit prospects. However, if the firm has already been successful in other foreign markets and understands what it takes to do business in other countries, these risks may not be that great. For example, having already gained great knowledge about operating internationally, the risk to McDonald's of entering yet another country is probably not that great. Also, green-field ventures are less risky than acquisitions in the sense that there is less potential for unpleasant surprises. A final disadvantage is the possibility of being preempted by more aggressive global competitors, who enter via acquisitions and build a big market presence that limits the market potential for the green-field venture.

GREEN-FIELD VENTURE OR ACQUISITION?

The choice between acquisitions and green-field ventures is not an easy one to make. Both modes have their advantages and disadvantages. In general, the choice will depend on the circumstances confronting the firm. If the firm is seeking to enter a market where there are already well-established incumbent enterprises and where global competitors are also interested in establishing a presence, it may pay the firm to enter via an acquisition. In such circumstances, a green-field venture may be too slow to establish a sizeable presence. However, if the firm is going to make an acquisition, its management should be cognizant of the risks associated with acquisitions that were discussed earlier and consider these when determining which firms to purchase. It may be better to enter by the slower route of a green-field venture than to make a bad acquisition.

If the firm is considering entering a country where there are no incumbent competitors to be acquired, then a green-field venture may be the only mode. Even when incumbents exist, if the competitive advantage of the firm is based on the transfer of organizationally embedded competencies, skills, routines, and culture, it may still be preferable to enter via a green-field venture. Things such as skills and organizational culture, which are based on significant knowledge that is difficult to articulate and codify, are much easier to embed in a new venture than they are in an acquired entity, where the firm may have to overcome the established routines and culture of the acquired firm. Thus, as our earlier examples suggest, firms such as McDonald's and Lincoln Electric prefer to enter foreign markets by establishing green-field ventures.

IMPLICATIONS FOR BUSINESS

The means through which companies can enter foreign markets have been detailed in this chapter. Here is an example of how this can take place.

When expanding abroad to certain countries, one condition of establishing a subsidiary will frequently entail the relinquishment of majority ownership to a host firm in the host country. Developing countries have been known to use this strategy to ensure that they benefit from foreign corporations operating within their borders, and that some profits remain as residuals.

Much focus in international trade is shifting towards China, which in spite of its opportunities is fraught with risks. Companies use different export strategies, some by choice, while others by necessity. To access the Chinese market, certain methods of entry are more successful than are others. For example, Canadian companies might use export, contractual joint venture, equity joint venture, or wholly owned modes of entry into the Chinese market. As for export and contractual joint ventures, these would be used for Canadian-based technology or manufacturing processes developed and manufactured in Canada. Normally, there would be no upfront Canadian investment required, yet the Canadian company would be responsible for training the Chinese users and ensuring that the product would work in the Chinese environment. The pay back to the Canadian company might be drawn out over years. Canadian companies could use their Canadian-based salespeople who travel often to China, to market products to the Chinese customers. Canadian companies might also use Chinese-based distributors to market their products to China since Chinese-based distributors have better access to Chinese market information and able to deliver better services to Chinese customers. The primary advantage of the export strategy is its low initial cost, given it does not require any upfront capital investment. Because it could withdraw quickly if local market conditions change, it is a low risk strategy for the Canadian company.

CONTRACTUAL JOINT VENTURES

The Chinese government usually prefers to have foreign companies use equity joint ventures to enter its markets. In this way, the Chinese government could be assured that the foreign companies would bring along capital, technology and managerial expertise. Until recently, many Canadian companies avoided such joint ventures in China because of China's frequently shifting regulations and convertibility of its currency along with concerns over skilled labour and quality raw materials, as well as infrastructure problems.

Despite the inconveniences of using equity joint ventures, many Canadian companies have stated that they had considerably higher sales in China than have other companies using other means of investment. The entry mode that achieved the second highest sales level was Canadian-based salespersons, an export mode. The experience gained with new business relations has enabled Canadian companies to bridge the confidence gap. Many companies preferred to test the Chinese market through exporting.

Wholly owned foreign operations were not allowed before 1986. Only in 1992 did they receive an equal tax status. Yet in the day-to-day operations of their business, they are completely on their own to deal with problems concerning taxation, foreign exchange, labour, and management.

There is no magic formula for Canadian companies seeking to do business in China. Each company has its own needs, perceptions, and realities. Companies with limited resources and international business experience should normally consider starting with an export strategy such as Canadian-based salespersons. Then, they should gradually progress in the direction of equity joint ventures.

CRITICAL SUCCESS FACTOR ISSUES WHEN DOING BUSINESS IN CHINA AND BEYOND

All companies should be adequately prepared with knowing the playing field. Companies should exhibit aggressiveness and above all, a strong commitment to patience. A company is only as good as its people. Therefore, all companies planning to do business internationally should have quality people willing and able to build business relationships in accordance with host-country norms.

In China, good relationships and connections are paramount, and are known as guanxi. If a company is unwilling to be flexible, then it is not guaranteed success. China is a huge market with which to contend. See Table 12.2 for the challenges facing Canadian businesspeople when dealing in China.

TABLE 12.2

Common Problems and Solutions Regardless of Entry Mode

Source: Department of Foreign Affairs and International Trade Canada, 2004. Reproduced with the permission of Her Majesty the Queen in Right of Canada, represented by the Minister of Public Works and Government Services Canada, 2005.

AREAS OF MAIN CONCERN	EVALUATION	HOW DID THE COMPANY DEAL WITH IT?
Culture difference	Large but manageable	Companies had executives who were extremely fond of the Chinese culture. Hire local Chinese to bridge the gap.
Foreign exchange	Extremely important	Help the Chinese apply for Export Development Corporation funding.
Quality of local employees	Very important	High quality local employees are available. Higher pay to attract quality people.
Training needs for the Chinese	Extremely important	Written into the employment contract for the Chinese employees to get training in Canada. Very good motivational tool.
High cost of doing business in China	The cost is reasonable	Hiring as many local Chinese as possible to lower the cost.
Expatriates	Not critical	None of the operations required full-time expatriate to be stationed in China. Each company had an individual who spent about six months out of a year in China.
Finding connections to help navigate the system	Very important	Connections and local employees help to do it.

KEY TERMS

cross-licensing agreement, p. 410

first-mover advantages, p. 402

first-mover disadvantages, p. 402

franchising, p. 410

joint venture, p. 412

licensing agreement, p. 408

pioneering costs, p. 402

strategic commitment, p. 404

timing of entry, p. 402

turnkey project, p. 408

wholly owned subsidiary, p. 413

SUMMARY

This chapter has been concerned with two related topics: (1) the decision of which foreign markets to enter, when to enter them, and on what scale, and (2) the choice of entry mode. This chapter made the following points:

1. Basic entry decisions include identifying which markets to enter, when to enter those markets, and on what scale.
2. The most attractive foreign markets tend to be found in politically stable developed and developing nations that have free market systems and where there is not a dramatic upsurge in either inflation rates or private-sector debt.

3. There are several advantages associated with entering a national market early, before other international businesses have established themselves. These advantages must be balanced against the pioneering costs that early entrants often have to bear, including the greater risk of business failure.
4. Large-scale entry into a national market constitutes a major strategic commitment that is likely to change the nature of competition in that market and limit the entrant's future strategic flexibility. The firm needs to think through the implications of such commitments before embarking on a large-scale entry. Although making major strategic commitments can yield many benefits, risks also are associated with such a strategy.
5. There are six modes of entering a foreign market: exporting, creating turnkey projects, licensing, franchising, establishing joint ventures, and setting up wholly owned subsidiaries.
6. Exporting has the advantages of facilitating the realization of experience curve economies and of avoiding the costs of setting up manufacturing operations in another country. Disadvantages include high transport costs and trade barriers and problems with local marketing agents. The latter can be overcome if the firm sets up a wholly owned marketing subsidiary in the host country.
7. Turnkey projects allow firms to export their process know-how to countries where FDI might be prohibited, thereby enabling the firm to earn a greater return from this asset. The disadvantage is that the firm may inadvertently create efficient global competitors in the process.
8. The main advantage of licensing is that the licensee bears the costs and risks of opening a foreign market. Disadvantages include the risk of losing technological know-how to the licensee and a lack of tight control over licensees.
9. The main advantage of franchising is that the franchisee bears the costs and risks of opening a foreign market. Disadvantages centre on problems of quality control of distant franchisees.
10. Joint ventures have the advantages of sharing the costs and risks of opening a foreign market and of gaining local knowledge and political influence. Disadvantages include the risk of losing control over technology and a lack of tight control.
11. The advantages of wholly owned subsidiaries include tight control over technological know-how. The main disadvantage is that the firm must bear all the costs and risks of opening a foreign market.
12. The optimal choice of entry mode depends on the firm's strategy.
13. When technological know-how constitutes a firm's core competence, wholly owned subsidiaries are preferred, since they best control technology.
14. When management know-how constitutes a firm's core competence, foreign franchises controlled by joint ventures seem to be optimal. This gives the firm the cost and risk benefits associated with franchising, while enabling it to monitor and control franchisee quality effectively.
15. When the firm is pursuing a global or transnational strategy, the need for tight control over operations to realize location and experience curve economies suggests wholly owned subsidiaries are the best entry mode.
16. When establishing a wholly owned subsidiary in a country, a firm must decide whether to do so by building a subsidiary from the ground up, the so-called green-field venture strategy, or by acquiring an established enterprise in the target market.
17. Relative to green-field ventures, acquisitions are quick to execute, may enable a firm to preempt its global competitors, and involve buying a known revenue and profit stream.
18. Acquisitions may fail when the acquiring firm overpays for the target, when the culture of the acquiring and acquired firms clash, when there is a high level of management attrition after the acquisition, and when there is a failure to integrate the operations of the acquiring and acquired firm.
19. The big advantage of establishing a green-field venture in a foreign country is that it gives the firm a much greater ability to build the kind of subsidiary company that it wants. For example, it is much easier to build an organization culture from scratch than it is to change the culture of an acquired unit.

CRITICAL THINKING AND DISCUSSION QUESTIONS

1. Review the opening case. ING chose to enter the U.S. financial services market via acquisitions rather than green-field ventures. What do you think are the advantages to ING of doing this? What might the drawbacks be? Does this strategy make sense? Why?
2. Licensing proprietary technology to foreign competitors is the best way to give up a firm's competitive advantage. Discuss.

3. What kinds of companies stand to gain the most from entering into strategic alliances with potential competitors? Why?
4. Discuss how the need for control over foreign operations varies with firms' strategies and core competencies. What are the implications for the choice of entry mode?
5. A small Canadian firm that has developed some valuable new medical products using its unique biotechnology know-how is trying to decide how best to serve the European Community market. Its choices are:
   a. Manufacture the product at home and let foreign sales agents handle marketing.
   b. Manufacture the products at home and set up a wholly owned subsidiary in Europe to handle marketing.
   c. Enter into a joint venture with a large European pharmaceutical firm. The product would be manufactured in Europe by the 50/50 joint venture and marketed by the European firm.

   The cost of investment in manufacturing facilities will be a major one for the Canadian firm, but it is not outside its reach. If these are the firm's only options, which one would you advise it to choose? Why?

RESEARCH TASK | globalEDGE™ globaledge.msu.edu

Use the globalEDGE™ site to complete the following exercises:

1. *Entrepreneur* magazine annually publishes a list of its ranking of America's top 200 franchisers seeking international franchisees. Provide a list of the top ten companies that pursue franchising as a mode of international expansion. Study one of these companies in detail and provide a description of its business model, its international expansion pattern, what qualifications it looks for in its franchisees, and what type of support and training it provides.
2. The U.S. Commercial Service prepares reports, titled the Country Commercial Guide, for each country of interest to U.S. investors. Utilize the Country Commercial Guide for Brazil to gather information on this country. Imagine that your company is producing laptop computers and is considering entering this country. Select the most appropriate entry method, supporting your decision with the information collected from the commercial guide.

Visit the *Global Business Today* Online Learning Centre at **www.mcgrawhill.ca/college/hill** to access quizzes, interactive exercises, a Business Around the World interactive map, and other learning and study tools related to this chapter.

Online LearningCentre

CLOSING CASE

CANADIAN BANKS IN THE USA

After intense lobbying by Canadian banks claiming that mergers would enable them to become bigger and more competitive at home and abroad, they began turning their attention to the lucrative south of the border markets to make up for the lacklustre Canadian banking scene. In 1998, the Government of Canada made known its aversion to various bank merger proposals. In the 1990s, there were on and off plans to merge the TD Bank with the CIBC, the RBC with the BMO, for example. As banks deal with the finances of Canadians from all lifestyles, their operations come under scrutiny by the minister of Finance, as required by the Bank Act. The Competition Bureau of Canada announced in July 1998, that it would deliver its assessment of bank mergers talks to the minister of Finance.

Canadians are typically averse to banks becoming fewer and bigger as it is feared that corporate interests will be served at the expense of diminishing services and increasing fees to retail customers. The bank industry has been frustrated by the anti-merger sentiment, apparent in Canada, since the idea was first floated in a significant manner more than 20 years ago. The bank industry is big business in Canada and touches the lives of citizens on a daily basis. According to 2002 Canadian Banker's Association statistics, over 175 000 Canadians were employed full time within the banking industry while providing part-time jobs for almost 41 000 individuals and contract work for nearly 24 000. There are almost 240 000 people directly employed by the banking industry in Canada.

Political parties have been repeatedly reminded by Canadian voters to shelve any merger and acquisition plans within the Canadian banking system. In 1998, the Liberals were all too well reminded in the pre-1998 election period to avoid the banking merger issue. For the time being, Canadian banks are increasingly busy setting up shop in the lucrative American markets, and Chicago and surrounding municipalities are one of the prime benefactors of BMO group expansion policy. During 2001, the Bank of Montreal group in the U.S. first acquired Harris Bank in Chicago followed by acquisition of the Credit Suisse's U.S. discount brokerage, CSFBdirect online firm, soon solidifying the BMO's status as Canada's largest bank in the United States valued at $830 million. By its acquisition of CSFBdirect, it increased its U.S. client base by 50 percent in what is the bank's biggest acquisition since it first took over the Chicago-based Harris Bank and expanded the Bank of Montreal's operations beyond the U.S. Midwest retail market.

The Bank of Montreal has used this platform to extend its sphere of business further within the United States Midwest. Shortly after the Harris Bank–BMO merger, this new entity quickly began shopping for more Chicago area banks and acquired the First National Bank of Joliet in the Chicago area, the 13th U.S. acquisition by BMO Financial Group since 1999.

The Harris Bank has been busy and since this time, plans to acquire yet another Chicago based bank—New Lenox State Bank (NLSB) (subject to approval) at a cost of US$228.5 million (or approximately Cdn$306 million). This proposed merger will increase the BMO's Chicago area presence to a network of 163 banks. The acquisition of NLSB will increase Harris Bank's network to 163 branches, which includes Harris' pending acquisition of Lakeland Community Bank, and over 450 ABMs throughout the greater Chicago area.

Other banks are responding to Canada's restrictive anti-bank merger sentiments by expanding south of the border. The Royal Bank of Canada is finding very green pastures in the southeastern states of Atlanta and Florida. It has every intent of continuing its expansion in this area and in 2004, the RBC opened about 30 branches in these markets. Another 20 to 30 branches are planned for 2005. It, like the BMO, has chosen its geographic area for expansion, even if both have a muted presence in other parts of the U.S.

Indicators and reports in 2004 still only attribute a marginal chance of Canadian bank mergers being allowed to happen over the next few years. Beyond Canada's borders bank merger activity is increasing at a dizzying pace, and the size of foreign banks in comparison to Canada's is staggering. It remains to be seen if and how Canada's stance on bank mergers influences its banking industry.

Sources: SNL at www.snl.com/bank/archive/20031110.asp; CRIC Information, "Quick Guide: Bank Mergers," www.cric.ca/en_html/guide/bank_mergers/bank_mergers.html; G. Berube, "Banks Need To Make Their Case," *CA Magazine*, June/July 2004, www.camagazine.com/index.cfm/ci_id/21540/la_id/1.htm; CBC at www.cba.ca/en/ViewDocument.asp?fl=6&sl=111&tl=&docid=420.

CASE DISCUSSION QUESTIONS

1. Given the increasing tendency towards bank mergers in today's world, and Canada's reticence to authorize them, does it make sense for Canadian banks to expand abroad?
2. What factors make Chicago and the southeastern U.S. so attractive for the BMO and the RBC, respectively?
3. Review the BMO's moves on Chicago, bearing in mind the timing and the scale of the entry along with the strategic commitments the BMO has made in the American Midwest? What are the potential benefits to the BMO? Apply the same principles to the RBC's expansion into the southeastern U.S.

PART FIVE

5

COMPETING IN A GLOBAL MARKETPLACE

Megahertz Communications

Established in 1982, U.K.-based Megahertz Communications is one of Great Britain's leading independent broadcasting system builders. The company's core skill is in the design, manufacture, and installation of TV and radio broadcast systems, including outside broadcast and news-gathering vehicles with satellite links. In 1998, Megahertz's managing director, Ashley Coles, set up a subsidiary company, Megahertz International, to sell products to the Middle East, Africa, and Eastern Europe.

While the EU market for media and broadcasting is both mature and well served by large established companies, the Middle East, Africa, and Eastern Europe are growth markets for media and broadcasting with significant long-term potential. They also were not well served by other companies, and all three lacked an adequate supply of local broadcast engineers.

Megahertz International's export strategy was simple. The company aimed to provide a turnkey solution to emerging broadcast and media entities in Africa, the Middle East, and Eastern Europe, offering to custom design, manufacture, install, and test broadcasting systems. To gain access to customers, Megahertz hired salespeople with significant experience in these regions and opened a foreign sales office in Italy. Megahertz also exhibited at a number of conferences that focused on the targeted regions, sent mailings and email messages to local broadcasters, and set up a Web page, which drew a number of international inquiries.

The response was swift. By early 2000, Megahertz had already been involved in projects in Namibia, Oman, Romania, Russia, Nigeria, Poland, South Africa, Iceland, and Ethiopia. The international operations had expanded to a staff of 75 and were generating £10 million annually. The average order size was about £250,000, and the largest £500,000. In recognition of the company's success, in January 2000 the British government picked Megahertz to receive a Small Business Export Award.

RF/Corbis.

CHAPTER 13

Exporting, Importing, and Countertrade

OPENING CASE

Despite the company's early success, however, it has not all been smooth sailing. According to Coles, preshipment financing has been a major headache. Coles describes his working life as a juggling act, with as much as 20 percent of his time spent chasing money. Due to financing problems, one week Megahertz can have next to nothing in the bank; the next it may have £300,000. The main problem is getting money to finance an order. Megahertz needs working capital to finance the purchase of component parts that go into the systems it builds for customers. The company has found that banks are very cautious, particularly when they hear that the customers are in Africa or Eastern Europe. The banks worry that Megahertz may not get paid on time, or at all, or that currency fluctuations may reduce the value of payments to Megahertz. Even when Megahertz has a letter of credit from the customer's bank and export insurance documentation, many lenders still see the risks as too great and decline to lend bridging funds to Megahertz. As a partial solution, Megahertz has turned to lending companies that specialize in financing international trade, but many of these companies charge interest rates significantly greater than those charged by banks, thereby squeezing Megahertz's profit margins.

Coles hopes these financing problems are temporary. Once Megahertz establishes a more sustained cash flow from its international operations, and once banks better appreciate the ability of Coles and his team to secure payment from foreign customers, he hopes that they will become more amenable to lending capital to Megahertz at rates that will help to protect the company's profit margins.

Source: www.megahertz.co.uk, and W. Smith, "Today Batley, Tomorrow the World?" *Director,* January 2000, pp. 42–49.

LEARNING OBJECTIVES

1. Understand the opportunities and risks associated with exporting.
2. Become familiar with the different steps companies can take to improve their export performance.
3. Learn about the information sources and municipal, provincial, and federal government programs that exist to support Canadian exporters.
4. Understand the basic steps involved in financing exporting.
5. Learn how countertrade can be used to facilitate exporting.

INTRODUCTION

In the previous chapter, we reviewed exporting from a strategic perspective. We considered exporting as just one of a range of strategic options for profiting from international expansion. This chapter is more concerned with the nuts and bolts of exporting (and importing). We take the choice of strategy as a given and look at how to export.

As we can see from the opening case, exporting is not just for large enterprises; many small firms such as Megahertz Communications have benefited significantly from the moneymaking opportunities of exporting. In the United States, for example, nearly 97 percent of firms that export are small businesses, and their share of total U.S. exports grew steadily over the last decade to reach 31 percent by the beginning of the new millennium.[1] The situation is similar in several other nations. In Germany, for example, companies with fewer than 500 employees account for about 30 percent of that nation's exports.[2]

The volume of export activity in the world economy is increasing as exporting has become easier. The gradual decline in trade barriers under the umbrella of GATT and now the WTO (see Chapter 6) along with regional economic agreements such as the European Union and the North American Free Trade Agreement (see Chapter 8) have significantly increased export opportunities. At the same time, modern communication and transportation technologies have alleviated the logistical problems associated with exporting. Firms are increasingly using fax machines, the World Wide Web, toll-free telephone numbers, and international air express services to reduce the costs of exporting. Consequently, it is no longer unusual to find small companies such as Megahertz Communications that are thriving as exporters.

Nevertheless, as the opening case illustrates, exporting remains a challenge for many firms. Smaller enterprises can find the process intimidating. The firm wishing to export must identify foreign market opportunities, avoid a host of unanticipated problems often associated with doing business in a foreign market, familiarize itself with the mechanics of export and import financing (a problem that Megahertz Communications has had to grapple with), learn where it can get financing and export credit insurance, and learn how it should deal with foreign exchange risk. The process is made more problematic by currencies that are not freely convertible. As a result, there is the problem of arranging payment for exports to countries with weak currencies. This brings us to the complex topic of countertrade, by which payment for exports is received in goods and services rather than money. In this chapter, we will discuss all these issues with the exception of foreign exchange risk, which was covered in Chapter 9. We open the chapter by considering the promise and pitfalls of exporting.

THE PROMISE AND PITFALLS OF EXPORTING

The great promise of exporting is that large revenue and profit opportunities are to be found in foreign markets for most firms in most industries. This was true for Megahertz

Communications, profiled in the opening case. The international market is normally so much larger than the firm's domestic market that exporting is nearly always a way to increase a company's revenue and profit base.

Studies have shown that while many large firms tend to be proactive about seeking opportunities for profitable exporting, systematically scanning foreign markets to see where the opportunities lie for leveraging their technology, products, and marketing skills in foreign countries, many medium-size and small firms are very reactive.[3] Typically, such reactive firms do not even consider exporting until their domestic market is saturated and the emergence of excess productive capacity at home forces them to look for growth opportunities in foreign markets. Also, many small and medium-size firms tend to wait for the world to come to them, rather than going out into the world to seek opportunities. Even when the world does come to them, they may not respond. An example is MMO Music Group, which makes sing-along tapes for karaoke machines. Foreign sales accounted for about 15 percent of MMO's revenues of $8 million in the mid-1990s, but the firm's CEO admits that this figure would probably have been much higher had he paid attention to building international sales during the 1980s and early 1990s. At that time, unanswered faxes and phone messages from Asia and Europe piled up while he was trying to manage the burgeoning domestic side of the business. By the time MMO turned its attention to foreign markets, other competitors had stepped in and MMO found it tough going to build export volume.[4]

MMO's experience is common, and it suggests a need for firms to become more proactive about seeking export opportunities. One reason more firms are not proactive is that they are unfamiliar with foreign market opportunities; they simply do not know how big the opportunities actually are or where they might lie. Simple ignorance of the potential opportunities is a huge barrier to exporting.[5] Also, many would-be exporters, particularly smaller firms, are often intimidated by the complexities and mechanics of exporting to countries where business practices, language, culture, legal systems, and currency are very different from the home market.[6] This combination of unfamiliarity and intimidation probably explains why exporters still account for only a tiny percentage of U.S. firms, less than 2 percent, according to the U.S. Small Business Administration.[7]

To make matters worse, many neophyte exporters have run into significant problems when first trying to do business abroad and this has soured them on future exporting ventures. Common pitfalls include poor market analysis, poor understanding of competitive conditions in the foreign market, failure to customize the product to the needs of foreign customers, lack of an effective distribution program, poorly executed promotion in the foreign market, and problems securing financing (again, see the opening case on Megahertz Communications for an example).[8] Novice exporters tend to underestimate the time and expertise needed to cultivate business in foreign countries.[9] Few realize the amount of management resources that have to be dedicated to this activity. Many foreign customers require face-to-face negotiations on their home turf. An exporter may have to spend months learning about a country's trade regulations, business practices, and more before a deal can be closed.

Exporters often face voluminous paperwork, complex formalities, and many potential delays and errors. According to a UN report on trade and development, a typical international trade transaction may involve 30 parties, 60 original documents,

ANOTHER PERSPECTIVE

Product naming may be tricky, even in English
Heublein had a cranberry liqueur that was popular in the United States called Boggs Cranberry Liqueur. For Americans, this name makes sense because we are aware that cranberries are grown in bogs, so the name communicates an authenticity and connects us to our heritage. When Heublein test-marketed Boggs Cranberry Liqueur in the United Kingdom, it quickly learned something about British slang: *bogs* is an informal term for what Americans call an outhouse or privy—an outdoor toilet. Boggs did not sell well.

and 360 document copies, all of which have to be checked, transmitted, reentered into various information systems, processed, and filed. The United Nations has calculated that the time involved in preparing documentation, along with the costs of common errors in paperwork, often amounts to 10 percent of the final value of goods exported.[10]

IMPROVING EXPORT PERFORMANCE

Inexperienced exporters have a number of ways to gain information about foreign market opportunities and avoid common pitfalls that tend to discourage and frustrate novice exporters.[11] In this section, we look at information sources that exporters can utilize to increase their knowledge of foreign market opportunities, we consider the pros and cons of using export management companies (EMCs) to assist in the export process, and we review various exporting strategies that can increase the probability of successful exporting. We begin, however, with a look at how several nations try to help domestic firms export.

AN INTERNATIONAL COMPARISON

One big impediment to exporting is the simple lack of knowledge of the opportunities available. Often there are many markets for a firm's product, but because they are in countries separated from the firm's home base by culture, language, distance, and time, the firm does not know of them. Identifying export opportunities is made even more complex by the fact that more than 192 countries with widely differing cultures compose the world of potential opportunities. Faced with such complexity and diversity, firms sometimes hesitate to seek export opportunities.

The way to overcome ignorance is to collect information. In Germany, one of the world's most successful exporting nations, trade associations, government agencies, and commercial banks gather information, helping small firms identify export opportunities. A similar function is provided by the Japanese Ministry of International Trade and Industry (MITI), which is always on the lookout for export opportunities. In addition, many Japanese firms are affiliated in some way with the *sogo shosha,* Japan's great trading houses. The *sogo shosha* have offices all over the world, and they proactively, continuously seek export opportunities for their affiliated companies large and small.[12] German and Japanese firms can draw on the large reservoirs of experience, skills, information, and other resources of their respective export-oriented institutions.

A number of private organizations are also beginning to provide more assistance to would-be exporters. Commercial banks and major accounting firms are more willing to assist small firms in starting export operations than they were a decade ago. In addition, large multinationals that have been successful in the global arena are typically willing to discuss opportunities overseas with the owners or managers of small firms.[13]

UTILIZING EXPORT MANAGEMENT COMPANIES

EXPORT MANAGEMENT COMPANY Export specialists who act as an export marketing department for client firms.

One way for first-time exporters to identify the opportunities associated with exporting and to avoid many of the associated pitfalls is to hire an **export management company** (EMC). EMCs are export specialists who act as the export marketing department or international department for their client firms. EMCs normally accept two types of export assignments. They start exporting operations for a firm with the understanding that the firm will take over operations after they are well established. In another type, start-up services are performed with the understanding that the EMC will have continuing responsibility for selling the firm's products. Many EMCs specialize in serving firms in particular industries and in particular areas of the world. Thus, one EMC may specialize in selling agricultural products in the Asian market, while another may focus on exporting electronics products to Eastern Europe.

Canadian and non-Canadian businesspeople can find useful information about international business at Strategis. Strategis, a part of Industry Canada, helps bring together suppliers of Canadian products and services with foreign businesses, and gives both groups the services they need to conduct successful business worldwide. Source: Strategis Home Page," Industry Canada. Reproduced with the permission of the Minister of Public Works and Government Services Canada, 2005.

In theory, the advantage of EMCs is that they are experienced specialists who can help the neophyte exporter identify opportunities and avoid common pitfalls. A good EMC will have a network of contacts in potential markets, have multilingual employees, have a good knowledge of different business mores, and be fully conversant with the ins and outs of the exporting process and with local business regulations. However, the quality of EMCs varies.[14] While some perform their functions very well, others appear to add little value to the exporting company. Therefore, it is important for an exporter to review carefully a number of EMCs and to check references. One drawback of relying on EMCs is that the company can fail to develop its own exporting capabilities in-house.

EXPORTING STRATEGY

In addition to using EMCs, a firm can reduce the risks associated with exporting if it is careful about its choice of exporting strategy. A few guidelines can help firms improve their odds of success. For example, one of the most successful exporting firms in the world, the Minnesota Mining and Manufacturing Co. (3M), has built its export success on three main principles–enter on a small scale to reduce risks, add additional product lines once the exporting operations start to become successful, and hire locals to promote the firm's products (3M's export strategy is profiled in the accompanying Management Focus). Also see the Country Focus on the Business Development Bank of Canada.

ANOTHER PERSPECTIVE

Networking towards success

Networking towards success is an important part of any international business strategy. There are many Canadian organizations that can help Canadian businesses build bridges towards solid and lasting relationships that translate into sales. The Brampton Board of Trade (BBOT) fosters business development relations at home and abroad. In late 2003, the Federation of Portuguese Canadian Business and Professionals Inc. (PCBP), in conjunction with the BBOT began discussing an inter-membership alliance between the organizations. The PCBP is the voice of the Portuguese business community within the GTA and this initiative holds hope for profitable business connections between Canadian and Portuguese businesses. Similar scenarios are played out at local levels, internationally. Without networking, there is little opportunity. Visit www.bramptonbot.com/. Source: *Brampton Board of Trade*, vol. 33, issue 5, 2004.

MANAGEMENT FOCUS

EXPORTING STRATEGY AT 3M

The Minnesota Mining and Manufacturing Co. (3M), which makes more than 40 000 products including tape, sandpaper, medical products, and the ever-present Post-it Notes, is one of the world's great multinational operations. In 2000, 51 percent of the firm's $17 billion in revenues was generated outside the United States. Although the bulk of these revenues came from foreign-based operations, 3M remains a major exporter with $1.5 billion in exports. The company often uses its exports to establish an initial presence in a foreign market, only building foreign production facilities once sales volume rises to a level where local production is justified.

The export strategy is built around simple principles. One is known as "FIDO," which stands for First In (to a new market) Defeats Others. The essence of FIDO is to gain an advantage over other exporters by getting into a market first and learning about that country and how to sell there before others do. A second principle is "make a little, sell a little," which is the idea of entering on a small scale with a very modest investment and pushing one basic product, such as reflective sheeting for traffic signs in Russia or scouring pads in Hungary. Once 3M believes it has learned enough about the market to reduce the risk of failure to reasonable levels, it adds additional products.

A third principle at 3M is to hire local employees to sell the firm's products. The company normally sets up a local sales subsidiary to handle its export activities in a country. It then staffs this subsidiary with local hires because it believes they are likely to have a much better idea of how to sell in their own country than American expatriates. Through the implementation of this principle, just 160 of 3M's 39 500 foreign employees are U.S. expatriates.

Another common practice at 3M is to formulate global strategic plans for the export and eventual overseas production of its products. Within the context of these plans, 3M gives local managers considerable autonomy to find the best way to sell the product within their country. Thus, when 3M first exported its Post-it Notes in 1981, it planned to "sample the daylights" out of the product, but it also told local managers to find the best way of doing this. Local managers hired office cleaning crews to pass out samples in Great Britain and Germany; in Italy, office products distributors were used to pass out free samples; while in Malaysia, local managers employed young women to go from office to office handing out samples. In typical 3M fashion, when the volume of Post-it Notes was sufficient to justify it, exports from the United States were replaced by local production. Thus, 3M found it worthwhile by 1984 to set up production facilities in France to produce Post-it Notes for the European market. As for 3M Canada, it is headquartered in London, Ontario, with five other manufacturing plants in Ontario and Manitoba. Up to 75 percent of 3M Canada's products are exported to the U.S. and to other 3M subsidiaries worldwide. There are currently 1202 3M employees in Canada.

Sources: R. L. Rose, "Success Abroad," *Wall Street Journal,* March 29, 1991, p. A1; T. Eiben, "US Exporters Keep on Rolling," *Fortune,* June 14, 1994, pp. 128–31; 3M's website at www.mmm.com; Industry Canada, "3M Canada," http://strategis.ic.gc.ca/ccc/search/navigate.do;jsessionid=0000k4fFFGN0zTtEOkUgel5BMIS: 1?language=eng&portal=1&profile=completeProfile&V_TOKEN=1095032668295&V_SEARCH.command=navigate&V_SEARCH.docsStart=1&V_SEARCH.resultsJSP=/profile.do&V_DOCUMENT.docRank=1&V_SEARCH.docsCount=3&estblmntNo=104659120000.

The probability of exporting successfully can be increased dramatically by taking a handful of simple strategic steps. First, particularly for the novice exporter, it helps to hire an EMC or at least an experienced export consultant to help identify opportunities and navigate through the web of paperwork and regulations so often involved in exporting. Second, it often makes sense to initially focus on one market or a handful of markets. The idea is to learn about what is required to succeed in those markets, before moving on to other markets. The firm that enters many markets at once runs the risk of spreading its limited management resources too thin. The result of such a "shotgun approach" to exporting may be a failure to become established in any one market. Third, as with 3M, it often makes sense to enter a foreign market on a small scale to reduce the costs of any subsequent failure. Most importantly, entering on a

COUNTRY FOCUS

ENHANCING FINANCING POSSIBILITIES — THE BUSINESS DEVELOPMENT BANK OF CANADA

Businesses and governments working together is not a new idea. For example, the Business Development Bank of Canada (BDC), formed on July 13, 1995 under the new *Business Development Bank of Canada Act,* has a broadened and dynamic public interest mandate, particularly focusing on Canadian exporting businesses in the technology sector. It does provide assistance to non-export ventures, but increasingly small businesses are using its services for export specific purposes.

The BDC took root during the end of World War II era when, in September 1944, the Canadian Parliament set into law the Industrial Development Bank of Canada (IDB), which was at that time an arm of the Bank of Canada. Its primary purpose was to assist manufacturing based companies. Over the next few years, the IDB Act was amended several times, expanding its ability to grant loans to many companies across a variety of industry sectors. By 1964, the bank had 22 cross-Canada branches.

The basic premise of the BDC's original set up in 1944 was to focus on providing financial loans to companies. During the 1970s, it began to acknowledge that companies needed more than money. It added to its roster of services to Canadian business areas such as counselling, training, and planning for small business owners. Another innovative concept to be injected into the IDB in the 1970s turned it into a sort of one stop shopping for small businesses in need of financing, export advice, and business planning counsel. It then evolved into a separate Crown corporation and the Federal Business Development Bank took over from the IDB in October 1975. The bank then decentralized and opened up more branches across Canada.

In April 2002, the BDC's mandate was renewed for a period of ten years and the partnership between Canadian small businesses and the BDC continues. Doing business abroad is difficult enough and most Canadian small businesses need all the help they can get. In 2005, the Business Development Bank of Canada boasts 80 branches cross-Canada as well as a virtual branch known as BDC Connex.

Its activities are similar to those of a regular chartered bank, such as the Canadian Imperial Bank of Commerce or the Royal Bank of Canada. The BDC's key activities involve granting flexible business loans with floating and fixed interest rates for up to 20 years. It also has a micro-business program. This arm of the bank assists small business owners with mentoring and continued management support for as long as two years after the initial signed agreement between the small business owner and the BDC. It can provide term financing of up to $25,000 to new businesses and up to $50,000 to existing companies with solid and realistic plans. The bank also offers a Young Entrepreneur Financing Program geared to 18- to 34-year-old entrepreneurs who show their mettle through strong business plans and character. Loans can amount to $25,000 and often come equipped with 50 hours of business specific consulting.

On a larger scale, the BDC provides Venture Loans® for higher risk companies, for financing amounts ranging between $100,000 and $1,000,000 for those well run niche companies with a proven high-quality management team and little money in the bank. Repayment of these loans is flexibly arranged to suit the company and can include repayment in part, through royalties on sales. Funds are also available to existing media related businesses, through the Cultural Industries Development Fund for the promotion of Canadian culture. Through this program, the BDC could loan to eligible companies $250,000 annually with a total commitment of $1 million over time.

There are several other types of services that enable eligible Canadian businesses to extend their business beyond Canada's borders. A Productivity Plus Loan assists well-established manufacturing companies to acquire various types of up-to-date equipment in the range of $100,000 to $5 million. In addition to this, the BDC might offer an extra 25 percent financing for installation, assembly, and personnel training.

Innovation Loans, geared primarily towards helping entrepreneurs grow their businesses, assist with the organizational logistics and implementation of innovation strategies, frequently in training for R&D, and International Organization for Standardization (ISO) standards training. Entrepreneurs can top up an Innovation loan for up to $100,000 with a Working Capital for Exporters loan for amounts up to $250,000.

BDC also provides Venture Capital loans in amounts ranging from $500,000 to $5,000,000 irrespective of the company lifecycle. The BDC Tourism Investment Fund has funds available to those entrepreneurs with good track records and future prospects in amounts ranging from $250,000 to $10,000,000 as well as Growth Capital for Aboriginal Business for loans ranging between $25,000 and $100,000, also with flexible repayment turns.

For costs relating to Web solutions, companies could be eligible to receive financing from $25,000 to $50,000 to meet the various costs related to the implementation of a Web solution.

Sources: BDC at www.bdc.ca/en/about/overview/history/default.htm; Canada-Ontario Business Service Centre at www.cbsc.org/ontario/english/search/display.cfm.

small scale provides the time and opportunity to learn about the foreign country before making significant capital commitments to that market. Fourth, the exporter needs to recognize the time and managerial commitment involved in building export sales and should hire additional personnel to oversee this activity. Fifth, in many countries, it is important to devote a lot of attention to building strong and enduring relationships with local distributors and/or customers. Sixth, as 3M often does, it is important to hire local personnel to help the firm establish itself in a foreign market. Local people are likely to have a much greater sense of how to do business in a given country than a manager from an exporting firm who has previously never set foot in that country. Seventh, several studies have suggested the firm needs to be proactive about seeking export opportunities.[15] Armchair exporting does not work! The world will not normally beat a path to your door.

Finally, it is important for the exporter to keep the option of local production in mind. Once exports reach a sufficient volume to justify cost-efficient local production, the exporting firm should consider establishing production facilities in the foreign market. Such localization helps foster good relations with the foreign country and can lead to greater market acceptance. Exporting is often not an end in itself, but merely a step on the road toward establishment of foreign production (again, 3M provides an example of this philosophy).

EXPORT AND IMPORT FINANCING

Mechanisms for financing exports and imports have evolved over the centuries in response to a problem that can be particularly acute in international trade: the lack of trust that exists when one must put faith in a stranger. In this section, we examine the financial devices that cope with this problem in the context of international trade: the letter of credit, the draft (or bill of exchange), and the bill of lading. Then we will trace the 14 steps of a typical export–import transaction.

LACK OF TRUST

Firms engaged in international trade have to trust someone they may have never seen, who lives in a different country, who speaks a different language, who abides by (or does not abide by) a different legal system, and who could be very difficult to track down if he or she defaults on an obligation. Consider a Canadian firm exporting to a distributor in France. The Canadian businessman might be concerned that if he ships the products to France before he receives payment for them from the French businesswoman, she might take delivery of the products and not pay him. Conversely, the French importer might worry that if she pays for the products before they are shipped, the Canadian firm might keep the money and never ship the products or might ship defective products. Neither party to the exchange completely trusts the other. This lack of trust is exacerbated by the distance between the two parties–in space, language, and culture–and by the problems of using an underdeveloped international legal system to enforce contractual obligations.

Due to the (quite reasonable) lack of trust between the two parties, each has his or her own preferences as to how they would like the transaction to be configured. To make sure he is paid, the manager of the Canadian firm would prefer the French distributor to pay for the products before he ships them (see Figure 13.1). Alternatively, to ensure she receives the products, the French distributor would prefer not to pay for them until they arrive (see Figure 13.2). Thus, each party has different preferences. Unless there is some way of establishing trust between the parties, the transaction might never take place.

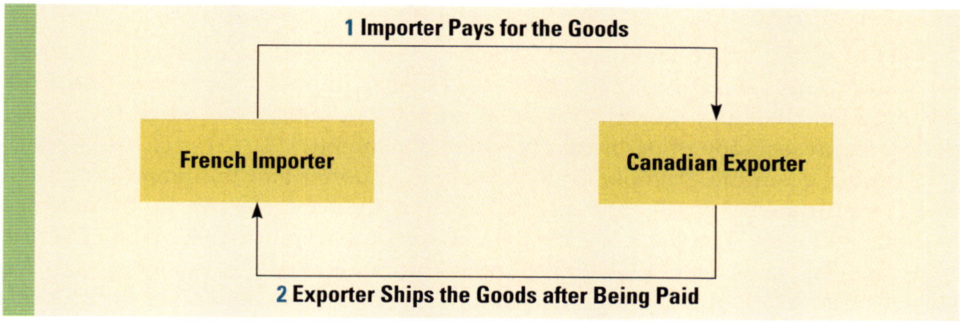

FIGURE 13.1
Preference of the Canadian Exporter

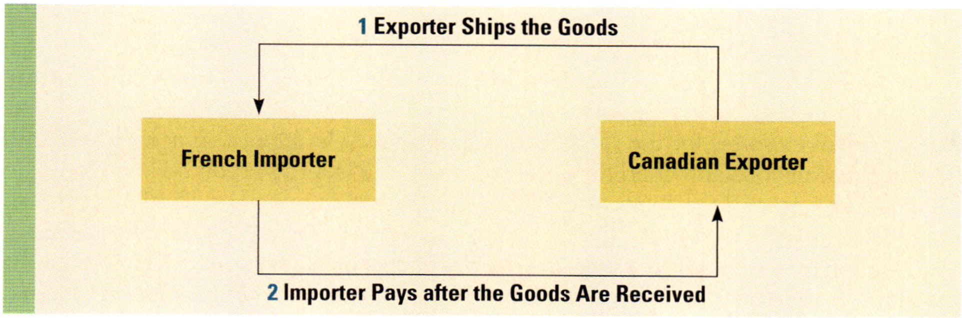

FIGURE 13.2
Preference of the French Importer

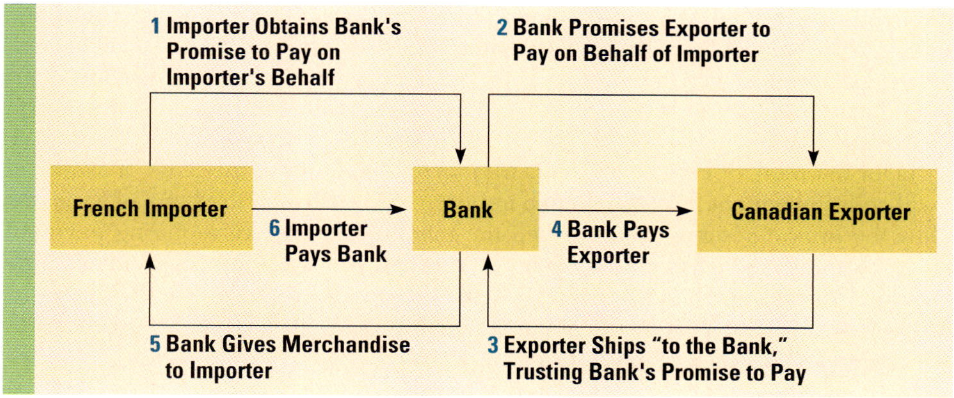

FIGURE 13.3
The Use of a Third Party

The problem is solved by using a third party trusted by both—normally a reputable bank—to act as an intermediary. What happens can be summarized as follows (see Figure 13.3). First, the French importer obtains the bank's promise to pay on her behalf, knowing the Canadian exporter will trust the bank. This promise is known as a letter of credit. Having seen the letter of credit, the Canadian exporter now ships the products to France. Title to the products is given to the bank in the form of a document called a bill of lading. In return, the Canadian exporter tells the bank to pay for the products, which the bank does. The document for requesting this payment is referred to as a draft. The bank, having paid for the products, now passes the title on to the French importer, whom the bank trusts. At that time or later, depending on their agreement, the importer reimburses the bank. In the remainder of this section, we examine how this system works in more detail.

LETTER OF CREDIT

LETTER OF CREDIT
Issued by a bank, indicating that the bank will make payments under specific circumstances.

A letter of credit, abbreviated as L/C, stands at the centre of international commercial transactions. Issued by a bank at the request of an importer, the **letter of credit** states the bank will pay a specified sum of money to a beneficiary, normally the exporter, on presentation of particular, specified documents.

Consider again the example of the Canadian exporter and the French importer. The French importer applies to her local bank, say the Bank of Paris, for the issuance of a letter of credit. The Bank of Paris then undertakes a credit check of the importer. If the Bank of Paris is satisfied with her creditworthiness, it will issue a letter of credit. However, the Bank of Paris might require a cash deposit or some other form of collateral from her first. In addition, the Bank of Paris will charge the importer a fee for this service. Typically this amounts to between 0.5 percent and 2 percent of the value of the letter of credit, depending on the importer's creditworthiness and the size of the transaction. (As a rule, the larger the transaction, the lower the percentage.)

Let us assume the Bank of Paris is satisfied with the French importer's creditworthiness and agrees to issue a letter of credit. The letter states that the Bank of Paris will pay the Canadian exporter for the merchandise as long as it is shipped in accordance with specified instructions and conditions. At this point, the letter of credit becomes a financial contract between the Bank of Paris and the Canadian exporter. The Bank of Paris then sends the letter of credit to the Canadian exporter's bank, say the Bank of Montreal. The Bank of Montreal tells the exporter that it has received a letter of credit and that he can ship the merchandise. After the exporter has shipped the merchandise, he draws a draft against the Bank of Paris in accordance with the terms of the letter of credit, attaches the required documents, and presents the draft to his own bank, the Bank of Montreal, for payment. The Bank of Montreal then forwards the letter of credit and associated documents to the Bank of Paris. If all the terms and conditions contained in the letter of credit have been complied with, the Bank of Paris will honour the draft and will send payment to the Bank of Montreal. When the Bank of Montreal receives the funds, it will pay the Canadian exporter.

As for the Bank of Paris, once it has transferred the funds to the Bank of Montreal, it will collect payment from the French importer. Alternatively, the Bank of Paris may allow the importer some time to resell the merchandise before requiring payment. This is not unusual, particularly when the importer is a distributor and not the final consumer of the merchandise, since it helps the importer's cash flow. The Bank of Paris will treat such an extension of the payment period as a loan to the importer and will charge an appropriate interest rate.

The great advantage of this system is that both the French importer and the Canadian exporter are likely to trust reputable banks, even if they do not trust each other. Once the Canadian exporter has seen a letter of credit, he knows that he is guaranteed payment and will ship the merchandise. Also, an exporter may find that having a letter of credit will facilitate obtaining pre-export financing. For example, having seen the letter of credit, the Bank of Montreal might be willing to lend the exporter funds to process and prepare the merchandise for shipping to France. This loan may not have to be repaid until the exporter has received his payment for the merchandise. As for the French importer, she does not have to pay for the merchandise until the documents have arrived and unless all conditions stated in the letter of credit have been satisfied. The drawback for the importer is the fee she must pay the Bank of Paris for the letter of credit. In addition, since the letter of credit is a financial liability against her, it may reduce her ability to borrow funds for other purposes.

DRAFT

A **draft,** sometimes referred to as a bill of exchange, is the instrument normally used in international commerce to effect payment. A draft is simply an order written by an exporter instructing an importer, or an importer's agent, to pay a specified amount of money at a specified time. In the example of the Canadian exporter and the French importer, the exporter writes a draft that instructs the Bank of Paris, the French importer's agent, to pay for the merchandise shipped to France. The person or business initiating the draft is known as the maker (in this case, the Canadian exporter). The party to whom the draft is presented is known as the drawee (in this case, the Bank of Paris).

DRAFT An order written by an exporter instructing an importer, or an importer's agent, to pay a specified amount of money at a specified time; also called a bill of exchange.

International practice is to use drafts to settle trade transactions. This differs from domestic practice in which a seller usually ships merchandise on an open account, followed by a commercial invoice that specifies the amount due and the terms of payment. In domestic transactions, the buyer can often obtain possession of the merchandise without signing a formal document acknowledging his or her obligation to pay. In contrast, due to the lack of trust in international transactions, payment or a formal promise to pay is required before the buyer can obtain the merchandise.

Drafts fall into two categories, sight drafts and time drafts. A **sight draft** is payable on presentation to the drawee. A **time draft** allows for a delay in payment–normally 30, 60, 90, or 120 days. It is presented to the drawee, who signifies acceptance of it by writing or stamping a notice of acceptance on its face. Once accepted, the time draft becomes a promise to pay by the accepting party. When a time draft is drawn on and accepted by a bank, it is called a banker's acceptance. When it is drawn on and accepted by a business firm, it is called a trade acceptance.

SIGHT DRAFT A draft payable on presentation to the drawee.

TIME DRAFT A promise to pay by the accepting party at some future date.

Time drafts are negotiable instruments; that is, once the draft is stamped with an acceptance, the maker can sell the draft to an investor at a discount from its face value. Imagine the agreement between the Canadian exporter and the French importer calls for the exporter to present the Bank of Paris (through the Bank of Montreal) with a time draft requiring payment 120 days after presentation. The Bank of Paris stamps the time draft with an acceptance. Imagine further that the draft is for $100,000.

The exporter can either hold onto the accepted time draft and receive $100,000 in 120 days or he can sell it to an investor, say the Bank of Montreal, for a discount from the face value. If the prevailing discount rate is 7 percent, the exporter could receive $96,500 by selling it immediately (7 percent per annum discount rate for 120 days for $100,000 equals $3,500, and $100,000 − $3,500 = $96,500). The Bank of Montreal would then collect the full $100,000 from the Bank of Paris in 120 days. The exporter might sell the accepted time draft immediately if he needed the funds to finance merchandise in transit and/or to cover cash flow shortfalls.

BILL OF LADING

The third key document for financing international trade is the bill of lading. The **bill of lading** is issued to the exporter by the common carrier transporting the merchandise. It serves three purposes: it is a receipt, a contract, and a document of title. As a receipt, the bill of lading indicates the carrier has received the merchandise described on the face of the document. As a contract, it specifies that the carrier is obligated to provide a transportation service in return for a certain charge. As a document of title, it can be used to obtain payment or a written promise of payment before the merchandise is released to the importer. The bill of lading can also function as collateral against which funds may be advanced to the exporter by its local bank before or during shipment and before final payment by the importer.

BILL OF LADING A document issued to an exporter by a common carrier transporting merchandise. It serves as a receipt, a contract, and a document of title.

A TYPICAL INTERNATIONAL TRADE TRANSACTION

Now that we have reviewed the elements of an international trade transaction, let us see how the process works in a typical case, sticking with the example of the Canadian exporter and the French importer. The typical transaction involves 14 steps (see Figure 13.4).

1. The French importer places an order with the Canadian exporter and asks the Canadian if he would be willing to ship under a letter of credit.
2. The Canadian exporter agrees to ship under a letter of credit and specifies relevant information such as prices and delivery terms.
3. The French importer applies to the Bank of Paris for a letter of credit to be issued in favour of the Canadian exporter for the merchandise the importer wishes to buy.
4. The Bank of Paris issues a letter of credit in the French importer's favour and sends it to the Canadian exporter's bank, the Bank of Montreal.
5. The Bank of Montreal advises the exporter of the opening of a letter of credit in his favour.
6. The Canadian exporter ships the goods to the French importer on a common carrier. An official of the carrier gives the exporter a bill of lading.
7. The Canadian exporter presents a 90-day time draft drawn on the Bank of Paris in accordance with its letter of credit and the bill of lading to the Bank of Montreal. The exporter endorses the bill of lading so title to the goods is transferred to the Bank of Montreal.
8. The Bank of Monreal sends the draft and bill of lading to the Bank of Paris. The Bank of Paris accepts the draft, taking possession of the documents and promising to pay the now-accepted draft in 90 days.

FIGURE 13.4

A Typical International Trade Transaction

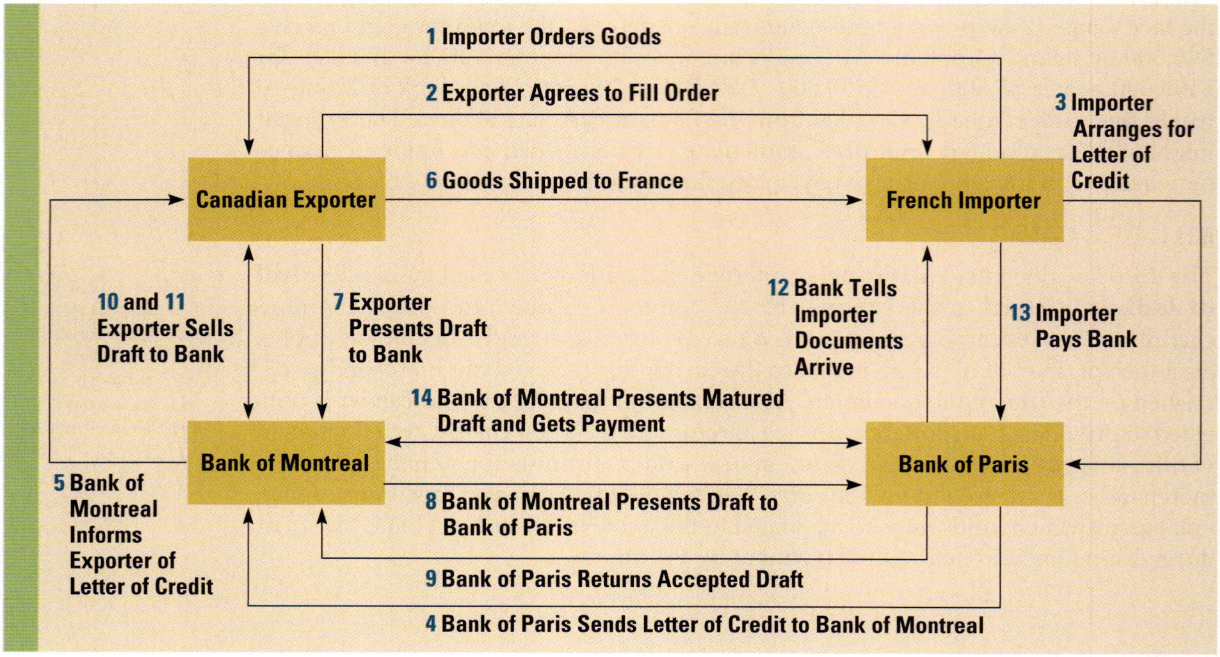

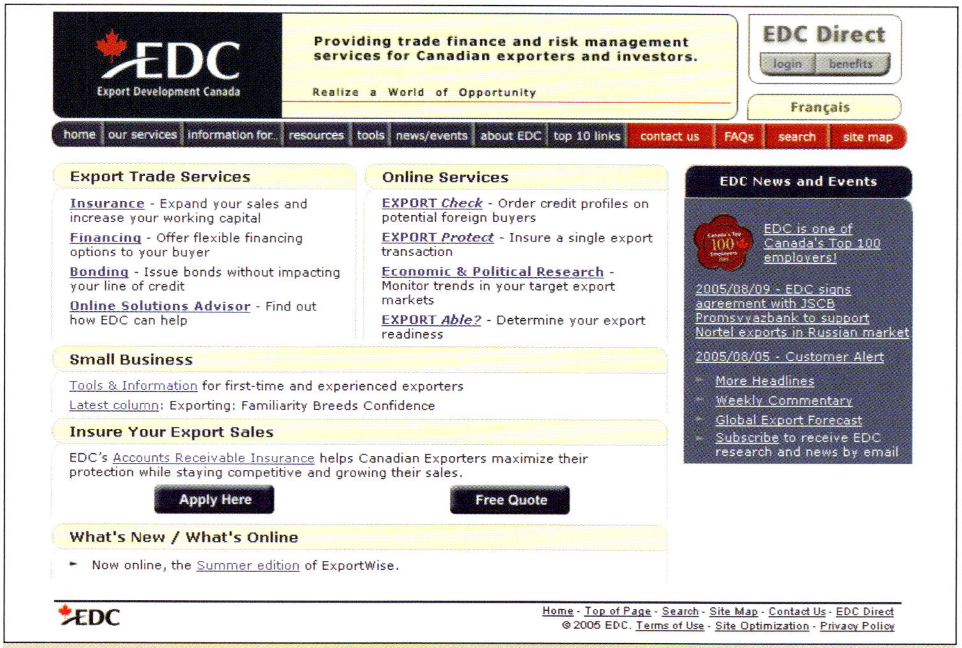

The Export Development Corporation is the only Canadian financial institution solely devoted to providing trade finance services in support of Canadian exporters and investors in up to 200 countries. Source: Founded in 1944, EDC is a Crown corporation that operates as a commercial financial institution. EDC at www.edc.ca/index_e.htm.

9. The Bank of Paris returns the accepted draft to the Bank of Montreal.
10. The Bank of Montreal tells the Canadian exporter that it has received the accepted bank draft, which is payable in 90 days.
11. The exporter sells the draft to the Bank of Montreal at a discount from its face value and receives the discounted cash value of the draft in return.
12. The Bank of Paris notifies the French importer of the arrival of the documents. She agrees to pay the Bank of Paris in 90 days. The Bank of Paris releases the documents so the importer can take possession of the shipment.
13. In 90 days, the Bank of Paris receives the importer's payment, so it has funds to pay the maturing draft.
14. In 90 days, the holder of the matured acceptance (in this case, the Bank of Montreal) presents it to the Bank of Paris for payment. The Bank of Paris pays.

Unlike their German and Japanese competitors, many Canadian firms are relatively blind when they seek export opportunities; they are less information disadvantaged than previously, but still prone to be more comfortable with the American market than beyond. Both Germany and Japan have long made their living as trading nations, whereas until recently, Canada had been a part of a relatively self-contained continental economy in which international trade played a minor role. This is changing; both imports and exports now play a much greater role in the Canadian economy than they did 20 years ago. However, Canada has not yet evolved an institutional structure to the degree that exists in Japan and Germany.

EXPORT INFORMATION SOURCES

Canadian firms are increasingly becoming aware of international business opportunities. There are many different sources of information available through municipal, provincial and federal governments. At the federal level, there is the Department of Foreign Affairs (Foreign Affairs Canada) (FAC) that helps Canadian tourists and businesspeople abroad, while striving towards a more peaceful and secure world.

The other federal department is International Trade Canada (previously combined as one department with the Department of Foreign Affairs). International Trade Canada (ITCan) supports the development of trade by providing services to exporters, developing policy, and attracting investment in the Canadian economy.[16]

Several Web-based sources provide information on international trade matters relating to Canada and the world. Strategis and Statistics Canada are extensive Web resources providing information on a plethora of international trade related subjects. Some reports and trade data are free, while others require payment of a small document access fee.

The Department of Foreign Affairs Web site provides extensive information about market reports, cultural reports, strategies for culture and trade, Infoexport, virtual trade commissioner, new exporters to border states, etc.

The Canadian government initiates international trade fairs, seminars, and conferences, at home and abroad, and trade visits in cooperation with various government agencies, including the International Trade Centres located across Canada, as well as Team Canada trade missions to other countries. In addition to ITC centres, trade commissioners working at Canadian high commissions, consuls general, and embassies around the world have teams of employees working to connect Canadian businesses to host country opportunities.

International Trade Centres also promote international trade training through the Forum for International Trade Training (FITT). FITT is an Ottawa-based international trade training organization belonging to the International Association of Trade Associations representing 32 country members. It offers eight international trade training modules and each module concludes with an exam:

- Global Entrepreneurship
- International Marketing
- International Trade Finance
- International Trade Logistics
- International Market Entry & Distribution
- International Trade Law
- International Trade Research
- International Trade Management

After successful completion of these eight modules, the student is then eligible to apply to write the "CITP" (Certified International Trade Professional) professional designation exam. On successful outcome, the student is awarded the CITP designation.

This synergy is played out at the provincial levels as well as municipal levels. Most provincial governments have trade representation offices, not only in other provinces, but in other countries as well aimed at attracting business in the home province.

At the municipal levels are local chambers of commerce, boards of trade, all linked to the provincial and Canadian Chamber of Commerce, the voice of Canadian business at the International Chamber of Commerce in Paris, and at World Trade Organization conferences, through the designate cabinet minister.

COUNTERTRADE

Countertrade is an alternative means of structuring an international sale when conventional means of payment are difficult, costly, or nonexistent. A government may restrict the convertibility of its currency to preserve its foreign exchange reserves so they can be used to service international debt commitments and purchase crucial imports.[17] This is problematic for exporters. Nonconvertibility implies that the exporter may not be able to be paid in his or her home currency; and few exporters would desire payment in a currency that is not convertible. Countertrade is often the solution.[18] **Countertrade** denotes a range of barterlike agreements; its principle is to trade goods and services for other goods and services when they cannot be traded for money. Some examples of countertrade are:

COUNTERTRADE
The trade of goods and services for other goods and services.

- An Italian company that manufactures power-generating equipment, ABB SAE Sadelmi SpA, was awarded a 720-million baht ($17.7 million) contract by the Electricity Generating Authority of Thailand. The contract specified that the company had to accept 218 million baht ($5.4 million) of Thai farm products as part of the payment.
- Saudi Arabia agreed to buy 10 747 jets from Boeing with payment in crude oil, discounted at 10 percent below posted world oil prices.
- General Electric won a contract for a $150-million electric-generator project in Romania by agreeing to market $150 million of Romanian products in markets to which Romania did not have access.
- The Venezuelan government negotiated a contract with Caterpillar under which Venezuela would trade 350 000 tonnes of iron ore for Caterpillar earthmoving equipment.
- Albania offered such items as spring water, tomato juice, and chrome ore in exchange for a $60-million fertilizer and methanol complex.
- Philip Morris ships cigarettes to Russia, for which it receives chemicals that can be used to make fertilizer. Philip Morris ships the chemicals to China, and in return, China ships glassware to North America for retail sale by Philip Morris.[19]

THE GROWTH OF COUNTERTRADE

In the modern era, countertrade arose in the 1960s as a way for the Soviet Union and the Communist states of Eastern Europe, whose currencies were generally nonconvertible, to purchase imports. During the 1980s, the technique grew in popularity among many developing nations that lacked the foreign exchange reserves required to purchase necessary imports. Today, reflecting their own shortages of foreign exchange reserves, many of the successor states to the former Soviet Union and the Eastern European Communist nations are engaging in countertrade to purchase their imports. Consequently, according to some estimates, more than 20 percent of world trade by value in 1998 was in the form of countertrade, up from only 2 percent in 1975.[20] There was a notable increase in the volume of countertrade after the Asian financial crisis of 1997. That crisis left many Asian nations with little hard currency to finance international trade. In the tight monetary regime that followed the 1997 crisis, many Asian firms found it difficult to get export credits to finance their own international trade. Consequently, they turned to the only option available–countertrade.

Given the importance of countertrade as a means of financing world trade, prospective exporters will have to engage in this technique from time to time to gain access to international markets. The governments of developing nations sometimes insist on a certain amount of countertrade.[21] For example, all foreign companies contracted by Thai state agencies for work costing more than 500 million baht ($12.3 million) are required to accept at least 30 percent of their payment in Thai agricultural products. Between 1994 and mid-1998, foreign firms purchased 21 billion baht ($517 million) in Thai goods under countertrade deals.[22]

TYPES OF COUNTERTRADE

With its roots in the simple trading of goods and services for other goods and services, countertrade has evolved into a diverse set of activities that can be categorized as five distinct types of trading arrangements: barter, counterpurchase, offset, switch trading, and compensation or buyback.[23] Figure 13.5 summarizes the popularity of each of these arrangements as indicated in a survey of multinational corporations. Many countertrade deals involve not just one arrangement, but elements of two or more.

Barter

BARTER The direct exchange of goods or services between two parties without a cash transaction.

Barter is the direct exchange of goods and/or services between two parties without a cash transaction. Although barter is the simplest arrangement, it is not common. Its problems are twofold. First, if goods are not exchanged simultaneously, one party ends up financing the other for a period. Second, firms engaged in barter run the risk of having to accept goods they do not want, cannot use, or have difficulty reselling at a reasonable price. For these reasons, barter is viewed as the most restrictive countertrade arrangement. It is primarily used for one-time-only deals in transactions with trading partners who are not creditworthy or trustworthy.

Counterpurchase

COUNTERPURCHASE A reciprocal buying agreement.

Counterpurchase is a reciprocal buying agreement. It occurs when a firm agrees to purchase a certain amount of materials back from a country to which a sale is made. Suppose a Canadian firm sells some products to China. China pays the Canadian firm

FIGURE 13.5

Countertrade Practice

Source: Reprinted from "The Do's and Don'ts of International Countertrade," by J. R. Carter and J. Gagne, *MIT Sloan Management Review,* Spring 1988, pp. 31–37, by permission of the publisher. Copyright © 1988 by Massachusetts Institute of Technology. All rights reserved.

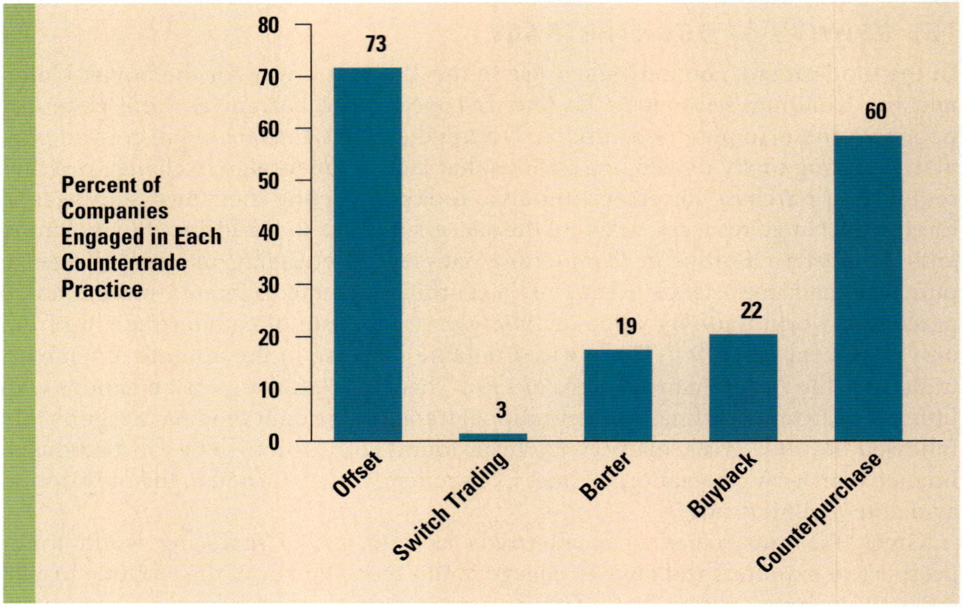

in dollars, but in exchange, the Canadian firm agrees to spend some of its proceeds from the sale on textiles produced by China. Thus, although China must draw on its foreign exchange reserves to pay the Canadian firm, it knows it will receive some of those dollars back because of the counterpurchase agreement. In one counterpurchase agreement, Rolls-Royce sold jet parts to Finland. As part of the deal, Rolls-Royce agreed to use some of the proceeds from the sale to purchase Finnish-manufactured TV sets that it would then sell in Great Britain.

Offset

Offset is similar to counterpurchase insofar as one party agrees to purchase goods and services with a specified percentage of the proceeds from the original sale. The difference is that this party can fulfill the obligation with any firm in the country to which the sale is being made. From an exporter's perspective, this is more attractive than a straight counterpurchase agreement because it gives the exporter greater flexibility to choose the goods that it wishes to purchase.

OFFSET A buying agreement similar to counterpurchase, but the exporting country can then fulfill the agreement with any firm in the country to which the sale is being made.

Switch Trading

Switch trading refers to the use of a specialized third-party trading house in a countertrade arrangement. When a firm enters a counterpurchase or offset agreement with a country, it often ends up with what are called counterpurchase credits, which can be used to purchase goods from that country. Switch trading occurs when a third-party trading house buys the firm's counterpurchase credits and sells them to another firm that can better use them. For example, a Canadian firm concludes a counterpurchase agreement with Poland for which it receives some number of counterpurchase credits for purchasing Polish goods. The Canadian firm cannot use and does not want any Polish goods, however, so it sells the credits to a third-party trading house at a discount. The trading house finds a firm that can use the credits and sells them at a profit.

SWITCH TRADING The use of a specialized third-party trading house in a countertrade arrangement.

In one example of switch trading, Poland and Greece had a counterpurchase agreement that called for Poland to buy the same U.S.-dollar value of goods from Greece that it sold to Greece. However, Poland could not find enough Greek goods that it required, so it ended up with a dollar-denominated counterpurchase balance in Greece that it was unwilling to use. A switch trader bought the right to 250,000 counterpurchase dollars from Poland for $225,000 and sold them to a European grape merchant for $235,000, who used them to purchase sultana grapes from Greece.

Buybacks

A **buyback** occurs when a firm builds a plant in a country—or supplies technology, equipment, training, or other services to the country—and agrees to take a certain percentage of the plant's output as partial payment for the contract. For example, Occidental Petroleum negotiated a deal with Russia under which Occidental would build several ammonia plants in Russia and as partial payment receive ammonia over a 20-year period.

BUYBACK When a firm builds a plant in a country and agrees to take a certain percentage of the plant's output as partial payment of the contract.

THE PROS AND CONS OF COUNTERTRADE

Countertrade's main attraction is that it can give a firm a way to finance an export deal when other means are not available. Given the problems that many developing nations have in raising the foreign exchange necessary to pay for imports, countertrade may be the only option available when doing business in these countries. Even when countertrade is not the only option for structuring an export transaction, many countries prefer countertrade to cash deals. Thus, if a firm is unwilling to enter a countertrade agreement, it may lose an export opportunity to a competitor that is willing to make a countertrade agreement.

ANOTHER PERSPECTIVE

A boatload of what?

In its early entry into the former Soviet Union, PepsiCo faced currency repatriation restrictions. Because the government would not allow foreign corporations to export currency, Pepsi could not take its popular beverage business profits out of the USSR. Instead, Pepsi received the export rights to Stolichnaya vodka from Russia. These exports were a way to take out part of its profits. Pepsi also set up a business to buy commodities in the USSR with rubles and export them to Europe for payment in currencies that could be converted to U.S. dollars. The company would buy discarded ships, including submarines, and sell them in Europe for scrap. Do you think Pepsi ever filled an old tanker with vodka for export? That's the rumour.

Today there is litigation in Russia over who owns the Stolichnaya brand. When the Russian government privatized its businesses, a group of Russian investors and businesspeople formed SPI as a private corporation in Russia and bought the brand and the company. But the minister of agriculture has ruled that the government still owns the company. Even though this is a Russian case being litigated in Russia, SPI's corporate lawyers are a Washington, D.C., law firm on K Street! (See www.hillnews.com/060502/ii_vodka.shtm for more details.)

In addition, a countertrade agreement may be required by the government of a country to which a firm is exporting goods or services. Boeing often has to agree to counterpurchase agreements to capture orders for its commercial jet aircraft. For example, in exchange for gaining an order from Air India, Boeing may be required to purchase certain component parts, such as aircraft doors, from an Indian company. Taking this one step further, Boeing can use its willingness to enter into a counterpurchase agreement as a way of winning orders in the face of intense competition from its global rival, Airbus Industrie. Thus, for firms such as Boeing, countertrade can become a strategic marketing weapon.

However, the drawbacks of countertrade agreements are substantial. Other things being equal, firms would normally prefer to be paid in hard currency. Countertrade contracts may involve the exchange of unusable or poor-quality goods that the firm cannot dispose of profitably. For example, a few years ago, one U.S. firm got burned when 50 percent of the television sets it received in a countertrade agreement with Hungary were defective and could not be sold. In addition, even if the goods it receives are of high quality, the firm still needs to dispose of them profitably. To do this, countertrade requires the firm to invest in an in-house trading department dedicated to arranging and managing countertrade deals. This can be expensive and time consuming.

Given these drawbacks, countertrade is most attractive to large, diverse multinational enterprises that can use their worldwide network of contacts to dispose of goods acquired in countertrading. The masters of countertrade are Japan's giant trading firms, the *sogo shosha,* which use their vast networks of affiliated companies to profitably dispose of goods acquired through countertrade agreements. The trading firm of Mitsui & Company, for example, has about 120 affiliated companies in almost every sector of the manufacturing and service industries. If one of Mitsui's affiliates receives goods in a countertrade agreement that it cannot consume, Mitsui & Company will normally be able to find another affiliate that can profitably use them. Firms affiliated with one of Japan's *sogo shosha* often have a competitive advantage in countries where countertrade agreements are preferred.

Western firms that are large, diverse, and have a global reach (e.g., General Electric, Philip Morris, and 3M) have similar profit advantages from countertrade agreements. Indeed, 3M has established its own trading company–3M Global Trading, Inc.–to develop and manage the company's international countertrade programs. Unless there is no alternative, small and medium-size exporters should probably try to avoid countertrade deals because they lack the worldwide network of operations that may be required to profitably utilize or dispose of goods acquired through them.[24]

IMPLICATIONS FOR BUSINESS

As Crown corporations, Export Development Corporation Canada and the Canadian Commercial Corporation play vital roles in providing export advisory and financial services to Canadian exporters.

If a company is eager to close a deal, it might even consider barter as an actual business transaction tool. Historically speaking, barter is one of the oldest forms of exchanging one product (or service) with another deemed to be of equal value. During the era of the Soviet Union and in some cases today, where poor countries don't have the disposable hard currency (U.S. dollars) to pay for goods, barter continues to serve as a commercial instrument for buying and selling.

During the export and import processes, accurate documentation is paramount. If waybills between the importer and exporter fail to match up, the merchandise could be refused entry into a foreign country. It has happened before that a detail, as seemingly insignificant as a missing comma, has scrapped an order. The buyer is not obliged to take delivery of orders where the paper work doesn't match up. The foreign buyer could feasibly tell a Canadian exporter that it will accept the product rather than having it returned to Canada, at 10 cents on the dollar. Of course this would jeopardize long term business relations between the two, yet it could happen.

In the world of exports and imports, goods can be detained at port of entry if the marking, labelling, packing and packaging are incompliant with exigencies in the host country.

There are many warning signs that an exporter can experience in the transaction and post-transaction processes. Should a Canadian shirt manufacturer succeed in exporting its shirts to another country and discover, after a period, that the importer wishes to change the current contract provisions, this should flag to the Canadian exporter that the importer is likely experiencing financial difficulties that could manifest in non-payment of shipped items. Extra vigilance and revision of terms of payment would be helpful.

Oftentimes, Canadian exporters use the CCC and EDC as safety nets. Canadian exporters frequently view developing countries as a source of the highest risk for non-payment on goods received, yet ironically this is not the case. The highest rate of defaults on commercial transactions for Canadian exporters is in fact the U. S. The reasons are varied, but can include the fact that certain American importers are aware that, up to a certain dollar amount (for example Cdn$70,000), Canadian exporters will not consider litigation due to the cost of retaining an American lawyer and other expenses of following up in a U.S. court of law to recover funds. The U.S. bankruptcy laws are more friendly (and quicker) to take advantage of than they are in Canada. Some American businesspeople might also know that the EDC or the CCC has covered the loss of the Canadian exporter and thus feel a sense of quasi entitlement to abscond without payment.

Tied in with international trade norms, are Incoterms, first formulated in Paris, in 1936 by the International Chamber of Commerce. Incoterms are a set of international trading rules that determine the rights and obligations of buyers and sellers in international trade transactions. Without Incoterms, international trade would not be possible.

KEY TERMS

barter, p. 442

bill of lading, p. 437

buyback, p. 443

counterpurchase, p. 442

countertrade, p. 441

draft, p. 437

export management company, p. 430

letter of credit, p. 436

offset, p. 443

sight draft, p. 437

switch trading, p. 443

time draft, p. 437

SUMMARY

In this chapter, we examined the steps that firms must take to establish themselves as exporters. This chapter made the following points:

1. One big impediment to exporting is ignorance of foreign market opportunities.
2. Neophyte exporters often become discouraged or frustrated with the exporting process because they encounter many problems, delays, and pitfalls.
3. The way to overcome ignorance is to gather information. In the United States, a number of institutions, most important of which is the Department of Commerce, can help firms gather information in the matchmaking process. Export management companies can also help an exporter identify export opportunities.
4. Many of the pitfalls associated with exporting can be avoided if a company hires an experienced export management company, or export consultant, and if it adopts the appropriate export strategy.
5. Firms engaged in international trade must do business with people they do not trust and people who may be difficult to track down if they default on an obligation. Due to the lack of trust, each party to an international transaction has a different set of preferences regarding the configuration of the transaction.
6. The problems arising from lack of trust between exporters and importers can be solved by using a third party that is trusted by both, normally a reputable bank.
7. A letter of credit is issued by a bank at the request of an importer. It states that the bank promises to pay a beneficiary, normally the exporter, on presentation of documents specified in the letter.
8. A draft is the instrument normally used in international commerce to effect payment. It is an order written by an exporter instructing an importer, or an importer's agent, to pay a specified amount of money at a specified time.
9. Drafts are either sight drafts or time drafts. Time drafts are negotiable instruments.
10. A bill of lading is issued to the exporter by the common carrier transporting the merchandise. It serves as a receipt, a contract, and a document of title.
11. U.S. exporters can draw on two types of government-backed assistance to help finance their exports: loans from the Export–Import Bank and export credit insurance from the FCIA.
12. Countertrade includes a range of barterlike agreements. It is primarily used when a firm exports to a country whose currency is not freely convertible and may lack the foreign exchange reserves required to purchase the imports.
13. The main attraction of countertrade is that it gives a firm a way to finance an export deal when other means are not available. A firm that insists on being paid in hard currency may be at a competitive disadvantage vis-à-vis one that is willing to engage in countertrade.
14. The main disadvantage of countertrade is that the firm may receive unusable or poor-quality goods that cannot be disposed of profitably.

CRITICAL THINKING AND DISCUSSION QUESTIONS

1. A firm based in British Columbia wants to export a shipload of finished lumber to the Philippines. The would-be importer cannot get sufficient credit from domestic sources to pay for the shipment but insists that the finished lumber can quickly be resold in the Philippines for a profit. Outline the steps the exporter should take to effect this export to the Philippines.
2. You are the assistant to the CEO of a small textile firm that manufactures high-quality, premium-priced, stylish clothing. The CEO has decided to see what the opportunities are for exporting and has asked you for advice as to the steps the company should take. What advice would you give the CEO?
3. An alternative to using a letter of credit is export credit insurance. What are the advantages and disadvantages of using export credit insurance rather than a letter of credit for exporting *(a)* a luxury yacht from California to Canada, and *(b)* machine tools from New York to the Ukraine?
4. How do you explain the popularity of countertrade? Under what scenarios might its popularity increase still further by the year 2010? Under what scenarios might its popularity decline by 2010?
5. How might a company make strategic use of countertrade schemes as a marketing weapon to generate export revenues? What are the risks associated with pursuing such a strategy?

RESEARCH TASK | globalEDGE™ globaledge.msu.edu

Use the globalEDGE™ site to complete the following exercises:

1. The Internet is rich with resources that provide guidance for companies that wish to expand their markets through exporting. GlobalEDGE provides links to these "tutorial" Web sites. Identify five of these sources and provide a description of the services available for new exporters through each of these sources.
2. Utilize the globalEDGE™ Glossary of International Business Terms to identify the definitions of the following exporting terms: air waybill, certificate of inspection, certificate of product origin, wharfage charge, and export broker.

Visit the *Global Business Today* Online Learning Centre at **www.mcgrawhill.ca/college/hill** to access quizzes, interactive exercises, a Business Around the World interactive map, and other learning and study tools related to this chapter.

CLOSING CASE

CAE TAKES ON THE WORLD

The Canadian aerospace industry consists of more than just the companies that make and operate aircraft. One such company is Montreal-based CAE Inc. It designs and manufactures flight simulators and ship control systems for two markets. CAE's civil simulation and training division builds and services flight simulators of commercial planes, including Boeing, Bombardier, and Airbus. Its flight-training unit serves flight schools, business aircraft, and helicopter operators, as well as major and regional airlines. CAE's other primary market is the military. It provides simulation and training systems for a variety of military aircraft, including helicopters, transport planes, and fighter jets. In total, sales for the company topped $1 billion in 2004, while it employs about 5000 people worldwide.

CAE operates in a truly global environment. Its military training systems are provided to more than 30 countries, making the company Canada's largest defence contractor. CAE has facilities and operations in 19 countries on five continents. Most recently, it entered such newly established markets as the Middle East and China through joint ventures with local partners Emirates and China Southern. More than 90 percent of the company's revenues have come from outside Canada, an amount that has been growing over time. The United States now makes up over 30 percent of CAE's revenue, while Europe provides an additional 40 percent.

Yet recent times have been challenging for the company. Its revenue has shrunk from about $1.13 billion in 2002, to $1.09 billion in 2004, due to both the downturn in civilian aviation as well as the recent strength of the Canadian dollar. On the military side, the company was hurt by the loss of a Canadian CF-18 contract, though 40 percent of this division's orders come from the United States military.

CAE has responded to these changing market conditions through an attempt to refocus on the company's key strengths. In February 2005, it sold its marine automation systems division, which provided systems to both naval and commercial shippers, to L-3 Communications Corp. The company also reduced its workforce by about 450 people, and consolidated its manufacturing facilities and global training network. It also shifted its emphasis from the manufacturing of equipment to the provision of potentially higher-profit services. In 2001, about 85 percent of the company's revenue came from equipment while only 15 percent came from training and services (these services included parts replacement and repairs, installations, relocations, upgrades, and technical training). By 2004, this had shifted dramatically, as about 45 percent of the company's revenue came from training and services.

Yet redirecting a $1-billion company doesn't always progress smoothly. As Robert Brown, president and CEO noted, "Those changes were creating serious conflicts within the organization. Our simulator people were continuing to design and manufacture highly customized equipment with relatively high costs, our training group was then challenged to make an acceptable return when they were deploying our high-cost equipment to our own training centres. And finally, the high cost of our own equipment also watered down our training proposition as we asked airlines to consider us over their own in-house training."

In its attempts to win business from the U.S. military market, CAE faces competition from U.S.-based companies like L-3 Communications and Environmental Tectonics Corp. "Politics is a fact of life in most defence markets," noted Robert Brown a few years, after CAE lost a US$1-billion contract, despite having a significantly lower bid. However, there are signs that the company's fortunes may have turned in this regard. In early 2005, CAE won two contracts from the U.S. military: a US$20-million contract for the Army's Special Operations Aviation Regiment, and a US$26-million contract for a Black Hawk simulator.

Sources: Robert Brown, president and CEO, *Remarks For Third-Quarter Results FY 2005*, www.cae.com, February 11, 2005; Editorial Board, "Canada's Military Can Be Relevant In A One-Superpower World," *Canadian Business*, November 24, 2003; Annual Report, Fact Sheet, Backgrounder, presentation "Restoring Shareholder Value," April 2005 from CAE's Web site, www.cae.com; Press releases, "CAE USA Awarded US $20 million in Additional Special OPS Contracts," April 26, 2005, "CAE USA Awarded US $26 million Contract for Special Ops Black Hawk Simulator, March 9, 2005, www.biz.yahoo.com.

CASE DISCUSSION QUESTIONS

1. How easy is it for a company operating around the globe to begin to refocus itself?
2. Should all purchasing decisions be based on who has submitted the lowest bid? Is national defence a special case? If it is, how far down the supply chain should preferences be given?

PART FIVE

5

COMPETING IN A GLOBAL MARKETPLACE

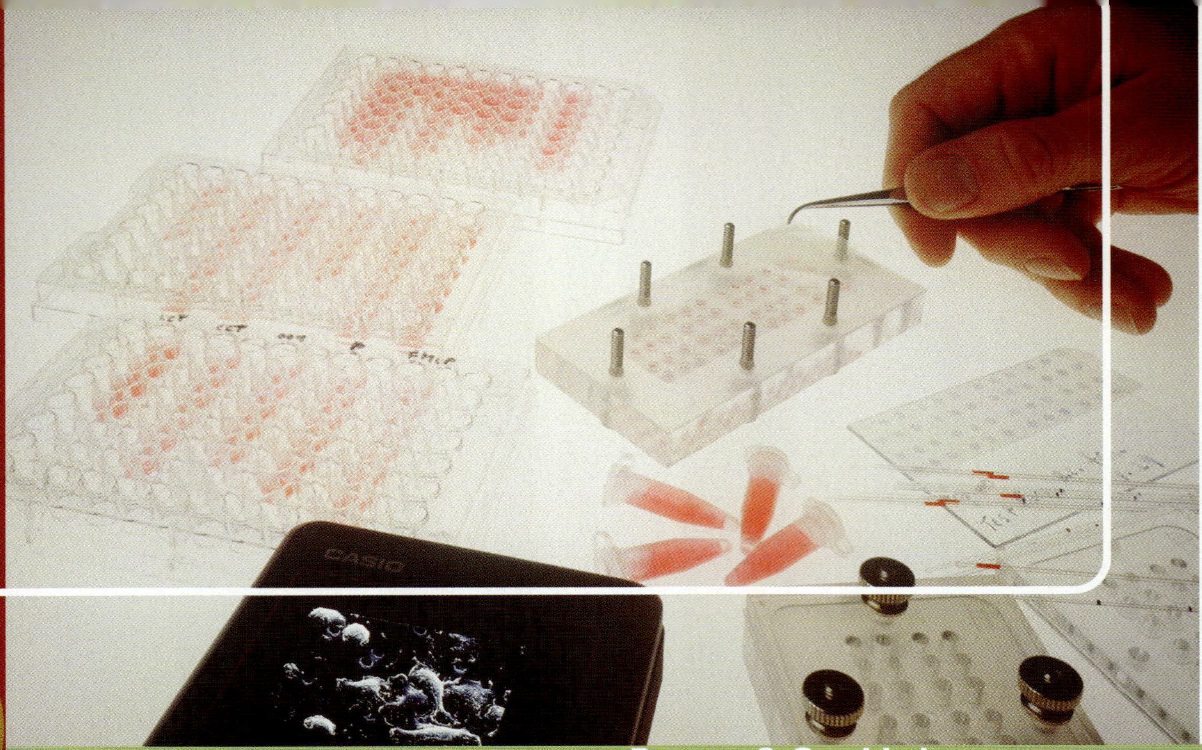

Procter & Gamble in Japan: from Marketing Failure to Success

Procter & Gamble (P&G), the large U.S. consumer products company, has a well-earned reputation as one of the world's best marketers. With its 80-plus major brands, P&G generates more than $37 billion in annual revenues worldwide. Along with Unilever, P&G is a dominant global force in laundry detergents, cleaning products, and personal care products. P&G expanded abroad after World War II by exporting its brands and marketing policies to Western Europe, initially with considerable success. Over the next 30 years, this policy of developing new products and marketing strategies in the United States and then transferring them to other countries became entrenched. Adaptation of marketing policies to accommodate country differences was minimal.

In Canada, P&G has had a prominent presence from 1915 when it opened its first manufacturing facility in Hamilton, Ontario, employing 75 people. Today P&G's Canadian head office is in Toronto, with manufacturing facilities located in Belleville, Brockville, as well as distribution centres in Hamilton and Brantford. Regional sales offices are in Halifax, Montreal, and Calgary. P&G Canada employs approximately 4000 people and its annual Canadian sales exceed $1 billion. P&G Canada is one of the top profit contributors in the P&G World—a global organization with operations in more than 70 countries.

The first signs that this policy was no longer effective emerged in the 1970s, when P&G suffered a number of major setbacks in Japan. By 1985, after 13 years in Japan, P&G was still losing $40 million a year there. It had introduced disposable diapers in Japan and at one time had commanded an 80-percent share of the market, but by the early 1980s it held a miserable 8 percent. Three large Japanese consumer products companies were dominating the market. P&G's diapers, developed in the United States, were too bulky for the tastes of Japanese consumers. Kao, a Japanese company, had developed a line of trim-fit diapers that appealed more to Japanese tastes. Kao introduced its product with a marketing blitz and was quickly rewarded

M. Freeman/PhotoLink/Getty Images.

CHAPTER 14

Global Marketing and R&D

OPENING CASE

with a 30-percent share of the market. P&G realized it would have to modify its diapers if it were to compete in Japan. It did, and the company now has a 30-percent share of the Japanese market. Plus, P&G's trim-fit diapers have become a bestseller in the United States.

P&G had a similar experience in marketing education in the Japanese laundry detergent market. In the early 1980s, P&G introduced its Cheer laundry detergent in Japan. Developed in the United States, Cheer was promoted in Japan with the U.S. marketing message—Cheer works in all temperatures and produces lots of rich suds. But many Japanese consumers wash their clothes in cold water, which made the claim of working in all temperatures irrelevant. Also, many Japanese add fabric softeners to their water, which reduces detergents' sudsing action, so Cheer did not suds as advertised. After a disastrous launch, P&G knew it had to adapt its marketing message. Cheer is now promoted as a product that works effectively in cold water with fabric softeners added, and it is one of P&G's bestselling products in Japan.

P&G's experience with disposable diapers and laundry detergents in Japan forced the company to rethink its product development and marketing philosophy. The company now admits that its U.S.-centred way of doing business no longer works. Since the late 1980s, P&G has been delegating more responsibility for product development and marketing to its major subsidiaries in Japan and Europe. The company is more responsive to local differences in consumer tastes and preferences and more willing to admit that good new products can be developed outside the United States.

Evidence that this new approach is working can again be found in the company's activities in Japan. Until 1995, P&G did not sell dish soap in Japan. By 1998, it had Japan's bestselling brand, Joy, which now has a 20-percent share of Japan's $400-million market for dish soap. It made major inroads against the products of two domestic firms, Kao and Lion Corp., each of which marketed multiple brands and controlled nearly 40 percent of the market before P&G's entry. P&G's success with Joy was due to its ability to develop a product formula that was specifically targeted at the unmet needs of Japanese consumers, to the design of a packaging format that appealed to retailers, and to the development of a compelling advertising campaign.

In researching the market in the early 1990s, P&G discovered an odd habit: Japanese homemakers, one after another, squirted out excessive amounts of detergent onto dirty dishes, a clear sign of dissatisfaction with existing products. On further inspection, P&G found that this behaviour resulted from the changing eating habits of Japanese consumers. The Japanese are consuming more fried food, and existing dish soaps did not effectively remove grease. Armed with this knowledge, P&G researchers in Japan went to work to create a highly concentrated soap formula based on a new technology developed by the company's scientists in Europe that was highly effective in removing grease. The company also designed a novel package for the product. The packaging of existing products had a clear weakness: the long-necked bottles wasted space on supermarket shelves. P&G's new dish soap containers were compact cylinders that took less space in stores, warehouses, and delivery trucks. This improved the efficiency of distribution and allowed supermarkets to use their shelf space more effectively, which made them receptive to stocking Joy. P&G also devoted considerable attention to developing an advertising campaign for Joy. P&G's ad agency, Dentsu Inc., created commercials in which a famous comedian dropped in on homemakers unannounced with a camera crew to test Joy on the household's dirty dishes. The camera focused on a patch of oil in a pan full of water. After a drop of Joy, the oil dramatically disappeared. With the product, packaging, and advertising strategy carefully worked out, P&G launched Joy throughout Japan in March 1996. The product almost immediately gained a 10-percent market share. Within three months, the product's share had increased to 15 percent, and by year-end it was close to 18 percent. Because of strong demand, P&G was also able to raise prices as were the retailers that stocked the product, all of which translated into fatter margins for the retailers and helped consolidate Joy's position in the market.

Sources: G. de Jonquieres and C. Bobinski, "Wash and Get into a Lather in Poland," *Financial Times,* May 28, 1992, p. 2; "Perestroika in Soapland," *The Economist,* June 10, 1989, pp. 69–71; "After Early Stumbles P&G Is Making Inroads Overseas," *Wall Street Journal,* February 6, 1989, p. B1; C. A. Bartlett and S. Ghoshal, *Managing across Borders: The Transnational Solution* (Boston: Harvard Business School Press, 1989); N. Shirouzu, "P&G's Joy Makes an Unlikely Splash in Japan," *Wall Street Journal,* December 10, 1997, p. B1; and www.pg.com/canada.

LEARNING OBJECTIVES

1. Understand why and how it may make sense to vary the attributes of a product among countries.
2. Appreciate why and how a firm's distribution strategy might vary among countries.
3. Understand why and how advertising and promotional strategies might vary among countries.
4. Understand why and how a firm's pricing strategy might vary among countries.
5. Understand how the globalization of the world economy is affecting new-product development within international businesses.

INTRODUCTION

This chapter focuses on how marketing and R&D can be performed in the international business so that they will reduce the costs of value creation and add value by better serving customer needs. In Chapter 11, we spoke of the tension existing in most international businesses between the needs to reduce costs and at the same time to respond to local conditions, which tends to raise costs. This tension continues to be a persistent theme in this chapter. A global marketing strategy that views the world's consumers as similar in their tastes and preferences is consistent with the mass production of a standardized output. By mass-producing a standardized output, the firm can realize substantial unit cost reductions from experience curve and other scale economies. But ignoring country differences in consumer tastes and preferences can lead to failure. Thus, an international business's marketing function needs to determine when product standardization is appropriate and when it is not, and to adjust the marketing strategy accordingly. Similarly, the firm's R&D function needs to be able to develop globally standardized products when appropriate as well as products customized to local requirements.

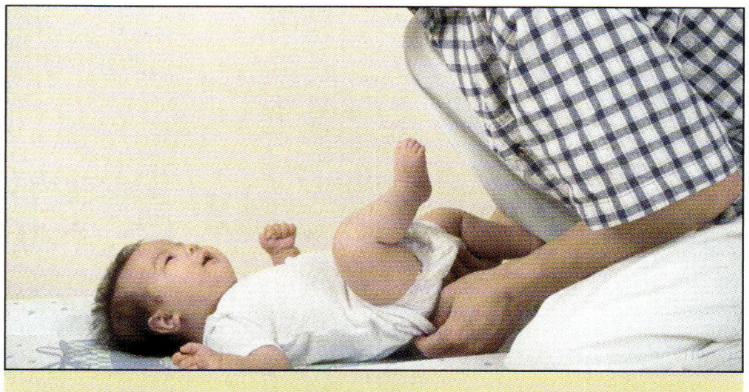

P&G realized that to effectively market diapers in Japan, they had to reduce the bulk of the diaper because Japanese consumers liked a more trim-fitting diaper. Research and development into consumer needs, along with the right marketing message, can lead to a successful launch of a product abroad. Do you think it is possible to launch a product abroad without sufficient research and development? Can you think of a product created domestically that has transferred to another country without any changes? © Jennie Woodcock Reflections Photolibrary/CORBIS.

We consider marketing and R&D within the same chapter because of their close relationship. A critical aspect of the marketing function is identifying gaps in the market so new products can be developed to fill those gaps. Developing new products requires R&D; thus, the linkage between marketing and R&D. New products should be developed with market needs in mind, and only marketing can define those needs for R&D personnel. Also, only marketing can tell R&D whether to produce globally standardized or locally customized products. Academic research has long maintained that a major factor of success for product introductions is the closeness of the relationship between marketing and R&D. The closer the linkage, the greater the success rate.[1]

The opening case illustrates some issues we will be debating in this chapter. Many of P&G's problems in Japan were caused by a failure to tailor its marketing strategy to the specific demands of the Japanese marketplace. P&G learned from its experience with disposable diapers and laundry detergent that a marketing approach that works in one context won't necessarily work in another. The company's subsequent success with Joy drives home the point that in many consumer product markets, it is important to customize the product offering, packaging, and advertising message to the specific needs of consumers in that country. Joy was developed by Procter & Gamble's R&D staff in Kobe, Japan, specifically to meet the evolving needs of Japanese consumers. This illustrates the benefits of locating R&D activities close to the market for the product when that market demands a customized product offering.

But it would be wrong to generalize too much from this case. For other firms in other industries, it may make sense to pursue a global strategy, producing a standardized product for global consumption and using the same basic market message to sell that product worldwide. Some product markets are truly global in their reach. The market for semiconductor chips, for example, is a global market where consumers demand the same standardized product worldwide so a global marketing strategy, supported by a global R&D strategy, might make sense.

In this chapter, we begin by reviewing the debate on the globalization of markets. Then we discuss the issue of market segmentation. Next we look at four elements that constitute a firm's **marketing mix:** product attributes, distribution strategy, communication strategy, and pricing strategy. The marketing mix is the set of choices the firm offers to its targeted markets. Many firms vary their marketing mix from country to country depending on differences in national culture, economic development, product standards, distribution channels, and so on. The chapter closes with a look at new-product development in an international business and at the implications of this for the organization of the firm's R&D function.

MARKETING MIX
Choices about product attributes, distribution strategy, communication strategy, and pricing strategy that a firm offers its targeted markets.

THE GLOBALIZATION OF MARKETS AND BRANDS

In a now-famous *Harvard Business Review* article, Theodore Levitt wrote lyrically about the globalization of world markets.[2] Levitt's arguments have become something of a lightning rod in the debate about the extent of globalization. According to Levitt:

Levitt mentions Hollywood movies as "confirmation" of the disappearance of national tastes due to the globalization of markets. Do you think this is so? How do movies differ from something like MTV in feeding this "standardization," as Levitt calls it.

> A powerful force drives the world toward a converging commonalty, and that force is technology. It has proletarianized communication, transport, and travel. The result is a new commercial reality–the emergence of global markets for standardized consumer products on a previously unimagined scale of magnitude.
>
> Gone are accustomed differences in national or regional preferences . . . The globalization of markets is at hand. With that, the multinational commercial world nears its end, and so does the multinational corporation. The multinational corporation operates in a number of countries and adjusts its products and practices to each–at high relative costs. The global corporation operates with resolute consistency–at low relative cost–as if the entire world were a single entity; it sells the same thing in the same way everywhere.
>
> Commercially, nothing confirms this as much as the success of McDonald's from the Champs Elysees to the Ginza, of Coca-Cola in Bahrain and Pepsi-Cola in Moscow, and of rock music, Greek salad, Hollywood movies, Revlon cosmetics, Sony television, and Levi's jeans everywhere.
>
> Ancient differences in national tastes or modes of doing business disappear. The commonalty of preference leads inescapably to the standardization of products, manufacturing, and the institutions of trade and commerce.

This is eloquent and evocative writing, but is Levitt correct? The rise of global media such as MTV and CNN, and the ability of such media to help shape a global culture, would seem to lend weight to Levitt's argument. If Levitt is correct, his argument has major implications for the marketing strategies pursued by international business. However, the current consensus among academics seems to be that Levitt overstates his case.[3] Although Levitt may have a point when it comes to many basic industrial products, such as steel, bulk chemicals, and semiconductor chips, globalization seems to be the exception rather than the rule in many consumer goods markets and industrial markets. Even a firm such as McDonald's, which Levitt holds up as the archetypal example of a consumer products firm that sells a standardized product worldwide, modifies its menu from country to country in light of local consumer preferences.[4]

Levitt is probably correct to assert that modern transportation and communications technologies, such as MTV, are facilitating a convergence of the tastes and preferences of consumers in the more advanced countries of the world. The popularity of sushi in Los Angeles, hamburgers in Tokyo, hip-hop music, and global media phenomena such as Pokémon, all support this. In the long run, such technological forces may lead to the evolution of a global culture. At present, however, the continuing persistence of cultural and economic differences between nations acts as a major brake on any trend toward global consumer tastes and preferences. In addition, trade barriers and differences in product and technical standards also constrain a firm's ability to sell a standardized product to a global market using a standardized marketing strategy. We discuss the sources of these differences in subsequent sections when we look at how products must be altered from country to country. Levitt's globally standardized markets seem a long way off in many industries.

MARKET SEGMENTATION

Market segmentation refers to identifying distinct groups of consumers whose purchasing behaviour differs from others in important ways. Markets can be segmented in numerous ways: by geography, demography (sex, age, income, race, education level, etc.), social-cultural factors (social class, values, religion, lifestyle choices), and psychological factors (personality). Because different segments exhibit different patterns of purchasing behaviour, firms often adjust their marketing mix from segment to segment. Thus, the precise design of a product, the pricing strategy, the distribution channels used, and the choice of communication strategy may all be varied from segment to segment. The goal is to optimize the fit between the purchasing behaviour of consumers in a given segment and the marketing mix, thereby maximizing sales to that segment. Automobile companies, for example, use a different marketing mix to sell cars to different socioeconomic segments. Thus, Toyota uses its Lexus division to sell high-priced luxury cars to high-income consumers, while selling its entry-level models, such as the Toyota Corolla, to lower-income consumers. Similarly, personal computer manufacturers will offer different computer models, embodying different combinations of product attributes and price points, precisely to appeal to consumers from different market segments (e.g., business users and home users).

MARKET SEGMENTATION
Identifying groups of consumers whose purchasing behaviour differs from others in important ways.

When managers in an international business consider market segmentation in foreign countries, they need to be cognizant of two main issues: the differences between countries in the structure of market segments and the existence of segments that transcend national borders. The structure of market segments may differ significantly from country to country. An important market segment in a foreign country may have no parallel in the firm's home country, and vice versa. The firm may have to develop a marketing mix to appeal to the unique purchasing behaviour of a segment in a given country. See the accompanying Management Focus, which looks at the marketing plan of the Jean Coutu Group. For example, a research project published in 1998 identified a segment of 45-to-55-year-old consumers in China that has few parallels in other countries.[5] This group came of age during China's violent and repressive Cultural Revolution in the late 1960s and early 1970s. The values of this group have been shaped by their experiences during the Cultural Revolution. They tend to be highly sensitive to price and respond negatively to new products and most forms of marketing.

ANOTHER PERSPECTIVE

Just a skin cream? Oil of Olay learns about itself in Malaysia

When Procter & Gamble prepared to introduce its Oil of Olay product line into the tropical country of Malaysia, a local Chinese Malay woman, who began by running focus groups of potential adopters, headed its marketing research efforts. Her research helped her to learn that local women wanted lighter skin. She found widespread use of skin bleaching products, some of them quite harsh, a product line P&G would not enter. One focus group respondent helped her to understand that many Malaysian women did not value tanned skin caused by sun exposure. They connected such darkening to outdoor manual labour, a sign of rural farming. P&G's Oil of Olay was just what they needed. Rather than bleach skin, it blocks UV rays, with an SPF of 15. That product now leads the skin cream market, not as a moisturizer, as in the United States and Europe, but as a skin protector. Who defines the product attributes?

MANAGEMENT FOCUS

JEAN COUTU GROUP—MARKETING TO THE NORTH AMERICAN CONSUMER

The Quebec-based Jean Coutu Group is unconventional in two ways. First, it is still very much a family-run company in an environment when many such businesses are disappearing. Jean Coutu, who founded the drugstore chain in 1969, is chairman of the board, while Francois Coutu is president and CEO of the company. Michel Coutu is president and CEO of The Jean Coutu Group USA Inc. with another member of the founding family as vice-president of Commercial Policies. Second, it is making money in the slow-growth field of drugstore retailing by slowly buying up its competitors. The company is now the fourth largest drugstore chain in North America and the second largest in both the eastern United States and Canada.

Jean Coutu's acquisition path began in the 1990s, a mere two decades after the company began. In 1994, it added the Brooks Pharmacy Network group of stores that operated in the U.S. northeast. Five years later, it added the 11-store City Drug chain in Vermont. By mid-2004, Jean Coutu operated 319 franchised stores in Canada and 336 stores in the United States.

The company's boldest move came in July 2004, when it purchased the 1549-store Eckerd group from J.C. Penney for a total cost of US$2.375 billion. The Eckerd drugstores, which would continue to be operated under the familiar Eckerd name, employs about 37 000 people. With this purchase, Jean Coutu will employ about 60 000 people in Canada and the United States. It is truly an example of a concentrated retail system.

Why make such a bold move? There are three factors in the company's favour. First, while there is always a risk associated with successfully integrating a new chain of stores within an existing corporate structure, Jean Coutu has a good record of successfully integrating its purchases made in the 1990s. The company's plans for the Eckerd stores include enhancing Eckerd's private label brands, adjusting product pricing, targetting local advertising through a 52-week flyer program, and increasing staffing levels and store operating hours. Second, the scale of the Eckerd purchase allows for true economies of scale to be present. In over 60 percent of the company's local U.S. markets, the stores will either hold the number one or number two position. Third, while there will be continued competition from supermarkets and other retailers, there is strong growth seen in the pharmacy side of the business. An aging population, increasing drug consumption on a per patient basis, more extensive prescription drug coverage, and high drug price inflation that is paid for by insurers and governments, and not the end consumer, drives this growth.

As with any strategy, there are risks associated with the purchase of Eckerd. The amount of debt that Jean Coutu has to take on to finance the Eckerd purchase will be on its balance sheet for many years. The Eckerd line, while having strong pharmacy sales, has suffered in its front-end (non-pharmacy) sales, as consumers have become confused by differing pricing strategies, and were frustrated to find items often out-of-stock.

Jean Coutu has a definite strategy to integrate and strengthen the Eckerd brand. Time will tell whether this big step will be a successful one for the company.

Sources: Jean Coutu at www.jeancoutu.com: Yahoo Finance, "Jean Coutu Group (PJCa.To)," Standard and Poor's, "Jean Coutu Group," *Credit Week*, July 19, 2004.

The existence of this group implies that firms doing business in China may need to customize their marketing mix to address the unique values and purchasing behaviour of the group. The existence of such a segment constrains the ability of firms to standardize their global marketing strategy.

In contrast, the existence of market segments that transcend national borders clearly enhances the ability of an international business to view the global marketplace as a single entity and pursue a global strategy, selling a standardized product worldwide and using the same basic marketing mix to help position and sell that product in a variety of national markets. For a segment to transcend national borders, consumers in that segment must have some compelling similarities along important dimensions–such as age, values, lifestyle choices–and those similarities must translate into similar purchasing behaviour. Although such segments exist in certain industrial markets, they are rare in consumer markets. However, one emerging global segment that is attracting the attention of international marketers of consumer goods is the so-called global youth segment. Global media are paving the way for a global youth segment. Evidence that such a segment exists comes from a study of the cultural attitudes and purchasing behaviour of more than 6500 teenagers in 26 countries.[6] The findings suggest that teens around the world are increasingly living parallel lives that share many common values. It follows that they are likely to purchase the same kind of consumer goods and for the same reasons. Even here though, marketing specialists argue that some customization in the marketing mix is required.

PRODUCT ATTRIBUTES

A product can be viewed as a bundle of attributes.[7] For example, the attributes that make up a car include power, design, quality, performance, fuel consumption, and comfort; the attributes of a hamburger include taste, texture, and size; a hotel's attributes include atmosphere, quality, comfort, and service. Products sell well when their attributes match consumer needs (and when their prices are appropriate). BMW cars sell well to people who have high needs for luxury, quality, and performance, precisely because BMW builds those attributes into its cars. If consumer needs were the same the world over, a firm could simply sell the same product worldwide. However, consumer needs vary from country to country depending on culture and the level of economic development. A firm's ability to sell the same product worldwide is further constrained by countries' differing product standards. In this section, we review each of these issues and discuss how they influence product attributes.

CULTURAL DIFFERENCES

We discussed countries' cultural differences in Chapter 3. Countries differ along a whole range of dimensions, including social structure, language, religion, and education. And as alluded to in Chapter 3, these differences have important implications for marketing strategy. For example, "hamburgers" do not sell well in Islamic countries,

Companies and their ads must be aware of the often-subtle differences in environment and culture. In this ad, Korean car manufacturer Daewoo touts the Italian design of its Leganza model in an ad created for the Australian market. Courtesy of The Campaign Palace.

where the consumption of ham is forbidden by Islamic law. The most important aspect of cultural differences is probably the impact of tradition. Tradition is particularly important in foodstuffs and beverages. For example, reflecting differences in traditional eating habits, the Findus frozen food division of Nestlé, the Swiss food giant, markets fish cakes and fish fingers in Great Britain, but beef bourguignon and coq au vin in France and vitéllo con funghi and braviola in Italy. In addition to its normal range of products, Coca-Cola in Japan markets Georgia, a cold coffee in a can, and Aquarius, a tonic drink, both of which appeal to traditional Japanese tastes.

For historical and idiosyncratic reasons, a range of other cultural differences exist between countries. For example, scent preferences differ from one country to another. S. C. Johnson Wax, a manufacturer of waxes and polishes, encountered resistance to its lemon-scented Pledge furniture polish among older consumers in Japan. Careful market research revealed that the polish smelled similar to a latrine disinfectant used widely in Japan in the 1940s. Sales rose sharply after the scent was adjusted.[8] In another example, Cheetos, the bright orange and cheesy-tasting snack from PepsiCo's Frito-Lay unit, do not have a cheese taste in China. Chinese consumers generally do not like the taste of cheese because it has never been part of traditional cuisine and because many Chinese are lactose-intolerant.[9]

There is some evidence of the trends Levitt talked about. Tastes and preferences are becoming more cosmopolitan. Coffee is gaining ground against tea in Japan and Great Britain, while American-style frozen dinners have become popular in Europe (with some fine-tuning to local tastes). Taking advantage of these trends, Nestlé has found that it can market its instant coffee, spaghetti bolognese, and Lean Cuisine frozen dinners in essentially the same manner in both North America and Western Europe. However, there is no market for Lean Cuisine dinners in most of the rest of the world, and there may not be for years or decades. Although some cultural convergence has occurred, particularly among the advanced industrial nations of North America and Western Europe, Levitt's global culture is still a long way off.

ECONOMIC DEVELOPMENT

Just as important as differences in culture are differences in the level of economic development. We discussed the extent of country differences in economic development in Chapter 2. Consumer behaviour is influenced by the level of economic development of a country. Firms based in highly developed countries such as Canada and the United States tend to build a lot of extra performance attributes into their products. These extra attributes are not usually demanded by consumers in less developed nations, where the preference is for more basic products. Thus, cars sold in less developed nations typically lack many of the features found in the West, such as air-conditioning, power steering, power windows, radios, and cassette players. For most consumer durables, product reliability may be a more important attribute in less developed nations, where such a purchase may account for a major proportion of a consumer's income, than it is in advanced nations.

Contrary to Levitt's suggestions, consumers in the most developed countries are often not willing to sacrifice their preferred attributes for lower prices. Consumers in the most advanced countries often shun globally standardized products that have been developed with the lowest common denominator in mind. They are willing to pay more for products that have additional features and attributes customized to

ANOTHER PERSPECTIVE

Careful: It's the old "Don't Judge a Book by its Cover" story

International business managers have to be careful when they see signs of cultural convergence, because the convergence may be only at the product or consumption level. Culture as it describes the way people give meaning is deep and enduring. If we go to Tokyo or Paris, we'll find certain surface-level similarities in fashion, food, and other products. But just because we are talking with someone who wears clothes that look like ours and perhaps even knows our language well enough to master slang is not evidence that person operates with the same set of assumptions about reality as we do. Deep-seated culture changes very slowly. Besides, not everyone wants to be like North Americans. Just ask them.

their tastes and preferences. For example, demand for top-of-the-line four-wheel-drive sport utility vehicles, such as Chrysler's Jeep, Ford's Explorer, and Toyota's Land Cruiser, is almost totally restricted to the United States. This is due to a combination of factors, including the high income level of U.S. consumers, the country's vast distances, the relatively low cost of gasoline, and the culturally grounded "outdoor" theme of American life.

PRODUCT AND TECHNICAL STANDARDS

Even with the forces that are creating some convergence of consumer tastes and preferences among advanced, industrialized nations, Levitt's vision of global markets may still be a long way off because of national differences in product and technological standards.

Differing government-mandated product standards can rule out mass production and marketing of a standardized product. For example, Caterpillar, the U.S. construction equipment firm, manufactures backhoe-loaders for all of Europe in Great Britain. These tractor-type machines have a bucket in front and a digger at the back. Several special parts must be built into backhoe-loaders that will be sold in Germany: a separate brake attached to the rear axle, a special locking mechanism on the backhoe operating valve, specially positioned valves in the steering system, and a lock on the bucket for travelling. These extras account for 5 percent of the total cost of the product in Germany.[10] The European Union is trying to harmonize such divergent product standards among its member nations. If the EU is successful, the need to customize products will be reduced within the boundaries of the EU.

Differences in technical standards also constrain the globalization of markets. Some of these differences result from idiosyncratic decisions made long ago, rather than from government actions, but their long-term effects are profound. For example, video equipment manufactured for sale in the United States will not play videotapes recorded on equipment manufactured for sale in Great Britain, Germany, and France (and vice versa). Different technical standards for frequency of television signals emerged in the 1950s that require television and video equipment to be customized to prevailing standards. RCA stumbled in the 1970s when it failed to account for this in its marketing of TVs in Asia. Although several Asian countries adopted the U.S. standard, Singapore, Hong Kong, and Malaysia adopted the British standard. People who bought RCA TVs in those countries could receive a picture but no sound![11]

DISTRIBUTION STRATEGY

A critical element of a firm's marketing mix is its distribution strategy: the means it chooses for delivering the product to the consumer. The way the product is delivered is determined by the firm's entry strategy, which we discussed in Chapter 13. In this section, we examine a typical distribution system, discuss how its structure varies between countries, and look at how appropriate distribution strategies vary from country to country.

A TYPICAL DISTRIBUTION SYSTEM

Figure 14.1 illustrates a typical distribution system consisting of a channel that includes a wholesale distributor and a retailer. If the firm manufactures its product in the particular country, it can sell directly to the consumer, to the retailer, or to the wholesaler. The same options are available to a firm that manufactures outside the country. Plus, this firm may decide to sell to an import agent, which then deals with the wholesale distributor, the retailer, or the consumer. The factors that determine the firm's choice of channel are considered later in this section.

FIGURE 14.1
A Typical Distribution System

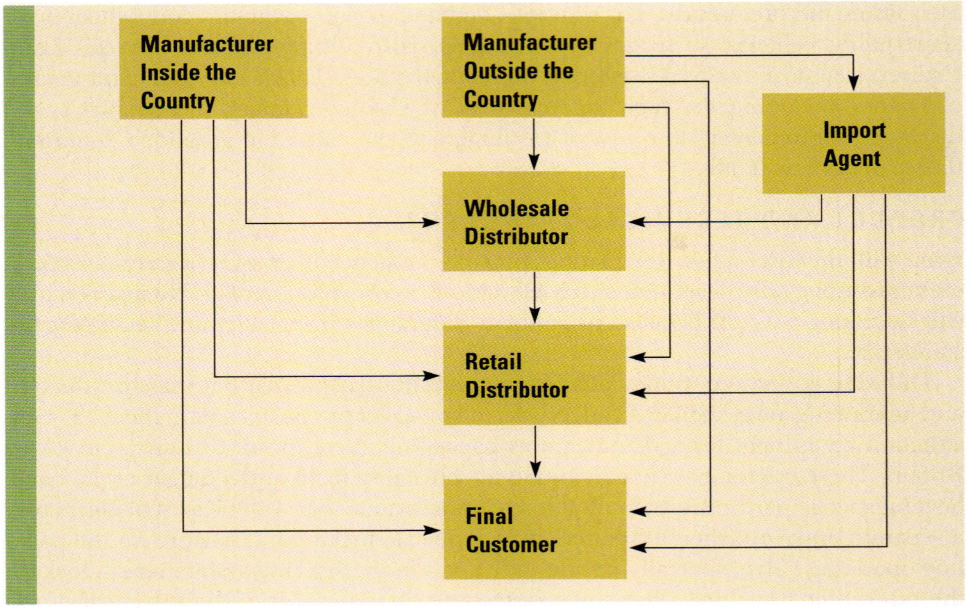

DIFFERENCES BETWEEN COUNTRIES

The three main differences between distribution systems are retail concentration, channel length, and channel exclusivity.

Retail Concentration

CONCENTRATED RETAIL SYSTEM A few retailers supply most of the market.

FRAGMENTED RETAIL SYSTEM Many retailers, with no one having a major share of the market.

In some countries, the retail system is very concentrated, but it is fragmented in others. In a **concentrated retail system,** a few retailers supply most of the market. A **fragmented retail system** is one in which there are many retailers, no one of which has a major share of the market. Many of the differences in concentration are rooted in history and tradition. In Canada and the United States, the importance of the automobile and the relative youth of many urban areas have resulted in a retail system centred around large stores or shopping malls to which people can drive. This has facilitated system concentration. Japan's much greater population density together with the large number of urban centers that grew up before the automobile have yielded a more fragmented retail system of many small stores that serve local neighbourhoods and to which people frequently walk. In addition, the Japanese legal system protects small retailers. Small retailers can block the establishment of a large retail outlet by petitioning their local government.

There is a tendency for greater retail concentration in developed countries. Three factors that contribute to this are the increases in car ownership, number of households with refrigerators and freezers, and number of two-income households. All these factors have changed shopping habits and facilitated the growth of large retail establishments sited away from traditional shopping areas. During the last decade there has been a tendency for consolidation in the global retail industry, with companies such as Wal-Mart and Carrefour attempting to become global retailers by acquiring retailers in different countries. This has increased retail concentration.

In contrast, retail systems are very fragmented in many developing countries, which can make for interesting distribution challenges. In India, for example, Unilever has to sell to retailers in 600 000 rural villages, many of which cannot be accessed via paved roads, which means that products can reach their destination only by bullock, bicycle, or cart. In neighbouring Nepal, the terrain is so rugged that even bicycles and carts are not practical, and businesses rely on yak trains and the human back to deliver products to thousands of small retailers.

Channel Length

Channel length refers to the number of intermediaries between the producer (or manufacturer) and the consumer. If the producer sells directly to the consumer, the channel is very short. If the producer sells through an import agent, a wholesaler, and a retailer, a long channel exists. The choice of a short or long channel is in part a strategic decision for the producing firm. However, some countries have longer distribution channels than others. The most important determinant of channel length is the degree to which the retail system is fragmented. Fragmented retail systems tend to promote the growth of wholesalers to serve retailers, which lengthens channels.

CHANNEL LENGTH The number of intermediaries that a product has to go through before it reaches the final consumer.

The more fragmented the retail system, the more expensive it is for a firm to make contact with each individual retailer. Imagine a firm that sells toothpaste in a country with more than a million small retailers, as in rural India and China. To sell directly to the retailers, the firm would have to build a huge sales force. This would be very expensive, particularly since each sales call would yield a very small order. But suppose there are a few hundred wholesalers in the country that supply retailers not only with toothpaste but also with all other personal care and household products. Because these wholesalers carry a wide range of products, they get bigger orders with each sales call, making it worthwhile for them to deal directly with the retailers. Accordingly, it makes economic sense for the firm to sell to the wholesalers and the wholesalers to deal with the retailers.

Because of such factors, countries with fragmented retail systems also tend to have long channels of distribution, sometimes with multiple layers. The classic example is Japan, where there are often two or three layers of wholesalers between the firm and retail outlets. In countries such as Canada, Germany, and the United States where the retail system is far more concentrated, channels are much shorter. When the retail sector is very concentrated, it makes sense for the firm to deal directly with retailers, cutting out wholesalers. A relatively small sales force is required to deal with a concentrated retail sector, and the orders generated from each sales call can be large. Such circumstances tend to prevail in the United States, where large food companies sell directly to supermarkets rather than going through wholesale distributors.

The rapid development of the Internet in recent years has helped to shorten channel length. For example, the Seattle-based outdoor equipment retailer REI sells its products in Japan via a Japanese-language website, thereby cutting out the need for a retail presence on the ground in Japan, which obviously shortens the channel length between REI and its customers. However, there are obvious drawbacks with such a strategy. In the case of REI, it is not possible to offer the same level of advice over the Web as it is in physical retail stores, where salespeople can help customers choose the right gear. So although REI benefits from a short channel in Japan, it may lose significant sales due to the lack of point-of-sale service.

Channel Exclusivity

An **exclusive distribution channel** is one that is difficult for outsiders to access. For example, new firms often have trouble getting access to shelf space in supermarkets. This occurs because retailers tend to prefer to carry the products of long-established manufacturers of foodstuffs with national reputations rather than gamble on the products of unknown firms. The exclusivity of a distribution system varies between countries. Japan's system is often held up as an example of a very exclusive system. In Japan, relationships between manufacturers, wholesalers, and retailers often go back

EXCLUSIVE DISTRIBUTION CHANNEL A distribution channel that outsiders find difficult to access.

decades. Many of these relationships are based on the understanding that distributors will not carry the products of competing firms. In return, the distributors are guaranteed an attractive markup by the manufacturer. As many U.S. and European manufacturers have learned, the close ties that result from this arrangement can make access to the Japanese market very difficult. But, as the opening case illustrates, it is possible to break into the Japanese market with a new consumer product, as Procter & Gamble did recently with its Joy brand of dish soap. P&G was able to overcome a tradition of exclusivity for two reasons. First, after a decade of lacklustre economic performance, Japan is changing. In their search for profits, retailers are far more willing than they have been historically to violate the old norms of exclusivity. Second, P&G has been in Japan long enough and has a broad enough portfolio of consumer products to give it considerable leverage with distributors, enabling it to push new products out through the distribution channel.

CHOOSING A DISTRIBUTION STRATEGY

The choice of distribution strategy determines which channel the firm will use to reach potential consumers. Should the firm try to sell directly to the consumer or should it go through retailers; should it go through a wholesaler; should it use an import agent? The optimal strategy is determined by the relative costs and benefits of each alternative. The relative costs and benefits of each alternative vary from country to country, depending on the three factors we have just discussed: retail concentration, channel length, and channel exclusivity.

Because each intermediary in a channel adds its own markup to the products, there is generally a critical link between channel length, the final selling price, and the firm's profit margin. The longer a channel, the greater is the aggregate markup, and the higher the price that consumers are charged for the final product. To ensure that prices do not get too high due to markups by multiple intermediaries, a firm might be forced to operate with lower profit margins. Thus, if price is an important competitive weapon, and if the firm does not want to see its profit margins squeezed, other things being equal, the firm would prefer to use a shorter channel.

However, the benefits of using a longer channel often outweigh these drawbacks. As we have seen, one benefit of a longer channel is that it cuts selling costs when the retail sector is very fragmented. Thus, it makes sense for an international business to use longer channels in countries where the retail sector is fragmented and shorter channels in countries where the retail sector is concentrated. Another benefit of using a longer channel is market access—the ability to enter an exclusive channel. Import agents may have long-term relationships with wholesalers, retailers, and/or important consumers and thus be better able to win orders and get access to a distribution system. Similarly, wholesalers may have long-standing relationships with retailers and be better able to persuade them to carry the firm's product than the firm itself would.

Import agents are not limited to independent trading houses; any firm with a strong local reputation could serve as well. For example, to break down channel exclusivity and gain greater access to the Japanese market, Apple Computer in 1991 and 1992 signed distribution agreements with five large Japanese firms including business equipment giant

ANOTHER PERSPECTIVE

Communication issues across cultures: a market research challenge

In the early 1980s, a manufacturer of packaged cake mixes began research for entry into Japan. The market researchers spoke fluent Japanese and set up their trial display in one of the early Western-style supermarkets in Tokyo. They offered the Japanese women tastes of the cakes and asked if they would serve these cakes to their families. Researchers had been concerned about whether the quality and taste of their product would meet the quality standards of Japanese consumers. They learned the consumers liked the cakes and would serve them to their families.

The product rollout was initiated, and much to the researchers' surprise, sales were very low. Only later did they learn why—Japanese homes tend to not have ovens. Their research had not asked the right questions!

Brother Industries, stationery leader Kokuyo, Mitsubishi, Sharp, and Minolta. These firms use their own long-established distribution relationships with consumers, retailers, and wholesalers to push Apple Macintosh computers through the Japanese distribution system. As a result, Apple's share of the Japanese market increased from less than 1 percent in 1988 to 6 percent in 1991 and 13 percent by 1994.[12]

If such an arrangement is not possible, the firm might want to consider other, less traditional alternatives to gaining market access. Frustrated by channel exclusivity in Japan, some foreign manufacturers of consumer goods have attempted to sell directly to Japanese consumers using direct mail and catalogues. REI had trouble persuading Japanese wholesalers and retailers to carry its products, so it began a direct-mail campaign and then Web-based strategy to enter Japan that is proving very successful.

COMMUNICATION STRATEGY

Another critical element in the marketing mix is communicating the attributes of the product to prospective customers. A number of communication channels are available to a firm, including direct selling, sales promotion, direct marketing, and advertising. A firm's communication strategy is partly defined by its choice of channel. Some firms rely primarily on direct selling, others on point-of-sale promotions or direct marketing, others on mass advertising; still others use several channels simultaneously to communicate their message to prospective customers. In this section, we will look first at the barriers to international communication. Then we will survey the various factors that determine which communication strategy is most appropriate in a particular country. After that we discuss global advertising.

BARRIERS TO INTERNATIONAL COMMUNICATION

International communication occurs whenever a firm uses a marketing message to sell its products in another country. The effectiveness of a firm's international communication can be jeopardized by three potentially critical variables: cultural barriers, source effects, and noise levels.

Cultural Barriers

Cultural barriers can make it difficult to communicate messages across cultures. We discussed some sources and consequences of cultural differences between nations in Chapter 3 and in the previous section of this chapter. Due to cultural differences, a message that means one thing in one country may mean something quite different in another. For example, when Procter & Gamble promoted its Camay soap in Japan in the 1980s it ran into unexpected trouble. In a TV commercial, a Japanese man walked into the bathroom while his wife was bathing. The woman began telling her husband all about her new soap, but the husband, stroking her shoulder, hinted that suds were not on his mind. This ad had been very popular in Europe, but it flopped in Japan because it is considered very bad manners there for a man to intrude on his wife.[13] Benetton, the Italian clothing manufacturer and retailer, is another firm that has run into cultural problems with its advertising. The company launched a worldwide advertising campaign in 1989 with the theme "United Colours of Benetton" that had won awards in France. One of its ads featured a black woman breast-feeding a white baby, and another one showed a black man and a white man handcuffed together. Benetton was surprised when the ads were attacked by U.S. civil rights groups for promoting white racial domination. Benetton withdrew its ads and fired its advertising agency, Eldorado of France.

The best way for a firm to overcome cultural barriers is to develop cross-cultural literacy (see Chapter 3). In addition, it should use local input, such as a local advertising agency, in developing its marketing message. If the firm uses direct selling rather than advertising to communicate its message, it should develop a local sales force whenever possible. Cultural differences limit a firm's ability to use the same marketing message and selling approach the world over. What works well in one country may be offensive in another.

Source and Country of Origin Effects

SOURCE EFFECTS When the receiver of the message evaluates the message based on the status or image of the sender.

Source effects occur when the receiver of the message (the potential consumer in this case) evaluates the message based on the status or image of the sender. Source effects can be damaging for an international business when potential consumers in a target country have a bias against foreign firms. For example, a wave of "Japan bashing" swept the United States in the early 1990s. Worried that U.S. consumers might view its products negatively, Honda responded by creating ads that emphasized the U.S. content of its cars to show how "American" the company had become. Many international businesses try to counter negative source effects by deemphasizing their foreign origins. When British Petroleum acquired Mobil Oil's extensive network of U.S. gas stations, it changed its name to BP, diverting attention away from the fact that one of the biggest operators of gas stations in the United States is a British firm.

COUNTRY OF ORIGIN EFFECTS The extent to which the place of manufacturing influences product evaluations.

A subset of source effects is referred to as **country of origin effects.** Country of origin effects refers to the extent to which the place of manufacturing influences product evaluations. Research suggests that country of origin is often used as a cue when evaluating a product, particularly if the consumer lacks more detailed knowledge of the product. For example, one study found that Japanese consumers tended to rate Japanese products more favourably than U.S. products across multiple dimensions, even when independent analysis showed that they were actually inferior.[14] When a negative country of origin effect exists, an international business may have to work hard to counteract this effect by, for example, using promotional messages that stress the positive performance attributes of the product. Thus, the Korean automobile company Hyundai tried to overcome negative perceptions about the quality of its vehicle in the United States by running advertisements that favourably compare the company's cars to more prestigious brands. See the accompanying Country Focus, which sheds light on the Canada–U.S. softwood lumber dispute.

Source effects and country of origin effects are not always negative. French wine, Italian clothes, and German luxury cars benefit from nearly universal positive source effects. In such cases, it may pay a firm to emphasize its foreign origins. In Japan, for example, there is strong demand for high-quality foreign goods, particularly those from Europe. It has become chic to carry a Gucci handbag, sport a Rolex watch, drink expensive French wine, and drive a BMW.

NOISE The amount of other messages competing for a potential consumer's attention.

Noise Levels

Noise tends to reduce the probability of effective communication. **Noise** refers to the amount of other messages competing for a potential consumer's attention, and this too varies across countries. In highly developed countries such as Canada and the United States, noise is extremely high. Fewer firms vie for the attention of prospective customers in developing countries, and the noise level is lower.

PUSH STRATEGY A marketing strategy emphasizing personal selling rather than mass media advertising.

PULL STRATEGY A marketing strategy emphasizing mass media advertising as opposed to personal selling.

PUSH VERSUS PULL STRATEGIES

The main decision with regard to communications strategy is the choice between a push strategy and a pull strategy. A **push strategy** emphasizes personal selling rather than mass media advertising in the promotional mix. Although very effective as a promotional tool, personal selling requires intensive use of a sales force and is relatively costly. A **pull strategy** depends more on mass media advertising to communicate the marketing message to potential consumers.

product through many layers of a distribution channel can be very expensive. In such circumstances, a firm may try to pull its product through the channels by using mass advertising to create consumer demand–once demand is created, intermediaries will feel obliged to carry the product.

In Japan, products often pass through two, three, or even four wholesalers before they reach the final retail outlet. This can make it difficult for foreign firms to break into the Japanese market. Not only must the foreigner persuade a Japanese retailer to carry her product, but she may also have to persuade every intermediary in the chain to carry the product. Mass advertising may be one way to break down channel resistance in such circumstances. However, in countries such as India, which has a very long distribution channel to serve its massive rural population, low literacy levels may imply that mass advertising may not work, in which case, the firm may need to fall back on direct selling, or rely on the good will of distributors.

Media Availability

A pull strategy relies on access to advertising media. In Canada and the United States, a large number of media are available, including print media (newspapers and magazines), broadcasting media (television and radio), and the Internet. For example, the rise of cable television in the United States has facilitated extremely focused advertising (e.g., MTV for teens and young adults, Lifetime for women, ESPN for sports enthusiasts). The same is true of the Internet, given that different Web sites attract different kinds of users. While this level of media sophistication is found in some other developed countries, it is not universal. Even many advanced nations have far fewer electronic media available for advertising than Canada and the United States. In Scandinavia, for example, no commercial television or radio stations existed in 1987; all electronic media were state owned and carried no commercials, although this has now changed with the advent of satellite television deregulation. In many developing nations, the situation is even more restrictive because mass media of all types are typically more limited. A firm's ability to use a pull strategy is limited in some countries by media availability. In such circumstances, a push strategy is more attractive.

Media availability is limited by law in some cases. Few countries allow advertisements for tobacco and alcohol products on television and radio, though they are usually permitted in print media. When the leading Japanese whisky distiller, Suntory, entered the U.S. market, it had to do so without television, its preferred medium. The firm spends about $50 million annually on television advertising in Japan.

The Push–Pull Mix

The optimal mix between push and pull strategies depends on product type and consumer sophistication, channel length, and media sophistication. Push strategies tend to be emphasized:

- For industrial products and/or complex new products.
- When distribution channels are short.
- When few print or electronic media are available.

Pull strategies tend to be emphasized:

- For consumer goods.
- When distribution channels are long.
- When sufficient print and electronic media are available to carry the marketing message.

GLOBAL ADVERTISING

In recent years, largely inspired by the work of visionaries such as Theodore Levitt, there has been much discussion about the pros and cons of standardizing advertising worldwide.[15] One of the most successful standardized campaigns in history was Philip Morris's promotion of Marlboro cigarettes. The campaign was instituted in the 1950s, when the brand was repositioned, to assure smokers that the flavour would be unchanged by the addition of a filter. The campaign theme of "Come to where the flavour is. Come to Marlboro country" was a worldwide success. Marlboro built on this when it introduced "the Marlboro man," a rugged cowboy smoking his Marlboro while riding his horse through the great outdoors. This ad proved successful in almost every major market around the world, and it helped propel Marlboro to the top in world market share.

For Standardized Advertising

The support for global advertising is threefold. First, it has significant economic advantages. Standardized advertising lowers the costs of value creation by spreading the fixed costs of developing the advertisements over many countries. For example, Levi Strauss paid an advertising agency $550,000 to produce a series of TV commercials. By reusing this series in many countries, rather than developing a series for each country, the company enjoyed significant cost savings. Similarly, Coca-Cola's advertising agency, McCann-Erickson, claims to have saved Coca-Cola $90 million over 20 years by using certain elements of its campaigns globally.

Second, there is the concern that creative talent is scarce and so one large effort to develop a campaign will produce better results than 40 or 50 smaller efforts. A third justification for a standardized approach is that many brand names are global. With the substantial amount of international travel today and the considerable overlap in media across national borders, many international firms want to project a single brand image to avoid confusion caused by local campaigns. This is particularly important in regions such as Western Europe, where travel across borders is almost as common as travel across state lines in the United States.

Against Standardized Advertising

There are two main arguments against globally standardized advertising. First, as we have seen repeatedly in this chapter and in Chapter 3, cultural differences between nations are such that a message that works in one nation can fail miserably in another. Due to cultural diversity, it is extremely difficult to develop a single advertising theme that is effective worldwide. Messages directed at the culture of a given country may be more effective than global messages.

Second, advertising regulations may block implementation of standardized advertising. For example, Kellogg could not use a television commercial it produced in Great Britain to promote its cornflakes in many other European countries. A reference to the iron and vitamin content of its cornflakes was not permissible in the Netherlands, where claims relating to health and medical benefits are outlawed. A child wearing a Kellogg T-shirt had to be edited out of the commercial before it could be used in France, because French law forbids the use of children in product endorsements. The key line, "Kellogg's makes their cornflakes the best they have ever been," was disallowed in Germany because of a prohibition against competitive claims.[16] Similarly, American Express ran afoul of regulatory authorities in Germany when it launched a promotional scheme that had proved very successful in other countries. The scheme advertised the offer of "bonus points" every time American Express cardholders used their cards. According to the advertisements, these "bonus points" could be used toward air travel on three airlines and for hotel accommodations. American Express was charged with breaking Germany's competition law, which prevents an offer of free gifts in connection with the sale of goods, and the firm had to withdraw the advertisements at considerable cost.[17]

Dealing with Country Differences

Some firms are experimenting with capturing some benefits of global standardization while recognizing differences in countries' cultural and legal environments. A firm may select some features to include in all its advertising campaigns and localize other features. By doing so, it may be able to save on some costs and build international brand recognition and yet customize its advertisements to different cultures.

Pepsi-Cola used this kind of approach in a 1980s advertising campaign. The company wanted to use music to connect its products with local markets. Pepsi hired U.S. singer Tina Turner and rock stars from six countries to team up in singing and performing the Pepsi-Cola theme song in a big rock concert. The commercials were customized for each market by showing Turner with the rock stars from that country. Except for the footage of the local stars, all the commercials were identical. By shooting the commercials all at once, Pepsi saved on production costs. The campaign was extended to 30 countries, which relieved the local subsidiaries or bottlers of having to develop their own campaigns.[18]

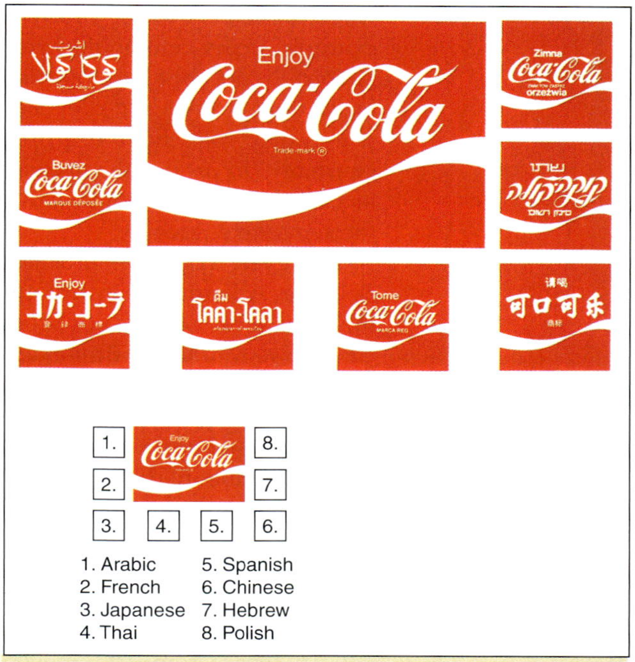

Coca-Cola's trademark varies from country to country, but in any country you would know it to be Coke. The overall look is retained through the use of similar letterforms and style, even with different alphabets. Courtesy of The Coca Cola Company.

PRICING STRATEGY

International pricing strategy is an important component of the overall international marketing mix.[19] In this section, we look at three aspects of international pricing strategy. First, we examine the case for pursuing price discrimination, charging different prices for the same product in different countries. Second, we look at what might be called strategic pricing. Third, we review regulatory factors, such as government-mandated price controls and antidumping regulations, that limit a firm's ability to charge the prices it would prefer in a country.

PRICE DISCRIMINATION

Price discrimination exists whenever consumers in different countries are charged different prices for the same product.[20] Price discrimination involves charging whatever the market will bear; in a competitive market, prices may have to be lower than in a market where the firm has a monopoly. Price discrimination can help a company maximize its profits. It makes economic sense to charge different prices in different countries.

Two conditions are necessary for profitable price discrimination. First, the firm must be able to keep its national markets separate. If it cannot do this, individuals or businesses may undercut its attempt at price discrimination by engaging in arbitrage. Arbitrage occurs when an individual or business capitalizes on a price differential for a firm's product between two countries by purchasing the product in the country where prices are lower and reselling it in the country where prices are higher. For example, many automobile firms have long practiced price discrimination in Europe. A Ford Escort once cost $2,000 more in Germany than it did in Belgium. This policy broke down when car dealers bought Escorts in Belgium and drove them to Germany, where they sold them at a profit for slightly less than Ford was selling Escorts in Germany. To protect the market share of its German auto dealers, Ford had to bring its German prices into line with those being charged in Belgium. Ford could not keep these markets separate.

However, Ford still practises price discrimination between Great Britain and Belgium. A Ford car can cost up to $3,000 more in Great Britain than in Belgium. In this case, arbitrage has not been able to equalize the price, because right-hand-drive cars are sold in Great Britain and left-hand-drive cars in the rest of Europe. Because there is no market for left-hand-drive cars in Great Britain, Ford has been able to keep the markets separate.

PRICE ELASTICITY OF DEMAND A measure of how responsive demand for a product is to changes in price.

ELASTIC When a small change in price produces a large change in demand.

INELASTIC When a large change in price produces only a small change in demand.

The second necessary condition for profitable price discrimination is different price elasticities of demand in different countries. The **price elasticity of demand** is a measure of the responsiveness of demand for a product to changes in price. Demand is said to be **elastic** when a small change in price produces a large change in demand; it is said to be **inelastic** when a large change in price produces only a small change in demand. Figure 14.2 illustrates elastic and inelastic demand curves. Generally, for reasons that will be explained shortly, a firm can charge a higher price in a country where demand is inelastic.

The Determinants of Demand Elasticity

The elasticity of demand for a product in a given country is determined by a number of factors, of which income level and competitive conditions are the two most important. Price elasticity tends to be greater in countries with low income levels. Consumers with limited incomes tend to be very price conscious; they have less to spend, so they look much more closely at price. Thus, price elasticities for products such as television sets are greater in countries such as India, where a television set is still a luxury item, than in Canada and the United States, where it is considered a necessity.

In general, the more competitors there are, the greater consumers' bargaining power will be and the more likely consumers will be to buy from the firm that charges the lowest price. Thus, many competitors cause high elasticity of demand. In such

FIGURE 14.2
Elastic and Inelastic Demand Curves

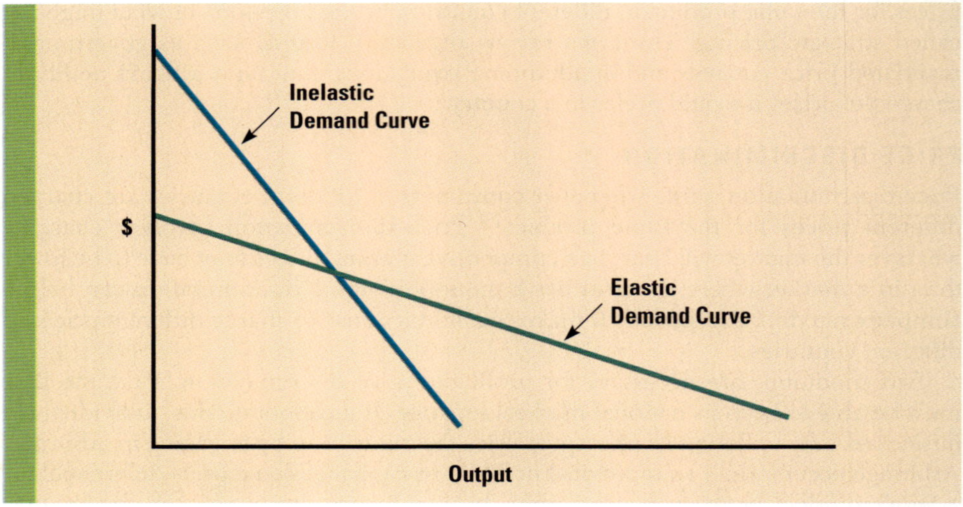

FIGURE 14.3

Price Discrimination

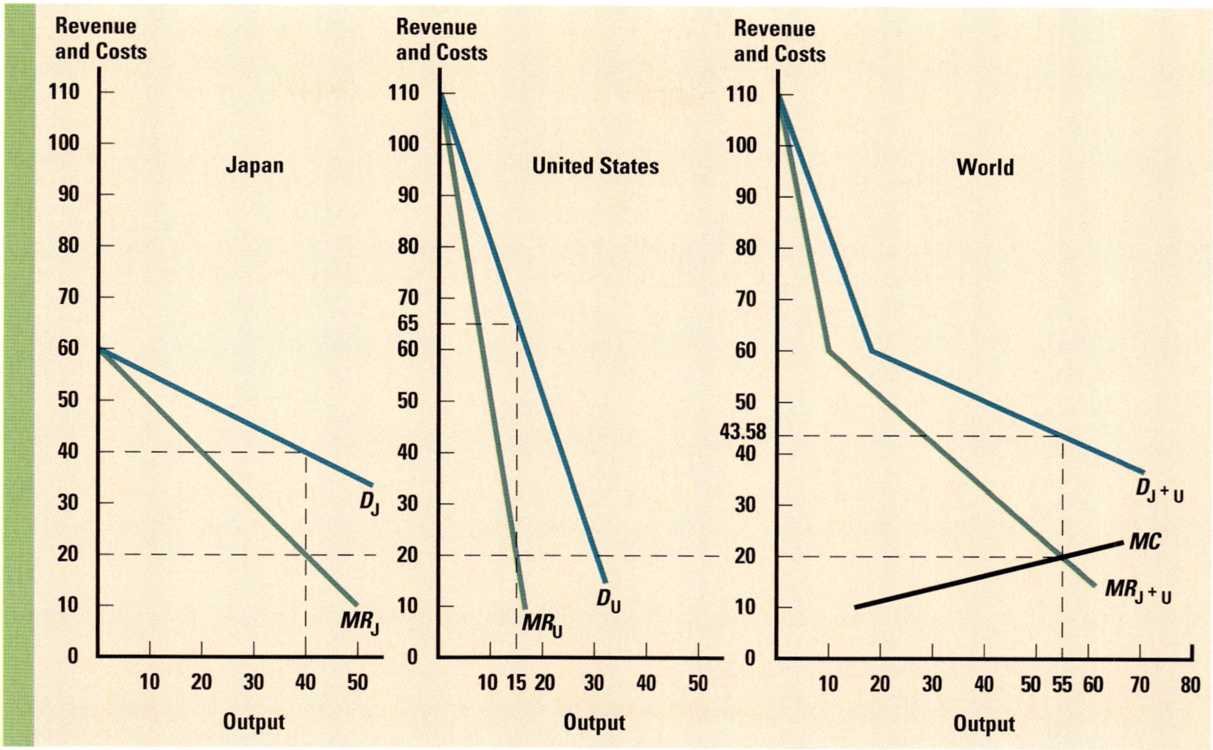

circumstances, if a firm raises its prices above those of its competitors, consumers will switch to the competitors' products. The opposite is true when a firm faces few competitors. When competitors are limited, consumers' bargaining power is weaker and price is less important as a competitive weapon. Thus, a firm may charge a higher price for its product in a country where competition is limited than in a country where competition is intense.

Maximizing Profit under Price Discrimination

For those readers with some grasp of economic logic, we can offer a more formal presentation of the above argument. (Readers unfamiliar with basic economic terminology may want to skip this subsection.) Figure 14.3 shows the situation facing a firm that sells the same product in only two countries: Japan and the United States. The Japanese market is very competitive, so the firm faces an elastic demand curve (Dj) and marginal revenue curve (MRj). The U.S. market is not competitive, so there the firm faces an inelastic demand curve (Du) and marginal revenue curve (MRu). Also shown in the figure are the firm's total demand curve (Dj + u), total marginal revenue curve (MRj + u), and marginal cost curve (MC). The total demand curve is simply the summation of the demand facing the firm in Japan and the United States, as is the total marginal revenue curve.

To maximize profits, the firm must produce at the output where MR = MC. In Figure 14.3, this implies an output of 55 units. If the firm does not practice price discrimination, it will charge a price of $43.58 to sell an output of 55 units. Thus, without price discrimination, the firm's total revenues are $43.58 × 55 = $2,396.90.

That changes when the firm decides to engage in price discrimination. It will still produce 55 units, since that is where MR = MC. However, the firm must now allocate this output between the two countries to take advantage of the difference in demand elasticity. Proper allocation of output between Japan and the United States can be determined graphically by drawing a line through their respective graphs at $20 to indicate that $20 is the marginal cost in each country (see Figure 14.3). To maximize profits, prices are now set in each country at that level where the marginal revenue for that country equals marginal costs. In Japan, this is a price of $40, and the firm sells 40 units. In the United States, the optimal price is $65, and it sells 15 units. Thus, reflecting the different competitive conditions, the price charged in the United States is over 50 percent more than the price charged in Japan. Look at what happens to total revenues. With price discrimination, the firm earns revenues of

$$\$40 \times 40 \text{ units} = \$1{,}600$$

in Japan and

$$\$65 \times 15 \text{ units} = \$975$$

in the United States. By engaging in price discrimination, the firm can earn total revenues of

$$\$1{,}600 + \$975 = \$2{,}575$$

which is $178.10 more than the $2,396.90 it earned before. Price discrimination pays!

STRATEGIC PRICING

STRATEGIC PRICING Pricing aimed at giving a company a competitive advantage over its rivals.

The concept of **strategic pricing** has three aspects, which we will refer to as predatory pricing, multipoint pricing, and experience curve pricing. Both predatory pricing and experience curve pricing may violate antidumping regulations. After we review predatory and experience curve pricing, we will look at antidumping rules and other regulatory policies.

Predatory Pricing

PREDATORY PRICING Reducing prices below fair market value as a competitive weapon to drive weaker competitors out of the market ("fair" being cost plus some reasonable profit margin).

Predatory pricing is the use of price as a competitive weapon to drive weaker competitors out of a national market. Once the competitors have left the market, the firm can raise prices and enjoy high profits. For such a pricing strategy to work, the firm must normally have a profitable position in another national market, which it can use to subsidize aggressive pricing in the market it is trying to monopolize. Many Japanese firms have been accused of pursuing such a policy. The argument runs like this: Because the Japanese market is protected from foreign competition by high informal trade barriers, Japanese firms can charge high prices and earn high profits at home. They then use these profits to subsidize aggressive pricing overseas, with the goal of driving competitors out of those markets. Once this has occurred, so it is claimed, the Japanese firms then raise prices. Matsushita was accused of using this strategy to enter the U.S. TV market. As one of the major TV producers in Japan, Matsushita earned high profits at home. It then used these profits to subsidize the losses it made in the United States during its early years there, when it priced low to increase its market penetration. Ultimately, Matsushita became the world's largest manufacturer of TVs.[21]

Multipoint Pricing Strategy

Multipoint pricing becomes an issue when two or more international businesses compete against each other in two or more national markets. For example, multipoint pricing is an issue for Kodak and Fuji Photo because both companies compete against each other in different national markets for film products around the world. **Multipoint pricing** refers to the fact a firm's pricing strategy in one market may have an impact on its rivals' pricing strategies in another market. Aggressive pricing in one market may elicit a competitive response from a rival in another market. In the case of Kodak and Fuji, Fuji launched an aggressive competitive attack against Kodak in the American company's home market in January 1997, cutting prices on multiple-roll packs of 35mm film by as much as 50 percent.[22] This price cutting resulted in a 28 percent increase in shipments of Fuji colour film during the first six months of 1997, while Kodak's shipments dropped by 11 percent. This attack created a dilemma for Kodak; the company did not want to start price discounting in its largest and most profitable market. Kodak's response was to aggressively cut prices in Fuji's largest market, Japan. This strategic response recognized the interdependence between Kodak and Fuji and the fact that they compete against each other in many different nations. Fuji responded to Kodak's counterattack by pulling back from its aggressive stance in the United States.

MULTIPOINT PRICING Occurs when a pricing strategy in one market may have an impact on a rival's pricing strategy in another market.

The Kodak story illustrates an important aspect of multipoint pricing–aggressive pricing in one market may elicit a response from rivals in another market. The firm needs to consider how its global rivals will respond to changes in its pricing strategy before making those changes. A second aspect of multipoint pricing arises when two or more global companies focus on particular national markets and launch vigorous price wars in those markets in an attempt to gain market dominance. In the Brazil market for disposable diapers, two U.S. companies, Kimberly-Clark Corp. and Procter & Gamble, entered a price war as each struggled to establish dominance in the market.[23] As a result, the cost of disposable diapers fell from $1 per diaper in 1994 to 33 cents per diaper in 1997, while several other competitors, including indigenous Brazilian firms, were driven out of the market. Kimberly-Clark and Procter & Gamble are engaged in a global struggle for market share and dominance, and Brazil is one battleground. Both companies can afford to engage in this behaviour, even though it reduces their profits in Brazil, because they have profitable operations elsewhere in the world that can subsidize these losses.

Pricing decisions around the world need to be centrally monitored. It is tempting to delegate full responsibility for pricing decisions to the managers of various national subsidiaries. However, because pricing strategy in one part of the world can elicit a competitive response in another part, central management needs to at least monitor and approve pricing decisions in a given national market, and local managers need to recognize that their actions can affect competitive conditions in other countries.

Experience Curve Pricing

We first encountered the experience curve in Chapter 11. As a firm builds its accumulated production volume over time, unit costs fall due to "experience effects." Learning effects and economies of scale underlie the experience curve. Price comes into the picture because aggressive pricing (along with aggressive promotion and advertising) can build accumulated sales volume rapidly and thus move production down the experience curve. Firms further down the experience curve have a cost advantage vis-à-vis firms further up the curve.

Many firms pursuing an experience curve pricing strategy on an international scale price low worldwide in attempting to build global sales volume as rapidly as possible, even if this means taking large losses initially. Such a firm believes that several years in the future, when it has moved down the experience curve, it will be making substantial profits and have a cost advantage over its less-aggressive competitors.

REGULATORY INFLUENCES ON PRICES

The ability to engage in either price discrimination or strategic pricing may be limited by national or international regulations. Most important, a firm's freedom to set its own prices is constrained by antidumping regulations and competition policy.

Antidumping Regulations

DUMPING Selling goods in a foreign market for less than their cost of production or below their "fair" market value.

Both predatory pricing and experience curve pricing can run afoul of antidumping regulations. **Dumping** occurs whenever a firm sells a product for a price that is less than the cost of producing it. Most regulations, however, define dumping more vaguely. For example, a country is allowed to bring antidumping actions against an importer under Article 6 of GATT as long as two criteria are met: sales at "less than fair value" and "material injury to a domestic industry." The problem with this terminology is that it does not indicate what is a fair value. The ambiguity has led some to argue that selling abroad at prices below those in the country of origin, as opposed to below cost, is dumping.

Such logic led the first Bush administration to place a 25 percent duty on imports of Japanese light trucks in 1988. The Japanese manufacturers protested that they were not selling below cost. Admitting that their prices were lower in the United States than in Japan, they argued that this simply reflected the intensely competitive nature of the U.S. market (i.e., different price elasticities). In a similar example, the European Commission found Japanese exporters of dot-matrix printers to be violating dumping regulations. To correct what they saw as dumping, the EU placed a 47 percent import duty on imports of dot-matrix printers from Japan and required that the import duty be passed on to European consumers as a price increase.[24]

Antidumping rules set a floor under export prices and limit firms' ability to pursue strategic pricing. The rather vague terminology used in most antidumping actions suggests that a firm's ability to engage in price discrimination also may be challenged under antidumping legislation.

Competition Policy

Most industrialized nations have regulations designed to promote competition and to restrict monopoly practices. These regulations can be used to limit the prices a firm can charge in a given country. For example, during the 1960s and 70s, the Swiss pharmaceutical manufacturer Hoffmann-LaRoche had a monopoly on the supply of Valium and Librium tranquilizers. The company was investigated in 1973 by the British Monopolies and Mergers Commission, which is responsible for promoting fair competition in Great Britain. The commission found that Hoffmann-LaRoche was overcharging for its tranquilizers and ordered the company to reduce its prices 35 to 40 percent. Hoffmann-LaRoche maintained unsuccessfully that it was merely engaging in price discrimination. Similar actions were later brought against Hoffmann-LaRoche by the German cartel office and by the Dutch and Danish governments.[25]

CONFIGURING THE MARKETING MIX

A firm might vary aspects of its marketing mix from country to country to take into account local differences in culture, economic conditions, competitive conditions, product and technical standards, distribution systems, government regulations, and the like. Such differences may require variation in product attributes, distribution strategy, communications strategy, and pricing strategy. The cumulative effect of these factors makes it rare for a firm to adopt the same marketing mix worldwide.

For example, financial services is often thought of as an industry where global standardization of the marketing mix is the norm. However, while a financial services company such as American Express may sell the same basic charge card service worldwide, utilize the same basic fee structure for that product, and adopt the same basic global advertising message ("never leave home without it"), differences in national regulations still mean it has to vary aspects of its communications strategy from country to country (as pointed out earlier, the promotional strategy it had developed in the United States was illegal in Germany). Similarly, while McDonald's is often thought of as the quintessential example of a firm that sells the same basic standardized product worldwide, in reality it varies one important aspect of its marketing mix–its menu–from country to country. McDonald's also varies its distribution strategy. In Canada and the United States, most McDonald's outlets are located in areas that are easily accessible by car, whereas in more densely populated and less automobile-reliant societies of the world, such as Japan and Great Britain, location decisions are driven by the accessibility of a restaurant to pedestrian traffic. Because countries typically still differ along one or more of the dimensions discussed above, some customization of the marketing mix is normal.

However, there are often significant opportunities for standardization along one or more elements of the marketing mix.[26] Firms may find that it is possible and desirable to standardize their global advertising message and/or core product attributes to realize substantial cost economies. They may find it desirable to customize their distribution and pricing strategy to take advantage of local differences. In reality, the "customization versus standardization" debate is not an all or nothing issue; it frequently makes sense to standardize some aspects of the marketing mix and customize others, depending on conditions in various national marketplaces. Decisions about what to customize and what to standardize should be driven by a detailed examination of the costs and benefits of doing so for each element in the marketing mix.

NEW-PRODUCT DEVELOPMENT

Firms that successfully develop and market new products can earn enormous returns. Examples include Du Pont, which has produced a steady stream of successful innovations such as cellophane, nylon, Freon, and Teflon (nonstick pans); Sony, whose successes include the Walkman and the compact disc; Merck, the drug company that during the 1980s produced seven major new drugs; 3M, which has applied its core competency in tapes and adhesives to developing a wide range of new products; Intel, which has consistently managed to lead in the development of innovative microprocessors to run personal computers; and Cisco Systems, which developed the routers that sit at the hubs of Internet connections, directing the flow of digital traffic.

In today's world, competition is as much about technological innovation as anything else. The pace of technological change has accelerated since the Industrial Revolution in the 18th century, and it continues to do so today. The result has been a dramatic shortening of product life cycles. Technological innovation is both creative and destructive.[27] An innovation can make established products obsolete overnight. But an innovation can also make a host of new products possible. Witness recent changes in the electronics industry. For 40 years before the early 1950s, vacuum valves were a major component in radios and then in record players and early computers. The advent of transistors destroyed the market for vacuum valves, but at the same time it created new opportunities connected with transistors. Transistors took up far less space than vacuum valves, creating a trend toward miniaturization that continues today. The transistor held its position as the major component in the electronics industry for just a decade.

Microprocessors were developed in the 1970s and the market for transistors declined rapidly. The microprocessor created yet another set of new-product opportunities–handheld calculators (which destroyed the market for slide rules), compact disc players (which destroyed the market for analog record players), personal computers (which destroyed the market for typewriters), to name a few.

This "creative destruction" unleashed by technological change makes it critical that a firm stay on the leading edge of technology, lest it lose out to a competitor's innovations. As we explain in the next subsection, this not only creates a need for the firm to invest in research and development, but it also requires the firm to establish R&D activities at those locations where expertise is concentrated. As we shall see, leading-edge technology on its own is not enough to guarantee a firm's survival. The firm must also apply that technology to developing products that satisfy consumer needs, and it must design the product so that it can be manufactured in a cost-effective manner. To do that, the firm needs to build close links between R&D, marketing, and manufacturing. This is difficult enough for the domestic firm, but it is even more problematic for the international business competing in an industry where consumer tastes and preferences differ from country to country. With all this in mind, we move on to examine locating R&D activities and building links between R&D, marketing, and manufacturing.

THE LOCATION OF R&D

Ideas for new products are stimulated by the interactions of scientific research, demand conditions, and competitive conditions. Other things being equal, the rate of new-product development seems to be greater in countries where:

- More money is spent on basic and applied research and development.
- Underlying demand is strong.
- Consumers are affluent.
- Competition is intense.[28]

Basic and applied research and development discovers new technologies and then commercializes them. Strong demand and affluent consumers create a potential market for new products. Intense competition between firms stimulates innovation as the firms try to beat their competitors and reap potentially enormous first-mover advantages that result from successful innovation.

For most of the post-World War II period, the country that ranked highest on these criteria was the United States. The United States devoted a greater proportion of its gross domestic product (GDP) to R&D than any other country did. Its scientific establishment was the largest and most active in the world. U.S. consumers were the most affluent, the market was large, and competition among U.S. firms was brisk. Due to these factors, the United States was the market where most new products were developed and introduced. Accordingly, it was the best location for R&D activities; it was where the action was.

Over the past 20 years, things have been changing quickly. The U.S. monopoly on new-product development has weakened considerably. Although U.S. firms are still at the leading edge of many new technologies, Japanese and European firms are also strong players, with companies such as Sony, Sharp, Ericsson, Nokia, and Philips NV driving product innovation in their respective industries. Both Japan and Germany are now devoting a greater proportion of their GDP to nondefense R&D than is the United States.[29] In addition, both Japan and the European Union are large, affluent markets, and the wealth gap between them and the United States is closing.

As a result, it is often no longer appropriate to consider the United States as the lead market. In video games, for example, Japan is often the lead market, with companies such as Sony and Nintendo introducing their latest video game players in Japan some six months before they introduce them in the United States. In wireless telecommunications, Europe is generally reckoned to be ahead of the United States. Some of the most advanced applications of wireless telecommunications services are being pioneered not in the United States, but in Finland, where 80 percent of the population has wireless telephones, compared to 40 percent of the U.S. population. However, it is questionable whether any developed nation can be considered the lead market. To succeed in today's high-technology industries, it is often necessary to simultaneously introduce new products in all major industrialized markets. When Intel introduces a new microprocessor, for example, it does not first introduce it in the United States and then roll it out in Europe a year later. It introduces it simultaneously around the world.

Because leading-edge research is now carried out in many locations around the world, the argument for centralizing R&D activity in the United States is much weaker than it was two decades ago. (It used to be argued that centralized R&D eliminated duplication.) Much leading-edge research is now occurring in Japan and Europe. Dispersing R&D activities to those locations allows a firm to stay close to the centre of leading-edge activity to gather scientific and competitive information and to draw on local scientific resources.[30] This may result in some duplication of R&D activities, but the cost disadvantages of duplication are outweighed by the advantages of dispersion.

For example, to expose themselves to the research and new-product development work being done in Japan, many U.S. firms have set up satellite R&D centres in Japan. Kodak's $65-million R&D centre in Japan employs about 200 people. The company hired about 100 professional Japanese researchers and directed the lab to concentrate on electronic imaging technology. U.S. firms that have established R&D facilities in Japan include Corning, Texas Instruments, IBM, Digital Equipment, Procter & Gamble, Upjohn, Pfizer, Du Pont, Monsanto, and Microsoft.[31] The National Science Foundation (NSF) has documented a sharp increase in the proportion of total R&D spending by U.S. firms that is now done abroad.[32] Motorola now has 14 dedicated R&D facilities located in seven countries, and Bristol-Myers Squibb has 12 facilities in six countries. At the same time, to internationalize their own research and gain access to U.S. talent, the NSF reports that many European and Japanese firms are investing in U.S.-based research facilities.

INTEGRATING R&D, MARKETING, AND PRODUCTION

Although a firm that is successful at developing new products may earn enormous returns, new-product development has a high failure rate. One study of product development in 16 companies in the chemical, drug, petroleum, and electronics industries suggested that only about 20 percent of R&D projects result in commercially successful products or processes.[33] Another in-depth case study of product development in three companies (one in chemicals and two in drugs) reported that about 60 percent of R&D projects reached technical completion, 30 percent were commercialized, and only 12 percent earned an economic profit that exceeded the company's cost of capital.[34] Similarly, a study by the consulting division of Booz, Allen & Hamilton found that more than one-third of 13 000 consumer and industrial products introduced between 1976 and 1981 failed to meet company-specific financial and strategic performance criteria.[35] A more recent study found that 45 percent of new products did not meet their profitability goals.[36] This evidence suggests that many R&D projects do not result in a commercial product, and that between 33 percent and 60 percent of all new products that do reach the marketplace fail to generate an adequate economic return. Two well-publicized product failures are Apple Computer's Newton, a personal digital assistant, and Sony's Betamax format in the video player and recorder market.

The reasons for such high failure rates are various and include development of a technology for which there is only limited demand, failure to adequately commercialize promising technology, and inability to manufacture a new product cost effectively. Firms can avoid such mistakes by insisting on tight cross-functional coordination and integration between three core functions involved in the development of new products: R&D, marketing, and production.[37] Tight cross-functional integration between R&D, production, and marketing can make sure

1. Product development projects are driven by customer needs.
2. New products are designed for ease of manufacture.
3. Development costs are kept in check.
4. Time to market is minimized.

Close integration between R&D and marketing is required to ensure that product development projects are driven by the needs of customers. A company's customers can be a primary source of new-product ideas. Identification of customer needs, particularly unmet needs, can set the context within which successful product innovation occurs. As the point of contact with customers, the marketing function of a company can provide valuable information in this regard. Integration of R&D and marketing are crucial if a new product is to be properly commercialized. Without integration of R&D and marketing, a company runs the risk of developing products for which there is little or no demand.

Integration between R&D and production can help a company design products with manufacturing requirements in mind. Designing for manufacturing can lower costs and increase product quality. Integrating R&D and production can also help lower development costs and speed products to market. If a new product is not designed with manufacturing capabilities in mind, it may prove too difficult to build. Then the product will have to be redesigned, and both overall development costs and the time it takes to bring the product to market may increase significantly. Making design changes during product planning could increase overall development costs by 50 percent and add 25 percent to the time it takes to bring the product to market.[38] Many quantum product innovations require new processes to manufacture them, which makes it all the more important to achieve close integration between R&D and production. Minimizing time to market and development costs may require the simultaneous development of new products and new processes.[39]

CROSS-FUNCTIONAL TEAMS

One way to achieve cross-functional integration is to establish product development teams composed of representatives from R&D, marketing, and production. Because these functions may be located in different countries, the team will sometimes have a multinational membership. The objective of a team should be to take a product development project from the initial concept development to market introduction. A number of attributes seem to be important for a product development team to function effectively and meet all its development milestones.[40]

First, the team should be led by a "heavyweight" project manager who has high status within the organization and the authority required to get the financial and human resources the team needs to succeed. The "heavyweight" leader should be dedicated primarily, if not entirely, to the project. The leader should be someone who believes in the project (a champion) and who is skilled at integrating the perspectives of different functions and at helping personnel from different functions and countries work together for a common goal. The leader should also be able to act as an advocate of the team to senior management.

Second, the team should be composed of at least one member from each key function. The team members should have a number of attributes, including an ability to contribute functional expertise, high standing within their function, a willingness to share responsibility for team results, and an ability to put functional and national advocacy aside. It is generally preferable if core team members are 100 percent dedicated to the project for its duration. This assures their focus on the project, not on the ongoing work of their function.

Third, the team members should be physically co-located if possible to create a sense of camaraderie and to facilitate communication. This presents problems if the team members are drawn from facilities in different nations. One solution is to transfer key individuals to one location for the duration of a product development project. Fourth, the team should have a clear plan and clear goals, particularly with regard to critical development milestones and development budgets. The team should have incentives to attain those goals, such as receiving pay bonuses when major development milestones are hit. Fifth, each team needs to develop its own processes for communication and conflict resolution. For example, one product development team at Quantum Corporation, a California-based manufacturer of disk drives for personal computers, instituted a rule that all major decisions would be made and conflicts resolved at meetings that were held every Monday afternoon. This simple rule helped the team meet its development goals. In this case, it was also common for team members to fly in from Japan, where the product was to be manufactured, to the U.S. development centre for the Monday morning meetings.[41]

IMPLICATIONS FOR BUSINESS

The need to integrate R&D and marketing to adequately commercialize new technologies poses special problems in the international business, since commercialization may require different versions of a new product to be produced for different countries.[42] We saw an example of this in the opening case, which described how Procter & Gamble's R&D centre in Kobe, Japan, developed a dish soap formula specifically for the Japanese market. To do this, the firm must build close links between its R&D centres and its various country operations. A similar argument applies to the need to integrate R&D and production, particularly in those international businesses that have dispersed production activities to different locations around the globe depending on a consideration of relative factor costs and the like.

Integrating R&D, marketing, and production in an international business may require R&D centres in North America, Asia, and Europe that are linked by formal and informal integrating mechanisms with marketing operations in each country in their regions and with the various manufacturing facilities. In addition, the international business may have to establish cross-functional teams whose members are dispersed around the globe. This complex endeavour requires the company to utilize formal and informal integrating mechanisms to knit its far-flung operations together so they can produce new products in an effective and timely manner.

While there is no one best model for allocating product development responsibilities to various centres, one solution adopted by many international businesses involves establishing a global network of R&D centres. Within this model, fundamental research is undertaken at **basic research centres** around the globe. These centres are normally located in regions or cities where valuable scientific knowledge is being created and where there is a pool of skilled research talent (e.g., Kanata and Markham, Ontario in Canada, Silicon Valley in the United States, Cambridge in England, Kobe in Japan). These centres are the innovation engines of the firm. Their job is to develop the basic technologies that become new products. These technologies are picked up by R&D units attached to global product divisions and are used to generate new products to serve the global marketplace. At this level, emphasis is placed on commercialization of the technology and design for manufacturing.

BASIC RESEARCH CENTRES Centres for fundamental research located in regions where valuable scientific knowledge is being created; they develop the basic technologies that become new products.

If further customization is needed so the product appeals to the tastes and preferences of consumers in individual markets, such redesign work will be done by an R&D group based in a subsidiary in that country or at a regional centre that customizes products for several countries in the region.

Hewlett-Packard (HP) has four basic research centres located in Palo Alto, California; Bristol, England; Haifa, Israel; and Tokyo, Japan.[43] These labs are the seedbed for technologies that ultimately become new products and businesses. They are the company's innovation engines. The Palo Alto centre, for example, pioneered HP's thermal ink-jet technology. The products are developed by R&D centres associated with HP's global product divisions. Thus, the Consumer Products Group, which has its worldwide headquarters in San Diego, California, designs, develops, and manufactures a range of imaging products using HP-pioneered thermal ink-jet technology. Subsidiaries might then customize the product so that it best matches the needs of important national markets. HP's subsidiary in Singapore, for example, is responsible for the design and production of thermal ink-jet printers for Japan and other Asian markets. This subsidiary takes products originally developed in San Diego and redesigns them for the Asian market. In addition, the Singapore subsidiary has taken the lead from San Diego in the design and development of certain portable thermal ink-jet printers. HP delegated this responsibility to Singapore because this subsidiary has built important competencies in the design and production of thermal ink-jet products, so it has become the best place in the world to undertake this activity.

Microsoft offers a similar example. The company has basic research sites in Redmond, Washington (its headquarters); Cambridge, England; Tokyo, Japan; and Silicon Valley, California. Staff members at these research sites work on the fundamental problems that underlie the design of future products. For example, a group at Redmond is working on natural language recognition software, while another works on artificial intelligence. These research centres don't produce new products; rather, they produce the technology that is used to enhance existing products or help produce new products. The products are produced by dedicated product groups (e.g., desktop operating systems, applications). Customization of the products to match the needs of local markets is sometimes carried out at local subsidiaries. Thus, the Chinese subsidiary in Singapore will do some basic customization of programs such as Microsoft Office, adding Chinese characters and customizing the interface.

KEY TERMS

basic research centres, p. 479

channel length, p. 461

concentrated retail system, p. 460

country of origin effects, p. 464

dumping, p. 474

elastic, p. 470

exclusive distribution channel, p. 461

fragmented retail system, p. 460

inelastic, p. 470

market segmentation, p. 455

marketing mix, p. 453

multipoint pricing, p. 473

noise, p. 464

predatory pricing, p. 472

price elasticity of demand, p. 470

pull strategy, p. 464

push strategy, p. 464

source effects, p. 464

strategic pricing, p. 472

SUMMARY

This chapter discussed the marketing and R&D functions in international business. A persistent theme of the chapter is the tension that exists between the need to reduce costs and the need to be responsive to local conditions, which raises costs. This chapter made the following points:

1. Theodore Levitt has argued that, due to the advent of modern communications and transport technologies, consumer tastes and preferences are becoming global, which is creating global markets for standardized consumer products. However, this position is regarded as extreme by many commentators, who argue that substantial differences still exist between countries.
2. Market segmentation refers to the process of identifying distinct groups of consumers whose purchasing behaviour differs from each other in important ways. Managers in an international business need to be aware of two main issues relating to segmentation: (*a*) the extent to which there are differences between countries in the structure of market segments, and (*b*) the existence of segments that transcend national borders.
3. A product can be viewed as a bundle of attributes. Product attributes need to be varied from country to country to satisfy different consumer tastes and preferences.
4. Country differences in consumer tastes and preferences are due to differences in culture and economic development. In addition, differences in product and technical standards may require the firm to customize product attributes from country to country.
5. A distribution strategy decision is an attempt to define the optimal channel for delivering a product to the consumer.
6. Significant country differences exist in distribution systems. In some countries, the retail system is concentrated; in others, it is fragmented. In some countries, channel length is short; in others, it is long. Access to distribution channels is difficult to achieve in some countries.
7. A critical element in the marketing mix is communication strategy, which defines the process the firm will use in communicating the attributes of its product to prospective customers.
8. Barriers to international communication include cultural differences, source effects, and noise levels.
9. A communication strategy is either a push strategy or a pull strategy. A push strategy emphasizes personal selling, and a pull strategy emphasizes mass media advertising. Whether a push strategy or a pull strategy is optimal depends on the type of product, consumer sophistication, channel length, and media availability.
10. A globally standardized advertising campaign, which uses the same marketing message all over the world, has economic advantages, but it fails to account for differences in culture and advertising regulations.
11. Price discrimination exists when consumers in different countries are charged different prices for the same product. Price discrimination can help a firm maximize its profits. For price discrimination to be effective, the national markets must be separate and their price elasticities of demand must differ.
12. Predatory pricing is the use of profit gained in one market to support aggressive pricing in another market to drive competitors out of that market.
13. Multipoint pricing refers to the fact a firm's pricing strategy in one market may affect rivals' pricing strategies in another market. Aggressive pricing in one market may elicit a competitive response from a rival in another market that is important to the firm.
14. Experience curve pricing is the use of aggressive pricing to build accumulated volume as rapidly as possible to quickly move the firm down the experience curve.
15. New-product development is a high-risk, potentially high-return activity. To build a competency in new-product development, an international business must do two things: (*a*) disperse R&D activities to those countries where new products are being pioneered and (*b*) integrate R&D with marketing and manufacturing.
16. Achieving tight integration among R&D, marketing, and manufacturing requires the use of cross-functional teams.

CRITICAL THINKING & DISCUSSION QUESTIONS

1. Imagine you are the marketing manager for a Canadian manufacturer of disposable diapers. Your firm is considering entering the Brazilian market. Your CEO believes the advertising message that has been effective in Canada will suffice in Brazil. Outline some possible objections to this. Your CEO also believes that the pricing decisions in Brazil can be delegated to local managers. Why might she be wrong?
2. Within 20 years, we will have seen the emergence of enormous global markets for standardized consumer products. Do you agree with this statement? Justify your answer.

3. You are the marketing manager of a food products company that is considering entering the South Korean market. The retail system in South Korea tends to be very fragmented. Also, retailers and wholesalers tend to have long-term ties with South Korean food companies, which makes access to distribution channels difficult. What distribution strategy would you advise the company to pursue? Why?
4. Price discrimination is indistinguishable from dumping. Discuss the accuracy of this statement.
5. You work for a company that designs and manufactures personal computers. Your company's R&D centre is in North Dakota. The computers are manufactured under contract in Taiwan. Marketing strategy is delegated to the heads of three regional groups: a North American group (based in Chicago), a European group (based in Paris), and an Asian group (based in Singapore). Each regional group develops the marketing approach within its region. In order of importance, the largest markets for your products are North America, Germany, Great Britain, China, and Australia. Your company is experiencing problems in its product development and commercialization process. Products are late to market, the manufacturing quality is poor, costs are higher than projected, and market acceptance of new products is less than hoped for. What might be the source of these problems? How would you fix them?

RESEARCH TASK | globalEDGE™ globaledge.msu.edu

Use the globalEDGE™ site to complete the following exercises:

1. Locate and retrieve the most current ranking of the global brands. Identify the criteria that are utilized in the ranking. Which country dominates the top 100 global brands list? Prepare a short report identifying the countries that possess global brands and the potential reasons for success.
2. Thorough planning is essential to export success. In this respect, pricing is one of the critical components for successful planning. Considering that your company tries to be price competitive, prepare an executive summary of how to do initial pricing analysis for international markets.

Visit the *Global Business Today* Online Learning Centre at **www.mcgrawhill.ca/college/hill** to access quizzes, interactive exercises, a Business Around the World interactive map, and other learning and study tools related to this chapter.

Online Learning Centre

CLOSING CASE

CELESTICA—ON A REBOUND?

Celestica is a worldwide provider of electronics manufacturing services (EMS) including the design, assembly, testing, and global distribution to its customers, who are mostly in the computing and communications fields. It provides its products and services to some household names, including IBM, Cisco Systems, Hewlett-Packard, Lucent Technologies, and Motorola. Headquartered in Toronto, the company has operations throughout Canada and the United States, as well as in Europe and Asia.

The 1990s was a good time for Celestica. It bought up original equipment manufacturing firms (OEMs) around the globe. Worldwide sales were continually increasing, and the industry seemed to be consolidating in the hands of a few players, such as Flextronics, Selectron and Sanmina-SCI, with Celestica taking the number four spot.

The popping of the technology bubble hit EMS companies hard. It brought with it a long-term slump in the industry and a worldwide glut in EMS capacity. Revenues at Celestica declined and losses mounted. Though the company, along with its competitors such as Flextronics, went into a program of cutting costs by closing facilities and laying off staff, for many years at the beginning of the decade, it looked as if times could only get worse. The end of 2003 brought another loss for the company, as well as the departure of their CEO Eugene Polistuk.

Recently, however, there are some signs of a turnaround. While the departure of Polistuk was called a retirement, it was widely rumoured that Celestica's board of directors forced his removal after years of failure to turn the company around. In early 2004, Stephen Delaney, who was previously the company's head of U.S. operations, was appointed interim CEO. Only 41 years old, Delaney moved quickly on a plan to close even more plants in North America and Europe and to lay off a further 5000 employees.

Such further drastic actions began to show a positive effect in the middle of 2004. The trimming of jobs and plant closings are expected to save Celestica about US$125 million a year. Sales have slowly begun to grow. These early successes resulted in Celestica's board of directors making Delaney the company's permanent CEO.

Has Delaney and his company turned a corner? Some analysts have said that the entire EMS sector has been down for so long that the only way to go is up. As the fortunes of their customers improve, they argue, so too will the fortunes of the EMS industry. However, there is still more that can be done to keep costs down. Celestica has promised to eliminate 20 percent of its senior management team. It is also attempting to tie the compensation that its senior executives receive to the overall performance of the company.

A key challenge is to keep product innovation strong in the face of cost containment. An encouraging sign is that Celestica recently received an "Excellence in B2B Collaboration in the EMS Sector, Supplier of the Year Award" from Cisco Systems, Inc. Celestica was selected for demonstrating the ability to significantly contribute innovation that has positively impacted the satisfaction level of Cisco's customers.

Outside analysts point to a range of possibilities for Celestica. For example, it could move away from the lower profit area of manufacturing into the high-margin world of electronics design. This could be done by either improving the company's in-house capabilities or by acquiring electronics design companies. Other analysts stress that keeping the lid on costs will be the key to Celestica's future success. Closing expensive plants in North America and opening new plants in low-cost China is an option for the company. Since OEMs often want their manufacturers to be in close proximity, a further option for Celestica is to open up new facilities in such future-growth areas as Eastern Europe and Mexico.

Whatever happens, there is little doubt that Stephen Delaney has some challenging years ahead of him.

Sources: Yahoo Finance, "Celestica Inc. (CLS)"; Forbes.com, "Four Picks Among EMS Companies," August 4, 2004; "Case Study: Celestica Inc.," *National Post Business*, July 2004.

CASE DISCUSSION QUESTIONS

1. Why are there so many past plant closures within Celestica? What reasons can be attributed to their current turnaround?
2. Is Celestica's optional plan for plant openings in China a cure-all for its financial woes/
3. How would you suggest Celestica turn itself around?

Donovan Reese/Getty Images.

Managing Timberland's Global Supply Chain

Timberland, a New Hampshire-based manufacturer of rugged, high-quality shoes and outdoor clothing, has built one of the world's premium footwear and apparel brands. From small beginnings in the late 1970s, Timberland has grown into a global business with sales of $1.15 billion in 2000. The company's global expansion began in 1979 when an Italian distributor walked into the then-small U.S. outfitter and expressed an interest in shoe #100-81, a hand-sewn moccasin with a lug sole. The Italian thought the shoe would sell well in Italy—land of high-style Gucci shoes. He was right; Timberland quickly became a phenomenon in Italy where Timberland shoes often sold for a 60-percent premium over prices in the United States. Expansion into other countries followed. Today, retailers sell its products through Timberland specialty stores, Timberland factory outlet stores, timberland.com, and franchisees in Europe. The products are sold throughout the United States, Canada, Europe, Asia, Latin America, and the Middle East.

Ignored during much of this rapid growth, however, was any attempt to build a tightly managed and coordinated global manufacturing and logistics system. By the early 1990s, Timberland was confronted with an extremely complex global manufacturing and logistics network. To take advantage of lower wage costs outside the United States, the company had established manufacturing facilities in the Dominican Republic and Puerto Rico. Timberland had also found it cost-efficient to source footwear and apparel from independent suppliers based in dozens of other low-wage countries in Asia, Europe, and Latin America. At the same time, Timberland's distribution network had grown to serve consumers in more than 50 countries. To complicate things further, the average shipment of footwear to retailers was for less than 12 pairs of each type of shoe, which made for an enormous volume of individual shipments to track.

Timberland found that its logistics system was breaking down under the strains imposed by rapid growth, a globally dispersed supply and distribution chain, and a large volume of individual shipments. The company simply lacked the information systems required to coordinate and control its dispersed production and distribution network. No common information

Global Manufacturing and Materials Management

CHAPTER 15

OPENING CASE

systems linked suppliers, Timberland, and retailers. Nor was there any attempt to consolidate shipments from different regions of the world to realize shipping economies. Products were shipped from six countries in Southeast Asia to the United States and Europe, as opposed to being consolidated at one location and then shipped. The consequences included an inability to match the demands of retailers with production, excess inventory, and high costs.

In the mid-1990s, Timberland decided to reorganize its global logistics system by streamlining its logistics information pipeline first and then its cargo pipeline. The information challenge was to come up with a system that would enable Timberland to track a product from the factory to its final destination, thereby better matching supply with demand. As Timberland's director of distribution explains it: "At every link in the chain, you can make a decision about cargo that would make it flow better, but only if you have the information about the product and the ability to communicate with that location in real time to direct the product." For example, when a product leaves the factory, Timberland can in theory direct a freight forwarder to send the product by air or by ocean carrier, depending on the urgency of the shipment. When a shipment lands in, say, Los Angeles, it can be shipped to a distribution centre or shipped directly to a customer, again depending on need. Until the mid-1990s, the company lacked the requisite information systems required to make such choices.

The company developed the required information system in conjunction with ACS, a freight forwarder, and The Rockport Group, a software house. To simplify its system at the physical distribution level and to make implementation of its information systems easier, Timberland consolidated regional warehousing. Timberland had separate warehouses in a dozen Asian countries, several in the United States, and three in Europe. Under the new Internet-based system, sources in Asia feed into one warehouse. The company also switched to single continental distribution centres in North America and Europe. By centralizing its warehousing at three locations, the company can better track where the product is located so that it can be routed quickly and flexibly to where it is needed. The result has been an improvement in Timberland's ability to deliver products to customers exactly when they need them, as opposed to delivering products too late or too soon. This has helped the company increase inventory turnover, thereby reducing the total amount of inventory it needs to hold. By centralizing warehousing, Timberland has also been able to consolidate shipments from a region into one transoceanic shipment, which has enabled the company to negotiate much better shipping rates.

In tandem with improvements in its global logistics system, Timberland also altered its supply base in response to changes in costs and import quotas. It reduced production from company-owned factories in the Dominican Republic and Puerto Rico from 28 percent of total sales in 1997 to 15 percent of total sales in 2000, preferring instead to source production from lower-cost suppliers in Southeast Asia. In response to the imposition of new European quotas on footwear imports from China, Timberland has also found it necessary to shift production destined for Europe from China to other Asian countries, such as Vietnam.

According to the company, better managing its global supply chain has helped Timberland increase its gross profit margins from 38 percent to 41 percent. The increase has been due to lower production costs and increased inventory turnover. Thanks to more efficient management of the supply chain, inventory now turns over four times a year, up from 2.9 times in 1997. Total inventory has fallen by 12 percent, implying that less working capital is tied up in inventory and fewer products remain unsold. Still, the company recognizes there is room for improvement. Currently the time between ordering and delivery of footwear is four months. Timberland wants to cut that to 45 days, which would allow the company to be much more responsive to short-term changes in consumer demands.

Sources: P. Buxbaum, "Timberland's New Spin on Global Logistics," *Distribution,* May 1994, pp. 33–36; A. E. Serwer, "Will Timberland Grow Up?" *Fortune,* May 29, 1995, p. 24; M. Tedeschi, "Timberland Vows to Get on the Ball," *Footwear News,* May 22, 1995, p. 2; *Timberland Annual Report,* 1997; A. Coia, "Timberland Keeps in Step with Changing Europe," *Logistics,* May 2001, pp. E4–E7; and S. Hill, "Timberland Heeds Consumers," *Apparel Industry Magazine,* December 2000, pp. 27–30.

LEARNING OBJECTIVES

1. Become familiar with the important influence that operations management can have on the competitive position of an international business.
2. Understand how country differences, manufacturing technology, and product features all affect the choice of where to locate production operations.
3. Appreciate the factors that influence a firm's decision of whether to source component parts from within the company or purchase them from a foreign supplier.
4. Understand what is required to efficiently coordinate a globally dispersed manufacturing system.

INTRODUCTION

As trade barriers fall and global markets develop, many firms increasingly confront a set of interrelated issues. First, where in the world should productive activities be located? Should they be concentrated in a single country, or should they be dispersed around the globe, matching the type of activity with country differences in factor costs, tariff barriers, political risks, and the like in order to minimize costs and maximize value added? Second, what should be the long-term strategic role of foreign production sites? Should the firm abandon a foreign site if factor costs change, moving production to another more favourable location, or is there value to maintaining an operation at a given location even if underlying economic conditions change? Third, should the firm own foreign productive activities, or is it better to outsource those activities to independent vendors? Fourth, how should a globally dispersed supply chain be managed, and what is the role of Internet-based information technology in the management of global logistics? Fifth, should the firm manage global logistics itself, or should it outsource the management to enterprises that specialize in this activity?

In this chapter we shall consider all these questions and discuss the various factors that influence decisions in this arena. The opening case on Timberland provides examples of the issues many firms struggle with in today's global economy. Timberland started to source production from foreign factories to reduce its cost structure. However, it soon found that it lacked the capability to manage the resulting supply chain. Most importantly, a lack of timely information meant that it was almost impossible for Timberland to closely match production schedules with demand from retailers around the world. The results included a shortage of some products and excess production of other products, which meant higher inventory and lower gross margins. Timberland responded by introducing information systems to better track the flow of products through the global supply chain. It also consolidated its global distribution systems at three warehouses. As a result, it is now better able to match supply and demand, which has increased inventory turnover and boosted profitability.

STRATEGY, MANUFACTURING, AND LOGISTICS

In Chapter 11, we introduced the concept of the value chain and discussed a number of value creation activities, including production, marketing, materials management (logistics), R&D, human resources, and information systems. In this chapter, we will focus on two of these activities–production and materials management (logistics)–and attempt to clarify how they might be performed internationally to (1) lower the costs of value creation and (2) add value by better serving customer needs. We will discuss the contributions of information technology, which has become particularly important in the era of the Internet.

In Chapter 11, we defined production as "the activities involved in creating a product." We used the term *production* to denote both service and manufacturing activities, since one can produce a service or produce a physical product. In this chapter, we focus more on manufacturing than on service activities, so we will use the term *manufacturing* rather than *production*. **Materials management** is the activity that controls the transmission of physical materials through the value chain, from procurement through production and into distribution. Materials management includes **logistics,** which refers to the procurement and physical transmission of material through the supply chain, from suppliers to customers. Manufacturing and materials management are closely linked, since a firm's ability to perform its manufacturing function efficiently depends on a continuous supply of high-quality material inputs, for which materials management is responsible.

MATERIALS MANAGEMENT The activity that controls the transmission of physical materials through the value chain, from procurement through production and into distribution.

LOGISTICS The procurement and physical transmission of material through the supply chain, from suppliers to customers.

The manufacturing and materials management functions of an international firm have a number of important strategic objectives.[1] One is to lower costs. Dispersing manufacturing activities to various locations around the globe where each activity can be performed most efficiently can lower costs. Costs can also be lowered by managing the global supply chain efficiently so as to better match supply and demand. Efficient supply chain management reduces the amount of inventory in the system and increases inventory turnover, which means the firm has to invest less working capital in inventory and is less likely to have excess inventory that cannot be sold and has to be written off.

A second strategic objective shared by manufacturing and materials management is to increase product quality by eliminating defective products from both the supply chain and the manufacturing process.[2] The objectives of reducing costs and increasing quality are not independent of each other. As illustrated in Figure 15.1, the firm that improves its quality control will also reduce its costs of value creation. Improved quality control reduces costs in three ways:

FIGURE 15.1

The Relationship between Quality and Costs

Source: Reprinted from "What Does Product Quality Really Mean?" by David A. Garvin, MIT *Sloan Management Review,* Fall 1984, p. 37, by permission of the publisher.

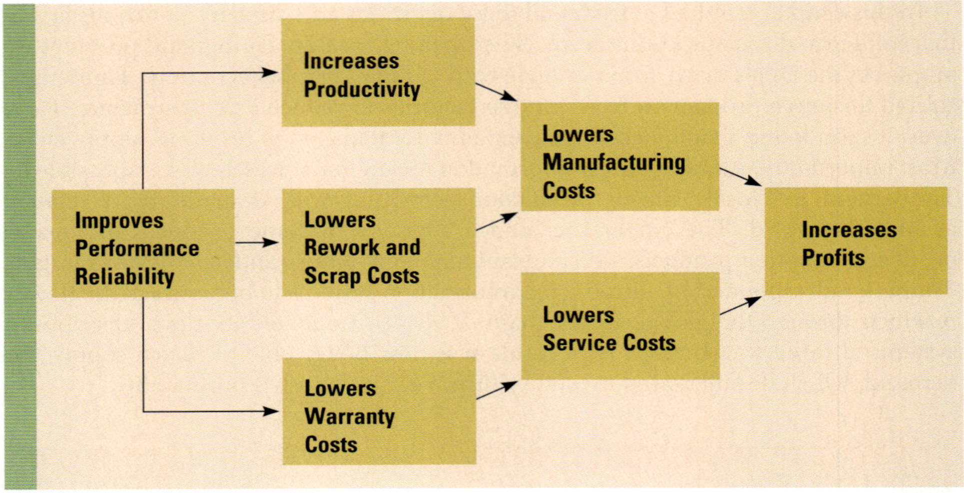

- Increases productivity because time is not wasted manufacturing poor-quality products that cannot be sold, leading to a direct reduction in unit costs.
- Lowers rework and scrap costs.
- Lowers warranty costs.

The effect is to lower the costs of value creation by reducing both manufacturing and service costs.

TOTAL QUALITY MANAGEMENT Management philosophy that takes as its central focus the need to improve the quality of a company's products and services.

Companies are utilizing **total quality management** (TQM) to boost their product quality. TQM takes as its central focus the need to improve the quality of a company's products and services. The TQM philosophy was developed by a number of American consultants such as the late W. Edward Deming, Joseph Juran, and A. V. Feigenbaum.[3] Deming identified a number of steps that should be part of any TQM program. He argued that management should embrace the philosophy that mistakes, defects, and poor-quality materials are not acceptable and should be eliminated. He suggested that the quality of supervision should be improved by allowing more time for supervisors to work with employees and by providing them with the tools they need to do the job. Deming recommended that management should create an environment in which employees will not fear reporting problems or recommending improvements. He believed that work standards should be defined not only as numbers or quotas, but also should include some notion of quality to promote the production of defect-free output. He argued that management has the responsibility to train employees in new skills to keep pace with changes in the workplace. In addition, he believed that achieving better quality requires the commitment of everyone in the company.

Li & Fung, one of the largest multinational trading companies in the developing world, manages a complex network of suppliers for a diverse group of customers, including The Limited, Gymboree, and Warner Brothers, with a customer-focused division for each of these customers. Overall costs are minimized because Li & Fung is able to break up the value chain and disperse activities to different manufacturers in different countries. William Taufic/The Stock Market.

The growth of international standards has also focused greater attention on the importance of product quality. In Europe, for example, the European

Union requires that the quality of a firm's manufacturing processes and products be certified under a quality standard known as **ISO 9000** before the firm is allowed access to the EU marketplace. Although the ISO 9000 certification process has proved to be a somewhat bureaucratic and costly process for many firms, it does focus management attention on the need to improve the quality of products and processes.[4]

ISO 9000
Certification process that requires certain quality standards that must be met.

In addition to the objectives of lowering costs and improving quality, two other objectives have particular importance in international businesses. First, manufacturing and materials management must be able to accommodate demands for local responsiveness. As we saw in Chapter 11, demands for local responsiveness arise from national differences in consumer tastes and preferences, infrastructure, distribution channels, and host-government demands. Demands for local responsiveness create pressures to decentralize manufacturing activities to the major national or regional markets in which the firm does business or to implement flexible manufacturing processes that enable the firm to customize the product coming out of a factory according to the market in which it is to be sold.

Second, manufacturing and materials management must be able to respond quickly to shifts in customer demand. In recent years, time-based competition has grown more important.[5] When consumer demand is prone to large and unpredictable shifts, the firm that can adapt most quickly to these shifts will gain an advantage. As we shall see, both manufacturing and materials management play critical roles here. The opening case illustrated how Timberland has been trying to reduce the time between the ordering and delivery of footwear so that it can better respond to changes in consumer demands.

WHERE TO MANUFACTURE

An essential decision facing an international firm is where to locate its manufacturing activities to achieve the goals of minimizing costs and improving product quality. For the firm contemplating international production, a number of factors must be considered. These factors can be grouped under three broad headings: country factors, technological factors, and product factors.[6]

COUNTRY FACTORS

We reviewed country-specific factors in some detail earlier in the book and we will not dwell on them here. Political economy, culture, and relative factor costs differ from country to country. In Chapter 4, we saw that due to differences in factor costs, certain countries have a comparative advantage for producing certain products. In Chapters 2 and 3, we saw how differences in political economy and national culture influence the benefits, costs, and risks of doing business in a country. Other things being equal, a firm should locate its various manufacturing activities where the economic, political, and cultural conditions, including relative factor costs, are conducive to the performance of those activities. In Chapter 11, we referred to the benefits derived from such a strategy as location economies. We argued that one result of the strategy is the creation of a global web of value creation activities.

Also important in some industries is the presence of global concentrations of activities at certain locations. In Chapter 7, we discussed the role of location externalities in influencing foreign direct investment decisions. Externalities include the

ANOTHER PERSPECTIVE

Production facilities on the move

Dell Computer recently decided to move its Asian production facilities from Kuala Lumpur, Malaysia, to China. Over the past five years, Singapore reports it has lost 42 000 jobs to China. What role do you think labour costs play in Dell's decision to move production? Do you think Dell and other companies want to ensure that their products are not kept out of the Chinese market in the future, so are establishing a foothold there for a centre of excellence via domestic production? (*International Herald Tribune,* June 29–30, 2002, p. 9.)

presence of an appropriately skilled labour pool and supporting industries.[7] Such externalities can play an important role in deciding where to locate manufacturing activities. For example, because of a cluster of semiconductor manufacturing plants in Taiwan, a pool of labour with experience in the semiconductor business has developed. In addition, the plants have attracted a number of supporting industries, such as the manufacturers of semiconductor capital equipment and silicon, which have established facilities in Taiwan to be near their customers. This implies that there are real benefits to locating in Taiwan, as opposed to another location that lacks such externalities. Other things being equal, the externalities make Taiwan an attractive location for semiconductor manufacturing facilities.

Of course, other things are not equal. Differences in relative factor costs, political economy, culture, and location externalities are important, but other factors also loom large. Formal and informal trade barriers obviously influence location decisions (see Chapter 6), as do transportation costs and rules and regulations regarding foreign direct investment (see Chapter 7). For example, although relative factor costs may make a country look attractive as a location for performing a manufacturing activity, regulations prohibiting foreign direct investment may eliminate this option. Similarly, a consideration of factor costs might suggest that a firm should source production of a certain component from a particular country, but trade barriers could make this uneconomical.

Another country factor is expected future movements in its exchange rate (see Chapters 9 and 10). Adverse changes in exchange rates can quickly alter a country's attractiveness as a manufacturing base. Currency appreciation can transform a low-cost location into a high-cost location. Many Japanese corporations had to grapple with this problem during the 1990s. The relatively low value of the yen on foreign exchange markets between 1950 and 1980 helped strengthen Japan's position as a low-cost location for manufacturing. Between 1980 and the mid-1990s, however, the yen's steady appreciation against the dollar increased the dollar cost of products exported from Japan, making Japan less attractive as a manufacturing location. In response, many Japanese firms moved their manufacturing offshore to lower-cost locations in East Asia.

TECHNOLOGICAL FACTORS

The technology we are concerned with in this subsection is manufacturing technology—the technology that performs specific manufacturing activities. The type of technology a firm uses in its manufacturing can be pivotal in location decisions. For example, because of technological constraints, in some cases it is necessary to perform certain manufacturing activities in only one location and serve the world market from there. In other cases, the technology may make it feasible to perform an activity in multiple locations. Three characteristics of a manufacturing technology are of interest here: the level of fixed costs, the minimum efficient scale, and the flexibility of the technology.

Fixed Costs

As we noted in Chapter 11, in some cases the fixed costs of setting up a manufacturing plant are so high that a firm must serve the world market from a single location or from a very few locations. For example, it now costs more than $1 billion to set up a state-of-the-art plant to manufacture semiconductor chips. Given this, serving the world market from a single plant sited at a single (optimal) location makes sense. Conversely, a relatively low level of fixed costs can make it economical to perform a particular activity in several locations at once. This allows the firm to better accommodate demands for local responsiveness. Manufacturing in multiple locations

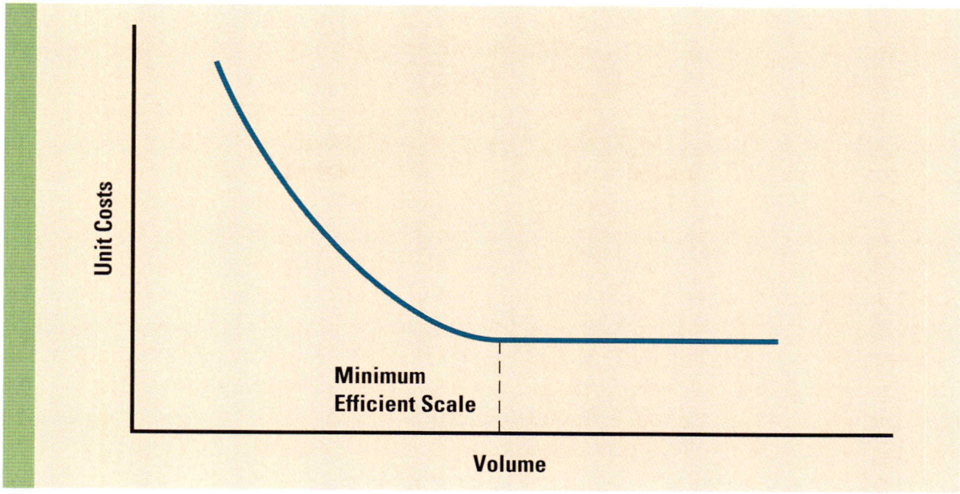

FIGURE 15.2
A Typical Unit Cost Curve

may also help the firm avoid becoming too dependent on one location. Being too dependent on one location is particularly risky in a world of floating exchange rates. Many firms disperse their manufacturing plants to different locations as a "real hedge" against potentially adverse moves in currencies.

Minimum Efficient Scale

The concept of economies of scale tells us that as plant output expands, unit costs decrease. The reasons include the greater utilization of capital equipment and the productivity gains that come with specialization of employees within the plant.[8] However, beyond a certain level of output, few additional scale economies are available. Thus, the "unit cost curve" declines with output until a certain output level is reached, at which point further increases in output realize little reduction in unit costs. The level of output at which most plant-level scale economies are exhausted is referred to as the minimum efficient scale of output. This is the scale of output a plant must operate at to realize all major plant-level scale economies (see Figure 15.2).

The implications of this concept are as follows: The larger the minimum efficient scale of a plant, the greater the argument for centralizing production in a single location or a limited number of locations. Alternatively, when the minimum efficient scale of production is relatively low, it may be economical to manufacture a product at several locations. As in the case of low fixed costs, the advantages are allowing the firm to accommodate demands for local responsiveness or to hedge against currency risk by manufacturing the same product in several locations.

Flexible Manufacturing and Mass Customization

Central to the concept of economies of scale is the idea that the best way to achieve high efficiency, and hence low unit costs, is through the mass production of a standardized output. The trade-off implicit in this idea is between unit costs and product variety. Producing greater product variety from a factory implies shorter production runs, which in turn implies an inability to realize economies of scale. That is, wide product variety makes it difficult for a company to increase its production efficiency and thus reduce its unit costs. According to this logic, the way to increase efficiency and drive down unit costs is to limit product variety and produce a standardized product in large volumes.

This view of production efficiency has been challenged by the rise of flexible manufacturing technologies. The term **flexible manufacturing technology**—or *lean production,* as it is often called—covers a range of manufacturing technologies designed to (1) reduce setup times for complex equipment, (2) increase the utilization of individual machines through better scheduling, and (3) improve quality control at all stages of the manufacturing process.[9] Flexible manufacturing technologies allow the company to produce a wider variety of end products at a unit cost that at one time could be achieved only through the mass production of a standardized output. Research suggests the adoption of flexible manufacturing technologies may actually increase efficiency and lower unit costs relative to what can be achieved by the mass production of a standardized output, while at the same time enabling the company to customize its product offering to a much greater extent than was once thought possible. The term **mass customization** has been coined to describe the ability of companies to use flexible manufacturing technology to reconcile two goals that were once thought to be incompatible—low cost and product customization.[10]

FLEXIBLE MANUFACTURING TECHNOLOGY Manufacturing technologies designed to improve job scheduling, reduce setup time, and improve quality control.

MASS CUSTOMIZATION The production of a variety of end products at a unit cost that could once be achieved only through mass production of a standardized output.

Flexible manufacturing technologies vary in their sophistication and complexity. One of the most famous examples of a flexible manufacturing technology, Toyota's production system, is relatively unsophisticated, but it has been credited with making Toyota the most efficient auto company in the world. Toyota's flexible manufacturing system was developed by one of the company's engineers, Ohno Taiichi. After working at Toyota for five years and visiting Ford's U.S. plants, Ohno became convinced that the mass production philosophy for making cars was flawed. He saw numerous problems with the mass production system.

First, long production runs created massive inventories that had to be stored in large warehouses. This was expensive, both because of the cost of warehousing and because inventories tied up capital in unproductive uses. Second, if the initial machine settings were wrong, long production runs resulted in the production of a large number of defects (i.e., waste). Third, the mass production system was unable to accommodate consumer preferences for product diversity.

In response, Ohno looked for ways to make shorter production runs economical. He developed a number of techniques designed to reduce setup times for production equipment (a major source of fixed costs). By using a system of levers and pulleys, he reduced the time required to change dies on stamping equipment from a full day in 1950 to 3 minutes by 1971. This made small production runs economical, which allowed Toyota to respond better to consumer demands for product diversity. Small production runs also eliminated the need to hold large inventories, thereby reducing warehousing costs. Furthermore, small product runs and the lack of inventory meant that defective parts were produced in small numbers and entered the assembly process immediately. This reduced waste and helped trace defects back to their source to fix the problem. In sum, Ohno's innovations enabled Toyota to produce a more diverse product range at a lower unit cost than was possible with conventional mass production.[11]

Flexible machine cells are another common flexible manufacturing technology. A **flexible machine cell** is a grouping of various types of machinery, a common materials handler, and a centralized cell controller (computer). Each cell normally contains four to six machines capable of performing a variety of operations. The typical cell is dedicated to the production of a family of parts or products. The settings on machines are computer controlled, which allows each cell to switch quickly between the production of different parts or products.

FLEXIBLE MACHINE CELL Flexible manufacturing technology in which a grouping of various machine types, a common materials handler, and a centralized cell controller produce a family of products.

Improved capacity utilization and reductions in work-in-progress inventory (that is, stockpiles of partly finished products) and in waste are major efficiency benefits of flexible machine cells. Improved capacity utilization arises from the reduction in setup times and from the computer-controlled coordination of production flow between machines, which eliminates bottlenecks. The tight coordination between machines also reduces work-in-progress inventory. Reductions in waste are due to the ability of computer-controlled machinery to identify ways to transform inputs into outputs while producing a minimum of unusable waste material. While freestanding machines might be in use 50 percent of the time, the same machines when grouped into a cell can be used more than 80 percent of the time and produce the same end product with half the waste. This increases efficiency and results in lower costs.

The efficiency benefits of installing flexible manufacturing technology can be dramatic. Avcorp Industries Inc., a public company based in Delta, B.C., is a supplier to the high technology and aerospace industries. Their products are flight structures, wing and fuselage components, flight control surfaces, and navigation and landing light lenses. In 1998, Avcorp worked with Dassault Aviation to engineer customized automated robotics. The automated assembly cell used in this robotic system performed coordinated movements for fastening operations, as well as independent movements for drilling and sealing for operational flexibility. This operation is unique to Avcorp; the design enables the robotic cells to work on more than one type of assembly, while traditional robotic cells are confined to only one application. Avcorp's robotic assembly time is estimated to be from 50 to 67 percent less than manual assembly time. Lowering the assembly time results in decreases in costs for the aero-structures supplier and the aircraft operator.[12] Similarly, Lexmark, a producer of computer printers, has also converted 80 percent of its 2700-employee factory in Lexington, Kentucky, to flexible manufacturing cells, and it too has seen productivity increase by about 25 percent.[13] Besides improving efficiency and lowering costs, flexible manufacturing technologies also enable companies to customize products to the unique demands of small consumer groups–at a cost that at one time could be achieved only by mass producing a standardized output. Thus, the technologies help a company achieve mass customization, which increases its customer responsiveness. Most important for an international business, flexible manufacturing technologies can help the firm customize products for different national markets. The importance of this advantage cannot be overstated. When flexible manufacturing technologies are available, a firm can manufacture products customized to various national markets at a single factory sited at the optimal location. And it can do this without absorbing a significant cost penalty. Thus, companies no longer need to establish manufacturing facilities in each major national market to provide products that satisfy specific consumer tastes and preferences, part of the rationale for a multidomestic strategy (Chapter 11).

Summary

A number of technological factors support the economic arguments for concentrating manufacturing facilities in a few choice locations or even in a single location. Other things being equal, when fixed costs are substantial, the minimum efficient scale of production is high, and/or flexible manufacturing technologies are available, the arguments for concentrating production at a few choice locations are strong. This is true even when substantial differences in consumer tastes and preferences exist between national markets, since flexible manufacturing technologies allow the firm to customize products to national differences at a single facility. Alternatively, when fixed costs are low, the minimum efficient scale of production is low, and flexible manufacturing technologies are not available, the arguments for concentrating production at one or a few locations are not as compelling. In such cases, it may make more sense to manufacture in each major market in which the firm is active if this helps the firm better respond to local demands. This holds only if the increased local responsiveness more than offsets the cost disadvantages of not concentrating manufacturing. With the advent of flexible

Products such as circuit boards have high value-to-weight ratios, meaning they are expensive in their worth, but do not weigh very much. This, in turn, means their transportation costs are a very small percentage of total costs, and thus, the products can be easily shipped across the world. AP Photo/ Mark Duncan.

manufacturing technologies and mass customization, such a strategy is becoming less attractive. In sum, technological factors are making it feasible, and necessary, for firms to concentrate manufacturing facilities at optimal locations. Trade barriers and transportation costs are major brakes on this trend.

PRODUCT FACTORS

Two product features affect location decisions. The first is the product's *value-to-weight ratio* because of its influence on transportation costs. Many electronic components and pharmaceuticals have high value-to-weight ratios; they are expensive and they do not weigh very much. Thus, even if they are shipped halfway around the world, their transportation costs account for a very small percentage of total costs. Given this, other things being equal, there is great pressure to manufacture these products in the optimal location and to serve the world market from there. The opposite holds for products with low value-to-weight ratios. Refined sugar, certain bulk chemicals, paint, and petroleum products all have low value-to-weight ratios; they are relatively inexpensive products that weigh a lot. Accordingly, when they are shipped long distances, transportation costs account for a large percentage of total costs. Thus, other things being equal, there is great pressure to manufacture these products in multiple locations close to major markets to reduce transportation costs.

The other product feature that can influence location decisions is whether the product serves **universal needs,** needs that are the same all over the world. Examples include many industrial products (e.g., industrial electronics, steel, bulk chemicals) and modern consumer products (e.g., handheld calculators and personal computers). Since there are few national differences in consumer taste and preference for such products, the need for local responsiveness is reduced. This increases the attractiveness of concentrating manufacturing at an optimal location.

UNIVERSAL NEEDS Needs that are the same all over the world, such as steel, bulk chemicals, and industrial electronics.

LOCATING MANUFACTURING FACILITIES

There are two basic strategies for locating manufacturing facilities: concentrating them in a centralized location and serving the world market from there, or decentralizing them in various regional or national locations that are close to major markets. The appropriate strategic choice is determined by the various country, technological, and product factors we have discussed in this section and are summarized in Table 15.1. As can be seen, concentrated manufacturing makes most sense when:

- Differences between countries in factor costs, political economy, and culture have a substantial impact on the costs of manufacturing in various countries.
- Trade barriers are low.
- Externalities arising from the concentration of like enterprises favour certain locations.
- Important exchange rates are expected to remain relatively stable.
- The production technology has high fixed costs, a high minimum efficient scale, or a flexible manufacturing technology exists.
- The product's value-to-weight ratio is high.
- The product serves universal needs.

COUNTRY FACTORS	CONCENTRATED MANUFACTURING FAVOURED	DECENTRALIZED MANUFACTURING FAVOURED
Differences in political economy	Substantial	Few
Differences in culture	Substantial	Few
Differences in factor costs	Substantial	Few
Trade barriers	Low	High
Location externalities	Important in industry	Not important in industry
Exchange rates	Stable	Volatile
Technological Factors		
Fixed costs	High	Low
Minimum efficient scale	High	Low
Flexible manufacturing technology	Available	Not available
Product Factors		
Value-to-weight ratio	High	Low
Serves universal needs	Yes	No

TABLE 15.1
Location Strategy and Manufacturing

Alternatively, decentralization of manufacturing is appropriate when:

- Differences between countries in factor costs, political economy, and culture do not have a substantial impact on the costs of manufacturing in various countries.
- Trade barriers are high.
- Location externalities are not important.
- Volatility in important exchange rates is expected.
- The production technology has low fixed costs, low minimum efficient scale, and flexible manufacturing technology is not available.
- The product's value-to-weight ratio is low.
- The product does not serve universal needs (that is, significant differences in consumer tastes and preferences exist between nations).

In practice, location decisions are seldom clear cut. For example, it is not unusual for differences in factor costs, technological factors, and product factors to point toward concentrated manufacturing while a combination of trade barriers and volatile exchange rates points toward decentralized manufacturing. For example, this seems to be the case in the world automobile industry. Although the availability of flexible manufacturing and cars' relatively high value-to-weight ratios suggest concentrated manufacturing, the combination of formal and informal trade barriers and the uncertainties of the world's current floating exchange rate regime (see Chapter 10) have inhibited firms' ability to pursue this strategy. For these reasons, several automobile companies have established "top-to-bottom" manufacturing operations in three major regional markets: Asia, North America, and Western Europe.

ANOTHER PERSPECTIVE

Ethics with outsourcing

As Nike has learned through its outsourced operations in Vietnam with a Korean-owned production company, the world citizen tends to see the ethical standards followed in production as a responsibility of the company. Imagine the challenge of monitoring such operations, many of which tend to be rural. As soon as you land at the regional airport for an on-site visit, the rural production site managers know you are there. They have time to pull together the face they know you want to see, the standards you included in your outsourcing contract. A long-term relationship with the supplier, insistence on acceptable production standards and human resource policies, including wage requirements, and the involvement of the supplier's local employees on workers councils are some ways to maintain knowledge of the actual standards in the production facility.

THE STRATEGIC ROLE OF FOREIGN FACTORIES

Whatever the rationale behind establishing a foreign manufacturing facility, the strategic role of foreign factories can evolve over time.[14] Initially, many foreign factories are established where labor costs are low. Their strategic role typically is to produce labour-intensive products at as low a cost as possible. For example, beginning in the 1970s, many U.S. firms in the computer and telecommunication equipment businesses established factories across Southeast Asia to manufacture electronic components, such as circuit boards and semiconductors, at the lowest possible cost. They located their factories in countries such as Malaysia, Thailand, and Singapore precisely because each of these countries offered an attractive combination of low labour costs, adequate infrastructure, and a favourable tax and trade regime. Initially, the components produced by these factories were designed elsewhere and the final product would be assembled elsewhere. Over time, however, the strategic role of some factories has expanded; they have become important centres for the design and final assembly of products for the global marketplace. An example is Hewlett-Packard's operation in Singapore. Originally established as a low-cost location for the production of circuit boards, the facility has become the centre for the design and final assembly of portable ink-jet printers for the global marketplace.

Such upward migration in the strategic role of foreign factories arises because many foreign factories upgrade their own capabilities.[15] This improvement comes from two sources. First, pressure from the center to improve a factory's cost structure and/or customize a product to the demands of consumers in a particular nation can start a chain of events that ultimately leads to development of additional capabilities at that factory. For example, to meet centrally mandated directions to drive down costs, engineers at HP's Singapore factory argued that they needed to redesign products so they could be manufactured at a lower cost. This led to the establishment of a design center in Singapore. As this design centre proved its worth, HP executives realized the importance of co-locating design and manufacturing operations. They increasingly transferred more design responsibilities to the Singapore factory. In addition, the Singapore factory ultimately became the centre for the design of products tailored to the needs of the Asian market. This too made good strategic sense because it meant products were being designed by engineers who were close to the Asian market and probably had a good understanding of the needs of that market, as opposed to engineers located in the United States.

A second source of improvement in the capabilities of a foreign factory can be the increasing abundance of advanced factors of production in the nation in which the factory is located. Many nations that were considered economic backwaters a generation ago have been experiencing rapid economic development during the 1980s and 1990s. Their communication and transportation infrastructures and the education level of the population have improved. While these countries once lacked the advanced infrastructure required to support sophisticated design, development, and manufacturing operations, this is often no longer the case. This has made it much easier for factories based in these nations to take on a greater strategic role.

Because of such developments, many international businesses are moving away from a system in which their foreign factories were viewed as nothing more than low-cost manufacturing facilities and toward one where foreign factories are viewed as globally dispersed centres of excellence. In this new model, foreign factories take the lead role for the design and manufacture of products to serve important national or regional markets or even the global market. The development of such dispersed centres of excellence is consistent with the concept of a transnational strategy, which we introduced in Chapter 11. A major aspect of a transnational strategy is a belief in global learning–the idea that valuable knowledge does not reside just in a firm's domestic operations; it may also be

MANAGEMENT FOCUS

HAVING FUN MAKING MONEY

Mad Science proves that learning can be fun. In homes across North America, Mad Science entertains at almost 20 000 children's birthday parties every year with high-energy shows displaying bubbling potions, slimy goo, and interactive chemical magic. In schools, Mad Science brings "the newest and coolest in cutting-edge science content" to classrooms, while meeting state and provincial requirements and costing schools less than what they would spend producing the curriculum themselves. At theme parks, Mad Science shows have been featured at Six Flags, Ontario Place, and Legoland. The company seems to be making good on its vision "To become the world leader in fun, wholesome and educational science entertainment, with a consumer brand, strong community support, and global operations that reach children in every facet of their lives."

The company was formed by Ariel and Ron Shlien, two Montreal-based brothers. Always interested in "cool stuff" like model rockets, the two bought a used helium-neon laser when they were only 15 (Ariel) and 13 (Ron). Their initial thought was to use it to produce a big finale for a Montreal YMCA where the two produced a weekly science show. They later earned money by renting the laser to local DJs for $50 a night. Just four years later the two registered the name "The Mad Science Group," with dreams of creating a company that would serve the educational and entertainment needs of children around the globe.

At first, growth came by hiring and training local teenagers to present a science-based show in local schools, camps, and birthday parties. Further growth came by franchising the idea. Initial locations came through word of mouth—in 1994 a franchise opened in Toronto and in Florida, where the younger brother Ron had relocated to in 1992. After setting up a U.S. office that replicated the operation in Montreal, and spending about $200,000 in legal expenses to establish a U.S. franchising system, the shoestring operation was able to sell franchises for under US$25,000.

While Mad Science is now an international company, a key part of its strategy is to maintain a local, community-based feel to its operations. Franchising is therefore an effective and low-cost way for the company to grow, while tapping into the local knowledge that franchisees bring. Though Mad Science operates in over 100 North American markets and 18 countries it deliberately does not seek out a global dominant position as does the Walt Disney Corporation. Instead, Mad Science requires a strong local base to tap into local events, clubs, camps, and birthday parties. As older brother Ariel states, "We don't make significant efforts to hide the fact that we're a national brand, but the franchisees are on the front line, judging science fairs, working with teachers and being part of the community. That's who people see."

With a proven business model, the continuing task is to grow the company without losing the local appeal. Mad Science has struck a book deal with U.S.-based Scholastic Inc. publishers to feature a series of books with a teenager and a white-haired science professor who use science to solve crimes. The brothers continue to look for other strategic partnerships with other firms that serve the children-based market.

Sources: Mad Science at www.madscience.org; L.Oliver, "The Method In Mad Science," *Profit Magazine*, December 2003, www.profitguide.com.

found in its foreign subsidiaries. Foreign factories that upgrade their capabilities over time are creating valuable knowledge that might benefit the whole corporation. See the accompanying Management Focus.

Managers of international businesses need to remember that foreign factories can improve their capabilities over time, and this can be of immense strategic benefit to the firm. Rather than viewing foreign factories simply as sweatshops where unskilled labour churns out low-cost goods, managers need to view them as potential centres of excellence and to encourage and foster attempts by local managers to upgrade the capabilities of their factories and, thereby, enhance their strategic standing within the corporation.

MAKE-OR-BUY DECISIONS

SOURCING DECISIONS Whether a firm should make or buy component parts.

International businesses frequently face **sourcing decisions,** decisions about whether they should make or buy the component parts that go into their final product. Should the firm vertically integrate to manufacture its own component parts, or should it outsource them, buying them from independent suppliers? Make-or-buy decisions are important factors in many firms' manufacturing strategies. In the automobile industry, for example, the typical car contains more than 10 000 components, so automobile firms constantly face make-or-buy decisions. Ford of Europe, for example, produces only about 45 percent of the value of a car in its own plants. The remaining 55 percent, mainly accounted for by component parts, comes from independent suppliers. In the athletic shoe industry, the make-or-buy issue has been taken to an extreme with companies such as Nike and Reebok having no involvement in manufacturing; all production has been outsourced, primarily to manufacturers based in low-wage countries. Similarly, as we saw in the opening case, Timberland outsources some 85 percent of shoe production to independent firms.

Make-or-buy decisions pose plenty of problems for purely domestic businesses but even more problems for international businesses. These decisions in the international arena are complicated by the volatility of countries' political economies, exchange rate movements, changes in relative factor costs, and the like. In this section, we examine the arguments for making components and for buying them, and we consider the trade-offs involved in these decisions. Then we discuss strategic alliances as an alternative to manufacturing component parts within the company.

THE ADVANTAGES OF MAKE

The arguments that support making component parts in-house–vertical integration –are fourfold. Vertical integration may be associated with lowering costs, facilitating investments in highly specialized assets, protecting proprietary product technology, and facilitating the scheduling of adjacent processes.

Lower Costs

It may pay a firm to continue manufacturing a product or component in-house if the firm is more efficient at that production activity than any other enterprise. Boeing, for example, has looked closely at its make-or-buy decisions with regard to commercial jet aircraft. It decided to outsource the production of some component parts but keep the production of aircraft wings in-house. Boeing's rationale was that it has a core competence in the production of wings, and it is more efficient at this activity than any other comparable enterprise in the world. Therefore, it makes little sense for Boeing to outsource this particular activity.

Facilitate Specialized Investments

We first encountered the concept of specialized assets in Chapter 7 when we looked at the economic theory of vertical foreign direct investment. A variation of that concept explains why firms might want to make their own components rather than buy them.[16] When one firm must invest in specialized assets to supply another, mutual dependency is created. In such circumstances, each party fears the other will abuse the relationship by seeking more favourable terms.

Imagine Ford of Europe has developed a high-performance, high-quality, and uniquely designed fuel-injection system. The fuel-injection system's increased fuel efficiency will help sell Ford cars. Ford must decide whether to make the system in-house or to contract out the manufacturing to an independent supplier. Manufacturing these uniquely designed systems requires investments in equipment that can be used only for this purpose; it cannot be used to make fuel-injection systems for any other auto firm. Thus, investment in this equipment constitutes an investment in specialized assets.

Let us first examine this situation from the perspective of an independent supplier who has been asked by Ford to make this investment. The supplier might reason that once it has made the investment, it will become dependent on Ford for business since Ford is the only possible customer for the output of this equipment. The supplier perceives this as putting Ford in a strong bargaining position and worries that once the specialized investment has been made, Ford might use this to squeeze down prices for the fuel-injection systems. Given this risk, the supplier declines to make the investment in specialized equipment.

Now take the position of Ford. Ford might reason that if it contracts out production of these systems to an independent supplier, it might become too dependent on that supplier for a vital input. Because specialized equipment is required to produce the fuel-injection systems, Ford cannot easily switch its orders to other suppliers who lack that equipment. (It would face high switching costs.) Ford perceives this as increasing the bargaining power of the supplier and worries that the supplier might use its bargaining strength to demand higher prices.

Thus, the mutual dependency that outsourcing would create makes Ford nervous and scares away potential suppliers. Neither party completely trusts the other to play fair. Consequently, Ford might reason that the only safe way to get the new fuel-injection systems is to manufacture them itself. It may be unable to persuade any independent supplier to manufacture them. Thus, Ford decides to make rather than buy.

In general, we can predict that when substantial investments in specialized assets are required to manufacture a component, the firm will prefer to make the component internally rather than contract it out to a supplier. A growing amount of empirical evidence supports this prediction.[17]

Protect Proprietary Product Technology

Proprietary product technology is technology unique to a firm. If it enables the firm to produce a product containing superior features, proprietary technology can give the firm a competitive advantage. The firm would not want this technology to fall into the hands of competitors. If the firm contracts out the manufacture of components containing proprietary technology, it runs the risk that those suppliers will expropriate the technology for their own use or that they will sell it to the firm's competitors. Thus, to maintain control over its technology, the firm might prefer to make such component parts in-house. Boeing has decided to outsource a number of important components that go toward the production of an aircraft, and has explicitly decided not to outsource the manufacture of wings and cockpits because it believes that doing so would give away key technology to potential competitors.

Improve Scheduling

The weakest argument for vertical integration is that production cost savings result from it because it makes planning, coordination, and scheduling of adjacent processes easier.[18] This is particularly important in firms with just-in-time inventory systems (which we discuss later in the chapter). In the 1920s, for example, Ford profited from tight coordination and scheduling made possible by backward vertical integration into steel foundries, iron ore shipping, and mining. Deliveries at Ford's foundries on the Great Lakes were coordinated so well that ore was turned into engine blocks within 24 hours. This substantially reduced Ford's production costs by eliminating the need to hold excessive ore inventories.

For international businesses that source worldwide, scheduling problems can be exacerbated by the time and distance between the firm and its suppliers. This is true whether the firms use their own subunits as suppliers or use independent suppliers. Ownership is not the issue here. As we saw in the opening case, Timberland can achieve tight scheduling with its globally dispersed parts suppliers without vertical integration. Thus, although this argument for vertical integration is often made, it is not compelling. See the accompanying Country Focus.

THE ADVANTAGES OF BUY

The advantages of buying component parts from independent suppliers are that it gives the firm greater flexibility, it can help drive down the firm's cost structure, and it may help the firm capture orders from international customers.

Strategic Flexibility

The great advantage of buying component parts from independent suppliers is that the firm can maintain its flexibility, switching orders between suppliers as circumstances dictate. This is particularly important internationally, where changes in exchange rates and trade barriers can alter the attractiveness of supply sources. One year Hong Kong might be the lowest-cost source for a particular component, and the next year, Mexico may be. Many firms source the same parts from suppliers based in two different countries, primarily as a hedge against adverse movements in factor costs, exchange rates, and the like.

Sourcing component parts from independent suppliers can also be advantageous when the optimal location for manufacturing a product is beset by political risks. Under such circumstances, foreign direct investment to establish a component manufacturing operation in that country would expose the firm to political risks. The firm can avoid many of these risks by buying from an independent supplier in that country, thereby maintaining the flexibility to switch sourcing to another country if a war, revolution, or other political change alters that country's attractiveness as a supply source.

However, maintaining strategic flexibility has its downside. If a supplier perceives the firm will change suppliers in response to changes in exchange rates, trade barriers, or general political circumstances, that supplier might not be willing to make specialized investments in plant and equipment that would ultimately benefit the firm.

Lower Costs

Although vertical integration is often undertaken to lower costs, it may have the opposite effect. When this is the case, outsourcing may lower the firm's cost structure. Vertical integration into the manufacture of component parts increases an organization's scope, and the resulting increase in organizational complexity can raise a firm's cost structure for three reasons.

First, the greater the number of subunits in an organization, the greater are the problems of coordinating and controlling those units. Coordinating and controlling subunits require top management to process large amounts of information about subunit activities. The greater the number of subunits, the more information top management must process and the harder it is to do well. Theoretically, when the firm becomes involved in too many activities, headquarters management will be unable to effectively control all of them, and the resulting inefficiencies will more than offset any advantages derived from vertical integration.[19] This can be particularly serious in an international business, where the problem of controlling subunits is exacerbated by distance and differences in time, language, and culture.

Second, the firm that vertically integrates into component part manufacture may find that because its internal suppliers have a captive customer in the firm, they lack an incentive to reduce costs. The fact that they do not have to compete for orders with other suppliers may result in high operating costs. The managers of the supply operation may

COUNTRY FOCUS

CANADIAN COMPANIES FIND PROFITS IN FOREIGN MARKETS

In the world of global manufacturing and materials management, ensuring that ordered products (and even services) arrive on time at their destination is important. Diverse methods and techniques have been fine-tuned over the past century. Just-in-time (JIT) is a great way, for example, to shorten time between the concept and the sales result. It's even better at keeping costs down because warehousing needs can be eliminated allowing for companies to save on wages, rent, insurance, and related factors. JIT practices get the goods to where they're supposed to be when they're needed. This sounds like a tall order but it has become a normal business practice. Imagine goods shipped and received, on time, originating, for example in Winnipeg and reaching their final destination in Saskatoon, with no breakage and no delays. Replicating this type of shipment, with the same JIT principles between Canada and an overseas destination is more difficult, yet done all the time!

Many larger businesses frequently have the in-house skills and know-how in the art of making the right business connections. Smaller companies that are new to exporting might need assistance.

Take, for example, the International Business Opportunities Centre (IBOC) that works with the Canadian Trade Commissioner Services. It recently connected the Montreal-based consulting firm of Steve Woloz Associates with the Caribbean Regional HRD Competitiveness Program (a consortium of government, industry, and education players in the Guyanese garment market). The Canadian government-sponsored IBOC's trade lead resulted in a contract worth Cdn$17,000, with encouraging signs for future business. To deliver a product or service to its destination, on time, at cost, and with quality is important, and an increasing number of smaller Canadian businesses are finding export-friendly solutions through a myriad of federal government-funded programs and agencies.

Being aware of one's environment is a key factor in global materials management. Consider Pestell Shavings in southern central Ontario (New Hamburg) where one company's waste becomes another company's treasure. It recycles more than 2.5 million bags of wood shavings each year, for use as livestock bedding, and gets this product to where it's needed on time. The process starts at selected lumber mills across North America where shavings are bagged and compressed.

Pestell's partnering with the IBOC team at the Canadian government trade office in Boston, was instrumental for clinching its first-time sale of chemical free, kiln-dried softwood shavings worth Cdn$4,000 to Blue View Nurseries of Massachusetts. As small as this transaction may appear, it bodes well for possible future business. Pestell's main export markets include the U.S., the U.K., and the United Arab Emirates. Its main Canadian market remains the province of Ontario.

As with all businesses, there are many layers of cooperation involved in exporting. Global manufacturing and materials management and selling into foreign markets is difficult enough, yet with the right alliances, inventory management techniques, and supplier reliability, global manufacturing and materials management can be an achievement within the grasp of all businesses. Being informed will open up the doors to provide partnering where and when it is needed.

Sources: ITC, "Canadian Company Turns Lumber Waste Into Wealth," www.e-leads.ca/sstories/viewstory-e.asp?intStoryId=40; Pestell at www.pestell.com/shavings.html.

be tempted to pass on cost increases to other parts of the firm in the form of higher transfer prices, rather than looking for ways to reduce those costs.

Third, vertically integrated firms have to determine appropriate prices for goods transferred to subunits within the firm. This is a challenge in any firm, but it is even more complex in international businesses. Different tax regimes, exchange rate movements, and headquarters' ignorance about local conditions all increase the complexity of transfer pricing decisions. This complexity enhances internal suppliers' ability to manipulate transfer prices to their advantage, passing cost increases downstream rather than looking for ways to reduce costs.

The firm that buys its components from independent suppliers can avoid all these problems and the associated costs. The firm that sources from independent suppliers has fewer subunits to control. The incentive problems that occur with internal suppliers do not arise when independent suppliers are used. Independent suppliers know they must continue to be efficient if they are to win business from the firm. Also, because independent suppliers' prices are set by market forces, the transfer pricing problem does not exist. In sum, the bureaucratic inefficiencies and resulting costs that can arise when firms vertically integrate backward and manufacture their own components are avoided by buying component parts from independent suppliers.

Offsets

Another reason for outsourcing some manufacturing to independent suppliers based in other countries is that it may help the firm capture more orders from that country. For example, before Air India places a large order with Boeing, the Indian government might ask Boeing to push some subcontracting work toward Indian manufacturers. This kind of quid pro quo is not unusual in international business, and it affects far more than just the aerospace industry. Representatives of the U.S. government have repeatedly urged Japanese automobile companies to purchase more component parts from U.S. suppliers to partially offset the large volume of automobile exports from Japan to the United States.

TRADE-OFFS

Trade-offs are involved in make-or-buy decisions. The benefits of manufacturing components in-house seem to be greatest when highly specialized assets are involved, when vertical integration is necessary for protecting proprietary technology, or when the firm is simply more efficient than external suppliers at performing a particular activity. When these conditions are not present, the risk of strategic inflexibility and organizational problems suggest it may be better to contract out component part manufacturing to independent suppliers. Since issues of strategic flexibility and organizational control loom even larger for international businesses than purely domestic ones, an international business should be particularly wary of vertical integration into component part manufacture. In addition, some outsourcing in the form of offsets may help a firm gain larger orders in the future.

STRATEGIC ALLIANCES WITH SUPPLIERS

Several international businesses have tried to reap some benefits of vertical integration without the associated organizational problems by entering strategic alliances with essential suppliers. For example, we have seen an alliance between Kodak and Canon, under which Canon builds photocopiers for sale by Kodak, and an alliance between Apple and Sony, under which Sony builds laptop computers for Apple. By these alliances, Kodak and Apple have committed themselves to long-term relationships with these suppliers, which have encouraged the suppliers to undertake specialized investments. Strategic alliances build trust between the firm and its suppliers. Trust is built when a firm makes a credible commitment to continue purchasing from a supplier on reasonable terms. For example, the firm may invest money in a supplier–perhaps by taking a minority shareholding–to signal its intention to build a productive, mutually beneficial long-term relationship.

In general, the increased utilization of just-in-time inventory systems (JIT), computer-aided design (CAD), and computer-aided manufacturing (CAM) over the past 15 years seems to have increased pressures for firms to establish long-term relationships with their suppliers. JIT, CAD, and CAM systems all rely on close links between firms and their suppliers supported by substantial specialized investment in equipment and information

Even though Italian auto-maker Fiat entered into a strategic alliance with General Motors in 2000, it is struggling to survive as an independent car company. Claudia Pap/REUTERS/Getty Images.

systems hardware. To get a supplier to agree to adopt such systems, a firm must make a credible commitment to an enduring relationship with the supplier–it must build trust with the supplier. It can do this within the framework of a strategic alliance.

Alliances are not all good. Like formal vertical integration, a firm that enters long-term alliances may limit its strategic flexibility by the commitments it makes to its alliance partners. As we saw in Chapter 10 when we considered alliances between competitors, a firm that allies itself with another firm risks giving away key technological know-how to a potential competitor.

IMPLICATIONS FOR BUSINESS

The implications for international businesses of the material discussed in this chapter fall into three main areas: co-ordination through materials management, just-in-time systems, and the importance of information technology.

COORDINATING A GLOBAL MANUFACTURING SYSTEM

Materials management, which encompasses logistics, embraces the activities necessary to get materials from suppliers to a manufacturing facility, through the manufacturing process, and out through a distribution system to the end user.[20] The twin objectives of materials management are to achieve this at the lowest possible cost and in a way that best serves customer needs, thereby lowering the costs of value creation and helping the firm establish a competitive advantage through superior customer service. The potential for reducing costs through more efficient materials management is enormous. For the typical manufacturing enterprise, material costs account for between 50 and 70 percent of revenues, depending on the industry. Even a small reduction in these costs can have a substantial impact on profitability. According to one estimate, for a firm with revenues of $1 million, a return on investment rate of 5 percent, and materials costs that are 50 percent of sales revenues, a $15,000 increase in total profits could be achieved either by increasing sales revenues 30 percent or by reducing materials costs by 3 percent.[21] In a saturated market, it would be much easier to reduce materials costs by 3 percent than to increase sales revenues by 30 percent.

As we saw in the opening case on Timberland, materials management is a major undertaking in a firm with a globally dispersed manufacturing system and global markets. In recent years, a number of international businesses have established reputations for superior materials management.

THE POWER OF JUST-IN-TIME

Pioneered by Japanese firms during the 1950s and 60s, just-in-time inventory systems now play a major role in most manufacturing firms. The basic philosophy behind just-in-time (JIT) systems is to economize on inventory holding costs by having materials arrive at a manufacturing plant just in time to enter the production process and not before. The major cost saving comes from speeding up inventory turnover. This reduces inventory holding costs, such as warehousing and storage costs. It also means the company is less likely to have excess unsold inventory that it has to write off against earnings or price low to sell. In addition to the cost benefits, JIT systems can also help firms improve product quality. Under a JIT system, parts enter the manufacturing process immediately; they are not warehoused. This allows defective inputs to be spotted right away. The problem can then be traced to the supply source and fixed before more defective parts are produced. Under a more traditional system, warehousing parts for months before they are used allows many defective parts to be produced before a problem is recognized.

The drawback of a JIT system is that it leaves a firm without a buffer stock of inventory. Although buffer stocks are expensive to store, they can tide a firm over shortages brought about by disruption among suppliers (such as a labour dispute). Buffer stocks can also help a firm respond quickly to increases in demand. However, there are ways around these limitations. To reduce the risks associated with depending on one supplier for an important input, some firms source these inputs from several suppliers. As for responding quickly to increases in consumer demand, the experience of Dell Computer shows that it is possible to do this while maintaining a JIT system.

THE ROLE OF INFORMATION TECHNOLOGY AND THE INTERNET

Web-based information systems play a crucial role in modern materials management. By tracking component parts as they make their way across the globe toward an assembly plant, information systems enable a firm to optimize its production scheduling according to when components are expected to arrive. By locating component parts in the supply chain precisely, good information systems allow the firm to accelerate production when needed by pulling key components out of the regular supply chain and having them flown to the manufacturing plant.

Firms increasingly use electronic data interchange to coordinate the flow of materials into manufacturing, through manufacturing, and out to customers. As at Dell, the ultimate goal here should be to replace inventory with information. EDI systems require computer links between a firm, its suppliers, and its shippers. Sometimes customers also are integrated into the system as at Dell. These electronic links are then used to place orders with suppliers, to register parts leaving a supplier, to track them as they travel toward a manufacturing plant, and to register their arrival. Suppliers typically use an EDI link to send invoices to the purchasing firm. One consequence of an EDI system is that suppliers, shippers, and the purchasing firm can communicate with each other with no time delay, which increases the flexibility and responsiveness of the whole supply system. A second consequence is that much of the paperwork between suppliers, shippers, and the purchasing firm is eliminated. Good EDI systems can help a firm decentralize materials management decisions to the plant level by giving corporate-level managers the information they need for coordinating and controlling decentralized materials management groups.

Before the emergence of the Internet as a major communication medium, firms and their suppliers normally had to purchase expensive proprietary software solutions to implement EDI systems. The ubiquity of the Internet and the availability of Web-based applications have made most of these proprietary solutions obsolete. Less-expensive Web-based systems that are much easier to install and manage now dominate the market for supply chain management software. These Web-based

ANOTHER PERSPECTIVE

Japanese supply chain management
Many Japanese manufacturers are vertically integrated to the point where they own their own shipping fleets. As the volume of their exports increased, Japanese auto manufacturers, for example, decided to buy their own ships. What are the benefits of such a move? What costs might it have?

systems are rapidly transforming the management of globally dispersed supply chains, allowing even small firms to achieve a much better balance between supply and demand, thereby reducing the inventory in their systems and reaping the associated economic benefits. With increasing numbers of firms adopting these systems, those that don't may find themselves at a significant competitive disadvantage.

KEY TERMS

flexible machine cell, p. 492

flexible manufacturing technology, p. 492

ISO 9000, p. 489

logistics, p. 487

mass customization, p. 492

materials management, p. 487

sourcing decisions, p. 498

total quality management, p. 488

universal needs, p. 494

SUMMARY

This chapter explained how efficient manufacturing and materials management functions can improve an international business's competitive position by lowering the costs of value creation and by performing value creation activities in such ways that customer service is enhanced and value added is maximized. We looked closely at three issues central to international manufacturing and materials management: where to manufacture, what to make and what to buy, and how to coordinate a globally dispersed manufacturing and supply system. This chapter made the following points:

1. The choice of an optimal manufacturing location must consider country factors, technological factors, and product factors.
2. Country factors include the influence of factor costs, political economy, and national culture on manufacturing costs, along with the presence of location externalities.
3. Technological factors include the fixed costs of setting up manufacturing facilities, the minimum efficient scale of production, and the availability of flexible manufacturing technologies that allow for mass customization.
4. Product factors include the value-to-weight ratio of the product and whether the product serves universal needs.
5. Location strategies either concentrate or decentralize manufacturing. The choice should be made in light of country, technological, and product factors. All location decisions involve trade-offs.
6. Foreign factories can improve their capabilities over time, and this can be of immense strategic benefit to the firm. Managers need to view foreign factories as potential centers of excellence and to encourage and foster attempts by local managers to upgrade factory capabilities.
7. An essential issue in many international businesses is determining which component parts should be manufactured in-house and which should be outsourced to independent suppliers.
8. Making components in-house facilitates investments in specialized assets and helps the firm protect its proprietary technology. It may improve scheduling between adjacent stages in the value chain, also. In-house production also makes sense if the firm is an efficient, low-cost producer of a technology.
9. Buying components from independent suppliers facilitates strategic flexibility and helps the firm avoid the organizational problems associated with extensive vertical integration. Outsourcing might also be employed as part of an "offset" policy, which is designed to win more orders for the firm from a country by pushing some subcontracting work to that country.
10. Several firms have tried to attain the benefits of vertical integration and avoid its associated organizational problems by entering long-term strategic alliances with essential suppliers.
11. Although alliances with suppliers can give a firm the benefits of vertical integration without dispensing entirely with the benefits of a market relationship, alliances have drawbacks. The firm that enters a strategic alliance may find its strategic flexibility limited by commitments to alliance partners.

12. Materials management encompasses all the activities that move materials to a manufacturing facility, through the manufacturing process, and out through a distribution system to the end user. The materials management function is complicated in an international business by distance, time, exchange rates, custom barriers, and other things.
13. Just-in-time systems generate major cost savings from reducing warehousing and inventory holding costs and from reducing the need to write off excess inventory. In addition, JIT systems help the firm spot defective parts and remove them from the manufacturing process quickly, thereby improving product quality.
14. Information technology, particularly Internet-based electronic data interchange, plays a major role in materials management. EDI facilitates the tracking of inputs, allows the firm to optimize its production schedule, allows the firm and its suppliers to communicate in real time, and eliminates the flow of paperwork between a firm and its suppliers.

CRITICAL THINKING AND DISCUSSION QUESTIONS

1. An electronics firm is considering how best to supply the world market for microprocessors used in consumer and industrial electronic products. A manufacturing plant costs about $500 million to construct and requires a highly skilled workforce. The total value of the world market for this product over the next ten years is estimated to be between $10 billion and $15 billion. The tariffs prevailing in this industry are currently low. Should the firm adopt a concentrated or decentralized manufacturing strategy? What kind of location(s) should the firm favour for its plant(s)?
2. A chemical firm is considering how best to supply the world market for sulfuric acid. A manufacturing plant costs approximately $20 million to construct and requires a moderately skilled workforce. The total value of the world market for this product over the next ten years is estimated to be between $20 billion and $30 billion. The tariffs prevailing in this industry are moderate. Should the firm favour concentrated manufacturing or decentralized manufacturing? What kind of location(s) should the firm seek for its plant(s)?
3. A firm must decide whether to make a component part in-house or to contract it out to an independent supplier. Manufacturing the part requires a nonrecoverable investment in specialized assets. The most efficient suppliers are located in countries with currencies that many foreign exchange analysts expect to appreciate substantially over the next decade. What are the pros and cons of *(a)* manufacturing the component in-house and *(b)* outsourcing manufacturing to an independent supplier? Which option would you recommend? Why?
4. Explain how an efficient materials management function can help an international business compete more effectively in the global marketplace.

RESEARCH TASK | globalEDGE™ globaledge.msu.edu

Use the globalEDGE™ site to complete the following exercises:

1. The U.S. Department of Labor's Bureau of International Labor Affairs publishes a Chartbook of International Labor Comparisons. Locate the latest edition of this report and identify the hourly compensation costs for manufacturing workers in the United States, Japan, Korea, Taiwan, Germany, and the United Kingdom.
2. *Industry Week* magazine ranks the world's largest manufacturing companies by sales revenue. Identify the largest Chinese manufacturing companies as provided in the most recent ranking, paying special attention to the industries in which these companies operate.

Visit the *Global Business Today* Online Learning Centre at **www.mcgrawhill.ca/college/hill** to access quizzes, interactive exercises, a Business Around the World interactive map, and other learning and study tools related to this chapter.

Online LearningCentre

CLOSING CASE

FOREIGN DIRECT INVESTMENT AT THE SOURCE OF RAW MATERIALS

The global mining industry extracts all sorts of minerals from the earth to refine into commodities that make our economies grow. It might be thought that there is little to organize in these cases—just dig out what you need and ship them to where they are needed. Nothing could be farther from the truth. Materials management starts right at the source of obtaining these raw materials. The example of Placer Dome Mines, like the "Another Perspective" about Nike earlier in this chapter, shows that there are ethical dimensions to managing resource extraction.

Placer Dome Mines, one of Canada's leading gold companies, operates in Papua New Guinea, at the Porgera mining site. Placer Dome has been receiving criticism for the manner in which it runs its Porgera gold mine facility, especially in the areas of ethics and the environment, along with the hurdles it must overcome to adapt culturally to local sensitivities.

"Placer Dome manages the Porgera mine on behalf of the Porgera Joint Venture (PJV), a joint venture of Placer Dome, two Australian mining companies, and the local Papua New Guinea government and landowners." Joint ventures are frequently used by companies to pool resources and to enter foreign markets. The question frequently arises as to whose laws one adheres when dealing with financial and other matters.

"The workforce at the mine comprises about 2000 employees, of which over 88 percent are Papua New Guinea nationals. Part of the PJV's agreement with the Papua New Guinea government calls for a multifaceted effort to help locals living near the mine.

One initiative is a tax credit scheme developed by the PJV and the government that allows the PJV and other resource companies to fund infrastructure projects from a proportion of their tax bills. These projects include roads, classrooms, hospitals and health centres, and miscellaneous facilities such as fishing cooperatives and libraries."

However, as part of its agreement with the Papua New Guinea government, the company has been dumping mine tailings, which can contain heavy metals such as lead and mercury, into a nearby river since 1992. "From Placer Dome's perspective, it has met, and continues to meet, its obligations regarding the sustainability of the Porgera mining operations." Others disagree. "Placer Dome knows that they would never have been allowed to do this in Canada, yet Placer Dome refuses to renounce the practice," says Dr. Catherine Coumans of MiningWatch Canada.

"Placer Dome says the Porgera Gold Mine is an important contributor to the Papua New Guinea national economy and living standards of citizens throughout the country. In 1998 the Porgera mine contributed 12.8 percent of Papua New Guinea's total exports." The financial impact that this mine operation has had on Papua New Guinea's economy is clear, but what about the operation's other impacts?

"To address initial perceptions about Placer Dome's overall ways of doing business in Papua New Guinea, Placer Dome has endeavoured to become more transparent." It issued sustainability reports for the Porgera mine, which gives the company's view on how it has addressed social and environmental concerns. After creating the multi-stakeholder group, Porgera Environmental Advisory Kommiti (PEAK), to address recommendations of an independent report, Placer Dome started a Web site to disclose PEAK's activities.

"One of the major issues of contention regarding the Porgera mine is that Placer Dome believes PEAK has addressed the recommendations of the Commonwealth Scientific and Industrial Research Organization (CSIRO), while critics such as MiningWatch Canada believe that PEAK has done virtually nothing to address the recommendations. Placer Dome's commitment to transparency might be perceived as being more sincere if it posted the complete CSIRO report on the PEAK Web site."

Source: Extracted from M. Thomsen, "Placer Dome's Efforts at Sustainability: Sincere or Greenwash?" SocialFunds.com, June 19, 2001, at www.socialfunds.com/news/article.cgi/article 603.html; Mining Technology, "Porgera Mine," www.mining-technology.com/projects/porgera/; M. Thomsen, "Placer Dome Mine Strikes Resentment in Papua New Guinea," SocialFunds.com, June 18, 2001, www.socialfunds.com/news/article.cgi/article602.html; Placer Dome at www.placerdome.com/operations/porgera/porgera.html; PEAK at www.peak-pjv.com/aboutpe/peakindex.htm.

CASE DISCUSSION QUESTIONS

1. Can you cite other Canadian mining companies that may not make the grade on foreign direct investment initiatives in other countries? Visit www.socialinvestment.ca.
2. If Canadian mining companies are adhering to the laws of business practice in other countries, should this be a sufficient control mechanism to ensure overall safe mining procedures in a host country? Explain your reply.
3. Placer Dome has generally preferred FDI to exports as a mode of entry into foreign markets. Why do you think this is the case?
4. What theory (or theories) best explains Placer Dome's decision to invest in Papua New Guinea: (a) the market imperfections approach, (b) the strategic behaviour approach, or (c) the location specific advantages approach?

PART FIVE

5

COMPETING IN A GLOBAL MARKETPLACE

Molex

Molex is a 65-year-old manufacturer of electronic components based in Chicago. The company established an international division to coordinate exporting in 1967, opened its first overseas plant in Japan in 1970, and a second in Ireland in 1971. From that base, Molex has evolved into a global business that generates about 65 percent of its $2.5 billion in annual revenues outside the United States. The company operates some 50 manufacturing plants in 21 countries and employs some 16 000 people worldwide, only one-third of which are located in the United States. Molex's competitive advantage is based on a strategy that emphasizes a combination of low costs and excellent customer service. Manufacturing sites are located in countries where cost conditions are favourable and major customers are close. Since the 1970s, a key goal of Molex has been to build a truly global company that is at home wherever in the world it operates, and which proactively shares valuable knowledge across operations in different countries. The human resources function of Molex has always played a central role in meeting this goal.

As Molex grew rapidly overseas, the human resource management (HRM) function made sure that every new unit did the same basic things whatever the country. Each new entity had to have an employee manual with policies and practices in writing, employee orientation programs, salary administration with a consistent grading system, written job descriptions, written promotion and grievance procedures, standard performance appraisal systems that were written down, and so on. Beyond these things, however, Molex views HRM as the most localized of functions. Different legal systems, particularly with regard to employment law, different compensation norms, different cultural attitudes to work, different norms regarding vacation, and so on, all imply that policies and programs must be customized to the conditions prevailing in a country. To make sure this occurs, Molex's policy is to hire experienced HRM professionals from other companies in the same country in which it has operations. The idea

S. Meltzer/PhotoLink/Getty Images.

CHAPTER

16

Global Human Resource Management

OPENING CASE

is to hire people who know the language, have credibility, know the law, and know how to recruit in that country.

Molex's strategy for building a global company starts with its staffing policy for managers and engineers. The company frequently hires foreign nationals who are living in the United States, have just completed MBAs, and are willing to relocate if required. These individuals will typically work in the United States for a while, becoming familiar with the company's culture. Some of them will then be sent back to their home country to work there. Molex also carefully screens its American applicants, favouring those who are fluent in at least one other language. Molex is unusual for an American company in having a language requirement as an important part of the interview process. However, with more than 15 languages spoken at its headquarters by native speakers, Molex is committed to the value of a multilingual competency. There is also significant hiring of managers and engineers at the local level. Here, too, a willingness to relocate internationally and foreign language competency are important, although this time English is the preferred foreign language. In a sign of how multinational Molex's management has become, it is not unusual to see foreign nationals holding senior positions at company headquarters. In addition to Americans, individuals of Greek, German, Austrian, Japanese, and British origin have all sat on the company's executive committee, its top decision-making body.

To help build a global company, Molex moves people around the world to give them experience in other countries and to help them learn from each other. It has five categories of expatriates: (1) regular expatriates who live in a country other than their home country for three-to-five-year assignments (there are approximately 50 of these at any one time), (2) "inpats" who come to the company's U.S. headquarters from other countries, (3) third-country nationals who move from one Molex entity to another (for example, Singapore to Taiwan), (4) short-term transfers who go to another Molex entity for six to nine months to work on a specific project, and (5) medium terms who go to another entity for 12 to 24 months, again to work on a specific project.

Having a high level of intracompany movement is costly. For an employee making $75,000 in base salary, the total cost of an expatriate assignment can run as high as $250,000 when additional employee benefits are included, such as the provision of schooling and housing, adjustments for higher costs of living, adjustments for higher tax rates, and so on. Molex also insists on treating all expatriates the same, whatever their country of origin, so a Singapore expatriate living in Taiwan is likely to be living in the same apartment building and sending his child to the same school as an American expatriate in Taiwan. This boosts the overall costs, but Molex believes that its extensive use of expatriates pays back dividends. It allows individuals to understand the challenges of doing business in different countries, it facilitates the sharing of useful knowledge across different business entities, and it helps to lay the foundation for a common company culture that is global in its outlook.

Molex also goes to great lengths to make sure that expatriates know why they are being sent to a foreign country, both in terms of their own career development and Molex's corporate goals. To make sure that expatriates don't become disconnected from their home office, the HRM department touches base with them on a regular basis through telephone, email, and direct visits. The company also encourages expatriates to make home office visits so that they do not become totally disconnected from their base and feel like a stranger when they return. Upon return, they are debriefed and their knowledge gained abroad is put to use by, for example, placing the expatriates on special task forces.

A final component of Molex's strategy for building a cadre of globally minded managers is the company's in-house management development programs. These are open to a wide range of managers who have worked at Molex for three years or more. Molex uses these programs not just to educate its managers in finance, operations, strategy, and the like, but also to bring together managers from different countries to build a network of individuals who know each other and can work together in a cooperative fashion to solve business problems that transcend borders.

Sources: J. Laabs, "Molex Makes Global HR Look Easy," *Workforce,* March 1999, pp. 42–46; C. M. Solomon; "Foreign Relations," *Workforce,* November 2000, pp. 50–56; C. M. Solomon, "Navigating Your Search for Global Talent," *Personnel Journal,* May 1995, pp. 94–100; and A. C. Poe, "Welcome Back," *HR Magazine,* March 2000, pp. 94–105.

LEARNING OBJECTIVES

1. Discuss the pros and cons of different approaches to staffing policy in international businesses.
2. Understand why managers may fail to thrive in foreign postings.
3. Understand what can be done to increase an executive's chance of succeeding in a foreign posting.
4. Appreciate the role that training, management development, and compensation practices can play in managing human resources within an international business.

INTRODUCTION

HUMAN RESOURCE MANAGEMENT
Activities an organization conducts to use its human resources effectively.

Continuing our survey of specific functions within an international business, this chapter examines international human resource management (HRM). **Human resource management** refers to the activities an organization carries out to use its human resources effectively.[1] These activities include determining the firm's human resource strategy, staffing, performance evaluation, management development, compensation, and labor relations. None of these activities is performed in a vacuum; all are related to the strategy of the firm because, as we will see, HRM has an important strategic component.[2] Through its influence on the character, development, quality, and productivity of the firm's human resources, the HRM function can help the firm achieve its primary strategic goals of reducing the costs of value creation and adding value by better serving customer needs.

The strategic role of HRM is complex enough in a purely domestic firm, but it is more complex in an international business, where staffing, management development, performance evaluation, and compensation activities are complicated by profound differences between countries in labour markets, culture, legal systems, economic systems, and the like (see Chapters 2 and 3). For example,

- Compensation practices may vary from country to country depending on prevailing management customs.
- Labour laws may prohibit union organization in one country and mandate it in another.
- Equal employment legislation may be strongly pursued in one country and not in another.

If it is to build a cadre of managers capable of managing a multinational enterprise, the HRM function must deal with a host of issues. It must decide how to staff key management posts in the company, how to develop managers so that they are familiar with the nuances of doing business in different countries, and how to compensate people in different nations. HRM must also deal with a host of issues related to expatriate managers. (An **expatriate manager** is a citizen of one country who is working abroad in one of the firm's subsidiaries.) It must decide whom to send on expatriate postings, be clear about why they are doing it, compensate expatriates appropriately, and make sure that they are adequately debriefed and reoriented once they return home.

EXPATRIATE MANAGER A national of one country appointed to a management position in another country.

The opening case detailed how Molex deals with some of these issues. Molex is quite explicit about using the HRM function to help attain the strategic goal of building a global company that has a low cost structure, provides excellent customer service, and is comfortable doing business in many different countries and cultures. Molex uses its staffing policy to recruit managers who are fluent in more than one language and willing to relocate to other countries. It makes liberal use of expatriates. Foreign postings are seen as a way of developing managers and a means for transferring valuable know-how between country operations. The benefits package for expatriates is designed to make sure there is no bonus for being an American, which sends the message that all employees are viewed equally, regardless of national origin. Finally, Molex proactively uses its own in-house management development programs to help establish a network of managers from different countries who know each other, can share valuable information with each other, and can work together in a cooperative fashion to solve business problems that transcend borders.

In this chapter, we will look closely at the role of HRM in an international business. We begin by briefly discussing the strategic role of HRM. Then we turn our attention to four major tasks of the HRM function: staffing policy, management training and development, performance appraisal, and compensation policy. We will point out the strategic implications of each of these tasks. The chapter closes with a look at international labour relations and the relationship between the firm's management of labour relations and its overall strategy.

THE STRATEGIC ROLE OF INTERNATIONAL HRM

In Chapter 11, we examined four strategies pursued by international businesses–the multidomestic, the international, the global, and the transnational. Multidomestic firms try to create value by emphasizing local responsiveness; international firms, by transferring core competencies overseas; global firms, by realizing experience curve and location economies; and transnational firms, by doing all these things simultaneously.

In this chapter, we will see that success also requires HRM policies to be congruent with the firm's strategy. For example, a transnational strategy imposes very different requirements for staffing, management development, and compensation practices than a multidomestic strategy does.

In many ways, Molex, which was profiled in the opening case, is pursuing a transnational strategy. Molex tries to drive down its cost structure by locating manufacturing plants in countries where cost conditions are favourable, but at the same time the firm devotes great attention to sharing valuable know-how among operations in different countries and uses management transfers (expatriates) and management development programs to facilitate that. Pursuing a transnational strategy requires a strong corporate culture and an informal management network for transmitting information within the organization. Through its employee selection, management development, performance appraisal, and compensation policies, the HRM function can help develop these things. For example, Molex's liberal use of expatriates, by creating a cadre of international managers with experience in various nations, should help to establish an informal management network. In addition, as at Molex, management development programs can build a corporate culture that supports strategic goals. In short, HRM has a critical role to play in implementing strategy. In each section that follows, we will review the strategic role of HRM in some detail.

STAFFING POLICY

STAFFING POLICY Strategy concerned with selecting employees for particular jobs.

CORPORATE CULTURE Organization's norms and value systems.

Staffing policy is concerned with the selection of employees for particular jobs. At one level, this involves selecting individuals who have the skills required to do particular jobs. At another level, staffing policy can be a tool for developing and promoting corporate culture.[3] By **corporate culture,** we mean the organization's norms and value systems. A strong corporate culture can help a firm pursue its strategy. General Electric, for example, is not just concerned with hiring people who have the skills required for performing particular jobs; it wants to hire individuals whose behavioral styles, beliefs, and value systems are consistent with those of GE. This is true whether an American is being hired, an Italian, a German, or an Australian and whether the hiring is for a U.S. operation or a foreign operation. The belief is that if employees are predisposed toward the organization's norms and value systems by their personality type, the firm will be able to attain higher performance.

TYPES OF STAFFING POLICY

Research has identified three types of staffing policies in international businesses: the ethnocentric approach, the polycentric approach, and the geocentric approach.[4] We will review each policy and link it to the strategy pursued by the firm. The most attractive staffing policy is probably the geocentric approach, although there are several impediments to adopting it.

The Ethnocentric Approach

ETHNOCENTRIC STAFFING POLICY A staffing approach within the MNE in which all key management positions are filled by parent-country nationals.

An **ethnocentric staffing policy** is one in which all key management positions are filled by parent-country nationals. This practice was very widespread at one time. Firms such as Procter & Gamble, Philips NV, and Matsushita originally followed it. In the Dutch firm Philips, for example, all important positions in most foreign subsidiaries were at one time held by Dutch nationals who were referred to by their non-Dutch colleagues as the Dutch Mafia. In many Japanese and South Korean firms today, such as Toyota, Matsushita, and Samsung, key positions in international operations are still often held by home-country nationals. According to the Japanese Overseas Enterprise Association, in 1996 only 29 percent of foreign subsidiaries of Japanese companies had presidents who were not Japanese. In contrast, 66 percent of the Japanese subsidiaries of foreign companies had Japanese presidents.[5]

Firms pursue an ethnocentric staffing policy for three reasons. First, the firm may believe the host country lacks qualified individuals to fill senior management positions. This argument is heard most often when the firm has operations in less developed countries. Second, the firm may see an ethnocentric staffing policy as the best way to maintain a unified corporate culture. Many Japanese firms, for example, prefer their foreign operations to be headed by expatriate Japanese managers because these managers will have been socialized into the firm's culture while employed in Japan.[6]

Coca-Cola tries to staff its local operations with local personnel, such as this Russian woman working in a local bottling plant. But expatriates are needed in the system in order to fill a need for specific skills that might not exist at a particular location, and to improve the employee's own skill base. STONE/Steven Weinberg.

Third, if the firm is trying to create value by transferring core competencies to a foreign operation, as firms pursuing an international strategy are, it may believe that the best way to do this is to transfer parent-country nationals who have knowledge of that competency to the foreign operation. Imagine what might occur if a firm tried to transfer a core competency in marketing to a foreign subsidiary without supporting the transfer with a corresponding transfer of home-country marketing management personnel.

Despite this rationale for pursuing an ethnocentric staffing policy, the policy is now on the wane in most international businesses for two reasons. First, an ethnocentric staffing policy limits advancement opportunities for host-country nationals. This can lead to resentment, lower productivity, and increased turnover among that group.

Second, an ethnocentric policy can lead to "cultural myopia," the firm's failure to understand host-country cultural differences that require different approaches to marketing and management. The adaptation of expatriate managers can take a long time, during which they may make major mistakes. For example, expatriate managers may fail to appreciate how product attributes, distribution strategy, communications strategy, and pricing strategy should be adapted to host-country conditions. The result may be costly blunders. They may also make decisions that are ethically suspect simply because they do not understand the culture in which they are managing.[7] In one highly publicized case in the United States, Mitsubishi Motors was sued by the federal Equal Employment Opportunity Commission for tolerating extensive and systematic sexual harassment in a plant in Illinois. The plant's top management, all Japanese expatriates, denied the charges. The Japanese managers may have failed to realize that behaviour that would be viewed as acceptable in Japan was not acceptable in the United States.[8]

Although one might cite corporate good will as a motivating force for ethical and equitable workplace hiring practices, there are also laws that in effect mandate good corporate citizenship. In Canada, for example, the Employment Equity Act was passed in 1995 and mandates equality in the workplace. Section 2 outlines the purpose of the Act:

> 2. The purpose of this Act is to achieve equality in the workplace so that no person shall be denied employment opportunities or benefits for reasons unrelated to ability and, in the fulfillment of that goal, to correct the conditions of disadvantage in employment experienced by women, aboriginal peoples, persons with disabilities and members of visible minorities by giving effect to the principle that employment equity means more than treating persons in the same way but also requires special measures and the accommodation of differences.[9]

Companies have to be compliant with these laws within the Dominion of Canada or they can be subject to a graded scale of monetary fines, depending on the size of the company.

The Polycentric Approach

POLYCENTRIC STAFFING POLICY
A staffing policy in an MNE in which host-country nationals are recruited to manage subsidiaries in their own country, while parent-country nationals occupy key positions at corporate headquarters.

A **polycentric staffing policy** requires host-country nationals to be recruited to manage subsidiaries, while parent-country nationals occupy key positions at corporate headquarters. In many respects, a polycentric approach is a response to the shortcomings of an ethnocentric approach. One advantage of adopting a polycentric approach is that the firm is less likely to suffer from cultural myopia. Host-country managers are unlikely to make the mistakes arising from cultural misunderstandings to which expatriate managers are vulnerable. A second advantage is that a polycentric approach may be less expensive to implement, reducing the costs of value creation. Expatriate managers can be very expensive to maintain.

A polycentric approach also has its drawbacks. Host-country nationals have limited opportunities to gain experience outside their own country and thus cannot progress beyond senior positions in their own subsidiary. As in the case of an ethnocentric policy, this may cause resentment. Perhaps the major drawback with a polycentric approach, however, is the gap that can form between host-country managers and parent-country managers. Language barriers, national loyalties, and a range of cultural differences may isolate the corporate headquarters staff from the various foreign subsidiaries. The lack of management transfers from home to host countries, and vice versa, can exacerbate this isolation and lead to a lack of integration between corporate headquarters and foreign subsidiaries.

ANOTHER PERSPECTIVE

Women in international assignments
We may think that women would be unsuitable expatriates in foreign cultures in which women's roles are somewhat limited in the public business sphere, such as Japan, Korea, and Latin America, yet research data tell us that women expatriates sent to these countries have met with substantial success. The tough part is actually getting the assignment; once in place, women are successful. This is in part because women expatriates in these cultures are seen first as expats. They fall outside the local role for women. Women also have salience in their new environment—they are noticed—and this can be a distinct business advantage. Locals often take pride in developing business relationships with women expatriates because by doing so they can suggest that the stereotype many Americans and Europeans have of women's roles in their culture is superficial and incomplete.

The Geocentric Approach

GEOCENTRIC STAFFING POLICY
A staffing approach where the best people are sought for key jobs throughout an MNE, regardless of nationality.

A **geocentric staffing policy** seeks the best people for key jobs throughout the organization, regardless of nationality. Molex is a good example of a company that has adopted a geocentric staffing policy (see the opening case). There are a number of advantages to this policy. First, it enables the firm to make the best use of its human resources. Second, and perhaps more important, a geocentric policy enables the firm to build a cadre of international executives who feel at home working in a number of cultures. Creation of such a cadre may be a critical first step toward building a strong unifying corporate culture and an informal management network, both of which are required for global and transnational strategies.[10] Firms pursuing a geocentric staffing policy may be better able to create value from the pursuit of experience curve and location economies and from the multidirectional transfer of core competencies than firms pursuing other staffing policies. In addition, the multinational composition of the management team that results from geocentric staffing tends to reduce cultural myopia and to enhance local responsiveness. Thus, other things being equal, a geocentric staffing policy seems the most attractive.

A number of problems limit the firm's ability to pursue a geocentric policy. Many countries want foreign subsidiaries to employ their citizens. To achieve this goal, they use immigration laws to require the employment of host-country nationals if they are available in adequate numbers and have the necessary skills. Most countries (including the United States) require firms to provide extensive documentation if they wish to hire a foreign national instead of a local national. This documentation can be time consuming, expensive, and at times futile. A geocentric staffing policy also can be very expensive to implement. Increased training and relocation costs are involved in transferring managers from country to country. The company may also need a compensation structure with a standardized international base pay level higher than national levels in many countries. In addition, the higher pay enjoyed by managers placed on an international "fast track" may be a source of resentment within a firm.

Summary

The advantages and disadvantages of the three approaches to staffing policy are summarized in Table 16.1. Broadly speaking, an ethnocentric approach is compatible with an international strategy, a polycentric approach is compatible with a multidomestic strategy, and a geocentric approach is compatible with both global and transnational strategies. (See Chapter 11 for details of the strategies.)

While the staffing policies described here are well known and widely used among both practitioners and scholars of international businesses, recently some critics have claimed that the typology is too simplistic and that it obscures the internal differentiation of management practices within international businesses. The critics claim that within some international businesses, staffing policies vary significantly from national subsidiary to national subsidiary; while some are managed on an ethnocentric basis, others are managed in a polycentric or geocentric manner.[11] Other critics note that the staffing policy adopted by a firm is primarily driven by its geographic scope, as opposed to its strategic orientation. Firms that have a very broad geographic scope are the most likely to have a geocentric mind-set.[12] Thus, Molex, which is involved in about 50 countries, is by this argument more likely to have a geocentric mind-set than a firm that is involved in only three countries.

Colgate-Palmolive's Lois D. Juliber joined the company in 1988 as general manager and later became president of the company's $800-million Far East/Canada Division. Under her leadership, Colgate's businesses in Asia and the Indian subcontinent grew rapidly, and the division became one of the company's strongest and most profitable. After her stint in Asia, she was promoted to chief operating officer of Colgate-Palmolive. Juliber is widely regarded as the successor to the current CEO, Reuben Mark. Spencer Grant/PhotoEdit.

EXPATRIATE MANAGERS

Two of the three staffing policies we have discussed–the ethnocentric and the geocentric–rely on extensive use of expatriate managers. As defined earlier, expatriates are citizens of one country who are working in another country. Sometimes the term *inpatriates* is used to identify a subset of expatriates who are citizens of a foreign country working in the home country of their multinational employer.[13] Thus, a citizen of Japan who moves to the United States to work at Molex would be classified as an inpatriate. With an ethnocentric policy, the expatriates are all home-country nationals who are transferred abroad. With a geocentric approach, the expatriates need not be home-country nationals; the firm does not base transfer decisions on nationality.

TABLE 16.1
Comparison of Staffing Approaches

STAFFING APPROACH	STRATEGIC APPROPRIATENESS	ADVANTAGES	DISADVANTAGES
Ethnocentric	International	Overcomes lack of qualified managers in host nation Unified culture Helps transfer core competencies	Produces resentment in host country Can lead to cultural myopia
Polycentric	Multidomestic	Alleviates cultural myopia Inexpensive to implement	Limits career mobility Isolates headquarters from foreign subsidiaries
Geocentric	Global and transnational	Uses human resources efficiently Helps build strong culture and informal management network	National immigration policies may limit implementation Expensive

EXPATRIATE FAILURE The premature return of an expatriate manager to the home country.

A prominent issue in the international staffing literature is **expatriate failure**–the premature return of an expatriate manager to his or her home country.[14] Here we briefly review the evidence on expatriate failure before discussing a number of ways to minimize the expatriate failure rate.

Expatriate Failure Rates

Expatriate failure represents a failure of the firm's selection policies to identify individuals who will not thrive abroad. The costs of expatriate failure are high. One estimate is that the average cost per failure to the parent firm can be as high as three times the expatriate's annual domestic salary plus the cost of relocation (which is affected by currency exchange rates and location of assignment).[15] Research suggests that between 16 and 40 percent of all American employees sent abroad to developed nations return from their assignments early, and almost 70 percent of employees sent to developing nations return home early.[16] Although detailed data are not available for other nationalities, one suspects that high expatriate failure is a universal problem. Estimates of the costs of each failure run between $250,000 and $1 million.[17] In addition, approximately 30 to 50 percent of American expatriates, whose average annual compensation package runs to $250,000, stay at their international assignments but are considered ineffective or marginally effective by their firms.[18] In a seminal study, R. L. Tung surveyed a number of U.S., European, and Japanese multinationals.[19] Her results suggested that 76 percent of U.S. multinationals experienced expatriate failure rates of 10 percent or more, and 7 percent experienced a failure rate of more than 20 percent. Tung's work also suggests that U.S.-based multinationals experience a much higher expatriate failure rate than either European or Japanese multinationals.

Tung asked her sample of multinational managers to indicate reasons for expatriate failure. For U.S. multinationals, the reasons, in order of importance, were

1. Inability of spouse to adjust.
2. Manager's inability to adjust.
3. Other family problems.
4. Manager's personal or emotional maturity.
5. Inability to cope with larger overseas responsibilities.

Managers of European firms gave only one reason consistently to explain expatriate failure: the inability of the manager's spouse to adjust to a new environment. For the Japanese firms, the reasons for failure were

1. Inability to cope with larger overseas responsibilities.
2. Difficulties with new environment.
3. Personal or emotional problems.
4. Lack of technical competence.
5. Inability of spouse to adjust.

The most striking difference between these lists is that "inability of spouse to adjust" was the top reason for expatriate failure among U.S. and European multinationals but only the number-five reason among Japanese multinationals. Tung comments that this difference is not surprising, given the role and status to which Japanese society traditionally relegates the wife and the fact that most of the Japanese expatriate managers in the study were men.

Since Tung's study, a number of other studies have consistently confirmed that the inability of a spouse to adjust, the inability of the manager to adjust, or other family problems remain major reasons for continuing high levels of expatriate failure. One study by International Orientation Resources, an HRM consulting firm, found that 60 percent of expatriate failures occur due to these three reasons.[20] Another study found that the most common reason for assignment failure is lack of partner (spouse) satisfaction, which was listed by 27 percent of respondents.[21] The inability of expatriate managers to adjust to foreign postings seems to be caused by a lack of cultural skills on the part of the manager being transferred. According to one HRM management consulting firm, this is because the expatriate selection process at many firms is fundamentally flawed. "Expatriate assignments rarely fail because the person cannot accommodate to the technical demands of the job. Typically, the expatriate selections are made by line managers based on technical competence. They fail because of family and personal issues and lack of cultural skills that haven't been part of the selection process."[22]

The failure of spouses to adjust to a foreign posting seems to be related to a number of factors. Often spouses find themselves in a foreign country without the familiar network of family and friends. Language differences make it difficult for them to make new friends. While this may not be a problem for the manager, who can make friends at work, it can be difficult for the spouse who might feel trapped at home. The problem is often exacerbated by immigration regulations prohibiting the spouse from taking employment. With the recent rise of two-career families in many developed nations, this has become a much more important issue. One recent survey found that 69 percent of expatriates are married, with spouses accompanying them 77 percent of the time. Of those spouses, 49 percent were employed before an assignment and only 11 percent were employed during an assignment.[23] Recent research suggests that a main reason managers now turn down international assignments is concern over the impact such an assignment might have on their spouse's career.[24]

Expatriate Selection

One way to reduce expatriate failure rates is by improving selection procedures to screen out inappropriate candidates. In a review of the research on this issue, Mendenhall and Oddou state that a major problem in many firms is that HRM managers tend to equate domestic performance with overseas performance potential.[25] Domestic performance and overseas performance potential are not the same thing. An executive who performs well in a domestic setting may not be able to adapt to managing in a different cultural setting. From their review of the research, Mendenhall and Oddou identified four dimensions that seem to predict success in a foreign posting: self-orientation, others-orientation, perceptual ability, and cultural toughness.

1. *Self-orientation.* The attributes of this dimension strengthen the expatriate's self-esteem, self-confidence, and mental well-being. Expatriates with high self-esteem, self-confidence, and mental well-being were more likely to succeed in foreign postings. Mendenhall and Oddou concluded that such individuals were able to adapt their interests in food, sport, and music; had interests outside of work that could be pursued (e.g., hobbies); and were technically competent.
2. *Others-orientation.* The attributes of this dimension enhance the expatriate's ability to interact effectively with host-country nationals. The more effectively the expatriate interacts with host-country nationals, the more likely he or she is to succeed. Two factors seem to be particularly important here: relationship development and willingness to communicate. Relationship development refers to the ability to develop long-lasting friendships with host-country nationals. Willingness to communicate refers to the expatriate's willingness to

use the host-country language. Although language fluency helps, an expatriate need not be fluent to show willingness to communicate. Making the effort to use the language is what is important. Such gestures tend to be rewarded with greater cooperation by host-country nationals.

3. *Perceptual ability.* This is the ability to understand why people of other countries behave the way they do; that is, the ability to empathize. This dimension seems critical for managing host-country nationals. Expatriate managers who lack this ability tend to treat foreign nationals as if they were home-country nationals. As a result, they may experience significant management problems and considerable frustration. As one expatriate executive from Hewlett-Packard observed, "It took me six months to accept the fact that my staff meetings would start 30 minutes late, and that it would bother no one but me." According to Mendenhall and Oddou, well-adjusted expatriates tend to be nonjudgmental and nonevaluative in interpreting the behaviour of host-country nationals and willing to be flexible in their management style, adjusting it as cultural conditions warrant.
4. *Cultural toughness.* This dimension refers to the fact that how well an expatriate adjusts to a particular posting tends to be related to the country of assignment. Some countries are much tougher postings than others because their cultures are more unfamiliar and uncomfortable. For example, many Americans regard Great Britain as a relatively easy foreign posting, and for good reason–the two cultures have much in common. But many Americans find postings in non-Western cultures, such as India, Southeast Asia, and the Middle East, to be much tougher.[26] The reasons are many, including poor health care and housing standards, inhospitable climate, lack of Western entertainment, and language difficulties. Also, many cultures are extremely male dominated and may be particularly difficult postings for female Western managers.

Mendenhall and Oddou note that standard psychological tests can be used to assess the first three of these dimensions, whereas a comparison of cultures can give managers a feeling for the fourth dimension. They contend that these four dimensions, in addition to domestic performance, should be considered when selecting a manager for foreign posting. However, current practice does not conform to Mendenhall and Oddou's recommendations. Tung's research, for example, showed that only 5 percent of the firms in her sample used formal procedures and psychological tests to assess the personality traits and relational abilities of potential expatriates.[27] Research by International Orientation Resources suggests that when selecting employees for foreign assignments, only 10 percent of the 50 Fortune 500 firms they surveyed tested for important psychological traits such as cultural sensitivity, interpersonal skills, adaptability, and flexibility. Instead, 90 percent of the time employees were selected on the basis of their technical expertise, not their cross-cultural fluency.[28]

Mendenhall and Oddou do not address the problem of expatriate failure due to a spouse's inability to adjust. According to a number of other researchers, a review of the family situation should be part of the expatriate selection process.[29] A survey by Windam International, another international HRM management consulting firm, found that spouses were included in preselection interviews for foreign postings only 21 percent of the time, and that only half of them receive any cross-cultural training. The rise of dual-career families has added an additional and difficult dimension to this long-standing problem.[30] Increasingly, spouses wonder why they should have to sacrifice their own career to further that of their partner.[31]

TRAINING AND MANAGEMENT DEVELOPMENT

Selection is just the first step in matching a manager with a job. The next step is training the manager to do the specific job. For example, an intensive training program might be used to give expatriate managers the skills required for success in a foreign posting. Management development is a much broader concept. It is intended to develop the manager's skills over his or her career with the firm. Thus, as part of a management development program, a manager might be sent on several foreign postings over a number of years to build her cross-cultural sensitivity and experience. At the same time, along with other managers in the firm, she might attend management education programs at regular intervals. The thinking behind job transfers is that broad international experience will enhance the management and leadership skills of executives. Recent research suggests this may be the case.[32]

Historically, most international businesses have been more concerned with training than with management development. Plus, they tended to focus their training efforts on preparing home-country nationals for foreign postings. Recently, however, the shift toward greater global competition and the rise of transnational firms have changed this. It is increasingly common for firms to provide general management development programs in addition to training for particular posts. In many international businesses, the explicit purpose of these management development programs is strategic. Management development is seen as a tool to help the firm achieve its strategic goals.

With this distinction between training and management development in mind, we first examine the types of training managers receive for foreign postings. Then we discuss the connection between management development and strategy in the international business.

TRAINING FOR EXPATRIATE MANAGERS

Earlier in the chapter we saw that the two most common reasons for expatriate failure were the inability of a manager's spouse to adjust to a foreign environment and the manager's own inability to adjust to a foreign environment. Training can help the manager and spouse cope with both these problems. Cultural training, language training, and practical training all seem to reduce expatriate failure.[33] Despite the usefulness of these kinds of training, evidence suggests that many managers receive no training before they are sent on foreign postings. One study found that only about 30 percent of managers sent on one- to five-year expatriate assignments received training before their departure.[34]

Cultural Training

Cultural training seeks to foster an appreciation for the host country's culture. The belief is that understanding a host country's culture will help the manager empathize with the culture, which will enhance her effectiveness in dealing with host-country nationals. It has been suggested that expatriates should receive training in the host country's culture, history, politics, economy, religion, and social and business practices.[35] If possible, it is also advisable to arrange for a familiarization trip to the host country before the formal transfer, as this seems to ease culture shock. Given the problems related to spouse adaptation, it is important that the spouse, and perhaps the whole family, be included in cultural training programs.

Language Training

English is the language of world business; it is quite possible to conduct business all over the world using only English. For example, at ABB Group, a Swiss electrical equipment giant, the company's top 13 managers hold frequent meetings in different countries. Because they share no common first language, they speak only English, a foreign tongue to all but one.[36] Despite the prevalence of English, however, an exclusive reliance on English diminishes an expatriate manager's ability to interact with host-country nationals. As noted earlier, a willingness to communicate in the language of the host country, even if the expatriate is far from fluent, can help build rapport with local employees and improve the manager's effectiveness. Despite this, J. C. Baker's study of 74 executives of U.S. multinationals found that only 23 believed knowledge of foreign languages was necessary for conducting business abroad.[37] Those firms that did offer foreign language training for expatriates believed it improved their employees' effectiveness and enabled them to relate more easily to a foreign culture, which fostered a better image of the firm in the host country.

Practical Training

Practical training is aimed at helping the expatriate manager and family ease themselves into day-to-day life in the host country. The sooner a routine is established, the better are the prospects that the expatriate and her family will adapt successfully. One critical need is for a support network of friends for the expatriate. Where an expatriate community exists, firms often devote considerable effort to ensuring the new expatriate family is quickly integrated into that group. The expatriate community can be a useful source of support and information and can be invaluable in helping the family adapt to a foreign culture.

REPATRIATION OF EXPATRIATES

A largely overlooked but critically important issue in the training and development of expatriate managers is to prepare them for reentry into their home-country organization.[38] Repatriation should be seen as the final link in an integrated, circular process that connects good selection and cross-cultural training of expatriate managers with completion of their term abroad and reintegration into their national organization. However, instead of having employees come home to share their knowledge and encourage other high-performing managers to take the same international career track, expatriates too often face a different scenario.[39]

Often when they return home after a stint abroad—where they have typically been autonomous, well-compensated, and celebrated as a big fish in a little pond—they face an organization that doesn't know what they have done for the last few years, doesn't know how to use their new knowledge, and doesn't particularly care. In the worst cases, reentering employees have to scrounge for jobs, or firms will create standby positions that don't use the expatriate's skills and capabilities and fail to make the most of the business investment the firm has made in that individual.

Research illustrates the extent of this problem. According to one study of repatriated employees, 60 to 70 percent didn't know what their position would be when they returned home. Also, 60 percent said their organizations were vague about repatriation, about their new roles, and about their future career progression within the company, while 77 percent of those surveyed took jobs at a lower level in their home organization than in their international assignments.[40] It is small wonder then that 15 percent of returning expatriates leave their firms within a year of arriving home, while 40 percent leave within three years.[41]

The key to solving this problem is good human resource planning. Just as the HRM function needs to develop good selection and training programs for its expatriates, it also needs to develop good programs for reintegrating expatriates back into work life within their home-country organization, for preparing them for changes in their physical and professional landscape, and for utilizing the knowledge they acquired while abroad. See accompanying Country Focus that looks at the home job market and the issue of outsourcing.

MANAGEMENT DEVELOPMENT AND STRATEGY

Management development programs are designed to increase the overall skill levels of managers through a mix of ongoing management education and rotations of managers through a number of jobs within the firm to give them varied experiences. They are attempts to improve the overall productivity and quality of the firm's management resources.

International businesses increasingly are using management development as a strategic tool. This is particularly true in firms pursuing a transnational strategy, as increasing numbers are. Such firms need a strong unifying corporate culture and informal management networks to assist in coordination and control. In addition, transnational firm managers need to be able to detect pressures for local responsiveness, and that requires them to understand the culture of a host country.

Management development programs help build a unifying corporate culture by socializing new managers into the norms and value systems of the firm. In-house company training programs and intense interaction during off-site training can foster esprit de corps–shared experiences, informal networks, perhaps a company language or jargon–as well as develop technical competencies. These training events often include songs, picnics, and sporting events that promote feelings of togetherness. These rites of integration may include "initiation rites" wherein personal culture is stripped, company uniforms are donned (e.g., T-shirts bearing the company logo), and humiliation is inflicted (e.g., a pie in the face). All these activities aim to strengthen a manager's identification with the company.[42]

Bringing managers together in one location for extended periods and rotating them through different jobs in several countries help the firm build an informal management network. Such a network can then be used as a conduit for exchanging valuable performance-enhancing knowledge within the organization.[43] Consider the Swedish telecommunications company L. M. Ericsson. Interunit cooperation is extremely important at Ericsson, particularly for transferring know-how and core competencies from the parent to foreign subsidiaries, from foreign subsidiaries to the parent, and between foreign subsidiaries. To facilitate cooperation, Ericsson transfers large numbers of people back and forth between headquarters and subsidiaries. Ericsson sends a team of 50 to 100 engineers and managers from one unit to another for a year or two. This establishes a network of interpersonal contacts. This policy is effective for both solidifying a common culture in the company and coordinating the company's globally dispersed operations.[44]

PERFORMANCE APPRAISAL

A particularly thorny issue in many international businesses is how best to evaluate its expatriate managers' performance.[45] In this section, we look at this issue and consider some guidelines for appraising expatriate performance.

PERFORMANCE APPRAISAL PROBLEMS

Unintentional bias makes it difficult to evaluate the performance of expatriate managers objectively. In most cases, two groups evaluate the performance of expatriate managers–host-nation managers and home-office managers–and both are subject to bias. The host-nation managers may be biased by their own cultural frame of reference and expectations. For example, Oddou and Mendenhall report the case of a U.S. manager who introduced participative decision making while working in an Indian

COUNTRY FOCUS

COUNTRIES WANT TO HOLD ON TO THEIR JOBS

Canadians and others in the developed world do not like to see jobs that could be given to their own citizens disappear to other countries. From China to India, developing countries are enticing companies from developed countries like Canada and the United States to take advantage of their cheap and skilled labour forces in areas from call centre operators to computer and pharmaceutical industry experts. In Canada, labour unions decry the loss of university jobs to foreigners and pin the blame for outsourcing and Canadian plant closures on lower cost foreign competitors.

High taxes, overbearing labour legislation, and unrealistically restrictive environmental regulations, according to some, are the real culprits of job loss and if given the choice, many Canadian companies will take flight to other business climates.

English linguists and culturalists are busy at work teaching the "right English" and colloquialisms to call centre employees in developing countries around the world, but the rumblings of discontent are heard frequently in home markets. Dell Computer for example, has allegedly received complaints from many North American consumers, expressing a low level of customer satisfaction with Indian call centres.

In reality though, low paid jobs, in relation to other countries, have been in existence for a long time, since well before the WTO agreements and NAFTA. The fact of cheap labour alone, although attractive, is not conclusively enough for a company to uproot and head to a new destination.

Thomas d'Acquino, chief executive of the Canadian Council for Chief Executives, referring to KPMG findings, points out that Canada has had the lowest cost of doing business among G-8 nations over the past five years. Ironically, the road to curbing job losses and making businesses less motivated to seek greener pastures abroad might not lie in the reduction of personal income taxes, but instead in the further reduction of corporate taxes. Jobs leave the country because of competitiveness issues, and one take on resolving this is through lower corporate taxes. Historically speaking, lower corporate taxes pave the way for more research and development, but the issue of jobs going to foreigners does not stop there.

But what to do when the home job market is being usurped by foreign nationals? In the bastions of academia, the calls for "made in Canada" professors has been constant ever since universities were first founded in Canada. For example, in one of the flare-ups over the past five years, it was highlighted that two-thirds of the zoology department of the University of British Columbia came from either Britain or the United States. At that time, one UBC faculty job that had become available received 35 Canadian applications and when an American was short-listed for the post, other applicants filed formal complaints.

Universities argue that they are quality specific, not nationality specific. Recently, the Canadian Association of University Teachers has taken up the cause. Thus far, the fervour has been of a nationalist leaning, and in spite of several attempts to litigate, it has been proven that nothing illegal has been done.

The notion of foreigners "taking away" jobs from one country can quickly become highly emotional. This issue will not disappear anytime soon. As the world increasingly becomes one marketplace, perhaps it might be best to expect the job markets to follow suit.

Sources: "Edge," *Financial Post*, May 3, 2004, p. FE1; CBC, "Canadian Academics Fight For University Jobs," November 30, 2001, www.cbc.ca/story/canada/national/2001/02/21/professors010221.html.

subsidiary.[46] The manager subsequently received a negative evaluation from host-country managers because the strong social stratification in India means managers are seen as experts who should not have to ask subordinates for help. The local employees apparently viewed the U.S. manager's attempt at participatory management as an indication that he was incompetent and did not know his job.

Home-country managers' appraisals may be biased by distance and by their own lack of experience working abroad. Home-office managers are often not aware of what is going on in a foreign operation. Accordingly, they tend to rely on hard data in evaluating an expatriate's performance, such as the subunit's productivity, profitability, or market share. Such criteria may reflect factors outside the expatriate manager's control (e.g., adverse changes in exchange rates, economic downturns). Also, hard data do not take into account many less-visible "soft" variables that are also important, such as an expatriate's ability to develop cross-cultural awareness and to work productively with local managers.

Due to such biases, many expatriate managers believe that headquarters management evaluates them unfairly and does not fully appreciate the value of their skills and experience. This could be one reason many expatriates believe a foreign posting does not benefit their careers. In one study of personnel managers in U.S. multinationals, 56 percent of the managers surveyed stated that a foreign assignment is either detrimental or immaterial to one's career.[47]

ANOTHER PERSPECTIVE

Rewarding the performance of a global team

Imagine that you are leading a global team composed of members from each of your company's seven operating regions: Asia, Southeast Asia, North America, South America, Europe, Eastern Europe and Russia, the Middle East and Africa. The team meets quarterly and communicates daily via computer and phone. How will you motivate and reward team performance on such a culturally diverse team? Team members from cultures that value the group before the individual may be motivated by group-level rewards and benefits, whereas team members from more individualist cultures, such as those found in North America, may well be motivated by individual-level rewards. In Japan, which values the group highly, a trip for salespeople who achieve the team's target for individual members may not motivate nearly as well as a reward for the entire group if the group goal is reached. North American managers who assume that they can motivate anyone with money incentives have learned the hard way that is not always the case. In some cultures, people work for the greater good first, and then for the individual. How would you motivate your team?

GUIDELINES FOR PERFORMANCE APPRAISAL

Several things can reduce bias in the performance appraisal process.[48] First, most expatriates appear to believe more weight should be given to an on-site manager's appraisal than to an off-site manager's appraisal. Due to proximity, an on-site manager is more likely to evaluate the soft variables that are important aspects of an expatriate's performance. The evaluation may be especially valid when the on-site manager is of the same nationality as the expatriate, since cultural bias should be alleviated. In practice, home-office managers often write performance evaluations after receiving input from on-site managers. When this is the case, most experts recommend that a former expatriate who served in the same location should be involved in the appraisal to help reduce bias. Finally, when the policy is for foreign on-site managers to write performance evaluations, home-office managers should be consulted before an on-site manager completes a formal termination evaluation. This gives the home-office manager the opportunity to balance what could be a very hostile evaluation based on a cultural misunderstanding.

COMPENSATION

Two issues are raised in every discussion of compensation practices in an international business. One is how compensation should be adjusted to reflect national differences in economic circumstances and compensation practices. The other issue is how expatriate managers should be paid.

NATIONAL DIFFERENCES IN COMPENSATION

Substantial differences exist in the compensation of executives at the same level in various countries. The results of a survey undertaken in 2000 by Towers Perrin are summarized in Table 16.2. This survey looked at average compensation for four positions across 26 countries.[49] The figures for CEOs and HR directors include both base compensation and performance-related pay bonuses, but do not include stock options. The figures for accountants and manufacturing employees just refer to base pay. As can be seen, wide variations exist across countries. The average compensation for a CEO in Canada was $742,228 and $1.4 million in the U.S., compared to $545,260 in Japan and $179,486 in Taiwan. These figures underestimate the true

TABLE 16.2

Compensation for Four Positions in 26 Countries

	CEO	HR DIRECTOR	ACCOUNTANT	MFG. EMPLOYEE
Argentina	$860,704	$326,874	$63,948	$17,884
Australia	646,316	235,316	57,129	29,703
Belgium	655,390	286,222	63,883	34,336
Brazil	597,454	287,683	44,605	10,480
Canada	742,228	188,070	44,866	36,289
China (Shanghai)	93,393	58,278	14,552	3,021
France	540,260	224,112	69,554	34,741
Germany	421,622	189,785	61,375	36,934
Hong Kong SAR	635,186	211,321	56,711	16,691
Italy	567,685	254,138	59,388	29,469
Japan	545,233	235,536	59,107	51,997
Malaysia	350,558	130,771	24,522	7,453
Mexico	648,695	239,028	41,582	14,302
Netherlands	621,153	217,142	48,838	27,892
New Zealand	258,114	111,803	38,382	15,931
Singapore	621,871	239,376	51,733	16,912
South Africa	406,263	179,268	43,234	7,974
South Korea	194,421	109,637	41,365	17,904
Spain	399,423	196,305	56,332	22,746
Sweden	440,265	166,312	43,438	32,564
Switzerland	448,422	175,008	66,121	41,104
Taiwan	179,486	102,491	30,652	11,924
Thailand	145,173	98,120	19,175	6,293
United Kingdom	719,665	268,302	107,839	28,874
United States	1,403,899	306,181	66,377	44,680
Venezuela	609,097	272,212	41,192	11,221

Source: Towers Perrin.

differential because many Canadian and U.S. executives earn considerable sums of money from stock options and grants.[50] According to Towers Perrin, in 1996 stock option grants were used in only 10 of the 26 countries in the survey. By 2000, however, this figure had risen to 19 out of 26, suggesting that North American-style compensation packages that include stock option grants are becoming more frequent.

These differences in compensation raise a perplexing question for an international business: Should the firm pay executives in different countries according to the prevailing standards in each country, or should it equalize pay on a global basis? The problem does not arise in firms pursuing ethnocentric or polycentric staffing policies. In ethnocentric firms, the issue can be reduced to that of how much home-country expatriates should be paid (which we will consider later). As for polycentric firms, the lack of managers' mobility among national operations implies that pay can and should be kept country-specific. There would seem to be no point in paying executives in Great Britain the same as U.S. executives if they never work side by side.

However, this problem is very real in firms with geocentric staffing policies. A geocentric staffing policy is consistent with a transnational strategy. One aspect of this policy is the need for a cadre of international managers that may include many different nationalities. Should all members of such a cadre be paid the same salary and the same incentive pay? For a U.S.-based firm, this would mean raising the compensation of foreign nationals to U.S. levels, which could be very expensive. If the firm does not equalize pay, it could cause considerable resentment among foreign nationals who are members of the international cadre and work with U.S. nationals. If a firm is serious about building an international cadre, it may have to pay its international executives the same basic salary irrespective of their country of origin or assignment. See the accompanying Management Focus that looks at Sony of Canada.

MANAGEMENT FOCUS

SHARING SONY'S VISION

Many companies say that their employees are an important part of their business. Sony of Canada goes the extra mile and says that its employees and a shared set of values are major keys to the company's success. These values include creating opportunities for employees to learn and grow. The company states that it supports individual empowerment and accountability. "Sony expects a lot from the people who work here, but in return provides a supportive and challenging work environment for everyone."

While Sony's employees have always been important to the company, the emphasis on providing work that is purposeful and challenging is relatively new. In 1995 Sony of Canada, which was a joint venture between Sony Tokyo and Gendis (a Canadian company founded in Calgary in 1939), was dissolved. The restructured company, Sony of Canada, became a wholly-owned subsidiary of Sony Corporation. This resulted in changes to the relationship of the company with its employees.

"(The old company) was a very paternalistic organization. It was the concept of 'employment for life' and the culture was old-fashioned," says the manager of human resources Lori Berenz.

The first step was to determine industry standards in terms of human resource management. The goal was "to take it from an organization where employees were told what to do, to an organization where the employees would be interactive," says Berenz.

The new approach to employee recognition was called the Total Rewards approach. The philosophy was based on the idea that people are not simply motivated by direct financial compensation, such as salary and benefits, but rather by a more complete package of rewards and benefits. This includes a broad range of programs such as performance-driven pay, a results-driven bonus program, a comprehensive benefit program, professional development opportunities, and a work environment conducive to both professional and personal fulfillment.

There were three key areas of concentration. The first was a visioning process, where human resources worked with management of each different division of the company, to develop a visioning statement and, later, a three-year strategy. The process focused on developing an understanding by each employee of his or her own individual role in attaining that vision.

The second step was to develop a system of communicating with the over 1100 employees across the country in branches in major cities and at over 70 Sony stores. An intranet site and companywide newsletter providing news, programs, electronic learning opportunities, and a message from the president, were established with the goals of uniting the company's divisions and providing employees with career information. Employees could map-out their career plans by thinking about making career moves across the entire organization, rather than merely moving upwards within their individual divisions.

The last step was to understand the role of leadership in empowering individuals. Unlike a management focus on day-to-day direction, strategic leadership was promoted by the company's management. The result was a roadmap of what the company and its divisions would be doing over the next three-year period, and how each employee would shape that plan.

The result was a complete program where employees are rewarded for their contribution to the organization. This is good for the employees as well as the company, its shareholders, and its customers.

Sources: Sony Canada at www.sony.ca/sonyca/view/english/careers.shtml and www.sony.ca/sonyca; "Profile," *Benefits and Pensions Monitor*, December 2001.

EXPATRIATE PAY

The most common approach to expatriate pay is the balance sheet approach. This approach equalizes purchasing power across countries so employees can enjoy the same living standard in their foreign posting that they enjoyed at home. In addition, the approach provides financial incentives to offset qualitative differences between assignment locations.[51] Figure 16.1 shows a typical balance sheet. Note that home-country outlays for the employee are designated as income taxes, housing expenses, expenditures for goods and services (food, clothing, entertainment, etc.), and reserves (savings, pension contributions, etc.). The balance sheet approach attempts to provide expatriates with the same standard of living in their host countries as they enjoy at home plus a financial inducement (i.e., premium, incentive) for accepting an overseas assignment.

The components of the typical expatriate compensation package are a base salary, a foreign service premium, allowances of various types, tax differentials, and benefits. We shall briefly review each of these components.[52] An expatriate's total compensation package may amount to three times what he or she would cost the firm in a home-country posting. Because of the high cost of expatriates, many firms have reduced their use of them in recent years. However, a firm's ability to reduce its use of expatriates may be limited, particularly if it is pursuing an ethnocentric or geocentric staffing policy.

Base Salary

An expatriate's base salary is normally in the same range as the base salary for a similar position in the home country. The base salary is normally paid in either the home-country currency or in the local currency.

Foreign Service Premium

A foreign service premium is extra pay the expatriate receives for working outside his or her country of origin. It is offered as an inducement to accept foreign postings. It compensates the expatriate for having to live in an unfamiliar country isolated from

FIGURE 16.1

A Typical Balance Sheet

Source: From J.J. Famularo, *Handbook of Human Resource Administration,* 2nd edition. Copyright © 1986 by The McGraw-Hill Companies, Inc. Reproduced with permission.

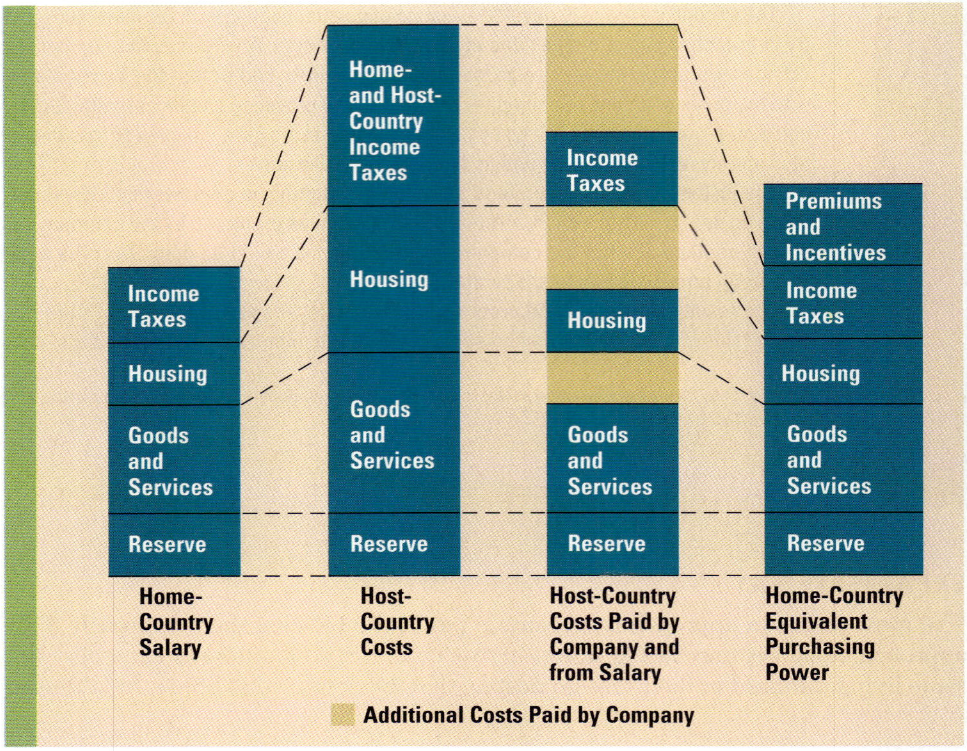

family and friends, having to deal with a new culture and language, and having to adapt to new work habits and practices. Many firms pay foreign service premiums as a percentage of base salary ranging from 10 to 30 percent after tax with 16 percent being the average premium.[53]

Expatriates receive an education allowance for their children so that they may receive the same standard of schooling as they would in their home country. Michael Newman/PhotoEdit.

Allowances

Four types of allowances are often included in an expatriate's compensation package: hardship allowances, housing allowances, cost-of-living allowances, and education allowances. A hardship allowance is paid when the expatriate is being sent to a difficult location, usually defined as one where such basic amenities as health care, schools, and retail stores are grossly deficient by the standards of the expatriate's home country. A housing allowance is normally given to ensure that the expatriate can afford the same quality of housing in the foreign country as at home. In locations where housing is very expensive (e.g., London, Tokyo), this allowance can be substantial–as much as 10 to 30 percent of the expatriate's total compensation package. A cost-of-living allowance ensures that the expatriate will enjoy the same standard of living in the foreign posting as at home. An education allowance ensures that an expatriate's children receive adequate schooling (by home-country standards). Host-country public schools are sometimes not suitable for an expatriate's children, in which case they must attend a private school.

Taxation

Unless a host country has a reciprocal tax treaty with the expatriate's home country, the expatriate may have to pay income tax to both the home- and host-country governments. When a reciprocal tax treaty is not in force, the firm typically pays the expatriate's income tax in the host country. In addition, firms normally make up the difference when a higher income tax rate in a host country reduces an expatriate's take-home pay.

Benefits

Many firms also ensure that their expatriates receive the same level of medical and pension benefits abroad that they received at home. This can be very costly for the firm, since many benefits that are tax deductible for the firm in the home country (e.g., medical and pension benefits) may not be deductible out of the country.

IMPLICATIONS FOR BUSINESS

The implications for international businesses fall into three categories: the concerns of organized labour regarding international enterprises, the strategy of organized labour, and the approaches to labour relations.

INTERNATIONAL LABOUR RELATIONS

The HRM function of an international business is typically responsible for international labour relations. From a strategic perspective, the key issue in international labour relations is the degree to which organized labour can limit the choices of an international business. A firm's ability to integrate and consolidate its global operations to realize experience curve and location economies can be limited by organized labour, constraining the pursuit of a transnational or global strategy. Prahalad and Doz cite the example

ANOTHER PERSPECTIVE

You make how much?

A global computer company with marketing division regional offices in New England brought three specialists from its East Asian operations in New Delhi to the United States for 18 months to work on a global team. This was an expatriate assignment for the Indian computer scientists, and their families accompanied them. Their initial excitement about their assignment began to wane when they realized that their U.S. colleagues were more highly paid. The salary differential between India and the United States in their job category can be as much as 100 percent. They had a salary boost for expatriation, but soon judged that they were underpaid. Meanwhile, their U.S. colleagues feared that the Indian computer scientists were brought into the project to replace them, at lower salaries. Imagine how this team functioned. What would be your approach to this HRM issue?

of General Motors, which bought peace with labour unions by agreeing not to integrate and consolidate operations in the most efficient manner.[54] In the early 1980s, General Motors made substantial investments in Germany—matching its new investments in Austria and Spain—at the demand of the German metalworkers' unions.

One task of the HRM function is to foster harmony and minimize conflict between the firm and organized labour. With this in mind, this section is divided into three parts. First, we review organized labour's concerns about multinational enterprises. Second, we look at how organized labour has tried to deal with these concerns. And third, we look at how international businesses manage their labour relations to minimize labour disputes.

THE CONCERNS OF ORGANIZED LABOUR

Labour unions generally try to get better pay, greater job security, and better working conditions for their members through collective bargaining with management. Unions' bargaining power is derived largely from their ability to threaten to disrupt production, either by a strike or some other form of work protest (e.g., refusing to work overtime). This threat is credible, however, only insofar as management has no alternative but to employ union labour.

A principal concern of domestic unions about multinational firms is that the company can counter its bargaining power with the power to move production to another country. Ford, for example, very clearly threatened British unions with a plan to move manufacturing to Continental Europe unless British workers abandoned work rules that limited productivity, showed restraint in negotiating for wage increases, and curtailed strikes and other work disruptions.[55]

Another concern of organized labour is that an international business will keep highly skilled tasks in its home country and farm out only low-skilled tasks to foreign plants. Such a practice makes it relatively easy for an international business to switch production from one location to another as economic conditions warrant. Consequently, the bargaining power of organized labour is once more reduced.

A final union concern arises when an international business attempts to import employment practices and contractual agreements from its home country. When these practices are alien to the host country, organized labour fears the change will reduce its influence and power. This concern has surfaced in response to Japanese multinationals that have been trying to export their style of labour relations to other countries. For example, much to the annoyance of the United Auto Workers (UAW), most Japanese auto plants in the United States are not unionized. As a result, union influence in the auto industry is declining.

THE STRATEGY OF ORGANIZED LABOUR

Organized labour has responded to the increased bargaining power of multinational corporations by taking three actions: (1) trying to establish international labour organizations, (2) lobbying for national legislation to restrict multinationals, and (3) trying to achieve international regulations on multinationals through such organizations as the United Nations. These efforts have not been very successful.

In the 1960s, organized labour began to establish international trade secretariats (ITSs) to provide worldwide links for national unions in particular industries. The long-term goal was to be able to bargain transnationally with multinational firms. Organized labour believed that by coordinating union action across countries through an ITS, it could counter the power of a multinational corporation by threatening to disrupt production on an international scale. For example, Ford's threat to move production from Great Britain to other European locations would not have been credible if the unions in various European countries had united to oppose it.

However, the ITSs have had virtually no real success. Although national unions may want to cooperate, they also compete with each other to attract investment from international businesses, and hence jobs for their members. For example, in attempting to gain new jobs for their members, national unions in the auto industry often court auto firms that are seeking locations for new plants. One reason Nissan chose to build its European production facilities in Great Britain rather than Spain was that the British unions agreed to greater concessions than the Spanish unions did. As a result of such competition between national unions, cooperation is difficult to establish.

A further impediment to cooperation has been the wide variation in union structure. Trade unions developed independently in each country. As a result, the structure and ideology of unions tend to vary significantly from country to country, as does the nature of collective bargaining. For example, in Great Britain, France, and Italy many unions are controlled by left-wing socialists, who view collective bargaining through the lens of "class conflict." In contrast, most union leaders in Germany, the Netherlands, Scandinavia, and Switzerland are far more moderate politically. The ideological gap between union leaders in different countries has made cooperation difficult. Divergent ideologies are reflected in radically different views about the role of a union in society and the stance unions should take toward multinationals.

Organized labour has also met with only limited success in its efforts to get national and international bodies to regulate multinationals. Such international organizations as the International Labour Organization (ILO) and the Organization for Economic Cooperation and Development (OECD) have adopted codes of conduct for multinational firms to follow in labour relations. However, these guidelines are not as far-reaching as many unions would like. They also do not provide any enforcement mechanisms. Many researchers report that such guidelines are of only limited effectiveness.[56]

APPROACHES TO LABOUR RELATIONS

International businesses differ markedly in their approaches to international labour relations. The main difference is the degree to which labour relations activities are centralized or decentralized. Historically, most international businesses have decentralized international labour relations activities to their foreign subsidiaries because labour laws, union power, and the nature of collective bargaining varied so much from country to country. It made sense to decentralize the labour relations function to local managers. The belief was that there was no way central management could effectively handle the complexity of simultaneously managing labour relations in a number of different environments.

Although this logic still holds, there is now a trend toward greater centralized control. This trend reflects international firms' attempts to rationalize their global operations. The general rise in competitive pressure in industry after industry has made it more important for firms to control their costs. Since labour costs account for such a large percentage of total costs, many firms are now using the threat to move production to another country in their negotiations with unions to change work rules and limit wage increases (as Ford did in Europe). Because such a move would involve major new investments and plant closures, this bargaining tactic requires the input of headquarters management. Thus, the level of centralized input into labour relations is increasing.

In addition, the realization is growing that the way work is organized within a plant can be a major source of competitive advantage. Much of the competitive advantage of Japanese automakers, for example, has been attributed to the use of self-managing teams, job rotation, cross-training, and the like in their Japanese plants.[57] To replicate their domestic performance in foreign plants, the Japanese firms have tried to replicate their work practices there. This often brings them into direct conflict with traditional work practices in those countries, as sanctioned by the local labour unions, so the Japanese firms have often made their foreign investments contingent on the local union accepting a radical change in work practices. To achieve this, the headquarters of many Japanese firms bargains directly with local unions to get union agreement to changes in work rules before committing to an investment. For example, before Nissan decided to invest in northern England, it got a commitment from British unions to agree to a change in traditional work practices. By its very nature, pursuing such a strategy requires centralized control over the labour relations function.

KEY TERMS

corporate culture, p. 512
ethnocentric staffing policy, p. 512
expatriate failure, p. 516
expatriate manager, p. 511
geocentric staffing policy, p. 514
human resource management, p. 510
polycentric staffing policy, p. 514
staffing policy, p. 512

SUMMARY

This chapter focused on human resource management in international businesses. HRM activities include human resource strategy, staffing, performance evaluation, management development, compensation, and labour relations. None of these activities is performed in a vacuum; all must be appropriate to the firm's strategy. This chapter made the following points:

1. Firm success requires HRM policies to be congruent with the firm's strategy.
2. Staffing policy is concerned with selecting employees who have the skills required to perform particular jobs. Staffing policy can be a tool for developing and promoting a corporate culture.
3. An ethnocentric approach to staffing policy fills all key management positions in an international business with parent-country nationals. The policy is congruent with an international strategy. A drawback is that ethnocentric staffing can result in cultural myopia.
4. A polycentric staffing policy uses host-country nationals to manage foreign subsidiaries and parent-country nationals for the key positions at corporate headquarters. This approach can minimize the dangers of cultural myopia, but it can create a gap between home- and host-country operations. The policy is best suited to a multidomestic strategy.
5. A geocentric staffing policy seeks the best people for key jobs throughout the organization, regardless of their nationality. This approach is consistent with building a strong unifying culture and informal management network and is well suited to both global and transnational strategies. Immigration policies of national governments may limit a firm's ability to pursue this policy.
6. A prominent issue in the international staffing literature is expatriate failure, defined as the premature return of an expatriate manager to his or her home country. The costs of expatriate failure can be substantial.
7. Expatriate failure can be reduced by selection procedures that screen out inappropriate candidates. The most successful expatriates seem to be those who have high self-esteem and self-confidence, get along well with others, are willing to attempt to communicate in a foreign language, and can empathize with people of other cultures.
8. Training can lower the probability of expatriate failure. It should include cultural training, language training, and practical training, and it should be provided to both the expatriate manager and the spouse.
9. Management development programs attempt to increase the overall skill levels of managers through a mix of ongoing management education and rotation of managers through different jobs within the firm to give them varied experiences. Management development is often used as a strategic tool to build a strong unifying culture and informal management network, both of which support transnational and global strategies.
10. It can be difficult to evaluate the performance of expatriate managers objectively because of unintentional bias. A number of steps can be taken to reduce this bias.
11. Country differences in compensation practices raise a difficult question for an international business: Should the firm pay executives in different countries according to the standards in each country or equalize pay on a global basis?
12. The most common approach to expatriate pay is the balance sheet approach. This approach aims to equalize purchasing power so employees can enjoy the same living standard in their foreign posting that they had at home.
13. A key issue in international labour relations is the degree to which organized labour can limit the choices available to an international business. A firm's ability to pursue a transnational or global strategy can be significantly constrained by the actions of labour unions.
14. A principal concern of organized labour is that the multinational can counter union bargaining power with threats to move production to another country.
15. Organized labour has tried to counter the bargaining power of multinationals by forming international labour organizations. In general, these efforts have not been effective.

CRITICAL THINKING AND DISCUSSION QUESTIONS

1. What are the main advantages and disadvantages of the ethnocentric, polycentric, and geocentric approaches to staffing policy? When is each approach appropriate?
2. Research suggests that many expatriate employees encounter problems that limit both their effectiveness in a foreign posting and their contribution to the company when they return home. What are the main causes and consequences of these problems, and how might a firm reduce the occurrence of such problems?
3. What is the link between an international business's strategy and its human resource management policies, particularly with regard to the use of expatriate employees and their pay scale?
4. In what ways can organized labour constrain the strategic choices of an international business? How can an international business limit these constraints?

RESEARCH TASK | globalEDGE™ globaledge.msu.edu

Use the globalEDGE™ site to complete the following exercises:

1. The U.S. Department of State prepares quarterly reports for living costs abroad. Using the most current report, identify the countries that are regarded as having a high cost of living and those that are perceived as risky. What are the living allowances and hardship differentials determined by the U.S. Department of State for those countries?
2. You work in the human resources department at the headquarters of a multinational corporation. Your company is about to send several American managers overseas as expatriates. Utilize resources available on the globalEDGE Web site regarding expatriate life to compile a short checklist of concerns and steps for your company to go through before sending its managers overseas.

Visit the *Global Business Today* Online Learning Centre at **www.mcgrawhill.ca/college/hill** to access quizzes, interactive exercises, a Business Around the World interactive map, and other learning and study tools related to this chapter.

Online Learning Centre

CLOSING CASE

HOW COCA-COLA RETAINS EMPLOYEES

The history of Coca-Cola in Canada is almost as long as the history of the product itself. Coca-Cola was developed as a drink sold at soda fountains in 1886. The first hint though of how widespread the drink would become came half a dozen years later in Vicksburg, Mississippi, when a candy storeowner bottled the product so that consumers could enjoy the drink away from the soda fountain setting. The idea grew rapidly. By 1909, there were nearly 400 Coca-Cola bottling plants in operation. Today there are bottling operations around the world, with new growth in Eastern Europe, and almost US$1.5 billion in new bottling facilities in Africa.

First sales of Coca-Cola were reported in Canada in 1897. Today the company bottles a wide variety of brands including Coca-Cola, Vanilla Coke, Diet Coke, and Cherry Coke; Sprite, Diet Sprite, and Fresca; Barq's Root Beer, Nestea iced tea, DASANI bottled water and Minute Maid juices, punches and lemonade. The products are produced and distributed by the Coca-Cola Bottling Company (CCBC), which is a wholly-owned subsidiary of Coca-Cola Enterprises Inc, based in Atlanta.

The continued growth of the company—including the integration of the Coca-Cola business in Canada with the Minute Maid Company of Canada in 2003—has made attracting and retaining world-class talent important for the company. CCBC employs about 6000 full-time employees, in nine facilities across the company. The company's benefits plan also includes 1300 retirees in every province. CCBC's strategy is to be an employer of choice in the marketplace—top people should actively seek out job opportunities with CCBC. But how do you create a benefits program that is consistent with head office goals, yet also responsive to local needs?

The company's benefits program, named Total Rewards Canada, was launched on July 1, 2001. It is based on three guiding principles:

1. provision of a base level of security so that all employees receive at least the minimum level of coverage in health, disability, life insurance, and pension;
2. additional value by enabling employees to tailor their benefits to their own particular circumstances;
3. choice through offering a range of options, from a basic package to one that is heavily enriched.

These three principles of security, value, and choice are the same ones followed by Coca-Cola Enterprises, the parent company of CCBC.

The company had four key objectives for the Total Rewards Canada program: to increase the number of employees who chose to participate in the pension plan, to change the employee perception of a group savings plan from one of saving for short-term needs to a longer-term approach focusing on retirement, to providing flexibility and more choice to employees, and to improving the value of the benefits program without increasing costs to the company.

The company's pension plan is a good example of the provision of security for employees, combined with the availability of choice of additional options. Employees are automatically enrolled in the pension plan when they become eligible. However, there is an opportunity now for employees to expand their individual tax-sheltered savings by contributing more money to an optional savings and investment program. This program offers competitive rates and an increased range of investment options for employees.

Health and welfare benefits were also aligned along these three principles. The result is what is called a "flex" benefits plan, which offers employees a core level of health coverage and a fixed number of credits to purchase optional benefits, ranging from vision care and prescription drug coverage to additional life and disability insurance.

CCBC spent significant effort to communicate the benefits of the plan to their employees, as well as to help them make informed decisions about their coverage. Increased employee participation in the program was one way to measure success. However, the company also conducted a satisfaction survey to measure the overall success of Total Rewards Canada. Employees rate the value provided by the benefits package very highly. "You can make huge investments into programs but, if employees don't appreciate the value of the programs, then you're not really getting the best return on your investment," says the manager of compensation and benefits for CCBC.

Sources: Coca-Cola Enterprises at www.cokecce.com; "Profile," *Benefits and Pensions Monitor*, February 2003.

CASE DISCUSSION QUESTIONS

1. How important do you think employee benefits packages are to employees, including those of the Coca-Cola Bottling Company?
2. Are CCBC's three principles of security, value, and choice the only ones a company can apply to its employee benefits program?
3. Does this package appeal to you? Would it attract you to CCBC? If you were an employee, would you be encouraged to remain at this company for a longer time?

INTERFACE: AN ENVIRONMENTALLY SUSTAINABLE COMMITMENT TO BUSINESS AND MATERIAL MANAGEMENT

The following case study describes a company's efforts to be both profitable and environmentally sustainable.

Interface, Inc., is the world's largest manufacturer of carpet tiles and upholstery fabrics for commercial interiors. But Interface's core vision is not about carpet or fabrics per se; it is about becoming a leading example of a sustainable and restorative enterprise by 2020 across five dimensions: people, place (the planet), product, process, and profits. That is a substantial challenge for a company that in 2000 had 27 factories, sales offices in 110 countries, annual sales of $1.3 billion, over 7000 employees, and a supply chain heavily dependent on petrochemicals.

Founder and Chairman Ray Anderson presented this challenge to the organization in 1994. "After 21 years of unwittingly plundering the earth, I read Paul Hawken's book *The Ecology of Commerce* (Harper 1993).... It convicted me on the spot, not only as a plunderer of Earth, but also as part of an industrial system that is destroying Earth's biosphere, the source and nurturer of all life.... I was struck to the core by Hawken's central point, that only business and industry, the major culprit, is also large enough, powerful enough, pervasive enough, wealthy enough, to lead humankind away from the abyss toward which we are plunging. It was an epiphanal experience for me, a 'spear in the chest.'... I myself became a recovering plunderer. At Interface we call this new direction, climbing Mount Sustainability, the point at its peak symbolically representing zero environmental 'footprint'—our definition of sustainability for ourselves, to reach a state in which our petro-intensive company (energy and materials) takes nothing from the earth that is not naturally and rapidly renewable, and does no harm to the biosphere: zero footprint."

As a result, Interface has undergone considerable transformation in its effort to reorient the entire organization. Some positive results were achieved in the beginning. Through its waste elimination drive, the company has saved $165 million over five years, paying for all of its sustainability work and delivering 27 percent of the group's operating income over the period. Over and above that, since 1994, Interface, Inc., has reduced its "carbon intensity"—its total supply chain virgin petrochemical material and energy use in raw pounds per dollar of revenue—by some 31 percent. However, Interface recognized that sustainability means far more than that.

The company developed a shift in strategic orientation based on a "seven-step" sustainability framework, using the systems thinking of The Natural Step (www.naturalstep.org/). These steps include eliminating waste (not just physical waste, but the whole concept of waste); eliminating harmful emissions; using only renewable energy; adopting closed loop processes; using resource-efficient transportation; energizing people (all stakeholders) around the vision; and redesigning commerce so that a service is sold that allows the company to retain ownership of its products and to maximize resource productivity.

Throughout the business, all employees were trained in the principles of systems thinking. They were required to examine the impact of their work and how they could work more sustainably in their business area. Training was necessary, according to Anderson, because traditional education "continues to teach economics students to trust the 'invisible hand' of the market, when the invisible hand is clearly blind to the externalities. . . . The truth is, we have an essentially illiterate populace when it comes to the environment." The feedback on this training has been very positive and a great deal of progress has been made as a result. However, there were three areas where Interface could have improved the process.

The first is always establishing a positive environment for inspired employees, fresh from their training courses, to return to. The company found that employees became passionate as their understanding of sustainability grew, and they needed an outlet for action. Although there were many areas of good supportive management across the business, there were also too many areas where local managers were not prepared well enough to facilitate motivated employees wanting to make a difference. Issues of management and leadership explain why some of the expected progress did not happen in certain areas.

Second, people engage in different ways with sustainability issues, and learning programs need to provide the space to explore these differences. Programs need to be flexible enough to go into detail on a hot issue such as climate change, while the next question may well be about equity of resource use. To keep people motivated, programs need to maintain this flexibility.

Third, follow-up was not quick enough; it takes much more than two days for people to really understand sustainability. Sustainability issues need to be revisited again and again, as employees begin to understand how it impacts their daily lives. It is a big commitment to revisit these issues on an ongoing basis, but the company recognized that it was vital for employees to continually buy in.

Interface has also learned the importance of making sustainability a "whole company" approach. Those who "got it" quickest were inevitably those working in either the manufacturing or the research areas of the business, people used to talking about the environment, systems, and material substitution. A high number of the company's early wins came on the manufacturing side: green energy purchase, waste elimination, and recycling. However, it took longer to really achieve the buy-in of the sales and marketing teams, with the result that "whole company" issues such as strategic product development planning and communicating sustainability externally took longer to be integrated.

For Interface this has been a comprehensive sustainability learning approach for the company; a great deal has been learned along the way, and the process has benefited from mistakes and successes. The company is now very aware that sustainability needs to become business as usual for everyone across the business, and these experiences have been a solid contribution to successful change. "A new paradigm is taking hold: waste-free, renewable, cyclical, resource efficient, benign, socially equitable, in harmony with nature," Anderson said. The company is now well on the course to achieve its 2020 vision.

Source: Case study reprinted with permission from the World Business Council for Sustainable Development at www.wbcsd.org. Quotes from Ray Anderson are from the chairman's speech at the National Council for Science and the Environment's 2003 conference. The full text of the speech is available at www.ncseonline.org/EFS.

GLOSSARY

absolute advantage A country has an absolute advantage in the production of a product when it is more efficient than any other country at producing it.

ad valorem tariff A tariff levied as a proportion of the value of an imported good.

administrative trade policies Administrative policies, typically adopted by government bureaucracies, that can be used to restrict imports or boost exports.

antidumping policies Policies designed to punish foreign firms that engage in dumping and thus protect domestic producers from unfair foreign competition.

arbitrage The purchase of securities in one market for immediate resale in another to profit from a price discrepancy.

balance-of-payments accounts National accounts that track both payments to and receipts from foreigners.

banking crisis A loss of confidence in the banking system that leads to a run on banks, as individuals and companies withdraw their deposits.

barter The direct exchange of goods or services between two parties without a cash transaction.

basic research centres Centres for fundamental research located in regions where valuable scientific knowledge is being created; they develop the basic technologies that become new products.

bill of lading A document issued to an exporter by a common carrier transporting merchandise. It serves as a receipt, a contract, and a document of title.

Bill S-21 Otherwise known as the Corruption of Foreign Officials Act that entered into force on February 14, 1999. It is Canadian legislation that makes the bribery, or other business corruption "tool" of a foreign official by a Canadian businessperson, a criminal offence.

business ethics Accepted principles of right or wrong governing the conduct of businesspeople.

buyback When a firm builds a plant in a country and agrees to take a certain percentage of the plant's output as partial payment of the contract.

capital flight Residents convert domestic currency into a foreign currency.

caste system A system of social stratification in which social position is determined by the family into which a person is born, and change in that position is usually not possible during an individual's lifetime.

channel length The number of intermediaries that a product has to go through before it reaches the final consumer.

civil law (system) A system of law based on a very detailed set of written laws and codes.

class consciousness A tendency for individuals to perceive themselves in terms of their class background.

class system A system of social stratification in which social status is determined by the family into which a person is born and by subsequent socioeconomic achievements. Mobility between classes is possible.

code of ethics A business's formal statement of ethical priorities.

collectivism A political system that emphasizes collective goals as opposed to individual goals.

command economy An economic system where the allocation of resources, including determination of what goods and services should be produced, and in what quantity, is planned by the government.

common law (system) A system of law based on tradition, precedent, and custom. When law courts interpret common law, they do so with regard to these characteristics.

communist totalitarianism A version of collectivism advocating that socialism can be achieved only through a totalitarian dictatorship.

communists Those who believe socialism can be achieved only through revolution and totalitarian dictatorship.

comparative advantage The theory that countries should specialize in the production of goods and services they can produce most efficiently. A country is said to have a comparative advantage in the production of such goods and services.

concentrated retail system A few retailers supply most of the market.

Confucian dynamism Theory that Confucian teachings affect attitudes toward time, persistence, ordering by status, protection of face, respect for tradition, and reciprocation of gifts and favours.

contract A document that specifies the conditions under which an exchange is to occur and details the rights and obligations of the parties involved.

contract law The body of law that governs contract enforcement.

Convention on Combating Bribery of Foreign Public Officials in International Business Transactions The convention obliges member states to make the bribery of foreign public officials a criminal offence.

copyrights Exclusive legal rights of authors, composers, playwrights, artists, and publishers to publish and dispose of their work as they see fit.

core competence Firm skills that competitors cannot easily match or imitate.

corporate culture Organization's norms and value systems.

counterpurchase A reciprocal buying agreement.

countertrade The trade of goods and services for other goods and services.

countervailing duties Antidumping duties.

country of origin effects The extent to which the place of manufacturing influences product evaluations.

cross-licensing agreement An arrangement in which a company licenses valuable intangible property to a foreign partner and receives a licence for the partner's valuable knowledge; reduces risk of licensing.

cultural relativism The belief that ethics are culturally determined and that firms should adopt the ethics of the cultures in which they operate.

currency board Means of controlling a country's currency.

currency crisis Occurs when a speculative attack on the exchange value of a currency results in a sharp depreciation in the value of the currency or forces authorities to expend large volumes of international currency reserves and sharply increase interest rates to defend the prevailing exchange rate.

currency speculation Involves short-term movement of funds from one currency to another in hopes of profiting from shifts in exchange rates.

currency swap Simultaneous purchase and sale of a given amount of foreign exchange for two different value dates.

current account In the balance of payments, records transactions involving the export or import of goods and services.

D'Amato Act Act passed in 1996, similar to the Helms–Burton Act, aimed at Libya and Iran.

democracy Political system in which government is by the people, exercised either directly or through elected representatives.

deregulation Removal of government restrictions concerning the conduct of a business.

dirty-float system A system under which a country's currency is nominally allowed to float freely against other currencies, but in which the government will intervene, buying and selling currency, if it believes that the currency has deviated too far from its fair value.

draft An order written by an exporter instructing an importer, or an importer's agent, to pay a specified amount of money at a specified time; also called a bill of exchange.

dumping Selling goods in a foreign market for less than their cost of production or below their "fair" market value.

eclectic paradigm Argument that combining location-specific assets or resource endowments and the firm's own unique assets often requires FDI; it requires the firm to establish production facilities where those foreign assets or resource endowments are located.

economic risk The likelihood that events, including economic mismanagement, will cause drastic changes in a country's business environment that adversely affect the profit and other goals of a particular business enterprise.

economies of scale Cost advantages associated with large-scale production.

efficient market A market where prices reflect all available information.

elastic When a small change in price produces a large change in demand.

ethical dilemma A situation in which there is no ethically acceptable solution.

ethical strategy A course of action that does not violate a company's business ethics.

ethical systems Cultural beliefs about what is proper behaviour and conduct.

ethnocentric behaviour Behaviour that is based on the belief in the superiority of one's own ethnic group or culture; often shows disregard or contempt for the culture of other countries.

ethnocentric staffing policy A staffing approach within the MNE in which all key management positions are filled by parent-country nationals.

exchange rate The rate at which one currency is converted into another.

exclusive distribution channel A distribution channel that outsiders find difficult to access.

expatriate failure The premature return of an expatriate manager to the home country.

expatriate manager A national of one country appointed to a management position in another country.

experience curve Systematic production cost reductions that occur over the life of a product.

export management company Export specialists who act as an export marketing department for client firms.

exporting Sale of products produced in one country to residents of another country.

externalities Knowledge spillovers.

externally convertible currency Nonresidents can convert their holdings of domestic currency into foreign currency, but the ability of residents to convert the currency is limited in some way.

external stakeholders Individuals or groups who have some claim on a firm such as customers, suppliers, and unions.

first-mover advantages Advantages accruing to the first to enter a market.

first-mover disadvantages Disadvantages associated with entering a foreign market before other international businesses.

fixed exchange rates A system under which the exchange rate for converting one currency into another is fixed.

flexible machine cell Flexible manufacturing technology in which a grouping of various machine types, a common materials handler, and a centralized cell controller produce a family of products.

flexible manufacturing technology Manufacturing technologies designed to improve job scheduling, reduce setup time, and improve quality control.

floating exchange rates A system under which the exchange rate for converting one currency into another is continuously adjusted depending on the laws of supply and demand.

flow of foreign direct investment The amount of foreign direct investment undertaken over a given time period (normally one year).

folkways Routine conventions of everyday life.

Foreign Corrupt Practices Act U.S. law regulating behaviour regarding the conduct of international business in the taking of bribes and other unethical actions.

foreign debt crisis Situation in which a country cannot service its foreign debt obligations, whether private-sector or government debt.

foreign direct investment (FDI) Direct investment in business operations in a foreign country.

foreign exchange market A market for converting the currency of one country into that of another country.

foreign exchange risk The risk that changes in exchange rates will hurt the profitability of a business deal.

forward exchange When two parties agree to exchange currency and execute a deal at some specific date in the future.

forward exchange rates The exchange rates governing forward exchange transactions.

fragmented retail system Many retailers, with no one having a major share of the market.

franchising A specialized form of licensing in which the franchiser sells intangible property to the franchisee and insists on rules to conduct the business.

free trade The absence of barriers to the free flow of goods and services between countries.

freely convertible currency A country's currency is freely convertible when the government of that country allows both residents and nonresidents to purchase unlimited amounts of foreign currency with the domestic currency.

fundamental analysis Draws on economic theory to construct sophisticated econometric models for predicting exchange rate movements.

General Agreement on Tariffs and Trade (GATT) International treaty that committed signatories to lowering barriers to the free flow of goods across national borders and led to the WTO.

geocentric staffing policy A staffing policy where the best people are sought for key jobs throughout an MNE, regardless of nationality.

global learning The flow of skills and product offerings from foreign subsidiary to home country and from foreign subsidiary to foreign subsidiary.

global web When different stages of value chain are dispersed to those locations around the globe where value added is maximized or where costs of value creation are minimized.

globalization Trend away from distinct national economic units and toward one huge global market.

globalization of markets Moving away from an economic system in which national markets are distinct entities, isolated by trade barriers and barriers of distance, time, and culture, and toward a system in which national markets are merging into one global market.

globalization of production Trend by individual firms to disperse parts of their productive processes to different locations around the globe to take advantage of differences in cost and quality of factors of production.

gold standard The practice of pegging currencies to gold and guaranteeing convertibility.

green-field investment Establishing a new operation in a foreign country.

gross fixed capital formation Summarizes the total amount of capital invested in factories, stores, office buildings, etc.

group An association of two or more individuals who have a shared sense of identity and who interact with each other in structured ways on the basis of a common set of expectations about each other's behaviour.

Helms-Burton Act Act passed in 1996 that allowed Americans to sue foreign firms that use Cuban property confiscated from them after the 1959 revolution.

Human Development Index (HDI) An attempt by the United Nations to assess the impact of a number of factors on the quality of human life in a country.

human resource management Activities an organization conducts to use its human resources effectively.

import quota A direct restriction on the quantity of a good that can be imported into a country.

individualism An emphasis on the importance of guaranteeing individual freedom and self-expression.

individualism versus collectivism Theory focusing on the relationship between the individual and his or her fellows. In individualistic societies, the ties between individuals are loose and individual achievement is highly valued. In societies where collectivism is emphasized, ties between individuals are tight, people are born into collectives, such as extended families, and everyone is supposed to look after the interests of his or her collective.

inefficient market One in which prices do not reflect all available information.

inelastic When a large change in price produces only a small change in demand.

inflows of FDI Flow of foreign direct investment into a country.

innovation Development of new products, processes, organizations, management practices, and strategies.

internalization theory Marketing imperfection approach to foreign direct investment.

internal stakeholders People who work for or own the business such as employees, directors, and stockholders.

international business Any firm that engages in international trade or investment.

International Fisher Effect For any two countries, the spot exchange rate should change in an equal amount but in the opposite direction to the difference in nominal interest rates between countries

International Monetary Fund (IMF) International institution set up to maintain order in the international monetary system.

international monetary system Institutional arrangements countries adopt to govern exchange rates.

international trade Occurs when a firm exports goods or services to consumers in another country.

joint venture A cooperative undertaking between two or more firms.

just distribution A distribution that is considered fair and equitable.

Kantian ethics Holds that people should be treated as ends, and never purely as means to the ends of others.

karoshi Japanese term meaning to die from overwork.

late-mover advantages Benefits enjoyed by a company that is late to enter a new market, such as consumer familiarity with the product or knowledge gained about a market.

late-mover disadvantages Handicap experienced by being a late entrant in a market.

law of one price In competitive markets free of transportation costs and barriers to trade, identical products sold in different countries must sell for the same price when their price is expressed in the same currency.

learning effects Cost savings from learning by doing.

legal risk The likelihood that a trading partner will opportunistically break a contract or expropriate intellectual property rights.

legal system System of rules that regulate behaviour and the processes by which the laws of a country are enforced and through which redress of grievances is obtained.

letter of credit Issued by a bank, indicating that the bank will make payments under specific circumstances.

licensing Occurs when a firm (the licensor) licenses the right to produce its product, use its production processes, or use its brand name or trademark to another firm (the licensee). In return for giving the licensee these rights, the licensor collects a royalty fee on every unit the licensee sells.

licensing agreement Arrangement in which a licensor grants the rights to intangible property to the licensee for a specified period and receives a royalty fee in return.

local content requirement A requirement that some specific fraction of a good be produced domestically.

location economies Cost advantages from performing a value creation activity at the optimal location for that activity.

location-specific advantages Advantages that arise from using resource endowments or assets that are tied to a particular foreign location and that a firm finds valuable to combine with its own unique assets (such as the firm's technological, marketing, or management know-how).

logistics The procurement and physical transmission of material through the supply chain, from suppliers to customers.

long-term versus short-term orientation Theory that deals with virtue regardless of truth; values associated with long-term orientation are thrift and perseverance; values associated with short-term orientation are respect for tradition, fulfilling social obligations, and protecting one's "face."

maquilladoras NAFTA-related Mexican work zones of cheap labour that are commonly found along the Texas–Mexican borders.

market economy An economic system in which the interaction of supply and demand determines the quantity in which goods and services are produced.

market segmentation Identifying groups of consumers whose purchasing behaviour differs from others in important ways.

marketing mix Choices about product attributes, distribution strategy, communication strategy, and pricing strategy that a firm offers its targeted markets.

masculinity versus femininity Theory of the relationship between gender and work roles. In masculine cultures, sex roles are sharply differentiated and traditional "masculine values" such as achievement and the effective exercise of power determine cultural ideals. In feminine cultures, sex roles are less sharply distinguished, and little differentiation is made between men and women in the same job.

mass customization The production of a variety of end products at a unit cost that could once be achieved only through mass production of a standardized output.

materials management The activity that controls the transmission of physical materials through the value chain, from procurement through production and into distribution.

mercantilism An economic philosophy advocating that countries should simultaneously encourage exports and discourage imports.

mixed economy Certain sectors of the economy are left to private ownership and free market mechanisms, while other sectors have significant government ownership and government planning.

Moore's Law The power of microprocessor technology doubles and its costs of production fall in half every 18 months.

moral hazard Arises when people behave recklessly because they know they will be saved if things go wrong.

mores Norms seen as central to the functioning of a society and to its social life.

Multilateral Agreement on Investment (MAI) An agreement that would make it illegal for signatory states to discriminate against foreign investors; would have liberalized rules governing FDI between OECD states.

multinational enterprise (MNE) A firm that owns business operations in more than one country.

multipoint competition Arises when two or more enterprises encounter each other in different regional markets, national markets, or industries.

multipoint pricing Occurs when a pricing strategy in one market may have am impact on a rival's pricing strategy in another market.

naïve immoralist Asserts that if a manager of a multinational sees that firms from other nations are not following ethical norms in a host nation, that manager should not either.

noise The amount of other messages competing for a potential consumer's attention.

nonconvertible currency A currency is not convertible when both residents and nonresidents are prohibited from converting their holdings of that currency into another currency.

norms Social rules and guidelines that prescribe appropriate behaviour in particular situations.

offset A buying agreement similar to counterpurchase, but the exporting country can then fulfill the agreement with any firm in the country to which the sale is being made.

oligopoly An industry composed of a limited number of large firms.

organization culture The values and norms shared among an organization's employees.

Organization for Economic Cooperation and Development (OECD) A Paris-based intergovernmental organization of "wealthy" nations whose purpose is to provide its 29 member states with a forum in which governments can compare their experiences, discuss the problems they share, and seek solutions that can then be applied within their own national contexts.

outflows of FDI Flow of foreign direct investment out of a country.

Paris Convention for the Protection of Industrial Property International agreement to protect intellectual property; signed by 96 countries.

patent Grants the inventor of a new product or process exclusive rights to the manufacture, use, or sale of that invention.

pegged exchange rate Currency value is fixed relative to a reference currency.

pioneering costs Costs an early entrant bears that later entrants avoid, such as the time and effort in learning the rules, failure due to ignorance, and the liability of being a foreigner.

political economy The political, economic, and legal systems of a country.

political risk The likelihood that political forces will cause drastic changes in a country's business environment that will adversely affect the profit and other goals of a particular business enterprise.

political system System of government in a nation.

polycentric staffing policy A staffing policy in an MNE in which host-country nationals are recruited to manage subsidiaries in their own country, while parent-country nationals occupy key positions at corporate headquarters.

positive-sum game A situation in which all countries can benefit even if some benefit more than others.

power distance Theory of how a society deals with the fact that people are unequal in physical and intellectual capabilities. High power distance cultures are found in countries that let inequalities grow over time into inequalities of power and wealth. Low power distance cultures are found in societies that try to play down such inequalities as much as possible.

predatory pricing Reducing prices below fair market value as a competitive weapon to drive weaker competitors out of the market ("fair" being cost plus some reasonable profit margin).

price elasticity of demand A measure of how responsive demand for a product is to changes in price.

private action The theft, piracy, blackmail, and the like by private individuals or groups.

privatization The sale of state-owned enterprises to private investors.

product liability Involves holding a firm and its officers responsible when a product causes injury, death, or damage.

product safety laws Set certain safety standards to which a product must adhere.

profit Difference between total revenues and total costs.

profitability A ratio or rate of return concept.

property rights Bundle of legal rights over the use to which a resource is put and over the use made of any income that may be derived from the resource.

public action The extortion of income or resources from property holders by public officials, such as politicians and government bureaucrats.

pull strategy A market strategy emphasizing mass media advertising as opposed to personal selling.

purchasing power parity (PPP) An adjustment in gross domestic product per capita to reflect differences in the cost of living.

push strategy A marketing strategy emphasizing personal selling rather than mass media advertising.

regional economic integration Agreements among countries in a geographic region to reduce and ultimately remove tariff and nontariff barriers to the free flow of goods, services, and factors of production between each other.

relatively efficient markets One in which few impediments to international trade and investment exist.

religion A system of shared beliefs and rituals concerned with the realm of the sacred.

representative democracy A political system in which citizens periodically elect individuals to represent them in government.

righteous moralist Claims that a multinational's home-country standards of ethics are the appropriate ones to follow in foreign countries.

rights theories A twentieth century theory that human beings have fundamental rights and privileges that transcend national boundaries and cultures.

right-wing totalitarianism A political system in which political power is monopolized by a party, group, or individual that generally permits individual economic freedom but restricts individual political freedom, including free speech, often on the grounds that it would lead to the rise of communism.

sight draft A draft payable on presentation to the drawee.

social democrats Those committed to achieving socialism by democratic means.

social mobility The extent to which individuals can move out of the social strata into which they are born.

social responsibility The idea that businesspeople should consider the social consequences of economic actions when making business decisions.

social strata Hierarchical social categories often based on family background, occupation, and income.

society Group of people who share a common set of values and norms.

source effects When the receiver of the message evaluates the message based on the status or image of the sender.

sourcing decisions Whether a firm should make or buy component parts.

specific tariff Tariff levied as a fixed charge for each unit of good imported.

spot exchange rate The exchange rate at which a foreign exchange dealer will convert one currency into another that particular day.

staffing policy Strategy concerned with selecting employees for particular jobs.

stakeholders The individuals or groups who have an interest, stake, or claim in the actions and overall performance of a company.

stock of foreign direct investment The total accumulated value of foreign-owned assets at a given time.

strategic alliances Cooperative agreements between two or more firms.

strategic commitment A decision that has a long-term impact and is difficult to reverse, such as entering a foreign market on a large scale.

strategic pricing Pricing aimed at giving a company a competitive advantage over its rivals.

strategy Actions managers take to attain the firm's goals.

subsidy Government financial assistance to a domestic producer.

switch trading The use of a specialized third-party trading house in a countertrade arrangement.

tariff A tax levied on imports.

technical analysis Uses price and volume data to determine past trends, which are expected to continue into the future.

theocratic law (system) A system of law based on religious teachings.

theocratic totalitarianism A political system in which political power is monopolized by a party, group, or individual that governs according to religious principles.

time draft A promise to pay by the accepting party at some future date.

timing of entry Entry is early when a firm enters a foreign market before other foreign firms and late when a firm enters after other international businesses have established themselves.

total quality management Management philosophy that takes as its central focus the need to improve the quality of a company's products and services.

totalitarianism Form of government in which one person or political party exercises absolute control over all spheres of human life and opposing political parties are prohibited.

trade creation Trade created due to regional economic integration; occurs when high-cost domestic producers are replaced by low-cost foreign producers in a free trade area.

trade diversion Trade diverted due to regional economic integration; occurs when low-cost foreign suppliers outside a free trade area are replaced by higher-cost foreign suppliers in a free trade area.

trademarks Designs and names, often officially registered, by which merchants or manufacturers designate and differentiate their products.

Trade Related Aspects of Intellectual Property Rights (TRIPS) An agreement among members of the WTO to enforce stricter intellectual property regulations, including granting and enforcing patents lasting at least 20 years and copyrights lasting 50 years.

transnational strategy Plan to exploit experience-based cost and location economies, transfer core competencies with the firm, and pay attention to local responsiveness.

tribal totalitarianism A political system in which a party, group, or individual that represents the interests of a particular tribe (ethnic group) monopolizes political power.

turnkey project A project in which a firm agrees to set up an operating plant for a foreign client and hand over the "key" when the plant is fully operational.

uncertainty avoidance Extent to which cultures socialize members to accept ambiguous situations and to tolerate uncertainty.

United Nations An international organization made up of 189 countries headquartered in New York City, formed in 1945 to promote peace, security, and cooperation.

United Nations Convention on Contracts for the International Sale of Goods (CIGS) A set of rules governing certain aspects of the making and performance of commercial contracts between sellers and buyers who have their places of businesses in different nations.

Universal Declaration of Human Rights A United Nations document that lays down the basic principles of human rights that should be adhered to.

universal needs Needs that are the same all over the world, such as steel, bulk chemicals, and industrial electronics.

utilitarian approaches Hold that the moral worth of actions or practices is determined by their consequences.

value creation Activities performed that increase the value of goods or services to consumers.

values Abstract ideas about what a society believes to be good, right, and desirable.

voluntary export restraint (VER) A quota on trade imposed from the exporting country's side, instead of the importer's; usually imposed at the request of the importing country's government.

wholly owned subsidiary A subsidiary in which the firm owns 100 percent of the stock.

World Bank International institution set up to promote general economic development in the world's poorer nations.

World Trade Organization (WTO) The organization that succeeded the General Agreement on Tariffs and Trade (GATT) as a result of the successful completion of the Uruguay Round of GATT negotiations.

zero-sum game A situation in which an economic gain by one country results in a economic loss by another.

END NOTES

CHAPTER 1

1. Hibernia at www.hibernia.ca/html/about_hibernia/.
2. T. Levitt, "The Globalization of Markets," *Harvard Business Review*, May–June 1983, pp. 92–102.
3. "Canada's Fastest-Growing Companies," *Profit*, June 2004, p. 32.
4. Supply Chain Alliance Inc. at www.supplychainalliance.ca/contact/shtml.
5. See F. T. Knickerbocker, *Oligopolistic Reaction and Multinational Enterprise* (Boston: Harvard Business School Press, 1973), and R. E. Caves, "Japanese Investment in the US: Lessons for the Economic Analysis of Foreign Investment," *The World Economy* 16 (1993), pp. 279–300.
6. Bombardier at www.bombardier.com.
7. Matrikon at www.matrikon.com.
8. United Nations, The UN in Brief, http://www.un.org/Overview/brief.html.
9. J. A. Frankel, "Globalization of the Economy," National Bureau of Economic Research, working paper no. 7858, 2000.
10. J. Bhagwati, *Protectionism* (Cambridge, MA: MIT Press, 1989).
11. F. Williams, "Trade Round Like This May Never Be Seen Again," *Financial Times*, April 15, 1994, p. 8.
12. UNCTAD, *Development and Globalization Facts and Figures*, 2004, p. 36.
13. World Trade Organization, *International Trade Trends and Statistics*, 2000 (Geneva: WTO, 2001).
14. UNCTAD, *Development and Globalization Facts and Figures*, 2004, p. 33.
15. World Trade Organization, *Annual Report 2000* (Geneva: WTO, 2000), and United Nations, *World Investment Report, 2001*.
16. United Nations, *World Investment Report, 2001*.
17. World Trade Organization, "Beyond Borders: Managing a World of Free Trade and Deep Interdependence," press release 55, September 10, 1996.
18. Moore's Law is named after Intel founder Gorden Moore.
19. Frankel, "Globalization of the Economy."
20. Data compiled from various sources and listed at http://www.euromktg.com/globstats.
21. UNCTAD, *E-Commerce and Development Report*, 2003, pp. 27-28, at www.unctad.org/en/docs//ecdr2003_en.pdf.
22. Statistics Canada, *The Daily*, July 8, 2004, at www.statcan.ca/Daily/English/today/d040708a.htm.
23. NUA, *Worldwide* B2B Revenues to Pass One Trillion, at www.nua.ie/surveys/index.cgi?f=VS&art_id=905358753&rel=true.
24. www.forrester.com/ER/Press/ForrFind/0,1768,0,00.html.
25. For a counterpoint, see "Geography and the Net: Putting It in Its Place," *The Economist*, August 11, 2001, pp. 18–20.
26. Frankel, "Globalization of the Economy."
27. Data from Bureau of Transportation Statistics, 2001.
28. Frankel, "Globalization of the Economy."
29. Interviews with Hewlett-Packard personnel by the author.
30. "War of the Worlds," *The Economist: A Survey of the Global Economy*, October 1, 1994, pp. 3–4.
31. Ibid.
32. United Nations, *Development Facts and Figures, United Nations Conference on Trade and Development*, 2004, p. 35.
33. Ibid, p. 33.
34. Oliver, Lee, "The Action Reaction," *Profit Magazine*, June 2004, at www.profitguide.com/profit100/2004/article.asp?ID=1299.
35. Sterner at www.sternerautomation.com/news.html.
36. International Trade Canada, *Why Trade Matters*, June 2004, at www.dfait-maeci.gc.ca/tna-nac/stories91-en.asp.
37. "Extreme Makeover: Carmanah Technologies: Bright Lights, Big City," *Canadian Business*, June 2004, pp. 64–66.
38. See, for example, Ravi Batra, *The Myth of Free Trade* (New York: Touchstone Books, 1993); William Greider, *One World, Ready or Not: The Manic Logic of Global Capitalism* (New York: Simon and Schuster, 1997); and D. Radrik, *Has Globalization Gone Too Far?* (Washington, DC: Institution for International Economics, 1997).

39. www.cbc.ca/stories/2004/01/21/business/roots210104. Retrieved: June 17, 2004.

40. D. Ticoll, "A Fine Balance, The Impact of Offshore IT Services on Canada's IT Landscape" *Pricewaterhouse Coopers*, p. 3.

41. Celestica, *Annual Report*, 2003, p. 24.

42. Peter Gottschalk and Timothy M. Smeeding, "Cross-National Comparisons of Earnings and Income Inequality," *Journal of Economic Literature* 35 (June 1997), pp. 633–87, and Susan M. Collins, *Exports, Imports, and the American Worker* (Washington, DC: Brookings Institution, 1998).

43. Organization for Economic Cooperation and Development, "Income Distribution in OECD Countries," OECD Policy Studies, no. 18 (October 1995).

44. "A Survey of Pay. Winner and Losers," The Economist, May 8, 1999, pp. 5–8.

45. See, Krugman, *Pop Internationalism*, and D. Belman and T. M. Lee, "International Trade and the Performance of US Labor Markets," in U.S. *Trade Policy and Global Growth*, ed. R. A. Blecker (New York: Economic Policy Institute, 1996).

46. See, Robert Lerman, "Is Earnings Inequality Really Increasing? Economic Restructuring and the Job Market," Brief No. 1 (Washington, DC: Urban Institute, March 1997).

47. "A Survey of Pay. Winner and Losers."

48. E. Goldsmith, "Global Trade and the Environment."

49. P. Choate, *Jobs at Risk: Vulnerable U.S. Industries and Jobs under NAFTA* (Washington, DC: Manufacturing Policy Project, 1993).

50. P. Choate, *Jobs at Risk: Vulnerable U.S. Industries and Jobs under NAFTA* (Washington, DC: Manufacturing Policy Project, 1993).

51. B. Lomborg, *The Skeptical Environmentalist* (Cambridge: Cambridge University Press, 2001).

52. H. Nordstrom and S. Vaughan, *Trade and the Environment, World Trade Organization Special Studies* No. 4 (Geneva: WTO, 1999).

53. Environment Canada, *Performance Report*, at www.ec.gc.ca/dpr/2003/en/c4a.htm.

54. OECD, *Key Environmental Indicators*, 2004, p.18.

55. Krugman, *Pop Internationalism.*

56. R. Kuttner, "Managed Trade and Economic Sovereignty," in *U.S. Trade Policy and Global Growth*, ed. R. A. Blecker (New York: Economic Policy Institute, 1996).

57. Maude Barlow speaking at the Seattle IFG Teach-In, at www.ratical.org/co-globalize/ifg112699MB.html p.3.

58. CBC at www.cbc.ca/news/indepth/water/barlow.html.

59. Lant Pritchett, "Divergence, Big Time," *Journal of Economic Perspectives*, 11, no. 3 (Summer 1997), pp. 3–18.

60. Ibid.

61. See, D. Ben-David, H. Nordstrom, and L. A. Winters, *Trade, Income Disparity and Poverty. World Trade Organization Special Studies* No. 5 (Geneva: WTO, 1999).

62. William Easterly, "Debt Relief," *Foreign Policy*, November/December 2001, pp. 20–26.

63. Jeffrey Sachs, "Sachs on Development: Helping the World's Poorest," *The Economist*, August 14, 1999, pp. 17–20.

64. Easterly, "Debt Relief."

65. WTO, *Understanding the WTO*, at www.wto.org/english/thewto_e/whatis_e/tif_e/fact1_e.htm.

66. GURN, Bilateral and Regional Trade Agreements, at www.gurn.info/topic/trade.

CHAPTER 2

1. Although as we shall see, there is not a strict one-to-one correspondence between political systems and economic systems. A. O. Hirschman, "The On-and-Off Again Connection between Political and Economic Progress," *American Economic Review* 84, no. 2 (1994), pp. 343–48.

2. For a discussion of the roots of collectivism and individualism, see H. W. Spiegel, *The Growth of Economic Thought* (Durham, NC: Duke University Press, 1991). An easily assessible discussion of collectivism and individualism can be found in M. Friedman and R. Friedman, *Free to Choose* (London: Penguin Books, 1980).

3. For a classic summary of the tenets of Marxism details, see A. Giddens, *Capitalism and Modern Social Theory* (Cambridge: Cambridge University Press, 1971).

4. J. S. Mill, *On Liberty* (London: Longman's, 1865), p. 6.

5. A. Smith, *The Wealth of Nations*, Vol. 1 (London: Penguin Books), p. 325.

6. R. Wesson, *Modern Government–Democracy and Authoritarianism*, 2nd ed. (Englewood Cliffs, NJ: Prentice Hall, 1990).

7. For a detailed but accessible elaboration of this argument, see Friedman and Friedman, *Free to Choose.* Also see P. M. Romer, "The Origins of Endogenous Growth," *Journal of Economic Perspectives* 8, no. 1 (1994), pp. 2–32.

8. T. W. Lippman, *Understanding Islam* (New York: Meridian Books, 1995).

9. L Hurst, "Sharia Law Approved in Ontario," *Indiamedia*, May 22, 2004, at www.vancouver.indymedia.org/news/2004/05/137382.php.

10. "Islam's Interest," *The Economist*, January 18, 1992, pp. 33–34.

11. This information can be found on the UN's Treaty website at www.untreaty.un.org/ENGLISH/bible/englishinternetbible/partl/chapterX/treaty17.asp.

12. International Court of Arbitration, www.iccwbo.org/index_court.asp.

13. D. North, *Institutions, Institutional Change, and Economic Performance* (Cambridge: Cambridge University Press, 1991).

14. P. Klebnikov, "Russia's Robber Barons," *Forbes*, November 21, 1994, pp. 74–84; C. Mellow, "Russia: Making Cash from Chaos," *Fortune*, April 17, 1995, pp. 145–51; and "Mr Tatum Checks Out," *The Economist*, November 9, 1996, p. 78.

15. "Godfather of the Kremlin?" *Fortune*, December 30, 1996, pp. 90–96.

16. M. Trickey, "Russian Takeover Spawns Suit From Canadian Oil Firm," *The Standard*, February 27, 2002, p. 23, at www.norexpetroleum.com/Rico%20case%20litigation/press%20about%20case/int_press/p23.

17. Ethics and International Business at www.witiger.com/internationalbusiness/ethics.htm.

18. K. van Wolferen, *The Enigma of Japanese Power* (New York: Vintage Books, 1990), pp. 100–5.

19. P. Bardhan, "Corruption and Development: A Review of the Issues," *Journal of Economic Literature*, September 1997, pp. 1320–46.

20. K. M. Murphy, A. Shleifer, and R. Vishny, "Why Is Rent Seeking So Costly to Growth," *American Economic Review* 83, no. 2 (1993), pp. 409–14.

21. Speech by John Sewell, Transparency International Inc. Symposium, "Corruption–Is Canada in Trouble?" Thursday, May 13, 2004 at Schulich School of Business, Room W136, York University Luncheon Speech, 12:45 p.m.

22. J. Coolidge and S. Rose Ackerman, "High Level Rent Seeking and Corruption in African Regimes," World Bank policy research working paper #1780, June 1997; and Murphy, Shleifer, and Vishny, "Why Is Rent Seeking So Costly to Growth."

23. Department of Justice Canada at, www.canada.justice.gc.ca/en/dept/pub/cfpoa/guide5.html, p. 2.

24. Ibid, p. 5.

25. For an interesting discussion of strategies for dealing with the low cost of copying and distributing digital information, see the chapter on rights management in C. Shapiro and H. R. Varian, *Information Rules* (Boston: Harvard Business School Press, 1999).

26. Douglass North has argued that the correct specification of intellectual property rights is one factor that lowers the cost of doing business and, thereby, stimulates economic growth and development. See North, *Institutions, Institutional Change, and Economic Performance.*

27. C. Webb, "Canada Puts Arctic Chill On Music Industry," *Washington Post*, April 1, 2004, at www.washingtonpost.com/ac2/wp-dyn?pagename=article&contentId=A41679-2004Apr1&notFound=true.

28. "Trade Tripwires," *The Economist*, August 27, 1994, p. 61.

29. World Bank at www.worldbank.org/data/aboutdata/working-meth.html.

30. World Bank at www.worldbank.org/data/databytopic/GNIPC.pdf.

31. A. Sen, *Development as Freedom* (New York: Alfred A. Knopf, 1999).

32. G. M. Grossman and E. Helpman, "Endogenous Innovation in the Theory of Growth," *Journal of Economic Perspectives* 8, no. 1 (1994), pp. 23–44, and P. M. Romer, "The Origins of Endogenous Growth," *Journal of Economic Perspectives* 8, no. 1 (1994), pp. 3–22.

33. F. A. Hayek, *The Fatal Conceit: Errors of Socialism* (Chicago: University of Chicago Press, 1989).

34. James Gwartney, Robert Lawson, and Walter Block, *Economic Freedom of the World: 1975–1995* (London: Institute of Economic Affairs, 1996).

35. North, *Institutions, Institutional Change, and Economic Performance.* See also Murphy, Shleifer, and Vishny, "Why Is Rent Seeking so Costly to Growth?" Also see K. E. Maskus, *Intellectual Property Rights in the Global Economy* (Institute for International Economics, 2000).

36. Hirschman, "The On-and-Off Again Connection between Political and Economic Progress," and A. Przeworski and F. Limongi, "Political Regimes and Economic Growth," *Journal of Economic Perspectives* 7, no. 3 (1993), pp. 51–59.

37. As an example, see "Why Voting Is Good for You," *The Economist*, August 27, 1994, pp. 15–17.

38. Ibid.

39. For details of this argument, see M. Olson, "Dictatorship, Democracy, and Development," *American Political Science Review*, September 1993.

40. For example, see Jarad Diamond's Pulitzer prize-winning book, *Guns, Germs, and Steel* (New York: W. W. Norton, 1997). Also see J. Sachs, "Nature, Nurture and Growth," *The Economist*, June 14, 1997, pp. 19–22.

41. Sachs, "Nature, Nurture and Growth."

42. "What Can the Rest of the World Learn from the Classrooms of Asia?" *The Economist*, September 21, 1996, p. 24.

43. J. Fagerberg, "Technology and International Differences in Growth Rates," *Journal of Economic Literature* 32 (September 1994), pp. 1147–75.

44. *2003 Annual Report*, Freedom House, p. 18.

45. Freedom House, "Democracies Century: A Survey of Political Change in the Twentieth Century, 1999." Available at http://www.freedomhouse.org.

46. F. Fukuyama, "The End of History," *The National Interest* 16 (Summer 1989), p. 18.

47. S. P. Huntington, *The Clash of Civilizations and the Remaking of World Order* (New York: Simon & Schuster, 1996).

48. Ibid., p. 116.

49. S. Fisher, R. Sahay, and C. A. Vegh, "Stabilization and the Growth in Transition Economies: the Early Experience," *Journal of Economic Perspectives* 10 (Spring 1996), pp. 45–66.

50. M. Miles, E. Feulner, M. O'Grady, and A. Eiris, *2004 Index of Economic Freedom* (Washington, DC: Heritage Foundation, 2004).

51. International Monetary Fund, *World Economic Outlook: Focus on Transition Economies* (Geneva: IMF, October 2000).

52. J. C. Brada, "Privatization Is Transition–Is It?" *Journal of Economic Perspectives*, Spring 1996, pp. 67–86.

53. See S. Zahra et al., "Privatization and Entrepreneurial Transformation," *Academy of Management Review* 3, no. 25 (2000), pp. 509–24.

54. Fischer, Sahay, and Vegh, "Stabilization and Growth in Transition Economies."

55. J. Nellis, "Time to Rethink Privatization in Transition Economies?" *Finance and Development* 36, no. 2 (1999), pp. 16–19.

56. M. S. Borish and M. Noel, "Private Sector Development in the Visegrad Countries," *World Bank*, March 1997.

57. See S. Fisher and R. Sahay, "The Transition Economies after Ten Years," IMF working paper 00/30 (Washington: International Monetary Fund, 2000).

58. International Monetary Fund, *World Economic Outlook: Focus on Transition Economies* (Geneva: IMF, October 2000).

59. "Lessons of Transition," *The Economist*, June 29, 1996, p. 81.

60. For a discussion of first-mover advantages, see M. Liberman and D. Montgomery, "First-Mover Advantages," *Strategic Management Journal* 9 (Summer Special Issue, 1988), pp. 41–58.

61. S. H. Robock, "Political Risk: Identification and Assessment," *Columbia Journal of World Business*, July/August 1971, pp. 6–20.

62. Steven L. Myers, "Report Says Business Interests Overshadow Rights," *New York Times*, December 5, 1996, p. A8.

63. Jo-Ann Mort, "Sweated Shopping," *The Guardian*, September 8, 1997, p. 11.

64. Bardhan Pranab, "Corruption and Development," *Journal of Economic Literature* 36 (September 1997), pp. 1320–46.

65. A. Shleifer and R. W. Vishny, "Corruption," *Quarterly Journal of Economics*, no. 108 (1993), pp. 599–617.

66. P. Mauro, "Corruption and Growth," *Quarterly Journal of Economics*, no. 110 (1995), pp. 681–712.

CHAPTER 3

1. See R. Dore, *Taking Japan Seriously* (Stanford, CA: Stanford University Press, 1987).

2. J. Monger, "International Comparisons of Labour Disputes in 2002," *National Statistics*, at www.statistics.gov.uk/CCI/article.asp?ID=886&Pos+&ColRank+2&Rank+672.

3. E. B. Tylor, *Primitive Culture* (London: Murray, 1871).

4. Geert Hofstede, *Culture's Consequences: International Differences in Work Related Values* (Beverly Hills, CA: Sage Publications, 1984), p. 21.

5. J. Z. Namenwirth and R. B. Weber, *Dynamics of Culture* (Boston: Allen & Unwin, 1987), p. 8.

6. R. Mead, *International Management: Cross Cultural Dimensions* (Oxford: Blackwell Business, 1994), p. 7.

7. "Iraq: Down But Not Out," *The Economist*, April 8, 1995, pp. 21–23.

8. S. P. Huntington, *The Clash of Civilizations* (New York, Simon & Schuster, 1996).

9. M. Thompson, R. Ellis, and A. Wildavsky, *Cultural Theory* (Boulder, CO: Westview Press, 1990).

10. M. Douglas, "Cultural Bias," in *Active Voice* (London: Routledge, 1982), pp. 183–254.

11. M. L. Dertouzos, R. K. Lester, and R. M. Solow, *Made in America* (Cambridge, MA: MIT Press, 1989).

12. C. Nakane, *Japanese Society* (Berkeley, CA: University of California Press, 1970).

13. Ibid.

14. For details, see M. Aoki, *Information, Incentives, and Bargaining in the Japanese Economy* (Cambridge: Cambridge University Press, 1988), and Dertouzos, Lester, and Solow, *Made in America.*

15. For an excellent historical treatment of the evolution of the English class system, see E. P. Thompson, *The Making of the English Working Class* (London: Vintage Books, 1966). See also R. Miliband, *The State in Capitalist Society* (New York: Basic Books, 1969), especially Chapter 2. For more recent studies of class in British societies, see Stephen Brook, Class: *Knowing Your Place in Modern Britain* (London: Victor Gollancz, 1997); A. Adonis and S. Pollard, *A Class Act: The Myth of Britain's Classless Society* (London: 1997); and J. Gerteis and M. Savage, "The Salience of Class in Britain and America: A Comparative Analysis," *British Journal of Sociology*, June 1998.

16. Adonis and Pollard, *A Class Act.*

17. N. Goodman, *An Introduction to Sociology* (New York: Harper Collins, 1991).

18. BBC at www.bbc.co.uk/. Retrieved: June 29, 2004.

19. M. Weber, *The Protestant Ethic and the Spirit of Capitalism* (New York: Scribner's Sons, 1958, original 1904–1905). For an excellent review of Weber's work, see A. Giddens, *Capitalism and Modern Social Theory* (Cambridge: Cambridge University Press, 1971).

20. Weber, *The Protestant Ethic and the Spirit of Capitalism*, p. 35.

21. A. S. Thomas and S. L. Mueller, "The Case for Comparative Entrepreneurship," *Journal of International Business Studies* 31, no. 2 (2000), pp. 287–302, and S. A. Shane, "Why Do Some Societies Invent More Than Others?" *Journal of Business Venturing* 7 (1992), pp. 29–46.

22. See S. M. Abbasi, K. W. Hollman, and J. H. Murrey, "Islamic Economics: Foundations and Practices," *International Journal of Social Economics* 16, no. 5 (1990), pp. 5–17, and R. H. Dekmejian, *Islam in Revolution: Fundamentalism in the Arab World* (Syracuse: Syracuse University Press, 1995).

23. T. W. Lippman, *Understanding Islam* (New York: Meridian Books, 1995).

24. Dekmejian, *Islam in Revolution.*

25. M. K. Nydell, *Understanding Arabs* (Yarmouth, ME: Intercultural Press, 1987).

26. Lippman, *Understanding Islam.*

27. The material in this section is based largely on Abbasi, Hollman, and Murrey, "Islamic Economics."

28. "Islam's Interest," *The Economist*, January 18, 1992, pp. 33–34.

29. For details of Weber's work and views, see Giddens, *Capitalism and Modern Social Theory.*

30. See, for example, the views expressed in "A Survey of India: The Tiger Steps Out," *The Economist*, January 21, 1995.

31. See R. Dore, *Taking Japan Seriously* (Stanford, CA: Stanford University Press, 1987), and C. W. L. Hill, "Transaction Cost Economizing as a Source of Comparative Advantage: The Case of Japan," *Organization Science* 6 (1995).

32. See Aoki, *Information, Incentives, and Bargaining in the Japanese Economy*, and J. P. Womack, D. T. Jones, and D. Roos, *The Machine That Changed the World* (New York: Rawson Associates, 1990).

33. For examples of this line of thinking, see the work by Mike Peng and his associates: M. W. Peng and P. S. Heath, "The Growth of the Firm in Planned Economies in Transition," *Academy of Management Review* 21 (1996), pp. 492–528; M. W. Peng, *Business Strategies in Transition Economies* (Thousand Oaks, CA: Sage, 2000); and M. W. Peng and Y. Luo, "Managerial Ties and Firm Performance in a Transition Economy," *Academy of Management Journal*, June 2000, pp. 486–501.

34. This hypothesis dates back to two anthropologists, Edward Sapir and Benjamin Lee Whorf. See E. Sapir, "The Status of Linguistics as a Science," Language 5 (1929), pp. 207–14, and B. L. Whorf, *Language, Thought, and Reality* (Cambridge, MA: MIT Press, 1956).

35. In fact, the tendency has been documented empirically. See A. Annett, "Social Fractionalization, Political Instability, and the Size of Government," *IMF Staff Papers* 48 (2001), pp. 561–92.

36. D. A. Ricks, *Big Business Blunders: Mistakes in Multinational Marketing* (Homewood, IL: Dow Jones-Irwin, 1983).

37. M. E. Porter, *The Competitive Advantage of Nations* (New York: Free Press, 1990).

38. Ibid., pp. 395–97.

39. UNCTAD, *Development and Globalization Facts and Figures*, UN Conference on Trade and Development, 2004, p. 12.

40. G. Hofstede, "The Cultural Relativity of Organizational Practices and Theories," *Journal of International Business Studies*, Fall 1983, pp. 75–89.

41. For a more detailed critique, see R. Mead, *International Management: Cross-Cultural Dimensions* (Oxford: Blackwell, 1994), pp. 73–75.

42. For example, see W. J. Bigoness and G. L. Blakely, "A Cross-National Study of Managerial Values," *Journal of International Business Studies*, December 1996, p. 739; D. H. Ralston, D. H. Holt, R. H. Terpstra, and Y. Kai-Cheng, "The Impact of National Culture and Economic Ideology on Managerial Work Values," *Journal of International Business Studies* 28, no. 1 (1997), pp. 177–208; and P. B. Smith, M. F. Peterson, and Z. Ming Wang, "The Manager as a Mediator of Alternative Meanings," *Journal of International Business Studies* 27, no. 1 (1996), pp. 115–37.

43. G. Hofstede and M. H. Bond, "The Confucius Connection," *Organizational Dynamics* 16, no. 4 (1988), pp. 5–12.

44. R. S. Yeh and J. J. Lawerence, "Individualism and Confucian Dynamism," *Journal of International Business Studies* 26, no. 3 (1995), pp. 655–66.

45. Mead, *International Management: Cross-Cultural Dimensions*, chap. 17.

46. "Free, Young, and Japanese," *The Economist*, December 21, 1991.

47. Namenwirth and Weber, *Dynamics of Culture.*

48. G. Hofstede, "National Cultures in Four Dimensions," *International Studies of Management and Organization* 13, no. 1, pp. 46–74.

49. Ibid.

50. See Aoki, *Information, Incentives, and Bargaining in the Japanese Economy*; Dertouzos, Lester, and Solow, *Made in America*; and Porter, *The Competitive Advantage of Nations*, pp. 395–97.

51. For empirical work supporting such a view, see Annett, "Social Fractionalization, Political Instability, and the Size of Government."

52. J. Goodwin and D. Goodwin, "Ethical Judgements Across Cultures," *Journal of Business Ethics* 18, no. 3 (February 1999), pp. 267–81.

53. T. Donaldson, "Values in Tension: Ethics Away from Home," *Harvard Business Review*, September–October 1996.

54. R. T. DeGeorge, "Ethics in International Business–A Contradiction in Terms?" *Business Credit*, September 2000, pp. 50–52.

55. S. Lovett, L. C. Simmons, and R. Kali, "Guanxi versus the Market: Ethics and Efficiency," *Journal of International Business Studies* 30, no. 2 (1999), pp. 231–48.

56. Donaldson, "Values in Tension: Ethics Away from Home."

57. R. J. Barnet and J. Cavanagh, *Global Dreams: Imperial Corporations and the New World Order* (New York: Touchstone Books, 1994), p. 33.

CHAPTER 4

1. Thomas Donaldson, "Values in Tension: Ethics Away From Home," *Harvard Business Review*, September–October 1996.

2. Students can hear some of the old news clip with speeches during this era on the CBC archives site at www.archives.cbc.ca/IDD-1-71-703/conflict_war/apartheid.

3. www.ivanhoe-mines.com/s/Home.asp.

4. Rowell, "Trouble Flares in the Delta of Death; Shell Has Polluted More Than Ken Saro Wiwa's Oroniland in Nigeria," *The Guardian*, November 8, 1995, p. 6.

5. Peter Singer, *One World: The Ethics of Globalization.* (New Haven, CT: Yale University Press, 2002).

6. Details can be found at www.oecd.org/EN/home/0,,EN-home-31-nondirectorate-no-no-no-31,00.html.

7. Bardhan Pranab, "Corruption and Development," *Journal of Economic Literature* 36 (September 1997), pp. 1320–46.

8. A. Shleifer and R.W. Vishny, "Corruption," *Quarterly Journal of Economics*, no. 108 (1993), pp. 599-617, and I. Ehrlich and F. Lui, "Bureaucratic Corruption and Endogenous Economic Growth," *Journal of Political Economy* 107 (December 1999), pp. 270–92.

9. S. A. Waddock and S. B. Graves, "The Corporate Social Performance-Finacial Performance Link," *Strategic Management Journal* 8 (1997), pp. 303–19.

10. Daniel Litvin, *Empires of Profit* (New York: Texere, 2003).

11. Details can be found at BP's Web site, www.bp.com.

12. This is known as the "when in Rome perspective." Donaldson, "Values in Tension: Ethics Away from Home."

13. Richard T. De George, *Competing with Integrity in International Business* (Oxford: Oxford University Press, 1993).

14. Donaldson, "Values in Tension: Ethics Away from Home."

15. Saul W. Gellerman, "Why Good Managers Make Bad Ethical Choices," in *Ethics in Practice: Managing the Moral Corporation*, ed. Kenneth R. Andrews (Cambridge, MA: Harvard Business School Press, 1989).

16. David Messick and Max H. Bazerman, "Ethical Leadership and the Psychology of Decision Making," *Sloan Management Review* 37 (Winter 1996), pp. 9–20.

17. Robert Bryce, *Pipe Dreams: Greed, Ego and the Death of Enron* (New York: Public Affairs, 2002).

18. Milton Friedman, "Social Responsibility of Business Is to Increase Profits," *The New York Times Magazine*, September 13, 1970. Reprinted in Tom L. Beauchamp and Norman E. Bowie, *Ethical Theory and Business*, 7th ed. (Prentice Hall, 2001).

19. Friedman, "Social Responsibility of Business Is to Increase Profits," p. 55.

20. For example, see Donaldson, "Values in Tension: Ethics Away from Home." See also Norman Bowie, "Relativism and the Moral Obligations of Multination Corporations," In Tom L. Beauchamp and Norman E. Bowie, *Ethical Theory and Business.*

21. For example, see De George. *Competing with Integrity in International Business.*

22. Details can be found at www.bp.com/sectiongenericarticle.do?category1d=79&contentId-2002369#2014689.

23. This example is often repeated in the literature on international business ethics. It was first outlined by Arthur Kelly in "Case Study–Italian Style Mores." Printed in Thomas Donaldson and Patricia Werhane, *Ethical Issues in Business* (Englewood Cliffs, NJ: Prentice Hall, 1979).

24. See Tom L. Beauchamp and Norman E. Bowie, *Ethical Theory and Business.*

25. Thomas Donaldson, *The Ethics of International Business.* (Oxford: Oxford University Press. 1989).

26. Found at www.un.org./Overview/rights.html.

27. Donaldson, *The Ethics of International Business.*

28. See Chapter 10 in Beauchamp and Bowie, *Ethical Theory and Business.*

29. John Rawls, *A Theory of Justice*, rev. ed. (Cambridge, MA: Belknap Press, 1999).

30. For example, see R. Edward Freeman and Daniel Gilbert, *Corporate Strategy and the Search for Ethics* (Englewood Cliffs, NJ: Prentice Hall, 1988); Thomas Jones, *Journal of Management Review* 16 (1991), pp. 366–95; and J. R. Rest, *Moral Development: Advances in Research and Theory* (New York Praeger, 1986).

31. Ibid.

32. See E. Freeman, *Strategic Management: A Stakeholder Approach* (Boston: Pitman Press, 1984); C. W. L. Hill and T. M. Jones, "Stakeholder–Agency Theory," *Journal of Management Studies* 29 (1992), pp. 131–54; and J. G. March and H. A. Simon, *Organizations* (New York: Wiley, 1958).

33. Hill and Jones, "Stakeholder–Agency Theory," and March and Simon, *Organizations* (New York: Wiley, 1958).

34. De George, *Competing with Integrity in International Business.*

35. The code can be accessed at United Technologies Web site, www.utc.com/profile/ethcis/index.htm.

36. Colin Grant, "Whistle Blowers: Saints of Secular Culture," *Journal of Business Ethics*, September 2002, pp. 391–400.

37. From www.rbc.com/governance/pdf/2003conduct.pdf.

CHAPTER 5

1. H. W. Spiegel, *The Growth of Economic Thought* (Durham, NC: Duke University Press, 1991).

2. G. de Jonquieres, "Mercantilists Are Treading on Thin Ice," *Financial Times*, July 3, 1994, p. 16.

3. Jarl Hagelstam, "Mercantilism Still Influences Practical Trade Policy at the End of the Twentieth Century," *Journal of World Trade*, 1991, pp. 95–105.

4. S. Hollander, *The Economics of David Ricardo* (Buffalo: The University of Toronto Press, 1979).

5. D. Ricardo, *The Principles of Political Economy and Taxation* (Homewood, IL: Irwin, 1967, first published in 1817).

6. For example, R. Dornbusch, S. Fischer, and P. Samuelson, "Comparative Advantage: Trade and Payments in a Ricardian Model with a Continuum of Goods," *American Economic Review* 67 (December 1977), pp. 823–39.

7. B. Balassa, "An Empirical Demonstration of Classic Comparative Cost Theory," *Review of Economics and Statistics*, 1963, pp. 231–38.

8. See P. R. Krugman, "Is Free Trade Passé?" *Journal of Economic Perspectives* 1 (Fall 1987), pp. 131–44.

9. P. Samuelson, "The Gains from International Trade Once Again," *Economic Journal* 72 (1962), pp. 820–29.

10. J. D. Sachs and A. Warner, "Economic Reform and the Process of Global Integration," *Brookings Papers on Economic Activity*, 1995, pp. 1–96.

11. Ibid., pp. 35–36.

12. J. A. Frankel and D. Romer, "Does Trade Cause Growth?" *American Economic Review* 89, no. 3 (June 1999), pp. 379–99.

13. A recent skeptical review of the empirical work on the relationship between trade and growth questions these results. See Francisco Rodriguez

and Dani Rodrik, "Trade Policy and Economic Growth: A Skeptics Guide to the Cross-National Evidence," *National Bureau of Economic Research*, Working Paper Series No. 7081, April 1999. Even these authors, however, cannot find any evidence that trade hurts economic growth or income levels.

14. B. Ohlin, *Interregional and International Trade* (Cambridge: Harvard University Press, 1933). For a summary, see R. W. Jones and J. P. Neary, "The Positive Theory of International Trade," in *Handbook of International Economics*, ed. R. W. Jones and P. B. Kenen (Amsterdam: North Holland, 1984).

15. W. Leontief, "Domestic Production and Foreign Trade: The American Capital Position Re-Examined," *Proceedings of the American Philosophical Society* 97 (1953), pp. 331–49.

16. R. M. Stern and K. Maskus, "Determinants of the Structure of U.S. Foreign Trade," *Journal of International Economics* 11 (1981), pp. 207–44.

17. See H. P. Bowen, E. E. Leamer, and L. Sveikayskas, "Multicountry, Multifactor Tests of the Factor Abundance Theory," *American Economic Review* 77 (1987), pp. 791–809.

18. D. Trefler, "The Case of the Missing Trade and Other Mysteries," *American Economic Review* 85 (December 1995), pp. 1029–46.

19. R. Vernon, "International Investments and International Trade in the Product Life Cycle," *Quarterly Journal of Economics*, May 1966, pp. 190–207, and R. Vernon and L. T. Wells, *The Economic Environment of International Business*, 4th ed. (Englewood Cliffs, NJ: Prentice Hall, 1986).

20. For a good summary of this literature, see E. Helpman and P. Krugman, *Market Structure and Foreign Trade: Increasing Returns, Imperfect Competition, and the International Economy* (Boston: MIT Press, 1985). Also see P. Krugman, "Does the New Trade Theory Require a New Trade Policy?" *World Economy* 15, no. 4 (1992), pp. 423–41.

21. A. A. Alchian, "Reliability of Progress Curves in Airframe Production," *Econometrica* 31 (1963), pp. 679–93.

22. M. B. Lieberman and D. B. Montgomery, "First-Mover Advantages," *Strategic Management Journal* 9 (Summer 1988), pp. 41–58.

23. A. D. Chandler, *Scale and Scope* (New York: Free Press, 1990).

24. Krugman, "Does the New Trade Theory Require a New Trade Policy?"

25. M. E. Porter, *The Competitive Advantage of Nations* (New York: Free Press, 1990). For a good review of this book, see R. M. Grant, "Porter's Competitive Advantage of Nations: An Assessment," *Strategic Management Journal* 12 (1991), pp. 535–48.

26. B. Kogut, ed., *Country Competitiveness: Technology and the Organizing of Work* (New York: Oxford University Press, 1993).

27. Porter, *The Competitive Advantage of Nations*, p. 121.

28. Lieberman and Montgomery, "First-Mover Advantages."

29. C. A. Hamilton, "Building Better Machine Tools," *Journal of Commerce*, October 30, 1991, p. 8, and "Manufacturing Trouble," *The Economist*, October 12, 1991, p. 71.

CHAPTER 6

1. CBC, "U.S. Threatening to Double Softwood Lumber Tariffs," at www.edmonton.cbc.ca/regional/servlet/View?filename=ca_softwood20030130.

2. CBC, "Talks Urged to End Softwood Lumber Dispute," at www.cbc.ca/stories/2003/08/13/business/lumberreax_030813.

3. For a detailed welfare analysis of the effect of a tariff, see P. R. Krugman and M. Obstfeld, *International Economics: Theory and Policy* (New York: Harper Collins, 2000), chap. 8.

4. Y. Sazanami, S. Urata, and H. Kawai, *Measuring the Costs of Protection in Japan* (Washington, DC: Institute for International Economics, 1994).

5. J. Bhagwati, *Protectionism* (Cambridge, MA: MIT Press, 1988), and "Costs of Protection," *Journal of Commerce*, September 25, 1991, p. 8A.

6. "A Not So Perfect Market," *The Economist: Survey of Agriculture and Technology*, March 25, 2000, pp. 8–10.

7. "From the Sublime to the Subsidy," *The Economist*, February 24, 1990, p. 71.

8. The study was undertaken by Kym Anderson of the University of Adelaide. See "A Not So Perfect Market."

9. R. W. Crandall, *Regulating the Automobile* (Washington, DC: Brookings Institute, 1986).

10. Quoted in Krugman and Obstfeld, *International Economics*.

11. G. Hufbauer and K. A. Elliott, *Measuring the Costs of Protectionism in the United States* (Washington, DC: Institute for International Economics, 1993).

12. A. Tanzer, "The Great Quota Hustle," *Forbes*, March 6, 2000, pp. 119–25.

13. Bhagwati, Protectionism, and "Japan to Curb VCR Exports," *New York Times*, November 21, 1983, p. D5.

14. Alan Goldstein, "Sematech Members Facing Dues Increase; 30% Jump to Make Up for Loss of Federal Funding," *Dallas Morning News*, July 27, 1996, p. 2F.

15. N. Dunne and R. Waters, "US Waves a Big Stick at Chinese Pirates," *Financial Times*, January 6, 1995, p. 4.

16. CBC, "The Breakdown of Government Protection," at www.cbc.ca/consumers/market/mp30/product_safety.html#.

17. Bill Lambrecht, "Monsanto Softens Its Stance on Labeling in Europe," *St. Louis Post-Dispatch*, March 15, 1998, p. E1.

18. Peter S. Jordan, "Country Sanctions and the International Business Community," *American Society of International Law Proceedings of the Annual Meeting* 20 no. 9 (1997), pp. 333–42.

19. "Waiting for China; Human Rights and International Trade," *Commonwealth*, March 11, 1994, and "China: The Cost of Putting Business First," *Human Rights Watch*, July 1996.

20. "Brazil's Auto Industry Struggles to Boost Global Competitiveness," *Journal of Commerce*, October 10, 1991, p. 6A.

21. For reviews, see J. A. Brander, "Rationales for Strategic Trade and Industrial Policy," in *Strategic Trade Policy and the New International Economics*, ed. P. R. Krugman (Cambridge, MA: MIT Press, 1986); P. R. Krugman, "Is Free Trade Passé?" *Journal of Economic Perspectives* 1 (1987), pp. 131–44; and P. R. Krugman, "Does the New Trade Theory Require a New Trade Policy?" *World Economy* 15, no. 4 (1992), pp. 423–41.

22. "Airbus and Boeing: The Jumbo War," *The Economist*, June 15, 1991, pp. 65–66.

23. For details see Krugman, *Is Free Trade Passé?* and Brander, "Rationales for Strategic Trade and Industrial Policy."

24. Krugman, "Is Free Trade Passé?"

25. This dilemma is a variant of the famous prisoner's dilemma, which has become a classic metaphor for the difficulty of achieving cooperation between self-interested and mutually suspicious entities. For a good general introduction, see A. Dixit and B. Nalebuff, *Thinking Strategically: The Competitive Edge in Business, Politics, and Everyday Life* (New York: W. W. Norton & Co., 1991).

26. Note that the Smoot-Hawley tariff did not cause the Great Depression. However, the beggar-thy-neighbour trade policies that it ushered in certainly made things worse. See Bhagwati, *Protectionism*.

27. Ibid.

28. World Bank, *World Development Report* (New York: Oxford University Press, 1987).

29. WTO, "Stronger than Expected Growth Spurs Modest Trade Recovery," at www.wto.org/english/news_e/pres04_e/pr373_e.htm.

30. Frances Williams, "WTO–New Name Heralds New Powers," *Financial Times*, December 16, 1993, p. 5, and Frances Williams, "GATT's Successor to Be Given Real Clout," *Financial Times*, April 4, 1994, p. 6.

31. Alan Cane, "Getting Through: Why Telecommunications Talks Matter," *Financial Times*, February 14, 1997.

32. Frances Williams, "Telecoms: World Pact Set to Slash Costs of Calls," *Financial Times*, February 17, 1997.

33. WTO press brief, Financial Services, September 1996.

34. G. De Jonquieres, "Happy End to a Cliff Hanger," *Financial Times*, December 15, 1997, p. 15.

35. "Overview of Developments in the International Trading Environment," Annual Report by the Director General (Geneva: World Trade Organization, 2001).

36. Ibid.

37. A. Tanzer, "Pill Factory to the World," *Forbes*, December 10, 2001, pp. 70–72.

38. W. Vieth, "Major Concessions Lead to Success for WTO Talks," *Los Angeles Times*, November 14, 2001, p. A1, and "Seeds Sown for Future Growth," *The Economist*, November 17, 2001, pp. 65–66.

CHAPTER 7

1. United Nations, *World Investment Report*, 2000 (New York and Geneva: United Nations, 2001).

2. UNCTAD, *World Investment Report, 2003 FDI Policies for Development: National and International Perspectives*, Chapter 1, p.17.

3. UNCTAD, *Development and Globalization: Facts and Figures United Nations Conference on Trade and Development*, 2004, p. 32.

4. UNCTAD, *World Investment Report, 2003 FDI Policies for Development: National and International Perspectives*, Chapter 1, p. 21.

5. CBC at www.cbc.ca/stories/2003/09/17/business/investment_030917.

6. *China Daily* at www2.chinadaily.com.cn/english/doc/2004-06/15/content_339450.htm.

7. Yahoo News, "China Leapfrogs U.S. to Claim Most FDI in 2003," at www.in.news.yahoo.com/040628/137/2eo34.html.

8. UNCTAD, *World Investment Report, 2003 FDI Policies for Development: National and International Perspectives*, Chapter 1, p. 23.

9. UNCTAD, *World Investment Report 2003 FDI Policies for Development: National and International Perspectives*, p. xiv.

10. Statistics Canada, "Economic Analysis and Forecasting," *EDC Economics*, August 2003, p.10.

11. See D. J. Ravenscraft and F. M. Scherer, *Mergers, Selloffs and Economic Efficiency* (Washington, DC: The Brookings Institution, 1987).

12. For example, see S. H. Hymer, *The International Operations of National Firms: A Study of Direct Foreign Investment* (Cambridge, MA: MIT Press, 1976); A. M. Rugman, *Inside the Multinationals: The Economics of Internal Markets* (New York: Columbia University Press, 1981), D. J. Teece, "Multinational Enterprise, Internal Governance, and Industrial Organization," *American Economic Review* 75 (May 1983), pp. 233–38; and C. W. L. Hill and W. C. Kim, "Searching for a Dynamic Theory of the Multinational Enterprise: A Transaction Cost Model," *Strategic Management Journal* 9 (special issue 1988), pp. 93–104.

13. J. P. Womack, D. T. Jones, and D. Roos, *The Machine that Changed the World* (New York: Rawson Associates, 1990).

14. The argument is most often associated with F. T. Knickerbocker, *Oligopolistic Reaction and Multinational Enterprise* (Boston: Harvard Business School Press, 1973).

15. R. E. Caves, *Multinational Enterprise and Economic Analysis* (Cambridge: Cambridge University Press, 1982).

16. See R. E. Caves, "Japanese Investment in the U.S.: Lessons for the Economic Analysis of Foreign Investment" *The World Economy* 16 (1993), pp. 279–300; B. Kogut and S. J. Chang, "Technological Capabilities and Japanese Direct Investment in the United States," *Review of Economics and Statistics* 73 (1991), pp. 401–43; and J. Anand and B. Kogut, "Technological Capabilities of Countries, Firm Rivalry, and Foreign Direct Investment," *Journal of International Business Studies*, Third Quarter 1997, pp. 445–65.

17. For the use of Vernon's theory to explain Japanese direct investment in the United States and Europe, see S. Thomsen, "Japanese Direct Investment in the European Community," *The World Economy* 16 (1993), pp. 301–15.

18. J. H. Dunning, *Explaining International Production* (London: Unwin Hyman, 1988).

19. P. Krugman, "Increasing Returns and Economic Geography," *Journal of Political Economy* 99, no. 3 (1991), pp. 483–99.

20. J. H. Dunning and R. Narula, "Transpacific Foreign Direct Investment and the Investment Development Path," *South Carolina Essays in International Business*, no. 10 (May 1995), CIBER: University of South Carolina.

21. W. Shan and J. Song, "Foreign Direct Investment and the Sourcing of Technological Advantage: Evidence from the Biotechnology Industry," *Journal of International Business Studies*, Second Quarter 1997, pp. 267–84.

22. For elaboration, see S. Hood and S. Young, *The Economics of the Multinational Enterprise* (London: Longman, 1979) and P. M. Sweezy and H. Magdoff, "The Dynamics of U.S. Capitalism," *New York: Monthly Review Press*, 1972.

23. UNCTAD, *World Investment Report 2003*, p. 21.

24. Government of Canada Competition Bureau at www.cb-bc.gc.ca/epic/internet/incb-bc.nsf/en/ct01737e.html.

25. CRTC at www.crtc.gc.ca/eng/NEWS/SPEECHES/2002/s021212.htm.

26. P. M. Romer, "The Origins of Endogenous Growth," *Journal of Economic Perspectives* 8, no. 1 (1994), pp. 3–22.

27. Wards Auto at www.subscribers.wardsauto.com/files/50/siteselection.pdf, pp. 6–7.

28. "Foreign Friends."

29. G. Hunya and K. Kalotay, *Privatization and Foreign Direct Investment in Eastern and Central Europe* (Geneva: UNCTAD, 2001).

30. P. R. Krugman and M. Obstfeld, *International Economics: Theory and Policy* (New York: Harper Collins, 1994), chap. 9. Also see, P. Krugman, *The Age of Diminished Expectations* (Cambridge, MA: MIT Press, 1990).

31. R. B. Reich, *The Work of Nations: Preparing Ourselves for the 21st Century* (New York: Alfred A. Knopf, 1991).

32. For a recent review, see John H. Dunning, "Re-evaluating the Benefits of Foreign Direct Investment," *Transnational Corporations* 3, no. 1 (February 1994), p. 23–51.

33. This idea has been articulated, although not quite in this form, by C. A. Bartlett and S. Ghoshal, *Managing across Borders: The Transnational Solution* (Boston: Harvard Business School Press, 1989).

34. P. Magnusson, "The Mexico Pact: Worth the Price?" *Business Week*, May 27, 1991, pp. 32–35.

35. C. Johnston, "Political Risk Insurance," in *Assessing Corporate Political Risk*, ed. D. M. Raddock (Totowa, NJ: Rowan & Littlefield, 1986).

36. J. Behrman and R. E. Grosse, *International Business and Government: Issues and Institutions* (Columbia: University of South Carolina Press, 1990).

37. G. De Jonquiers and S. Kuper, "Push to Keep Alive Effort to Draft Global Investment Rules," *Financial Times*, April 29, 1988, p. 5.

38. See Caves, *Multinational Enterprise and Economic Analysis.*

39. Tim Hortons at www.timhortons.com/english/english.html.

40. For a good general introduction to negotiation strategy, see M. H. Bazerman, *Negotiating Rationally* (New York: Free Press, 1999), A. Dixit and B. Nalebuff, *Thinking Strategically: The Competitive Edge in Business, Politics, and Everyday Life* (New York: W. W. Norton, 1991), and H. Raiffa, *The Art and Science of Negotiation* (Cambridge, MA: Harvard University Press, 1982).

CHAPTER 8

1. Information taken from World Trade Organization website as of July 2002, www.wto.org.

2. BBC News, "Q&A EU Enlargement," at www.news.bbc.co.uk/1/hi/world/europe/2266385.stm.

3. H. Smith, "France to Oppose Turkish EU Entry," The Guardian, April 8, 2004, www.guardian.co.uk/turkey/story/0,12700,1188109,00.html.

4. World Trade Organization, *Annual Report*, 2002 (WTO: Geneva, 2002).

5. The Andean Pact has been through a number of changes since its inception. The latest version was established in 1991. See "Free-Trade Free for All," *The Economist*, January 4, 1991, p. 63.

6. D. Swann, *The Economics of the Common Market*, 6th ed. (London: Penguin Books, 1990).

7. See J. Bhagwati, "Regionalism and Multilateralism: An Overview," Columbia University discussion paper 603, Department of Economics, Columbia University, New York; A. de la Torre and M. Kelly, "Regional Trade Arrangements," occasional paper 93, Washington, DC: International Monetary Fund, March 1992; and J. Bhagwati, "Fast Track to Nowhere," *The Economist*, October 18, 1997, pp. 21–24.

8. N. Colchester and D. Buchan, *Europower: The Essential Guide to Europe's Economic Transformation in 1992* (London: The Economist Books, 1990); and Swann, *The Economics of the Common Market.*

9. CBC News at www.cbc.ca/news/background/eu/.

10. Swann, *The Economics of the Common Market*; Colchester and Buchan, Europower; "The European Union: A Survey," *The Economist*, October 22, 1994; and "The European Community: A Survey," *The Economist*, July 3, 1993.

11. Department of Justice Canada at www.laws.justice.gc.ca/en/C-34/index.html.

12. EUROPA, "European Merger Control," at www.europa.eu.int/comm/competition/mergers/cases/stats.html.

13. "One Europe, One Economy," *The Economist*, November 30, 1991, pp. 53–54, and "Market Failure: A Survey of Business in Europe," *The Economist*, June 8, 1991, pp. 6–10.

14. See C. Wyploze, "EMU: Why and How It Might Happen," *Journal of Economic Perspectives* 11 (1997), pp. 3–22, and M. Feldstein, "The Political Economy of the European Economic and Monetary Union," *Journal of Economic Perspectives* 11 (1997), pp. 23–42.

15. "One Europe, One Economy," and Feldstein, "The Political Economy of the European Economic and Monetary Union."

16. Feldstein, "The Political Economy of the European Economic and Monetary Union."

17. "The Confused Muddle," *The Economist*, December 11, 1999, pp. 44–45, and "Currency Crossroads," *The Economist*, December 4, 1999, pp. 17–18.

18. International Monetary Funds, *World Economic Outlook*, October 2000.

19. "The Darling Dollar," *The Economist*, April 7, 2001.

20. "What Are They Building? Survey of Europe's Internal Market," *The Economist*, July 8, 1989, pp. 5–7, and Colchester and Buchan, *Europower.*

21. EU, " European International Transactions," *Luxembourg Office for Official Publications of the European Communities*, 2003, p. 14.

22. World Trade Organization, *Regionalism and the World Trading System* (Geneva: World Trade Organization, 1995).

23. "What Is NAFTA?" *Financial Times*, November 17, 1993, p. 6, and S. Garland, "Sweet Victory," *Business Week*, November 29, 1993, pp. 30–31.

24. J. Berger, "Canada and Mexico Improving Economies on Both Sides of U.S. Border," at www.bizsites.com/2004/july/article.asp?id=683.

25. Statistics Canada, CANSIM tables 282-0069 and 282-0073.

26. "NAFTA: The Showdown," *The Economist*, November 13, 1993, pp. 23–36.

27. "Happy Ever NAFTA?" *The Economist*, December 10, 1994, pp. 23–24, and D. Harbrecht, "What Has NAFTA Wrought? Plenty of Trade?" *Business Week*, November 21, 1994, pp. 48–49.

28. P. B. Carroll and C. Torres, "Mexico Unveils Program of Harsh Fiscal Medicine," *Wall Street Journal*, March 3, 1995, pp. A1, A6.

29. N. C. Lustog, "NAFTA: Setting the Record Straight," *The World Economy*, 1997, pp. 605–14.

30. R. H. Ojeda, C. Dowds, R. McCleery, S. Robinson, D. Runsten, C. Wolff, and G. Wolff, "NAFTA–How Has It Done? North American Integration Three Years after NAFTA," North American Integration and Development Center at UCLA, December 1996.

31. "NAFTA Is Not Alone," *The Economist*, June 18, 1994, pp. 47–48; B. Sweeney, "First Latin American Customs Union Looms over Venezuela," *Journal of Commerce*, September 26, 1991, p. 5A; and "The Business of the American Hemisphere," *The Economist*, August 24, 1991, pp. 37–38.

32. The comment was made by the Colombian ambassador. See K. G. Hall, "Andean Pact Nations to Work Together at Talks," *Journal of Commerce*, April 8, 1998, p. 2A.

33. "Business of the American Hemisphere."

34. "NAFTA Is Not Alone."

35. "Murky MERCOSUR," *The Economist*, July 26, 1997, pp. 66–67.

36. See M. Philips, "South American Trade Pact Under Fire," *Wall Street Journal*, October 23, 1996, p. A2; A. J. Yeats, *Does MERCOSUR's Trade Performance Justify Concerns about the Global Welfare-Reducing Effects of Free Trade Arrangements? Yes!* (Washington, DC: World Bank, 1996); and D. M. Leipziger et al., "MERCOSUR: Integration and Industrial Policy," *The World Economy*, 1997, pp. 585–604.

37. "Another Blow to MERCOSUR," *The Economist*, March 31, 2001, pp. 33–34.

38. "Aimless in Seattle," *The Economist*, November 13, 1993, pp. 35–36.

39. G. de Jonquieres, "Different Aims, Common Cause," *Financial Times*, November 18, 1995, p. 14.

40. G. de Jonquieres, "APEC Grapples with Market Turmoil," *Financial Times*, November 21, 1997, p. 6, and G. Baker, "Clinton Team Wins Most of the APEC Tricks," *Financial Times*, November 27, 1997, p. 5.

41. M. Turner, "Trio Revives East African Union," *Financial Times*, January 16, 2001, p. 4.

42. "World Economic Survey," *The Economist*, September 19, 1992, p. 17.

43. 3M Canada, "The 3M Canada Story," at www.cms.3m.com/cms/CA/en/1-30/criRRFI/view.jhtml.

44. Ibid.

45. P. Davis, "A European Campaign: Local Companies Rush for a Share of EC Market While Barriers Are Down," *Minneapolis-St. Paul City Business*, January 8, 1990, p. 1.

46. "The Business of Europe," *The Economist*, December 7, 1991, pp. 63–64.

47. E. G. Friberg, "1992: Moves Europeans Are Making," *Harvard Business Review*, May–June 1989, pp. 85–89.

CHAPTER 9

1. For a good general introduction to the foreign exchange market, see R. Weisweiller, *How the Foreign Exchange Market Works* (New York: New York Institute of Finance, 1990). A detailed description of the economics of foreign exchange markets can be found in P. R. Krugman and M. Obstfeld, *International Economics: Theory and Policy* (New York: Harper-Collins, 1994).

2. XE.com at www.xe.com.

3. Photius, "Exports 2003," at www.photius.com/rankings/exports_2003_0.html.

4. Bank for International Settlements, *Central Bank Survey of Foreign Exchange and Derivatives Market Activity, April 2001* (Basle, Switzerland: BIS, 2002).

5. Ibid.

6. CRB, *CRB Commodity Yearbook*, 2004, pp. 40T.

7. For a comprehensive review, see M. Taylor, "The Economics of Exchange Rates," *Journal of Economic Literature* 33 (1995), pp. 13–47.

8. Krugman and Obstfeld, *International Economics.*

9. M. Friedman, *Studies in the Quantity Theory of Money* (Chicago: University of Chicago Press, 1956). For an accessible explanation, see M. Friedman and R. Friedman, *Free to Choose* (London: Penguin Books, 1979), chap. 9.

10. Juan-Antino Morales, "Inflation Stabilization in Bolivia," in *Inflation Stabilization: The Experience of Israel, Argentina, Brazil, Bolivia, and Mexico,* ed. Michael Bruno et al. (Cambridge, MA: MIT Press, 1988), and The Economist, *World Book of Vital Statistics* (New York: Random House, 1990).

11. For reviews and recent articles, see L. H. Officer, "The Purchasing Power Parity Theory of Exchange Rates: A Review Article," International Monetary Fund staff papers, March 1976, pp. 1–60; Taylor, "The Economics of Exchange Rates"; H. J. Edison, J. E. Gagnon, and W. R. Melick, "Understanding the Empirical Literature on Purchasing Power Parity," *Journal of International Money and Finance* 16 (February 1997), pp. 1–18; J. R. Edison, "Multi-Country Evidence on the Behavior of Purchasing Power Parity under the Current Float," *Journal of International Money and Finance* 16 (February 1997), pp. 19–36; and K. Rogoff, "The Purchasing Power Parity Puzzle," *Journal of Economic Literature* 34 (1996), pp. 647–68.

12. M. Obstfeld and K. Rogoff, "The Six Major Puzzles in International Economics," *National Bureau of Economic Research* working paper 7777, July 2000.

13. Ibid.

14. See M. Devereux and C. Engel, "Monetary Policy in the Open Economy Revisited: Price Setting and Exchange Rate Flexibility," *National Bureau of Economic Research* working paper 7665, April 2000. Also P. Krugman, "Pricing to Market When the Exchange Rate Changes," in *Real Financial Economics*, ed. S. Arndt and J. Richardson (Cambridge, MA: MIT Press).

15. For a summary of the evidence, see the survey by Taylor, "The Economics of Exchange Rates."

16. R. E. Cumby and M. Obstfeld, "A Note on Exchange Rate Expectations and Nominal Interest Differentials: A Test of the Fisher Hypothesis," *Journal of Finance*, June 1981, pp. 697–703.

17. Taylor, "The Economics of Exchange Rates."

18. See H. L. Allen and M. P. Taylor, "Charts, Noise, and Fundamentals in the Foreign Exchange Market," *Economic Journal* 100 (1990), pp. 49–59, and T. Ito, "Foreign Exchange Rate Expectations: Micro Survey Data," *American Economic Review* 80 (1990), pp. 434–49.

19. For example, see E. Fama, "Forward Rates as Predictors of Future Spot Rates," *Journal of Financial Economics*, October 1976, pp. 361–77.

20. R. M. Levich, "The Efficiency of Markets for Foreign Exchange," in *International Finance*, ed. G. D. Gay and R. W. Kold (Richmond, VA: Robert F. Dane, Inc., 1983).

21. J. Williamson, *The Exchange Rate System* (Washington, DC: Institute for International Economics, 1983).

22. R. M. Levich, "Currency Forecasters Lose Their Way," *Euromoney*, August 1983, p. 140.

23. Rogoff, "The Purchasing Power Parity Puzzle."

24. C. Engel and J. D. Hamilton, "Long Swings in the Dollar: Are They in the Data and Do Markets Know It?" *American Economic Review*, September 1990, pp. 689–713.

25. J. R. Carter and J. Gagne, "The Do's and Don'ts of International Countertrade," *Sloan Management Review*, Spring 1988, pp. 31–37.

26. D. S. Levine, "Got a Spare Destroyer Lying Around?" *World Trade* 10 (June 1997), pp. 34–35, and Dan West, "Countertrade," *Business Credit*, April 2001, pp. 64–67.

CHAPTER 10

1. The argument goes back to 18th century philosopher David Hume. See D. Hume, "On the Balance of Trade," reprinted in *The Gold Standard in Theory and in History*, ed. B. Eichengreen (London: Methuen, 1985).

2. J. Powell, *A History of the Canadian Dollar*, (Ottawa: Bank of Canada, nd) p. 14.

3. Ibid., p.18.

4. Ibid., p. 23.

5. Ibid., p. 25.

6. R. Solomon, *The International Monetary System*, 1945–1981 (New York: Harper & Row, 1982).

7. International Monetary Fund, *World Economic Outlook*, 1998 (Washington, DC: IMF, May 1998).

8. For a feel for the issues contained in this debate, see P. Krugman, *Has the Adjustment Process Worked?* (Washington, DC: Institute for International Economics, 1991); "Time to Tether Currencies," *The Economist*, January 6, 1990, pp. 15–16; P. R. Krugman and M. Obstfeld, *International Economics: Theory and Policy* (New York: Harper Collins, 1994); J. Shelton, Money Meltdown (New York: Free Press, 1994); and S. Edwards, "Exchange Rates and the Political Economy of Macroeconomic Discipline," *American Economic Review* 86, no. 2 (May 1996), pp. 159–63.

9. The argument is made by several prominent economists, particularly Stanford's Robert McKinnon. See R. McKinnon, "An International Standard for Monetary Stabilization," *Policy Analyses in International Economics* 8 (1984). The details of this argument are beyond the scope of this book. For a relatively accessible exposition, see P. Krugman, *The Age of Diminished Expectations* (Cambridge, MA: MIT Press, 1990).

10. A. R. Ghosh and A. M. Gulde, "Does the Exchange Rate Regime Matter for Inflation and Growth?" *Economic Issues*, no. 2, (1997).

11. "The ABC of Currency Boards," *The Economist*, November 1, 1997, p. 80.

12. International Monetary Fund, *World Economic Outlook*, 1998.

13. Ibid.

14. For a summary of the arguments for debt reductions, see "And Forgive Us Our Debts: A Survey of the IMF and the World Bank," The Economist, October 12, 1991, pp. 23–33, and Krugman, *Age of Diminished Expectations.*

15. See P. Carroll and C. Torres, "Mexico Unveils Program of Harsh Fiscal Medicine," *Wall Street Journal*, March 10, 1995, pp. A1, A6, and "Putting Mexico Together Again," *The Economist*, February 4, 1995, p. 65.

16. S. Erlanger, "Russia Will Test a Trading Band for the Ruble," New York Times, July 7, 1995, p. 1; C. Freeland, "Russia to Introduce a Trading Band for Ruble against Dollar," *Financial Times*, July 7, 1995, p. 1; J. Thornhill, "Russians Bemused by 'Black Tuesday,'" *Financial Times*, October 12, 1994, p. 4; R. Sikorski, "Mirage of Numbers," *Wall Street Journal*, May 18, 1994, p. 14; "Can Russia Fight Back?" *The Economist*, June 6, 1998, pp. 47–48; and J. Thornhill, "Russia's Shrinking Options," *Financial Times*, August 19, 1998, p. 19.

17. World Trade Organization, *Annual Report*, 1997, vol. II, table III, p. 69.

18. World Bank, 1997 *World Development Report* (Oxford: Oxford University Press), Table 11.

19. Ridding and Kynge, "Complacency Gives Way to Contagion."

20. Burton and Baker, "The Country That Invested Its Way into Trouble."

21. World Bank, 1997 *World Development Report*, Table 2.

22. International Monetary Fund, press release no. 97/37, August 20, 1997.

23. T. S. Shorrock, "Korea Starts Overhaul; IMF Aid Hits $60 Billion," *Journal of Commerce*, December 8, 1997, p. 3A.

24. www.imf.org/external/np/exr/facts/glance.htm.

25. Sachs, "Power unto Itself."

26. S. Poloz, "EDC Economics Letter," *EDC*, September 2, 2004.

27. Martin Wolf, "Same Old IMF Medicine," *Financial Times*, December 9, 1997, p. 12.

28. Sachs, "Power unto Itself."

29. P. Gumbel and B. Coleman, "Daimler Warns of Severe 95 Loss Due to Strong Mark," *New York Times*, June 29, 1995, pp. 1, 10, and M. Wolf, "Daimler-Benz Announces Major Losses," *Financial Times*, June 29, 1995, p. 1.

CHAPTER 11

1. The concept of consumer surplus is an important one in economics. For a more detailed exposition, see D. Besanko, D. Dranove, and M. Shanley, *Economics of Strategy* (New York: John Wiley & Sons, 1996).

2. However, P-V only in the special case where the company has a perfect monopoly, and where it can charge each customer a unique price that reflects the value of the product to that customer (i.e., where perfect price discrimination is possible). More generally, except in the limiting case of perfect price discrimination, even a monopolist will see most consumers capture some of the value of a product in the form of a consumer surplus.

3. This point is central to the work of Michael Porter, *Competitive Advantage* (New York: Free Press, 1985). See also chap. 4 in P. Ghemawat, *Commitment: The Dynamic of Strategy* (New York: Free Press, 1991).

4. M. E. Porter, *Competitive Strategy* (New York: Free Press, 1980).

5. Porter, *Competitive Advantage.*

6. Canarm at http://www.canarm.com/about.html.

7. G. Hall and S. Howell, "The Experience Curve from an Economist's Perspective," *Strategic Management Journal* 6 (1985), pp. 197–212.

8. A. A. Alchain, "Reliability of Progress Curves in Airframe Production," *Econometrica* 31 (1963), pp. 693–697.

9. Hall and Howell, "The Experience Curve from an Economist's Perspective."

10. For a full discussion of the source of scale economies, see D. Besanko, D. Dranove, and M. Shanley, *Economics of Strategy* (New York: Wiley & Sons, 1996).

11. This estimate was provided by the Pharmaceutical Manufacturers Association.

12. "Matsushita Electrical Industrial in 1987," in *Transnational Management*, eds. C. A. Bartlett and S. Ghoshal (Homewood, IL: Richard D. Irwin, 1992).

13. This concept has been popularized by G. Hamel and C. K. Prahalad, *Competing for the Future* (Boston: Harvard Business School Press, 1994). The concept is grounded in the resource-based view of the firm. For a summary, see J. B. Barney, "Firm Resources and Sustained Competitive Advantage," *Journal of Management* 17 (1991), pp. 99–120, and K. R. Conner, "A Historical Comparison of Resource-Based Theory and Five Schools of Thought within Industrial Organization Economics: Do We Have a New Theory of the Firm?" *Journal of Management* 17 (1991), pp. 121–54.

14. J. P. Womack, D. T. Jones, and D. Roos, *The Machine that Changed the World* (New York: Rawson Associates, 1990).

15. "Canadian Tire Corp To Open Shanghai Office," *Taipei Times* at www.taipeitimes.com/News/biz/archives/2004/06/27/2003176753.

16. See J. Birkinshaw and N. Hood, "Multinational Subsidiary Evolution: Capability and Charter Change in Foreign-Owned Subsidiary Companies," *Academy of Management Review* 23 (October 1998), pp. 773–95, and A. K. Gupta and V. J. Govindarajan, "Knowledge Flows within Multinational Corporations," *Strategic Management Journal* 21 (2000), pp. 473–96.

17. K. Ferdows, "Making the Most of Foreign Factories," *Harvard Business Review*, March–April 1997, pp. 73–88.

18. C. K. Prahalad and Yves L. Doz, *The Multinational Mission: Balancing Local Demands and Global Vision* (New York: Free Press, 1987). Prahalad and Doz actually talk about local responsiveness rather than local customization.

19. "The Tire Industry's Costly Obsession with Size," *The Economist*, June 8, 1993, pp. 65–66.

20. T. Levitt, "The Globalization of Markets," *Harvard Business Review*, May–June 1983, pp. 92–102.

21. C. A. Bartlett and S. Ghoshal, *Managing across Borders* (Boston: Harvard Business School Press, 1989).

22. C. J. Chipello, "Local Presence Is Key to European Deals," *Wall Street Journal*, June 30, 1998, p. A15.

23. This section is based on Bartlett and Ghoshal, *Managing across Borders*.

24. Bartlett and Ghoshal, *Managing across Borders*.

25. A recent empirical study seems to confirm this hypothesis. See J. Birkinshaw, N. Hood, and S. Jonsson, "Building Firm-Specific Advantages in Multinational Corporations: The Role of Subsidiary Initiative," *Strategic Management Journal* 19 (1998), pp. 221–41.

26. See P. Marsh and S. Wagstyle, "The Hungry Caterpillar," *Financial Times*, December 2, 1997, p. 22, and T. Hout, M. E. Porter, and E. Rudden, "How Global Firms Win Out," *Harvard Business Review*, September–October 1982, pp. 98–108.

27. Guy de Jonquieres, "Unilever Adopts a Clean Sheet Approach," *Financial Times*, October 21, 1991, p. 13.

28. See K. Ohmae, "The Global Logic of Strategic Alliances," *Harvard Business Review*, March–April 1989, pp. 143–54; G. Hamel, Y. L. Doz, and C. K. Prahalad, "Collaborate with Your Competitors and Win!" *Harvard Business Review*, January–February 1989, pp. 133–39; W. Burgers, C. W. L. Hill, and W. C. Kim, "Alliances in the Global Auto Industry," *Strategic Management Journal* 14 (1993), pp. 419–32; and P. Kale, H. Singh, and H. Perlmutter, "Learning and Protection of Proprietary Assets in Strategic Alliances: Building Relational Capital," *Strategic Management Journal* 21 (2000), pp. 217–37.

29. Cinram at www.cinram.com/index.html.

30. "Asia Beckons," *The Economist*, May 30, 1992, pp. 63–64.

31. P. M. Reilly, "Sony's Digital Audio Format Pulls ahead of Philips's," *Wall Street Journal*, August 6, 1993, p. B1.

32. Kale, Singh, Perlmutter, "Learning and Protection of Proprietary Assets."

33. R. B. Reich and E. D. Mankin, "Joint Ventures with Japan Give Away Our Future," *Harvard Business Review*, March–April 1986, pp. 78–90.

34. J. Bleeke and D. Ernst, "The Way to Win in Cross-Border Alliances," *Harvard Business Review*, November–December 1991, pp. 127–35.

35. W. Roehl and J. F. Truitt, "Stormy Open Marriages Are Better," *Columbia Journal of World Business*, Summer 1987, pp. 87–95.

36. McQuade and Gomes-Casseres, "Xerox and Fuji-Xerox." HBC Case: Harvard Business School.

37. See T. Khanna, R. Gulati, and N. Nohria, "The Dynamics of Learning Alliances: Competition, Cooperation, and Relative Scope," *Strategic Management Journal* 19 (1998); pp. 193–210, and Kale, Singh, and Perlmutter, "Learning and Protection of Proprietary Assets."

38. Kale, Singh, and Perlmutter, "Learning and Protection of Proprietary Assets."

39. Hamel, Doz, and Prahalad, "Collaborate with Competitors," and Khanna, Gulati, and Nohria, "The Dynamics of Learning Alliances."

40. B. Wysocki, "Cross-Border Alliances Become Favorite Way to Crack New Markets," *Wall Street Journal*, March 4, 1990, p. A1.

41. Hamel, Doz, and Prahalad, "Collaborate with Competitors," p. 138.

CHAPTER 12

1. For interesting empirical studies that deal with the issues of timing and resource commitments, see T. Isobe, S. Makino, and D. B. Montgomery, "Resource Commitment, Entry Timing, and Market Performance of Foreign Direct Investments in Emerging Economies," *Academy of Management Journal* 43, no. 3, (2000), pp. 468–84, and Y. Pan and P. S. K. Chi, "Financial Performance and Survival of Multinational Corporations in China," *Strategic Management Journal* 20, no. 4, (1999), pp. 359–74.

2. This can be reconceptualized as the resource base of the entrant, relative to indigenous competitors. For work that focuses on this issue, see W. C. Bogenr, H. Thomas, and J. McGee, "A Longitudinal Study of the Competitive Positions and Entry Paths of European Firms in the U.S. Pharmaceutical Market," *Strategic Management Journal* 17 (1996), pp. 85–107; D. Collis, "A Resource-Based Analysis of Global Competition," *Strategic Management Journal* 12 (1991), pp. 49–68; and S. Tallman, "Strategic Management Models and Resource-Based Strategies among MNEs in a Host Market," *Strategic Management Journal* 12 (1991), pp. 69–82.

3. For a discussion of first-mover advantages, see M. Liberman and D. Montgomery, "First-Mover Advantages," *Strategic Management Journal* 9 (Summer Special Issue, 1988), pp. 41–58.

4. J. M. Shaver, W. Mitchell, and B. Yeung, "The Effect of Own Firm and Other Firm Experience on Foreign Direct Investment Survival in the United States, 1987–92," *Strategic Management Journal* 18 (1997), pp. 811–24.

5. S. Zaheer and E. Mosakowski, "The Dynamics of the Liability of Foreignness: A Global Study of Survival in the Financial Services Industry," *Strategic Management Journal* 18 (1997), pp. 439–64.

6. Shaver, Mitchell, and Yeung, "The Effect of Own Firm and Other Firm Experience on Foreign Direct Investment Survival in the United States."

7. P. Ghemawat, *Commitment: The Dynamics of Strategy* (New York: Free Press, 1991).

8. R. Luecke, *Scuttle Your Ships before Advancing* (Oxford: Oxford University Press, 1994).

9. Isobe, Makino, and Montgomery, "Resource Commitment, Entry Timing, and Market Performance," and Pan and Chi, "Financial Performance and Survival of Multinational Corporations in China."

10. Christopher Bartlett and Sumantra Ghoshal, "Going Global: Lessons from Late Movers," *Harvard Business Review*, March–April 2000, pp. 132–45.

11. This section draws on several studies, including C. W. L. Hill, P. Hwang, and W. C. Kim, "An Eclectic Theory of the Choice of International Entry Mode," *Strategic Management Journal* 11 (1990), pp. 117–28; C. W. L. Hill and W. C. Kim, "Searching for a Dynamic Theory of the Multinational Enterprise: A Transaction Cost Model," *Strategic Management Journal* 9 (Special Issue on Strategy Content, 1988), pp. 93–104; E. Anderson and H. Gatignon, "Modes of Foreign Entry: A Transaction Cost Analysis and Propositions," *Journal of International Business Studies* 17 (1986), pp. 1–26; F. R. Root, *Entry Strategies for International Markets* (Lexington, MA: D. C. Heath, 1980); A. Madhok, "Cost, Value and Foreign Market Entry: The Transaction and the Firm," *Strategic Management Journal* 18 (1997), pp. 39–61; K. D. Brouthers and L. B. Brouthers, "Acquisition or Greenfield Start-up?" *Strategic Management Journal* 21, no. 1 (2000), pp. 89–97.

12. For a general discussion of licensing, see F. J. Contractor, "The Role of Licensing in International Strategy," *Columbia Journal of World Business*, Winter 1982, pp. 73–83.

13. See E. Terazono and C. Lorenz, "An Angry Young Warrior," *Financial Times*, September 19, 1994, p. 11, and K. McQuade and B. Gomes-Casseres, "Xerox and Fuji–Xerox," Harvard Business School Case #9-391-156.

14. O. E. Williamson, *The Economic Institutions of Capitalism* (New York: Free Press, 1985).

15. J. H. Dunning and M. McQueen, "The Eclectic Theory of International Production: A Case Study of the International Hotel Industry," *Managerial and Decision Economics* 2 (1981), pp. 197–210.

16. Andrew E. Serwer, "McDonald's Conquers the World," *Fortune*, October 17, 1994, pp. 103–16.

17. For an excellent review of the basic theoretical literature of joint ventures, see B. Kogut, "Joint Ventures: Theoretical and Empirical Perspectives," *Strategic Management Journal* 9 (1988), pp. 319–32. More recent studies include T. Chi, "Option to Acquire or Divest a Joint Venture," *Strategic Management Journal* 21, no. 6 (2000), pp. 665–88; H. Merchant and D. Schendel, "How Do International Joint Ventures Create Shareholder Value?" *Strategic Management Journal* 21, no. 7 (2000), pp. 723–37; and H. K. Steensma and M. A. Lyles, "Explaining IJV Survival in a Transitional Economy through Social Exchange and Knowledge Based Perspectives," *Strategic Management Journal* 21, no. 8 (2000), pp. 831–51.

18. D. G. Bradley, "Managing against Expropriation," *Harvard Business Review*, July–August 1977, pp. 78–90.

19. Speech given by Tony Kobayashi at the University of Washington Business School, October 1992.

20. A. C. Inkpen and P. W. Beamish, "Knowledge, Bargaining Power, and the Instability of International Joint Ventures," *Academy of Management Review* 22 (1997), pp. 177–202, and S. H. Park and G. R. Ungson, "The Effect of National Culture, Organizational Complementarity, and Economic Motivation on Joint Venture Dissolution," *Academy of Management Journal* 40 (1997), pp. 279–307.

21. Inkpen and Beamish, "Knowledge, Bargaining Power, and the Instability of International Joint Ventures."

22. See Brouthers and Brouthers, "Acquisition or Greenfield Start-up?" and J. F. Hennart and Y. R. Park, "Greenfield versus Acquisition: The Strategy of Japanese Investors in the United States," *Management Science*, 1993, pp. 1054–70.

23. This section draws on Hill, Hwang, and Kim, "An Eclectic Theory of the Choice of International Entry Mode."

24. C. W. L. Hill, "Strategies for Exploiting Technological Innovations: When and When Not to License," *Organization Science* 3 (1992), pp. 428–41.

25. United Nations, *World Investment Report, 2000: Cross-Border Mergers and Acquisitions and Development* (New York and Geneva: United Nations, 2000).

26. Ibid.

27. Ibid.

28. For evidence on acquisitions and performance, see R. E. Caves, "Mergers, Takeovers, and Economic Efficiency," *International Journal of Industrial Organization* 7 (1989), pp. 151–74; M. C. Jensen and R. S. Ruback, "The Market for Corporate Control: The Scientific Evidence," *Journal of Financial Economics* 11 (1983), pp. 5–50; R. Roll, "Empirical Evidence on Takeover Activity and Shareholder Wealth," in Knights, Raiders and Targets, ed. J. C. Coffee, L. Lowenstein, and S. Rose (Oxford: Oxford University Press, 1989); A. Schleifer and R. W. Vishny, "Takeovers in the 60s and 80s: Evidence and Implications," *Strategic Management Journal* 12 (Winter 1991) Special Issue, pp. 51–60; and T. H. Brush, "Predicted Changes in Operational Synergy and Post Acquisition Performance of Acquired Businesses," *Strategic Management Journal* 17 (1996), pp. 1–24.

29. J. Warner, J. Templeman, R. Horn, "The Case against Mergers," *Business Week*, October 30, 1995, pp. 122–34.

30. D. J. Ravenscraft and F. M. Scherer, *Mergers, Selloffs, and Economic Efficiency* (Washington, DC: Brookings Institution, 1987).

31. See P. Ghemawat and F. Ghadar, "The Dubious Logic of Global Mega-mergers," *Harvard Business Review*, July–August 2000, pp. 65–72.

32. R. Roll, "The Hubris Hypothesis of Corporate Takeovers," *Journal of Business* 59 (1986), pp. 197–216.

33. "Marital Problems," *The Economist*, October 14, 2000.

34. See J. P. Walsh, "Top Management Turnover Following Mergers and Acquisitions," *Strategic Management Journal* 9 (1988), pp. 173–83.

35. B. Vlasic and B. A. Stertz, *Taken for a Ride: How Daimler-Benz Drove off with Chrysler* (New York: Harper Collins, 2000).

36. See A. A. Cannella and D. C. Hambrick, "Executive Departure and Acquisition Performance," *Strategic Management Journal* 14 (1993), pp. 137–52.

37. P. Haspeslagh and D. Jemison, *Managing Acquisitions* (New York: Free Press, 1991).

38. Ibid.

39. McCain at www.mccain.com/MediaDesk/MediaReleases/HTMLView.asp?ID=39; K. McArthur, "McCain Set To Build Fry Plant in China in August," *The Globe and Mail*, July 24, 2004, p. B3, www.globetechnology.com/servlet/ArticleNews/TPStory/LAC/20040624/RMCCAIN24/TPTechInvestor.

CHAPTER 13

1. M. Dickerson and L. Romney, "US Exports Get a Big Boost from Small Firms," *Los Angeles Times*, November 17, 1999, p. 10.

2. W. J. Holstein, "Why Johann Can Export, but Johnny Can't," *Business Week*, November 4, 1991, pp. 64–65.

3. S. T. Cavusgil, "Global Dimensions of *Marketing*," in Marketing, ed. P. E. Murphy and B. M. Enis (Glenview, IL: Scott, Foresman, 1985), pp. 577–99.

4. S. M. Mehta, "Enterprise: Small Companies Look to Cultivate Foreign Business," *Wall Street Journal*, July 7, 1994, p. B2.

5. W. Pavord and R. Bogart, "The Dynamics of the Decision to Export," Akron B*usiness and Economic Review*, 1975, pp. 6–11.

6. W. J. Burpitt and D. A. Rondinelli, "Small Firms' Motivations for Exporting: To Earn and Learn?" *Journal of Small Business Management*, October 2000, pp. 1–14.

7. J. Norman, "Small Businesses Have Big Role in Export Field," *Orange Country Register*, April 27, 1998, p. D15.

8. A. O. Ogbuehi and T. A. Longfellow, "Perceptions of U.S. Manufacturing Companies Concerning Exporting," *Journal of Small Business Management*, October 1994, pp. 37–59.

9. R. W. Haigh, "Thinking of Exporting?" *Columbia Journal of World Business* 29 (December 1994), pp. 66–86.

10. F. Williams, "The Quest for More Efficient Commerce," *Financial Times*, October 13, 1994, p. 7.

11. See Burpitt and Rondinelli, "Small Firms' Motivations for Exporting," and C. S. Katsikeas, L. C. Leonidou, and N. A. Morgan, "Firm Level Export Performance Assessment," *Academy of Marketing Science* 28 (2000), pp. 493–511.

12. M. Y. Yoshino and T. B. Lifson, *The Invisible Link* (Cambridge, MA: MIT Press, 1986).

13. L. W. Tuller, *Going Global* (Homewood, IL: Business One-Irwin, 1991).

14. Haigh, "Thinking of Exporting?"

15. J. Francis and C. Collins-Dodd, "The Impact of Firms' Export Orientation on the Export Performance of High-Tech Small and Medium Sized Enterprises," *Journal of International Marketing* 8, no. 3 (2000), pp. 84–103.

16. Foreign Affairs Canada at www.dfait-maeci.gc.ca/.

17. *Exchange Agreements and Exchange Restrictions* (Washington, DC: International Monetary Fund, 1989).

18. It's also sometimes argued that countertrade is a way of reducing the risks inherent in a traditional money-for-goods transaction, particularly with entities from emerging economies. See C. J. Choi, S. H. Lee, and J. B. Kim, "A Note of Countertrade: Contractual Uncertainty and Transactional Governance in Emerging Economies," *Journal of International Business Studies* 30, no. 1 (1999), pp. 189–202.

19. J. R. Carter and J. Gagne, "The Do's and Don'ts of International Countertrade," *Sloan Management Review*, Spring 1988, pp. 31–37, and W. Maneerungsee, "Countertrade: Farm Goods Swapped for Italian Electricity," *Bangkok Post*, July 23, 1998.

20. Estimate from the American Countertrade Association at http://freedonia.tpusa.com/infosrc/aca/. See also D. West, "Countertrade," *Business Credit* 104, no. 4 (2001), pp. 64–67.

21. Carter and Gagne, "The Do's and Don'ts of International Countertrade."

22. Maneerungsee, "Countertrade: Farm Goods Swapped for Italian Electricity."

23. For details, see Carter and Gagne, "Do's and Don'ts"; J. F. Hennart, "Some Empirical Dimensions of Countertrade," *Journal of International Business Studies*, 1990, pp. 240–60; and West, "Countertrade."

24. D. J. Lecraw, "The Management of Countertrade: Factors Influencing Success," *Journal of International Business Studies*, Spring 1989, pp. 41–59.

CHAPTER 14

1. See R. W. Ruekert and O. C. Walker, "Interactions between Marketing and R&D Departments in Implementing Different Business-Level Strategies," *Strategic Management Journal* 8 (1987), pp. 233–48, and K. B. Clark and S. C. Wheelwright, *Managing New Product and Process Development* (New York: Free Press), 1993.

2. T. Levitt, "The Globalization of Markets," *Harvard Business Review*, May–June 1983, pp. 92–102. Reprinted by permission of *Harvard Business Review*, an exerpt from "The Globalization of Markets," by Theodore Levitt, May–June 1983. Copyright © 1983 by the President and Fellows of Harvard College. All rights reserved.

3. For example, see S. P. Douglas and Y. Wind, "The Myth of Globalization," *Columbia Journal of World Business*, Winter 1987, pp. 19–29, and C. A. Bartlett and S. Ghoshal, *Managing across Borders: The Transnational Solution* (Boston: Harvard Business School Press, 1989).

4. "Slow Food," *The Economist*, February 3, 1990, p. 64.

5. J. T. Landry, "Emerging Markets: Are Chinese Consumers Coming of Age?" *Harvard Business Review*, May–June 1998, pp. 17–20.

6. C. Miller, "Teens Seen as the First Truly Global Consumers," *Marketing News*, March 27, 1995, p. 9.

7. This approach was originally developed in K. Lancaster, "A New Approach to Demand Theory," *Journal of Political Economy* 74 (1965), pp. 132–57.

8. V. R. Alden, "Who Says You Can't Crack Japanese Markets?" *Harvard Business Review*, January–February 1987, pp. 52–56.

9. T. Parker-Pope, "Custom Made," *Wall Street Journal*, September 26, 1996, p. 22.

10. A. Rawthorn, "A Bumpy Ride over Europe's Traditions," *Financial Times*, October 31, 1988, p. 5.

11. "RCA's New Vista: The Bottom Line," *Business Week*, July 4, 1987, p. 44.

12. N. Gross and K. Rebello, "Apple? Japan Can't Say No," *Business Week*, June 29, 1992, pp. 32–33.

13. "After Early Stumbles P&G Is Making Inroads Overseas," *Wall Street Journal*, February 6, 1989, p. B1.

14. Z. Gurhan-Cvanli and D. Maheswaran, "Cultural Variation in Country of Origin Effects," *Journal of Marketing Research*, August 2000, pp. 309–17.

15. See M. Laroche, V. H. Kirpalani, F. Pons, and L. Zhou, "A Model of Advertising Standardization in Multinational Corporations," *Journal of International Business Studies*, 32 (2001), pp. 249–66, and D. A. Aaker and E. Joachimsthaler, "The Lure of Global Branding," *Harvard Business Review*, November–December 1999, pp. 137–44.

16. "Advertising in a Single Market," *The Economist*, March 24, 1990, p. 64.

17. D. Waller, "Charged up over Competition Law," *Financial Times*, June 23, 1994, p. 14.

18. J. Lumbin, "Advertising: Tina Turner Helps Pepsi's Global Effort," *New York Times*, March 10, 1986, p. D13.

19. R. J. Dolan and H. Simon, *Power Pricing* (New York: Free Press, 1999).

20. B. Stottinger, "Strategic Export Pricing: A Long Winding Road," *Journal of International Marketing* 9, (2001), pp. 40–63.

21. These allegations were made on a PBS "Frontline" documentary telecast in the United States in May 1992.

22. G. Smith and B. Wolverton, "A Dark Moment for Kodak," *Business Week*, August 4, 1997, pp. 30–31.

23. R. Narisette and J. Friedland, "Disposable Income: Diaper Wars of P&G and Kimberly-Clark Now Heat up in Brazil," *Wall Street Journal*, June 4, 1997, p. A1.

24. "Printers Reflect Pattern of Trade Rows," *Financial Times*, December 20, 1988, p. 3.

25. J. F. Pickering, *Industrial Structure and Market Conduct* (London: Martin Robertson, 1974).

26. S. P. Douglas, C. Samuel Craig, and E. J. Nijissen. "Integrating Branding Strategy across Markets," *Journal of International Marketing* 9, no 2, (2001), pp. 97–114.

27. The phrase was first used by economist Joseph Schumpeter in Capitalism, *Socialism, and Democracy* (New York: Harper Brothers, 1942).

28. See D. C. Mowery and N. Rosenberg, *Technology and the Pursuit of Economic Growth* (Cambridge, UK: Cambridge University Press, 1989), and M. E. Porter, *The Competitive Advantage of Nations* (New York: The Free Press, 1990).

29. C. Farrell, "Industrial Policy," *Business Week*, April 6, 1992, pp. 70–75.

30. W. Kuemmerle, "Building Effective R&D Capabilities Abroad," *Harvard Business Review*, March–April 1997, pp. 61–70.

31. "When the Corporate Lab Goes to Japan," *New York Times*, April 28, 1991, sec. 3, p. 1.

32. D. Shapley, "Globalization Prompts Exodus," *Financial Times*, March 17, 1994, p. 10.

33. E. Mansfield, "How Economists See R&D," *Harvard Business Review*, November–December, 1981, pp. 98–106.

34. Ibid.

35. Booz, Allen, & Hamilton, "New Products Management for the 1980s," privately published research report, 1982.

36. A. L. Page, "PDMA's New Product Development Practices Survey: Performance and Best Practices," PDMA 15th Annual International Conference, Boston, October 16, 1991.

37. K. B. Clark and S. C. Wheelwright, *Managing New Product and Process Development* (New York: Free Press, 1993), and M. A. Shilling and C. W. L. Hill, "Managing the New Product Development Process," *Academy of Management Executive* 12, no. 3 (1998), pp. 67–81.

38. O. Port, "Moving Past the Assembly Line," *Business Week Special Issue: Reinventing America*, 1992, pp. 177–80.

39. K. B. Clark and T. Fujimoto, "The Power of Product Integrity," *Harvard Business Review*, November–December 1990, pp. 107–18; Clark and Wheelwright, *Managing New Product and Process Development*; S. L. Brown and K. M. Eisenhardt, "Product Development: Past Research, Present Findings, and Future Directions," *Academy of Management Review* 20 (1995), pp. 348–78; and G. Stalk and T. M. Hout, *Competing against Time* (New York: Free Press, 1990).

40. Shilling and Hill, "Managing the New Product Development Process."

41. C. Christensen, "Quantum Corporation-Business and Product Teams," *Harvard Business School* Case # 9-692-023.

42. R. Nobel and J. Birkinshaw, "Innovation in Multinational Corporations: Control and Communication Patterns in International R&D Operations," *Strategic Management Journal* 19 (1998), pp. 479–96.

43. Information comes from the company's website, and from K. Ferdows, "Making the Most of Foreign Factories," *Harvard Business Review*, March–April 1997, pp. 73–88.

CHAPTER 15

1. B. C. Arntzen, G. G. Brown, T. P. Harrison, and L. L. Trafton, "Global Supply Chain Management at Digital Equipment Corporation," *Interfaces* 25 (1995), pp. 69–93.

2. D. A. Garvin, "What Does Product Quality Really Mean," *Sloan Management Review* 26 (Fall 1984), pp. 25–44.

3. For general background information, see "How to Build Quality," *The Economist*, September 23, 1989, pp. 91–92; A. Gabor, *The Man Who Discovered Quality* (New York: Penguin, 1990); and P. B. Crosby, *Quality Is Free* (New York: Mentor, 1980).

4. M. Saunders, "U.S. Firms Doing Business in Europe Have Options in Registering for ISO 9000 Quality Standards," *Business America*, June 14, 1993, p. 7.

5. G. Stalk and T. M. Hout, *Competing Against Time* (New York: Free Press, 1990).

6. M. A. Cohen and H. L. Lee, "Resource Deployment Analysis of Global Manufacturing and Distribution Networks," *Journal of Manufacturing and Operations Management* 2 (1989), pp. 81–104.

7. P. Krugman, "Increasing Returns and Economic Geography," *Journal of Political Economy* 99, no. 3 (1991), pp. 483–99, and J. M. Shaver and F. Flyer, "Agglomeration Economies, Firm Heterogeneity, and Foreign Direct Investment in the United States," *Strategic Management Journal* 21 (2000), pp. 1175–93.

8. For a review of the technical arguments, see D. A. Hay and D. J. Morris, *Industrial Economics: Theory and Evidence* (Oxford: Oxford University Press, 1979). See also C. W. L. Hill and G. R. Jones, *Strategic Management: An Integrated Approach* (Boston: Houghton Mifflin, 1995).

9. See P. Nemetz and L. Fry, "Flexible Manufacturing Organizations: Implications for Strategy Formulation," *Academy of Management Review* 13 (1988), pp. 627–38; N. Greenwood, *Implementing Flexible Manufacturing Systems* (New York: Halstead Press, 1986); J. P. Womack, D. T. Jones, and D. Roos, *The Machine That Changed the World* (New York: Rawson Associates, 1990); and R. Parthasarthy and S. P. Seith, "The Impact of Flexible Automation on Business Strategy and Organizational Structure," *Academy of Management Review* 17 (1992), pp. 86–111.

10. B. J. Pine, *Mass Customization: The New Frontier in Business Competition* (Boston: Harvard Business School Press, 1993); S. Kotha, "Mass Customization: Implementing the Emerging Paradigm for Competitive Advantage," *Strategic Management Journal* 16 (1995), pp. 21–42; and J. H. Gilmore and B. J. Pine II, "The Four Faces of Mass Customization," *Harvard Business Review*, January–February 1997, pp. 91–101.

11. M. A. Cusumano, *The Japanese Automobile Industry* (Cambridge, MA: Harvard University Press, 1989); T. Ohno, *Toyota Production System* (Cambridge, MA: Productivity Press, 1990); and Womack, Jones, and Roos, *The Machine That Changed the World.*

12. Industry Canada Web site, "Avcorp," http://strategis.ic.gc.ca/ccc/search/navigate.do?language=eng&portal=1&estblmntNo=123456165234&profile=completeProfile.

13. "The Celling Out of America," *The Economist*, December 17, 1994, pp. 63–64.

14. K. Ferdows, "Making the Most of Foreign Factories," *Harvard Business Review*, March–April 1997, pp. 73–88.

15. This argument represents a simple extension of the dynamic capabilities research stream in the strategic management literature. See D. J. Teece, G. Pisano, and A. Shuen, "Dynamic Capabilities and Strategic Management," *Strategic Management Journal* 18 (1997), pp. 509–33.

16. The material in this section is based primarily on the transaction cost literature of vertical integration; for example, O. E. Williamson, *The Economic Institutions of Capitalism* (New York: The Free Press, 1985).

17. For a review of the evidence, see Williamson, *The Economic Institutions of Capitalism.*

18. A. D. Chandler, *The Visible Hand* (Cambridge, MA: Harvard University Press, 1977).

19. For a review of these arguments, see C. W. L. Hill and R. E. Hoskisson, "Strategy and Structure in the Multiproduct Firm," *Academy of Management Review* 12 (1987), pp. 331–41.

20. See R. Narasimhan and J. R. Carter, "Organization, Communication and Coordination of International Sourcing," *International Marketing Review* 7 (1990), pp. 6–20, and Arntzen, Brown, Harrison, and Trafton, "Global Supply Chain Management at Digital Equipment Corporation."

21. H. F. Busch, "Integrated Materials Management," IJPD & MM 18 (1990), pp. 28–39.

CHAPTER 16

1. P. J. Dowling and R. S. Schuler, *International Dimensions of Human Resource Management* (Boston: PSW-Kent, 1990).

2. J. Millman, M. A. von Glinow, and M. Nathan, "Organizational Life Cycles and Strategic International Human Resource Management in Multinational Companies," *Academy of Management Review* 16 (1991), pp. 318–39.

3. E. H. Schein, *Organizational Culture and Leadership* (San Francisco: Jossey-Bass, 1985).

4. H. V. Perlmutter, "The Tortuous Evolution of the Multinational Corporation," *Columbia Journal of World Business* 4 (1969), pp. 9–18; D. A. Heenan and H. V. *Perlmutter, Multinational Organizational Development* (Reading, MA: Addison-Wesley, 1979); and D. A. Ondrack, "International Human Resources Management in European and North American Firms," *International Studies of Management and Organization* 15 (1985), pp. 6–32.

5. V. Reitman and M. Schuman, "Men's Club: Japanese and Korean Companies Rarely Look Outside for People to Run Their Overseas Operations," *Wall Street Journal*, September 26, 1996, p. 17.

6. S. Beechler and J. Z. Yang, "The Transfer of Japanese Style Management to American Subsidiaries," *Journal of International Business Studies* 25 (1994), pp. 467–91.

7. M. Banai and L. M. Sama, "Ethical Dilemma in MNCs' International Staffing Policies," *Journal of Business Ethics*, June 2000, pp. 221–35.

8. Reitman and Schuman, "Men's Club: Japanese and Korean Companies Rarely Look Outside for People to Run Their Overseas Operations."

9. Employment Equity Act at www.laws.justice.gc.ca/en/E-5.401/50057.html#rid-50066.

10. S. J. Kobrin, "Geocentric Mindset and Multinational Strategy," *Journal of International Business Studies* 25 (1994), pp. 493–511.

11. P. M. Rosenzweig and N. Nohria, "Influences on Human Resource Management Practices in Multinational Corporations," *Journal of International Business Studies* 25 (1994), pp. 229–51.

12. Kobrin, "Geocentric Mindset and Multinational Strategy."

13. M. Harvey and H. Fung, "Inpatriate Managers: The Need for Realistic Relocation Reviews," *International Journal of Management* 17 (2000), pp. 151–59.

14. S. Black, M. Mendenhall, and G. Oddou, "Towards a Comprehensive Model of International Adjustment," *Academy of Management Review* 16 (1991), pp. 291–317, and J. Shay and T. J. Bruce, "Expatriate Managers," *Cornell Hotel & Restaurant Administration Quarterly*, February 1997, p. 30–40.

15. M. G. Harvey, "The Multinational Corporation's Expatriate Problem: An Application of Murphy's Law," *Business Horizons* 26 (1983), pp. 71–78.

16. Shay and Bruce, "Expatriate Managers." Also see J. S. Black and H. Gregersen, "The Right Way to Manage Expatriates," *Harvard Business Review*, March–April 1999, pp. 52–63.

17. S. Caudron, "Training Ensures Overseas Success," *Personnel Journal*, December 1991, p. 27.

18. Black, Mendenhall, and Oddou, "Towards a Comprehensive Model of International Adjustment."

19. R. L. Tung, "Selection and Training Procedures of U.S., European, and Japanese Multinationals," *California Management Review* 25 (1982), pp. 57–71.

20. C. M. Solomon, "Success Abroad Depends upon More Than Job Skills," *Personnel Journal*, April 1994, pp. 51–58.

21. C. M. Solomon, "Unhappy Trails," *Workforce*, August 2000, pp. 36–41.

22. Solomon, "Success Abroad Depends upon More Than Job Skills."

23. Solomon, "Unhappy Trails."

24. M. Harvey, "Addressing the Dual Career Expatriation Dilemma," *Human Resource Planning* 19, no. 4 (1996), pp. 18–32.

25. M. Mendenhall and G. Oddou, "The Dimensions of Expatriate Acculturation: A Review," *Academy of Management Review* 10 (1985), pp. 39–47.

26. I. Torbiorin, *Living Abroad: Personal Adjustment and Personnel Policy in the Overseas Setting* (New York: John Wiley & Sons, 1982).

27. R. L. Tung, "Selection and Training of Personnel for Overseas Assignments," *Columbia Journal of World Business* 16 (1981), pp. 68–78.

28. Solomon, "Success Abroad Depends upon More Than Job Skills."

29. S. Ronen, "Training and International Assignee," in *Training and Career Development*, ed. I. Goldstein (San Francisco: Jossey-Bass, 1985), and Tung, "Selection and Training of Personnel for Overseas Assignments."

30. Solomon, "Success Abroad Depends upon More Than Job Skills."

31. Harvey, "Addressing the Dual Career Expatriation Dilemma"; and J. W. Hunt, "The Perils of Foreign Postings for Two," *Financial Times*, May 6, 1998, p. 22.

32. C. M. Daily, S. T. Certo, and D. R. Dalton, "International Experience in the Executive Suite: A Path to Prosperity?" *Strategic Management Journal* 21 (2000), pp. 515–23.

33. Dowling and Schuler, *International Dimensions of Human Resource Management.*

34. Ibid.

35. G. Baliga and J. C. Baker, "Multinational Corporate Policies for Expatriate Managers: Selection, Training, and Evaluation," *Advanced Management Journal*, Autumn 1985, pp. 31–38.

36. C. Rapoport, "A tough Swede Invades the U.S.," *Fortune*, June 20, 1992, pp. 67–70.

37. J. C. Baker, "Foreign Language and Departure Training in U.S. Multinational Firms," *Personnel Administrator*, July 1984, pp. 68–70.

38. A 1997 study by the Conference Board looked at this in depth. For a summary, see L. Grant, "That Overseas Job Could Derail Your Career," *Fortune*, April 14, 1997, p. 166. Also see J. S. Black and H. Gregersen, "The Right Way to Manage Expatriates," *Harvard Business Review*, March–April 1999, pp. 52–63.

39. J. S. Black and M. E. Mendenhall, *Global Assignments: Successfully Expatriating and Repatriating International Managers* (San Francisco: Jossey-Bass, 1992).

40. Ibid.

41. Figures from the Conference Board study. For a summary, see Grant, "That Overseas Job Could Derail Your Career."

42. S. C. Schneider, "National v. Corporate Culture: Implications for Human Resource Management," *Human Resource Management* 27 (Summer 1988), pp. 231–46.

43. I. M. Manve and W. B. Stevenson, "Nationality, Cultural Distance and Expatriate Status," *Journal of International Business Studies* 32 (2001), pp. 285–303.

44. Bartlett and Ghoshal, *Managing across Borders.*

45. See G. Oddou and M. Mendenhall, "Expatriate Performance Appraisal: Problems and Solutions," in *International Human Resource*

Management, ed. Mendenhall and Oddou (Boston: PWS-Kent, 1991); Dowling and Schuler, International Dimensions; R. S. Schuler and G. W. Florkowski, "International Human Resource Management," in *Handbook for International Management Research*, ed. B. J. Punnett and O. Shenkar (Oxford: Blackwell, 1996); and K. Roth and S. O'Donnell, "Foreign Subsidiary Compensation Strategy: An Agency Theory Perspective," *Academy of Management Journal* 39, no. 3 (1996), pp. 678–703.

46. Oddou and Mendenhall, "Expatriate Performance Appraisal."

47. "Expatriates Often See Little Benefit to Careers in Foreign Stints, Indifference at Home," *Wall Street Journal*, December 11, 1989, p. B1.

48. Oddou and Mendenhall, "Expatriate Performance Appraisal;" and Schuler and Florkowski, "International Human Resource Management."

49. "Towers Perrin & Mercer examine pay levels and increases in 26 countries," *Ioma's Report on Salary Surveys*, January 2001, pp. 2–4.

50. R. C. Longworth, "US Executives Sit on Top of the World," *Chicago Tribune*, May 31, 1998, p. C1.

51. C. Reynolds, "Compensation of Overseas Personnel," in *Handbook of Human Resource Administration*, ed. J. J. Famularo (New York: McGraw-Hill, 1986).

52. M. Helms, "International Executive Compensation Practices," in *International Human Resource Management*, ed. M. Mendenhall and G. Oddou (Boston: PWS-Kent, 1991).

53. G. W. Latta, "Expatriate Incentives," *HR Focus* 75, no. 3 (March 1998), p. S3.

54. C. K. Prahalad and Y. L. Doz, *The Multinational Mission* (New York: The Free Press, 1987).

55. Ibid.

56. Schuler and Florkowski, "International Human Resource Management."

57. See J. P. Womack, D. T. Jones, and D. Roos, *The Machine that Changed the World* (New York: Rawson Associates, 1990).

NAME/COMPANY INDEX

A
Abacha, Sani, 56
ABB Group, 519
ABB SAE Sadelmi SpA, 441
Abbott Laboratories, 230*t*
ABN AMRO, 292, 293
ACCION International, 292, 293
Acres International Limited, 52–53, 131, 132
ACS, 485
Adidas-Salomon, 38
Adolph Coors Co., 232, 236*f*
Aetna Financial Services, 399
AGF, 259, 260
Ahold, 2, 3, 4
Air Canada, 86, 393
Air India, 444, 502
Air Touch Communications, 416
Air Wisconsin, 221
Airbus Industrie, 178, 179, 208, 209, 444
Aircatel, 230*t*
Alcoa, 230*t*
Alfa Group, 52
Allianz, 259, 260
Amerada Hess Corporation, 230*t*
American Consumers for Affordable Homes, 196
American Express, 375, 468–469, 475
American Futures Exchange, 304
American United Steelworkers, 130
Amgen, 410
Amnesty International, 123
Amstrad, 379
Anderson, David, 122
Anderson, Ray, 533–534
AOL Time Warner, 388
Apple Computer, 186, 187, 240, 303, 462, 463, 477, 502
Applied Materials, 310
Arcand, Denys, 345
Aristotle, 45
Armed Forces, 133
Asarco, 130
Asda, 2
Asner, Ed, 345
Assemble Conferencing, 404
Association of Russian Banks, 347
AT Kearney, 229
AT&T, 389, 409
Aung San Suu Kyi, 129
Avcorp Industries Inc., 493
Axa, 259, 260

B
Baker, J.C., 520
Bam, Zalisiwonga, 52–53, 132
Banco ABN AMRO Real, 292
Bank 24, 290
Bank of Montreal, 424, 425
Barings, 399
Barlow, Maude, 28, 30–31, 268
Barrick Gold, 298, 300
Bartlett, Christopher, 379, 386, 387, 406
Batignolles, Spie, 132
Baultar, Inc., 268
Bavaria Brewery, 393
BBC, 126
B.C. Hydro, 158
BDC Tourism Investment Fund, 433
Bell, Alexander Graham, 122
Bell Canada Enterprises, 229, 230t, 405
Bell Laboratories, 409
Ben & Jerry's Homemade, 403
Benetton, 463
Bentham, Jeremy, 144
Berenz, Lori, 525
Bernard, Jean-Rene, 121
Binns, Pat, 383*f*
Black, Conrad, 139–140, 141
Blue View Nurseries, 501
BMO Financial Group, 425
BMW, 457, 464
Boeing, 8, 11, 166, 178, 179, 180, 207, 208, 209, 294, 389, 391, 412, 441, 444, 498, 502
Bombardier, 7, 8, 11, 23, 178, 179, 199, 221, 222, 380
Bon Appetit Group, 225
Bono, 32, 343*f*
Booz, Allen & Hamilton, 477
Boston Pizza, 410f
Bove, Jose, 27
BP, 134–135, 142–143, 144, 230t, 464
Brady, Nicholas, 343
Brampton Board of Trade (BBOT). *See* 3M Company
Bravado! Designs Inc., 24
Bristol-Myers Squibb, 477
British American Tobacco Plc, 230t
British Petroleum, 464
see also BP
British Telecom (BT), 73
Broadbent, Ed, 124
Brooks Pharmacy Network, 456
Brother Industries, 463
Brown, Robert, 447–448, 448
Bryce, Robert, 137, 139, 140
Bundesbank, 331
Burlington Industries, 266
Bush, George, 198, 466
Buss, Trevor, 113
Byers, 216

C
CAE Inc., 447–448
Calvert, Lorne, 383*f*
Cambridge Mercantile Corp., 320
Cambridge University, 95
Cameron, James, 345
Canada Hibernia Holding Corporation, 5
Canadian Armature Works, 370
Canadian Association of University Teachers, 522
Canadian Bankers Association, 328, 425
Canadian Evaluation Society, 124
Canadian Film Centre, 345
Canadian Imperial Bank of Commerce. *See* CIBC
Canadian Marketing Association, 149
Canadian Press, 127
Canadian Tire, 375
Canarm Ltd., 370, 371, 372
Canon, 502
Cargill Inc., 37
Caribbean Regional HRD Competitiveness Program, 501
Carlson Hospitality Group, 234
Carmanah Technologies Inc., 24
Carrefour, 2, 3, 4, 6, 7, 460
Caterpillar Inc., 7, 310, 317, 355, 358–359, 368, 386–387, 386*f*, 441, 459
CBC, 132, 153, 345
Celestica, 28, 482–483
Centre for Research and Information on Canada, 92
Chandler, Alfred, 179
Channel 1, 52
Chen, Steve, 231
Chevron Canada Resources, 5
Chicago Mercantile Exchange, 304
Chiquita Brands, 192
Chrètien, Jean, 55, 129, 132, 139, 383*f*
Christian Dior, 55
Chrysler Corporation, 355, 416, 418, 459
CIBC, 424, 433

Cinram, 388–389
Cinram UK Limited, 388
Cisco Systems, 64, 475, 482, 483
Citicorp, 7, 290, 375
Citigroup, 102
City Drug Chain, 456
Clearwater Seafoods, 200, 201
Clinton, Bill, 78
Clinton Cards, 17
CNN, 16, 125, 126, 454
Coca-Cola Bottling Company, 531–532
Coca-Cola Enterprises Inc., 5, 7, 58, 70, 78, 87, 230*t*, 364, 375, 379, 409, 454, 458, 468, 469*f*, 531–532
Coffee Partners, 226
Coles, Ashley, 426, 427
Colgate-Palmolive, 515*f*
Commonwealth Scientific and Industrial Research Organization (CSIRO), 507
Computer Associates, 189
Cone Mills, 266
Confucius, 104
Coors. *See* Adolph Coors Co.
Copps, Sheila, 345
Corning, 477
Cortès, Hernán, 406
Coumans, Catherine, 507
Coutu, Francois, 456
Coutu, Michel, 456
Crawfish Promotion and Research Board, 165
Credit Commercial de France, 400
Credit Suisse, 425
CRJ, 8
Cronenberg, David, 345
CRTC, 203
CryptoLogic Inc., 59
CSFBdirect, 425
Custom House, 320
CVS Corporation, 3

D

d'Acquino, Thomas, 522
Daewoo, 457*f*
Daimler-Benz, 355, 416, 418
DaimlerChrysler, 5, 355, 416, 418–419
Dalai Lama, 32
D'Alessandro, Dominic, 256
Dalfen, Charles, 242
Daly, Herman, 360
Danor Manufacturing Co. Ltd., 370
Dassault Aviation, 493
Debien, M.P.M., 124
DeHavilland, 180
Delaney, Stephen, 483
Dell Computer Corp., 64, 298, 489, 504, 522
Delors, Jacques, 272
Demers, Rock, 345
Deming, W. Edward, 488
Dentsu Inc., 452
Deutsche Bank, 290, 291
Deutsche Telekom AG, 230*t*, 416
Diana, Princess of Wales, 382
Diaz, Manuel, 27
Digital Equipment, 477
Disney. *See* Walt Disney Corporation
Distributing Centres B.V., 388
Doer, Gary, 383*f*
Dole Food Co., 192
Domi, Dash, 53
Donaldson, Thomas, 118
Doz, Yves, 392, 393, 527
Dresdner Bank, 290
Du Pont, 475, 477
Du Yu Zhou, 206
Duncan, Pat, 383*f*
Dunning, John, 239–240, 251
Duplication France, S.A., 388

E

East India Company, 134
Eckerd Group, 456
The Economist, 92, 306–307
Eggplant Interactive, 268
Egoyan, Atom, 345
E.I. du Pont, 266
El Cortes, 17
Eldorado, 463
Elliott, Kim, 197
Embraer, 7, 178, 179, 221, 222
EMI, 271
Enron Corp., 137–139, 139, 140, 141, 148
The Entertainment Network Ltd., 388
Environmental Tectonics Corp., 448
Equitable Life Insurance Company, 399
Ericsson LM, 183, 184, 230t, 379, 476, 520
Ernst & Young, 190
ESPN, 467
Eton, 95
Euro-Disneyland, 121
Excel Communications, 416
Exxon Mobil Canada, 5, 23
Exxonmobil Corporation, 230*t*

F

Fastow, Andrew, 139
Federal Express, 201
Federation of Portuguese Canadian Business 431. *See* 3M Company
Feigenbaum, A.V., 488
Felix, David, 360
Findus, 458
First National Bank of Joliet, 425
Fisher, Irvin, 311
Flextronics, 482
Fokker, 180
Ford Motor Company, 7, 12, 23, 230*t*, 247, 378, 392, 396, 416, 459, 470, 528
Ford of Europe, 498–499, 529
Forrester Research, 13
Four Seasons Hotel Budapest, 234, 411
Four Seasons Hotels and Resorts, 234
Fox Broadcasting Company, 17
Frankel, Jeffrey, 174
Fraser, Sheila, 132
Freedom House, 71
Freeport McMoran Copper and Gold, 300
Frefone, 404
Freston, Tom, 362
Friedman, Milton, 141–142
Frito-Lay, 458
Fruit of the Loom Inc., 266
Fuji Photo Film Co., 23, 236, 238, 239, 252, 388, 390, 392, 409, 412, 413, 473
Fujifilm, 202
Fukuyama, Francis, 69, 70

G

Gandhi, Mahatma, 103
Gap, 79
Gautama, Siddhartha, 103
Gendis, 525
General Electric, 230t, 317, 391, 441, 444, 512
General Motors, 12, 23, 106, 230t, 247, 378, 392–393, 503*f*, 528
General Motors Corporation of Canada, 396
Generali, 259, 260
Genesis Organic Inc., 383
Ghoshal, Sumantra, 379, 386, 387, 406
Giant, 4
Gilligan, Carol, 147
Globalive, 403, 404–405
Gomery, John H., 132
Graham, Bill, 129
Grameen Bank, 292
GreenBud Manufacturing Ltd., 28
Groening, Matt, 17
Grupo Mexico, 130
Gucci, 464, 484
Gymboree, 488*f*

H

Haagen Dazs, 403
Hagelstam, Jarl, 167
Hamburg-Mannheimer, 259
Hamel, Gary, 392, 393
Hamilton, Alexander, 206
Hamm, John, 383*f*
Harris Bank, 425
Harvard Business Review, 453
Hawken, Paul, 533
Hawker Siddely, 180
HBO, 16
Heckscher, Eli, 163, 164, 166, 174, 175, 179, 181, 182, 185, 194
Heller, George, 206
Heritage Foundation, 71
Heublein, 429
Hewlett-Packard (HP), 15, 230*t*, 240, 376, 480, 482, 496, 518
High Liner Foods Inc., 201
Hilton, 411, 411*f*
Hilton Hotel Corp., 411
Hitachi, 114, 374, 386, 387
H.J. Heinz, 375
Hoffmann-LaRoche, 474
Hofstede, Geert, 88, 109–110, 111, 112
Holland, Robert, 403
Hollinger International, 140
Honda Motor Co., 198, 238, 243, 356, 464
Houghton Mifflin, 27
HSBC, 102
Hufbauer, Gary, 197
Human Rights Watch, 78
Hume, David, 45, 144, 167
Huntington, Samuel, 70, 90
Hurtig, Mel, 28
Husky Oil, 86
Hussein, Saddam, 205
Hyundai Electronics, 202
Hyundai Motor Co., 464

I

IBM, 58, 78, 109, 111, 186, 187, 189, 381, 390, 477, 482
IKEA, 381, 381*f*, 383, 384–385
Impregilo, 132
ING Direct, 400
ING Direct Canada, 400
ING Group, 398–400, 400, 401, 402, 403, 404, 405, 413, 416
Intel Corporation, 17, 204, 240, 374–375, 385, 475, 477
Interclear, 404
Interface, Inc., 533–534
Interfor, 466*f*
International Federation of the Phonographic Industry, 57
International Orientation Resources, 517, 518
International Paper Company, 230t
Ipsos Reid Group, 158
Isuzu, 247
Ivanhoe Mines, 129

J

Jackson, Craig, 287
Jackson, Michael, 362
Jakobek, Tom, 53
Jamieson, Don, 128
Japan Airlines (JAL), 294–295, 296, 302
Japanese Overseas Enterprise Association, 512
J.C. Penney, 456
Jean Coutu Group, 455, 456
The Jean Coutu Group USA Inc., 456
Jefferson, Thomas, 165
Jewison, Norman, 345
John Hancock Financial Services, 255–256
John Paul II, Pope, 32
Johnson, Lyndon, 331

Jones, Jim, 100
Jospin, Lionel, 27
Juliber, Lois D., 515*f*
Juran, Joseph, 488
JVC, 12, 389

K

Kahn, Joseph, 156
Kaiser Breweries, 393
Kamprad, Ingvar, 384
Kant, Immanuel, 145
Kao, 450, 451
The Keg, 201
Kellogg, 3, 375, 381, 468
KFC, 403, 411, 420
Killgallon, William, 156, 157
Kim Young-Sam, 314
Kimberly-Clark Corp., 473
Kin Ki Industrial, 156–157
Kirin, 410
Kiriyenko, Sergei, 347
Kivelidi, Ivan, 52
Klein, Pam, 268
Klein, Ralph, 383*f*
Kmart, 2
Knickerbocker, F.T., 238, 253
Kobayashi, Tony, 413
Kodak, 12, 202, 236, 252, 473, 477, 502
Kokuyo, 463
Komatsu, 7, 310, 358, 359, 386, 387
Koresh, David, 100
KPMG, 522
Krugman, Paul, 166, 208, 209, 245
K'ung-Fu-tzu, 104

L

L-3 Communications Corp., 447–448, 448
Lacavera, Tony, 404
Lahmeyer International, 132
Lakeland Community Bank, 425
Lay, Kenneth, 137, 139, 140, 141
Lay, Mark, 137–139
Lean Cuisine, 458
Lee Kuan Yew, 65
Legoland, 497
Leontief, 175
Lerman, Robert, 29
Levi Strauss, 13, 16, 57, 114, 118, 127, 379, 454
Levitt, Theodore, 379, 453–454, 455, 458, 459, 468
Lexmark, 493
LG Semicon, 202
Li, Victor, 86
Li & Fung, 488*f*
Li Ka-shing, 84–85
Life Savers, 171
Lifetime, 467
The Limited, 488*f*
Lincoln Electric, 420
Lion Corp., 451
Listiev, Vladislav, 52
Littlewoods Gaming, 59
London Metal Exchange, 129
L'Oreal, 403*f*
Lucent Technologies, 482
Lucky Call, 404
LVHM Moët-Hennessy Louis Vuitton SA, 230t
Lyons, Jeff, 53

M

Macdonald, Colin, 201
Mad Science, 497
Madonna, 362
Mandela, Nelson, 128–129
Mankin, Eric, 389–390, 391
Manulife Financial, 255–256
Maple Leaf Foods, 59
Marcos, Ferdinand, 53
Maritime Life, 256
Mark, Reuben, 515*f*
Marks & Spencer, 201
Martin, Paul, 343*f*, 466
Marx, Karl, 44, 45
Masayoshi Son, 116
Massachusetts Institute of Technology, 92
Matrex Company, 7
Matrikon, 8, 11
Matsushita, 12, 23, 116, 236, 374, 379, 384, 389, 407, 410, 415, 472, 512
Maxblue, 290
Mazda, 247, 392
McCain Foods Ltd., 420
McCann-Erickson, 468
McDonald's Corporation, 5, 7, 16, 27, 37, 76, 84–86, 87, 135, 250, 252–253, 306, 375, 376, 379, 381, 403, 410, 411, 415, 420, 454, 475
Megahertz Communications, 426–427, 428, 429
Mehta, Deepa, 345
Mendenhall, 517, 518, 521
Mercedes-Benz, 349, 355
Mercer Management Consulting, 418
Merck & Co., 230*t*, 475
Merrill Lynch, 12, 290, 375
Mesa, Carlos, 417
Metro-Goldwyn-Mayer Studios Inc., 389
MFP Financial Services, 53
Micron Technology, 202, 204
Microsoft Corp., 58, 64, 114, 173, 189, 190, 310, 311, 381, 383, 477, 480
Mill, John Stuart, 45, 144
Mining Association of Canada, 122
MiningWatch Canada, 507
Minnesota Mining and Manufacturing Co. *See* 3M Company
Minolta, 463
Minute Maid Company, 531
Mirant Corp, 230*t*
Mitsubishi Heavy Industries, 179, 412
Mitsubishi Motors, 463, 513
Mitsui & Company, 444
MMO Music Group, 429
Mobil Oil, 464
Molex, 508–510, 511, 512, 514, 515
Molson Brewers, 232, 236*f*, 393
Mondavi, Robert, 27
Monsanto, 477
Moody's Investors Service Inc., 347
Morales, Eva, 417
Motorola Inc., 183, 184, 186, 230t, 379, 385, 389, 390, 392, 477, 482
MTV Europe, 362, 383
MTV Networks, 13, 16, 70, 362–364, 365, 369, 375, 376, 378, 379, 387, 454*f*, 467
MuchArgentina, 363
MuchBogota, 363
MuchMusic, 363
Muhammed, 99, 101
Mun, Thomas, 167
Murdoch, Rupert, 134
Murphy Oil, 5

N

Nakane, 93
Namenwirth, Zvi, 88
Napster, 57
the Nation, 118
National Association of Software and Service Companies, 189
National Grid Transco, 230*t*
National Science Foundation, 477
Nationale-Nederlanden, 399
The Natural Step, 533
NEC Corporation, 389
Nestlé, 458
New Lenox State Bank, 425
New United Motor Manufacturing, Inc., 393
New York Times, 156
News Corporation, 17, 134
Nickelodeon, 362
Nike, 79, 495, 498
Nintendo, 7, 476
Nissan Motor Co., 238, 243, 416, 529
Nixon, Richard, 331
Nkrumah, Kwame, 160
Nokia, 5, 183, 184, 185, 186, 379, 476
Norex Petroleum, 52
Norsk Hydro, 5
Nortel Corporation, 229
Nortel Networks, 5, 122, 230t
North, Douglass, 65

O

Obstfeld, 245
Oddou, 517, 518, 521
Ohio Art Company, 156–157
Ohlin, Bertil, 163, 164, 166, 174, 175, 179, 181, 182, 185, 194
Ohno Taiichi, 492
Okalik, Paul, 383*f*
One 2 One, 416
One Connect, 404
Ontario Place, 497
Oracle, 64, 189, 190
Orthodox Church, 98
Oxford University, 95

P

Peeling, Gordon, 122
PeopleSoft, 190
PepsiCo, 7, 231, 444, 454, 458, 469
Perot, Ross, 279
Perry, William, 151
Pestell Shavings, 501
Petunias, Susan, 196
Pfizer Inc., 137, 138, 230*t*, 477
Pheonix Group, 268
Philip Morris, 441, 444, 468
Philips NV, 12, 374, 384, 389, 476, 512
Pinault-Printemps Redoute SA, 230*t*
Placer Dome Mines, 246, 300, 507
Plato, 45
Plaza Hotel, 334
Polistuk, Eugene, 482
PolyGram Manufacturing, 388
Porgera Environmental Advisory Kommiti, 507
Porter, Michael, 107, 166, 181–182, 183, 185, 187
Prahalad, C.K., 392, 393, 527
PricewaterhouseCoopers, 28
Procter & Gamble, 3, 12, 23, 230t, 310, 349, 375, 381, 450–452, 453, 455, 462, 463, 473, 477, 479, 512
Profit Magazine, 404

Q

Quantum Corporation, 479

R

Rank, 239
Ravenscraft, David, 418
Rawls, John, 146–147, 149, 150
RCA, 236, 410, 459
RCA Corporation, 409–410
RCMP, 132
Real Microcredito, 292–293
Recording Industry Association of America (RIAA), 57
Red Cross, 124
Reebok, 498
REI, 461, 463
Reich, Robert, 246, 389–390, 391
Reitman, Ivan, 345
ReliaStar Financial Services, 399
Renault, 49, 416
Revlon, 454
Ricardo, David, 163, 164, 166, 167, 169, 171, 172, 174, 175, 194, 208, 210, 211, 241
Risley, John, 201
The Rockport Group, 485
Rodriguez, Eduardo, 417
Rolex, 57, 464
Rolls-Royce, 443
Roman Catholic Church, 98

Romer, David, 174
Roots Canada Ltd., 28
Rose, Lewis, 59
Royal Bank of Canada, 424, 425, 433
Royal Dutch/Shell Group, 230*t*
Royal Insurance, 259
Ruggiero, Renato, 13

S

Sachs, Jeffrey, 32, 66, 174, 340, 354
Samsung, 407, 512
Sanmina-SCI, 482
SAP, 190
Saskatchewan Wheat Pool, 144
S.C. Johnson Wax, 458
Scherer, Mike, 418
Schmidt, Rodney, 360
Scholastic Inc., 497
Schor, Juliet, 360
Schulich School of Business, 53
Schwarzenegger, Arnold, 249, 345
Screen Actors Guild, 345
Seagram, 272*f*
Seattle Coffee, 225, 226
Sega, 7
Seko, Mobutu Sese, 340
Selectron, 482
Selz, Furman, 399
Sematech, 203–204
Sen, Amartya, 62, 65, 66
Sewell, John, 53
Shapiro, Joe, 121
Sharp, Isadoe, 234
Sharp Corporation, 463, 476
Shell Canada, 5
Shiseido Group, 403*f*
Shlien, Ariel, 497
Shlien, Ron, 497
Six Flags, 497
Skilling, Jeff, 140
Smith, Adam, 45, 46, 117, 163, 164, 166, 167, 168, 169, 194, 208, 210, 241, 373
SNC-Lavalin, 376
Snecma, 391
Sobeys, 201
Softbank, 116
Sole, Masupha Ephraim, 53, 132
Sony Corporation, 5, 7, 12, 13, 16, 23, 114, 116, 186, 236, 374, 379, 389, 390, 407, 410, 454, 475, 476, 477, 502
Sony Music Entertainment (UK) Limited, 388
Sony of Canada, 524, 525
Sony Tokyo, 525
Spahn, Paul Bernd, 360
Sprint, 271
Stalin, Joseph, 265
Standard & Poor's, 315
Star TV, 134
Starbucks, 224–225, 226, 227, 246
Starbucks Coffee of Japan, 224
State of Louisiana, 165
Statistics Canada, 13, 440
STC (Sistema de Transporte Colectivo), 268
Sterner Automation Ltd., 23
Steve Woloz Associates, 501
Stolichnaya, 444
Stop & Shop, 4
Strategis, 431
Suharto, Mohamed, 53, 351
Sun Alliance, 259
Sunbeam Corporation, 106
Suntory, 467
Supply Chain Alliance Inc., 7
Swift, 37

T

Talisman Energy, 123–124
the Tans, 127
Tao, Johnson, 156
Target, 2
Taylor, Betsy, 360
TCS, 190
TD Bank, 424
Telefonica, 416
Teleglobe, 416
TEN, 388
Tesco, 2, 3, 4, 6, 7
Tessier, Yvan, 127
Texas Instruments, 186, 385, 412–413, 477
Texas Utilities Company, 230*t*
Thatcher, Margaret, 73
Thomas Cook, 320
Thomson, 389
Thomson Corporation, 229, 230*t*
3M Company, 287, 431, 432, 434, 444, 475
3M Global Trading, Inc., 444
Ticoll, David, 28
Tim Hortons, 114, 253
Timberland, 484–486, 487, 489, 498, 500, 504
Time magazine, 17
Time Warner, 271
Tobin, Brian, 221
Tobin, James, 360
Tokyo Disneyland, 121
Toshiba, 186, 389, 390, 392
TotalFinaElf, 230*t*
Towers Perrin, 523–524
Toyota Motor Co., 7, 21, 198, 237, 238, 243, 244, 247, 249, 356, 375, 378, 392–393, 455, 459, 492, 512
Toys "R" Us, 62, 156, 248
Travelex, 320
Trudeau, Pierre Elliot, 253
TRW, Inc., 391
Tung, R.L., 516, 518
Turner, Tina, 469
Twentieth Century Fox Home Entertainment Inc., 389
Tylor, Edward, 88
Tyson Foods, 37
Tyumen Oil Company, 52

U

UAP, 259, 260
Unilever, 3, 23, 152, 310, 387, 403, 450, 460
United Auto Workers (UAW), 528
United Technologies, 151–152
Universal Pictures, 27
University of British Columbia, 522
University of New Brunswick, 127
University of Windsor, 396
Upjohn, 477
Urban Institute, 29

V

Vajpayee, Atal Behari, 42
Verizon Communications, 230*t*
Vernon, Raymond, 166, 176, 238–239
VH1, 362
Viacom, 362
Victoria Insurance, 259
Vivendi, 27, 272*f*
Vivendi Universal, 230t, 272*f*
Vodafone, 230*t*, 416
Volvo, 416
von Finkelstein, Konrad, 57

W

Wal-Mart, 2, 3, 4, 6, 7, 79, 156, 375, 381, 460
Wall, Howard, 197
Walt Disney Corporation, 79, 114, 120–121, 497
Warner, Andrew, 174
Warner Brothers, 488*f*
Warnex, 382
Watanabe, Junko, 16
Weber, Max, 98–99, 103, 117
Weber, Robert, 88
William Hill, 59
Windam International, 518
WorldCom, 271

X

Xerox Corporation, 239, 388, 390, 392, 408–409, 412, 413

Y

Yahoo!, 125, 301
Yeats, Alexander, 282
YMCA, 497
Yugraneft, 52

SUBJECT INDEX

A

absolute advantage, 167–168, 169*f*
ad valorem tariffs, 195
administrative trade policies, 200–202
advertising, 468–469
aerospace industry, 178–179
agriculture, protectionism in, 214–215
allowances, 527
American Funds Exchange, 304
Andean Pact, 281–282
antidumping policies, 202, 214, 215*f*, 474
antiglobalization, 20, 26–28
APEC (Asia-Pacific Economic Cooperation), 261, 284–285, 284*f*
arbitrage, 304–305
Arbitration Act, 51
ASEAN (Association of Southeast Nations), 33, 284
Asia-Pacific Economic Cooperation. *See* APEC
Asian Development Bank, 351
Association of Southeast Nations. *See* ASEAN (Association of Southeast Nations)
attractiveness of a country, 75, 78
AU (African Union), 33
Auto Pact, 198
autonomy, 246

B

balance of payments, adverse effects of, 246
balance-of-payments accounts, 245, 315
balance sheet approach, 525–526, 526f
banana war, 192–194
bandwagon effects, 312–313
banking crisis, 339–342
  See also financial crises
barter, 442
base salary, 526
basic research centres, 479–480
benefits
  acquisitions, 416–418
  of doing business in a country, 76
  of ethical behaviour, 153
  of the euro, 274–275
  foreign direct investment (FDI), 243–245, 246–247
  home-country effects, 246–247
  host-country effects, 243–245
benefits (employee), 527
Big Mac index, 64, 306–307, 307t
bilateral investment treaties (BIT), 228, 241
bilingualism, 105
bill of lading, 437
Bill S-21, 55, 79, 87
biotechnology, 204
Brady Plan, 343
Bretton Woods system, 326, 329–331, 332
bribery, 55, 131
British Monopolies and Mergers Commission, 474
broadcasting industry, 242
Bundesbank, 275
business clusters, 185
Business Development Bank of Canada (BDC), 433
business ethics, 126
  see also ethics
buybacks, 443

C

CAFTA (Central American Free Trade Agreement), 33
Canada
  see also NAFTA (North American Free Trade Agreement)
  cultural content policies, 203
  film industry in, 345
  gold standard, 327–329
  import tariffs, 196
  lumber industry, 465–466
  major religious denominations, 98*t*
  subsidies to foreign companies, 198
  Toronto, financial city status of, 304
  total exports, all industries, 19*t*
  total imports, all industries, 20*f*
  United States, largest trading partner of, 18–19
Canadian Bankers Association, 328
Canadian Chamber of Commerce, 440
Canadian Commercial Corporation, 445
Canadian Competition Tribunal, 271
Canadian dollar, 298–299, 304
Canadian Radio-Television and Telecommunications Commission, 242
Canadian Trade Commissioner Services, 501
capital flight, 317
CARICOM (Caribbean Community), 33, 283
caste system, 94
CEMAC (Communauté Economique et Monétaire de l'Afrique Centrale), 33
Central American common market, 283
channel exclusivity, 461–462
channel length, 461
Chicago Mercantile Exchange, 304
child labour, 142
CITP (Certified International Trade Professional), 440
civil law, 50
class consciousness, 96
class system, 94–95
code of ethics, 148–149
collectivism, 44–45
command economy, 49
Common Agricultural Policy (CAP), 198
common law, 50
common market, 263
communication barriers, 463–464
communication issues, 462
communication strategy, 464-474
communist totalitarianism, 47
communists, 44
comparative advantage, 169-173
compensation, 523-527
Competition Act (Canada), 271
competition policy, 474
competitive advantage
  technological know-how, 414–415
The Competitive Advantage of Nations (Porter), 181
competitive pressure, 376–380, 415–416
computer-aided design (CAD), 502
computer-aided manufacturing (CAM), 502
concentrated manufacturing, 494
concentrated retail system, 460
Confucian dynamism, 111–112
Confucianism, 104–105
consumer preferences, 378–379
consumer protection, 204–205

consumer sophistication, 466
consumer tastes, 378–379
containerization, 14
contract, 51
contract law, 51–52
contractual joint venture, 421
Convention on Combating Bribery of Foreign Public Officials in International Business Transactions (OECD Convention), 55, 131
convertibility of currency. *See* currency convertibility
copyrights, 55
core competence
  and entry mode, 414–416
  and global expansion, 375–376
  management know-how, 415
  technological know-how, 414–415
Corn Laws, 210
corporate culture, 512, 521
corporate-government relations, 356
corruption
  and ethics, 79, 131–134
  exporters, and "corrupt politician" perceptions, 132–134
  Nigeria, 56
  and property rights, 53–54, 54t, 56
cost-of-living allowances, 527
cost reduction pressures, 376–378, 377f, 415–416
counterpurchase, 442–443
countertrade, 442–444
  currency convertibility, 317–318
countervailing duties, 202
country differences
  distribution strategy, 460–462
  economic development, determinants of, 60–68
  economic systems, 48–49
  and global advertising, 469
  introduction, 42–43
  legal systems, 49–60
  political systems, 44–48
country of origin effects, 464
Court of Justice, 272
crawfish wars, 165
creative destruction, 476
cross-border mergers and acquisitions, 228f
cross-cultural literacy, 115
cross-functional teams, 478–479
cross-licensing agreement, 410
cultural barriers to communication, 463–464
cultural change, 112–114
cultural convergence, 458
cultural differences
  see also culture
  education, 107
  ethical systems, 96–105
  gestures, 106
  implications of, 115–118
  introduction, 86–87
  language, 105–107
  manufacturing, location of, 489–490
  product attributes, 457–458
  religion, 96–105
  significance of, 116–117
  the workplace, 109–112
cultural myopia, 513
cultural relativism, 117, 127, 142–143
cultural toughness, 518
cultural training, 519
Currency Act (Canada), 328
currency boards, 338–339
currency conversion, 297–298
currency convertibility
  capital flight, 317
  countertrade, 317–318
  externally convertible currency, 316
  freely convertible currency, 316
  and government policy, 316–317
  nonconvertible currency, 316
currency crisis, 339
  See also financial crises
currency speculation, 298
currency swaps, 302–304
current account, 245
custom, 50
customs union, 263

D

D'Amato Act (U.S.), 205
debt relief movement, 32
decentralized manufacturing, 495
decision-making processes, and ethics, 149–151
deficit on balance-of-payments accounts, 315
Delors Commission, 272
demand conditions, 181, 182–183
demand elasticity, 470–471
democracy, 46, 65–66, 67–69
demographics
  changing, 16–26
  foreign direct investment, 20–23
  multinational enterprise (MNE), 23–24
  world order, 24–25
  world output and trade, 16–20, 17t
Department of Foreign Affairs (Canada), 268, 440
deregulation, 71–72
developing world, drug testing in, 138
dharma, 101
dictators, 65
difference principle, 147
differences. *See* country differences
direct selling. *See* push strategy
dirty-float system, 325
distribution channels, 380, 466–467
distribution strategy
  choosing, 462–463
  country differences, 460–462
distribution system, 459, 460*f*
Doha Development Agenda, 33
Doha talks, 216–217
double taxation treaties (DTT), 228
draft, 437
drivers of globalization
  declining trade and investment barriers, 10–13
  technological change, 13–16
drug patents, 217
dumping, 202, 474

E

early entry. *See* first-mover advantages
East African Community. *See* EAC (East African Community)
eclectic paradigm, 235, 239–240
economic development
  broader conceptions of, 62
  democracy and, 65–66
  determinants of, 60–68
  differences in, 60–61
  and education, 66
  entrepreneurship, 62–65
  and geography, 66
  Human Development Index (HDI), 62, 63f
  innovation, 62–65
  and political economy, 62–66
  product attributes, 458–459
economic freedom, 71, 72*f*
economic growth
  comparative advantage, 173–174
  from 1947-1979, 210–211
  and trade, link between, 174
economic integration. *See* regional economic integration
economic risk, 77
economic systems
  command economy, 49
  global changes in, 75
  market-based systems, spread of, 70–71
  market economy, 48
  mixed economy, 49
economic theories of exchange rate determination, 305–313
economic transformation
  deregulation, 71–72
  implications, 75
  and legal systems, 74
  privatization, 73
  rocky road of, 74–75
  underlying rationale for, 71
economic union, 263–264
economies of scale, 178
EDI systems, 504
education allowances, 527
efficient market, 306, 313
elastic demand, 470
employee benefits, 527
employment effects, 244
Employment Equity Act (Canada), 513
employment practices, 127
entrepreneurship
  as engine of growth, 62–64
  and innovation, 62
  market economy, 64
  required political system, 65
  strong property rights, 64–65
entry into foreign market
  basic entry decisions, 401–406
  foreign markets, choice of, 401–402
  pioneering costs, 402–403
  scale of entry, 403–406
  strategic commitments, 404–406
  timing of entry, 402–403
"environments" affecting ethics, 125–126
Equal Employment Opportunity Commission (U.S.), 513
ethical behaviour, 136*f*
ethical decision making
  decision-making processes, 149–151
  ethics officers, 151–152
  hiring, 148
  job seeker's ethics audit, 149*t*
  and leadership, 148–149
  moral courage, 152
  organization culture, 148–149
  promotion, 148
  summary of decision-making steps, 152
ethical dilemmas, 135–136
ethical strategy, 126
ethical systems, 96
ethics officers, 151–152
ethnocentric behaviour, 115
ethnocentric staffing policy, 512–513
the euro
  benefits of, 274–275
  conversion, and tipping the taxi driver, 274
  costs of, 275–276
  early experience, 276
  establishment of, 273–277
  hold-outs, 286
Europe, and regional economic integration. *See* European Union
European Central Bank (ECB), 258, 275, 276
European Commission, 270–271
European Community (EC), 265
European Competition Commissioner, 271
European Free Trade Association (EFTA), 262–263

European insurance market, 258–260
European Union
banana tariff, 192, 194
beginnings of, 263
Common Agricultural Policy (CAP), 198
Council of Ministers, 271
countries and applicants, 269–270, 270*f*
Court of Justice, 272
the euro, 273–277
European Parliament, 271
evolution of, 269–270
External Trade, 33
ISO 9000, 489
Maastricht Treaty, 269, 275
partial political union, 264
political structure, 270–272
protectionism, fear of, 276–277
Single European Act, 272–273
Treaty of Rome, 269
U.S. steel tariff, 186
excess capacity, 349
exchange rate determination
bandwagon effects, 312–313
described, 305–306
economic theories of, 305–313
empirical tests of PPP theory, 310–311
Fisher Effect, 311–312
interest rates, and exchange rates, 311–312
International Fisher Effect (IFE), 312
and investor psychology, 312–313
law of one price, 306
money supply, 308–310
price inflation, 308–310
prices, and exchange rates, 306–311
purchasing power partly (PPP), 306–311
exchange rate forecasting
efficient market school, 313
fundamental analysis, 315–316
inefficient market school, 313–314
need for, 313
technical analysis, 316
exchange rates, 296
see also foreign exchange market
exclusive distribution channel, 461–462
expanding trade agreements, 213–214
expatriate failure, 516–517
expatriate manager
compensation, 525–527
defined, 511
dimensions predicting success, 517–518
expatriate failure, 516–517
expatriate selection, 517–518
inpatriates, 515
repatriation, 520–521
training, 519–520
women in international assignments, 514
expatriate selection, 517–518
experience curve, 372–375, 373*f*
experience curve pricing, 473
export and import financing
bill of lading, 437
draft, 437
letter of credit, 436
trust, lack of, 434–435
typical international trade transaction, 438–439
Export Development Canada (EDC), 268, 439*f*, 445
export management companies (EMCs), 430–431
exporters, and "corrupt politician" perceptions, 132–134
exporting
advantages, 407
defined, 235
disadvantages, 407–408
as entry mode, 407–408
export management companies (EMCs), 430–431
improving export performance, 430–434
information sources, 440
international comparison, 430
limitations of, 235–236
pitfalls, 428–429
promise of, 428–429
strategy, 431–434
exports of harmonized system (HS) total, 18*t*
external stakeholders, 150
externalities, 240
externally convertible currency, 316

F

factor endowments, 181, 182
Finance Act (Canada), 328–329
financial services industry, 213–214, 474–475
financing. *See* countertrade; export and import financing
firm as value chain
described, 367*f*
primary activities, 367–368
support activities, 368–369
firm strategy, structure and rivalry, 182, 183–185
first-mover advantages, 76, 186, 402
first-mover disadvantages, 402–403
Fisher Effect, 311–312
fixed costs, 490–491
fixed exchange rate, 325, 331-336
flexible machine cell, 492–493
flexible manufacturing, 491–493
floating exchange rate
case for, 334–335
defined, 325
flow of FDI, 226
folkways, 89
Food and Drug Administration (FDA), 138
food retailers, 2
Foreign Affairs Canada, 440
Foreign Corrupt Practices Act (U.S.), 54–55, 79, 87, 131, 142
foreign debt crisis, 342
see also financial crises
foreign direct investment (FDI)
acquisitions, 226, 230–232
advantages, 237–238
and Africa, 242
alternatives to, 235–236
autonomy, 246
balance-of-payment effects, 245
balance of payments, adverse effects of, 246
benefits (home-country effects), 246–247
benefits (host-country effects), 243–245
bilateral investment treaties, 228
and Canada, 229, 232–235, 233f, 233*t*
changes in national regulations, 1991-2002, 228*f*
changing trends in, 20–23
and China, 229, 231–232
competition, adverse effects on, 245–246
costs (home-country effects), 247
costs (host-country effects), 245–246
cross-border mergers and acquisitions, share of, 228*f*
decision framework, 252*f*
defined, 10, 226
eclectic paradigm, 235, 239–240
employment effects, 244
and externalities, 240
flow of FDI, 226
flows, 227*f*
form of, 230–232
free market view, 241–242
government policy, 253
and government policy instruments, 248–250
green-field investment, 226, 230–232
growth of, 227–229
home-country policies, 248–249
host-country effects, 243–246
host-country policies, 249–250
inflows, 22f
inflows of FDI, 226
internalization theory, 236
international institutions, and liberalization of FDI, 250–251
inward FDI, encouragement of, 249
inward FDI, restriction of, 250
location-specific advantages, 239
mergers, 226
and modern day colonialism, 246
multipoint competition, 238
national sovereignty, 246
by non-U.S. firms, 20–21
offshore production, 248
outflows, 22*f*
outflows of FDI, 226
outward FDI, encouragement of, 248
outward FDI, restriction of, 249
pattern of, 238–240
and political ideology, 240–243
pragmatic nationalism, 242–243
product life cycle, 238–239
prospects for FDI flows, 232*f*
radical view, 240–241
reasons for, 235–238
resource-transfer effects, 243–244
role in global economy, 11
shifting ideology, 243
source of, 229
at source of raw materials (case), 507
Starbuck's (case), 224–225
of stock, inward, 21*f*
of stock, outward, 21*f*
stock of FDI, 226, 229
stock of foreign direct investment, 22–23
strategic behaviour, 238
theory of, 235–240, 251–253
and trade theory, 248
types of changes in FDI laws and regulations, 2002, 229*f*
in world economy, 226–235
foreign drug testing, 138, 140
foreign exchange market
see also exchange rates
arbitrage, 304–305
Canadian dollar, status of, 298–299, 304
currency conversion, 297–298
currency convertibility, 316–318
currency speculation, 298
currency swaps, 302–304
defined, 296
foreign exchange quotations, 302*t*
foreign exchange risk, insuring against, 299–303
forward exchange rates, 301–302
functions of, 297–303
geographical distribution of global foreign exchange activity, 303f

government intervention, 311
major participants in, 297–298
nature of, 303–305
spot exchange rate, 301
Foreign Investment in Canada Act (FICA), 370
Foreign Investment Review Act (FIRA) (Canada), 203
Foreign Investment Review Agency (FIRA), 242
foreign policy objectives, 205
foreign service premium, 526–527
Forum for International Trade Training (FITT), 440
forward exchange, 301
forward exchange rates, 301–302
fragmented retail system, 460
franchising, 410–411
free market view, 241–242
free trade
see also international trade
arguments for free trade, 208–209
comparative advantage, 169–174
defined, 163, 194
and domestic politics, 209
effects of, 29–30
retaliation and trade war, 208–209
world trading system, development of, 209–217
free trade agreements, 262
free trade area, 262
freely convertible currency, 316
Friedman doctrine, 141–142
FTAA (Free Trade Agreement of the Americas), 261, 283
fundamental analysis, 315–316
fundamentalism, 100–102

G

gains from trade
and absolute advantage, 169f
comparative advantage, 170–172, 171*t*
Ghana and South Korea, 160–162, 168
gambling, 59
General Agreement on Tariffs and Trade (GATT)
antidumping actions, 474
circumvention of, 211
defined, 8
establishment of, 210–211
function of, 195
goal of, 10
infant industry argument, 207
intellectual property, 212
intellectual property and, 57
services, 212
Uruguay Round, 33, 212
genetic pollution, 205
genetical engineering, 204–205
geocentric staffing policy, 514–515
geography, and economic development, 66
gestures, 106
gift giving, 118
global advertising, 468–469
global economy
changing demographics, 16–26
of the twenty-first century, 25–26
global institutions. *See* international institutions
global learning, 386
global marketing
communication issues across cultures, 462
communication strategy, 463–469
distribution strategy, 459–463
globalization of markets and brands, 453–455
market segmentation, 455–457
marketing mix, 453, 474–475
new-product development, 475–479
product attributes, 457–459
global outlook in summary, 2002-2006, 12t
global strategy, 384–385
see also strategy
global trading system. *See* world trading system
global web, 371–372
globalization
antiglobalization, 20, 26–28
and cultural change, 114
debate about, 26–32
declining trade and investment barriers, 10–13
defined, 7
drivers of, 10–16
emergence of global institutions, 8–9
and the environment, 29–30
implications for business, 33–34
and income, 28–29
introduction to, 5–6
and jobs, 28–29
and labour policies, 29–30
management in global marketplace, 32–33
of markets and brands, 453–455
and national sovereignty, 30–31
opposition to, 20
risks of, 26
and technological change, 13–16
and world poverty, 31–32
globalization of markets, 7-8
globalization of production, 8
GNI (gross national income), 61, 61t
GNP (gross national product), 60–61
gold standard
defined, 327
described, 326
end of era, 328–329
mechanics of, 327
period between the wars (1918-1939), 327–329
strength of, 327
government
corporate-government relations, 356
host-government demands, 380
intervention. *See* government intervention
market economy, role in, 48
mixed economies, role in, 72–73
policy. *See* trade policy
government intervention
see also trade policy
Canadian cultural content policies, 203
case for intervention, 202–208
consumers, protection of, 204–205
domestic politics, 209
economic arguments for intervention, 206–208
economic case for regional integration, 264–265
in foreign exchange market, 311
foreign policy objectives, 205
free trade arguments, 208–209
human rights, protection of, 206
industries, protection of, 203
infant industry argument, 206–207
job protection, 203
national security, 203–204
political arguments for intervention, 203–206
retaliation, 204, 208–209
strategic trade policy, 207–208
trade war, 208–209
government policy
competition policy, 474
and currency convertibility, 316–318
monetary policy autonomy, 334–335
trade policy. *See* trade policy
Great Depression, 10, 210
green-field investment, 226, 230–232, 419–420
see also foreign direct investment (FDI)
green revolution, 173
gross domestic product (GDP), 476
gross fixed capital formation, 228
Group of Five, 334
groups, 91, 93–94
growth. *See* economic growth
guanxi, 84–86, 87, 117
guanxiwang, 85, 118

H

hardship allowances, 527
Heckscher-Ohlin theory, 174–175, 179
Helms-Burton Act (U.S.), 205
hierarchy of concepts, 116
highly indebted poorer countries (HIPCs), 31–32
hiring, and ethical decision making, 148
home-country effects
benefits, 246–247
costs, 247
home-country policies, 248–249
host-country effects
autonomy, 246
balance-of-payment effects, 245
balance of payments, adverse effects of, 246
competition, adverse effects on, 245–246
costs, 245–246
employment effects, 244
foreign direct investment (FDI), 243–245
national sovereignty, 246
resource-transfer effects, 243–244
host-country policies, 249–250
host-government demands, 380
housing allowances, 527
hubris hypothesis, 418
Human Development Index (HDI), 62, 63*f*
human resource management (HRM)
compensation, 523–527
defined, 510
expatriate manager, 511
expatriate managers, 515–518
management development and strategy, 521
performance appraisal, 521–523
repatriation of expatriates, 520–521
staffing policy, 512–518
strategic role of, 511–512
training, 519–520
human rights
and ethics, 127–130
issues, 78
protection of, and government intervention, 206

I

identified cultures, 126
illiteracy rates, 107, 108*f*
IMF conspiracy theory, 329
immobile resources, 173
import financing. *See* export and import financing

import quotas, 199–200
imports of harmonized system (HS) total, 19*t*
In a Different Voice (Gilligan), 147
income, and globalization, 28–29
income taxes, 527
Incoterms, 445
individualism, 45–46, 92
individualism versus collectivism, 110
individuals, 91–92
Indonesia, financial crisis in, 348–351
inefficient market, 313–314
inelastic demand, 470
infant industry argument, 206–207, 245
inflation
  described, 308
  and exchange rates, 308–310
  and pegged exchange rates, 338
  in Southeast Asia, 353*t*
inflows of FDI, 226
informal administrative barriers, 201–202
infrastructure differences, 379
innovation
  defined, 62
  as engine of growth, 62–64
  market economy, 64
  required political system, 65
  strong property rights, 64–65
inpatriates, 515
intellectual property
  copyrights, 55
  described, 55
  drug patents, 217
  as economic value, 55
  extension of GATT rules, 212
  Paris Convention for the Protection of Industrial Property, 57
  patent, 55
  philosophy behind, 55–57
  protection of, 215–216
  Trade Related Aspects of Intellectual Property Rights (TRIPS), 57
  trademarks, 55
interest rates, and exchange rates, 311–312
internal stakeholders, 150
internalization theory, 236
International Association of Trade Associations, 440
International Bank for Reconstruction and Development (IBRD). *See* World Bank
international business
  defined, 32
  vs. domestic business, 86
international business management
  attractiveness of a country, 75, 78
  benefits of doing business in a country, 76
  China, doing business in, 421–422
  contractual joint venture, 421
  corporate-government relations, 356
  costs of doing business in a country, 76
  cultural differences, implications of, 115–118
  currency management, 355
  described, 32–33
  entry into foreign markets, 421–422
  ethical behaviour, 152–153
  ethics, 78–79
  and exchange rates, 318
  export and import processes, 445
  first-mover implications, 186
  foreign direct investment (FDI), 251–253
  and foreign exchange market, 318
  global manufacturing system, coordination of, 503–504
  global marketing, 479–480
  information technology, 504–506
  and international monetary system, 355–356
  Internet gambling, 59
  just-in-time inventory systems (JIT), 504
  labour relations, 527–529
  location implications, 186
  policy implications, 187
  political economy, implications of, 75–79
  regional economic integration, implications of, 286–288
  research and development, 479–480
  risks, 77–78
  strategy and, 393
  trade barriers and firm strategy, 217–218
  trade policies, implication of, 218
  trade theory, implications of, 185–187
international business opportunities, 440
International Business Opportunities Centre, 501
International Chamber of Commerce, 52
International Court of Arbitration, 52
International Development Association, 132
International Finance Corporation, 132
International Fisher Effect (IFE), 312
international labour relations, 527–529
international marketing. *See* global marketing
International Monetary Fund (IMF)
  accountability, lack of, 354
  Articles of Agreement, 329–330, 332
  austerity programs, 326
  crisis management, 339–354
  Democratic Republic of the Congo, 340–341
  described, 8, 9
  evaluation of policy prescriptions, 352–354
  inappropriate policies, 352–353
  Mexican currency crisis, 1995, 344
  moral hazard, 353–354
  observations about, 354
  on pegged exchange rates, 338
  role of, 326, 329–330
  Russian ruble crisis, 344–347
  Southeast Asian crisis, 348–351
  Third World debt crisis, 343
  Turkey, 322–324
international monetary system
  Bretton Woods system, 326, 329–331, 332
  currency boards, 338–339
  defined, 324
  dirty-float system, 325
  exchange rate regimes in practice, 337–339, 337*f*
  financial crises, 339–354
  financial crisis in post-Bretton Woods era, 339–342
  fixed exchange rate, 325, 331–332, 334–336
  floating exchange rate, 325, 332–336
  gold standard, 326–329
  IMF crisis management, 339–354
  International Monetary Fund (IMF), role of, 329–330
  pegged exchange rate, 325, 337–338
  World Bank, role of, 330–331
international strategy, 381–383
  see also strategy
international trade
  benefits of trade, 163–164
  defined, 10
  and economic growth, link between, 174
  gains from trade, 160–162
  national competitive advantage, 181–185
  pattern of international trade, 164–166
  trade theory. *See* trade theory
  typical transaction, 438–439
International Trade Canada (ITCan), 440
International Trade Commission, 164, 165, 202
Internet
  and distribution channel length, 461
  EDI systems, 504
  gambling, 59
  impact of, 13–14
  low-cost global communications networks, 16
  and manufacturing, 504–506
interunit cooperation, 521
investment barriers, 10–13
Investment Canada Act (ICA), 370
investor psychology, 312–313
invisible barrier to trade, 202
Iraq, 205
Islam, 99–101
Islamic banking, 102
Islamic fundamentalism, 100–101
Islamic law, 50–51
ISO 9000, 489

J

Jamaica agreement, 332
Japanese Overseas Enterprise Association, 512
jobs
  globalization, effects of, 28–29
  outsourcing and, 28
joint ventures, 412–413, 421
JSEPA (Japan/Singapore Economic Partnership Agreement), 33
just distribution, 146–147
just-in-time inventory systems (JIT), 502, 504
justice theories, 146–147

K

Kantian ethics, 145
karma, 102
karoshi, 93–94, 117

L

labour
  learning effects, 178
  policies, and globalization, 29–30
labour relations, 527–529
language
  bilingualism, 105
  spoken language, 105–106
  unspoken language, 106–107
late-mover disadvantages, 76
law of one price, 306
leadership, and ethical decision making, 148–149
lean production, 492
learning effects, 178, 372–373
legal risk, 77–78
legal system
  Bill S-21, 55
  civil law, 50
  common law, 50

contract law, 51–52
corruption, 53–54, 54*t*, 56
defined, 49
and economic transformation, 74
Foreign Corrupt Practices Act (U.S.), 54–55
intellectual property, 55–58
political influences on, 50
and pricing strategy, 474
private action, 52–53
product liability, 60
product safety laws, 60
property rights, 52–55
public action, 53–54
theocratic law, 50–51
types of, 50–51
Leontief paradox, 175
letter of credit, 436
licensing
advantages, 409
cross-licensing agreement, 410
defined, 235
disadvantages, 409–410
as entry mode, 408–410
limitations of, 236–237
licensing agreement, 408
living standards, comparison of, 61
local content requirements, 200
local responsiveness
pressures, 376–377, 377*f*, 378–380
location economies, 371
location-specific advantages, 239
logistics, 487–489
long-term versus short-term orientation, 110

M

Maastricht Treaty, 269, 275
Mafia problems, 52, 53
make-or-buy decisions
buy, advantages of, 500–502
described, 498
make, advantages of, 498–500
strategic alliances with suppliers, 502–503
trade-offs, 502
Malaysia
financial crisis, 348–351
and IMF conspiracy theory, 329
Oil of Olay in, 455
and pegged exchange rates, 338
management development and strategy, 521
management know-how, 415
maquilladoras, 268
market-based systems, 70–71
market economy, 48, 64
market entry. See entry into foreign market
market segmentation, 455–457
marketing. *See* global marketing
marketing mix
communication strategy, 463–469
configuration, 474–475
defined, 453
distribution strategy, 459–463
pricing strategy, 469–474
product attributes, 457–459
markets. *See* globalization of markets
Marshall Plan, 330
masculinity versus femininity, 110
mass customization, 491–493
materials management, 487
"mean and lean" argument, 299
media availability, 467
Mercado Comun del Sur. *See* MERCOSUR (Mercado Comun del Sur)
mercantilism, 163, 166–167
MERCOSUR (Mercado Comun del Sur), 33, 261, 282–283
mergers
cross-border mergers and acquisitions, share of, 228*f*
and foreign direct investment (FDI), 226
Mexico
see also NAFTA
currency crisis, 1995, 344
environmental protection regulations, 30
microprocessors, 13
mini-multinationals, 23–24
minimum efficient scale, 491
mining, 122–124
Ministry of International Trade and Industry (MITI) (Japan), 430
mixed economy, 49
monetary discipline, and fixed exchange rates, 335–336
monetary policy autonomy, 334–335
money supply, 308–310
monopoly, 48, 64
Moore's Law, 13
moral courage, 152
moral hazard, 353–354
moral obligations, 134–135
mores, 89
most-favoured-nation (MFN) status, 206
multidomestic strategy, 383–384
see also strategy
Multilateral Agreement on Investment (MAI), 251
multinational enterprise (MNE)
changing nature of, 23
defined, 23, 226
mini-multinationals, 23–24
non-U.S. multinationals, 23
performance requirements, 250
radical view of, 240–241
multipoint competition, 238
multipoint pricing, 472–473
Myanmar, 129

N

NAFTA (North American Free Trade Agreement)
case against, 279
case for, 278–279
contents of, 277–278
critics, 279, 280
detractors of, 261
enlargement of, 281
environmental concerns, 279
experience so far, 280–281
impact of, on Canadian business, 268
job loss and, 265, 280–281
opposition to, 29–30
and U.S. textile industry, 266
naive immoralist, 143–144
NASDAQ, 274
nation-state, 89–90
national competitive advantage (Porter's diamond)
demand conditions, 181, 182–183
described, 181–182
determinants of, 181f
evaluation of Porter's theory, 185
factor endowments, 181, 182
firm strategy, structure and rivalry, 182, 183–185
related industries, 182, 183
supporting industries, 182, 183
national security, 203–204
national sovereignty, 30–31, 246, 265–267
networking, 431
new-product development, 475–479
new trade theory
aerospace example, 178–179
described, 166
economies of scale, 178
emergence of, 176
implications, 179–180
new world order, 69–70
nirvana, 102
noblesse oblige, 134
noise, 464
non-U.S. multinationals, 23
nonconvertible currency, 316
see also currency convertibility
nonverbal communication, 106–107
norms, 88–89
north-south divide, 34

O

OECD Convention, 55
offset, 443
offsets, 502
offshore production, 248
oligopoly, 238
online gambling, 59
OPEC, 343
organization culture
defined, 137
and ethical decision making, 148–149
Organization for Economic Cooperation and Development (OECD), 29, 30, 54–55, 79, 131, 229, 251
organized labour, 527–529
others-orientation, 517–518
outflows of FDI, 226
outsourcing, 28–29, 495, 500–502

P

Paris Convention for the Protection of Industrial Property, 57
patent, 55
pegged exchange rate, 325, 337–338
perceptual ability, 518
performance appraisal, 521–523
performance requirements, 250
personal selling. *See* push strategy
personal space, 106–107
pioneering costs, 402–403
policy. *See* government policy; trade policy
political economy
defined, 43
and economic progress, 62–66
economic systems, 48–49
legal systems, 49–60
manufacturing, location of, 489–490
political systems, 44–48
states in transition, 67–75
political environment, 125
political freedom, 2003, 67, 68*f*
political ideology, and foreign direct investment (FDI), 240–243
political risk, 77
political systems
collectivism, 44–45
communist totalitarianism, 47
communists, 44
defined, 44
democracy, 46
global changes in, 75
individualism, 45–46
required, for innovation and entrepreneurship, 65
right-wing totalitarianism, 47–48
social democrats, 44–45
socialism, 44–45
theocratic totalitarianism, 47
totalitarianism, 46–48
tribal totalitarianism, 47
pollution
corporate right to pollute, issue of, 130–131
and ethics, 130–131
polycentric staffing policy, 514
Porter's diamond, 181–185
positive-sum game, 167
post-Communist states
gross domestic product, 74

"shock therapy" economic policy, 74–75
poverty. *See* world poverty
power, morally neutral, 134
power distance, 110
practical training, 520
pragmatic nationalism, 242–243
precedent, 50
predatory pricing, 472
price discrimination, 469–470, 471*f*
price elasticity of demand, 470–471
price inflation. *See* inflation
prices
and exchange rates, 306–311
law of one price, 306
pricing strategy, 469-474
Principles of Political Economy (Ricardo), 169
private action, 52–53
privatization, 64, 73, 417
product attributes, 457-459
product factors, 494
product liability, 60
product life-cycle theory, 166, 176, 177f, 238–239
product naming, 429
product safety laws, 60, 79
product standards, 459
production
defined, 487
described, 368
globalization of production. *See* globalization of production
integration with R&D and marketing, 477–478
lean production, 492
offshore production, 248
scheduling, 499–500
profit, 366
profit maximization, and price discrimination, 471–472
profitability
defined, 366
global expansion, 370–376
promotion, and ethical decision making, 148
property rights, 52-58
and innovation, 64–65
proprietary product technology, 499
protectionism, 197
see also trade policy
Protestant work ethic, 98–99
psychology, investor, 312–313
public action, 53–54
public health measures, 217
pull strategy, 464-467
purchasing power parity (PPP), 61, 64, 306–311, 335
push strategy, 464-466

Q

quality
ISO 9000, 489
quality-cost relationship, 488*f*
total quality management (TQM), 488
quality-cost relationship, 488*f*

R

radical view, 240–241
regional economic integration
Africa, 287
in the Americas, 277–283
APEC, 284–285
ASEAN, 284
attempts at, 283
case against, 267–269
case for, 264–265
defined, 260
economic case for integration, 264–265
in Europe, 269–277
impediments, 265–267
levels of economic integration, 262–264, 263*f*
movement towards, 261–262
opportunities of, 286–287
political case for integration, 265
threats, 287–288
related industries, 182, 183
relational capital, 392
relatively efficient markets, 306
religion, 96
research and development
basic research centres, 479–480
creative destruction, 476
cross-functional teams, 478–479
gross domestic product (GDP), 476
implications for business, 479–480
integration with marketing and production, 477–478
location of, 476–477
resource-transfer effects, 243–244
retail concentration, 460–461
retailers
late mover in global arena, 6
top global retailers, 3–4
retaliation, 204, 208–209
Ricardian model, 169–174
right-wing totalitarianism, 47–48
righteous moralist, 143
rights theories, 145–146
risks
economic risk, 77
of ethical behaviour, 153
of failure, 419
foreign exchange risk, 297, 299–303
legal risk, 77–78
political risk, 77
Russian Mafia, 52

S

SAFTA (South American Free Trade Area), 261
SARS, 125
scale of entry, 403–406
scheduling, 499–500
selection of expatriates, 517–518
self-orientation, 517
September 11 terrorist attacks, 100–101
"shock therapy" economic policy, 74–75
sight draft, 437
Single European Act, 271, 272–273
social-cultural environment, 125
social democrats, 44–45
social investments, 134
social mobility, 94–96
social responsibility, 134–135
social strata, 94
social stratification, 94-96
social structure, 91-96
socialism, 44–45
society, 88, 89–90
source effects, 464
sourcing decisions, 498–503
specialized investments, 498–499
specific tariffs, 195
speculation, 335–336
spoken language, 105–106
sponsorship scandal, 132–133
spot exchange rate, 301
staffing policy, 512-518
stages of ethical development, 151
stakeholders, 150
standardized advertising, 468–469
states in transition
democracy, spread of, 67–69
economic transformation, 71–75
market-based systems, spread of, 70–71
new world order, 69–70
stock of FDI
defined, 22, 226
described, 22–23
rise in actual world FDI stock, 229
strategic alliances
advantages, 388–389
defined, 388
disadvantages of, 389–390
strategic behaviour, and foreign direct investment (FDI), 238
strategic commitments, 404–406
strategic flexibility, 500
strategic pricing
defined, 472
experience curve pricing, 473
multipoint pricing strategy, 472–473
predatory pricing, 472
strategic trade policy, 207–208
Strategis, 440
strategy
choices, 380–388, 381f
communication strategy, 463–469
comparisons of, 387–388, 388t
core competence, 375–376
cost reduction pressures, 376–378, 377*f*
defined, 365
distribution strategy, 459–463
and experience curve, 374–375
exporting, 431–434
and the firm, 365–370
firm as value chain, 367–369
and foreign factories, 496–497
global strategy, 384–385
global web, 371–372
and international human resource management (HRM), 511–512
international strategy, 381–383
local responsiveness, 376–377, 377f, 378–380
and location economies, 371
and logistics, 487–489
and manufacturing, 487–489
multidomestic strategy, 383–384
pricing strategy, 469–474
and profitability, 366
profiting from global expansion, 370–376
role of, 369–370
subsidiary skills, 376
transnational strategy, 386–387
and value creation, 366–367
straw men approaches to ethics
cultural relativism, 142–143
described, 141
Friedman doctrine, 141–142
naive immoralist, 143–144
righteous moralist, 143
subsidiaries
subsidiary skills, 376
wholly owned subsidiaries, 413–414, 416–420
subsidies, 198–199, 221–222
sugar industry, 199–200
suppliers, 502–503
supply-chain management, 38
supporting industries, 182, 183
sweatshop labour, 79
switch trading, 443

T

tariffs, 10, 195–198
taxes
income taxes, 527
tax incentives, 221–222
Tobin tax, 360
Team Canada trade mission, 382–383
teams, and individualism, 92
technical analysis, 316
technical standards, 379, 459
technological change
creative destruction, 476
and globalization of markets, 16
and globalization of production, 14–15
Internet and World Wide Web, 13–14
microprocessors, 13
Moore's Law, 13

research and development, 476–479
role of, 13–16, 34
telecommunications, 13
transportation technology, 14
technological environment
described, 125
and ethics, 126–127
technological factors
fixed costs, 490–491
flexible manufacturing, 491–493
mass customization, 491–493
minimum efficient scale, 491
technological know-how, 414–415
telecommunications, 13, 213, 379
textile industry, 200, 266
theocratic law, 50–51
theocratic totalitarianism, 47
Third World debt crisis, 343
time draft, 437
timing of entry, 402–403
Tobin tax, 360
totalitarianism, 46–48, 65
trade balance adjustments, 335, 336
trade barriers
see also trade policy
administrative trade policies, 200–202
antidumping policies, 202
declining, and globalization, 10–13
and firm strategy, 217–218
invisible barrier to trade, 202
subsidies, 198–199
tariffs, 10, 195–198
voluntary export restraints (VERs), 211
Trade Commissioner Service (Canada), 268
trade creation, 267
trade diversion, 267–268
trade fortress, 288
trade liberalization, 210–211
trade-offs, 502
Trade Related Aspects of Intellectual Property Rights (TRIPS), 57, 212
trade theory
absolute advantage, 167–168, 169f
benefits of trade, 163–164
business clusters, 185
comparative advantage, 169–174
first-mover implications, 186
and foreign direct investment (FDI), 248
and government policy, 166
Heckscher-Ohlin theory, 174–175, 179
Leontief paradox, 175
location implications, 186
mercantilism, 163, 166–167
new trade theory, 166, 176–180
overview of, 163–166
pattern of international trade, 164–166
policy implications, 187
product life-cycle theory, 166, 176, 177*f*
trade unions, 527–529
trade war, 208–209
trademarks, 55
tradition, 50
traditional practices, 379
tragedy of the commons, 130–131
training, 519–520
transnational strategy, 386–387
see also strategy
transportation technology, 14
Treaty of Rome, 269
tribal totalitarianism, 47
trust, 392, 434–435
turnkey projects, 408

U

UN Charter, 9
UN Conference on Trade and Development, 241
UN Universal Declaration of Human Rights, 117–118, 145–146, 148–149
UN World Investment Report on FDI Policies for Development, 228
uncertainty, 336
uncertainty avoidance, 110
unethical behaviour, 136–141
unions, 527–529
unit cost curve, 491*f*
United Nations, 8, 9
United Nations Conference on Trade and Development, 107
United Nations Convention on Contracts for the International Sale of Goods (CIGS), 51–52
United States
see also NAFTA
Brady Plan, 343
Buy America Act, 200
Canada, largest trading partner of, 18–19
Canadian banks in, 424–425
crawfish wars, 165
"culturally impoverished" interests and values, 26
dominant industrial power, 11
and fixed exchange rate system breakup, 331–332
gold standard, 327
individual performance, focus on, 92
Marshall Plan, 330
persistent trade deficit, and world trading system, 211
protectionism, costs of, 197
research and development, post World War II, 476
television networks, 16
textile industry, and NAFTA, 266
world output, 16–17
Universal Declaration of Human Rights. *See* UN Universal Declaration of Human Rights
universal needs, 494
unspoken language, 106–107
Uruguay Round, 213
U.S. Federal Reserve, 29
utilitarian approaches, 144–145

V

value creation, 366–367, 487
value-to-weight ratio, 494
values, 88
veil of ignorance, 146–147
volatility of exchange rates, 332–333
voluntary export restraint (VER), 199–200
voluntary export restraints (VERs), 211

W

The Wealth of Nations (Smith), 46, 167
wholly owned subsidiaries, 413–414, 416–420
women in international assignments, 514
work-related values, 109–111, 111t
work safety standards, 79
the workplace
Confucian dynamism, 111–112
culture and, 109–112
Hofstede's results, 109–111
individualism versus collectivism, 110
long-term versus short-term orientation, 110
masculinity versus femininity, 110
power distance, 110
uncertainty avoidance, 110
work-related values, 111*t*
World Bank, 8, 9, 60–61, 326, 330–331, 343, 351
world order, changing, 24–25
world output and trade, 16–20, 17*t*
world poverty
debt relief movement, 32
and globalization, 31–32
highly indebted poorer countries (HIPCs), 31–32
World Trade Center, 100–101
World Trade Organization
agriculture, protectionism in, 214–215
anti-global movement and, 10–11
antidumping policies, 214
banana tariff, ruling on, 194–195
creation of, 8, 10, 195, 212–213
defined, 9
dispute settlement, 212–213
Doha Development Agenda, 33
Doha talks, 216–217
financial services industry, 213–214
function of, 195
future of, 214–217
General Agreement on Trade in Services (GATS), 212
intellectual property, protection of, 215–216
intellectual property regulations, 57
liberalization of regulations governing FDI, 250–251
lower trade barriers, calls for, 5
members in, 33
north-south divide, 34
public health measures, 217
regional trade agreements, notification of, 260–261
role of, 250
Seattle protests, 26
as target, 30–31
telecommunications reform, 213
and trade diversion, 267–269
Trade Related Aspects of Intellectual Property Rights (TRIPS), 212
"WTO club," 33
world trading system
see also World Trade Organization
development of, 209–217
disturbing trends (1980-1993), 211
economic growth, 210–211
expanding trade agreements, 213–214
future of WTO, 214–217
General Agreement on Tariffs and Trade (GATT), 210–211
Japan's economic success, 211
from Smith to the Great Depression, 210
trade liberalization, 210–211
Uruguay Round, 213
U.S.'s persistent trade deficit, 211
World Trade Organization, creation of, 212–213
"WTO club," 33

Z

zero-sum game, 167